W9-CRI-787

COMBAT AIRCRAFT
OF WORLD WAR TWO

Elke C. Weal, John A. Weal and Richard F. Barker
Editorial Consultant: J. M. Bruce,
R A F Museum, Hendon

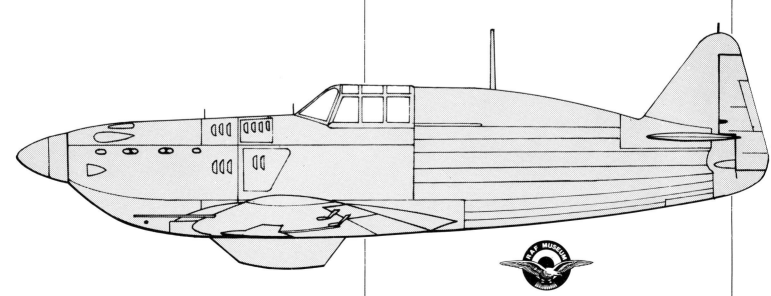

The publishers are pleased to acknowledge
the invaluable assistance of the R.A.F. Museum, Hendon,
during the production of this book.

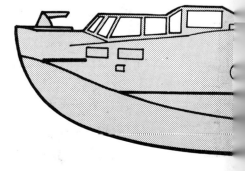

COMBAT AIRCRAFT
OF WORLD WAR TWO

Compiled by Elke C. Weal. Colour plates by John A. Weal

Line drawings by Richard F. Barker

Editorial consultant: J. M. Bruce, Keeper of Aircraft and Aviation Records,

Royal Air Force Museum, Hendon

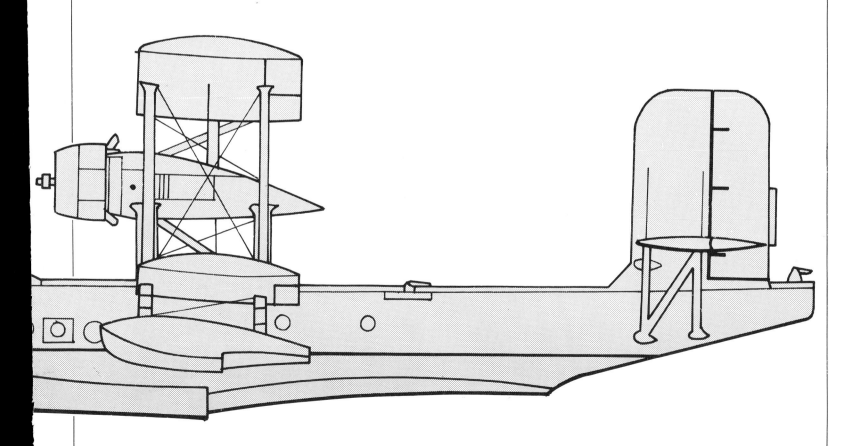

MACMILLAN PUBLISHING CO., INC.
New York

Copyright © Lionel Leventhal Limited, 1977.
All rights reserved. No part of this book may be reproduced or transmitted in any form or by any means, electronic or mechanical, including photocopying, recording or by any information storage and retrieval system, without permission in writing from the Publisher.

Macmillan Publishing Co., Inc., 866 Third Avenue, New York, N.Y. 10022.

First printing 1977.

Library of Congress Cataloging in Publication Data:
Main entry under title:

Combat Aircraft of World War Two.

Bibliography: p.
Includes index.
1. Airplanes, Military. 2. World War, 1939-1945--
Aerial operations. I. Weal, Elke C. II. Weal, John A.
UG1240.C65 623.74'6'09044 77-961
ISBN 0-02-624660-0

Acknowledgments: The compilation of a work such as this would not have been possible without the kind assistance of a great number of people. Special thanks are due to the following individuals, all of whom gave very freely of their time and expertise: the staff of the Royal Air Force Museum, Hendon, and in particular to J. M. Bruce (Keeper of Aircraft and Aviation Records) for much valuable advice and comment throughout the preparation of the manuscript; the staff of the Museum library, especially Richard Barker and his colleagues Peter Murton, Fred Flower, Dave Greenwood and Richard Simpson; Eric Turner, Mr. Coles and Mr. Gately of the Air Historical Branch of the Ministry of Defence; Prof. Dr. Gley and Herr Herbert Walther of the Bundesarchiv/Bildarchiv, Koblenz; Malcolm Passingham, who performed the wearisome task of checking the manuscript, and who provided many nuggets of additional information in the process; William Green and Gordon Swanborough, who kindly loaned much otherwise unobtainable reference material; Steven Bryant, Graham Denley, Adrian Harris, Derek Linington and Jack Selwyne; the late Generalleutnant Bruno Maass a.D, from whose files came much of the German information; Indulis Ozols and Wolfgang Weber; to the many friends both at home and abroad, who offered such valuable assistance in the preparation of the foreign sections — Paul E. Branke, Harri Habel, Jan Frumerie, Bo Widfeldt, Ermanno Cimenti, Franco Tripoli, Alex Vanags, Jean Mességué, Masatoshi Mituhashi and Wing-Chee Leung; Richard Barker, for his carefully researched and excellently executed line profile drawings, and who helped in preparing the colour section and the index; Brian Turner and Charles Wooldridge, who also provided valuable assistance with the colour plates; and last, but by no means least, special thanks to a gallant band of typists — Mary Emmett, Jenny Jerrum, Janet Smith and Rosemary Daniels — whose powers of deciphering the most complex of manuscripts never ceased to amaze.

E.C.W., Cookham, Berkshire

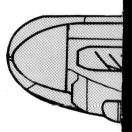

Designed by David Gibbons.
Printed and bound in Great Britain by Cox & Wyman Limited, Fakenham, England.

CONTENTS

LIST OF
ORDERS OF BATTLE

The illustration on the cover of this book is "Easy Skip, Sparks is bad" by John Young, M.S.I.A., G.Av.A. It depicts a familiar scene in the North of England during the latter days of the Second World War, as a damaged Lancaster, with wounded crew members, returns from a night raid on Germany. On the far right of the picture, the runway controller fires a red flare from his caravan, to warn the following aircraft that the strip may not be cleared in time for his landing. The painting was acquired by the R.A.F. Museum, Hendon, in 1975.
Illustrations on the preliminary pages of the book are as follows.
Page 1: the Yugoslavian Rogožarski IK-3 fighter, which, although produced in tiny numbers, achieved considerable initial success in defence of Belgrade, during the Axis invasion of 1941. (See page 220.)
Page 3: the French Bre 521 Bizerte long-range reconnaissance flying-boat, a development of the British Short Calcutta. (See page 88.)
Page 5: the British de Havilland Mosquito N.F.Mk30 night-fighter, which destroyed over 600 German raiders in a space of three years. (See page 137.)
Page 7: the United States Boeing B-17C "Flying Fortress", America's most famous high-altitude heavy bomber of the Second World War. (See page 189.)

On pages 17 to 80,
the scale of the aircraft
depicted is indicated
by this 6ft figure

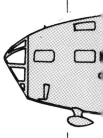

FOREWORD

by J. M. Bruce
Keeper of Aircraft and Aviation Records
R.A.F. Museum, Hendon

In the Royal Air Force Museum at Hendon, the Departments of Printed Books and of Aviation Records between them house much unique and valuable archive material relating to the aircraft of the world. This material has provided a substantial part of the foundations underlying the massive research task that has gone into the making of *Combat Aircraft of World War Two*. The assembling of data for this volume has necessitated checking and re-checking facts from many sources and in many languages; and such has been the thoroughness of the compiler's research that it has been possible to identify and eliminate a number of misconceptions (some of which had arisen by the repetition of errors from one book to another).

This volume, in my view, presents the optimum compilation of hard fact. The very proliferation of books dealing, in varying degrees of accuracy and thoroughness, with the aviation of the 1939-45 war makes essential the compilation of a single, compact book providing the basic data on all the combat aircraft of that conflict. In fact, nothing did more to emphasize the need for such a book than the research undertaken in its preparation.

Research is one problem: presenting the fruits of that research is another. There is (and always will be) room for argument about how best to do this, while still achieving reasonable uniformity of treatment. The greatest difficulty often lies in deciding what must be left out. In this aspect, the compiler's skill and judgment have produced a well-balanced and informative distillation of information which should satisfy the most fastidious devotees of the subject.

Excellent likenesses of many of the aircraft are provided, in line drawings and in colour, and themselves represent untold hours of research and highly talented work. How admirably they complement and illustrate the text will become evident to the reader however he chooses to use this volume.

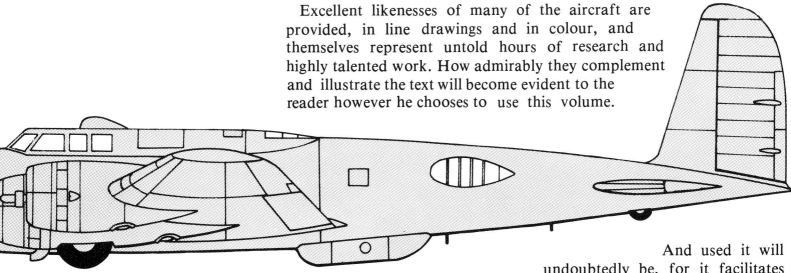

And used it will undoubtedly be, for it facilitates reference as few other works do. My own copy is going to earn its keep, and my pleasure in using it will be commensurate with my opinion of its accuracy and reliability.

J. M. Bruce, Hendon, 1977.

INTRODUCTION

Combat Aircraft of World War Two, the end-product of over five years' intensive research, represents an attempt to gather together — for the first time between one set of covers — concise yet comprehensive details of every combat aircraft actively engaged on operations during the Second World War. The material for this book has been culled from both official sources and private archives and, in fact, encompasses far more than its title would at first suggest.

After much deliberation, it was decided that the many transport, reconnaissance, liaison, and other ancillary types of aircraft (including civil impressments) which played such an integral — yet relatively unrecorded — part in the pursuance of hostilities, should also be included. As a result, the yardstick applied during the course of compilation was for the inclusion of every machine, other than those used solely for training purposes, known to have been employed by the combatant (and peripheral neutral) air forces of the Second World War. Such a rule of thumb is obviously open to an element of individual interpretation, and the compiler apologizes in advance to any reader whose own favourite aircraft has slipped through so necessarily ill-defined a net, and has thus escaped inclusion in the pages that follow.

Nor is the phrase 'Second World War' quite as clear-cut in aviation terms as the history books would have us believe. To make the book as complete as possible, details of the types that received their baptisms of fire in the skies over Spain or China during those occidental and oriental dress-rehearsals for the major conflict to come, the Spanish Civil War and the Second Sino–Japanese 'Incident' respectively, have also been recorded.

For ease of reference, the main text is arranged alphabetically by country, and each national section is, in turn, divided alphabetically by manufacturer. Their products have then been listed chronologically (apart from a few exceptions where a complete design series is dealt with sequentially to facilitate understanding). Each individual aircraft type is represented by one standard entry (or more, if production complexity so warrants). Performance figures quoted in the specifications are not necessarily compatible for any one configuration, but are intended rather to give maximum data wherever possible. The 'in service' entry lists all known users of the aircraft type concerned during the period of hostilities from 1939 to 1945 (and, in relevant cases, during the Spanish and Chinese conflicts). Unless otherwise indicated, the name of the country alone is taken to mean that nation's air force. And, in order to minimize the confusion that would arise from the use of the official abbreviations of the world's air arms,

a standard AF/NAF system (indicating Air Force and Navy Air Force respectively) has been employed throughout. Captured types which were subsequently taken on to the official strength of an air force for evaluation, propaganda, or operational purposes are also·included in these entries, but it has obviously proven impracticable to itemize those ex-enemy machines 'liberated' by front-line squadrons for their own private and personal uses.

The production breakdown into variants itemizes significant structural, design and/or role differences, as well as listing alternative names and/or designations for foreign service and licence-production. The numbers of each individual variant produced (as far as it has been possible to ascertain) are bracketed at the close of the relevant entry; numbers shown in italics indicate either conversions or redesignations from totals already quoted against an entry above.

Lastly, the 'remarks' entry gives brief mention of service career, operational deployment, and claims to fame (or infamy), if any. For a more detailed study of the operational uses of any aircraft listed, the reader is referred to the bibliography at the end of the book. To give some perspective to scope of employment, however, a number of carefully-selected and inter-related 'orders of battle' for various air forces are to be found at intervals in the main text. Thus it is possible, for example, to compare the opposing air forces engaged in the Battle for Normandy.

Of the eight-hundred-plus individual specifications itemized, over one hundred of the more important types have been illustrated in full colour. In the preparation of these plates (each page of which has been scaled to a common six-foot figure as depicted), we have selected, wherever possible, colour schemes of an unusual nature or of special interest, and many of the aircraft are shown in finishes not hitherto illustrated in colour. A detailed description of each camouflage scheme and the details of the unit to which this applied can be found in the text entry for the particular aircraft concerned, under the heading 'Colour Reference'. In addition, some 250 further types and/or variants are depicted by line profiles.

Such are the ingredients that together make up *Combat Aircraft of World War Two*. In any work of this nature, discrepancies from previously published documentation inevitably arise. And, although every possible care has been taken to ensure that the following pages contain the most comprehensive and accurate information available at the present time, the compiler would welcome any suggestions for additional types, or authenticated data currently lacking, to fill gaps in any possible future edition.

Notes on the Colour Plates

AUSTRALIA

Plates 1, 2: Commonwealth CA–13 Boomerang II QE.Z (A46–137) of No 4 Army Co-operation Squadron, No 10 (Operational) Group, RAAF, Nadzab, New Guinea, Feb 1944; standard foliage green/dark earth/sky blue finish (see Bristol Beaufighter Mk 21, plate 53, for altn overall foliage green scheme); all-white tail surfaces (in this instance with foliage green tip) and wing leading edges (two-thirds span on No 4 Squadron aircraft) official SWPA theatre recognition markings. [Data reference: page 81.]

CANADA

Plate 3: Noorduyn UC–64A Norseman (43–5179) of 1st Air Commando Group, USAAF, Hailakandi, India, April 1944; assigned aerial support second Wingate 'Chindit' expedition into Burma, March–May 1944, majority 1st Air Commando Group aircraft (inc P–51s, B–25s, and C–47s) identified by five white diagonals around rear fuselage as illustrated. [Data reference: page 82.]

CZECHOSLOVAKIA

Plates 4, 5: Avia B 534.IV (M–19) of 13. stíhakí letka (fighter squadron), Slovak Air Force, Zhitomir-Kiev (Ukraine), Oct 1941; standard dark green/pale blue finish; late style national insignia; yellow nose/fuselage band and wingtips Axis Eastern Front recognition markings. [Data reference: page 83.]

Plate 6: Letov Š 328 (S–76) of Combined Squadron, Slovak Insurgent Air Force, Tri Duby, Sept 1944; note Insurgent AF wing/tail markings (Combined Sqn also operated Š 328s Nos S–27 and B–10 with Slovak AF insignia (see plates 4–5 above) and Soviet Red Star markings resp); S–76 (and S–27) destroyed by Luftwaffe bombing raid on Tri Duby, 10 Sept 1944. [Data reference: page 84.]

FRANCE

Plates 7, 8: Lioré-et-Olivier Leo 451 B4 (No 482) of Escadrille 6B, Flotille 4F, Aéronavale, Tafaroui-Lartigue, Algeria, Nov 1942; standard finish with Vichy nacelle/tail striping, plus Aéronavale anchor insignia centered on roundels and rudder tricolour; all thirteen aircraft of Flotille 4F's two component Escadrilles (6B/7B) either destroyed or captured by US forces in first hours of 'Torch' landings, 8 Nov 1942. [Data reference: page 95.]

Plate 9: Amiot 143M (No 56) of GB II/34, Armée de l'Air; Roye-Amy, May 1940; standard brown overall (except natural metal nacelles); machine flown by Commandant de Laubier, No 56 destroyed over Sedan bridgeheads, 14 May 1940. [Data reference: page 85.]

Plates 10, 11: Bloch 152 recently of 4ème Escadrille, GC II/9, Armée de l'Air de l'Armistice, Aulnat, Southern France, Nov 1942; this machine one of number seized by Luftwaffe's 'Monte-Rosa' special detachment for flight testing and transfer to German fighter schools; standard Vichy AF finish with Luftwaffe call-sign (07+11) and markings superimposed; note anomalous retention French rudder and underwing tricolour striping. [Data reference: page 87.]

Plate 12: Dewoitine D.520 of 6. Orliak (Air Regiment), Royal Bulgarian Air Force, Karlovo, Winter 1943–44; compare much-simplified post-Oct 1940 national markings with elaborate earlier style insignia as carried by P.Z.L. P.43A circa 1939 (see plates 121–122). [Data reference: page 91.]

Plate 13: Breguet Bre 695 AB2 of 1ére Escadrille, GBA I/151, Armée de l'Air de l'Armistice; Lézignan-Corbières, Southern France, June 1942; standard three-tone finish. Vichy AF nacelle and tail striping, plus white roundel surround and fuselage bar; subsequently (early 1943) to Regia Aeronautica. [Data reference: page 88.]

Plates 14, 15: Potez 630 C3 No 44 (C5–56) assigned to 3ème Escadrille, GC II/1, Armée de l'Air, Buc (nr Paris), May 1940; current FAF practice to attach two or three multi-seat command and fighter-direction machines to each single-seat Groupe de Chasse (GC II/1 equipped with Bloch 152), hence 3ème Escadrille's 'Grim Reaper' emblem on fuselage; note small size upper surface wing roundels. [Data reference: page 99.]

Plates 16, 17: Morane-Saulnier M.S.406 (MS–311) of 1./LeLv 14, Finnish Air Force, Tiiksjärvi, Finland, Sept 1943; standard two-tone camouflage scheme, personal shark mouth insignia. [Data reference: page 96.]

Plate 18: D–3801 (J–292) of Überwachungsgeschwader (Surveillance Wing), Swiss Air Force, Dübendorf, 1944–45; standard two-tone camouflage scheme, personal shark mouth insignia. [Data reference: page 97.]

GERMANY

Plates 19, 20: Arado Ar 66C (6A + TN) of NSGr 12, Riga-Spilve, Latvia, Sept 1944; representative of mixed bag both indigenous and foreign second-line types pressed into service with Luftwaffe's night ground-attack wings, 6A+TN operated by Latvian-manned NSGr 12 on Northern (Baltic) Sector of Russian Front, Feb-Oct 1944; note black/white night camouflage finish and flame damper exhaust. [Data reference: page 100.]

Plate 21: Focke-Wulf FW 189A–4 (W7+WM) of II./NIG 100, Jafü Ostpreussen, Powunden, East Prussia, Nov 1944; interim night-fighter adaptation operated by Ju 88/Bf 109-equipped NJG 100 exclusively on Eastern Front, Fw 189s intended primarily to combat Soviet Polikarpov U-2 (Po-2) night harassment of Wehrmacht transportation system; note FuG 212 Lichtenstein C–1 nose radar array and 15 mm MG 151 dorsal cannon. [Data reference: page 108.]

Plate 22: Heinkel He 177A–5/R2 Greif (V4+LN) of II./KG 1 Hindenburg, Prowehren, East Prussia, July 1944; subordinated directly to Lfl.Kdo.6, II. Gruppe deployed total 67 Heinkel He 177s; note combination night undersurface finish with mottled upper surfaces. [Data reference: page 115.]

Plate 23: Focke-Wulf FW 200C–3 Condor (F8+GH) of 1./KG 40; Bordeaux-Mérignac, Aug 1941; primarily employed Atlantic anti-shipping operations, this particular machine served briefly Mediterranean area, late Summer 1941; note 20 mm MG 151 in nose of ventral gondola and tally of two earlier attacks on UK recorded on tailfin. [Data reference: page 109.]

Plates 24, 25: Arado Ar 234B–2 Blitz flown by Oberstleutnant Robert Kowalewski, Kommodore KG 76, Karstedt, Schleswig-Holstein, May 1945; note abbreviated fuselage code (reduced from standard F1+AA to single individual aircraft letter 'A' in Stab colour), common late-war practice remaining Luftwaffe bomber units; Kowalewski's machine one of number Ar 234s captured intact by RAF and test-flown post-war. [Data reference: page 101.]

Plate 26: Dornier Do 217J–2 of 235ª squadriglia. 60° gruppo autonomo CN (Independent night-fighter wing), Regia Aeronautica, Lonate Pozzolo, Aug–Sept 1943; one of eight Do 217 night-fighters on strength 235ª squadriglia immediately prior Armistice; note matt black overall, no national markings on wing surfaces. [Data reference: page 106.]

Plate 27: Fully-armed Heinkel He 111P–4 (VG+ES) assigned Korpskette X. Fliegerkorps (X Air Corps HQ Flight); Mediterranean theatre, 1941–42; desert finish VG+ES employed by successive Fliegerführer Afrika, Generalmajor Fröhlich and Generalleutnant Hoffmann von Waldau, in Western Desert campaigns of Winter 1941–42. [Data reference: page 114.]

Plates 28, 29: Dornier Do 17Z–2 (5K+BU) of 10.(kroat)/KG 3 Blitz; Central Sector Russian Front, Dec 1941; Croatian volunteer-manned 10.Staffel, operational Winter 1941–42; this particular machine (Bruno-Ulrich) participated first all-Croatian attack on Moscow; note temporary Winter finish, Croatian (Ustachi) shield below cockpit; (for subsequent independent Croatian national markings see Junkers Ju 52, plates 36–37). [Data reference: page 104.]

Plates 30, 31: Focke-Wulf Fw 190F (G5+02) of 101. Csatarepülö Osztály (Assault Group), Royal Hungarian Air Force, Börgönd, Hungary, Nov 1944; component part of Lfl.Kdo.4's Fliegerführer 102 ungarn based Lake Balaton area; fuselage code indicates this machine second Fw 190 supplied to Hungarian AF for advanced training duties; note late style markings (compare with Caproni-Reggiane Re.2000, plates 86–87). [Data reference: page 109.]

Plate 32: Focke-Wulf Fw 190D–9 of Stabskette IV./JG 3 Udet, Prenzlau (nr Berlin), Feb 1945; previous Fw 190A–8-equipped Reichs-defence Sturmgruppe, IV./JG 3 re-assigned Lfl.Kdo.6 in Feb 1945 for operations against Soviet forces advancing on capital; note early style straight canopy. [Data reference: page 109.]

Plates 33, 34: Henschel Hs 129B–1 of II./Sch1G 2; Tunis-El Aouina, May 1943; slightly damaged in earlier crash-landing, Red 'C' abandoned/captured intact by Allied forces; sand-brown mirror wave over standard two-tone green; note replacement starboard spinner. [Data reference: page 116.]

Plate 35: Junkers Ju 87D–7 (HH) of 1./NSGr. 9; Caselle Torino. NE Italy, April 1944; night ground-attack finish comprising grey mottle/ mirror wave over standard two-tone green; note extended wingtips, flame damper exhaust, and Mk 250Bk flare canister on ventral pylon. [Data reference: page 118.]

Plates 36, 37: Junkers Ju 52/3m g6e attached to 1. kroat.Stukastaffel; Eichwalde, East Prussia, Nov 1944; assigned for transport duties with Ju 87-equipped Croatian dive-bomber Staffel (itself part specialized anti-tank formation under control Stab SG 9 at nearby Schippenbeil); note standard Luftwaffe finish, definitive Croatian wing/fuselage crosses and Ustachi tail emblem. [Data reference: page 117.]

Plate 38: Junkers Ju 86Z–7 (No 640) of No 12 (Bomber) Squadron, SAAF, Mogadishu, Italian Somaliland, March 1941; modified ex-South African Airways airliners, SAAF Ju 87Z–7s finished bright green overall. [Data reference: page 118.]

Plates 39, 40: Unusual example of markings applied not for recognition/camouflage purposes but for deception, painted transparencies on nose of heavy fighter intended to represent bomber version; Junkers Ju 88C–6a (F1+XM) of 4.(Z)/KG 76; Southern Sector of Russian Front, Winter 1942–43; employed primarily 'train-busting' missions. [Data reference: page 119.]

Plate 41: Junkers Ju 88G–7a (2Z+AW) of IV./ NJG 6, Neubiberg (nr Münich), Feb 1945; second example of Ju 88 markings applied for purposes of deception (see also Ju 88C–6a above), 2Z+AW has angular fin and rudder outline overpainted to resemble contours of earlier Ju 88C night-fighters – presumably intended to confuse Bomber Command air-gunners. [Data reference: page 119.]

Plates 42, 43: Messerschmitt Bf 109G–14/U4 of Major Friedrich-Karl Müller, Kommandeur I./NJG 11, Bonn-Hangelar, Feb 1945; special anti-Mosquito single-seat night-fighter Gruppe, note unusual dapple finish, lack of fuselage tactical markings, and installation single rearward-firing 20 mm MG 151/20 cannon in dorsal 'Schräge Musik' mounting. [Data reference: page 123.]

Plate 44: Messerschmitt Bf 109K–4 (Red '10') of I./JG 300 flown by Fw. Wolfgang Hundsdorfer.

Borkheide (nr Berlin), Jan 1945; note personal insignia below cockpit, and Reichs-defence bands around rear fuselage. [Data reference: page 123.]

Plates 45, 46: Messerschmitt Me 210A–1 (2H+DA) of Versuchsstaffel (Test Squadron) 210, Soesterberg, Netherlands, Aug 1942; standard day-fighter finish; Versuchsst.210 redesignated 16./KG 6 by end Aug 1942, suffering first operational losses (to RAF Typhoons) over UK during first week Sept. [Data reference: page 124.]

Plate 47: Messerschmitt Bf 110G–4d (G9+AA: Werk-Nr.140 655) flown by Oberstleutnant Hans-Joachim Jabs, Kommodore NJG 1, Eggebeck, Schleswig-Hostein, April 1945; note 'Schräge Musik' installation, FuG 218 Neptun V, and FuG 350 Naxos; on 1 May 1945 G9+AA scheduled to be ferried from Lüneburg to Neumünster by two NCO pilots who instead defected to Sweden, belly-landing at Hammerlöv (Trelleborg). [Data reference: page 123.]

Plates 48, 49: Messerschmitt Me 163B–1a Komet of II./JG 400, Husum, Schleswig-Holstein, May 1945; Yellow '10' belonged to 7.Staffel, only Komet unit remaining on Luftwaffe order of battle at close WWII (on paper forming part of 2.Jagddivision headquartered at nearby Hackstedt, in reality grounded from lack of fuel and completely ineffectual). [Data reference: page 124.]

Plate 50: Messerschmitt Me 262A–1a flown by Gruppen-Adjutant, Stab III./JG 7 Nowotny, Parchim, March 1945; note non-standard over-sprayed camouflage effect, Geschwader badge, Adjutant's chevron, Reichs-defence rear fuselage bands, and unusual treatment tail swastika. [Data reference: page 125.]

GREAT BRITAIN

Plates 51, 52: Ikarus-built Bristol Blenheim Mk 1 of 11th Independent Bomber Group, Yugoslav Royal Air Force, Belgrade, April 1941; note three-tone upper surface camouflage scheme (peculiar to Yugoslav licence-built machines) and lack of wing upper surface roundels; this machine captured intact close of hostilities, April 1941, and subsequently supplied to Croatia. [Data reference: page 133.]

Plate 53: Australian (DAP)-built Bristol Beaufighter T.F. Mk 21 N.SK (A8-116) of No 93 'Green Ghost' Squadron, No 86 Attack Wing, RAAF, Labuan, North Borneo, Aug 1945; overall foliage green finish (compare with Commonwealth Boomerang, plates 1–2); personal 'Pistol Packin' Gremlin' emblem on rudder. [Data reference: page 134.]

Plate 54: Fairey Battle (K9254) PM.L of No 103 Squadron, AASF, St Lucien Ferme, France; May 1940; note overpainted canopy centre section and unusual aft fuselage positioning of hastily hand-painted roundels. [Data reference: page 139.]

Plates 55, 56: De Havilland Mosquito P.R.Mk XVI (NS710) of 653rd Squadron, 25th Bomb Group (Reconnaissance), 8th USAAF, Watton, Norfolk, March 1945; overall RAF PR-blue, all-red tail surfaces; 653rd BS identified by circle round individual aircraft letter 'L', 654th sister squadron applied letter directly on background red; (652nd equipped with B–17G). [Data reference: page 136.]

Plate 57: Fairey Swordfish Mk III (NF374) NH.M of No 119 Squadron, No 16 Group, RAF Coastal Command, Belgium, April 1945; based Belgian coastal airstrips, all-black Swordfish and Albacores of No 119 Squadron employed closing weeks WWII against German midget submarines off Dutch coast; note ventral ASV housing, underwing weapons racks. [Data reference: page 138.]

Plates 58, 59: Fairey Barracuda Mk II (BV952) '4S', of No 826 Squadron, Fleet Air Arm, HMS Indefatigable, July 1944; '4S' returned safely from Operation 'Mascot', strike on Tirpitz, 17 July 1944, but was damaged beyond repair in hangar fire aboard Indefatigable following day. [Data reference: page 140.]

Plates 60, 61: Fairey Firefly F.Mk I (MB522) 279 'Y', of No 837 Squadron, Fleet Air Arm; HMS *Glory*, British Pacific Fleet, Aug 1945; note distinctive US-style barred BPF roundels carried port upper/starboard lower wing stations only, (compare location/size with British East Indies Fleet markings, see Grumman Avenger, plate 141). [Data reference: page 141.]

Plate 62: Fairey Fulmar Mk I (N1877) 'H' flown by Sub-Lt S. G. Orr of No 806 Squadron, Fleet Air Arm, HMS *Illustrious*, Mediterranean, Oct 1940; note 'Black Panther' squadron emblem; (Lt-Cdr Orr ended war with 12 'kills' as FAA's third-ranking Ace). [Data reference: page 140.]

Plate 63: Gloster Gladiator Mk II (J 8A) of Flygflottilj F 19, Swedish volunteer squadron, Lake Kemi, Northern Finland, Jan 1940; attached Finnish AF for Winter War operations, all twelve Swedish Gladiators of F 19 (individual aircraft letters 'A'–'L') had Swedish AF triple-crown insignia overpainted with solid black disc; unofficial F 19 squadron emblem was skull-and-crossbones (applied either to fuselage disc or on vertical tail surfaces), wing motif on Gladiator 'F' personal marking. [Data reference: page 141.]

Plates 64, 65: Gloster Meteor Mk III (EE239) YQ.Q of No 616 'South Yorkshire' Squadron, RAF, on detachment Melsbroek, Belgium, March 1945; temporary overall white finish (obscuring all codes) instant recognition aid in attempt to reduce risk from friendly anti-aircraft gunners (to whom every approaching jet was much publicized Messerschmitt Me 262, see plate 50). [Data reference: page 141.]

Plate 66: Avro Lancaster B.I (Special) (PD133) YZ.P of No 617 Squadron, RAF, Woodhall Spa, Lincs, March 1945; modified to carry 22,000 lb (9,979 kg) 'Grand Slam' bomb; note special Day Scheme camouflage finish unique to such conversions, plus 'YZ' code (as distinct from Dam Busters' standard 'KC') in reversed colours (and also carried across upper/lower tailplane surfaces) as further aid to differentiate between squadron aircraft. [Data reference: page 130.]

Plate 67: Handley Page Halifax B.Mk II Series IA (JP275) 'N' of No 614 'County of Glamorgan' Squadron, RAF, Celone, Italy, March 1944; re-numbered from No 462 Squadron, RAAF (first Middle East Halifax squadron), No 614 employed pathfinder duties southern Europe until re-equipment with Consolidated Liberator early 1945; note standard night finish undersides with Middle East dark earth/mid-stone upper surfaces. [Data reference: page 142.]

Plate 68: Hawker Hurricane Mk I (Z4177) 'Q' of No 806 Squadron, Fleet Air Arm, Sidi Haneish (LG 102), Egypt, Oct 1941; component of Royal Naval Fighter Squadron posted ashore and operating in support RAF in Western Desert after damage to carrier HMS *Formidable* previous May; Hurricane Flight (formed from No 806 Squadron) in standard temperate day fighter scheme; note individual aircraft letter 'Q', serial, and 'Royal Navy' in dark blue; (Compare with overall azure blue of Grumman Martlet Flight, see plate 145). [Data reference: page 143.]

Plates 69, 70: Hawker Hurricane Mk IIC (HV538) 'B' of No 3 Squadron, Indian Air Force, Assam, Dec 1943; forming part No 167 Wing, Indian AF (Nos 2 and 3 Squadrons on Hurricanes, No 7 Squadron Vengeance), participated Second Arakan, Dec 1943–Jan 1944; standard

SEAC finish; note white wing/tail bands and Tiger's Head personal insignia. [Data reference: page 144.]

Plates 71, 72: Hawker Typhoon Mk IA (R7596) US. M of No 56 Squadron, RAF, Duxford, Cambs, Oct 1941; standard day fighter finish; note early Type A1 fuselage roundels, 'solid' canopy aft fairing, and twelve wing machine-guns. [Data reference: page 144.]

Plate 73: Westland Whirlwind (P6969) HE.V of No 263 Squadron, RAF, on detachment St Eval, Cornwall, Jan 1941; one of squadron's earliest machines (delivered July 1940), well-worn P6969, flown by PO Graham, failed to return from patrol 8 Feb 1941, which scored squadron's first confirmed Whirlwind victory, Arado Ar 196 floatplane shot down south of Dodman Point. [Data reference: page 151.]

Plates 74, 75: Short Stirling Mk IV (LK117) V8.F of No 570 Squadron, No 38 Group, RAF, Harwell, Berks, Sept 1944; participated Operation 'Market-Garden', Arnhem assault and back-up supply sorties; note under-fuselage invasion striping and four daggers below cockpit, symbol employed by squadron to indicate number of special operations supply missions; pink square port upper wing surface marks dinghy stowage. [Data reference: page 147.]

Plate 76: Short Sunderland Mk III (JM673) 'P' flown by Wg Cdr D. K. Bednall, CO No 230 Squadron, No 222 Group, RAF, Koggala, Ceylon, 1944–45; unique all-black JM673 (known to squadron as 'Black Peter') so camouflaged for dawn/dusk anti-shipping patrols Bay of Bengal. [Data reference: page 147.]

Plate 77: Supermarine Spitfire Mk VB (AB502) IR.G flown by Wg Cdr Ian Richard Gleed, DFC, CO No 244 Wing. Desert Air Force, Tunisia, April 1943; standard Middle East finish; Abouqir filter; in addition to distinctive Wing Commander's markings (pennant beneath cockpit and initials (IR.G) in place of normal squadron code), AB502 also carried Gleed's personal 'Figaro the Cat' emblem on starboard side of fuselage below windscreen; 'Widge' Gleed failed to return from patrol Cap Bon area, 16 April 1943 (shot down by Messerschmitt Bf 109s of JG 77); 'Figaro' panel later recovered from crash-site and now in possession RAF Museum Hendon. [Data reference: page 148.]

Plates 78, 79: Supermarine Spitfire H.F.VIII (JF404) GZ.M of No 32 Squadron, RAF, Foggia-Main, Italy, April 1944; Aero-Vee filter; note extended wingtips, enlarged fin and rudder, reduced span ailerons; special high-altitude finish comprising medium sea grey upper surfaces, PRU-blue undersides; no underwing roundels. [Data reference: page 148.]

Plate 80: Vickers Wellington Mk X (HZ950) 'Z' of No 99 'Madras Presidency' Squadron on detachment from Jessore, India, to Burma for emergency supply-dropping duties with Troop Carrier Command during Japanese siege of Imphal, May–June 1944; standard night bomber finish, SEAC-style roundels. [Data reference: page 150.]

Plates 81, 82: Armstrong Whitworth Whitley Mk V (Z6795) JL.W of No 10 (Bomber) O.T.U. on loan from Bomber Command to No 19 Group, RAF Coastal Command, Feb 1943; during period of service with Coastal Command (up to July 1943) No 10 O.T.U. operated anti-U-boat role, sinking one boat (U-564) for total loss 35 aircraft, inc Z6795 (ex-'A'-Able of No 102 'Ceylon' Squadron, note crudely overpainted fuselage code DY.A) subsequently salved from French Atlantic Coast shallows by Luftwaffe recovery team. [Data reference: page 128.]

ITALY

Plate 83: Fiat CR.32 quater (M.M.4666) '10' of 160ª squadriglia, 12° gruppo assalto, Regia Aeronautica, Tobruk, Italian Cyrenaica, Oct 1940; standard North African desert dapple finish. [Data reference: page 155.]

Plates 84, 85: Fiat CR.42 Falco (No 26) of 4/II/2 (4e Escadrille, II Groupe, 2e Régiment d'Aéronautique (chasse)), Brusthem (nr St Trond), 10 May 1940, one of six CR.42s evacuated to France towards close Belgian campaign, No 26 subsequently damaged during Luftwaffe bombing raid on Chartres; standard Italian-style dapple finish; individual aircraft number on rudder, repeated under lower wing ('R' starboard/'26' port); 4e Escadrille red 'Cocotte' insignia on fuselage. [Data reference: page 157.]

Plates 86, 87: Caproni-Reggiane Re.2000 Serie I (Héja I) (V.417) of special Héja Flight attached to Air Force Brigade in support Hungarian Fast Corps' advance across Ukraine, June-Dec 1941; compare early style Hungarian national markings with post-1941 insignia (see Focke-Wulf Fw 190F, plates 30–31). [Data reference: page 159.]

Plate 88: Fiat (CMASA) G.50bis Serie IV of 20° gruppo, 56° stormo caccia terrestre (fighter of the Corpo Aereo Italiano, Maldeghem, Belgium, Oct 1940; part of Italian Corps based Belgium for abortive aerial assault on UK, Oct 1940–April 1941; note yellow tactical recognition markings, 'Black Cat' unit badge on tail fin and Commandante di Gruppo pennant below cockpit. [Data reference: page 156.]

Plate 89: Macchi MC.200 Saetta of 362ª squadriglia, 22° gruppo autonomo, CSIR (Italian Expeditionary Corps in Russia), Zaporozhe, Ukraine, Aug 1941; standard Regia Aeronautica finish; yellow cowling, wingtip, and fuselage band theatre markings applicable all Axis aircraft operational Eastern Front, white wing leading edge chevrons unique CSIR fighters; note abbreviated tail cross and uncommon position Spauracchio (Scarecrow) gruppo insignia. [Data reference: page 157.]

Plates 90, 91: Macchi MC.205V Veltro (White '17') of II./JG 77; Viterbo, Central Italy. Nov 1943; only Luftwaffe Jagdgruppe to operate MC.205V; standard Regia Aeronautica mirror wave finish; note unusual incorporation German cross into white fuselage band, non-standard (narrow-width) tail swastika, II.Gruppe horizontal bar identification, and typical Luftwaffe spinner spiral. [Data reference: page 157.]

Plates 92, 93: Savoia-Marchetti S.M.79–II (mod) Sparviero (No '5') of 2° gruppo, 3° stormo trasporto, Regia Aeronautica cobelligerante, Lecce-Galatina, Southern Italy, Nov 1944; standard RA mid-green overall; note overpainted wing fasces, rear fuselage band, and tail cross; (compare with near-contemporary S.M.81 transport of RSIAF below). [Data reference: page 162.]

Plate 94: Savoia-Marchetti S.M.81 Pipistrello (M.M.24147) 8Q+FK of 1° gruppo aerotrasporti 'Terracciano', Aeronautica Nazionale Repubblicana; Riga-Spilve, Latvia, June 1944; RSIAF transport group operating under Luftwaffe control (as 1.Staffel/Transportfliegergruppe 10(ital)), Northern/Baltic Sector of Russian Front; standard RA mid-green overall; Luftwaffe-style national markings and unit codes, RSIAF tricolour aft of cockpit. [Data reference: page 162.]

JAPAN

Plates 95, 96: Aichi D3A1 'Val' (Navy Type 99 Carrier Bomber, Model 11) No 31 aboard IJN carrier Soryu, Second Koku Sentai for attack on Pearl Harbor, 7 Dec 1941; overall sky grey finish, tail code: B=Second Koku Sentai, I=First Carrier (Soryu), −2=Carrier Bomber. [Data reference: page 162.]

Plate 97: Nakajima B5N2 'Kate' (Navy Type 97 Carrier Attack Bomber, Model 12) No 15 aboard IJN carrier Kaga, First Koku Sentai, Battle of Midway, June 1942; dark green upper surfaces, light grey undersides; tail code: A=First Koku Sentai, II=Second Carrier (Kaga, sunk during battle), −3=Carrier Attack Bomber. [Data reference: page 173.]

Plate 98: Mitsubishi Ki-46–III 'Dinah' (Army Type 100 Command Reconnaissance Plane, Model 3) of 3rd Chutai, 81st Sentai, IJAAF; Burma, Aug 1944; overall brown, deep yellow wing leading edge panels. [Data reference: page 171.]

Plates 99, 100: Kawasaki Ki-45 KAIc Toryu 'Nick' (Army Type 2 Two-seat Fighter, Model C) of 3rd Chutai, 53rd Sentai, IJAAF, Matsudo (Chiba Prefecture), NW of Tokyo, Winter 1944–45; white ground to national markings (Hinomaru) indicates home-defence deployment. [Data reference: page 166.]

Plate 101: Nakajima Ki-27b 'Nate' (Army Type 97 Fighter, Model B) of Manchurian Air Force, Mukden, Manchoukuo, Sept 1942; overall light grey finish; Manchurian AF roundels upper and lower wing stations; one of number Ki-27s purchased by public donations, fuselage inscription reads 'Defence of the Homeland, Anto (Province) No 4'. [Data reference: page 172.]

Plates 102, 103: Kawasaki Ki-61–I KAI Hien 'Tony' (Army Type 3 Fighter, Model 1) of HQ Chutai (Flight), 244th Sentai, IJAAF; Chofu (Tokyo Prefecture), Aug 1945; fuselage/tail lightning flashes are Chutai/Sentai markings, all-red tail indicates HQ Chutai; note white home-defence wing bands do not extend over aileron upper surfaces. [Data reference: page 167.]

Plates 104, 105: Mitsubishi G3M2 'Nell' (Navy Type 96 Attack Bomber, Model 22) No 23 of Mihoro Kokutai (Mihoro Naval Air Corps), 22nd Koku Sentai, IJNAF; Saigon, French Indo-China, Dec 1941; participated sinking Prince of Wales and Repulse, South China Sea; tail code: M=Mihoro (Naval Air Corps), −3=Attack Bomber. [Data reference: page 169.]

Plate 106: Mitsubishi Ki-67–I KAI Hiryu 'Peggy' (Army Type 4 Special Attack Plane) No 05 of 1st Chutai, 7th Sentai, IJAAF; Formosa, April 1945; standard olive green/light grey finish; employed Kamikaze role against Okinawan invasion forces, April-July, 1945. [Data reference: page 172.]

Plates 107, 108: Mitsubishi A6M2 Reisen 'Zero' (Navy Type O Carrier Fighter, Model 21) No 08 aboard IJN carrier Ryujo, Fourth Koku Sentai, Aleutians attack force, June 1942; flown by Flight Petty Officer Tadayoshi Koga, No 08 participated attack on Dutch Harbor, Unalaska Island, 4 June 1942; with oil-pressure gauge indicator line severed by single bullet from PBY Catalina, Koga attempted wheels-down landing nearby Akutan Island; machine recovered intact by US Navy team one month later; tail code: D=Fourth Koku Sentai, I=First Carrier (Ryujo), −1=Carrier Fighter. [Data reference: page 170.]

Plate 109: Mitsubishi J2M3 Raiden 'Jack' (Navy Interceptor Fighter, Model 21) No 02 of 302nd Kokutai, IJNAF; Yokosuka (Tokyo Prefecture), Aug 1945; standard dark green/light grey finish (note IJNAF machines did not follow IJAAF practice of marking home-defence aircraft with white wing/fuselage bands around Hinomaru stations, see plates 99–100 and 102–103); late style tail code identifies Kokutai (3D), indicates naval land-based interceptor fighter (1100-series), and individual aircraft number. [Data reference: page 172.]

Plate 110: Mitsubishi Ki–21–IIb 'Sally' (Army Type 97 Heavy Bomber, Model 2B) of 1st Chutai, 14th Sentai. IJAAF, Philippines, June 1944; olive green dapple over natural metal; note stylized '14' Sentai insignia across vertical tail surfaces. [Data reference: page 170.]

Plate 111: Mitsubishi G4M1 'Betty' (Navy Type 1 Attack Bomber, Model 11) No 39 of 1st Kokutai, 21st Koku Sentai, IJNAF, Formosa, Dec 1941; standard early style camouflage scheme dark green/tan upper surfaces (separated by narrow light blue strips), light grey undersides; participated attack on Philippines across Luzon Strait; tail code: Z=1st Kokutai, −7=Naval land-based Attack Bomber. [Data reference: page 171.]

Plates 112, 113: Nakajima Ki–43–Ia Hayabusa 'Oscar' (Army Type 1 Fighter, Model 1A) of Royal Thai Air Force, Chiengmai, Northern Thailand, Summer 1944; brown/light blue dapple over standard IJAAF olive green finish; national insignia as carried during period of Japanese occupation only. [Data reference: page 173.]

Plate 114: Nakajima Ki–44–IIb Shoki 'Tojo' (Army Type 2 Single Seat Fighter, Model 2B) of Shinten (Sky Shadow) air superiority flight of 47th Sentai, 10th Hikoshidan, IJAAF, Narimasu (Toyko Prefecture), Winter 1944–45; 47th Home Defence Sentai formed special Shinten flight late 1944 for aerial ramming attack against USAAF B–29 bombers; note red fuselage flash and Shinten emblem, stylized '47' Sentai insignia across vertical tail surfaces. [Data reference: page 173.]

NETHERLANDS

Plates 115, 116: Fokker D.XXI (No 241) of 1e Ja.V.A. (1st Fighter Group), L.V.A. (Netherlands Air Force), De Kooy (nr Den Helder), 10 May 1940; flown by Luitenant-vlieger (Fl Lt) Bosch, No 241 destroyed by Luftwaffe Bf 109Es while attempting to land at De Kooy on first day of hostilities; note post-Oct 1939 national insignia (compare with Fokker G.IA below), and 'Three White Mice' Group insignia on engine cowling. [Data reference: page 180.]

Plate 117: Fokker G.IA (No 313) of 4e Ja.V.A. (4th Fighter Group), L.V.A. (Netherlands Air Force), Bergen, Oct 1939; No 313 (shown here in early style national markings prior re-painting as Fokker D.XXI above) destroyed in hangar during Luftwaffe bombing attack on Bergen, 10 May 1940. [Data reference: page 180.]

POLAND

Plates 118, 119: P.Z.L. P.11c (8.13) No 3 of un-identified operational fighter unit, Polish AF (Lotnictwo Wojskowe); Sept 1939; note three-tone 'splinter' camouflage finish reportedly being applied Polish AF fighter squadrons immediately prior outbreak WWII, also asymmetrical upper wing insignia. [Data reference: page 183.]

Plate 120: P.Z.L. P.24G (Delta 127) of 22 Mira (sqn), EVA (Royal Hellenic AF); Ptolemaïs, Greece, Dec 1940; standard olive green/sand-brown finish; saw extensive action against Regia Aeronautica aerial defence Salonika, Winter 1940–41. [Data reference: page 184.]

Plates 121, 122: P.Z.L. P.43A Tchaika of 1st Orliak (Air Regiment), Royal Bulgarian Air Force, Sofia-Bojourishté, Sept 1939; early style fuselage/wing markings with non-standard rudder tricolour striping; (see Dewoitine D.520, plate 12, for 1940–44 pro-Axis period national insignia). [Data reference: page 184.]

Plate 123: P.Z.L. P.37B Los B of 1st Air Regiment, Polish Air Force (Lotnictwo Wojskowe), Warsaw-Okecie, Sept 1939. [Data reference: page 184.]

RUMANIA

Plates 124, 125: IAR 81C (No 391) of Grupul 3 picaj (3rd Dive-bomber Group), Corpul 1 Aerien (1st Air Corps), FARR (Royal Air Forces of Rumania), Cioara Dolcesti, Rumania, Aug 1944; subordinated to Luftwaffe Lfl.Kdo.4 (currently headquartered Debrecen, Hungary), IAR 81C No 391 carries pro-Axis wing/fuselage national insignia (compare with post-Aug 1944 markings on IAR 39 below). [Data reference: page 186.]

Plate 126: IAR 39 (No 204) army co-operation aircraft attached Corpul 1 Aerien (1st Air Corps), FARR (Royal Air Forces of Rumania); Slovakian Front, Jan 1945; now subordinated 5th Soviet Air Force, all machines of Corpul 1 Aerien have had earlier pro-Axis wing/fuselage cross insignia (see IAR 81C above) supplanted by re-introduction pre-war roundels; rudder tricolour striping retained. [Data reference: page 185.]

USA

Plate 127: Brewster Buffalo I (W8153) GA.P of No 21 Squadron, RAAF; shown in late NEIAF markings (roundels overpainted with Dutch tri-colour flag) as captured by Japanese forces upon occupation Netherlands East Indies, Andir (Bandoeng), Java, March 1942. [Data reference: page 190.]

Plates 128, 129: Vought F4U–1A Corsair (NZ5339) of No 22 Squadron, RNZAF, Bougain-ville, late 1944; note US-style (barred) RNZAF roundels all six wing/fuselage stations, plus narrow fin flash unique to RNZAF, and one of few instances of red being used in markings by Allied forces in Pacific area post-1942. [Data reference: page 211.]

Plate 130: Martin PBM–3D Mariner (P–9) of VP–202 'Leeman's Demons', Tarawa, Central Pacific, Jan 1944; named after CO, Commander Leeman, VP-202 was one of first Mariner squad-rons to achieve operational status; standard non-specular blue fuselage/white undersurfaces; note squadron insignia, winged 'Napoleon' (well-known US canine comic-strip hero) below cockpit. [Data reference: page 204.]

Plates 131, 132: Consolidated (Vickers) OA–10A Catalina (44–33882) of 2nd ERS (Emergency Rescue Squadron), 13th USAAF, Middelburg Island, Netherlands New Guinea, late 1944; relatively rare example of AAF aircraft sporting naval-style colour scheme, ERS Catalinas usually finished either dark-blue upper surfaces as illustrated (Pacific theatre), or white overall (Pacific/European theatres). [Data reference: page 191.]

Plate 133: Curtiss Mohawk IV (BS798) 'B' of 'A'-Flight, No 155 Squadron, Agartala, Bengal, Aug 1943; participated Imphal fighting Feb–March 1943, subsequently engaged dive-bomber Army support duties India/Burma theatre, May–Dec 1943; early style SEAC insignia; note retention sky rear fuselage band. [Data reference: page 194.]

Plates 134, 135: Curtiss P–40N Warhawk (42–105120?) '51' of 80th Fighter Group, 10th USAAF, Nagaghuli (Upper Assam), India, May 1944; although less well-known than famous P–40s of 'Flying Tigers', each 80th FG machine bore individual interpretation of Group's macabre grinning skull marking; few examples were as elaborately shaded or as extensive (joining across top of carburettor intake fairing) as that carried by No 51; note also over-painted fin and rudder,

evidence of previous ownership. [Data reference: page 195.]

Plates 136, 137: Douglas Dakota Mk.III (KG496) of No 267 'Pegasus' Squadron, RAF, Bari, Italy, Oct 1943; standard Middle East camouflage scheme; note squadron badge on nose; employed in support SOE operations in Balkans. [Data reference: page 197.]

Plate 138: Curtiss C–46A Commando (41–12322) of Air Transport Command, USAAF, assigned CBI theatre for operations over 'Hump', Kunming, Western China, Summer 1944; standard olive-drab finish, no unit markings. [Data reference: page 195.]

Plates 139, 140: Douglas SBD Dauntless (No 3) of VS–6 aboard carrier USS *Enterprise* (CV-6), prior raid on Marcus Island, Central Pacific, 4 March 1942; standard late-1941 blue/grey finish; note earlier red/white rudder striping overpainted, also deletion ship's number from fuselage ship/mission/aircraft number coding (full code would previously have read 6–S–3), and variation in size wing upper surface markings. [Data reference: page 197.]

Plate 141: Grumman Avenger Mk II (JZ512) K1.B of No 832 Squadron, Fleet Air Arm; HMS *Begum*, British East Indies Fleet, Indian Ocean, 1944–45; standard FAA dark slate grey/extra dark sea grey/sky finish; note overpainted roundels (six stations) with new reduced diameter SEAC blue/white roundels superimposed; (compare with British Pacific Fleet markings, see Fairey Firefly, plates 60–61). [Data reference: page 200.]

Plates 142, 143: Douglas A–20G Havoc (42–54255) of Soviet Air Force, Tula, Central (Moscow) Sector, Russian Front, March 1944; representative of the many thousands Allied aircraft supplied to the Soviet AF during WWII; note (local) dorsal turret modification, also over-painting US bars four of six stations; white tail tip and rudder tab tactical/unit marking; rudder motifs, corresponding to rank and branch badges as worn by Colonel of Soviet AF, presumably indicate pilot's status/rank. [Data reference: page 198.]

Plate 144: Douglas A–26B Invader (41–39272) AN.V of 553rd Bomb Squadron, 386th Bomb Group (Medium), 9th USAAF; St Trond, Belgium, April 1945; natural metal finish; horizontal yellow tail band (outlined in black) group marking, fuselage code (AN) and yellow engine cowlings indicate squadron. [Data reference: page 198.]

Plate 145: Grumman Martlet I (AX730) 'L' of No 805 Squadron, Fleet Air Arm, Sidi Haneish (LG 102), Egypt, Sept 1941; forming one flight of Royal Naval Fighter Squadron in Western Desert, No 805's Martlets finished light azure blue overall; (compare with Hawker Hurricane Mk I, plate 68). [Data reference: page 200.]

Plates 146, 147: Grumman F6F–5 Hellcat (No 73) of VF–15 aboard carrier USS *Randolph* (CV–15), Task Force 58, off Okinawa, May 1945; representative example late-war white geometrical squadron markings assigned by COMNAVAIR-PAC, 27 Jan 1945, to twenty-eight USN Pacific Fleet carriers, Randolph's squadrons' identifying symbols comprised horizontal bars across tailfin/rudder and solid white ailerons. [Data reference: page 200.]

Plates 148, 149: Lockheed P38L Lightning (No 210) 'Rickie Boy' of 18th Fighter Group, 13th USAAF, Zamboanga (Mindanao), Philippine Islands, June 1945; employed bomber-escort duties length and breadth South China Sea, attacking targets in Borneo, French Indo-China, and Formosa; natural metal overall, light blue

Group/Squadron markings, red checkerboard trim. [Data reference: page 203.]

Plate 150: Northrop P–61B Black Widow (42–39405) of 6th Night Fighter Squadron, 7th USAAF, Kagman Field, Saipan, late 1944; overall gloss black finish, individual nose artwork. [Data reference: page 206.]

Plates 151, 152: North American B–25J Mitchell (No 192) of 498th 'Falcon' Squadron, 345th Bomb Group (Medium) 'Air Apaches', 5th USAAF, Clark Field (Luzon), Philippine Islands, May 1945; one of most distinctively marked of all USAAF units, 'Air Apache' Mitchells carried variety colourful nose/fin motifs; Aircraft No 192 brought down by anti-aircraft fire over target during low-level attack on Formosan oil refinery, 26 May 1945. [Data reference: page 205.]

Plate 153: Martin B–26B Marauder (42–43304) of 444th Bomb Squadron, 320th Bomb Group (Medium), 12th USAAF, Sardinia, Summer 1944; standard olive drab finish; group identification yellow tail band; squadron within Group indicated officially by Battle Number '95' on vertical tail surfaces, and unofficially by Shark's Nose which decorated all 44th Marauders during closing year of war. [Data reference: page 205.]

Plate 154: Consolidated B–24H Liberator (42–52106) 'Sunshine' of 716th Bomb Squadron, 449th Bomb Group (Heavy), 15th USAAF, Grottaglie, Italy, March 1944; standard olive drab finish; early style 15th AF rudder markings: upper triangle denoting 47th Bomb Wing, lower '3' Group (449th) within Wing, plus individual aircraft number '5' on rudder (note evidence of overpainting on tailfin); 'Sunshine' captured intact after landing in error at Venegono airfield (25 miles n. Milan), April 1944; subject much propaganda footage before repainting in German markings for clandestine service with Luftwaffe's KG 200. [Data reference: page 192.]

Plate 155: Boeing B–17F Flying Fortress (41–24587) GN.P 'Bad Check' of 427th Bomb Squadron, 303rd Bomb Group (Heavy) 'Hell's Angels', 8th USAAF, Molesworth, Hunts, late 1943; olive drab upper surfaces with medium green dapple over fuselage and tail surfaces; standard Group (triangle 'C') tail markings and Squadron/aircraft fuselage codes, plus Squadron 'Bugs Bunny' emblem on port side of nose; 'Bad Check' one of ten B–17s lost by 303rd to German defences over Oschersleben, 11 Jan 1944. [Data reference: page 190.]

Plate 156: North American Mustang I (AG565) HB.A of No 239 Squadron, RAF; primarily engaged Army co-operation exercises in UK, AG565 failed to return from cross-Channel sortie (crash-landing Occupied Europe) in July 1943, two months prior to Squadron's re-mustering for night-fighter role. [Data reference: page 206.]

Plate 157, 158: North American P–51D Mustang (44–14292) QP.A 'Man o'War' of 334th Fighter Squadron, 4th Fighter Group, 8th USAAF, Debden, Essex, late 1944; flown by Lt Col C. H. Kinnard, 44–14292 featured unusual dark green camouflage pattern over natural metal finish; note also victory scoreboard around canopy frame. [Data reference: page 206.]

Plate 159: Republic P–47M Thunderbolt (44–21225) UN.K 'Fire Ball' of 63rd Fighter Squadron, 56th Fighter Group, 8th USAAF, Boxted, Essex, early 1945; flown by Lt P. G. Kuhn, 44–21225 finished in distinctive dark blue/sky blue shadow shading camouflage scheme adopted by 63rd FS upon re-equipping with P–47M model; Group's other two squadrons, 61st and 62nd, featured overall matt-black and dark green/light grey shadow shading resp. [Data reference: page 208.]

Plates 160, 161: Republic P–47N Thunderbolt (No 107) 'The Shell Pusher' of 463rd Fighter Squadron, 507th Fighter Group, 20th USAAF, Ie Shima, Western Pacific, July 1945; all-yellow tail served group identification, blue triangle on both vertical and horizontal surfaces denoted 463rd FS; flown by Capt R. T. Forrest, 'The Shell Pusher' can claim to have carried out one of very last operational missions of WWII, hostilities between Japan and Allies having officially ceased prior to his landing back from patrol over Korea, 14 Aug 1945. [Data reference: page 208.]

USSR

Plates 162, 163: Ilyushin Il–2m3 of V–VS (Air Forces of the USSR), 1st Belorussian Front (Berlin area), May 1945; note tailfin/rudder tactical/unit markings. [Data reference: page 214.]

Plate 164: Tupolev SB–2bis (0202) of Nationalist Chinese Air Force; standard Soviet AF olive green/light blue camouflage finish; the pilot of this particular aircraft defected to Japanese-controlled Cochin China in Nov 1941. [Data reference: page 218.]

Plates 165, 166: Mikoyan-Gurevich MiG–3 (No 35) of 12th IAP (Fighter Aviation Regiment), assigned to Moscow Army Region IAP–VO (Anti-aircraft defence Fighter Aviation), Winter 1941–42; note high-visibility wing upper surfaces, intended to facilitate location downed aircraft, a luxury soon discarded in face of Luftwaffe fighter opposition. [Data reference: page 213.]

Plate 167: Lavochkin La–7 (No 47) of 1st Czechoslovak Fighter Regiment, Balice (nr Cracow), Poland, April 1945; note standard Soviet blue/grey shadow shading camouflage scheme and national markings, but no manufacturer's 'La-7' stencils on tailfin tip or engine cowling. [Data reference: page 215.]

Plate 168: Polikarpov I–15 (No 7) of V–VS (Air Forces of the USSR) captured intact on advanced landing ground near Kowno (Kaunus). Lithuania, by German 30.I.D. June 1941; standard olive green/light blue scheme. [Data reference: page 216.]

Plates 169, 170: Polikarpov I–16 Type 10 (1–W–20) of Grupo núm 26, Spanish Air Force, Tablada, summer 1944; light grey fuselage, natural metal cowling, wings, and tail surfaces. [Data reference: page 216.]

Plate 171: Tupolev TB–3 (ANT–6) No 9 bomber-transport of V–VS (Air Forces of the USSR) abandoned intact in woods outside Smolensk, Central Sector Russian Front, Aug 1941; black/green camouflage scheme, early style fuselage/wing insignia; note outlined Red Star on extreme nose. [Data reference: page 218.]

Plates 172, 173: Petlyakov Pe–8 (TB–7) No 14 of V–VS (Air Forces of the USSR), Southern Sector of Russian Front, Autumn 1944; standard Soviet AF night-bomber camouflage scheme. [Data reference: page 216.]

Plate 174: Yakovlev Yak–1 (No 2) of V–VS (Air Forces of the USSR), Leningrad Front, Spring 1942; standard black/green shadow shading camouflage scheme. [Data reference: page 219.]

Plates 175, 176: Yakovlev Yak–3 (No 11) of 1ère Escadrille, Normandie-Niémen, East Prussia, Germany, May 1945; French volunteer unit attached V–VS (Air Forces of the USSR), Normandie-Niémen machines finished dark earth/olive green upper surfaces with Soviet national insignia on fuselage and wing undersides; note French tricolour spinner markings, but absence white Cross of Lorraine on tailfin as normally carried by fighters operated by this unit. [Data reference: page 219.]

1, 2. Commonwealth CA-13 Boomerang II.

3. Noorduyn UC-64A Norseman.

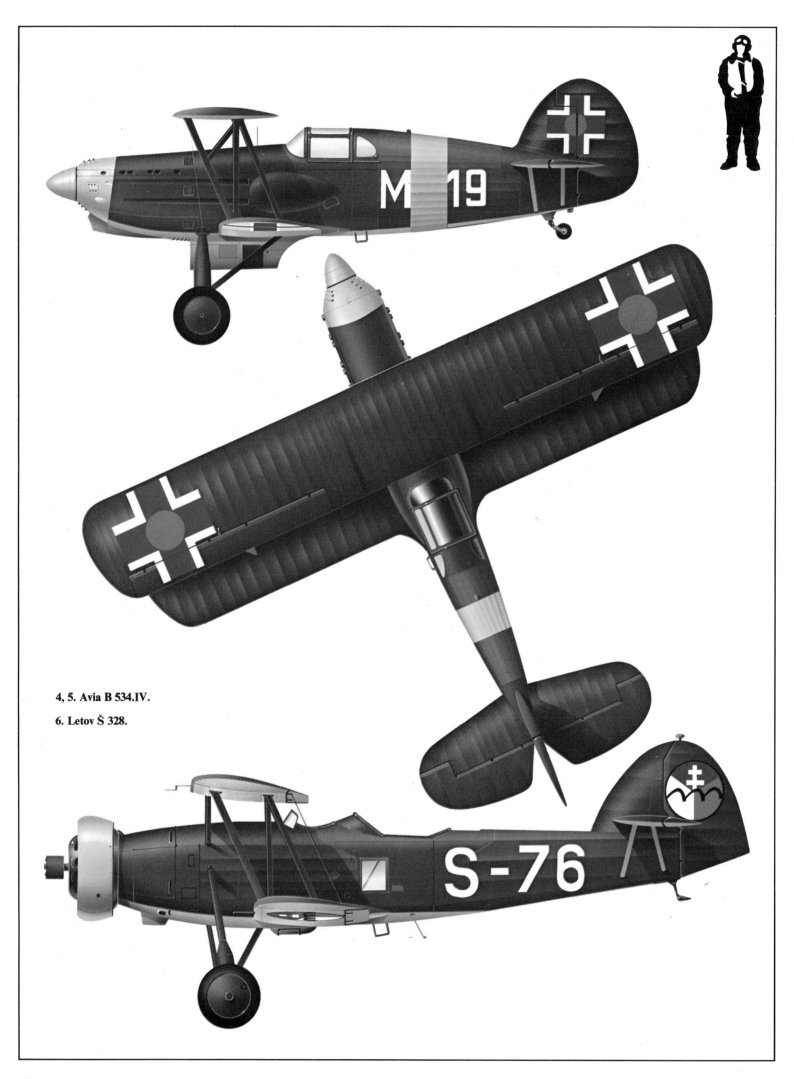

4, 5. Avia B 534.IV.

6. Letov Š 328.

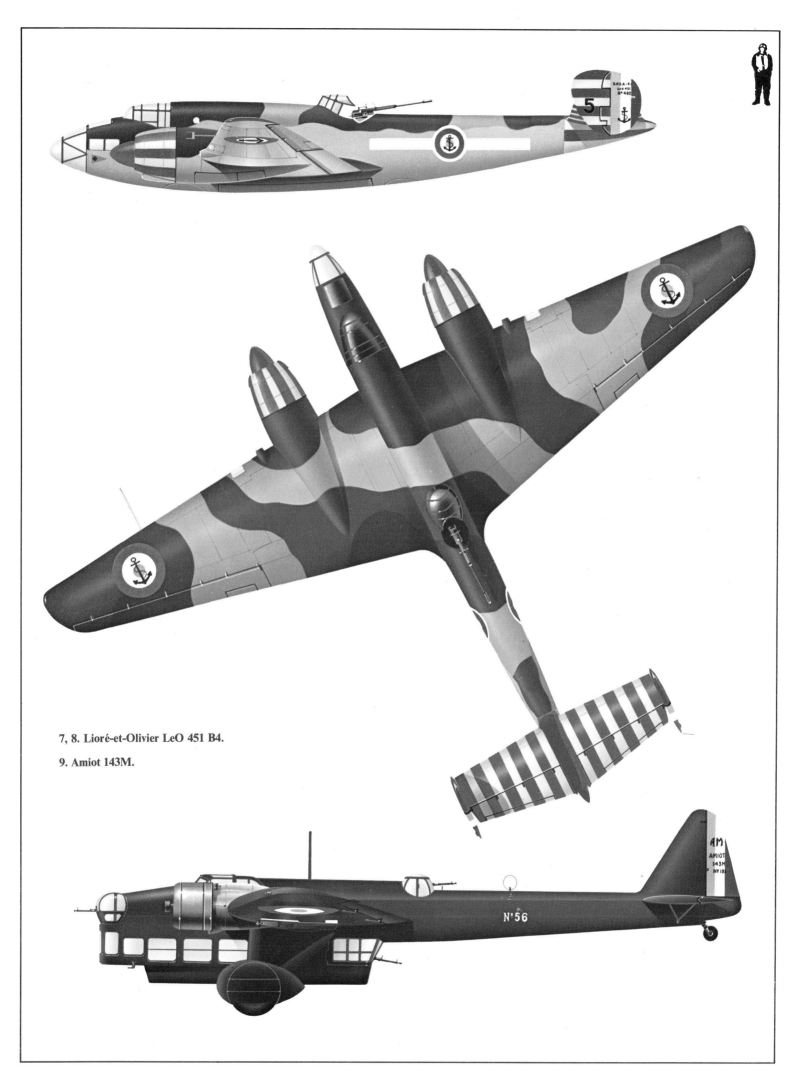

7, 8. Lioré-et-Olivier LeO 451 B4.

9. Amiot 143M.

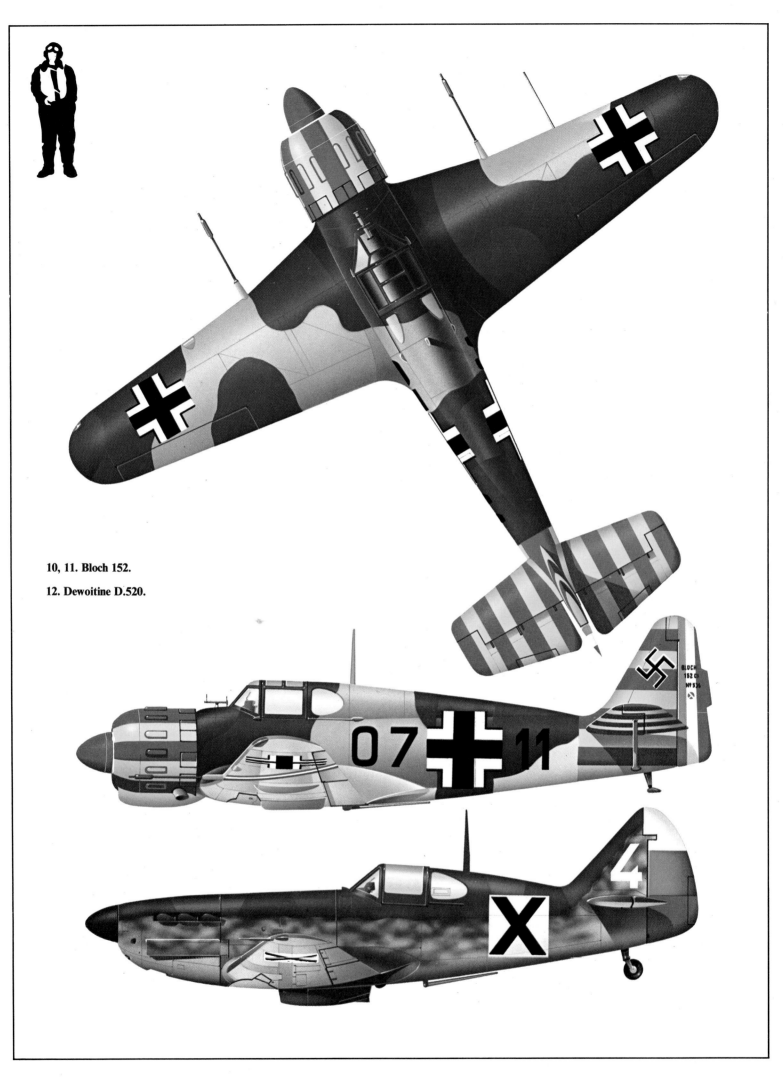

10, 11. Bloch 152.

12. Dewoitine D.520.

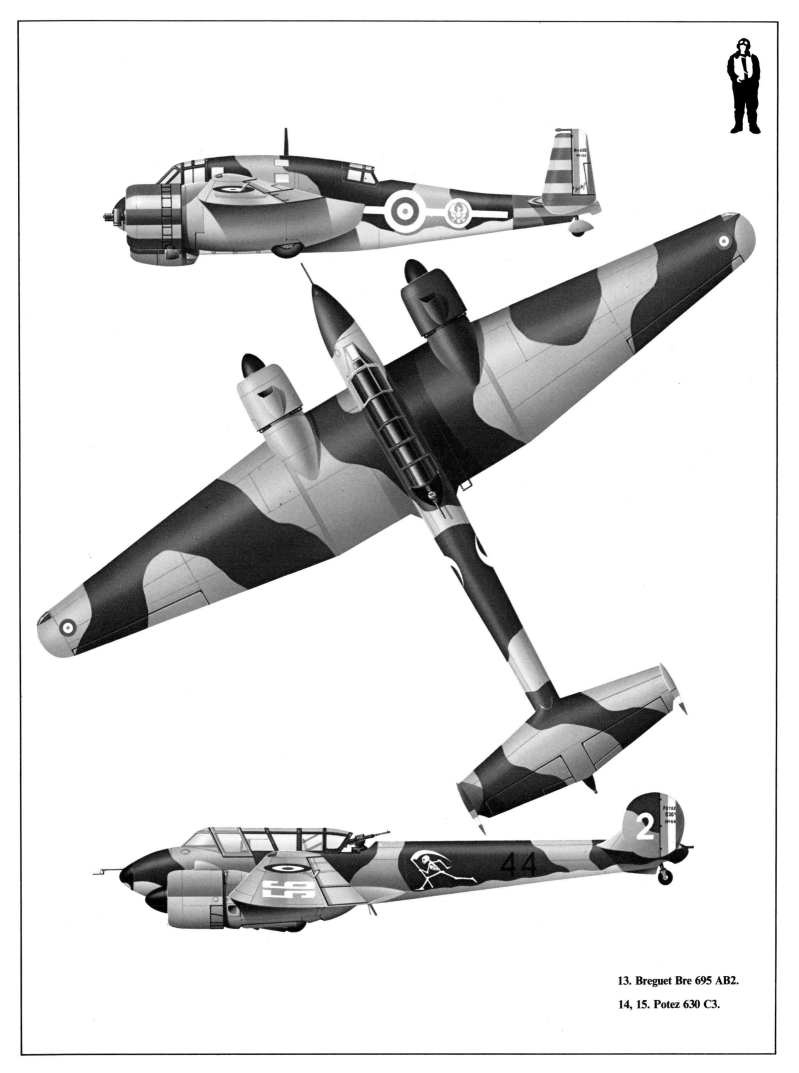

13. Breguet Bre 695 AB2.

14, 15. Potez 630 C3.

16, 17. Morane-Saulnier M.S. 406.

18. D-3801.

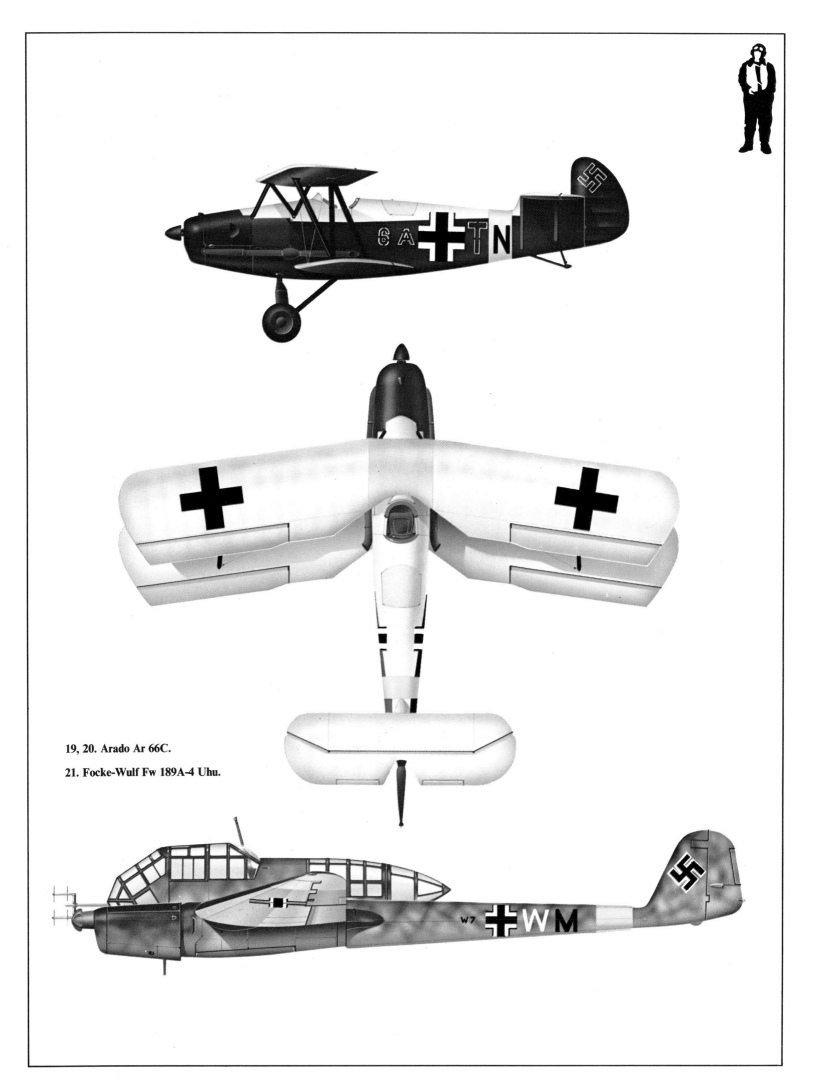

19, 20. Arado Ar 66C.

21. Focke-Wulf Fw 189A-4 Uhu.

22. Heinkel 177 A-5/R2 Greif.

23. Focke-Wulf Fw 200C-3 Condor.

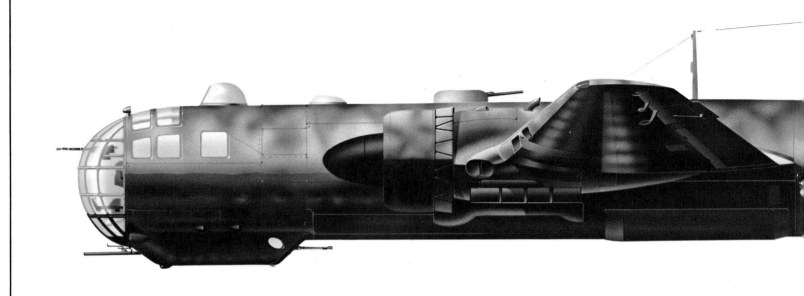

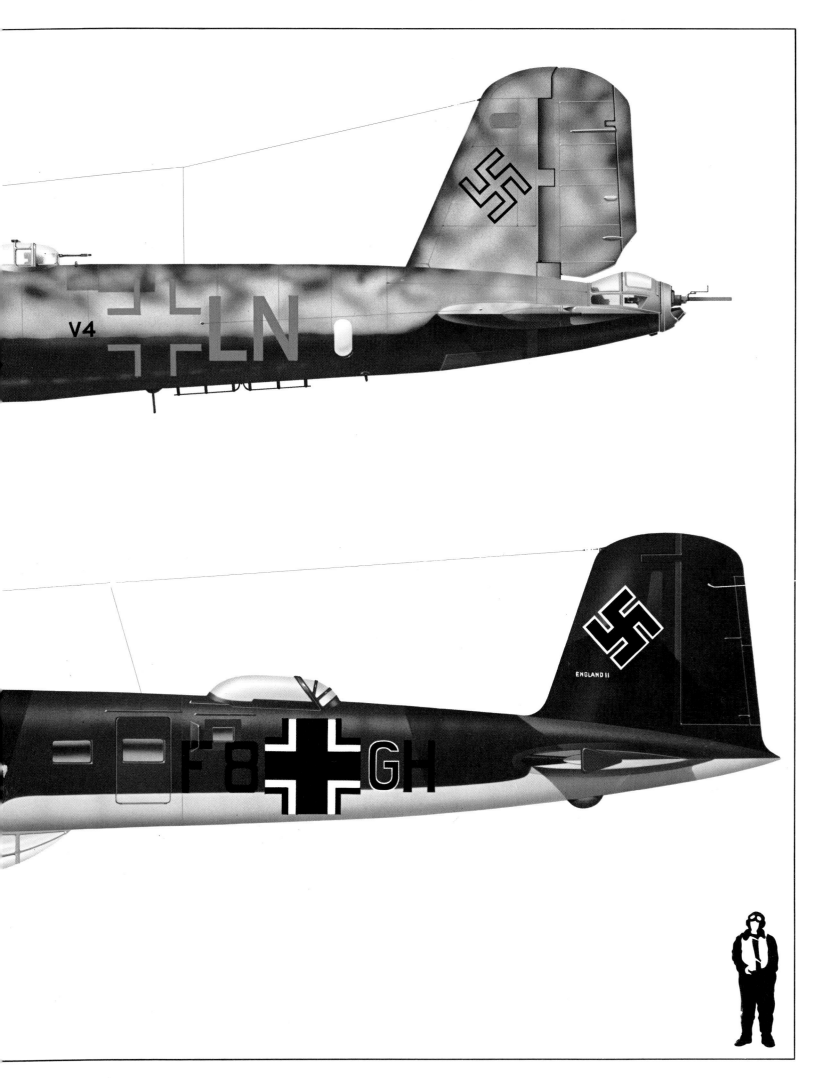

V4+LN

F8+GH

ENGLAND II

24, 25. Arado Ar 234B-2.

26. Dornier Do 217J-2.

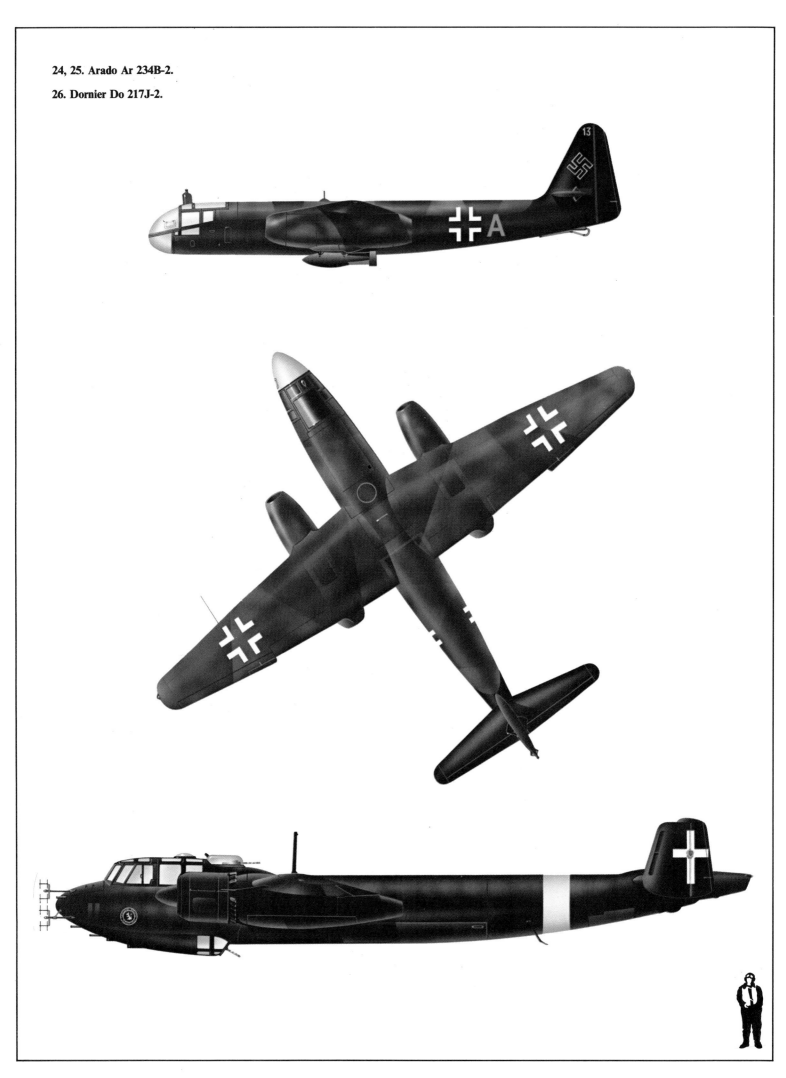

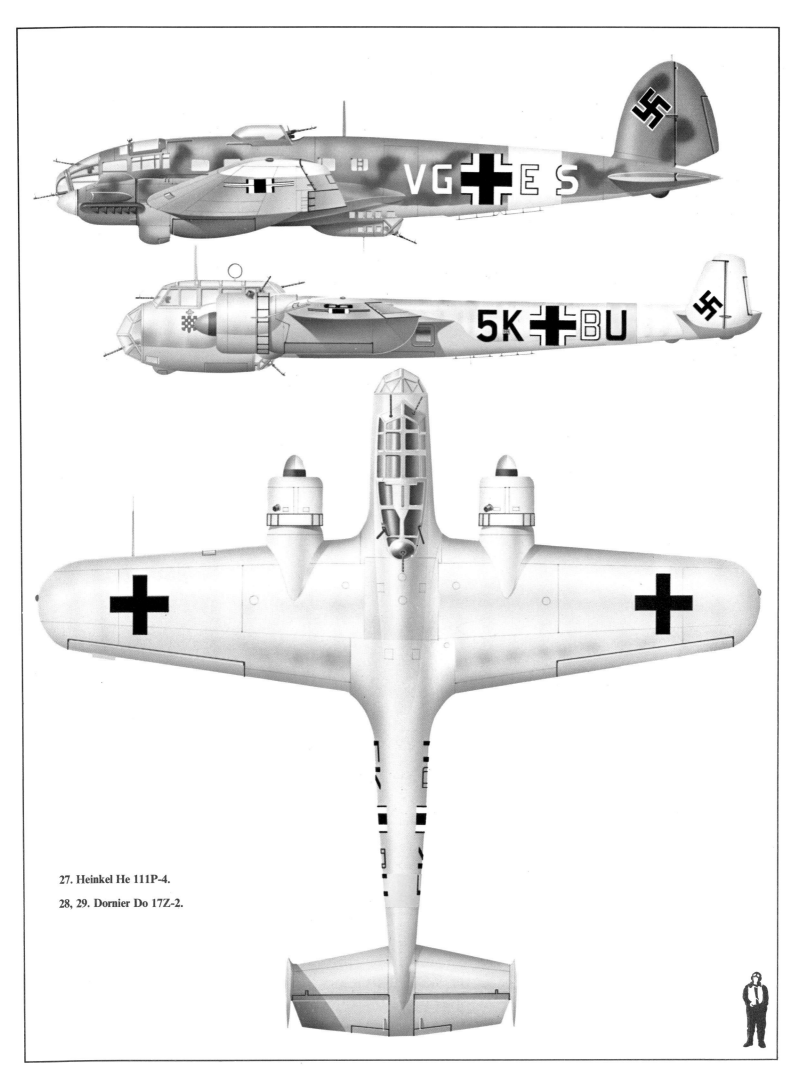

27. Heinkel He 111P-4.

28, 29. Dornier Do 17Z-2.

30, 31. Focke-Wulf Fw 190F.

32. Focke-Wulf Fw 190D-9.

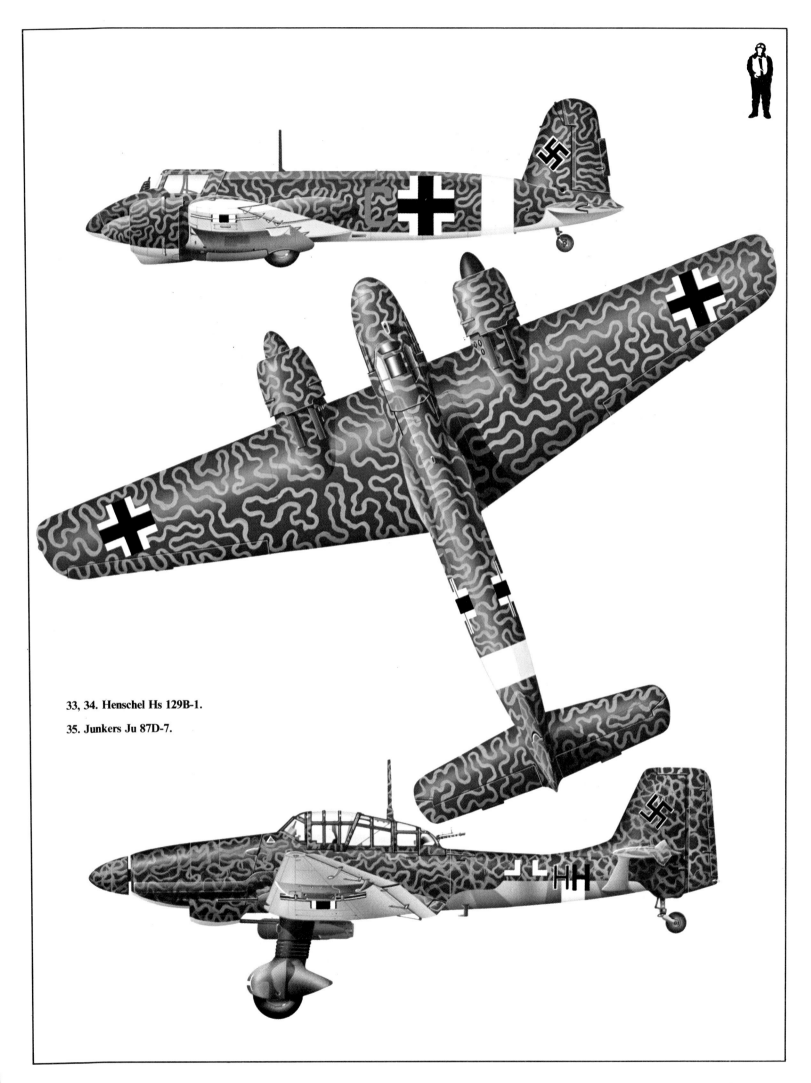

33, 34. Henschel Hs 129B-1.

35. Junkers Ju 87D-7.

36, 37. Junkers Ju 52/3m g6e.

38. Junkers Ju 86Z-7.

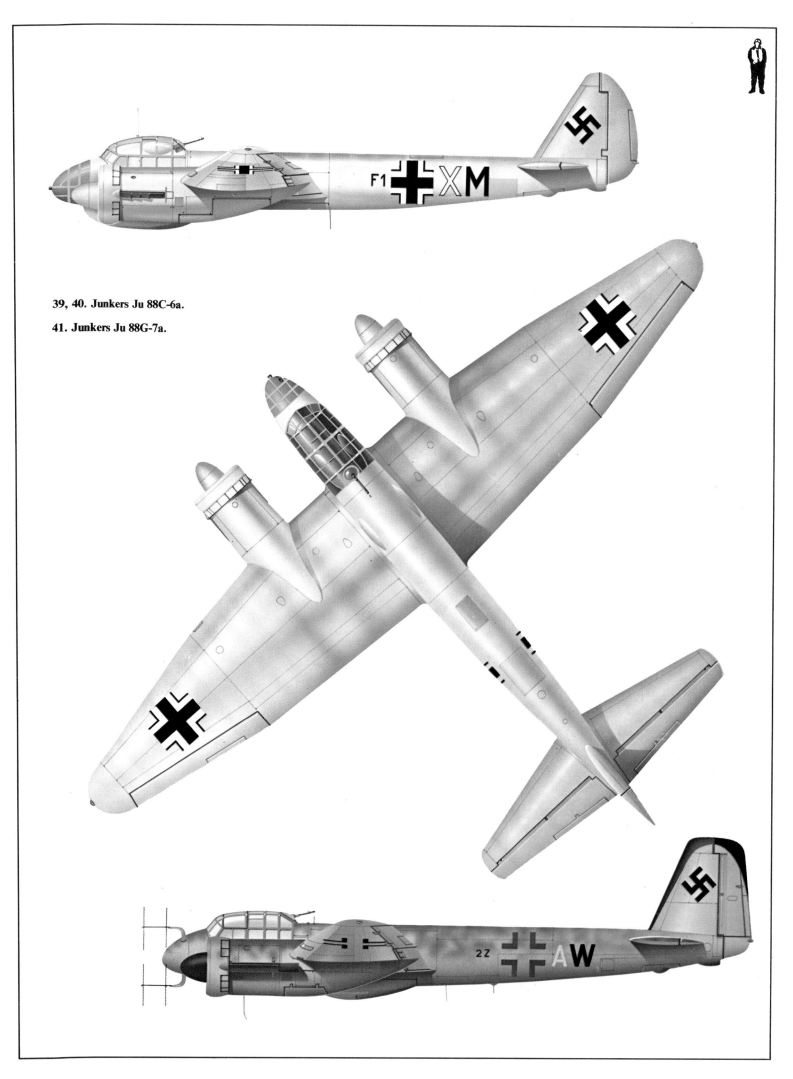

39, 40. Junkers Ju 88C-6a.

41. Junkers Ju 88G-7a.

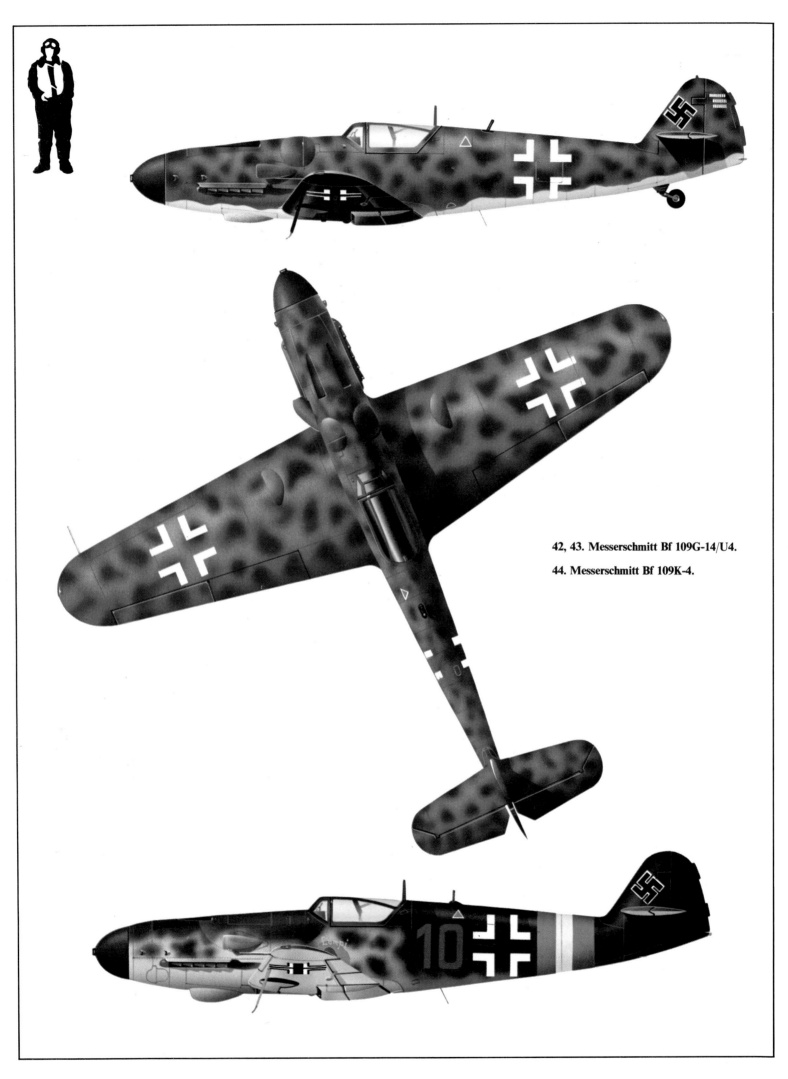

42, 43. Messerschmitt Bf 109G-14/U4.

44. Messerschmitt Bf 109K-4.

45, 46. Messerschmitt Me 210A-1.

47. Messerschmitt Bf 110G-4d.

48, 49. Messerschmitt Me 163B-1a Komet.

50. Messerschmitt Me 262A-1a.

51, 52. Bristol (Ikarus) Blenheim Mk I.

53. Bristol Beaufighter T.F. Mk 21.

54. Fairey Battle.

55, 56. De Havilland Mosquito P.R. Mk XVI.

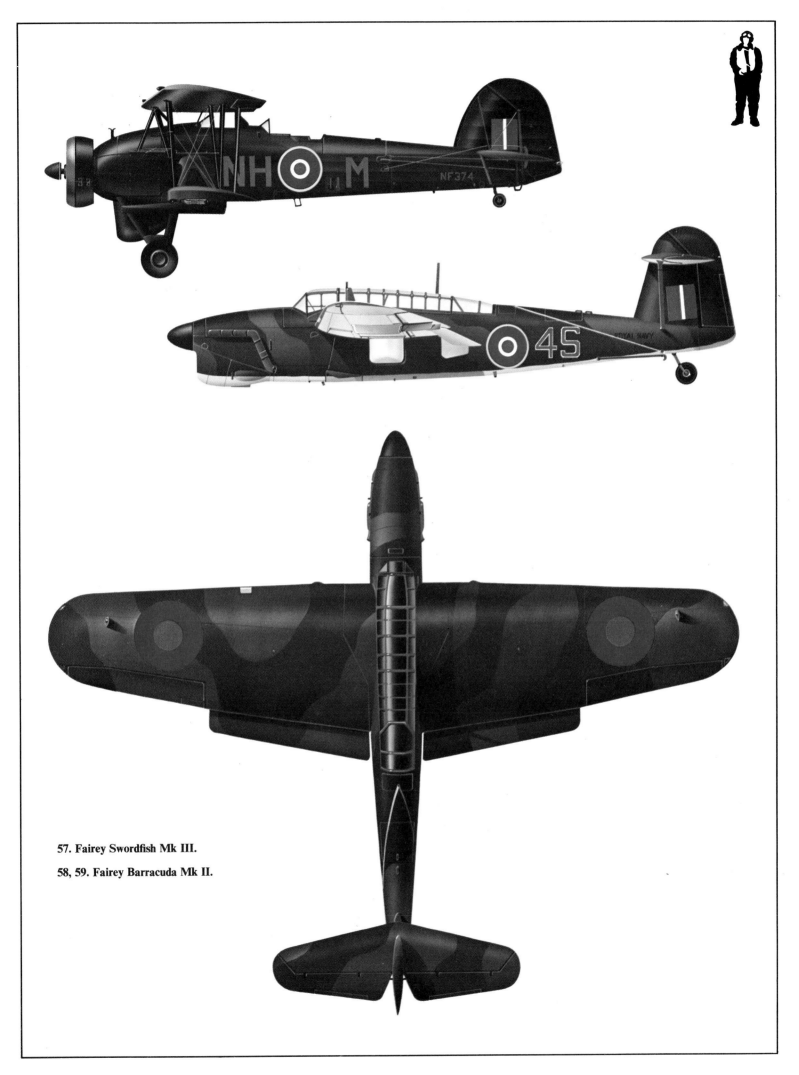

57. Fairey Swordfish Mk III.

58, 59. Fairey Barracuda Mk II.

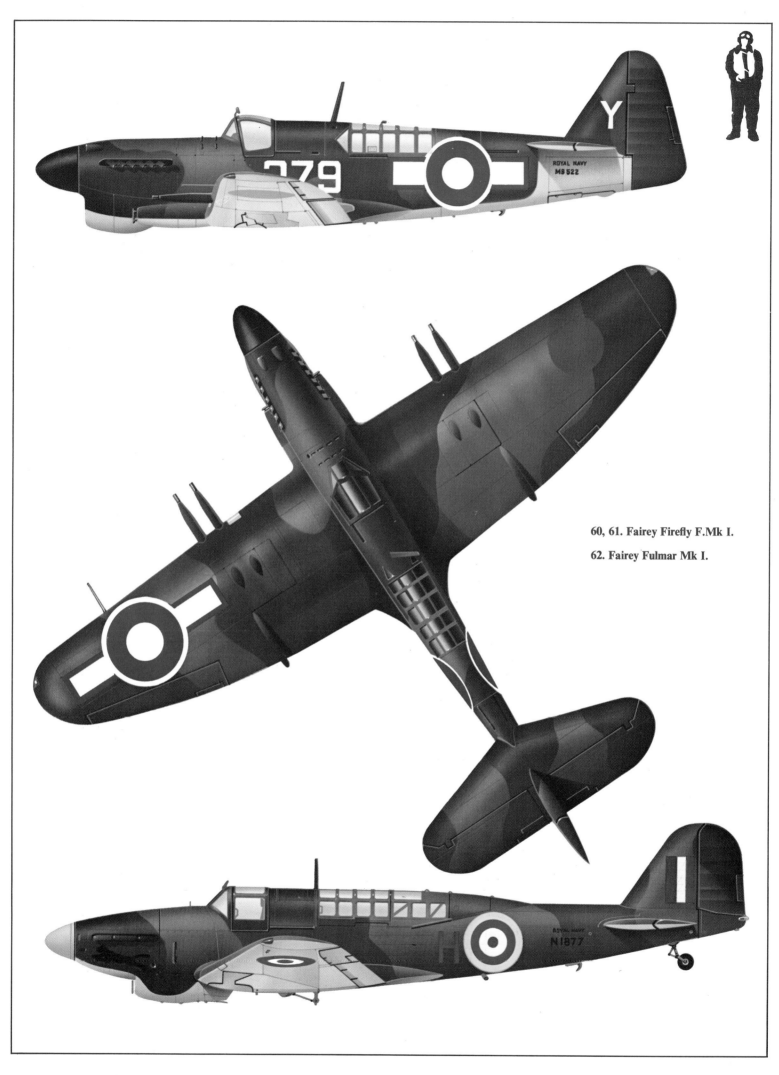

60, 61. Fairey Firefly F.Mk I.

62. Fairey Fulmar Mk I.

63. Gloster Gladiator Mk II (J 8A).

64, 65. Gloster Meteor Mk III.

66. Avro Lancaster B.I (special).

67. Handley Page Halifax B.Mk II Series IA.

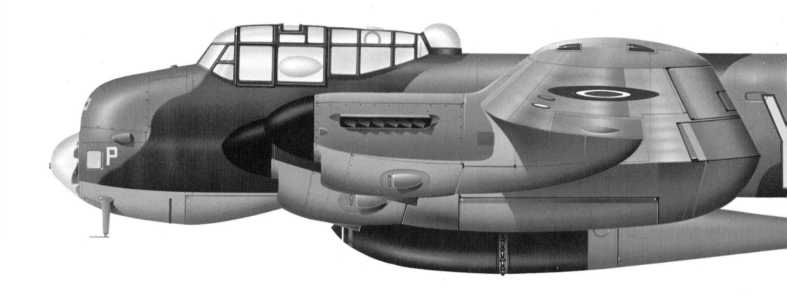

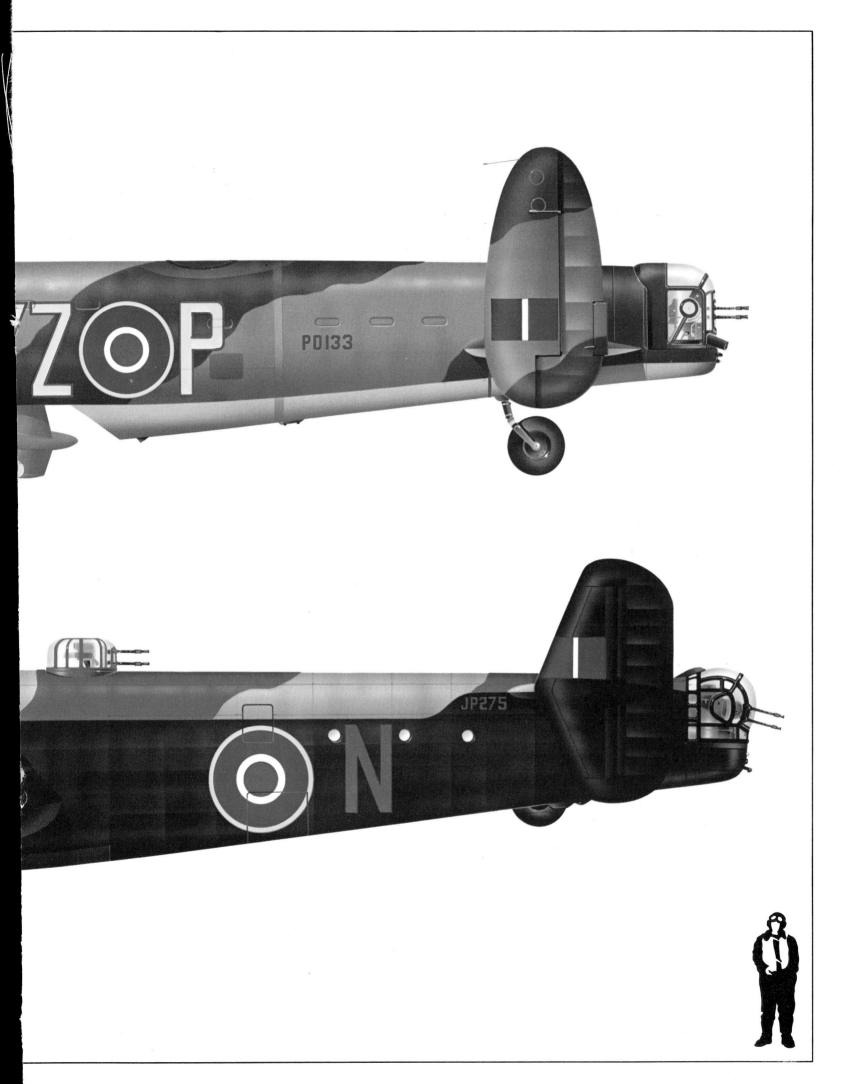

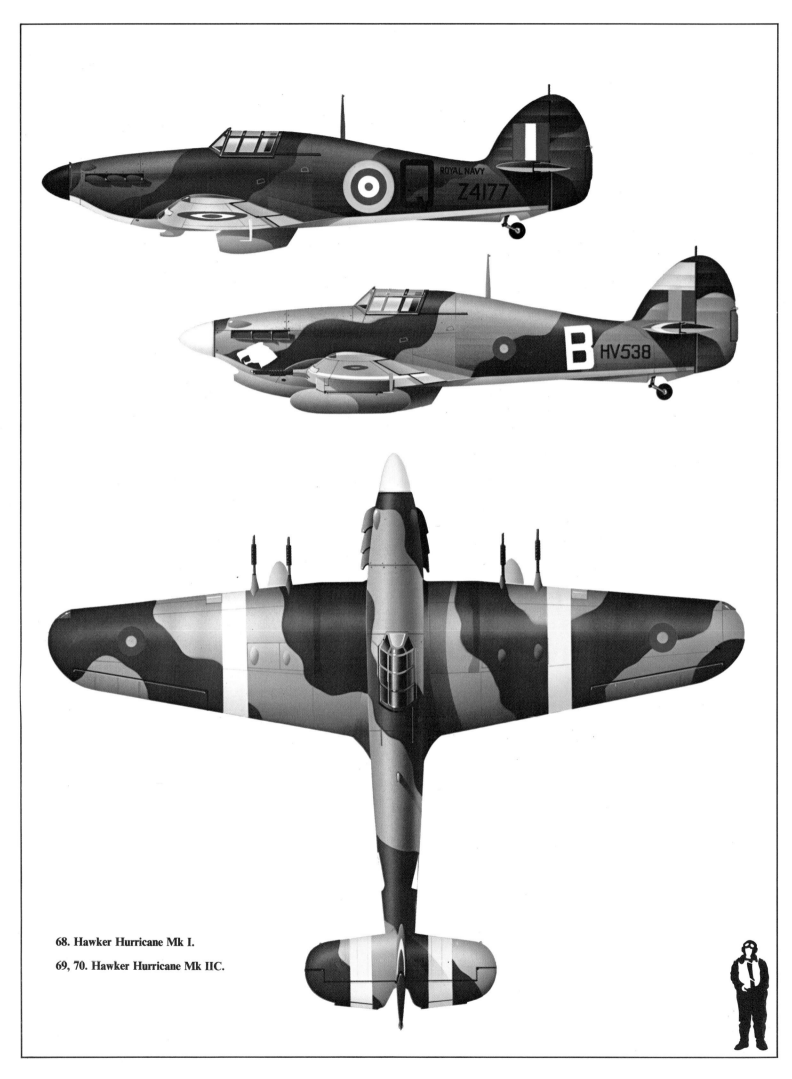

68. Hawker Hurricane Mk I.

69, 70. Hawker Hurricane Mk IIC.

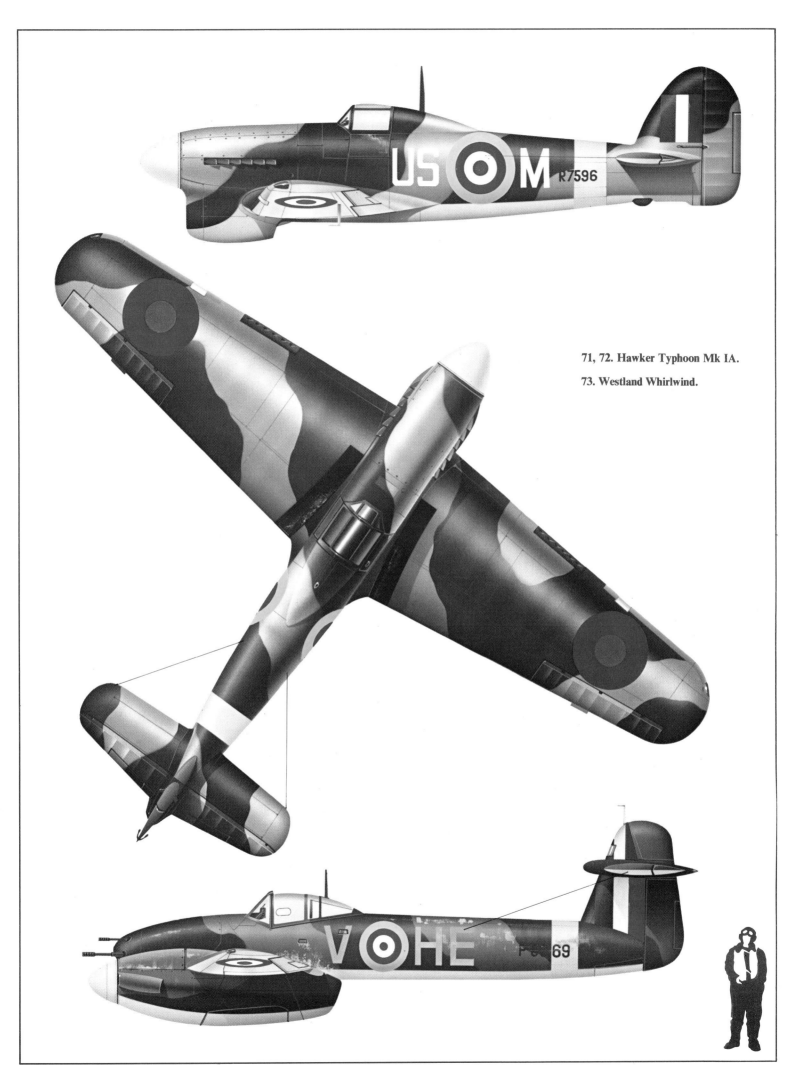

71, 72. Hawker Typhoon Mk IA.

73. Westland Whirlwind.

74, 75. Short Stirling Mk IV.

76. Short Sunderland Mk III.

77. Supermarine Spitfire Mk VB (Mod).

78, 79. Supermarine Spitfire H.F.VIII.

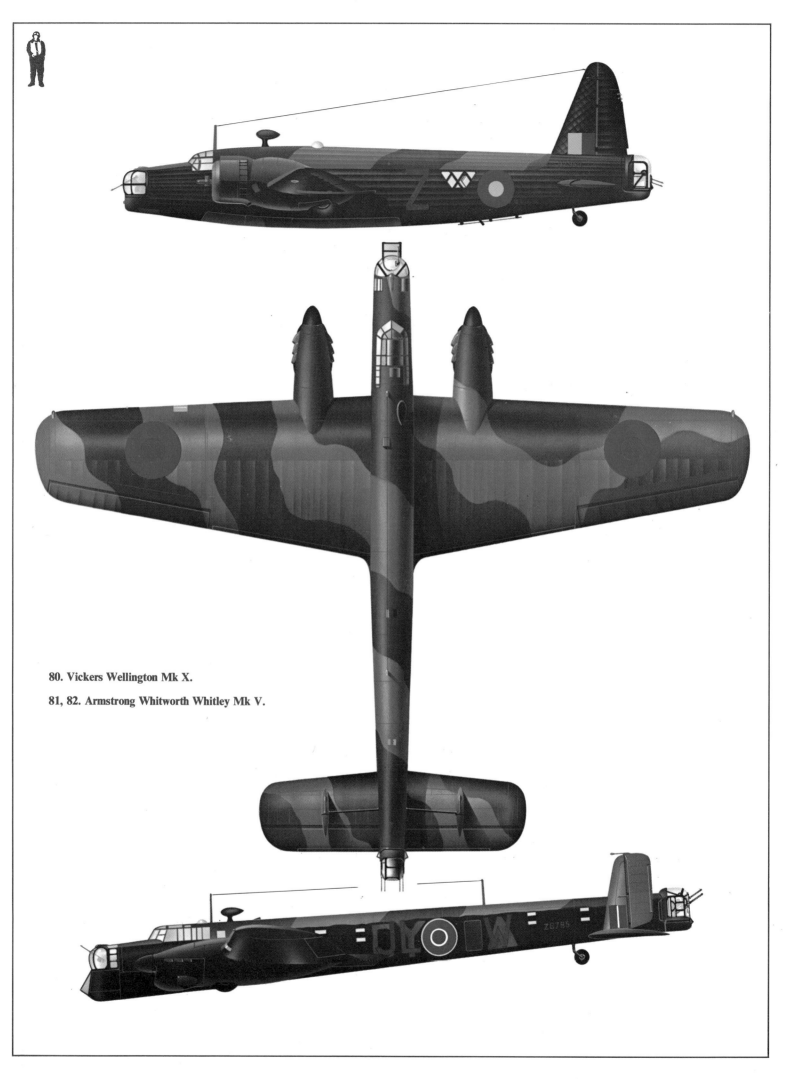

80. Vickers Wellington Mk X.

81, 82. Armstrong Whitworth Whitley Mk V.

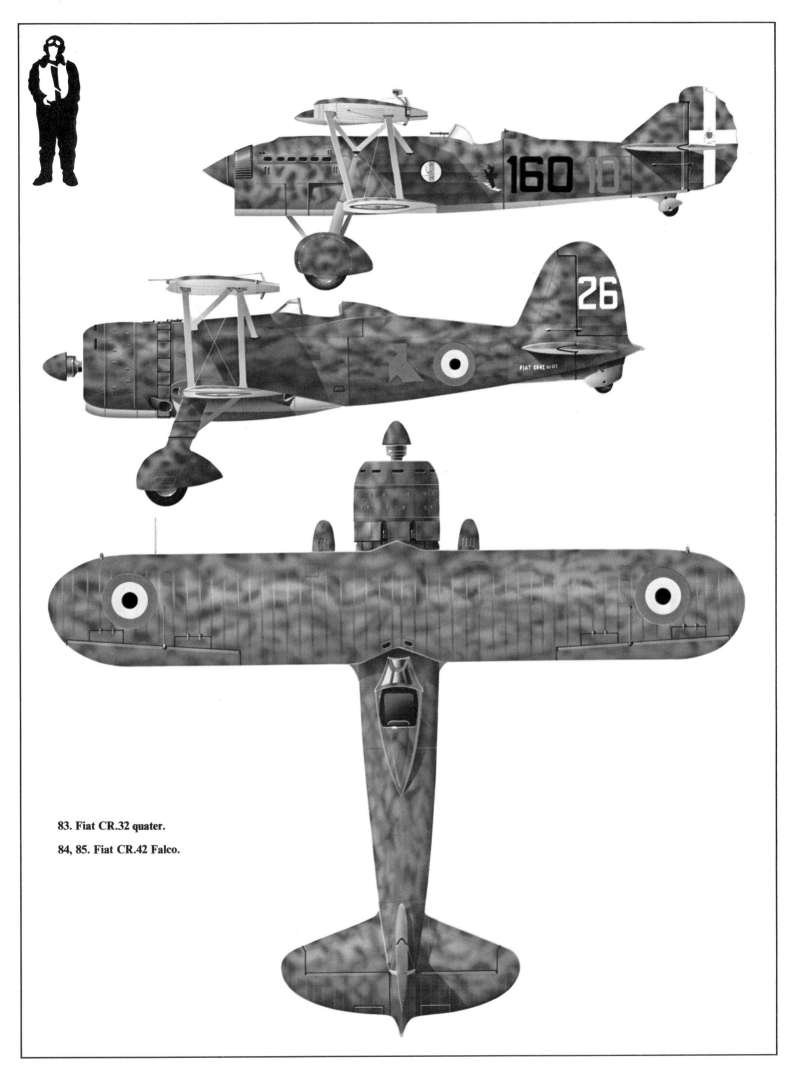

83. Fiat CR.32 quater.

84, 85. Fiat CR.42 Falco.

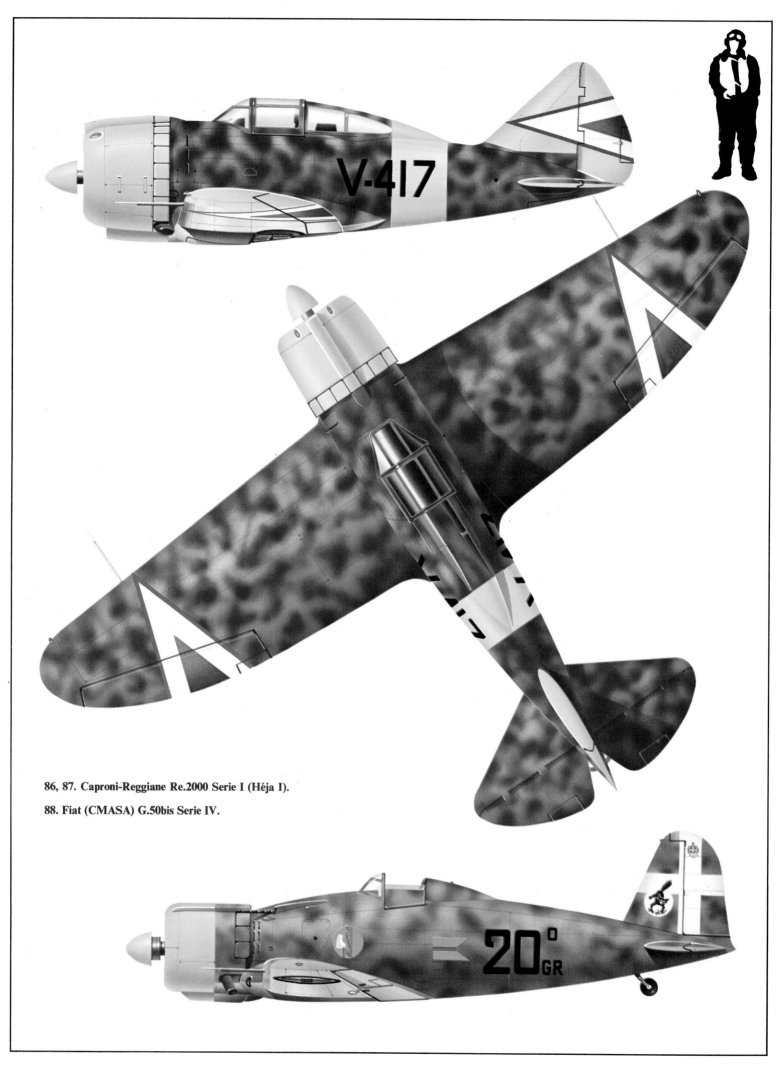

86, 87. Caproni-Reggiane Re.2000 Serie I (Héja I).

88. Fiat (CMASA) G.50bis Serie IV.

89. Macchi MC.200 Saetta.

90, 91. Macchi MC.205V Veltro.

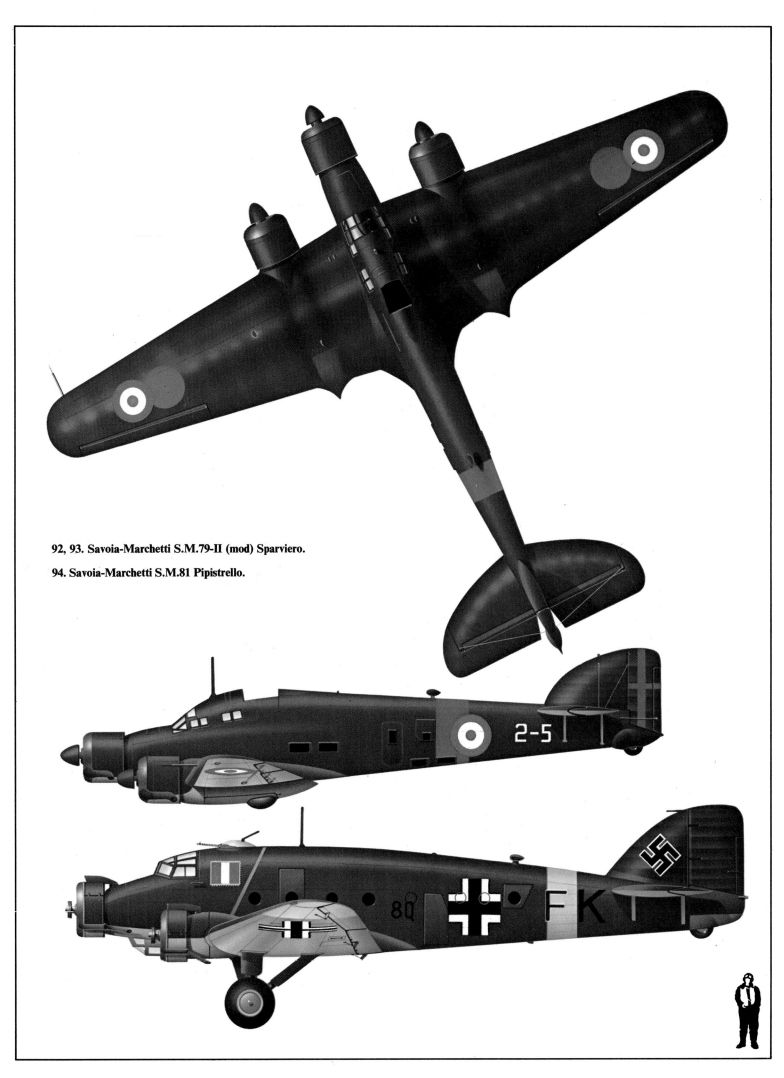

92, 93. Savoia-Marchetti S.M.79-II (mod) Sparviero.

94. Savoia-Marchetti S.M.81 Pipistrello.

95, 96. Aichi D3A1 'Val' (Navy Type 99 Carrier Bomber, Model 11).

97. Nakajima B5N2 'Kate' (Navy Type 97 Carrier Attack Bomber, Model 12).

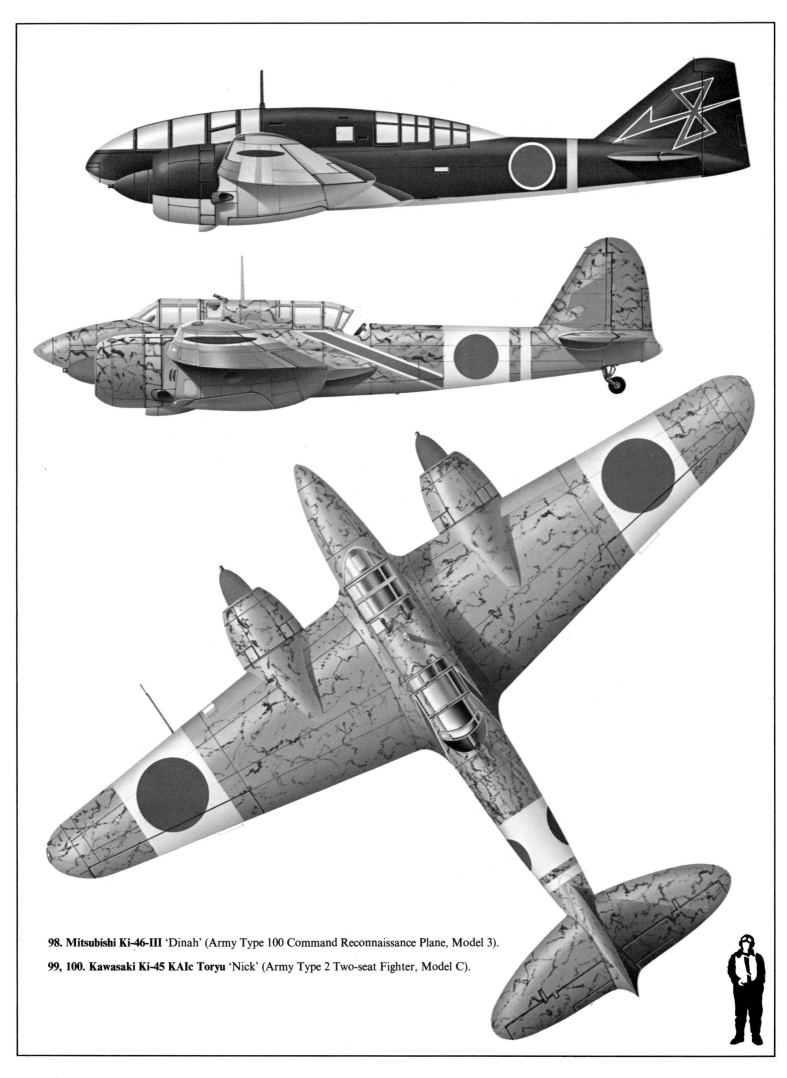

98. Mitsubishi Ki-46-III 'Dinah' (Army Type 100 Command Reconnaissance Plane, Model 3).

99, 100. Kawasaki Ki-45 KAIc Toryu 'Nick' (Army Type 2 Two-seat Fighter, Model C).

101. Nakajima Ki-27b 'Nate' (Army Type 97 Fighter, Model B).

102, 103. Kawasaki Ki-61-I KAI Hien 'Tony' (Army Type 3 Fighter, Model 1).

104, 105. Mitsubishi G3M2 'Nell' (Navy Type 96 Attack Bomber, Model 22).

106. Mitsubishi Ki-67-I KAI Hiryu 'Peggy' (Army Type 4 Special Attack Plane).

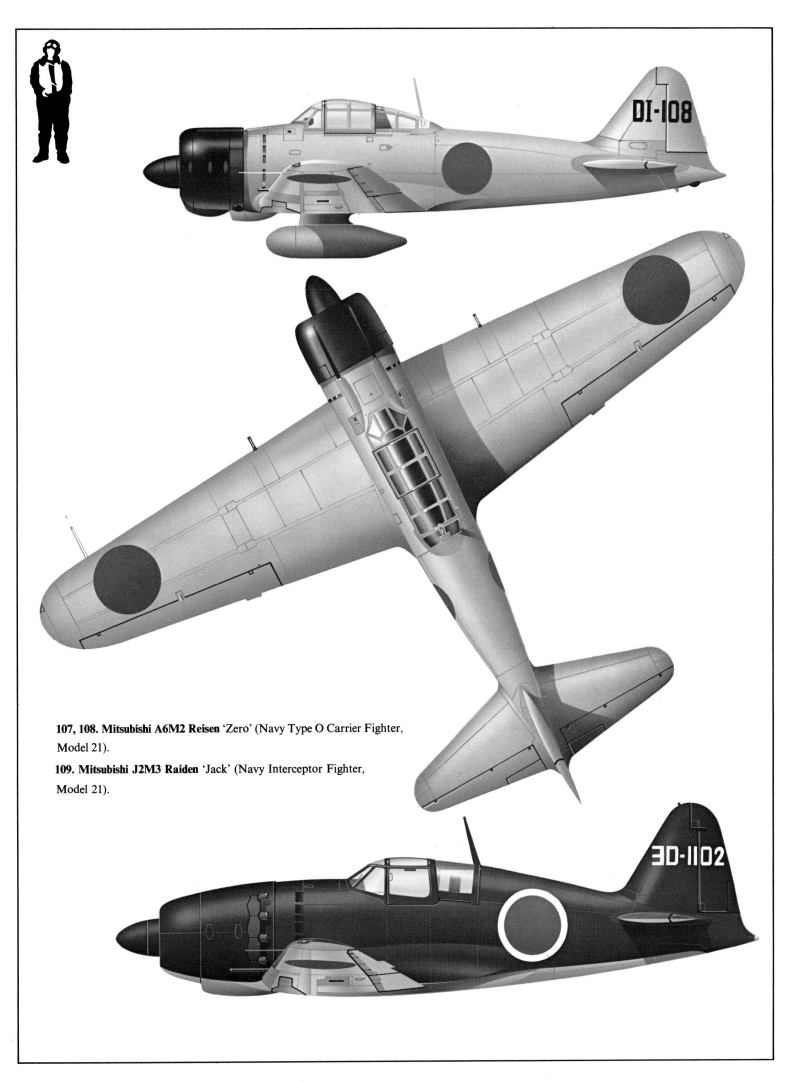

107, 108. Mitsubishi A6M2 Reisen 'Zero' (Navy Type O Carrier Fighter, Model 21).

109. Mitsubishi J2M3 Raiden 'Jack' (Navy Interceptor Fighter, Model 21).

110. Mitsubishi Ki-21-IIb 'Sally' (Army Type 97 Heavy Bomber, Model 2B).

111. Mitsubishi G4M1 'Betty' (Navy Type 1 Attack Bomber, Model 11).

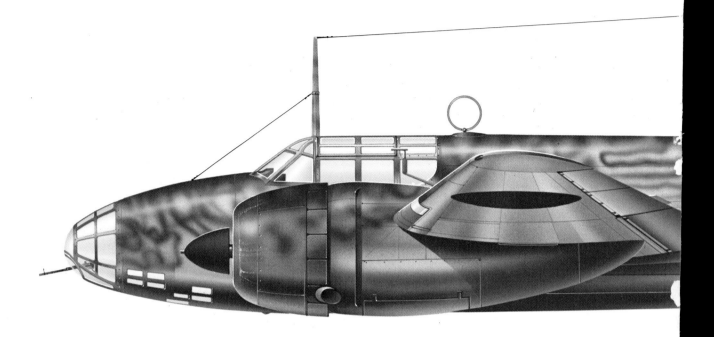

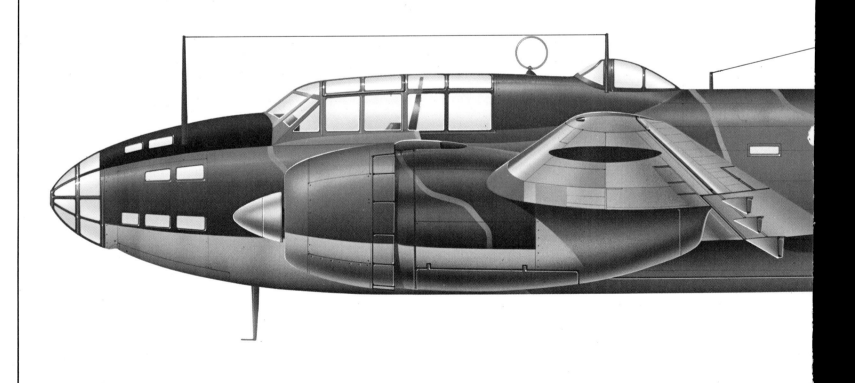

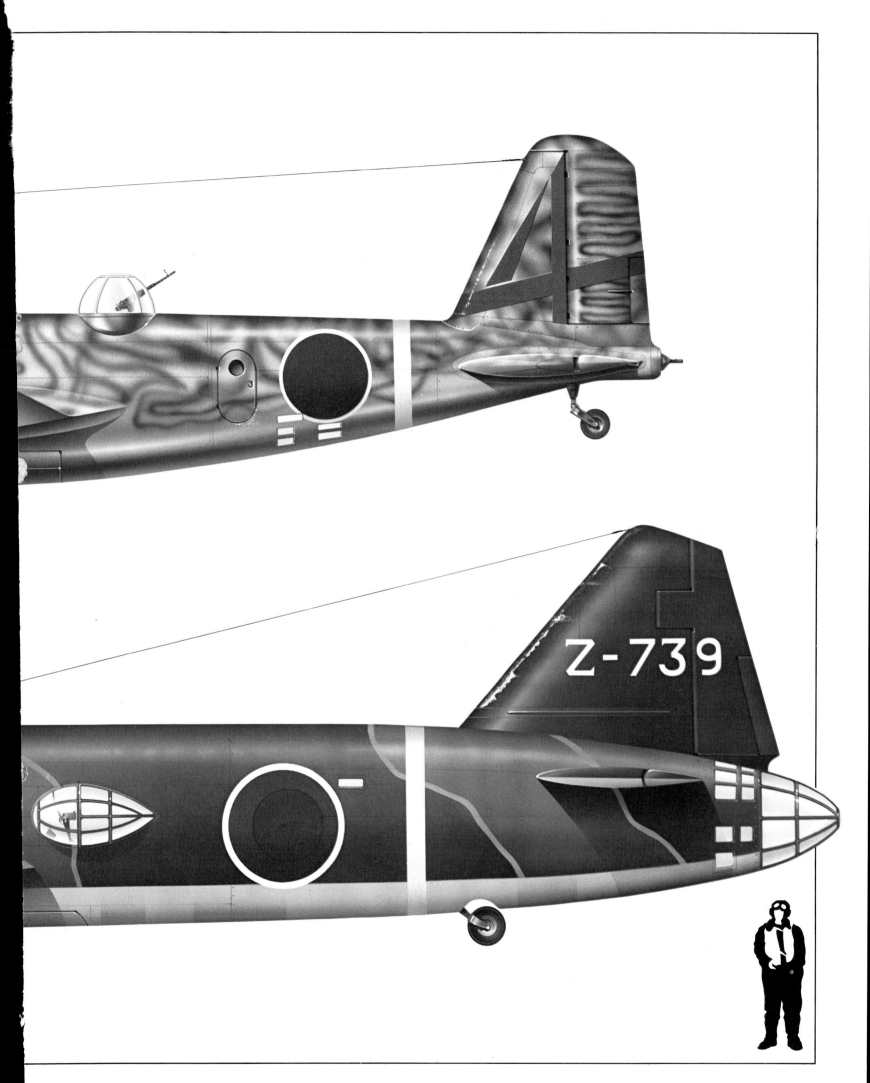

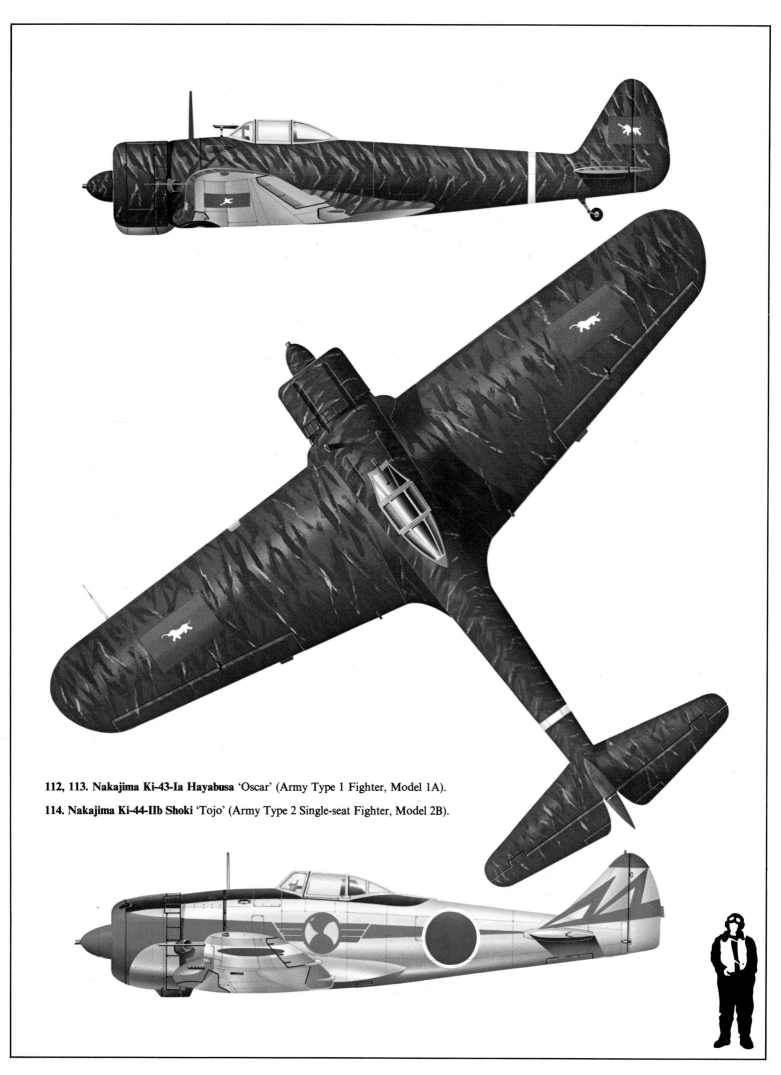

112, 113. Nakajima Ki-43-Ia Hayabusa 'Oscar' (Army Type 1 Fighter, Model 1A).

114. Nakajima Ki-44-IIb Shoki 'Tojo' (Army Type 2 Single-seat Fighter, Model 2B).

115, 116. Fokker D.XXI.

117. Fokker G.IA.

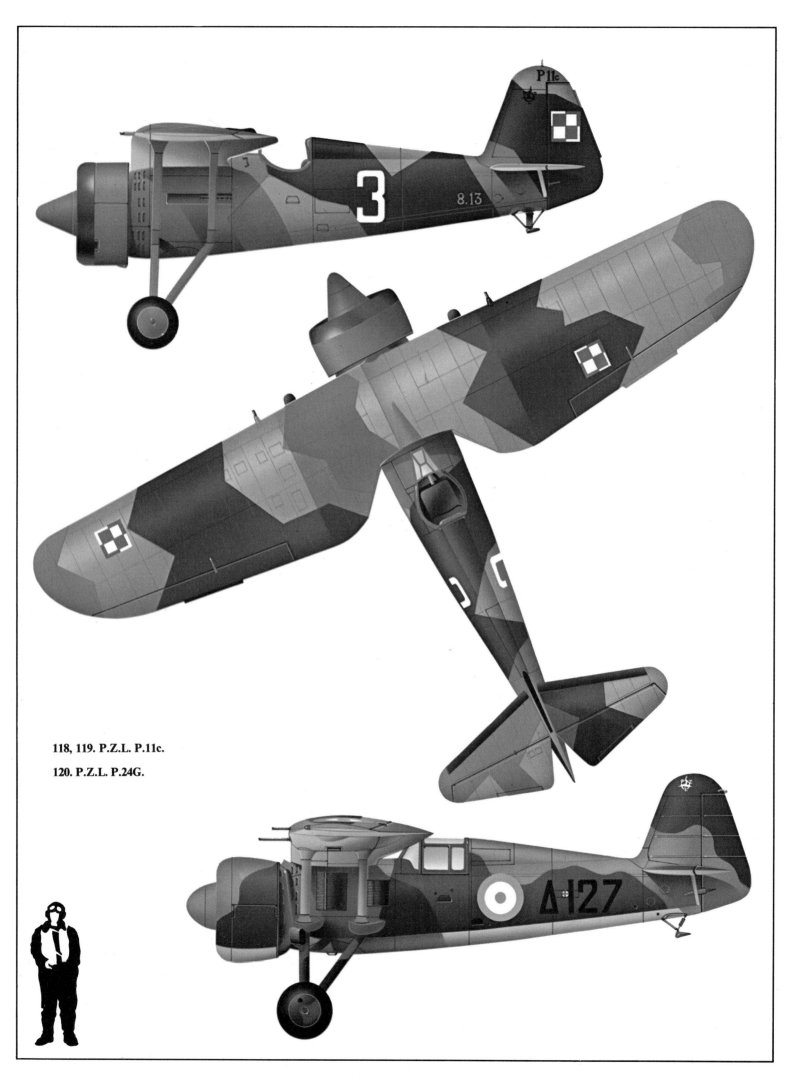

118, 119. P.Z.L. P.11c.

120. P.Z.L. P.24G.

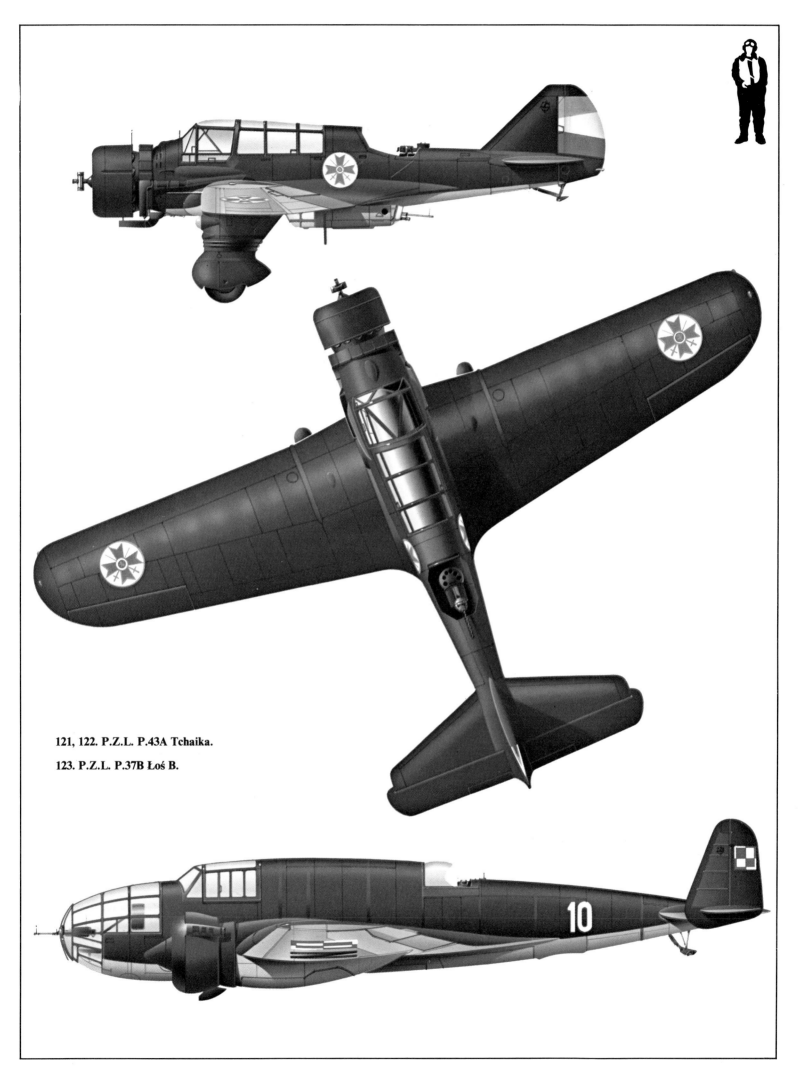

121, 122. P.Z.L. P.43A Tchaika.

123. P.Z.L. P.37B Łoś B.

124, 125. IAR 81C.

126. IAR 39.

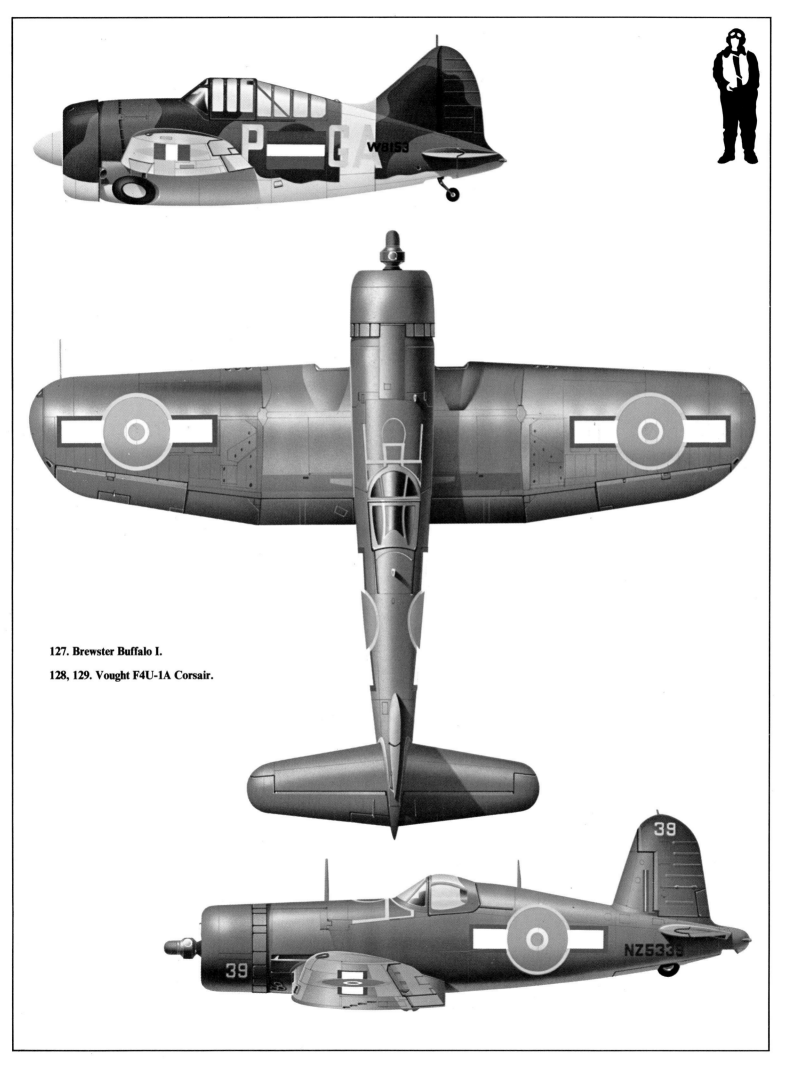

127. Brewster Buffalo I.

128, 129. Vought F4U-1A Corsair.

130. Martin PBM-3D Mariner.

131, 132. Consolidated (Vickers) 0A-10A Catalina.

133. Curtiss Mohawk IV.

134, 135. Curtiss P-40N Warhawk.

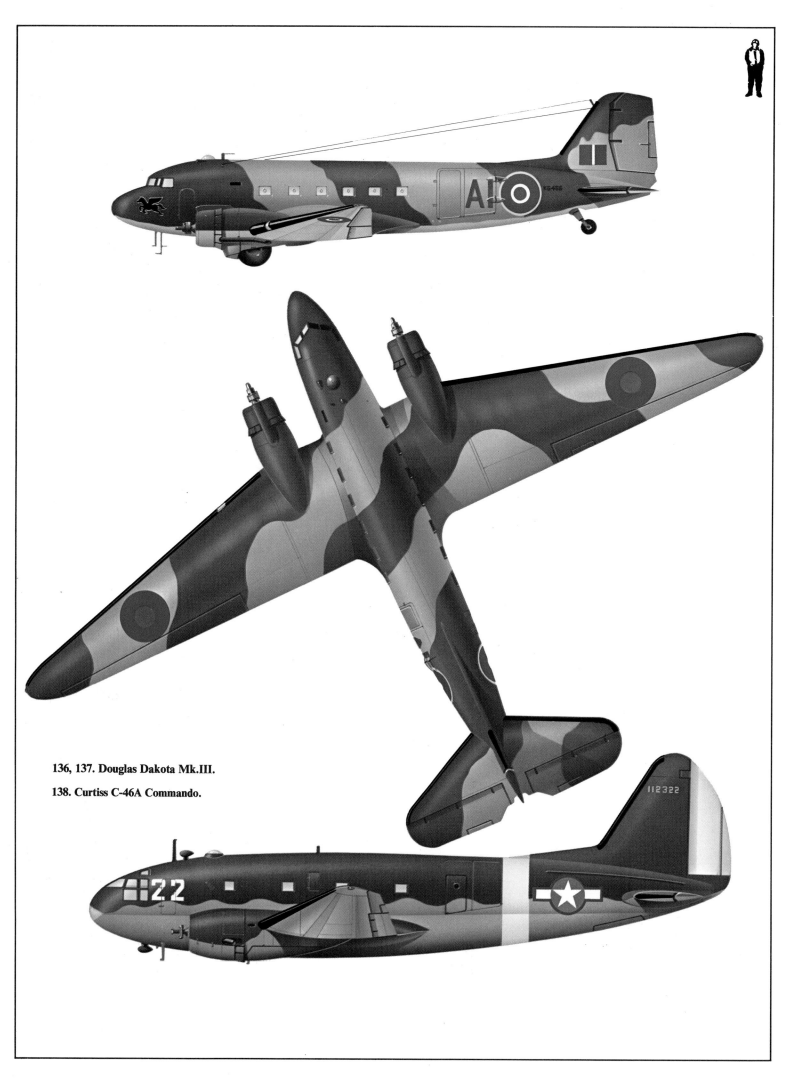

136, 137. Douglas Dakota Mk.III.

138. Curtiss C-46A Commando.

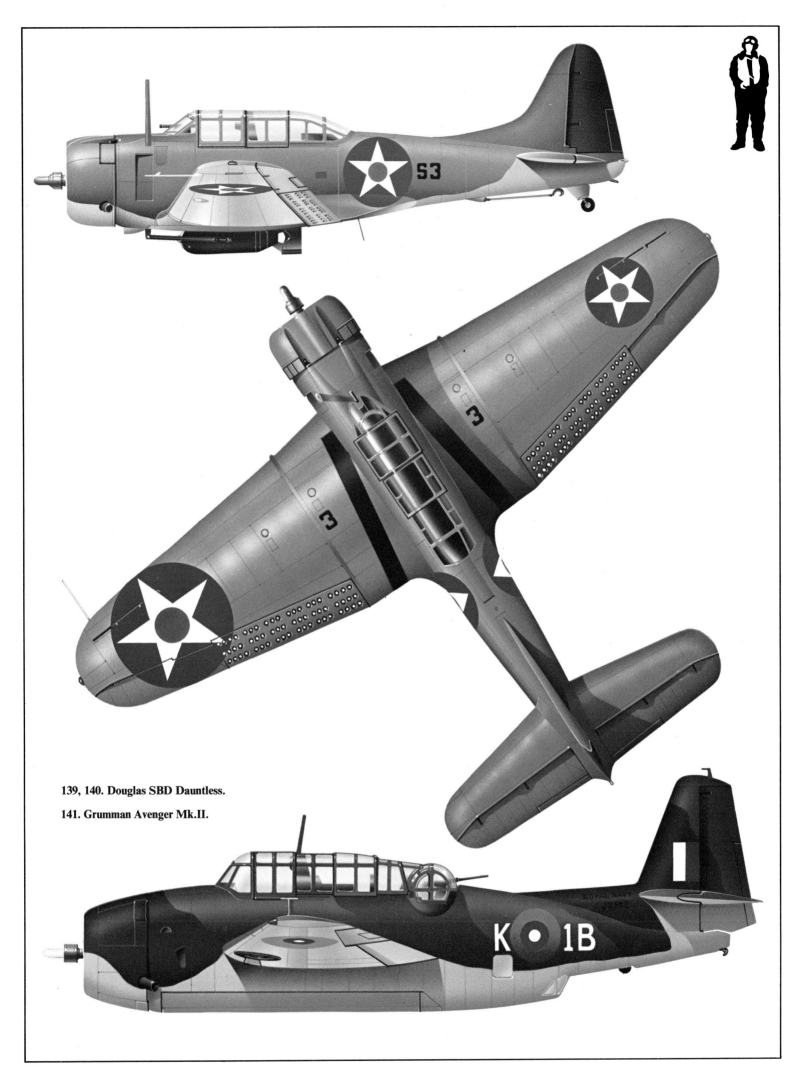

139, 140. Douglas SBD Dauntless.

141. Grumman Avenger Mk.II.

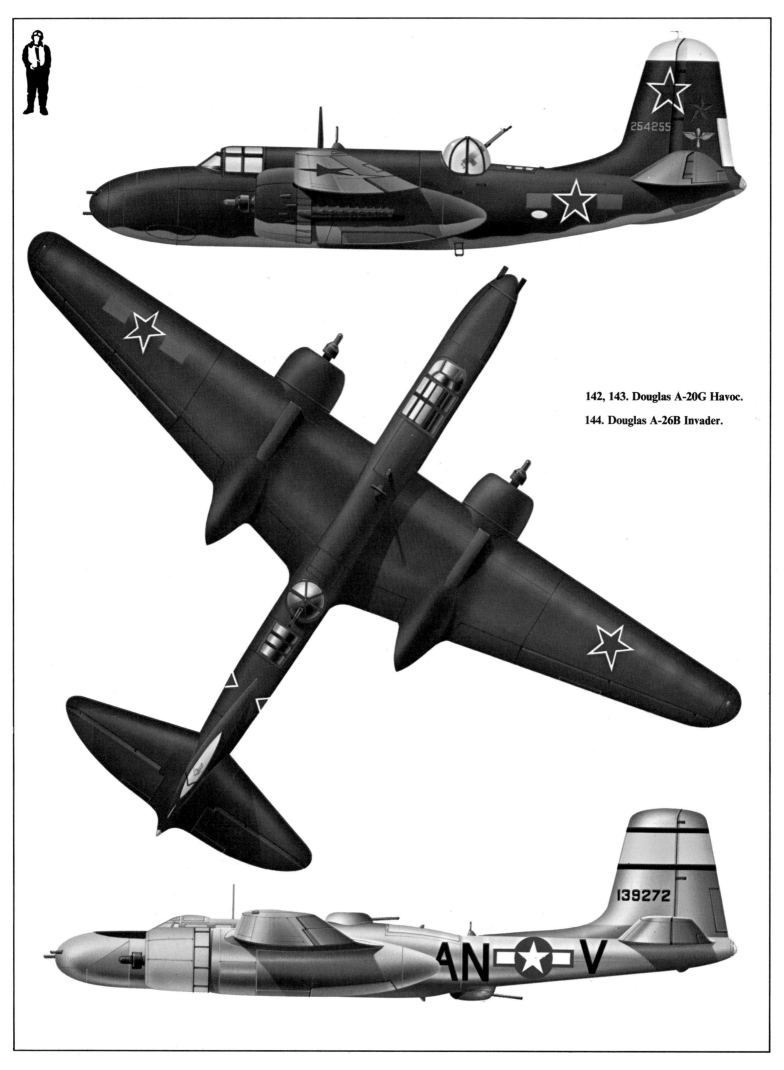

142, 143. Douglas A-20G Havoc.

144. Douglas A-26B Invader.

145. Grumman Martlet I.

146, 147. Grumman F6F-5 Hellcat.

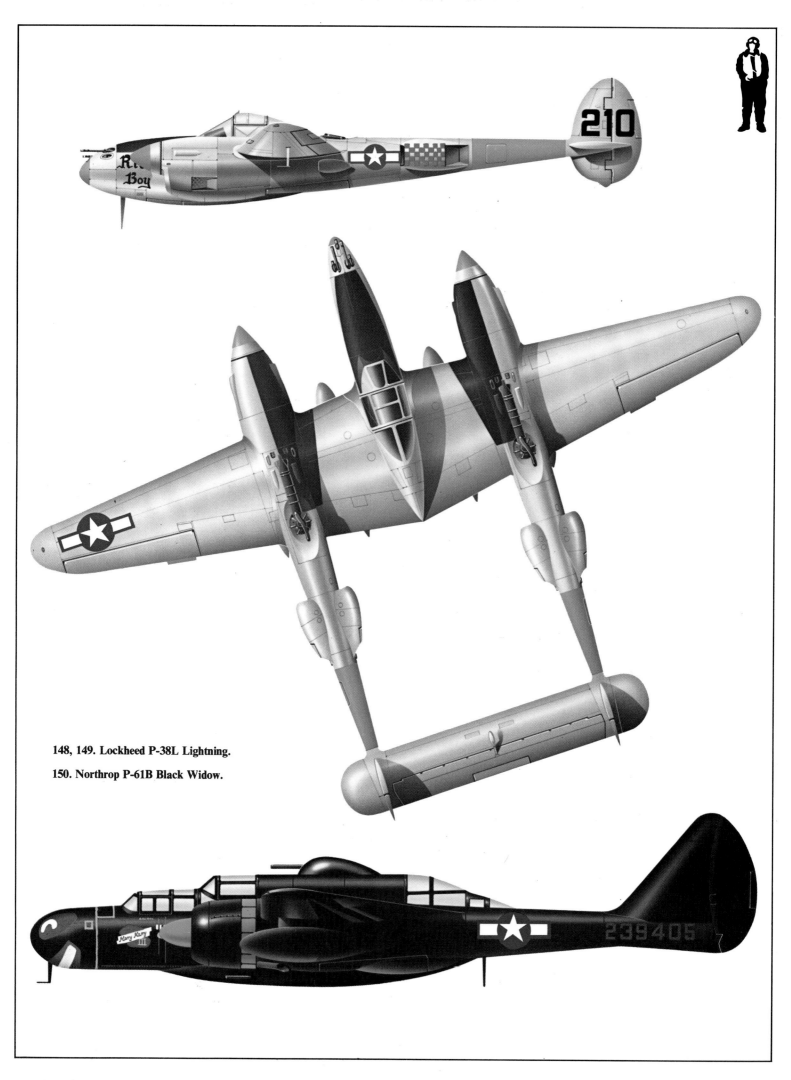

148, 149. Lockheed P-38L Lightning.

150. Northrop P-61B Black Widow.

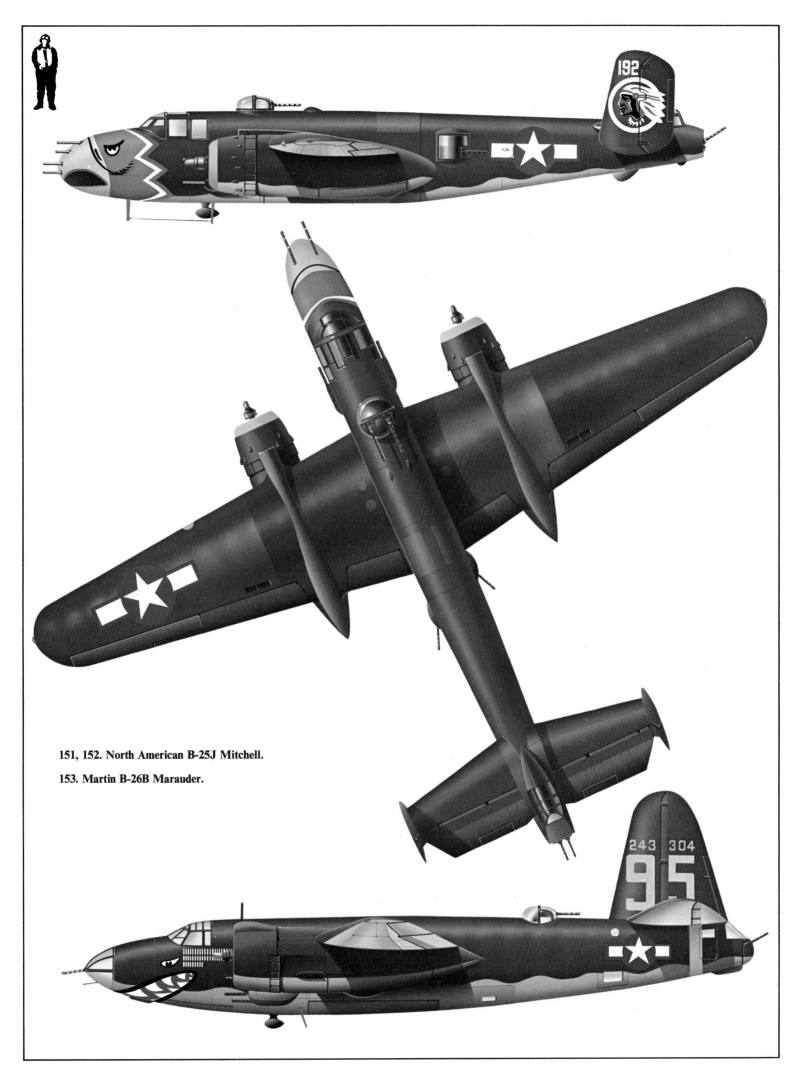

151, 152. North American B-25J Mitchell.

153. Martin B-26B Marauder.

154. Consolidated B-24H Liberator.

155. Boeing B-17F Flying Fortress.

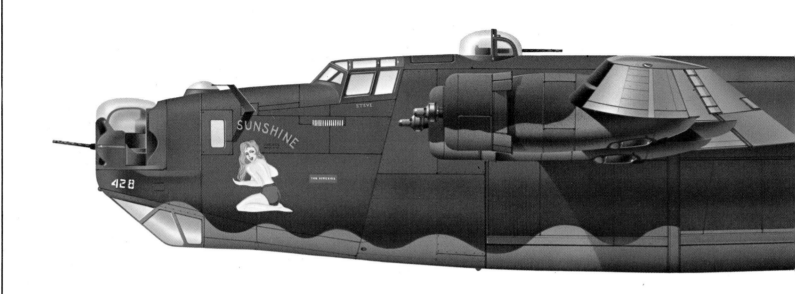

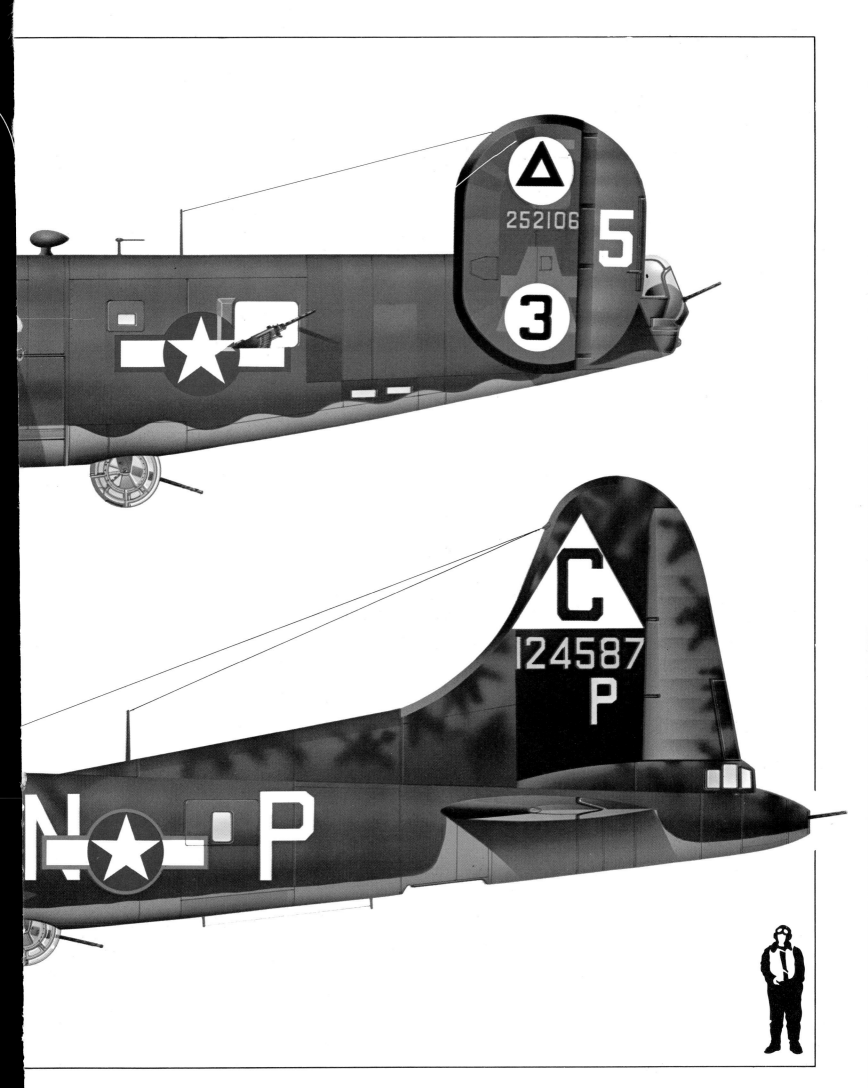

156. North American Mustang I.

157, 158. North American P-51D Mustang.

159. Republic P-47M Thunderbolt.

160, 161. Republic P-47N Thunderbolt.

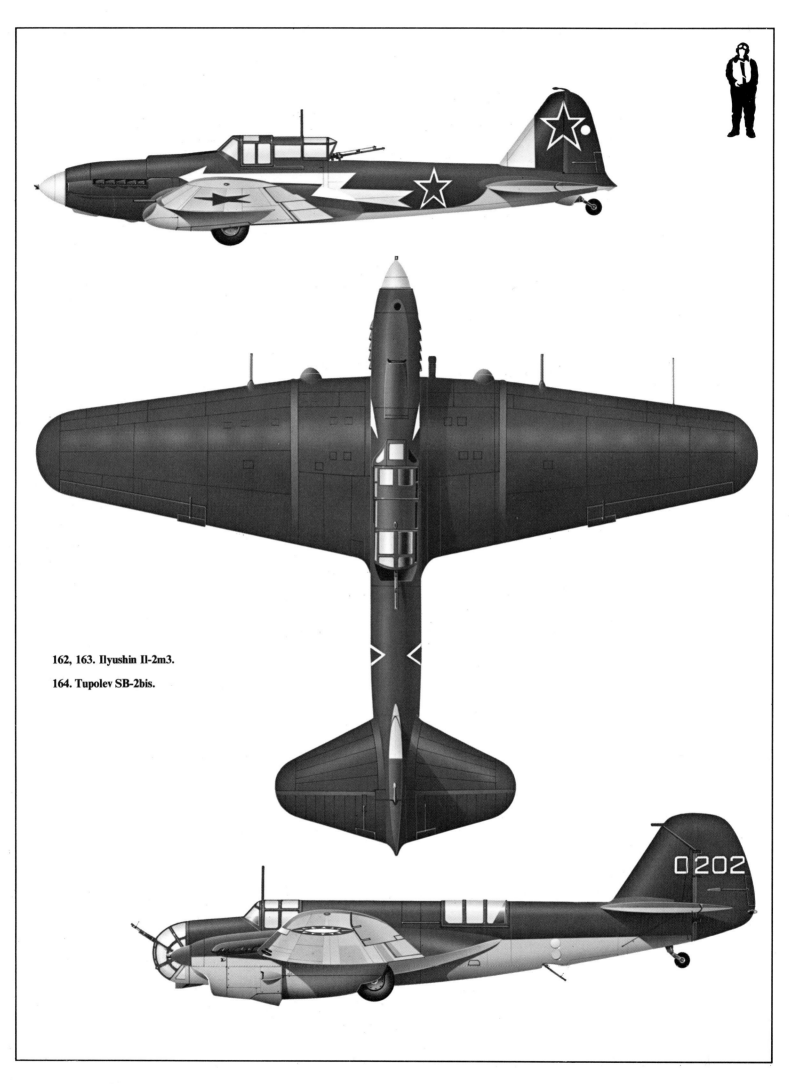

162, 163. Ilyushin Il-2m3.

164. Tupolev SB-2bis.

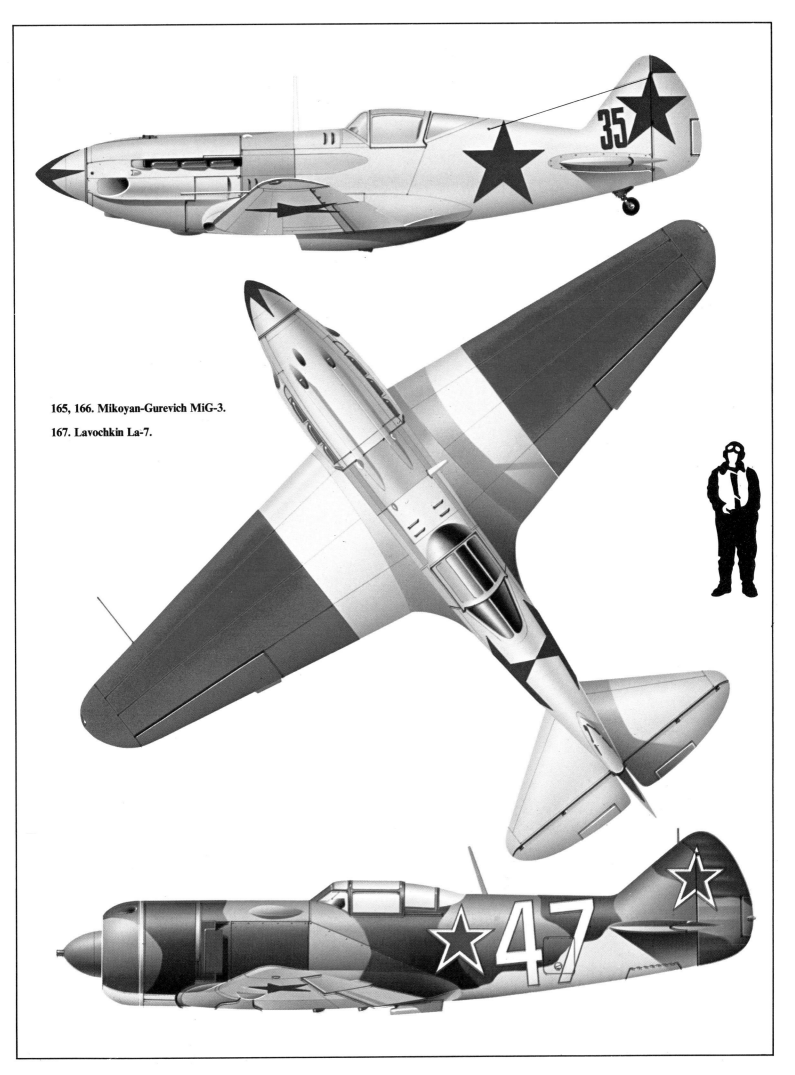

165, 166. Mikoyan-Gurevich MiG-3.

167. Lavochkin La-7.

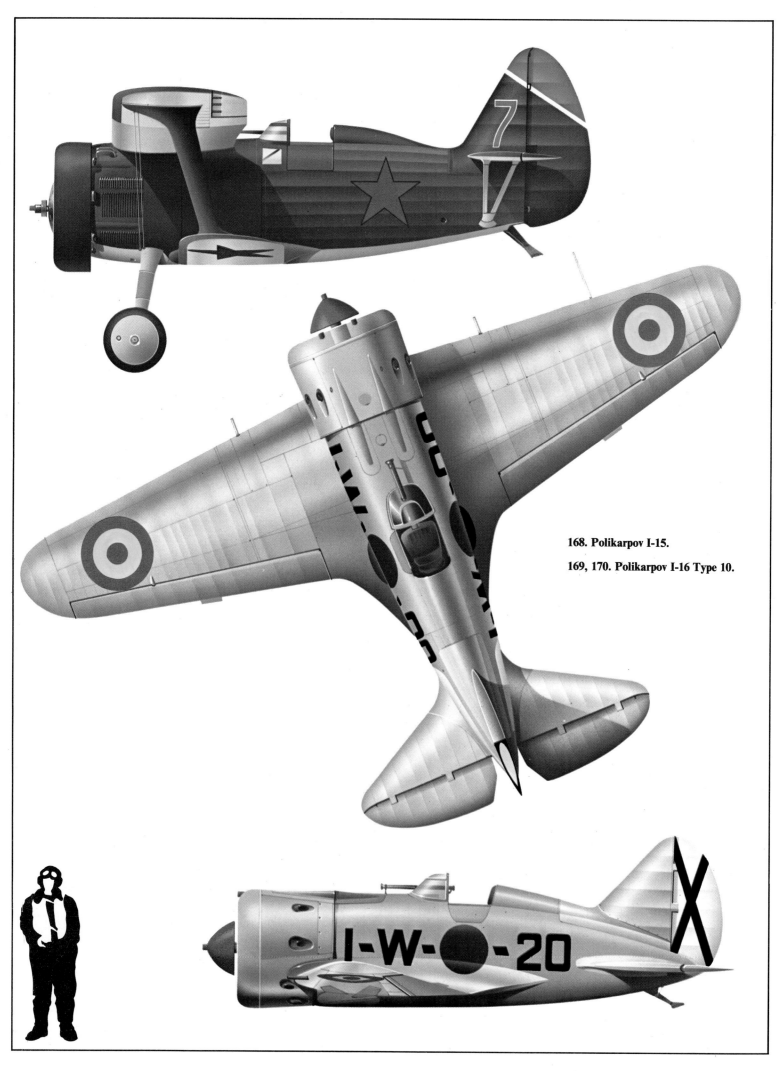

168. Polikarpov I-15.

169, 170. Polikarpov I-16 Type 10.

171. Tupolev TB-3 (ANT-6).

172, 173. Petlyakov Pe-8 (TB-7).

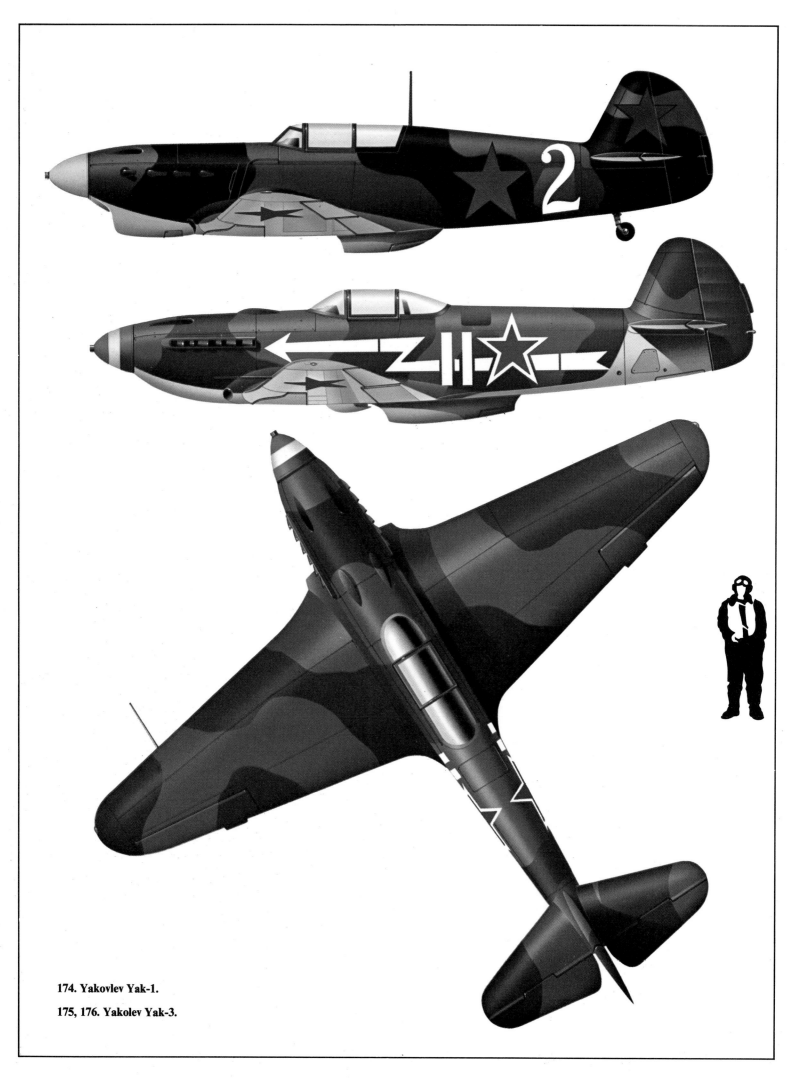

174. Yakovlev Yak-1.

175, 176. Yakolev Yak-3.

AUSTRALIA

Commonwealth CA–5 Wirraway

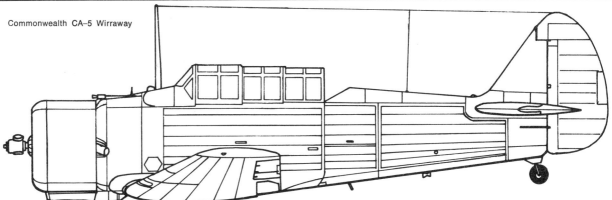

Manufacturer: Commonwealth.
Model: CA–1 Wirraway (Challenge).
Type: General-purpose/trainer.
Power Plant: One 600hp Common-
wealth-built Pratt and Whitney
S1H1–G Wasp.
Performance:
maximum speed 205mph (330km/hr).
cruising speed 182mph (283km/hr).
normal range 720 miles (1,158km).
initial rate of climb 1,950ft/min
  (594m/min).
service ceiling 23,000ft (7,010m).
Weights:
empty 3,980lb (1,805kg).
loaded 6,353lb (2,881kg).
Dimensions:
wing span 43ft 0in (13.11m).
length 27ft 10in (8.48m).
height 12ft 0in (3.66m).
wing area 255.75sq ft (23.76sq m).
Armament: Two fixed forward-
firing .303in Vickers Mk V
machine-guns in upper cowling;
one flexible .303in Vickers Mk I
machine-gun in rear cockpit; max
(underwing) bomb load 500lb
(227kg), plus (optional) ventral
stores/flares.
Crew: 2.
In Service: Australia, Netherlands
(NEIAF 1).
Variants (with no. built):
Prototypes: Two imported North
American NA–32/33 trainers (2).
Production model: Modified NA–33;
redesigned (strengthened) wings
and tail; addn armament/equip-
ment; produced in seven blocks;
CA–1, 3, 5, 7–9, 16 (CA–20 post-
war RAN trainer conversions)
(755).
Total Production: 755.
Remarks: First flown March 1939,
Wirraway general-purpose intermediate trainer pressed into
immediate operational service
opening weeks Pacific War, fought
rearguard actions Rabaul/Malaya,
Dec 1941–March 1942, participated
New Guinea campaign, late 1942–
mid 1943, primarily army co-
operation and tactical reconnaissance duties; replaced by

Boomerang (though not before
claiming destruction of one
Mitsubishi 'Zero'), Wirraway
resumed original training role until
final retirement 1959.

Manufacturer: Commonwealth.
Model: CA–13 Boomerang II.
Type: Interceptor/reconnaissance-
fighter.
Power Plant: One 1,200hp (Com-
monwealth-built) Pratt and Whitney
R–1830 S3C4–G Twin Wasp.
Performance:
maximum speed at sea level 273mph
  (439km/hr).
maximum speed at 15,500ft
  (4,724m) 305mph (490km/hr).
cruising speed 190mph (306km/hr).
maximum range 1,600 miles
  (2,574km).
initial rate of climb 2,940ft/min
  (896m/min).
service ceiling 34,000ft (10,363m).
Weights:
empty 5,373lb (2,437kg).
maximum 8,249lb (3,742kg).
Dimensions:
wing span 36ft 0in (10.97m).
length 26ft 9in (8.15m).
height 13ft 0in (3.96m).

wing area 225sq ft (20.9sq m).
Armament: Two 20mm Hispano
Mk II (or CAC) cannon and four
.303in Browning Mk II machine-
guns in wings; provision for four
20lb (9kg) smoke bombs.
Crew: 1.
In Service: Australia.
Variants (with no. built):
CA–12 Boomerang I: Prototype and
initial production model (105).
CA–13 Boomerang II: Improved
CA–12; flame-damper exhaust;
minor detail modifications; some
equipped for PR role (95).
CA–14/14A: Experimental prototype; General Electric turbo-
supercharger; extended tailfin;
modified wing root (CA–14A
extensive fuselage, vertical tail
surface redesign) (1).
CA–19 Boomerang II: As CA–13;
minor detail modifications; final
39 examples with F24 PR camera
as standard equipment (49).
Total Production: 250.
Remarks: Designed and developed
around basic CA–1 Wirraway
structure (to which was mated
new forward fuselage and cockpit),
CA–12 Boomerang entered service

late 1942; replacing former in
first-line units from mid-1943;
employed both aerial defence
western and northern Australia,
and in army co-operation role New
Guinea/SWPA campaigns, 1943–
45; although probably only WWII
fighter to enjoy two-year operational career without being able to
claim single enemy aircraft
destroyed, Boomerang performed
valuable ground-support, artillery
spotter and target-marker duties as
integral part Allied land/air
offensive.
Colour Reference: Plates 1, 2. Commonwealth CA–13 Boomerang II
QE.Z (A46–137) of No 4 Army
Co-operation Squadron, No 10
(Operational) Group, RAAF,
Nadzab, New Guinea, Feb 1944;
standard foliage green/dark earth/
sky blue finish (see Bristol Beaufighter Mk 21, plate 53, for
altn overall foliage green scheme);
all-white tail surfaces (in this
instance with foliage green tip) and
wing leading edges (two-thirds span
on No 4 Squadron aircraft) official
SWPA theatre recognition
markings.

Manufacturer: Tugan (Wackett).
Model: Gannet.
Type: Survey/ambulance.
Power Plant: Two 200hp
de Havilland Gypsy Six.
Performance:
maximum speed 150mph (241km/hr).
range 550 miles (885km).
initial rate of climb 850ft/min
  (260m/min).
service ceiling 17,000ft (5,180m).
Weights:
empty 3,242lb (1,471kg).
loaded 5,400lb (2,449kg).
Dimensions:
wing span 52ft 0in (15.85m).
length 34ft 6in (10.51m).
Crew/Accommodation: 2/2–4 litters
plus medic/s.
In Service: Australia.
Variants:
Gannet: High-wing fixed-under-
carriage cartographic survey
aircraft.
Remarks: Originally built by
Tugan (but renamed after designer
upon take-over by Commonwealth),
six Gannets employed by RAAF
for general-purpose survey/
ambulance/light transport duties,
1936–46.

BELGIUM

Renard R–31

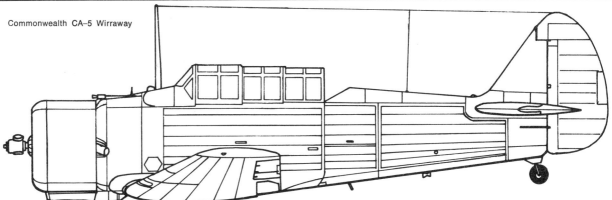

Manufacturer: Renard.
Model: R–31.
Type: Tactical reconnaissance/army
co-operation.
Power Plant: One 485hp Rolls-
Royce Kestrel IIS.
Performance:
maximum speed at sea level 169mph
  (272km/hr).
maximum speed at 19,685ft
  (6,000m) 199mph (320km/hr).
cruising speed 174mph (280km/hr).
normal range 621 miles (1,000km).
service ceiling 29,530ft (9,000m).
Weights:
empty 2,734lb (1,240kg).
loaded 4,410lb (2,000kg).
Dimensions:
wing span 47ft 3in (14.4m).
length 30ft 2¼in (9.2m).
height 9ft 7½in (2.93m).
wing area 344.45sq ft (32sq m).
Armament: One or two fixed
forward-firing 7.62mm Vickers
machine-gun/s plus one flexible
7.62mm Vickers 'K' gun in rear
cockpit.
Crew: 2.
In Service: Belgium.
Variants (with no. built):
R31: Prototype; one Rolls-Royce
Kestrel IIS (1).
R–31: Production model; two-seat
reconnaissance version; open
cockpits; Renard-built (12);
SABCA licence-built (22).
R–32: Modified R–31; Enclosed
pilot's cockpit; one 870hp Gnome-
Rhône 14Krsd (subsequently one
860hp Hispano-Suiza 12Ydrs);
one R–31 conversion/reconversion.
Total Production: 35.
Remarks: First flown Oct 1932,
twenty-one R–31s still equipped two
Escadrilles Belgian AF at time of
German invasion, 10 May 1940;
operated tactical reconnaissance
role throughout ensuing eighteen-
day campaign; despite heavy

attrition responsible for carrying
out final Belgian AF mission prior
capitulation, reconnaissance sortie
Ostende area.

Manufacturer: Stampe-et-Vertongen.
Model: RSV 32/90.
Type: Trainer/liaison.
Power Plant: One 90hp Anzani
10C.
Performance:
maximum speed at sea level
  78mph (125km/hr).
time to 3,280ft (1,000m) 7min 0sec.
service ceiling 16,400ft (5,000m).
Weights:
empty 1,168lb (530kg).
loaded 1,808lb (820kg).
Dimensions:
wing span 36ft 9in (11.2m).
length 24ft 1½in (7.35m).

height 9ft 2½in (2.8m).
wing area 344.45sq ft (32.0sq m).
Crew/Accommodation: 1/1.
In Service: Belgium.
Variants:
RSV 32/90: Civil and military
trainer versions: one Anzani 10C.
RSV 32/100, 32/105, 32/120: Civil
trainer versions; one 100hp Renard,
105hp Hermes, and 120hp Gipsy
resp.
RSV 32/110: Military trainer
version; one 110hp Lorraine-
Dietrich.
Total Production: 57.
Remarks: Built between 1923 and
1932, majority RSV 32s served pre-
war Belgian AF; all military
examples long obsolete by outbreak WWII, but several late
model civil RSV 32/120s impressed

for liaison/communications duties during 'eighteen-day war' (May 1940).

Manufacturer: Stampe-et-Vertongen.
Model: S.V.4B.
Type: Trainer/liaison.
Power Plant: One 130hp de Havilland Gipsy Major I.
Performance:
maximum speed at sea level 127mph (205km/hr).
cruising speed 109mph (175km/hr).
normal range 248miles (400km).
time to 3,280ft (1,000m) 4min 0sec.
service ceiling 17,060ft (5,200m).
Weights:
empty 1,058lb (480kg).
loaded 1,720lb (780kg).
Dimensions:
wing span 27ft 6¾in (8.4m).
length 21ft 11¾in (6.7m).
height 8ft 0¼in (2.45m).
wing area 193.75sq ft (18sq m).
Crew/Accommodation: 1/1.
In Service: Belgium, Germany (captured ex-Belgian), Great Britain (1 escapee/impressed).
Variants (with no. built):
S.V.4: Prototype and initial production model; one 120hp de Havilland Gipsy III (6).
S.V.4A: Advanced aerobatics version; one 140hp Renault 4–PO5.
S.V.4B: Improved S.V.4; Reduced dimensions; redesigned wings; pre- and post-war production; latter with enclosed cockpits (35 pre-, and 66 post-war).
S.V.4C: As S.V.4B; one 140hp Renault 4-Pei; inc French (SNCA du Nord) and Algerian (AIAA) licence-production (approx 940).
S.V.4D: Post-war model. One 175hp Mathis C7R (1).
Total Production: approx 1,000.
Remarks: Prototype first flown 1933, approx twenty S.V.4Bs completed for Belgian AF prior German invasion, 10 May 1940; these, plus several impressed civil models, employed emergency liaison role; majority former escaped France, number latter seized by Germany; production both S.V.4B/C resumed post-war; extensive military trainer/civil aerobatic use into seventies.

Manufacturer: Stampe-et-Vertongen.
Model: S.V.5.
Type: Trainer/reconnaissance.
Power Plant: One 340hp Armstrong-Siddeley Cheetah IX or X.
Performance:
maximum speed at 8,530ft (2,600m) 172mph (277km/hr).
time to 13,120ft (4,000m) 10min 30sec.
service ceiling 23,786ft (7,250m).
Weights:
empty 2,250lb (1,020kg).
loaded 3,461lb (1,570kg).
Dimensions:
wing span 34ft 5½in (10.5m).
length 25ft 6¼in (7.78m).
height 9ft 6¼in (2.9m).
wing area 287.4sq ft (26.7sq m).
Armament: One fixed forward-firing machine-gun; one flexible machine-gun in rear cockpit; provision for light bombs.
Crew/Accommodation: 1/1.
In Service: Belgium, Germany. (ex-Latvia), Latvia.
Variants:
S.V.5: Two-seat advanced trainer biplane; provision for one camera in rear cockpit.
Total Production: approx 30.
Remarks: Enlarged and more powerful development of earlier S.V.4, re-engined S.V.5 enjoyed far less success; twenty ordered by Belgian AF, plus ten exported Latvian AF; latter served trainer role prior Soviet annexation, Summer 1940; post-1941 survivor/s incorporated into Luftwaffe as part autonomous Latvian-manned Staffel for reconnaissance/communications duties.

BULGARIA

Manufacturer: State Aircraft Workshop.
Model: LAZ-3a (D.A.R.3a) Garvan (Raven).
Type: Reconnaissance.
Crew: 2.
In Service: Bulgaria.
Variants:
LAZ-3: Initial production model. Two-seat reconnaissance biplane; one 400hp Lorraine-Dietrich or (later models) 480hp Gnome-Rhône Jupiter; open cockpit.
LAZ-3a (D.A.R.–3a): Re-engined LAZ-3; one 655hp Wright Cyclone or 750hp Alfa Romeo 126; late models with enclosed cockpit.
Remarks: First built 1929, improved LAZ-3a (D.A.R.–3a) appeared 1939–40; rejected first-line reconnaissance duties, served primarily training, liaison, and ancillary roles.

Manufacturer: State Aircraft Workshop.
Model: D.A.R.6 Sinigier (Titmouse).
Type: Trainer/communications.
Power Plant: One 145hp Walter Mars.
Performance:
maximum speed at sea level 111mph (178km/hr).
cruising speed 96mph (155km/hr).
normal range 445 miles (715km).
time to 9,840ft (3,000m) 12min 0sec.
Weights:
empty 1,124lb (510kg).
normal 1,698lb (770kg).
Dimensions:
wing span 29ft 8¼in (9.05m).
length 22ft 5¾in (6.85m).
height 9ft 4¼in (2.85m).
wing area 207.75sq ft (19.3sq m).
Crew/Accommodation: 1/1.
In Service: Bulgaria.
Variants:
D.A.R.6: Prototype and initial production model; basic trainer version; one 85hp Walter Vega.
D.A.R.6: Elementary/conversion trainer version; uprated engine; Townend ring.
Remarks: Two-seat trainer biplane first flown 1929, some half-dozen D.A.R.6s still on strength Bulgarian AF, Spring 1940; equipped one training Eskadra attached to mixed fighter/bomber Regt for training and communications duties.

Manufacturer: State Aircraft Workshop.
Model: D.A.R.10F.
Type: Light bomber/dive-bomber.
Power Plant: One 960hp Fiat A.74 RC 38.
Performance:
maximum speed at sea level 236mph (380km/hr).
maximum speed at 16,400ft (5,000m) 282mph (454km/hr).
normal range 870 miles (1,400km).
service ceiling 29,500ft (8,990m).
Weights:
empty 4,475lb (2,030kg).
loaded 6,390lb (2,900kg).
Dimensions:
wing span 41ft 6in (12.65m).
length 32ft 3in (9.83 m).
wing area 246.28sq ft (22.8sq m).
Armament: Two fixed forward-firing 7.92mm MG 17 machine-guns; two 20mm MG FF cannon in wings; one flexible 7.92mm MG 15 machine-gun in rear cockpit; max bomb load 1,100lb (500kg).
Crew: 2.
In Service: Bulgaria.
Variants:
D.A.R.–10: Prototype; light reconnaissance-bomber/general-purpose version.
D.A.R.–10F: Production model; dive-bomber version; modified D.A.R.–10; structural strengthening; revised armament.
Remarks: First flown early 1941, limited number D.A.R.–10Fs supplied Bulgarian AF; brief first line service prior replacement by Junkers Ju 87D–5; subsequently employed in close-support anti-partisan ground operations in Yugoslavia.

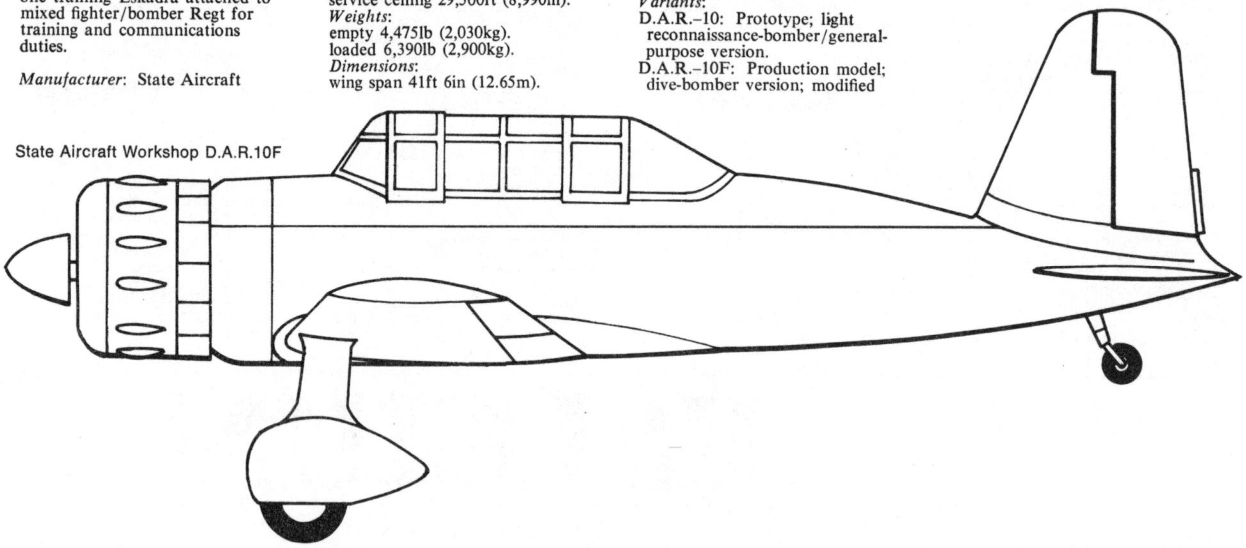
State Aircraft Workshop D.A.R.10F

CANADA

Manufacturer: Fleet.
Model: 50K.
Type: Light transport.
Power Plant: Two 330hp Jacobs L–6MB.
Performance (landplane):
maximum speed at sea level 148mph (238km/hr).
cruising speed 128mph (206km/hr).
normal range 660 miles (1,062km).
initial rate of climb 1,000ft/min (304.8m/min).
service ceiling 15,000ft (4,572m).
Weights:
empty 4,665lb (2,116kg).
loaded 8,327lb (3,777kg).
Dimensions:
wing span 45ft 0in (13.72m).
length 35ft 10in (10.92m).
height 13ft 1in (3.99m).
wing area 528sq ft (49.05sq m).
Crew/Payload/Accommodation: 2/2,960lb (1,343kg)/12.
In Service: Canada.
Variants:
Model 50K: Light cargo or passenger transport biplane; altn wheel, float or ski undercarriage.
Total Production: 2.
Remarks: First flown 1938, both Model 50Ks impressed RCAF service 1942–44; operated as 50K Freighters in cargo and passenger transport roles.

Manufacturer: Noorduyn.
Model: UC-64A Norseman.
Type: General-purpose transport.
Power Plant: One 600hp Pratt & Whitney R–1340–AN–1 Wasp.
Performance:
maximum speed at 5,000ft (1,525m) 165mph (266km/hr).
normal range 600 miles (966km).
service ceiling 17,000ft (5,182m).
Weights:
maximum 7,400lb (3,357kg).
Dimensions:
wing span 51ft 8in (15.75m).
length 31ft 9in (9.68m).
height 10ft 1in (3.07m).
wing area 325sq ft (30.2sq m).
Crew/Accommodation: 1/8.
In Service: Australia (14 UC–64A), Brazil (17 UC–64A), Canada, USA (USAAF, USNAF).
Variants (with no. built):
Norseman: Prototype; civil transport version; one (Canadian) Wright R–975–E3 (1).
Norseman MK I–III: Civil transport versions.
Norseman MK IV: Dual-control military trainer/flying classroom (*38*).
Norseman MK V: Post-war civil/military transport version; CCF-built.
Norseman MK VI: Military general-purpose transport version.
Norseman MK VII: Improved Mk V; lengthened fuselage; post-war; prototype only; CCF-built.
(Total Norseman MK I–VII: 158).
YC–64/UC–64A (C–64A): USAAF designation for military general-purpose transport version; inc 34 Lend-Lease to RCAF as Mk VI (753).
C–64B: Floatplane version of C–64A (6).
JA–1: USN designation for UC–64A (*3*).
Total Production: 918.
Remarks: First flown early 1935, built in limited numbers prior outbreak WWII; bulk of major wartime production to USAAF; used in all theatres, primarily passenger/cargo transport duties, also staff/station communications; employed ambulance (casualty evacuation), Burma-India; equipped several Allied AFs (Lend-Lease); continued post-war production (until 1960) and extensive use both civil and ex-military models.
Colour Reference: Plate 3: Noorduyn UC–64A Norseman (43–5179) of 1st Air Commando Group, USAAF, Hailakandi, India, April 1944; assigned aerial support second Wingate 'Chindit' expedition into Burma, March–May 1944, majority 1st Air Commando Group aircraft (inc P–51s, B–25s, and C–47s) identified by five white diagonals around rear fuselage as illustrated.

CZECHOSLOVAKIA

Manufacturer: Aero.
Model: A 32.
Type: Close-support/light bomber.
Power Plant: One 450hp Walter Jupiter IV.
Performance:
maximum speed at 8,200ft (2,500m) 140mph (225km/hr).
normal range 497 miles (800km).
time to 16,400ft (5,000m) 29min 11sec.
service ceiling 18,000ft (5,500m).
Weights:
empty 2,301lb (1,046kg).
loaded 4,225lb (1,915kg).
Dimensions:
wing span 40ft 8in (12.1m).
length 26ft 11in (8.2m).
height 10ft 2in (3.1m).
wing area 329.89sq ft (36.5sq m).

Armament: Two fixed forward-firing Vickers machine-guns; twin flexible Lewis machine-guns in rear cockpit; max bomb load 264lb (120kg) underwing.
Crew: 2.
In Service: Finland (16).
Variants (with no. built):
A 32: Prototype and initial production model; close-support/light bomber biplane; one Walter Jupiter IV (32).
A 32 IF: Finnish order; re-engined A 32; one 500hp Isotta-Fraschini Asso Caccia (1).
A 32 GR: Finnish order; re-engined A 32; one 450hp Gnome-Rhône Jupiter (15).
Ap 32, Apb 32: Improved versions; redesigned undercarriage (68).
Total Production: 116.
Remarks: Development of 1923-vintage A–11, sixteen A 32s supplied Finnish AF, 1929–30; remained in service until close Continuation War, 1944, primarily relegated training roles but also some limited-scale light-reconnaissance/communications use.

Manufacturer: Aero.
Model: A 100.
Type: Long-range reconnaissance/medium bomber.
Power Plant: One 650hp Avia Vr–36.
Performance:
maximum speed 167mph (269km/hr).
normal range 590 miles (950km).
time to 16,400ft (5,000m) 20min 0sec.
service ceiling 21,300ft (6,500m).
Weights:
empty 4,488lb (2,040kg).
loaded 7,098lb (3,220kg).
Dimensions:
wing span 48ft 2¾in (14.7m).
length 34ft 9¼in (10.6m).
height 11ft 5¾in (3.5m).
wing area 476.85sq ft (44.3sq m).
Armament: Two fixed forward-firing 7.7mm Mk 30 machine-guns; twin flexible 7.7mm Mk 30 machine-guns in rear cockpit; max bomb load 1,320lb (600kg).
Crew: 2.
In Service: Spain (RepAF approx 20 A 100, NatAF approx 5 A 100), Slovakia.
Variants (with no. built):
A 100: Prototype and initial production model; long-range single-engined reconnaissance/medium bomber biplane (44).
A 101: Medium bomber version; modified A 100; one 800hp Praga Asso; enlarged rudder; increased dimensions (29).
Ab 101: Bomber version; modified A 101; one 860hp (CKD–Praga-built) Hispano-Suiza 12Ydrs; increased dimensions (64).
Total Production: 137.
Remarks: Evolved from earlier A 30 (originally proposed as A 430), prototype A 100 reconnaissance-bomber first flown 1933; served mid-thirties Czech AF; approx 20 supplied Spanish RepAF for Civil War use, 1937 (of which approx 5 captured and subsequently employed trainer role by NatAF); post-German annexation Czechoslovakia, March 1939, number A 100/101s equipped newly-established Slovak AF, initially as light bomber, later relegated training/ancillary roles.

Manufacturer: Aero.
Model: A 304.
Type: Light bomber/reconnaissance.
Power Plant: Two 430hp Walter Super Castor I–MR.
Performance:
Maximum speed at sea level 186mph (300km/hr).
maximum speed at 5,740ft (1,750m) 201mph (323km/hr).
normal range 745 miles (1,200km).
time to 13,120ft (4,000m) 19min 0sec.
service ceiling 20,700ft (6,310m).
Weights:
empty 6,614lb (3,000kg).
loaded 9,600lb (4,350kg).
Dimensions:
wing span 63ft 0in (19.2m).
length 43ft 3¾in (13.2m).
height 11ft 2in (3.4m).
wing area 489.76sq ft (45.5sq m).
Armament: One fixed forward-firing 7.7mm Mk 30 machine-gun in nose; one flexible 7.7mm Mk 30 machine-gun in dorsal turret; max bomb load 705lb (320kg).
Crew: 3.
In Service: Bulgaria (1), Germany (12+).
Variants (with no. built):
A 204: Prototype; 8-passenger civil transport version; two 360hp Walter Pollux IIR (1).
A 300: Prototype: fast medium bomber version; A 204 development; two 830hp Bristol Mercury IX; redesigned fuselage; fully-glazed nose; twin fins and rudders; max bomb-load 2,204lb (1,000kg) (1).
A 304: Reconnaissance/light bomber version; modified A 204; uprated engines; modified glazed nose; dorsal turret (15).
Total Production: 17 (all Marks).
Remarks: Basic adaptation of unsuccessful A 204 civil transport of 1936, (even to retaining latter's cabin windows), fifteen A 304s built 1938 for Czech AF; seized by Germany following year; majority employed staff transport role, inc one supplied Bulgarian AF; more extensively modified A 300 prototype used trials purposes only.

Manufacturer: Avia.
Model: BH 25J.
Type: Transport.
Power Plant: One 450hp Bristol Jupiter IV.
Performance:
maximum speed 119mph (190km/hr).
cruising speed 99mph (160km/hr).
normal range 373 miles (600km).
time to 6,560ft (2,000m) 20min 0sec.
service ceiling 13,450ft (4,100m).
Weights:
empty 4,056lb (1,840kg).
loaded 6,834lb (3,100kg).
Dimensions:
wing span 50ft 2¼in (15.3m).
length 41ft 4½in (12.61m).
wing area 672.7sq ft (62.5sq m).
Crew/Payload/Accommodation: 2/1,278lb (580kg)/6 passengers.
In Service: Rumania (2).
Variants (with no. built):
BH 25L: Prototype; two-crew (open cockpit)/six-passenger civil transport biplane; one 450hp (Skoda-built) Lorraine-Dietrich (1).
BH 25J: Production model; one (Walter-built) Bristol Jupiter IV; lengthened nose; revised vertical tail surfaces (approx 8).
Total Production: approx 9.
Remarks: Prototype first flown 1926; two of four civil models delivered Rumanian operator/s 1931 subsequently (1937) supplied Rumanian AF; served military transport role late thirties and reportedly into early months WWII.

Manufacturer: Avia.
Model: B 534.IV.
Type: Fighter.
Power Plant: One 830hp (Avia-built) Hispano-Suiza 12Ydrs.
Performance:
maximum speed at 14,435ft (4,400m) 252mph (405km/hr).
cruising speed 214mph (345km/hr).
normal range 360 miles (580km).
initial rate of climb 2,953ft/min (900m/min).
time to 16,400ft (5,000m) 5min 0sec.
service ceiling 34,776ft (10,600m).
Weights:
empty 3,219lb (1,460kg).
loaded 4,376lb (1,985kg).
Dimensions:
wing span 30ft 10in (9.4m).
length 26ft 11in (8.2m).
height 10ft 2in (3.1m).
wing area 253.6sq ft (23.56sq m).
Armament: Four 7.7mm Mk 30 machine-guns in forward fuselage.
Crew: 1.
In Service: Bulgaria (48), Croatia, Germany, Greece (6), Hungary (1 ex-Slovak), Slovakia (SlovAF/InsAF), USSR (ex-Slovak), Yugoslavia (14).
Variants (with no. built):
B 34: Prototypes (2) and initial production model; single-seat fighter biplane; various power plants (14).
B 534/1, 534/2: Prototypes; modified B 34; one 860hp Hispano-Suiza 12Ybrs; two 7.7mm machine-guns. B 534/2 with redesigned vertical tail surfaces and modified rear fuselage decking; cockpit canopy; main wheel spats; inc 1 B 34 conversion) (1).
B 534.I: As B 534/2; one (Avia-built) HS 12Tdrs; canopy and wheel spats deleted; two 7.7mm Mk 30 machine-guns each in fuselage and lower wings (47).
B 534.II: As B 534.I; four 7.7mm Mk 30 machine-guns in fuselage (99).
B 534.III: Improved B 534.II; enlarged supercharger air intake; wheel spats; inc 6 Greek/14 Yugoslav orders (46).
B 534.IV: Major production model; sliding cockpit canopy; raised dorsal decking; number subsequently modified reduced decking/all-round vision canopy (272).
Bk 534: Modified B 534.II; one 7.7mm Mk 30 machine-gun firing through propeller hub plus two 7.7mm Mk 30 machine-guns in forward fuselage (35).
Total Production: 514 (all Marks).
Remarks: Comparable with best of world's contemporary designs, Avia B 534 was standard pre-war Czech fighter (also flown by Air Police unit); post-German occupation Czechoslovakia, March 1939, number retained newly-activated Slovak AF, remainder seized by Germany; latter equipped one Luftwaffe fighter Staffel early months WWII (subsequently modified and relegated target-towing duties); others supplied Bulgarian AF; opposed early incursions USAAF heavy bombers, inc second Ploesti raid; Slovak machines participated Carpathian dispute Spring 1939 (one captured by Hungary employed communications duties), later serving southern (Ukraine) sector of Soviet Front, 1941–42; still operational Autumn 1944, three examples flown by Slovak Insurgent AFs combined sqn in action against German forces.
Colour Reference: Plates 4, 5; Avia B 534.IV (M–19) of 13. stíhakí letka (fighter squadron), Slovak Air Force; Zhitomir-Kiev (Ukraine), Oct 1941; standard dark green/pale blue finish; late style national insignia; yellow nose/fuselage band and wingtips Axis Eastern Front recognition markings.

Manufacturer: Avia.
Model: B 135.
Type: Fighter.
Power Plant: One 860hp (Avia-built) Hispano-Suiza 12Ycrs.
Performance:
maximum speed 332 mph(535km/hr).
cruising speed 286mph (460km/hr).
normal range 342 miles (550km).
initial rate of climb 2,657ft/min (810m/min).
service ceiling 27,890ft (8,500m).
Weights:
empty 4,241lb (1,924kg).
loaded 5,428lb (2,462kg).
Dimensions:
wing span 35ft 7in (10.85m).
length 28ft 3⅓in (8.62m).
height 8ft 2¾in (2.7m).
wing area 182.99sq ft (17.0sq m).
Armament: One 20mm Oerlikon cannon firing through propeller hub; two 7.7mm Mk 30 machine-guns in upper cowling; max bomb load 485lb (220kg).
Crew: 1.
In Service: Bulgaria.
Variants (with no. built):
B 35/1–/3: Prototypes; single-seat fighter version; one 860hp (Avia-built) Hispano-Suiza 12Ycrs; B 35/1–2 with two 7.7mm Mk 30 machine guns; fixed spatted undercarriage; B 35/3 with one addn (engine-mounted) 20mm Oerlikon cannon; retractable undercarriage (3).
B 135: Prototype; Improved B 35/3; redesigned wing; enlarged rudder (1).
B 135: Production model; Bulgarian order (12).
Total Production: 16.
Remarks: First prototype produced 1938; B 135 prototype completed post-German annexation; twelve supplied Bulgarian AF; served homeland defence/interceptor role against USAAF heavy bombers en route Rumanian oilfields.

Manufacturer: Benes-Mráz.
Model: Be 51 Beta-Minor.
Type: Liaison/communications.
Power Plant: One 95hp Walter Minor 4–I.
Performance:
maximum speed at sea level 127mph (205km/hr).
cruising speed 112mph (180km/hr).
maximum range 500 miles (800km).
time to 3,280ft (1,000m) 6min 0sec.
service ceiling 16,400ft (5,000m).
Weights:
empty 1,058lb (480kg).
loaded 1,675lb (760kg).
Dimensions:
wing span 37ft 6½in (11.44m).
length 25ft 5½in (7.76m).
height 6ft 8¾in (2.05m).
wing area 164.69sq ft (15.3sq m).
Crew/Accommodation: 1/1.
In Service: Germany.
Variants:
Be 50 Beta-Minor: Prototype and initial production; low-wing two-seat light civil tourer; open cockpits; fixed (trousered) undercarriage.
Be 51 Beta-Minor: Modified Be 50; enclosed cockpits; raised dorsal decking; reduced span.
Remarks: Popular pre-war Czech light tourers, number (primarily enclosed-cockpit Be 51) seized Germany post-annexation and employed Luftwaffe training and communications roles.

Manufacturer: Letov.
Model: Š 218 Smolik.
Type: Trainer/communications.
Power Plant: One 120hp Walter.
Performance:
maximum speed 93mph (150km/hr).
time to 3,280ft (1,000m) 5min 22sec.
Weights:
empty 1,124lb (510kg).
loaded 1,636lb (742kg).
Dimensions:
wing span 32ft 9⅔in (10.00m).
length 22ft 8in (6.91m).
height 10ft 2in (3.10m).
Crew/Accommodation: 1/1.
In Service: Estonia, Finland, Latvia, Lithuania.
Variants:
Š218: Two-seat training biplane.
Remarks: Built late twenties and named after designer, Smolik designs exported to all three Baltic States; ten Š 218 also purchased by Finland (plus twenty-nine built under licence) and used throughout Winter and Continuation Wars in training/communications roles.

Manufacturer: Letov.
Model: Š 231.
Type: Fighter.
Power Plant: One 560hp Bristol Mercury IV S2.
Performance:
maximum speed at sea level 176mph (283km/hr).
maximum speed at 16,400ft (5,000m) 216mph (348km/hr).
normal range 280 miles (450km).
time to 16,400ft (5,000m) 8min 28sec.
service ceiling 29,530ft (9,000m).
Weights:
empty 2,822lb (1,280kg).
loaded 3,902lb (1,770kg).
Dimensions:
wing span 33ft 0in (10.06m).
length 25ft 9in (7.85m).
height 9ft 10in (3.00m).
wing area 321.43sq ft (21.50sq m).
Armament: Four 7.92mm Model

Aero A 100

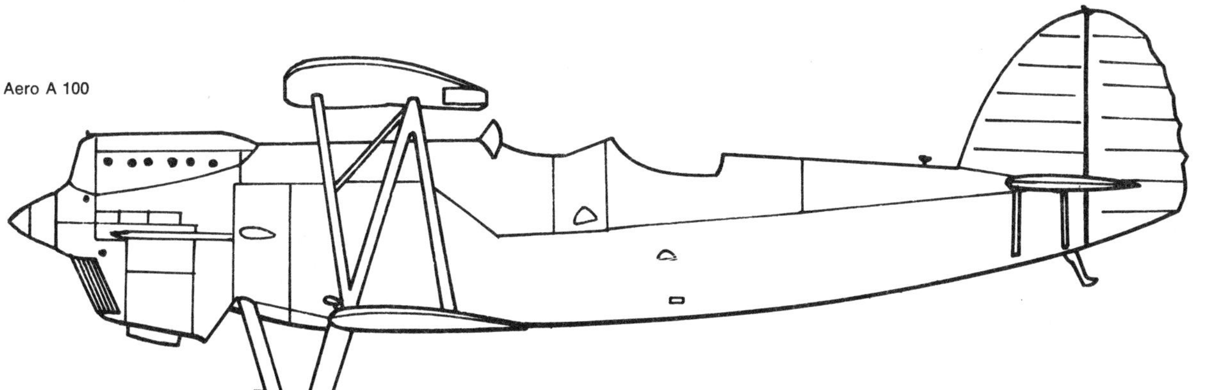

Avia B 135

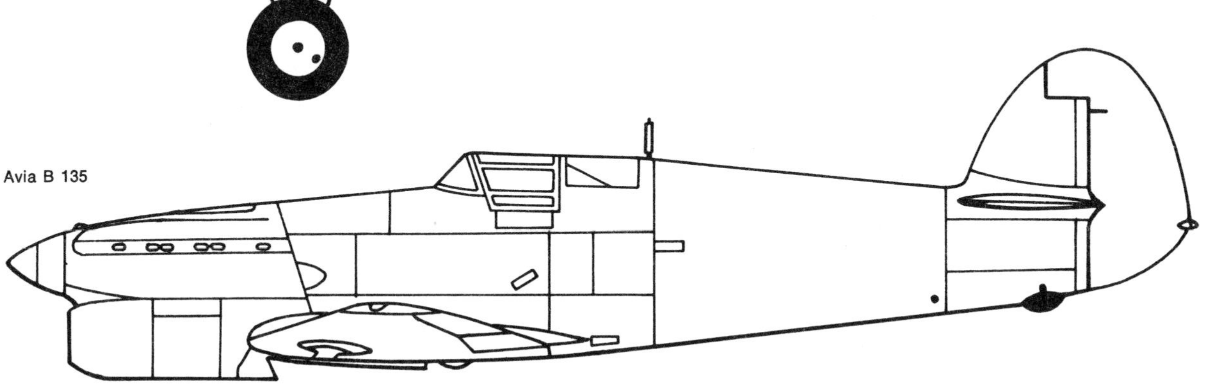

28 machine-guns.
Crew: 1.
In Service: Spain.
Variants (with no. built):
Š 31: Prototype and initial pro-
 duction model; one 450hp Walter
 Jupiter VI.
Š 231: Prototypes; improved S 31;
 one 560hp Bristol Mercury; first/
 second prototypes with armament
 mounted in upper/lower wings
 resp (2).
Š 231: Production model; as second
 prototype (25).
Š 331/431: Prototypes; re-engined
 Š 231; one 900hp Walter K–14 II
 and one 680hp Armstrong Siddeley
 Tiger resp (2).
Remarks: Ten Š 231s delivered
Spanish RepAF 1936; seven lost
during Civil War, survivors taken
over by NatAF and served into
early months WWII.

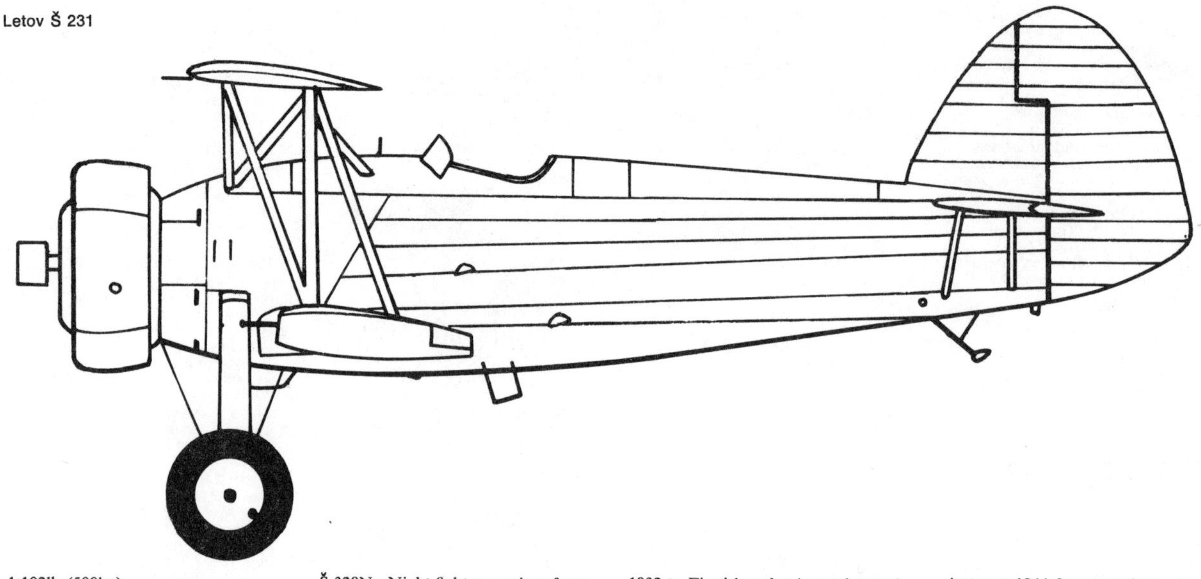

Manufacturer: Letov.
Model: Š 328.
Type: Reconnaissance-bomber.
Power Plant: One 635hp (Walter-
built) Bristol Pegasus IIM–2.
Performance:
maximum speed at 5,905ft (1,800m)
 174mph (280km/hr).
normal range 435 miles (700km).
time to 16,400ft (5,000m)
 17min 0sec.
service ceiling 23,622ft (7,200m).
Weights:
empty 3,696lb (1,680kg).
loaded 5,820lb (2,675kg).
Dimensions:
wing span 44ft 11¼in (13.7m).
length 34ft 1¼in (10.4m).
height 11ft 2in (3.4m).
wing area 722.26sq ft (67.1sq m).
Armament: Two 7.7mm Mk 30
machine-guns in wings; twin
flexible 7.7mm Mk 30 machine-guns
in rear cockpit; max bomb load

Letov Š 231

1,102lb (500kg).
Crew: 2.
In Service: Bulgaria (30+),
Germany, Slovakia (SlovAF/InsAF),
USSR (ex Slovak).
Variants (with no. built):
Š 328F: Prototype; two-seat recon-
 naissance-bomber biplane; one
 580hp Bristol Pegasus IIM–2; two
 fixed plus two flexible 7.7mm Mk
 30 machine-guns; original Finnish
 order (1).
Š 328: Initial production model;
 uprated engine (445).

Š 328N: Night-fighter version; four
 fixed and two flexible machine-guns
 (13).
Š 328V: Twin-float target-tug
 seaplane version (4).
Š 428: Prototype; Modified S 328;
 one 650hp (Hispano-Suiza 12 Nbr)
 Avia Vr–36; four fixed machine-
 guns (1).
Š 528: Re-engined S 328; one 800hp
 Gnome-Rhône Mistral-Major;
 NACA engine cowling (6).
Total Production: 470 (all Marks).
Remarks: Originally designed in

1932 to Finnish order (not taken up),
Š 328 entered production for Czech
AF two years later; extensive pre-
war service, all seized by Germany
(inc continuing production) upon
annexation, March 1939; operated
considerable numbers Luftwaffe
training purposes only; also supplied
Slovak/Bulgarian AFs; former participated Axis invasions Poland and
USSR, 1939, 1941 resp, latter
employed primarily Black Sea
coastal patrol duties; three Slovak
examples joined Insurgent AF

Autumn 1944 for operations
against German forces.
Colour Reference: Plate 6.
Letov S 328 (S–76) of Combined
Squadron, Slovak Insurgent Air
Force, Tri Duby, Sept 1944; note
Nos. S–27 and B–10 with Slovakian
AF insignia (see plates 4–5 above)
and Soviet Red Star markings
resp); S–76 (and S–27) destroyed by
Luftwaffe bombing raid on Tri
Duby, 10 Sept 1944.

DENMARK

Manufacturer: Royal Army Aircraft
Factory.
Model: I O.
Type: Trainer/communications.
Power Plant: One 220hp BMW.
Performance:
maximum speed 124mph
 (200km/hr).
cruising speed 93mph (150km/hr).
normal range 310 miles (500km).
service ceiling 19,685ft (6,000m).
Weights:
empty 2,207lb (1,000kg).
loaded 3,087lb (1,400kg).
Dimensions:
wing span 34ft 11¾in (10.66m).
length 27ft 6¾in (8.40m).
height 8ft 10¼in (2.70m).
Armament: Provision for two 8mm
machine-guns.
Crew/Accommodation: 1/1.
In Service: Denmark.
Variants (with no. built):
I O; Prototype and initial production model; two-seat advanced
 training biplane (15).
II O: Single-seat version; one 160hp
 Mercedes (7).

Royal Army Aircraft Factory II O

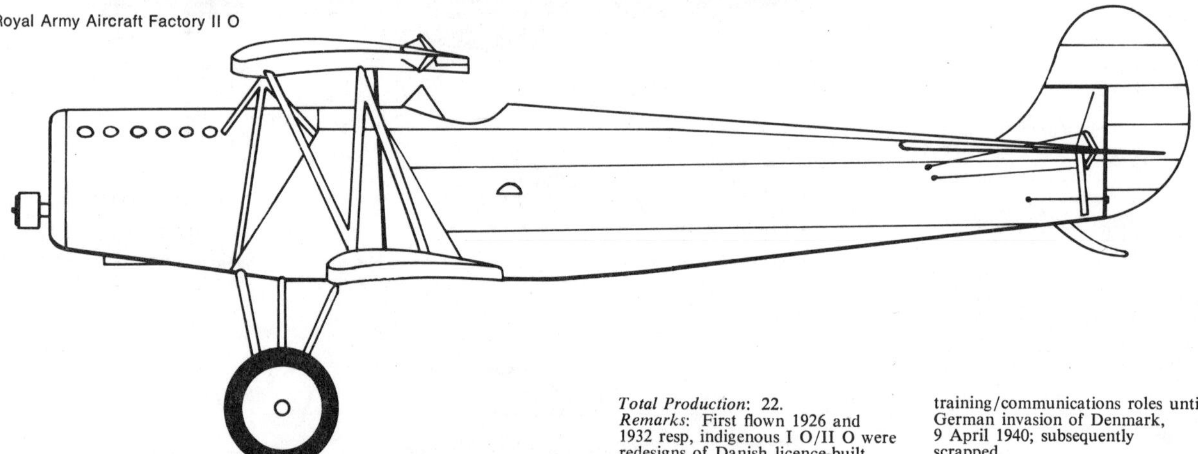

Total Production: 22.
Remarks: First flown 1926 and
1932 resp, indigenous I O/II O were
redesigns of Danish licence-built
Fokker C.I.; served advanced

training/communications roles until
German invasion of Denmark,
9 April 1940; subsequently
scrapped.

ESTONIA

Manufacturer: Military Workshops.
Model: PTO–4.
Type: Trainer/communications.
Power Plant: 120hp de Havilland
Gipsy.

Crew: 1.
In Service: Estonia, Germany
(approx 1).
Variants:
PTO–4: Single-/two-seat low-wing

monoplane; altn wheel, ski fixed
undercarriage.
Total Production: approx 2.
Remarks: Single examples both
versions operated pre-war Estonian

ADF; evidence suggests at least one
(two seat) model survived Soviet
annexation, 1940–41, subsequently
to serve Estonian-manned volunteer
Staffel of German Luftwaffe as

trainer/liaison, and for submarine-
tracking duties over Baltic coast.

FINLAND

Manufacturer: VL.
Model: Sääski II.
Type: Trainer/communications.
Power Plant: One 120hp Siemens.
Performance:
maximum speed 90mph (145km/hr).
Weights:
loaded 2,013lb (913kg).
Dimensions:
wing span 32ft 5¾in (9.9m).
length 25ft 11in (7.9m).

Armament: One 7.7mm machine-
gun.
Crew/Accommodation: 1/1.
In Service: Finland.
Variants (with no. built):
Sääski I: Prototype; two-seat trainer
 biplane; Sääski-built (1).
Sääski II: Initial production model;
 VL-built (10+).
Sääski IIA: Improved Sääski II
 (22+).

Total Production: 33+
Remarks: Sääski-designed and built
prototype first flown 1928; production models employed during
thirties by Finnish Customs Service,
(as floatplane), Civil Air Guard, and
civilian flying clubs; Finnish AF
examples (operated pre-war interim
reconnaissance/close support duties)
in use until 1941; equipped Winter
War, 1939–40, training units, plus

opening months Continuation War
in communications role.

Manufacturer: VL.
Model: Kotka II.
Type: Maritime reconnaissance.
Power Plant: One 575hp Wright
R–1820–E Cyclone.
Performance:
maximum speed 140mph (225km/hr).
Weights:

loaded 5,688lb (2,580kg).
Dimensions:
wing span 41ft 8in (12.7m).
length 33ft 9½in (10.3m).
Armament: One fixed forward-firing
machine-gun; one flexible machine-
gun in rear cockpit; provision for
max 661lb (300kg) bomb load
underwing.
Crew: 2.
In Service: Finland.

Variants (with no. built):
Kotka I: Prototype; two-seat maritime reconnaissance biplane; one Bristol Jupiter; altn wheel, ski, or float undercarriage (1).
Kotka II: Production model; one Wright R–1820–E Cyclone (6).
Total Production: 7.
Remarks: Entering service 1931 as maritime reconnaissance/light day-bomber, Kotka II remained in use throughout Winter and Continuation Wars, 1939–40/1941–44 resp, latterly relegated second-line duties, inc trainer, target-tug; withdrawn 1945.

Manufacturer: VL.
Model: Tuisku II.
Type: Advanced trainer/light reconnaissance.
Power Plant: One 215hp Armstrong Siddeley Lynx.
Performance:
maximum speed 129mph (207km/hr).
maximum speed 106mph (170km/hr).
maximum range 715 miles (1,150km).
time to 6,560ft (2,000m) 11min 55sec.
service ceiling 14,436ft (4,400m).
Weights:
empty 2,183lb (990kg).
loaded 3,582lb (1,625kg).
Dimensions:
wing span 39ft 8⅓in (12.1m).
length 30ft 8¼in (9.35m).
height 10ft 8⅓in (3.26m).
wing area 362.21sq ft (33.65sq m).
Armament: One flexible machine-gun in rear cockpit; provision for light bombs underwing.
Crew/Accommodation: 1/1.
In Service: Finland.
Variants (with no. built):
Tuisku: Prototypes; two-seat advanced training biplane (2).
Tuisku I: Initial production model; advanced trainer/light reconnaissance; altn one 240hp Lycoming R–680–BA wheel, ski, or float undercarriage (13).
Tuisku II: Improved Tuisku I (16).
Total Production: 31.
Remarks: First flown 1933, entered Finnish AF service 1939; in use throughout Winter and Continuation Wars, 1939–40/1941–44 resp, primarily assigned school and operational training units, but also employed limited scale reconnaissance, communications, and ancillary duties.

Manufacturer: VL.
Model: Viima II.
Type: Elementary trainer/ liaison.
Power Plant: One 150hp Siemens Sh 14A.
Performance:
maximum speed at sea level 121mph (195km/hr).
cruising speed 93mph (150km/hr).
normal range 311 miles (500km).
time to 9,840ft (3,000m) 19min 0sec.
service ceiling 14,760ft (4,500m).
Weights:
loaded 1,929lb (875kg).
Dimensions:
wing span 30ft 2in (9.2m).
length 24ft 1in (7.34m).
height 9ft 0in (2.74m).
wing area 215.3sq ft (20.0sq m).
Crew/Accommodation: 1/1.
In Service: Finland.
Variants (with no. built):
Viima I: Prototype/s and initial production; two-seat trainer biplane (2).
Viima II: Production model; improved Viima I; reduced dimensions; revised fuel tankage; VL-built (approx 22).

VL Pyry II

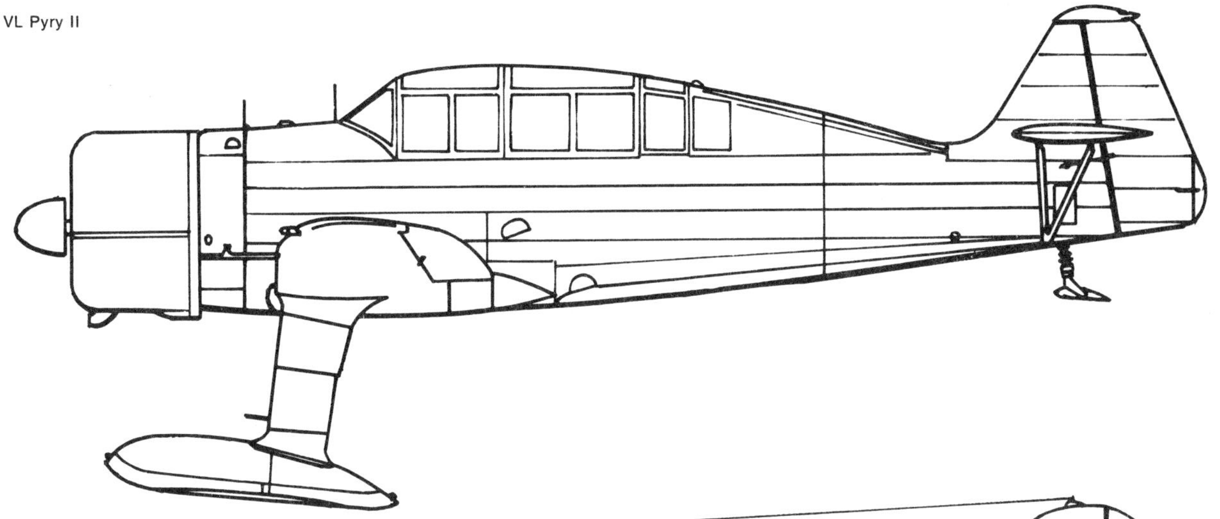

VL Myrsky II

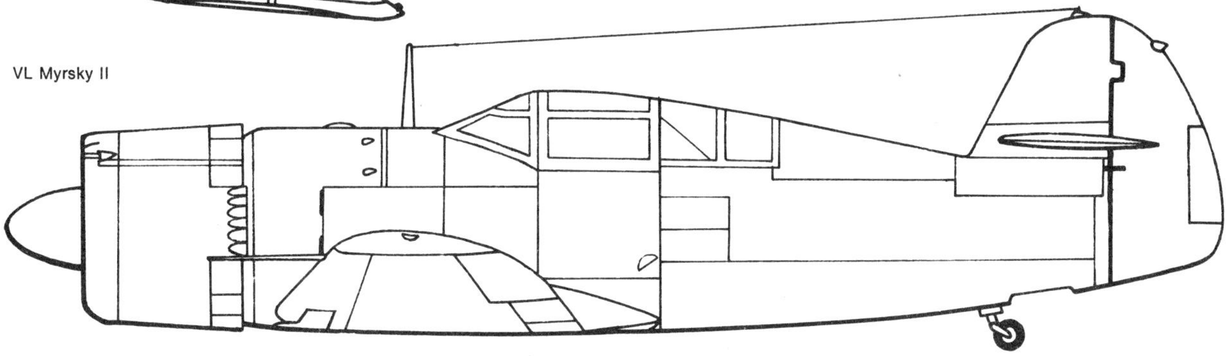

Total Production: approx 24.
Remarks: First flown late 1935, production Viima IIs operated by Finnish AF 1939–62; served throughout Winter and Continuation Wars, primarily training role but latterly also ancillary liaison duties; post-war (early fifties) modified with enclosed cockpits.

Manufacturer: VL.
Model: Pyry II (Thunderstorm).
Type: Advanced trainer/liaison.
Power Plant: One 420hp Wright Whirlwind.
Performance:
maximum speed 205mph (330km/hr).
cruising speed 180mph (290km/hr).
normal range 466 miles (750km).
time to 3,280ft (1,000m) 2min 30sec.
service ceiling 19,029ft (5,800m).
Weights:
loaded 3,197lb (1,450kg).
Dimensions:
wing span 32ft 2in (9.80m).
length 24ft 9¼in (7.55m).
height 8ft 2½in (2.50m).
wing area 136.70sq ft (12.70sq m).
Armament: One fixed forward-firing 7.7mm KSP machine-gun in upper cowling.
Crew/Accommodation: 1/1.
In Service: Finland.
Variants (with no. built):
Pyry I: Prototype; two-seat advanced training low-wing monoplane (1).
Pyry II: Modified Pyry I; revised cockpit canopy/tail bracing; altn wheel/ski undercarriage (40).
Total Production: 41.
Remarks: Prototype first flown 1939, Pyry remained in Finnish AF service until 1962; employed throughout Continuation War, 1941–44, as advanced trainer and in variety liaison and ancillary roles.

Manufacturer: VL.
Model: Myrsky II (Storm).
Type: Fighter.
Power Plant: One 1,065hp (SFA-built) Pratt & Whitney, R–1830–S1C3–G Twin Wasp.
Performance:
maximum speed at 10,665ft (3,250m) 329mph (530km/hr).
cruising speed 260mph (418km/hr).
normal range 311 miles (500km).
service ceiling 29,530ft (9,000m).
Weights:
empty 5,141lb (2,332kg).
normal 6,504lb (2,950kg).
Dimensions:
wing span 36ft 1in (11.0m).
length 27ft 4¾in (8.35m).
height 9ft 10in (3.0m).
wing area 190.4sq ft (17.69sq m).
Armament: Four 12.7mm Browning MG 53 machine-guns in upper cowling.
Crew: 1.
In Service: Finland.
Variants (with no. built):
Myrsky: Initial prototype; single-seat low-wing fighter monoplane (1).
Myrsky I: Prototype and pre-production models (3).
Myrsky II: Production model; modified Myrsky I; redesigned wing; strengthened undercarriage (47).
Myrsky III: Improved Myrsky II (10); none completed.
Pyörremyrsky (Whirlwind): Myrsky development; one 1,475hp Daimler-Benz DB 605; prototype only (1).
Total Production: 52 (all Marks).
Remarks: Only indigenous Finnish fighter to see WWII combat, Myrsky got off to inauspicious start, all four first machines crashing during test programme; much modified Myrsky II entered service 1943; employed post-Sept 1944 Armistice in close-support role against retiring German ground-forces.

Order of Battle November 1939

FINNISH AIR FORCE (Ilmavoimat)

Lentorykmentti 1 (Flight Regiment 1)		
Close-support:		
PLeLv 10 (3 sqns)	Lappeenranta	12 Fokker C.X
TLeLv 12 (3 sqns)	Suur-Merijoki	13 Fokker C.X
TLeLv 14 (3 sqns)	Laikko	4 Fokker C.X
		7 Fokker C.V–E
		2 Fieseler Fi 156C Storch
TLeLv 16 (3 sqns)	Värtsilä	9 Blackburn Ripon IIF
		5 Junkers K 43
		3 VL Sääski
		1 VL Kotka
TLeLv 36 (2 sqns)	Kallvik	6 Blackburn Ripon IIF
TLeLv 39 (1 flight)	Mariehamina	2 Junkers K 43
Lentorykmentti 2 (Flight Regiment 2)		
Fighters:		
HLeLv 24 (5 sqns)	Immola	36 Fokker D.XXI
		2 de Havilland Moth
HLeLv 26 (1 sqn)	Raulampi	10 Bristol Bulldog IVA
Lentorykmentti 4 (Flight Regiment 4)		
Bombers:		
PLeLv 44 (3 sqns)	Luonetjärvi	8 Bristol Blenheim I
		1 de Havilland Moth
PLeLv 46 (3 sqns)	Luonetjärvi	8 Bristol Blenheim I

FRANCE

Manufacturer: Amiot.
Model: 143M.
Type: Reconnaissance bomber.
Power Plant: Two 870hp Gnome-Rhône 14 Kirs/jrs Mistral-Major.
Performance:
maximum speed at 13,120ft (4,000m) 193mph (310km/hr).
cruising speed 154mph (248km/hr).
maximum range 1,240 miles (2,000km).
time to 13,120ft (4,000m) 14min 20sec.
service ceiling 25,920ft (7,900m).
Weights:
empty 13,448lb (6,100kg).
maximum 21,385lb (9,700kg).
Dimensions:
wing span 80ft 5¾in (24.53m).
length 59ft 11in (18.24m).
height 18ft 7¾in (5.68m).
wing area 1,076.39sq ft (100sq m).
Armament: One or two 7.5mm MAC 1934 machine-gun/s each in nose and dorsal turrets; one flexible 7.5mm MAC 1934 machine-gun each in fore and aft of ventral gondola; max bomb load (internal and external) 3,960lb (1,800kg).
Crew: 4–6.
In Service: France (FAF, FFAF, FVAF).
Variants (with no. built):
Amiot 140MX: Initial prototypes; day- and night-reconnaissance bomber version; two 700hp Lorraine 18Gad; open cockpits (2).
Amiot 142: As Amiot 140MX; two Hispano-Suiza 12Yers (1).
Amiot 143–01: Prototype; two 800hp Gnome-Rhône 14Kdrs/Kgrs (1).
Amiot 143M: Production model; two supercharged Gnome-Rhône 14Kirs/Kjrs; auxiliary fuel tanks (jettisonable in Nos. 1–40); three (or five) .303in Lewis guns, or four 7.5mm MAC 1934 machine-guns; lengthened nose commencing No. 31 (138).
Amiot 144M: Modified 143M; redesigned wings; retractable undercarriage; prototype only (1).
Amiot 145, 146: Re-engined 144M versions; projects only.
Amiot 147: Modified 144M; two 880hp Hispano-Suiza 12Ydrs/frs; twin fins and rudders; test aircraft only.
Amiot 150BE: Reconnaissance/torpedo-bomber version of 143M; interchangeable wheel/float undercarriage; redesigned wings; two 740hp Gnome-Rhône 14Krsd (1).
Total Production: 144 (all Marks).
Remarks: First flown Spring 1935, obsolescent Amiot 143M still equipped six bomber Groupes on outbreak WWII; carried out night-reconnaissance and leaflet raids over Germany, Sept 1939–May 1940; Battle of France, May–June 1940, night attacks on German lines of communications; suffered severe losses by day over German bridge-heads at Sedan, 14 May 1940; subsequently served with Vichy AF in transport role, North Africa 1941–44.
Colour Reference: Plate 9: Amiot 143M (No. 56) of GB II/34, Armée de l'Air; Roye-Amy, May 1940; standard brown overall (except natural metal nacelles); machine flown by Commandant de Laubier, No. 56 destroyed over Sedan bridge-heads, 14 May 1940.

Manufacturer: Amiot.
Model: 354 B4.
Type: Medium bomber.
Power Plant: Two 1,060hp Gnome-Rhône 14N 48/49.
Performance:
maximum speed at sea level 255mph (410km/hr).
maximum speed at 13,120ft (4,000m) 298mph (480km/hr).
cruising speed 217mph (349km/hr).
normal range 1,553 miles (2,500km).

Amiot 354 B4

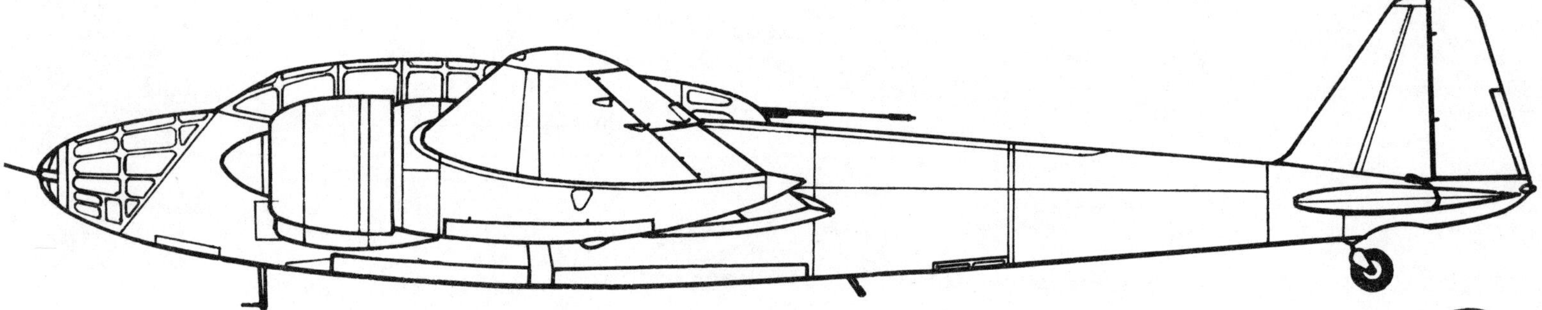

Bloch 131 RB4

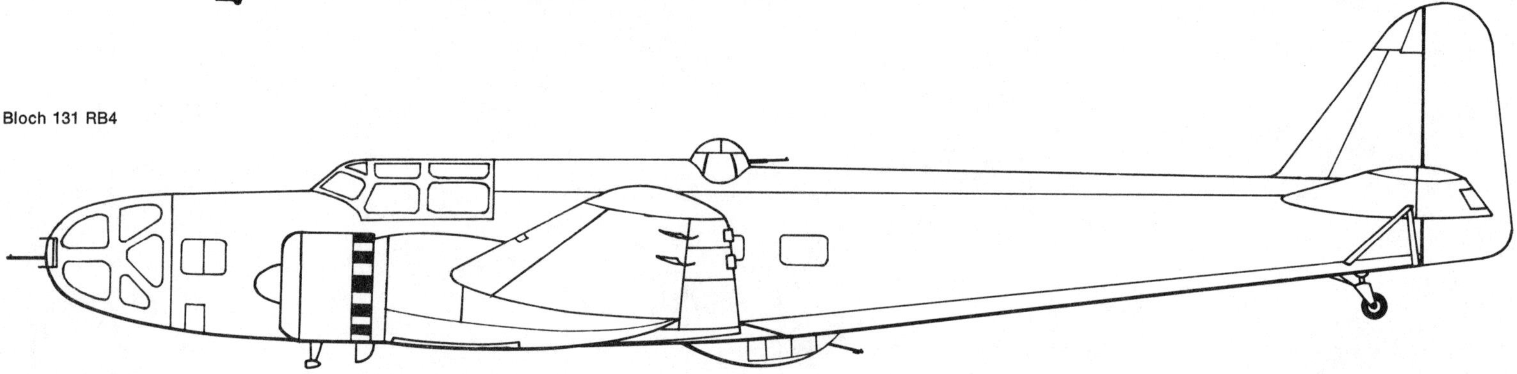

time to 13,120ft (4,000m) 8min 42sec.
service ceiling 32,810ft (10,000m).
Weights:
empty 10,417lb (4,725kg).
maximum 24,912lb (11,300kg).
Dimensions:
wing span 74ft 10¾in (22.83m).
length 47ft 6¾in (14.5m).
height 13ft 4½in (4.07m).
wing area 721.18sq ft (67.0sq m).
Armament: One flexible 20mm Hispano-Suiza HS 404 cannon, (or one 7.5mm Darne machine-gun) in dorsal position; plus one flexible 7.5mm MAC 1934 machine-gun each in nose and ventral positions; max bomb load 2,646lb (1,200kg).
Crew: 4.
In Service: France (FAF, FVAF), Germany.
Variants (with no. built):
Amiot 341: Long-range mail plane; two 920hp Gnome-Rhône 14N 0/1. 3 crew; single fin and rudder (1).
Amiot 340-01: Prototype; 3-seat bomber version; Amiot 341 conversion.
Amiot 350: Modified Amiot 340-01; two Hispano-Suiza 12Y 28/29; project only.
Amiot 351-01: Re-engined Amiot 340-01; two 1,020hp Gnome-Rhône 14N 20/21. 4 crew; modified engine cowling; twin fin and rudder; one 7.5mm MAC 1934 machine-gun in ventral hatch; 1 conversion.
Amiot 351 B4: Initial production model; reduced wing span; enlarged vertical tail surfaces; enlarged cockpit; two 950hp Gnome-Rhône 14N 38/39; increased armament (approx 17).
Amiot 352 B4: Two 1,100hp Hispano-Suiza 12Y 50/51; not completed.
Amiot 353 B4: Two 1,030hp Rolls-Royce Merlin III; not completed.
Amiot 354 B4: Two 1,070hp Gnome-Rhône 14N 48/49; single fin and rudder (approx 45).
Amiot 355-01: Prototype; two supercharged 1,200hp Gnome-Rhône 14R 2/3 (1).
Amiot 356-01: Prototype; re-engined Amiot 354 B4; two 1,130hp Rolls-Royce Merlin X (1).
Amiot 357 B4: High-altitude bomber version; two turbo-supercharged Hispano-Suiza 12Z; pressurised cabin; not completed.
Total Production: approx 65.
Remarks: Developed from Amiot 341 long-range civil mailplane (itself evolved from Amiot 370 world speed record-holder), Amiot 351/354 series was potentially among finest French AF bomber aircraft, but production difficulties restricted deliveries to little more than 50 of almost 900 on order; saw limited use, solely by night, during Battle of France, May-June 1940; several subsequently converted as high-speed civil transports and operated by Vichy-controlled Air France; four examples later taken over by Germany for Luftwaffe use as special-duties transport.

Manufacturer: Arsenal.
Model: VG 33 C1.
Type: Lightweight interceptor-fighter.
Power Plant: One 860hp Hispano-Suiza 12Y31.
Performance:
maximum speed at sea level 367mph (590km/hr).
maximum speed at 17,060ft (5,200m) 347mph (558km/hr).
normal range 746 miles (1,200km).
service ceiling 36,090ft (11,000m).
Weights:
empty 4,519lb (2,050kg).
loaded 5,853lb (2,655kg).
Dimensions:
wing span 35ft 5½in (10.8m).
length 28ft 0⅝in (8.55m).
height 10ft 10¼in (3.31m).
wing area 150.7sq ft (14.0sq m).
Armament: One 20mm Hispano-Suiza 404 cannon firing through propeller hub; four 7.5mm MAC 1934 M39 machine-guns in wings.
Crew: 1.
In Service: France.
Variants (with no. built):
VG 30: Initial prototype; single-seat fighter; one 690hp Hispano-Suiza 12Xcrs (1).
VG 32: Prototype; re-engined VG 30; one 1,040hp Allison V-1710-C15 (1).
VG 33: Production model; modified VG 30; inc 4 prototypes (44).
VG 34, 35: Prototypes; re-engined VG 33s; one 910hp Hispano-Suiza 12Y45 and 1,000hp Hispano-Suiza 12Y51 resp inc one (VG 35) VG 33 conversion (1).
VG 36: Modified VG 35; redesigned rear fuselage and radiator bath (1).
VG 39: Modified VG 33; one 1,200hp Hispano-Suiza Type 89ter; modified wing with two addn machine-guns (1).
Total Production: 49.
Remarks: VG 33 prototype first flown May 1939; out of total 720 machines ordered, only 40 completed—19 taken on charge by FAF prior Armistice, June 1940, 21 seized by Germany, fate unknown.

Manufacturer: Blériot SPAD.
Model: S.510.
Type: Fighter.
Power Plant: One 690hp Hispano-Suiza 12Xbrs.
Performance:
maximum speed at 16,405ft (5,000m) 230mph (370km/hr).
normal range 543 miles (875km).
time to 9,840ft (3,000m) 3min 22sec.
Weights:
empty 2,755lb (1,250kg).
maximum 4,034lb (1,830kg).
Dimensions:
wing span 29ft 0in (8.84m).
length 24ft 5⅞in (7.46m).
height 12ft 2¼in (3.72m).
wing area 236.81sq ft (22.0sq m).
Armament: Four fixed forward-firing 7.5mm MAC 1934 machine-guns in underwing fairings.
Crew: 1.
In Service: France (FAF), Spain (RepAF).
Variants (with no. built):
Blériot SPAD S.510 prototype; Hispano-Suiza 12Xbrs (1).
Blériot SPAD S.510 production model: As prototype; last two re-engined with HS 12Xcrs and with one 20mm Hispano-Suiza cannon in place of two machine-guns; (60).
Total Production: 61.
Remarks: FAF's last fighter biplane, Blériot SPAD S.510 entered service early 1936; some examples delivered Spain for use by Republican AF during Civil War; obsolescent by Sept 1939, 510s served briefly with ERCs during early months of WWII, before replacement by more modern types and relegation to overseas (North African) units.

Manufacturer: Bloch.
Model: 81.
Type: Ambulance/light transport.
Power Plant: One 175hp Salmson 9 Nd.
Performance:
maximum speed at sea level 117mph (188km/hr).
cruising speed 100mph (161km/hr).
range 407 miles (655km).
time to 8,200ft (2,500m) 11min 0sec.
service ceiling 21,000ft (6,400m).
Weights:
empty 1,281lb (581kg).
loaded 1,940lb (880kg).
Dimensions:
wing span 41ft 3⅜in (12.59m).
length 27ft 6¾in (8.4m).
height 9ft 6in (2.9m).
wing area 191.6sq ft (17.8sq m).
Crew/Accommodation: 1/2 or 1 litter.
In Service: France (FAF, FVAF).
Variants (with no. built):
Bloch 80: Prototype (1).
Bloch 81: Production model; various power plants (20).
Total Production: 21.
Remarks: First flown early thirties; several remained in service in North Africa and during Syrian campaign, 1940-41.

Manufacturer: Bloch.
Model: 200.
Type: Medium bomber.
Power Plant: Two 900hp Gnome-Rhône 14 Kirs/Kjrs.
Performance:
maximum speed at sea level 149mph (240km/hr).
maximum speed at 14,110ft (4,300m) 176mph (283km/hr).
normal range 620 miles (1,000km).
time to 19,685ft (6,000m) 23min 6sec.
Weights:
empty 9,840lb (4,300kg).
maximum 16,490lb (7,480kg).
Dimensions:
wing span 73ft 8in (22.45m).
length 52ft 6in (16.00m).
height 12ft 10in (3.92m).
wing area 721.18sq ft (67.0sq m).
Armament: One 7.5mm MAC 1934 machine-gun each in nose and dorsal turret and in ventral gondola; max bomb load 2,746lb (1,200kg).
Crew: 4.
In Service: Bulgaria (12 ex-Czech), Croatia (ex-Czech), France (FAF, FNAF, FVAF), Germany (ex-Czech/French), Rumania (25 ex-Czech).
Variants (with no. built):
Bloch 200-01: Prototype; two 760hp Gnome-Rhône 14Krsd (1).
Bloch 200: Production model; uprated engines; modified nose; wheel spats; Bloch-built (4); Potez-built (111); Hanriot-built (45); Loire-built (19); Breguet-built (19); Sud-Ouest-built (10); also Czech licence-built by Aero and Avia (124).
Total Production: 333.
Remarks: First flown 1933, elderly MB 200 still equipped seven bomber Groupes on outbreak WWII, four in metropolitan France and three overseas; saw limited service opening weeks of war before relegation to training role, Winter 1939-40; retained by Vichy AF in Syria until mid-1941; Czech licence-built machines appropriated by Luftwaffe; served alongside captured French examples on crew-trainer and general duties; number allocated to German satellite AFs.

Manufacturer: Bloch.
Model: 210 BN5.
Type: Medium night bomber.
Power Plant: Two 910hp Gnome-Rhône 14N 10/11.
Performance:
maximum speed at 11,480ft (3,500m) 200mph (322km/hr).
cruising speed 149mph (240km/hr).
maximum range 1,056 miles (1,700km).
time to 13,120ft (4,000m) 12min 0sec.
service ceiling 32,480ft (9,900m).
Weights:
empty 14,109lb (6,400kg).
maximum 22,487lb (10,200kg).
Dimensions:
wing span 74ft 10in (22.8m).
length 62ft 0in (18.9m).
height 21ft 11⅜in (6.69m).
wing area 672.74sq ft (62.5sq m).
Armament: One 7.5mm MAC 1934 machine-gun each in nose and retractable dorsal and ventral turrets; max bomb load 3,527lb (1,600kg) plus underwing flares.
Crew: 5.
In Service: Bulgaria (6), France (FAF, FVAF), Germany (37 ex-France), Rumania (24), Spain (RepAF 35).
Variants (with no. built):
Bloch 210 Prototype: Private venture; medium night bomber; two 800hp Gnome-Rhône 14 Kdrs/grs; fixed undercarriage; subsequently fitted with twin floats as torpedo-bomber (1).
Bloch 210 BN4: Production model; two 900hp Gnome-Rhône 14Kirs/jrs; modified tail and wings; re-positioned dorsal turret; retractable ventral turret; retractable undercarriage; majority subsequently re-engined with Gnome-Rhône 14N 10/11s; Bloch-built.
Bloch 210 BN5: Modified Bloch BN4; one addn crew: Bloch 210 BN4, BN5 production: Bloch-, Potez-CAMS-, Renault-, Hanriot-, and ANF-Mureaux-built (inc 24 Rumanian order) (281).
Bloch 211 Verdun: Prototype; as Bloch 210 prototype; two 860hp Hispano-Suiza 12Y; retractable undercarriage (1).
Total Production: 283.
Remarks: Low-wing, retractable undercarriage development of marginally earlier MB 200, Bloch 210 was numerically most important FAF bomber on outbreak of WWII, equipping total of twelve Groupes: despite intensive 1939-40 replacement programme, still accounted for one third of French medium bomber force (five Groupes) at time of German offensive, 10 May 1940; participated Battle of France, May-June 1940, attacking German lines of communication in Rhineland and Belgium; six out of thirty-seven examples later seized by Germany in Unoccupied France (late 1942) passed to Bulgarian AF; pre-war French deliveries to Rumania (24) and Spain (35), latter serving with Republican AF in Civil War.

Manufacturer: Bloch.
Model: 220.
Type: Transport.
Power Plant: Two 985hp Gnome-Rhône 14N 16/17.
Performance:
maximum speed 205mph (330km/hr).
cruising speed 174mph (280km/hr).
normal range 869 miles (1,400km).
service ceiling 22,965ft (7,000m).
Weights:
empty 14,799lb (6,713kg).
loaded 20,943lb (9,500kg).
Dimensions:
wing span 74ft 10¼in (22.82m).
length 63ft 1¾in (19.25m).
wing area 807.29sq ft (75.0sq m).
Crew/Accommodation: 4/16.
In Service: France.
Variants (with no. built):
Bloch 220.01: Prototype; civil transport version; 16 passengers (1).
Bloch 220: Production model (16).
Bloch 221: Re-engined Bloch 220; two Wright Cyclone R-1820-97; five post-war conversions.
Total Production: 17.
Remarks: First flown late 1935, Bloch 220 airliner entered Air France service 1937; at least one example impressed for military transport duties with FAF after outbreak WWII; 3/4 commandeered 1943 for wartime operation by DLH.

Manufacturer: Bloch.
Model: 131 RB4.
Type: Reconnaissance-bomber.
Power Plant: Two 950hp Gnome-Rhône 14N 10/11.
Performance:
maximum speed at sea level 188mph (302km/hr).
maximum speed at 12,300ft

(3,750m) 217mph (349km/hr).
cruising speed 168mph (270km/hr).
maximum range 808 miles (1,300km).
time to 13,120ft (4,000m) 13min 0sec.
service ceiling 23.785ft (7,250m).
Weights:
empty 10,340lb (4,690kg).
maximum 18,960lb (8,600kg).
Dimensions:
wing span 66ft 6in (20.27m).
length 58ft 6½in (17.85m).
height 13ft 5in (4.09m).
wing area 581.25sq ft (54.0sq m).
Armament: One flexible 7.5mm MAC 1934 machine-gun each in nose, dorsal turret and ventral gondola; max bomb load 1,764lb (800kg).
Crew: 4.
In Service: France (FAF, FFAF, FVAF).
Variants (with no. built):
Bloch 131 RB4 No 1, RB5 No 2: 4 and 5-seat prototypes resp; reconnaissance-bomber version; two 900hp Gnome-Rhône 14K Mistral-Major; subsequently re-engined with Gnome-Rhône 14N 10/11; one flexible 20mm cannon or one 7.5mm MAC 1934 machine-gun in nose resp; dorsal turret; No 2 with semi-retractable ventral gun position (2).
Bloch 131 R4: Initial production model; reconnaissance version; 4 crew; Gnome-Rhône 14N; ventral gondola with one 7.5mm MAC 1934 machine-gun (13).
Bloch 131 Ins: Dual-control trainer version (5).
Bloch 131 RB4: Production model; reconnaissance-bomber version; modified R4; internal bomb-bay; revised equipment (119).
Bloch 133: Prototype; modified Bloch 131; redesigned tail (1).
Bloch 134: Prototype; two 1,100hp Hispano-Suiza L4AA (1).
Total Production: 143.
Remarks: Entered service Autumn 1938; Bloch 131s equipped six reconnaissance Groupes in metropolitan France (plus a seventh in North Africa) by Sept 1939; after heavy losses suffered in early attempts at daylight reconnaissance of Germany's western borders, Bloch 131s restricted to operating by night; by May 1940 all French-based Groupes converted to Potez 63.11, the only MB 131s remaining in first-line service being those deployed overseas; limited number subsequently served Vichy AF as target-tugs.

Manufacturer: Bloch.
Model: 151.
Type: Fighter.
Power Plant: One 920hp Gnome-Rhône 14N-35.
Performance:
maximum speed at 13,120ft (4,000m) 301mph (485km/hr).
normal range 398 miles (640km).
time to 16,400ft (5,000m) 7min 0sec.
service ceiling 32,800ft (10,000m).

Weights:
empty 4,576lb (2,073kg).
maximum 6,173lb (2,800kg).
Dimensions:
wing span 34ft 7in (10.54m).
length 29ft 10½in (9.1m).
height 9ft 11½in (3.03m).
wing area 186.43sq ft (17.32sq m).
Armament: Four 7.5mm MAC 1934 machine-guns in wings; or two 7.5mm MAC 1934 machine-guns and two 20mm Hispano-Suiza HS 404 cannon, all in wings.
Crew: 1.
In Service: France (FAF, FNAF, FVAF), Germany (ex-France), Greece (9), Rumania (20 Bloch 151/152).
Variants (with no. built):
Bloch 151 prototype and pre-production models: one 920hp Gnome-Rhône 14N-11 (25).
Bloch 151 production model: Gnome-Rhône 14N-35; minor modifications (115).
Total Production: 140.
Remarks: Developed from earlier Bloch 150-01, itself an unsuccessful contender in 1934 fighter programme, the Bloch 151 (first flown Aug 1938) had poor performance; despite being classified as unsuitable for first-line combat duties and relegated to fighter training role, Bloch 151s did operate with both FAF and FNAF; in latter service sustained heavy losses in action against Italian AF in southern France, June 1940; nine supplied to Greece also employed against Italian AF during October 1940 Balkans campaign; captured French 151/152s passed to Rumania as trainers.

Manufacturer: Bloch.
Model: 152.
Type: Fighter.
Power Plant: One 1,000hp Gnome-Rhône 14N-25.
Performance:
maximum speed at 14,765ft (4,500m) 316mph (509km/hr).
normal range 335 miles (540km).
time to 6,560ft (2,000m) 3min 24sec.
Weights:
empty 4,758lb (2,158kg).
maximum 6,173lb (2,800kg).
Dimensions:
wing span 34ft 7in (10.54m).
length 29ft 10½in (9.1m).
height 9ft 11½in (3.03m).
wing area: 186.43sq ft (17.32sq m).
Armament: Four 7.5mm MAC 1934 machine-guns in wings; or two 7.5mm MAC 1934 machine-guns and two 20mm Hispano-Suiza HS 404 cannon, in wings.
Crew: 1.
In Service: France (FAF, FNAF, FVAF), Germany (ex-France), Rumania (20 Bloch 151/152).
Variants (with no. built):
Bloch 152-01: Prototype; modified MB-151; one 1,030hp Gnome-Rhône 14N-21; modified engine cowling; revised (belt-fed) armament (1).
Bloch 152: Production model;

Gnome-Rhône 14N-21 or 1,060hp 14N-49 (481).
Bloch 153-01: Prototype; modified Bloch 152; one 1,050hp Pratt and Whitney R1830 SC3-G 'Twin Wasp' (1).
Bloch 154: Proposed re-engined Bloch 152; one 1,200hp Wright GR-1820 'Cyclone' not completed.
Total Production: 483.
Remarks: Manufactured in parallel with Bloch 151, the Bloch 152 was fitted with more powerful engine and modified armament; equipped only one (non-operational) Groupe on outbreak of WWII; of nearly 300 machines delivered to FAF by Jan 1940, almost two-thirds remained non-operational for lack of correct propellers; eventually served nine Groupes, plus two naval and several defence Escadrilles; Bloch 152s claimed 146 enemy aircraft destroyed (for 86 of own number lost in action) before June 1940 armistice; subsequently served with Vichy AF, others taken over by Luftwaffe as trainers (inc twenty 151/152s to Rumania).
Colour Reference: Plates 10, 11: Bloch 152 recently of 4ème Escadrille, GC II/9, Armée de l'Air de l'Armistice; Aulnat, Southern France, Nov 1942; this machine one of number seized by Luftwaffe's 'Monte-Rosa' special detachment for flight testing and transfer to German fighter schools; standard Vichy AF finish with Luftwaffe call-sign (07 + 11) and markings superimposed; note anomalous retention French rudder and under-wing tricolour striping.

Manufacturer: Bloch.
Model: 155.
Type: Fighter.
Power Plant: One 1,100hp Gnome-Rhône 14N-49.
Performance:
maximum speed at 14,765ft (4,500m) 323mph (520km/hr).
normal range 652 miles (1,050km).
time to 13,125ft (4,000m) 6min 55sec.
Weights:
empty 4,718lb (2,140kg).
maximum 6,393lb (2,900kg).
Dimensions:
wing span 34ft 7in (10.54m).
length 29ft 8½in (9.05m).
height 10ft 6in (3.21m).
wing area 186.43sq ft (17.32sq m).
Armament: Two 20mm Hispano-Suiza HS 404 cannon, plus two or four 7.5mm MAC 1934 machine-guns in wings; or six 7.5mm MAC 1934 machine-guns in wings.
Crew: 1.
In Service: France (FVAF), Germany.
Variants (with no. built):
Bloch 155 prototype: Modified Bloch 152; redesigned forward fuselage (1 conversion).
Bloch 155 production model: As prototype; re-positioned

cockpit; increased fuel capacity; inc 3 pre-production models (33).
Total Production: 33.
Remarks: Re-engined Bloch 152, involving major design changes to cowling and forward fuselage, plus additional armament and armour; only 8 Bloch 155s completed prior to Franco-German armistice of 25 June 1940; production subsequently resumed for Vichy AF; several captured examples employed by Luftwaffe as fighter-trainers, 1942–44.

Manufacturer: Bloch.
Model: 162.
Type: Long-range heavy bomber.
Power Plant: Four 1,100hp Gnome-Rhône 14N-48/49.
Performance:
maximum speed at 18,045ft (5,500m) 342mph (550km/hr).
normal range 1,490 miles (2,400km).
time to 6,560ft (2,000m) 5min 48sec.
ceiling 29,530ft (9,000m).
Weights:
empty 26,158lb (11,865kg).
loaded 41,888lb (19,000kg).
Dimensions:
wing span 92ft 2in (28.1m).
length 71ft 10½in (21.9m).
height 12ft 4in (3.76m).
wing area 1,173.27sq ft (109sq m).
Armament: One flexible 7.5mm MAC 1934 machine-gun each in nose and ventral positions, plus one 20mm Hispano-Suiza cannon each in dorsal (flexible) and ventral positions; max bomb load 7,937lb (3,600kg).
Crew: 5.
In Service: Germany.
Variants:
Bloch 160, 161: Initial long-range civil transport versions; four 720hp Hispano-Suiza 12Xirs or four 900hp Gnome-Rhône 14N resp.
Bloch 162 Raid: Mailplane/long-range communications version of Bloch 160; redesigned fuselage; four Gnome-Rhône 14N.
Bloch 162-01: Prototype; long-range heavy bomber version; modified Bloch 162 Raid; 5 crew; two 7.5mm MAC 1934s plus two 20mm cannon.
Bloch 162 B5: Projected production model.
Total Production: 1.
Remarks: First flown June 1940; sole Bloch 162-01 prototype fell into German hands following Armistice later same month; after extensive flight testing, aircraft transferred to Germany for clandestine long-range special duties, 1943–44.

Manufacturer: Bloch.
Model: 174 A3.
Type: Reconnaissance/light bomber.
Power Plant: Two 1,140hp Gnome-Rhône 14N 48/49.
Performance:
maximum speed at sea level

248mph (400km/hr).
maximum speed at 17,060ft (5,200m) 329mph (530km/hr).
cruising speed 248mph (400km/hr).
maximum range 1,025 miles (1,650km).
time to 26,250ft (8,000m) 11min 0sec.
service ceiling 36,090ft (11,00m).
Weights:
empty 12,346lb (5,600kg).
loaded 15,784lb (7,160kg).
Dimensions:
wing span 58ft 9½in (17.92m).
length 40ft 1½in (12.23m).
height 11ft 7½in (3.55m).
wing area 442.73sq ft (41.13sq m).
Armament: Two fixed forward-firing 7.5mm MAC 1934 machine-guns in wings; two flexible 7.5mm MAC 1934 machine-guns in rear cockpit; plus three rearward-firing 7.5mm MAC 1934 M39 machine-guns in ventral positions; max bomb load 1,102lb (500kg).
Crew: 3.
In Service: France (FAF, FFAF, FVAF).
Variants (with no. built):
Bloch 170 AB2 A3 No. 01, B3 No. 02: Prototypes; assault bomber and high-speed bomber versions resp; two 950hp Gnome-Rhône 14N 6/7; one 20mm Hispano-Suiza cannon and four/three 7.5mm MAC 1934 machine-guns resp; No. 01 with ventral gondola; No. 02 increased canopy area, enlarged vertical tail surfaces (2).
Bloch 171, 172, 173: Projects only.
Bloch 174 No. 01: Prototype; reconnaissance/light bomber version; modified Bloch 170 B3 No.02; two 1,030hp Gnome-Rhône 14N 20/21; redesigned fuselage; fully-glazed nose; re-positioned cockpit (1).
Bloch 174 A3: Pre-production and production models; two Gnome-Rhône 14N 48/49; three (pre-production) or seven (production) 7.5mm MAC 1934 machine-gun armament (56).
Bloch 174Z: Two 1,600hp Hispano-Suiza 12Z; one post-war conversion.
Total Production: 59 (all Marks).
Remarks: Developed from original Bloch 170 bomber design, Bloch 174 used solely in reconnaissance role during Batte of France; entered service half March 1940; carried out long-range reconnaissance penetration German airspace; over half 49 operational models lost by capitulation, majority being destroyed on ground to prevent capture; equipped one Groupe FVAF based Tunisia; number subsequently employed in bomber role against German forces closing stages Tunisian campaign, Spring 1943.

Manufacturer: Bloch.
Model: 175 B3.
Type: Light bomber/attack.
Power Plant: Two 1,140hp

Bloch 155

Bloch 174 A3

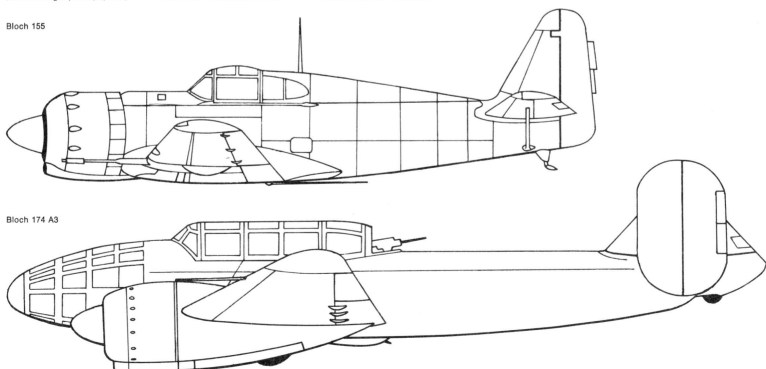

Gnome-Rhône 14N 48/49.
Performance:
maximum speed at sea level 248mph (400km/hr).
maximum speed at 17,060ft (5,200m) 335mph (540km/hr).
cruising speed 244mph (393km/hr).
range 993 miles (1,600km).
time to 26,250ft (8,000m) 13min 30sec.
Weights:
empty 12,478lb (5,660kg).
maximum 17,688lb (8,023kg).
Dimensions:
wing span 58ft 11in (17.95m).
length 40ft 9¼in (12.43m).
height 11ft 7¾in (3.55m).
wing area 442.72sq ft (41.13sq m).
Armament: Two fixed forward-firing 7.5mm MAC 1934 M39 machine-guns in wings; two flexible 7.5mm MAC 1934 machine-guns in rear cockpit; three 7.5mm MAC 1934 M39 machine-guns in ventral positions; max bomb load 1,323lb (600kg).
Crew: 3.
In Service: France (FAF, FFAF, FVAF), Germany.
Variants (with no. built):
Bloch 175 No. 01: Prototype; bomber version; modified Bloch 174; enlarged bomb-bay; redesigned fuselage/wing centre section (1).
Bloch 175 B3: Production model; inc 56 completed as trainers for Germany (79).
Bloch 175 A,B: Torpedo-bomber and heavy fighter versions resp; modified Bloch 175; projects only.
Bloch 175 T: Naval torpedo-bomber version; modified Bloch 175; two 1,150hp Gnome-Rhône 14N 54/55, 66/67, or 70/71; post-war production for FNAF (80).
Bloch 176 No. 01: Prototype; re-engined Bloch 174; two 1,050hp Pratt & Whitney R-1830 SC3-G Twin Wasps; one conversion.
Bloch 176 B3: Production model; modified Bloch 175 (5).
Bloch 177: Modified Bloch 175; two 830hp Hispano-Suiza 12Y 31; prototype only (1).
Bloch 178: High-altitude bomber version; project only.
Total Production: Approx 166 (all Marks).
Remarks: Modified Bloch 174 designed specifically for light bomber role, twenty Bloch 175s delivered FAF prior to Armistice, none being used in action; subsequently equipped one Groupe FVAF based Algeria, majority destroyed during 'Torch' landings, Nov 1942; survivors (plus single Bloch 176) transferred to Bloch 174-equipped Groupe for Tunisian operations early 1943; over 50 examples supplied to Luftwaffe as operational trainers; bulk of remaining production stripped of engines for use in Messerschmitt Me 323 programme; post-war development, Bloch 175T served FNAF until early fifties.

Manufacturer: Breguet.
Model: Bre XIX B.2.
Type: Bomber.
Power Plant: One 500hp Hispano-Suiza 12Hb.
Performance:
maximum speed at 9,840ft (3,000m) 143mph (230km/hr).
maximum range 497 miles (800km).
service ceiling 21,982ft (6,700m).
Weights:
normal 4,850lb (2,200kg).
Dimensions:
wing span 48ft 7¾in (14.83m).
length 31ft 2in (9.5m).
height 10ft 11½in (3.34m).
Armament: One fixed forward-firing 7.5mm Darne (or 7.7mm Vickers) machine-gun in upper cowling; one (or two) flexible 7.5mm Darne (or 7.7mm Vickers) machine-gun/s in rear cockpit; one rearward-firing machine-gun in ventral position; max bomb load (external) 970lb (440kg).
Crew: 2.
In Service: China, Croatia, Greece (Bre XIX A.2/B.2), Poland, Spain (Rep./Nat.AFs), Turkey, Yugoslavia.
Variants (with no. built):
Bre XIX: Prototype; one 420hp Renault 12Kb; subsequently (Lorraine) re-engined.
Bre XIX A.2.: Production model; observation/reconnaissance version; various 400/860hp power plant/armament combinations; alt land/floatplane.
Bre XIX B.2.: Bomber version of Bre XIX A.2., external bomb-load.
Bre XIX GR: Reconnaissance version; various power plants and armament as A.2.
Bre XIX production: Breguet-built (approx 1,100); Belgian (SABCA) licence-built (approx 150); Greek licence-built, Japanese (Nakajima) licence-built, Spanish (CASA) licence-built (approx 100); also Yugoslav (Ikarus) licence-built.
Bre XIX bis, ter, T, T bis and Bre 191, 192, 197/199: Further development; various power plants, armament, dimensions.
Total Production: approx 1,500 (Bre XIX inc licence-production).
Remarks: Successor to Bre XIV bomber of WWI vintage, Bre XIX first flown May 1922; subsequently produced in multiplicity of versions, inc extensive licence-production, Bre XIX exported Europe, South America, Middle, and Far East; last of FAF models withdrawn from first-line service latter half of thirties, but fought on both sides during Spanish Civil War; number still operational with foreign AFs into early forties; equipped two Mire (sqns) Greek AF during opening weeks Italian invasion; Oct-Nov 1940, employed in light bomber/ground-attack role against advancing Alpini.

Manufacturer: Breguet.
Model: Bre 270.
Type: Observation.
Power Plant: One 500hp Hispano-Suiza 12Hb.
Performance:
maximum speed at sea level 147mph (216km/hr).
maximum speed at 9,840ft (3,000m) 140mph (225km/hr).
range 621 miles (1,000km).
time to 19,685ft (6,000m) 29min 0sec.
service ceiling 25,920ft (7,900m).
Weights:
empty 3,871lb (1,756kg).
normal 6,378lb (2,893kg) (with bomb load).
Dimensions:
wing span 55ft 9¾in (17.01m).
length 32ft 0¼in (9.76m).
height 11ft 9in (3.58m).
wing area 534.65sq ft (49.67sq m).
Armament: One fixed forward-firing 7.7mm machine-gun; one flexible 7.7mm machine-gun in rear cockpit; provision for max 265lb (120kg) bombs.
Crew: 2.
In Service: France.
Variants (with no. built):
Bre 270: Prototypes and initial production model; 2-seat general-purpose/reconnaissance version (inc 10 export models) (100).
Bre 271: Modified Bre 270; various power plants (inc prototypes) (50).
Bre 272: Prototype; modified Bre 270 (1).
Bre 273: Prototype and production models; long-range reconnaissance/bomber version; one 650hp Hispano-Suiza 12Nb or one supercharged Hispano-Suiza 12 Ybrs; production model for export only (22).
Bre 274: Prototype; re-engined Bre 273; one 700hp supercharged Gnome-Rhône 14 Krsd (1).
Bre 330 R2: Prototypes; re-engined Bre 270; one 650hp Hispano-Suiza 12Nb (2).
Total Production: 176.
Remarks: First flown late twenties, Bre 270 observation sesquiplane still equipped three GAOs (Groupes Aériens d'Observation) upon outbreak WWII; suffered heavy losses over Western Front/Rhineland before withdrawal from service Winter 1939–40.

Manufacturer: Breguet.
Model: Bre 521 Bizerte.
Type: Long-range reconnaissance flying-boat.
Power Plant: Three 900hp Gnome-Rhône 14 Kirs 1.
Performance:
maximum speed at 3,280ft (1,000m) 151mph (243km/hr).
cruising speed 102mph (165km/hr).
maximum range 1,864 miles (3,000km).
time to 6,560ft (2,000m) 8min 46sec.
service ceiling 19,685ft (6,000m).
Weights:
empty 20,878lb (9,470kg).
maximum 36,597lb (16,600kg).
Dimensions:
wing span 115ft 4in (35.15m).
length 67ft 2¼in (20.48m).
height 24ft 6½in (7.48m).
wing area 1,827.17sq ft (169.7sq m).
Armament: One flexible 7.5mm Darne machine-gun each, in two forward lateral, two waist, and one tail position; max bomb load (external) 660lb (300kg).
Crew: 8.
In Service: France (FNAF, FFNAF, FVNAF), Germany (8).
Variants (with no. built):
Bre 521-01: Prototype; three 845hp Gnome-Rhône 14 Kdrs; open bow gun position (1).
Bre 521: Production model; extended forward canopy; uprated engines; last three with three 900hp Gnome-Rhône 14N-11 and improved equipment (30).
Bre 522: Re-engined Bre 521; three 1,000hp Hispano-Suiza 14AA (1).
Bre 530 Saïgon: 19/20-passenger civil version of Bre 521; three 785hp Hispano-Suiza 12Ybr (2).
Total Production: 34.
Remarks: Development of Short Calcutta (four of which licence-built by Breguet 1931–32), Bre 521 Bizerte entered service mid-thirties; twenty examples equipped four Escadrilles FNAF outbreak WWII; operated Atlantic/Mediterranean reconnaissance Sept 1939–June 1940; subsequently served two FVNAF Escadrilles; eight seized by Germany, Nov 1942; performed ASR duties based French Atlantic coast.

Manufacturer: Breguet.
Model: Bre 693 AB2.
Type: Light attack bomber.
Power Plant: Two 700hp Gnome-Rhône 14M 6/7 Mars.
Performance:
maximum speed at sea level 265mph (426km/hr).
maximum speed at 6,560ft (2,000m) 295mph (475km/hr).
cruising speed 186mph (300km/hr).
maximum range 840 miles (1,350km).
time to 13,120ft (4,000m) 7min 12sec.
Weights:
empty 6,636lb (3,010kg).
maximum 12,125lb (5,500kg).
Dimensions:
wing span 50ft 5in (15.36m).
length 31ft 8¾in (9.67m).
height 10ft 5½in (3.19m).
wing area 310.0sq ft (28.8sq m).
Armament: One fixed forward-firing 20mm Hispano-Suiza HS 404 cannon; and two fixed forward-firing 7.5mm MAC 1934 machine-guns in nose; one flexible 7.5mm MAC 1934 machine-gun in rear cockpit and one oblique fixed rearward-firing 7.5mm MAC 1934 machine-gun in ventral position; plus (late models only) one fixed rearward-firing 7.5mm MAC 1934 machine-gun in tail of each engine nacelle; max bomb load 880lb (400kg).
Crew: 2.
In Service: France (FAF, FVAF), Germany (ex-France), Italy (ex-Germany).
Variants (with no. built):
Bre 690-01: Prototype; 3-seat fighter version; two 680hp Hispano-Suiza 14AB 02/03; two 20mm cannon, plus one 7.5mm machine-gun (1).
Bre 691-01: Prototype; 2-seat attack bomber version; two 700hp Hispano-Suiza 14AB 10/11; revised armament; centre-section bomb-bay; max load 880lb (400kg); detail modifications (1).
Bre 691 AB2: Initial production model; 2-seat attack bomber version; as prototype (78).
Bre 692 AB2: As Bre 691 AB2; two 980hp Gnome-Rhône 14N; project only.
Bre 693-01: Prototype; re-engined Bre 691 AB2; two 700hp Gnome-Rhône 14M 6/7 (1 conversion).
Bre 693 AB2: Production model; 2-seat attack bomber version; late models with addn rearward-firing 7.5mm MAC 1934 machine-gun in tail of each engine nacelle (254).
Bre 694-01: Prototype; 3-seat reconnaissance or 2-seat bomber version; two 710hp Gnome-Rhône 14M 4/5; centre-section bomb-bay replaced by third crew position (as Bre 690), plus camera; reduced armament (1).
Bre 695-01: Prototype; modified Bre 690-01; two 825hp Pratt & Whitney SB4G Twin Wasp Junior; redesigned engine nacelle and cowling (1 conversion).
Bre 695 AB2: Production model; 2-seat attack bomber version (50).
Bre 696-01: Prototype; 2-seat light bomber version; Two 700hp Gnome-Rhône 14M 6/7; enlarged bomb-bay; (Bre 696 B2 production cancelled) (1).
Bre 697-01: Prototype; re-engined Bre 691 AB2; two 1,070hp Gnome-Rhône 14N 48/49; development for Bre 700 C2 project (1 conversion).
Bre 698 Bp2, Bre 699 B2, Bre 700 C2: 2-seat dive-bomber, bomber, and heavy destroyer versions resp; projects only.
Total Production: 386.
Remarks: Operational debut 12 May 1940, attacking German columns advancing through Belgium, ten out of eleven Bre 693s destroyed, crash-landed, or damaged beyond repair; nevertheless, continued low-level bombing attacks throughout remainder of campaign, losing almost fifty per cent of the 106 delivered prior to Armistice; subsequently equipped two Groupes FVAF (inc some Bre 695s); number of both types seized by Germany after occupation Vichy Zone, Nov 1942; majority then passed to Italy for operational training purposes.
Colour Reference: Plate 13: Breguet Bre 695 AB2 of 1ère Escadrille, GBA I/151, Armée de l'Air de l'Armistice; Lézignan-Corbières, Southern France, June 1942; standard three-tone finish. Vichy AF nacelle and tail striping, plus white roundel surround and fuselage bar; subsequently (early 1943) to Regia Aeronautica.

Manufacturer: C.A.M.S.
Model: 37.2.
Type: Ship-borne observation/patrol flying boat.
Power Plant: One 450hp Lorraine 12 Ed.
Performance:
maximum speed at sea level 109mph (175km/hr).
maximum speed at 6,560ft (2,000m) 105mph (170km/hr).
normal range 497 miles (800km).
time to 6,560ft (2,000m) 19min 0sec.
service ceiling 11,155ft (3,400m).
Weights:
empty 4,784lb (2,170kg).
loaded 6,614lb (3,000kg).
Dimensions:
wing span 47ft 6¾in (14.5m).
length 37ft 6in (11.43m).
height 13ft 9½in (4.19m).
wing area 644.76sq ft (59.9sq m).
Armament: Two .303in Lewis machine-guns each in open nose and dorsal positions; provision for max 660lb (300kg) bomb load underwing.
Crew: 3.
In Service: France (FNAF, FFNAF, FVNAF, FVAF).
Variants (with no. built):
C.A.M.S.37 R3b: Initial prototype; 3-seat ship-borne reconnaissance flying boat; one 400hp Lorraine 12Db (1).
C.A.M.S.37A: Prototype and production model; one 450hp Lorraine 12Eb; amphibian; modified vertical tail surfaces; inc 7 for Portuguese NAF with 450hp Hispano-Suiza 50 (12 Gb) (23).
C.A.M.S.37C: Modified 37A; 4-seat civil transport version.
C.A.M.S.37 GR: Modified 37C; military communications (1 conversion).
C.A.M.S.37.2, 37.6: 3-seat observation version of 37A, and 4-seat military communications/liaison version of 37C resp; amphibious undercarriage deleted from former; 37.6 alt designation 37 Lia.
C.A.M.S.37.3, 37.7, 37.12, 37.13: Projects only.
C.A.M.S.37.9: 4-seat transport amphibian (4).
C.A.M.S.37.11 (37E): 4-seat trainer flying boat.
Remarks: First flown 1926, C.A.M.S.37 was oldest French flying boat to see operational use WWII; despite previous relegation purely training/communications duties, two FNAF Escadrilles mobilised on C.A.M.S.37s and employed coastal patrol role until Aug 1940; single examples reportedly remained in use overseas territories 1941–42.

Manufacturer: C.A.M.S.
Model: 55.10.
Type: Maritime reconnaissance flying boat.
Power Plant: Two 530hp Gnome-Rhône 9 Kbr.
Performance:
maximum speed at sea level 134mph (215km/hr).
maximum speed at 3,280ft (1,000m) 118mph (190km/hr).
cruising speed 94mph (150km/hr).
normal range 808 miles (1,300km).
time to 3,280ft (1,000m) 7min 30sec.
service ceiling 11,155ft (3,400m).
Weights:
empty 10,231lb (4,640kg).
normal/loaded 14,396lb (6,530kg).
Dimensions:
wing span 66ft 11in (20.39m).
length 49ft 2½in (15.0m).
height 17ft 9in (5.41m).
wing area 1,221.18sq ft (113.45sq m).
Armament: Two .303in Lewis machine-guns each in open bow and dorsal positions; max bomb load 330lb (150kg) underwing.
Crew: 5.
In Service: France (FNAF, FFNAF).
Variants (with no. built):
C.A.M.S.55: Prototypes; two 480hp Gnome-Rhône 9Akx Jupiter or 600hp Hispano-Suiza 12 Lbr (5).
C.A.M.S.55.1: Initial production model; two Hispano-Suiza 12 Lbr; all-wood construction (43).
C.A.M.S.55.2: Re-engined C.A.M.S.55.1; two Gnome-Rhône Jupiters (29).
C.A.M.S.55.3: As C.A.M.S.55.2; metal hull.
C.A.M.S.55.4: Two 600hp Lorraine 12Fa; project only.
C.A.M.S.55.5: Project only.
C.A.M.S.55.6: As C.A.M.S.55.2; metal fuselage and floats; reduced weight (1).
C.A.M.S.55.10: Re-engined C.A.M.S.55.2; two 530hp Gnome-Rhône 9 Kbr (inc 16 with metal floats) (28).
C.A.M.S.55.10 Coloniaux: Long-range version of C.A.M.S.55.10; improved radio equipment (4).
C.A.M.S.55.12/13: Four-engined Lorraine/Gnome-Rhône versions resp; projects only.
C.A.M.S.55.14: As C.A.M.S.6; two 535hp supercharged Gnome-Rhône 9 Kdrsl (1).
Total Production: 112.
Remarks: Military development of earlier C.A.M.S.53 civil flying boat, C.A.M.S.55 entered service 1930; largely relegated training/second-line duties by outbreak WWII, twenty-four C.A.M.S.55.2/10s still on strength FNAF employed maritime reconnaissance role; all scrapped after Armistice, except two operated FFNAF in South Pacific, 1940–41.

Manufacturer: Caudron.
Model: C.272 'Luciole'.
Type: Communications/liaison.
Power Plant: One 140/150hp Renault 'Bengali' 4Pei.
Performance:
maximum speed 108mph (173km/hr).
cruising speed 93mph (150km/hr).
normal/maximum range 389 miles (625km).
service ceiling 11,154ft (3,400m).
Weights:
empty 1,067lb (485kg).
normal/loaded 1,848lb (840kg).
Dimensions:
wing span 32ft 5¾in (9.9m).
length 25ft 2in (7.67m).
height 9ft 0¾in (2.76m).
wing area 258.2sq ft (24.0sq m).
Crew: 2.
In Service: France (FAF, FFAF, FVAF), Germany (ex-France), Great Britain (1+ ex-France/impressed).
Variants:
C.270: Prototype; one 95hp Salmson 7 Ac.
C.272: Production model; improved C.270; alternative Renault 4 Pei, 120hp Bengali Junior, or 105hp Hirth HM 504A power plants.
Remarks: Pre-war light sportsplane; number employed on auxiliary communications/liaison duties by French forces for duration WWII; several examples also believed used in similar roles by both RAF and Luftwaffe.

Manufacturer: Caudron.
Model: C.400.
Type: Liaison.
Power Plant: One 120hp Renault 4 Pdi.
Performance:
maximum speed at sea level 116mph (186km/hr).
cruising speed 93mph (150km/hr).
normal range 513 miles (825km).
time to 9,840ft (3,000m) 32min 0sec.
service ceiling 13,940ft (4,250m).
Weights:
empty 1,300lb (590kg).
loaded 2,470lb (1,120kg).
Dimensions:
wing span 38ft 1½in (11.62m).
length 27ft 9in (8.46m).
height 7ft 3in (2.21m).
wing area 249.72sq ft (23.2sq m).
Crew/Accommodation: 1/3.
In Service: France (FAF, FVAF).
Variants (with no. built):
C.282 'Phalene': 4-seat civil light tourer; various power plants.
C.400: Militiary liaison/trainer version of C.282. (40).
Remarks: Development of civil 'Phalene', C.400 ordered by FAF prior WWII for liaison and ancillary

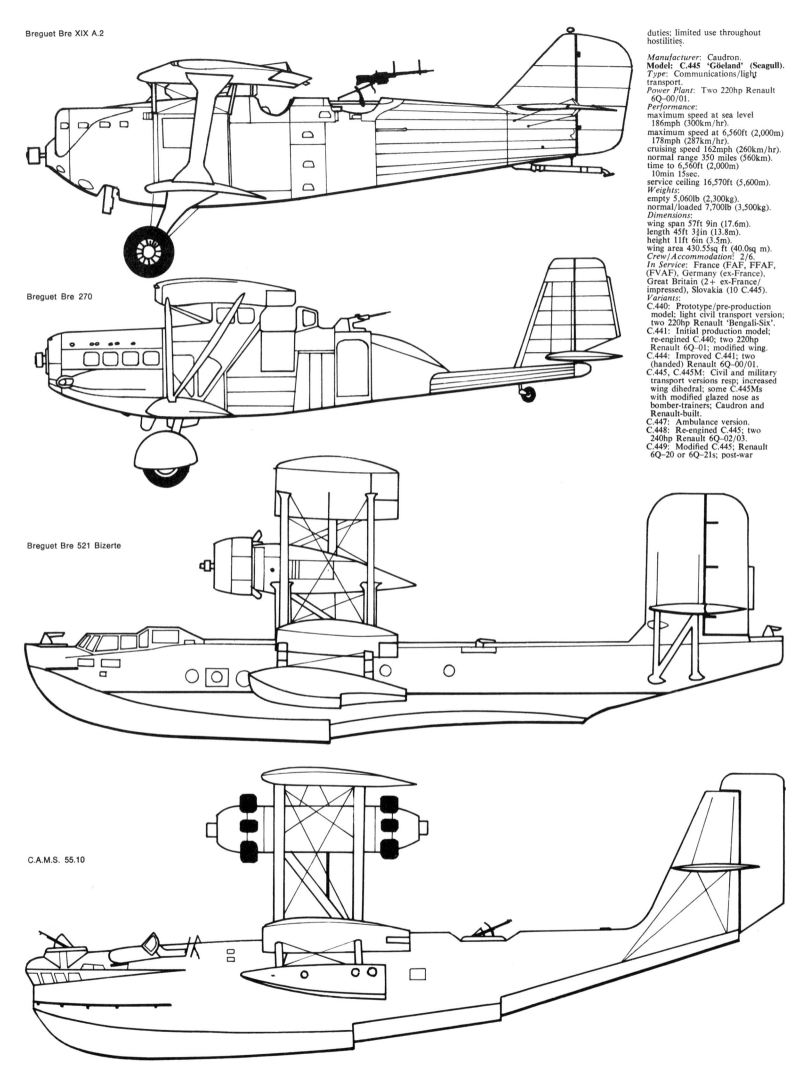

Breguet Bre XIX A.2

Breguet Bre 270

Breguet Bre 521 Bizerte

C.A.M.S. 55.10

duties; limited use throughout
hostilities.

Manufacturer: Caudron.
Model: C.445 'Göeland' (Seagull).
Type: Communications/light
transport.
Power Plant: Two 220hp Renault
6Q–00/01.
Performance:
maximum speed at sea level
186mph (300km/hr).
maximum speed at 6,560ft (2,000m)
178mph (287km/hr).
cruising speed 162mph (260km/hr).
normal range 350 miles (560km).
time to 6,560ft (2,000m)
10min 15sec.
service ceiling 16,570ft (5,600m).
Weights:
empty 5,060lb (2,300kg).
normal/loaded 7,700lb (3,500kg).
Dimensions:
wing span 57ft 9in (17.6m).
length 45ft 3¾in (13.8m).
height 11ft 6in (3.5m).
wing area 430.55sq ft (40.0sq m).
Crew/Accommodation: 2/6.
In Service: France (FAF, FFAF,
(FVAF), Germany (ex-France),
Great Britain (2 + ex-France/
impressed), Slovakia (10 C.445).
Variants:
C.440: Prototype/pre-production
model; light civil transport version;
two 220hp Renault 'Bengali-Six'.
C.441: Initial production model;
re-engined C.440; two 220hp
Renault 6Q–01; modified wing.
C.444: Improved C.441; two
(handed) Renault 6Q–00/01.
C.445, C.445M: Civil and military
transport versions resp; increased
wing dihedral; some C.445Ms
with modified glazed nose as
bomber-trainers; Caudron and
Renault-built.
C.447: Ambulance version.
C.448: Re-engined C.445; two
240hp Renault 6Q–02/03.
C.449: Modified C.445; Renault
6Q–20 or 6Q–21s; post-war

Caudron C.714 C1 Cyclone

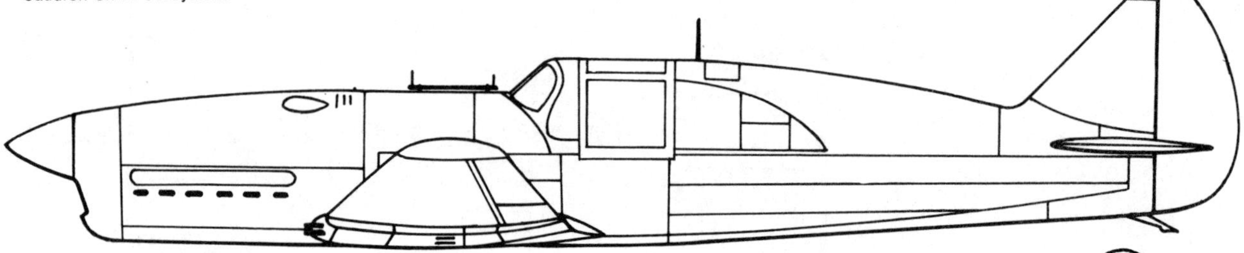

Dewoitine D.510

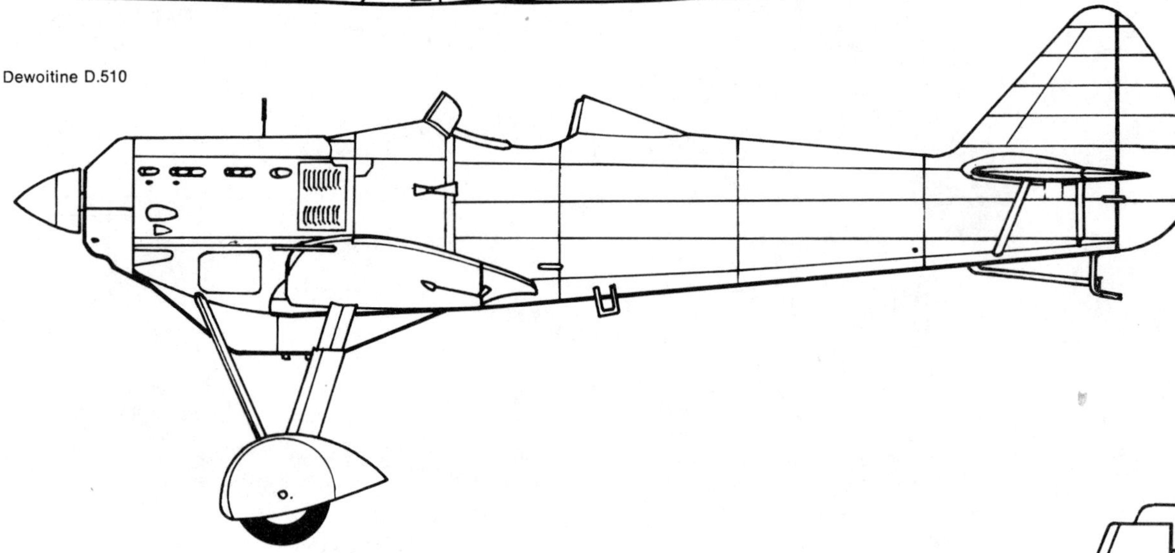

Farman (Centre) NC 223.4

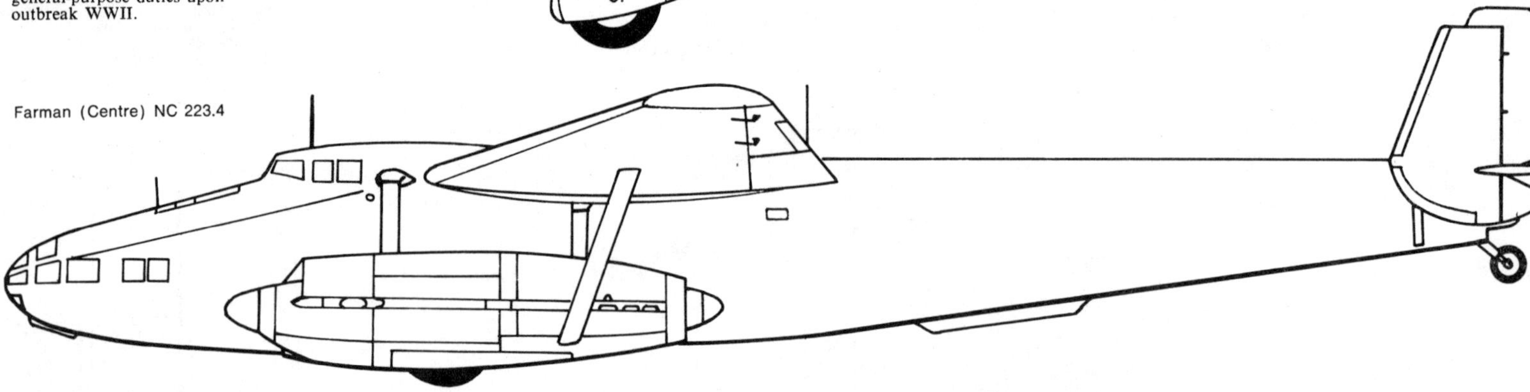

production-alternative designation AA.1.
Total Production: 1,702.
Remarks: Twin-engined light civil transport first flown 1935; extensive pre-war use Europe and Africa; military C.445M ordered 1937; served French forces throughout WWII most fronts; production continued during war (for both FVAF and Germany) and after, as AA.1; employed by Luftwaffe in variety ancillary roles—trainer, communications, light transport, air ambulance; also supplied Slovak AF as crew-trainer.

Manufacturer: Caudron.
Model: C.510 'Pelican'.
Type: Liaison/ambulance.
Power Plant: One 100hp Renault 4 Pei.
Performance:
maximum speed at sea level 110mph (177km/hr).
cruising speed 103mph (165km/hr).
range 435 miles (700km).
time to 1,180ft (360m) 2min 40sec.
service ceiling 14,765ft (4,500m).
Weights:
empty 1,367lb (620kg).
loaded 2,529lb (1,147kg).
Dimensions:
wing span 38ft 9½in (11.82m).
length 27ft 11½in (8.52m).
height 7ft 4½in (2.25m).
wing area 255.11sq ft (23.7sq m).
Crew/Accommodation: 1 or 2/2.
In Service: France.
Variants:
C.510: Four-seat civil tourer/ambulance; provisions for addn fuel as 3-seat long-range transport.
Remarks: First flown 1935, number civil C.510s impressed liaison/general-purpose duties upon outbreak WWII.

Manufacturer: Caudron.
Model: C.600 'Aiglon'.
Type: Liaison.
Power Plant: One 140hp Renault 'Bengali'.
Performance:
maximum speed 140mph (225km/hr).
cruising speed 124mph (200km/hr).
normal range 336 miles (540km).
service ceiling 19,685ft (6,000m).
Weights:
empty 1,279lb (580kg).
loaded 1,940lb (880kg).
Dimensions:
wing span 37ft 4in (11.38m).
length 24ft 2½in (7.62m).
height 6ft 6½in (2.0m).
wing area 156.08sq ft (14.50sq m).
Crew/Accommodation: 1/3.
In Service: France (FAF, FVAF, FFAF), Germany.
Variants:
C.600, 601: 2-seat light touring monoplane; one 100hp Renault 4 Pei or 140hp Renault 'Bengali'.
Remarks: First flown 1935, number C.600 civil tourers impressed military liaison duties upon outbreak WWII; served throughout hostilities, inc post-liberation 1944–45 as single-seaters.

Manufacturer: Caudron.
Model: C.630 'Simoun'.
Type: Transport.
Power Plant: One 220hp Renault 'Bengali-Six'.
Performance:
maximum speed 193mph (310km/hr).
cruising speed 174mph (280km/hr).
maximum range 764 miles (1,230km).
service ceiling 23,945ft (7,300m).
Weights:
empty 1,881lb (885kg).
normal/loaded 2,970lb (1,350kg).
Dimensions:
wing span 34ft 1in (10.4m).
length 28ft 6in (8.7m).
height 7ft 4in (2.25m).
wing area 172.16sq ft (16.0sq m).
Crew/Accommodation: 1/3.

In Service: France (FAF, FFAF, FVAF), Germany (ex-France), Great Britain (2+ ex-France, impressed).
Variants:
C.620: Initial production model; civil transport version; one 220hp Renault 'Bengali-Six'.
C.630: Improved C.620; one 180hp Renault 6Q or 6 Pdi, or 220hp Renault 'Bengali-Six'.
C.631: Re-engined C.630; one 220hp Renault 'Bengali-Six'.
C.633,634,635: Modified C.630s; various power plants; C.633 modified fuselage; C.634 modified wings and increased weight; C.635M militarised.
Total Production: 550+.
Remarks: First flown 1934, original civil C.620 4-seat cabin monoplane subject of FAF order 1937; in wide service by outbreak WWII, many captured intact by Germany and subsequently used in courier and liaison roles; at least two known escapes, one to UK, other to RAF Middle East.

Manufacturer: Caudron.
Model: C.714 C1 'Cyclone'.
Type: Lightweight interceptor-fighter.
Power Plant: One 450hp Renault 12R 03.
Performance:
maximum speed at 16,400ft (5,000m) 299mph (465km/hr).
maximum range 559 miles (900km).
time to 13,120ft (4,000m) 6min 45sec.
service ceiling 29,855ft (9,100m).
Weights:
empty 3,086lb (1,400kg).
loaded 3,858lb (1,750kg).
Dimensions:
wing span 29ft 5in (8.96m).
length 28ft 3½in (8.63m).
height 9ft 5in (2.87m).
wing area 134.55sq ft (12.5sq m).
Armament: Four 7.5mm MAC 1934 machine-guns in wings.
Crew: 1.
In Service: Finland (6), France

(FAF, FPAF, FVAF), Germany.
Variants (with no. built):
C.710–01: Prototype; experimental lightweight fighter; one 450hp Renault 12R 01; two 20mm cannon (1).
C.712R: Civil racer; one 730hp Renault 12R (1).
C.713 C1: Lightweight fighter version; modified C.710–01; retractable undercarriage; redesigned vertical tail surfaces (1).
C.714–01: Prototype; modified C.713; strengthened fuselage; revised armament; improved wing.
C.714 C1: Production model; as C.714–01 (92).
C.720 Trainer version of C.714; one 220hp Renault 'Bengali' 6Q or 100hp Renault 4 Pei.
C.760, C.770: Prototypes; modified C.714; one 750hp Isotta-Fraschini Delta RC.40, or one 800hp Renault 626 resp (3).
C.780: Project only.
Total Production: 98.
Remarks: Development of pre-war civil racing series, C.714 'Cyclone' lightweight fighter entered FAF service early 1940; only six of intended fifty allocated to Finnish AF delivered before end of Winter War; brief employment one sqn, 1940; only FAF unit to fly C.714 during Battle of France was single Groupe of Polish volunteers; operated 2–13 June 1940, destroying twelve German aircraft at cost of thirteen 'Cyclones'; after Armistice 9 C.714s to FVAF, 20+ to Germany.

Manufacturer: Dewoitine.
Model: D.338.
Type: Transport.
Power Plant: Three 575hp Hispano-Suiza 9Vd.
Performance:
maximum speed at sea level 196mph (315km/hr).
cruising speed 174mph (280km/hr).
normal range 547 miles (880km).
time to 6,560ft (2,000m)

11min 59sec.
service ceiling 16,400ft (5,000m).
Weights:
empty 14,890lb (6,754kg).
loaded 24,471lb (11,100kg).
Dimensions:
wing span 96ft 4½in (29.38m).
length 72ft 7½in (22.13m).
height 18ft 3½in (5.57m).
wing area 1,065.64sq ft (99.0sq m).
Crew/Accommodation: 3/24.
In Service: France.
Variants (with no. built):
D.338: Civil airliner (approx 20).
D.339: Projected military transport/ambulance version.
Total Production: approx 20.
Remarks: First flown 1936, several D.338s impressed by FAF for transport duties after outbreak of WWII.

Manufacturer: Dewoitine.
Model: D.376.
Type: Ship-borne fighter.
Power Plant: One 930hp Gnome-Rhône 14 Kfs.
Performance:
maximum speed 249mph (400km/hr).
normal range 435 miles (700km).
service ceiling 32,800ft (10,000m).
Weights:
loaded 4,342lb (1,970kg).
Dimensions:
wing span 36ft 10in (11.22m).
length 24ft 5in (7.44m).
height 11ft 2½in (3.42m).
Armament: Two fixed forward-firing 7.5mm MAC 1934 machine-guns in fuselage; two fixed forward-firing 7.5mm machine-guns in wings.
Crew: 1.
In Service: France (FAF, FNAF), Spain (RepAF D.27/372), Switzerland (11 D.26, 66 D.27).
Variants (with no. built):
D.26/27: Initial production models; single-seat fighter; 250hp Wright/300–500hp Hispano-Suiza 12 resp; Swiss (EKW) licence-built (96); D.27 also Rumanian and Yugoslav licence-built.

D.271/274: Modified D.27, prototypes only; Dewoitine-built (4).
D.37: Prototype; D.27 development; increased dimensions; strengthened wing; one 750hp Gnome-Rhône 14 Kbrs (1).
D.371: Production model; one 800hp Gnome-Rhône 14 Kes; wing dihedral; two cannon or four machine-gun armament (20+).
D.372: As D.371; one 930hp Gnome-Rhône 14 Kfs; increased weight (D.371 conversions).
D.373: Navalised D.371; Gnome-Rhône 14 Kfs; arrester hook; structural strengthening (40).
D.376: As D.373; Folding wings.
Total Production: approx 75 (exc D.26/27).
Remarks: Final variants of a long line of parasol-wing fighters dating back to D–1 of early twenties, Swiss-built D.26/27 remained in service 1930–50; both D.27 and French-built D.372 participated Spanish Civil War; twenty-seven D.376s comprised sole fighter strength FNAF upon outbreak WWII; limited employment opening weeks hostilities before replacement by Potez 631, Winter, 1939–40.

Manufacturer: Dewoitine.
Model: D.501.
Type: Fighter.
Power Plant: One 690hp Hispano-Suiza 12Xcrs.
Performance:
maximum speed at sea level 196mph (315km/hr).
maximum speed at 6,560ft (2,000m) 207mph (334km/hr).
cruising speed 140mph (226km/hr).
normal range 540 miles (870km).
time to 9,840ft (3,000m) 4min 0sec.
service ceiling 33,165ft (10,200m).
Weights:
empty 4,222lb (1,287kg).
maximum 6,234lb (1,900kg).
Dimensions:
wing span 39ft 8in (12.09m).
length 24ft 10in (7.57m).
height 8ft 10½in (2.7m).

wing area 177.6sq ft (16.5sq m).
Armament: One 20mm Hispano-Suiza HS9 cannon firing through propeller hub; plus two 7.5mm Darne 33 (or 7.5mm MAC 1934) machine-guns in wings.
Crew: 1.
In Service: China (24 D.510C), France (FAF, FNAF, FVAF), Lithuania (14 D.501L), Spain (RepAF, 2 D.510T).
Variants (with no. built):
D.500 No.01: Prototype; one 660hp Hispano-Suiza 12 Xbrs; two 7.7mm Vickers machine-guns in fuselage (1).
D.500: Initial production model; late models with Vickers guns replaced by 7.5mm Darne machine-guns (inc three D.500V Venezuelan order); Dewoitine-built and Lioré-et-Olivier-built (101).
D.501: Re-engined D.500; increased armament; (inc 14 D.501L Lithuanian order); Dewoitine-built, Lioré-et-Olivier-built and Loire-built (157).
D.502: Catapult-launched fighter floatplane version; project only.
D.503: Re-engined D.511; one Hispano-Suiza 12Xcrs (1).
D.504: Parachute trials aircraft; project only.
D.505/509: Modified D.500; various power plants; projects only.
D.510: Improved D.501; one 860hp Hispano-Suiza 12Ycrs; lengthened nose; increased fuel capacity; modified undercarriage; late models with 7.5mm Darne machine-guns replaced by 7.5mm MAC 1934 machine-guns (inc 24 D.510C Chinese order and 36 D.510T original Turkish order); Lioré-et-Olivier-built and SNCASE-built (120).
D.511: Modified D.510; reduced wing span; revised (cantilever) undercarriage; prototype only (1).
Total Production: 381.
Remarks: Successful early thirties design, D.500 series subject of extensive pre-war evaluation/export orders, inc South America and Far East; saw action both second Sino-Japanese conflict and Spanish Civil War; sixty D.510s equipped three FAF Groupes upon outbreak WWII, plus number earlier D.500/501s deployed by ERCs (regional defence sqns); majority replaced or withdrawn overseas (North Africa) prior to German Blitzkrieg of 10 May 1940.

Manufacturer: Dewoitine.
Model: D.520.
Type: Fighter.
Power Plant: One 920hp Hispano-Suiza 12Y 45.
Performance:
maximum speed at sea level 264mph (425km/hr).
maximum speed at 19,685ft (6,000m) 332mph (535km/hr).
cruising speed 230mph (370km/hr).
maximum range 553 miles (900km).
time to 13,120ft (4,000m) 5min 49sec.
service ceiling 36,090ft (11,000m).
Weights:
empty 4,612lb (2,092kg).
loaded 6,134lb (2,783kg).
Dimensions:
wing span 33ft 5½in (10.2m).
length 28ft 8¾in (8.76m).
height 8ft 5¼in (2.57m).
wing area 171.69sq ft (15.95sq m).
Armament: One fixed 20mm Hispano-Suiza HS 404 cannon firing through propeller hub; four fixed forward-firing 7.5mm MAC 1934 M39 machine-guns in wings.
Crew: 1.
In Service: Bulgaria (approx 100), France (FAF, FNAF, FFAF, FVAF, FVNAF), Germany (approx 50), Great Britain (3), Italy (60), Rumania (approx 150).
Variants (with no. built):
D.520–01/03: Prototypes; one 890hp Hispano-Suiza 12Y 21, 1000hp 12Y 51, and 830hp 12Y 31 resp; wing, vertical tail, canopy modifications; 02 one 20mm cannon, two 7.5mm wing machine-guns; 03 with tailwheel in place of skid (3).
D.520: Production model; 920hp Hispano-Suiza 12Y 45 or 12Y 49; lengthened fuselage; armour; increased wing armament (905).
D.520Z: As D.520; Modified coolant/exhaust systems; improved undercarriage (1 conversion).
D.521: Re-engined D.520; 990hp Rolls-Royce Merlin III (1 conversion).
D.523/524: Re-engined D.520/521 resp; 1,000hp Hispano-Suiza 12Y 51/1,200hp 12Z 89 (2 conversions).
SE 520Z: Improved D.520; 1,200/1,600hp Hispano-Suiza 12Z; modified (lengthened) forward fuselage; revised armament; prototype only (1).
HD–780: Floatplane version; modified D.520 (1).
Total Production: 910.
Remarks: Arguably FAF's finest fighter, only 36 D.520s (of total 2,320 on order) delivered prior to German attack, 10 May 1940; equipped five Groupes (plus three Escadrilles FNAF) by Armistice, having scored 114 confirmed 'kills' for loss of 85 own number; production resumed under Vichy régime; operated FVAF, FVNAF units; saw action against Allied forces North African, Middle East (Syrian) campaigns; over 400 seized by Germany after occupation Vichy France, Nov 1942; employed Luftwaffe training Geschwader; also supplied Italian, Rumanian, and Bulgarian AFs; used by latter in home-defence role against incursions US 9th/15th AFs; resumed FAF (FFI) service latter half 1944, engaged in reduction German pockets SE France; continued limited post-war use until early fifties.
Colour Reference: Plate 12: Dewoitine D.520 of 6. Orliak (Air Regiment), Royal Bulgarian Air Force, Karlovo, Winter 1943–44; compare much-simplified post-Oct 1940 national markings with elaborate earlier style insignia as carried by P.Z.L. P.43A circa 1939 (see plates 121–122).

Manufacturer: Farman (Centre).
Model: F.222.2.
Type: Heavy night bomber.
Power Plant: Four 950hp Gnome-Rhône 14N 11/15.
Performance:
maximum speed at 13,120ft (4,000m) 224mph (360km/hr).
cruising speed 196mph (315km/hr).
normal range 1,240 miles (2,000km).
time to 9,840ft (3,000m) 9min 40sec.
service ceiling 26,250ft (8,000m).
Weights:
empty 23,122lb (10,500kg).
maximum 41,226lb (18,700kg).
Dimensions:
wing span 118ft 1⅓in (36.0m).
length 70ft 4½in (21.45m).
height 17ft 0⅓in (5.19m).
wing area 2,002.08sq ft (186.0sq m).
Armament: One 7.5mm MAC 1934 Type T machine-gun each in manually-operated nose and dorsal turrets and ventral 'dustbin'; max bomb load (internal) 9,240lb (4,190kg).
Crew: 5.
In Service: France (FAF, FNAF, FFAF, FVAF).
Variants (with no. built):
F. 220.01: Initial prototype; four (tandem pair) 600hp Hispano-Suiza 12 Lbr (1).
F 221.01: Prototype; four (tandem pair) 800hp Gnome-Rhône 14 Kbrs; redesigned nose (1).
F 221 BN5: Production model; as 221.01 (10).
F 222 BN5 No. 01: Prototype; converted F 221.01; retractable undercarriage; modified engine nacelles (one conversion).
F 222.1 BN5: Production model (11).
F 222.2 BN5: Modified F 222.1; redesigned (lengthened) nose; outer wing dihedral (24).
F 224: Civil/military transport version; development of F 222; four 815hp Gnome-Rhône 14K (6).
Total Production: 53 (all Marks).
Remarks: The only four-engined bombers in operational service upon outbreak WWII, twenty-nine F 221/222s equipped three FAF Groupes—two in Metropolitan France and one in West Africa; former employed leaflet-dropping, Winter 1939–40, subsequently attacking targets in Western Germany, inc BMW plant in Munich; only one bomber lost (accidentally) during entire Battle of France; FNAF examples performed Atlantic patrol duties, plus night bombing Sardinia/NW Italy; after Armistice served FVAF Farman-equipped transport Groupe (with 224s/223.3s); based Morocco, number destroyed on ground by USN fighters during 'Torch' landings, Nov 1942; finally withdrawn FFAF service end 1944; F 224 civil transports, rejected by Air France, taken over by FAF 1939.

Manufacturer: Farman (Centre).
Model: NC 223.3 BN5.
Type: Heavy bomber.
Power Plant: Four 910hp Hispano-Suiza 12Y 29.
Performance:
maximum speed at 13,120ft (4,000m) 248mph (400km/hr).
cruising speed 174mph (280km/hr).
normal range 1,490 miles (2,400km).
time to 13,120ft (4,000m) 10min 0sec.
ceiling 26,240ft (8,000m).
Weights:
empty 23,258lb (10,550kg).
maximum 42,329lb (19,200kg).
Dimensions:
wing span 110ft 2in (33.6m).
length 72ft 2in (22.0m).
height 16ft 8in (5.1m).
wing area 1,425sq ft (132.4sq m).
Armament: One flexible 7.5mm MAC 1934 machine-gun in nose; one 20mm Hispano 404 cannon each in dorsal and ventral turrets; max bomb load (internal) 9,240lb (4,200kg).
Crew: 5–6.
In Service: France (FAF, FNAF, FFAF, FVAF).
Variants (with no. built):
F 223.1 No.01: Initial prototype; long-range mailplane; four (tandem pair) 720hp Hispano-Suiza 12 Xirsl (1).
NC 223 No.01: Prototype; bomber version; four (tandem pair) 1,000hp Hispano-Suiza 14AA; modified equipment; subsequently re-engined Hispano-Suiza 12Y (as NC 223.3 No.01) (1).
NC 223.2: Proposed bomber version; Gnome-Rhône 14 Ns.
NC 223.3 BN5: Initial production model; as re-engined NC 223.3 No. 01 (8+).
NC 223.4: Long-range mailplane version of NC 223.3 BN5; four (tandem pair) 910hp Hispano-Suiza 12Y 39; redesigned fuselage, modified tail surfaces; subsequently re-engined (970hp Hispano-Suiza 12Y 37) and converted maritime reconnaissance role; one 7.5mm Darne machine-gun; eight 551lb (250kg) bombs underwing (3).
Total Production: 13+.
Remarks: Entered service at height Battle of France; first four NC 223.3s participated night raids on Germany, late May–June, 1940; subsequently converted civil (Air France) and military (FVAF) transport duties; in contast, NC 223.4 (evolved specifically as transatlantic mailplane) converted for military role; intended maritime reconnaissance, in fact served as night bomber, claiming distinction first Allied bomber to attack Berlin, 7–8 June 1940; after Armistice restored civil use.

Manufacturer: Farman (Centre).
Model: NC 470.
Type: Reconnaissance/trainer floatplane.
Power Plant: Two 480hp Gnome-Rhône 9Akx Jupiter.
Performance:
maximum speed 143mph (230km/hr).
cruising speed 118mph (190km/hr).
time to 6,560ft (2,000m) 9min 40sec.
service ceiling 19,685ft (6,000m).
Weights:
empty 8,179lb (3,710kg).
loaded 13,228lb (6,000kg).
Dimensions:
wing span 80ft 2½in (24.45m).
length 52ft 10in (16.1m).
height 15ft 11in (4.85m).
wing area 1,022.57sq ft (95.0sq m).
Armament: One 7.5mm Darne machine-gun in open dorsal position; max bomb load 440lb (200 kg).
Crew: 6.
In Service: France (FNAF, FVNAF).
Variants (with no. built):
NC 470: Prototype and production model; trainer floatplane; two 480hp Gnome-Rhône 9 Akx Jupiter (23+).
NC 471-01: Prototype; as NC 470; two 500hp Gnome-Rhône 9Kgr (1).
NC 472: Modified NC 470; two 600hp Pratt & Whitney S3H1-G Wasp; project only.
Total Production: 24+.
Remarks: First flown as landplane late 1937; NC 470 trainer floatplane pressed into service maritime reconnaissance role early weeks WWII; returned training duties; 14 seized by Germany Nov 1942.

Manufacturer: Gourdou-Leseurre.
Model: GL–810 Hy.
Type: Ship-borne observation/scout floatplane.
Power Plant: One 420hp Gnome-Rhône 9Ady Jupiter.
Performance:
maximum speed at sea level 112mph (180km/hr).
cruising speed 98mph (158km/hr).
time to 9,840ft (3,000m) 16min 0sec.
service ceiling 18,045ft (5,500m).
Weights:
empty 3,682lb (1,670 kg).
normal/loaded 5,423lb (2,460kg).
Dimensions:
wing span 52ft 6in (16.0m).
length 34ft 5in (10.5m).
height 13ft 11¾in (4.2m).
wing area 462.85sq ft (43.0sq m).
Armament: One fixed forward-firing 7.7mm Vickers machine-gun; two flexible 7.7mm Lewis guns; max bomb load 330lb (150kg).
Crew: 3.
In Service: France (FNAF, FVNAF).
Variants (with no. built):
L 2-01: Prototype; 2-seat land-based or ship-borne reconnaissance floatplane; 380hp Gnome-Rhône Jupiter (1).
L 3: Pre-production model; one addn crew; uprated engine (6).
GL-810 Hy: Production model; lengthened floats (24).
GL-811: Modified GL 810; folding wing; dual controls (20).
GL-812: Modified GL-810; redesigned, enlarged tail surfaces (29).
GL-813: As GL-812; dual controls (13).
Total Production: 93.
Remarks: Pre-war battleship-borne, heavy cruiser-borne, and seaplane carrier-borne observation floatplane; GL-810/812s relegated shore-based units prior WWII; seventeen of latter (plus nine GL-810s) still on FNAF strength Sept 1939; limited employment Channel coastal patrol, before being pressed into service as emergency evacuation transport (at least four men plus essential equipment) during final stages of French retreat along Atlantic coast late June 1940; West Indies-based examples in Vichy employ until mid-1943.

Manufacturer: Gourdou-Leseurre.
Model: GL–832 Hy.
Type: Ship-borne observation/scout floatplane.
Power Plant: One 230hp Hispano-Suiza 9Qb.
Performance:
maximum speed at 9,840ft (3,000m) 114mph (184km/hr).
normal range 348 miles (560km).
time to 9,840ft (3,000m) 17min 30sec.
service ceiling 15,750ft (4,800m).
Weights:
empty 2,443lb (1,108kg).
maximum 3,858lb (1,750kg).
Dimensions:
wing span 42ft 7¾in (13.0m).
length 28ft 7¾in (8.7m).
height 9ft 1½in (2.78m).
wing area 322.92sq ft (28.0sq m).
Armament: One flexible .303in Lewis machine-gun in rear cockpit.
Crew: 2.
In Service: France.
Variants (with no. built):
GL-831-01: Prototype; 250hp Hispano-Suiza 9Qa (1).
GL-832 Hy: Production model; re-engined; modified floats and tail surfaces (22).
Total Production: 23.
Remarks: Smaller version of earlier GL-810/812 series, GL-832 Hy served as catapult aircraft aboard French cruisers, as well as equipping colonial sloops, during mid-thirties; by Sept 1939 less than a dozen remained on charge, inc five with Far East Fleet (Indo-China), at least two aboard home-based units; others in French West Indies waters.

Manufacturer: Hanriot.
Model: H.436.
Type: General-purpose/trainer.
Power Plant: One 230hp Salmson 9Ab.
Performance:
maximum speed 112mph (180km/hr).
normal range 280 miles (450km).
service ceiling 13,451ft (4,100m).
Weights:
empty 2,050lb (930kg).
loaded 3,130lb (1,420kg).
Dimensions:
wing span 37ft 4¾in (11.4m).
length 25ft 4in (7.72m).
height 10ft 9½in (3.29m).
wing area 325.5sq ft (30.24sq m).
Armament: Provision for one 7.7mm machine-gun in rear

Gourdou-Leseurre GL–810 Hy

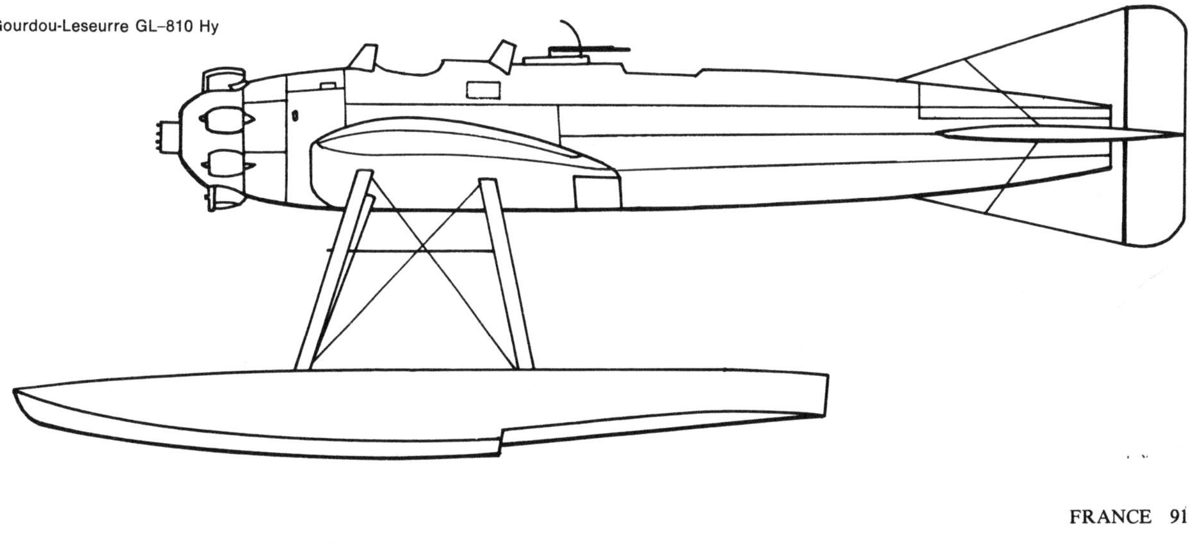

Order of Battle 10 May 1940

FRENCH AIR FORCE (Armée de l'Air)

ZONE D'OPERATIONS AÉRIENNES NORD (AIR ZONE NORTH)

Fighters
Groupement de Chasse 21:

GC I/1	Chantilly-les-Aigles	Bloch 152
GC II/1	Buc	Bloch 152
GC III/3	Beauvais-Tillé	Morane-Saulnier M.S.406
GC II/10	Rouen-Boos	Bloch 151
		Bloch 152
GC III/10	Le Havre-Octeville	Bloch 151
		Bloch 152

Groupement de Chasse 23:

GC II/2	Laon-Chambry	Morane-Saulnier M.S.406
GC III/2	Cambrai-Niergnies	Morane-Saulnier M.S.406
GC I/4	Wez-Thuisy	Curtiss Hawk 75
GC I/5	Suippes	Curtiss Hawk 75
ECMJ I/16	Wez-Thuisy	Potez 631

Groupement de Chasse 25:

GC III/1	Norrent-Fontés	Morane-Saulnier M.S.406
GC II/8	Calais-Marck	Bloch 152

Night fighters

ECN I/13	Le Plessis-Belleville	Potez 631
ECN II/13	Meaux-Esbly	Potez 631
ECN III/13	Melun-Villaroche	Potez 631
ECN IV/13	Betz-Bouillancy	Potez 631

Bombers
Groupement de Bombardement 6:

GB I/12	Soissons-Saconin	Lioré-et-Olivier LeO 451
GB II/12	Persan-Beaumont	Lioré-et-Olivier LeO 451

Groupement de Bombardement 9:

GB I/34	Montdidier	Amiot 143
GB II/34	Roye-Amy	Amiot 143

Attack bombers
Groupement de Bombardement d'Assaut 18:

GBA I/54	La Ferté-Gaucher	Breguet Bre 693
GBA II/54	Nangis	Breguet Bre 693

Strategic reconnaissance

GR II/33	Athies-sous-Laon	Potez 637
		Bloch 174
GR I/35	St. Omer-Wizerne	Potez 63.11
GR I/14	St. Simon-Clastres	Potez 63.11
GR II/52	Couvron	Potez 637
		Potez 63.11
GR II/22	Chatel-Chéhéry	Potez 63.11

Tactical reconnaissance (Army co-operation)
I Land Army:

FA 2 (GAO 502)	La Fère-Courbes	Potez 63.11
		Mureaux 115
FA 3 (GAO 503)	Valenciennes	Potez 63.11
		Mureaux 115
FA 4 (GAO 504)	Denain-Prouvy	Potez 63.11
		Mureaux 115
FA 5 (GAO 505)	Vertain-Le Quesnoy	Potez 63.11
		Potez 39
FA 34 (GAO 544)	Villers-les-Guise	Potez 63.11
		Mureaux 115

II Land Army:

FA 10 (GAO 510)	Attigny	Potez 63.11
		Mureaux 115
		Potez 39
FA 18 (GAO 518)	Challerange	Potez 63.11
		Breguet Bre 270
		Potez 25
FA 26 (GAO 2/520)	Challerange	Potez 63.11
		Mureaux 115
FA 35 (GAO 507)	Attigny	Potez 63.11
		Mureaux 115

VII Land Army:

FA 1 (GAO 501)	Dunkerque-Mardyck	Potez 63.11
		Mureaux 115
FA 16 (GAO 516)	Calais-St. Inglevert	Potez 63.11
		Breguet Bre 270
FA 28 (GAO 552)	St. Omer-Wizerne	Potez 63.11
		Mureaux 117

IX Land Army:

FA 11 (GAO 511)	Villers-les Guise	Potez 63.11
		Potez 39
FA 25 (GAO 2/551)	Tournès-Belval	Potez 63.11
		Mureaux 117
FA 30 (GAO 4/551)	Le Quesnoy	Potez 63.11
		Mureaux 117
FA 32 (GAO 547)	Mézières-Tournès-Belval	Potez 63.11
		Breguet Bre 270
FA 33 (GAO 545)	Denain-Prouvy	Potez 63.11
		Breguet Bre 270

Land Army Group Reserve:

FA 42 (GAO 515)	Connantre	Potez 63.11
		Mureaux 115

ZONE D'OPERATIONS AÉRIENNES EST (AIR ZONE EAST)

Fighters
Groupement de Chasse 22:

GC I/2	Toul-Ochey	Morane-Saulnier M.S.406
GC II/4	Xaffévillers	Curtiss Hawk 75
GC II/5	Toul-Croix-de-Metz	Curtiss Hawk 75
GC II/6	Anglure-Vouarces	Morane-Saulnier M.S.406
GC III/7	Vitry-le-Francois-Vauxclerc	Morane-Saulnier M.S.406
GC I/8	Velaine-en-Haye	Bloch 152

Bombers
Groupement de Bombardement 10:

GB I/38	Troyes	Amiot 143
GB II/38	Auxerre	Amiot 143

Groupement de Bombardement 15:

GB I/15	Reims-Courcy	Farman 221 and 222
GB II/15	Reims-Courcy	Farman 221 and 222

Strategic reconnaissance

GR I/22	Metz-Frescaty	Potez 63.11
GR I/36	Martigny-les-Gerbonveaux	Potez 63.11
GR II/36	Neufchateau-Azelot	Potez 63.11
		Bloch 174

GR I/52	St. Dizier	Potez 637
		Bloch 174

Tactical reconnaissance (Army co-operation)
III Land Army:

FA 6 (GAO 2/506)	Chambley	Potez 63.11
		Mureaux 115
FA 21 (GAO 1/551)	Etain-Buzy	Potez 63.11
		Mureaux 115
FA 22 (GAO 2/508)	Mars-la-Tour	Potez 63.11
		Breguet Bre 270
		Potez 25
FA 23 (GAO 1/506)	Conflans-Doncourt	Potez 63.11
		Mureaux 115
FA 27 (GAO 3/551)	Senon-Spincourt	Potez 63.11
		Mureaux 115

IV Land Army:

FA 9 (GAO 509)	Delme-Essey	Potez 63.11
		Breguet Bre 270
FA 20 (GAO 520)	Morhange	Potez 63.11
		Mureaux 115

V Land Army:

FA 8 (GAO 548)	Epinal-Dogneville	Potez 63.11
		Mureaux 117
FA 12 (GAO 512)	La Perthe	Potez 63.11
		Breguet Bre 270
FA 17 (GAO 517)	Neufchateau	Potez 63.11
		Potez 39
FA 24 (GAO 553)	Nancy-Azelot	Potez 63.11
		Mureaux 115

Land Army Group Reserve:

FA 31 (GAO 546)	Sézanne	Potez 63.11
		Breguet Bre 270

ZONE D'OPERATIONS AÉRIENNES SUD (AIR ZONE SOUTH)

Fighters
Groupement de Chasse 24:

GC III/6	Chissey	Morane-Saulnier M.S.406
GC II/7	Luxeuil-St. Sauveur	Morane-Saulnier M.S.406

Strategic reconnaissance

GR I/33	Dôle	Potez 637
		Bloch 174
GR I/55	Lure-Malbouhans	Potez 63.11

Tactical reconnaissance (Army co-operation)
VIII Land Army:

FA 7 (GAO 543)	Luxeuil-St. Sauveur	Potez 63.11
		Potez 540
		Breguet Bre 270
FA 13 (GAO 513)	Belfort-Chaux	Potez 63.11
		Potez 39
		Potez 25

ZONE D'OPERATIONS AÉRIENNES DES ALPES (AIR ZONE ALPS)

Fighters

GC I/3	Cannes	Dewoitine D.520
GC II/3	Le Luc	Morane-Saulnier M.S.406
		Dewoitine D.520
GC I/6	Marseille-Marignane	Morane-Saulnier M.S.406
GC II/9	Marseille-Marignane	Morane-Saulnier M.S.406
		Bloch 152
GC III/9	Lyon-Bron	Bloch 151
GAM 550	Ghisonaccia (Corsica)	Morane-Saulnier M.S.406
		Potez 63.11
GC (Pol.)	Lyon-Bron	Morane-Saulnier M.S.406
		Caudron C.714

Night fighters

ECN V/13	Lyon-Bron	Potez 631

Bombers
Groupement de Bombardement 1:

GB I/62	Orange-Plan de Dieu	Martin 167F
GB I/63	Orange-Plan de Dieu	Martin 167F

Groupement de Bombardement 6:

GB I/31	Lézignan	Lioré-et-Olivier LeO 451
GB II/31	Lézignan	Lioré-et-Olivier LeO 451

Groupement de Bombardement 7:

GB I/23	Istres-Le Vallon	Bloch 210
GB II/23	Istres-Le Vallon	Bloch 210
		Lioré-et-Olivier LeO 451

Groupement de Bombardement 9:

GB I/21	Avignon	Amiot 351
		Amiot 354
		Bloch 210
GB II/21	Avignon	Amiot 351
		Amiot 354
		Bloch 210

Groupement de Bombardement 11:

GB I/11	Istres-Mas de Rue	Lioré-et-Olivier LeO 451
		Bloch 210
GB II/11	Istres-Mas de Rue	Lioré-et-Olivier LeO 451
		Bloch 210

Attack bombers
Groupement de Bombardement d'Assaut 19:

GBA II/35	Briare	Potez 633
		Breguet Bre 691
GBA I/51	Le Luc	Potez 633
		Breguet Bre 691 & 693
GBA II/51	Le Luc	Potez 633
		Breguet Bre 691 & 693

Strategic reconnaissance

GR II/14	Valence	Potez 63.11
GR II/55	Chambarand-Marciolles	Potez 63.11

Tactical reconnaissance (Army co-operation)

FA 14 (GAO 2/514)	St. Etienne-de-St. Geoirs	Potez 63.11
		Mureaux 117
FA 36 (GAO 1/514)	Montbard-Touillon	Potez 63.11
		Mureaux 115
FA 37 (GAO 1/584)	Valence	Potez 63.11

Reserve:

FA 39 (GAO 581)	Marignane	Potez 63.11
FA 40 (GAO 582)	Valence-Chabeuil	Potez 63.11
FA 41 (GAO 1/589)	Fayence-Sisteron	Potez 63.11

---

cockpit.
Crew: 2.
In Service: France.
Variants (with no. built):
H.43: Prototypes; single-seat liaison version; various power plants (2).
LH.431 (H.431): Prototype and production model; dual-control advanced trainer version; one 420hp Lorraine 'Mizar' (51).
LH.432,433,H.436: Modified H.43; general-purpose versions, various power plants (78).
H.434: Prototype; trainer version (1).
LH.437: Prototypes; advanced trainer/ambulance version; one Lorraine 'Mizar' (2).
H.438: Export reconnaissance version (12).
H.439: Trainer version (14).
Total Production: 160.
Remarks: Prolific series general-purpose/trainer biplanes dating back to late twenties, several still serving FAF upon outbreak WWII.

Manufacturer: Hanriot.
Model: H.16-1.
Type: Observation/liaison.
Power Plant: One 120hp Renault 4 Pdi.
Performance:
maximum speed at sea level 96mph (155km/hr).
normal range 233 miles (375km).
service ceiling 13,780ft (4,200m).
Weights:
empty 1,343lb (609kg).
loaded 2,083lb (945kg).
Dimensions:
wing span 39ft 0½in (11.9m).
length 26ft 11¾in (8.22m).
height 8ft 7in (2.62m).
wing area 336.81sq ft (22.0sq m).
Crew/Accommodation: 1/1.
In Service: France.
Variants (with no. built):
H.16: 2-seat trainer version (15).
H.16–1: 2-seat observation and liaison version; modified H.16 (29).
Total Production: 44.
Remarks: Development of earlier LH.12 high-wing primary trainer, H.16 first flown 1934, several still in FAF service early months WWII.

Manufacturer: Hanriot.
Model: H.185 L2.
Type: Liaison/communications.
Power Plant: One 140hp Renault 4 Pei.
Performance:
maximum speed 118mph (190km/hr).
normal range 497 miles (800km).
service ceiling 18,040ft (5,500m).
Weights:
empty 1,433lb (650kg).
loaded 2,037lb (924kg).
Dimensions:
wing span 39ft 4½in (12.0m).
length 23ft 8½in (7.22m).
height 10ft 4in (3.15m).
wing area 204.19sq ft (18.97sq m).
Crew/Accommodation: 1/1.
In Service: France (FAF, FNAF, FVAF, FVNAF).
Variants (with no. built):
H.170, 171, 172B: Prototypes; 2-seat observation, tourer and trainer versions resp; one 180hp Salmson 6TE (3).
H.172N: Pre-production trainer version; modified H.172B (7).
H.173, 174: Prototypes; 2-seat and 3-seat aerobatic trainer versions resp (2).
H. 175: Modified H.170; navalised observation version (FNAF) (10).
H.180T, 180M, 181: Prototypes; 3-seat tourer, observation and ambulance versions resp; one 140hp Renault 4 Pei (3).
H.182: Production model; 2-seat military trainer version; modified H.180M (346).
H.183, 184: Prototypes; aerobatic and 3-seat trainer versions resp; one Renault 4 Pei (2).
H.185: 2-seat liaison version for FNAF (6).
H.190M, 191, 192B: Prototypes; observation, 3-seat tourer and 2-seat trainer versions resp; one 180hp Régnier R6 (3).
H.192N: Production model; trainer version; modified H.192B (9).
H.195: 2-seat liaison version; modified H.190M (1).
Total Production: 392.
Remarks: Extensive and versatile mid-thirties series, both civil and military; major production version, H.182, extensively used trainer and liaison roles; H.175/185 employed by FNAF observation/liaison duties, 1939–40.

Manufacturer: Hanriot.
Model: H.232.
Type: Liaison/advanced trainer.
Power Plant: Two 220hp Renault

6Q.
Performance:
maximum speed 199mph (320km/hr).
Dimensions:
wing span 42ft 0in (12.8m).
length 26ft 8in (8.13m).
height 11ft 7¾in (3.55m).
Crew/Accommodation: 1/1.
In Service: Finland.
Variants:
H.230/231: 2-seat advanced trainer versions; two 170hp Salmson 6TE or 250hp Salmson 6AF2/AF3; fixed undercarriage.
H.232: Improved H.230; uprated engines; modified wing-flaps; retractable undercarriage.
Remarks: First flown 1938; three captured H.232s sold by Germany to Finland 1941; employed by Finnish AF as advanced trainer (Continuation War 1941/44), and liaison duties.

Manufacturer: Latécoère.
Model: Laté 29.0.
Type: Torpedo-bomber floatplane.
Power Plant: One 650hp Hispano-Suiza 12Nbr.
Performance:
maximum speed at sea level 131mph (210km/hr).
cruising speed 94mph (151km/hr).
normal range 435 miles (700km).
time to 4,920ft (1,500m) 7min 37sec.
service ceiling 13,450ft (4,100m).

Latécoère Laté 298D

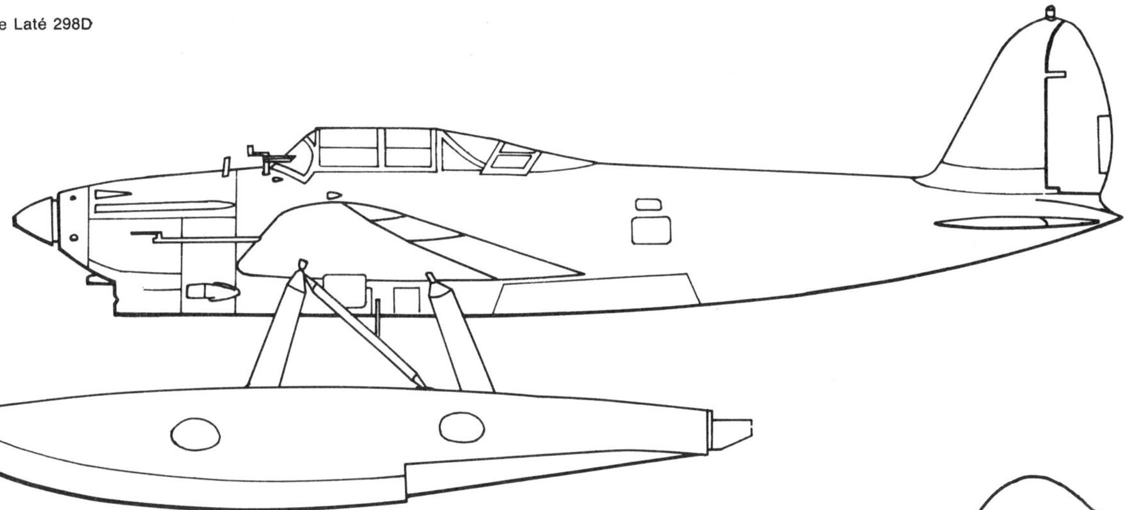

Latécoère Laté 302

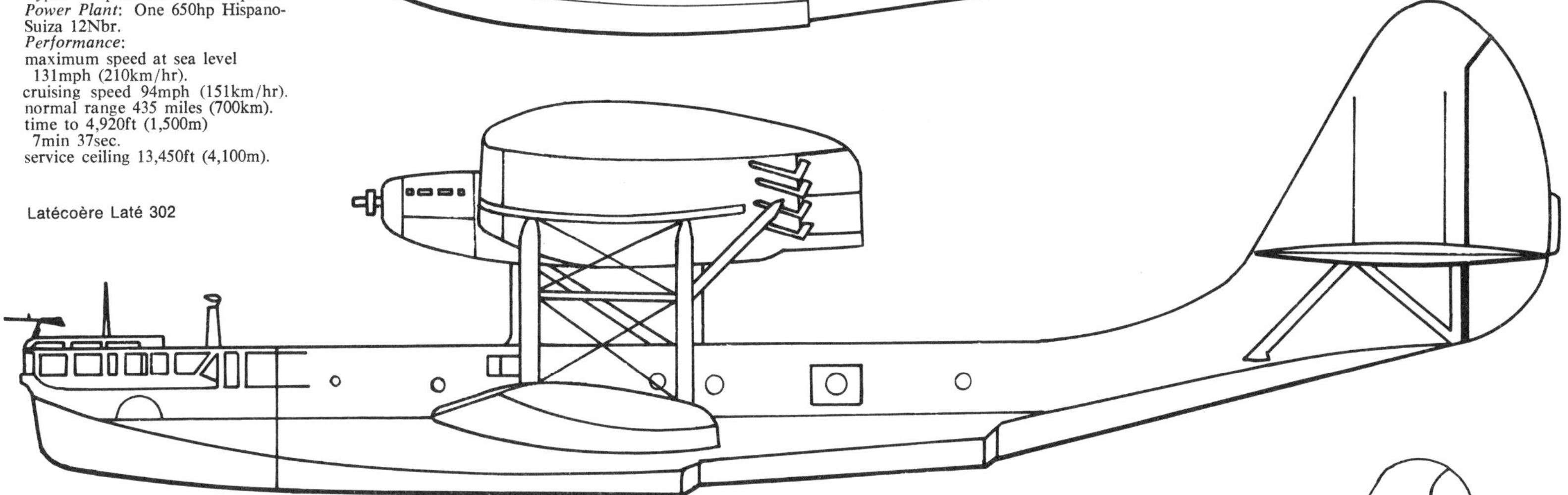

Latécoère Laté 523

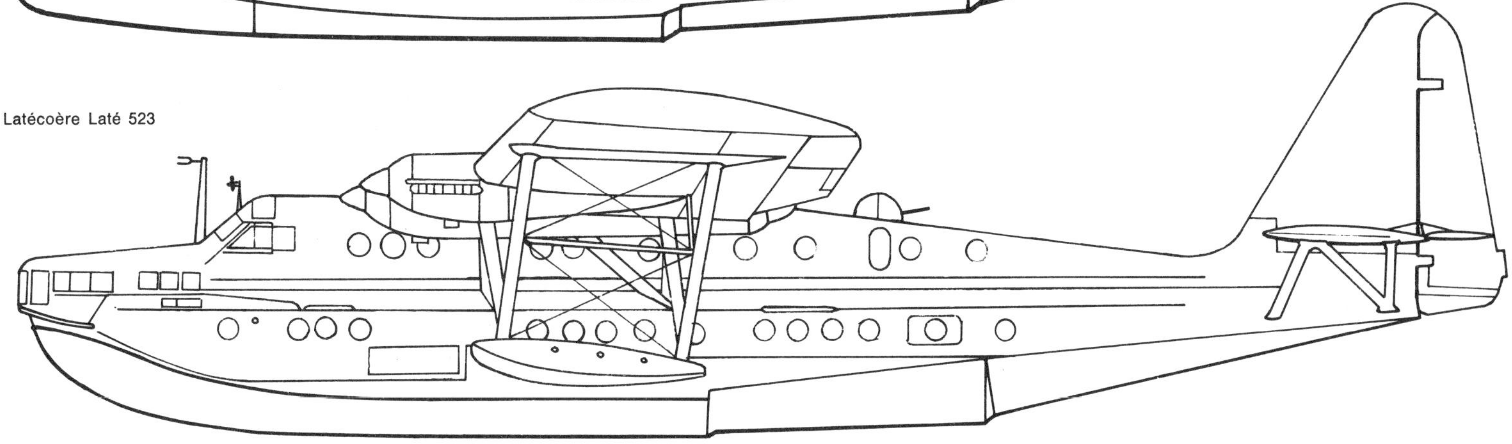

Weights:
empty 6,595lb (2,990kg).
loaded 10,582lb (4,800kg).
Dimensions:
wing span 63ft 1¾in (19.25m).
length 47ft 6in (14.48m).
height 18ft 2½in (5.55m).
wing area 626.46sq ft (58.2sq m).
Armament: One fixed forward-firing 7.7mm Vickers machine-gun; two 7.7mm Lewis guns in dorsal turret; max bomb load 660lb (300kg) or one Type 1926 DA torpedo.
Crew: 3.
In Service: France (FNAF).
Variants (with no. built):
Laté 29.0–01/2: Prototypes (2).
Laté 29.0: Initial production model; Laté 29.3, 4, 6, experimental versions; 800hp Gnome-Rhône 14Krs, 830hp 14Kdrs, and 840hp Hispano-Suiza 12 Ycrs resp (total approx 33).
Total Production: approx 35.
Remarks: First flown 1931, Laté 29.0 torpedo-bomber floatplanes withdrawn from first-line service Winter 1938–39; four examples returned to operations immediately prior outbreak WWII; equipped one naval Escadrille for Channel coastal patrol duties, Sept 1939–June 1940; dive-bombed German naval units during retreat along Channel and Atlantic seaboards, subsequently serving as emergency evacuation/transports (5 troops), before final immobilisation on lake north of Bordeaux, 25 June 1940.

Manufacturer: Latécoère.
Model: Laté 298D.
Type: Torpedo-bomber/reconnaissance floatplane.
Power Plant: One 880hp Hispano-Suiza 12 Ycrs1.
Performance:
maximum speed at 6,560ft (2,000m) 180mph (290km/hr).
cruising speed 149mph (240km/hr).
maximum range (reconnaissance) 1,367 miles (2,200km).
time to 4,920ft (1,500m) 5min 39sec.
service ceiling 21,325ft (6,500m).
Weights:
empty 6,770lb (3,071kg).
maximum 10,582lb (4,800kg).
Dimensions:
wing span 50ft 10¼in (15.5m).
length 41ft 2½in (12.56m).
height 17ft 1¼in (5,23m).
wing area 340.14sq ft (31.6sq m).
Armament: Two fixed forward-firing 7.5mm Darne machine-guns in wings; one flexible 7.5mm Darne machine-gun in rear cockpit; max bomb load 1,100lb (500kg), or one 1,477lb (700kg) torpedo, or depth-charges.
Crew: 2–3.
In Service: France (FNAF, FFNAF, FVNAF), Germany.
Variants (with no. built):
Laté 298–01: Prototype; three-seat torpedo-bomber floatplane (1).
Laté 298A: Initial production model; modified canopy; land-based fixed wing; dual controls (24).
Laté 298B: Seaplane carrier-borne; folding wing; four crew (27+).
Laté 298C: Project only.
Laté 298D: Modified 298B; fixed wing (approx 60).
Laté 298E: Observation/coastal patrol version; torpedo/bomb crutch replaced by ventral observation gondola; increased canopy area; 298D conversion.
Laté 298F: As 298D; minor modifications; German controlled wartime productions; 30 ordered.
Laté 299: Prototypes; carrier-borne reconnaissance/torpedo-bomber version of Laté 298B; retractable undercarriage; lengthened fuselage; 970hp Hispano-Suiza 12 Y43 (2).
Total Production: 130+.
Remarks: Entered service end 1938, equipping four Escadrilles by outbreak of WWII; during Battle of France employed not as naval torpedo-bomber, but primarily in ground-attack role in support of French Army; also engaged in southern France and Mediterranean areas against Italy; after French capitulation continued to serve FVNAF, and later FFNAF, from Mediterranean and West African bases; latterly co-operated RAF Coastal Command Wellingtons as U-boat hunter/killer team; late 1944 returned mainland France, participated actions against German-held strongpoints on Atlantic/Biscay coasts; immediate post-war months performed policing duties as part occupation forces southern Germany; retired FNAF first-line service Spring 1946.

Manufacturer: Latécoère.
Model: Laté 302.
Type: Long-range maritime reconnaissance flying boat.
Power Plant: Four 930hp Hispano-Suiza 12 Ydrs2.
Performance:
maximum speed at 6,560ft (2,000m) 149mph (240km/hr).
cruising speed 115mph (185km/hr).
maximum range 2,050 miles (3,300km).
time to 6,560ft (2,000m) 12min 30sec.
service ceiling 16,400ft (5,000m).
Weights:
empty 31,548lb (14,310kg).
loaded 52,911lb (24,000kg).
Dimensions:
wing span 144ft 4¼in (44.0m).
length 85ft 9¼in (26.1m).
height 26ft 2in (7.97m).
wing area 2,755.56sq ft (256.0sq m).
Armament: One flexible 7.5mm Darne machine-gun each in nose and two beam positions; one or two flexible 7.5mm Darne machine-gun/s above each tandem engine nacelle; max bomb load 660lb (300kg).
Crew: 8.
In Service: France (FNAF, FVNAF).
Variants (with no. built):
Laté 300: Prototype; long-range civil transport flying boat; 4 crew; 2,200lb (1,000kg) payload (1).
Laté 301: Initial production model; four 650hp Hispano-Suiza 12 Nbr; modified wing and vertical tail surfaces inc one subsequently militarized for FNAF (3).
Laté 302: Military reconnaissance version; four 930hp supercharged Hispano-Suiza 12 Ydrs2; modified equipment; provision for external bomb load (3).
Total Production: 7.
Remarks: Parallel pre-war civil/military flying boat development, Laté 301/302s entered service mid-thirties; all three FNAF examples (plus fourth Laté 301 conversion) equipped single Escadrille at outbreak WWII; based French West Africa for shipping patrol duties 1939–40, continuing in role as part FVNAF (minus Laté 301) until grounded from lack of spares during course of 1941; single example very similar Laté 381 also reported brief wartime service.

Manufacturer: Latécoère.
Model: Laté 523.
Type: Long-range maritime reconnaissance flying boat.
Power Plant: Six 900hp Hispano-Suiza 12 Y27.
Performance:
maximum speed at 3,280ft (1,000m) 162mph (260km/hr).
cruising speed 112mph (180km/hr).

Lioré-et-Olivier LeO H-258

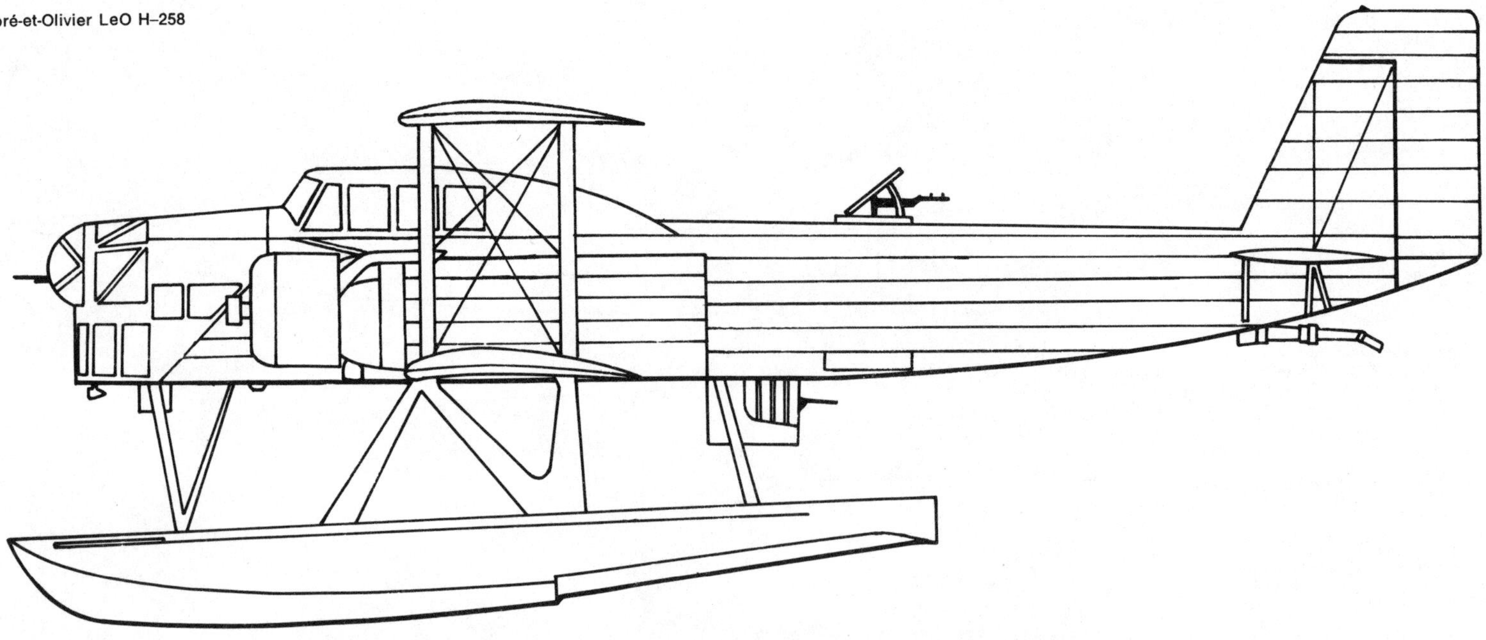

Weights:
empty 45,944lb (20,840kg).
maximum 92,594lb (42,000kg).
Dimensions:
wing span 161ft 9⅓in (49.31m).
length 103ft 9in (31.62m).
height 31ft 10in (9.7m).
wing area 3,552.09sq ft (330.0sq m).
Armament: One 7.5mm Darne machine-gun each in dorsal turret and four beam positions; max bomb load 2,645lb (1,200kg).
Crew: 14.
In Service: France (FNAF, FVNAF).
Variants (with no. built):
Laté 520: Prototype; 8 crew, 30 passenger long-range civil transport flying boat; four 1,000hp Hispano-Suiza 18 Sbr; not completed.
Laté 521: Modified Laté 520; six 860hp Hispano-Suiza 12 Ybrs; subsequently re-engined—six 650hp Hispano-Suiza 12 Nbr/970hp 12 Y37s/900hp 12 Y27s (1).
Laté 522: Improved Laté 521; six 970hp Hispano-Suiza 12 Y37; subsequently militarised and temporarily re-engined with Hispano-Suiza 12 Y27s (1).
Laté 523: Long-range maritime reconnaissance version; Hispano-Suiza 12 Y27s; single-stepped nose; provision for external bomb load (3).
Total Production: 5.
Remarks: All five examples (inc impressed/militarised 521/522) operated Atlantic long-range reconnaissance patrols, 1939–40; only one Laté 523 survived after June 1940; served FVNAF in West Africa, 1941–42.

Manufacturer: Latécoère.
Model: Laté 611.
Type: Long-range maritime reconnaissance flying boat.
Power Plant: Four 1,010hp Gnome-Rhône 14N30/31.
Performance:
maximum speed at 3,280ft (1,000m) 217mph (350km/hr).
maximum range 2,640 miles (4,250km).
time to 6,560ft (2,000m) 10min 0sec.
Weights:
empty 35,274lb (16,000kg).
maximum 68,343lb (31,000kg).
Dimensions:
wing span 133ft 0½in (40.55m).
length 88ft 9in (27.05m).
height 25ft 1in (7.65m).
wing area 2,098.96sq ft (195.0sq m).
Armament: Two 7.5mm Darne (or subsequently .5in Browning) machine-guns each in dorsal turret and (retractable) tail position; one 7.5mm Darne machine-gun in each wing leading-edge (centre section) and four beam positions; max bomb load 1,764lb (800kg).
In Service: France (FNAF, FFNAF, FVNAF).
Variants (with no. built):
Laté 611: Prototype; four 1,010hp Gnome-Rhône 14N4/5; subsequently re-engined Gnome-Rhône 14N30/31; various armament (1).
Laté 612: Proposed production model; four Pratt & Whitney S3C4–G; none built.
Total Production: 1.
Remarks: Unlike earlier Laté 300/520 boats, Laté 611 designed from outset for militarv role; first flown Spring 1939, entered FNAF service April, 1940; chequered wartime career, operating with both FVNAF in West Africa, and subsequently as part of FFNAF (alongside Sunderlands) on South Atlantic patrols, before finally returning to France and communications duties with FNAF, 1945–47.

Manufacturer: Levasseur.
Model: P.L.7 Series 2.
Type: Long-range carrier-borne torpedo-bomber.
Power Plant: One 600hp Hispano-Suiza 12 Lbr.
Performance:
maximum speed at sea level 106mph (170km/hr).
range 400 miles (650km).
service ceiling 9,432ft (2,875m).
Weights:
empty 6,173lb (2,800kg).
loaded 12,690lb (3,950kg).
Dimensions:
wing span 54ft 1⅔in (16.5m).
length 38ft 4in (11.68m).
height 15ft 4¼in (4.86m).
wing area 764.67sq ft (71.04sq m).
Crew: 3.
In Service: France (FNAF).
Variants (with no. built):
P.L.7.01/02: Prototypes; 3-seat long-range torpedo-bomber biplane; alternative wheel- or float-undercarriage; folding upper wing; P.L.7.02 with reduced wing span (2).
P.L.7 series 1: Production model; as P.L.7.01 (9).
P.L.7 series 2: Production model; as P.L.7.02 (30).
Total Production: 41.
Remarks: First flown 1926, still in service one Escadrille FNAF upon outbreak WWII.

Manufacturer: Levasseur.
Model: P.L.101.
Type: Carrier-borne reconnaissance.
Power Plant: One 600hp Hispano-Suiza 12Lb.
Performance:
maximum speed at sea level 137mph (220km/hr).
range 342 miles (550km).
service ceiling 1,280ft (4,200m).
Weights:
empty 4,453lb (2,020kg).
loaded 6,945lb (3,150kg).
Dimensions:
wing span 46ft 7in (14.2m).
length 31ft 11¾in (9.75m).
height 12ft 5⅔in (3.8m).
wing area 611.93sq ft (56.85sq m).
Armament: Two flexible Lewis guns in centre cockpit; provision for bomb/s or one torpedo.
Crew: 3.
In Service: France (FNAF).
Variants (with no. built):
P.L.10: Initial production model; reconnaissance biplane (30).
P.L.101: Modified P.L.10; redesigned widetrack undercarriage (30).
Total Production: 60.
Remarks: P.L.10 first flown 1929; improved P.L.101 still operated by one FNAF Escadrille Sept 1939.

Manufacturer: Levasseur.
Model: P.L.14.
Type: Torpedo-bomber/reconnaissance floatplane.
Power Plant: One 650hp Hispano-Suiza 12Nb.
Performance:
maximum speed at sea level 103mph (165km/hr).
normal range 597 miles (960km).
service ceiling 10,663ft (3,250m).
Weights:
empty 6,614lb (3,000kg).
loaded 9,370lb (4,250kg).
Dimensions:
wing span 59ft 0¾in (18.0m).
length 42ft 2in (12.85m).
height 16ft 1in (4.9m).
wing area 801.9sq ft (74.5sq m).
Crew: 2.
In Service: France (FNAF).
Variants (with no. built):
P.L.14 prototypes: 2-seat torpedo-bomber/reconnaissance floatplane (2).
P.L.14 production model: As prototypes; various power plants; a number subsequently converted as landplanes (28).
Total Production: 30.
Remarks: First flown 1929, several examples (since converted to landplane configuration) still in FNAF service (in support role), Sept 1939.

Manufacturer: Levasseur.
Model: P.L.15.
Type: Torpedo-bomber/reconnaissance floatplane.
Power Plant: One 650hp Hispano-Suiza 12Nbr (or Nb), or one 600hp Hispano-Suiza 12Lbr.
Performance:
maximum speed at sea level 118mph (190km/hr).
cruising speed 99mph (160km/hr).
maximum range 932 miles (1,500km).
time to 3,280ft (1,000m) 5min 30sec.
service ceiling 13,120ft (4,000m).
Weights:
empty 6,724lb (3,050kg).
loaded 9,590lb (4,350kg).
Dimensions:
wing span 59ft 0¾in (18.0m).
length 42ft 1¾in (12.8m).
height 16ft 8¾in (5.1m).
wing area 801.9sq ft (74.5sq m).
Armament: One fixed forward-firing 7.7mm Vickers; two flexible 7.7mm Lewis machine-guns in rear cockpit; max bomb load 992lb (500kg) or one 1,653lb (750kg) torpedo.
Crew: 2–4.
In Service: France (FNAF).
Variants (with no. built):
P.L.15: 2-seat torpedo-bomber, 3-seat observation or 4-seat reconnaissance floatplane versions (16).
P.L.151: Modified P.L.15; redesigned (inverted sesquiplane) wing (1).
P.L.154: One P.L.15 conversion; wheel undercarriage.
Total Production: 17.
Remarks: First flown 1932, P.L.15 one of oldest floatplanes to see service in WWII, five equipping one Escadrille for Mediterranean coastal patrol duties Sept 1939–June 1940; scrapped after Armistice.

Manufacturer: Lioré-et-Olivier.
Model: LeO H–43.
Type: Observation/scout floatplane.
Power Plant: One 650hp Hispano-Suiza 9Vb.
Performance:
maximum speed at 3,280ft (1,000m) 130mph (209km/hr).
cruising speed 93mph (150km/hr).
normal range 512 miles (825km).
time to 6,560ft (2,000m) 9min 0sec.
service ceiling 19,685ft (6,000m).
Weights:
loaded 7,496lb (3,400kg).
Dimensions:
wing span 52ft 6in (16.0m).
length 35ft 8½in (10.88m).
height 15ft 4¼in (4.68m).
wing area 387.5sq ft (36.0sq m).
Armament: One fixed forward-firing 7.5mm Darne machine-gun; one flexible 7.5mm Darne machine-gun in dorsal hatch; max bomb load 330lb (150kg).
Crew: 3.
In Service: France (FNAF).
Variants (with no. built):
LeO H–43–01: Prototype; seaplane carrier-borne observation floatplane; one 575hp Hispano-Suiza 9Va; subsequently re-engined 650hp 9Vb; modified vertical tail surfaces; dorsal turret (1).
LeO H–43: Production model; Hispano-Suiza 9Vb; redesigned fuselage upper contours; dorsal turret replaced by sliding hatch; cowling and float modifications (20).
Total Production: 21.
Remarks: Prototype first flown late 1934, extensive modifications and production delays preventing acceptance of first service models until Feb 1940; fifteen examples equipped two Escadrilles based French Mediterranean coast, 10 May 1940; limited employment prior capitulation.

Manufacturer: Lioré-et-Olivier.
Model: LeO 206.
Type: Heavy bomber.
Power Plant: Four 350hp Gnome-Rhône 7Kds.
Performance:
maximum speed at 10,000ft (3,050m) 146mph (235km/hr).
normal range 1,245 miles (2,000km).
time to 9,850 ft (3,000m) 15min 0sec.
service ceiling 24,940ft (7,600m).
Weights:
loaded 18,628lb (8,500kg).
Dimensions:
wing span 80ft 6¼in (24.54m).
length 48ft 5½in (14.77m).
height 19ft 7½in (5.98m).
Armament: Two 7.7mm machine-guns each in nose and dorsal positions; one 7.7mm machine-gun at rear of ventral gondolas; max bomb load 2,210lb (1,000kg).
Crew: 4–5.
In Service: France.
Variants (with no. built):
LeO 203: Prototype; four 300/350hp Gnome-Rhône 7Kb/Kds (1).
LeO 204: Prototype; floatplane version of LeO 203 (1).
LeO 205: Prototype; four 300/350hp Renault 9 Ca; not completed.
LeO 206: Production model; modified LeO 203; ventral gondola (37).
LeO 207: As LeO 206; four Gnome-Rhône Titan-Major (3).
LeO 208: Modified LeO 206; two supercharged 790hp Gnome-Rhône 14Krsd; redesigned wing; retractable undercarriage (1).
Total Production: 43 (all Marks).
Remarks: Four-engined (two tractor/two pusher) development of earlier twin-engined LeO 20, LeO 206 first flew 1933; 25 of original 40 series production still in service outbreak WWII, equipping two Groupes based North Africa.

Manufacturer: Lioré-et-Olivier (Sud-Est).
Model: LeO H–246.1.
Type: Maritime reconnaissance flying boat.
Power Plant: Four 720hp Hispano-Suiza 12Xgrs 12Xhrs 1.
Performance:
maximum speed at 6,560ft (2,000m) 205mph (330km/hr).
cruising speed 161mph (260km/hr).
normal range 1,240 miles (2,000km).
time to 11,480ft (3,500m) 15min 0sec.
service ceiling 22,965ft (7,000m).
Weights:
empty 19,842lb (9,000kg).
loaded 33,070lb (15,000kg).
Dimensions:
wing span 104ft 0½in (31.7m).
length 71ft 2¾in (21.7m).
height 23ft 10¼in (7.22m).
wing area 1,410sq ft (131.0sq m).
Armament: One flexible 7.5mm Darne machine-gun in each of four fore and aft beam positions; max bomb load 1,322lb (600kg).
Crew: 6–8.
In Service: Bulgaria (1), Finland (2), France (FVNAF), Germany (3).
Variants (with no. built):
LeO H–246.1: 26-passenger civil transport flying boat; No. 03 militarised for maritime reconnaissance role (6).
Total Production: 6.
Remarks: 1935 commercial design intended for Mediterranean passenger routes; third production model militarised for maritime reconnaissance duties; first flown at time of Armistice, subsequently served FVNAF, 1940–42; at least three of remaining civil examples, having operated France–North Africa service, seized by Germany, Nov 1942; employed by Luftwaffe in armed transport role (21 troops/14 litters); also brief use by Bulgaria for medical evacuation and as ambulance, 1943, and by Finnish AF for transport duties, 1944.

Manufacturer: Lioré-et-Olivier.
Model: LeO H–257bis.
Type: Torpedo-bomber floatplane.
Power Plant: Two 870hp Gnome-Rhône 14 Knrs/ors.
Performance:
maximum speed at 11,480ft (3,500m) 143mph (230km/hr).
cruising speed 115mph (185km/hr).
maximum range 932 miles (1,500km).

Lioré-et-Olivier LeO H-470

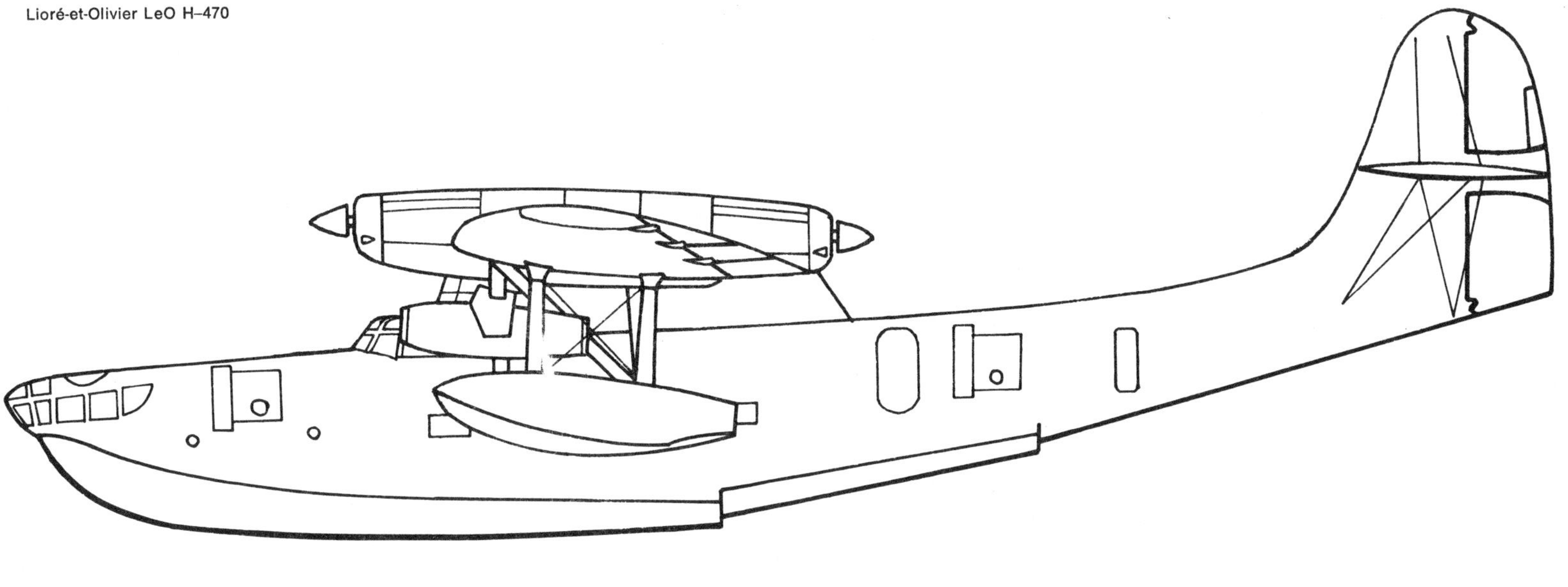

Weights:
empty 11,684lb (5,300kg).
loaded 21,076lb (9,560kg).
Dimensions:
wing span 83ft 7in (25.47m).
length 58ft 2¾in (17.75m).
height 22ft 2in (6.76m).
wing area 1,284.7sq ft (119.35sq m).
Armament: One flexible 7.5mm Darne machine-gun each in nose, dorsal and ventral positions; max bomb load 2,888lb (1,310kg) or one 1,477lb (670kg) torpedo.
Crew: 6.
In Service: France (FAF, FNAF, FF(N)AF, FVNAF).
Variants (with no. built):
LeO H-254-01: Prototype; two 500hp Hispano-Suiza 12Mbr (1).
LeO 255-01: Prototype; as H-254-01; two 690hp Hispano-Suiza 12Xbrs; alt land-/floatplane undercarriage (1).
LeO H-256-01: Prototype; Modified H-254-01; two 650hp Hispano-Suiza 12Nbr; increased wing area (1).
LeO H-257-01: Production prototype; as H-256-01; two 800hp Gnome-Rhône 14Kbr; enclosed cockpit (1).
LeO H-257bis: Production model: two supercharged 870hp Gnome-Rhône 14Kirs/jrs; some later re-engined Gnome-Rhône 14Knrs/ors; strengthened wing (60).
LeO H-258: Initial production model; two 650hp Hispano-Suiza 12Nbr (26).
LeO H-258bis: As H-258; two Hispano 12Ys; project only.
LeO H-259-01: Prototype; alt land-/floatplane; modified rear fuselage and wing struts; two Hispano-Suiza 12Ydrs/frs (1).
Total Production: 91 (all Marks).
Remarks: LeO 250 series last of long line of twin-engined LeO biplane bombers dating back to LeO 7 of immediate post-WWI vintage; entered service (H-258) mid-1935; operating in both land-plane/floatplane versions, equipped three Escadrilles FNAF plus single Groupe FAF outbreak WWII; employed maritime patrol Channel, Atlantic, Mediterranean areas, as well as in day and night bombing roles during latter stages of Battle of France; subsequent limited use training and communications duties FVNAF and FF(N)AFs, latter (as landplane) until late 1944.

Manufacturer: Lioré-et-Olivier.
Model: LeO 451 B4.
Type: Medium bomber.
Power Plant: Two 1,140hp Gnome-Rhône 14N 48/49 or 14N 38/39.
Performance:
maximum speed at sea level 227mph (365km/hr).
maximum speed at 15,748ft (4,800m) 298mph (480km/hr).
cruising speed 231mph (372km/hr).
maximum range 1,802 miles (2,900km).
time to 16,400ft (5,000m) 14min 0sec.
service ceiling 29,530ft (9,000m).
Weights:
empty 16,600lb (7,530kg).
maximum 25,128lb (11,398kg).
Dimensions:
wing span 73ft 10½in (22.52m).
length 56ft 4in (17.17m).
height 17ft 2¼in (5.24m).
wing area 710.4sq ft (66.0sq m).
Armament: One fixed forward-firing 7.5mm MAC 1934 M39 machine-gun; one 20mm Hispano-Suiza HS 404 cannon (plus, in later conversions, two addn 7.5mm MAC 1934 machine-guns) in retractable dorsal turret; one 7.5mm MAC 1934 machine-gun in retractable ventral turret; max bomb load 4,410lb (2,000kg).
Crew: 4.
In Service: France (FAF, FNAF, FFAF, FVAF, FVNAF), Germany (approx 100), Italy.
Variants (with no. built):
LeO 45-01, 02: Prototypes; two 1,080hp Hispano-Suiza 14 AA 06/07; modified engine cowlings; redesigned vertical tail surfaces; No. 01 re-engined 1,030hp Gnome-Rhône 14N 20/21s (redesignated LeO 451-01 prototype (2).
LeO 451 B4: Initial production model; Gnome-Rhône 14N 48/49 or 38/39; progressive minor modifications and improvements in equipment and to structure; number test and trials installations on various individual machines; also subsequent conversions as follows (approx 580).
LeO 451C: 12-passenger civil transport version; 12 LeO 451 conversions.
LeO 451E: Flying test-bed; 3 LeO 451C conversions.
LeO 451G: As LeO 451 B4; 7.92mm Browning machine-guns; max 1,920lb (870kg) internal bomb load; Greek order—not fulfilled (12).
LeO 451M: Redesignation of LeO 456.
LeO 451T: 17-troop or fuel military transport version; 15+ LeO 451 conversions.
LeO 452: As LeO 45; two 1,150hp Hispano-Suiza 14AA 12/13; project only.
LeO 453: Unarmed communications/ASR version; two 1,200hp Pratt & Whitney R-1830-67; 40 LeO 451 post-war conversions.
LeO 454-01: Prototype; two 1,150hp Bristol Hercules II; not completed.
LeO 455-01: Prototype; two 1,375hp Gnome-Rhône 14R 0/1; subsequently fitted with 1,320hp Gnome-Rhône 14R 4/5 'power eggs'; modified nacelles; enlarged vertical tail surfaces (redesignated LeO 451.01GS) (1).
LeO 455: Production model; as LeO 451.01GS; 1/3 LeO 451 late/post-war conversions.
LeO 455Ph: Photographic-reconnaissance version of LeO 455; 5 LeO 451 post-war conversions.
LeO 456: Navalised (land-based) version of LeO 451; flotation gear; 7.5mm MAC 1934 machine-guns replaced by 7.5mm Darne machine-guns; subsequently redesignated LeO 451M (1).
Total Production: 584.
Remarks: LeO 451 entered service upon outbreak WWII (only 5 on first-line strength as of 3 Sept 1939), constituted only modern bomber available to FAF in any quantity; equipped ten Groupes by 10 May 1940, operating both as low-level assault and strategic night bomber; attacked targets in Germany, northern Italy, and Sicily (latter from North Africa); had suffered some 130 losses by close Battle of France; initially operated seven FVAF Groupes post-Armistice, participated raids on Gibraltar, Sept 1940, and subsequent campaigns Syria, North Africa; over ninety seized by Germany, Nov 1942, served primarily transport role (inc special LeO 451T conversion, at least one of which captured and used as sqn hack by USAAF), but also limited number for clandestine special-duties; some also passed to Italy for brief service one bomber Gruppo; post-war FAF/FNAF use various roles until latter half fifties.
Colour Reference: Plates 7, 8: Lioré-et-Olivier LeO 451 B4 (No. 482) of Escadrille 6B, Flotille 4F, Aéronavale, Tafaroui-Lartigue, Algeria, Nov 1942; standard finish with Vichy nacelle/tail striping, plus Aéronavale anchor insignia centered on roundels and rudder tricolour; all thirteen aircraft of Flotille 4F's two component Escadrilles (6B/7B) destroyed or captured by US forces in first hours of 'Torch' landings, 8 Nov 1942.

Manufacturer: Lioré-et-Olivier (Sud-Est).
Model: LeO H-470.
Type: Long-range maritime reconnaissance flying boat.
Power Plant: Four 880hp Hispano-Suiza 12Y-34/35.
Performance:
maximum speed at 6,560ft (2,000m) 219mph (352km/hr).
maximum range 2,300 miles (3,700km).
time to 6,560ft (2,000m) 8min 15sec.
Weights:
empty 23,148lb (10,500kg).
maximum 44,533lb (20,200kg).
Dimensions:
wing span 104ft 4in (31.8m).
length 71ft 3¼in (21.72m).
height 23ft 5¼in (7.15m).
wing area 1,453.13sq ft (135.0sq m).
Armament: One flexible 7.5mm Darne machine-gun in each of four fore and aft beam positions; max bomb load 1,322lb (600kg).
Crew: 9.
In Service: France (FNAF, FFNAF, FVNAF).
Variants (with no. built):
LeO H-47: Prototype; long-range civil transport flying boat; 880hp Hispano-Suiza 12 Yrs 1/frs 1 (1).
LeO H-470: Production model; improved hull; modified vertical tail surfaces; subsequently militarised for maritime reconnaissance (5).
Total Production: 6.
Remarks: Undergoing Air France acceptance trials upon outbreak WWII, all five LeO H-470s impressed/militarised for maritime reconnaissance role; operated Biscay and Mediterranean patrols, 1939–40; after capitulation served as FVNAF communications/transport; finally, brief employment with Free French in West Africa on convoy-escort and shipping protection duties 1943.

Manufacturer: Loire.
Model: 46 C1.
Type: Fighter.
Power Plant: One 900hp Gnome-Rhône 14Kfs Mistral-Major.
Performance:
maximum speed at 3,280ft (1,000m) 199mph (312km/hr).
normal range 466 miles (750km).
time to 3,280ft (1,000m) 1min 26sec.
Weights:
empty 3,197lb (1,450kg).
maximum 4,630lb (2,100kg).
Dimensions:
wing span 38ft 9¾in (11.83m).
length 25ft 10½in (7.88m).
height 16ft 10in (4.13m).
wing area 209.9sq ft (19.5sq m).
Aramament: Four 7.5mm MAC 1934 machine-guns in wings.
Crew: 1.
In Service: France (FAF), Spain (approx 4 RepAF).
Variants (with no. built):
Loire 43, 45: Initial prototypes; 600hp Hispano-Suiza 12Xbrs and 800hp Gnome-Rhône 14Kds Mistral-Major (re-engined Gnome-Rhône 14Kes) resp (2).
Loire 46.01: Prototype; 880hp Gnome-Rhône 14 Kes; two 20mm cannon in underwing gondolas; (re-engined 900hp Gnome-Rhône 14Kfs Mistral-Major) (1).
Loire 46 C1: Production model; revised armament; modified cowling (60).
Total Production: 63 (all Marks).
Remarks: Brief pre-war operational career 1936–38, majority Loire 46s in storage upon outbreak WWII; returned to service Winter 1939–40, operated fighter-trainer/emergency (second-line) fighter roles prior and during Battle of France; continued limited use training duties FVAF units overseas.

Manufacturer: Loire.
Model: 501.
Type: Communications/liaison flying boat.
Power Plant: One 350hp Hispano-Suiza 9Qd.
Performance:
maximum speed at 3,280ft (1,000m) 121mph (195km/hr).
cruising speed 87mph (140km/hr).
maximum range 683 miles (1,100km).
time to 3,280ft (1,000m) 4min 0sec.
service ceiling 15,910ft (4,850m).
Weights:
empty 3,053lb (1,385kg).
loaded 4,740lb (2,150kg).
Dimensions:
wing span 52ft 6in (16.0m).
length 36ft 4⅞in (11.1m).
height 14ft 8in (4.47m).
wing area 424.10sq ft (39.4sq m).
Crew/Accommodation: 1/2–3.
In Service: France (FNAF).
Variants (with no. built):
Loire 50: Prototype; 230hp Salmson 9AB; subsequently modified (as amphibian), re-engined (Hispano-Suiza 9Qd), and redesignated Loire 50bis (1).
Loire 501: Production model; as Loire 50bis (6).
Loire 502: Re-engined Loire 501; one 300hp Lorraine 9Na; project only.
Total Production: 7.
Remarks: First flown 1931, several Loire 501 light communications/liaison flying boats still in FNAF service early months WWII.

Manufacturer: Loire.
Model: 70.
Type: Maritime reconnaissance flying boat.
Power Plant: Three 740hp Gnome-Rhône 9Kfr.
Performance:
maximum speed at sea level 146mph (235km/hr).
maximum speed at 6,560ft (2,000m) 143mph (230km/hr).
cruising speed 103mph (165km/hr).
range 1,865 miles (3,000km).
time to 6,560ft (2,000m) 13min 48sec.
service ceiling 13,120ft (4,000m).
Weights:
empty 14,330lb (6,500kg).
maximum 25,353lb (11,500kg).
Dimensions:
wing span 98ft 5in (30.0m).
length 63ft 11¾in (19.5m).
height 22ft 1½in (6.75m).
wing area 1,463.89sq ft (136.0sq m).
Armament: One 7.5mm Darne machine-gun each in forward and dorsal turrets, two lateral bow positions, and two beam positions; max bomb load 1,323lb (600kg).
Crew: 8.
In Service: France (FNAF).
Variants (with no. built):
Loire 70: Prototype; three 500hp Gnome-Rhône 9Kbr (two tractor, one pusher); subsequently modified to production standard (1).
Loire 70: Production model; uprated engines; bow gun deleted; enlarged tail surfaces; increased fuel capacity (7).
Loire 701: As Loire 70; three 750hp Hispano-Suiza 9Vbrs (1 conversion/reconversion).
Total Production: 8.
Remarks: Entered service mid-1937, operated Sept 1939–June 1940 on Mediterranean patrol duties; all but one lost through accident/enemy (Italian) action by Armistice.

Manufacturer: Loire.
Model: 130M.
Type: Ship-borne or land-based observation/communications flying boat.
Power Plant: One 720hp Hispano-Suiza 12Xirsl.
Performance:
maximum speed at 6,890ft (2,100m) 137mph (220km/hr).
cruising speed 102mph (165km/hr).
time to 9,840ft (3,000m) 11min 0sec.
service ceiling 19,685ft (6,000m).
Weights:
empty 4,519lb (2,050kg).
maximum 7,716lb (3,500kg).
Dimensions:
wing span 52ft 6in (16.0m).
length 37ft 1in (11.3m).
height 12ft 7½in (3.85m).
wing area 410.86sq ft (40.8sq m).
Armament: One 7.5mm Darne machine-gun each in bow and dorsal positions; provision for two 165lb (75kg) bombs.
Crew/Accommodation: 3/0 or (communications) 1/6.
In Service: France (FAF, FVAF, FNAF, FFNAF, FVNAF).
Variants (with no. built):
Loire 130 prototype: 3-seat observation or 4-seat communications flying boat; one 720hp

Hispano-Suiza 12Xbrsl; folding wings (1).
Loire 130M (Métropole): Production model; Hispano-Suiza 12Xirsl; two Darne machine-guns; max bomb load 330lb (150kg).
Loire 130C (Colonial): Tropicalised (dive-bomber) version; structural strengthening; enlarged radiator (Total Loire 130M and 130C, 124).
Total Production: 125.
Remarks: Most numerous among the proliferation of pre-war French boats, Loire 130 widely used on all fronts; served aboard seaplane carrier, battleships, and cruisers, as well as equipping naval Escadrilles mainland France, West Indies, West and North Africa, and Far East; also served FAF (one Escadrille) in Indo-China; post-1942 FVNAF machines restricted shore-bases only, used in coastal patrol/communications roles; several escapes to neighbouring Allied-held territory; also served with FFNAF in West Africa; continued post-war employment training duties.

Manufacturer: Loire.
Model: 210.
Type: Ship-borne fighter floatplane.
Power Plant: One 980hp Hispano-Suiza 9Vbs.
Performance:
maximum speed at sea level 174mph (280km/hr).
maximum speed at 9,840ft (3,000m) 186mph (300km/hr).
normal range 466 miles (750km).
time to 9,840ft (3,000m) 5min 19sec.
service ceiling 26,250ft (8,000m).
Weights:
empty 3,174lb (1,440kg).
loaded 4,740lb (2,150kg).
Dimensions:
wing span 38ft 8in (11.78m).
length 31ft 2¼in (9.52m).
height 12ft 5¼in (3.79m).
wing area 218.5sq ft (20.3sq m).
Armament: Four 7.5mm Darne machine-guns in wings.
Crew: 1.
In Service: France (FNAF).
Variants (with no. built):
Loire 210: Prototype; ship-borne fighter floatplane; two 7.5mm Darne machine-guns in wings (1).
Loire 210: Production model; increased armament (20).
Loire 211: Re-engined Loire 210; one Gnome-Rhône 14M–2; project only.
Total Production: 21.
Remarks: Unsuccessful fighter floatplane design intended for service aboard French Navy battleships; equipped two shore-based Escadrilles opening weeks WWII, before high accident rate from wing failure led to premature grounding and disbandment, Nov 1939.

Manufacturer: Loire-Nieuport.
Model: LN 401.
Type: Ship-borne dive-bomber.
Power Plant: One 690hp Hispano-Suiza 12Xcrs.
Performance:
maximum speed at sea level 199mph (320km/hr).
maximum speed at 13,120ft (4,000m) 236mph (380km/hr).
cruising speed 186mph (300km/hr).
maximum range 746 miles (1,200km).
service ceiling 31,168ft (9,500m).
Weights:
empty 4,945lb (2,243kg).
loaded 6,250lb (2,835kg).
Dimensions:
wing span 45ft 11in (14.0m).
length 31ft 11¾in (9.75m).
height 11ft 5¾in (3.5m).
wing area 266.4sq ft (24.75sq m).
Armament: One 20mm Hispano-Suiza cannon firing through propeller hub; two 7.5mm Darne machine-guns in wings; max bomb load 496lb (225kg).
Crew: 1.
In Service: France (FNAF, FVAF), Germany (12).
Variants (with no. built):
LN 40 No. 01: Prototype; ship-borne dive-bomber version; semi-retractable undercarriage; folding-wing (1).
LN 410: Initial production model; modified wing (23+).
LN 402: As LN 401; 860hp Hispano-Suiza 12Y–31; prototype only (1).
LN 411: Land-based dive-bomber version of LN 401; arrester hook, floatation bags, and wing-fold mechanism deleted (23+).
LN 420: Re-engined LN 411; 1,100hp Hispano-Suiza 12Y–51; redesigned wing; modified tail (1 conversion).
Total Production: approx 72.
Remarks: Prototype first flown mid-1938; only three LN 401s in

FNAF service by outbreak WWII, two Escadrilles converting before capitulation; operated as land-based dive-bomber during Battle of France, suffering heavy casualties (on one occasion half of twenty-strong force attacking German armour failed to return, all others damaged to varying degree); subsequently relegated reconnaissance, night-attack roles on southern (Italian) front; twelve of twenty-four examples produced under Vichy control later seized by Germany.

Manufacturer: Maillet.
Model: 201.
Type: Liaison/trainer.
Power Plant: One 185hp Régnier 6B–01.
Performance:
maximum speed at sea level 180mph (290km/hr).
cruising speed 153mph (246km/hr).
normal range 932 miles (1.500km).
service ceiling 21,000ft (6.400m).
Weights:
empty 1,500lb (680kg).
loaded 2,646lb (1,200kg).
Dimensions:
wing span 33ft 9½in (10.3m).
length 25ft 2¼in (7.68m).
height 9ft 2¼in (2.8m).
wing area 185.14sq ft (17.2sq m).
Crew/Accommodation: 1/2.
In Service: France.
Variants (with no. built):
Maillet 20: Prototypes; 3-seat civil tourer/trainer; one Renault 6Q–06 (4).
Maillet 201: Production model; re-engined Maillet 20 (31).
Total Production: 35.
Remarks: Prototype first flown 1933, several civil 201s impressed by FAF for liaison and ancillary duties upon outbreak WWII.

Manufacturer: Morane-Saulnier.
Model: M.S.225.
Type: Fighter.
Power Plant: One 500hp Gnome-Rhône 9Kbrs Mistral.
Performance:
maximum speed at sea level 174mph (280km/hr).
maximum speed at 13,125ft (4,000m) 207mph (333km/hr).
time to 29,500ft (9,000m) 24min 30sec.
service ceiling 32,500ft (9,900m).
Weights:
loaded 3,476lb (1,577kg).
Dimensions:
wing span 34ft 7in (10.54m).
length 23ft 9in (7.23m).
Armament: Two fixed forward-firing 7.7mm Vickers machine-guns.
Crew: 1.
In Service: France.
Variants (with no. built):
M.S. 225: Prototype and initial production model; one 500hp Gnome-Rhône 9Kbrs Mistral (75).
M.S. 226: Navalised M.S. 225; arrester hook; tailwheel (in place of skid) (1).
M.S. 226bis: As M.S. 226; folding wing (1).
M.S. 227, 275, 278: Experimental prototypes (3).
Total Production: 80.
Remarks: Gnome-Rhône (M.S. 255) and Hispano-Suiza-powered (M.S. 227) prototypes first flown 1932–33 resp; former selected for production, of which at least nine were included among those obsolescent types inducted from training establishments into front-line inventory as part of French mobilisation programme immediately prior WWII; based South of France, Winter 1939–40.

Manufacturer: Morane-Saulnier.
Model: M.S.406 C1.
Type: Fighter.
Power Plant: One 860hp Hispano-Suiza 12Y 31.
Performance:
maximum speed at 14,764ft (4,500m) 304mph (490km/hr).
cruising speed 248mph (400km/hr).
normal range 466 miles (750km).
time to 16.405ft (5,000m) 6min 30sec.
service ceiling 30,840ft (9,400m).
Weights:
empty 4,127lb (1,872kg).
loaded 5,448lb (2,471kg).
Dimensions:
wing span 34ft 9½in (10.62m).
length 26ft 9½in (8.17m).
height 10ft 8in (3.25m).
wing area 172.22sq ft (16.0sq m).
Armament: One 20mm Hispano-Suiza S9 (or HS 404) cannon firing through propeller hub; two 7.5mm MAC 1934 machine-guns in wings.
Crew: 1.
In Service: Croatia (approx 35 M.S.406), Finland (78 M.S.406, 9 M.S.410, plus approx 40 Mörkö Moraani conversions), France (FAF, FNAF, FFAF, FVAF), Great Britain (8+ FAF/FVAF escapees), Switzerland (2 M.S. 406H, plus licence-production), Turkey (45 M.S.406).
Variants (with no. built):
M.S.405–01/02: Prototypes; one 860hp Hispano-Suiza 12 Ygrs/12 Ycrs resp; 02 with modified wing (2).
M.S.405 C1: Pre-production model; as prototype 02; semi-retractable radiator; (inc 7 as further prototypes/special purpose) (15).
M.S.406 C1: Production model; as M.S.405 No. 04. 860hp Hispano-Suiza 12Y-31. (1,077).
M.S.406H: Pattern aircraft; as M.S.406 C1; Swiss order (2).
M.S.407 LP: As re-engined M.S.405 No. 14; 930hp Hispano-Suiza 12 Ycrs 2; high-speed (supply) parachute-dropping model; 1 conversion (2).
M.S.408: Re-engined M.S.405 No. 13; 1,000hp Hispano-Suiza 12Y 51; originally as test night-fighter; four landing lights; 1 conversion.
M.S.409: Repositioned radiator; project only.

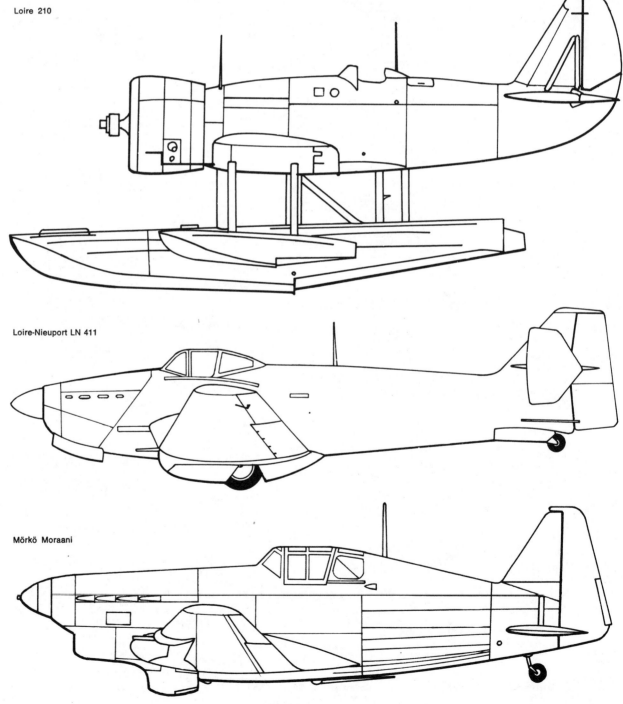

Loire 210

Loire-Nieuport LN 411

Mörkö Moraani

Mureaux 115 R2 B2

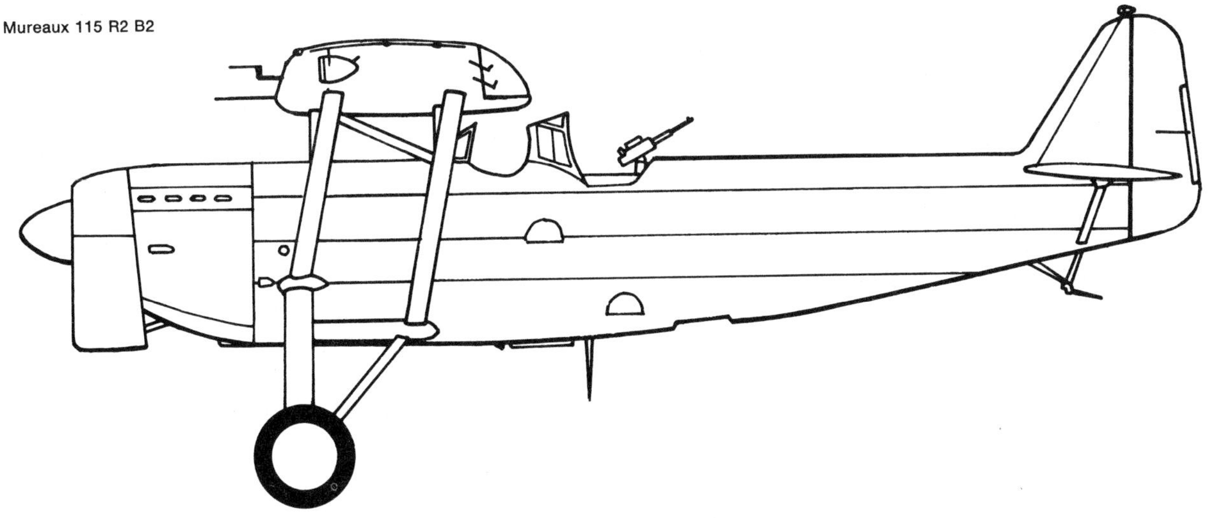

Potez 25

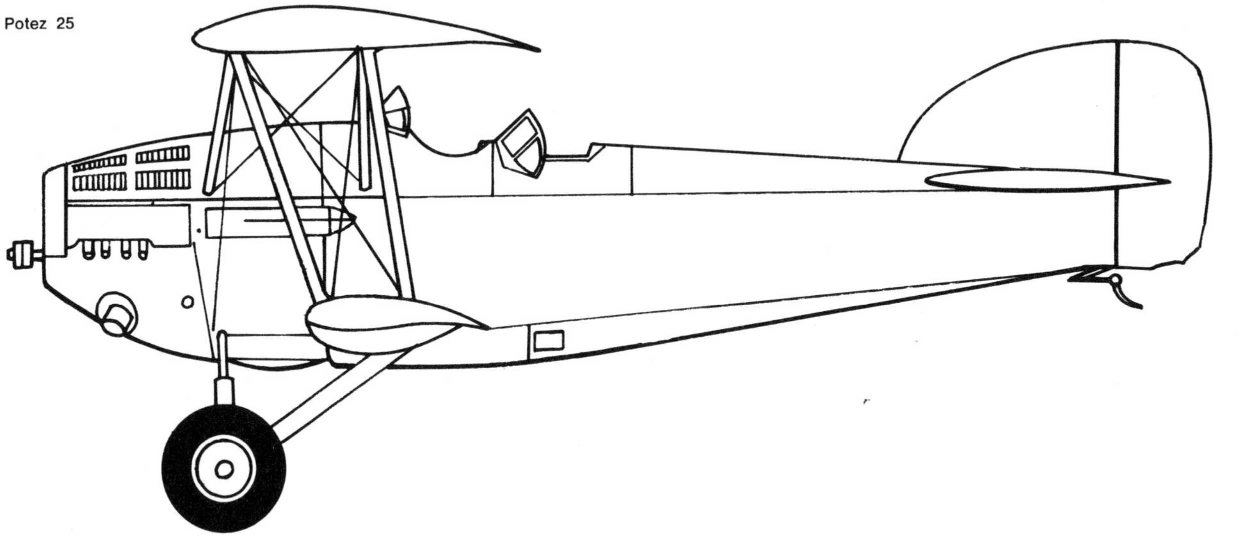

M.S.410: Modified M.S.406; strengthened wing; four belt-fed 7.5mm MAC 1934 machine-guns; 79 conversions.
M.S.411: Re-engined M.S.405 No. 12; 950hp Hispano-Suiza 12Y 45; non-retractable radiator; 1 conversion.
M.S.420: As M.S.406; fully retractable radiator; 1 conversion.
M.S.450: M.S.406 development; 1,100hp Hispano-Suiza 12Y 51; prototypes only (3).
D–3800: Swiss equivalent of M.S.406H; 860hp Saurer/SLM-built Hispano-Suiza 12Y 31; minor modifications; EFW-licence-built (82).
D–3801: Re-engined D–3800; 1,020hp Saurer/SLM-built Hispano-Suiza 12Y 51; fixed radiator; addn armour; EFW-, Dornier-, Pilatus licence-built (207).
D–3802: Swiss equivalent of M.S.450; one 1,250hp Hispano-Suiza 12Y–52; wing guns replaced by two 20mm FFK-HS cannon (12).
D–3803: Prototype; improved D–3802; one 1,500hp Hispano-Suiza 12Y–53; redesigned rear fuselage and cockpit hood (1).
Mörkö Moraani (Werewolf Morane): Finnish designation for M.S.406 conversions; 1,100hp Soviet Klimov M–105P; engine-mounted 12.7mm Beresin UB machine-gun (*15*).
Total Production: approx 1,403 (all Marks).
Remarks: First flown 1937, M.S.406 subject number pre-war export orders, only those of Switzerland and Turkey being fulfilled; numerically most important FAF fighter upon outbreak WWII, equipped sixteen Groupes (plus three Escadrilles) at home and overseas; markedly inferior performance against opposing German fighters enabled 406s to claim only some 175 confirmed victories for loss of over 400 own number from all causes; retained by only one Groupe FVAF after Armistice; later saw limited action against Allies in Syria and over Madagascar; also engaged Thai AF over French Indo-China; almost fifty M.S.406s seized by Germany after occupation Vichy France; majority passed to Croatian AF for home-defence duties; others to Finland (inc some 410s) to supplement earlier 1939 French delivery of thirty M.S.406s, plus ground personnel, for Winter War operations; employment by Finnish AF during Continuation War, 1941–44, and after (against German forces, 1944–45) inc Soviet-engined Mörkö Moraani conversions, latter remaining in use until early fifties; Swiss-built D 3800/3801 operated 1940–59.
Colour Reference: Plates 16, 17: Morane-Saulnier M.S.406 (MS–311) of 1./LeLv 14 Finnish Air Force; Tiiksjärvi, Finland, Sept 1943; standard two-tone camouflage scheme, personal shark mouth insignia.
Plate 18: D–3801 (J–292) of Überwachungsgeschwader (Surveillance Wing), Swiss Air Force, Dübendorf, 1944–45; standard two-tone camouflage scheme, personal shark mouth insignia.

Manufacturer: Mureaux.
Model: 115 R2 B2.
Type: Observation.
Power Plant: One 650hp Hispano-Suiza 12Ycrs.
Performance:
maximum speed 211mph (340km/hr).
normal range 930 miles (1,500km).
time to 16,400ft (5,000m) 8min 10sec.
service ceiling 34,100ft (10,400m).
Weights:
loaded 5,643lb (2,560kg).
Dimensions:
wing span 50ft 6in (15.4m).
length 32ft 7¾in (9.95m).
height 11ft 9in (3.58m).
Armament: One 20mm cannon firing through propeller hub (subsequently replaced by either one wing-mounted, or two fuselage-mounted, 7.5mm MAC machine-guns); plus two flexible 7.5mm MAC machine-guns in rear cockpit; max bomb load 660lb (300kg).
Crew: 2.
In Service: France.
Variants (with no. built):
Mureaux 110/112: Prototypes; 2-seat reconnaissance version (6).
Mureaux 113: Initial production; reconnaissance model; one 650hp Hispano-Suiza 12Ybrs (49).
Mureaux 114 CN2: Night-fighter version; modified 113 (inc 2 conversions) (2).
Mureaux 115 R2: Reconnaissance version; 860hp Hispano-Suiza 12Ycrs; repositioned radiator; one cannon in nose (inc prototype) (3).
Mureaux 115 R2 B2: Reconnaissance-bomber version of Mureaux 115 R2; revised armament (120).
Mureaux 117 R2: As Mureaux 113; 860hp Hispano-Suiza 12Ycrs; strengthened wing (57).
Mureaux 117 R2 B2: Reconnaissance-bomber version; as Mureaux 117 R2; provision for four 110lb (50kg) bombs underwing (60).
Mureaux 200 A3: 3-seat assault version; one Mureaux 115 conversion.
Total Production: 297.
Remarks: Mureaux 113 first flown Spring 1931, but obsolescent by Sept 1939, over half having been replaced by later models; Mureaux 115/117 most modern army observation aircraft available upon outbreak WWII (first flown March/Jan 1935 resp); equipped nineteen out of forty-five GAOs (army observation groups); provided Luftwaffe with first FAF 'kill' of war, one 115 being brought down on sixth day of hostilities; in process of replacement by Potez 63.11, over one hundred 115/117s still in service 10 May 1940; many destroyed during ensuing Battle of France, inc some reportedly employed in emergency light bomber role.

Manufacturer: Mureaux (Besson).
Model: MB–411.
Type: Submarine-borne observation floatplane.
Power Plant: 175hp Salmson 9 ND.
Performance:
maximum speed at 3,280ft (1,000m) 115mph (185km/hr).
cruising speed 81mph (130km/hr).
maximum range 215 miles (345km).
time to 4,920ft (1,500m) 8min 0sec.
Weights:
empty 1,521lb (690kg).
maximum 2,513lb (1,140kg).
Dimensions:
wing span 39ft 4½in (12.0m).
length 27ft 0¾in (8.25m).
height 9ft 4¼in (2.85m).
wing area 236.81sq ft (22.0sq m).
Crew: 2.
In Service: France (FNAF, FFNAF).
Variants (with no. built):
MB–410–01: Initial prototype: 130hp Salmson 9NC (1).
MB–411: Prototypes; uprated engine; originally delivered as single-seater; ANF-built (2).
Total Production: 3.
Remarks: Intended specifically for service aboard 2,880-ton French submarine *Surcouf*, Marcel Besson-designed and built MB–410 prototype destroyed during acceptance trials; Mureaux-completed MB–411s entered service 1937; one example aboard *Surcouf* at time of latter's arrival in UK, June 1940, to continue fight under Free French flag; subsequently damaged during Luftwaffe raid on Plymouth, MB-411 was not re-embarked (*Surcouf* later sunk in collision en route Bermuda-Tahiti) but served instead for limited period at FAA shore establishment.

Manufacturer: Nieuport-Delage.
Model: Ni–D.622.
Type: Fighter.
Power Plant: One 500hp Hispano-Suiza 12Md.
Performance:
maximum speed 168mph (270km/hr).
normal range 310 miles (500km).
service ceiling 26,900ft (8,200m).
Weights:
loaded 4,148lb (1,880kg).
Dimensions:
wing span 39ft 4½in (12.0m).
length 24ft 7¼in (7.5m).
height 9ft 10in (3.0m).
wing area 332.066sq ft (30.85sq m).
Armament: Two 7.7mm Vickers machine-guns in upper cowling.
Crew: 1.
In Service: France, Spain (RepAF, NatAF).
Variants (with no. built):
Ni–D.42: Initial production; various power plants.
Ni–D.52: Development of Ni–D.42; one 500hp Hispano-Suiza 12Mb; all-metal construction; Nieuport-Delage and Spanish Hispano licence-built (125+).
Ni–D.62: Modified Ni–D.42; 590hp Hispano-Suiza 12Hb; repositioned radiator; enlarged tailplane (349).
Ni–D.621: Floatplane version (3 conversions).
Ni–D.622: Modified Ni–D.62; 500hp Hispano-Suiza 12Md (approx 330).
Ni–D.623/626, 628: Experimental and export versions; various power plants; Ni–D.624 with stub wing deleted (approx 16).
Ni–D.629: Re-engined Ni–D.622; supercharged Hispano-Suiza 12Mdsh; improved undercarriage (approx 50).
Total Production: 730+ (exl' Ni–D.42, 52).
Remarks: Developments of 1924-vintage Ni–D.42, Spanish licence-built Ni–D.52s saw service both sides during Civil War; FAF/FNAF's original Ni–D.62s long obsolete by outbreak WWII, but both 622/629 models still in FAF service Sept 1939, equipping one metropolitan Escadrille/one metropolitan Escadrille plus one overseas (North Africa) Groupe resp; latter still in operation 10 May 1940, French-based 622/629s having been relegated ERC (regional defence sqn) duties Winter 1939–40.

Manufacturer: Potez.
Model: 25 TOE.
Type: Reconnaissance-bomber/army co-operation.
Power Plant: One 450hp Lorraine-Dietrich 12Eb.
Performance:
maximum speed at 16,400ft (5,000m) 106mph (170km/hr).
normal range 391 miles (630km/hr).
time to 3,280ft (1,000m) 4min 0sec.
service ceiling 19,030ft (5,800m).
Weights:
empty 2,926lb (1,327kg).
loaded 4,930lb (2,240kg).
Dimensions:
wing span 46ft 5in (14.15m).
length 30.29ft 10¼in (9.1m).
height 11.12ft 0½in (3.67m).
wing area 505.9sq ft (47.0sq m).
Armament: One fixed forward-firing 7.5mm MAC or Vickers machine-gun; two flexible 7.5mm machine-guns in rear cockpit; max bomb load 440lb (200kg).
Crew: 2.
In Service: France (FAF, FFAF, FVAF).
Variants:
Potez 25: Prototype and production models; 87 individual variants, civil and military; various 450/500hp power plant (inc Gnome-Rhône, Hispano-Suiza, Lorraine, Renault) and/or armament/equipment modifications.
Total Production: 3,500+.
Remarks: First flown 1925, Potez 25 subsequently produced in multiplicity of versions; widely exported (supplied approx 20 foreign AFs), also extensive FAF service in variety reconnaissance, army co-operation, training and ancillary roles both at home and overseas; equipped single army reconnaissance Groupe, plus number of observation Groupes upon outbreak WWII, disappearing from all but four of latter (three based metropolitan France, one North Africa) by time of German invasion (10 May 1940); individual examples continued perform second-line duties with overseas FFAF/FVAF units, inc North Africa and Middle and Far East (one of latter reportedly captured/used by IJAAF in Indo-China as late as 1945).

Manufacturer: Potez.
Model: 29–2.
Type: Transport.
Power Plant: One 450hp Lorraine-Dietrich 12Eb.
Performance:
maximum speed at 6,560ft (2,000m) 130mph (210km/hr).
normal range 310 miles (500km).
service ceiling 17,060ft (5,200m).
Weights:
empty 3,306lb (1,500kg).
Dimensions:
wing span 47ft 7in (14.5m).
length 35ft 0½in (10.68m).
wing area 519.5sq ft (48.27sq m).
Crew/Accommodation: 2/5 (or 3 litters plus 1 medic).
In Service: France (FAF, FFAF)

Potez-C.A.M.S. 141

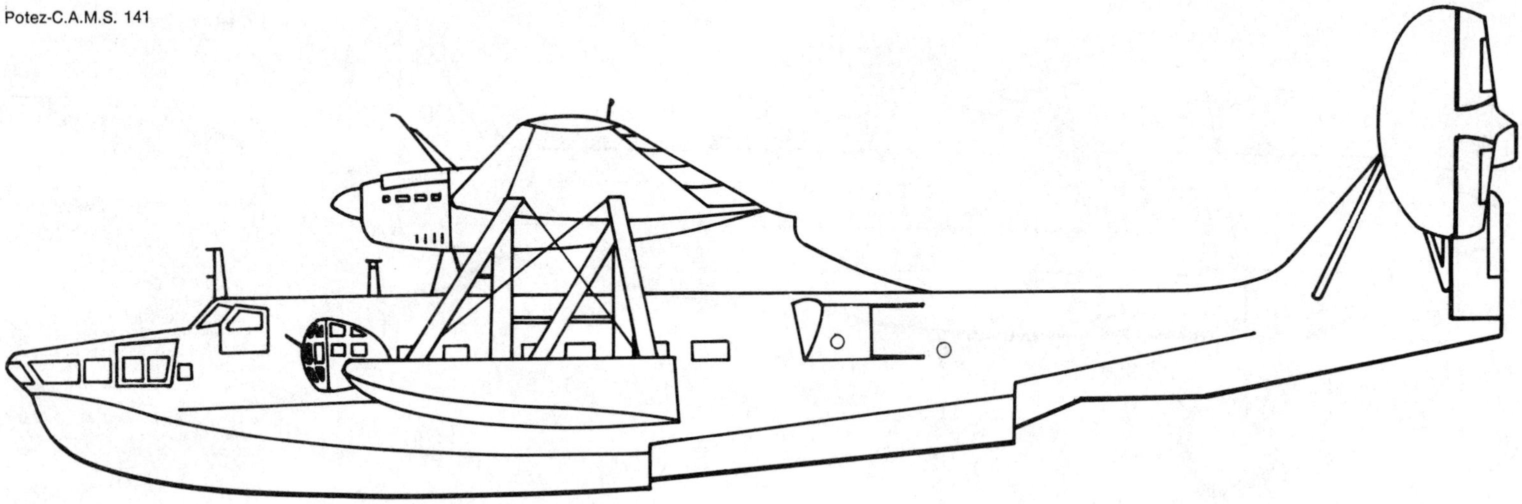

Potez 637 A3

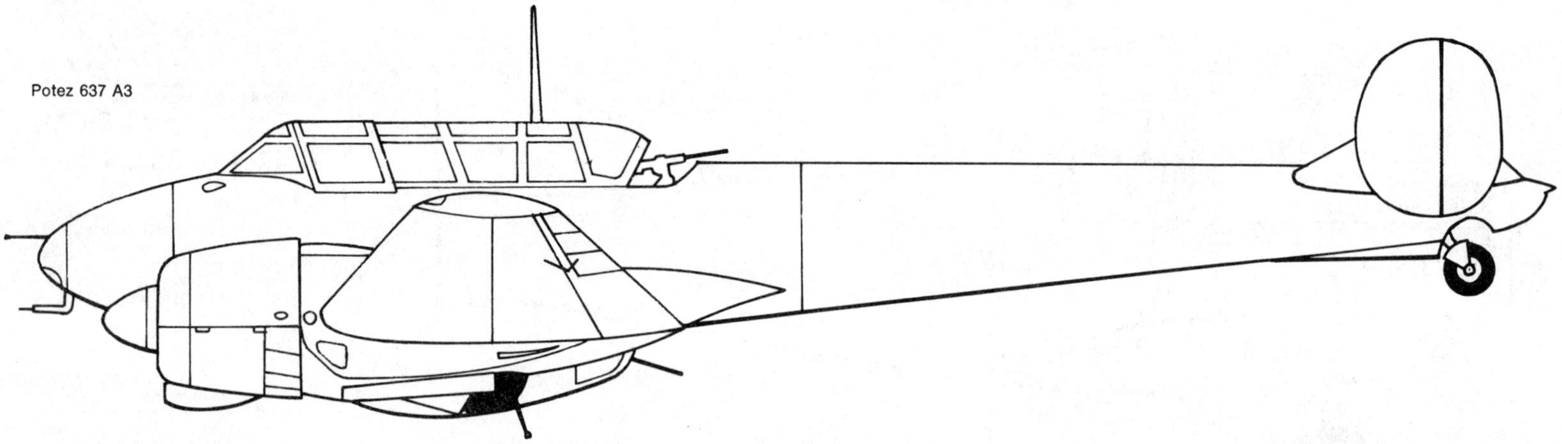

Variants (with no. built):
Potez 29: Prototype and production models; civil airliner and military transport/ambulance versions; majority with either 450hp Lorraine-Dietrich 12Eb (Potez 29–2), or 420hp (480hp) Gnome-Rhône Jupiter 9 (Potez 29–4). (Civil production, approx 25, Military production, approx 125).
Total Production: approx 150.
Remarks: 6/8-passenger enclosed cabin development of basic Potez 25 reconnaissance-bomber design, Potez 29 first flown 1927; bulk of production delivered FAF for light transport/ambulance duties, several still employed these and other ancillary roles early months WWII.

Manufacturer: Potez.
Model: 33.
Type: Observation/liaison.
Power Plant: One 230hp Salmson A.B.9.
Performance:
maximum speed 112mph (180km/hr).
normal range 416 miles (670km).
ceiling 14,765ft (4,500m).
Weights:
empty 2,094lb (950kg).
loaded 3,858lb (1,750kg).
Dimensions:
wing span 47ft 6¾in (14.5m).
length 33ft 3¾in (10.15m).
wing area 376.74sq ft (35.0sq m).
Armament: Twin flexible Lewis gun in dorsal position; provision for 22–26lb (10–12kg) bombs internally.
Crew/Accommodation: 2/4 (or two litters).
In Service: France (FAF, FVAF).
Variants:
Potez 32: 6-seat civil transport; various power plants; 23 variants.
Potez 33: Military advanced trainer/liaison/observation version of Potez 32; modified cabin and equipment.
Remarks: First flown 1928, several Potez 33s, still serving FAF colonial units light transport/liaison duties upon outbreak of WWII.

Manufacturer: Potez.
Model: 39 A2.
Type: Observation.
Power Plant: One 720hp Hispano-Suiza 12 Xbrs.
Performance:
maximum speed at 16,400ft (5,000m) 178mph (286km/hr).
maximum range 472 miles (760km).
time to 11,480ft (3,500m) 7min 0sec.
Weights:
empty 3,600lb (1,633kg).
maximum 5,842lb (2,650kg).
Dimensions:
wing span 52ft 6in (16.0m).
length 32ft 9¾in (10.0m).
height 11ft 2in (3.4m).
wing area 376.74sq ft (35.0sq m).
Armament: Two fixed forward-firing Vickers machine-guns, twin flexible Lewis guns in rear cockpit; one rearward-firing machine-gun in ventral position.
Crew: 2.
In Service: France.
Variants:
Potez 39 A2: Two-seat high-wing observation monoplane; various power plants inc 650hp Hispano-Suiza 12 Ybrs, Hispano-Suiza 12 Xbrs, and Lorraine 12 Hars.
Total Production: approx 250.
Remarks: Standard mid-thirties reconnaissance/observation machine, number still employed by FAF for general-purpose duties upon outbreak WWII.

Manufacturer: Potez.
Model: 402.
Type: Colonial transport/ambulance.
Power Plant: Three 300hp Lorraine 'Algol'.
Performance:
maximum speed at sea level 143mph (230km/hr).
maximum speed at 6,560ft (2,000m) 137mph (220km/hr).
cruising speed 118mph (190km/hr).
normal range 708 miles (1,140km).
time to 6,560ft (2,000m) 7min 0sec.
Weights:
empty 7,158lb (3,247kg).
loaded 10,461lb (4,745kg).
Dimensions:
wing span 66ft 3¼in (20.2m).
length 47ft 1in (14.35m).
height 11ft 9¾in (3.6m).
wing area 710.42sq ft (66.0sq m).
Armament: Provision for light bombs.
Crew/Accommodation: 2/8 (or litters).
In Service: France.
Variants:
Potez 400: Initial version; colonial military troop/ambulance/cargo transport; various power plants.
Potez 402: Modified Potez 400; three 300hp Lorraine 'Algol'.
Potez 403: 10-seat civil transport version of Potez 402; modified fuselage; three 350hp Gnome-Rhône 'Titan-Major'.
Remarks: Potez 400 first flown 1930; several 402s still on active colonial service upon outbreak WWII.

Manufacturer: Potez.
Model: 438.
Type: Liaison.
Power Plant: One 120hp Renault 4 Pdi.
Performance:
maximum speed at sea level 106mph (170km/hr).
cruising speed 92mph (148km/hr).
normal range 435 miles (700km).
service ceiling 16,400ft (5,000m).
Weights:
empty 1,235lb (560kg).
loaded 2,028lb (920kg).
Dimensions:
wing span 37ft 0¾in (11.3m).
length 25ft 1in (7.65m).
height 7ft 9in (2.36m).
wing area 193.75sq ft (18.0sq m).
Crew/Accommodation: 1/1.
In Service: France.
Variants (with no. built):
Potez 43: Civil light tourer; various power plants (167).
Potez 438: Liaison version; militarized Potez 43 (33).
Total Production: 200.
Remarks: Development of civil prototype first flown 1932, several military Potez 438s still on FAF strength early months WWII.

Manufacturer: Potez.
Model: 452.
Type: Ship-borne observation flying boat.
Power Plant: One 350hp Hispano-Suiza 9Qd.
Performance:
maximum speed at sea level 121mph (195km/hr).
maximum speed at 6,560ft (2,000m) 135mph (217km/hr).
time to 6,560ft (2,000m) 7min 15sec.
service ceiling 18,040ft (5,500m).
Weights:
empty 2,426lb (1,100kg).
normal 3,571lb (1,620kg).
Dimensions:
wing span 42ft 7⅔in (13.0m).
length 33ft 6¾in (10.24m).
height 11ft 2in (3.4m).
wing area 261.56sq ft (24.3sq m).
Armament: One flexible 7.5mm Darne machine-gun in rear cockpit.
Crew: 2.
In Service: France (FNAF, FVNAF).
Variants (with no. built):
Potez 450: Prototype; one 230hp Salmson 9AB; various subsequent modifications, inc re-engined 350hp Hispano-Suiza 9Qd (redesignated Potez 452) (1).
Potez 452: Production model; as definitive prototype; enlarged rudder; original .303in Lewis machine-gun replaced by 7.5mm Darne (16).
Total Production: 17.
Remarks: Built to 1930 requirement for folding-wing ship-borne observation seaplane, ten Potez 452s on FNAF strength outbreak WWII, majority serving aboard light cruisers, colonial sloops in Far Eastern/foreign waters; remained in FVNAF use North Africa until late 1942.

Manufacture: Potez–C.A.M.S.
Model: 141.
Type: Long-range maritime reconnaissance flying boat.
Power Plant: Four 930hp Hispano-Suiza 12Y 26/27.
Performance:
maximum speed at 3,280ft (1,000m) 199mph (320km/hr).
cruising speed 162mph (260km/hr).
maximum range 1,490 miles (2,400 km).
service ceiling 18,370ft (5,600m).
Weights:
empty 33,069lb (15,000kg).
maximum 57,096lb (25,900kg).
Dimensions:
wing span 134ft 6in (41.0m).
length 82ft 8in (25.2m).
height 25ft 9in (7.85m).
wing area 1,840.62sq ft (171.0sq m).
Armament: Two 7.5mm Darne machine-guns in dorsal turret; one flexible 7.5mm Darne machine-gun each in two lateral barbettes and two waist positions; max bomb load 3,308lb (1,500kg).
Crew: 9–12.
In Service: France (FNAF, FFNAF, FVNAF).
Variants:
Potez–C.A.M.S. 141–01: Prototype.
Potez–C.A.M.S. 141: Production model; one 25mm cannon in dorsal turret; none completed.
Total Production: 1.
Remarks: First flown early 1938, sole prototype operated long-range Atlantic patrols 1939–40; subsequently equipped FVNAF, FFNAF based West Africa, claiming destruction German U-boat during latter service; scrapped late 1943.

Manufacturer: Potez.
Model: 540.
Type: Bomber/reconnaissance.
Power Plant: Two 690hp Hispano-Suiza 12 Xirs/Xjrs.
Performance:
maximum speed 193mph (310km/hr).
normal range 777 miles (1,250km).
time to 13,120ft (4,000m) 9min 24sec.
service ceiling 19,685ft (6,000m).
Weights:
loaded 13,025lb (5,900kg).
Dimensions:
wing span 72ft 6in (22.1m).
length 53ft 2¾in (16.22m).
height 12ft 9in (3.88m).
wing area 818.06sq ft (76.0sq m).
Armament: One 7.5mm Darne machine-gun each in nose, dorsal and ventral turrets; max bomb load 1,987lb (900kg).
Crew: 5.
In Service: France (FAF, FNAF, FFAF, FVAF), Rumania (8 Potez 543), Spain (Rep.AF: 49 Potez 540, 4 Potez 543).
Variants (with no. built):
Potez 54: Prototype; two 660hp Hispano-Suiza 12 Xbrs; twin fins and rudders (1).
Potez 540: Initial production model; re-engined; single fin and rudder (192).
Potez 541: Prototype; two 700hp Gnome-Rhône 14Ks (1).
Potez 542: Re-engined Potez 540; two 780hp Lorraine 12 Hfrs/Hgrs Pétrel (later 860hp Hispano-Suiza 12 Ybrs) (67).
Potez 543: Production (export) model; as Potez 541; two 700hp Gnome-Rhône 13Kdrs (10+).
Potez 544: Civil mailplane version; two 860hp Hispano-Suiza 12Ybrs (1).
Total Production: 272+.
Remarks: Potez 540 series first flown 1933, saw widespread pre-war FAF use; also supplied considerable numbers Spain, and to Rumania; approx 70 still on first-line FAF/FNAF strength (equipping 3 bomber and 2 army co-op Groupes, plus single overseas Escadrille FNAF) upon outbreak WWII; relegated transport/liaison role soon after commencement hostilities, continuing similar duties with FVAF, FFAF after Armistice; 5 reportedly seized by Germany Nov 1942, subsequent deployment, if any, unknown; ultimate fate of FVNAF 542s based French Indo-China at time of Japanese occupation likewise obscure.

Manufacturer: Potez.
Model: 56.
Type: Transport.
Power Plant: Two 185hp Potez 9AB.
Performance:
maximum speed 174mph (280km/hr).
maximum range 932 miles (1,500km).
time to 6,560ft (2,000m) 11min 0sec.
Weights:
empty 4,319lb (1,959kg).
loaded 6,570lb (2,980kg).
Dimensions:
wing span 52ft 6in (16.0m).
length 38ft 10in (11.84m).
height 10ft 2in (3.10m).
wing area 355.21sq ft (33.0sq m).
Crew/Accommodation: 1/6.
In Service: France.
Variants (with no. built):
Potez 56, 561: Initial production models; six-passenger civil transport versions; various power plants (20).
Potez 565/568: Military developments, inc liaison general-duties, day/night reconnaissance, advanced trainer, target-tug versions (52).
Total Production: 72 (all Marks).
Remarks: Civil prototype first flown June 1934; number military variants employed by FAF general-purpose/ancillary duties early months WWII.

Manufacturer: Potez.
Model: 585.
Type: Liaison.
Power Plant: One 130hp Potez 6Ba.
Performance:
maximum speed 118mph (190km/hr).
cruising speed 99mph (160km/hr).
normal range 466 miles (750km).
service ceiling 19,030ft (5,800m).
Weights:
empty 1,157lb (525kg).
loaded 2,116lb (960kg).
Dimensions:
wing span 37ft 1in (11.3m).
length 24ft 5¼in (7.45m).
height 7ft 9in (2.36m).
wing area 193.75sq ft (18.0sq m).
Crew/Accommodation: 1/1.
In Service: France (FAF, FVAF).
Variants (with no. built):
Potez 58: Prototype; three-seat light tourer (1).
Potez: 580, 582, 584, 586: Civil versions of Potez 58; various power plants.
Potez 585: Civil tourer/military liaison version; modified Potez 58. (Total Potez 580, 582, 584, 586, 585: 200.)
Total Production: 201.
Remarks: Prototype first flown Sept 1934; considerable number Potez 585s on FAF strength general liaison duties, 1939–40.

Manufacturer: Potez.
Model: 631 C3.
Type: Heavy fighter/night-fighter.
Power Plant: Two 700hp Gnome-Rhône 14 M4/M5 or M6/M7.
Performance:
maximum speed at sea level 224mph (360km/hr).
maximum speed at 14,764ft (4,500m) 275mph (442km/hr).
cruising speed 149mph (240km/hr).
maximum range 758 miles (1,220km).
time to 13,120ft (4,000m) 5min 56sec.
Weights:
empty 5,401lb (2,450kg).
loaded 8,289lb (3,760kg).
Dimensions:
wing span 52ft 6in (16.0m).
length 36ft 4in (11.07m).
height 11ft 10½in (3.62m).
wing area 351.98sq ft (32.7sq m).
Armament: Two fixed forward-firing 20mm Hispano-Suiza 404 (or HS9) cannon in nose (or one cannon and one 7.5mm machine-gun); one flexible 7.5 MAC 1934 machine-gun in rear cockpit; plus (optional) four 7.5mm MAC 1934 machine-guns in underwing fairings.
Crew: 3.
In Service: France (FAF, FNAF, FVAF, Rumania (1 Potez 631), Switzerland (2 Potez 630), Yugoslavia (1 Potez 630).
Variants (with no. built):
Potez 630 No. 01: Initial prototype; private venture; two 580hp Hispano-Suiza 14 Hbs; 3 crew (1).
Potez 630 CN2 No. 02 and C3 No. 03: Prototypes; 2-seat night-fighter/3-seat day-fighter versions respectively (2).
Potez 630 C3 No. 01/02: Pre-production models; 3-seat day-fighter version (2).
Potez 630 C3: Production model; 3-seat fighter version; two 20mm cannon plus one 7.5mm machine-gun; alt two 650/700hp Hispano-Suiza 14 Ab 02/03 or 14 Ab 10/11 (inc 1 each Switzerland/Yugoslavia) (82).
Potez 630 DC No.04: Pre-production dual-control trainer version; original Yugoslav order (1).
Potez 631 C3 No. 01, 02, 04 INS: Prototypes; day-fighter version; modified Potez 630; two 570hp Gnome-Rhône 14 Mars; revised nacelles; No.02 re-engined Hispano-Suiza 14 AB 02/03s (Potez 631 No. 04 Ins. trainer to Rumania) (3).
Potez 631 C3: Production model; two Gnome-Rhône 14 M4/M5 or M6/M7; alt armament arrangements (202).
Potez 631 Ins. (634): Pre-production dual-control trainer version (10).
Total Production: approx 1,360 (all Marks).
Remarks: First flown Spring 1936, majority Potez 630s grounded/withdrawn front-line service by outbreak WWII; Potez 631s equipped 8 Escadrilles FAF/FNAF during Battle of France; served both night and day-fighter roles; claimed total 29 confirmed victories, but suffered heavily at hands of friendly forces due striking resemblance to Messerschmitt Bf 110; limited service FVAF southern France and North Africa; subsequently employed by FFAF (FFI) against German forces in Tunisia and on French Atlantic coast.
Colour Reference: Plates 14, 15: Potez 630 C3 No.44 (C5–56) assigned to 3ème Escadrille, GC II/I, Armée de l'Air, Buc (nr Paris), May 1940; current FAF practice to attach two or three multi-seat command and fighter-direction machines to each single-seat Groupe de Chasse (GC II/1 equipped with Bloch 152), hence 3ème Escadrille's 'Grim Reaper' emblem on fuselage; note small size upper surface wing roundels.

Manufacturer: Potez.
Model: 633 B2.
Type: Light bomber.
Power Plant: Two 700hp Gnome-Rhône 14 M4/M5 or M6/M7.
Performance:
maximum speed at sea level 244mph (393km/hr).
maximum speed at 13,780ft (4,200m) 273mph (439km/hr).
cruising speed 199mph (320km/hr).
maximum range 810 miles (1,300km).
time to 13,120ft (4,000m) 8min 30sec.
service ceiling 26,250ft (8,000m).
Weights:
empty 5,401lb (2,450kg).
normal/loaded 9,921lb (4,500kg).
Dimensions:
wing span 52ft 6in (16.0m).
length 36ft 4in (11.07m).
height 11ft 10½in (3.62m).
wing area 351.98sq ft (32.7sq m).
Armament: One fixed forward-firing 7.5mm MAC 1934 machine-gun in nose; one flexible 7.5mm MAC 1934 machine-gun in rear cockpit; max bomb load (internal) 880lb (400kg).
Crew: 2.
In Service: France (FAF, FVAF), Greece (13), Rumania (20), Switzerland (1).
Variants (with no. built):
Potez 632 No.01: Prototype; light bomber; modified Potez 630 CN2 No.02 (1 conversion).
Potez 633 No. 01/02: Prototypes; light bomber version; modified Potez 631 C3; bomb-bay; 2 crew; revised nose and armament (2).
Potez 633 B2: Production model; original Chinese (4) and Swiss (1) orders; former retained FAF, latter Hispano-Suiza power plants, Swiss armament (5).
Potez 633 Grec: As Potez 633 B2. Greek order; increased 1,322lb (600kg) max bomb load (inc 11 retained by FAF) (24).
Potez 633 Roumain: Rumanian order; 7.5mm MAC 1934 machine-guns replaced by three 7.7mm FN-Browning machine-guns (inc one addn ventral rearward-firing); provision for bomb-bay camera (20).
Potez 633 Franco-Roumain: Addn Rumanian order; as 633 Roumain; (all retained by FAF) (20).
Potez 633 C3: Three-seat fighter version; projected Czech (Avia) licence-production.
Potez 637 No.01: Prototype; reconnaissance version of Potez 633 B2; ventral observation gondola; 3 crew; addn ventral 7.5mm MAC 1934 machine-gun; external (underwing) 220lb (100kg) bomb load only (1).
Potez 637 A3: Production model (60).
Potez 639 No.01: Prototype; low-level ground-attack version; 2 crew; fixed forward-firing 20mm Hispano-Suiza cannon plus max 1,100lb (500kg) bomb load (1).
Total Production: approx 1,360 (all Marks).
Remarks: Subject number export orders (majority of which sequestrated prior delivery), Potez 633 light bomber served FAF primarily in training role (only one recorded instance operational use, strafing German columns vicinity Arras, 20 May 1940); in contrast, Potez 637 models heavily committed reconnaissance/observation duties from outbreak WWII until Armistice, suffering over 75% casualties of total 60 produced. Potez 633 Grec equipped one Greek AF Mira in action against Italian forces in Albania, Winter 1940; Potez 633 Roumain employed army co-operation/tactical reconnaissance roles in support Rumanian advance into Soviet Union, 1941–42.

Manufacturer: Potez.
Model: 63.11.
Type: Tactical reconnaissance/army co-operation.
Power Plant: Two 700hp Gnome-Rhône 14M 4/5.
Performance:
maximum speed at sea level 230mph (370km/hr).
maximum speed at 16,400ft (5,000m) 264mph (425km/hr).
maximum range 932 miles (2,500km).
time to 6,560ft (2,000m) 4min 0sec.
Weights:
empty 6,911lb (3,135kg).
maximum 9,987lb (4,530kg).
Dimensions:
wing span 52ft 6in (16.0m).
length 36ft 1in (11.0m).
height 11ft 10½in (3.62m).
wing area 351.98sq ft (32.7sq m).
Armament: One fixed forward-firing and one fixed rearward-firing ventral 7.5mm MAC 1934 machine-gun, plus one flexible 7.5mm MAC 1934 machine-gun in rear cockpit; or three fixed forward-firing and three fixed rearward-firing ventral 7.5mm machine-guns, plus two 7.5mm MAC 1934 machine-guns in rear cockpit, plus (optional) addn four 7.5mm MAC 1934 machine-guns in underwing fairings; max bomb load 616lb (280kg).
Crew: 3.
In Service: France (FAF, FFAF, FVAF, FVNAF), Germany (approx 250), Great Britain (2+ escapes), Hungary, Rumania (63).
Variants (with no. built):
Potez 63.11 A3 No.01/03: Prototypes; tactical reconnaissance/army co-operation version of modified Potez 630; redesigned (fully glazed) nose and fuselage centre section; No.01 rounded nose panels; Nos.02/03 optically flat panelling; two 700hp Gnome-Rhône 14M 4/5 (3).
Potez 63.11: Production model; as nos. 02/03; two Gnome-Rhône 14M 4/5 or 14M 6/7; alt two/three-blade propellers; progressive (addn) armament/equipment modifications (approx 925).
Potez 63.12 C3 No.01: Experimental 3-seat fighter prototype; two Pratt & Whitney SB4G Twin Wasp Juniors (one Potez 631 C3 conversion).
Potez 63.13 Bp2 No.01: Experimental 2-seat dive-bomber prototype; air brakes; two ventral fixed forward-firing 20mm cannon plus max 440lb (200kg) bomb load underwing (one Potez 633 B2 conversion).
Potez 63.16 T3 No.01: Experimental 3-seat army co-operation crew trainer prototype; modified Potez 63.11; increased wing span/area. (One Potez 63.11 conversion).
Total Production: approx 1,360 (all Marks).
Remarks: Numerically by far most important of entire series, Potez 63.11 entered service Nov 1939, rapidly supplanted variety obsolescent observation types remaining on FAF inventory; equipped forty Groupes by 10 May 1940; lacking adequate fighter cover, Potez 63.11 sustained more casualties than any other single type, 225 being lost out of total 700+ delivered; subsequent extensive use both FFAF/FVAF Middle East and North Africa, participating Western Desert, Syrian, and NW Africa/Tunisian campaigns; considerable numbers acquired by Germany, 80+ captured 1940 post-Armistice, 120 completed during 1941, and 50+ seized upon occupation Vichy France 1942; served Luftwaffe schools/training units; also supplied (ex-Vichy) Rumanian (and reportedly Hungarian) AFs for similar duties, 1942/43 resp.

Manufacturer: Potez.
Model: 65.
Type: Transport/light bomber.
Power Plant: Two 720hp Hispano-Suiza 12Xbrs 1/Xgrs 1.
Performance:
maximum speed at 6,560ft (2,000m) 186mph (300km/hr).
cruising speed 155mph (250km/hr).
normal range 510 miles (800km).
service ceiling 19,680ft (6,000m).
Weights:
empty 9,570lb (4,340kg).
loaded 16,280lb (7,380kg).
Dimensions:
wing span 73ft 7¼in (22.44m).
length 56ft 9½in (17.31m).
height 12ft 9in (3.88m).
Armament: Provision for 22lb (10kg), 221lb (100kg) or 441lb (200kg) bombs.
Crew/Accommodation: 2/14 troops (or six litters, four seated wounded, plus one medic).
In Service: (FAF, FFAF, FVAF), Germany (ex-France), Rumania (5).
Variants (with no. built):
Potez 62–0, 62–1: Initial prototype and production models; civil transports; various power plants; 62–1 modified wing (23).
Potez 65–01: Prototype; military troop transport version; Potez 62 development (1).
Potez 65: Production model; as prototype; alt trooper, ambulance (or light bomber) configurations (approx 55).
Total Production: approx 80 (all Marks).
Remarks: Development of earlier Potez 62 civil airliner, Potez 65 (originally intended for colonial use) first flew mid-1937; 25 examples on FAF strength outbreak WWII; served variety transport/ancillary roles; several captured by Germany; also supplied pre-war Rumanian AF; at least one civil 62–1 impressed FFAF military transport duties.

Manufacturer: Potez.
Model: 662.
Type: Transport.
Power Plant: Four 680hp Gnome-Rhône 14 Mars.
Performance:
maximum speed 292mph (470km/hr).
cruising speed 248mph (400km/hr).
maximum range 621 miles (1,000km).
service ceiling 29,500+ft (9,000+m).
Weights:
empty 12,125lb (5,500kg).
loaded 18,474lb (8,380kg).
Dimensions:
wing span 73ft 10in (22.5m).
length 54ft 5½in (16.6m).
wing area 688.8sq ft (64sq m).
Crew/Accommodation: 2/12.
In Service: France (FAF, FVAF).
Variants (with no. built):
Potez 661.01: Prototype; civil transport version; four 220hp Renault 6Q 02/03 (1).
Potez 662.01: Prototype; military transport version; re-engined Potez 661 (1).
Total Production: 2.
Remarks: Potez 661 four-engined civil transport based upon military Potez 63 series, first flown late 1937; employed post-Armistice FVAF liaison duties; Potez 662, also originally envisaged as civil airliner, served military role from outset; operated by FAF/FVAF, 1939–41.

Manufacturer: SNCAO.
Model: C.A.O.200.
Type: Interceptor fighter.
Power Plant: One 860hp Hispano-Suzia 12Y–31.
Performance:
maximum speed at sea level 277mph (445km/hr).
maximum speed at 16,400ft (5,000m) 342mph (550km/hr).
time to 19,685ft (6,000m) 7min 50sec.
service ceiling 36,090ft (11,000m).
Weights:
loaded 5,512lb (2,500kg).
Dimensions:
wing span 31ft 2in (9.5m).
length 29ft 2¼in (8.9m).
height 11ft 5¼in (3.49m).
wing area 143.16sq ft (13.3sq m).
Armament: One 20mm Hispano-Suiza 404 cannon firing through propeller hub; two 7.5mm MAC 1934 machine-guns in wings.
Crew: 1.
In Service: France.
Variants (with no. built):
C.A.O.200 prototype: Development of Nieuport Ni–161; one 860hp Hispano-Suiza 12Y–31 (1).
C.A.O.200: Pre-production model; 1,100hp Hispano-Suiza 12Y–51; 12 ordered, none completed.
Total Production: 1.
Remarks: Produced as competitor to Dewoitine D.520, prototype C.A.O.200 first flew 31 Jan 1939; none of initial Service Trials order completed before capitulation; sole prototype returned SNCAO works as part of factory defence flight.

Manufacturer: (SNCA du) Sud-Est.
Model: SE 200.
Type: Transport flying boat.
Power Plant: Six 1,600hp Gnome-Rhône 14R 26/27.
Performance:
maximum speed at sea level 220mph (354km/hr).
maximum speed at 8,200ft (2,500m) 235mph (378km/hr).
cruising speed 190mph (305km/hr).
maximum range 3,765 miles (6,060km).
Weights:
empty 72,192lb (32,746kg).
maximum 158,733lb (72,000kg).
Dimensions:
wing span 171ft 3in (52.2m).
length 131ft 8¾in (40.15m).
wing area 3,659.73sq ft (340sq m).
Crew/Accommodation: 8/40.
In Service: Germany (1).
Variants (with no. built):
SE 200 Nos.01/03: Prototypes; civil transport flying boat; six 1,500hp Wright R–2600 Cyclone 14 or 1,600hp Gnome-Rhône 14R 26/27 (3).
Total Production: 3.
Remarks: Ordered 1938, first Wright-powered SE 200 completed after Armistice; first flown Aug 1943, subsequently taken over by Luftwaffe and assigned operational test unit; destroyed at moorings by RAF raid; No.02 likewise destroyed prior first flight, No.03 completed post-war.

Manufacturer: Wibault.
Model: 283T.
Type: Transport.
Power Plant: Three 350hp Gnome-Rhône 7Kd.
Performance:
maximum speed 177mph (285km/hr).
normal range 696 miles (1,120km).
service ceiling 17,060ft (5,200m).
Weights:
empty 9,921lb (4,500kg).
loaded 14,330lb (6,500kg).
Dimensions:
wing span 74ft 1¾in (22.60m).
length 55ft 9¼in (17.00m).
height 18ft 10½in (5.75m).
wing area 686.74sq ft (63.8sq m).
Crew/Accommodation: 2/10.
In Service: France.
Variants (with no. built):
280T: Prototypes; civil transport/airliner; three 300hp Hispano-Suiza 9Qa and 350hp Gnome-Rhône 7Kd (2).
281T: Prototype; re-engined 280T (1 conversion).
282T: Improved 281T; engine cowlings; modified tail (inc converted 280T and 281T) (6).
283T: Modified 282T; increased weight; addn fuel capacity; various subsequent modifications to undercarriage and tail; some as long-range transport (12).
Total Production: 20.
Remarks: Entered commercial service 1932–33, twelve impressed FAF upon outbreak WWII; served transport role 1939–40, inc liaison/support duties for RAF; similarity to German Junkers Ju 52 transport resulted in all suffering damage from friendly AA fire, inc one destroyed.

GERMANY

Manufacturer: Arado.
Model: Ar 66C.
Type: Trainer/communications.
Power Plant: One 240hp Argus As
10C.
Performance:
maximum speed at sea level
 130mph (210km/hr).
cruising speed 109mph (175km/hr).
normal range 444 miles (715km).
time to 3,280ft (1,000m) 4min 6sec.
service ceiling 14,765ft (4,500m).
Weights:
empty 1,995lb (905kg).
maximum 2,932lb (1,330kg).
Dimensions:
wing span 32ft 9¾in (10.0m).
length 27ft 2¾in (8.30m).
height 9ft 7½in (2.93m).
wing area 318.94sq ft (29.63sq m).
Crew: 2.
In Service: Germany.
Variants (with no. built):
Ar 66a: Prototype; landplane
 version (1).
Ar 66b: Prototype; floatplane
 version (1).
Ar 66B: Production model;
 floatplane version (10).
Ar 66C: Main production model;
 as Ar 66a; provision for blind- and
 night-flying equipment; many
 subsequently converted for night
 ground-attack role.
Remarks: Entered service 1933,
remained standard Luftwaffe trainer
until well after outbreak WWII;
Winter 1942–43 modified to carry
4.4lb (2kg) or 8.8lb (4kg) anti-
personnel bombs and employed as
night ground-attack aircraft against
Soviet forces along Eastern Front
and in Finland; equipped sixteen
Staffeln, inc one manned by
Estonian volunteers, two by Latvian,
and one by Russian (ex-PoW).
Colour Reference: Plates 19, 20:
Arado Ar 66C (6A + TN) of NSGr
12; Riga-Spilve, Latvia, Sept 1944;
representative of mixed bag both
indigenous and foreign second-line
types pressed into service with
Luftwaffe's night ground-attack
wings, 6A + TN operated by
Latvian-manned NSGr 12 on
Northern (Baltic) Sector of Russian
Front, Feb–Oct 1944; note black/
white night camouflage finish and
flame damper exhaust.

Manufacturer: Arado.
Model: Ar 68E-1.
Type: Fighter.
Power Plant: One 690hp Junkers
Jumo 210 Ea.
Performance:
maximum speed at sea level
 190mph (306km/hr).
maximum speed at 8,695ft (2,650m)
 208mph (335km/hr).
normal range 310 miles (500km).
initial rate of climb 2,480ft/min
 (776m/min).
service ceiling 26,575ft (8,100m).
Weights:
empty 3,527lb (1,600kg).
loaded 4,453lb (2,020kg).
Dimensions:
wing span—upper 36ft 1in (11.00m).
 lower 26ft 2½in (8.00m).
length 31ft 2in (9.50m).
height 10ft 10in (3.30m).
wing area 293.85sq ft (27.30sq m).
Armament: Two fuselage-mounted
7.9mm MG 17 machine-guns; max
(optional) bomb load 132lb (60kg).
Crew: 1.
In Service: Germany.
Variants (with no. built):
Ar 68a/e (V1/5): Prototypes;
 various power plants (5).
Ar 68E-0: Pre-production model;
 690hp Jumo 210 Da.
Ar 68E-1: Main production model;
 re-engined.
Ar 68F-1: Initial production model;
 750hp BMW VI.
Ar 68G: Project only.
Ar 68H: Redesigned E-1; 850hp
 supercharged BMW 132Da; sliding
 cockpit canopy; two addn 7.9mm
 MG 17 (upper) wing guns;
 prototypes only (1).
Remarks: Service debut late
Summer 1936 as replacement for
Heinkel He 51; relatively brief
first-line fighter service, as itself
superseded by Bf 109 monoplane
fighter from 1937–38; two examples
sent to Spain 1938 for operational
trials (attached NatAF); by outbreak
WWII Ar 68 equipped only three
provisional night-fighter Staffeln;
Spring 1940 relegated advanced
trainer role.

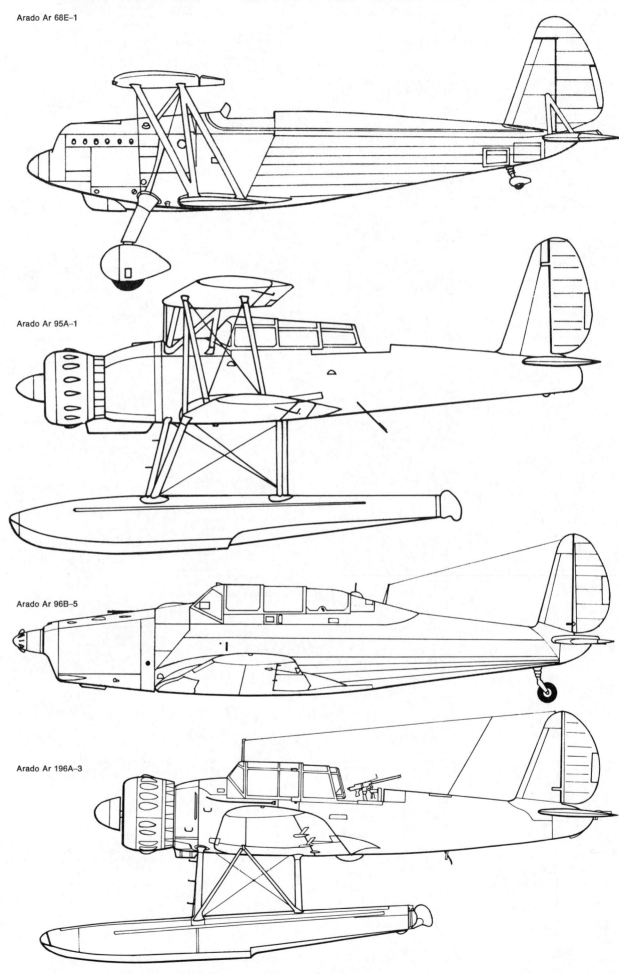

Arado Ar 68E–1

Arado Ar 95A–1

Arado Ar 96B–5

Arado Ar 196A–3

Manufacturer: Arado.
Model: Ar 79.
Type: Communications.
Power Plant: One 105hp Hirth HM 504A–2.
Performance:
maximum speed at sea level 143mph (230km/hr).
cruising speed 127mph (205km/hr).
normal range 637 miles (1,025km).
time to 3,280ft (1,000m) 3min 48sec.
service ceiling 14,764ft (4,500m).
Weights:
empty 1,160lb (526kg).
loaded 1,764lb (800kg).
Dimensions:
wing span 32ft 9½in (10.0m).
length 24ft 11¼in (7.6m).
height 6ft 10¾in (2.1m).
wing area 150.7sq ft (14.0sq m).
Crew: 2.
In Service: Germany, Hungary (5).
Variants:
Ar 79: Light sports tourer/trainer; dual controls.
Remarks: Holder of a number of pre-war international speed and distance records, majority Ar 79 tourers impressed by Luftwaffe on outbreak of war for communications/liaison duties.

Manufacturer: Arado.
Model: Ar 95A–1.
Type: Torpedo-bomber/reconnaissance floatplane.
Power Plant: One 880hp BMW 132 Dc.
Performance:
maximum speed at sea level 171mph (275km/hr).
cruising speed 157mph (253km/hr).
maximum range 680 miles (1,095km).
time to 3,280ft (1,000m) 2min 18sec.
service ceiling 23,950ft (7,300m).
Weights:
empty 5,588lb (2,535kg).
loaded 7,843lb (3,558kg).
Dimensions:
wing span 41ft 0in (12.5m).
length 36ft 5in (11.1m).
height 17ft 0½in (5.2m).
wing area 488.5sq ft (45.38sq m).
Armament: One fixed forward-firing 7.9mm MG 17 machine-gun in upper cowling; one flexible 7.9mm MG 17 machine-gun in rear cockpit; max weapon load one 1,487lb (700kg) torpedo, or one 1,102lb (500kg) bomb.
Crew: 2.
In Service: Chile (3 Ar 95B), Germany, Spain (NatAF 3Ar 95A–0).
Variants (with no. built):
Ar 95 V1/5: Prototypes; BMW 132 or Jumo 210. V1 and V2 2-seaters; V4 with wheeled undercarriage (5).
Ar 95A–0: Pre-production model; floatplane; three-man crew; uprated engine (6).
Ar 95A–1: Production model; two crew (12+).
Ar 95B: Landplane version (to Chile as Ar 95L) (3).
Total Production: 26+.
Remarks: First flown 1936, and combat-tested with Condor Legion during Spanish Civil War (3 of 6 examples sent subsequently transferred to Spanish NatAF, serving in patrol and reconnaissance roles throughout WWII). Ar 95 floatplane not accepted by Luftwaffe; instead offered for export in either land-(Ar 95L) or floatplane (Ar 95W) versions; ordered by Chile and Turkey resp; latter contract taken over by Luftwaffe (as Ar 95A–1) on outbreak WWII; employed primarily as floatplane trainer, sole operational deployment maritime reconnaissance Baltic Sea/Gulf of Finland by Estonian volunteer Staffel.

Manufacturer: Arado.
Model: Ar 96B–5.
Type: Advanced trainer/communications.
Power Plant: One 485hp Argus As 410MA–1.
Performance:
maximum speed at 9,840ft (3,000m) 205mph (330km/hr).
cruising speed 171mph (275km/hr).
normal range 615 miles (990km).
service ceiling 22,965ft (7,000m).
Weights:
empty 2,690lb (1,220kg).
maximum 3,858lb (1,750kg).
Dimensions:
wing span 36ft 1in (11.0m).
length 29ft 11½in (9.13m).
height 8ft 8in (2.64m).
wing area 182.99sq ft (17.10sq m).
Armament: One fixed forward-firing 7.9mm MG 17 machine-gun in upper cowling.
Crew: 2.
In Service: Germany, Hungary (35), Rumania.
Variants (with no. built):
Ar 96 V1/4, 6: Prototypes; various power plants; cockpit and engine cowling modifications (5).
Ar 96A–1: Initial production model; 240hp As 10C–3.
Ar 96 V5: Prototype; 465hp As 410A–1; dual controls; increased length (1).
Ar 96B–1: Production model as V5; unarmed.
Ar 96B–2: As B–1; one MG 17 machine-gun in forward fuselage.
Ar 96B–5: As B–2; improved radio equipment.
(Total Ar 96B–1, –2, –5; Arado-, Ago-, Letov-, and Avia-built: approx 10,000).
Ar 96 V9: Export prototype; open cockpit; one flexible and one fixed MG 17; provision for three light bombs underwing. Bulgarian order (1).
Ar 96C: Bomb-aimer trainer; project only.
Ar 296: Project only.
Ar 396: Mixed wood/metal development of Ar 96B; 580hp As 411A–1; redesigned cockpit and undercarriage;/prototypes: (French) SIPA-built (3); (Czech) Letov-built (approx 5).
SIPA S.10, S.11, S.12, S.121: French designations for late-post war Ar 396 versions; SIPA-built (181).
C.2B–1: Czech designation for post-war Ar 96B production; Avia- and Letov-built (394).
Total Production: 11,546 (exc post-war foreign production).
Remarks: Standard Luftwaffe advanced trainer of WWII; formed mainstay all fighter-training and replacement-fighter wings; also served ancillary reconnaissance, liaison, and communications roles; some examples field-modified with two MG 17 machine-guns in underwing gondolas; Ar 396 under development in both Occupied France and Czechoslovakia at time of liberation; continued post-war production both models.

Manufacturer: Arado.
Model: Ar 196A–3.
Type: Shipboard reconnaissance floatplane.
Power Plant: One 900hp BMW 132K.
Performance:
maximum speed at 13,120ft (4,000m) 193mph (310km/hr).
cruising speed 166mph (266km/hr).
maximum range 665 miles (1,070km).
initial rate of climb 1,358ft/min (414m/min).
service ceiling 23,026ft (7,020m).
Weights:
empty 5,148lb (2,335kg).
loaded 7,282lb (3,303kg).
Dimensions:
wing span 40ft 9½in (12.40m).
length 36ft 0½in (11.0m).
height 14ft 7¼in (4.45m).
wing area 304.62sq ft (28.3sq m).
Armament: Two fixed forward-firing 20mm MG FF cannon in wings; one fixed forward-firing 7.9mm MG 17 machine-gun in upper cowling; plus either one flexible 7.9mm MG 15, or two paired 7.9mm MG 17 (MG 81Z) machine-guns in rear cockpit; max bomb load 220lb (100kg).
Crew: 2.
In Service: Bulgaria (12), Finland (2), Germany, Rumania (28).
Variants (with no. built):
Ar 196 V1/2: Prototypes; twin floats; 880hp BMW 132 Dc (2).
Ar 196 V3/5: Prototypes; single central float version (3).
Ar 196A–0: Pre-production twin float model; uprated engine (10).
Ar 196A–1: Initial production model; two 7.9mm MG 17 machine-guns; structural strengthening for catapult launching (20).
Ar 196A–2: Modified A–1; two addn 20mm wing cannon; increased weight.
Ar 196A–3: Improved version; addn strengthening; major production variant.
Ar 196A–4: As A–3; addn radio equipment.
(Total Ar 196A–2, –3, –4: Arado-built (392); SNCA-built (23).
Ar 196A–5: Revised armament; improved radio equipment; Arado-built (22); Fokker-built (69).
Ar 196B–0: Pre-production single float model (approx 5).
Total Production: 546.
Remarks: Service debut Autumn 1939; standard equipment aboard all Germany's capital ships, *Tirpitz* and *Bismarck* each carrying six, *Scharnhorst* and *Gneisenau* four, heavy cruisers three, pocket-battleships and some light cruisers two; one of Admiral *Graf Spee*'s two Arados destroyed on catapult by gunfire during Battle of River Plate, 13 Dec 1939; also equipped ten coastal-based Staffeln; active North Sea (captured HMS/M *Seal* in Kattegat, 5 May 1940), Baltic, Channel and Biscay coasts; subsequently deployed Eastern Mediterranean and Aegean; employed by Rumanian and Bulgarian units on reconnaissance and convoy-escort duties over Black Sea.

Manufacturer: Arado.
Model: Ar 232B–0.
Type: General-purpose transport.
Power Plant: Four 1,200hp BMW-Bramo 323R–2 Fafnir.
Performance:
maximum speed at 13,120ft (4,000m) 191mph (307km/hr).
cruising speed 180mph (290km/hr).
normal range 830 miles (1,335km).
time to 13,120ft (4,000m) 15min 48sec.
service ceiling 22,640ft (6,900m).
Weights:
empty 28,175lb (12,780kg).
loaded 44,090lb (20,000kg).
Dimensions:
wing span 109ft 10¾in (33.50m).
length 77ft 2in (23.52m).
height 18ft 8¼in (5.70m).
wing area 1,535sq ft (142.6sq m).
Armament: One flexible forward-firing 13mm MG 131 machine-gun in nose; one 20mm MG 151/20 cannon in dorsal turret; one (or two) 13mm MG 131 machine-gun/s at rear of fuselage pod; provision for max eight hand-held 7.9mm MG 34s firing through side-windows.
Crew/Payload: 4–5/10,097lb (4,580kg).
In Service: Germany.
Variants (with no. built):
Ar 232 V1/2: Twin-engined prototypes; two 1,600hp BMW 801MA (2).
Ar 232 V3: Four BMW-Bramo 323R–2; increased wing span (1).
Ar 232B–0(V4/22): Pre-production models (as V3 prototype); one with four Gnome-Rhône 14Ms; one with fixed ski undercarriage (approx 19).
Total Production: approx 22.
Remarks: Innovatory twin-engined transport design first flown early 1941; subsequent four-engined configuration dictated by unavailability BMW 801 power plants (reserved for Fw 190 fighter programme); exact number pre-production B–0 series completed not certain; less than ten Ar 232s believed accepted by Luftwaffe; dubbed 'Tausendfüssler' (Millipede) by crews, saw limited service on Eastern Front, initially in transport role, latterly with special-duties unit.

Manufacturer: Arado.
Model: Ar 234B–2 Blitz (Lightning).
Type: Reconnaissance-bomber.
Power Plant: Two 1,980lb.s.t. Junkers Jumo 004B.
Performance:
maximum speed at 19,685ft (6,000m) 457mph (735km/hr).
maximum range 1,013 miles (1,630km).
time to 19,685ft (6,000m) 12min 48sec.
service ceiling 32,810ft (10,000m).
Weights:
empty 11,464lb (5,200kg).
maximum 21,715lb (9,800kg).
Dimensions:
wing span 47ft 3¾in (14.41m).
length 41ft 5¾in (12.64m).
height 14ft 1¼in (4.30m).
wing area 284.17sq ft (26.4sq m).
Armament: Two fixed rearward-firing 20mm MG 151/20 cannon; max bomb load 3,308lb (1,500kg).
Crew: 1.
In Service: Germany.
Variants (with no. built):
Ar 234 V1/18: Prototypes; various turbojet power plant arrangements; V1/8 with take-off trolley/landing skids; some with pressurised cabin, ejection seat, and RATOG (18).
Ar 234A: Projected initial production model; as V1/8.
Ar 234B–0: Pre-production model; conventional retractable undercarriage; reconnaissance version; Jumo 004B–1s (20).
Ar 234B–1: Initial production model; Patin PDS autopilot; drop tanks.
Ar 234B–2: Reconnaissance-bomber version; improved Ar 234B–1; bomb-sight, cameras, and drop tanks.
(Total 234B–1, –2: 210).
Ar 234B–3: Bomber version; project only.
Ar 234 V19/30: Prototypes; four-engined reconnaissance/multi-purpose versions; various equipment; V26 and V30 not completed (12).
Ar 234C–1: Production model; reconnaissance version; modified B–1; four 1,760hp BMW 003A–1s.
Ar 234C–3: Pre-production model; bomber/ground-attack version; revised armament.
(Total Ar 234C–1, –3: 14).
Ar 234C–2, 4/8: Projects only.
Total Production: 274.
Remarks: World's first operational jet bomber, and only one of its kind to see service in WWII (if discount misuse of Me 262); operational debut in reconnaissance role, July 1944; operated over UK, 1944–45; also employed in Northern Italy; equipped three reconnaissance Staffeln, plus number experimental/special units; bomber version first employed during Ardennes counter-offensive, Winter 1944–45; continued operations over Western Front until Spring 1945, culminating in attacks on Allied-held bridge over Rhine at Remagen; two examples also equipped experimental night-fighter unit assigned to Reich defence closing weeks of war.
Colour Reference: Plates 24, 25: Arado Ar 234B–2 Blitz flown by Oberstleutnant Robert Kowalewski, Kommodore KG 76, Karstedt, Schleswig-Holstein, May 1945; Note abbreviated fuselage code (reduced from standard F1+AA to single individual aircraft letter 'A', in Stab colour), common late-war practice remaining Luftwaffe bomber units; Kowalewski's machine one of number Ar 234s captured intact by RAF and test-flown post-war.

Manufacturer: Arado.
Model: Ar 240A–0.
Type: Long-range reconnaissance.
Power Plant: Two 1,175hp Daimler-Benz DB 601E.
Performance:
maximum speed at 19,685ft (6,000m) 384mph (618km/hr).
cruising speed 345mph (555km/hr).
maximum range 1,243 miles (2,000km).
time to 19,685ft (6,000m) 11min 0sec.
service ceiling 34,450ft (10,500m).
Weights:
empty 13,669lb (6,200kg).
loaded 20,834lb (9,450kg).
Dimensions:
wing span 43ft 9in (13.33m).
length 42ft 0¼in (12.81m).
height: 12ft 11½in (3.95m).
wing area 336.91sq ft (31.3sq m).
Armament: Two fixed forward-firing 7.9mm MG 17 machine-guns; two 7.9mm MG 81 machine-guns each in dorsal and ventral remotely-controlled barbettes.
Crew: 2.
In Service: Germany.
Variants (with no. built):
Ar 240 V1/2: Prototypes; armed multi-purpose version; 1,075hp DB 601As (2).
Ar 240 V3; Major redesign; armed reconnaissance version; remotely-controlled armament barbettes (1).
Ar 240 V4: Prototype; dive-bomber version; 1,750hp DB 603As (1).
Ar 240A–0 (inc. V5/6): Pre-production Service Trials models; reconnaissance version; DB 601Es; one subsequently re-engined with supercharged 1,880hp BMW 801TJs; two unarmed (5).
Ar 240B–0 (V7/8): Modified Ar 240A–0; revised armament; 1,475hp DB 605AMs (2).
Ar 240C–0 (V9/12): Zerstörer, Kampfzerstörer and night-fighter prototypes; 1,750hp DB 603A–2s; various armament (4).
Total Production: 15.
Remarks: Original multi-purpose design first flown May 1940; protracted and troublesome development/trials programme finally abandoned Dec 1942; Ar 240 nevertheless saw limited service with Luftwaffe between 1941–44, being operated at various times by four reconnaissance, one experimental, and one fighter Staffeln; served on Eastern Front, both central and far northern (Murmansk railway) sectors, in Mediterranean theatre (based Italy), and over UK.

Manufacturer: Blohm und Voss.
Model: Bv 138A–1.
Type: Long-range maritime reconnaissance flying boat.
Power Plant: Three 600hp Junkers Jumo 205C–4.
Performance:
maximum speed at sea level 165mph (265km/hr).
cruising speed 155mph (250km/hr).
maximum range 2,442 miles (3,930km).
time to 6,560ft (2,000m) 8min 30sec.
service ceiling 11,810ft (3,600m).
Weights:
empty 23,810lb (10,800kg).
loaded 30,313lb (13,750kg).
Dimensions:
wing span 88ft 4in (26.94m).
length 65ft 1¼in (19.85m).
height 19ft 4¼in (5.90m).
wing area 1,205.56sq ft (112sq m).
Armament: One 20mm (MG 204) cannon in nose turret; one 7.9mm MG 15 machine-gun each in two open fuselage positions, one aft of

Arado Ar 240A–O

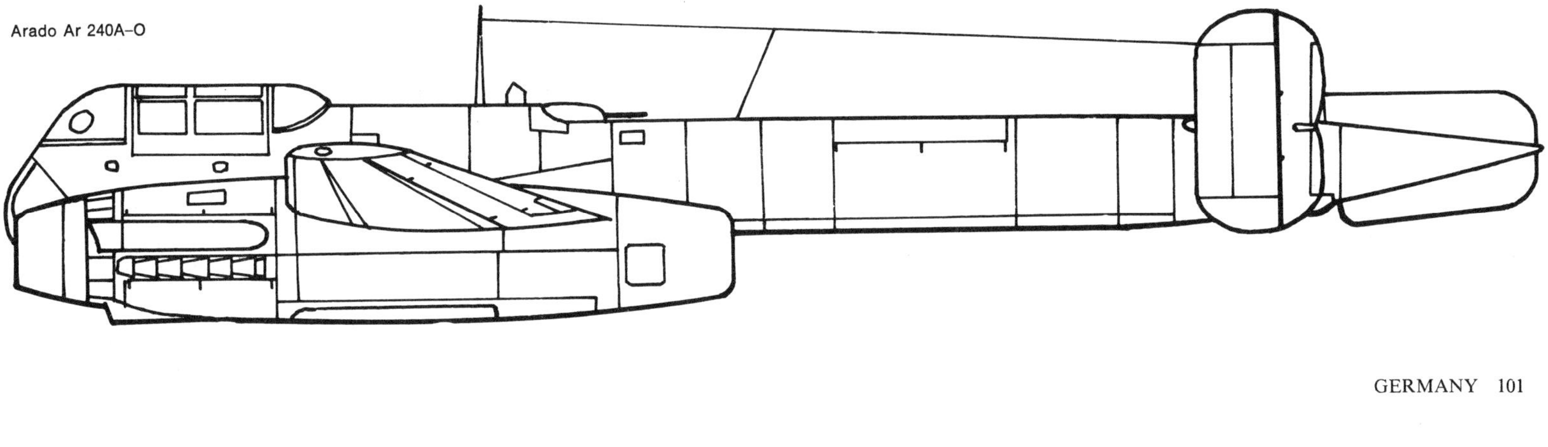

central engine nacelle and one at rear of hull; max bomb load 330lb (150kg).
Crew/Accommodation: 5–6/10.
In Service: Germany.
Variants (with no. built):
Ha 138 V1/V2: Prototypes; three Jumo 205s (2).
Bv 138A–0: Pre-production model; redesigned Ha 138 V; three Jumo 205C–4s; redesigned hull; armed; four subsequently converted to Bv 138B standard (6).
Bv 138A–1: Initial production model (25).
Bv 138B–0: Modified Bv 138A; strengthened structure; increased weight (6).
Bv 138B–1: Production model; three 880hp Jumo 205Ds; increased armament; optional addn bomb load (BV 138B–1/U1) (14).
Bv 138C–1: Major production model; further structural strengthening; revised (turreted) armament plus addn 13mm MG 131 and (optional) 7.9mm MG 15 machine-gun(s); optional addn bomb load (BV 138C–1/U1); Blohm & Voss-built (approx 160); Wesser-built (approx 67).
Bv 138MS: Mine-sweeper version; large dural hoop; no armament; Bv 138B conversions.
Total Production: 279.
Remarks: Operational debut, in transport role, during invasion of Norway, April 1940; despite poor serviceability record, Bv 138s subsequently served over wide area, Arctic and Atlantic Oceans, Biscay, Mediterranean, North Sea, Baltic and Black Sea, equipping a total of some twenty maritime reconnaissance Staffeln; on one occasion claimed destruction of Soviet flying boat over Black Sea by cannon fire at range of 2,187yds (2km); production ceased 1943; continued to operate until very end of war, being one of the last aircraft to fly into beleaguered Berlin, May 1945, landing on one of city's many lakes to evacuate casualties.

Manufacturer: Blohm und Voss.
Model: Ha 139B/MS.
Type: Long-range maritime reconnaissance/mine-sweeping floatplane.
Power Plant: Four 660hp Junkers Jumo 205C.
Performance:
maximum speed at 9,840ft (3,000m) 179mph (288km/hr).
cruising speed 124mph (200km/hr).
maximum range 3,075 miles (4,950km).
time to 3,280ft (1,000m) 4min 0sec.
service ceiling 16,400ft (5,000m).
Weights:
loaded 41,888lb (19,000kg).
Dimensions:
wing span 96ft 9¼in (29.5m).
length 65ft 10¼in (20.07m).
height 15ft 9in (4.8m).
wing area 1,399.31sq ft (130.0sq m).
Armament: One 7.9mm MG 15 machine-gun in nose; one 7.9mm MG 15 machine-gun in forward dorsal hatch; one 7.5mm MG 15 each in two rear fuselage lateral mountings.
Crew: 5–6.
In Service: Germany.
Variants (with no. built):
Ha 139A (Ha 139 V1/2): Initial civil prototypes; long-range floatplanes (2).
Ha 139B (Ha 139 V3): Prototype; modified; increased wing span, lengthened fuselage; increased weight (1).
Ha 139B/MS (Ha 139 V3/U1): Lengthened glazed nose; enlarged vertical tail surfaces; degaussing loop; armament; V3 conversion.
Total Production: 3.
Remarks: Pre-war long-range civil floatplanes used by Deutsche Lufthansa on South Atlantic mail routes; all three impressed late 1939; V3 extensively modified for reconnaissance/mine-sweeping roles; V1/2 retained as unarmed troop-freight transports; saw limited employment during invasion of Norway, April 1940, and after.

Manufacturer: Blohm und Voss.
Model: Bv 142 V2/U1.
Type: Long-range maritime reconnaissance.
Power Plant: Four 880hp BMW 132H–1.
Performance:
maximum speed at sea level 233mph (375km/hr).
cruising speed 202mph (325km/hr).
maximum range 2,425 miles (3,900km).
initial rate of climb 122ft/min (400m/min).
service ceiling 29,527ft (9,000m).
Weights:
empty 24,250lb (11,000kg).
loaded 36,376lb (16,500kg).
Dimensions:
wing span 96ft 10½in (29.53m).
length 67ft 1in (20.45m).
height 14ft 6¾in (4.44m).
wing area 1,399.3sq ft (130.0sq m).
Armament: One 7.9mm MG 15 machine-gun each in nose, ventral cupola, two fuselage lateral positions, and in dorsal turret; max bomb load 882lb (400kg).
Crew: 6.
In Service: Germany.
Variants (with no. built):
Ha 142 V1, Bv 142 V2/4: Prototypes; long-range civil transports (4).
Bv 142 V/U1: Armed maritime-reconnaissance version; two conversions (Bv 142 V1/2).
Total Production: 4.
Remarks: Intended for trans-atlantic mail routes, Ha(Bv) 142 was landplane version of earlier Ha 139 floatplane; on outbreak of WWII V1 and V2 prototypes fully militarized for maritime reconnaissance role; limited use late 1940–42; V3 and V4 not converted; served as transports during Norwegian campaign, April 1940.

Manufacturer: Blohm und Voss.
Model: Bv 222C–0 Wiking (Viking).
Type: Long-range reconnaissance flying-boat.
Power Plant: Six 1,000hp Jumo 207C.
Performance:
maximum speed at 16,400ft (5,000m) 242mph (390km/hr).
cruising speed 214mph (345km/hr).
maximum range 3,790 miles (6,100km).
time to 19,685ft (6,000m) 52min 0sec.
service ceiling 23,950ft (7,300m).
Weights:
empty 67,572lb (30,650kg).
maximum 108,026lb (50,000kg).
Dimensions:
wing span 150ft 11in (46.0m).
length 121ft 4¾in (37.0m).
height 35ft 9in (10.90m).
wing area 2,745sq ft (255sq m).
Armament: One 20mm MG 151 cannon each in forward dorsal turret and two wing turrets; one 13mm MG 131 machine-gun in bow; four 13mm MG 131 (or 7.9mm MG 81) machine-guns in beam positions.
Crew/Accommodation: 10/110 troops.
In Service: Germany.
Variants (with no. built):
Bv 222 V1/8: Prototypes; civil (1) and military transport/reconnaissance (7) flying boats; 1,200hp Bramo Fafnir 323R or (V7) Jumo 207C; various armament arrangements (8).
Bv 222B: Civil transport version; project only.
Bv 222C–09/012: Pre-production model; as Bv 222 V7 (4).
Bv 222C–013: Jumo 205Cs.
Bv 222C–014/017: Not completed.
Total Production: 12.
Remarks: Originally a civil design intended for transatlantic service, Bv 222 was largest operational flying boat of WWII; service debut, in transport role, mid-1941; equipped specially-activated maritime transport Staffel, operating primarily Mediterranean theatre; early 1943 modified for reconnaissance duties, inc addn armament plus search/rear warning radar; four pre-production models delivered latter half 1943; together with surviving prototypes deployed French Atlantic coast, Baltic and Norwegian waters; in use until close of war despite steady rate of attrition, both in the air and at moorings; last two prototypes scuttled at war's end; sole two remaining pre-production examples evaluated post-war UK and USA.

Manufacturer: Bücker.
Model: Bü 131B Jungmann (Youth).
Type: Primary trainer/night ground-attack.
Power Plant: One 105hp Hirth HM 504A–2.
Performance:
maximum speed at sea level 114mph (183km/hr).
cruising speed 104mph (170km/hr).
normal range 398 miles (650km).
time to 3,280ft (1,000m) 6min 18sec.
service ceiling 9,842ft (3,000m).
Weights:
empty 860lb (390kg).
loaded 1,500lb (680kg).
Dimensions:
wing span 24ft 3⅓in (7.4m).
length 21ft 8½in (6.62m).
height 7ft 4½in (2.25m).
wing area 145.3sq ft (13.5sq m).
Crew: 2.
In Service: Finland, Germany, Great Britain (1+ captured), Hungary (100), Japan (licence-production), Lithuania, Netherlands (NEIAF 6), Rumania (approx 150), Spain, Sweden, Switzerland (80, inc 75 licence-built).
Variants (with no. built):
Bü 131: Prototype; 80hp Hirth HM 60R.
Bü 131A: Initial production model; primary trainer.
Bü 131B: Modified Bü 131A; uprated engine.
Bü 131C: 90hp Cirrus Minor; experimental only.
Kokusai Ki–86: Japanese licence production for IJAAF (1,037).
Kyushu K9W1: Japanese licence production for IJNAF (217).
C4: Czech designation for post-war Bü 131 production (Aero-built).
Remarks: Aerobatic/sports biplane first flown April 1934; Luftwaffe primary trainer 1935–45, latterly supplanted by Bü 181; examples thus released from training duties, together with similar types, formed initial equipment earliest night ground-attack auxiliary sqns (Behelfsnachtkampfstaffeln), activated in answer to Soviet U–2's nocturnal harassment of German ground-forces; Bü 131 performed similar role over Russian lines, usually with ground-crewman dropping 2.2lb (1kg) and 4.4lb (2kg) bombs from rear cockpit by hand; subsequently fitted with light underwing racks for service with established Nachtschlachtgruppen. Extensive foreign use as trainer; also licence-produced both during and post-war.

Manufacturer: Bücker.
Model: Bü 133C Jungmeister (Young Champion).
Type: Trainer/liaison.
Power Plant: One 160hp Siemens Sh 14A–4.
Performance:
maximum speed at sea level 137mph (220km/hr).
cruising speed 124mph (200km/hr).
normal range 311 miles (500km).
time to 3,280ft (1,000m) 2min 48sec.
service ceiling 14,764ft (4,500m).
Weights:
empty 937lb (425kg).
loaded 1,356lb (615kg).
Dimensions:
wing span 21ft 7⅞in (6.6m).
length 19ft 9in (6.02m).
height 7ft 2½in (2.2m).
wing area 129.2sq ft (12.0sq m).
Crew: 1.
In Service: Germany, Lithuania (4), Spain (50), Switzerland (51).
Variants:
Bü 133 V1: Prototype; 135hp Hirth HM 6.
Bü 133A: Initial production.
Bü 133B: 160hp Hirth HM 506; licence-production only.
Bü 133C: Standard production model; also Swiss (Dornier) and Spanish (CASA) licence-built.
Remarks: Smaller single-seat aerobatic version of Bü 131; extensive use Luftwaffe training and fighter-pilot school establishments; also employed in liaison role; limited foreign service.

Manufacturer: Bücker.
Model: Bü 181D Bestmann.
Type: Basic trainer/communications.
Power Plant: One 150hp Hirth HM 504A.
Performance:
maximum speed at sea level 130mph (210km/hr).
cruising speed 126mph (200km/hr).
normal range 534 miles (850km).
time to 3,280ft (1,000m) 5min 18sec.
service ceiling 16,404ft (5,000m).
Weights:
empty 1,047lb (475kg).
loaded 1,687lb (765kg).
Dimensions:
wing span 34ft 9¼in (10.6m).
length 25ft 9in (7.85m).
height 6ft 9¼in (2.06m).
wing area 145.3sq ft (13.5sq m).
Crew: 2.
In Service: Germany, Sweden (125 licence-built as Sk 25), Switzerland (7 interned/impressed), USSR (1+ captured).
Variants (with no. built):
Bü 181: Prototype.
Bü 181A: Initial production model; 105hp Hirth HM 504.
Bü 181D: Modified Bü 181A.
Remarks: Basic trainer monoplane; Luftwaffe service debut late 1940, gradually supplanting previous Bücker types during course of war; also served as communications, light transport and glider-tug; several thousand produced by Bücker, plus extensive licence-production in Holland (708), Sweden (125) and Czechoslovakia (180), latter continuing post-war as C.6/106 and Zlin Z.281/381 for both military and civil use.

Manufacturer: DFS.
Model: DFS 230B–1.
Type: Assault transport glider.
Performance:
maximum gliding speed 180mph (290km/hr).
normal towing speed 112mph (180km/hr).
Weights:
empty 1,896lb (860kg).
loaded 4,630lb (2,100kg).
Dimensions:
wing span 72ft 1¾in (21.98m).
length 36ft 10½in (11.24m).
height 9ft 6¼in (2.90m).
wing area 444.12sq ft (41.3sq m).
Armament: One 7.9mm MG 15 machine-gun in upper fuselage decking; two fixed forward-firing 7.9mm MG 34 machine-guns.
Crew/Accommodation: 2/8.
In Service: Germany.
Variants (with no. built):
DFS 230 V1/6: Prototypes (6).
DFS 230A–0: Production model.
DFS 230A–1: Initial production model; major variant.
DFS 230A–2: Dual-control version of A–1.
DFS 230B–1: Improved version; structural strengthening; braking parachute; provision for one MG 15 and two MG 34 machine-guns.
DFS 230B–2: Dual-control version of B–1.
DFS 230A/B: DFS-, Gotha, Hartig- and Erla-built (approx 1,095); Czechoslovak/Mraz licence-built (410).
DFS 230C–1: DFS 230B–1 conversions; redesigned nose with three Rheinmetall-Borsig braking rockets.
DFS 230D–1: As C–1; one DFS 230 V conversion.
DFS 230 V7: Prototype for projected F–1; enlarged fuselage; increased (15 troop) payload (1).
Total Production: approx 1,510.
Remarks: Standard Luftwaffe assault glider; by very nature of its role, participated several well-documented actions, inc reduction of Belgian fortress of Eben-Emael, 10 May 1940, airborne invasion of Crete, May 1941, and rescue of Mussolini from Gran Sasso redoubt, 12 Sept 1943; but DFS 230 also mounted number less well known, but equally exacting, supply/relief missions both in Mediterranean theatre and, more importantly, on Eastern Front; latter commenced with supplying encircled defenders of Cholm pocket, Jan–May 1942; subsequently supported Kuban bridgehead operations; final months of war undertook near-suicidal arms supply missions into beleaguered Budapest, Jan. and Breslau, March 1945.

Manufacturer: Dornier.
Model: Do 11D.
Type: Medium bomber.
Power Plant: Two 650hp Siemens Sh 22B–2.
Performance:
maximum speed at sea level 161mph (260km/hr).
cruising speed 140mph (225km/hr).
maximum range 596 miles (960km).
time to 3,280ft (1,000m) 7min 0sec.
service ceiling 13,450ft (4,100m).
Weights:
empty 13,173lb (5,975kg).
maximum 18,080lb (8,200kg).
Dimensions:
wing span 86ft 3¼in (26.3m).
length 61ft 8in (18.8m).
height 18ft 0in (5.49m).
wing area 1,160.3sq ft (107.8sq m).
Armament: One flexible 7.9mm MG 15 machine-gun each in nose, dorsal and ventral positions; max bomb load 2,205lb (1,000kg).
Crew: 4.
In Service: Bulgaria (12).
Variants (with no. built):
Do F (Do 11a): Prototype; two 550hp (Siemens-built) Bristol Jupiters (1).
Do 11C: Initial production model; two 650hp Siemens Sh 22B–2s; retractable undercarriage; all subsequently converted to Do 11D standard.
Do 11D: Improved version; modified shorter-span wings; fixed undercarriage; inc converted Do 11Cs (150).
Do 13a–c: Prototypes; simplified Do 11; fixed spatted undercarriage; 750hp BMW VIs (3).
Do 13C: Production model; (approx 12).
Do 13e: Prototype; redesigned Do 23.
Total Production: approx 166 (inc Do 13).
Remarks: Formed initial bomber equipment (together with numerically superior Ju 52) of the then still clandestine Luftwaffe, 1934; long obsolete by outbreak of WWII, twelve Do 11Ds supplied to Bulgarian AF in 1937 remained in service until replaced by Do 17s in 1940.

Manufacturer: Dornier.
Model: Do 15 Wal (Whale).
Type: Reconnaissance flying boat.
Power Plant: Two 750hp BMW VI.
Performance:
maximum speed 143mph (230km/hr).
cruising speed 124mph (200km/hr).
normal range 1,180 miles (1,900km).
time to 3,280ft (1,000m) 7min 0sec.
service ceiling 9,842ft (3,000m).
Weights:
empty 10,362lb (4,700kg).
loaded 17,637lb (8,000kg).
Dimensions:
wing span 76ft 1½in (23.2m).
length 60ft 0⅓in (18.3m).
height 17ft 6⅔in (5.35m).
wing area 1,033.34sq ft (96sq m).
Armament: One flexible 7.9mm MG 15 machine-gun in open bow position; one flexible 7.9mm MG 15 machine-gun each in two open dorsal positions; max bomb load 440lb (200kg).
Crew: 4.
In Service: Netherlands (NAF approx 6 Do J Wal), Spain (NAF, NatNAF 40+ Do J Wal, Do R Super-Wal).
Variants (with no. built):
Do J 'Wal': Prototype; two 300hp Hispano-Suiza; Pisa-built (1).
Do J 'Wal': Production; civil and military models; various power plants and wing span dimensions; Italian Pisa (CMASA) and Piaggio licence-built (150+); Spanish (CASA) licence-built (40); Dutch (Aviolanda) licence-built (approx 40); Japanese (Kawasaki) licence-built (3); Dornier-built.
Do JII 'Wal': Do J development; first produced by CMASA as MF.5; Dornier-built; two versions 8 ton and 10 ton (metric gross weight).
Do 15 'Wal': Luftwaffe designation of militarized 8 ton variant; original designation 'Militär-Wal 33'.
(Total Dornier production of Do J, J11, Do 15: 50).
Do R 'Super-Wal': Prototype; modified and enlarged Do J: two 650hp Rolls-Royce Condors.
Do R 'Super-Wal': Production; majority with four (two tandem) engines; civil model; Dornier built (16+); Military model: Spanish (CASA) licence-built.
Total Production: approx 300.
Remarks: First flown late 1922. Do J/JII Wal series saw extensive service, both civil and military, throughout late twenties and thirties; employed by Spanish NatNAF during Civil War; six (of original 46) still on Netherlands NAF's inventory on outbreak of WWII.

Manufacturer: Dornier.
Model: Do 17F–1
Type: Long-range reconnaissance.
Power Plant: Two 750hp BMW VI 7,3.
Performance:
maximum speed at sea level 222mph (357km/hr).
maximum speed at 13,120ft (4,000m) 196mph (315km/hr).
cruising speed 165mph (265km/hr).
maximum range 1,275 miles (2,050km).
service ceiling 19,685ft (6,000m).
Weights:
empty 9,920lb (4,500kg).
loaded 15,430lb (7,000kg).
Dimensions:
wing span 59ft 0⅔in (18.00m).
length 53ft 3¾in (16.25m).
height 14ft 2in (4.32m).
wing area 592.01sq ft (55.0sq m).
Armament: One forward-firing 7.9mm MG 15 machine-gun each on semi-flexible mounting in starboard windscreen panel and (optional) in lower nose; plus one flexible rearward-firing 7.9mm MG 15 machine-gun each in dorsal blister and ventral hatch positions.
Crew: 3.
In Service: Croatia (Do 17Es), Germany, Spain (NatAF Do 17F).
Variants (with no. built):
Do 17 V1/3: Civil prototypes; single fin and rudder (3).
Do 17 V4/15: Military prototypes; twin fin and rudder; various power plants; nose and tail modifications; armament and equipment changes (12).
Do 17E–1: Initial production model; bomber version; BMW VI

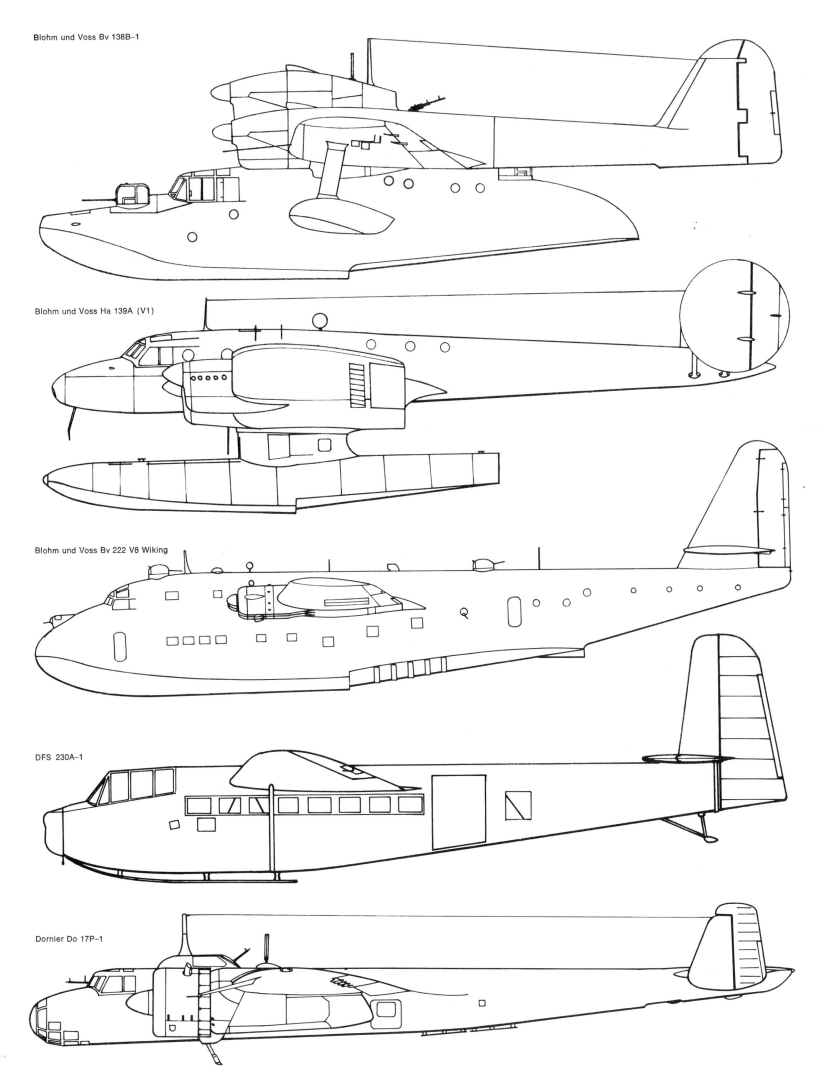

Blohm und Voss Bv 138B–1

Blohm und Voss Ha 139A (V1)

Blohm und Voss Bv 222 V8 Wiking

DFS 230A–1

Dornier Do 17P–1

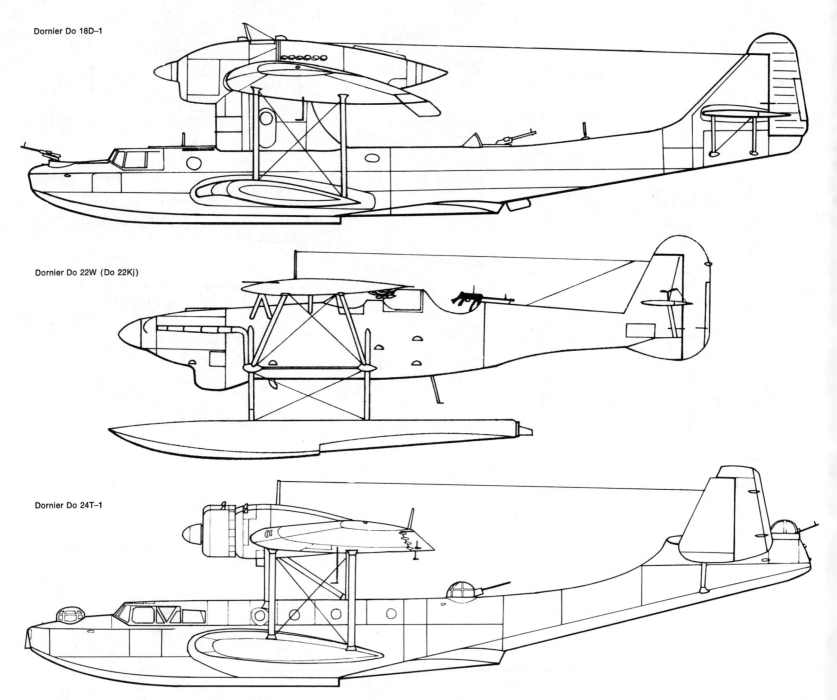

Dornier Do 18D–1

Dornier Do 22W (Do 22Kj)

Dornier Do 24T–1

7,3s; shortened glazed nose;
armament as F–1; max bomb load
1,650lb (750kg).
Do 17F–1: Long-range reconnaissance version; modified Do
17E–1; two Rb 50/30 (or 75/30)
cameras in bomb-bay, plus addn
fuel.
Do 17L V1/2: Prototypes; four-
crew pathfinder bomber version;
900hp Bramo Fafnir;
redesignation of Do 17 V11 and
V12.
Do 17R V1/2: Engine test-beds;
various power plants (2).
Total Production: approx 1.200 (all
Marks).
Remarks: Initial variants of prolific
Dornier twin-engined medium
bomber family, whose twelve-year
period of development neatly
mirrors Luftwaffe's changing for-
tunes from 1933 to 1945; original
civil prototypes rejected due to
cramped conditions within extremely
slim fuselage, a feature which was
to earn early military versions
nickname of 'Flying Pencil'; E–1
and F–1 both entered service at
beginning of 1937, fifteen examples
of latter being despatched to
Condor Legion in Spain by early
Spring; soon followed by twenty
E–1 bombers; Dorniers' speed
ensured near-immunity from interception until advent of more
modern Soviet Republican fighters;
remaining aircraft (plus some later
Do 17Ps) passed to Spanish NatAF,
Aug 1938; remained in Spanish
service until mid-40s; Croatian AF
also employed Do 17E–1 bombers
in anti-partisan role during 1942.

Manufacturer: Dornier.
Model: Do 17M–1.
Type: Medium bomber.
Power Plant: Two 900hp BMW-
Bramo 323A–1 Fafnir.
Performance:
maximum speed at 13,120ft (4,000m)
255mph (410km/hr).
cruising speed 218mph (350km/hr).
maximum range 845 miles
(1,360km).
service ceiling 22,965ft (7,000m).
Weights:
loaded 17,640lb (8,000kg).
Dimensions:
wing span 59ft 0½in (18.00m).
length 52ft 9¾in (16.09m).
height 14ft 11in (4.54m).
wing area 592.01sq ft (55.0sq m).
Armament: One forward-firing
7.9mm MG 15 machine-gun each
on semi-flexible mounting on starboard windscreen panel and
(optional) in lower nose; plus one
flexible rearward-firing 7.9mm MG
15 machine-gun each in dorsal
fairing and ventral hatch positions;
max bomb load 2,205lb (1,000kg).
Crew: 3.
In Service: Croatia (Do 17Ks; ex-
Yugoslav), Germany, Spain
(NatAF approx 8 Do 17Ps),
Yugoslavia (70+ Do 17Ka/b).
Variants (with no. built):
Do 17M V1/3: Prototypes; 1,000hp
DB 600As (M V1) and 900hp
Bramo 323A–1s (M V2/3);
redesignation of Do 17 V8, 13
and 14 resp.
Do 17M–1: Production model;
bomber version; re-engined Do
17E; improved equipment.
Do 17P V1: Prototype; 865hp BMW

132Ns; redesignation of Do 17 V15.
Do 17P–1: Production model; long-
range reconnaissance version; re-
engined Do 17F–1; two cameras
plus flares.
Do 17M–1/U1: Modified M–1;
enlarged bomb-bay; inflatable
dinghy.
Do 17M–1/Trop, Do 17P–1/Trop:
As Do 17M–1 and Do 17P–1 resp;
tropicalized; Do 17E, F, M and P
(excl prototypes) (565).
Do 17Kb–1: Export bomber version; Yugoslav order; redesigned
nose; 980hp Gnome-Rhône 14
Na/2s; one 7.92mm FN Browning
machine-gun and one 20mm
Hispano-Suiza 404 cannon in nose,
plus one 7.92mm FN Browning
machine-gun each in windscreen,
dorsal, and ventral positions.
Do 17Ka–2: Export reconnaissance/
bomber version; modified Do
17Kb–1; revised equipment;
Yugoslav order.
Do 17Ka–3: As Do 17Ka–2; modified camera equipment; 20mm
cannon deleted; Yugoslav order.
(Total Do 17Ks: Dornier-built
20; Yugoslav licence-built 50+).
Total Production: approx 1,200 (all
Marks).
Remarks: Do 17M/P were BMW
radial re-engined developments
of earlier Do 17E/F bomber
and reconnaissance models respectively; entering service in 1938, Do
17M soon supplanted in first-line
bomber units by improved Do 17Z;
Do 17P retained in reconnaissance
role early years WWII; both types
subsequently served in training and
ancillary duties; over one-third of

Yugoslavia's 70 available Do 17s
destroyed on ground in initial phase
of German invasion, (6 April 1941);
remainder decimated in attacks on
Axis targets both sides of Yugoslav-
Bulgarian border; two Do 17Ka's
escaped to Egypt (loaded with
bullion) to serve briefly under RAF
in Middle East; others captured
intact by Germany and passed to
Croatian AF, 1942.

Manufacturer: Dornier.
Model: Do 17Z–2.
Type: Medium bomber.
Power Plant: Two 1,000hp BMW
Bramo 323P Fafnir.
Performance:
maximum speed at sea level
214mph (345km/hr).
maximum speed at 13,120ft (4,000m)
255mph (410km/hr).
cruising speed 168mph (270km/hr).
maximum range 932 miles (1,500km).
service ceiling 26,900ft (8,200m).
Weights:
empty 11,465lb (5,200kg).
maximum 18,940lb (8,590kg).
Dimensions:
wing span 59ft 0½in (18.00m).
length 51ft 9¾in (15.80m).
height 15ft 1in (4.60m).
wing area 592.01sq ft (55.0sq m).
Armament: Four (later optional six
or eight) 7.9mm MG 15 machine-
guns in windscreen, nose, dorsal,
and ventral positions; max bomb
load 2,205lb (1,000kg).
Crew: 4–5.
In Service: Croatia, Finland (3 Do
17Z–1, 3 Do 17Z–2, 9 Do 17Z–3),
Germany.
Variants (with no. built):

Do 17S–0: High-speed long-range
reconnaissance version; deepened
forward fuselage; fully glazed
'beetle-eye' nose; improved cockpit; 4 crew; DB 600Gs (3).
Do 17U–0/1: Pathfinder/bomber
versions of Do 17S; 5 crew; DB
600As (15).
Do 17Z–0: Pre-production model;
4 crew bomber version; modified
Do 17U–1; Bramo 323A–1s;
addn armament (1).
Do 17Z–1: Production model;
1,102lb (500kg) max bomb load.
Do 17Z–2: Improved version; uprated engines; increased bomb load.
(Total Do 17Z–1, –2: 500).
Do 17Z–3: Reconnaissance-bomber
version; as Z–2; two RB 20/30
cameras; reduced bomb load (22).
Do 17Z–4: Dual-control trainer
version; Do 17Z conversions.
Do 17Z–5: Long-range maritime
reconnaissance version; inflatable
flotation-bags; survival equipment;
Do 17Z–1/2 conversions.
Do 17Z–6 Kauz I (Screech Owl):
Long-range night-fighter version;
modified Do 17Z–3 with Ju 88C–2
nose cone; addn armament; 3 crew;
one conversion.
Do 17Z–10 Kauz II: Improved
Do 17Z–3; redesigned nose; four
7.9mm MG 17 machine-guns plus
two 20mm MG FF cannon; infra-
red sensor; nine conversions.
Total Production: approx 1,200 (all
Marks).
Remarks: Three Service Trials Do
17S models first to feature fully
glazed 'beetle-eye' nose transparencies synonymous with Dornier's
WWII bombers; major production

variant, Do 17Z, entered service late 1938; accounted for 70% of the 500 Dorniers available to Luftwaffe by close of 1939; participated all early campaigns—Poland, Norway (Do 17P), Low Countries, France, Battle of Britain; phased out by mid-1940, but took part Balkans campaign and subsequent invasion of Soviet Union, June 1941; finally disappeared from first-line bomber service Nov 1942; continued use in other roles, inc night reconnaissance and glider-tug (employed on latter duties until war's end); Z–10 night-fighters saw brief service late 1940; last of 15 Finnish examples retired 1948.
Colour Reference: Plates 28, 29: Dornier Do 17Z–2 (5K + BU) of 10.(kroat)/KG 3 Blitz; Central Sector Russian Front, Dec 1941; Croatian volunteer-manned 10.Staffel operational Winter 1941–42; this particular machine (Bruno-Ulrich) participated first all-Croatian attack on Moscow; note temporary Winter finish, Croatian (Ustachi) shield below cockpit; (for subsequent independent Croatian national markings see Junkers Ju 52, plates 36, 37).

Manufacturer: Dornier.
Model: Do 18G–1.
Type: Maritime reconnaissance/patrol flying boat.
Power Plant: Two 880hp Junkers Jumo 205D.
Performance:
maximum speed at 6,560ft (2,000m) 166mph (267km/hr).
cruising speed 142mph (228km/hr).
maximum range 2,175 miles (3,500km).
time to 3,280ft (1,000m) 7min 48sec.
service ceiling 13,800ft (4,200m).
Weights:
empty 13,180lb (5,980kg).
maximum 23,800lb (10,800kg).
Dimensions:
wing span 77ft 9¼in (23.70m).
length 63ft 7in (19.37m).
height 17ft 5½in (5.32m).
wing area 1,054.86sq ft (98.0sq m).
Armament: One 13mm 131 machine-gun in nose plus one 20mm MG 151 cannon in dorsal turret; bomb load 220lb (100kg).
Crew: 4.
In Service: Germany.
Variants (with no. built):
Do 18 V1/3 (Do 18a/c): Civil prototypes; various power plants (3).
Do 18 D–1/3: Military production models; maritime reconnaissance flying boat; 600hp Jumo 205Cs; two 7.9mm MG 15 machine-guns; provision for two underwing bomb-racks; Dornier- and Weser-built (approx 75).
Do 18E: Civil flying boat; inc one Weser-built (2).
Do 18F: Modified Do 18E; increased wing span (1).
Do 18G–1: Improved Do 18D; modified nose; revised armament; provision for RATOG.
Do 18H–1: 6-seat unarmed trainer version.
(Total Do 18G–1, H–1: 71).
Do 18L: Modified Do 18F; 865hp BMW 132Ns; one conversion.
Do 18N–1: Air/sea-rescue version; Do 18G conversions.
Total Production: approx 152.
Remarks: Originally ordered by DLH as Dornier Wal replacement, aerodynamically refined Do 18 first flew March 1935, featuring similar tandem-mounted engine layout as predecessor, only six civil models were delivered; bulk of production went to Luftwaffe, commencing 1938; equipped six maritime Staffeln for patrol duties early part WWII; number subsequently modified for ASR role, 1941–42.

Manufacturer: Dornier.
Model: Do 22.
Type: Reconnaissance/torpedo-bomber floatplane.
Power Plant: One 860hp Hispano-Suiza 12 Ybrs.
Performance:
maximum speed at 13,120ft (4,000m) 217mph (350km/hr).
cruising speed 186mph (300km/hr).
normal range 1,430 miles (2,300km).
time to 3,280ft (1,000m) 2min 6sec.
service ceiling 26,247ft (8,000m).
Weights:
empty 5,610lb (2,545kg).
loaded 8,800lb (3,990kg).
Dimensions:
wing span 53ft 2in (16.2m).
length 43ft 1¾in (13.15m).
height 15ft 11in (4.85m).
wing area 484.2sq ft (44.98sq m).
Armament: One fixed forward-firing 7.9mm machine-gun in upper cowling; two flexible 7.9mm machine-guns in rear cockpit and one in ventral fuselage step; max bomb load 440lb (200kg) or one 1,760lb (800kg) torpedo.
Crew: 2–3.
In Service: Finland (4), Greece (12), Yugoslavia (Yugoslav NAF 12).
Variants (with no. built):
Do C3: Prototypes; twin-float seaplane; Swiss Dornier-built (2).
Do 22W: Production floatplane; ordered by Greece, Yugoslavia and Latvia (as Do 22Kg, Kj, and Kl resp) (28).
Do 22L: Modified Do 22W; landplane version; fixed spatted undercarriage (2).
Total Production: 31.
Remarks: First designed in 1934, Do 22 not accepted for Luftwaffe service; released for export 1938; both Greek and Yugoslav models participated defence of Balkans against Italo-German invasion; four Yugoslav survivors escaped to Egypt, April 1941; subsequently serving under Allied command in Mediterranean; four ex-Latvian order purchased by Finland; took part in Continuation War, 1941–44.

Manufacturer: Dornier.
Model: Do 23G.
Type: Medium bomber.
Power Plant: Two 750hp BMW VIU.
Performance:
maximum speed at 3,937ft (1,200m) 161mph (260km/hr).
cruising speed 130mph (209km/hr).
maximum range 840 miles (1,350km).
initial rate of climb 886ft/min (270m/min).
time to 3,280ft (1,000m) 4min 0sec.
service ceiling 13,780ft (4,200m).
Weights:
empty 12,346lb (5,600kg).
maximum 20,282lb (9,200kg).
Dimensions:
wing span 84ft 0in (25.60m).
length 61ft 8¼in (18.80m).
height 17ft 8½in (5.40m).
wing area 1,147.43sq ft (106.6sq m).
Armament: One flexible 7.9mm MG 15 machine-gun each in nose, dorsal, and ventral positions; max bomb load 2,205lb (1,000kg).
Crew: 4.
In Service: Germany.
Variants (with no. built):
Do 23 (Do 13e): Prototype; improved Do 13 (see Do 11); strengthened airframe; shortened wing span (1).
Do 23F: Initial production model; two 750hp BMW VId.
Do 23G: Re-engined Do 23F; major series.
(Total Do 23F, G: approx 210).
Total Production: approx 210.
Remarks: Brief first-line Luftwaffe service, 1935–36; subsequently relegated training and other ancillary duties; employed as aerial minesweepers (fitted with large degaussing ring) early months WWII.

Manufacturer: Dornier.
Model: Do 24T–1.
Type: Air/sea-rescue flying boat.
Power Plant: Three 1,000hp BMW-Bramo 323R–2 Fafnir.
Performance:
maximum speed at 9,840ft (3,000m) 211mph (340km/hr).
cruising speed 137mph (220km/hr).
maximum range 2,920 miles (4,700km).
time to 6,560ft (2,000m) 6min 0sec.
service ceiling 24,605ft (7,500m).
Weights:
empty 20,723lb (9,400kg).
maximum 35,715lb (16,207kg).
Dimensions:
wing span 88ft 7in (27.0m).
length 72ft 4in (22.0m).
height 18ft 10¼in (5.75m).
wing area 1,162.5sq ft (108.0sq m).
Armament: One 7.9mm MG 15 machine-gun each in nose and tail turrets; one 20mm Hispano-Suiza 404 cannon in dorsal turret.
Crew: 6.
In Service: Australia (6 Do 24 K–1/2, ex NEINAF), France (FNAF 22 Do 24T–1), Germany, Holland (NEINAF 37 Do 24K–1/2), Spain (NAF 12 Do 24T–3), Sweden (1 Do 24T–1).
Variants (with no. built):
Do 24 V1/2: Prototypes; Junkers Jumo 205Cs; general-purpose flying boat (2).
Do 24K–1: Initial production model; 875hp Wright Cyclone R–1820–F52s; Dutch order. (Dornier-built (inc V3) 2; Swiss Dornier-built 10).
Do 24K–2: As Do 24K–1; uprated engines; one 7.9mm Browning plus one 20mm Solothurn cannon; max bomb load 2,642lb (1,200kg); Dutch licence-built by Aviolanda (28).
Do 24N–1: Air/sea-rescue version; modified Do 24K–2; revised armament; addn rescue hatches in upper decking; (Dutch (Fokker)-assembled 11).
Do 24T–1: Air/sea-rescue/transport version; modified Do 24N–1; BMW-Bramo Fafnirs; (Dutch-built 110; French (CAMS)-built 70).
Do 24T–2: As T–1. Minor equipment changes; (Dutch-built 49).
Do 24T–3: As T–2. Spanish order; (Dutch-built 12).
Total Production: 294.
Remarks: Originally built to Dutch requirement; only 25 of 48 licence-production K–2 models despatched to Netherlands East Indies before German invasion of Holland, May 1940; majority destroyed during opening weeks Pacific War, only one survivor (plus five of original K–1s) escaping to Australia; production resumed in Occupied Holland, 170 examples being built for Luftwaffe ASR duties; remained in service until end of War, having equipped some 15 ASR Staffeln as well as performing many other roles, inc reconnaissance, convoy-escort, transport and troop evacuation, the latter particularly in the Eastern Mediterranean, Black Sea, and Baltic campaigns; also produced in France—48 delivered to Luftwaffe prior to liberation, a further 22 completed 1944–45 for FNAF; French (and sole Swedish) models remained in service until early fifties, Spanish T–3s until seventies.

Manufacturer: Dornier.
Model: Do 26D–0.
Type: Long-range maritime reconnaissance/transport flying boat.
Power Plant: Four 800hp Junkers Jumo 205D.
Performance:
maximum speed at 8,530ft (2,600m) 201mph (323km/hr).
cruising speed 160mph (257km/hr).
normal range 2,980 miles (4,800km).
time to 6,560ft (2,000m) 16min 30sec.
service ceiling 14,760ft (4,500m).
Weights:
empty 24,912lb (11,300kg).
maximum 49,600lb (22,500kg).
Dimensions:
wing span 98ft 5in (30.0m).
length 80ft 8½in (24.60m).
height 22ft 5¾in (6.85m).
wing area 1,291.67sq ft (120.0sq m).
Armament: One 20mm MG 151 cannon in nose turret; one rearward-firing 7.9mm MG 15 machine-gun in each of two waist blisters and in rear hull ventral position.
Crew/Accommodation: 4/10–12 troops.
In Service: Germany.
Variants (with no. built):
Do 26 V1/2: Prototypes; civil mail-plane flying boat. Jumo 205C (V1) and 205D (V2) (2).
Do 26D–0 (V3/6): Modified prototypes; armed military transport/reconnaissance versions (4).
Total Production: 6.
Remarks: Last of a long line of Dornier boats, Do 26's four engines mounted in tandem pairs; first two saw pre-war civil use on South Atlantic mail routes; remaining four modified prior to completion (as planned B and C civil passenger models), for military service; (V2 also to Luftwaffe); participated Norwegian campaign in troop-transport role; two destroyed by RAF fighters; survivors subsequently relegated to communications duties.

Manufacturer: Dornier.
Model: Do 215B–4.
Type: Long-range reconnaissance/bomber.
Power Plant: Two 1,075hp Daimler-Benz DB 601A.
Performance:
maximum speed at 17,220ft (5,250m) 326mph (525km/hr).
maximum range 1,523 miles (2,500km).
time to 3,280ft (1,000m) 2min 0sec.
service ceiling 29,850ft (9,100m).
Weights:
empty 12,740lb (5,800kg).
maximum 20,282lb (9,200kg).
Dimensions:
wing span 59ft 0¾in (18.00m).
length 51ft 9¾in (15.79m).
height 14ft 11½in (4.56m).
wing area 592.01sq ft (55.0sq m).
Armament: Six 7.9mm MG 15 machine-guns in windscreen, nose, cockpit, lateral, dorsal, and ventral positions; max bomb load 1,102lb (500kg).
Crew: 4.
In Service: Germany, Hungary (4 Do 215B–4), USSR (2 Do 215B–3).
Variants (with no. built):
Do 215 V1: Prototype; redesignated Do 17Z–0; export demonstration model (*1*).
Do 215 V2/3: Prototype; modified Do 17Z airframes; Gnome-Rhône 14N 1/2s and DB 601As resp (*2*).
Do 215A–1: Production model; four crew bomber version; 1,075hp DB 601As; Swedish order (18).
Do 215B–0/1: Long-range reconnaissance bomber version; inc Do 215A–1 conversion.
Do 215B–2: Bomber version; project only.
Do 215B–3: Export version of Do 215B–1; Soviet order (2).
Do 215B–4: Modified Do 215B–1; improved camera equipment; Do 215B–1 and B–4 production (92).
Do 215B–5: Night-fighter/intruder version; four 7.9mm MG 17s plus two 20mm MG FF cannon in Do 17Z–10-type nose cone; infra-red sensor; Do 215B–0/1 and 4 conversions.
Total Production: 112.
Remarks: Intended export version of basic Do 17Z design; sole pre-war order (from Sweden) suffered export embargo prior to completion; all 18 aircraft modified for Luftwaffe reconnaissance duties; Do 215Bs equipped six reconnaissance Staffeln, serving 1940–42; two supplied USSR under terms of Soviet-German Agreement, early 1940; four to Hungary, 1942; B–5 night-fighter/intruder conversions served in limited numbers 1940–44, operated by elements of five Gruppen.

Manufacturer: Dornier.
Model: Do 217E–2.
Type: Heavy bomber.
Power Plant: Two 1,580hp BMW 801ML.
Performance:
maximum speed at sea level 273mph (440km/hr).
maximum speed at 17,060ft (5,200m) 320mph (515km/hr).
cruising speed 245mph (395km/hr).
maximum range 1,740 miles (2,800km).
service ceiling 29,530ft (9,000m).
Weights:
empty 19,522lb (8,855kg).
loaded: 33,070lb (15,000kg).
Dimensions:
wing span 62ft 4in (19.0m).
length 59ft 8½in (18.2m).
height 16ft 6in (5.03m).
wing area 613.54sq ft (57.0sq m).
Armament: One fixed forward-firing 15mm MG 151 cannon in nose; one 13mm MG 131 machine-gun each in dorsal turret and ventral position; one flexible forward-firing 7.9mm MG 15 machine-gun; two flexible lateral-firing 7.9mm MG 15s; two remotely-controlled rearward-firing 7.9mm MG 81s in tail cone; max bomb load 8,818lb (4,000kg).
Crew: 4.
In Service: Germany.
Variants (with no. built):
Do 217 V1/14, V1E: Prototypes; various power plants; some with tail-mounted dive-brake (15).
Do 217A–0: Pre-production model; long-range reconnaissance version; redesigned fuselage; three 7.9mm MG 15s; two cameras (8).
Do 217C V1: Bomber prototype; 1,075hp DB 601As (1).
Do 217C–0: Bomber version of Do 217A–0; fuselage as prototypes V1/8; two addn 7.9mm MG 15s plus one 15mm MG 151; max bomb load 6,615lb (3,000kg) (4).
Do 217E–0: Pre-production model; bomber version; 1,550hp BMW 801MAs; deepened fuselage.
Do 217E–1: Initial production model; bomber/anti-shipping version; five 7.9mm MG 15s plus one 15mm MG 151 cannon; bomb-bay with max bomb load; 4,410lb (2,000kg); 2 cameras.
Do 217E–2: Bomber version; improved E–1; BMW 801MLs; revised armament; dorsal turret; alternative tail dive-brake or fixed cone.
(Total Do 217E–0, –1, –2: approx 200).
Do 217E–3: Modified Do 217E–1; armour plating; seven 7.9mm machine-guns plus one 20mm MG FF cannon (100).
Do 217E–4: As E–3, 1,500hp BMW 801Cs; balloon-cable cutters on wings (approx 500).
Do 217E–5: Do 2174–E conversions; 2 X Henschel Hs 293A missiles.
(/R1 to /R25): Designation suffixes applicable to majority Do 217 bomber models, indicating use of various Rüstsätze (field conversion kits) providing altn or additional armament (inc torpedoes, bombs, and missiles), camera equipment, auxiliary fuel tanks, or tail braking-chute.
Total Production: approx 1,750 (all Marks).
Remarks: First flown 1938, Do 217 was progressive development of earlier Do 17; pre-production A–O models first employed clandestine surveillance USSR early 1940; bomber versions served mainly Western Europe, 1941–43; participated so-called 'Baedeker' raids on UK, Spring–Summer 1942, attacking such targets as Bath, York, Exeter and Canterbury; also employed anti-shipping role over North Sea and Biscay; Aug 1943, combat debut of Do 217E–5 model equipped with two Hs 293A missiles on underwing racks; minimal success against Allied warships in Biscay, two vessels damaged.

Manufacturer: Dornier.
Model: Do 217M–1.
Type: Heavy night bomber.
Power Plant: Two 1,750hp DB 603A.
Performance:
maximum speed at sea level 294mph (473km/hr).
maximum speed at 18,700ft (5,700m) 348mph (600km/hr).
cruising speed 248mph (400km/hr).
maximum range 1,555 miles (2,500km).
initial rate of climb 690ft/min (210m/min).
max service ceiling 31,180ft (9,500m).
Weights:
empty 19,985lb (9,065kg).
maximum 36,817lb (16,700kg).
Dimensions:
wing span 62ft 4in (19.0m).
length 55ft 9¼in (17.0m).
height 16ft 3¼in (4.96m).
wing area 613.54sq ft (57.0sq m).
Armament: Two forward-firing 7.9mm MG 81 machine-guns in nose; one 13mm MG 131 machine-gun each in dorsal turret and ventral position; plus two (later four) 7.9mm MG 81 machine-guns in rear cockpit lateral positions; max bomb load 8,818lb (4,000kg).
Crew: 4.
In Service: Germany.
Variants (with no. built):
Do 217K V1/3: Prototypes (3).
Do 217K–1: Night-bomber version; redesigned unstepped and fully glazed nose; 1,700hp BMW 801Ds; revised armament; some with provision for four L5 torpedoes.
Do 217K–2: Modified Do K–1; increased wing span; two FX 1400 (Fritz X) rocket-propelled missiles underwing; FuG 203a transmitter; four rearward-firing 7.9mm MG 81s in tail cone.
Do 217K–3: As K–2, Hs 293A or FX 400 missiles; FuG 203c or 203d transmitter.
Do 217L V1/2: Modified Do 217K; revised cockpit and armament; BMW 801Ds; prototypes (2).
Do 217M–1: Re-engined Do 217K–1; 1,750hp DB 603As.
Do 217M–5, –11: Missile-carrier versions; single Hs 293A below fuselage, or as K–3 resp).
Do 217P V1/3: Prototypes; high-altitude reconnaissance/bomber version; two 1,750hp DB 603Bs plus 1,475hp DB 605T within fuselage to drive supercharger; pressurised cabin; V2/3 increased wing span (3).
Do 217P–0: Pre-production model; 3 crew (3).
Do 217R: Prototypes; missile-carrier version; two Hs 293 underwing; revised armament inc 15mm MG 151 cannon in nose and addn 13mm 131 dorsal machine-gun; five Do 317 conversions.
Total Production: approx 1,750 (all Marks).
Remarks: Do 217E development distinguished by completely redesigned forward fuselage with unstepped fully glazed nose section, Do 217K's combat debut Autumn 1942; limited service night-bombing role over UK by both K and M models, culminating participation Operation 'Steinbock' in attacks on London, early 1944; missile-carrying K–2s sank Italian battleship *Roma* off Corsica, 9 Sept 1943 (the day following announcement of Italian armistice); subsequently operated against Salerno and Anzio beach-heads, sinking a cruiser and destroyer, and damaging a battleship and two more cruisers; Summer 1944 participated Normandy campaign, using missiles to attack invasion ports and Allied-held bridges; final employment closing weeks of war similarly against

Oder bridges in last-ditch attempt to halt Soviet advance on Berlin.

Manufacturer: Dornier.
Model: Do 217N-2.
Type: Night-fighter interceptor/intruder.
Power Plant: Two 1,850hp Daimler-Benz DB 603A.
Performance:
maximum speed at sea level 267mph (430km/hr).
maximum speed at 19,685ft (6,000m) 320mph (515 km/hr).
cruising speed 264mph (425km/hr).
normal range 1,088 miles (1,750km).
time to 19,685ft (6,000m) 15min 0sec.
Weights:
empty 22,665lb (10,280kg).
loaded 29,101lb (13,200kg).
Dimensions:
wing span 62ft 4in (19.0m).
length 62ft 0in (18.9m).
height 16ft 4¾in (5.0m).
wing area 613.54sq ft (57.0sq m).
Armament: Four 20mm MG 151 cannon; four 7.9mm MG 17 machine-guns in nose.
Crew: 4.
In Service: Germany, Italy (Do 217J-2).
Variants (with no. built):
Do 217H: High-altitude conversion of Do 217E bomber; turbo-supercharged DB 601s (*1*).
Do 217J-1: Night-fighter/intruder version of Do 217E-2; BMW 801MLs; redesigned nose cone with four 20mm MG FF cannon plus four 7.9mm MG 17 machine-guns; provision for addn fuel tank in forward bomb-bay.
Do 217J-2: As J-1; night-fighter; FuG 202 Lichtenstein radar; aft bomb-bay deleted.
(Total Do 217J-1, -2: 157).
Do 217N-1: Night-fighter/intruder version of Do 217M-1; armament as J-1/2; DB 603As; FuG 202 or FuG 212 radar.
Do 217N-1/U1: Modified N-1; dorsal turret deleted; MG FF cannon replaced by four 20mm MG 151 cannon; ventral gun position faired over.
Do 217N-1/U3: As N-1/U1; addn two (or four) oblique upward-firing 20mm MG 151 cannon in dorsal 'Schräge Musik' installation; three conversions.
Do 217N-2: As N-1/U1; FuG 202 or FuG 212 plus FuG 220 and, later FuG 227 and FuG 350.
(Total Do 217N-1, U1, U3, -2: 207).
Do 217N/-2/R22: As N-2; addn four oblique upward-firing 20mm MG 151 cannon in dorsal 'Schräge Musik' installation; N-2 conversions.
Total Production: approx 1,750 (all Marks).
Remarks: Do 217J and N night-fighter/intruders entered service early and end 1942 resp; J-1 models (lacking radar) soon relegated training duties; radar (and later 'Schräge Musik')-equipped J-2/N-2s operational throughout 1943, before phasing out early months 1944; never completely equipping any one unit, Do 217 night-fighters employed in conjunction with other types (usually Bf 110Gs or Ju 88Cs) by some fifteen Nachtjagdgruppen; operated in Defence of Reich, over Eastern Front, and in Mediterranean area; also supplied Italian AF for defence northern Italian industrial centres (Milan, Turin, Genoa), Spring–Autumn 1943.
Colour Reference: Plate 26: Dornier Do 217J-2 of 235ª squadriglia, 60° gruppo autonomo CN (Independent night-fighter group), riglia, 60° gruppo autonomo CN Aug–Sept 1943; one of eight Do 217 night-fighters on strength 235ª squadriglia immediately prior Armistice; note matt black overall, no national markings on wing surfaces.

Manufacturer: Dornier.
Model: Do 317 V1.
Type: High-altitude heavy bomber.
Power Plant: Two 1,750hp Daimler-Benz DB 603A.
Performance:
maximum speed at sea level approx 328mph (approx 528km/hr).
Dimensions:
wing span 67ft 8½in (20.64m).
length 55ft 1¼in (16.80m).
height 17ft 10¾in (5.45m).
Crew: 4.
In Service: Germany.
Variants (with no. built):
Do 317 VI: Prototype; Do 217M development; pressurized cabin; triangular twin fins and rudders; unarmed (1).
Do 317 V2/6: Prototypes; unpressurized; completed as missile-carriers redesignated Do 217R (5).
Do 317A: High-altitude bomber; DB 603As; project only.
Do 317B: Improved Do 317A; DB 610s; remotely-controlled armament; project only.
Total Production: 6.
Remarks: Do 217 development originally designed to Luftwaffe's 'Bomber B' specification of 1939, Do 317 project resuscitated in 1941, first prototype flying two years later; marginal performance improvement over existing Do 217P-0; remaining five prototypes completed as missile-carriers; redesignated Do 217R and assigned to Do 217K-2 equipped Kampfgruppe in France, Summer 1944.

Manufacture: Dornier.
Model: Do 335A-1 Pfeil (Arrow).
Type: Fighter-bomber.
Power Plant: Two 1,800hp Daimler-Benz DB 603E-1.
Performance:
maximum speed at 21,325ft (6,500m) 474mph (763km/hr).
cruising speed 281mph (452km/hr).
normal range 870 miles (1,400km).
time to 3,280ft (1,000m). 0min 55sec.
service ceiling 37,400ft (11,400m).
Weights:
empty 16,005lb (7,260kg).
loaded 21,165lb (9,600kg).
Dimensions:
wing span 45ft 3¼in (13.80m).
length 45ft 5¼in (13.85m).
height 16ft 4¾in (5.00m).
wing area 414.41sq ft (38.50sq m).
Armament: One 30mm MK 103 cannon firing through propeller hub; two 15mm MG 151 cannon in upper cowling; max bomb load 1,102lb (500kg).
Crew: 1.
In Service: Germany.
Variants (with no. built):
Do 335 V1/14: Prototypes; progressive equipment and (from V5) armament changes; single and 2-seat versions (14)
Do 335A-0: Pre-production model; fighter-bomber version; 1,750hp DB 603A-2s (10).
Do 335A-1: Initial production model; re-engined (11).
Do 335A-2/3: Projects only.
Do 335A-4: Unarmed long-range reconnaissance version; two Rb 50/30(18) cameras in bomb bay; 1,900hp DB 603Gs; one A-0 conversion; not completed.
Do 335A-6, A-10: 2-seat night-fighter/trainer versions resp; not completed (other than V10, V11 prototypes).
Do 335A-12: 2-seat trainer version; DB 603E-1s (2).
Do 335B: Zerstörer version; not completed (other than V13, V14 prototypes).
Total Production: 37.
Remarks: Unique tandem-engined tractor/pusher fighter design first flown Autumn 1943; pre-production A-0 models commenced service evaluation trials late Summer 1944, joined by production A-1s to form special operational test Kommando early in 1945.

Manufacturer: Fieseler.
Model: Fi 103 (V1).
Type: Pilotless flying-bomb.
Power Plant: One 660lb s.t. Argus As 109-014 pulse-jet.
Performance:
maximum speed approx 400mph (approx 644km/hr).
maximum range 220 miles (355km).
ground-launch velocity 20,700ft/min (6,300m/min).
service ceiling 8,202ft (2,500m).
Weights:
loaded 4,806lb (2,180kg).
Dimensions:
wing span: metal 16ft 0in (4.87m); wooden 17ft 4¼in (5.3m).
length 25ft 11in (7.9m).
Armament: 1,874lb (850kg) Trialen (Amatol) warhead.
In Service: Germany.
Variants (with no. built):
Fi 103 (V1): Pilotless flying-bomb; metal (later wooden) wing structure (30,000+).
Fi 103R (Reichenberg)–I: Single-seat unpowered test vehicle; V1 conversions. –II: Tandem cockpit unpowered trainer; V1 conversions. –III: Single-seat advanced trainer; Argus 109–014 pulse-jet; nose ballast; landing skid; V1 conversions. –IV Single-seat operational version; 1,874lb (850kg) Amatol warhead; V1 conversions. (Total approx 175).
Total Production: 30,000+.
Remarks: Ground (later air)-launched medium-range pilotless winged missile first employed against London week following D-Day; nearly 2,500 V1s hit London before final incident recorded 29 March, 1945; similar number fell on Allies' supply port of Antwerp, Oct 1944–March 1945; many thousands more hit far wide of intended target areas, were destroyed by Allied defences, or malfunctioned on or after launch; planned use of converted V1s as piloted expendable attack aircraft quashed by more level-headed faction among Luftwaffe hierarchy towards close of 1944.

Manufacturer: Fieseler.
Model: Fi 156C-2 Storch (Stork).
Type: Army Co-operation/liaison.
Power Plant: One 240hp Argus As 10C.
Performance:
maximum speed at sea level 109mph (175km/hr).
cruising speed 80mph (128km/hr).
normal range 239 miles (385km).
time to 3,280ft (1,000m) 3min 24sec.
service ceiling 16,700ft (5,090m).
Weights:
empty 2,050lb (930kg).
loaded 2,910lb (1,320kg).
Dimensions:
wing span 46ft 9in (14.25m).
length 32ft 5¾in (9.90m).
height 10ft 0in (3.05m).
wing area 279.9sq ft (26.0sq m).
Armament: One 7.9mm MG 15 machine-gun in rear cockpit glazing.
Crew/Accommodation: 2/(provision for 1 litter).
In Service: Bulgaria (20), Croatia (approx 6), Finland (2), Germany, Great Britain (impressments and captured), Hungary (approx 40), Italy, Rumania (45), Slovakia (10), Spain (approx 10), Sweden (19), Switzerland (6), USA (captured), USSR (1+).
Variants (with no. built):
Fi 156 V1/4: Prototypes; inc 1 with military equipment (V3), and 1 with ski undercarriage (V4); 3-seat (4).
Fi 156 V5: Pre-production prototype; militarized (as V3) (1).
Fi 156A-0: Service Trials model; as V3 (10).
Fi 156A-1: Initial production model.
Fi 156B: Civil model; project only.
Fi 156C-0: Modified A-1; raised rear cabin glazing; one 7.9mm MG 15; improved radio equipment.
Fi 156C-1: Liaison/staff transport version.
Fi 156C-2: 2-seat reconnaissance (and ambulance) version; provision for one camera, or one litter in rear cockpit.
Fi 156C-3: General-purpose light transport; alternative As 10P power plant; some tropicalized, as Fi 156C-3/Trop.
Fi 156C-5: As C-3; Ventral drop tank; max range 631 miles (1,015km); Argus As 10P; some tropicalized, as Fi 156C-5/Trop.
Fi 156D-0: Ambulance version; pre-production model; modified interior for one litter; enlarged loading hatch; Argus As 10C.
Fi 156 D-1: As D-0; Argus As 10P.
Fi 156 E-0: Pre-production model; as C-1; experimental rubber-tracked tandem-wheel under-carriage (10).
Fi 156A/E production: Fieseler-built (approx 1,900); French (Morane-Saulnier) licence-built (784); Czech (Mraz) licence-built (approx 150).
Fi 156P: Factory designation; police (anti-partisan) version; two under-wing bomb-racks; max 48 SD-2 light anti-personnel bombs.
Fi 256: Prototypes; 5-seat civil model; Fi 156 development. Argus As 10P; (French (Morane-Saulnier) licence-built 2).
Total Production: approx 2,900 (exc post-war licence prod).
Remarks: First flown Spring 1936, Storch's exceptional STOL capabilities made it ideal machine for wide variety of army co-operation and allied duties; served on all fronts throughout WWII, performing tactical-reconnaissance, emergency rescue (principally in North Africa), liaison, staff transport, and many other roles; played vital part in German invasion of France (10 May 1940), some 125 Storch landing shock-troops ahead of armour in Belgium and Luxembourg to secure lines of advance; better-known Storch exploits include rescue of Mussolini, 12 Sept 1943, and flight of General Ritter von Greim into beleaguered Berlin twelve days before German surrender; many Storchs also supplied Axis satellite and neutral AFs; production continued after the war in both Franee (as M.S.500 and 502 'Criquet') and Czechoslovakia (as K-65 'Cap').

Manufacturer: Fieseler.
Model: Fi 167A-0.
Type: Carrier-borne attack/reconnaissance.
Power Plant: One 1,100hp Daimler-Benz DB 601B.
Performance:
maximum speed 199mph (320km/hr).
cruising speed 155mph (250km/hr).
maximum range 932 miles (1,500km).
time to 3,280ft (1,000m) 2min 42sec.
service ceiling 26,900ft (8,200m).
Weights:
empty 6,173lb (2,800kg).
maximum 10,690lb (4,850kg).
Dimensions:
wing span 44ft 3½in (13.5m).
length 37ft 4¾in (11.4m).
height 15ft 9in (4.5m).
wing area 489.76sq ft (45.5sq m).
Armament: One fixed forward-firing 7.9mm MG 17 machine-gun in upper cowling; one flexible 7.9mm MG 15 machine-gun in rear cockpit; max bomb load 2,205lb (1,000kg), or one 1,686lb (750kg) torpedo.
Crew: 2.
In Service: Germany, Rumania (9).
Variants (with no. built):
Fi 167 V1, V2: Prototypes (2).
Fi 167A-0: Pre-production model; minor modifications; jettisonable main undercarriage; inflatable dinghy (12).
Total Production: 14.
Remarks: Specifically designed for service aboard German carrier *Graf Zeppelin*, Fi 167 displayed even more remarkable STOL characteristics than earlier Storch, being capable of near-vertical descent; with work on *Graf Zeppelin* halted, Fi 167s transferred to Netherlands for advanced coastal Service Trials; despite subsequent resumption carrier construction, Fi 167s deemed surplus (role to be filled by 'navalised', Ju 87E), nine examples then being passed to Rumanian AF for operations over Black Sea.

Order of Battle 1 September 1939

GERMAN AIR FORCE (Luftwaffe)

Luftwaffe Lehrdivision (Operational Training and Development Division)

Tactical reconnaissance:		
9.(H)/LG 2	Jüterbog-Damm	11 Henschel Hs 126
Strategic reconnaissance:		
7.(F)/LG 2	Jüterbog-Damm	12 Dornier Do 17
8.(F)/LG 2	Jüterbog-Damm	12 Dornier Do 17
Single-engined fighters:		
Stab/LG 2	Jüterbog-Damm	3 Messerschmitt Bf 109
I.(J)/LG 2	Garz	36 Messerschmitt Bf 109
11.(N)/LG 2	Garz	10 Messerschmitt Bf 109
Zerstörer (heavy fighters):		
I.(Z)/LG 1	Barth	32 Messerschmitt Bf 110
Bombers:		
Stab(K)/LG 1	Greifswald	10 Heinkel He 111
II.(K)/LG 1	Neubrandenburg; Schwerin	41 Heinkel He 111
III.(K)/LG 1	Greifswald	40 Heinkel He 111
10.(See)/LG 2	Travemünde	9 Heinkel He 111
Dive-bombers:		
IV.(St.)/LG 1	Barth	39 Junkers Ju 87 3 Dornier Do 17

Luftflotte 1 (Air Fleet 1) North-East Germany

Tactical reconnaissance:		
1.(H)/10	Neuhausen	11 Henschel Hs 126
2.(H)/10	Neuhausen	12 Henschel Hs 126
1.(H)/11	Grossenhain	9 Henschel Hs 126 3 Heinkel He 46
1.(H)/21	Stargard	12 Henschel Hs 126
2.(H)/21	Stargard	12 Henschel Hs 126
3.(H)/21	Stargard	11 Henschel Hs 126
4.(H)/21	Stargard	9 Heinkel He 45
1.(H)41	Reichenberg	12 Henschel Hs 126
2.(H)/41	Reichenberg	11 Henschel Hs 126
3.(H)/41	Reichenberg	9 Henschel 126 2 Heinkel He 46
Strategic reconnaissance:		
3.(F)/10	Neuhausen	12 Dornier Do 17
2.(F)/11	Grossenhain	12 Dornier Do 17
3.(F)/11	Grossenhain	10 Dornier Do 17
4.(F)/11	Grossenhain	11 Dornier Do 17
1.(F)/120	Neuhausen	13 Dornier Do 17
1.(F)/121	Prenzlau	11 Dornier Do 17
2.(F)/121	Prenzlau	10 Dornier Do 17
3.(F)/121	Prenzlau	12 Dornier Do 17
4.(F)/121	Prenzlau	11 Dornier Do 17
Single-engined fighters:		
I./JG 1	Seerappen	54 Messerschmitt Bf 109
I./JG 21	Jesau	29 Messerschmitt Bf 109
I./JG 2	Döberitz	42 Messerschmitt Bf 109
10.(N)/JG 2	Fürstenwalde	9 Messerschmitt Bf 109
1./JG 20 & 2./JG 20	Fürstenwalde	21 Messerschmitt Bf 109
Stab/JG 3	Bernburg	3 Messerschmitt Bf 109
I./JG 3	Zerbst	48 Messerschmitt Bf 109
Zerstörer (heavy fighters):		
I./ZG 1	Jüterbog-Damm	32 Messerschmitt Bf 110
II./ZG 1 (JGr. 101)	Fürstenwalde	36 Messerschmitt Bf 109
I./ZG 2 (JGr. 102)	Bernburg	44 Messerschmitt Bf 109
Bombers:		
Stab/KG 1	Neubrandenburg	7 Heinkel He 1
I./KG 152 (II./KG 1)	Neubrandenburg	37 Heinkel He 1
I./KG 1	Kolberg	38 Heinkel He 1
Stab/KG 2	Cottbus	11 Dornier Do 1
I./KG 2	Liegnitz	37 Dornier Do 1
II./KG 2	Liegnitz	35 Dornier Do 1
Stab/KG 3	Elbing	9 Dornier Do 1
II./KG 3	Heiligenbeil	36 Dornier Do 1
III./KG 3	Heiligenbeil	39 Dornier Do 17
I./KG 25	Rechlin	18 Junkers Ju 88
Stab/KG 4	Erfurt	6 Heinkel He 111
I./KG 4	Gotha	31 Heinkel He 111
II./KG 4	Erfurt	32 Heinkel He 111
III./KG 4	Nordhausen	33 Heinkel He 111
Dive-bombers:		
I./St.G 1	Insterburg	35 Junkers Ju 87 3 Dornier Do 17
I./St.G 2	Cottbus	38 Junkers Ju 87
II./St.G 2	Stolp-Reitz	38 Junkers Ju 87
III./St.G 2	Langensalza	40 Junkers Ju 87
Ground-attack:		
II.(Schl.)/LG 2	Tutow	40 Henschel Hs 12

Luftflotte 2 (Air Fleet 2) North-West Germany

Tactical reconnaissance:		
1.(H)/12	Münster-Loddenheide	12 Henschel Hs 12
2.(H)/12	Münster-Loddenheide	12 Henschel Hs 12
3.(H)/12	Münster-Loddenheide	9 Henschel Hs 12 1 Heinkel He 46
4.(H)/12	Münster-Loddenheide	9 Heinkel He 46 3 Heinkel He 45
4.(H)/22	Kassel-Rothwesten	12 Henschel Hs 12
Strategic reconnaissance:		
1.(F)/22	Kassel-Rothwesten	11 Dornier Do 1
2.(F)/22	Kassel-Rothwesten	12 Dornier Do 1
3.(F)/22	Kassel-Rothwesten	12 Dornier Do 1
1.(F)/122	Goslar	6 Dornier Do 1
2.(F)/122	Goslar	12 Dornier Do 1
3.(F)/122	Goslar	12 Dornier Do 1
Single-engined fighters:		
I./JG 26	Cologne-Ostheim	48 Messerschmi Bf 109
II./JG 26	Düsseldorf	48 Messerschmi Bf 109
10.(N)/JG 26	Düsseldorf	9 Messerschmi Bf 109

Fiesler Fi 156C–3 Storch

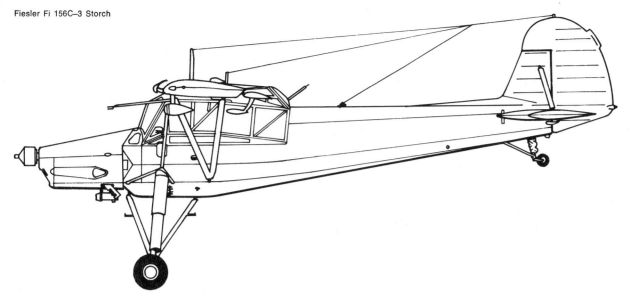

Manufacturer: Flettner.
Model: Fl 282 Kolibri (Hummingbird).
Type: AOP/anti-submarine helicopter.
Power Plant: One 160hp BMW-Bramo Sh 14A.
Performance:
maximum speed at sea level 93mph (150km/hr).
cruising speed 71mph (115km/hr).
maximum range 186 miles (300km).
initial rate of climb (vertical) 300.2ft/min (91.5m/min).
service ceiling 10,800ft (3,300m).
Weights:
empty 1,675lb (760kg).
loaded 2,205lb (1,000kg).
Dimensions:
rotor diameter 39ft 2½in (11.96m).
length 21ft 6½in (6.56m).
height 7ft 2½in (2.2m).
rotor disc area 1,280.9sq ft (119sq m).

Crew: 1–2.
In Service: Germany.
Variants (with no. built):
Fl 282 V1/3: Prototypes; single-seat; enclosed cockpit (3).
Fl 282 V4/24: Prototypes; 2-seat; open fore-and-aft crew positions (21).
Total Production: 24.
Remarks: Intended 2-seat development of earlier Fl 265 design, Fl 282—leading German helicopter of WWII—first flew 1941; only initial 24 of planned 30 prototypes (plus 15 pre-production models, and subsequent production order for 1,000 examples), completed by war's end; after Service Trials aboard cruiser in Baltic, several Kolibris employed in convoy-escort role in Eastern Mediterranean/Aegan areas; also operated by specialised Transportstaffel Spring 1945.

Manufacturer: Focke-Achgelis.
Model: Fa 223 Drachen (Kite).
Type: General-purpose/transport helicopter.
Power Plant: One 1,000hp BMW-Bramo 323 Q3.
Performance:
maximum speed at sea level 109mph (176km/hr).
cruising speed 75mph (120.5km/hr).
maximum range 435 miles (700km).
initial rate of climb (vertical) 800.5ft/min (244m/min).
service ceiling 16,000ft (4,880m).
Weights:
empty 7,055lb (3,200kg).
maximum 9,480lb (4,300kg).
Dimensions:
span across rotors 80ft 4½in (24.5m).
length 40ft 2½in (12.25m).
height 14ft 3¾in (4.36m).
rotor disc area 2,432.7sq ft (226sq m).

Crew/Accommodation: 2/4 (or freight).
In Service: Germany.
Variants (with no. built):
Fa 266 Hornisse (Hornet): Prototype; 6-seat civil transport; militarized as a Fa 223 (1).
Fa 223: Pre-production model (18).
Total Production: 19.
Remarks: Outrigger-mounted twin-rotor civil prototype, designed for DLH, completed just after outbreak of WWII; adopted for military use, lengthy period of development, plus destruction of two factories by Allied bombing, meant that only 18 of 30 pre-production models (and none of production order for 100 machines) actually completed; of less than dozen Fa 223s flown, at least three served in transport/communications role alongside Flettner Fl 282s in special transport unit during closing weeks of war; world's first true transport helicopter, Fa 223 subject of post-war development in both France and Czechoslovakia.

Manufacturer: Focke-Achgelis.
Model: Fa 330 Bachstelze (Wagtail).
Type: Observation gyrokite.
Performance:
maximum towing speed 25 + mph (40 + km/hr).
service ceiling 328 + ft (100 + m).
Weights:
empty 181lb (82kg).
normal 363lb (165kg).
Dimensions:
rotor diameter 23ft 11½in (7.31m).
length 14ft 6in (4.42m).
rotor disc area 450.47sq ft (41.85sq m).
Crew: 1.
In Service: Germany (NAF).
Variants (with no. built):
Fa 330: Prototype and production (150+).
Total Production: 150+.
Remarks: Ingenious but unpopular scheme to increase a surfaced U-boat's normal 5 mile (8km) range of vision up to as much as 25 miles (40km), Fa 330 was simply a rotor-kite, launched by tilting off the U-boat's after casing and towed at speed at the end of a 492ft (150m) cable; operational debut mid-1942, Fa 330 first saw limited service in South Atlantic, but mainly used over Indian Ocean and in Far Eastern waters by Type IXD 2 ocean-going boats of the 'Monsun' (Monsoon) groups; obvious disadvantages of surprise attack while gyrokite deployed led to early abandonment.

Manufacturer: Focke-Wulf.
Model: Fw 44C Stieglitz (Goldfinch).
Type: Trainer/liaison.
Power Plant: One 150hp Siemens Sh 14A.
Performance:
maximum speed at sea level 115mph (185km/hr).
cruising speed 107mph (172km/hr).
maximum range 419 miles (675km).
time to 3,280ft (1,000m) 5min 30sec.
service ceiling 12,795ft (3,900m).
Weights:
empty 1,158lb (525kg).

Zerstörer (heavy fighters):

Unit	Base	No.	Type
./ZG 26	Dortmund	52	Messerschmitt Bf 109
./ZG 26	Werl	48	Messerschmitt Bf 109
II.(ZG 26 (JGr. 126)	Lippstadt	49	Messerschmitt Bf 109

Bombers:

Unit	Base	No.	Type
Stab/KG 26	Lüneburg	8	Heinkel He 111
./KG 26	Lübeck-Blankensee	32	Heinkel He 111
./KG 26	Lüneburg	35	Heinkel He 111
Stab/KG 27	Hannover-Langenhagen	6	Heinkel He 111
./KG 27	Hannover-Langenhagen	34	Heinkel He 111
./KG 27	Wunstorf	26	Heinkel He 111
./KG 27	Delmenhorst	28	Heinkel He 111
./KG 28	Gütersloh	35	Heinkel He 111

Luftflotte 3 (Air Fleet 3) South-West Germany

Tactical reconnaissance:

Unit	Base	No.	Type
.(H)/13	Göppingen	12	Henschel Hs 126
.(H)/13	Göppingen	11	Henschel Hs 126
.(H)/13	Göppingen	12	Henschel Hs 126
.(H)/13	Göppingen	9	Henschel Hs 126
		3	Heinkel He 46
.(H)/13	Göppingen	9	Henschel Hs 126
		3	Heinkel He 45
.(H)/23	Eschwege	12	Henschel Hs 126
.(H)/23	Eschwege	12	Heinkel He 46
.(H)/23	Eschwege	9	Heinkel He 46
		3	Heinkel He 45

Strategic reconnaissance:

Unit	Base	No.	Type
.(F)/123	Würzburg	12	Dornier Do 17
.(F)/123	Würzburg	12	Dornier Do 17
.(F)/123	Würzburg	13	Dornier Do 17

Single-engined fighters:

Unit	Base	No.	Type
/JG 51	Bad Aibling	47	Messerschmitt Bf 109
/JG 52	Böblingen	39	Messerschmitt Bf 109
/JG 53	Wiesbaden-Erbenheim	51	Messerschmitt Bf 109
/JG 53	Mannheim-Sandhofen	43	Messerschmitt Bf 109
/JG 70 & 2./JG 70	Nürnberg	24	Messerschmitt Bf 109
/JG 71	Friedrichshafen	15	Messerschmitt Bf 109
/JG 71	Friedrichshafen	24	Messerschmitt Bf 109
.(N)/JG 72	Mannheim-Sandhofen	16	Arado Ar 68
.(N)/JG 72	Stuttgart-Echterdingen	12	Arado Ar 68

Zerstörer (heavy fighters):

Unit	Base	No.	Type
/ZG 52 (JGr. 152)	Illesheim	44	Messerschmitt Bf 109

Bombers:

Unit	Base	No.	Type
tab/KG 51	Landsberg	6	Heinkel He 111
		3	Dornier Do 17
/KG 51	Landsberg	36	Heinkel He 111
./KG 51	Memmingen	36	Heinkel He 111
tab/KG 53	Ansbach	6	Heinkel He 111
/KG 53	Ansbach	32	Heinkel He 111
/KG 53	Schwäbisch-Hall	32	Heinkel He 111

Unit	Base	No.	Type
III./KG 53	Giebelstadt	35	Heinkel He 111
Stab/KG 54	Fritzlar	9	Heinkel He 111
I./KG 54	Fritzlar	36	Heinkel He 111
Stab/KG 55	Giessen	9	Heinkel He 111
I./KG 55	Langendiebach	33	Heinkel He 111
II./KG 55	Giessen	31	Heinkel He 111

Dive-bombers:

Unit	Base	No.	Type
III./St.G 51	Wertheim	40	Junkers Ju 87
		3	Dornier Do 17

Luftflotte 4 (Air Fleet 4) South-East Germany; Austria; Czechoslovakia

Tactical reconnaissance:

Unit	Base	No.	Type
1.(H)/14	Köttingbrunn	9	Henschel Hs 126
		3	Heinkel He 46
2.(H)/14	Köttingbrunn	12	Henschel Hs 126
3.(H)/14	Köttingbrunn	9	Henschel Hs 126
		3	Heinkel He 46
1.(H)/31	Brieg	9	Henschel Hs 126
2.(H)/31	Brieg	8	Heinkel He 46
4.(H)/31	Brieg	9	Heinkel He 46
		3	Heinkel He 45

Strategic reconnaissance:

Unit	Base	No.	Type
4.(F)/14	Köttingbrunn	11	Dornier Do 17
3.(F)/31	Brieg	12	Dornier Do 17
1.(F)/124	Wiener Neustadt	11	Dornier Do 17

Single-engined fighters:

Unit	Base	No.	Type
I./JG 76	Wien-Aspern	49	Messerschmitt Bf 109
I./JG 77	Breslau	50	Messerschmitt Bf 109
II.JG 77	Pilsen	50	Messerschmitt Bf 109

Zerstörer (heavy fighters):

Unit	Base	No.	Type
I./ZG 76	Olmütz	31	Messerschmitt Bf 110
II./ZG 76 (JGr. 176)	Gablingen	40	Messerschmitt Bf 109

Bombers:

Unit	Base	No.	Type
Stab/KG 76	Wiener-Neustadt	9	Dornier Do 17
I./KG 76	Wiener-Neustadt	36	Dornier Do 17
III./KG 76	Wels	39	Dornier Do 17
Stab/KG 77	Prag-Kbely	9	Dornier Do 17
I./KG 77	Prag-Kbely	37	Dornier Do 17
II./KG 77	Brünn	39	Dornier Do 17
III./KG 77	Olmütz	34	Dornier Do 17

Dive-bombers:

Unit	Base	No.	Type
Stab/St.G 77	Breslau-Schöngarten	3	Junkers Ju 87
I./St.G 77	Brieg	40	Junkers Ju 87
II./St.G 77	Breslau-Schöngarten	42	Junkers Ju 87
I./St.G 76	Graz	39	Junkers Ju 87
		3	Dornier Do 17

Transport Units

Unit	Base	No.	Type
Stab/KGzbV 1	Fürstenwalde; Burg		
I./KGzbV 1	Burg		
II./KGzbV 1	Stendal		
III./KGzbV 1	Berlin-Tempelhof		
IV./KGzbV 1	Braunschweig		
Stab/KGzbV 2	Neuruppin		
I./KGzbV 2	Tutow		
II./KGzbV 2	Fassberg		} 496 Junkers Ju 52
III./KGzbV 2	Lechfeld		
I./KGzbV 172	Berlin-Tempelhof		
II./KGzbV 172	Berlin-Tempelhof		
10./KGzbV 172	Berlin-Tempelhof		
KGr.zbV 9	Berlin-Tempelhof		} 56 Junkers Ju 52
			2 Focke-Wulf Fw 200
			2 Junkers Ju 90
			1 Junkers G 38b

Maritime Units

North Sea:
Coastal squadrons:

Unit	Base	No.	Type
Stab/KüFlGr.106	Norderney		
1.(M)/KüFlGr.106	Norderney		
2.(F)/KüFlGr.106	Norderney		
3.(Mz)/KüFlGr.106	Borkum		} 31 Heinkel He 59
1.(M)/KüFlGr.306	Norderney		54 Heinkel He 60
Stab/KüFlGr.406	List / Sylt		36 Dornier Do 18
1.(M)/KüFlGr.406	List / Sylt		8 Heinkel He 115
2.(F)/KüFlGr.406	List / Sylt		
3.(Mz)/KüFlGr.406	List / Sylt		

Ship-borne squadron:

Unit	Base	No.	Type
1./BFlGr.196	Wilhelmshaven	6	Arado Ar 196

Baltic:
Coastal squadrons:

Unit	Base	No.	Type
Stab/KüFlGr.506 (KGr.806)	Dievenow		
1.(M)/KüFlGr.506	Dievenow		
2.(F)/KüFlGr.506	Dievenow		} 27 Heinkel He 60
3.(Mz)/KüFlGr.506	Dievenow		27 Dornier Do 18
Stab/KüFlGr.706	Kamp bei Kolberg		21 Heinkel He 111
1.(M)/KüFlGr.706	Kamp bei Kolberg		
3.(Mz)/KüFlGr.706	Kamp bei Kolberg		
2.(F)/KüFlGr.606	Kamp bei Kolberg		

Ship-borne squadrons:

Unit	Base	No.	Type
5./BFlGr.196	Kiel-Holtenau	6	Arado Ar 196
4.(St.)/TrGr.186	Kiel-Holtenau	12	Junkers Ju 87
5.(J)/TrGr.186	Kiel-Holtenau	12	Messerschmitt Bf 109
6.(J)/TrGr.186	Kiel-Holtenau	12	Messerschmitt Bf 109

NOTE:
The bases quoted in the above table are mainly peace-time home stations. Many units were deployed to forward fields upon mobilisation in late August, 1939.

Focke-Wulf Fw 44C Stieglitz

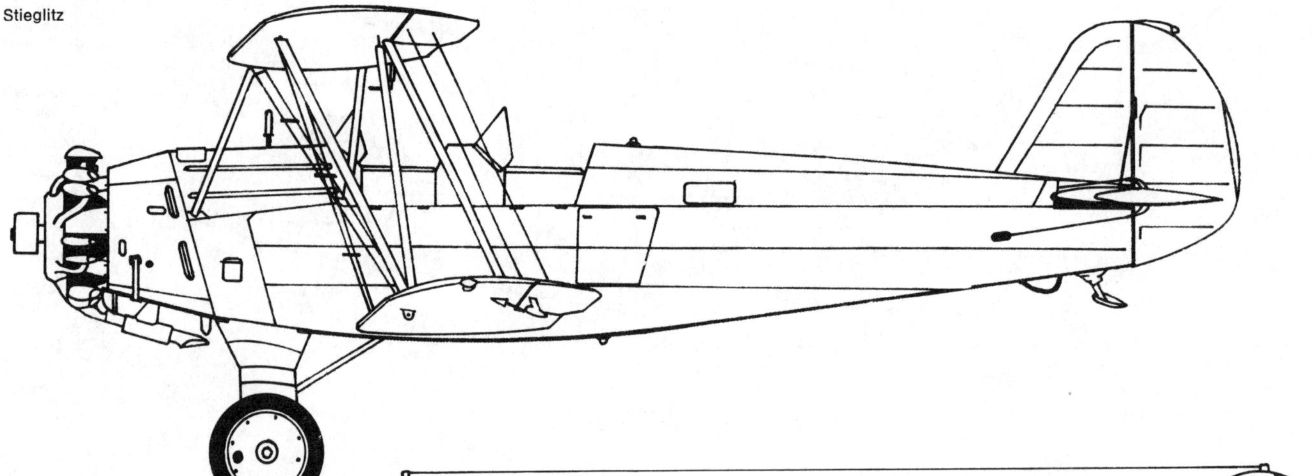

Focke-Wulf Fw 58C Weihe

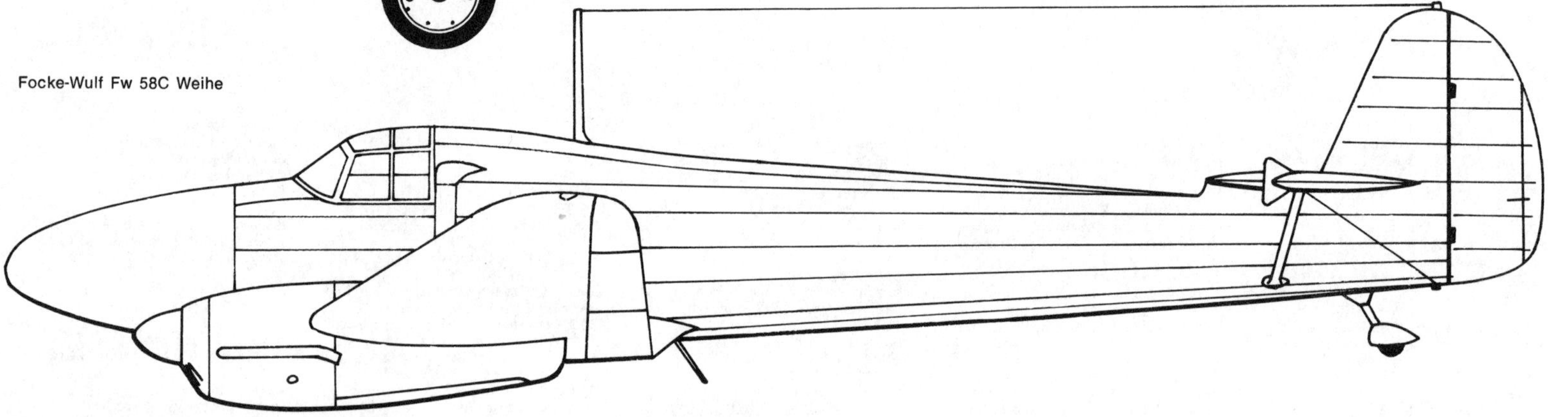

loaded 1,918lb (870kg).
Dimensions:
wing span 29ft 6¼in (9.0m).
length 23ft 11¼in (7.3m).
height 8ft 10¼in (2.7m).
wing area 215.28sq ft (20.0sq m).
Crew: 2.
In Service: Bulgaria, China, Finland (34), Germany, Rumania, Slovakia (30), Sweden (85+ inc licence-production), Turkey.
Variants (with no. built):
Fw 44A: Prototype; 150hp Siemens Sh 14A.
Fw 44B: Initial production model; 120hp Argus As 8.
Fw 44C: Major production model; 150hp Siemens Sh 14A (5).
Remarks: First flown 1932, Fw 44 widely exported (and licence-built) pre-war throughout Europe and South America; used by Luftwaffe duration WWII both as trainer and in variety ancillary reconnaissance, liaison roles.

Manufacturer: Focke-Wulf.
Model: Fw 56 Stösser (Hawk).
Type: Fighter/ advanced fighter-trainer.
Power Plant: One 240hp Argus As 10C.
Performance:
maximum speed at sea level 166mph (267km/hr).
cruising speed 152mph (245km/hr).
normal range 230 miles (370km).
initial rate of climb 1,650ft/min (503m/min).
service ceiling 20,340ft (6,200m).
Weights:
empty 1,477lb (670kg).
loaded 2,171lb (985kg).
Dimensions:
wing span 34ft 5¼in (10.50m).
length 24ft 11½in (7.60m).
height 8ft 6¼in (2.60m).
wing area 150.7sq ft (14.0sq m).
Armament: One (or two) 7.9mm MG 17 machine-guns in upper cowling; provision for three 22lb (10kg) bombs.
Crew: 1.
In Service: Germany, Hungary (18).
Variants (with no. built):
Fw 56 V1/3: Prototypes; under-carriage and wing modifications (3).
Fw 56A–0 (V4/6): Pre-production model; armament (3).
Fw 56A–1: Production model (approx 900).
Total Production: approx 900.
Remarks: First prototype (original designation Fw 56a) flown late 1933; extensive production 1935–40; pre-war deliveries to Austria (12) and Hungary; employed mainly as advanced trainer, but also served as emergency fighter and experimental glider-tug.

Manufacturer: Focke-Wulf.
Model: Fw 58C Weihe (Kite).
Type: Transport/communications.
Power Plant: Two 240hp Argus As 10C.
Performance:
maximum speed at sea level 162mph (260km/hr).
cruising speed 149mph (240km/hr).
range 497 miles (800km).
time to 3,280 ft (1,000m) 3min 48sec.
service ceiling 17,716ft (5,400m).
Weights:
empty 5,290lb (2,400kg).
loaded 7,937lb (3,600kg).
Dimensions:
wing span 68ft 10¾in (21.0m).
length 45ft 11in (14.0m).
height 12ft 9½in (3.9m).
wing area 505.91sq ft (47.0sq m).
Crew/Accommodation: 2/6.
In Service: Bulgaria (17), China, Croatia, Finland (1), Germany, Hungary (9), Rumania, Slovakia, Sweden, Turkey, USSR (1+ captured, ex-Slovak).
Variants:
Fw 58 V1/13: Prototypes; progressive civil, military and experimental series.
Fw 58A: Initial production model; general-purpose military trainer/ transport version; one 7.9mm MG 15 each in open nose and dorsal positions.
Fw 58B: Improved Fw 58A; glazed nose, with 7.9mm MG 15 mounting.
Fw 58BW: Float plane version of Fw 58B.
Fw 58C: Major production model; military (and civil) transport version; modified Fw 58B; solid nose-fairing.
Remarks: Designed as light transport; saw extensive Luftwaffe service in variety of crew/gunnery training, communications, ambulance, transport and other roles; widespread pre-war exports (military and civil) to Europe and South America (licence-built in Brazil); employed by Bulgarian AF as anti-partisan light bomber 1944.

Manufacturer: Focke-Wulf.
Model: Fw 187A–0 Falke (Falcon).
Type: Heavy fighter.
Power Plant: Two 700hp Junkers Jumo 210Ga.
Performance:
maximum speed at sea level 322mph (518km/hr).
maximum speed at 13,780ft (4,200m) 329mph (530km/hr).
initial rate of climb 3,445ft/min (1,050m/min).
service ceiling 32,810ft (10,000m).
Weights:
empty 8,157lb (3,700kg).
loaded 11,023lb (5,000kg).
Dimensions:
wing span 50ft 2¼in (15.30m).
length 36ft 5¼in (11.10m).
height 12ft 7½in (3.85m).
wing area 327.22sq ft (30.4sq m).
Armament: Four fixed forward-firing 7.9mm MG 17 machine-guns; two 20mm MG FF cannon.
Crew: 2.
In Service: Germany.
Variants (with no. built):
Fw 187 V1/V2: Initial prototypes; single-seat; 680hp Jumo 210Da or 670hp 210Gs; two 7.9mm MG 17 (2).
Fw 187 V3/V5: Prototypes; 2-seat, provision for addn two 20mm MG FF cannon; design changes, inc lengthened canopy, engine nacelles; Jumo 210 Gs (3).
Fw 187 V6: As V3. 1,000hp Daimler-Benz DB 600As (1).
Fw 187A–0: Pre-production model; two addn MG 17s; minor equipment changes (3).
Total Production: 9.
Remarks: Originally designed 1936 as twin-engined single-seat fighter, subsequent attempt to adapt Fw 187 for 2-seat 'Zerstörer' role proved unsuccessful; three A–0s served as 'Industrie-Schutzstaffel' (Industrial defence sqn) manned by Focke-Wulf test pilots in defence of their own Bremen plant during Summer 1940 before brief, and completely unofficial, sojourn for evaluation with operational fighter unit in Norway; later relegated experimental trials/ development duties.

Manufacturer: Focke-Wulf.
Model: Fw 189A–1 Uhu (Owl).
Type: Tactical reconnaissance/ liaison.
Power Plant: Two 465hp Argus As 410A–1.
Performance:
maximum speed at 8,202ft (2,500m) 214mph (344km/hr).
cruising speed 197mph (317km/hr).
maximum range 584 miles (940km).
initial rate of climb 1,017ft/min (310m/min).
service ceiling 22,966ft (7,000m).
Weights:
empty 5,930lb (2,690kg).
loaded 8,708lb (3,950kg).
Dimensions:
wing span 60ft 4½in (18.40m).
length 39ft 1in (11.90m).
height 10ft 2in (3.10m).
wing area 409.03sq ft (38.0sq m).
Armament: Two fixed forward-firing 7.9mm MG 17 machine-guns in wing roots; plus one flexible 7.9mm MG 15 machine-gun each in dorsal and fuselage tail cone positions; max bomb load 440lb (200kg).
Crew: 3.
In Service: Germany, Hungary (approx 30 Fw 189A–2s), Slovakia (14 Fw 189A–1s).
Variants (with no. built):
Fw 189 V1/6: Prototypes; various armament, design changes (6).
Fw 189A–0: Pre-production model (10).
Fw 189A–1: Production model; as V4; modified cowlings; increased armament.
Fw 189 A–1/Trop: As A–1; tropicalized; desert survival equipment.
Fw 189 A–1/U2–3: VIP staff transports; two A–1 conversions.
Fw 189 A–2: As A–1; MG 15s replaced by MG 81Zs.
Fw 189A–3: Dual-control trainer version.
Fw 189A–4: Tactical reconnaissance /ground-support version; as A–2; wing root MG 17s replaced by 20mm MG FF cannon; ventral armour.
(Total Fw 189A–0/4: Focke-Wulf-built 188; French (SNCASO)-built 293; Czechoslovakian (Aero)-built 337).
Fw 189 B–0/1: Trainer version; as V5 (13).
Fw 189C: Assault version; project only (modified Vlb/V6 prototypes).
Fw 189D: Dual-control floatplane trainer; project only.
Fw 189E: As A–1; 700hp Gnome-Rhône 14Ms; one conversion.
Fw 189F–1: Modified A–2; 580hp Argus As 411MA–1s; French-built (17).
Fw 189G: Improved version; 950hp Argus As 402s; project only.
Total Production: 864.
Remarks: Entering service late 1940, twin-boom Fw 189 slowly supplanted Henschel Hs 126 as standard Luftwaffe tactical reconnnaissance aircraft; served primarily on Eastern Front, 1942–45, but also operated in Finland and North Africa; interim employment in both night ground-attack and night-fighter roles, latter equipped with FuG 212 radar and single oblique upward firing 15mm MG 151 cannon in dorsal 'Schräge Musik' installation; supplied to Hungarian and Slovak AFs for Eastern Front service, a single Slovak example subsequently being flown by Insurgent AF's combined sqn against German forces during Slovak National Uprising, Autumn 1944.
Colour Reference: Plate 21: Focke-Wulf Fw 189A–4 (W7+WM) of II./NJG 100, Jafü Ostpreussen, Powunden, East Prussia, Nov 1944; interim night-fighter adaptation operated by Ju 88/Bf 109-equipped NJG 100 exclusively on Eastern Front, Fw 189s intended primarily to combat Soviet Polikarpov U–2 (Po–2) night harassment of Wehrmacht transportation system; note FuG 212 Lichtenstein C–1 nose radar array and 15mm MG 151 dorsal cannon.

Manufacturer: Focke-Wulf.
Model: Fw 190A–3.
Type: Fighter.
Power Plant: One 1,700hp BMW 801D–2.
Performance:
maximum speed at sea level 312mph (502km/hr).
maximum speed at 19,685ft (6,000m) 382mph (615km/hr).
cruising speed 278mph (447km/hr).
maximum range 497 miles (800km).
initial rate of climb 2,830ft/min (863m/min).
service ceiling 34,775ft (10,600m).
Weights:
empty 6,393lb (2,900kg).
loaded 8,770lb (3,980kg).
Dimensions:
wing span 34ft 5½in (10.5m).
length 28ft 10½in (8.8m).
height 12ft 11½in (3.95m).
wing area 196.98sq ft (18.3sq m).
Armament: Two 7.9mm MG 17 machine-guns in upper cowling; two 20mm MG 151 and two 20mm MG FF cannon in wings.
Crew: 1.
In Service: Germany (inc Spanish vol sqn), Great Britain (3+ evaluation), Turkey (75 Fw 190A–3s).
Variants (with no. built):
Fw 190 V1, 2, 5k: Initial prototypes; BMW 139 or (V5k) BMW 801C–0; V5k subsequently modified with increased wing span (redesignated V5g) (3).
Fw 190A–0: Pre-production model; as Fw 190 V5g. BMW 801C–0; first seven examples with reduced wing span (and inc 14 used for experimental purposes with V-designations) (40).
Fw 190A–1: Initial production model; 1,600hp BMW 801C–1; four 7.9mm MG 17s plus (optional) two 20mm MG FFs; Focke-Wulf-, Ago-, and Arado-built (100).
Fw 190A–2: Modified A–1; increased wing span; two MG 17s replaced by MG 151s; BMW 801C–2; addn radio equipment; Focke-Wulf-, Ago-, and Arado-built (426).
Fw 190A–3: Uprated engine; modified cowling; Focke-Wulf-, Ago-, Fieseler-, and Arado-built (509).
Fw 190A–3/U1, 3, 4, 7: Fighter-bomber and (Fw 190A–3/U4) reconnaissance versions; modified armament; bomb-racks and

camera equipment resp A–3 conversions.
Fw 190A–4: As A–3; addn MW power booster; revised radio equipment.
Fw 190A–4/U1, 3, 8: Fighter-bomber, ground-support fighter, and long-range fighter-bomber versions resp; various (reduced) armament; bomb-racks and drop-tanks; A–4 conversions.
Fw 190A–5: Revised engine mounting; some tropicalized, as Fw 190A–5/Trop.
Fw 190A–5/U2 to U4, U8: Night fighter-bomber, ground-support fighter, reconnaissance-fighter, and long-range fighter-bomber versions resp; A–5 conversions.
Fw 190A–5/U9 to U17: Zerstörer, fighter, heavy fighter, Zerstörer, long-range fighter-bomber, torpedo-fighter (U14 and U15), and ground-support fighter (U16 and U17) versions resp; various revised armament. U10 with modified wing; A–5 conversions.
Fw 190A–4/R6, A–5/R6: As A–4 and A–5 resp; equipped with Rüstsätze (field conversion kits); two addn 21cm Wfr.Gr.21 mortars underwing.
(Total Fw 190A–5 series; Focke-Wulf-, Ago-, Fieseler-, and Arado-built 723).
Fw 190A–6: Modified A–5; two MG 17s in fuselage plus four 20mm MG 151s; revised wing structure; some converted to fighter-bomber (Fw 190A–6/U3).
Fw 190A–6/R1 to R6: A–6 conversions with Rüstsätze (field conversion kits) for alternative or addn armament; A–6/R4 with modified wings and GM 1 power booster.
Fw 190A–7: Improved radio equipment; MG 17s replaced by 13mm MG 131s; some conversions to heavy fighter and Zerstörer configuration with alternative or addn armament (Fw 190A–7/R1, R2, R6); Focke-Wulf-, Arado, Ago- and Fieseler-built (80).
Fw 190A–8: Major production model; Modified A–7; MW 50 power booster. Revised radio equipment; inc 3 trainer conversions Fw 190–8/U1); Focke-Wulf-, Ago-, Arado, and Fieseler-built (1,334).
Fw 190A–8/R1 to R3, R7, R8, R11, R12: A–8 conversions with Rüstsätze (field conversion kits) for alternative or addn armament (R11 and R12 projected all-weather fighters).
Fw 190A–9: Assault-fighter version; 2,000hp BMW 801F; armoured wing leading-edges; prototype only (Fw 190 V34); subsequently re-engined GMW 801TS.
Fw 190A–10: Project only.
Fw 190S–5, S–8: Modified A–5 and A–8 resp; trainer versions.
Fw 190 V13: Prototype; modified Fw 190A–0; 1,750hp DB 603A–1; GM 1 power booster, pressurized cockpit.
Fw 190B–0 (V24, 26, 28, 29): Pre-production models; 1,700hp BMW 801D–2; GM 1 power booster; V24 with increased wing span (4).
Fw 190B–1: Production model; two MG 17s, two MG 151s plus two MG FF cannon (1).
Fw 190 V16, 18/U1, 29 to 33: Prototypes; DB 603A or G; pressurized cockpit; supercharger in redesigned lower fuselage; 4-blade prop.
Fw 190C–0: Pre-production model; high-altitude fighter version.
Fw 190C–1: Project only.
NC 900: French designation for Fw 190A–8 post-war production; SNCA-built (64).
Total Production: approx 19,500 (all Marks).
Remarks: Germany's finest wartime fighter, Fw 190's combat debut on Channel Front early autumn 1941; claiming three Spitfires in first engagement, Fw 190 quickly gained ascendancy over RAF, a supremacy not seriously challenged until advent of improved Spitfire Mk IX some twelve months later; Fw 190s participated Operation 'Cerberus/Donnerkeil', the escape up-channel of German battle-cruisers *Scharnhorst* and *Gneisenau* and heavy cruiser *Prinz Eugen*, 12 Feb 1942; shot down all six attacking Swordfish of one strike; during 1942–43 Fw 190s appeared in increasing numbers on all major fronts—Russia, Mediterranean, Arctic, and Defence of Reich; in West played both defensive (opposition Allied landings at Dieppe), and offensive (fighter-bomber raids on southern England) roles; heavily committed in Normandy campaign, June–Aug 1944; latter war years principal home defence fighter against US day bombers, inc especially activated 'Sturm' (ramming) Gruppen; also limited employment night-fighter role; sole export order to Turkey, 1943; brief post-war use by FAF (as NC 900).

Manufacturer: Focke-Wulf.
Model: Fw 190D–9.
Type: Fighter/fighter-bomber.
Power Plant: One 1,770hp Junkers Jumo 213A–1.
Performance:
maximum speed at sea level 357mph (575km/hr).
maximum speed at 21,650ft (6,600m) 426mph (685km/hr).
maximum range 520 miles (835km).
time to 6,560ft (2,000m) 2min 6sec.
Weights:
empty 7,694lb (3,490kg).
maximum 10,670lb (4,840kg).
Dimensions:
wing span 34ft 5½in (10.5m).
length 33ft 5¼in (10.2m).
height 11ft 0¼in (3.36m).
wing area 196.98sq ft (18.3sq m).
Armament: Two 13mm MG 131 machine-guns in upper cowling, two 20mm MG 151 cannon in wings; max bomb load 1,102lb (500kg).
Crew: 1.
In Service: Germany.
Variants (with no. built):
Fw 190 V17, 19–23, 25–28: Experimental prototypes; modified Fw 190As; redesigned wing; 1,170hp Jumo 213A(C) in lengthened nose; plus lengthened fuselage.
Fw 190D–0: Service trials model; converted Fw 190A–1s; two MG 17s in fuselage plus four MG 151s in wings.
Fw 190D–1: Project only.
Fw V17/U1, V54: Prototypes; modified D–0s; increased fin area; revised armament; provision for bomb load.
Fw 190D–9: Production model; majority with bubble canopy.
Fw 190D–10: Modified D–9; Jumo 213C; one 30mm MK 108 cannon firing through propeller hub plus one 20mm MG 151 in port wing (2).
Fw 190 V55–V61: Prototypes; 1,750hp 213E; two 20mm MG 151 cannon in wings (6).
Fw 190D–11: Production model; Jumo 213F with MW 50 injection; project only.
Fw 190D–12: Ground-attack fighter; modified armoured cowling; 2,060hp Jumo 213F–1; one 30mm MK 108 cannon firing through propeller hub plus two 20mm MG 151s in wings; project only.
Fw 190D–9/R11, D–12/R11: All-weather fighter versions of D–9 and D–12 resp; Rüstsätze (field conversion kits) with PKS 12 auto-pilot and FuG 125 Hermine D/F blind-landing equipment.
Fw 190 V65, V71: Prototypes for projected D–13; as D–12; revised armament; A–8 conversions.
Fw 190 V76, V77: Prototypes; 1,800 DB 603A and DB 603E; modified D–9 and D–12 resp.
Fw 190D–14. Project only.
Fw 190D–15: 1,800hp DB 603E/G; D–9 conversion/s; one completed.
(Total Fw 190D production: 674).
Total Production: approx 19,500 (all Marks).
Remarks: Entering service Autumn 1944, Fw 190D–9 (popularly known as 'Langnase' (long-nose) or 'Dora-9') initially employed in airfield defence of experimental Me 262 jet-fighter unit, covering latter during highly vulnerable periods of take-off and landing; subsequently participated Operation 'Bodenplatte', Luftwaffe's last-fling attack on Allied airfields in Low Countries, 1 Jan 1945; despite increasing tempo of deliveries, majority D–9s grounded due to lack of fuel in closing weeks of war.
Colour Reference: Plate 32: Focke-Wulf Fw 190D–9 of Stabskette IV./JG 3 Udet; Prenzlau (nr Berlin), Feb 1945; previous Fw 190A–8-equipped Reichs-defence Sturmgruppe, IV./JG 3 re-assigned Lfl.Kdo.6 in Feb 1945 for operations against Soviet forces advancing on capital; note early style straight canopy.

Manufacturer: Focke-Wulf.
Model: Fw 190F–3.
Type: Ground-attack fighter.
Power-Plant: One 1,700hp BMW 801D–2.
Performance:
maximum speed at sea level 326mph (525km/hr).
maximum speed at 18,045ft (5,000m) 368mph (592km/hr).
normal range 330 miles (530km).
initial rate of climb 2,110ft/min (645m/min).
Weights:
empty 7,328lb (3,224kg).
maximum 10,850lb (4,920kg).
Dimensions:
wing span 34ft 5½in (10.5m).
length 29ft 4½in (8.95m).
height 12ft 11½in (3.93m).
wing area 196.98sq ft (18.3sq m).
Armament: Two 7.9mm MG 17 machine-guns in upper cowling; two 20mm MG 151 cannon in wings; max bomb load 551lb (250kg).
Crew: 1.
In Service: Germany, Hungary (approx 35).
Variants (with no. built):
Fw 190F–1: Ground-support fighter version; BMW 801D–2; two MG 17s in fuselage plus two MG 151s in wings; 20+ Fw 190A–4 conversions.
Fw 190F–2: Modified A–5; improved (blown) cockpit canopy; ETC 501 bomb-rack (271).
Fw 190F–3: Modified F–2; revised wing structure; SC 250 bomb-rack; some tropicalized; Arado-built (approx 250).
Fw 190F–3/R1, R3: F–3 conversions with Rüstsätze (field conversion kits); four addn ETC 50 bomb-racks or two addn underwing 30mm MK 103 cannon resp.
Fw 190F–4, –5, –6: Projected production models; subsequently redesignated F–8, –9, –10 resp.
Fw 190F–8: Modified A–7; two MG 131s plus two MG 151s; bomb-racks as F–3/R1; some tropicalized; Arado- and Dornier-built (385).
Fw 190F–8/U1: 2-seat trainer version; project only.
Fw 190F–8/U2, U3, U14: Torpedo-bomber versions; F–8 conversions; one 1,543lb (700kg) BT 700, one 3,086lb (1,400kg) BT 1400, or one LT F5 torpedo resp.
Fw 190F–8/R14 to R16; Projected production versions of F–8/U14, F–8/U2 and /U3 resp.
Fw 190 V75: Prototype; anti-tank version; SG 113A (four vertically downwards-firing 77mm recoilless wing guns); one F–8 conversion.
Fw 190F–9: Re-engined F–8; 2,270hp turbo-supercharged BMW 801TS; MW 50 power booster; Arado- and Dornier-built.
Fw 190 F–10, –15, –16: Projects only.
Total Production: approx 19,500 (all Marks).
Remarks: Evolved directly from Fw 190A fighter-bomber variants, Fw 190F ground-attack models (distinguishable from parallel Fw 190G development by clear-blown bulged cockpit canopy) entered service Winter 1942–43 at time of Battle of Stalingrad; replacing earlier Ju 87 in both day- (and, subsequently, night-) ground-assault Gruppen, Fw 190Fs operated principally on Eastern Front, participating all major actions in German retreat from the Don to the Oder, 1943–45; also limited employment eastern Mediterranean and Italian campaigns; supplied to Hungarian AF, 1944–45.
Colour Reference: Plates 30, 31: Focke-Wulf Fw 190F (G5+02) of 101. Csatarepülö Osztály (Assault Group), Royal Hungarian Air Force, Börgönd, Hungary, Nov 1944; component part of Lfl.Kdo.4's Fliegerführer 102 ungarn based Lake Balaton area; fuselage code indicates this machine second Fw 190 supplied to Hungarian AF for advanced training duties; note late style markings (compare with Caproni-Reggiane Re.2000, plates 86, 87).

Manufacturer: Focke-Wulf.
Model: Fw 190G–3.
Type: Long-range fighter-bomber.
Power Plant: One 1,700hp BMW 801D–2.
Performance:
maximum speed at sea level 356mph (573km/hr).
cruising speed 262mph (422km/hr).
normal range 395 miles (635km).
Weights:
loaded 10,480lb (4,754kg).
Dimensions:
wing span 34ft 5½in (10.5m).
length 29ft 4½in (8.95m).
wing area 196.5sq ft (18.25sq m).
Armament: Two 20mm MG 151 cannon in wings; max bomb load 2,755lb (1,250kg).
Crew: 1.
In Service: Germany, USA (1 + evaluation).
Variants (with no. built):
Fw 190G–1: Long-range fighter-bomber version; modified A–4/U8; 1,700hp BMW 801D–2; two 20mm MG 151 cannon in wings; bomb load 1,102lb (500kg); underwing drop tanks; Focke-Wulf-, Arado-, and Fieseler-built (49).
Fw 190G–2: Modified G–1; revised engine mounting as A–5; minor equipment changes (468).
Fw 190G–3: Improved G–2; PKS 11 autopilot; modified bomb racks; balloon-cable cutter in wings; later models with addn booster; several subsequent modifications, inc night-flying equipment, revised armament, deletion of bomb-racks.
Fw 190G–2/Trop, G–3/Trop: As G–2 and G–3 resp; tropicalized.
Fw 190G–8: To A–8 standard; modified G–3; re-positioned bomb-rack.
Fw 190G–8/R1, R4, R5: G–8 conversions with Rüstsätze (field conversion kits) for addn auxiliary fuel tanks, GM–1 power booster, and wing-racks resp.
Fw 190G–9, –10: Projects only.
Total Production: approx 19,500 (all Marks).
Remarks: Continuation of Fw 190A series specifically as long-range fighter-bomber, Fw 190G had bomb-racks fitted as standard equipment and fuselage machine-guns deleted; operational debut closing stages North African (Tunisian) campaign; subsequently served mainly Eastern Front against advancing Soviets; participated Battle of Kursk, July 1943; final months of war one night ground-assault Gruppe flew Fw 190G–1s, each equipped to carry single 3,968lb (1,800kg) bomb, in attacks on Allied-held bridges on Western Front, inc Ludendorff bridge across Rhine at Remagen, captured intact by US forces 7 March 1945.

Manufacturer: Focke-Wulf.
Model: Fw 200C–8 Condor.
Type: Long-range maritime reconnaissance/bomber.
Power Plant: Four 1,200hp BMW-Bramo 323 R–2 Fafnir.
Performance:
maximum speed at sea level 190mph (305km/hr).
maximum speed at 15,750ft (4,800m) 224mph (360km/hr).
cruising speed 155mph (250km/hr).
maximum range 2,175 miles (3,500km).
service ceiling 19,030ft (5,800m).
Weights:
empty 29,367lb (12,950kg).
loaded 50,044lb (22,700kg).
Dimensions:
wing span 109ft 1in (33.25m).
length 78ft 3in (23.85m).
height 20ft 4in (6.2m).
wing area 1,270.2sq ft (118sq m).
Armament: One 20mm MG 151 cannon in forward dorsal turret; one 13mm MG 131 machine-gun each in rear dorsal and two beam positions; one 13mm MG 131 machine-gun in nose, and one 7.9mm MG 15 at rear of ventral gondola; one Hs 293A missile under each outboard engine nacelle.
Crew: 6.
In Service: Germany, Great Britain (1 ex-Denmark, interned/impressed).
Variants (with no. built):
Fw 200 V1/3: Prototypes; civil transport; Pratt & Whitney S1E–G Hornets or BMW 132G–1s (licence-built P. & W. Hornets); V3 personal aircraft of Adolf Hitler (3).
Fw 200A–0: Pre-production model (9).
Fw 200 V10: Prototype; subsequently converted as long-range maritime reconnaissance version; one 7.9mm MG 15 in dorsal turret plus one hand-held MG 15; original Japanese order (1).
Fw 200B–1/2: Production models; civil transport versions; 850hp BMW 132Dcs or 830hp BMW 132Hs resp (4).
Fw 200C–0: Pre-production model; maritime reconnaissance-bomber(6) and unarmed military transport(4) versions; modified Fw 200B–2s; Nacelle modifications (10).
Fw 200C–1: Production model; maritime reconnaissance/bomber version; two 7.9 MG 15s in fore and aft dorsal positions, one MG 15 plus one 20mm MG FF cannon in ventral gondola; max bomb load 3,757lb (1,750kg).
Fw 200C–2: As C–1; modified outboard engine nacelles; faired underwing bomb racks.
Fw 200C–3: Improved version; BMW-Bramo 323R–2 Fafnirs; 1 addn crew; structural strengthening; increased weight and bomb load; three addn 7.9mm MG 15s in dorsal turret and two beam positions.
Fw 200C–3/U1: As C–3; one 20mm MG 151 cannon in nose of ventral gondola and one 15mm MG 151 cannon in enlarged forward dorsal turret.
Fw 200C–3/U2: As C–3; 20mm MG 151 in nose of ventral gondola replaced by one 13mm MG 131; Lotfe 7D bomb sight.
Fw 200C–3/U3: As C–3; one 13mm MG 131 each in forward turret and rear dorsal position.
Fw 200C–3/U4: As C–3; one addn crew; beam 7.9mm MG 15s replaced by 13mm MG 131s.
Fw 200C–4: Main production model; addn FuG Rostock and/or FuG 200 Hohentwiel radar; enlarged forward dorsal turret as C–3/U1; ventral gondola as C–3/U1 or U2.
Fw 200C–4/U1 and U2: Transport versions; 11- and 14-passengers resp., abbreviated ventral gondola; four 7.9mm MG 15s.
Fw 200C–6: Missile-carrier version; one Hs 293 missile under each outboard engine nacelle; FuG 203B Kehl III (missile control) transmitter; Fw 200C–3/U1 and U2 conversions.
Fw 200C–8: Missile-carrier version; as C–6.
Total Production: 276.
Remarks: Original civil transport design, DLH operated Fw 200 Condor from introduction in 1938 until closing month of war (last scheduled flight, Barcelona to Berlin, completed 14 April 1945); also pre-war deliveries to Danish (2) and Brazilian (2) airlines; impressed/produced for military transport role. Fw 200 participated Norwegian campaign; later took part supply/evacuation flights into beleaguered Stalingrad; also employed as personal VIP transport by Nazi

Focke-Wulf Fw 190A–3

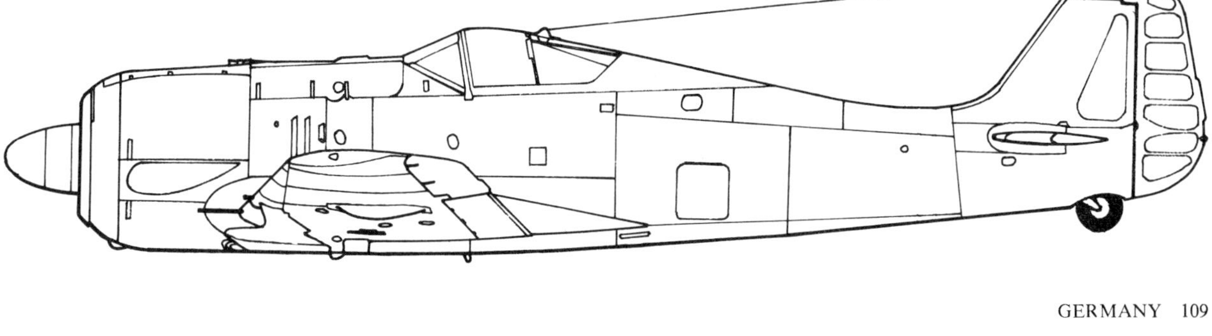

hierarchy, inc Adolf Hitler (V3) and Heinrich Himmler (C–4/U1); but it was fortuitous availability of Fw 200 as only aircraft suitable for armed conversion at time when Germany's first specialized long-range anti-shipping Staffel was being formed which led to Condor's most famous role, that of maritime reconnaissance-bomber; despite structural weakness, Fw 200s early successes (85 Allied merchantmen sunk in just over six months, 1940–41) soon earned it title 'Scourge of the Atlantic'; remained in maritime service until early 1944, never in any great numbers, but ranging Atlantic from Norway to Biscay, latterly armed with Henschel Hs 293 missiles.
Colour Reference: Plate 23: Focke-Wulf Fw 200C–3 Condor (F8+GH) of 1./KG 40; Bordeaux-Mérignac, Aug 1941; primarily employed Atlantic anti-shipping operations, this particular machine served briefly Mediterranean area, late Summer 1941; note 20mm MG 151 in nose of ventral gondola and tally of two earlier attacks on UK recorded on tailfin.

Manufacturer: Focke-Wulf.
Model: Ta 152H–1.
Type: High-altitude fighter.
Power Plant: One 1,750hp Jumo 213E.
Performance:
maximum speed at sea level 332mph (534km/hr).
maximum speed at 40,010ft (12,500m) 472mph (760km/hr).
cruising speed 311mph (500km/hr).
maximum range 1,250 miles (2,000km).
initial rate of climb 3,445ft/min (1,050m/min).
service ceiling 48,550ft (14,800m).
Weights:
empty 8,642lb (3,920kg).
maximum 11,502lb (5,217kg).
Dimensions:
wing span 47ft 4½in (14.44m).
length 35ft 1½in (10.71m).
height 11ft 0¼in (3.36m).
wing area 250.8sq ft (23.3sq m).
Armament: One 30mm MK 108 cannon firing through propeller hub; two 20mm MG 151 cannon in wings.
Crew: 1.
In Service: Germany.
Variants (with no. built):
Fw 190 V18/U2, V29/U1, V30/U1, V32/U2, V33/U1: Development prototypes; high-altitude fighter version; Jumo 213E; various armament; Fw 190C conversions.
Ta 152 V3–V5, V25, V26: Prototypes; Jumo 213E; one 30mm MK 108 cannon firing through propeller hub, plus two 20mm MG 151 cannon in wings; V25 not completed (4).
Ta 152H–0: Pre-production model; high-altitude fighter version; pressurised cabin; auxiliary drop tank; inc one with all-weather equipment H–0/R11 (20).
Ta 152H–1: Production model; addn fuel capacity; MW 50 and GM 1 power boosters; majority with all-weather equipment (H–1/R11) (approx 190).
Ta 152H–2, –10/–12: Projects only.
Total Production: approx 215.
Remarks: Long-span, Jumo 213E-powered development of earlier Fw 190C high-altitude fighter proposal, first Ta 152Hs delivered to Service Trials unit opening weeks 1945; few production models were to see operational service (mainly in defence of Me 262 jet bases), the majority of the almost 200 reportedly built being destroyed on the ground prior to Luftwaffe acceptance; parallel Ta 152B/C short-span medium-altitude escort/heavy fighter series had not progressed beyond prototype/development stage by time of German surrender.

Manufacturer: Focke-Wulf.
Model: Ta 154A–1.
Type: Night-fighter.
Power Plant: Two 1,750hp Junkers Jumo 213E.
Performance:
maximum speed at sea level 332mph (535km/hr).
maximum speed at 26,250ft (8,000m) 404mph (650km/hr).
maximum range 1,156 miles (1,860km).
time to 26.250ft(8,000m) 14min 30sec.
service ceiling 35,760ft (10,900m).
Weights:
loaded 19,687lb (8,930kg).
Dimensions:
wing span 53ft 6in (16.0m).
length 41ft 2¾in (12.6m).
height 11ft 9¾in (3.6m).
wing area 348.75sq ft (32.4sq m).
Armament: Four fixed forward-firing cannon (two 20 mm MG 151, and two 30mm MK 108) in fuselage sides.
Crew: 2.
In Service: Germany.
Variants (with no. built):
Ta 154 V1/2: Prototypes and pre-production models; two 1,350hp Jumo 211Rs (2).
Ta 154A–0 (Ta 154 V3/15): Pre-production model; supercharged Jumo 213Es; fully armed; various radar equipment (13).
Ta 154A–1: Production model (10).
Ta 154C: Improved version; project only.
Ta 254: High-altitude day and night fighter version; project only.
Total Production: 25.
Remarks: First flown mid-1943, wooden construction Ta 154 plagued by production difficulties; whole programme (initial order called for output of 250 aircraft per month) cancelled 1944 due to failure of adhesive bonding, two production machines literally disintegrating in mid-air; nonetheless saw limited operational service with two night-fighter Gruppen; number of air-frames converted for 'Mistel' and 'Sturm' programmes but not used.

Manufacturer: Gotha.
Model: Go 145C.
Type: Trainer/night ground-attack.
Power Plant: One 240hp Argus As 10C.
Performance:
maximum speed at sea level 132mph (212km/hr).
cruising speed 112mph (180km/hr).
normal range 391 miles (630km/hr).
time to 3,280ft (1,000m) 5min 30sec.
service ceiling 12,140ft (3,700m).
Weights:
empty 1,940lb (880kg).
loaded 3,043lb (1,380kg).
Dimensions:
wing span 29ft 6¼in (9.0m).
length 28ft 6¾in (8.7m).
height 9ft 6in (2.9m).
wing area 234.12 sq ft (21.75sq m).
Armament: One 7.9mm MG 15 machine-gun in rear cockpit; provision for up to 154lb (70kg) bomb load.
Crew: 2.
In Service: Germany, Great Britain (1), Slovakia (30), Spain, Turkey.
Variants (with no. built):
Go 145: Prototype.
Go 145A: Initial production; dual-control trainer version; open cockpit.
Go 145B: Experimental; enclosed cockpit; wheel spats.
Go 145C: As Go 145A; gunnery trainer; one 7.9mm MG 15.
(Total Gotha-, Ago, BFW, Focke-Wulf and licence-built: 9,500+).
Total Production: 9,500+.
Remarks: Service debut 1935, Go 145 remained standard Luftwaffe trainer throughout WWII; also supplied to Slovak AF, and licence-built in Spain and Turkey; from 1943 increasingly employed in night ground-attack role, equipping (either wholly or partially) some fifteen Staffeln, inc one manned by Russian volunteers; served exclusively on Eastern Front, remaining in action until very end of war.

Manufacturer: Gotha.
Model: Go 242A–1.
Type: Transport/assault glider.
Performance:
maximum gliding speed 180mph (290km/hr).
maximum towing speed 149mph (240km/hr).
cruising speed under tow 130mph (210km/hr).
time under tow to 3,280ft (1,000m) 15min 0sec.
Weights:
empty 7,055lb (3,200kg).
loaded 14,991 lb (6,800kg).
Dimensions:
wing span 80ft 4½in (24.50m).
length 51ft 10¼in (15.80m).
height 14ft 0in (4.26m).
wing area 693.194sq ft (64.40sq m).
Armament: Four 7.9mm MG 15 machine-guns plus (optional) four hand-held 7.9mm MG 34 machine-guns.
Crew/Accommodation: 2/23 troops.
In Service: Germany, Rumania (4).
Variants (with no. built):
Go 242 V1/2: Prototypes; steel skid undercarriage/twin-wheel jettisonable dolly (2).
Go 242A–0: Pre-production model; modified vertical tail surfaces and wings.
Go 242A–1: Initial production model; deepened tailbooms; braking 'plough' incorporated in nose skid: 5.9ton towline coupling in nose.
Go 242A–2: Assault-glider version; 10 ton towline coupling in nose; braking chute in rear fuselage; addn doors in hinged tail section.
Go 242B–1: As A–1; fixed-wheel undercarriage.
Go 242B–2: Modified B–1; revised undercarriage; semi-retractable enlarged nose-wheel.
Go 242B–3/4: Paratroop transport versions of B–1 and B–2 resp; addn drop-doors at rear of fuselage.
Go 242B–5: Modified B–2; dual controls.
Go 242C–1: Modified A–1; twin-wheel jettisonable dolly; planing hull; underwing stabilizing floats; floatation bags.
Total Production: 1,528.
Remarks: Standard Luftwaffe transport glider during latter half of war, twin-boom Go 242's operational debut Mediterranean theatre early 1942; initially equipped six so-called Gotha-Staffeln later incorporated into Schleppgruppen (glider wings); extensive use on Eastern Front, inc supply/evacuation missions into Cholm pocket and Odessa; Go 242C version specifically designed to alight on water and intended for projected attack on British Home Fleet at Scapa Flow.

Manufacturer: Gotha.
Model: Go 244B–2.
Type: Transport.
Power Plant: Two 715hp Gnome-Rhône 14M.
Performance:
maximum speed 180mph (290km/hr).
cruising speed 155mph (250km/hr).
normal range 435 miles (740km).
initial rate of climb 886ft/min (270m/min).
service ceiling 25,100ft (7,650m).
Weights:
empty 11,244lb (5,100kg).
maximum 17,196lb (7,800kg).
Dimensions:
wing span 80ft 4½in (24.50m).
length 51ft 10¼in (15.80m).
height 15ft 1in (4.60m).
wing area 693.194sq ft (64.40sq m).
Armament: Four (or six) 7.9mm MG 15 machine-guns.
Crew: 2/23 troops.
In Service: Germany.
Variants (with no. built):
Go 244V: Prototypes; converted Go 242B–2; two 750hp Shvetsov M–25A, 660hp BMW 132Z, or 700hp Gnome-Rhône 14M.
Go 244B–1/5: Modified Go 242B–1/5s; majority with Gnome-Rhône 14M (43).
Total Production: 43 (plus 133 Go 242B–1/5 conversions).
Remarks: Go 244 represented attempt to motorize standard Go 242 glider from captured stocks of French (Gnome-Rhône) and Soviet (Shvetsov) engines; resulting aircraft proved both underpowered and highly vulnerable to Allied fighters, seeing but limited service in Mediterranean and on southern sector of Russian front during 1942.

Manufacturer: Gotha-Kalkert.
Model: Ka 430A–0.
Type: Assault/transport glider.
Performance:
maximum gliding speed 199mph (320km/hr).
maximum towing speed 186mph (300km/hr).
Weights:
empty 3,990lb (1,810kg).
maximum 10,140lb (4,600kg).
Dimensions:
wing span 63ft 11¾in (19.5m).
length 43ft 4½in (13.22m).
height 13ft 8in (4.16m).
wing area 429.48sq ft (39.9sq m).
Armament: One 13mm MG 131 machine-gun in forward dorsal turret.
Crew/Accommodation: 2/12 troops (or cargo).
In Service: Germany.
Variants (with no. built):
Ka 430 V: Prototype; converted Go 242A–2; redesigned rear fuselage; single fin and rudder; loading ramp (*1*).
Ka 430A–0: Pre-production model; Mitteldeutsche Maschinenwerke-built (12).
Total Production: 12.
Remarks: Last German transport glider to be produced, only 12 Ka 430's completed before cancellation of project; delivered Winter 1944–45, at least one employed in unarmed transport role prior to end of war in Europe.

Manufacturer: Heinkel.
Model: He 8.
Type: Reconnaissance floatplane.
Power Plant: One 450hp Armstrong-Siddeley Jaguar.
Performance:
maximum speed 134mph (215/km/hr).
cruising speed 106mph (170km/hr).
maximum range 621 miles (1,000km).
time to 3,280ft (1,000m) 3min 0sec.
service ceiling 19,685ft (6.000m).
Weights:
empty 3,693lb (1,675kg).
loaded 5,126lb (2,325kg).
Dimensions:
wing span 55ft 1in (16.8m).
length 38ft 2¼in (11.65m).
height 14ft 5¼in (4.40m).
wing area 507sq ft (47.0sq m).
Crew: 2.
In Service: Denmark (DNAF).
Variants (with no. built):
He 8: Prototype. Reconnaissance floatplane (1).
H.M.II: Danish NAF designation; Heinkel-built (6); Danish (Naval Shipyards) licence-built (16).
Total Production: 22+.
Remarks: Early Heinkel floatplane design first flown 1927; purchased by Danish NAF, continued in use on reconnaissance/survey duties until April 1940; thirteen remaining examples dismantled and stored during German occupation; reported destroyed by Danish underground 1943.

Focke-Wulf Ta 152H–1

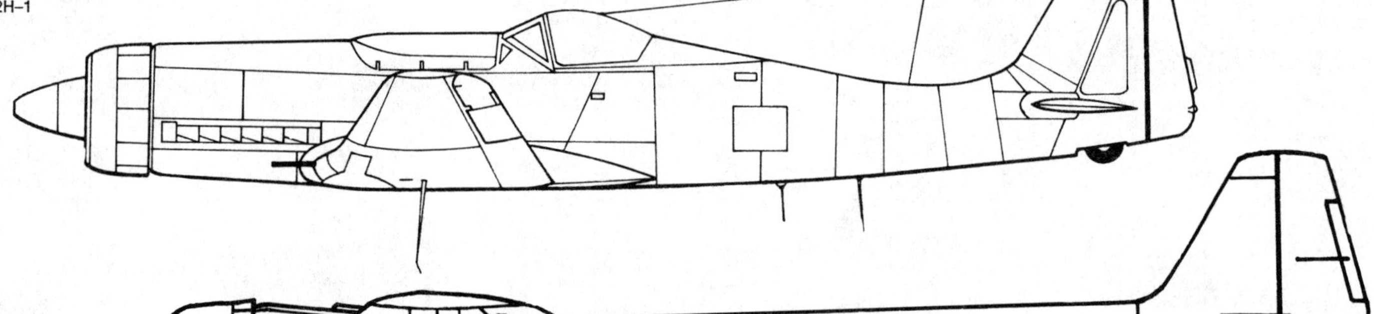

Gotha Go 244B–1

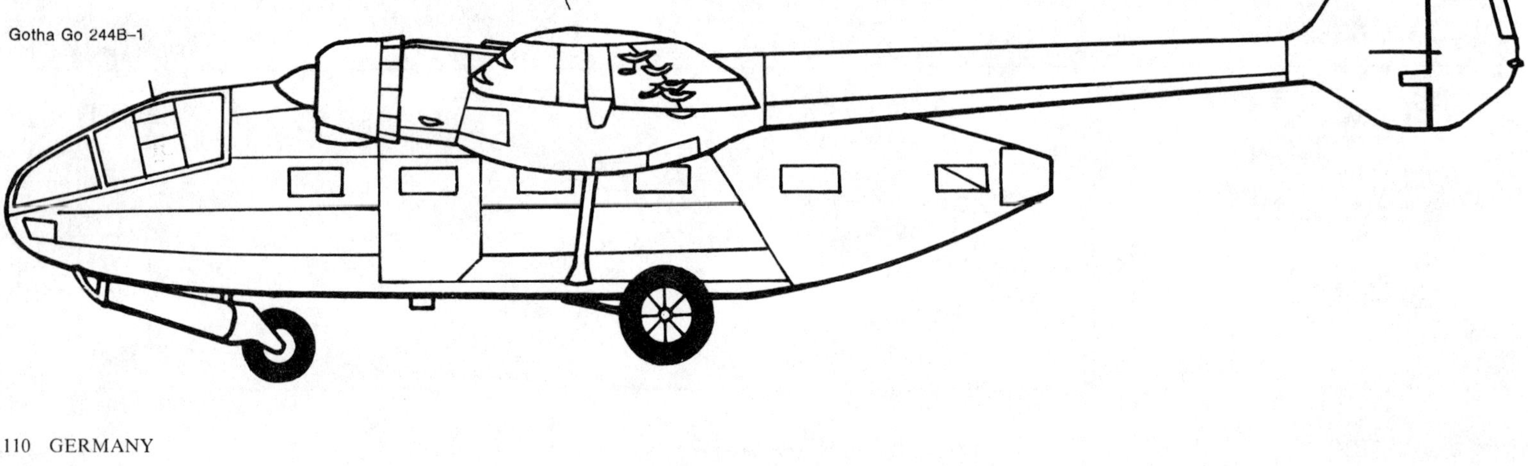

Manufacturer: Heinkel.
Model: He 42C–2.
Type: Maritime reconnaissance/air-sea-rescue floatplane.
Power Plant: One 380hp Junkers Jumo L–5Ga.
Performance:
maximum speed at sea level 124mph (200km/hr).
cruising speed 115mph (185km/hr).
maximum range 652 miles (1,050km).
time to 6,560ft (2,000m) 13min 24sec.
service ceiling 14,700ft (4,180m).
Weights:
empty 2,980lb (1,352kg).
maximum 5,336lb (2,420kg).
Dimensions:
wing span 45ft 11in (14.0m).
length 34ft 10in (10.6m).
height 14ft 1in (4.29m).
wing area 603sq ft (56.0sq m).
Armament: One flexible 7.9mm MG 15 (or 7.9mm MG 17) machine-gun in rear cockpit.
Crew: 2.
In Service: Bulgaria (2), Germany.
Variants (with no. built):
He 42: Prototype; dual-control trainer floatplane (1).
He 42A: Initial production model; 300hp Junkers L–5 (31).
He 42B–0: Uprated Junkers L–5G; trainer version (10).
He 42B–1: Improved B–0; structural strengthening for catapult-launching; inc two B–0 conversions (34).
He 42C–1: Final trainer variant.
He 42C–2: Armed reconnaissance version.
(Total He 42C–1, –2: 10+).
Total Production: 85+.
Remarks: First flown 1931, saw extensive service pre-war Luftwaffe maritime training units; remained in Luftwaffe service until near end of war; at least two examples supplied to Bulgarian AF for Black Sea ASR duties.

Heinkel He 45C

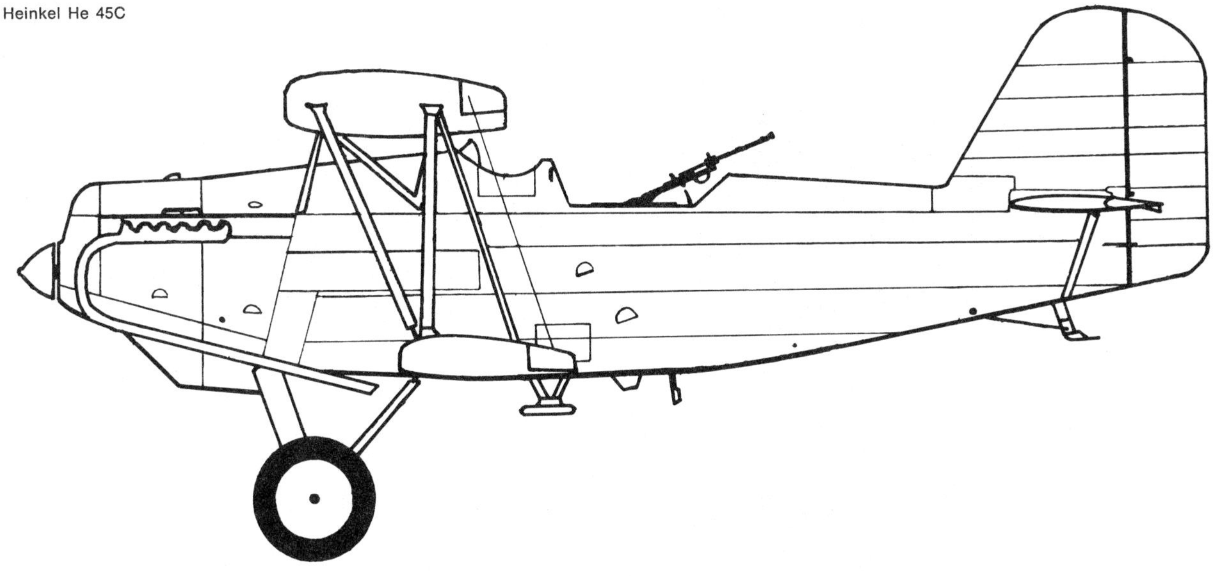

Heinkel He 46C–1

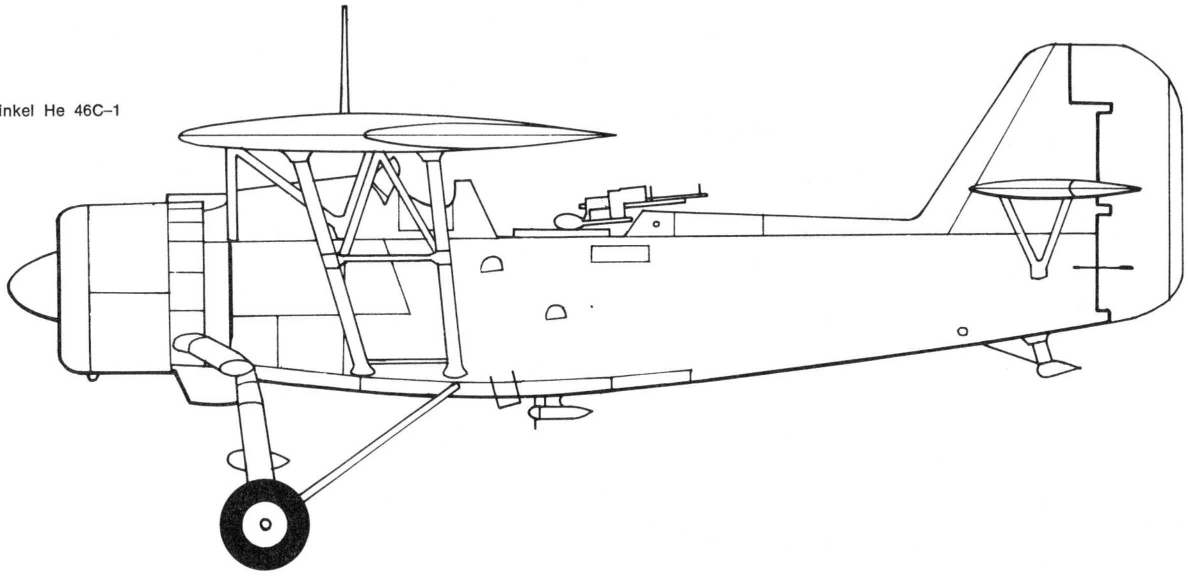

Manufacturer: Heinkel.
Model: He 45C.
Type: General purpose/light reconnaissance-bomber.
Power Plant: One 750hp BMW VI 7,3.
Performance:
maximum speed at sea level 180mph (290km/hr).
maximum speed at 6,560ft (2,000m) 168mph (270km/hr).
cruising speed 130mph (210km/hr).
maximum range 746 miles (1,200km).
time to 3,280ft (1,000m) 2min 24sec.
service ceiling 18,045ft (5,500m).
Weights:
empty 4,641lb (2,105kg).
loaded 6,052lb (2,745kg).
Dimensions:
wing span 37ft 8¾in (11.5m).
length 32ft 9¾in (10.0m).
height 11ft 9¾in (3.6m).
wing area 372.33sq ft (34.59sq m).
Armament: One fixed forward-firing 7.9mm MG 17 machine-gun; one flexible 7.9mm MG 15 machine-gun in rear cockpit; max bomb load 660lb (300kg).
Crew: 2.
In Service: Bulgaria (12+), Germany, Hungary (2).
Variants (with no. built):
He 45a, b, c: Prototypes (3).
He 45A–1, –2: Initial production models; unarmed trainer/reconnaissance versions; (Focke-Wulf-built 159; BFW-built 126; Gotha-built 68).
He 45B–1, –2: Reconnaissance/light bomber versions; one 7.9mm MG 17 machine-gun; max bomb load 220 lb (100kg); Focke-Wulf-built 60; BFW-built 30).
He 45C: Modified He 45B; uprated engine; enlarged rudder.
He 45D: As He 45C; minor equipment changes; (Heinkel-built (A/D) 66).
He 61: Export development; 660hp BMW VI; to China.
Total Production: 512 (exc He 61).
Remarks: Operated by pre-war Luftwaffe in tactical-reconnaissance role; served with Condor Legion in Spanish Civil War; by outbreak of WWII only twenty-one examples remaining in Luftwaffe first-line service (with five Staffeln); Winter 1942–43 reappeared on Eastern Front as night ground-attack aircraft; subsequently relegated training duties; also supplied Bulgaria and Hungary.

Manufacturer: Heinkel.
Model: He 46C–1.
Type: Tactical reconnaissance/army co-operation.
Power Plant: One 650hp Bramo 322B (SAM 22B).
Performance:
maximum speed at 2,625ft (800m) 161mph (260km/hr).
cruising speed 137mph (220km/hr).
maximum range 615 miles (1,000km).
time to 6,560ft (2,000m) 5min 30sec.
service ceiling 19,685ft (6,000m).
Weights:
empty 3,890lb (1,765kg).
maximum 5,070lb (2,300kg).
Dimensions:
wing span 45ft 11¼in (14.0m).
length 31ft 2in (9.5m).
height 11ft 1¾in (3.4m).
wing area 354.13sq ft (32.9sq m).
Armament: One flexible 7.9mm MG 17 machine-gun in rear cockpit; max (optional) bomb load 440lb (200kg).
Crew: 2.
In Service: Bulgaria (18), France (FFAF), Germany, Hungary (36), Spain (20 He 46C–1).
Variants (with no. built):
He 46a: Initial prototype; 450hp Siemens-built Bristol Jupiter; biplane (1).
He 46b/c: Improved prototype/pre-production models; parasol monoplane; increased wing area; Bristol Jupiter/650hp SAM 22B resp (2).
He 46C–1: Major production model; Heinkel-built (194); MIAG-built (32); Siebel-built (159); Fieseler-built (12); Gotha-built (6).
He 46C–2: As C–1; NACA engine cowling; to Bulgaria; Gotha-built (18).
He 46D–0, –1: Unarmed reconnaissance versions; seven He 46C conversions.
He 46e: Prototype; one He 46D–1 conversion.
He 46E–1/3: Production models; inc 36 MIAG-built E–2s to Hungary (43).
He 46f: Prototype; 560hp Siddeley Panther; one He 46C conversion.
He 46f–1/2: Production models; unarmed trainers; MIAG-built (14).
Total Production: 481.
Remarks: Standard Luftwaffe tactical reconnaissance aircraft of mid-thirties; by Sept 1939 only two Staffeln still fully equipped with type, plus nine partially equipped (total 62 aircraft); brief service Polish campaign; subsequently employed training duties; reinstated first-line service in night ground-attack role on Eastern Front, 1943; supplied to Spain (employed by NatAF during civil war), Bulgaria, and Hungary (served Eastern Front as both reconnaissance and bomber, 1941–43).

Manufacturer: Heinkel.
Model: He 50A.
Type: Dive-bomber/ground-attack bomber.
Power Plant: One 650hp Bramo 322B (SAM 22B).
Performance:
maximum speed at sea level 143mph (230km/hr).
maximum speed at 2,625ft (800m) 146mph (235km/hr).
cruising speed 118mph (190km/hr).
normal range 373 miles (600km).
time to 3,280ft (1,000m) 3min 0sec.
service ceiling 21,000ft (6,400m).
Weights:
empty 3,527lb (1,600kg).
loaded 5,776lb (2,620kg).
Dimensions:
wing span 37ft 8¾in (11.5m).
length 31ft 6in (9.6m).
height 14ft 5¼in (4.4m).
wing area 374.58sq ft (34.8sq m).
Armament: One fixed forward-firing 7.9mm MG 15, or 7.9mm MG 17 machine-gun; max bomb load 1,100lb (500kg).
Crew: 1.
In Service: China (12), Germany, Japan (IJNAF licence-production).
Variants (with no. built):
He 50aW: Prototype; twin-float seaplane; 390hp Junkers L–5 (1).
He 50aL: Prototype and service test models; 490hp Siemens-built Bristol Jupiter VI or (uncowled) SAM 21B resp; interchangeable fuselage decking for dive-bomber or reconnaissance roles; landplanes (4).
He 50A: Initial production model; as He 50aL; uncowled SAM 22B; Heinkel-built (25); BFW-built (35).
He 50b (He 66): Export version; pattern aircraft; engine cowling; Jupiter VI; subsequently re-engined, 580hp Nakajima Kotobuki II-Kai; Japanese order; Heinkel-built (1); D1A1/2: IJNAF designations; Japanese licence-built by Aichi (590).
He 66aCh: As He 50b; initial Chinese order (12).
He 66bCh: As He 50A; 650hp SAM 22B; NACA engine cowling; second Chinese order; commandeered by Luftwaffe as He 50B (12).
Total Production: 90 (exc D1A1/2 licence-production).
Remarks: Formed initial equipment Luftwaffe's first dive-bomber (Stuka) Gruppe, 1935; already being phased out following year, completely disappearing by April 1937; remained in use in training roles, whence returned to active service end of 1943 equipping Estonian volunteer-manned Nachtschlacht-gruppe on northern sector of Russian Front; extensive licence-production for IJNAF, seeing widespread use throughout second Sino-Japanese conflict; no corroborated evidence of any encounter between Japanese and Chinese (Heinkel-built) machines discovered to date.

Manufacturer: Heinkel.
Model: He 51B–1.
Type: Fighter.
Power Plant: One 750hp BMW VI 7,3 Z.
Performance:
maximum speed at sea level 205mph (330km/hr).
cruising speed 174mph (280km/hr).
normal range 354 miles (570km).
time to 13,120ft (4,000m) 7min 48sec.
service ceiling 25,262ft (7,700m).
Dimensions:
wing span 36ft 1in (11.00m).
length 27ft 6¾in (8.40m).
height 10ft 6in (3.20m).
wing area 292.778sq ft (27.2sq m).
Armament: Two fixed forward-firing 7.9mm MG 17 machine-guns in upper cowling.
Crew: 1.
In Service: Spain.
Variants (with no. built):
He 51a: Prototype; modified He 49; single-seat fighter biplane; one 750hp BMW VI 7,3 Z (1).
He 51A–0: Pre-production model; improved He 51a; two 7.9mm MG 17 machine-guns (9).
He 51A–1: Initial production model; As A–0; Heinkel-built (75); Arado-built (75).
He 51A–2: Floatplane version of A–1; 1 conversion.
He 51B–0: Pre-production model; modified A–1; undercarriage bracing; ventral jettisonable fuel tank (12).
He 51B–1: Production model; as B–0; Arado-built (150); Erla-built (200); Fieseler-built (100).
He 51B–2: Floatplane version of B–1; 46 completed from B–1 contracts, inc 8 airframe conversions.
He 51B–3: Experimental high-altitude version; increased wing span (1).
He 51C–1: Ground-attack/fighter version; provision for six 22lb (10kg) bombs underwing; Fieseler-built (79).
He 51C–2: As C–1; Improved radio equipment; Fieseler-built (21).
He 51W: Floatplane prototype; modified He 49c; 1 conversion.
He 52B/D: Prototypes; high-altitude land/floatplane resp; as He 51B–3 (2).
He 52E: High-altitude interceptor; project only.
Total Production: 725.
Remarks: Served pre-war Luftwaffe fighter and ground-attack Gruppen; relegated fighter-training role by outbreak WWII; 135 examples

Heinkel He 51B–1

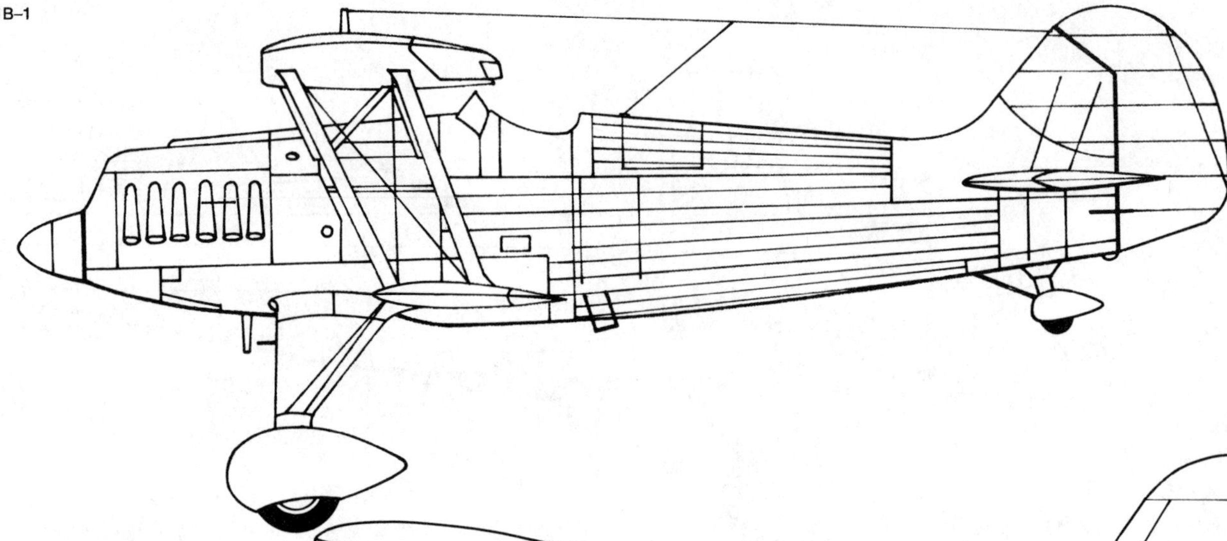

Heinkel He 59D–1

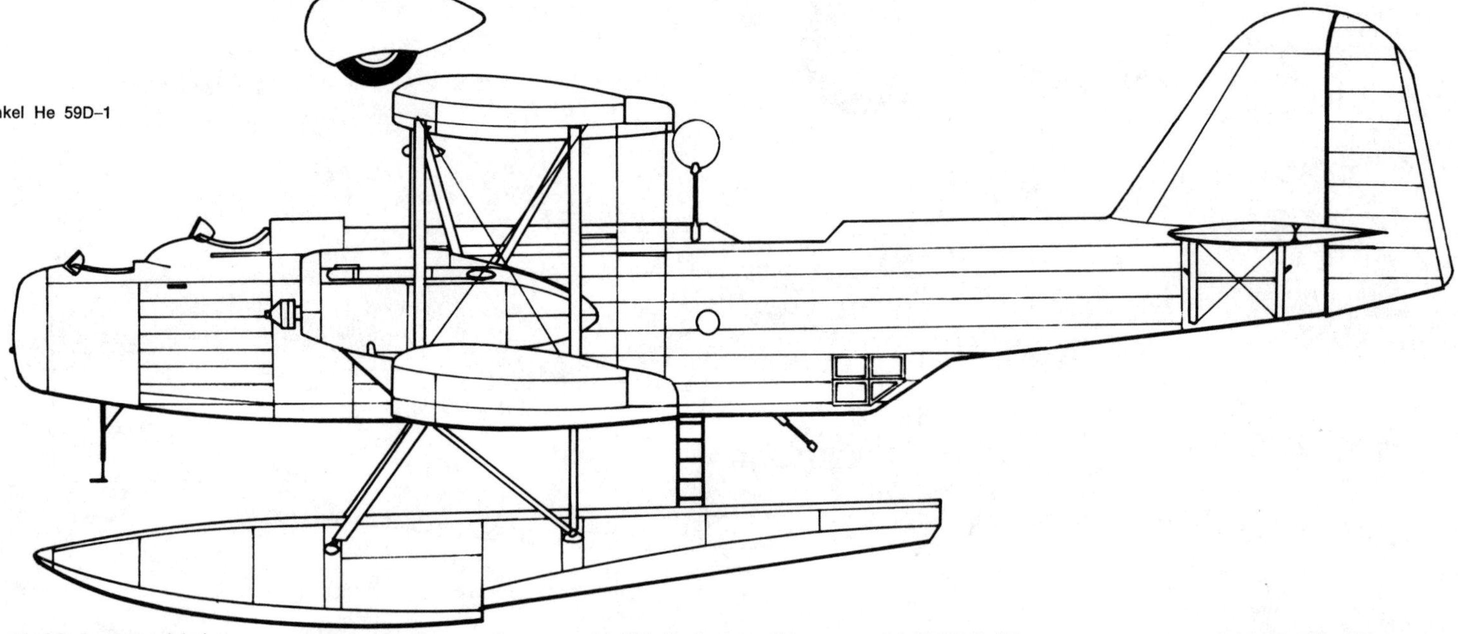

despatched Spain, operated during Civil War both by Condor Legion and by Spanish NatAF; survivors among latter remained in Spanish AF service early years WWII.

Manufacturer: Heinkel.
Model: He 59B–2.
Type: Torpedo-bomber/reconnaissance floatplane.
Power Plant: Two 660hp BMW VI 6,0 ZU.
Performance:
maximum speed at sea level 137mph (220km/hr).
maximum speed at 3,280ft (1,000m) 130mph (210km/hr).
cruising speed 111mph (180km/hr).
maximum range 950 miles (1,530km).
time to 3,280ft (1,000m) 4min 42sec.
service ceiling 11,480ft (3,475m).
Weights:
empty 11,023lb (5,000kg).
loaded 20,062lb (9,100kg).
Dimensions:
wing span 77ft 9in (23.7m).
length 57ft 1in (17.4m).
height 23ft 3½in (7.1m).
wing area 1,645sq ft (152.8sq m).
Armament: One flexible 7.9mm MG 15 machine-gun each in open nose, dorsal, and ventral positions; max bomb load 2,205lb (1,000kg) or one torpedo.
Crew: 4.
In Service: Germany, Spain (3).
Variants (with no. built):
He 59a/b: Prototypes; float- and landplane versions resp (2).
He 59A: Service Trials model; as He 59a.
He 59B–1: Pre-production model; armed; modified He 59a (16).
He 59B–2: Initial production model; as B–1; improved equipment; increased armament; Arado-built.
He 59B–3: Long-range maritime patrol version; one MG 15 machine-gun deleted.
(Total He 59B–2, –3: 126).
He 59C–1: Unarmed trainer version.
He 59C–2: Unarmed air/sea-rescue version; external folding ladder; medical equipment.
He 59D–1: Air/sea-rescue/trainer version; redesigned nose.
He 59E–1/2: Torpedo-bomber and reconnaissance trainer versions resp.
He 59N: Navigational trainer version; D–1 conversions.
(Total production He 59C–N Bachmann-built
Remarks: Equipped pre-war Luftwaffe's maritime reconnaissance and general-purpose Staffeln; approx 15 sent to Spain 1936, participating Civil War in anti-shipping and night-bomber roles; three subsequently operated by Spanish AF throughout WWII; extensive Luftwaffe employment early months WWII, inc anti-shipping and coastal patrols North Sea and Baltic areas, participation Norwegian campaign (addn auxiliary transport duties), landing of storm-troops on River Maas to capture Rotterdam bridges in combined assault with paratroops, 10 May 1940, minelaying in Thames Estuary, and as ASR aircraft over English Channel during Battle of Britain; also performed similar ASR duties over Black Sea, 1941–43; subsequently relegated training roles.

Manufacturer: Heinkel.
Model: He 60C.
Type: Reconnaissance floatplane.
Power Plant: One 660hp BMW VI 6,0 ZU.
Performance:
maximum speed at 3,280ft (1,000m) 140mph (225km/hr).
cruising speed 118mph (190km/hr).
normal range 447 miles (720km).
time to 3,280ft (1,000m) 3min 48sec.
service ceiling 16,400ft (5,000m).
Weights:
empty 5,313lb (2,410kg).
maximum 7,840lb (3,555kg).
Dimensions:
wing span 42ft 4¾in (12.9m).
length 37ft 8¾in (11.5m).
height 16ft 2½in (4.9m).
wing area 581.25sq ft (53.97sq. m).
Armament: One flexible 7.9mm MG 15 machine-gun in rear cockpit.
Crew: 2.
In Service: Germany, Spain (6).
Variants (with no. built):
He 60a/c: Prototypes; various power plants; He 60c with catapult hooks (3).
He 60A: Pre-production model; 660hp BMW VI 6,0 ZU (21).
He 60B: Production model; as He 60A; minor equipment changes; armed.
He 60C: Improved He 60B.
He 60D: As He 60C; one 7.9mm MG 17; subsequently modified as unarmed trainer.
He 60E: Export version of original He 60D; Spanish order (6).
(Total He 60B/E; Heinkel-built, Arado-built (100); Weser-built (100).
Total Production: approx 250.
Remarks: Pre-war shipboard deployment on all Kriegsmarine capital vessels; participated Spanish Civil War (4 survivors served Spanish AF throughout WWII); by outbreak of WWII equipped shore-based Luftwaffe maritime units only; employed coastal reconnaissance role 1939–43 in North Sea, Baltic and Eastern Mediterranean areas; subsequently relegated ancillary training and communications duties.

Manufacturer: Heinkel.
Model: He 70F–2.
Type: Light bomber/reconnaissance.
Power Plant: One 750hp BMW VI 7,3 Z.
Performance:
maximum speed at 3,280ft (1,000m) 224mph (360km/hr).
cruising speed 208mph (335km/hr).
normal range 560 miles (900km).
time to 3,280ft (1,000m) 2min 30sec.
service ceiling 17,880ft (5,500m).
Weights:
empty 5,203lb (2,360kg).
loaded (bomber) 7,630lb (3,460kg).
Dimensions:
wing span 48ft 6¾in (14.79m).
length 39ft 4½in (12.0m).
height 10ft 2in (3.1m).
wing area 392.88sq ft (36.5sq m).
Armament: One flexible 7.9mm MG 15 machine-gun in rear cockpit; max bomb load 660lb (300kg).
Crew: 3.
In Service: Germany, Spain (NatAF 12 F–2).
Variants (with no. built):
He 70: Prototype; 637hp BMW VI 6,0 Z (1).
He 70a/d: Civil (a/b) and military (c/d) prototypes (4).
He 70D–0: Pre-production model; 3 civil, 9 military; 750hp BMW VI 7,3 Z (12).
He 70D–1: Initial (military) production; high-speed communications aircraft.
He 70e/f: Light bomber/reconnaissance-bomber prototypes (2).
He 70E–1: Light bomber; limited production.
He 70F–1: Reconnaissance-bomber; initial production model.
He 70F–2/3: Improved F–1; equipment changes.
(Total He 70E–1, F–1, –2, –3: 265).
He 70G–1: Domestic airliner development; 750hp BMW VI 7,3 Z; inc one exported to UK with Rolls-Royce Kestrel V (22).
He 170: Re-engined export version; to Hungary (see He 170).
He 270: Light bomber/reconnaissance; 1,175hp DB 601A; one He 70F conversion.
Total Production: 306 (excl He 170).
Remarks: Spurred by appearance of Lockheed Orion on neighbouring Swissair routes, He 70 was advanced high-speed four-passenger transport designed for DLH's domestic routes; preponderance subsequent production for Luftwaffe as strategic reconnaissance aircraft; operational debut with Condor Legion Autumn 1936; 12 of 18 examples despatched later transferred to Spanish NatAF; remained in use until early fifties, latterly in VIP-transport role; Luftwaffe WWII employment restricted communications duties; sole He 270 first flown 1938.

Manufacturer: Heinkel.
Model: He 72B–1 Kadett (Cadet).
Type: Primary trainer/liaison.
Power Plant: One 160hp Siemens Sh 14A.
Performance:
maximum speed at sea level 115mph (185km/hr).
cruising speed 106mph (170km/hr).
normal range 295 miles (475km).
time to 3,280ft (1,000m) 6min 0sec.
service ceiling 11,483ft (3,500m).
Weights:
empty 1,190lb (540kg).
loaded 1,907lb (865kg).
Dimensions:
wing span 29ft 6¼in (9.0m).
length 24ft 7¼in (7.5m).
height 8ft 10¼in (2.7m).
wing area 222.8sq ft (20.7sq m).
Crew: 2.
In Service: Germany, Slovakia (SlovAF/InsAF).
Variants (with no. built):
He 72: Prototype; 140hp Argus As 8B (1).
He 72A: Initial production model; 150hp Argus As 8R; 2-seat trainer
He 72B–1: Improved He 72A; major production model.
He 72BW: Floatplane version of B–1; prototype only (1).
He 72B–3 Edelkadett (Honour-Cadet): Improved civil model (30).
He 172: Development of He 72B; NACA cowling; wheel fairings; prototype only (1).
Remarks: Extensive use mid-thirties both civil and military flying schools; examples operated WWII in light communications/liaison roles; ex-Slovak AF trainer/s employed by Slovak Insurgent AF's combined sqn for reconnaissance duties, Aug–Sept 1944.

Manufacturer: Heinkel.
Model: He 100D–1.
Type: Interceptor fighter.
Power Plant: One 1,175hp Daimler-Benz DB 601Aa.
Performance:
maximum speed at 16,400ft (5,000m) 415mph (668km/hr).
cruising speed 342mph (550km/hr).
normal range 553 miles (900km).
time to 6,560ft (2,000m) 2min 12sec.
service ceiling 36,090ft (11,000m).
Weights:
empty 3,990lb (1,810kg).
loaded 5,511lb (2,500kg).
Dimensions:
wing span 30ft 10¾in (9.41m).
length 26ft 10¾in (8.2m).
height 11ft 9¾in (3.6m).
wing area 155.0sq ft (14.4sq m).
Armament: One 20mm MG FF cannon in nose; two 7.9mm MG 17 machine-guns in wings.
Crew: 1.
In Service: Germany, Japan (IJNAF 3), USSR (7).
Variants (with no. built):
He 100 V1/2: Prototypes; DB 601/601M (2).
He 100 V3 and 8: Prototypes; Boosted DB 601; reduced wing span; special high-speed (World

Record) models (2).
He 100 V4/5: Prototypes; projected He 100B production model (2).
He 100 V6/7 and 9: Prototypes; projected He 100C production model; V9 armed (3).
He 100 V10: Static-test airframe (1).
He 100D–0: Pre-production model; enlarged vertical tail surfaces; redesigned cockpit (3).
He 100D–1: Production model; enlarged horizontal tail surfaces (12).
Total Production: 25.
Remarks: Subject of much pre-war and wartime propaganda, specially designated (non-sequential) He 100 represented determined attempt on part of Heinkel to regain lead in fighter-design, lost by earlier He 112 to Messerschmitt's Bf 109, by offering dramatic increase in speed; He 100 V8 in fact established new absolute world speed record, 30 March 1939, under false 'He 112U' designation; type not accepted by Luftwaffe however, as DB 601 production already fully committed to other (mainly Messerschmitt) types; instead offered for export—six prototypes to USSR, and the three D–0s to Japan, (IJNAF designation AXHe1); D–1s employed as factory-defence Staffel; flown by Heinkel test-pilots, and sporting variety of spurious unit badges and markings, D–1s received wide coverage as He 113, Luftwaffe's latest operational fighter, a propaganda fiction which survived into post-war aviation literature.

Manufacturer: Heinkel.
Model: He 111B–2.
Type: Medium Bomber.
Power Plant: Two 950hp Daimler-Benz DB 600CG.
Performance:
maximum speed at sea level 186mph (300km/hr).
maximum speed at 13,120ft (4,000m) 230mph (370km/hr).
cruising speed 214mph (345km/hr).
maximum range 1,030 miles (1,660km).
service ceiling 22,966ft (7,000m).
Weights:
empty 12,875lb (5,840kg).
maximum 22,046lb (10,000kg).
Dimensions:
wing span 74ft 1¾in (22.6m).
length 57ft 5in (17.5m).
height 14ft 5¼in (4.4m).
wing area 942.92sq ft (87.60sq m).
Armament: One 7.9mm MG 15 machine-gun each on nose mounting and flexible dorsal mounting; one 7.9mm MG 15 machine-gun in retractable ventral 'dustbin'; max bomb load 3,307lb (1,500kg).
Crew: 4.
In Service: China (10 He 111A–0), Germany, Spain (He 111B, E), Turkey (30 He 111F–1, 5 He 111G–5).
Variants (with no. built):
He 111a (V1): Initial prototype for both civil transport and bomber versions; two 660hp BMW 6,0Z (1).
He 111 V2, 4: Prototype; civil transport version (1).
He 111 V3: Prototype; bomber version (1).
He 111A–0: Pre-production model; as V3; lengthened glazed fuselage nose; three MG 15s; bomb load 2,205lb (1,000kg) (10).
He 111 V5: Prototype; 1,000hp DB 600s; increased weight; He 111A–0 airframe (1).
He 111B–0: Pre-production model.
He 111B–1: Initial production model; modified rudder and wing tips; DB 600As or DB 600Cs; increased bomb load.
He 111B–2: Re-engined B–1; surface coolant radiators.
(Total He 111B–0, –1, –2: approx 300).
He 111 V6: Prototype; B–0 conversion; test-bed for Jumo 210 and 211.
He 111C–0: Two crew, 10 passenger civil transport version; modified V4 (5).
He 111 V9: Prototype; re-engined B–0; 950hp DB 600 Ga; redesigned cooling system.
He 111D–0: Pre-production model; modified exhaust and radiator system; surface radiators deleted.
He 111D–1: Production model of D–0; limited series; Heinkel and Dornier-built.
He 111 V10: Prototype; modified D–1; redesigned semi-retractable coolant radiators; modified exhaust system; 1,000hp Jumo 211A–1s; one D–0 conversion.
He 111E–0: Pre-production model; bomb load 3,747lb (1,700kg); increased weight.
He 111E–1: Production model; bomb load 4,410lb (2,000kg).
He 111E–3: Principal He 111E production model; as E–1; minor equipment changes.
He 111E–4: Modified E–3; external racks for 2,205lb (1,000kg) bombs, plus internal bomb load 2,205lb (1,000kg).
He 111E–5: As E–4; auxiliary fuel tanks within fuselage.
(Total He 111E–0/–5: approx 190).
He 111 V11: Prototype; modified B–1; redesigned straight-tapered wings; DB 600CGs; armament and equipment as E–1; one conversion.
He 111F–0: Re-engined V11; 1,100hp Jumo 211A–3s; auxiliary fuel tanks.
He 111F–1: Production model; Turkish order (30).
He 111F–4: As F–1; bomb load as E–4 (40).
He 111G–0 (V12, 13): Modified C–0; civil transport version; straight-taper wing; BMW VI 6,0 ZUs (2).
He 111G–3 (V14, 15): As G–O; BMW 132Ds or 132H–1s resp; (2).
He 111G–4 (V16): Re-engined G–3; up-rated DB 600Gs; personal transport of General-Feldmarschall Milch (1).
He 111G–5: Production model; Turkish order; DB 600Gas (5).
He 111J–0: Pre-production model; torpedo-bomber version; modified F–4; bomb-bays deleted.
He 111J–1: Production model; torpedo-bomber version; as J–0; internal bomb-bays; 950hp DB 600CGs (90).
Total Production: 7,300+ (all Marks).
Remarks: Perhaps best remembered of all Germany's wartime bombers, Heinkel's He 111—unlike Dornier Do 17 and Junkers Ju 88 series—did not undergo progressive development, but instead retained its basic configuration until very end of WWII; entering service late 1936, operational debut (30 He 111B–1s) with Condor Legion in Spain early following year; by Sept 1939 most early stepped-cockpit models withdrawn from Luftwaffe first-line service; saw limited action Polish and Norwegian campaigns (latterly in transport role), before relegation to training and secondary duties; remained in service with both Spanish and Turkish AFs throughout war years; operational details of Chinese AF's ten He 111A–0s obscure.

Manufacturer: Heinkel.
Model: He 111H–16.
Type: Medium bomber.
Power Plant: Two 1,350hp Junkers Jumo 211F–2.
Performance:
maximum speed at sea level 217mph (330km/hr).
maximum speed at 19,685ft (6.000m) 252mph (405km/hr).
normal range 1,200 miles (1,930km).
time to 19,685ft (6,000m) 42min 0sec.
max service ceiling 27,890ft (8,500m).
Weights:
empty 19,136lb (8,680kg).
maximum 30,865lb (14,000kg).
Dimensions:
wing span 74ft 1¾in (22.6m).
length 53ft 9½in (16.4m).
height 13ft 1½in (3.4m).
wing area 931.07sq ft (86.5sq m).
Armament: One 20mm MG FF cannon and one (optional) 7.9mm MG 15 machine-gun in nose; one 13mm MG 131 machine-gun in dorsal position; two 7.9mm MG 81 machine-guns in ventral gondola; one 7.9mm MG 15 or MG 81, or two MG 81 machine-guns in two beam positions; max bomb load (external and internal) 7,165lb (3,250kg).
Crew: 5.
In Service: Germany, Great Britain (2+ evaluation), Hungary (1 He 111H), Rumania (65 He 111H–3), Slovakia (+ He 111H–3).
Variants (with no. built):
He 111 V19: Prototype; re-engined He 111P–0; 1,010hp Jumo 211A–1s; 4-crew bomber version.
He 111H–0: Pre-production model; as P–2 Jumo 211A–1s; three MG 15s.
He 111H–1: Production model; as H–0.
He 111H–2: Re-engined H–1; 1,100hp Jumo 211A–3s; later models with increased armament as P–4.
He 111H–3: Bomber/anti-shipping version; 1,200hp Jumo 211D–1s; modified H–2; one/two addn crew; max bomb load (internal) 4,410lb (2,000kg); auxiliary fuel tanks; one 20mm MG FF cannon in ventral gondola; major series, inc licence-production in Rumania (30).
He 111H–4: Jumo 211D–1s or (late models) 1,400hp supercharged Jumo 211F–1s; 2,205kg bomb load (starboard bomb bay), plus 3,968lb (1,800kg) externally to port.
He 111H–5: Improved H–4; Jumo 211D–1s; increased fuel capacity; external bomb load only.
He 111H–6: Bomber/torpedo-bomber version; modified H–5; Jumo 211F–1s; max bomb load 5,512lb (2,500kg) or torpedoes or mines; five MG 15s, one MG FF plus (optional) one MG 17 in tail cone; five crew; major series.
He 111H–7, 9: As H–6; minor equipment changes.
He 111H–8: As H–3 and H–5; balloon-cable fender and cutting array forward of nose; increased weight; reduced bomb load (30 H–3 and H–5 conversions); some subsequently converted to glider-tugs (H–8/R2).
He 111H–10: Night-bomber version; modified H–6; increased armour plating; Jumo 211F–2s; integral balloon-cable cutters (Kuto-Nase); MG FF cannon in nose, and MG 15 in ventral gondola; otherwise armament as H–6.
He 111H–11: Modified H–10; revised armament; MG 131 in enclosed dorsal position; MG 15 in gondola replaced by two 7.9mm MG 81s; increased armour plating; bomb load (external) 2,755lb (1,250kg).
He 111H–11/R1,/R2: MG 15s in beam positions replaced by MG 81s, and glider-tug version resp; H–11 conversions.
He 111H–12: Four-crew missile-carrier version; two Henschel Hs 293A; ventral gondola deleted; FuG 203b 'Kehl', plus FuG 230b 'Strassburg' in missiles; four MG 15s.
He 111H–14: Pathfinder version; modified H–10; FuG 'Samos' and FuG 351 'Korfu'; one MG FF, 4–5 MG 15s or 81s; twenty completed without special radio equipment as glider-tugs (H–14/R2).
He 111H–15: Carrier version for three 3 BV glider bombs; subsequently converted as night-bomber with 2 BV.
He 111H–16: Improved H–6; Jumo 211F–2s; armour plating as H–11; revised armament; major series.
He 111H–16/R1, /R2, /R3: As H–16; dorsal turret with MG 131, glider-towing coupling, and increased armour plating/reduced bomb load (Pathfinder) resp.
He 111H–18: Night-bomber version; as H–16/R3; improved radio equipment; armament as H–14; 6 crew.
He 111H–20/R1: Paratroop-transport version; modified H–16; ventral jump hatch; 3 crew, 16 paratroops; increased armament.
He 111H–20/R2: Glider-tug version; armament as H–16; 5 crew.
He 111H–20/R3: Night-bomber version; as H–20/R2; provision for 4,410lb (2,000kg) bomb load.
He 111H–20/R4: Night-bomber/interceptor version; as H20/R3; provision for 2,204lb (1,000kg) external bomb load.
He 111H–21: Night-bomber version; re-engined H–20/R3; 1,750hp Jumo 213E–1s or (early models) 211Fs; three MG 131s plus two MG 81Z; max bomb load 6,615lb (3,000kg).
He 111H–22: Missile-carrier version; one Fi 103 (V1) underwing; 100+ H–21 conversions.
He 111H–23: Transport version; 8 paratroops; 1,776hp Jumo 213A–1s.
(Total He 111H–0/–23 production: approx 6,150).
He 111 V32: Prototype; high-altitude bomber version; two supercharged DB 601U.
He 111R–1/–2: High-altitude bomber versions; Jumo 211Fs or DB 603Us resp; projects only.
He 111Z V1, 2: Prototypes; glider-tug version for Me 321 heavy transport glider; two H–6 fuselages connected by addn wing centre section five Jumo 211F–2s; H–6 conversions.
He 111Z–1 'Zwilling' (Twin): Production model; 9 crew; various armament; three converted from H–6 and five from H–16 airframes.
He 111Z–2/–3: Long-range bomber/reconnaissance versions; projects only.
Total Production: 7,300+ (all Marks).
Remarks: Major production variant, He 111H was re-engined development of chronologically earlier P-model; served alongside He 111P

Heinkel He 60A

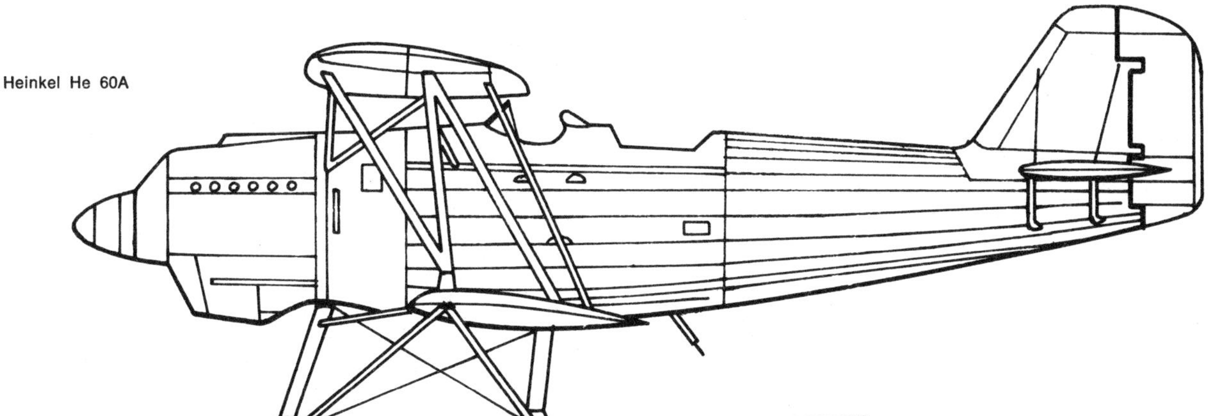

Heinkel He 70F–1

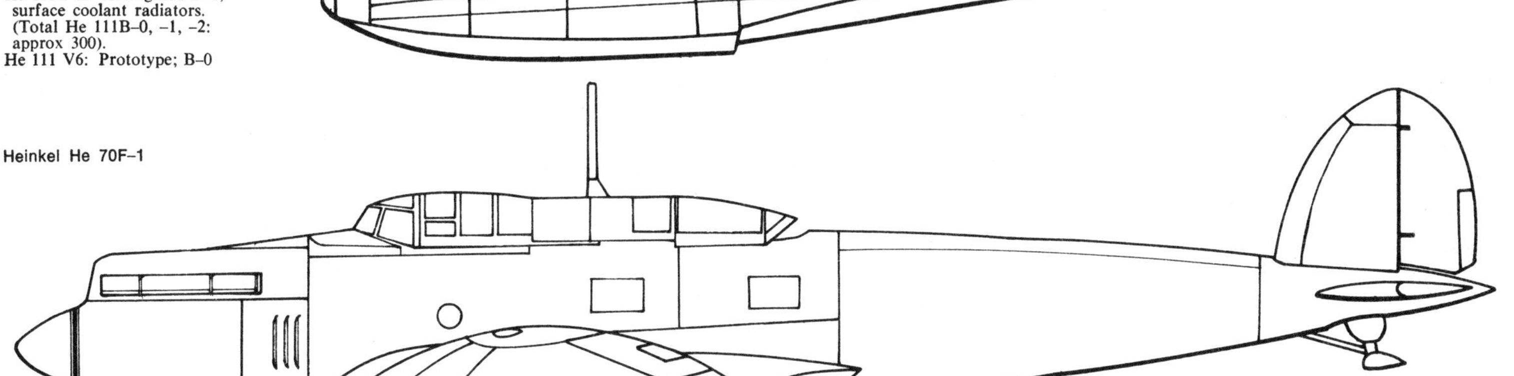

Heinkel He 112B–1

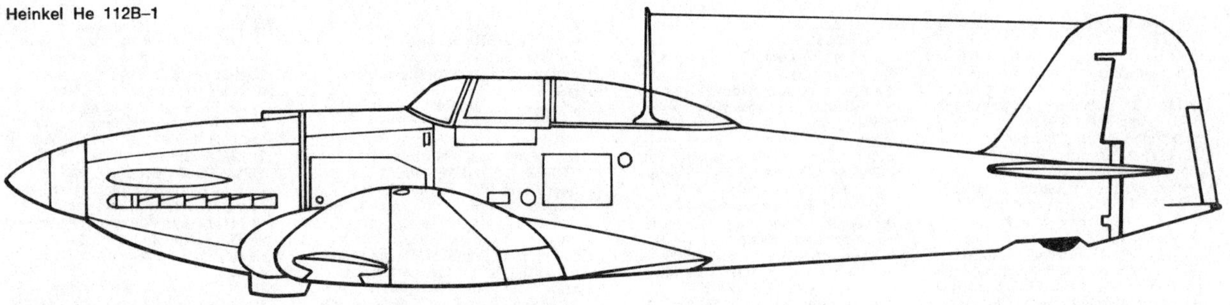

throughout all major offensives early part WWII—Poland, Scandinavia, Low Countries and France, Battle of Britain, and night Blitz of 1940–41; subsequently operated Mediterranean and Eastern Fronts; also employed in anti-shipping torpedo-bomber role, particularly against Arctic convoys, 1942; scored one of last major successes of Luftwaffe's strategic bomber arm on night of 21–22 June 1944—destruction of nearly 60 US heavy bombers and fighters on ground at Poltava in USSR after shuttle-bombing of Berlin; 1944–45 used as missile-carriers (H–22) to air-launch V1 rockets against UK; approx 1,200 missiles launched for loss of nearly 80 carriers; from 1942 He 111 also played increasing part in transport role and as glider-tug; participated aerial supply Stalingrad, Winter 1942–43 (over 150 Heinkels lost); employed as paratroop-transport during Battle of Ardennes; closing stages of war supplied German garrisons isolated in French Channel and Atlantic ports; altogether equipped over thirty Kampfgruppen, ten Transportgruppen, plus number of reconnaissance and experimental units.

Manufacturer: Heinkel.
Model: He 111P–2.
Type: Medium bomber.
Power Plant: Two 1,020hp Daimler-Benz DB 601Aa.
Performance:
maximum speed 249mph (400km/hr).
cruising speed 224mph (360km/hr).
maximum range 1,243 miles (2,000km).
service ceiling 24,278ft (7,400m).
Weights:
empty 17,673lb (8,015kg).
normal 29,326lb (13,300kg).
Dimensions:
wing span 73ft 9¾in (22.5m).
length 53ft 9¾in (16.4m).
height 13ft 2¼in (4.02m).
wing area 931.09sq ft (86.5sq m).
Armament: One 7.9mm MG 15 machine-gun each in nose, dorsal position and ventral gondola; max bomb load 4,410lb (2,000kg).
Crew: 4.
In Service: Germany, Hungary (10 He 111P–6).
Variants (with no. built):
He 111 V7, 8: Prototypes; modified B–0; two DB 601A or 600A resp; wing as He 111F; redesigned fully glazed nose and cockpit area; V7 ventral gondola in lieu of retractable 'dustbin' turret; glazed faring over dorsal gun position; two B–0 conversions.
He 111P–0: Pre-production model; as V7; three MG 15s; max bomb load (internal) 4,410lb (2,000kg).
He 111P–1: Production model; FuG III radio.
He 111P–2: As P–1; FuG III replaced by FuG X.
He 111P–3: Dual-control trainer version; P–0 and P–1 conversions.
He 111P–4: Modified P–2; armour plating; increased armament; two MG 15s in nose, one MG 15 each in two beam positions, dorsal position, and ventral gondola plus (optional) one MG 17 in tail cone; max bomb load (internal) 2,205lb (1,000kg), provision for 2,205lb (1,000kg) external bomb load; auxiliary fuel tanks.
He 111P–6: Re-engined P–4; 1,175hp DB 601Ns; internal bomb load as P–0; modified dorsal gun position.
He 111P–6/R2: Transport glider-tug conversions of P–6; He 111P–0/–6 production; Heinkel, Dornier and Arado-built (approx 400).
Total Production: 7,300+ (all Marks).
Remarks: First model to feature asymmetrical fully-glazed nose, He 111P series curtailed due to near-total commitment of Daimler-Benz engine production to fighter programme; after extensive service early campaigns of WWII, gradually supplanted by improved Jumo-powered He 111H models; continued use in transport and glider-tug roles (latter towing Gotha Go 242) primarily Mediterranean and Eastern Front theatres.
Colour Reference: Plate 27: Fully-armed Heinkel He 111P–4 (VG+ES) assigned Korpskette X. Fliegerkorps (X Air Corps HQ Flight); Mediterranean theatre, 1941–42; desert finish VG+ES employed by successive Fliegerführer Afrika, Generalmajor Fröhlich and Generalleutnant Hoffman von Waldau, in Western Desert campaigns of Winter 1941–42.

Manufacturer: Heinkel.
Model: He 112B–1.
Type: Fighter.
Power Plant: One 700hp Junkers Jumo 210G.
Performance:
maximum speed 317mph (510km/hr).
normal range 684 miles (1,100km).
time to 19,685ft (6,000m) 10min 0sec.
service ceiling 27,887ft (8,500m).
Weights:
empty 3,570lb (1,620kg).
loaded 4,960lb (2,250kg).
Dimensions:
wing span 29ft 10¼in (9.1m).
length 30ft 6in (9.3m).
height 12ft 7½in (3.85m).
wing area 182.99sq ft (17.0sq m).
Armament: Two 20mm MG FF cannon in wings; two 7.9mm machine-guns in fuselage; provision for four 22lb (10kg) bombs.
Crew: 1.
In Service: Germany, Hungary (V9,3 B–1s), Japan (IJNAF V12, 12 B–0), Rumania (13 B–0, 11 B–1), Spain (17 B–0).
Variants (with no. built):
He 112 V1/6: Prototypes; projected He 112A; various power plants and armament; wing and tail design changes (6).
He 112 V7/12: Prototypes; redesigned fuselage, wing and tail surfaces; various power plants, inc one B–0 conversion to V11 (5).
He 112B–0: Pre-production model; 680hp Jumo 210Ea (43).
He 112B–1: Production model; as B–0 Jumo 210G; revised exhaust system (14).
He 112E: Export version; Jumo 210G, 210Ea or DB 601Aa; project only.
A7He1: IJNAF designation for He 112B–0 (*12*).
Total Production: 68.
Remarks: Loser to Bf 109 in 1935 competition to determine He 51/Ar 68 replacement, Heinkel's He 112 subsequently offered for export; 12 delivered to IJNAF, Spring 1938; after briefly equipping one Luftwaffe Gruppe during time of München (Sudeten) crisis, further export deliveries to Spain (operated by NatAF during and post-Civil War). Rumania (employed over Russian front, 1941–42), and Hungary (evaluation only, again losing out to Bf 109 competitor).

Manufacturer: Heinkel.
Model: He 114A–2.
Type: Maritime reconnaissance floatplane.
Power Plant: One 960hp BMW 132K.
Performance:
maximum speed at 3,280ft (1,000m) 208mph (335km/hr).
cruising speed 183mph (295km/hr).
maximum range 571 miles (920km).
time to 3,280ft (1,000m) 4min 18sec.
service ceiling 16,075ft (4,900m).
Weights:
empty 5,070lb (2,300kg).
maximum 8,090lb (3,670kg).
Dimensions:
wing span 44ft 7½in (13.6m).
length 38ft 2¼in (11.65m).
height 17ft 2in (5.23m).
wing area 455sq ft (42.3sq m).
Armament: One fixed forward-firing 7.9mm MG 17 machine-gun; 7.9mm MG 17 machine-gun in rear cockpit; max bomb load 220lb (100kg).
Crew: 2.
In Service: Germany, Rumania (18), Spain (NAF approx 3), Sweden (14).
Variants (with no. built):
He 114 V1/5: Prototypes; various power plants; wingtip, float and canopy modifications (5).
He 114A–0: Service Trials and pre-production model; clipped wings; 880hp BMW 132Dc or uprated BMW 132K; some with catapult points (10).
He 114A–1: Initial production model; trainer version; 865hp BMW 132N; redesigned vertical tail surfaces; modified cockpit; 2- or 3-blade propeller; Weser-built (33).
He 114A–2: As A–1; strengthened fuselage; catapult points; BMW 132K; (early models BMW 132N); subsequently converted to export version.
He 114B–1/2: Export versions of A–2; Swedish (14) and Rumanian (6) orders resp; Weser-built (20).
He 114B–3: Export version; Rumanian order; two addn fixed 7.9mm MG 17s; Weser-built (12).
He 114C–1: As A–2; one addn fixed forward-firing 7.9mm MG 17 (14).
He 114C–2: Unarmed A–2; ship-borne (commerce raider) version (4).
Total Production: approx 98.
Remarks: Twin-float sesquiplane design first flown 1936; limited WWII Luftwaffe service Baltic, Black Sea and Eastern Mediterranean areas, 1941–43; exported to Sweden and Rumania (Black Sea coastal reconnaissance); several also supplied to Spain to replace earlier He 60 aboard Spanish Navy cruisers.

Manufacturer: Heinkel.
Model: He 115C–1.
Type: General-purpose/torpedo-bomber floatplane.
Power Plant: Two 960hp BMW 132K.
Performance:
maximum speed at 3,280ft (1,000m) 186mph (300km/hr).
maximum range 1,740 miles (2,800km).
time to 3,280ft (1,000m) 5min 6sec.
Weights:
empty 15,146lb (6,870kg).
loaded 23,545lb (10,680kg).
Dimensions:
wing span 73ft 1in (22.28m).
length 56ft 9¾in (17.3m).
height 21ft 7¾in (6.59m).
wing area 933.23sq ft (86.7sq m).
Armament: One flexible 7.9mm MG 15 machine-gun and one fixed forward-firing 15 mm MG 151 cannon in nose; one fixed rearward-firing 7.9mm MG 17 machine-gun in each engine nacelle; plus one flexible 7.9mm MG 15 machine-gun in rear cockpit; max bomb load 2,756lb (1,250kg) or one 1,102lb (500kg) torpedo, or mines.
Crew: 3.
In Service: Germany, Finland (1 He 115A–2 ex-Norway), Great Britain (2 He 115A–2 ex-Norway, 1 He 115B–1 ex-Germany), Norway (15 He 115A–2, plus 2 captured He 115B–1), Sweden (10 He 115A–2).
Variants (with no. built):
He 115 V1/4: Prototypes; various control surface and cockpit modifications (4).
He 115A–0: Pre-production model; general-purpose floatplane; max bomb load 2,756lb (1,250kg) (10).
He 115A–1: Initial production model; torpedo-carrier version; increased weight (34).
He 115A–2: Export version; as A–1; minor equipment changes; revised armament (18).
He 115A–3: Improved A–1; revised radio equipment; modified bomb bay; torpedo-release mechanism.
He 115 V5: Prototype; modified He 115A–0; increased fuel capacity; structural strengthening; one conversion.
He 115B–0: Pre-production model; as V5; modified wings; Weser-built (10).
He 115B–1: Production model.
He 115B–1/R1: As B–1; photo-graphic-reconnaissance; two addn cameras.
He 115B–1/R2: As B–1; provision for one 1,102lb (500kg) bomb.
He 115B–1/R3: As B–1; provision for one 2,028lb (920kg), or two 1,102lb (500kg) mines.
He 115B–2, B–2/R1 to R3: As B–1, B–1/R1 to R3 resp; reinforced floats; eighteen B–1 conversions.
He 115C–1, C–1/R1 to R3: As B–1/R1 to R3 resp; one addn 15mm MG 151 cannon in nose, plus one addn rearward-firing 7.9mm MG 17 in each engine nacelle.
He 115C–2, C–2/R1 to R3: As C–1, C–1/R1 to R3 resp; reinforced floats.
He 115C–3, C–3/R1 to R3: Mine-laying version; as C–1, C–1/R1 to R3 resp.
He 115C–4, C–4/R1 to R3: Arctic torpedo-bomber version; modified C–1, C–1/R1 to R3 resp; nose

Heinkel He 115B–2

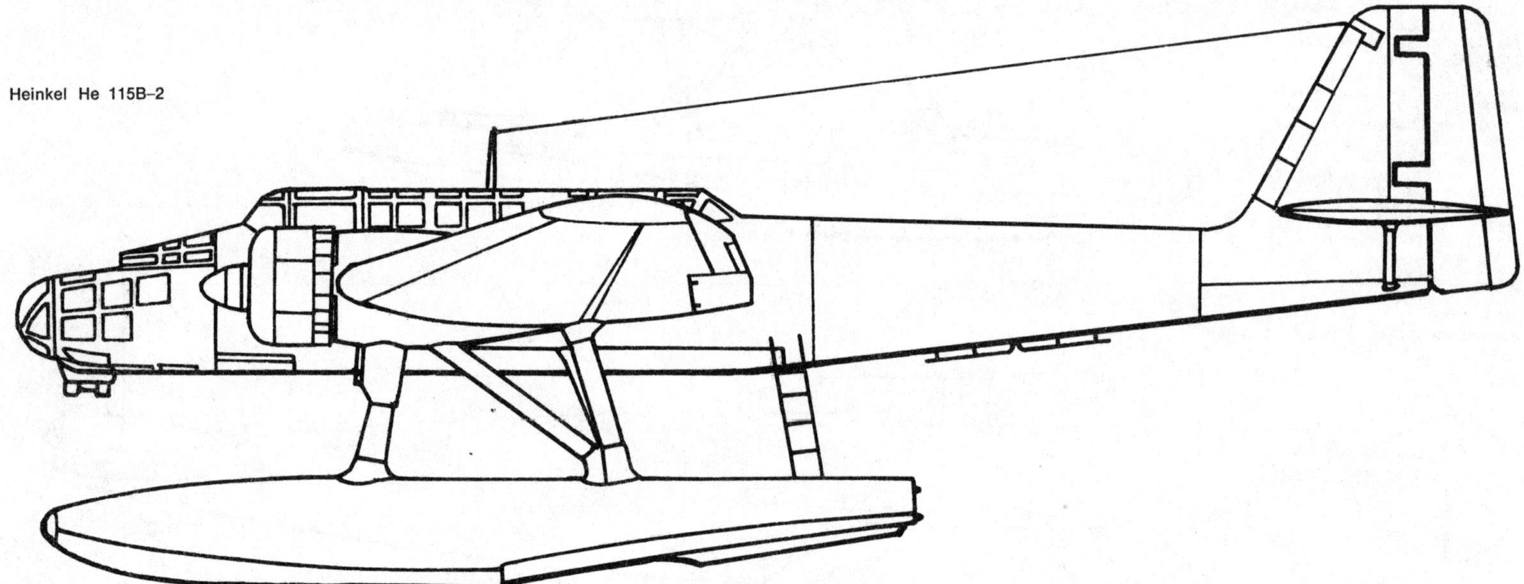

guns deleted.
He 115C–1/R4, C–2/R4, C–3/R4, C–4/R4: As C–1, C–2, C–3, C–4 resp; convoy-escort versions; smoke-laying equipment.
(Total He 115B–1 to He 115C–4/R4, Weser-built: 66).
He 1150: Improved version; 1,600hp BMW 801 Mas; one addn crew; revised armament; one conversion.
Total Production: 142.
Remarks: Standard Luftwaffe attack and reconnaissance floatplane for most of WWII; carried out aerial minelaying UK coastal waters, Winter 1939–40; participated invasion of Norway and subsequent North Sea actions, culminating in attack on Arctic Convoy PQ 17 in July 1942; remained in first-line service in Far North until mid-1944; also limited employment Mediterranean area on convoy-escort duties; equipped total of 12 Staffeln (sqns); pre-war exports to Sweden and Norway, latter (each reportedly delivered with one fuel tank full of Schnapps) subsequently saw action against Luftwaffe He 115B–1s during April–June 1940 campaign; three Norwegian examples escaped, taken in charge by RAF, and later employed on special-duties missions in Mediterranean.

Manufacturer: Heinkel.
Model: He 116B.
Type: Communications/ cartographic-reconnaissance.
Power Plant: Four 240hp Hirth HM 508H.
Performance:
maximum speed at sea level 178mph (286km/hr).
maximum speed at 9,840ft (3,000m) 202mph (325km/hr).
cruising speed 164mph (264km/hr).
normal range 2,120 miles (3,400km).
time to 3,280ft (1,000m) 4min 12sec.
service ceiling 21,680ft (6,600m).
Weights:
empty 8,862lb (4,020kg).
loaded 15,533lb (7,045kg).
Dimensions:
wing span 72ft 2in (22.0m).
length 46ft 11in (14.3m).
height 10ft 10in (3.3m).
wing area 677.06sq ft (62.9sq m).
Crew: 4.
In Service: Germany.
Variants (with no. built):
He 116A (V1/8): Prototypes; long-range civil mail plane (8).
He 116B (V9/14): Prototypes; militarised; long-range reconnaissance; fully-glazed unstepped nose (6).
He 116R: Designation given to V3(A–03) modified for long-distance international record flight.
Total Production: 14.
Remarks: Designed as long-range mail carrier for DLH's South Atlantic and Far Eastern routes; two (V5/6) supplied Manchurian Air Lines of Japan; He 116Bs' Luftwaffe service limited to internal photographic-mapping and communications duties over Germany and German-held territories.

Manufacturer: Heinkel.
Model: He 162A–2.
Type: Interceptor fighter.
Power Plant: One 1,764lb s.t. BMW 003E–1 or E–2.
Performance:
maximum speed at 19,685ft (6,000m) 562mph (905km/hr).
maximum range 606 miles (975km).
initial rate of climb 1,950ft/min (595m/min).
service ceiling 39,400ft (12,000m).
Weights:
empty 3,666lb (1,663kg).
normal 5,744lb (2,605kg).
Dimensions:
wing span 23ft 7½in (7.2m).
length 29ft 8¼in (9.05m).
height 8ft 6½in (2.6m).
wing area 120.56sq ft (11.2sq m).
Armament: Two 20mm MG 151 cannon in fuselage sides.
Crew: 1.
In Service: Germany.
Variants (with no. built):
He 162A–0 (V1/10): Prototypes and pre-production model; BMW 003A–1 'Sturm' turbojet; FuG 25a and FuG 24R/T; two 30mm MK 108 or (V8/10) MG 151; modified tail and (from V3) anhedral wingtips (10).
He 162A–1: Initial production model; two MK 108s; superseded by A–2.
He 162A–2: Major production model; as A–1. MG 151s; increased tailplane span: BMW 003E, inc V18 to V24.
He 162A–3: As A–2; MK 108s; none completed.
He 162V25/30: Prototypes; lengthened fuselage; MK 108s; V29 armament test aircraft; V30 experimental gunsight.
He 162A–6: As V25/28; project only.
He 162 V11, V12: Prototypes; A–2 airframes; Jumo 004D turbojet.
He 162A–8: As V11 and V12; project only.
He 162 V14, V15: A–2 test airframes.
He 162A–9, –14: Projects only.
He 162B/E: Projects only.
He 162 V16, V17: Prototypes; dual-control training glider version; modified A–2.
He 162S: As V16 and V17; project only.
Total Production: 270+.
Remarks: Variously known as 'Spatz' (Sparrow), 'Salamander', or more popularly 'Volksjäger' (People's Fighter), He 162 prototype was built and flown in space of just over ten weeks late in 1944; emphasis placed on mass-production, both of aircraft (planned output of 4,000 per month), and of pilots to fly them (to be culled from ranks of Hitler Youth); neither of these grandiose schemes came to fruition however, and sole operational unit to receive 'Volksjäger', one reconstituted Jagdgruppe, was formed only four days prior to official cessation of hostilities in Europe.

Manufacturer: Heinkel.
Model: He 170A.
Type: Short/medium-range reconnaissance.
Power Plant: One 910hp Manfred Weiss WM–K–14.
Performance:
maximum speed at 11,155ft (3,400m) 258mph (415km/hr).
maximum cruising speed 236mph (380km/hr).
maximum range 570 miles (920km).
time to 3,280ft (1,000m) 2min 42sec.
service ceiling 27,200ft (8,290m).
Weights:
empty 5,071lb (2,300kg).
loaded 7,804lb (3,540kg).
Dimensions:
wing span 48ft 6¾in (14.8m).
length 37ft 4¾in (11.5m).
height 10ft 7½in (3.24m).
wing area 392.88sq ft (36.5sq m).
Armament: Two flexible 8mm Gebauer machine-guns in rear cockpit.
Crew: 3.
In Service: Hungary.
Variants (with no. built):
He 170 V1: Re-engined He 70F–3; one conversion.
He 170A: Production model; A–01/2 with French-built engines (18).
Total Production: 18.
Remarks: Re-engined (Hungarian licence-built Gnome-Rhône 14K Mistral-Major) and re-numbered export version of pre-war He 70 Blitz (Lightning) high-speed civil transport and military reconnaissance aircraft, He 170's operational debut was in action against newly-created state of Slovakia during Hungarian re-occupation of Carpatho-Ruthenia, March 1939; subsequently saw limited service opening weeks German invasion of Soviet Union, June–July 1941, flying less than 30 sorties before lack of adequate defensive armament and insufficient range forced its withdrawal.

Manufacturer: Heinkel.
Model: He 177A–1/R1 Greif (Griffon).
Type: Heavy bomber.
Power Plant: Two 2,700hp Daimler-Benz DB 606 (two DB 601).
Performance:
maximum speed at 19,030ft (5,800m) 317mph (510km/hr).
cruising speed 267mph (430km/hr).
maximum range 3,480 miles (5,600km).
service ceiling 22,966ft (7,000m).
Weights:
empty 35,494lb (16,100kg).
maximum 66,139lb (30,000kg).
Dimensions:
wing span 103ft 1¾in (31.44m).
length 66ft 11in (20.4m).
height 20ft 11¾in (6.39m).
wing area 1,097.92sq ft (102.0sq m).
Armament: One 7.9mm MG 81J machine-gun in nose; one forward-firing 20mm MG FF cannon and two rearward-firing 7.9mm MG 81 machine-guns in ventral gondola; plus one 13mm MG 131 each in dorsal barbette and tail position; max bomb-load 13,230lb (6,000kg).
Crew: 5.
In Service: Germany.
Variants (with no. built):
He 177 V1/8: Prototypes; progressive modifications to nose section, tail surfaces, and (from V5) armament. 3/4 crew (8).
He 177A–0: Pre-production model; three 7.9mm MG 81, one 13mm MG 131, plus one 20mm MG FF; Heinkel-built (30); Arado-built (5).
He 177A–1/R1–R4: Production models; various armament; R4 with addn dorsal turret; Arado-built (130).
He 177A–3/R1: Modified A–1; lengthened fuselage; addn dorsal turret.
He 177A–3/R2–R5, R7: Various equipment and armament modifications; R3 with three HS 293 missiles; R5 (Stalingrad type) with 75mm 7.5 anti-tank gun; R7 with LT 50 torpedoes; all He 117A–3s: Heinkel and Arado-built (170).
He 117A–4: High-altitude version; project only; re-designated He 274 and completed (post-war) by French as AAS 01A.
He 177A–5/R2–R8: Bomber/ anti-shipping versions; 2,900hp DB 610A–1/B–1; modified under-carriage; Fowler flaps deleted; three torpedoes or mines; triple bomb-bay; various addn armaments (565).
He 177A–6/R1: Long-range bomber version; addn armament; tail turret in lieu of rear dorsal turret; He 117A–5 conversions (6).
He 177 V22: Modified A–6; redesigned nose; revised armament; one conversion.
He 177A–7: High-altitude bomber version; two DB 613; increased wing span; one He 177A–5 conversion.
He 177B: Redesigned He 117A–3; four separate DB 603A; pressurized cabin; revised armament; one He 177A–3 conversion; (7 subsequently built as He 277).
Total Production: 909.
Remarks: Only purpose-built four-engined strategic heavy bomber to see widespread Luftwaffe service in WWII, He 177 featured unique coupled power plants, whose propensity to ignite plagued its operational career; combat debut Summer 1942, sporadic bombing raids on U.K.; participated supply missions to Stalingrad early 1943; also operated in anti-shipping role (with Hs 293 missiles) over Atlantic and Mediterranean, Winter 1943–44; reappeared over UK during Operation 'Steinbock', Jan–May 1944; employed against Soviets on Eastern Front, Summer 1944, missions ranging from massed 90-bomber raids down to individual low-level attacks on Russian armour; altogether operated by nine Kampfgruppen, plus several experimental units.
Colour Reference: Plate 22: Heinkel He 177A–5 Greif (V4+LN) of II./KG 1 Hindenburg; Prowehren, East Prussia, July 1944; subordinated directly to Lfl.Kdo.6, II. Gruppe deployed total of 67 Heinkel He 177s; note combination night undersurface finish with mottled upper surfaces.

Manufacturer: Heinkel.
Model: He 219A–5/R2 Uhu (Owl).
Type: Night-fighter.
Power Plant: Two 1,800hp Daimler-Benz DB 603E.
Performance:
maximum speed at sea level 391mph (630km/hr).
cruising speed 310mph (500km/hr).
maximum range 1,740 miles (2,800km).
initial rate of climb 1,772ft/min (540m/min).
service ceiling 37,073ft (11,300m).
Weights:
empty 21,826lb (9,900kg).
loaded 28,990lb (13,150kg).
Dimensions:
wing span 60ft 8¼in (18.5m).
length 50ft 11¾in (15.54m).
height 13ft 5¼in (4.10m).
wing area 478.99sq ft (44.5sq m).
Armament: Two 20mm MG 151 cannon in wings; two 30mm MK 108 cannon in ventral tray; two oblique upward-firing 30mm MK 108 cannon in rear fuselage.
Crew: 2.
In Service: Germany.
Variants (with no. built):
He 219 V1/10: Prototypes; 1,750hp DB 603As; various armament; modified fuselage and tail V4/10 with FuG 212 Lichtenstein radar (10).
He 219A–0: Pre-production model; two 20mm MG 151s in wings, four MG 151s in ventral tray, plus one 13mm MG 131 in rear cockpit.
He 219A–0/R–1 to R–6: As A–0; various ventral armament and/or oblique upward-firing dorsal 'Schräge Musik' installation.
(Total He 219A–0, A–0/R–1: 130).
He 219A–1: Proposed production model DB 603 with GM 1 power booster (2).
He 219A–2: Initial production model; DB 603As; two MG 151s in wings, two MK 108 'Schräge Musik'; plus two MG 151s (or MK 103s) in ventral tray; He 219A–2/R1 (or R2) resp (40).
He 219A–3, –4: 3-seat fighter bomber and high-altitude reconnaisance-bomber versions resp; projects only.
He 219A–5: Modified A–2; alternative DB 603E, G, or Aa; two MG 151 cannon in wings, plus two MK 108s each in ventral tray and in 'Schräge Musik' installation.
He 219A–5/R1 to R4: As A–5; various ventral armament or (A–5/R4); one addn crew; modified canopy.
He 219A–6: Re-engined A–5; anti-mosquito interceptor version; DB 603Ls with GM 1; ventral and wing armament only; reduced weight.
He 219A–7: High-altitude version; DB 603Gs; increased armour plating; addn SN–2 search radar and FuG 218 Neptun; improved radio equipment; two MK 108s in wings plus two MK 103 and two MG 151 cannon in ventral tray; various altn or addn armament in Rüstsätzen (He 219A–7/R1 to R4), or alt power plants (He 219A–7/R5, R6).
He 219B–1: High-altitude version; 1 addn crew; lengthened fuselage; increased wing area; modified canopy (1).
He 219B–2: Anti-Mosquito interceptor version; modified A–6; DB 603Aa or L.
He 219B–3: Modified B–2; project only.
He 219C–1, –2: Night-fighter and fighter-bomber versions resp; re-designed fuselage; 4 crew; ventral tray deleted; C–2 with three 1,102lb (500kg) bombs; prototypes only.
Total Production: 294.

Heinkel He 162A–2

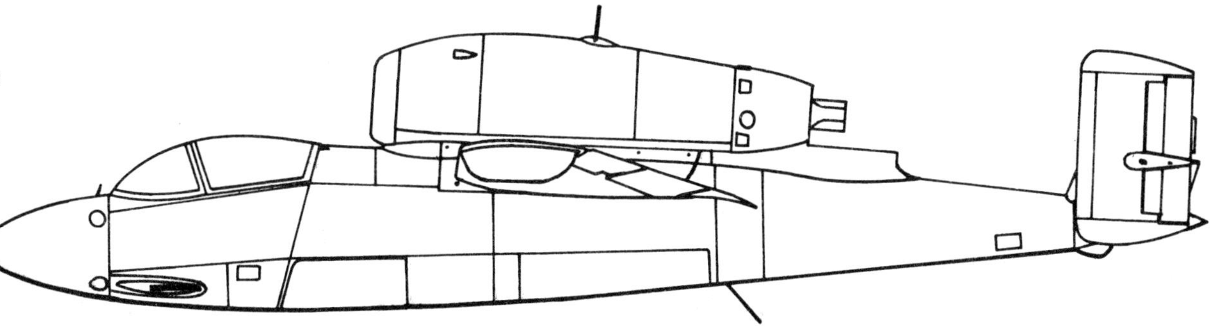

Heinkel He 219A–7/R4 Uhu

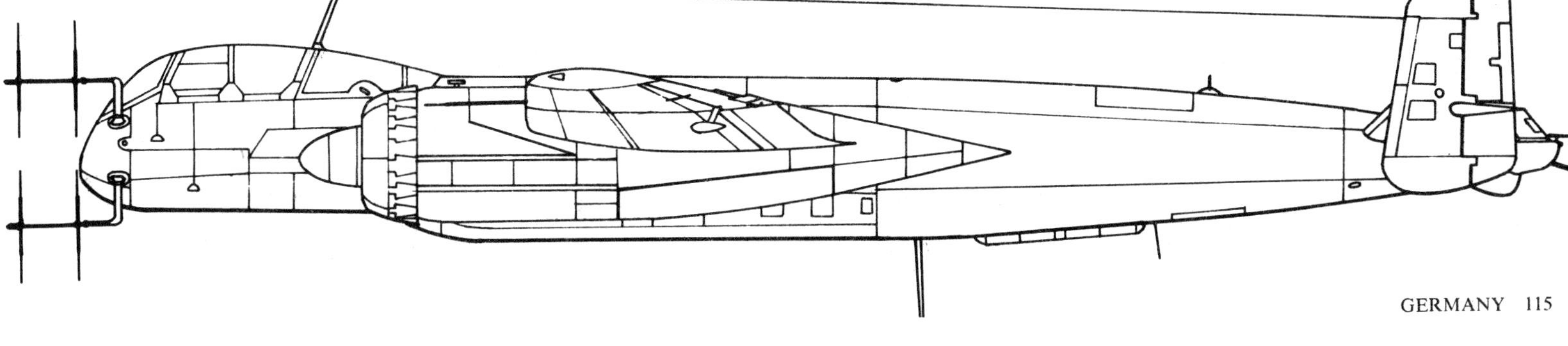

Henschel Hs 123A–1

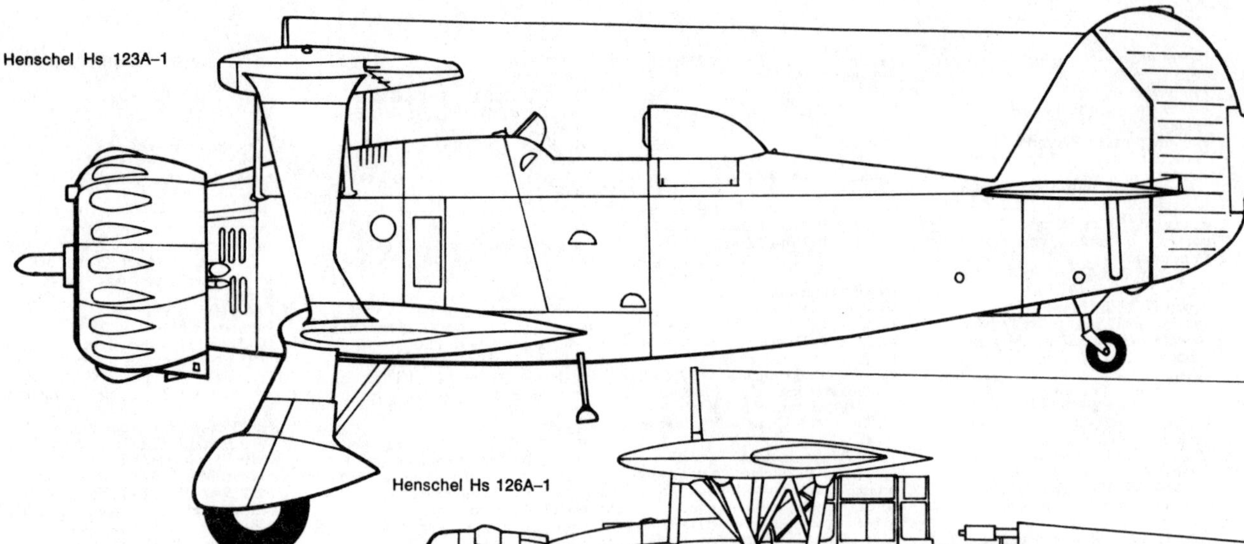

Henschel Hs 126A–1

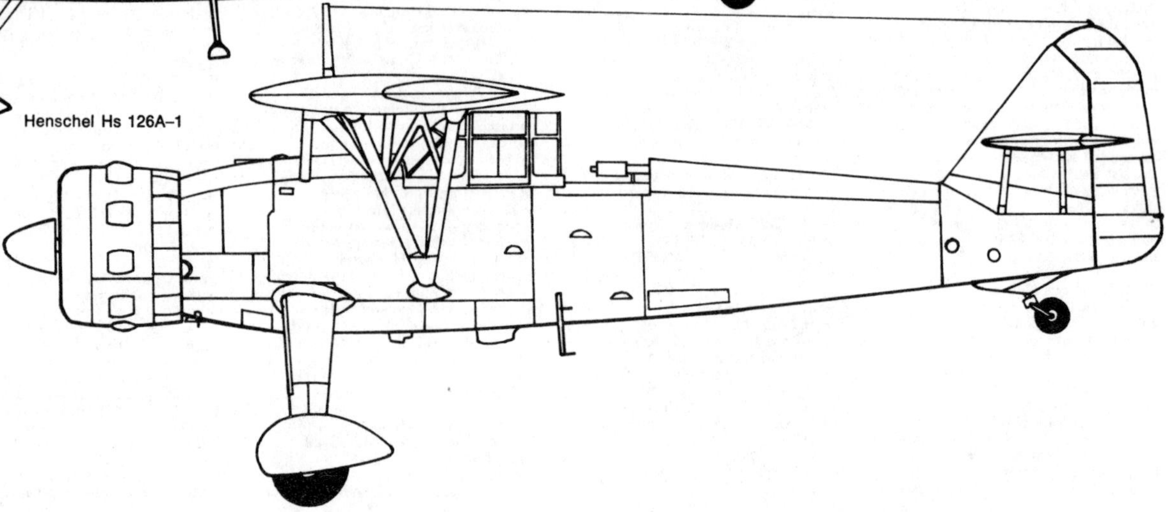

Remarks: Germany's first night-fighter (combat debut marked by a single example's claiming the destruction of five RAF Lancasters in thirty minutes), the He 219's operational career was dogged by political irresolution; launched as a private venture, and despite acclaim from service personnel, its development was finally abandoned in favour of two other designs, both complete failures; continued limited production by Heinkel, in the face of official interference, ensured its remaining in service until the end of the war, albeit in far fewer numbers than either the Ju 88 or Bf 110; only two night-fighter Gruppen, plus a specialized anti-Mosquito unit, being fully equipped with the type.

Manufacturer: Henschel.
Model: Hs 123A–1.
Type: Dive-bomber/ground-attack.
Power Plant: One 880hp BMW 132Dc.
Performance:
maximum speed at 3,940ft (1,200m) 213mph (342km/hr).
cruising speed 197mph (317km/hr).
range 534 miles (860km).
initial rate of climb 2,950ft/min (900m/min).
service ceiling 29,525ft (9,000m).
Weights:
empty 3,316lb (1,504kg).
normal 4,888lb (2,217kg).
Dimensions:
wing span—upper 34ft 5½in (10.50m).
lower 26ft 3in (8.00m).
length 27ft 4in (8.33m).
height 10ft 6½in (3.21m).
wing area 267.483sq ft (24.85sq m).
Armament: Two fixed forward-firing 7.9mm MG 17 machine-guns; two (optional) 20mm MG FF cannon on underwing racks; max bomb load 992lb (450kg).
Crew: 1.
In Service: Germany, Spain (NatAF 16).
Variants (with no. built):
Hs 123 V1/V4: Prototypes; 650hp BMW 132A–3; cowling modifications; two- or three-blade propeller (4).
Hs 123A–1: Production model; uprated engine (604).
Hs 123 V5/V6: Prototypes for projected B- and C-series resp; 960hp BMW 132K or 132DC; one (V6) with two addn 7.9mm MG 17 machine-guns and enclosed cockpit (2).
Total Production: 60+.
Remarks: Entering service 1936, Hs 123 biplane briefly equipped pre-war Luftwaffe dive-bomber units; five examples despatched to Spain late 1936; operational experience with Condor Legion revealed true close-support potential; (sixteen Hs 123As, inc ex-Condor Legion machines, subsequently supplied to Spanish AF); on outbreak of WWII forty Hs 123As equipped Luftwaffe's sole specialized ground-attack Gruppe; participated Polish, French, and Balkan campaigns; continued to serve on Eastern Front until mid-1944; demands from front-line that production of obsolescent but highly-effective Hs 123 (terminated in 1938) be resumed proved impracticable.

Manufacturer: Henschel.
Model: Hs 126B–1.
Type: Tactical reconnaissance.
Power Plant: One 850hp BMW-Bramo Fafnir 323A–1 or Q–1, or one 900hp 323A–2 or Q–2.
Performance:
maximum speed at sea level 193mph (310km/hr).
maximum speed at 9,840ft (3,000m) 221mph (356km/hr).
normal range 360 miles (560km).
time to 13,130ft (4,000m) 7min 14sec.
service ceiling 27,000ft (8,230m).
Weights:
empty 4,480lb (2,032kg).
maximum 7,209lb (3,270kg).
Dimensions:
wing span 47ft 6¾in (14.5m).
length 35ft 7in (10.84m).
height 12ft 3¼in (3.74m).
wing area 340.14sq ft (31.6sq m).
Armament: One fixed forward-firing 7.9mm MG 17 machine-gun in fuselage; one flexible 7.9mm MG 15 machine-gun in rear cockpit; max bomb load 331lb (150kg).
Crew: 2.
In Service: Germany, Greece (16 Hs 126A–1s), Spain (5 Hs 126A–1s).
Variants (with no. built):
Hs 126 V1: Initial prototype; modified Hs 122B–0 airframe; 610hp Junkers Jumo 210C (1).
Hs 126 V2/3: Prototypes; redesigned rudder; addn tailplane bracing struts; 850hp supercharged Bramo Fafnir 323A–1 (2).
Hs 126A–0: Pre-production model (10).
Hs 126A–1: Initial production model; 880hp BMW 132Dc.
Hs 126 B–1: Re-engined A–1; improved radio equipment; FuG 17 VHF.
(Total Hs 126A–1, B–1: approx 800).
Total Production: 810+.
Remarks: Operational debut with Condor Legion 1938 (five examples subsequently transferred to Spanish NatAF), Hs 126 was Luftwaffe's standard tactical reconnaissance aircraft by outbreak WWII, equipping 80% all such units; extensive use early campaigns, up to and including invasion of Soviet Union, before replacement by Fw 189 during 1942; Hs 126 thereafter employed in glider-tug role, and by night ground-attack Gruppen in Balkans (for anti-partisan operations), and in Baltic (by Estonian and Latvian volunteer units); Greek export models (delivered 1939) saw intensive action during Italian invasion, Winter 1940–41.

Manufacturer: Henschel.
Model: Hs 129B–2.
Type: Ground-attack/anti-tank aircraft.
Power Plant: Two 700hp Gnome-Rhône 14M 4/5.
Performance:
maximum speed at 12,570ft (3,830m) 253mph (407km/hr).
cruising speed 196mph (315km/hr).
range 429 miles (690km).
initial rate of climb 1,595ft/min (486m/min).
service ceiling 29,530ft (9,000m).
Weights:
empty 8,400lb (3,810kg).
maximum 11,574lb (5,250kg).
Dimensions:
wing span 46ft 7in (14.20m).
length 31ft 11¾in (9.75m).
height 10ft 8in (3.25m).
wing area 312.153sq ft (29.0sq m).
Armament: Two 7.9mm MG 17 (or two 13mm MG 131) machine-guns in wings; two fixed forward-firing 20mm MG 151 cannon in fuselage; one (optional) 30mm MK 101 (or MK 103) cannon in ventral pack; or (B–2/R3) two fixed forward-firing 20mm MG 151 cannon in fuselage; one 37mm BK 3.7in ventral pack; max bomb load 771lb (350kg).
Crew: 1.
In Service: Germany, Rumania (62 Hs 129B).
Variants (with no. built):
Hs 129 V1/3: Prototypes; two 465hp Argus 410A–1s (3).
Hs 129A–0: Pre-production model; two subsequently re-engined with Gnome-Rhône 14 Ms (8).
Hs 129B–0: Pre-production model; modified Hs 129A–0; revised armament; improved canopy; Gnome-Rhône 14 Ms (16).
Hs 129B–1: Initial production model; minor equipment changes.
Hs 129B–2: Modified B–1; various armament; some with specialised anti-tank armament (B–2/R3 and /R4).
(Total Hs 129B–1, –2: 843).
Hs 129B–3: As Hs 129B–2/R4; 75mm BK 7.5 (modified 75mm Pak 40L) in jettisonable ventral fairing; no wing guns; approx 25 Hs 129B–2 conversions.
Hs 129C: Improved version; 840hp Isotta-Fraschini Delta RCs; project only.
Total Production: 870.
Remarks: Heavily-armoured Hs 129 plagued throughout operational career by power plant troubles; original A-models seriously under-powered; captured Gnome-Rhônes utilized in re-engined B-series prone to seizure and highly vulnerable even to small-arms fire; limited service closing stages North African campaign; primarily employed against Soviet armour on Eastern front; participated Operation 'Zitadelle', German offensive against Kursk salient, July 1943, claiming large proportion of over 1,000 Russian tanks destroyed from the air; also appeared briefly over Normandy; more than half total number Hs 129Bs supplied to Rumanian AF in 1943 later used against Axis (German and Hungarian) ground forces following Rumanian capitulation of Aug 1944 and subsequent pursuance of war on side of Soviets.
Colour Reference: Plates 33, 34: Henschel Hs 129B–1 of II./Schl.G 2: Tunis-El Aouina, May 1943; slightly damaged in earlier crash-landing, red 'C' abandoned/captured intact by Allied forces; sand-brown mirror wave over standard two-tone green; note replacement starboard spinner.

Manufacturer: Junkers.
Model: F 13.
Type: Transport.
Power Plant: 280hp Junkers–L5.
Performance:
cruising speed 106mph (170km/hr).
range 528 miles (850km).
service ceiling 16,732ft (5,100m).
Weights:
empty 3,263lb (1,480kg).
loaded 5,512lb (2,500kg).
Dimensions:
wing span 58ft 2¾in (17.75m).
length 34ft 5⅓in (10.5m).
wing area 473.62sq ft (44.0sq m).
Crew/Accommodation: 2/4.
In Service: Finland.
Variants (with no. built):
F 13: Prototype; 160hp Mercedes D.IIIa (1).
F 13a–k: Production models; various power plants; landplane/floatplane versions; 60–70 individual variants (321).
F 13L, S, W: Alternative generic designations for wheeled, ski, or float undercarriage versions resp.
Total Production: 322.
Remarks: Reportedly born of a design meeting held on Armistice Day, 1918, highly-advanced, all-metal F 13 first flew June 1919; true pioneer of air transport, extensive use Europe, South Africa, and the Americas; two Finnish Coast Guard examples employed during Winter War of 1939–40; joined by third, arriving early 1940 with Swedish volunteer sqn; latter subsequently taken over by Finnish AF; served in Continuation War, 1941–44.

Manufacturer: Junkers.
Model: G 31.
Type: Freighter.
Power Plant: Three 525hp BMW Hornet.
Performance:
maximum speed 133mph (214km/hr).
range 740 miles (1,190km).
service ceiling 14,107ft (4,300m).
Weights:
empty 11,400lb (5,171kg).
loaded 18,740lb (8,500kg).
Dimensions:
wing span 99ft 5in (30.3m).
length 56ft 8¼in (17.28m).
wing area 1,097sq ft (102sq m).
Crew/Payload: 2/5,800lb (2,630kg).
In Service: Australia.
Variants (with no. built):
G 31: Prototype; three 28/310hp Junkers–L5 (1).
G 31a–f, h: Civil airliners; 11–15 passengers; three 450hp Gnome-Rhône Jupiters or three 525hp BMW Hornets (9).
G 31g: Freighter version/s; inc modified prototype (4).
Total Production: 13.
Remarks: 1926 development of earlier, smaller, G 24 trimotor, G 31 operated pre-war both by German and Austrian airlines; four examples delivered New Guinea early thirties for freighting supplies and heavy equipment into Bulolo goldfields; three subsequently destroyed by enemy action early months Pacific war, fourth impressed into RAAF 1942.

Manufacturer: Junkers.
Model: W 34h.
Type: Transport/communications.
Power Plant: 660hp BMW 132.
Performance:
maximum speed 165mph (265km/hr).
normal range 560 miles (900km).
time to 3,280ft (1,000m) 3min 14sec.
service ceiling 20,670ft (6,300m).
Weights:
empty 3,748lb (1,700kg).
loaded 7,055lb (3,200kg).
Dimensions:
wing span 58ft 2¾in (17.75m).
length 33ft 8¼in (10.27m).
height 11ft 7in (3.53m).
wing area 462.85sq ft (43.0sq m).
Crew/Accommodation: 2/6 (or cargo).
In Service: Australia (1 W 34d, 1 W 34f), Croatia, Finland (6 W 34, 6 K 43), Germany, Rumania, Slovakia (6 W 34), USSR (1+ ex-Slovak).
Variants (with no. built):
W 33: Prototype; modified F 13; 280hp Junkers–L5; 1 conversion.
W 33a–h: Production model; various power plants; landplane/floatplane versions; 30 individual variants (199).
W 34: Prototype; modified F 13;

420hp Gnome-Rhône Jupiter VI; 1 conversion.
W 34a–h: Production models; various power plants; landplane/floatplane versions; civil and military; 70+ individual variants (1,791).
K 43: Military export model; light reconnaissance-bomber; various power plants; three 7.62mm machine-guns; max bomb load 660lb (300kg); landplane/floatplane (K 43L/W) versions; Junkers (and AB Flygindustri licence)-built.
Tp 2A: Swedish AF designation of W 34h; 605hp Bristol Mercury VIA; AB Flygindustri licence-built.
Total Production: 1,991 (excl K 43).
Remarks: In-line and radial-engined developments of earlier F 13 resp, W 33 and W 34 general-purpose cargo/passenger transports saw world-wide service throughout late twenties and thirties; extensively employed by Luftwaffe duration WWII in communications/training roles, (plus limited use original Störkampfstaffeln early 1943); W 34s also supplied to Croatia, Slovakia, Rumania, and Finland (latter in use until 1952); two (believed ex-Guinea) impressed into RAAF, 1942; one Swedish Tp 2A used for air-ambulance duties, 1935–61; pre-war K 43 deliveries inc Argentina, Bolivia, Finland, and Portugal (NAF).

Manufacturer: Junkers.
Model: G 38b 'Hindenburg'.
Type: Heavy transport.
Power Plant: Four 750hp Junkers Jumo 204.
Performance:
maximum speed 134mph (215km/hr).
cruising speed 129mph (208km/hr).
normal range 1,181miles (1,900km).
service ceiling 12,140ft (3,700m).
Weights:
empty 32,804lb (14,880kg).
loaded 52,910lb (24,000kg).
Dimensions:
wing span 144ft 4¼in (44.0m).
length 76ft 1⅓in (23.20m).
height 23ft 7½in (7.20m).
wing area 3,229.2sq ft (300sq m).
Crew/Accommodation: 7/34.
In Service: Germany.
Variants (with no. built):
G 38: Prototype; civil transport; two 400hp Junkers–L 8, plus two 800hp Junkers–L 88 (1).
G 38b: Production model; deepened fuselage; double-deck passenger cabin (1).
Total Production: 2.
Remarks: First flown 1929, ambitious G 38 based upon early Junkers 'Nurflügel' (wing-only) concept; first prototype crashed at Dessau, 1936; G 38b, named 'Generalfeldmarschall von Hindenburg', impressed by Luftwaffe on outbreak WWII; participated Norwegian campaign, April 1940, and in Balkans April 1941; destroyed in RAF bombing raid on Athens airfield, 17 May 1941.

Manufacturer: Junkers.
Model: Ju 52/3m g3e.
Type: Medium bomber/transport.
Power Plant: Three 725hp BMW 132A–3.
Performance:
maximum speed at sea level 165mph (265km/hr).
cruising speed 130mph (209km/hr).
normal range 620 miles (1,000km).
time to 9,840ft (3,000m) 17min 30sec.
service ceiling 19,360ft (5,900m).
Weights:
empty 12,610lb (5,720kg).
maximum 23,146lb (10,500kg).
Dimensions:
wing span 95ft 11½in (29.24m).
length 62ft 0in (18.9m).
height 18ft 2½in (5.55m).
wing area 1,189.41sq ft (110.5sq m).
Armament: One 7.9mm MG 15 machine-gun each in open dorsal position and semi-retractable ventral 'dustbin'; max bomb load 1,102lb (500kg).
Crew: 4.
In Service: Germany, Portugal (10 Ju 52/3m g3e), Spain, Switzerland (3 Ju 52/3m g4e).
Variants (with no. built):
Ju 52: Prototype; civil cargo transport version; one 725hp BMW VII (1).
Ju 52a–d: Initial production; as prototype; various alternative power plants; progressive modifications; land/floatplanes (4).
Ju 52/3m ce, de, fe: Redesigned Ju 52; three-engined civil transport versions; various power plants; Ju 52/3m de minus engine cowlings and wheel spats.
Ju 52/3m ge: Initial 17-passenger transport version; three 660hp BMW 132A–1s; majority subsequently completed as auxiliary bombers.
Ju 52/3m g3e: Initial bomber-transport version; uprated engines; improved radio equipment; two 7.9mm MG 15s; Junkers-, Weser-, and ATG-built.
Ju 52/3m g4e: Bomber-transport version; heavier load capacity tailskid replaced by tailwheel; improved equipment; some with ventral 'dustbin' deleted; 12 converted as convoy-escorts. (Total Ju 52/3m g3e, g4e: 500+).
Total Production: approx 4,850 (all Marks).
Remarks: Vying with Douglas DC–3/C–47 series for pride of place as world's most famous transport aircraft, Ju 52 first flew as single-engined cargo transport; developed as tri-motor airliner, nearly 200 saw world-wide service with almost 30 airlines prior WWII; formed initial equipment Luftwaffe's first bomber Gruppen, subsequently participating Spanish Civil War; equipped both Condor Legion and Spanish NatAF; by outbreak WWII formed backbone German transport strength, all but 5 of 613 transport aircraft on charge as at 1 Sept 1939, being Ju 52s, inc 59 DLH impressments; pre-war military deliveries to Portugal (as night-bomber), and Switzerland (served in transport role 1939–69).

Manufacturer: Junkers.
Model: Ju 52/3m g7e.
Type: Medium transport.
Power Plant: Three 830hp BMW 132T–2.
Performance:
maximum speed at sea level 169mph (272km/hr).
maximum speed at 4,590ft (1,400m) 178mph (286km/hr).
cruising speed 160mph (257km/hr).
normal range 930 miles (1,500km).
time to 9,840ft (3,000m) 19min 0sec.
service ceiling 18,000ft (5,500m).
Weights:
empty 14,328lb (6,500kg).
loaded 24,320lb (11,030kg).
Dimensions:
wing span 95ft 10in (29.2m).
length 62ft 0in (18.9m).
height 14ft 10in (4.52m).
wing area 1,189.41sq ft (110.5sq m).
Armament: One 7.9mm MG 15 (or 13mm MG 131), in open aft dorsal position; one (optional) 7.9mm MG 15 machine-gun each in forward upper and two beam positions.
Crew/Accommodation: 3/18 troops or 12 litters.
In Service: Bulgaria (2), Croatia, France, Germany, Great Britain (2+ captured), Hungary (7), Norway (NorNAF 1), Rumania (31), Slovakia (2), South Africa (11 impressed), USA (1 captured/impressed as C–79), USSR (80+ captured).
Variants:
Ju 52/3m g5e: Re-engined Ju 52/3m g4c; three 830hp BMW 132T–2s; interchangeable wheel, ski, or float undercarriage; ventral gun replaced by two beam guns.
Ju 52/3m g6e: Transport version; as g5e; improved radio equipment; some completed as floatplanes.
Ju 52/3m g7e: Modified Ju 52/3m g5e; transport version; autopilot; enlarged loading hatch; extended cowlings; some with addn MG 15 in cockpit upper glazing (Condor-Haube).
Ju 52/3m g8e: Modified Ju 52/3 g6e; addn loading hatch in cabin roof; alternative BMW 132Z engines; some with 13mm MG 131 in lieu of dorsal MG 15.
Ju 52/3m g8e(E), (F), (H), (N), (R), (S): Modified Ju 52/3m g8e with standard conversion kits for cargo; paratroop transport; flying-classroom; supply; courier; and squadron support transport duties.
Ju 52/3m (MS): Mine-sweeper; Ju 52/3m g4e to g8e conversions; KK-Gerät (anti-acoustic explosives device), or braced dural hoop.
Ju 52/3m g9e: Three BMW 132Zs; strengthened undercarriage; glider-towing couplings.
Ju 52/3m g12e: Civil and military transport version; three 800hp BMW 132L.
Ju 52/3m g14e: Transport version; armour-plating; revised armament; cockpit cupola.
All Ju 52/3m g5e–g14e: Junkers, and Weser-built, plus French (AAC)-, Spanish (CASA)-, and Hungarian (PIRT)- licence production/assembly.
Total Production: approx 4,850 (all Marks).
Remarks: Progressive development of original Ju 52/3m, the 'Tante Ju' (Auntie Junkers) served as Wehrmacht workhorse throughout WWII; performing multiplicity of roles, predominantly as transport, played active part every campaign and on every front; suffered heavy losses invasions of Norway, France and Low Countries, and airborne assault on Crete; as war progressed increasingly engaged supply/evacuation operations, inc Stalingrad and Tunisia, again taking heavy casualties; also supplied many satellite AFs; but second largest user (after Germany) was USSR, repairing over eighty Ju 52s captured at time of Stalingrad for service with wartime para-military Aeroflot; continued post-war production in both France (as AAC.1 Toucan), and Spain (as CASA 352); extensive post-war use both military, and as civil transport

Order of Battle 26 June 1944, Western Front

GERMAN AIR FORCE (Luftwaffe)

LUFTFLOTTE 3 (AIR FLEET 3) PARIS:

Strategic reconnaissance:			
Stab/FAGr.123	Toussus le Buc		Focke-Wulf Fw 190 Junkers Ju 188
4.(F)/123	St. André	9	Messerschmitt Bf 109
5.(F)/123	Monchy-Breton	8	Messerschmitt Bf 109
1.(F)/121	Toussus le Buc	7	Messerschmitt Me 410

II.Fliegerkorps (II Flying Corps) Chartres
Fl. Fü. West (Schlacht) (Flying Leader West (Ground-attack)):

Tactical reconnaissance:			
Stab/NAGr.13	Chartres		Messerschmitt Bf 109 Focke-Wulf Fw 190
1./NAGr.13	Chartres	11	Messerschmitt Bf 109 Focke-Wulf Fw 190
3./NAGr.13	Laval	10	Messerschmitt Bf 109 Focke-Wulf Fw 190
Ground-attack:			
III./SG 4 III./SG 4 (det)	Clermont-Ferrand Averd	52	Focke-Wulf Fw 190

IX.Fliegerkorps (IIX Flying Corps) Beauvais-Tille

Strategic reconnaissance:			
3.(F)/122	Soesterberg	7	Junkers Ju 188
6.(F)/123	Cormeilles	6	Junkers Ju 88 Junkers Ju 188
Bombers:			
Stab/KG 2	Gilze Rijen	4	Junkers Ju 188
I./KG 2	Gilze Rijen	10	Junkers Ju 188
II./KG 2	Gilze Rijen		Junkers Ju 188
III./KG 2	Hesepe	6	Dornier Do 217
5./KG 76	Gilze Rijen		Junkers 88
III./KG 3	Hesepe		Heinkel He 111
Stab/KG 6	Melun-Villaroche		Junkers Ju 188
I./KG 6	Melun-Villaroche	16	Junkers Ju 188
II./KG 6	Melun-Villaroche		Junkers Ju 188
III./KG 6	Melun-Villaroche	7	Junkers Ju 188
Stab/KG 30	Zwischenahn		Junkers Ju 88
I./KG 30	Leck	20	Junkers Ju 88
4.KG 51 & 6./KG 51	Soesterberg	14	Messerschmitt Me 410
5./KG 51	Gilze Rijen		Messerschmitt Me 410
Stab/KG 54	Eindhoven	2	Junkers Ju 88
I./KG 54	Eindhoven	14	Junkers Ju 88
III./KG 54	Eindhoven	13	Junkers Ju 88
I./KG 66	Montdidier	6	Junkers Ju 88 Junkers Ju 188
Eins.St.IV./KG 101	St. Dizier	6	Junkers Ju 88
Stab/LG 1	Melsbroek	1	Junkers Ju 88
I./LG 1	Le Culot	13	Junkers Ju 88
II./LG 1	Melsbroek	13	Junkers Ju 88
Fighter-bombers:			
I./SKG 10	Tours	19	Focke-Wulf Fw 190

X.Fliegerkorps (X Flying Corps) Angers

Strategic/maritime reconnaissance:			
Stab/FAGr.5 1.(F)/5 2.(F)/5	Mont de Marsan Mont de Marsan Mont de Marsan	15	Junkers Ju 290
4.(F)/5	Nantes	4	Junkers Ju 290
3.(F)/123	Corme Ecluse	7	Junkers Ju 88
1.(F)/SAGr.129	Biscarosse	4	Blohm und Voss Bv 222
Bombers:			
Stab/KG 40	Bordeaux-Mérignac		Focke-Wulf Fw 200
1./KG 40 & 2./KG 40	Toulouse-Blagnac	12	Heinkel He 177
II./KG 40	Bordeaux-Mérignac	12	Heinkel He 177
7./KG 40 8./KG 40 & 9./KG 40	St. Jean d'Angely Cognac	23	Focke-Wulf Fw 200

2.Fliegerdivision (2nd Flying Division) Montfrin:

Strategic/tactical/maritime reconnaissance:			
1.(F)/33	St. Martin	11	Junkers Ju 88 Messerschmitt Me 410
2./NAGr.13	Cuers	10	Messerschmitt Bf 109 Focke-Wulf Fw 190
2./SAGr.128	Berre	4	Arado Ar 196
Bombers:			
Stab/KG 26	Montpellier		Junkers Ju 88
II./KG 26 (LT)	Valence	27	Junkers Ju 88
III./KG 26 (LT)	Montpellier	22	Junkers Ju 88
III./KG 26 (LT)(det)	Valence		Junkers Ju 88
Stab/KG 77	Salon	1	Junkers Ju 88
I./KG 77 (LT)	Orange-Caritat	18	Junkers Ju 88
III./KG 77 (LT)	Orange-Caritat	16	Junkers Ju 88
6./KG 77	Istres	8	Junkers Ju 88
4./KG 76 & 6./KG 76	Istres	7	Junkers Ju 88
Stab/KG 100	Toulouse-Francazals	2	Dornier Do 217 Heinkel He 177
III./KG 100	Toulouse-Francazals	26	Dornier Do 217

II.Jagdkorps (II Fighter Corps) Chantilly
4.Jagddivision (4th Fighter Division) Metz:
(Jafü 4) – (Fighter-leader 4) St. Pol-Brias

Fighters:			
Stab/JG 1	St. Quentin-Clastres	3	Focke-Wulf Fw 190
I./JG 3	St. Quentin-Clastres	14	Messerschmitt Bf 109
I./JG 5	Mons en Chaussée	14	Messerschmitt Bf 109
II./JG 11	Mons en Chaussée	19	Messerschmitt Bf 109
I./JG 301	Epinoy	13	Messerschmitt Bf 109
Stab/JG 27	Champfleury	6	Messerschmitt Bf 109
I./JG 27	Vertus	39	Messerschmitt Bf 109
III./JG 27	Connantre	32	Messerschmitt Bf 109
IV./JG 27	Champfleury	31	Messerschmitt Bf 109
Night-fighters:			
Stab/NJG 4	Chenay	2	Messerschmitt Bf 110
I./NJG 4	Florennes	38	Junkers Ju 88
III./NJG 4	Junvincourt	18	Junkers Ju 88
Stab/NJG 5	Hagenau		Messerschmitt Bf 110
I./NJG 5	St. Dizier	15	Messerschmitt Bf 110
III./NJG 5	Athies s. Laon		Messerschmitt Bf 110

5.Jagddivision (5th Fighter Division) Jouy-en-Josas:
(Jafü 5)–(Fighter-leader 5) Bernay

Fighters:			
Stab/JG 2	Creil	2	Focke-Wulf Fw 190
I./JG 2	Creil	16	Focke-Wulf Fw 190
II./JG 2	Creil	46	Messerschmitt Bf 109
III./JG 2	Creil	18	Focke-Wulf Fw 190
Stab/JG 3	Evreux	3	Messerschmitt Bf 109 Focke-Wulf Fw 190
II./JG 3	Guyancourt		Re-equipping
III./JG 3	Mareilly	23	Messerschmitt Bf 109
II./JG 5	Evreux	51	Messerschmitt Bf 109
Stab/JG 11	Le Mans		Focke-Wulf Fw 190
I./JG 11	Le Mans	19	Focke-Wulf Fw 190
10./JG 11	Le Mans		Focke-Wulf Fw 190
I./JG 1	Alençon	17	Focke-Wulf Fw 190
II./JG 1	Alençon		Focke-Wulf Fw 190
Stab/JG 26	Guyancourt	3	Focke-Wulf Fw 190
I./JG 26	Guyancourt	27	Focke-Wulf Fw 190
II./JG 26	Guyancourt	12	Focke-Wulf Fw 190
Night-fighters:			
Stab/NJG 2	Coulommiers	4	Junkers Ju 88
I./NJG 2	Chateaudun	10	Junkers Ju 88
II./NJG 2	Coulommiers	24	Junkers Ju 88
II./NJG 4	Coulommiers	13	Junkers Ju 88

(Jafü Bretagne) – (Fighter-leader Brittany) Brest:

Fighters:			
II./JG 53	Vannes	32	Messerschmitt Bf 109

(Jafü Südfrankreich) – (Fighter-leader Southern France) Aix:

Fighters:			
1./JGr.200 & 3./JGr. 200 2./JGr.200	Orange-Caritat Avignon	34	Focke-Wulf Fw 190 Focke-Wulf Fw 190
Jagdlehrer–Gr. (Eins.Teile)	Marignane		Focke-Wulf Fw 190

(Fighter Instructors' Wing; operational detachments)

(Jagdabschnittsführer Bordeaux) – (Fighter sector-leader Bordeaux) Bordeaux-Mérignac:

Zerstörer (heavy fighters):			
Stab/ZG 1	Bordeaux-Mérignac	1	Junkers Ju 88
1./ZG 1 & 3./ZG 1	Corme Ecluse	4	Junkers Ju 88
2./ZG 1	Chateauroux	10	Junkers Ju 88
III./ZG 1	Cazaux	7	Junkers Ju 88

by many national airlines.
Colour Reference: Plates 36, 37: Junkers Ju 52/3m g6e attached to 1. kroat. Stukastaffel: Eichwale, East Prussia, Nov 1944; assigned for transport duties with Ju 87-equipped Croatian dive-bomber Staffel (itself part specialized anti-tank formation under control Stab SG 9 at nearby Schippenbeil); note standard Luftwaffe finish, definitive Croatian wing/fuselage crosses and Ustachi tail emblem.

Manufacturer: Junkers.
Model: Ju 86D-1.
Type: Medium bomber.
Power Plant: Two 600hp Jumo 205C-4.
Performance:
maximum speed at sea level 186mph (300km/hr).
maximum speed at 9,840ft (3,000m) 202mph (325km/hr).
cruising speed 171mph (275km/hr).
maximum range 932 miles (1,500km).
service ceiling 19,360ft (5,900m).
Weights:
empty 11,354lb (5,150kg).
loaded 17,770lb (8,060kg).
Dimensions:
wing span 73ft 10in (22.50m).
length 58ft 7½in (17.87m).
height 16ft 7¼in (5.06m).
wing area 882.64sq ft (82.0sq m).
Armament: One flexible 7.9mm MG 15 machine-gun each in dorsal position and semi-retractable ventral 'dustbin'; one hand-held 7.9mm MG 15 in nose; max bomb load 2,204lb (1,000kg).
Crew: 4.
In Service: Germany, Hungary (66 Ju 86 K-2), Manchuria (5 Ju 86Z-2), Portugal (10 Ju 86K-6), South Africa (17 Ju 86Z-7 impressments, 1 Ju 86K-1 evaluation), Sweden (60 Ju 86K, inc licence-production).
Variants (with no. built):
Ju 86a (V1): Initial prototype; two Siemens SAM 22 radials; subsequently armed (1).
Ju 86 V2, 5: Prototypes; bomber version; SAM 22s or Junkers Jumo 205Cs resp; various armament; modified wing (12).
Ju 86 V3, 4: Prototypes; civil transport version; Jumo 205Cs (2).
Ju 86A-0: Pre-production model; bomber version; modified Ju 86 V5 (13).
Ju 86A-1: Production model; revised nose; semi-retractable ventral gun position (approx 20).
Ju 86B-0: Pre-production civil transport (2).
Ju 86C-1: Modified Ju 86B-0; extended tail-cone (6).
Ju 86 V6: Modified Ju 86A-0; extended tail-cone; 1 conversion.
Ju 86D-1: Production model; as Ju 86 V6 (approx 140).
Ju 86 V9: Prototype; bomber version; modified Ju 86D-1; two 810hp BMW 132Fs; increased fuel capacity; 1 conversion.
Ju 86E-1: Production model; as Ju 86 V9 (30).
Ju 86E-2: As Ju 86E-1; two 865hp BMW 132N (approx 20).
Ju 86F-0/1: Civil transport versions; re-engined Ju 86C; two 770hp BMW 132D.
Ju 86 V10: Prototype; bomber version; modified Ju 86E-1; redesigned (hemispherical) fully-glazed nose; 1 conversion.
Ju 86G-1: Production model; as Ju 86 V10; BMW 132Fs or Ns; improved blind-flying equipment (40).
Ju 86K-1: Export bomber version of Ju 86E; 875hp Pratt & Whitney Hornets; 3 to Sweden (as B3) and 1 to South Africa (4).
Ju 86K-2: Hungarian order; Manfred Weiss-built Gnome-Rhône 14Ks (66).
Ju 86K-4: As K-1; 820hp Nohab-built Bristol Pegasus IIIs; Swedish order (B3A) (20).
Ju 86K-5: As K-1; 920hp Nohab-built Pegasus XIIs; Swedish order (B3B) (17).
Ju 86K-6: Portuguese, Chilean and Brazilian orders; Pratt & Whitney Hornets (25+).
Ju 86K-13: As K-1; 980hp Nohab-built Pegasus XXIVs or 835hp PZL-built Pegasus XIXs (B3C/D resp); Swedish (Saab) licence-built (16).
JU 86Z-1, 2, 7: Export versions; civil transports; Jumo 205s, BMW 132s, and Pratt & Whitney Hornets resp (33).
Total Production: 470 (all Marks).
Remarks: Less than completely successful Junkers design, first Jumo (diesel)-powered Ju 86s entered Luftwaffe service Spring 1936 as replacement for interim Ju 52 bomber, but had themselves completely disappeared from first-line inventory by outbreak WWII; continued to serve in ancillary training roles, plus participation Stalingrad airlift, Winter 1942–43, and brief use Balkans anti-partisan operations; export versions employed by Swedish AF 1937–1958, latterly in transport role; also equipped para-military Manchuria Air Transport; operational use in WWII by Hungary (on Eastern Front 1941–1942), and by South Africa (impressed Ju 86Z-7s converted for coastal patrol and for service as bombers against Italian forces in East Africa, 1941).
Colour Reference: Plate 38: Junkers Ju 86Z-7 (No 640) of No. 12 (Bomber) Squadron, SAAF; Mogadishu, Italian Somaliland, March 1941; modified ex-South African Airways airliners, SAAF Ju 87Z-7s finished bright green overall.

Manufacturer: Junkers.
Model: Ju 86R.
Type: High-altitude bomber/reconnaissance.
Power Plant: Two 1,000hp Junkers Jumo 207B-3.
maximum speed at 29,527ft (9,000m) 261mph (420km/hr).
maximum range 1,085 miles (1,750km).
service ceiling 47,250ft (14,400m).
Weights:
empty 14,947lb (6,780kg).
maximum 25,420lb (11,530kg).
Dimensions:
wing span 104ft 11¾in (32.0m).
length 54ft 0in (16.46m).
height 13ft 4¼in (4.07m).
wing area 1,049.48sq ft (97.5sq m).
Armament: One (optional) remotely-controlled rearward-firing 7.9mm MG 17 machine-gun; max bomb load 2,204lb (1,000kg).
Crew: 2.
In Service: Germany.
Variants:
Ju 86P V1/3: Prototypes; high-altitude version; 950hp Jumo 207A-1s; redesigned (pressurized) nose section; increased wing span; armament deleted; 3 Ju 86D conversions.
Ju 86P-1: Production model; high-altitude bomber version; max bomb load 2,204lb (1,000kg).
Ju 86P-2: High-altitude reconnaissance version; 3 cameras; some subsequently fitted with one remote-controlled 7.9mm MG 17 in rear fuselage:
(Total: Ju 86P-1/2:) approx 40 Ju 886D conversions:
Ju 86R-1: Ultra-high-altitude reconnaissance version; 1,000hp supercharged Jumo 207B-3s; further wing span increase; Ju 86P-2 conversions.
Ju 86R-2: High-altitude bomber version; Ju 86P-1 conversions.
Ju 86R-3: Improved Ju 86R-1; 1,500hp supercharged Jumo 208s; project only.
Total Production: approx 470.
Remarks: New lease of life afforded obsolescent Ju 86 bomber by conversion into high-altitude reconnaissance bomber; limited service P-1/2 variants over UK, 1940, over USSR prior to June 1941 invasion, and over North Africa, 1942–43; immunity challenged by specially modified high-altitude Spitfire Vs; three Ju 86Ps shot down over Mediterranean; led to introduction of improved Ju 86R, a few examples of which served with experimental Staffel 1943–44.

Manufacturer: Junkers.
Model: Ju 87A-1.
Type: Dive-bomber.
Power Plant: One 640hp Junkers Jumo 210Ca.
Performance:
maximum speed at 12,140ft (3,700m) 199mph (320km/hr).
cruising speed 171mph (275km/hr).
maximum range 620 miles (1,000km).
service ceiling 22,965ft (7,000m).
Weights:
empty 5,104lb (2,315kg).
maximum 7,495lb (3,400kg).
Dimensions:
wing span 45ft 3¼in (13.8m).
length 35ft 5¼in (10.78m).
height 12ft 9½in (3.89m).
wing area 343.37sq ft (31.9sq m).
Armament: One fixed forward-firing 7.9mm MG 17 machine-gun in starboard wing; one flexible 7.9mm MG 15 machine-gun in rear cockpit; max bomb load 551lb (250kg).
Crew: 2.
In Service: Germany, Japan (evaluation).
Variants (with no. built):
Ju 87 V1: Prototype; 640hp Rolls-Royce Kestrel V, twin fins and rudders (1).
Ju 87 V2/3: Prototypes; 610hp Junkers Jumo 210Aa; single fin and rudder (2).
Ju 87 V4: Production prototype; increased vertical tail surfaces; one 7.9mm MG 17 machine-gun in starboard wing (1).
Ju 87A-0: Pre-production model; 640hp Jumo 210Ca; one 7.9mm MG 15 in rear cockpit; simplified wing (10).
Ju 87A-1: Initial production model; as A-0.
Ju 87A-2: Improved A-1; 680hp Jumo D 210DA.
(Total Ju 87A-1, -2: 200).
Total Production: 5,709 (all Marks).
Remarks: Synonymous with Blitzkrieg campaigns of 1939–40, word 'Stuka'—although strictly the generic abbreviation for any dive-bomber type of aircraft—now indissolubly linked with Junkers inverted gull-winged Ju 87; prototype first flew 1935; A-1's operational debut Spring 1937; three examples despatched to Spain for service with Condor Legion late 1937; all A-models withdrawn from first-line service by outbreak WWII.

Manufacturer: Junkers.
Model: Ju 87B-1.
Type: Dive-bomber.
Power Plant: One 1,200hp Junkers Jumo 211Da.
Performance:
maximum speed at sea level 211mph (340km/hr).
maximum speed at 13,410ft (4,090m) 238mph (383km/hr).
cruising speed 175mph (282km/hr).
maximum range 490 miles (790km).
time to 6,560ft (2,000m) 4min 18sec.
service ceiling 26,150ft (8,000m).
Weights:
empty 5,980lb (2,710kg).
maximum 9,560lb (4,340kg).
Dimensions:
wing span 45ft 3¼in (13.8m).
length 36ft 5in (11.1m).
height 13ft 2in (4.01m).
wing area 343.368sq ft (31.9sq m).
Armament: Two fixed forward-firing 7.9mm MG 17 machine-guns in wings; one flexible 7.9mm MG 15 machine-gun in rear cockpit; max bomb load 1,102lb (500kg).
Crew: 2.
In Service: Bulgaria (12 Ju 87R-2, R-4), Germany, Great Britain (captured/evaluation), Hungary (approx 10 Ju 87B-2), Italy (Ju 87B-2, B-2/Trop), Rumania (approx 50 Ju 87B).
Variants (with no. built):
Ju 87 V6: Engine test-bed; 1,000hp Junkers Jumo 211A; one A-1 conversion.
Ju 87 V7: Prototype; modified A-2; Jumo 211A; redesigned canopy; enlarged vertical tail surfaces; undercarriage fairings replaced by spats (1).
Ju 87B-0: Pre-production model; as V7 (10).
Ju 87B-1: Production model; uprated Jumo 211Da; one addn MG 17 in (port) wing; Junkers- and Weser-built.
Ju 87B-1/U2: B-1 conversions; improved radio equipment.
(Total Ju 87B-1, B-1/U2: approx 350).
Ju 87B-2: Improved B-1; max bomb load 2,205lb (1,000kg); some tropicalized (B-2/Trop); Weser-built.
Ju 87B-2/U2, U3 U4: Modified B-2s; improved radio equipment, addn armour, and ski-undercarriage resp.
Ju 87C-0: Pre-production model; carrier-based dive-bomber version; navalised Ju 87B; catapult spools, arrestor hook; manually folding wings; jettisonable undercarriage.
Ju 87C-1: Production model; none completed; converted to B-2s.
Ju 87R-1: Long-range anti-shipping version; modified B-2; addn fuel capacity, inc underwing drop tanks; one 551lb (250kg) bomb.
Ju 87R-2/-4: Modified R-1s; minor equipment changes.
Total Production: 5,709 (all Marks).
Remarks: After combat debut with Condor Legion, Oct 1938, Ju 87B-1 quickly became standard Luftwaffe dive-bomber; by outbreak WWII equipped all nine Stukagruppen (342 aircraft); played major, if not decisive, part Polish and French campaigns; intervening invasion of Norway involved only one long-range Ju 87R Gruppe; suffered first serious reverses at hands of RAF Fighter Command over Channel/Southern England opening rounds Battle of Britain, Aug 1940; withdrawn at height of Battle, Ju 87B reappeared over Mediterranean early 1941; initially employed in anti-shipping role, subsequently participated Balkan, Crete and North African campaigns (inc reduction of Tobruk and Bir Hacheim), and attacks on Malta (by both Luftwaffe and Italian AF); nine Stukagruppen (inc one Rumanian, and totalling 361 aircraft) deployed for invasion of Soviet Union, 22 June 1941; faced with little aerial opposition, recaptured great measure earlier success before being replaced by first Ju 87Ds towards close of year.

Manufacturer: Junkers.
Model: Ju 87D-1.
Type: Dive-bomber/close-support.
Power Plant: One 1,400hp Junkers Jumo 211J-1.
Performance:
maximum speed at 13,500ft (4,100m) 255mph (410km/hr).
cruising speed 115mph (185km/hr).
maximum range 954 miles (1,535km).
time to 16,400ft (5,000m) 19min 48sec.
service ceiling 23,900ft (7,290m).
Weights:
empty 8,600lb (3,900kg).
maximum 14,550lb (6,600kg).
Dimensions:
wing span 45ft 3¼in (13.8m).
length 37ft 8¾in (11.5m).
height 12ft 9½in (3.88m).
wing area 343.37sq ft (31.9sq m).
Armament: Two fixed forward-firing 7.9mm MG 17 machine-guns in wings; one flexible 7.9mm twin MG 81Z in rear cockpit; max bomb load 3,968lb (1,800kg).
Crew: 2.
In Service: Bulgaria (approx 32 Ju 87D-5), Croatia (approx 15 Ju 87D), Germany, Great Britain (captured/evaluation), Hungary (approx 40 Ju 87D-1, approx 30 87D-5), Rumania (115 Ju 87D-1, -3, -5).
Variants (with no. built):
Ju 87 V21/25: Prototypes.
Ju 87D-1: Dive-bomber/close-support version; improved B-2; 1,400hp Jumo 211J-1; redesigned engine cowling and canopy; simplified undercarriage; enlarged vertical tail surfaces; increased armour/fuel capacity; two 7.9mm MG 17s in wings plus two MG 17s, or MG 81s, in rear cockpit; some tropicalized (D-1/Trop).
Ju 87D-2: Modified D-1; strengthened fuselage; glider-towing hook.
Ju 87D-3: As D-1; ground-attack version; increased armour plating.
Ju 87D-4: Intended torpedo-carrier version; D-1 and D-3 conversions/reconversions.
Ju 87D-5: Close-support/ground-attack version; increased wing span; jettisonable undercarriage; dive-brakes deleted.
Ju 87D-7: Night ground-attack version; modified D-3/D-5s; 1,500hp Jumo 211P; two 7.9mm MG 17s in wings replaced by 20mm MG 151 cannon; night-flying equipment; flame dampers.
Ju 87D-8: As D-7; night-flying equipment and flame-dampers deleted; D-5 conversions.
All Ju 87Ds Junkers- and Weser-built.
Ju 87E: Carrier-borne version; navalized Ju 78D; project only.
Ju 87F: Redesignated Ju 87D; increased wing span; 1,750hp Jumo 213; project only.
Ju 87G-1: D-5 conversions; anti-tank version; two 37mm BK 3.7 (Flak 18) cannon underwing.
Ju 87H-1, -3, -5, -7, -8: Dual-control trainer conversions of D-1, -3, -5, -7 and -8 resp; modified rear cockpit; bomb-racks and armament deleted.
Ju 187: Modified Ju 87F; 1,776hp Jumo 213A; retractable undercarriage; modified wing; project only.
Total Production: 5,709 (all Marks).
Remarks: Entered service late 1941, improved Ju 87D unable to sustain fearsome reputation of previous models for more than few months before growing strength Allied fighter power virtually drove it from daylight skies (with notable exception several areas where Luftwaffe still held local air superiority); employed mainly on Soviet Front, but also served North African, Italian and Eastern Mediterranean theatres; post-1943 equipped growing number night ground-attack Gruppen on Eastern Front, in Balkans, Italy and in West; specialised Ju 87G anti-tank version remained in action, almost exclusively against Soviet armour, until very end of hostilities; Axis satellite AF machines also operated predominantly against Russian ground-forces; many of those supplied to Rumania in 1943 subsequently employed against German targets after the Rumanian armistice of Aug 1944, while others, seized by Luftwaffe units, were in turn used against their erstwhile owners.
Colour Reference: Plate 35: Junkers Ju 87D-7 (HH) of 1./NSGr. 9, Caselle Torino, NE Italy, April 1944; night ground-attack finish comprising extensive grey mottle/mirror wave over standard two-tone green; note extended wingtips, flame damper exhaust, and Mk 250Bk flare canister on ventral pylon.

Manufacturer: Junkers.
Model: Ju 88A-4.
Type: Medium bomber/dive-bomber.
Power Plant: Two 1,340hp Junkers Jumo 211J-1 or J-2.
Performance:
maximum speed at 19,685ft (6,000m) 280mph (450km/hr).
cruising speed 230mph (370km/hr).
maximum range 1,696 miles (2,730km).
time to 17,716ft (5,400m) 23min 0sec.
service ceiling 26,900ft (8,200m).
Weights:
empty 21,737lb (9,860kg).
maximum 30,865lb (14,000kg).
Dimensions:
wing span 65ft 7½in (20.0m).
length 47ft 2¾in (14.4m).
height 15ft 11in (4.85m).
wing area 586.63sq ft (54.5sq m).
Armament: One fixed (or flexible) forward-firing 7.9mm MG 81 machine-gun in front cockpit; one flexible forward-firing 13mm MG 131 (or two 7.9mm MG 81) machine-guns in fuselage nose; two rearward-firing 7.9mm MG 81 machine-guns in rear cockpit; plus one 13mm MG 131 (or two 7.9mm MG 81) machine-guns, at rear of ventral nose gondola; max bomb load (internal and external) 7,935lb (3,600kg).
Crew: 4.
In Service: Finland (24 Ju 88A-4), France (FAF, FFAF), Germany, Hungary (approx 40 Ju 88A-4), Italy (Ju 88A-4), Rumania (50 Ju 88A-4/D-1).
Variants (with no. built):
Ju 88 V1/5: Initial prototypes; two 1,000hp DB 600A (V1, V2), 1,000hp Jumo 211A (V3, V4) or 1,200hp Jumo 211B-1 (V5); 3 or (V4) 4 crew; various armament; V5 subsequently converted to two-seat high-speed record-breaker (5).
Ju 88 V6/10: Prototypes; dive-bomber and Zerstörer versions; two 1,200hp Jumo 211B-1; four crew; three MG 15s plus provision for internal and (V10) external bomb load; V7 subsequently converted to transport (5).
Ju 88A-0: Pre-production model; dive-bomber version; as V6; modified cockpit; max bomb load 2,205lb (1,000kg) (20).
Ju 88A-1: Initial production model; as A-0; Jumo 211B-1s or G-1s; max bomb load (internal and external) 3,967lb (1,800kg); three or five MG 15s.
Ju 88A-2: As A-1; rocket-assisted take-off equipment.
Ju 88A-3: Unarmed 3-seat dual-control trainer version; A-1 conversions.
Ju 88A-4: Improved A-1; early models with two Jumo 211F; increased wing span; strengthened undercarriage; increased bomb load; revised armament.
Ju 88A-4/Trop: As A-4; tropicalized; redesignated Ju 88A-11; A-4 conversions.
Ju 88A-4/Torp: Torpedo-bomber version; A-4 conversions.
Ju 88A-5: Preceded A-4; modified A-1; two 1,200hp Jumo 211G-1; increased wing span.
Ju 88A-6: As A-5; nose/wing-mounted balloon-cable cutting fender; reduced bomb load; majority subsequently converted to maritime reconnaissance version; ventral cupola deleted; FuG 200 Hohentwiel radar (Ju 88A-6/U).
Ju 88A-7: Dual-control trainer version of A-5; two 1,200hp Jumo 211H-1.
Ju 88A-8: Re-engined A-6; Jumo 211Hs; Kuto-Nase (balloon-cable cutters) in wing leading edges.
Ju 88A-9/-11: Redesignations of A-1/Trop, A-5/Trop, and A-4/Trop resp.
Ju 88A-12: Unarmed dual-control trainer version; ventral cupola and dive-brakes deleted; A-4 conversions.
Ju 88A-13: Low-level ground-attack version; max 16 fixed forward-

firing 7.9mm MG 17 machine-guns; increased armour plating; max bomb load 1,102lb (500kg); A–4 conversions.
Ju 88A–14: Anti-shipping version; modified A–4; increased armour plating; Kuto-Nase (balloon-cable cutters); some with 20mm MG FFs in ventral gondola; two 1,200hp Jumo 211J.
Ju 88A–15: Enlarged (bulged) wooden bomb-bay for max 6,614lb (3,000kg) load; ventral gondola deleted; three crew; two 7.9mm MG 15 machine-guns.
Ju 88A–16: Unarmed dual-control trainer version; ventral gondola deleted; modified A–14.
Ju 88A–17: Torpedo-bomber version of A–14; two 1,686lb (765kg) LT F5b torpedoes underwing; some with ventral gondola deleted.
(Total Ju 88A production: Junkers-, Arado-, Heinkel-, Henschel-, Dornier-, and VW-built: 7,000+).
Total Production: approx 15,000 (all Ju 88 Marks).
Remarks: Arguably most important Luftwaffe bomber of WWII, Ju 88A remained in front-line service from first weeks of war until last; operational debut 26 Sept 1939, attacking British warships in Firth of Forth; participated Norwegian and French campaigns; played major role Battle of Britain; subsequently saw action on all fronts from Arctic to North Africa; scored notable successes against Allied convoys to Russia and against Royal Navy in Mediterranean; heavily committed against Soviet Union (inc bombing of Moscow), over Malta, and in Italy, before reappearing over UK during Operation 'Steinbock' (the Little Blitz), Jan 1944; towards end of war many early Ju 88As, supplanted by improved models, utilized in 'Mistel' development/operational programme; number Ju 88As supplied Axis satellite AFs, those of Finland and Rumania later used against Germany after separate armistices with Soviet Union.

Manufacturer: Junkers.
Model: Ju 88C–6c.
Type: Night-fighter.
Power Plant: Two 1,340hp Junkers Jumo 211J–1 (or J–2).
Performance:
maximum speed at 19,685ft (6,000m) 303mph (488km/hr).
cruising speed 263mph (423km/hr).
maximum range 1,230 miles (1,980km).
time to 19,685ft (6,000m) 12min 42sec.
service ceiling 32,480ft (9,900m).
Weights:
empty 19,973lb (9,060kg).
normal 27,225lb (12,350kg).
Dimensions:
wing span 65ft 7½in (20.0m).
length 47ft 1¼in (14.36m).
height 16ft 7¼in (5.06m).
wing area 586.63sq ft (54.5sq m).
Armament: Three fixed forward-firing 20mm MG FF/M cannon; three fixed forward-firing 7.9mm MG 17 machine-guns; one flexible 13mm MG 131 machine-gun at rear of cockpit.
Crew: 3.
In Service: Germany, Great Britain (2+ evaluation).
Variants (with no. built):
Ju 88C V1: Prototype; Zerstörer version; modified V7.
Ju 88C–0: Pre-production model; A–1 conversions.
Ju 88C–1: Planned production model; Zerstörer version; two 1,600hp BMW 801MA; none completed.
Ju 88C–2: Initial production model; Zerstörer version; modified A–1; redesigned non-glazed nose; two 1,200hp Jumo 211B–1; 3 crew; three fixed forward-firing 7.9mm MG 17 machine-guns and one 20mm MG FF cannon, plus two (defensive) 7.9mm MG 15 machine-guns in dorsal and ventral positions; max bomb load 1,102lb (500kg).
Ju 88C–3: Modified C–2; two 1,600hp BMW 801MA; one conversion.
Ju 88C–4: Zerstörer/reconnaissance version; modified A–4; solid nose; two Jumo 211F–1 (later models 211J–1 or J–2); increased armament; two 20mm MG FF cannon in ventral gondola exchangeable with cameras for reconnaissance role; increased weight; strengthened undercarriage.
Ju 88C–5: Zerstörer version; modified C–4; two 1,700hp BMW 801–D2; 3 crew; ventral gondola replaced by 'Waffentropfen' weapon pack below fuselage with two MG 17s; MG FF cannon replaced by MG 151; 10 pre-production models only.
Ju 88C–6a: Day-Zerstörer version; modified C–5; two Jumo 211J–1 or J2; increased armour plating; fixed armament, three MG 17s, three MG FFs plus (defensive) one MG 15; ventral gondola re-introduced; various armament modifications.
Ju 88C–6b: Night-fighter version; as C–6a; FuG 202 Lichtenstein BC or FuG 212 Lichtenstein C–1 radar.
Ju 88C–6c: As C–6b; FuG 220 Lichtenstein SN–2 plus (some models) Lichtenstein C–1; defensive armament one MG 131; some with addn two oblique upward-firing 20mm MG 151s in dorsal 'Schräge Musik' installation; alternative power-plant Jumo 211H).
Ju 88C–7a: Intruder version; two Jumo 211J–1; 2–3 crew; ventral gondola replaced by jettisonable weapon pack with two MG FF/M; three fixed forward-firing MG 17s; max bomb load 1,102lb (500kg).
Ju 88C–7b: As C–7a; underwing bomb-racks; max bomb load 3,305lb (1,500kg).
Ju 88C–7c: Zerstörer version; modified C–7a; two 1,600hp BMW 801MA; MG FF in nose replaced by MG 151; no series production.
(Total Ju 88C production: 3,200+).
Ju 88P V1: Anti-tank prototype; modified A–4; one 75mm KwK 39 anti-tank cannon forward, plus twin 7.9mm MG 81Z aft of large ventral fairing; two 1,340hp Jumo 211J.
Ju 88P–1: Production model; as Ju 88P V1; solid unglazed nose; KwK 39 replaced by 75mm PaK 40 anti-tank cannon; 3 crew; one forward-firing MG 81 plus two twin MG 81Zs.
Ju 88P–2: As P–1; two 37mm BK 3.7 (Flak 38) cannon in ventral fairing; A–4 conversions.
Ju 88P–3: As P–2; increased armour plating; two Jumo 211H; A–4 conversions.
Ju 88P–4: Heavy fighter/anti-tank version; two Jumo 211J–2; offensive armament reduced to single 50mm BK 5 cannon; abbreviated ventral fairing.
Ju 88R–1: Night fighter version; re-engined C–6b; two 1,600hp BMW 801MA; FuG 212 Lichtenstein C–1 radar.
Ju 88R–2: As R–1; two 1,700hp BMW 801D; addn FuG 202 Lichtenstein BC, plus FuG 217 Neptun tail-warning and FuG 350 Naxos Z passive radar.
Total Production: approx 15,000 (all Ju 88 Marks).
Remarks: First of many such modifications to adapt basic Ju 88A bomber for various fighter roles, C–0's operational debut during Polish campaign of Sept 1939; C–2 served as night-intruder over both UK and Mediterranean areas; C–6s operated in both day and night versions, principally in Russia/Eastern Mediterranean and in Defence of Reich resp, latter being replaced by improved Ju 88G from mid-1944; Ju 88C–7 and BMW-powered Ju 88R 'Wilde Sau' models appeared 1943; specialized but vulnerable Ju 88P served limited numbers on Eastern Front in anti-tank and 'train-busting' roles late 1943 before relegation to night ground-attack operations during 1944.
Colour Reference: Plates 39, 40: Unusual example of markings applied not for recognition/ camouflage purposes but for deception, painted transparencies on nose of heavy fighter intended to represent bomber version; Junkers Ju 88C–6a (F1+XM) of 4.(Z)/KG 76; Southern Russian Front, Winter 1942–43; employed primarily 'train-busting' missions.

Manufacturer: Junkers.
Model: Ju 88D–1.
Type: Long-range reconnaissance.
Power Plant: Two 1,340hp Junkers Jumo 211J.
Performance:
maximum speed at 15,750ft (4,800m) 301mph (485km/hr).
normal range 2,980 miles (4,800km).
initial rate of climb 1,066ft/min (325m/min).
service ceiling 26,250ft (8,000m).
Weights:
empty 19,510lb (8,850kg).
loaded 27,230lb (12,350kg).
Dimensions:
wing span 65ft 10½in (20.08m).
length 47ft 1¼in (14.36m).
height 15ft 9in (4.80m).
wing area 586.64sq ft (54.50sq m).
Armament: One 7.9mm MG 15 machine-gun each in nose, dorsal, and ventral positions.
Crew: 4.
In Service: Germany, Great Britain (1+ ex-Rumania/evaluation), Hungary (approx 40 Ju 88D–1), Rumania (Ju 88D–1).
Variants (with no. built):
Ju 88B V1: Prototype; bomber version; modified Ju 88A–1; two 1,600hp BMW 801MA; modified forward fuselage with fully-glazed unstepped nose; addn underwing bomb-racks (1).
Ju 88B–0: Pre-production model; modified A–4; BMW 801MAs; lengthened forward fuselage; three twin 7.9mm MG 81Z machine-guns in nose, dorsal and ventral positions; max bomb load 5,510lb (2,500kg) (10).
Ju 88D–0: Pre-production model; long-range reconnaissance version of A–4; two 1,200hp Jumo 211B–1; two cameras; increased fuel capacity.
Ju 88D–1: Production model; Jumo 211Js; three MG 15s; two cameras.
Ju 88D–2: Initial service version; modified A–5; Jumo 211B–1s, G–1s, or H–1s; underwing ETC racks; drop tanks; three MG 15s; two cameras.
Ju 88D–3, –4: Redesignated Ju 88D–1/Trop and D–2/Trop resp; tropicalized.
Ju 88D–5: As D–1; Jumo 211Gs or 211Js; three cameras; some tropicalized (D–5/Trop).
(Total Ju 88D–0/5 production: 1,450+).
Ju 88E–0: Re-engined B–0. BMW 801Cs; one 13mm MG 131 machine-gun each in dorsal turret, in nose, and at rear of cockpit, plus rearward-firing twin 7.9mm MG 81Z in ventral position; subsequently as Ju 188 development prototype; 1 conversion.
Total Production: approx 15,000 (all Ju 88 Marks).
Remarks: Neither B nor E model entered production; reconnaissance Ju 88D operational debut Summer 1940; participated all subsequent campaigns until closing months WWII, inc Mediterranean, Russia, and West; also employed over Atlantic in anti-shipping reconnaissance role; supplied Hungarian and Rumanian AFs 1943 for service on Eastern Front.

Manufacturer: Junkers.
Model: Ju 88G–7b.
Type: Night-fighter.
Power Plant: Two 1,725hp Junkers Jumo 213E.
Performance:
maximum speed at sea level 270mph (434km/hr).
maximum speed at 33,500ft (10,200m) 363mph (585km/hr).
normal range 1,400 miles (2,250km).
time to 30,200ft (9,200m) 26min 24sec.
service ceiling 32,800ft (10,000m).
Weights:
loaded 28,900lb (13,100kg).
maximum 32,350lb (14,670kg).
Dimensions:
wing span 65ft 7½in (20.0m).
length 47ft 8¾in (22.77m).
height 15ft 11in (4.85m).
wing area 586.63sq ft (54.5sq m).
Armament: Four fixed forward-firing 20mm MG 151 cannon in ventral tray; two fixed oblique upward-firing 20mm MG 151 cannon in dorsal position; one flexible 13mm MG 131 machine-gun at rear of cockpit.
Crew: 4.
In Service: Germany, Great Britain (1+ Ju 88G–1, evaluation).
Variants (with no. built):
Ju 88G V1: Prototype; night-fighter version; modified R–2; two 1,700hp BMW 801D; 3 crew; two fixed MG 151s in fuselage nose and four fixed MG 151s in ventral gun tray, plus one MG 131 at rear of cockpit; FuG 212 Lichtenstein C–1 radar.
Ju 88G–0: Pre-production model; reduced (four MG 151) armament; FuG 220 Lichtenstein SN–2; angular vertical tail surfaces.
Ju 88G–1: Production model; as G–0; modified equipment; four MG 151s in ventral gun tray; Lichtenstein SN–2, FuG 227 Flensburg.
Ju 88G–4: Improved G–1; some with two oblique upward-firing 20mm MG 151 in dorsal 'Schräge Musik' installation.
Ju 88G–6a: As G–4; two 1,700hp BMW 801G; improved equipment.
Ju 88G–6b: As G–6a; two ('Schräge Musik') 20mm MG 151/20s in dorsal position; FuG 350 Naxos Z.
Ju 88G–6c: Two 1,750hp Jumo 213A 'Schräge Musik' installation immediately aft of cockpit; reduced fuel capacity.
Ju 88G–7a: Re-engined G–6c; two 1,725hp Jumo 213E with MW 50 power booster; 3 crew; FuG 220 Lichtenstein SN–2 radar.
Ju 88G–7b: As G–7a; FuG 228 Lichtenstein SN–3 radar, or FuG 218 Neptun VR, in (optional) pointed wooden nose cone.
Ju 88G–7c: As G–7a; FuG 240/1 Berlin N–1a in blunt wooden nose cone.
(Total Ju 88G production: 2,800+).
Total Production: approx 15,000 (all Ju 88 Marks).
Remarks: Definitive night-fighter development, Ju 88G entered service early Summer 1944, replacing earlier C and R models as well as ageing Bf 110; standard equipment nearly all Nachtjagdgruppen by end of year, flown by many leading Aces in closing months Defence of Reich; carried out 'final fling' night-intruder missions over UK, March 1945, suffering heavy casualties (inc last enemy aircraft to be destroyed over Great Britain); number early G–1s employed as part 'Mistel' programme.
Colour Reference: Plate 41: Junkers Ju 88G–7a (2Z+AW) of IV./NJG 6; Neubiberg (nr Münich), Feb 1945; second example of Ju 88 markings applied for purposes of deception (see also Ju 88C–6a above), 2Z+AW has angular fin and rudder outline overpainted to resemble contours of earlier Ju 88C night-fighters—presumably intended to confuse Bomber Command air-gunners.

Manufacturer: Junkers.
Model: Ju 88S–1.
Type: High-speed bomber.
Power Plant: Two 1,730hp BMW 801G–2.
Performance:
maximum speed at 26,250ft (82,000m) 379mph (610km/hr).
cruising speed 289mph (465km/hr).
service ceiling 38,000ft (11,500m).
Weights:
empty 18,250lb (8,280kg).
maximum 30,400lb (13,800kg).
Dimensions:
wing span 65ft 7½in (20.0m).
length 48ft 8¾in (14.85m).
height 15ft 8½in (4.78m).
wing area 586.63sq ft (54.5sq m).
Armament: One flexible rearward-firing 13mm MG 131 machine-gun; max bomb load 4,410lb (2,000kg).
Crew: 3.
In Service: Germany, Great Britain (1+captured/evaluation).
Variants (with no. built):
Ju 88H–1: Long-range reconnaissance version; two 1,700hp BMW 801D; lengthened fuselage; tail as Ju 88D–1; wings as G–1; FuG 200 Hohentwiel radar; cameras in rear fuselage; 3 crew; one twin 7.9mm WT 81Z plus two 7.9mm MG 81s (10).
Ju 88H–2: Long-range maritime fighter version; as H–1; six MG 151s plus one MG 131; radar and camera equipment deleted (10).
Ju 88H–3/4: Ultra-long-range versions of H–1/2 resp; two 1,776hp Jumo 213A–12; addn increase fuselage length; enlarged angular tail surfaces.
Ju 88S V1: Prototype; high-speed bomber version; modified A–4; two 1,700hp BMW 801Ds; smooth glazed nose; bomb racks deleted; 1 conversion.
Ju 88S–0: Pre-production model; as Ju 88S V1; 4 crew; one forward-firing MG 81, one rearward-firing twin MG 81Z in ventral gondola plus one MG 131 at rear of cockpit; max bomb load 1,764lb (800kg).
Ju 88S–1: Production model; modified S–0; two BMW 801G–2 with GM 1 booster; ventral gondola deleted; 3 crew; reduced armament; underwing bomb racks.
Ju 88S–2: As S–1; two 1,810hp supercharged BMW 801TJ; enlarged (bulged) wooden bomb bay (as A–15); max bomb load 6,614lb (3,000kg); two addn MG 81s; increased fuel capacity.
Ju 88S–3: Re-engined S–1; two Jumo 213A–12 with GM 1 booster (max 2,125hp at take-off).
Ju 88T–1: Long-range reconnaissance version; modified S–1; two MG 15s or MG 81s; increased fuel capacity; various camera equipment.
Ju 88T–3: Long-range reconnaissance version; modified S–3; two Jumo 213E; increased fuel capacity; 3 cameras; pre-production models only.
(Total Ju 88H/S/T: approx 550).
Total Production: approx 15,000 (all Ju 88 Marks).
Remarks: Very-long-range 'stretched' H–1/H–2 models saw brief service based French Atlantic coast; those few H–3/H–4 variants completed assigned to 'Mistel' programme; Ju 88S high-speed bomber, distinguished from A-series by smooth glazed nose, entered service early 1944; employed primarily in West, in pathfinder role; participated attacks on UK cities and southern ports, March–May 1944; Ju 88T reconnaissance version likewise limited employment Western Front, 1944.

Manufacturer: Junkers.
Model: Mistel 1 (Mistletoe).
Type: Unmanned expendable (composite) attack aircraft.
Power Plant: Two 1,340hp Junkers Jumo 211J–2 or J–2; plus one (optional) 1,350hp Daimler-Benz DB 601E–1.
Armament: One 8,380lb (3,800kg) warhead.
Crew: 1.
In Service: Germany.
Variants (with no. built):
Prototype: One Bf 109F–4 (upper) coupled to one Ju 88A–4 (lower) by DFS-designed connecting/ release structure.
Mistel 1: Bf 109F–4/Ju 88A–4 combination; Ju 88 nose section replaced by 8,380lb (3,800kg) hollow-charge warhead with impact fuze projection; strengthened structure.
Mistel S1: Trainer version of Mistel 1; addn forward bracing struts.
Mistel 2: Improved Mistel 1; Fw 190A–6 (or F–8)/Ju 88G–1 combination; inc some trainer conversions (Mistel S2) (125).
Mistel 3: Improved Mistel 2; addn jettisonable third main-wheel under fuselage.
Mistel S3A: Trainer version; Fw 190A–6/Ju 88A–4 (or A–6) combination.
Mistel 3B: Fw 190A–8/Ju 88H–4 combinations.
Mistel 3C: Fw 190A–8 (or F–8)/Ju 88G–10 (or H–4) combinations; addn fuel capacity.
Mistel Führungsmaschine: Long-range pathfinder version of Mistel 3B; Ju 88H–4 with 3 crew, one rearward-firing 13mm MG 131, and centimetric radar in extended nose.
Mistel 4: Projected Me 262/Ju 287 combination.
Mistel 5: Projected Me 262 (or He 162)/Ju 268 (or Arado E–377A) combination.
Total Production: 250+.
Remarks: Unorthodox 'pick-a-back' composite arrangement originally envisaged for aerial-tug purposes, Mistel trials commenced mid-1943; comprising an upper (Bf 109F–4 single-engined fighter) component mounted above converted Ju 88A–4 bomber (lower component), the whole was flown to vicinity of target area where latter was aimed and released by parent fighter; Mistel 1 was only version to be employed operationally; planned attack on Scapa Flow diverted against Allied shipping off Normandy invasion beaches, 24–25 June, 1944; even more ambitious scheme for massed (100 Misteln) raid on Soviet power stations likewise overtaken by war situation, majority Misteln being used during closing weeks of war against bridges on Eastern Front in vain attempt to halt advancing Soviets.

Manufacturer: Junkers.
Model: Ju 89 V2.
Type: Long-range heavy bomber/ transport.
Power Plant: Four 960hp Daimler-Benz DB 600A.
Performance:
maximum speed at 16,400ft (5,000m) 242mph (390km/hr).
cruising speed 196mph (315km/hr).
maximum range 1,240 miles (2,000km).
service ceiling 22,965ft (7,000m).
Weights:
empty 37,480lb (17,000kg).
maximum 61,290lb (27,800kg).
Dimensions:
wing span 115ft 8½in (35.26m).
length 86ft 11¼in (26.5m).
height 24ft 11¼in (7.6m).
wing area 1,980.56sq ft (184.0sq m).
Crew/Payload: 5–6/22,000+lb (1,000+kg).
In Service: Germany.

Variants (with no. built):
Ju 89 V1/2: Prototypes; four 1,075hp Junkers Jumo 211A and 960hp DB 600A resp (2).
Ju 89 V3: Not completed.
Ju 89A: Production model; project only.
Total Production: 2.
Remarks: Pre-war four-engined heavy bomber design first flown late 1936; programme cancelled 1937, prototypes subsequently converted for transport role; brief service early months WWII, inc invasion of Norway April 1940.

Manufacturer: Junkers.
Model: Ju 90B–1.
Type: Long-range transport.
Power Plant: Four 830hp BMW 132H.

Performance:
maximum speed at 8,200ft (2,500m) 217mph (350km/hr).
cruising speed 199mph (320km/hr).
normal range 1,243 miles (2,000km).
time to 3,280ft (1,000m) 4min 12sec.
service ceiling 18,044ft (5,500m).
Weights:
empty 31,526lb (14,300kg).

loaded 50,706lb (23,000kg).
Dimensions:
wing span 114ft 10in (35.00m).
length 86ft 3½in (26.30m).
height 24ft 7¼in (7.50m).
wing area 1,980.6sq ft (184.0sq m).
Crew/Accommodation: 4/40.
In Service: Germany.
Variants (with no. built):
Ju 90 V1: Prototype; civil transport;

redesigned Ju 89 V3; four 1,000hp Daimler-Benz DB 600s (1).
Ju 90 V2/4: Prototypes; four 830hp BMW 132Hs; Ju 90 V4 subsequently re-engined with 1,740hp BMW 801MAs (3).
Ju 90B–1 (V5/7, 10/14): Production model; 38–40 passenger civil transport; BMW 132Hs (8).
Ju 90Z–2 (V8/9): as B–1 (Pratt and

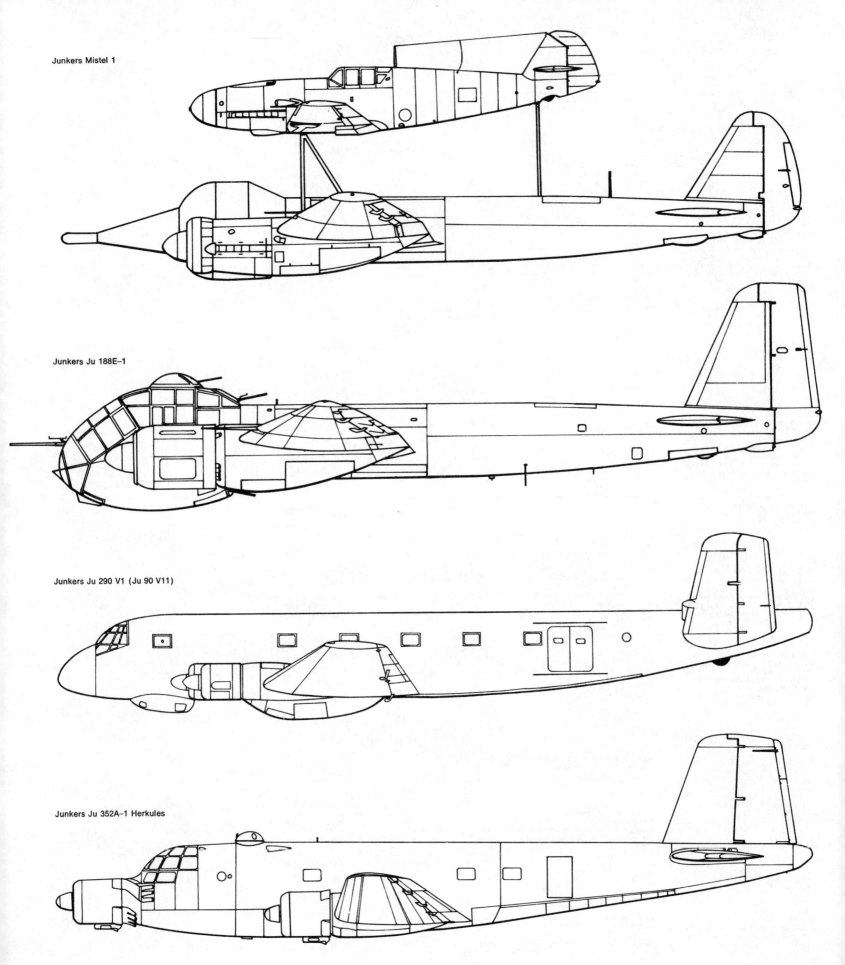

Junkers Mistel 1

Junkers Ju 188E–1

Junkers Ju 290 V1 (Ju 90 V11)

Junkers Ju 352A–1 Herkules

Whitney Twin Wasps); original South African Airways order; completed but not delivered (2).
Ju 90 V7: Prototype; lengthened fuselage; ventral loading ramp; subsequently re-engined BMW 801C; one Ju 90B–1 conversion.
Ju 90 V8: Transport/maritime reconnaissance version of V7; one 20mm MG 151 cannon and one 13mm MG 131 machine-gun fore and aft of ventral gondola, plus one 20mm MG 151 each in dorsal turret and tail position; one Ju 90Z–2 conversion.
Ju 90 V11: Redesigned wing; modified (angular) fins and rudders; subsequently redesignated Ju 290 V1; one Ju 90B–1 conversion.
Total Production: 14.
Remarks: Completely new fuselage mated to wings and tail of abandoned Ju 89 V3 bomber prototype, Ju 90 V1 developed as civil airliner for DLH. Majority taken over by Luftwaffe after outbreak WWII; served in military transport role 1940–43; operational debut invasion of Norway, April 1940; subsequently employed Balkans/Mediterranean areas, inc Greek and short-lived Iraqi campaigns, and supply/evacuation Tunisia; also operated southern sector of Russian Front during latter stages Battle of Stalingrad; several prototypes served in Ju 290 development programme.

Manufacturer: Junkers.
Model: Ju 160.
Type: Communications/transport.
Power Plant: One 660hp BMW 132E.
Performance:
maximum speed at sea level 211mph (340km/hr).
cruising speed 196mph (315km/hr).
normal range 683 miles (1,100km).
time to 3,280ft (1,000m) 3min 42sec.
service ceiling 17,060ft (5,200m).
Weights:
empty 5,114lb (2,320kg).
loaded 7,606lb (3,450kg).
Dimensions:
wing span 46ft 11¾in (14.32m).
length 39ft 4¼in (12.0m).
height 11ft 3¾in (3.45m).
wing area 374.59sq ft (34.8sq m).
Crew/Accommodation: 2/6.
In Service: Germany.
Variants (with no. built):
Ju 160 V1: Prototype; high-speed medium-range civil transport/mailplane (1).
Ju 160A: Initial production; modified rudder; tailskid replaced by tailwheel.
Ju 160B–D: Improved versions; inc 1 with one 7.9mm MG 15 machine-gun for military reconnaissance.
(Total Ju 160A–D: 47).
Total Production: 48.
Remarks: Direct development of earlier Ju 60, itself built to counter competition from Lockheed Orion ordered by neighbouring Switzerland, Ju 160 entered domestic DLH service 1935; majority impressed by Luftwaffe upon outbreak of WWII and used for transport/communications duties.

Manufacturer: Junkers.
Model: Ju 188E–1.
Type: Medium bomber.
Power Plant: Two 1,700hp BMW 801D–2.
Performance:
maximum speed at 19,685ft (6,000m) 310mph (500km/hr).
cruising speed 233mph (375km/hr).
normal range 1,210 miles (1,950km).
service ceiling 30,665ft (9,350m).
Weights:
empty 21,737lb (9,860kg).
loaded 31,989lb (14,510kg).
Dimensions:
wing span 72ft 2in (22.0m).
length 49ft 0½in (14.9m).
height 14ft 7in (4.44m).
wing area 602.78sq ft (56.0sq m).
Armament: One 20mm MG 151 cannon in nose; one 13mm MG 131 machine-gun each in dorsal turret and at rear of cockpit; one rearward-firing twin 7.9mm MG 81Z machine-gun in ventral position; max bomb load 6,615lb (3,000kg).
Crew: 4.
In Service: Germany.
Variants:
Ju 188 V1/2: Prototypes; modified Ju 88E–0; redesigned vertical tail surfaces; extended pointed wingtips; two 1,600hp BMW 810MA; V1 ex-Ju 88 V44.
Ju 188A–0: Pre-production model; bomber version; two 1,776hp Jumo 213A–1.
Ju 188A–2: Production model; as A–0; uprated engines; one 20mm MG 151 cannon each in dorsal turret and nose, one 13mm MG 131 at rear of cockpit, plus twin 7.9mm MG 81Z in ventral position; dive brakes deleted.
Ju 188A–3: Torpedo-bomber version; outboard centre section, wing racks deleted; Jumo 213A–1s; two 1,686lb (765kg) or two 1,764lb (800kg) torpedoes underwing; FuG 200 radar in nose.
Ju 188C–0: Modified Ju 188A; two remote controlled 13mm MG 131s in tail barbette; 1 conversion.
Ju 188D–1/2: Reconnaissance versions; modified Ju 188A; 20mm MG 151 in nose deleted; 3 crew; various camera equipment; D–2 with FuG 200 Hohentwiel search radar.
Ju 188E–0: Pre-production model; bomber version; two 1,600hp BMW 801ML.
Ju 188E–1: Production model; as E–0; later models with BMW 801D–2s or G–2s.
Ju 188E–2: Torpedo-bomber version; equipment and armament as A–3.
Ju 188F–1/2: Reconnaissance versions; as D–1/2; BMW 801Ds/Gs resp; F–2 with FuG 200 Hohentwiel search radar.
Ju 188G–0: Pre-production model; bomber version; manual tail turret; deepened rear fuselage; Ju 188 V2 conversion.
Ju 188G–2: Production model; project only.
Ju 188H–2: Reconnaissance version of Ju 188G; project only.
Ju 188J/L: Projected high-altitude bad weather interceptor, bomber, and reconnaissance versions resp; developed as Ju 388J/L.
Ju 188M–1/2: Long-range reconnaissance versions; projects only.
Ju 188R–0: Pre-production model; experimental night-fighter version; modified Ju 188E; two BMW 801G–2; three crew; four 20mm MG 151, or two 30mm MK 103, fixed forward-firing cannon; radar.
Ju 188S–1: Unarmed high-altitude intruder version; redesigned forward fuselage; pressurized cabin; two 1,750hp Jumo 213E–1; max (internal) bomb load 1,764lb (800kg); number completed as close-support aircraft; one 50mm BK 5 cannon in ventral fairing; armoured; pressurization deleted; redesignated as Ju 188S–1/U.
Ju 188T–1: Long-range high-altitude reconnaissance version of S–1; two Rb cameras.
Total Production: approx 1,100.
Remarks: Private venture development of basic Ju 88 design, initial BMW-powered Ju 188E model entered service mid-1943; operated in pathfinder role over UK, Winter 1943–44; continued limited use (equipping, either wholly or partially, some half-dozen Gruppen) mainly on Western Front until early 1945; over half total production comprised D and F reconnaissance models; widely employed Eastern Front, Italy, Arctic, and in West; brief post-war use Ju 188E torpedo-bomber by FNAF.

Manufacturer: Junkers.
Model: Ju 252A–1.
Type: Medium transport.
Power Plant: Three 1,340hp Junkers Jumo 211F.
Performance:
maximum speed at 19,030ft (5,800m) 272mph (437km/hr).
cruising speed 208mph (335km/hr).
normal range 4,100 miles (6,600km).
time to 3,280ft (1,000m) 4min 18sec.
service ceiling 20,670ft (6,300m).
Weights:
empty 28,880lb (13,100kg).
maximum 52,911lb (24,000kg).
Dimensions:
wing span 111ft 10in (34.08m).
length 82ft 4½in (25.1m).
height 18ft 10½in (5.75m).
wing area 1,319.65sq ft (122.6sq m).
Armament: One 13mm MG 131 machine-gun in forward dorsal turret; two 7.9mm MG 15 machine-guns in beam positions.
Crew/Accommodation: 3/25–32 (or cargo).
In Service: Germany.
Variants (with no. built):
Ju 252 V1/4: Prototypes (V4 armed; modified rudder (4).
Ju 252A–1 (V5/15): Service Trials model; As V4 (11).
Total Production: 15.
Remarks: Ordered by DLH as intended Ju 52 replacement, Ju 252 development overtaken by war situation; only 15 produced of initial order for 25; A–1s delivered to Luftwaffe as special-duties/cargo transports; served 1943–44 in trooper, freighter, and clandestine (agent-dropping) roles.

Manufacturer: Junkers.
Model: Ju 288B.
Type: Medium bomber.
Power Plant: Two 2,700hp Daimler-Benz DB 606A–1/B–1.
Performance (estimates):
maximum speed at 17,700ft (5,400m) 387mph (623km/hr).
normal range 1,680 miles (2,700km).
time to 13,120ft (4,000m) 10min 0sec.
service ceiling 30,500ft (9,300m).
Weights:
maximum 46,200lb (20,950kg).
Dimensions:
wing span 74ft 4in (22.66m).
length 58ft 4¾in (17.8m).
wing area 696.42sq ft (64.7sq m).
Armament: Two 13mm MG 131 machine-guns each in remotely-controlled forward dorsal and chin barbettes; one 15mm MG 151 cannon (or two 13mm MG 131 machine-guns) in remotely-controlled tail barbette; max bomb load (internal) 6,614lb (3,000kg).
Crew: 4.
In Service: Germany.
Variants (with no. built):
Ju 288 V1/5: Initial prototypes; A-series; two 1,600hp BMW 801MA or (V5) 2,500hp Jumo 222A/B; three crew, various wing, dive-brake and (projected) armament modifications (5).
Ju 288 V6/8: Prototypes; B-series; two 2,500hp Jumo 222A/B or (V7) BMW 801C; four crew; redesigned wing; V7 and V8 enlarged tail surfaces (3).
Ju 288A–1/–2: Production models; two 13mm MG 131 machine-guns each in remotely-controlled forward dorsal and aft ventral barbettes; max bomb load (internal) 6,614lb (3,000kg); projects only.
Ju 288 V9, V11/14: Prototypes; modified V8; redesigned forward fuselage; enlarged cockpit; V12 retained A-series forward fuselage section; V11 and V13 with two 2,700hp DB 606A/B; revised armament (5).
Ju 288B: Production model; project only.
Ju 288 V101/108: Prototypes; 2,700hp DB 606A/Bs or 29,950hp 610A/Bs; redesigned, lengthened nose; addn ventral barbette; improved equipment (8).
Ju 288C–1/–2: Proposed bomber versions; various armament.
Ju 288C–3: Proposed night-bomber version.
Total Production: 21.
Remarks: Junkers contender for 1939 Bomber B contract, Ju 288 was officially recognised as Ju 88 replacement (as opposed to private venture Ju 188); in event, after long and troublesome four-year development period, mainly attributed non-availability Jumo 222 power plants, whole programme cancelled; of those few prototypes still serviceable number subsequently fitted with 50mm BK 5 (KwK 39) cannon in ventral pod (similar to Ju 88P–4 and Ju 188S–1) and issued operational units closing stages WWII.

Manufacturer: Junkers.
Model: Ju 290A–5.
Type: Long-range maritime reconnaissance.
Power Plant: Four 1,700hp BMW 801D.
Performance:
maximum speed at 19,030ft (5,800m) 273mph (440km/hr).
cruising speed 224mph (360km/hr).
maximum range 4,620 miles (7,450km).
time to 6,090ft (1,850m) 9min 48sec.
service ceiling 19,685ft (6,000m).
Weights:
loaded 90,323lb (40,970kg).
maximum 99,140lb (44,970kg).
Dimensions:
wing span 137ft 9½in (42.00m).
length 93ft 11¾in (28.64m).
height 22ft 4¾in (6.83m).
wing area 2,191.5sq ft (204.0sq m).
Armament: One 20mm MG 151 cannon each in two dorsal turrets and two waist positions; one 20mm MG 151 cannon in tail; one 20mm MG 151 in nose of ventral gondola; one 13mm MG 131 machine-gun in tail of ventral gondola.
Crew: 9.
In Service: Germany.
Variants (with no. built):
Ju 290 V1: Prototype; redesignated Ju 90 V11.
Ju 290A–0: Pre-production model; modified Ju 90 transport version; four 1,600hp BMW 801L (2).
Ju 290A–1: Production model; defensive armament as Ju 90 V8; plus two addn 7.9mm MG 15 machine-guns (5).
Ju 290A–2: Martitime reconnaissance version; as A–1; one 20mm MG 151 cannon in addn aft dorsal turret; increased fuel capacity; FuG 200 Hohentwiel search radar (3).
Ju 290A–3: As A–2; low-drag aft dorsal turret; gun-blister in tail; two with 1,700hp BMW 801Ds (3).
Ju 290A–4: As A–3, low-drag forward and aft dorsal turrets (5).
Ju 290A–5: Improved version; increased armour protection; beam 13mm MG 131 machine-guns replaced by two 20mm MG 151 cannon; two addn crew; BMW 801Ds; Junkers-built (11); (Ju 290A) Letov-built (18).
Ju 290A–6: 50-passenger transport version; initially intended for service Hitler's personal transport flight (1).
Ju 290A–7: Reconnaissance-bomber version; modified A–5; increased weight and range; addn 20mm MG 151 cannon in redesigned glazed nose; three ETC racks; max bomb load 6,615lb (3,000kg) or three Hs 293, or Fritz X missiles (approx 12).
Ju 290A–8: Modified A–7; revised armament; four dorsal turrets; 13 crew; BMW 801Gs (1).
Ju 290A–9: Long-range reconnaissance version; increased fuel capacity; reduced armament (3).
Ju 290B–1: Long-range high-altitude heavy bomber version; bomb load as A–7; pressurized nose, dorsal, and tail turrets; increased armament; prototype only (1).
Ju 290B–2: Unpressurized B–1; revised armament; none completed.
Ju 290B MS, C/E: Projects only.
Total Production: 65+.
Remarks: Development of Ju 90, enlarged Ju 290 long-range transport entered service early 1943; maritime reconnaissance versions equipped French-based FAGr (long-range reconnaissance wing) for operations over Atlantic; Spring 1944 three aircraft this unit modified for ultra-long-range transport flights to Japanese-held Manchuria; Summer 1944 FAGr disbanded, majority Ju 290s transferred special-duties transport Gruppe for agent-dropping and other clandestine roles; close WWII involved in evacuation Nazi leaders to neutral territory; sole 290A–6, after flight to Barcelona end April 1945, used by Spanish AF until mid-fifties; one 290A–8 completed post-war by Czech Letov plant as modified transport (L 290 Orel).

Manufacturer: Junkers.
Model: Ju 352A–1 Herkules.
Type: Transport.
Power Plant: Three 1,000hp BMW Bramo 323R–2.
Performance:
maximum speed at sea level 205mph (330km/hr).
cruising speed 152mph (245km/hr).
maximum range 1,852 miles (2,980km).
time to 3,280ft (1,000m) 3min 12sec.
service ceiling 19,685ft (6,000m).
Weights:
empty 27,558lb (12,500kg).
loaded 43,034lb (19,520kg).
Dimensions:
wing span 112ft 2¼in (34.2m).
length 79ft 4¾in (24.2m).
height 21ft 7¾in (6.6m).
wing area 1,379.93sq ft (128.2sq m).
Armament: One 20mm MG 151 cannon in forward dorsal turret; two (optional) lateral-firing 13mm MG 131 machine-guns.
Crew/Payload: 4–5/8,820–9,500lb (4,000–4,300kg).
In Service: Germany.
Variants (with no. built):
Ju 352 V1/2: Prototypes; redesigned Ju 252; three 1,000hp Bramo 323R–2s; unarmed (2).
Ju 352A–0 (V3/12): Pre-production model; armed (10).
Ju 352A–1: Production model; final 8 examples with structural modifications; weight reduction/increase load capacity (33).
Ju 352 B–1/2: Projects only.
Total Production: 45.
Remarks: Attempt to conserve strategic materials, Ju 352 was re-engined, mixed wood and steel--tube construction development of earlier Ju 252; in service 1944–45, performed special-duties missions plus regular transport/supply roles over Courland/East Prussian fronts during closing months WWII.

Manufacturer: Junkers.
Model: Ju 388L–1.
Type: Photographic-reconnaissance.
Power Plant: Two 1,800hp BMW 801TJ.
Performance:
maximum speed at 40,300ft (12,300m) 383mph (616km/hr).
cruising speed 280mph (450km/hr).
maximum range 2,160 miles (3,500km).
initial rate of climb 1,330ft/min (405m/min).
time to 36,100ft (11,000m) 30min 0sec.
service ceiling 44,100ft (13,450m).
Weights:
maximum 32,350lb (14,670kg).
Dimensions:
wing span 72ft 2in (22.0m).
length 49ft 0½in (14.95m).
height 14ft 7¼in (4.45m).
wing area 602.78sq ft (56.0sq m).
Armament: Two 13mm MG 131 machine-guns in remotely-controlled tail barbette.
Crew: 3.
In Service: Germany.
Variants (with no. built):
Ju 388L V1: Prototype; high-altitude long-range reconnaissance version; converted Ju 188T–1 airframe (1).
Ju 388 V2, 4, 5: Prototypes; high-altitude night/all-weather fighter version; various armament and radar equipment; V4/5 pointed wooden nose cone; V2 tail barbette (3).
Ju 388 V3: Prototype; high-altitude bomber version; max bomb load 6,610lb (3,000kg) (1).
Ju 388J–1: Projected production model; high-altitude night/all-weather fighter version; two 30mm MK 108 and two 20mm MG 151 cannon in ventral fairing, plus two oblique upward-firing 20mm MG 151 cannon in 'Schräge Musik' dorsal installation; none completed.
Ju 388J–2/4: Modified J–1 sub-variants; projects only.
Ju 388K–0: Pre-production model; high-altitude bomber version (10).
Ju 388K–1: Production model; as K–0; FA 15 tail barbette (5).
Ju 388K–2/3: Re-engined K–1 versions; projects only.
Ju 388L–0: Pre-production model; converted Ju 88S–1 airframes; two rearward-firing 7.9mm MG 81s in ventral WT 81Z Waffentropfen fairing (10).
Ju 388L–1: Production model; modified L–0; FuG 217 Neptun tail-warning radar; wooden ventral pannier with two cameras and auxiliary fuel tank; remotely-controlled FA 15 tail barbette; Junkers-built (35); Weser-built (10).
Ju 388L–1/b: As L–1; one addn 13mm MG 131 machine-gun in rear of cockpit; four crew; Ju 388L–1 conversions.
Ju 388L–3: Re-engined L–1; 1,750hp Jumo 213E–1s (2).
Ju 388M–1: Torpedo-carrier version; none completed.
Total Production: 77.
Remarks: Based upon earlier Ju 188S/T designs, development of Ju 388K/L high-altitude bomber/long-range reconnaissance projects (and parallel Ju 388J high-altitude night-fighter/all-weather interceptor, afforded top priority Autumn 1943; first and only variant to see service, Ju 388L–1 deliveries commenced late 1944; at least three examples operated by special experimental reconnaissance unit closing weeks WWII.

Manufacturer: Junkers.
Model: Ju 390A–1.
Type: Long range heavy bomber/reconnaissance
Power Plant: Six 1,970hp BMW 801E.
Performance (estimated):
maximum speed at 20,340ft (6,200m) 314mph (505km/hr).
cruising speed 222mph (357km/hr).
maximum range (reconnaissance) 6,030 miles (9,700km).
Weights:
empty 81,350lb (36,900kg).
maximum 166,450lb (53,112kg).
Dimensions:
wing span 165ft 1in (50.32m).
length 112ft 2¼in (34.2m).
height 22ft 7in (6.88m).
wing area 2,729.73sq ft (253.6sq m).
Armament: Four 13mm MG 131 machine-guns each in nose and tail turrets; two 20mm MG 151 cannon each in forward and rear dorsal turrets and ventral barbette, plus two lateral-firing 20mm MG 151 cannon in beam positions; max bomb load: 15,872lb (7,200kg), or four Hs 293, Hs 294, or FX 1400 missiles.
In Service: Germany.
Variants (with no. built):
Ju 390 V1: Prototype; long range transport version; redesigned Ju 290A; lengthened fuselage; increased wing span; six 1,700hp

Messerschmitt Bf 109E–4

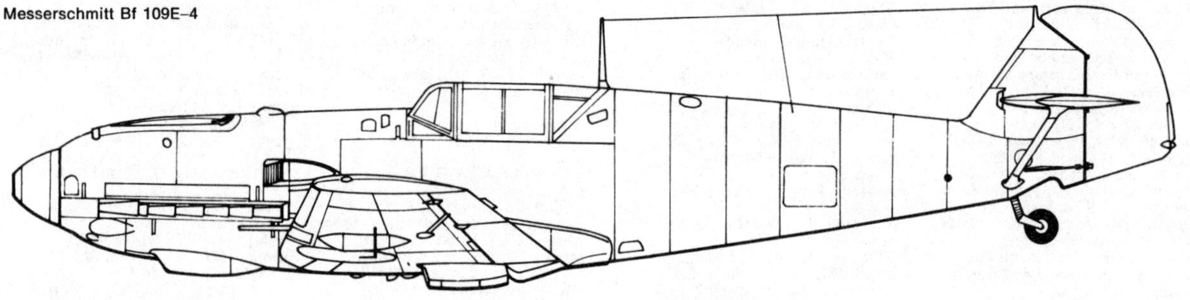

BMW 801Ds (1).
Ju 390 V2: Prototype; long range maritime reconnaissance version; modified V1; extended forward fuselage; one 20mm MK 151 cannon each in forward and rear dorsal turrets, nose of ventral gondola, and in tail; two 13mm MG 131 machine-guns in beam positions, plus one 13mm MG 131 at rear of ventral gondola; FuG 200 Hohentwiel search radar (1).
Ju 390A-1: Projected long range reconnaissance-bomber version; modified V2; revised armament; provision for underwing bomb load BMW 801Es.
Total Production: 2.
Remarks: V1 and V2 first flown Aug/Oct 1943 resp; latter, forerunner of projected A–1 production model, delivered to long range reconnaissance Gruppe based French Biscay coast for operational evaluation early 1944; made at least one recorded transatlantic flight, approaching to within twelve miles of American coatstline north of New York.

Manufacturer: Klemm.
Model: L 25D.
Type: Trainer/liaison.
Power Plant: One 80hp Hirth HM 60R.
Performance:
maximum speed at sea level 99mph (160km/hr).
cruising speed 87mph (140km/hr).
normal range 404 miles (650km).
time to 3,280ft (1,000m) 5min 48sec.
service ceiling 15,748ft (4,800m).
Weights:
empty 926lb (420kg).
loaded 1,587lb (720kg).
Dimensions:
wing span 42ft 7¾in (13.0m).
length 24ft 7¼in (7.5m).
height 6ft 8¾in (2.05m).
wing area 215sq ft (20.0sq m).
Crew/Accommodation: 1/1.
In Service: Germany, Great Britain (15+ impressments), Hungary (6).
Variants (with no. built):
L 25a/b: Prototypes; civil lightplane/trainer versions; one 22hp Mercedes.
L 25 I/IW: Initial production model; land and floatplane versions resp 45hp Salmson AD9.
L 25a I: Modified L 25 I; 45hp Salmson AD 9.
L 25b VII: Re-engined L 25a I; 80hp Hirth HM 60.
L 25d II: 88hp Siemens Sh 13a.
L 25D VIIR: Major production model.
(Total: L 25 Klemm-built: (approx 600); L 25 British Klemm (British Aircraft) licence-built: 134).
Total Production: approx 600 (excl UK licence-production).
Remarks: Built between 1927–1939, Klemm L 25s equipped number pre-war school/training establishments, both civil and military; continued use into WWII, inc liaison/light communications roles; several UK licence-produced examples impressed into RAF/FAA for similar duties (see British Aircraft Swallow 2).

Manufacturer: Klemm.
Model:: Kl 31.
Type: Liaison.
Power Plant: One 150hp Siemens Sh 14a.
Performance:
maximum speed at sea level 118mph (190km/hr).
cruising speed 102mph (165km/hr).
normal range 457 miles (735km).
initial rate of climb 459ft/min (140m/min).
service ceiling 12,467ft (3,800m).
Weights:
empty 1,521lb (690kg).
loaded 2,756lb (1,250kg).
Dimensions:
wing span 44ft 3½in (13.5m).
length 28ft 2¾in (8.6m).
height 7ft 6½in (2.3m).
wing area 223.89sq ft (20.8sq m).
Crew/Accommodation: 1/3.
In Service: Germany, Hungary (1 Kl 31).
Variants:
Kl 31V(a): Prototype; 120hp Argus As 8.
Kl 31a XIV: Standard production model; metal (steel tube) fuselage construction.
Kl 32A XII: Modified Kl 31; 3-seat; wooden fuselage construction; Hirth HM 150.
Kl 32B XIV: As Kl 32A XII; 160hp BMW-Bramo Sh 14a.
Remarks: 4 and 3-seat resp, Kl 31/32 enclosed cabin tourers built early thirties; several employed in liaison role during WWII.

Manufacturer: Klemm.
Model: Kl 35D.
Type: Trainer/communications.
Power Plant: One 80hp Hirth HM 60R.
Performance:
maximum speed at sea level 132mph (212km/hr).
cruising speed 118mph (190km/hr).
normal range 413 miles (665km).
time to 3,280ft (1,000m) 6min 0sec.
service ceiling 14,272ft (4,350m).
Weights:
empty 1,014lb (460kg).
loaded 1,654lb (750kg).
Dimensions:
wing span 34ft 1½in (10.4m).
length 24ft 7¼in (7.5m).
height 6ft 8¾in (2.05m).
wing area 163.61sq ft (15.2sq m).
Crew/Accommodation: 1/1.
In Service: Germany, Hungary, Rumania, Slovakia (30 Kl 35D), Sweden (inc licence-production).
Variants:
Kl 35a/b: Prototypes; civil lightplane/trainer; 80hp Hirth HM 60R.
Kl 35B: Initial production model; Hirth HM 504A–2.
Kl 35BW: Floatplane version of Kl 35B.
Kl 35D: Improved Kl 35B; military trainer version; strengthened, braced undercarriage; spats deleted; altn ski/float/undercarriage.
Remarks: First flown 1935, Kl 35(D) became standard Luftwaffe trainer; also used in variety ancillary roles, inc liaison, courier, and field-postal service; pre-war deliveries to Hungary (5), Rumania, Lithuania (3 to National Guard), Czechoslovakia and Sweden (plus licence-production); equipped wartime Slovak AF, inc two examples employed by Combined Sqn, Slovak Insurgent AF.

Manufacturer: Messerschmitt.
Model: Bf 108B Taifun (Typhoon).
Type: Liaison/communications.
Power Plant: One 240hp Argus As 10C.
Performance:
maximum speed at sea level 186mph (300km/hr).
cruising speed 165mph (265km/hr).
normal range 590 miles (950km).
initial rate of climb 1,132ft/min (345m/min).
service ceiling 15,750ft (4,800m).
Weights:
empty 1,896lb (860kg).
loaded 3,086lb (1,400kg).
Dimensions:
wing span 34ft 10in (10.62m).
length 27ft 2¼in (8.29m).
height 6ft 10¾in (2.1m).
wing area 176.53sq ft (16.4sq m).
Crew/Accommodation: 1/3.
In Service: Bulgaria, Germany, Great Britain (2+ impressed/captured), Hungary (approx 120), Rumania (approx 30), Yugoslavia.
Variants (with no. built):
Bf 108: Original prototype; M 37 International sports tourer.
Bf 108A: Prototypes and (A) initial production models; one 250hp Hirth HM 8U or one 210hp Argus As 17.
Bf 108B: Improved Bf 108A; civil (tourer) and military (liaison/communications) versions; modified tail surfaces; tailwheel.
Bf 108C: Re-engined Bf 108B; 400hp Hirth HM 512; one conversion.
Bf 108 production: Messerschmitt- and French (SNCA)-built (885).
Me 208 V1/2: Prototypes; modified Bf 108B; 240hp Renault 6Q–10; retractable (tricycle) undercarriage; French (SNCA)-built (2).
Nord 1001/1002 Pingouin (Penguin) I/II: Post-war French production of Bf 108; Renault 6Q–10/6Q–11 resp; (approx 285).
Nord 1003/1004: 240/305hp Potez 6 resp.
Nord 1101 Ramier (Wood Pigeon)/ 1101 Noralpha: Post-war French production of Bf 208; military and civil versions resp; Renault 6Q.
Total Production: 887 (excl post-war).
Remarks: Designed as 1934 International Tourist Trophy Challenge contender, Bf 108 developed into standard Luftwaffe liaison/light communications aircraft; served throughout WWII in these and other ancillary roles; exported pre-war Japan, Switzerland, USSR and Yugoslavia, as well as equipping number wartime Axis satellite AFs; French production/development (of both 108 and 208) continued post-war into early fifties; many still flying.

Manufacturer: Messerschmitt.
Model: Bf 109D–1.
Type: Fighter.
Power Plant: One 986hp Daimler-Benz DB 600Aa.
Performance:
maximum speed at sea level 298mph (480km/hr).
maximum range 348 miles (600km).
initial rate of climb 2,985ft/min (910m/min).
service ceiling 32,810ft (10,000m).
Weights:
empty 3,964lb (1,800kg).
loaded 5,335lb (2,420kg).
Dimensions:
wing span 32ft 4½in (9.87m).
length 28ft 2¼in (8.6m).
height 8ft 4¾in (2.56m).
wing area 176.53sq ft (16.4sq m).
Armament: One 20mm MG FF cannon firing through propeller hub; two 7.9mm MG 17 machine-guns in upper cowling.
Crew: 1.
In Service: Germany, Hungary (3 Bf 109D–1, evaluation), Spain, Switzerland (10 Bf 109C–1).
Variants (with no. built):
Bf 109 V1/3: Prototypes; 610hp Jumo 210A or (V1) 697hp Rolls-Royce Kestrel V (3).
Bf 109B–0 (V4/13): Pre-production model; various Jumo 210 (A/G), or (V10/12) 950/960hp DB 600/600A, or (V13) 1,650 DB 601; various machine-gun and/or cannon armament (10).
Bf 109B–1: Initial production model; 680hp Jumo 210Da; two 7.9mm MG 17 machine-guns in upper cowling (approx 30).
Bf 109B–2: Modified B–1; variable-pitch metal propeller; late models with 700hp Jumo 210G; Messerschmitt- and Fieseler-built.
Bf 109C–1: As B–2; Jumo 210Ga; deeper intake; two addn 7.9mm MG 17 machine-guns in wing; Messerschmitt-, Fieseler-, Focke-Wulf-, and Erla-built.
Bf 109C–2: As C–1; one addn engine-mounted 7.9mm MG 17 machine-gun.
Bf 109C–4: As C–2; engine-mounted MG 17 replaced by 20mm MG FF cannon; project only.
Bf 109D–0: Pre-production model; 960hp DB 600A; two 7.9mm MG 17 machine-guns plus one 20mm MG FF cannon.
Bf 109D–1: Production model; structural strengthening; deep radiator bath deleted; increased fuel capacity (approx 175).
Bf 109D–2/3: As D–1; increased armament; projects only.
Bf 109C–2 to D–1: Messerschmitt-, Focke-Wulf-, Fieseler-, Erla-, and Arado-built.
Total Production: 30,500+ (all Bf–109 Marks except foreign prod).
Remarks: Epitome of German Luftwaffe of WWII, Bf 109 involved on every fighting front from first day of war until last; prototype first flown Sept 1935; V4/6 service evaluation with Condor Legion in Spain early 1937; followed by B–1/2 (40) and C–1 (12) models; despite intensive conversion to improved E–1 variant during Spring and Summer 1939, number of earlier examples remained on first-line strength upon outbreak WWII; participated Polish campaign, and as interim night-fighter in defence northern Germany until Spring 1940, after which relegated training role.

Manufacturer: Messerschmitt.
Model: Bf 109E–3.
Type: Fighter.
Power Plant: One 1,175hp Daimler-Benz DB 601Aa.
Performance:
maximum speed at sea level 290mph (467km/hr).
maximum speed at 14,560ft (4,440m) 348mph (560km/hr).
cruising speed 300mph (483km/hr).
maximum range 410 miles (660km).
time to 3,280ft (1,000m) 1min 6sec.
service ceiling 34,450ft (10,500m).
Weights:
empty 4,189lb (1,900kg).
loaded 5,875lb (2,665kg).
Dimensions:
wing span 32ft 4½in (9.87m).
length 28ft 4¼in (8.64m).
height 8ft 2¼in (2.50m).
wing area 174.05sq ft (16.17sq m).
Armament: Two 20mm MG FF cannon in wings; two 7.9mm MG 17 machine-guns in upper cowling; one 20mm MG FF/M cannon firing through propeller hub.
Crew: 1.
In Service: Bulgaria (19 Bf 109E–4), Croatia, Germany, Great Britain (2+ captured/evaluation), Japan (3 Bf 109E–4 evaluation), Rumania (69 Bf 109E–4), Slovakia (14 Bf 109E–7), Spain, Switzerland (89 Bf 109E), USSR (5 Bf 109E–3, evaluation), Yugoslavia (73 Bf 109E).
Variants (with no. built):
Bf 109 V14/15: Prototypes; 1,050hp DB 601A–1; two 7.9mm MG 17 machine-guns plus (V14) two 20mm MG FF cannon (2).
Bf 109E–0: Pre-production model; four 7.9mm MG 17s (10).
Bf 109E–1: Production model; two 7.9mm MG 17s in upper cowling, plus two 20mm MG FF cannon in wings.
Bf 109E–1/B: Fighter-bomber version; provision for max bomb load 551lb (250kg).
Bf 109E–3: Re-engined E–1; one addn (engine-mounted) 20mm MG FF cannon (usually deleted in service); improved canopy; armour plating.
Bf 109E–4: As E–1; modified armament; nose cannon deleted.
Bf 109E–4/B: Fighter-bomber version; as E–4; max bomb load 551lb (250kg).
Bf 109E–4/N: Modified E–4; 1,200hp DB 601N.
Bf 109E–5: Reconnaissance fighter version; modified E–4; one Rb 50/30 camera; wing cannon deleted.
Bf 109E–4/Trop., E–5/Trop: As E–4 and E–5 resp; tropicalized.
Bf 109E–6: Reconnaissance-fighter version; as E–5; 1,200hp DB 601N.
Bf 109E–7: As E–4/N; provision for one 551lb (250kg) SC 250 bomb or 66 Imp gal drop tank; some tropicalized (E–7/Trop), others with addn armour plating (E–7/U2).
Bf 109E–7/Z: As E–7; addn GM 1 power booster.
Bf 109E–8: Re-engined E–7; 1,350hp DB 601E.
Bf 109E–9: Reconnaissance-fighter version of E–8; one Rb 50/30, or two Rb 32/7 cameras; wing cannon deleted.
(Total Bf 109E–0/9, Messerschmitt, AGO-, Fieseler-, Erla, and (Austrian) WNF-built: 4,000+).
Bf 109T–0: Pre-production model; carrier-borne fighter version; catapult points; arrester hook; redesigned (folding) wing; ten E–1 conversions.
Bf 109T–2: Production model; land-based fighter-bomber version; 1,200hp DB 601N; carrier equipment deleted; provision for max 551lb (250kg) bomb load or 66 Imp gal drop tank; Fieseler-built (60).
Total Production: 30,500+ (all Bf 109 Marks, excl foreign prod).
Remarks: Entering service end 1938, Bf 109E quickly supplanted majority earlier models, accounting for approx 75% of over 1,100 Messerschmitt fighters on Luftwaffe strength upon outbreak WWII; particpated Polish, Norwegian, and Low Countries/French campaigns, but undoubtedly most closely associated with epic struggle against RAF Fighter Command during 1940 Battle of Britain; equal, if not superior in certain respects, of both Spitfire and Hurricane (610 Messerschmitts lost on operations during Battle, as against 1,043 of latter), Bf 109 units bested by own tactical dictates—close escort of bombers, and enforced conversion to fighter-bomber role; subsequently engaged Balkan (against Bf 109Es of Yugoslav AF), and North African campaigns; also opening phases invasion of Soviet Union, before gradual withdrawal from front-line fighter inventory; continued to equip number of satellite AFs (and volunteer sqns) on Eastern Front into 1942; specialized (intended carrier-borne) Bf 109T service restricted Norway, 1941–42.

Manufacturer: Messerschmitt.
Model: Bf 109F–2.
Type: Fighter.
Power Plant: One 1,200hp Daimler-Benz DB 601N.
Performance:
maximum speed at 19,685ft (6,000m) 373mph (600km/hr).
cruising speed 328mph (528km/hr).
maximum range 528 miles (650km).
time to 16,400ft (5,000m) 5min 12sec.
service ceiling 36,090ft (11,000m).
Weights:
empty 5,188lb (2,353kg).
loaded 6,173lb (2,800kg).
Dimensions:
wing span 32ft 5¾in (9.9m).
length 29ft 0½in (8.85m).
height 8ft 6in (2.59m).
wing area 174.38sq ft (16.2m).
Armament: One 15mm MG 151 cannon firing through propeller hub; two 7.9mm MG 17 machine-guns in upper cowling.
Crew: 1.
In Service: Croatia, Germany, Great Britain (2+captured/evaluation), Hungary (20 Bf 109F–4), Italy (Bf 109F–4), Spain (15+ Bf 109F–4), Switzerland (2 interned/impressed).
Variants (with no. built):
Bf 109 V21/24: Prototypes; 1,175hp DB 601Aa (V21) or 1,350hp DB 601E; modified (symmetrical) cowling; rounded wingtips (V23) and unbraced tailplane (4).
Bf 109F–0: Pre-production model; 1,200hp DB 601N; two 7.9mm MG 17 plus one 20mm MG FF/M cannon (10).
Bf 109F–1: Production model; as F–0; modified supercharger intake.
Bf 109F–2: As F–1; MG FF/M cannon replaced by one 15mm MG 151.
Bf 109F–3: Re-engined F–2; 1,350hp DB 601E; increased weight.
Bf 109F–4: Modified F–3; 15mm MG 151 replaced by 20mm MG 151 cannon; increased armour plating.
Bf 109F–2/Z, F–4/Z: As F–2 and F–4 resp; addn GM 1 power booster.
Nf 109F–2/Trop, F–4/Trop: Tropicalized versions of F–2 and F–4 resp.
Bf 109F–4/B: Fighter-bomber version; one 551lb (250kg) bomb.
Bf 109F–4/R1 to F–4/R6: Modified F–4s; various Rüstsätze (field conversion kits) for addn armament, bombs, or drop tanks.
Bf 109F–5: Reconnaissance version; 20mm MG 151 cannon deleted; one camera; provision for addn drop tank.
Bf 109F–6: Unarmed reconnaissance version; camera bay; interchangeable Rb 20/30, Rb 50/30, Rb 75/30 cameras.
(Total Bf 109F–0/6, Messerschmitt-, Erla-, and (Austrian) WNF-built:

approx 2,200).
Bf 109Z: (Zwilling): Experimental heavy fighter/fighter-bomber version; two Bf 109F airframes connected by parallel-chord wing centre-section to form 'twin' configuration; two 1,350hp DB 601E–1; span 43ft 6¼in (13.27m); prototype only.
Total Production: 30,500+ (all Bf 109 Marks, excl foreign prod).
Remarks: Re-engined, aerodynamically refined Bf 109F entered service Channel Front Spring 1941, partly redressing ascendancy being gained by RAF's newly-introduced Spitfire V; equipped almost two-thirds Luftwaffe fighter force upon invasion Soviet Union; also employed North Africa at height of Western Desert campaigns; although eventful, operational career relatively brief, replacement by Bf 109G commencing mid-1942; continued service Hungarian and Spanish AFs (former engaged on Eastern Front, 1942–43, together with similarly-equipped Spanish and Croatian volunteer Staffeln); sole Bf 109 Zwilling (Twin) prototype damaged by Allied air attack prior to first flight.

Manufacturer: Messerschmitt.
Model: Bf 109G–2.
Type: Fighter.
Power Plant: One 1,475hp Daimler-Benz DB 605A.
Performance:
maximum speed at sea level 317mph (510km/hr).
maximum speed at 28,540ft (9,000m) 406mph (653km/hr).
maximum range 528 miles (850km).
time to 6,560ft (2,000m) 1min 30sec.
service ceiling 39,370ft (12,000m).
Weights:
empty 4,968lb (2,253kg).
maximum 7,055lb (3,200kg).
Dimensions:
wing span 32ft 6½in (9.92m).
length 29ft 0½in (8.85m).
height 8ft 2½in (2.50m).
wing area 173.3sq ft (16.1sq m).
Armament: One 20mm MG 151/20 cannon firing through propeller hub; two 7.9mm MG 17 machine-guns in upper cowling.
Crew: 1.
In Service: Bulgaria (29 Bf 109G–2, 50+ Bf 109G–6/G–10), Croatia (Bf 109G–2/G–6/G–10), Finland (1 Bf 109G–1, 47 Bf 109G–2, 30 Bf 109G–6, 3 Bf 109G–8, 81 Bf 109G–10), Germany, Great Britain (2+ captured/evaluation), Hungary (approx 59 Bf 109G–2/G–4, plus approx 300 G–2/G–6/G–14 licence production), Italy (RSI 28 Bf 109G–6, 97 Bf 109G–10, 4 Bf 109G–12), Rumania (135 Bf 109G–2/G–6/G–8, plus approx 16 licence-production), Slovakia (30 Bf 109G–6), Switzerland (12 Bf 109G–6, plus 2 interned/impressed), USA (1+ evaluation), USSR (1+ captured/evaluation).
Variants (with no. built):
Bf 109G–0: Pre-production model; 1,350hp DB 601E; revised cowling; enlarged oil cooler; pressurized cockpit.
Bf 109G–1: Production model; as G–0; 1,475hp DB 605A; two 7.9mm MG 17s plus one 20mm MG 151 cannon; provision for GM 1 power booster.
Bf 109G–1/Trop: Tropicalized version of G–1; MG 17s replaced by two 13mm MG 131 machine-guns.
Bf 109G–2: As G–1; unpressurized; one converted as fighter-bomber with redesigned undercarriage and one 1,102lb (500kg) bomb (Bf 109G–2/R1).
Bf 109G–3/4: As G–1 and G–2 resp; revised radio equipment.
Bf 109G–5: As G–1; alt DB 605A/605As (with GM 1 power booster/addn supercharging resp; one 20mm MG 151 cannon plus two 13mm MG 131 machine-guns.
Bf 109G–5/U2: As G–5; wooden tailplane.
Bf 109G–6: 'Standard' model; unpressurized; various alt DB 605A/D power plants; late models with engine-mounted 20mm MG 151 replaced by 30mm MK 108 cannon.
Bf 109G–6/R1 to R6: As G–6; various 'Rüstsätze' (field conversion kits) for addn/alt underwing armament or ventral stores.
Bf 109G–6/U2: As G–6; wooden tailplane; some with enlarged wooden vertical tail surfaces.
Bf 109G–6/U4: Modified G–6; semi-retractable tailwheel.
Bf 109G–6/N: Night-fighter version of G–6; FuG 350 Naxos Z; two 20mm MG 151 cannon in underwing gondolas (as G–6/R–6).
Bf 109G–7: Projected 'standardization' G–6/R–2 and R–4 versions.
Bf 109G–8: Reconnaissance-fighter version; modified G–6; alt DB 605A–1/AS; one engine-mounted 30mm MK 108 (or 20mm MG 151) cannon; one camera.
Bf 109G–10: Improved G–6; 1,850hp DB 605D; one engine-mounted 30mm MK 108 (or 20mm MG 151) cannon plus two 13mm MG 131 machine-guns in upper cowling.
BF 109G–10/R1 to R6: As G–10; various 'Rüstsätze' (field conversion kits) for addn/alt underwing armament, camera, or ventral stores.
Bf 109G–10/U2: As G–10; wooden tailplane.
Bf 109G–10/U4: As G–10/U2; addn enlarged wooden vertical tail surfaces.
Bf 109G–12: 2-seat trainer version; Bf 109G conversions.
Bf 109G–14: Modified G–6; alt DB 605AM/605AS; improved-vision canopy; fixed (lengthened) tailwheel; one engine-mounted 20mm MG 151 cannon plus two 13mm MG 131s; some with wooden tail surfaces (Bf 109G–14/U4); provision for underwing armament/ventral stores.
Bf 109G–16: As G–14; 1,850hp DB 605D; addn armour; two 20mm MG 151 cannon in underwing gondolas plus ventral ETC bomb rack.
(Total Bf 109G–0/16: Messerschmitt-, Erla, (Austrian) WNF-, (Hungarian) MAVAG-, and (Rumanian) Brasov-built: approx 23,500).
Total Production: 30,500– (all Bf 109 Marks, except foreign prod).
Remarks: Numerically by far most important of entire series, Bf 109G's operational debut early Summer 1942 with Channel-based JGs (fighter groups); bore brunt latter war years' heavy attritional campaigning, serving extensively on all fronts, Russian, Mediterranean, Western, and Defence of Reich; subject numerous field conversions/modifications, employed in wide variety interceptor, bomber-destroyer, and ground-attack roles; suffered increasingly severe losses final months 1944–45; last major operation, only recorded mass-sortie by specially-activated 'Rammkommando', 7 April 1945, resulted in over 90% casualties among 120-strong attacking force; equipped all Axis Satellite AFs deployed Eastern Front, principally Hungarian, Rumanian, and Finnish (two latter subsequently using Bf 109G in considerable numbers against erstwhile allies); Finnish AF employment until mid-fifties; post-war development by both Czechoslovakia (S 99/199) and Spain (HA–1109/1112).
Colour Reference: Plates 42, 43: Messerschmitt Bf 109G–14/U4 of Major Friedrich-Karl Müller, Kommandeur I./NJG 11; Bonn-Hangelar, Feb 1945; special anti-Mosquito single-seat night-fighter Gruppe; note unusual dapple finish, lack of fuselage tactical markings, and installation single rearward-firing 20mm MG 151/20 cannon in dorsal 'Schräge Musik' mounting.

Manufacturer: Messerschmitt.
Model: Bf 109K–4.
Type: Fighter.
Power Plant: One 2,00hp Daimler-Benz DB 605ASCM.
Performance:
maximum speed at sea level 378mph (608km/hr).
maximum speed at 19,685ft (6,000m) 452mph (727km/hr).
normal range 366 miles (590km).
time to 32,810ft (10,000m) 6min 42 sec.
service ceiling 41,000ft (12,500m).
Weights:
empty 4,886lb (2,380kg).
maximum 7,937lb (3,600kg).
Dimensions:
wing span 32ft 8¼in (9.97m).
length 29ft 0½in (8.85m).
height 8ft 2½in (2.5m).
wing area 173.3sq ft (16.1sq m).
Armament: One 30mm MK 108 (or MK 103) cannon firing through propeller hub; two 15mm MG 151 cannon in upper cowling.
Crew: 1.
In Service: Germany, Italy (RSI 19 Bf 109K–4).
Variants:
Bf 109 V49, 50 and 109H V54, 55: Prototypes; high altitude/performance fighter; 1,490hp DB 628A or (V55) 1,600hp DB 605B; enlarged Bf 109G airframes.
Bf 109H–0: Pre-production model; high-altitude fighter version; modified F–4 airframes; addn parallel chord wing centre section; 1,350hp DB 603E–1 with GM 1 power booster; one engine-mounted 20mm MG 151 cannon plus two 7.9mm MG 17s.
Bf 109H–1: Service Trials model; modified G–5 airframes; 1,475hp DB 605A plus GM 1 power booster; pressurized cockpit; armament as H–0, plus provision for one camera.
Bf 109H–2/4: Projected heavy, and light high-altitude fighter and unarmed reconnaissance versions resp.
Bf 109K–0: Pre-production model; improved Bf 109G–10; 1,850hp DB 605D(B) plus GM 1; refined cowling and spinner; enlarged (wooden) tail surfaces with modified rudder; improved-vision canopy; semi-retractable tailwheel; three cannon armament.
Bf 109K–2, 4: Production models; 2,000hp DB 605ASCM/DCM; K–4 pressurized cockpit; late models with engine-mounted 30mm MK 103 cannon.
Bf 109K–6: As K–4; two addn MK 103s in underwing gondolas; 20mm MG 151 cannon in upper cowling replaced by two 13mm MG 131 machine-guns.
Bf 109K–14: 1,725hp DB 605L; two 13mm MG 131 machine-guns in upper cowling plus one engine-mounted 30mm MK 108 (or MK 103) cannon.
Total Production: 30,500+ (all Bf 109 Marks, except foreign prod).
Remarks: Short-lived Bf 109H programme abandoned in favour of Focke Wulfe Ta 152H; brief operational appearance one Channel-based long-range reconnaissance Staffel, Spring 1944; last of ten-year line, Bf 109K represented belated attempt standardization after multiplicity Bf 109G sub-variants; entering service late 1944, participated Operation 'Bodenplatte' (lit 'Ground-plate'), last-ditch attack on Allied airfields in Low Countries and France, 1 Jan 1945; subsequent sporadic use by some half-dozen Jagdgruppen prior final surrender, 8 May, 1945.
Colour Reference: Plate 44: Messerschmitt Bf 109K–4 (red '10') of I./JG 300 flown by Fw. Wolfgang Hundsdorfer; Borkheide (nr Berlin), Jan 1945; note personal insignia below cockpit, and Reichs-defence bands around rear fuselage.

Manufacturer: Messerschmitt.
Model: Bf 110C–1.
Type: Heavy fighter.
Power Plant: Two 1,100hp Daimler-Benz DB 601A–1.
Performance:
maximum speed at 13,120ft (4,000m) 326mph (525km/hr).
cruising speed 217mph (350km/hr).
maximum range 680 miles (1,100km).
initial rate of climb 2,165ft/min (660m/min).
time to 19,685ft (6,000m) 10min 12sec.
service ceiling 32,810ft (10,000m).
Weights:
empty 9,755lb (4,425kg).
maximum 14,880lb (6,750kg).
Dimensions:
wing span 53ft 3¾in (16.25m).
length 39ft 7⅞in (12.7m).
height 13ft 6½in (4.13m).
wing area 413.33sq ft (38.4sq m).
Armament: Four fixed forward-firing 7.9mm MG 17 machine-guns and two fixed forward-firing 20mm MG FF cannon in nose; plus one flexible 7.9mm MG 15 machine-gun in rear cockpit.
Crew: 2–3.
In Service: Germany, Great Britain (2+ captured/evaluation).
Variants (with no. built):
Bf 110 V1/3: Prototypes; long-range fighter; two 910hp DB 600A; V3 armed (3).
Bf 110A–0: Pre-production model; two 680hp Junkers Jumo 210Da (4).
Bf 110B–0: Pre-production model; two 700hp Jumo 210Ga; refined nose contours; unarmed (10).
Bf 110B–1: Initial production model; as B–0; four 7.9mm MG 17s and two 20mm MG FF cannon in nose, plus one 7.9mm MG 15 in rear cockpit.
Bf 110B–2: Reconnaissance version; nose cannon deleted; camera equipment.
(Total Bf 110B–1, –2: 45).
Bf 110B–3: 2-seat trainer version; nose cannon and machine-guns deleted; B–1/2 conversions.
Bf 110C–0: Pre-production model; re-engined (1,100hp DB 601A) Bf 110B–1; modified radiators; revised (angular) wingtips (10).
Bf 110C–1: Production model; as C–0; DB 601A–1s.
Bf 110C–1/U1: Modified C–1; Me 321 glider-tug.
Bf 110C–2: As C–1; improved electrics and rear gunner's position.
Bf 110C–3: As C–2; improved MG FF nose cannon; Messerschmitt-, Focke-Wulf-, Gotha-, (Austrian) WNF-built (approx 1,300).
Bf 110C–4: As C–3; armour protection.
Bf 110C–4B: Fighter-bomber version; ventral ETC 250 racks; max bomb load 1,102lb (500kg); two 1,200hp DB 601N.
Bf 110C–5: Reconnaissance version; nose cannon deleted; one Rb 50/30 camera; 1,100hp DB 601A–1s.
Bf 110C–5/N: As C–5; 1,200hp DB 601Ns.
Bf 110C–6: Heavy fighter-version; modified C–4; MG 151 nose cannon replaced by single 30mm MK 101.
Bf 110C–7: Fighter-bomber version; DB 601Ns; two ETC 500 racks; max bomb load 2,205lb (1,000kg); strengthened undercarriage.
Total Production: approx 6,000 (all Marks).
Remarks: First flown May, 1936, Bf 110 equipped three Gruppen upon outbreak WWII; participated Polish, Norwegian, and Low Countries/French campaigns, before suffering first major reversal at hands of Fighter Command during Battle of Britain (over 200 Bf 110s lost, Aug–Sept 1940); defeat by day led to new career as night-fighter, role in which Bf 110 was to be employed for remainder of hostilities; first night-fighter Gruppe in fact formed July, 1940, initial victories being gained by purely visual means in Bf 110Cs 'modified' by addition flame dampers but lacking all radar.

Manufacturer: Messerschmitt.
Model: Bf 110F–2.
Type: Heavy fighter.
Power Plant: Two 1,350hp Daimler-Benz DB 601F.
Performance:
maximum speed at 17,700ft (5,400m) 352mph (566km/hr).
cruising speed 248mph (400km/hr).
maximum range 745 miles (1,200km).
time to 19,685ft (6,000m) 9min 18sec.
service ceiling 35,760ft (10,900m).
Weights:
empty 12,346lb (5,600kg).
maximum 15,653lb (7,000kg).
Dimensions:
wing span 53ft 3¾in (16.25m).
length 39ft 7⅛in (12.0m).
height 13ft 6½in (4.13m).
wing area 413.33sq ft (38.4sq m).
Armament: Four fixed forward-firing 7.9mm MG 17 machine-guns and two fixed forward-firing 20mm MG FF cannon in nose; plus one flexible 7.9mm MG 15 machine-gun in rear cockpit.
Crew: 2.
In Service: Germany.
Variants (with no. built):
Bf 110D–0: Pre-production model; long-range heavy fighter version of Bf 110C; 264 Imp gal auxiliary fuel tank in large (plywood/fabric) ventral fairing; 20mm MG FF nose cannon deleted; 1,100hp DB 601A–1s; Bf 110C–3 conversions.
Bf 110D–1/R1: Production model; as Bf 110D–0.
Bf 110D–1/R2: Modified D–1/R–1; ventral tank deleted; two 198 Imp gal underwing drop tanks; nose cannon reinstated.
Bf 110D–1/U1: Night-fighter version; nose-mounted 'Spanner-Anlage' (infra-red sensor).
Bf 110D–2: Fighter-bomber version; as Bf 110D–1/R2; two 66 Imp gal drop tanks plus max 2,205lb (1,000kg) bomb load; some tropicalized (D–2/Trop).
Bf 110D–3: Long-range convoy-escort; as D–2 (alt 66/198 Imp gal drop tanks); addn oil tank; dinghy in extended tail section; 1,200hp DB 601Ns.
Bf 110E–0: Pre-production model; improved D–2; four underwing ETC 50 racks; max bomb load 2,645lb (1,200kg).
Bf 110E–1: Production model; alt DB 601As or DB 601Ns; some as night-fighter with 'Spanner-Anlage' (infra-red sensor) (E–1/U1), or as 3-seat formation leader (E–1/U2), or with addn ETC 1000 racks for max 4,410lb (2,000kg) bomb load (E–1/R2).
Bf 110E–2: Fighter-bomber version; as E–1; 1,200hp DB 601Ns; dinghy in extended tail as D–3.
Bf 110E–3: Long-range reconnaissance version; modified E–1; nose cannon and ventral ETC racks deleted; two rearward-firing 7.9mm MG 17 machine-guns in fuselage sides; one camera.
Bf 110F–0: Pre-production model; modified Bf 110E–1; two 1,350hp DB 601F.
Bf 110F–1: Production model; fighter-bomber version; as F–0; addn armour; ventral/underwing ETC 500/50 racks.
Bf 110F–2: Fighter version; as F–1; ETC racks deleted.
Bf 110F–3: Long-range reconnaissance version; as E–3; DB 601Fs.
Bf 110F–4: 3-seat night-fighter version; addn two forward-firing 30mm MK 108 cannon in ventral tray; revised (enlarged) vertical tail surfaces.
Bf 110F–4/U1: As F–4; Ventral tray deleted; 30mm MK 108 cannon in oblique upward-firing 'Schräge Musik' installation in rear cockpit; 7.9mm MG 15 machine-gun deleted.
Bf 110F–4a: As F–4; ventral tray deleted; forward-firing 20mm MG FF cannon replaced by 20mm MG 151s; FuG 202 Lichtenstein radar.
(All Bf 110D/F: Messerschmitt-, Gotha-, and MIAG-built).
Total Production: approx 6,000 (all Marks).
Remarks: Early long-range Bf 110Ds, based Norway, participated Battle of Britain; sustained heavy losses in only major cross-North Sea raid of Battle, 15 Aug 1940; later models subsequently participated Balkans/Mediterranean campaigns in variety fighter-bomber, reconnaissance, and shipping-escort roles; also employed as fighter-bomber Eastern Front (along with remaining Bf 110Cs); F–4, fore-runner specialized radar-equipped night-fighter series, entered service early 1942 as interim measure prior advent improved Bf 110G.

Manufacturer: Messerschmitt.
Model: Bf 110G–4.
Type: Night-fighter.
Power Plant: Two 1,475hp Daimler-Benz DB 605B.
Performance:
maximum speed at 22,950ft (7,000m) 342mph (550km/hr).
maximum range 1,305 miles (2,100km).
initial rate of climb 2,170ft/min (661m/min).
service ceiling 26,250ft (8,000m).
Weights:
empty 11,220lb (5,090kg).
loaded 20,700lb (9,390kg).
Dimensions:
wing span 53ft 4¾in (16.27m).
length 41ft 6¾in (12.65m).
height 13ft 1¼in (3.99m).
wing area 413.33sq ft (38.4sq m).
Armament: Four fixed forward-firing 7.9mm MG 17 machine-guns and two fixed forward-firing 20mm MG 151 (or 30mm MK 108) cannon in nose; plus one flexible 7.9mm twin MG 81Z machine-gun in rear cockpit.
Crew: 3.
In Service: Germany, Great Britain (1+ evaluation), Hungary (6), Italy, Rumania, Switzerland (1 interned/impressed).
Variants:
Bf 110G–0: Pre-production model; heavy fighter version; as Bf 110F; two 1,574hp DB 605B–1.
Bf 110G–1: Production model; forward-firing 20mm MG FF cannon replaced by 20mm MG 151s; ETC racks deleted.
Bf 110G–2: Improved G–1; revised vertical tail surfaces as F–4; strengthened undercarriage; 7.9mm MG 15 in rear cockpit replaced by 7.9mm twin MG 81Z; alt ventral ETC racks/two 20mm MG 151 gun tray.
Bf 110G–2/R1 to R5: 'Rüstsäze' (field conversion kits) for alt/addn armament (inc ventral 37mm BK 3.7 (Flak 18) cannon), power boosting, or armour protection.
Bf 110G–3: Long-range reconnaissance-fighter version; nose cannon deleted; one fixed rearward-firing 20mm MG 151 cannon in ventral blister; two cameras.
Bf 110G–3/R3: As G–3; four fixed forward-firing 7.9mm MG 17 machine-guns replaced by two fixed forward-firing 30mm MK 108 cannon.
Bf 110G–4: Standard night-fighter version; subject multiplicity modifications, 'Rüstsätze' (field conversion kits), or 'Umrüst-Bausätze (factory conversion sets) as follows: Bf 110G–4a to 4d: Altn FuG 212/220b Lichtenstein C–1/SN–2 intercept radar; plus Bf 110G–4/R1 to G–4/R8 for altn/addn armament, power boosting and/or fuel; or Bf 110G–

4/U1 to G-4/U8 for altn/addn armament, radar, power boosting and fuel.
Bf 110H-1 to H-4: As Bf 110G-1 to G-4 resp; two DB 605Es; strengthened undercarriage and rear fuselage; retractable tailwheel; Bf 110H-3 armament as G-3/R3.
Total Production: approx 6,000 (all Marks).
Remarks: Complete failure of Me 210 as intended Bf 110 replacement led to reinstatement of latter in full-scale production and appearance definitive Bf 110G/H models in 1942; employed primarily in defence of Reich, both against USAAF by day (in bomber-destroyer role, some models equipped with 210mm WGr 21 air-to-air rocket tubes underwing), but in far greater numbers against RAF Bomber Command by night; at peak, Spring 1944, over 300 Bf 110s accounted for 60% Luftwaffe's night-fighter force; by year's end numbers declined to half that figure, but Bf 110Gs still operational with elements four Nachtjagdgeschwader, plus two Eastern Front reconnaissance Staffeln, at war's end.
Colour Reference: Plate 47: Messerschmitt Bf 110G-4d (G9+AA: Werk-Nr.140 655) flown by Oberstleutnant Hans-Joachim Jabs, Kommodore NJG 1, Eggebeck, Schleswig-Hostein, April 1945; note 'Schräge Musik' installation, FuG 218 Neptun V, and FuG 350 Naxos; on 1 May 1945 G9+AA scheduled to be ferried from Lüneburg to Neumünster by two NCO pilots who instead defected to Sweden, belly-landing at Hammerlöv (Trelleborg).

Manufacturer: Messerschmitt.
Model: Me 163B-1a Komet (Comet).
Type: Interceptor fighter.
Power Plant: One 3,750lb s.t. Walter HWK 509A-2.
Performance:
maximum speed at sea level 515mph (829km/hr).
maximum speed at 9,840ft (3,000m) 596mph (960km/hr).
normal range 50 miles (80km).
time to 30,000ft (9,100m) 2min 36sec.
service ceiling 39,500ft (12,000m).
Weights:
empty 4,190lb (1,900kg).
maximum 9,500lb (4,300kg).
Dimensions:
wing span 30ft 7¼in (9.33m).
length 19ft 2¼in (5.85m).
height 9ft 0½in (2.76m).
wing area 199.13sq ft (18.5sq m).
Armament: Two 30mm MK 108 cannon in wings.
Crew: 1.
In Service: Germany.
Variants (with no. built):
Me 163A V1/6: Prototypes; 1,653lb s.t. HWK RII-203b rocket (6).
Me 163A-0: Pre-production model; unpowered (glider) trainer version; Hirth-built (10).
Me 163B V1/6: Prototypes; extensive redesign fuselage, vertical tail surfaces, addn ventral fairing (extendable landing skid/tailwheel), fully blown canopy; 3,750lb.t. RII-211 (HWK 509A) (6).
Me 163Ba-1 (V7/41): Pre-production, and service test, models; two 20mm MG 151 cannon in wings (70).
Me 163B-1a: Initial production model; two 30mm MK 108 cannon in wings; armour plating; FuG 16zy plus addn FuG 25a; cockpit, rear fuselage modifications; Klemm-built.
Me 163S: 2-seat trainer glider version of Me 163B.
(Total Me 163B-1a, 163S: approx 300).
Me 163C V1/3: Prototypes; lengthened fuselage; auxiliary cruising chamber; twin rocket pipes; fuselage-mounted armament (3).
Me 163D V1: Improved Me 163B; further fuselage length increase; retractable nosewheel undercarriage; unarmed (1).
Me 263 V1: Me 163D development; wing-mounted armament (1).
MXY8 Akigusa (Autumn Grass): IJNAF equivalent of Me 163A training glider; Yokosuka-, Maeda-built.
Ki-13 Shusui (Swinging Sword): IJAAF equivalent of Me 163A training glider; Yokoi-built.
(Total MXY8, Ki-13: approx 60).
J8MI Shusui (Swinging Sword): IJNAF equivalent of Me 163B.
Ki-200 Shusui (Swinging Sword): IJAAF equivalent of Me 163B.
(Total J8MI, Ki-200; Mitsubishi-built: 7).
Total Production: approx 400 (excl Japanese).
Remarks: Developed from long line Lippisch tailless (powered) gliders, unique rocket-powered Me 163 entered service May, 1944; assigned defence nearby synthetic fuel plants, Komet's combat debut late July, attacking USAAF B-17s without result; equipped one operational Jagdgruppe mid-1944/Spring 1945, but limited period/radius of action, plus increasing shortages rocket fuels and trained pilots, restricted number confirmed 'kills' to just nine for loss of fourteen Komets in action; Japanese development programme terminated by Pacific surrender, Aug 1945; only one prototype J8M1 flown.
Colour Reference: Plates 48, 49: Messerschmitt Me 163B-1a Komet of II./Jg 400, Husum, Schleswig-Holstein, May 1945; yellow '10' belonged to 7.Staffel, only Komet unit remaining on Luftwaffe order of battle at close WWII (on paper forming part of 2.Jagddivision headquartered at nearby Hackstedt, in reality grounded from lack of fuel and completely ineffectual).

Manufacturer: Messerschmitt.
Model: Me 210A-1.
Type: Heavy fighter (Zerstörer)/fighter-bomber.
Power Plant: Two 1,350hp Daimler-Benz DB 601F.
Performance:
maximum speed at 17,820ft (5,430m) 350mph (563km/hr).
cruising speed 385mph (620km/hr).
maximum range 1,130miles (1,820km).
time to 13,120ft (4,000m) 7min 30sec.
service ceiling 22,970ft (7,000m).
Weights:
empty 15,586lb (7,070kg).
maximum 21,390lb (9,700kg).
Dimensions:
wing span 53ft 7¼in (16.34m).
length 39ft 9¼in (12.12m).
height 14ft 0½in (4.28m).
wing area 389.657sq ft (36.2sq m).
Armament: Two fixed forward-firing 7.9mm MG 17 machine-guns; two fixed forward-firing 20mm MG 151 cannon; plus two rearward-firing 13mm MG 131 machine-guns in remotely-controlled FDL 131 barbettes; max (optional) bomb load 2,204lb (1,000kg).
Crew: 2.
In Service. Germany, Hungary (159 Me 210C-1/Ca-1), Japan (1 Me 210A-2, evaluation).
Variants (with no. built):
Me 210V1/V15: Prototypes and service test models; two 1,050hp DB 601A-1, DB-601Bf, or DB 601F; progressive tail (twin and single), wing, cockpit, and equipment modifications (15).
Me 210A-0: Pre-production model; DB 601Fs; armament plus max 2,204lb (1,000kg) bomb load (94).
Me 210A-1: Initial production model; Zerstörer/fighter-bomber version (optional bomb load as A-0); late models with modified (lengthened) rear fuselage.
Me 210A-2 Dive-bomber/Zerstörer version; max bomb load 4,408lb (2,000kg); all models with modified (lengthened) rear fuselage.
(Total Me 210A-1A-2: Messerschmitt-, MIAC-built: approx 175).
Me 210B-0: Reconnaissance version; two cameras; forward-firing MG 17s deleted; two A-0 conversions.
Me 210B-1: Production model; as B-0 (2).
Me 210 V17: Me 410 (and Me 210C) prototype; lengthened rear fuselage; automatic leading-edge slots; one A-0 conversion.
Me 210C V1: Prototype; as V17; two 1,475hp DB 605B; one A-0 conversion.
Me 210C-1: Reconnaissance/Zerstörer version; as late model Me 210A; two 1,475hp DB 605B.
Me 210Ca-1: Zerstörer/dive-bomber version; as C-1; max bomb load 2,204lb (1,000kg).
(Total Me 210C-1/Ca-1 (Hungarian): DAF built: 262).
Me 210D: Improved Me 210C; project only.
Total Production: approx 550.
Remarks: As intended successor to Bf 110 Zerstörer, Me 210 proved complete failure; early models (184 Me 210A-0/A-1s produced) saw brief service as heavy-fighter on Eastern Front, Spring 1942; modified A-1/A-2s resumed operations Autumn 1942; limited use fighter-bomber role over UK, majority employed Mediterranean area by Zerstörer and long-range reconnaissance units; improved Hungarian-built Me 210C (inc 108 delivered Luftwaffe) equipped Hungarian AF sqns on Eastern Front as dive-bomber, close-support aircraft, and as day/night-fighter for home-defence.
Colour Reference: Plates 45, 46: Messerschmitt Me 210A-1 (2H+DA) of Versuchsstaffel (Test Squadron) 210; Soesterberg, Netherlands, Aug 1942; standard day-fighter finish; Versuchsst.210 redesignated 16./KG 6 by end Aug 1942, suffering first operational losses (to RAF Typhoons) over UK during first week Sept.

Manufacturer: Messerschmitt.
Model: Me 261 V3.
Type: Long-range reconnaissance.
Power Plant: Two 2,950hp Daimler-Benz DB 610A-1/B-1.
Performance:
maximum speed at sea level 305mph (490km/hr).
maximum speed at 21,325ft (6,500m) 385mph (620km/hr).
cruising speed 248mph (400km/hr).
range 6,830 miles (11,000km).
service ceiling 27,100ft (8,260m).
Dimensions:
wing span 88ft 2in (26.87m).
length 54ft 9¼in (16.69m).
height 15ft 6in (4.72m).
wing area 818.06sq ft (76.0sq m).
Crew: 5-7.
In Service: Germany.
Variants (with no. built):
Me 261 V1, V2: Prototypes; two 2,700hp DB 606A-1/B-1; 5 crew (2).
Me 261 V3: Prototype; DB 610s; 2 addn crew (1).
Total Production: 3.
Remarks: Unofficially dubbed 'Adolfine' in recognition of Führer's personal interest in project,

Order of Battle 26 June 1944, East Front

GERMAN AIR FORCE (Luftwaffe)

FAR NORTHERN SECTOR: Luftflotte 5 (Air Fleet 5) Oslo
Kom.Gen.d.dtsch.Lw.i.Finnland (General OC German Air Force in Finland) Rovaniemi
Fl.Fü. 3 (Flying Leader 3) Kirkenes:

Strategic reconnaissance:			
1.(F)/124	Kirkenes	20	Junkers Ju 88 Messerschmitt Bf 109
1.(F)/32	Kemijärvi	15	Focke-Wulf Fw 189 Messerschmitt Bf 109
Maritime reconnaissance:			
3.(F)/SAGr.130	Kirkenes	8	Blohm und Voss Bv 138
Ground-attack:			
I./SG 5	Kirkenes	51	Focke-Wulf Fw 190 Junkers Ju 87

Jafü Norwegen (Fighter-leader Norway) Petsamo:

Fighters:			
III./JG 5	Petsamo	24	Messerschmitt Bf 109
Zerstörer (heavy fighters):			
13.(zerst.)/JG 5	Kirkenes	16	Messerschmitt Bf 110

NORTHERN (BALTIC) SECTOR: Luftflotte 1 (Air Fleet 1)
Malpils (Latvia):

Strategic reconnaissance:			
Stab/FAGr.1	Riga-Spilve		
3.(F)/22	Riga-Spilve	7	Junkers Ju 188
5.(F)/122	Mitau	9	Junkers Ju 88
NSt.3	Riga-Spilve	15	Dornier Do 217
Maritime reconnaissance:			
1./SAGr.127	Reval-Uleministe	12	Arado Ar 96 Henschel Hs 126 Junkers Ju 60
Bombers:			
14.(Eis.)/KG 55	Jakobstadt	9	Heinkel He 111

3.Fliegerdivision (3rd Flying Division) Petseri:

Tactical reconnaissance:			
Stab/NAGr.5	Petseri	4	Messerschmitt Bf 109 Focke-Wulf Fw 189
1./NAGr.5	Idriza	13	Messerschmitt Bf 109 Focke-Wulf Fw 189
1./NAGr.31	Wesenberg	11	Focke-Wulf Fw 189 Henschel Hs 126
Ground-attack:			
II./SG 3	Jakobstadt	35	Junkers Ju 87 Focke-Wulf Fw 190
Night ground-attack:			
Stab/NSGr.1 3./NSGr.1	Idriza Idriza	28	Gotha Go 145 Junkers W 34
1./NSGr.1 & 2./NSGr.1	Kovno		Re-equipping
Stab/NSGr.3 1./NSGr.3 & 2./NSGr.3	Vecumi Vecumi	49	Gotha Go 145 Arado Ar 66
1./NSGr.12	Vecumi	18	Arado Ar 66
Stab/NSGr.11 1./NSGr.11 & 2./NSGr.11	Rahkla Rahkla	31	Heinkel He 50 Fokker C.V
2./NSGr.12	Libau		Forming

Jagdabschnittsführer Ostland (Fighter sector-leader Baltic States) Riga-Spilve (Latvia):

Fighters:			
Stab/JG 54	Dorpat	12	Focke-Wulf Fw 190
1./JG 54	Turku (Finland)		Focke-Wulf Fw 190
2./JG 54 & 3./JG 54	Reval-Laksberg	22	Focke-Wulf Fw 190

Gefechtsverband Kulmey (Battle-unit Kulmey) Immola (Finland)

Tactical reconnaissance:			
1./NAGr.5	Immola		Messerschmitt Bf 109
Fighters:			
II./JG 54	Immola		Focke-Wulf Fw 190
Ground-attack:			
Stab/SG 3	Immola		Junkers Ju 87
1./SG 3	Immola		Focke-Wulf Fw 190
2./SG 3 & 3.SG 3	Immola		Junkers Ju 87

CENTRAL SECTOR: Luftflotte 6 (Air Fleet 6) Priluki:

Strategic reconnaissance:			
Stab/FAGr.2	Baranovichi		
4.(F)/11	Baranovichi	2	Junkers Ju 188 Heinkel He 111
4.(F)/14	Baranovichi	15	Junkers Ju 188 Dornier Do 217
NSt.4	Bobruisk		
Bombers:			
14.(Eis.)/KG 3	Puchivichi		
Stab/KG 1	Prohwehren		
II./KG 1	Prohwehren		

IV.Fliegerkorps (IV Flying Corps) Bre

Strategic reconnaissance:	
1.(F)/100	Pinsk
Tactical reconnaissance:	
Stab/NAGr.4	Biala-Podlaska
3./NAGr.4	Kobryn
12./NAGr.3	Brest-Litovsk
Bombers:	
Stab/KG 4	Bialystock
II./KG 4	Baranovichi
III./KG 4	Baranovichi
Stab/KG 27	Krosno
I./KG 27	Krosno
III./KG 27	Mielec
Stab/KG 53	Radom
I./KG 53	Radom
II./KG 53	Piastov
III./KG 53	Radom
Stab/KG 55	Deblin-Irena
I./KG 55	Deblin-Ulez
II./KG 55	Deblin-Irena
III./KG 55	Groyek

1.Fliegerdivision (1st Flying Division

Tactical reconnaissance:	
Stab/NAGr.15	Uretsye
1./NAGr.4	Bobruisk
11./NAGr.11	Uretsye
11./NAGr.12	Uretsye
Ground-attack:	
Stab/SG 1	Pastovichi
III./SG 1	Pastovichi
I./SG 10	Bobruisk

4.Fliegerdivision (4th Flying Division

Tactical reconnaissance:	
Stab/NAGr.10	Toloschin
2./NAGr.4	Orscha
13./NAGr.14	Toloschin
Ground-attack:	
I./SG 1	Toloschin
II./SG 1	Vilna
10.(Pz)/SG 1	Boyari
10.(Pz)/SG 3	Toloschin
Stab/SG 10	Dokudovo
III./SG 10	Dokudovo

Fl.Fü. 1 (Flying-leader 1) Minsk:

Tactical reconnaissance:	
12./NAGr.12	Mogilev
2./NAGr.5	Budsslav
4./NAGr.31	Budsslav
Night ground-attack:	
Stab/NSGr.2	Lida
1./NSGr.2	Bobruisk
3./NSGr.2	Lida
4./NSGr.2	Mogilev
1.Ostfl.St(Russ.) Eastern Volunteer Sqn. (Russian)	Lida
1./NSGr.1 & 2./NSGr.1	Kovno
Stab I./Eins.Gr.Fl. Sch.Div.	Borrissov
Flying Sch. Div. Operational Wing	
2. & 3./Eins.Gr.Fl. Sch.Div.	Borrissov

Me 261 conceived 1937 for non-stop prestige flight carrying 1940 Olympic Torch from Berlin to Tokyo; development halted prior outbreak WWII; three prototypes subsequently completed, one (V3) being employed in long-range reconnaissance role latter half 1943.

Manufacturer: Messerschmitt.
Model: Me 262A–1a.
Type: Interceptor fighter.
Power Plant: Two 1,980lb s.t. Junkers Jumo 004B–1, B–2, or B–3.
Performance:
maximum speed at 19,685ft (6,000m) 540mph (870km/hr).
normal range 525 miles (845km).
time to 19,685ft (6,000m) 6min 48sec.
service ceiling 37,565ft (11,450m).
Weights:
empty 8,378lb (3,800kg).
loaded 14,108lb (6,400kg).
Dimensions:
wing span 40ft 11½in (12.48m).
length 34ft 9½in (10.6m).
height 12ft 7in (3.83m).
wing area 234sq ft (21.7sq m).
Armament: Four 30mm MK 108 cannon in nose.
Crew: 1.
In Service: Germany.
Variants (with no. built):
Me 262 V1/5: Initial prototypes; two 1,850lb s.t. Jumo 004A turbojets; V1 originally with one 1,200hp Jumo 210G; unarmed (5).
Me 262A–0: Pre-production model (and prototypes); pressurized cockpit and canopy; some with provision for max 2,205lb (1,000kg) bomb load or rockets (23).
Me 262A–1a: Initial production model; four 30mm MK 108s.
Me 262A–1a/U1: Modified A–1a; two 20mm MG 151, two 30mm MK 108, plus two 30mm MK 103 cannon in nose (3).
Me 262A–1a/U3: Reconnaissance version; two cameras in addn nose bay; reduced (to two 30mm MK 108 cannon) armament (2).
Me 262–1b: As A–1a; plus provision for max twenty-four 55mm R4M rockets underwing.
Me 262A–2a: Fighter-bomber version; as A–1a; two pylons for max 1,102lb (500kg) bomb load.
Me 262A–2a/U1: Dive-bomber version; TSA (low-flying/diving device); two 30mm MK 108 nose cannon deleted; test models only (2).
Me 262A–2a/U2: Modified A–2a; redesigned (bombardier) glazed nose; Lofte 7H bomb sight; bomb load as A–2a; armament deleted; test model only (1).
Me 262A–3: Projected ground-attack version.
Me 262A–5a: Reconnaissance-fighter version; camera nose bay and armament as A–1/U3; two drop tanks.
Me 262B–1a: 2-seat dual control

	No.	Aircraft
7		Junkers Ju 88 / Junkers Ju 188
?3		Junkers Ju 88
1		Junkers Ju 88
?3		Junkers Ju 88

Litovsk:

	No.	Aircraft
?4		Junkers Ju 88
		Messerschmitt Bf 109
		Focke-Wulf Fw 189
		Henschel Hs 126
8		Messerschmitt Bf 109 / Henschel Hs 126 / Focke-Wulf Fw 189
8		Heinkel He 111 / Junkers Ju 88
34		Heinkel He 111
40		Heinkel He 111
1		Heinkel He 111
41		Heinkel He 111
35		Heinkel He 111
1		Heinkel He 111
37		Heinkel He 111
36		Heinkel He 111
1		Heinkel He 111
35		Heinkel He 111
35		Heinkel He 111
36		Heinkel He 111

...bruisk:

	No.	Aircraft
		Focke-Wulf Fw 189
12		Focke-Wulf Fw 189
9		Focke-Wulf Fw 189
7		Focke-Wulf Fw 189
5		Focke-Wulf Fw 190
?8		Focke-Wulf Fw 190

...rscha:

	No.	Aircraft
		Messerschmitt Bf 109 / Focke-Wulf Fw 189 / Henschel Hs 126
?3		Messerschmitt Bf 109 / Focke-Wulf Fw 189 / Henschel Hs 126
7		Messerschmitt Bf 109 / Focke-Wulf Fw 189 / Henschel Hs 126
?4		Junkers Ju 87
?3		Focke-Wulf Fw 190 / Junkers Ju 87
?0		Junkers Ju 87
?9		Focke-Wulf Fw 190
2		Messerschmitt Bf 109
6		Focke-Wulf Fw 189
2		Junkers Ju 87 / Arado Ar 66
4		Junkers Ju 87
1		Junkers Ju 87
7		Junkers Ju 87 / Arado Ar 66 / Gotha Go 145 / Arado Ar 66 / Polikarpov U-2

Re-equipping

42

1./Eins.Gr.Fl.Sch.Div. Dubinskaya
Jagdabschnittsführer 6 (Fighter sector-leader 6) Priluki:

Fighters:

Unit	Base	No.	Aircraft
Stab/JG 51	Orscha	5	Messerschmitt Bf 109 / Focke-Wulf Fw 190
Stab/St.JG 51	Orscha	12	Messerschmitt Bf 109 / Focke-Wulf Fw 190
I./JG 51	Orscha	35	Messerschmitt Bf 109
III./JG 51	Bobruisk	31	Messerschmitt Bf 109
IV./JG 51	Mogilev		Messerschmitt Bf 109
III./JG 11	Dokudovo		Messerschmitt Bf 109

Night-fighters:

Unit	Base	No.	Aircraft
Stab I./NJG 100			
1./NJG 100	Baranovichi		
1./NJG 100 (detachment)	Biala-Podlaska		
1./NJG 100 (detachment)	Baranovichi		Focke-Wulf Fw 189 / Dornier Do 217
1./NJG 100 (detachment)	Dokudovo		
3./NJG 100	Radom	51	Junkers Ju 88
3./NJG 100 (detachment)	Dokudovo		
4./NJG 100	Puckovichi		Junkers Ju 88

SOUTHERN SECTOR: Luftflotte 4 (Air Fleet 4) Morczyn:

Strategic reconnaissance:

Unit	Base	No.	Aircraft
2.(F)/11	Jasionka	9	Junkers Ju 88
2.(F)/22	Focsani	8	Junkers Ju 88
2.(F)/100	Lublin	7	Junkers Ju 188

I.Fliegerkorps (I Flying Corps) Focsani (Rumania):

Strategic reconnaissance:

Unit	Base	No.	Aircraft
3.(F)/121	Zilistea	8	Junkers Ju 88
NSt.1	Focsani	14	Dornier Do 217 / Heinkel He 111

Tactical reconnaissance:

Unit	Base	No.	Aircraft
Stab/NAGr.1	Kizhinev	3	Messerschmitt Bf 109 / Focke-Wulf Fw 189
2./NAGr.16	Kizhinev	10	Messerschmitt Bf 109 / Focke-Wulf Fw 189
Stab/NAGr.14	Comrat	3	Messerschmitt Bf 109
1./NAGr.14	Comrat	12	Messerschmitt Bf 109
2./NAGr.14	Bacau	15	Messerschmitt Bf 109

Maritime reconnaissance:

Stab/FAGr.125 (See) Constanza

Unit	Base	No.	Aircraft
1.(F)/125 (See)	Varna (Bulgaria)	9	Blohm und Voss Bv 138 / Arado Ar 196
3.(F)/125 (See)	Mamaia	8	Blohm und Voss Bv 138 / Arado Ar 196
Rum.A.St.22/1	Ciocarlia (Rumania)	8	
Rum.101.A.St.	Mamaia	12	
Bulg.See A.St.	Varna (Bulgaria)	12	

Fighters:

Unit	Base	No.	Aircraft
Stab/JG 52	Manzar	1	Messerschmitt Bf 109
I./JG 52	Leipzig (Rumania)	23	Messerschmitt Bf 109
II./JG 52	Manzar	11	Messerschmitt Bf 109
III./JG 52	Roman	19	Messerschmitt Bf 109
15.(Kroat.)/JG 52	Zilistea		Re-equipping

Ground-attack:

Unit	Base	No.	Aircraft
Stab/SG 2	Husi	1	Junkers Ju 87
I./SG 2	Husi	29	Junkers Ju 87
II./SG 2	Zilistea	27	Focke-Wulf Fw 190
III./SG 2	Husi	43	Junkers Ju 87
10.(Pz)/SG 2	Husi	16	Junkers Ju 87
II./SG 10	Culm	29	Focke-Wulf Fw 190
10.(Pz)/SG 9	Trotus	15	Henschel Hs 129
14.(Pz)/SG 9	Trotus	15	Henschel Hs 129

Night ground-attack:

Unit	Base	No.	Aircraft
Stab/NSGr.5	Manzar		Gotha Go 145 / Arado Ar 66
1./NSGr.5	Roman	21	Gotha Go 145 / Arado Ar 66
2./NSGr.5	Kizhinev	40	Gotha Go 145 / Arado Ar 66
3./NSGr.5	Kizhinev		

Bombers:

Unit	Base	No.	Aircraft
I./KG 4	Focsani	43	Heinkel He 111

VIII.Fliegerkorps (VIII Flying Corps) Lubien (Poland):

Strategic reconnaissance:

Unit	Base	No.	Aircraft
2.(F)/11	Jasionka	9	Junkers Ju 88
2.(F)/100	Lublin	7	Junkers Ju 188

Tactical reconnaissance:

Unit	Base	No.	Aircraft
Stab/NAGr.2	Strunybaby	5	Messerschmitt Bf 109
1./NAGr.2	Stry	11	Messerschmitt Bf 109
2./NAGr.2	Strunybaby	13	Messerschmitt Bf 109

Ground-attack:

Unit	Base	No.	Aircraft
StabIV.(Pz)/SG 9	Lysiatycze	6	Henschel Hs 129
12.(Pz)/SG 9	Stry		Henschel Hs 129
13.(Pz)/SG 9	Lysiatycze	16	Henschel Hs 129
Stab/SG 77	Jasionka		Re-equipping
I./SG 77	Jasionka		Re-equipping
II./SG 77	Lemberg	33	Focke-Wulf Fw 190
III./SG 77	Cuniov	42	Junkers Ju 87
10.(Pz)/SG 77	Starzava	19	Junkers Ju 87
Ung.S.St.102/1	Cuniov	11	

Night ground-attack:

Unit	Base	No.	Aircraft
Stab/NSGr.4	Hordinia	4	Gotha Go 145
1./NSGr.4	Hordinia	28	Gotha Go 145

Bombers:

Unit	Base	No.	Aircraft
14.(Eis.)/KG 27	Krosno	15	Heinkel He 111

Fliegerführer 102 Ungarn (Flying-leader 102 Hungary) Labunia:

Tactical reconnaissance:

Unit	Base	No.	Aircraft
Ung.N.A.St.102/1	Labunia	8	
7./NAGr.32	Labunia	11	Messerschmitt Bf 109 / Focke-Wulf Fw 189

Fighters:

Unit	Base	No.
Ung.JSt.102/1	Zamocz	8

Bombers:

Unit	Base	No.
Ung.KSt.102/1	Klemensova	5

Fast-bombers:

Unit	Base	No.
Ung.SKSt.		12

Rum.I.Fliegerkorps (I Rumanian Flying Corps) Tecuci (Rumania):

Strategic/tactical reconnaissance

Unit	Base	No.
Rum.2.(F)A.St.	Ivesti	5
Rum.102.A.St.	Vilkov	11

Fighters:

Unit	Base	No.	Aircraft
Rum.II./JG 3 (65., 66., 67.JSt.)	Bacau	18	IAR 80
Stab Rum.IV.JGr.	Janca		
Rum.45.JSt.	Janca		
Rum.46.JSt.	Janca		
Rum.49.JSt.	Janca		Re-equipping
Rum.IX.JGr. (47., 48., 56.JSt.)	Tecuci	23	Messerschmitt Bf 109

Dive-bombers:

Unit	Base	No.
Rum.III.St.Gr.	Carlamanesti	24
Rum.VI.St.Gr.	Husi	23
Rum.VIII.SGr.	Matca	39

Bombers:

Unit	Base	No.
Rum.II.KGr.	Tandarei	10
Rum.IV.KGr. (76., 78.KSt.)	Janca	15
Rum.V.KGr.	Ivesti	16
Rum.KSt.1./3	Ciocarlia	9

Kom.Gen.d.dtsch.Lw.i.Rum. (General OC German Air Force in Rumania)
Bucharest
Jagdabschnittsführer Rum. (Fighter sector-leader Rumania) Bucharest:

Fighters:

Unit	Base	No.	Aircraft
I./JG 53	Targsorul-Nou	28	Messerschmitt Bf 109
III./JG 77	Mizil	28	Messerschmitt Bf 109
Rum.I./JG 2 (43., 63., 64.JSt.)	Rosiori		IAR 80
Rum.VI./JG 2 (59., 61., 62.JSt.)	Popesti-Leordeni	16	IAR 80
Rum.VII.JGr. (53., 57.JSt.)	Boteni	12	Messerschmitt Bf 109
Rum.51.JSt.	Tepes-Voda	21	
Rum.52.JSt.	Mamaia	14	
Rum.58.JSt.	Pipera	4	

Night-fighters:

Unit	Base	No.	Aircraft
10./NJG 6 & 12./NJG 6	Otopeni	25	Messerschmitt Bf 110
11./NJG 6	Zilistea		Messerschmitt Bf 110
2./NJG 100	Otopeni		Junkers Ju 88 / Dornier Do 217 / Focke-Wulf Fw 189
4./JG 301	Mizil	6	Messerschmitt Bf 109
6./JG 301	Targsorul-Nou	7	Messerschmitt Bf 109
Rum.1.NJSt.	Otopeni	4	

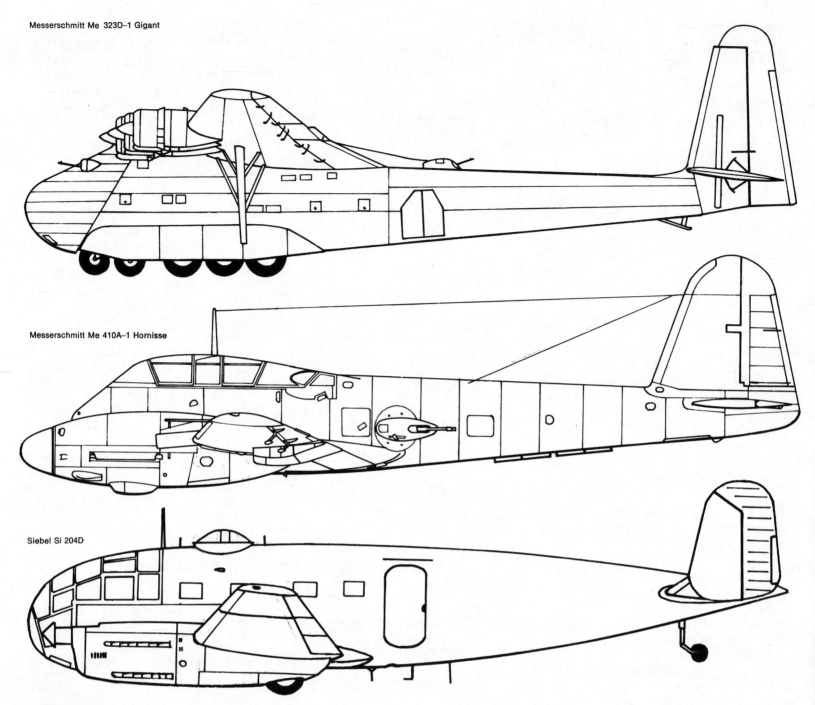

Messerschmitt Me 323D–1 Gigant

Messerschmitt Me 410A–1 Hornisse

Siebel Si 204D

(conversion) trainer version; armament as A–1a (approx *15*).
Me 262B–1a/U1: Interim 2-seat night fighter version; armament as A–1a; FuG 218 Neptun and FuG 350 Naxos (B–1a conversions).
Me 262B–2a: Night-fighter version; modified B–1a; lengthened fuselage; increased fuel capacity; radar and armament as B–1a/U1, plus provision for two addn oblique upward-firing 30mm MK 108 cannon in dorsal 'Schräge Musik' installation (1).
Me 262C–1a, Heimatschützer I: Addn Walter RII–211/3 booster rocket in tail; one Me 262A–1a conversion.
Me 262C–2b, Heimatschützer II: Two 1,760lb s.t. BMW 003A/ 2,700lb thrust BMW 718 rocket motors; one Me 262–1a conversion.
Me 262C–3: Modified C–1a; external (ventral) Walter RII–211/ 3 booster rocket; project only.
Total Production: approx 1,100.
Remarks: World's first operational jet aircraft, Me 262 entered service with experimental test unit early Summer 1944, result Hitler's insistence upon development as 'Blitzbomber', first operational deployment (as bomber) on Western Front, Aug 1944; subsequent anullment Führer's strict 'bombers-only' decree permitted continued development and increasing emphasis fighter production; equipped number Jagdgruppen closing months WWII, inc elite unit composed pick of veteran pilots; also operated at Staffel

strength in specialized short-range reconnaissance and night-fighter roles, latter in defence of Berlin; planned conversion of four complete Kampfgeschwader on to Me 262A 'Schwalbe' (Swallow) fighters brought to halt by war's end; likewise development of rocket-boosted Me 262C 'Heimatschützer' (Homeland-Protector) versions; limited post-war production (by Avia) for Czech AF both single/ 2-seat trainer variants (S–92/CS–92) in service until mid-fifties.
Colour Reference: Plate 50: Messerschmitt Me 262A–1a flown by Gruppen-Adjutant, Stab III./JG 7 Nowotny, Parchim, March 1945; note non-standard oversprayed camouflage effect, Geschwader badge, Adjutant's chevron, Reichs-defence rear fuselage bands, and unusual treatment tail swastika.

Manufacturer: Messerschmitt.
Model: Me 264 V3.
Type: Long-range maritime reconnaissance-bomber.
Power Plant: Four 1,700hp BMW 801D.
Performance (Estimated):
maximum speed at 27,230ft (8,300m) 351mph (565km/hr).
cruising speed 217mph (350km/hr).
maximum range 9,320 miles (15,000km).
initial rate of climb 453ft/min (138m/min).
service ceiling 26,250ft (8,000m).
Weights:
empty 46,627lb (21,150kg).

maximum 123,460lb (56,000kg).
Dimensions:
wing span 141ft 1in (43.0m).
length 68ft 6½in (20.9m).
height 14ft 1¼in (4.3m).
wing area 1,374.55sq ft (127.7sq m).
Armament: One 13mm MG 131 machine-gun each in forward dorsal position, nose, and two beam positions; one 20mm MG 151 cannon each in aft dorsal turret and in ventral positions; max bomb load (internal) 4,410lb (2,000kg).
Crew: 8.
In Service: Germany.
Variants (with no. built):
Me 264 V1: Initial prototype; four 1,340hp Junkers Jumo 211J–1; max bomb load 3,968lb (1,800kg) (1).
Me 264 V2: Modified V1; BMW 801Ds; armour protection; provision for defensive armament; extended wing tips (1).
Me 264 V3: As V2; armed; RATOG; not completed.
Total Production: 2.
Remarks: So-called 'Amerika-Bomber', V1 prototype first flown Dec 1942; subsequently assigned special transport Staffel operating miscellany large multi-engined types (inc Ar 232, Ju 252, Ju 290, and Italian Piaggio P.108T); finally destroyed on ground by Allied bombing (as was V2 prior to first flight); further work on V3 halted upon cancellation of project.

Manufacturer: Messerschmitt.
Model: Me 321B–2 Gigant (Giant).
Type: Heavy transport glider.

Performance:
maximum towing speed 112mph (180km/hr).
gliding speed 87mph (140km/hr).
Weights:
empty 26,896lb (12,200kg).
loaded 74,956lb (34,000kg).
Dimensions:
wing span 180ft 5¼in (55.00m).
length 92ft 4¼in (28.15m).
height 33ft 3½in (10.15m).
wing area 3229.2sq ft (300sq m).
Armament: Two flexible 7.9mm MG 15 machine-guns in nose doors; plus provision (as troop transport) for hand-held 7.9mm MG 34 machine-guns firing from hold windows.
Crew/Payload: 3/22 tons (22.35 Tonnen) or troops or vehicle.
In Service: Germany.
Variants (with no. built):
Me 321 V1: Prototype; heavy transport glider.
Me 321A–1: Initial production model; 1 crew.
Me 321B–1: Modified A–1; armed; enlarged flight deck; 3 crew. (Total Me 321 V1, A–1, B–1: 200).
Total Production: 200.
Remarks: Initially towed by trio of Bf 110C fighters (interim solution pending delivery of specially developed He 111Z glider-tug), Me 321 entered service Russian Front late 1941; complex towing arrangement restricted use primarily rear-area logistic support, although some assault operations mounted on northern (Baltic) sector; with abandonment of planned 1942 airborne assault on Malta, majority

321s returned limited period ferrying duties Eastern Front before final withdrawal mid-1943.

Manufacturer: Messerschmitt.
Model: Me 323E–2 Gigant (Giant).
Type: Heavy transport.
Power Plant: Six 1,140hp Gnome-Rhône 14N 48/49.
Performance:
maximum speed at sea level 157mph (253km/hr).
maximum speed at 9,840ft (3,000m) 137mph (220km/hr).
cruising speed 140mph (225km/hr).
normal range 745 miles (1,200km).
initial rate of climb 866ft/min (264m/min).
service ceiling 14,760ft (4,500m).
Weights:
empty 65,260lb (29,600kg).
maximum 99,210lb (45,000kg).
Dimensions:
wing span 180ft 5¼in (55.0m).
length 93ft 6in (28.5m).
height 31ft 6in (9.6m).
wing area 3,229sq ft (300.0sq m).
Armament: One 20mm MG 151 cannon in each of two upper-surface wing turrets; one 13mm MG 131 machine-gun each at rear of flight deck, in two nose-door and four (fore and aft) beam positions; plus provision for additional hand-held 7.9mm MG 34 machine-guns firing from hold windows.
Crew/Accommodation: 7–11/ 120 troops (or 60 litters plus medics, or freight).
In Service: Germany.
Variants (with no. built):
Me 323 V1/2: Prototypes; four/

six 1,140hp Gnome-Rhône 14Ns resp; structural strengthening; multi-wheel undercarriage; two Me 321B conversions.
Me 323D–0 (V3/12): Pre-production model; six Gnome-Rhône 14N; four 7.9mm MG 15 machine-guns in nose and dorsal positions; RATOG (10).
Me 323D–1: Initial production model; as D–0.
Me 323D–2: As D–1; two-blade fixed-pitch propellers; weight/performance reductions.
Me 323D–6: As D–1; modified cowlings; increased armament to five 13mm MG 131.
Me 323 V13/14: Prototypes; improved Me 323Ds; structural strengthening; increased fuel capacity; revised armament; V14 with four 1,350hp Jumo 211F.
Me 323E–1: Production model; as V13; Heinkel- and Zeppelin-built.
Me 323E–2: As E–1; two addn, low-drag wing turrets; Zeppelin-built.
Me 323E–2/WT: Weapon-carrier (gunship); eleven 20mm MG 151s, four 13mm MG 131s; four wing turrets; power-operated nose turrets; one E–2 conversion.
Me 323 V16: Prototype; as E–2; six 1,350hp Jumo 211R (1).
(Total Me 323D–1, –2, –6, Me 323 V13/14, E–1, E–2: 201).
Me 323F/G: Projects only.
Total Production: 211.
Remarks: Powered development of basic Me 321 heavy transport glider, six-engined Me 323 entered service end 1942 on cross-Mediterranean supply routes to North Africa; suffered heavy casualties Spring 1943 during closing stages Tunisian campaign; subsequently (late 1943 to mid-1944) employed Russian Front, inc Crimean airlift/evacuation and northern (Baltic) sector logistic support.

Manufacturer: Messerschmitt.
Model: Me 410A–1/U2 Hornisse (Hornet).
Type: Heavy fighter (Zerstörer).
Power Plant: Two 1,750hp Daimler-Benz DB 603A.
Performance:
maximum speed at sea level 315mph (507km/hr).
maximum speed at 26,250ft (8,000m) 373mph (600km/hr).
cruising speed 365mph (587km/hr).
maximum range 1,050 miles (1,690km).
time to 22,000ft (6,700m) 10min 42sec.
service ceiling 32,810ft (10,000m).
Weights:
empty 16,574lb (7,518kg).
loaded 21,276lb (9,650kg).
Dimensions:
wing span 53ft 7¾in (16.35m).
length 40ft 11½in (12.48m).
height 14ft 0½in (4.28m).
wing area 389.687sq ft (36.20sq m).
Armament: Two fixed forward-firing 7.9mm MG 17 machine-guns and two fixed forward-firing 20mm MG 151 cannon in nose; two rearward-firing 13mm MG 131 machine-guns in lateral barbettes; plus two forward-firing 20mm MG 151 cannon in bomb-bay.
Crew: 2.
In Service: Germany, Great Britain (1 evaluation).
Variants (with no. built):
Me 210 V17: Design prototype; one Me 210A–0 conversion.
Me 410 V1: Prototype; re-engined Me 210A–0; 1,750hp DB 603As.
Me 410 V2/22: Development prototypes; armament/equipment modifications.
Me 410A–1: Production model; high-speed bomber version; armament as Me 210A–1; max bomb load 2,205lb (1,000kg).
Me 410A–1/U1: Reconnaissance version; as A–1; forward-firing 7.9mm MG17s deleted; one camera.
Me 410A–1/U2, A–1/U4: Zerstörer version; as A–1; two addn forward-firing 20mm MG 151, or one 50mm BK5, cannon in bomb-bay resp; A–1/U4 with standard forward-firing MG 17s and MG 151 deleted.
Me 410A–2: Zerstörer version; as A–1; dive-bombing sight and (optional) underwing ETC racks deleted.
Me 410A–2/U4: As A–1/U4; standard forward-firing armament retained.
Me 410A–3: Long-range reconnaissance version; modified (deepened) forward fuselage; two cameras; forward-firing 7.9mm MG 17s deleted.
Me 410B–1: High-speed bomber version; as A–1; two 1,900hp DB 603G; increased (external) bomb load.
Me 410B–1/U2, B–1/U4: As A–1/U2, A–1/U4 resp.
Me 410B–2: Zerstörer version; as A–2; two 1,900hp DB 603G.
Me 410B–2/U2, B–2/U4: As B–1/U2, B–1/U4 resp; B–2/U4 with standard forward-firing armament replaced by two 30mm MK 103 cannon.
Me 410B–2/U2/R2 to U2/R5: As B–2/U2 with Rüstsätze (field conversion kits) for addn/altn (bomber-destroyer) 20mm/30mm cannon.
Me 410B–3: Long-range reconnaissance version; as A–3; two 1,900hp DB 603G.
Me 410B–5: Torpedo-bomber version; forward-firing 7.9mm MG 17s deleted; one 1,984lb (900kg) torpedo, or 3,968lb (1,800kg) bomb load; FuG 200 Hohentwiel search radar; test models only.
Me 410B–6: Zerstörer version; forward-firing 7.9mm MG 17s replaced by 13mm MG 131 machine-guns; two addn 30mm MK 103 cannon in bomb-bay; FuG 200 Hohentwiel search radar.
Me 410B–7/–8: Day/night reconnaissance versions resp; test models.
Me 410C, D, H: Projects only.
(Production: Messerschmitt-built 902; Dornier-built: 258).
Total Production: 1,160.
Remarks: Successful development of disastrous Me 210, re-engined Me 410 entered service early Summer 1943; initially employed as nocturnal fighter-bomber over UK, also operated long-range reconnaissance and Zerstörer roles in Mediterranean; from Spring 1944 replaced Bf 110 in Zerstörer units' daylight defence of Reich; suffered heavy casualties at hands of US single-engined fighters; also saw limited service anti-shipping role (based French Atlantic coast) and as night-fighter on Eastern Front.

Manufacturer: Siebel.
Model: Fh 104A Hallore.
Type: Communications/liaison.
Power Plant: Two 280hp Hirth HM 508D.
Performance:
maximum speed at sea level 217mph (350km/hr).
cruising speed 194mph (312km/hr).
normal range 572 miles (920km).
time to 3,280ft (1,000m) 1min 54sec.
service ceiling 21,653ft (6,600m).
Weights:
empty 3,330lb (1,510kg).
loaded 5,180lb (2,350kg).
Dimensions:
wing span 39ft 6¾in (12.06m).
length 31ft 2in (9.5m).
height 8ft 7¾in (2.64m).
wing area 240.04sq ft (22.30sq m).
Crew/Accommodation: 1/4.
In Service: Germany.
Variants (with no. built):
Fh 104 V1/2: Prototypes; minor differences; 270hp HM 508Cs (2).
Fh 104A: Production model; light civil/military transport (46).
Total Production: 48.
Remarks: Esoterically named 'Hallore' (worker at the Halle salt-mines), designed by Klemm, first flown 1937; produced at Siebel's Halle plant, won several pre-war competitions; majority served Luftwaffe in communications/liaison and light VIP-transport roles; employed post-war by Czech AF.

Manufacturer: Siebel.
Model: Si 202C Hummel (Bumble-bee).
Type: Communications/trainer.
Power Plant: One 60hp Hirth HM 515.
Performance:
maximum speed at sea level 112mph (180km/hr).
cruising speed 93mph (150km/hr).
normal range 497 miles (800km).
time to 3,280ft (1,000m) 9min 0sec.
service ceiling 10,827ft (3,300m).
Weights:
empty 739lb (335kg).
loaded 1,367lb (620kg).
Dimensions:
wing span 34ft 9⅓in (10.6m).
length 21ft 4in (6.5m).
height 6ft 4¼in (1.94m).
wing area 150.7sq ft (14.0sq m).
Crew/Accommodation: 1/1.
In Service: Germany, Hungary (2).
Variants:
Si 202A: Initial production model; 2-seat sports tourer/trainer; one 45hp Salmson 7Ad.
Si 202B: Modified Si 202A; 50hp Zündapp.
Si 202C: Improved Si 202B; modified wings and tail surfaces; addn fuel capacity.
Remarks: Pre-war light sports plane/trainer; many impressed for light-liaison duties with operational Luftwaffe units.

Manufacturer: Siebel.
Model: Si 204A.
Type: General-purpose/light transport/trainer.
Power Plant: Two 360hp Argus As 410.
Performance:
maximum speed at 9,842ft (3,000m) 200mph (322km/hr).
cruising speed 186mph (300km/hr).
normal range 621 miles (1,000km).
initial rate of climb 846ft/min (258m/min).
service ceiling 20,997ft (6,400m).
Weights:
empty 7,628lb (3,460kg).
loaded 11,023lb (5,000kg).
Dimensions:
wing span 69ft 11¾in (21.33m).
length 42ft 8½in (13.02m).
height 13ft 11⅓in (4.25m).
wing area 495.1sq ft (46.0sq m).
Crew/Accommodation: 2/8.
In Service: Germany, Slovakia, Switzerland (1 interned/impressed).
Variants (with no. built):
Si 204A: Initial production model; light transport; Siebel-, BMM-, Aero-, and SNCAC-built.
Si 204D: Military trainer version; fully-glazed unstepped nose; 600hp Argus As 411s; Siebel-, BMM-, Aero- and SNCAC-built.
(Total Si 204A, D: 1,000+).
NC 701/702 Martinet: Post-war French equivalent of Si 204D/A; 590hp Renault 12S–00s; SNCAC-built (300+).
C.3A/B: Post-war Czech production of Si 204D trainer/bomber versions; Aero/CKD-built (179).
Total Production: 1,500+.
Remarks: Designed as light civil transport easily adaptable to military usage, Si 204 was scaled-up and much-modified development of earlier Fh 104; extensively employed by Luftwaffe in wide variety of training roles (Si 204D), as well as for VIP-transport, communications, light freight, and ambulance duties; also operated limited numbers by at least one night ground-attack Staffel (sqn) on Eastern Front, late 1944; licence-production in both France and Czechoslovakia continued well into post-war years.

GREAT BRITAIN

Manufacturer: Airspeed.
Model: AS.5A Courier.
Type: Light transport/communications.
Power Plant: One 240hp Armstrong Siddeley Lynx IVC.
Performance:
maximum speed at sea level 154mph (246km/hr).
cruising speed 132mph (212km/hr).
maximum range 600 miles (965km).
initial rate of climb 730ft/min (222m/min).
service ceiling 13,500ft (4,120m).
Weights:
empty 2,344lb (1,064kg).
loaded 3,900lb (1,771kg).
Dimensions:
wing span 47ft 0in (14.3m).
length 28ft 6in (8.68m).
wing area 250sq ft (23.2sq m).
Crew/Payload: 2/1,200lb (545kg).
In Service: Great Britain.
Variants (with no. built):
Prototype (1).
AS.5A: Short-stage version (1).
AS.5B: Long-distance version with 350hp Armstrong Siddeley Cheetah V; later converted to 5A (2).
AS.5C: Engine test-bed; one 325hp Napier Rapier IV (1).
AS.5D: Private order (1).
Total Production: 16.
Remarks: Pre-war light transport; one RAF machine plus 9 impressments used for communications and transport duties.

Manufacturer: Airspeed.
Model: A.S.6 Envoy III.
Type: Communications.
Power Plant: Two 350hp Armstrong Siddeley Cheetah IX.
Performance:
maximum speed at 7,300ft (2,226m) 210mph (338km/hr).
cruising speed 192mph (309km/hr).
normal range 650 miles (1,045km).
time to 5,000ft (1,525m) 3min 30sec.
service ceiling 22,500ft (6,860m).
Weights:
empty 4,057lb (1,842kg).
loaded 6,300lb (2,860kg).
Dimensions:
wing span 52ft 4in (15.94m).
length 34ft 6in (10.53m).
height 9ft 6in (2.9m).
wing area 339sq ft (31.5sq m).
Crew/Accommodation: 1/6.
In Service: China (Kwangsi 2), Finland, Great Britain (RAF, FAA), South Africa (7), Spain.
Variants (with no. built):
Prototype: With 240hp Armstrong Siddeley Lynx IVCs (1).
Envoy I: Initial production model; various power plants; Airspeed-built (14); Japanese licence-built by Mitsubishi (3).
Envoy II: Modified Mk I (incl 3 military models with one fixed forward-firing gun and dorsal turret) (13).
Envoy III: Improved Mk II variant (incl two Mk II conversions) (19).
Total Production: 50.
Remarks: Pre-war twin-engined development of Courier; employed during both Spanish Civil War and Sino-Japanese conflict; WWII use by RAF (Comms in UK and India) and SAAF.

Manufacturer: Airspeed.
Model: A.S.10 Oxford II.
Type: Trainer/light transport and communications.
Power Plant: Two 375hp Armstrong Siddeley Cheetah X or 250hp de Havilland Gipsy Queens.
Performance:
maximum speed at 8,300ft (2,530m) 188mph (301km/hr).
time to 10,000ft (3,048m) 12min.
service ceiling 19,500ft (5,945m).
Weights:
empty 5,380lb (2,440kg).
loaded 7,600lb (3,447kg).
Dimensions:
wing span 53ft 4in (16.25m).
length 34ft 6in (10.5m).
height 11ft 1in (3.38m).
wing area 348sq ft (32.34sq m).
Crew: 3–6.
In Service: Australia (389), Canada, France (FFAF), Great Britain (RAF, FAA), New Zealand, Portugal, South Africa (approx 700), Southern Rhodesia, USA.
Variants (with no. built):

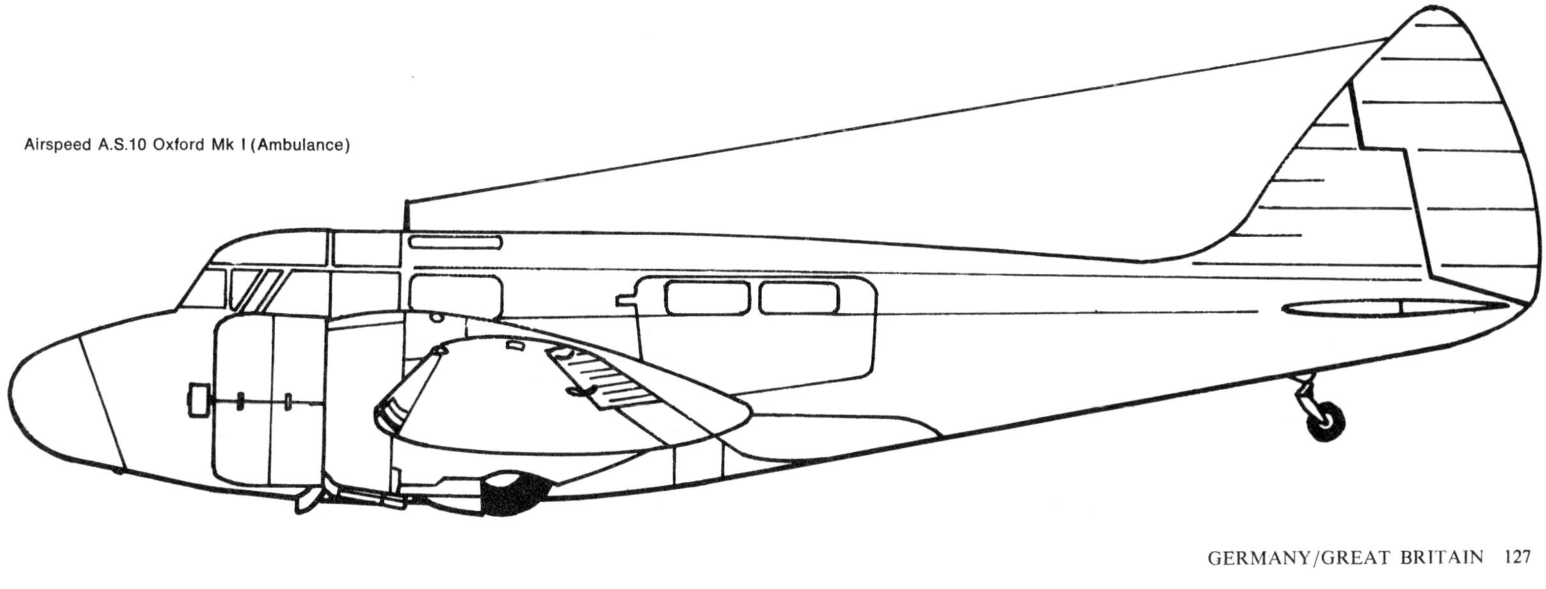
Airspeed A.S.10 Oxford Mk I (Ambulance)

Prototype (1).
Mk I: General-purpose trainer; some with dorsal turret; Airspeed-built (3,784); De Havilland-built (75); Standard Motor-built (750); Percival-built (775).
Mk II: Pilot trainer; Airspeed-built (989); De Havilland-built (1,440); Percival-built (575).
T.Mk II: Mk I variant (incl eight Mk I conversions) (9).
Mk III: Cheetah XVs (1).
Mk IV: Modified Mk III; project only.
Mk V: Navigation, pilot and radio trainer, 450hp Pratt & Whitney Wasp Juniors.
A.S.40: Modified Mk II civil version.
A.S.41: Post-war conversion.
A.S.42: Redesigned Mk I for RNZAF.
A.S.43: A.S.42 Survey version.
Total Production: 8,586.
Remarks: Advanced trainer, but also used for communications, ambulance, radar-calibration and other ancillary duties during WWII.

Manufacturer: Airspeed.
Model: Horsa I.
Type: Transport-glider.
Performance:
maximum towing speed 150mph (241km/hr).
normal gliding speed 100mph (161km/hr).
Weights:
empty 8,370lb (3,800kg).
loaded 15,500lb (7,030kg).
Dimensions:
wing span 88ft 0in (26.8m).
length 67ft 0in (20.4m).
height 19ft 6in (5.9m).
wing area 1,104sq ft (102.5sq m).
Crew/Accommodation: 2.
In Service: Great Britain, USA.
Variants (with no. built):
Prototypes (7).
Horsa Mk I: Troop-carrier version; Airspeed-built (470); Austin-built (300); Harris Lebus built (inc RAF-assembled) (1,461).
Mk II: Modified Mk I; hinged nose for heavy cargo, Airspeed-built (225); Austin-built (65); Harris Lebus-built (inc RAF-assembled) (1,271).
A.S.52: Bomb-carrying version; project only.
A.S.53 and 54: Vehicle-carrying versions; projects only.
Total Production: 3,785.
Remarks: Standard British troop-carrying/transport glider; first operated Sicilian invasion, later extensively employed by both British and US during D-Day landings; also took part Arnhem and Rhine Crossing operations.

Manufacturer: Armstrong Whitworth.
Model: Atlas I.
Type: Army co-operation.
Power Plant: One 400hp Armstrong Siddeley Jaguar IVC.
Performance:
maximum speed at sea level 142mph (229km/hr).
maximum speed at 15,000ft (4,572m) 124mph (200km/hr).
normal range 480 miles (772km).
time to 15,000ft (4,572m) 28min 0sec.
service ceiling 16,800ft (5,120m).
Weights:
empty 2,250lb (1,157kg).
maximum 4,020lb (1,824kg).

Dimensions:
wing span 39ft 7in (12.07m).
length 28ft 7in (8.71m).
height 10ft 6in (3.20m).
wing area 391sq ft (36.23sq m).
Armament: One fixed Vickers gun in propeller arc; one Lewis gun in rear cockpit; four 120lb (54kg) bombs.
Crew: 2.
In Service: Canada (16), China (14 Mk II), Egypt (1 ex-RAF), Great Britain, Greece (2), Japan (1).
Variants (with no. built):
Prototype: (private venture) (1).
Atlas I: Production model.
Atlas II: 2-seat fighter/day bomber; prototype (converted from Mk I) (14).
Remarks: Pre-war army co-operation machine; Mk II used in Sino-Japanese conflict; employed by RCAF on coastal patrol duties 1939–40.

Manufacturer: Armstrong Whitworth.
Model: Scimitar.
Type: Fighter-trainer.
Power Plant: One 605hp Armstrong Siddeley Panther VII.
Performance:
maximum speed at sea level 172mph (277km/hr).
maximum speed at 20,000ft (6,096m) 215mph (346km/hr).
time to 20,000ft (6,096m) 11min 45sec.
service ceiling 30,600ft (9,330m).
Weights:
empty 2,814lb (1,276kg).
loaded 4,100lb (1,860kg).
Dimensions:
wing span 33ft 0in (10.06m).
length 25ft 0in (7.62m).
height 12ft 0in (3.66m).
wing area 261.35sq ft (24.28sq m).
Armament: Two .303in Vickers Type E machine-guns; four 20lb (9.07kg) bombs.
Crew: 1.
In Service: Norway.
Variants (with no. built):
Prototypes (2).
Production model (730hp Panther XI A) (4).
Total Production: 6.
Remarks: Employed as fighter-trainers by Norwegian AF 1936–39; subsequently saw brief service in armed neutrality patrols of Norway's northern borders.

Manufacturer: Armstrong Whitworth.
Model: A.W. XV Atalanta.
Type: Transport.
Power Plant: Four 340hp Armstrong Siddeley Serval III.
Performance:
maximum speed at 3,000ft (914m) 156mph (251km/hr).
cruising speed 118mph (190km/hr).
range 640 miles (1,030km).
time to 9,000ft (2,743m) 21min 30sec.
service ceiling 14,200ft (4,328m).
Weights:
empty 14,832lb (6,727kg).
maximum 21,000lb (9,525kg).
Dimensions:
wing span 90ft 0in (27.43m).
length 71ft 0in (21.79m).
height 14ft 4½in (4.37m).
wing area 1,285sq ft (119.38sq m).
Payload/Accommodation: 5,500lb (2,495kg)/9–17 passengers.
In Service: Great Britain, India.
Total Production: 8.

Remarks: Civil airliner; 5 impressed as troop transports (RAF); subsequently to Indian AF for coastal reconnaissance.

Manufacturer: Armstrong Whitworth.
Model: A.W.27 Ensign Mk I.
Type: Transport.
Power Plant: Four 850hp Armstrong Siddeley Tiger IXC.
Performance:
maximum speed at 7,200ft (2,195m) 200mph (322km/hr).
cruising speed 170mph (274km/hr).
range 860 miles (1,384km).
time to 3,000ft (914m) 3min 6sec.
service ceiling 22,000ft (6,106m).
Weights:
empty 32,920lb (14,932kg).
maximum 48,500lb (21,999kg).
Dimensions:
wing span 123ft 0in (37.49m).
length 111ft 0in (33.83m).
height 23ft 0in (7.01m).
wing area 2,450sq ft (227.61sq m).
Payload/Accommodation: 9,500lb (4,309kg)/40.
In Service: Germany (1 captured, 1 from Vichy France, re-engined with Daimler-Benz), Great Britain, Vichy France (one taken over after forced-landing West Africa, later sent to Germany).
Variants (with no. built):
Mk I: Initial production model (12).
Mk II: Four 950hp Wright Cyclones (2).
Total Production: 14.
Remarks: Pre-war civil airliner; used to supply BEF in France, May/June 1940; later as transport on West Africa/Egypt supply route.

Manufacturer: Armstrong Whitworth.
Model: A.W.38 Whitley Mk V.
Type: Heavy night-bomber/maritime-reconnaissance.
Power Plant: Two 1,145hp Rolls-Royce Merlin X.
Performance:
maximum speed at 16,400ft (4,999m) 230mph (370km/hr).
cruising speed 210mph (338km/hr).
time to 15,000ft (4,572m) 16min 0sec.
service ceiling 26,000ft (7,925m).
Weights:
empty 19,350lb (8,777kg).
maximum 33,500lb (15,196kg).
Dimensions:
wing span 84ft 0in (25.60m).
length 69ft 3in (21.11m).
height 15ft 0in (4.57m).
wing area 1,137sq ft (105.63sq m).
Armament: One .303in machine-gun in nose turret; four .303in machine-guns in powered tail turret; max bomb load 7,000lb (3,175kg).
Crew: 5.
In Service: Great Britain.
Variants (with no. built):
Prototypes (2).
Mk I: Initial production model (34).
Mk II: As Mk I; 845hp Tiger VIII (46).
Mk III: Power-operated nose turret; new bomb racks (80).
Mk IV: R.R. Merlin IV; power-operated tail turret (33).
Mk IVA: As Mk IV; two Merlin X (1).
Mk V: Lengthened tail-section; re-designed fins and rudders; increased fuel capacity (1,466).
Mk V Freighter: Mk V conversions as civil freighters (15).
Mk VI: Project only.

Mk VII: Coastal Command maritime reconnaissance version with A.S.V. Mk II air-to-surface radar (146).
Total Production: 1,814.
Remarks: Along with Vickers Wellington and Handley-Page Hampden formed mainstay of Bomber Command's early offensive; scored notable succession of 'firsts'—equal first to drop bombs on German soil, equal first to bomb Germany proper, first British bomber over Berlin (leaflet dropping), first British bomber to attack Italy; retired from Bomber Command April 1942; continued in Coastal Command until August 1942; also served as glider-tugs and paratroop trainers.
Colour Reference: Plates 81, 82: Armstrong Whitworth Whitley Mk V (Z6795) JL.W of No 10 (Bomber) O.T.U. on loan from Bomber Command to No 19 Group, RAF Coastal Command, Feb 1943; during period of service with Coastal Command (up to July 1943) No 10 O.T.U. operated anti-U-boat role, sinking one boat (U 564) for total loss 35 aircraft, inc Z6795 (ex-'A'-Able of No 102 'Ceylon' Squadron, note crudely overpainted fuselage code DY.A) subsequently salved from French Atlantic Coast shallows by Luftwaffe recovery team.

Manufacturer: Armstrong Whitworth.
Model: A.W.41 Albemarle Mk II.
Type: Special transport.
Power Plant: Two 1,590hp Bristol Hercules XI.
Performance:
maximum speed at 10,500ft (3,200m) 265mph (427km/hr).
cruising speed 170mph (274km/hr).
range 1,300 miles (2,092km).
initial rate of climb 980ft/min (279m/min).
service ceiling 18,000ft (5,486m).
Weights:
loaded 22,600lb (10,250kg).
maximum 36,500lb (16,556kg).
Dimensions:
wing span 77ft 0in (23.47m).
length 59ft 11in (18.26m).
height 15ft 7in (4.75m).
wing area 803.5sq ft (74.65sq m).
Armament: Bomber: Four guns in electrically-operated dorsal turret; two guns in manually-operated turret under fuselage.
Transport: Two hand-operated Vickers K-guns in dorsal position.
Crew: 4.
In Service: Great Britain, Russia (10+).
Variants (with no. built):
Mk I: Prototype (2).
Initial production bomber; later converted to glider-tug (80) and special transport (78) (200).
Mk II: Special transport version (99); Glider-tug version (1).
Mk IV: Prototype (Wright Double-Cyclones) (1).
Mk V: Glider-tug version (49).
Mk VI: Special transport version (133); Glider-tug version (117).
Total Production: 600.
Remarks: Initially designed as reconnaissance bomber, but served solely in glider-tug and special transport roles—Sicily (1943), Normandy and Arnhem (1944); 10+ supplied to Russia.

Manufacturer: Avro.
Model: Tutor Mk I.
Type: Trainer/communications.
Power Plant: One 240hp Armstrong Siddeley Lynx IVC.
Performance:
maximum speed 120mph (192km/hr).
cruising speed 97mph (156km/hr).
range 250 miles (402km).
initial rate of climb 910ft/min (277m/min).
service ceiling 16,000ft (4,877m).
Weights:
empty 1,844lb (836kg).
maximum 2,493lb (1,131kg).
Dimensions:
wing span 36ft 0in (10.97m).
length 26ft 4½in (8.04m).
height 9ft 7in (2.92m).
wing area 301sq ft (27.96sq m).
Crew: 2.
In Service: Canada (7), China (Kwangsi 5), Denmark (5), Eire (3), Great Britain, Greece (40), Hong Kong (4), Poland (2), South Africa (59).
Variants (with no. built):
Prototypes.
Mk I: Alternative 155hp Armstrong Siddeley Mongoose IIIA.
Sea Tutor: Float-equipped Mk I.
Mk II: As Mk I; fitted with bay wings; one only.
(Total Mk I, Sea Tutor and Mk II: 795).
P.W.S. 18: Polish designation for Tutor; Polish (P.W.S.) licence-built (40).
Total Production: 835.
Remarks: Trainer; also served on communications; 57 licence-built in South Africa and 3 in Denmark; extensive foreign use.

Manufacturer: Avro.
Model: 626.
Type: General-purpose.
Power Plant: One 260hp Armstrong Siddeley Cheetah V.
Performance:
maximum speed 130mph (209km/hr).
cruising speed 108mph (174km/hr).
normal range 210 miles (338km).
initial rate of climb 10,000ft/min (3,048m/min).
service ceiling 16,800ft (5,121m).
Weights:
empty 1,844lb (835kg).
maximum 2,493lb (1,121kg).
Dimensions:
wing span 34ft 0in (10.36m).
length 26ft 6in (8.07m).
height 9ft 7in (2.92m).
wing area 300sq ft (27.87sq m).
Crew: 2.
In Service: Pre-war deliveries to Argentina, Austria, Belgium, Brazil, Canada, Chile, China (Kwangsi eight 637), Czechoslovakia, Egypt (15), Estonia (4), Great Britain, Greece, Ireland, Lithuania (4), New Zealand (4 Prefects).
Variants (with no. built):
Avro 626: Prototype (1).
Production model; land/seaplane; alternative 240hp Lynx XIVC; Civil (19); Military (168).

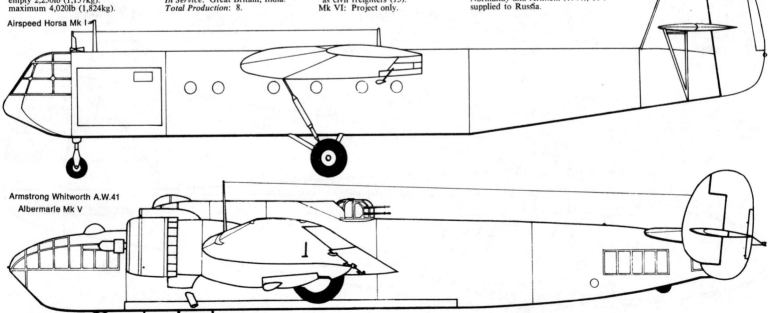

Airspeed Horsa Mk I

Armstrong Whitworth A.W.41
Albermarle Mk V

Avro Prefect: Modified Tutor (12).
Avro 637: As 626 with additional fuel tanks; light armed patrol (8).
Total Production: 208.
Remarks: World-wide trainer use; also employed on reconnaissance duties.

Manufacturer: Avro.
Model: 641 Commodore.
Type: Trainer/communications.
Power Plant: One 240hp Armstrong Siddeley Lynx IVC.
Performance:
maximum speed 130mph (209km/hr).
cruising speed 110mph (177km/hr).
range 500 miles (805km).
initial rate of climb 700ft/min (213m/min).
service ceiling 11,500ft (3,505m).
Weights:
empty 2,237lb (1,015kg).
maximum 3,500lb (1,588kg).
Dimensions:
wing span 37ft 4in (11.38m).
length 27ft 3in (8.30m).
height 10ft 0in (3.05m).
wing area 307sq ft (28.52sq m).
Crew/Accommodation: 2/2–3.
In Service: Egypt (2), Great Britain.
Total Production: 6.
Remarks: Initially built as trainer/private transport; 2 impressed by RAF as transports; 2 used by Egyptian AF in communications role.

Manufacturer: Avro.
Model: Type 642/4m.
Type: VIP transport.
Power Plant: Four 240hp Armstrong Siddeley Lynx.
Performance:
maximum speed 150mph (241km/hr).
maximum range 560 miles (907km).
Weights:
loaded 12,250lb (5,557kg).
Dimensions:
wing span 71ft 3in (21.72m).
length 54ft 6in (16.61m).
Crew/Accommodation: 2/7.
In Service: Great Britain.
Variants (with no. built):
Type 642/2m: Initial production model; two 450hp Armstrong Siddeley Jaguar VID (1).
Type 642/4m: VIP-transport version; reduced seating; four-engined (1).
Total Production: 2.
Remarks: Civil airliner Type 642/2m first built 1933, improved 642/4m (for use Viceroy of India) following year; latter impressed RAF transport duties, India, 1939–40; former destroyed by Japanese action, New Guinea, March 1942.

Manufacturer: Avro.
Model: 652A Anson Mk I.
Type: General reconnaissance.
Power Plant: Two 335hp Armstrong Siddeley Cheetah IX or 395hp Cheetah XIX.
Performance:
maximum speed 188mph (302km/hr).
cruising speed 158mph (254km/hr).
range 660 miles (1,062km).
initial rate of climb 960ft/min (293m/min).
service ceiling 19,000ft (5,791m).
Weights:
empty 5,375lb (2,438kg).
maximum 8,000lb (3,629kg).
Dimensions:
wing span 56ft 6in (17.22m).
length 42ft 3in (12.87m).
height 13ft 1in (3.99m).
wing area 463sq ft (43.01sq m).
Armament: One fixed .303in gun forward; one .303in gun in dorsal turret; max bomb load 360lb (163kg).
Crew: 3.
In Service: Australia (1,021), Canada, Egypt, Finland (3), Germany (captured ex-Greek), Greece (12), Great Britain (RAF, FAA), Ireland (2 Mk I), South Africa (approx 750), Turkey (6 Mk II), United States (50).
Variants (with no. built):
Prototypes: 1 civil, 1 military (2).
Mk I and GR Mk I: Initial production version (6,704).
Mk II: Re-designed nose section; licence-built by Canadian Car, de Havilland (Canada), Federal, National Steel and Ottawa Car (1,050).
Mk III: Trainer; two 330hp Jacobs L6MB.
Mk IV: British airframes; two 300hp Wright Whirlwinds fitted in Canada (223).
Mk V prototype: Conversion of Mk I and Mk IV.
Mk V: American-built trainer; two Pratt & Whitney Wasp Juniors (1,070).
Mk VI: Gunnery trainer; as Mk V but with Bristol turret (1).

Order of Battle September 1939

ROYAL AIR FORCE

Home Commands

Bomber Command:

No. 2 Bomber Group:		
21 Sqn.	Watton	Bristol Blenheim IV
82 Sqn.	Watton	Bristol Blenheim IV
101 Sqn.	West Raynham	Bristol Blenheim IV
107 Sqn.	Wattisham	Bristol Blenheim IV
110 Sqn.	Wattisham	Bristol Blenheim IV
114 Sqn.	Wyton	Bristol Blenheim IV
139 Sqn.	Wyton	Bristol Blenheim IV
No. 3 Bomber Group:		
9 Sqn.	Honington	Vickers Wellington
37 Sqn.	Feltwell	Vickers Wellington
38 Sqn.	Marham	Vickers Wellington
99 Sqn.	Mildenhall	Vickers Wellington
115 Sqn.	Marham	Vickers Wellington
149 Sqn.	Mildenhall	Vickers Wellington
214 Sqn.	Feltwell	Vickers Wellington
215 Sqn.	Bassingbourn	Vickers Wellington
No. 4 Bomber Group:		
10 Sqn.	Dishforth	Armstrong Whitworth Whitley
51 Sqn.	Linton-on-Ouse	Armstrong Whitworth Whitley
58 Sqn.	Linton-on-Ouse	Armstrong Whitworth Whitley
77 Sqn.	Driffield	Armstrong Whitworth Whitley
78 Sqn.	Dishforth	Armstrong Whitworth Whitley
102 Sqn.	Driffield	Armstrong Whitworth Whitley
No. 5 Bomber Group:		
44 Sqn.	Waddington	Handley Page Hampden
49 Sqn.	Scampton	Handley Page Hampden
50 Sqn.	Waddington	Handley Page Hampden
61 Sqn.	Hemswell	Handley Page Hampden
83 Sqn.	Scampton	Handley Page Hampden
106 Sqn.	Cottesmore	Handley Page Hampden
144 Sqn.	Hemswell	Handley Page Hampden
185 Sqn.	Cottesmore	Handley Page Hampden

Fighter Command:

No. 11 Fighter Group:		
3 Sqn.	Biggin Hill	Hawker Hurricane Mk I
17 Sqn.	North Weald	Hawker Hurricane Mk I
25 Sqn.	Northolt	Bristol Blenheim IF
32 Sqn.	Biggin Hill	Hawker Hurricane Mk I
43 Sqn.	Tangmere	Hawker Hurricane Mk I
54 Sqn.	Hornchurch	Supermarine Spitfire Mk I
56 Sqn.	North Weald	Hawker Hurricane Mk I
65 Sqn.	Hornchurch	Supermarine Spitfire Mk I
74 Sqn.	Hornchurch	Supermarine Spitfire Mk I
79 Sqn.	Biggin Hill	Hawker Hurricane Mk I
111 Sqn.	Northolt	Hawker Hurricane Mk I
151 Sqn.	North Weald	Hawker Hurricane Mk I
501 Sqn.	Filton	Hawker Hurricane Mk I
600 Sqn.	Northolt	Bristol Blenheim IF
601 Sqn.	Hendon	Bristol Blenheim IF
604 Sqn.	Hendon	Bristol Blenheim IF
605 Sqn.	Tangmere	Gloster Gladiator
615 Sqn.	Kenley	Gloster Gladiator
No. 12 Fighter Group:		
19 Sqn.	Duxford	Supermarine Spitfire Mk I
23 Sqn.	Wittering	Bristol Blenheim IF
29 Sqn.	Debden	Bristol Blenheim IF
46 Sqn.	Digby	Hawker Hurricane Mk I
66 Sqn.	Duxford	Supermarine Spitfire Mk I
213 Sqn.	Wittering	Hawker Hurricane Mk I
504 Sqn.	Hucknall	Hawker Hurricane Mk I
610 Sqn.	Hooton Park	Hawker Hurricane Mk I
611 Sqn.	Duxford	Supermarine Spitfire Mk I
616 Sqn.	Finningley	Gloster Gauntlet
No. 13 Fighter Group:		
41 Sqn.	Catterick	Supermarine Spitfire Mk I
64 Sqn.	Church Fenton	Bristol Blenheim IF
72 Sqn.	Church Fenton	Supermarine Spitfire Mk I
602 Sqn.	Abbotsinch	Supermarine Spitfire Mk I
603 Sqn.	Turnhouse	Supermarine Spitfire Mk I
607 Sqn.	Usworth	Gloster Gladiator
609 Sqn.	Yeadon	Supermarine Spitfire Mk I Hawker Hind

Coastal Command:

No. 15 GR Group:		
204 Sqn.	Mount Batten	Short Sunderland I Saro London II
210 Sqn.	Pembroke Dock	Short Sunderland I Saro London II
217 Sqn.	Warmwell	Avro Anson De Havilland Tiger Moth
228 Sqn.	Pembroke Dock	Short Sunderland I
502 Sqn.	Aldergrove	Avro Anson G.R.Mk I
No. 16 GR Group:		
22 Sqn.	Thorney Island	Vickers Vildebeest IV
42 Sqn.	Bircham Newton	Vickers Vildebeest I and IV
48 Sqn.	Thorney Island	Avro Anson G.R.Mk I
206 Sqn.	Bircham Newton	Avro Anson G.R.Mk I
500 Sqn.	Detling	Avro Anson Hawker Hind Avro Tutor
No. 18 GR Group:		
201 Sqn.	Calshot	Saro London II
209 Sqn.	Invergordon	Supermarine Stranraer
220 Sqn.	Bircham Newton	Avro Anson Lockheed Hudson
224 Sqn.	Leuchars	Lockheed Hudson Avro Anson
233 Sqn.	Leuchars	Lockheed Hudson Avro Anson
240 Sqn.	Invergordon	Saro London II Saro Lerwick
269 Sqn.	Montrose	Avro Anson
608 Sqn.	Thornaby	Avro Anson
612 Sqn.	Dyce	Avro Anson Hawker Hector Hawker Hind

Advanced Air Striking Force:

1 Sqn.	Octeville (Tangmere)	Hawker Hurricane Mk I
12 Sqn.	Berry-au-Bac (Bicester)	Fairey Battle
15 Sqn.	Bétheniville (Abingdon)	Fairey Battle
40 Sqn.	Bétheniville (Abingdon)	Fairey Battle
73 Sqn.	Le Havre (Digby)	Hawker Hurricane Mk I
103 Sqn.	Challerange (Benson)	Fairey Battle
105 Sqn.	Rheims (Harwell)	Fairey Battle
142 Sqn.	Berry-au-Bac (Bicester)	Fairey Battle
150 Sqn.	Challerange (Benson)	Fairey Battle
218 Sqn.	Auberive-sur-Suippes (Boscombe Down)	Fairey Battle
226 Sqn.	Rheims (Harwell)	Fairey Battle

(Fairey Battle Units ex-No. 1 Bomber Group)

Air Component BEF:

4 Sqn.	— (Hawkinge)	Westland Lysander Mk I (Army Co-opn)
18 Sqn.	Beauvraignes (Upper Heyford)	Bristol Blenheim I (Recce)
53 Sqn.	— (Oatham)	Bristol Blenheim IV (Army Co-opn)
57 Sqn.	Amy (Upper Heyford)	Bristol Blenheim I (Recce)
59 Sqn.	— (Old Sarum)	Bristol Blenheim IV (Army Co-opn)
85 Sqn.	Lille (Debden)	Hawker Hurricane Mk I
87 Sqn.	Boos (Debden)	Hawker Hurricane Mk I

Army Co-operation:

No. 22 (Army Co-operation) Group:		
2 Sqn.*	Hawkinge	Westland Lysander Mk I
13 Sqn.*	Odiham	Westland Lysander Mk II
16 Sqn.**	Old Sarum	Westland Lysander Mk II
26 Sqn.*	Catterick	Westland Lysander Mk II
613 Sqn.	Ringway	Hawker Hind and Hind (T) Avro Tutor
614 Sqn.	Cardiff	De Havilland Tiger Moth Westland Lysander Hawker Hind and Hector Avro Tutor

* To Air Component BEF; October, 1939.
** To Air Component BEF; April, 1940.

Overseas Commands:

RAF Middle East:

Egypt Group:		
14 Sqn.	Ismailia	Vickers Wellesley
30 Sqn.	Ismailia	Bristol Blenheim I
33 Sqn.	Qasaba	Gloster Gladiator I
45 Sqn.	Fuka	Bristol Blenheim I
55 Sqn.	Ismailia	Bristol Blenheim I
70 Sqn.	Helwan	Vickers Valentia
113 Sqn.	Heliopolis	Bristol Blenheim I
208 Sqn.	Heliopolis	Westland Lysander Mk I
211 Sqn.	Ismailia/El Daba	Bristol Blenheim I
216 Sqn.	Heliopolis	Vickers Valentia
No. 252 Wing:		
80 Sqn.	Amriya, Egypt	Gloster Gladiator I
112 Sqn.	Helwan, Egypt	Gloster Gladiator I
Sudan Wing:		
47 Sqn.	Khartoum	Vickers Vincent Vickers Wellesley
223 Sqn.	Summit	Vickers Wellesley

RAF in Palestine and Transjordan:

6 Sqn.	Ramleh/Haifa	Hawker Hardy Gloster Gauntlet Westland Lysander

British Forces in Iraq:

84 Sqn.	Shaibah	Bristol Blenheim

British Forces in Aden:

8 Sqn.	Khormaksar	Bristol Blenheim I Vickers Vincent
94 Sqn.	Sheik Othman	Gloster Sea Gladiator (Int) Vickers Vincent
203 Sqn.	Basra	Short Singapore III

Royal Air Force Mediterranean:

202 Sqn.	Kalafrana, Malta	Saro London II

Air Forces in India:

No. 1 (Indian) Group:		
5 Sqn. (Army Co-op)	Risalpur	Westland Wapiti IIA and V
20 Sqn. (Army Co-op)	Peshawar	Hawker Audax
27 Sqn.	Kohat/Juhu (Bombay) /St. Thomas' Mount (Madras)	Westland Wapiti IIA and V
60 Sqn.	Ambala/Dum Dum (Calcutta)	Bristol Blenheim I
28 Sqn. (Army Co-op)	Ambala	Hawker Audax
31 Sqn.	Lahore	Vickers Valentia Westland Wapiti IIA and V
Indian Air Force:		
1 Sqn. (Ind.)	Risalpur/Bannu	Westland Wapiti IIA

Royal Air Force Far East:

11 Sqn.	Tengah, Singapore	Bristol Blenheim I
34 Sqn.	Tengah, Singapore (en route)	Bristol Blenheim I
36 Sqn.	Seletar	Vickers Vildebeest III
39 Sqn.	Tengah, Singapore	Bristol Blenheim I
62 Sqn.	Tengah, Singapore (en route)	Bristol Blenheim I
100 Sqn.	Seletar	Vickers Vildebeest III
205 Sqn.	Seletar	Short Singapore III
230 Sqn.	Seletar	Short Sunderland I
273 Sqn.	China Bay, Ceylon	Vickers Vildebeest Fairey Seal

Avro 652A Anson Mk I

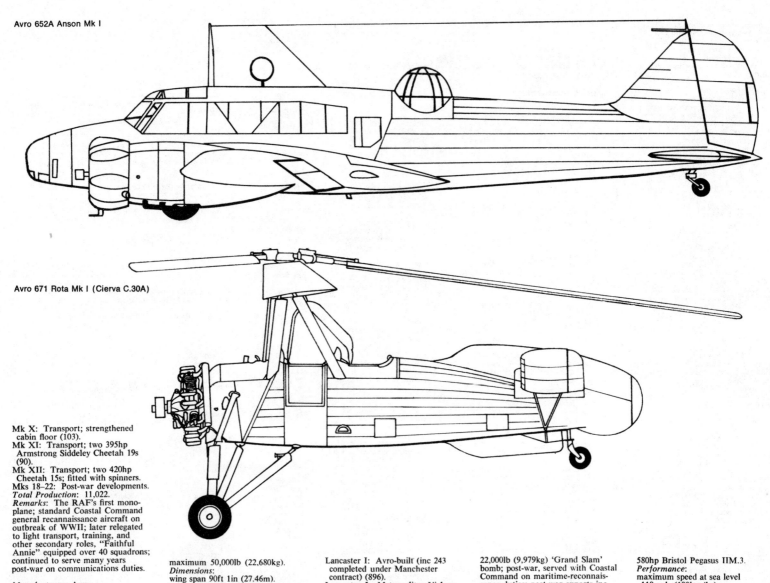

Avro 671 Rota Mk I (Cierva C.30A)

Mk X: Transport; strengthened
cabin floor (103).
Mk XI: Transport; two 395hp
Armstrong Siddeley Cheetah 19s
(90).
Mk XII: Transport; two 420hp
Cheetah 15s; fitted with spinners.
Mks 18–22: Post-war developments.
Total Production: 11,022.
Remarks: The RAF's first monoplane; standard Coastal Command
general reconnaissance aircraft on
outbreak of WWII; later relegated
to light transport, training, and
other secondary roles, "Faithful
Annie" equipped over 40 squadrons;
continued to serve many years
post-war on communications duties.

Manufacturer: Avro.
**Model: 671 Rota Mk 1 (Cierva
C.30A).**
Type: Autogyro.
Power Plant: One 140hp Armstrong
Siddeley Genet Major IA (Civet).
Performance:
maximum speed 110mph
(177km/hr).
cruising speed 95mph (153km/hr).
range 285 miles (465km).
initial rate of climb 700ft/min
(213m/min).
service ceiling 8,000ft (2,438m).
Weights:
empty 1,220lb (553kg).
maximum 1,800lb (816kg).
Dimensions:
rotor diameter 37ft 0in (11.28m).
length 19ft 8½in (6.00m).
Crew: 2.
In Service: France (FAF/FNAF
C.30/C.301), Great Britain,
Yugoslavia.
Variants (with no. built):
C.30P: Pre-production model (3).
Rota Mk I and Mk II: Production
versions; development of C.30A;
folding rotor blades (70).
Sea Rota: Twin floats (1).
C.30(A): German (Focke-Wulf)
licence-built (40).
C.30/301: French (Lioré-et-Olivier)
licence-built (64).
Total Production: 178.
Remarks: Initial Cierva model
(C.30A) licence-built and re-
designed by Avro; re-designated
Avro Rota; saw RAF service on
coastal radar-calibration and
liaison duties; 52 LeO C.30/301s on
strength FAF/FNAF outbreak
WWII; employed coastal/estuary
patrol until Armistice, June 1940.

Manufacturer: Avro.
Model: Manchester I.
Type: Medium bomber.
Power Plant: Two 1,760hp Rolls-
Royce Vulture I.
Performance:
maximum speed at 17,000ft
(5,182m) 265mph (426km/hr).
range 1,630 miles (2,623km).
service ceiling 19,200ft (5,852m).
Weights:
empty 29,432lb (13,350kg).

maximum 50,000lb (22,680kg).
Dimensions:
wing span 90ft 1in (27.46m).
length 68ft 10in (20.98m).
height 19ft 6in (6.04m).
wing area 1,131sq ft (105.07sq m).
Armament: Two .303in Browning
machine-guns each in nose and
dorsal turrets; 4-gun tail turret;
max bomb load 10,350lb (4,695kg).
Crew: 7.
In Service: Canada, Great Britain.
Variants (with no. built):
Prototypes (2).
Mk I: Initial production model;
triple fins (20).
Mk IA: Modified Mk I; larger fins
and rudders; centre fin deleted
(20).
Mk II: Prototype only (1).
Mk III: Four-engined bomber
(subsequently redesignated
Lancaster).
Total Production: 43.
Remarks: Entered service Nov 1940;
participated 1,000-bomber raid on
Cologne, but Vulture unreliable, and
withdrawn mid-1942 to make way for
4-engined successor.

Manufacturer: Avro.
Model: Lancaster I.
Type: Heavy bomber.
Power Plant: Four 1,640hp Rolls-
Royce Merlin 24.
Performance:
maximum speed at sea level
245mph (394km/hr).
maximum range 2,530 miles
(4,070km).
service ceiling 22,000ft (6,706m).
Weights:
empty 37,000lb (16,780kg).
normal 65,000lb (29,480kg).
Dimensions:
wing span 102ft 0in (31.09m).
length 69ft 6in (21.18m).
height 20ft 0in (6.10m).
wing area 1,297sq ft (120.49sq m).
Armament: Two .303in Browning
machine-guns each in nose and
dorsal turrets; four .303in Browning
machine-guns in tail turret; max
bomb load 18,000lb (8,165kg).
Crew: 7.
In Service: Australia, Canada,
Great Britain.
Variants (with no. built):
Prototype: (Manchester III) 1,130hp
Merlin X (2).

Lancaster I: Avro-built (inc 243
completed under Manchester
contract) (896).
Lancaster I: Metropolitan-Vickers
built, inc 57 completed under
Manchester contract (944).
Lancaster I: Vickers-Armstrong
built (535).
Lancaster I: Austin Motors built
(150).
Lancaster I: Armstrong-Whitworth
built (919).
Lancaster B.I. (Special): Converted
Mk Is; extended bomb-bay
(without doors) to carry 22,000lb
(9,979kg) 'Grand Slam' bomb (33).
Lancaster I (F.E.): Tropicalised;
intended for Far-Eastern service.
Lancaster P.R.I.: Post-war
conversions for photographic
reconnaissance duties.
Lancaster Mk II: Prototypes;
improved Mk I; Bristol Hercules
VI or XVI (2).
Lancaster Mk III: Production model;
Armstrong-Whitworth built (300).
Lancaster Mk III: Prototype (con-
verted Mk I) Packard-built Merlin
engines (*J*).
Lancaster III: Major production
model; Avro-built (2,774).
Lancaster III: Metropolitan-Vickers
built (136).
Lancaster III: Armstrong-
Whitworth built (110).
Lancaster Mk IV: Renamed
Lincoln I before first flight.
Lancaster Mk V: Renamed Lincoln
II before first flight.
Lancaster Mk VI: Converted
Mk I(2) and MkIII(7) airframes;
Merlin 85s and 87s (9).
Lancaster Mk VII: Austin Motors-
built; Martin dorsal turret; final
production model (180).
Lancaster Mk X: Canadian
production (of basic Mk III) by
Victory Aircraft Ltd (430).
Total Production: 7,378.
Remarks: 4-engined development of
Manchester; first operations March
1942, soon became mainstay of
Bomber Command's offensive
against Germany, by Summer 1944
equipping over 40 sqns; participated
in many famous raids, inc daylight
attack on Augsburg, the destruction
of the Möhne and Eder dams, and
the sinking of the *Tirpitz*, only
bomber capable of carrying the

22,000lb (9,979kg) 'Grand Slam'
bomb; post-war, served with Coastal
Command on maritime-reconnaissance duties; post-war exports inc
Egypt, France, Sweden.
Colour Reference: Plate 66:
Avro Lancaster B.I. (Special)
(PD133) YZ.P of No 617 Squadron,
RAF, Woodhall Spa, Lincs, March
1945; modified to carry 22,000lb
(9,979kg) 'Grand Slam' bomb; note
special Day Scheme camouflage
finish unique to such conversions,
plus 'YZ' code (as distinct from
Dam Busters' standard 'KC') in
reversed colours (and also carried
across upper/lower tailplane
surfaces) as further aid to differentia-
tion between squadron aircraft.

Manufacturer: Avro.
Model: York C.Mk 1.
Type: Transport.
Power Plant: Four 1,620hp Rolls-
Royce Merlin T.24 or Merlin 502.
Performance:
maximum speed 298mph (479km/hr).
cruising speed 223mph (375km/hr).
range 2,700 miles (4,344km).
initial rate of climb 1,500ft/min
(457m/min).
service ceiling 26,000ft (7,925m).
Weights:
empty 42,040lb (19,069kg).
maximum 68,000lb (30,845kg).
Dimensions:
wing span 102ft 0in (31.09m).
length 78ft 6in (23.92m).
height 16ft 6in (5.03m).
wing area 1,205sq ft (112sq m).
Payload: 10,000lb (4,536kg).
In Service: Great Britain, South
Africa.
Variants (with no. built):
Prototypes (4).
C.Mk 1: Production model (253).
C.Mk 2: 1 converted prototype;
four 1,650hp Bristol Hercules VI.
Total Production: 257 (inc 208 RAF).
Remarks: Used for VIP transport
and freighter duties during WWII;
post-war production for civil
airlines.

Manufacturer: Blackburn.
Model: Ripon IIF.
Type: Reconnaissance landplane.
Power Plant: One 480hp Gnome-
Rhône Jupiter VI 9AK or 535hp
Armstrong Siddeley Panther IIA or

580hp Bristol Pegasus IIM.3.
Performance:
maximum speed at sea level
118mph (190km/hr).
maximum speed at 5,000ft (1,524m)
128mph (206km/hr).
range 1,127 miles (1,814km).
initial rate of climb 510ft/min
(155m/min).
service ceiling 8,700ft (2,652m).
Weights:
empty 3,850lb (1,746kg).
maximum 7,000lb (3,175kg).
Dimensions:
wing span: upper 44ft 10in (13.67m).
lower 45ft 6½in (13.88m).
length 36ft 9in (11.20m).
height 12ft 10in (3.91m).
wing area 683sq ft (63.45sq m).
Armament: One forward-firing
Vickers gun; plus one Lewis gun in
rear cockpit, later replaced by
Finnish-manufactured L–33
machine-guns.
Crew: 2.
In Service: Finland.
Variants (with no. built):
Ripon I, II, IIA, IIC and III:
Pre-war FAA models. Obsolete by
1939 (95).
Ripon IIF: Initial Finnish export
model; Blackburn-built (1); licence-
built by VL; alt land/floatplane
versions (25).
Ripon V: Prototype with torpedo
(2).
Total Production: 123.
Remarks: Finnish licence-built by
Valton Lentokonetehdas; served
with 3 reconnaissance sqns during
Russo-Finnish Winter War of
1939–40; also undertook night anti
U-boat patrols during Continuation
War of 1941–44.

Manufacturer: Blackburn.
Model: Baffin.
Type: Torpedo-bomber/
reconnaissance.
Power Plant: One 565hp Bristol
Pegasus I.M3.
Performance:
maximum speed at sea level
125mph (201km/hr).
maximum speed at 6,500ft (1,981m)
136mph (219km/hr).
initial rate of climb 480ft/min
(146m/min).
service ceiling 15,000ft (4,572m).
Weights:

empty 3,184lb (1,444kg).
maximum 7,610lb (3,451kg).
Dimensions:
wing span: upper 44ft 10in (13.67m);
lower 45ft 6½in (13.88m).
length 38ft 3½in (11.67m).
height 12ft 10in (3.91m).
wing area 683sq ft (63.45sq m).
Armament: One forward-firing
Vickers gun and one Lewis gun in
rear cockpit; one Mk VIII
torpedo.
Crew: 2.
In Service: Great Britain (FAA),
New Zealand (29).
Variants (with no. built):
Prototypes: Private venture (2).
Pre-production model (2).

229mph (369km/hr).
service ceiling 19,100ft (5,822m).
Weights:
empty 5,496lb (2,493kg).
maximum 8,228lb (3,732kg).
Dimensions:
wing span 46ft 2in (14.07m).
length 35ft 7in (10.84m).
height 12ft 6in (3.808m).
wing area 319sq ft (29.64sq m).
Armament: Four fixed Browning
Mk II guns; one Lewis Mk IIIE
machine-gun; one 500lb (227kg)
SAP bomb; eight 30lb (19kg)
practice bombs (optional).
Crew: 2.
In Service: Great Britain (FAA),
Sweden (2 interned).

Variants (with no. built):
Skua I: Prototype (2).
Skua II: Production version (190).
Total Production: 192.
Remarks: First FAA combat
monoplane; equipped 4 sqns; sank
German cruiser *Königsberg*,
Norway, April 1940; operated over
Dunkirk as fighter; served in
Mediterranean 1940–41;
subsequently used in training roles.

Manufacturer: Blackburn.
Model: Roc.
Type: Naval fighter.
Power Plant: One 890hp Bristol
Perseus XII.
Performance:

maximum speed at sea level
190mph (306km/hr).
cruising speed 135mph (217km/hr).
maximum range 810 miles
(1,304km).
initial rate of climb 1,500ft/min
(457m/min).
service ceiling 18,000ft (5,486m).
Weights:
empty 6,124lb (2,778kg).
maximum 7,950lb (3,606kg).
Dimensions:
wing span 46ft 0in (14.02m).
length 35ft 7in (10.84m).
height 12ft 1in (3.68m).
wing area 310sq ft (28.80sq m).
Armament: Four .303in Browning
guns in dorsal turret; one 250lb

(113kg) bomb; eight 30lb (14kg)
practice bombs underwing.
Crew: 2.
In Service: Great Britain (FAA).
Total Production: 136.
Remarks: Limited operational use,
shore-based only; subsequently
relegated to second-line duties.

Manufacturer: Blackburn.
Model: Botha I.
Type: Reconnaissance bomber.
Power Plant: Two 880hp Bristol
Perseus X.
Performance:
maximum speed at 15,000ft
(4,572m) 253mph (407km/hr).
cruising speed 212mph (341km/hr).

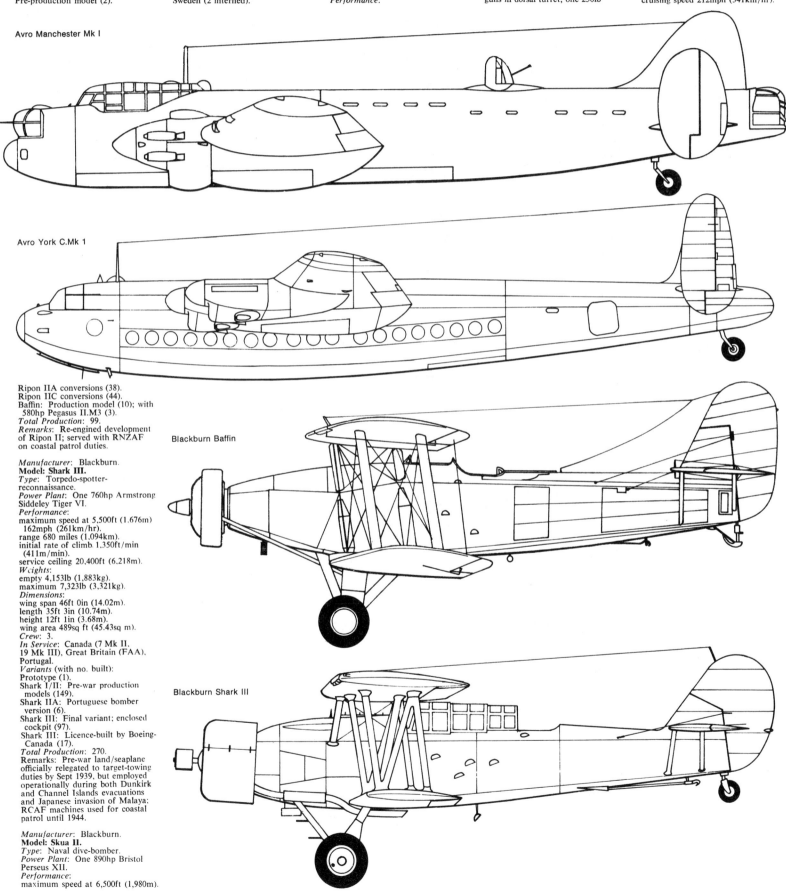

Avro Manchester Mk I

Avro York C.Mk 1

Ripon IIA conversions (38).
Ripon IIC conversions (44).
Baffin: Production model (10); with
580hp Pegasus II.M3 (3).
Total Production: 99.
Remarks: Re-engined development
of Ripon II; served with RNZAF
on coastal patrol duties.

Manufacturer: Blackburn.
Model: Shark III.
Type: Torpedo-spotter-
reconnaissance.
Power Plant: One 760hp Armstrong
Siddeley Tiger VI.
Performance:
maximum speed at 5,500ft (1.676m)
162mph (261km/hr).
range 680 miles (1.094km).
initial rate of climb 1,350ft/min
(411m/min).
service ceiling 20,400ft (6.218m).
Weights:
empty 4,153lb (1,883kg).
maximum 7,323lb (3,321kg).
Dimensions:
wing span 46ft 0in (14.02m).
length 35ft 3in (10.74m).
height 12ft 1in (3.68m).
wing area 489sq ft (45.43sq m).
Crew: 3.
In Service: Canada (7 Mk II,
19 Mk III), Great Britain (FAA),
Portugal.
Variants (with no. built):
Prototype (1).
Shark I/II: Pre-war production
models (149).
Shark IIA: Portuguese bomber
version (6).
Shark III: Final variant; enclosed
cockpit (97).
Shark III: Licence-built by Boeing-
Canada (17).
Total Production: 270.
Remarks: Pre-war land/seaplane
officially relegated to target-towing
duties by Sept 1939, but employed
operationally during both Dunkirk
and Channel Islands evacuations
and Japanese invasion of Malaya;
RCAF machines used for coastal
patrol until 1944.

Manufacturer: Blackburn.
Model: Skua II.
Type: Naval dive-bomber.
Power Plant: One 890hp Bristol
Perseus XII.
Performance:
maximum speed at 6,500ft (1,980m).

Blackburn Baffin

Blackburn Shark III

initial rate of climb 820ft/min
   (250m/min).
time to 15,000ft (4,572m)
   24min 0sec.
service ceiling 23,600ft (7,193m).
Weights:
empty 11,830lb (5,366kg).
maximum 17,628lb (7,996kg).
Dimensions:
wing span 59ft 0in (17.98m).
length 51ft 0½in (15.56m).
height 14ft 7½in (4.46m).
wing area 518sq ft (48.12sq m).
Armament: One fixed .303in
   Browning machine-gun and two
   .303in Browning machine-guns in
   dorsal turret; plus one Mk XII or
   XIV torpedo (or max bomb load
   2,000lb (907kg)).
Crew: 4.
In Service: Great Britain.
Variants:
Botha I: Sole production model;
   alternative 930hp Perseus XAs.
Botha II: Project only.
Total Production: 580.
Remarks: Underpowered; limited
operational use 1939–41 (two sqns);
relegated training duties 1941–44.

Manufacturer: Blackburn.
Model: Firebrand T.F. Mk II.
Type: Torpedo strike fighter.
Power Plant: One 2,305hp Napier
Sabre III.
Performance:
maximum speed at sea level
   314mph (505km/hr).
cruising speed 274mph (441km/hr).
range 770 miles (1,239km).
initial rate of climb 2,300ft/min
   (701m/min).
Weights:
maximum 15,049lb (6,826kg).
Dimensions:
wing span 51ft 3½in (15.63m).
length 38ft 2in (11.63m).

height 13ft 4in (4.06m).
wing area 383sq ft (35.58sq m).
Armament: Four 20mm Hispano
cannon; one 1,850lb (839kg) torpedo
or two 500lb (227kg) bombs.
Crew: 1.
In Service: Great Britain (FAA).
Variants (with no. built):
Prototypes (3).
F. Mk I: Initial production model
   (9).
T.F. Mk II: As F. Mk I; provision
   for one torpedo (12).
T.F. Mk III, TF Mk 4, 5 and 5A;
   post-war developments (201).
Total Production: 225.
Remarks: Entered service 1944
(T.F. Mk II) with shore-based trials
squadron.

Manufacturer: Boulton Paul.
Model: Defiant N.F. Mk I.
Type: Night-fighter.
Power Plant: One 1,030hp Rolls-
Royce Merlin III.
Performance:
maximum speed at sea level
   250mph (402km/hr).
maximum speed at 17,000ft (5,182m)
   304mph (489km/hr).
cruising speed 259mph (416km/hr).
range 465 miles (748km).
initial rate of climb 1,900ft/min
   (579m/min).
service ceiling 30,350ft (9,250m).
Weights:
empty 6,078lb (2,757kg).
maximum 8,600lb (3,900kg).
Dimensions:
wing span 39ft 4in (11.99m).
length 35ft 4in (10.77m).
height 12ft 2in (3.71m).
wing area 250sq ft (23.23sq m).
Armament: Four .303in Browning
machine-guns in power-operated
turret.
Crew: 2.

In Service: Great Britain (RAF,
FAA), USA (approx 2).
Variants (with no. built):
Prototypes: 1,030hp Merlin I or II (2).
F. Mk I: Day-fighter.
N.F. Mk I: Night-fighter; converted
   F. Mk I.
Mk IA: With A.I. Mk IV and
   VI radar.
   (Total F. Mk I, N.F. Mk I,
   Mk IA: 723).
Mk II: Improved day fighter
   version; 1,260hp Merlin XX; many
   as night-fighters with radar;
   prototypes; production model; 40
   subsequently
   converted to T.T. Mk I (210).
T.T. Mk I: Modified Mk II target-
   tug without turret (140).
T.T. Mk III: Target-tug; approx
   150 Mk I conversions.
Total Production: 1,075.
Remarks: Initially equipped one
day-fighter squadron; scored notable
successes over Dunkirk, May 1940;
suffered even more notable reverses
in opening stages of Battle of
Britain; withdrawn from service
Aug 1940; subsequently served in
night-fighter role; performed well
1940–41, equipped 13 UK-based sqns;
later relegated to target-tug (UK,
Middle and Far East), training,
Army co-operation, and ASR (3
sqns) duties.

Manufacturer: Bristol.
Model: Bulldog IVA.
Type: Fighter.
Power Plant: One 640hp Bristol
Mercury VIS.2.
Performance:
maximum speed 224mph (360km/hr).
service ceiling 33,400ft (10,180m).
Weights:
empty 2,690lb (1,220kg).
maximum 4,010lb (1,820kg).

Dimensions:
wing span 33ft 8in (10.26m).
height 9ft 1in (2.77m).
wing area 294sq ft (27.31sq m).
Armament: Two synchronised
Vickers machine-guns; four 20lb
(9kg) bombs.
Crew: 1.
In Service: Australia (8), Denmark
(4 Mk III), Estonia (12 Mk II),
Finland (2 Mk IIA and 17 Mk
IVA), Great Britain, Japan
(2 J.S.S.F.), Latvia (12 Mk II),
Sweden (3 Mk II, 8 Mk IIA).
Variants (with no. built):
Prototype (1).
Mk I: 440hp Bristol Jupiter VII (2).
Mk II: Modified Mk I; lengthened
   fuselage; Jupiter VII (92).
Mk IIA: Re-designed oil system
   and strengthened structure for
   additional load; Jupiter VIIF (268).
Mk III (105D): Danish order; as
   Mk IIA but with 450hp Jupiter
   VIFH and two 8mm Madsens (4).
Mk IIIA: Mk IIA version;
   improved performance (2).
Mk IVA: Finnish order; alternative
   ski-wheeled undercarriage plus
   armament heating system (18).
H.A.: As Mk II with increased
   rudder area (1).
T.M.: 2-seat trainer version (59).
J.S.S.F.: Japanese licence-built by
   Nakajima (2).
Total Production: 449.
Remarks: RAF Bulldogs withdrawn
from service 1937; Finnish Mk
IVA's employed on Karelian Front
during Soviet-Finnish 'Winter War'
of 1939–40.

Manufacturer: Bristol.
Model: Bombay.
Type: Troop-carrier/bomber-
transport.

Power Plant: Two 1,010hp Bristol
Pegasus XXII.
Performance:
maximum speed at 6,500ft (1,981m)
   192mph (309km/hr).
cruising speed 160mph (257km/hr).
initial rate of climb 750ft/min
   (229m/min).
service ceiling 25,000ft (7,620m).
Weights:
empty 13,800lb (6,260kg).
maximum 20,000lb (9,072kg).
Dimensions:
wing span 95ft 9in (29.18m).
length 69ft 3in (21.11m).
height 19ft 6in (5.94m).
wing area 1,340sq ft (124.49sq m).
Armament: One manually-operated
Vickers 'K' gun each in nose and
tail turrets; max bomb load 2,000lb
(907kg).
Crew/Accommodation: 3/24.
In Service: Great Britain.
Variants (with no. built):
Type 130: Prototype (1).
Bombay: Production model (50).
Total Production: 51.
Remarks: Served primarily in
Mediterranean theatre; participated
British evacuation of Greece, and
Iraqi campaign of 1941; employed as
night-bomber in Western Desert.

Manufacturer: Bristol.
Model: Blenheim I.
Type: Medium bomber.
Power Plant: Two 840hp Bristol
Mercury VIII.
Performance:
maximum speed at sea level
   240mph (386km/hr).
maximum speed at 15,000ft (4,572m)
   285mph (459km/hr).
range 1,125 miles (1,810km).
time to 15,000ft (4,572m)
   11min 30sec.
service ceiling 27,280ft (8,315m).

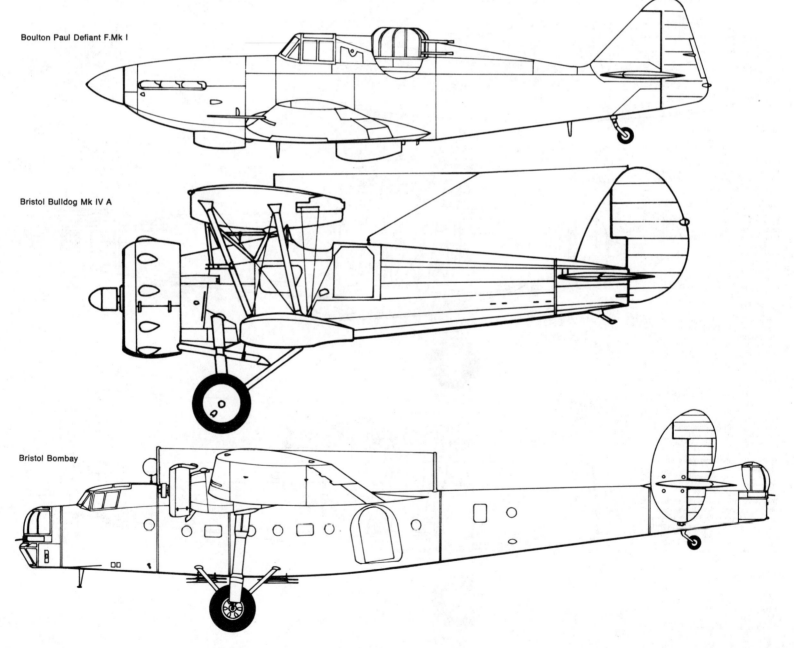

Boulton Paul Defiant F.Mk I

Bristol Bulldog Mk IV A

Bristol Bombay

Weights:
empty 8,100lb (3,674kg).
loaded 12,500lb (5,670kg).
Dimensions:
wing span 56ft 4in (17.17m).
length 39ft 9in (12.11m).
height 12ft 10in (3.91m).
wing area 469sq ft (43.57sq m).
Armament: One .303in Browning machine-gun in wing; one .303 Vickers 'K' gun in dorsal turret; max bomb load 1,000lb (454kg).
Crew: 3.
In Service: Canada, Croatia (ex-Yugoslav), Finland (75 Mk I), Great Britain, Greece (6 Mk I), Hungary (1 ex-Yugoslavia), Rumania (13 Mk I), Turkey (30 Mk I), Yugoslavia (18 Mk I).
Variants (with no. built):
Prototype (1).
Mk I: Standard Bristol-built bomber version (693); Avro-built (250); Rootes-built (422); Finnish (VLT) licence-built (45); Yugoslav licence-built by Ikarus (16).
Mk IF: Interim night-fighter version; 4 additional Browning machine-guns in ventral pack and AI Mk III or Mk IV radar equipment; approx 200 conversions of Mk I.
Mk II: General reconnaissance; Mk I variant; prototype (conversion) only.
Mk III: Project only.
Total Production: 1,427.
Remarks: RAF bomber variant employed in North Africa and Greece, 1941; UK-based Mk IF night-fighters pioneered airborne radar during German 'Blitz' of 1940–41; Blenheim I bombers saw extensive foreign use in both Allied (Yugoslav) and Axis (Croatian, Finnish and Rumanian) camps, the latter exclusively against Soviet

forces.
Colour Reference: Plates 51, 52: Ikarus-built Bristol Blenheim Mk I of 11th Independent Bomber Group, Yugoslav Royal Air Force, Belgrade April 1941; note three-tone upper surface camouflage scheme (peculiar to Yugoslav licence-built machines) and lack of wing upper surface roundels; this machine captured intact close of hostilities, April 1941, and subsequently supplied to Croatia.

Manufacturer: Bristol.
Model: Blenheim IVF.
Type: Long-range fighter.
Power Plant: Two 920hp Bristol Mercury XV.
Performance:
maximum speed at 12,000ft (3,658m) 260mph (418km/hr).
cruising speed 220mph (354km/hr).
range 1,460miles (2,349km).
initial rate of climb 1,500ft/min (457m/min).
service ceiling 24,600ft (7,498m).
Weights:
empty 9,200lb (4,173kg).
loaded 13,800lb (6,260kg).
maximum 14,500lb (6,580kg).
Dimensions:
wing span 56ft 4in (17.17m).
length 42ft 7in (12.98m).
height 9ft 10in (2.99m).
wing area 469sq ft (43.57sq m).
Armament: Four .303in Browning machine-guns in ventral pack; one fixed .303in Browning machine-gun in wing; one .303in Vickers 'K' gun in dorsal turret.
Crew: 2.
In Service: Canada (Bolingbroke), Finland (21 Mk IV), France (FFAF), Greece (12 Mk IV), Great Britain, New Zealand, Portugal, South Africa, Turkey.

Variants (with no. built):
Blenheim Mk IV: Bomber prototype; converted from Mk I (1); Bristol-built (300); Avro-built (755); Rootes-built (2,230).
Mk IVF: Fighter variant (conversions of above).
Mk IV: (Greek) Export version (12); (Finnish) licence-built by VLT (10).
Bolingbroke: RCAF designation; Canadian (Fairchild) licence production (676).
Total Production: 3,983.
Remarks: Blenheim IV bombers saw extensive service from the very first day of WWII, crossing the German frontier during an armed reconnaissance sortie, until finally phased out in Aug, 1942; altogether they equipped 25 UK-based Bomber Command sqns; plus 19 in the Middle East and 1 in the Far East, in defence of Singapore; Mk IVF fighters served primarily in the anti-shipping strike role with 10 Coastal Command sqns, with two home, and one overseas fighter units; Finnish and Greek AF bombers both saw action, against the Soviet Union and Germany resp; in the Western Desert the Mk IV was flown by the Free French.

Manufacturer: Bristol.
Model: Blenheim V.
Type: High-altitude bomber/trainer.
Power Plant: Two 950hp Bristol Mercury 25 or 30.
Performance:
maximum speed 260mph (418km/hr).
range 1,600 miles (2,574km).
service ceiling 31,000ft (9,449m).
Weights:
empty 11,000lb (4,990kg).
maximum 17,000lb (7,710kg).
Dimensions:

wing span 56ft 1in (17.09m).
length 43ft 11in (13.38m).
height 12ft 10in (3.91m).
wing area 469sq ft (43.57sq m).
Armament: Two rearward-firing .303in Browning guns; two .303in Browning guns in dorsal turret; max bomb load 1,000lb (454kg).
Crew: 3.
In Service: France (FFAF), Great Britain, Portugal Turkey.
Variants (with no. built):
Prototypes: Bisley I; original solid nose close-support version (2).
Blenheim V; high-altitude bomber version (1).
Blenheim V: Production model; inc VA basic bomber version; VB ground-attack version; VC operational trainer; VD major variant; tropicalised VA; Rootes-built (942).
Total Production: 945.
Remarks: Originally designed as 2-seat support bomber; specification changed to high-altitude bomber; equipped with oxygen and tropicalised for Middle and Far-Eastern theatres; first saw action in North Africa, Nov 1942; poor performance and consequent high rate of loss soon led to replacement; in Far East equipped 4 sqns, remaining operational until late 1943.

Manufacturer: Bristol.
Model: Beaufort I.
Type: Torpedo-bomber.
Power Plant: Two 1,130hp Bristol Taurus VI, XII or XVI.
Performance:
maximum speed at 6,000ft (1,829m) 265mph (426km/hr).
range 1,600 miles (2,574km).
service ceiling 16,500ft (5,029m).
Weights:

empty 13,100lb (5,942kg).
maximum 21,230lb (9,630kg).
Dimensions:
wing span 57ft 10in (17.62m).
length 44ft 3in (13.49m).
height 14ft 3in (4.34m).
wing area 503sq ft (46.73sq m).
Armament: Two .303in guns each in nose and dorsal turret, some with two .303in 'K'-guns in extreme nose and two beam guns; original rearward-firing Brownings in undernose blister normally discarded; max bomb load 1,500lb (680kg), or one semi-enclosed 1,605lb (728kg) torpedo.
Crew: 4.
In Service: Australia (700 Mk V–IX), Canada, Great Britain (RAF, FAA (Mk II)), Turkey.
Variants (with no. built):
Prototype (1).
Mk I: Initial British production model; some with A.S.V. radar (965).
Mk II: Prototype; conversion of Mk I (1).
Production model; two 1,130hp Bristol Taurus VI, XII or XVI (12 as dual-control trainers) (164).
Mk IV: Conversion of Mk II; prototype only (1).
Mks V–IX: Australian (DAP) licence-built (700).
Total Production: 1,130.
Remarks: Standard Coastal Command torpedo-bomber, 1940–43; extensive service North Sea, English Channel, and French Atlantic Coast; also attacked Axis supply convoys in Mediterranean; replaced by torpedo-equipped Beaufighters. Over half total production to RAAF.

Manufacturer: Bristol.
Model: Beaufighter IF.
Type: Night-fighter.

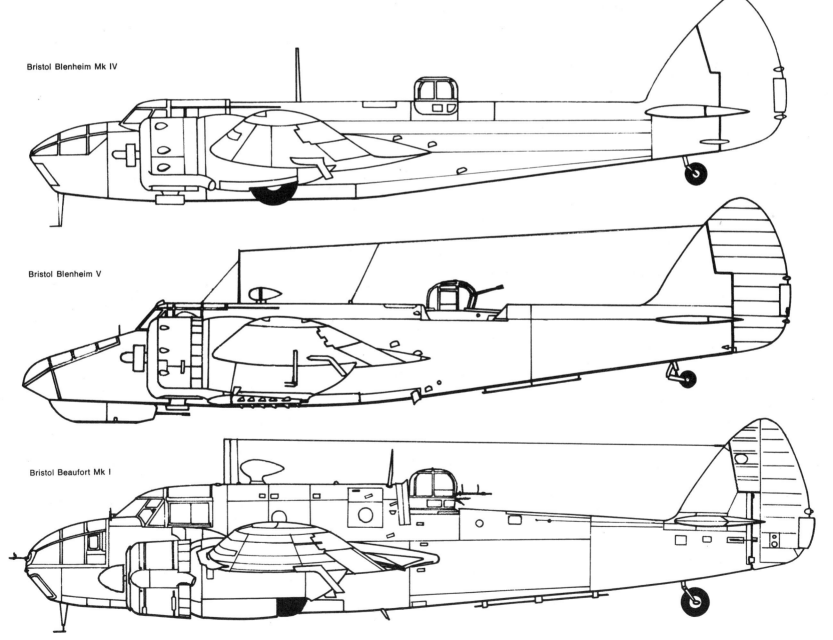

Bristol Blenheim Mk IV

Bristol Blenheim V

Bristol Beaufort Mk I

Bristol Beaufighter Mk IIF

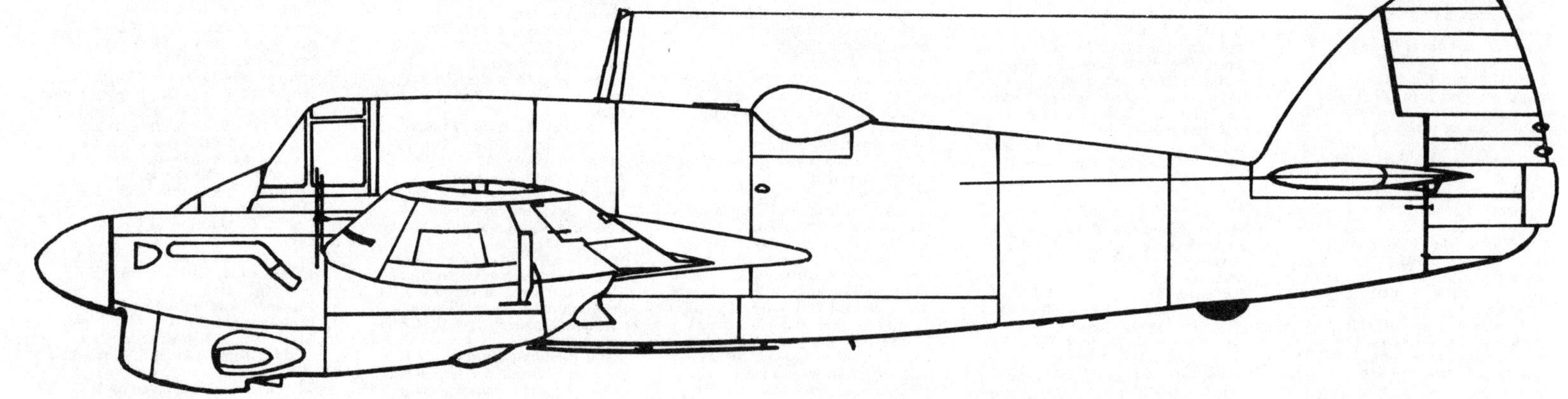

Power Plant: Two 1,590hp Bristol Hercules VI.
Performance:
maximum speed at sea level 306mph (492km/hr).
normal range 1,500 miles (2,414km).
initial rate of climb 1,850ft/min (564m/min).
service ceiling 28,900ft (8,809m).
Weights:
empty 14,069lb (6,381kg).
maximum 21,100lb (9,435kg).
Dimensions:
wing span 57ft 10in (17.63m).
length 41ft 4in (12.60m).
height 15ft 10in (4.82m).
wing area 503sq ft (46.73sq m).
Armament: Four 20mm Hispano cannon in fuselage nose; six wing-mounted .303in Browning machine-guns, two to port and four to starboard.
Crew: 2.
In Service: Australia (76 Mk IC), Canada, Italy (1+ captured), Great Britain (RAF, FAA), New Zealand.
Variants (with no. built):
Prototypes: Radar equipped (4).
Mk IF: Initial night-fighter production version; Bristol-built (528): Fairey-built (25).
Mk IC: Coastal Command version with additional radio and navigational equipment; Bristol-built (97); Fairey-built (300).
Mk II: Prototypes (3).
Mk IIF: Re-engined night-fighter; two 1,280hp Rolls-Royce Merlin XXs (597).
Mk III: Project only.
Mk IV: Project only.
Mk V: Mk II conversion with turret containing four .303in machine-guns in place of wing guns (2).
Total Production: 5,918 (all Marks).
Remarks: Entered service Sept 1940; equipped with AI Mk IV radar, bore brunt of Luftwaffe's 1940–41 'Blitz'; first successful night intercept, Nov 1940; Coastal Command's Mk ICs began operations Spring 1941, ranging from Norwegian to French Biscay coasts; also served Middle East.

Manufacturer: Bristol.
Model: Beaufighter T.F. Mk X.
Type: Anti-shipping strike-fighter.
Power Plant: Two 1,770hp Bristol Hercules XVII.
Performance:
maximum speed at 13,000ft (3,962m) 303mph (488km/hr).
range 1,470 miles (2,366km).
time to 5,000ft (1,524m) 3min 30sec.
service ceiling 15,000ft (4,572m).
Weights:
empty 15,592lb (7,072kg).
maximum 25,400lb (11,521kg).
Dimensions:
wing span 57ft 10in (17.63m).
length 41ft 8in (12.70m).
height 15ft 10in (4.82m).
wing area 503sq ft (46.73sq m).
Armament: Four 20mm Hispano cannon in nose; one .303in Vickers 'K' gun in dorsal position; one 1,650lb (748kg) or 2,127lb (965kg) torpedo; two 250lb (113.4kg) bombs or eight 90lb (41kg) rockets.
Crew: 2 or 3.
In Service: Australia, Canada, Great Britain (RAF, FAA), New Zealand, South Africa, USA.
Variants (with no. built):
Mk VIC: Torpedo fighter; two 1,600hp Hercules VI; one 22.5in (572mm) US, or one 18in (457mm) British torpedo; Bristol-built (518); Fairey-built (175).
Mk VIF: Two 1,635hp Hercules VI; 'Thimble' nose with AI Mk VII radar; Bristol-built (729); Rootes-built (150).
Mk VI (I.T.F.): With eight under-wing rockets in place of wing guns (60).
Mk VII–IX: Projects only.
T.F. Mk X: As Mk VIC but Hercules XVII engines; A.I. Mk VIII radar; 60 converted from Mk VI (I.T.F.); Bristol-built (2,095); Rootes-built (110).
Mk XI C: As T.F. Mk X but without torpedo gear (163).
T.F. Mk 21: Australian licence-built T.F. Mk X (364); some with Sperry auto-pilot.
Total Production: 5,918 (all Marks).
Remarks: Hercules VI-powered Mk VIs entered service early 1942; Coastal Command machines first employed rocket projectiles May 1943; night-fighter variant equipped 4 US sqns in Mediterranean theatre; T.F. Mk Xs—organized into formidable Strike Wings—scoured North Sea and English Channel 1944–45; sank 5 U-Boats in two days, March 1945; also employed Far East; post-war many converted for target-towing duties (T.T.10); also served Portuguese and Dominican AFs post-war.
Colour Reference: Plate 53: Australian (DAP)-built Bristol Beaufighter T.F. Mk 21 N.SK (A8–116) of No 93 'Green Ghost' Squadron, No 86 Attack Wing, RAAF, Labuan, North Borneo, Aug 1945; overall foliage green finish (compare with Commonwealth Boomerang, (plates 1, 2); personal 'Pistol Packin' Gremlin' emblem on rudder.

Manufacturer: Bristol.
Model: Buckingham.
Type: High-speed transport.
Power Plant: Two 2,400hp Bristol Centaurus IV, VII or XI.
Performance:
maximum speed at 12,000ft (3,658m) 336mph (541km/hr).
cruising speed 294mph (473km/hr).
range 2,360 miles (3,797km).
service ceiling 25,000ft (7,620m).
Weights:
empty 24,040lb (10,905kg).
maximum 36,900lb (16,738kg).
Dimensions:
wing span 71ft 10in (21.89m).
length 46ft 10in (14.27m).
height 17ft 7in (5.36m).
wing area 708sq ft (65.77sq m).
Crew/Accommodation: 3/4.
In Service: Great Britain.
Variants (with no. built):
Prototype (4).
Production version (119).
Total Production: 123.
Remarks: Originally intended as tactical day-bomber; last 65 aircraft of production run completed as high-speed transports; remainder retrospectively modified.

Manufacturer: British Aircraft.
Model: B.A. Swallow 2.
Type: Communications.
Power Plant: One 90hp Pobjoy Cataract III.
Performance:
maximum speed at sea level 112mph (180km/hr).
cruising speed 98mph (158km/hr).
range 420 miles (676km).
initial rate of climb 800ft/min (244m/min).
service ceiling 17,000ft (5,182m).
Weights:
empty 990lb (449kg).
maximum 1,500lb (680kg).
Dimensions:
wing span 42ft 8½in (13.01m).
length 26ft 0in (7.92m).
height 7ft 0in (2.13m).
wing area 215sq ft (19.97sq m).
Crew/Accommodation: 1/1.
In Service: Great Britain (RAF/FAA).
Variants (with no. built):
Prototype: British version of German Klemm L–25; 75hp Salmson A.D.9 (1).
B.K. (British Klemm) Swallow: Initial production models; various power plants (28).
B.A. Swallow 2: Modified B.K. 90hp Pobjoy Cataract III or Blackburn Cirrus Minor 1 (105).
Total Production: 134.
Remarks: Original German design; first flown 1927; many UK machines impressed as instructional airframes; others (15+) for communications duties, inc at least one with FAA in Ceylon.

Manufacturer: British Aircraft.
Model: B.A. Eagle 2.
Type: Communications.
Power Plant: One 130hp de Havilland Gipsy Major.
Performance:
maximum speed 148mph (238km/hr).
cruising speed 130mph (209km/hr).
normal range 650 miles (1,046km).
initial rate of climb 700ft/min (213m/min).
service ceiling 16,000ft (4,877m).
Weights:
empty 1,450lb (658kg).
maximum 2,400lb (1,089kg).
Dimensions:
wing span 39ft 3in (11.96m).
length 26ft 0in (7.92m).
height 6ft 9in (2.05m).
wing area 200sq ft (18.58sq m).
Crew/Accommodation: 1/2.
In Service: Great Britain, Kenya (1), Malaya (1).
Variants (with no. built):
Prototype (1).
B.K.1 Eagle: Initial production model (5).
B.A. Eagle 2: Improved B.K.1; deepened rear fuselage; modified rudder (36).
Total Production: 42.
Remarks: Pre-war low-wing cabin monoplane; 16 exported; eleven WWII impressments—seven UK, two India (RAF), one Kenya and one Malayan VolAF; latter destroyed by enemy action.

Manufacturer: British Burnelli.
Model: OA–1.
Type: Transport.
Power Plant: Two 710hp Bristol Perseus XIVC.
Performance:
maximum speed at sea level 225mph (362km/hr).
cruising speed 195mph (314km/hr).
range 1,950 miles (3,138km).
initial rate of climb 1,250ft/min (381m/min).
Weights:
empty 9,500lb (4,309kg).
maximum 19,000lb (8,618kg).
Dimensions:
wing span 73ft 6in (22.40m).
length 44ft 2in (13.46m).
height 12ft 0in (3.66m).
wing area 826.5sq ft (76.78sq m).
Accommodation: 15.
In Service: France (FFAF).
Variants (with no. built):
OA–1: Redesigned American Burnelli UB–14; Cunliffe-Owen-built (1).
Total Production: 1.
Remarks: Original American 'Flying Wing' (lifting fuselage) design of 1936; British version built 1938; impressed May 1941; served in French Equatorial Africa as troop and freight transport with FFAF.

Manufacturer: British Taylorcraft.
Model: Auster IV.
Type: A.O.P.
Power Plant: One 130hp Lycoming 0–290–3.
Performance:
maximum speed at sea level 130mph (209km/hr).
cruising speed 112mph (180km/hr).
normal range 250 miles (402km).
Weights:
empty 1,100lb (499kg).
maximum 1,850lb (839kg).
Dimensions:
wing span 36ft 0in (10.97m).
length 22ft 5in (6.83m).
height 8ft 0in (2.44m).
wing area 167sq ft (15.51sq m).
Crew: 3.
In Service: Canada, Great Britain, Netherlands (20 Mk III).
Variants (with no. built):
Plus C, D: Licence-built American light plane design (32).
Auster Mk I: Modified Plus D. Military version, A.O.P. 90hp Cirrus Minor I (100).
Mk II: 130hp Lycoming (2).
Mk III: Modified Mk I; 130hp Gipsy Major I (470).
Mk IV: 130hp Lycoming; enlarged cabin; one additional seat (254).
Mk V: Modified Mk IV; blind-flying panel; inc 3 floatplane conversions (804).
Mk VI: Post-war development (381).
Model H: Experimental wartime glider variant (1).
Total Production: 2,044.
Remarks: 14+ civil Plus Cs impressed on outbreak of war for communications duties; 1940 eight Plus Ds likewise taken over for early AOP experiments; resulted in first of long line of military variants; entered service July 1941; equipped 9 sqns Mediterranean theatre; also 10 sqns with 2nd TAF from D-Day until end of war; some modified for tactical (photographic) reconnaissance in Normandy and after; some Mk Vs also served in communications role; equipped Dutch communications sqn from Jan 1945.

Manufacturer: de Havilland.
Model: Cirrus II Moth.
Type: Communications.
Power Plant: One 85hp A.D.C. Cirrus II.
Performance:
maximum speed 95mph (153km/hr).
cruising speed 85mph (137km/hr).
range 430 miles (692km).
initial rate of climb 650ft/min (198m/min).
service ceiling 17,000ft (5,182m).
Weights:
empty 890lb (404kg).
maximum 1,550lb (703kg).
Dimensions:
wing span 30ft 0in (9.14m).
length 23ft 8½in (7.29m).
height 8ft 9½in (2.67m).
wing area 243sq ft (22.57sq m).
Crew: 2.
In Service: Great Britain.
Variants (with no. built):
Cirrus II Moth: Alternative power plants; 75hp Armstrong Siddeley Genet I; 105hp A.D.C. Cirrus Hermes I (38).
Remarks: Pre-war light sports-plane; 20 employed as trainers; others impressed for communications duties.

Manufacturer: de Havilland.
Model: Gipsy Moth.
Type: Communications.
Power Plant: One 120hp de Havilland Gipsy II.
Performance:
maximum speed at sea level 105mph (169km/hr).
cruising speed 85mph (137km/hr).
normal range 320 miles (515km).
initial rate of climb 500ft/min (152m/min).
service ceiling 14,500ft (4,420m).
Weights:
empty 920lb (417kg).
maximum 1,750lb (794kg).
Dimensions:
wing span 30ft 0in (9.14m).
length 23ft 11in (7.29m).
height 8ft 9½in (2.67m).
wing area 243sq ft (22.57sq m).
Crew: 1 or 2.
In Service: Australia, Denmark (NAF), Egypt, Finland, France, Great Britain, Hungary, Iraq, Malaya, South Africa.
Variants (with no. built):
Moth and Gipsy Moth: Production models; alternative power plants: 100hp Gipsy I, 105hp Cirrus Hermes I, 120hp Gipsy III, 85hp General Aircraft V.4; de Havilland-built (595); French licence-built by Morane-Saulnier (40); US licence-built by Moth Aircraft Corp (18); Australian licence-built by Larkin Aircraft Supply Co (32); Finnish licence-built by VL (re-engined with 85hp Cirrus II) (22).
Total Production: 707.
Remarks: Pre-war light sports-plane; trainer version widely exported; several hundred impressed RAF, Commonwealth, and foreign AFs for communications and training duties during WWII.

Manufacturer: de Havilland.
Model: Moth Major.
Type: Communications.
Power Plant: One 133hp de Havilland Gipsy Major IIIA or 130hp Gipsy Major.
Performance:
maximum speed 112mph (180km/hr).
cruising speed 96mph (154km/hr).
range 300 miles (483km).
initial rate of climb 892ft/min (272m/min).
service ceiling 20,000ft (6,096m).
Weights:
empty 1,040lb (472kg).
maximum 1,750lb (794kg).
Dimensions:
wing span 30ft 0in (9.14m).
length 23ft 11in (7.29m).
height 8ft 9½in (2.67m).
wing area 243sq ft (22.57sq m).
Crew: 2.
In Service: Australia, Great Britain, Malaya.
Variants (with no. built):
60GIII Moth: Initial production variant; one 120hp Gipsy III (57).
Moth Major: Standard model (87).
Total Production: 144.
Remarks: Pre-war sports-plane and trainer; many sold abroad; majority impressed for communications duties in UK and Commonwealth during WWII; most either lost to enemy action or written off.

Manufacturer: de Havilland.
Model: Puss Moth.
Type: Communications/light-bomber.
Power Plant: One 120hp de Havilland Gipsy III, or 130hp Gipsy Major, or 147hp Gipsy Major h.c.
Performance:
maximum speed 128mph (206km/hr).
cruising speed 108mph (174km/hr).
range 300 miles (483km).
initial rate of climb 610ft/min (185m/min).
service ceiling 17,500ft (5,334m).
Weights:
empty 1,265lb (574kg).
maximum 2,050lb (930kg).
Dimensions:
wing span 36ft 9in (11.20m).
length 25ft 0in (7.62m).
height 7ft 0in (2.13m).
wing area 222sq ft (20.62sq m).
Crew: 3.
In Service: Great Britain, Iraq (4), Manchuria (6).
Variants (with no. built):
D.H. 80: Prototype (1).
D.H. 80A: Production model as land or seaplane (264).

Total Production: 265.
Remarks: Pre-war long-distance sports-plane; only 1 produced for RAF; many impressed during WWII for communications duties; three Royal Iraqi AF machines fitted with bomb-racks and W/T equipment; these, together with five earlier D.H. 60M Moths. believed destroyed by RAF action during Iraqi rebellion, May 1941; Manchurian civil examples employed para-military light transport role.

Manufacturer: de Havilland.
Model: Tiger Moth II.
Type: Anti-submarine bomber/ambulance.
Power Plant: One 130hp de Havilland Gipsy Major I.
Performance:
maximum speed 104mph (167km/hr).
cruising speed 90mph (145km/hr).
range 300 miles (483km).
initial rate of climb 635ft/min (194m/min).
service ceiling 14,000ft (4,267m).
Weights:
empty 1,115lb (506kg).
maximum 1,825lb (828kg).
Dimensions:
wing span 29ft 4in (8.94m).
length 23ft 11in (7.29m).
height 8ft 9½in (2.67m).
wing area 239sq ft (22.20sq m).
Armament: Eight 20lb (9.07kg) bombs on underwing racks.
Crew: 2.
In Service: Burma, Great Britain (RAF, FAA).
Variants (with no. built):
D.H. 82, D.H. 82A, D.H. 82C: Elementary trainers, inc licence-production (8,280).
Total Production: 8,280.
Remarks: Basic elementary trainer; used by Air Forces throughout the world; 1,500 sets of underwing bomb-racks supplied to RAF schools for emergency conversion to anti-submarine role during post-Dunkirk invasion crisis; other aircraft later converted for ambulance duties during Burma campaign, the original Tiger Moths of Burma Volunteer Air Force having been destroyed within days of Japanese invasion; extensive post-war private use.

Manufacturer: de Havilland.
Model: Fox Moth.
Type: Light transport.
Power Plant: One 130hp Gipsy Major.
Performance:
maximum speed 123mph (198km/hr).
cruising speed 105mph (169km/hr).
range 375 miles (603km).
initial rate of climb 605ft/min (184m/min).
service ceiling 15,000ft (4,572m).
Weights:
empty 1,100lb (499kg).
maximum 2,070lb (939kg).
Dimensions:
wing span 30ft 10.6in (9.41m).
length 25ft 9in (7.66m).
height 8ft 9½in (2.67m).
wing area 261.5sq ft (24.29sq m).
Crew/Accommodation: 1/4 or 5.
In Service: Canada, Great Britain.
Variants (with no. built):
D.H. 83 Fox Moth: De Havilland British-built (98); Australian-built (2).
D.H. 83C: Post-war Canadian-built (54).
Total Production: 154.
Remarks: Civil light transport; extensive foreign use; 7 British examples impressed for communications and radar-calibration trials.

Manufacturer: de Havilland.
Model: Dragon Mk 2.
Type: Army Co-operation/light transport.
Power Plant: Two 130hp de Havilland Gipsy Major I.
Performance:
maximum speed 134mph (216km/hr).
cruising speed 114mph (183km/hr).
range 545 miles (877km).
initial rate of climb 565ft/min (172m/min).
service ceiling 14,500ft (4,420m).
Weights:
empty 2,336lb (1,060kg).
maximum 4,500lb (2,041kg).
Dimensions:
wing span 47ft 4in (14.43m).
length 34ft 6in (10.51m).
height 10ft 1in (3.07m).
wing area 376sq ft (34.93sq m).
Crew/Accommodation: 1/6–8.
In Service: Great Britain.
Variants (with no. built):
Dragon Mk 1: Pre-war all-purpose civil and military transport (62).
Mk 2: Improved land- or seaplane

version; de Havilland British-built (53); Australian-built (87).
Total Production: 202.
Remarks: Pre-war light transport; military variants exported to Denmark (5), Iraq (8) and Portugal (3); 17 impressed in UK 1940; used for parachute training and on army co-operation night flights; one abandoned in France; another (civil) destroyed by enemy action.

Manufacturer: de Havilland.
Model: Leopard Moth.
Type: Communications.
Power Plant: One 130hp de Havilland Gipsy Major, or one 230hp Gipsy Six R.
Performance:
maximum speed 137mph (220km/hr).
cruising speed 119mph (191km/hr).
range 715 miles (1,150km).
initial rate of climb 550ft/min (168m/min).
service ceiling 21,500ft (6,553m).
Weights:
empty 1,290lb (585kg).
maximum 2,225lb (1,009kg).
Dimensions:
wing span 37ft 6in (11.43m).
length 24ft 6in (7.47m).
height 8ft 9in (2.66m).
wing area 206sq ft (19.14sq m).
Crew/Accommodation: 1/2.
In Service: Great Britain, India, South Africa, Southern Rhodesia.
Variants (with no. built):
D.H. 85 and D.H. 85A Leopard Moth (133).
Total Production: 133.
Remarks: Pre-war light private tourer; 44 British examples impressed for communications duties with RAF and ATA; others similarly impressed in India, Rhodesia and South Africa.

Manufacturer: de Havilland.
Model: D.H. 86B.
Type: General-purpose transport/trainer.
Power Plant: Four 205hp de Havilland Gipsy Six I.
Performance:
maximum speed 166mph (267km/hr).
cruising speed 142mph (228km/hr).
range 800 miles (1,287km).
initial rate of climb 925ft/min (282m/min).
service ceiling 17,400ft (5,304m).
Weights:
empty 6,489lb (2,943kg).
maximum 10,250lb (4,649kg).
Dimensions:
wing span 64ft 6in (19.66m).
length 46ft 1in (14.05m).
height 13ft 0in (3.624m).
wing area 641sq ft (59.55sq m).
Crew/Accommodation: 2/8–16.
In Service: Australia, Finland, Germany (1 + captured/impressed), Great Britain, New Zealand, Southern Rhodesia.
Variants (with no. built):
D.H. 86: Initial production variant; single pilot version (3); two-crew version (29).
D.H. 86A: Improved model; alternative 205hp Gipsy Six II engines (converted to 86B in 1937) (20).
D.H. 86B: As D.H. 86A with auxiliary fins on tailplane (10).
Total Production: 62.
Remarks: Pre-war civil airliner; extensive foreign sales; many impressed during WWII: RAF (22), RAAF (8), RNZAF (3); employed on transport, VIP-transport, and training duties in UK; single Finnish example used as air ambulance; similar duties performed by RAAF in Middle East; at least one lost to Luftwaffe over Western Desert.

Manufacturer: de Havilland.
Model: Hornet Moth.
Type: Communications.
Power Plant: One 130hp de Havilland Gipsy Major 1 or 1F.
Performance:
maximum speed 124mph (200km/hr).
cruising speed 105mph (169km/hr).
range 640 miles (1,030km).
initial rate of climb 690ft/min (210m/min).
service ceiling 14,800ft (4,511m).
Weights:
empty 1,240lb (562kg).
maximum 2,000lb (907kg).
Dimensions:
wing span 31ft 11in (9.72m).
length 24ft 11½in (7.60m).
height 6ft 7in (2.00m).
wing area 244.5sq ft (22.71sq m).
Crew: 2.
In Service: Great Britain.
Variants (with no. built):
D.H. 87: Prototype (1).
D.H. 87A and 87B: Production versions; 87B with re-designed wings (164).
Total Production: 165.
Remarks: Pre-war touring aircraft in world-wide use; many impressed in Britain and used for communications and radar-calibration duties; one escaped from German-occupied Denmark to join RAF.

Manufacturer: de Havilland.
Model: Dominie Mk 2.
Type: Communications.
Power Plant: Two 200hp de Havilland Gipsy Queen 3.
Performance:
maximum speed at 1,000ft (304m) 157mph (253km/hr).
cruising speed 132mph (212km/hr).
range 570 miles (917km).
initial rate of climb 867ft/min (264m/min).
service ceiling 16,700ft (5,090m).
Weights:
empty 3,276lb (1,486kg).
maximum 5,500lb (2,495kg).

Dimensions:
wing span 48ft 0in (14.63m).
length 34ft 6in (10.36m).
height 10ft 3in (3.05m).
wing area 336sq ft (31.21sq m).
Crew/Accommodation: 1/9.
In Service: Great Britain (RAF, FAA), Kenya (AuxAF), Lithuania (2), New Zealand, South Africa, Spain (3), USAAF (UK).
Variants (with no. built):
Dragon Rapide D.H. 89: Light civil airliner; initial production model (inc prototype) (59).
D.H. 89M: Coastal Command armed reconnaissance version with 280lb (127kg) bomb load; Prototype (British) 1 conversion; Spanish export model (3); Lithuanian export model (2).
D.H. 89A: As D.H. 89 with nose landing light, modified wingtips and cabin heating (inc 100 post-war Dominie conversions) (240).
Dominie D.H. 89B: Mk 1—Military trainer variant of civil Dragon Rapide; Mk 2—Communications model; de Havilland-built (188); Brush-built (236).
Total Production: 728.
Remarks: Pre-war civil airliner; extensive foreign sales; 9 British civil machines lost on supply flights to BEF, May–June 1940; majority Dragon Rapides subsequently impressed; employed for communications and light transport duties, supplemented by wartime Dominie production; both types disposed of post-war to civil operators; 3 FAA machines still on charge early 1960s.

Manufacturer: de Havilland.
Model: Dragonfly.
Type: Communications/light transport.
Power Plant: Two 130hp de Havilland Gipsy Major 1, or two 142hp Gipsy Major 1C or D, or two 145hp Gipsy Major 10.
Performance:
maximum speed 144mph (232km/hr).
cruising speed 125mph (201km/hr).
range 900 miles (1,448km).
initial rate of climb 730ft/min (223m/min).
service ceiling 18,100ft (5,516m).
Weights:
empty 2,487lb (1,128kg).
maximum 4,000lb (1,814kg).
Dimensions:
wing span 43ft 0in (13.11m).
length 31ft 8in (9.65m).
height 9ft 2in (2.94m).
wing area 256sq ft (23.78sq m).
Crew/Accommodation: 2/3.
In Service: Canada, Denmark (AF), Great Britain.
Variants (with no. built):
Dragonfly: Prototype (1).
Production model; alternative land or seaplane (66).
Total Production: 67.

Remarks: Pre-war luxury touring aircraft; 6 impressed in Canada for transport and communications duties; 15 British impressments used as industrial hacks; 2 Danish AF machines in service 1937–40.

Manufacturer: de Havilland.
Model: Albatross.
Type: Long-range transport.
Power Plant: Four 525hp de Havilland Gipsy Twelve.
Performance:
maximum speed 213mph (343km/hr).
cruising speed 205mph (330km/hr).
range 3,230 miles (5,197km).
initial rate of climb 620ft/min (199m/min).
service ceiling 16,800ft (5,121m).
Weights:
empty 20,314lb (9.214kg).
maximum 28,500lb (12,928kg).
Dimensions:
wing span 104ft 8in (31.90m).
length 70ft 0in (21.34m).
height 20ft 2in (6.15m).
wing area 1,078sq ft (100.15sq m).
Crew/Payload: 2/1,000lb (454kg).
In Service: Great Britain.
Variants (with no. built):
Albatross: Prototypes (experimental mailplanes (2).
Production passenger version (5).
Total Production: 7.
Remarks: Pre-war long-range mailplane and airliner; two mailplanes impressed by RAF for transport duties UK/Iceland; one civil passenger aircraft destroyed by enemy action.

Manufacturer: de Havilland.
Model: Don.
Type: Communications.
Power Plant: One 525hp de Havilland Gipsy King I.
Performance:
maximum speed at 8,750ft (2,667m) 189mph (304km/hr).
range 890 miles (1,432km).
initial rate of climb 830ft/min (253m/min).
service ceiling 23,300ft (7,102m).
Weights:
empty 5,050lb (2,291kg).
maximum 6,530lb (2,962kg).
Dimensions:
wing span 47ft 6in (14.48m).
length 37ft 4in (11.38m).
height 9ft 5in (2.87m).
wing area 304sq ft (28.24sq m).
Crew/Accommodation: 2.
In Service: Great Britain.
Variants (with no. built):
Don: Prototype (1).
Production model (29).
Total Production: 30.
Remarks: Pre-war general-purpose trainer; 12 + used briefly for communications duties before relegation to ground instructional airframes.

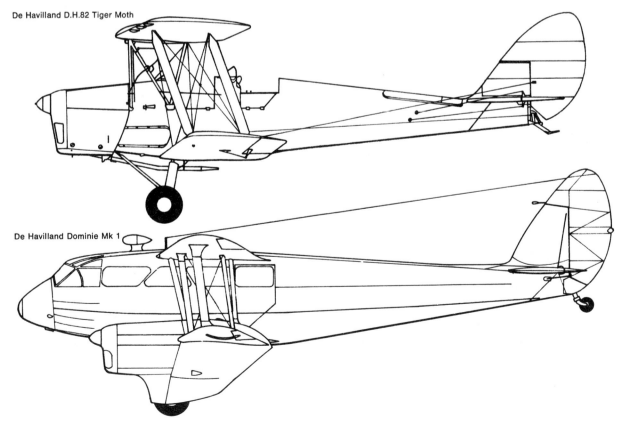

De Havilland D.H.82 Tiger Moth

De Havilland Dominie Mk 1

Manufacturer: de Havilland.
Model: Moth Minor.
Type: Light transport/communications.
Power Plant: One 80hp de Havilland Gipsy Minor.
Performance (Open Cockpit model):
maximum speed 118mph (190km/hr).
cruising speed 100mph (161km/hr).
range 300 miles (483km).
initial rate of climb 590ft/min (180m/min).
service ceiling 18,400ft (5,608m).
Weights:
empty 960lb (435kg).
maximum 1,150lb (522kg).
Dimensions:
wing span 36ft 7in (10.97m).
length 24ft 5in (7.44m).
height 6ft 4in (1.93m).
wing area 162sq ft (15.05sq m).
Crew: 2.
In Service: Australia (40), Great Britain (RAF, FAA), India, Malaya, USA (1).
Variants (with no. built):
Moth Minor: Prototype (1).
Production model (with open or closed cockpit) (100+).
Completed in Australia (40+).
Total Production: approx 150.
Remarks: Pre-war light sports plane; used by RAAF as interim trainer; 30+ impressed in UK as general-purpose liaison aircraft; many issued to Station Flights; one FAA impressment employed East Africa, another procured by USAAF for use in Middle East.

Manufacturer: de Havilland.
Model: Flamingo.
Type: Light transport.
Power Plant: Two 890hp Bristol Perseus XIIC.
Performance:
maximum speed 243mph (391km/hr).
cruising speed 204mph (328km/hr).
range 1,345 miles (2,164km).
initial rate of climb 1,470ft/min (448m/min).
service ceiling 20,900ft (6,370m).
Weights:
empty 11,325lb (5,137kg).
maximum 17, 600lb (7,983kg).
Dimensions:
wing span 70ft 0in (21.34m).
length 51ft 7in (15.72m).
height 15ft 3in (4.65m).
wing area 651sq ft (60.48sq m).
Crew/Accommodation: 3/12–17.
In Service: Great Britain (RAF, FAA).
Variants (with no. built):
Flamingo: Prototype (1).
Civil production model (12).
Military production model (3).
Hertfordshire: Military version; modified cabin windows; prototype only (1).
Total Production: 17.
Remarks: All-metal civil airliner evaluated pre-war as military transport; prototype and first two production models impressed as VIP transports; 8 to BOAC for Middle East routes; last two impressed by FAA for UK communications; three military models to King's Flight.

Manufacturer: de Havilland.
Model: Mosquito P.R. Mk IX (Reconnaissance variants).
Type: High-altitude photographic reconnaissance.
Power Plant: Two 1,680hp Rolls-Royce Merlin 72.
Performance:
maximum speed 408mph (656km/hr).
cruising speed 250mph (402km/hr).
maximum range 2,450 miles (3,942km).
initial rate of climb 2,850ft/min (869m/min).
service ceiling 38,000ft (11,582m).
Weights:
empty 14,569lb (6,608kg).
maximum 22,000lb (9,980kg).
Dimensions:
wing span 54ft 2in (16.51m).

Order of Battle 6 June 1944

ROYAL AIR FORCE (Home Commands)

BOMBER COMMAND

No. 1 Bomber Group:

12 Sqn.	Wickenby	Avro Lancaster I and III
100 Sqn.	Grimsby	Avro Lancaster I and III
101 Sqn.	Ludford Magna	Avro Lancaster I and III
103 Sqn.	Elsham Wolds	Avro Lancaster I and III
166 Sqn.	Kirmington	Avro Lancaster I and III
300 Sqn. (Polish)	Faldingworth	Avro Lancaster I and III
460 Sqn. (RAAF)	Binbrook	Avro Lancaster I and III
550 Sqn.	North Killingholme	Avro Lancaster I and III
576 Sqn.	Elsham Wolds	Avro Lancaster I and III
625 Sqn.	Kelstern	Avro Lancaster I and III
626 Sqn.	Wickenby	Avro Lancaster I and III

No. 3 Bomber Group:

15 Sqn.	Mildenhall	Avro Lancaster I and III
75 Sqn. (RNZAF)	Mepal	Avro Lancaster I and III
90 Sqn.	Tuddenham	Short Stirling III Avro Lancaster I and III
115 Sqn.	Witchford	Lancaster I and III
138 Sqn. (SD)	Tempsford	Handley Page Halifax Short Stirling
149 Sqn.	Methwold	Short Stirling III
161 Sqn. (SD)	Tempsford	Lockheed Hudson Westland Lysander Handley Page Halifax
218 Sqn.	Woolfox Lodge	Short Stirling III
514 Sqn.	Waterbeach	Avro Lancaster II
622 Sqn.	Mildenhall	Avro Lancaster I and III

No. 4 Bomber Group:

10 Sqn.	Melbourne	Handley Page Halifax B. Mk III
51 Sqn.	Snaith	Handley Page Halifax B. Mk III
76 Sqn.	Holme-on-Spalding-Moor	Handley Page Halifax B. Mk III
77 Sqn.	Full Sutton	Handley Page Halifax B. Mk III
78 Sqn.	Breighton	Handley Page Halifax B. Mk III
102 Sqn.	Pocklington	Handley Page Halifax B. Mk III
158 Sqn.	Lissett	Handley Page Halifax B. Mk III
346 Sqn. (French)	Elvington	Handley Page Halifax B. Mk III and Mk V
466 Sqn. (RAAF)	Driffield	Handley Page Halifax B. Mk III
578 Sqn.	Burn	Handley Page Halifax B. Mk III
640 Sqn.	Leconfield	Handley Page Halifax B. Mk III

No. 5 Bomber Group:

9 Sqn.	Bardney	Avro Lancaster I and III
44 Sqn.	Dunholme Lodge	Avro Lancaster I and III
49 Sqn.	Fiskerton	Avro Lancaster I and III
50 Sqn.	Skellingthorpe	Avro Lancaster I and III
57 Sqn.	East Kirkby	Avro Lancaster I and III
61 Sqn.	Skellingthorpe	Avro Lancaster I and III
83 Sqn.	Coningsby	Avro Lancaster I and III
97 Sqn.	Coningsby	Avro Lancaster I and III
106 Sqn.	Metheringham	Avro Lancaster I and III
207 Sqn.	Spilsby	Avro Lancaster I and III
463 Sqn. (RAAF)	Waddington	Avro Lancaster I and III
467 Sqn. (RAAF)	Waddington	Avro Lancaster I and III
617 Sqn.	Woodhall Spa	Avro Lancaster I and III De Havilland Mosquito B. Mk IV
619 Sqn.	Dunholme Lodge	Avro Lancaster I and III
627 Sqn.	Woodhall Spa	De Havilland Mosquito B. Mk IV
630 Sqn.	East Kirkby	Avro Lancaster I and III

No. 6 (RCAF) Bomber Group:

408 Sqn. (RCAF)	Linton-on-Ouse	Avro Lancaster II
419 Sqn. (RCAF)	Middleton St. George	Avro Lancaster X
420 Sqn. (RCAF)	Tholthorpe	Handley Page Halifax B. Mk III
424 Sqn. (RCAF)	Skipton-on-Swale	Handley Page Halifax B. Mk III
425 Sqn. (RCAF)	Tholthorpe	Handley Page Halifax B. Mk III
426 Sqn. (RCAF)	Linton-on-Ouse	Handley Page Halifax B. Mk III
427 Sqn. (RCAF)	Leeming	Handley Page Halifax B. Mk III
428 Sqn. (RCAF)	Middleton St. George	Handley Page Halifax Mk II Avro Lancaster X
429 Sqn. (RCAF)	Leeming	Handley Page Halifax B. Mk III
431 Sqn. (RCAF)	Croft	Handley Page Halifax B. Mk III
432 Sqn. (RCAF)	East Moor	Handley Page Halifax B. Mk III and B. Mk VII
433 Sqn. (RCAF)	Skipton-on-Swale	Handley Page Halifax B. Mk III
434 Sqn. (RCAF)	Croft	Handley Page Halifax B. Mk III

No. 8 Pathfinder Group:

7 Sqn.	Oakington	Avro Lancaster I and III
35 Sqn.	Graveley	Avro Lancaster I and III
105 Sqn.	Bourn	De Havilland Mosquito B. Mk IX
109 Sqn.	Little Staughton	De Havilland Mosquito B. Mk IX and Mk XVI
139 Sqn.	Upwood	De Havilland Mosquito B. Mk IV and Mk IX
156 Sqn.	Upwood	Avro Lancaster I and III
405 Sqn. (RCAF)	Gransden Lodge	Avro Lancaster I and III
571 Sqn.	Oakington	De Havilland Mosquito B. Mk XVI
582 Sqn.	Little Staughton	Avro Lancaster I and III
635 Sqn.	Downham Market	Avro Lancaster I and III
692 Sqn.	Graveley	De Havilland Mosquito B. Mk IV and Mk XVI
1409 Flight (Met.)	Wyton	De Havilland Mosquito

No. 100 Bomber Support (Special Duties) Group:

23 Sqn.	Little Snoring	De Havilland Mosquito Mk VI
85 Sqn.	Swannington	De Havilland Mosquito N.F. Mk XIX
141 Sqn.	West Raynham	De Havilland Mosquito Mk VI
157 Sqn.	Swannington	De Havilland Mosquito N.F. Mk XVII
169 Sqn.	Great Massingham	De Havilland Mosquito Mk II
192 Sqn.	Foulsham	Vickers Wellington Mk X Handley Page Halifax B.Mk III De Havilland Mosquito B.Mk IV
199 Sqn.	North Creake	Short Stirling III
214 Sqn.	Oulton	Boeing Fortress II and III
239 Sqn.	West Raynham	De Havilland Mosquito Mk VI
515 Sqn.	Little Snoring	De Havilland Mosquito Mk VI
1692 Flight	Great Massingham	Bristol Beaufighter
1699 Flight	Oulton	Boeing Fortress

ALLIED EXPEDITIONARY AIR FORCE

Air Defence of Great Britain

No. 10 Fighter Group:

1 Sqn.	Predannack	Supermarine Spitfire F.Mk IX
41 Sqn.	Bolt Head	Supermarine Spitfire Mk XII
68 Sqn.	Fairwood Common	Bristol Beaufighter Mk VIF
126 Sqn.	Culmhead	Supermarine Spitfire F.Mk IX
131 Sqn.	Culmhead	Supermarine Spitfire Mk VII
151 Sqn.	Predannack	De Havilland Mosquito N.F. Mk XIII
165 Sqn.	Predannack	Supermarine Spitfire F.Mk IX
263 Sqn.	Harrowbeer	Hawker Typhoon IB
275 Sqn. (ASR)	Warmwell	Supermarine Walrus Supermarine Spitfire Mk V
276 Sqn. (ASR) ('A' Flight)	Portreath	Vickers Warwick Avro Anson Supermarine Walrus
276 Sqn. (ASR) ('B' Flight)	Bolt Head	Supermarine Spitfire Supermarine Walrus
406 Sqn. (RCAF)	Winkleigh	Bristol Beaufighter Mk VIF De Havilland Mosquito N.F. Mk XII
610 Sqn.	Harrowbeer	Supermarine Spitfire F.Mk XIV
616 Sqn.	Culmhead	Supermarine Spitfire Mk VII

No. 11 Fighter Group:

33 Sqn.	Lympne	Supermarine Spitfire F.Mk IX
64 Sqn.	Deanland	Supermarine Spitfire Mk VB
74 Sqn.	Lympne	Supermarine Spitfire F.Mk IX
80 Sqn.	Detling	Supermarine Spitfire F.Mk IX
96 Sqn.	West Malling	De Havilland Mosquito N.F. Mk XIII
125 Sqn.	Hurn	De Havilland Mosquito N.F. Mk XVII
127 Sqn.	Lympne	Supermarine Spitfire F.Mk IX
130 Sqn.	Horne	Supermarine Spitfire Mk VB
137 Sqn.	Manston	Hawker Typhoon IB
219 Sqn.	Bradwell Bay	De Havilland Mosquito N.F. Mk XVII
229 Sqn.	Detling	Supermarine Spitfire F.Mk IX
234 Sqn.	Deanland	Supermarine Spitfire Mk VB
274 Sqn.	Detling	Supermarine Spitfire F.Mk IX
277 Sqn. (ASR) ('A' Flight)	Shoreham	Supermarine Spitfire Supermarine Sea Otter Supermarine Walrus
277 Sqn. (ASR) ('B' Flight)	Hawkinge	Supermarine Spitfire Supermarine Walrus
278 Sqn. (ASR) ('A' Flight)	Bradwell Bay	Vickers Warwick
278 Sqn. (ASR) ('B' Flight)	Martlesham Heath	Supermarine Spitfire Supermarine Walrus
303 Sqn. (Polish)	Horne	Supermarine Spitfire Mk VB
345 Sqn. (French)	Shoreham	Supermarine Spitfire Mk VB
350 Sqn. (Belgian)	Friston	Supermarine Spitfire Mk VB
402 Sqn. (RCAF)	Horne	Supermarine Spitfire Mk VB
418 Sqn. (RCAF)	Holmsley South	De Havilland Mosquito Mk VI
456 Sqn. (RAAF)	Ford	De Havilland Mosquito N.F. Mk XVII
501 Sqn.	Friston	Supermarine Spitfire F.Mk IX
605 Sqn.	Manston	De Havilland Mosquito Mk VI
611 Sqn.	Deanland	Supermarine Spitfire Mk VB

No. 12 Fighter Group:

25 Sqn.	Coltishall	De Havilland Mosquito N.F. Mk XVII
309 Sqn. (Polish) 'B' (Flight)	Hutton Cranswick	
316 Sqn. (Polish)	Coltishall	
504 Sqn. ('A' Flight)	Digby	
504 Sqn. ('B' Flight)	Coltishall	
1426 (EA) Flight	Collyweston	

No. 13 Fighter Group:

118 Sqn. ('A' Flight)	Sumburgh
118 Sqn. ('B' Flight)	Skeabrae
309 Sqn. (Polish) ('A' Flight)	Drem
899 Sqn. (FAA) (attached)	Peterhead

No. 38 Airborne Forces Group:

190 Sqn.	Fairford
196 Sqn.	Keevil
295 Sqn.	Harwell
296 Sqn.	Brize Norton
297 Sqn.	Brize Norton
298 Sqn.	Tarrant Rushton
299 Sqn.	Keevil
570 Sqn.	Harwell
620 Sqn.	Fairford
644 Sqn.	Tarrant Rushton

2nd Tactical Air Force

No. 2 Bomber Group:

137 Wing:	
88 Sqn.	Hartford Bridge
226 Sqn.	Hartford Bridge
342 Sqn. (French)	Hartford Bridge
138 Wing:	
107 Sqn.	Lasham
305 Sqn. (Polish)	Lasham
613 Sqn.	Lasham
139 Wing:	
98 Sqn.	Dunsfold
180 Sqn.	Dunsfold
320 Sqn. (Dutch)	Dunsfold
140 Wing:	
21 Sqn.	Gravesend
464 Sqn. (RAAF)	Gravesend
487 Sqn. (RNZAF)	Gravesend

No. 83 Composite Group:

39 (Recce) Wing:	
168 Sqn.	Odiham
400 Sqn. (RCAF)	Odiham
414 Sqn. (RCAF)	Odiham
430 Sqn. (RCAF)	Odiham
121 Wing:	
174 Sqn.	Holmsley South
175 Sqn.	Holmsley South
245 Sqn.	Holmsley South
122 Wing:	
19 Sqn.	Funtington
65 Sqn.	Funtington
122 Sqn.	Funtington
124 Wing:	
181 Sqn.	Hurn
182 Sqn.	Hurn
247 Sqn.	Hurn
125 Wing:	
132 Sqn.	Ford
453 Sqn. (RAAF)	Ford
602 Sqn.	Ford
126 Wing:	
401 Sqn. (RCAF)	Tangmere
411 Sqn. (RCAF)	Tangmere
412 Sqn. (RCAF)	Tangmere
127 Wing:	
403 Sqn. (RCAF)	Tangmere
416 Sqn. (RCAF)	Tangmere
421 Sqn. (RCAF)	Tangmere
129 Wing:	
184 Sqn.	Westhampnett
143 Wing:	
438 Sqn. (RCAF)	Hurn
439 Sqn. (RCAF)	Hurn
440 Sqn. (RCAF)	Hurn

length 44ft 6in (13.56m).
height 12ft 6in (3.81m).
wing area 454sq ft (42.18sq m).
Crew: 2.
In Service: Great Britain, USA (P.R.Mk XVI and F–8).
Variants (with no. built):
P.R.Mk I: Prototype (1); Production model (10).
P.R.Mk IV: 32 B.Mk IV conversions.
P.R.Mk VIII: As Mk IV with Merlin 61s (5).
P.R.Mk IX: B.Mk IX variant (90).
P.R.Mk XVI: Prototype; one B.Mk IX conversion; Production model (pressurized cabin) (432).
P.R.Mk 32: Five conversions (lightened; increased wingspan) with Merlin 113s.

P.R.Mk 34: Very-long-range version (50).
P.R.Mks 35 and 40: Post-war conversions.
T.Mk III: Dual-control trainer version (343).
T.Mks 22, 27 and 43, T.R.Mks 33 and 37, T.T.Mks 35 and 39: Post-war trainers and target tugs.
F–8: USAAF designation; 40 conversions from Canadian B.Mk XX.
Total Production: 7,785 (all Marks).
Remarks: P.R. version was last of three original Mosquito prototypes to fly, but first variant to enter service; first operational sortie 20 Sept 1941, daylight reconnaissance of French Atlantic ports; by mid-1942 ranging Europe from Norway to Czechoslovakia, later (1943) staging via North Africa or Gibraltar for refuelling before return flight. 1944–45 equipped one sqn in Far East; also served two sqns US 8th AAF, April 1944– May 1945.
Colour Reference: Plates 55, 56: De Havilland Mosquito P.R.Mk XVI (NS710) of 653rd Bomb Squadron, 25th Bomb Group (Reconnaissance), 8th USAAF, Watton, Norfolk, March 1945; overall RAF PR-blue, all-red tail surfaces; 653rd BS identified by circle round individual aircraft letter 'L', 654th sister squadron applied letter directly on background red; (652nd equipped with B–17G).

Manufacturer: de Havilland.
Model: Mosquito B.Mk XVI (Bomber variants).
Type: High-altitude light bomber.
Power Plant: Two 1,680hp Rolls-Royce Merlin 72.
Performance:
maximum speed at 26,000ft (7,925m) 408mph (656km/hr).
cruising speed 245mph (394km/hr).
maximum range 1,485 miles (2,389km).
initial rate of climb 2,800ft/min (835m/min).
service ceiling 37,000ft (11,278m).
Weights:
empty 14,635lb (6,638kg).
maximum 23,000lb (10,433kg).
Dimensions:
wing span 54ft 2in (16.51m).
length 44ft 6in (13.56m).
height 12ft 6in (3.81m).
wing area 454sq ft (42.18sq m).
Armament: Four 500lb (227kg) bombs internally plus two 500lb (227kg) bombs underwing, or one 4,000lb (1,814kg) bomb.
In Service: Australia, Canada, Great Britain, New Zealand, South Africa, USA.
Variants (with no. built):
Mk I: Prototype; two 1,250hp Rolls-Royce Merlin 21; (1).
B.Mk IV: Initial production bomber with four 500lb (227kg) bombs; 54 converted to carry one 4,000lb (1,814kg) bomb; some fitted with Oboe radar (273).
B.Mk V: Prototype (1).
B.Mk VII: With 1,418hp Packard Merlin 31s; Canadian-built by D.H. (25).

(continued aircraft list, left column)

Hawker Hurricane Mk IIC
North American Mustang III
Supermarine Spitfire Mk VB
Supermarine Spitfire Mk VB

Supermarine Spitfire Mk VB
Supermarine Spitfire Mk VB

Hawker Hurricane Mk IIC

Supermarine Seafire

Short Stirling IV/ Airspeed Horsa
Short Stirling IV/ Airspeed Horsa
Armstrong Whitworth Albemarle/Airspeed Horsa
Armstrong Whitworth Albemarle/Airspeed Horsa
Armstrong Whitworth Albemarle/Airspeed Horsa
Handley Page Halifax Mk V /Airspeed Horsa; G.A. Hamilcar
Short Stirling IV/ Airspeed Horsa
Armstrong Whitworth Albemarle/Airspeed Horsa
Short Stirling IV/ Airspeed Horsa
Handley Page Halifax Mk V /Airspeed Horsa; G.A. Hamilcar

Douglas Boston IIIA/IV
North American Mitchell II
Douglas Boston IIIA/IV
De Havilland Mosquito F.B. Mk VI
De Havilland Mosquito F.B. Mk VI
De Havilland Mosquito F.B. Mk VI
North American Mitchell II
North American Mitchell II
North American Mitchell II
De Havilland Mosquito F.B. Mk VI
De Havilland Mosquito F.B. Mk VI
De Havilland Mosquito F.B. Mk VI

North American Mustang I
Supermarine Spitfire P.R. Mk XI
North American Mustang I
North American Mustang I

Hawker Typhoon IB
Hawker Typhoon IB
Hawker Typhoon IB

North American Mustang III
North American Mustang III
North American Mustang III

Hawker Typhoon IB
Hawker Typhoon IB
Hawker Typhoon IB

Supermarine Spitfire Mk IX
Supermarine Spitfire Mk IX
Supermarine Spitfire Mk IX

Supermarine Spitfire Mk IX
Supermarine Spitfire Mk IX
Supermarine Spitfire Mk IX

Supermarine Spitfire Mk IX
Supermarine Spitfire Mk IX
Supermarine Spitfire Mk IX

Hawker Typhoon IB

Hawker Typhoon IB
Hawker Typhoon IB
Hawker Typhoon IB
Hawker Typhoon IB

---

144 Wing:

Squadron	Base	Aircraft
441 Sqn. (RCAF)	Ford	Supermarine Spitfire Mk IX
442 Sqn. (RCAF)	Ford.	Supermarine Spitfire Mk IX
443 Sqn. (RCAF)	Ford	Supermarine Spitfire Mk IX
653 Sqn.	Penshurst	British Taylorcraft Auster IV
658 Sqn.	Collyweston	British Taylorcraft Auster IV
659 Sqn.	Hammerwood	British Taylorcraft Auster IV
662 Sqn.	Westley	British Taylorcraft Auster III and IV

No. 84 Composite Group:

35 (Recce) Wing:

Squadron	Base	Aircraft
2 Sqn.	Gatwick	North American Mustang IA
4 Sqn.	Gatwick	Supermarine Spitfire P.R. Mk XI
168 Sqn.	Gatwick	North American Mustang IA

123 Wing:

Squadron	Base	Aircraft
198 Sqn.	Thorney Island	Hawker Typhoon IB
609 Sqn.	Thorney Island	Hawker Typhoon IB

131 Wing:

Squadron	Base	Aircraft
302 Sqn. (Polish)	Chailey	Supermarine Spitfire Mk IX
308 Sqn. (Polish)	Chailey	Supermarine Spitfire Mk IX
317 Sqn. (Polish)	Chailey	Supermarine Spitfire Mk IX

132 Wing:

Squadron	Base	Aircraft
66 Sqn. (Norwegian)	Bognor	Supermarine Spitfire Mk IX
331 Sqn. (Norwegian)	Bognor	Supermarine Spitfire Mk IX
332 Sqn. (Norwegian)	Bognor	Supermarine Spitfire Mk IX

133 Wing:

Squadron	Base	Aircraft
129 Sqn.	Coolham	North American Mustang III
306 Sqn. (Polish)	Coolham	North American Mustang III
315 Sqn. (Polish)	Coolham	North American Mustang III

134 Wing:

Squadron	Base	Aircraft
310 Sqn. (Czech)	Appledram	Supermarine Spitfire Mk IX
312 Sqn. (Czech)	Appledram	Supermarine Spitfire Mk IX
313 Sqn. (Czech)	Appledram	Supermarine Spitfire Mk IX

135 Wing:

Squadron	Base	Aircraft
222 Sqn.	Selsey	Supermarine Spitfire Mk IX
349 Sqn. (Belgian)	Selsey	Supermarine Spitfire Mk IX
485 Sqn. (RNZAF)	Selsey	Supermarine Spitfire Mk IX

136 Wing:

Squadron	Base	Aircraft
164 Sqn.	Thorney Island	Hawker Typhoon IB
183 Sqn.	Thorney Island	Hawker Typhoon IB

145 Wing:

Squadron	Base	Aircraft
329 Sqn. (French)	Merston	Supermarine Spitfire Mk IX
340 Sqn. (French)	Merston	Supermarine Spitfire Mk IX
341 Sqn. (French)	Merston	Supermarine Spitfire Mk IX

146 Wing:

Squadron	Base	Aircraft
193 Sqn.	Needs Oar Point	Hawker Typhoon IB
197 Sqn.	Needs Oar Point	Hawker Typhoon IB
257 Sqn.	Needs Oar Point	Hawker Typhoon IB
266 Sqn.	Needs Oar Point	Hawker Typhoon IB
652 Sqn.	Cobham	British Taylorcraft Auster IV
660 Sqn.	Westenhangar	British Taylorcraft Auster IV
661 Sqn.	'Fairchildes'	British Taylorcraft Auster IV

No. 85 Base Group:

141 Wing:

Squadron	Base	Aircraft
264 Sqn.	Hartford Bridge	De Havilland Mosquito N.F. Mk XIII
322 Sqn. (Dutch)	Hartford Bridge	Supermarine Spitfire Mk XIV

148 Wing:

Squadron	Base	Aircraft
29 Sqn.	West Malling	De Havilland Mosquito N.F. Mk XIII
91 Sqn.	West Malling	Supermarine Spitfire Mk XIV
409 Sqn. (RCAF)	West Malling	De Havilland Mosquito N.F. Mk XIII
3 Sqn.	Newchurch	Hawker Tempest Mk V
56 Sqn.	Newchurch	Supermarine Spitfire Mk IX
410 Sqn. (RCAF)	Hunsdon	De Havilland Mosquito N.F. Mk XIII
486 Sqn. (RNZAF)	Newchurch	Hawker Tempest Mk V
488 Sqn. (RNZAF)	Zeals	De Havilland Mosquito N.F. Mk XIII
604 Sqn.	Hurn	De Havilland Mosquito N.F. Mk XIII

TRANSPORT COMMAND

No. 46 Transport Group:

Squadron	Base	Aircraft
48 Sqn.	Down Ampney	Douglas Dakota/ Airspeed Horsa
233 Sqn.	Blakehill Farm	Douglas Dakota/ Airspeed Horsa
271 Sqn.	Down Ampney	Douglas Dakota/ Airspeed Horsa
512 Sqn.	Broadwell	Douglas Dakota/ Airspeed Horsa
575 Sqn.	Broadwell	Douglas Dakota/ Airspeed Horsa
1697 Flight (ADLS)	Northolt	Hawker Hurricane Mk II / Avro Anson
Harrow/Sparrow Flight	Doncaster	Handley Page Harrow / Handley Page Sparrow
Sparrow Ambulance Flight	Watchfield	Handley Page Sparrow

COASTAL COMMAND

No. 15 (GR) Group:

Squadron	Base	Aircraft
59 Sqn.	Ballykelly	Consolidated Liberator V
120 Sqn.	Ballykelly	Consolidated Liberator V
281 Sqn. (ASR) (HQ)	Tiree	Vickers Warwick / Supermarine Sea Otter
422 Sqn. (RCAF)	Castle Archdale	Short Sunderland III
423 Sqn. (RCAF)	Castle Archdale	Short Sunderland III
518 Sqn. (Met.)	Tiree	Handley Page Halifax
1402 Flight (Met.)	Aldergrove	Gloster Gladiator / Supermarine Spitfire Mk VI

No. 16 (GR) Group:

Squadron	Base	Aircraft
143 Sqn.	Manston	Bristol Beaufighter Mk X
236 Sqn.	North Coates	Bristol Beaufighter Mk X
254 Sqn.	North Coates	Bristol Beaufighter Mk X
279 Sqn. (ASR)	Bircham Newton	Lockheed Hudson
280 Sqn. (ASR)	Strubby	Vickers Warwick
280 Sqn. (ASR) (det.)	Thornaby	Vickers Warwick
415 Sqn. (RCAF)	Bircham Newton	Vickers Wellington XIII
455 Sqn. (RAAF)	Langham	Bristol Beaufighter Mk X
489 Sqn. (RNZAF)	Langham	Bristol Beaufighter Mk X
521 Sqn. (Met.)	Docking	Lockheed Ventura / Gloster Gladiator
1401 Flight (Met.)	Manston	Supermarine Spitfire Mk IX
819 Sqn. (FAA)	Manston	Fairey Swordfish
848 Sqn. (FAA) (attached)	Manston	Grumman Avenger
854 Sqn. (FAA) (attached)	Hawkinge	Grumman Avenger
855 Sqn. (FAA) (attached)	Hawkinge	Grumman Avenger

No. 18 (GR) Group:

Squadron	Base	Aircraft
86 Sqn.	Tain	Consolidated Liberator
210 Sqn.	Sullom Voe	Consolidated Catalina
281 Sqn. (ASR) (det.)	Leuchars	Vickers Warwick
281 Sqn. (ASR) (det.)	Wick	Vickers Warwick
281 Sqn. (ASR) (det.)	Sumburgh	Vickers Warwick
330 Sqn. (Norwegian)	Sullom Voe	Short Sunderland III
333 Sqn. (Norwegian)	Leuchars	De Havilland Mosquito F.B. Mk VI
333 Sqn. (Norwegian) (det.)	Sumburgh	De Havilland Mosquito F.B. Mk VI
333 Sqn. (Norwegian) (det.)	Woodhaven	Consolidated Catalina IB
519 Sqn. (Met.)	Skitten	Lockheed Ventura V / Supermarine Spitfire Mk VI
544 Sqn. (PR) (det.)	Leuchars	De Havilland Mosquito P.R. Mk IX
618 Sqn. (SD)	Turnberry	De Havilland Mosquito B. Mk IV (mod.)

No. 19 (GR) Group:

Squadron	Base	Aircraft
10 Sqn. (RAAF)	Mount Batten	Short Sunderland III
53 Sqn.	St. Eval	Consolidated Liberator V
58 Sqn.	St. Davids	Handley Page Halifax Mk II
144 Sqn.	Davidstowe Moor	Bristol Beaufighter Mk X
172 Sqn.	Chivenor	Vickers Wellington Mk XIV
172 Sqn. (det.)	Davidstowe Moor	Vickers Wellington Mk XIV
179 Sqn.	Predannack	Vickers Wellington Mk XIV
201 Sqn.	Pembroke Dock	Short Sunderland III
206 Sqn.	St. Eval	Consolidated Liberator VI
224 Sqn.	St. Eval	Consolidated Liberator V
228 Sqn.	Pembroke Dock	Short Sunderland III
235 Sqn.	Portreath	Bristol Beaufighter Mk X
248 Sqn.	Portreath	Bristol Beaufighter Mk X
282 Sqn. (ASR)	Davidstowe Moor	Vickers Warwick Mk I
304 Sqn. (Polish)	Chivenor	Vickers Wellington Mk XIV
311 Sqn. (Czech)	Predannack	Consolidated Liberator V
404 Sqn. (RCAF)	Davidstowe Moor	Bristol Beaufighter Mk X
407 Sqn. (RCAF)	Chivenor	Vickers Wellington Mk XIV
415 Sqn. (RCAF) (det.)	Winkleigh	Fairey Albacore
461 Sqn. (RAAF)	Pembroke Dock	Short Sunderland III
502 Sqn.	St. Davids	Handley Page Halifax Mk II
517 Sqn. (Met.)	Brawdy	Handley Page Halifax
524 Sqn.	Davidstowe Moor	Vickers Wellington Mk XIII
541 Sqn. (PR) ('B' Flight)	St. Eval	Supermarine Spitfire P.R. Mk XI
547 Sqn.	St. Eval	Consolidated Liberator V
612 Sqn.	Chivenor	Vickers Wellington Mk XIV
816 Sqn. (FAA) (attached)	Perranporth	Fairey Swordfish Mk II
838 Sqn. (FAA) (attached)	Harrowbeer	Fairey Swordfish
849 Sqn. (FAA) (attached)	Perranporth	Grumman Avenger I
850 Sqn. (FAA) (attached)	Perranporth	Grumman Avenger I

No. 106 (PR) Group:

540 Sqn.	Benson	De Havilland Mosquito P.R.Mk IX
541 Sqn. ('A' Flight)	Benson	Supermarine Spitfire P.R. Mk XI
542 Sqn.	Benson	Supermarine Spitfire P.R. Mk XI
544 Sqn.	Benson	De Havilland Mosquito P.R.Mk IX

B.Mk IX: As B.Mk IV but with 1,680hp Merlin 72s and two additional 500lb (227kg) bombs; some later modified with bulged bomb-bays to carry 4,000lb (1,814kg) bomb load (54).
B.Mk XVI: B.Mk IX development with pressurized cabin (1,200).
B. Mk XX: With American equipment; Canadian-built by D.H. (40 converted to F–8 for USAAF) (145).
B.Mk 23: Project only.
B.Mk 25: With 1,620hp Merlin 225s; Canadian-built by D.H. (400).
B.Mk 35: Post-war development; Airspeed licence-built (122).
Total Production: 7,785 (all Marks).
Remarks: One of the most successful British aircraft of the war, de Havilland's "Wooden Wonder" was RAF's fastest piston-engined bomber; entered squadron service in May 1942; employed initially on daylight pin-point raids, subsequently as Pathfinders spearheading Bomber Command's night offensive; only light bomber able to deliver 4,000lb (1,814kg) 'block-buster' bomb; carried out last Bomber Command raid of WWII, against Kiel on 2 May 1945; equipped thirty-eight squadrons during and after the war.

Manufacturer: de Havilland.
Model: Mosquito N.F.Mk XIX (Night-fighter variants).
Type: Night-fighter.
Power Plant: Two 1,635hp Rolls-Royce Merlin 25.
Performance:
maximum speed at 13,200ft (4,023m) 378mph (608km/hr).
cruising speed 295mph (475km/hr).
initial rate of climb 2,700ft/min (823m/min).
service ceiling 28,000ft (8,534m).
Weights:
empty 15,550lb (7,052kg).
maximum 21,750lb (9,866kg).
Dimensions:
wing span 54ft 2in (16.51m).
length 41ft 2in (12.55m).
height 15ft 3in (4.65m).
wing area 454sq ft (42.18sq m).
Armament: Four 20mm British Hispano cannon.
Crew: 2.
In Service: Australia, Canada, Great Britain, New Zealand.
Variants (with no. built):
N.F.Mk II: With four 20mm Hispano cannon, four machine-guns and A.I.Mk IV radar, Prototype (Mk II) (1); Production model (467).
N.F.Mk XII: With 20mm cannon in nose in lieu of machine-guns and A.I.Mk VIII radar; 97 Mk II conversions.
N.F.Mk XIII: As Mk XII but modified wing and additional fuel tanks (270).
N.F. Mk XV: Five B.Mk IV high-altitude conversions with extended wing-span, A.I.Mk VIII radar and 4-gun pack under fuselage.
N.F. Mk XVII: 100 Mk II conversions with A.I. Mk X radar.
N.F.Mk XIX: Mk XVII derivative; increased weight (220).
N.F.Mk 30: With Merlin 76s rated for high-altitude (526).
N.F.Mk 31: Project only.
N.F.Mk 36: Post-war development with American A.I.Mk X radar (266).
N.F.Mk 38: Mk 36 modified for British A.I.Mk IX radar (50).
Total Production: 7,785 (all Marks).
Remarks: Entered service May 1942, supplanting Bristol Beaufighter as standard home-defence night-fighter; claimed over 600 German raiders in three years, and 600 V–1 flying bombs in just 60 nights; from mid-1944 also used by Bomber Support Group to protect RAF's heavy bombers from German night-fighter attack; by war's end Mosquito night-fighters equipped 7 home defence sqns, and 6 bomber support sqns; also saw service in Middle Eastern (4 sqns) and Far Eastern (3 sqns) theatres.

Manufacturer: de Havilland.
Model: Mosquito F.B.Mk VI (Fighter-bomber variants).
Type: Fighter bomber.
Power Plant: Two 1,460hp Rolls-Royce Merlin 21 or 23, or two 1,635hp Merlin 25.
Performance:
maximum speed at 13,000ft (3,962m) 380mph (611km/hr).
cruising speed 255mph (410km/hr).
normal/maximum range 1,885 miles (2,985km).
initial rate of climb 2,850ft/min (869m/min).
service ceiling 33,000ft (10,058m).
Weights:
empty 14,344lb (6,506kg).
maximum 22,258lb (10,096kg).
Dimensions:
wing span 54ft 2in (16.51m).
length 40ft 6in (12.34m).
height 12ft 6in (3.81m).
wing area 452sq ft (42.18sq m).
Armament: Four forward-firing 20mm cannon plus four .303in guns; two 250lb (113kg) bombs in bomb-bay plus two underwing; or two 500lb (227kg) bombs in bomb-bay plus two underwing; some with 60lb (27kg) rocket projectiles.
Crew: 2.
In Service: Australia, Canada, Germany (evaluation), Great Britain (RAF, FAA), New Zealand, USA.
Variants (with no. built):
F.Mk II: Prototype; Fighter version (1).
F.B.Mk VI: Prototype; converted Mk II (1); Production model; de Havilland-built (1,218); Standard Motor-built (1,200); Airspeed-built (300).
F.B.Mks X and XI: Projects only.
F.B. Mk XVIII: Coastal Command version; one 57mm Molins gun in lieu of four 20mm cannon; alternative load of eight rockets (25).
F.B.Mk 21: As Mk VI but with Merlin 31s and 33s; Canadian-built by DH (3).
F.B.Mk 24: With Merlin 301s; Canadian-built by D.H. (2).
F.B.Mk 26: With Merlin 225s; Canadian-built by D.H. (338).
T.R.Mk 37 (Sea Mosquito): FAA version with one 18in torpedo plus two (optional) rocket projectiles (50).
F.B.Mk 40: Post-war development; Australian-built by D.H. (178).
F.B.Mk 42: One F.B.Mk 40 conversion.
Total Production: 7,785 (all Marks).
Remarks: Last of the versatile Mosquito family to enter service, the fighter-bomber was employed both by Fighter Command (from May 1943) in the day/night intruder and tactical ground-support roles, and by Coastal Command (from early 1944) on anti-shipping strikes; also re-equipped a number of Bomber Command sqns for low-level daylight attacks, including those on Amiens (18 Feb 1944), and the Gestapo offices in the Hague (11 April 1944) and Copenhagen (21 March 1945); served in Burma (6 sqns) 1944–45; at least one example captured by Luftwaffe, Nov 1944.

Manufacturer: Fairey (Avions Fairey).
Model: Fox VI.
Type: Reconnaissance-fighter.
Power Plant: One 860hp Hispano-Suiza 12Ydrs.
Performance:
maximum speed at 13,120ft (4,000m) 227mph (365km/hr).
maximum range 373 miles (600km).
time to 16,400ft (5,000m) 6min 30sec.
service ceiling 36,745ft (11,200m).
Weights:
loaded 4,950lb (2,245kg).
Dimensions:
wing span 38ft 0in (11.58m).
length 30ft 1in (9.17m).
height 11ft 0in (3.35m).
Armament: One or two fixed forward-firing machine-guns; one flexible machine-gun in rear cockpit; provision for light bombs.
Crew: 2.
In Service: Belgium, Switzerland (2).
Variants (with no. built):
Fox I: Original prototype and production model; 2-seat day bomber biplane; one 450hp Curtiss D–12 (Felix) (28).
Fox IA: Re-engined Fox I; one Rolls-Royce Kestral (Conversions).
Fox II: Prototype; 3-seat day bomber version; one 480hp Rolls-Royce F.XIB (Kestrel IB) (1).
Fox II: Initial production model; fixed (ventral) radiator; one Kestrel IIS; Fairey-built (12); Belgian (Avions Fairey) licence-built (31).
Fox III: Private venture demonstrator (subsequently designated Fox IV) (1).
Fox III: As Fox II; one 340hp Armstrong Siddeley Serval; (subsequently with Kestrel IIMS as prototype Fox IIIS) (1).
Fox III: Production model; 2-seat reconnaissance-fighter version; Belgian (Avions Fairey) licence-built (13).
Fox IIIC: Modified Fox II; enclosed cockpits; one Kestrel V; (inc one as Fox IIICS dual-control trainer); Belgian (Avions Fairey) licence-built (48).
Fox IIIS: Dual-control trainer version; Belgian (Avions Fairey) licence-built (4).
Fox IV Floatplane: Peruvian order (6).
Fox V: Prototype; modified Fox II; one 650hp Hispano 12Ybrs; (1 conversion).
Fox VI: Production model; 2-seat reconnaissance-fighter version; (inc 4 as dual-control trainers and 2 Swiss order); Belgian (Avions Fairey) licence-built (approx 85).
Fox VII: Single-seat fighter version of Fox VI; max six machine-guns; Belgian (Avions Fairey) licence-built (2).
Fox VIII: Improved Fox VI; Belgian (Avions Fairey) licence-built (12).
Total Production: approx 245.
Remarks: Second-generation Fox II entered Belgian AF service early 1932; after lengthy and complex production history, some 90 licence-built Foxes equipped 9 escadrilles (sqns) Belgian AF at time of German invasion, 10 May 1940; despite obsolescence are reported to have mounted nearly one hundred individual sorties during 18-day campaign; 2 examples Fox VI operated by Swiss AF, 1935–45, latterly in target-tug role.

Manufacturer: Fairey (Avions Fairey).
Model: Firefly IIM.
Type: Fighter.
Power Plant: One 480hp Rolls-Royce F.XIS (Kestrel IIS).
Performance:
maximum speed at sea level 175mph (282km/hr).
time to 19,685ft (6,000m) 10min 55sec.
service ceiling 30,840ft (9,400m).
Weights:
empty 2,387lb (1,083kg).
loaded 3,285lb (1,490kg).
Dimensions:
wing span 31ft 6in (9.6m).
length 24ft 8in (7.52m).
height 9ft 4in (2.85m).
wing area 236sq ft (22.0sq m).
Armament: Two fixed forward-firing machine-guns.
Crew: 1.
In Service: Belgium.
Variants (with no. built):
Firefly I: Original prototype; single-seat fighter biplane; one 450hp Curtiss D–12 (Felix) (1).
Firefly II: Prototype; single-seat fighter biplane; one Rolls-Royce F.XIS (Kestrel IIS) (1).
Firefly IIM: Modified (metal construction) Firefly II (1 conversion).
Firefly IIM: Initial production model; as modified prototype; Fairey-built (25); Belgian (Avions Fairey) licence-built (63).
Firefly III: Prototype; naval fighter version; increased wing span; one Rolls-Royce F.XIMS (1).
Firefly IIIM: Modified Firefly III; one Rolls-Royce F.XIS; alt land/floatplane (1 conversion).
Firefly IV: Re-engined Firefly IIM; one 758hp Hispano-Suiza 12Xbrs (2 conversions).
Total Production: 91.
Remarks: Original prototype first flown late 1925; re-designed Firefly II, 1929; production model of latter selected by Belgian AF, entering service late 1931; withdrawn first-line use prior outbreak WWII, approx 50 still on strength during German invasion, 10 May 1940; limited participation ensuing 18-day campaign, after which majority survivors evacuated to France.

Manufacturer: Fairey.
Model: Seal.
Type: Carrier-borne reconnaissance.
Power Plant: One 525hp Armstrong Siddeley Panther IIA.
Performance:
maximum speed 138mph (222km/hr).
time to 5,000ft (1,524m) 5min 20sec.
service ceiling 17,000ft (5,182m).
Weights:
loaded 6,000lb (2,722kg).
Dimensions:
wing span 45ft 9in (13.94m).
length 33ft 8in (10.26m).
height 12ft 9in (3.88m).
wing area 443.5sq ft (41.20sq m).
Armament: One fixed forward-firing Vickers gun; one Lewis gun; provision for max bomb load 500lb (227kg) underwing.
Crew: 3.
In Service: Great Britain, Latvia (4).
Variants (with no. built):
Prototype: Fairey IIIF conversion.
Production Model: Land or seaplane versions (90); Dual-control trainer prototype (1).
Total Production: 91.
Remarks: FAA equivalent of RAF's Fairey Gordon (both derivatives of earlier Fairey IIIF, and originally designated IIIF Mk VI and Mk V respectively); although phased out of front-line FAA service by 1938, the Seal was only one of series to equip during WWII, equipping one RAF sqn for maritime-patrol duties over Indian Ocean 1939–42.

Manufacturer: Fairey.
Model: Swordfish Mk I.
Type: Carrier-based reconnaissance/torpedo-bomber.
Power Plant: One 690hp Bristol Pegasus IIIM3.
Performance:
maximum speed 154mph (248km/hr).
maximum speed at 4,750ft (1,448m) 139mph (224km/hr).
cruising speed 129mph (208km/hr).
maximum range 1,030 miles (1,657km).
time to 5,000ft (1,524m) 10min 0sec.
service ceiling 10,700ft (3,261m).
Weights:
empty 4,195lb (1,903kg).
loaded 7,720lb (3,502kg).
Dimensions:
wing span 45ft 6in (13.87m).
length 35ft 8in (10.87m).
height 12ft 4in (3.76m).
wing area 607sq ft (56.39sq m).
Armament: One fixed .303in Vickers machine-gun firing through propeller hub; one .303in Lewis or Vickers 'K' gun; provision for one 18in torpedo, or one 1,500lb (680kg) mine, or 1,500lb (680kg) bomb load underwing or under fuselage.
Crew: 2–3.
In Service: Canada, Great Britain (RAF, FAA).
Variants (with no. built):
Prototype: T.S.R.II (1).
Swordfish: Pre-production model; Pegasus IIIM3 (3).
Mk I: Initial production model; land or seaplane versions; Fairey-built (689); Blackburn-built (300).
Mk II: Modified Mk I; strengthened lower mainplane for eight 60lb (27kg) rockets; Pegasus IIIM3 or XXX; land or seaplane versions; Blackburn-built (1,080).
Mk III: Modified Mk II; A.S.V. Mk X radar; Blackburn-built (320).
Mk IV: Mk II conversions; enclosed cockpit for use in Canada.
Total Production: 2,393.
Remarks: Universally known as the 'Stringbag', Swordfish was FAA's equivalent of the Spitfire, not in appearance—and certainly not in performance—but in longevity of service and in the affection in which it was held by its pilots; entering service in 1936, Swordfish equipped 13 sqns by outbreak of WWII; participated in many famous actions—Second Battle of Narvik, Oran, Malta, Taranto, Cape Matapan and, above all, attack on German capital ships *Scharnhorst*, *Gneisenau* and *Prinz Eugen* during the historic 'Channel Dash'; subsequently employed primarily on anti-submarine duties with depth-charges and, later, rocket projectiles in Battle of Atlantic and North Russian convoys; continued in service until VE-Day, equipping grand total of 26 FAA sqns, 2 RAF sqns, and numerous training units.
Colour Reference: Plate 57: Fairey Swordfish Mk III (NF374) NH.M of No 119 Squadron, No 16 Group, RAF Coastal Command, Belgium, April 1945; based Belgian coastal airstrips, all-black Swordfish and Albacores of No 119 Squadron employed closing weeks WWII against German midget submarines off Dutch coast; note ventral ASV housing, underwing weapons racks.

De Havilland Mosquito F.B.Mk VI

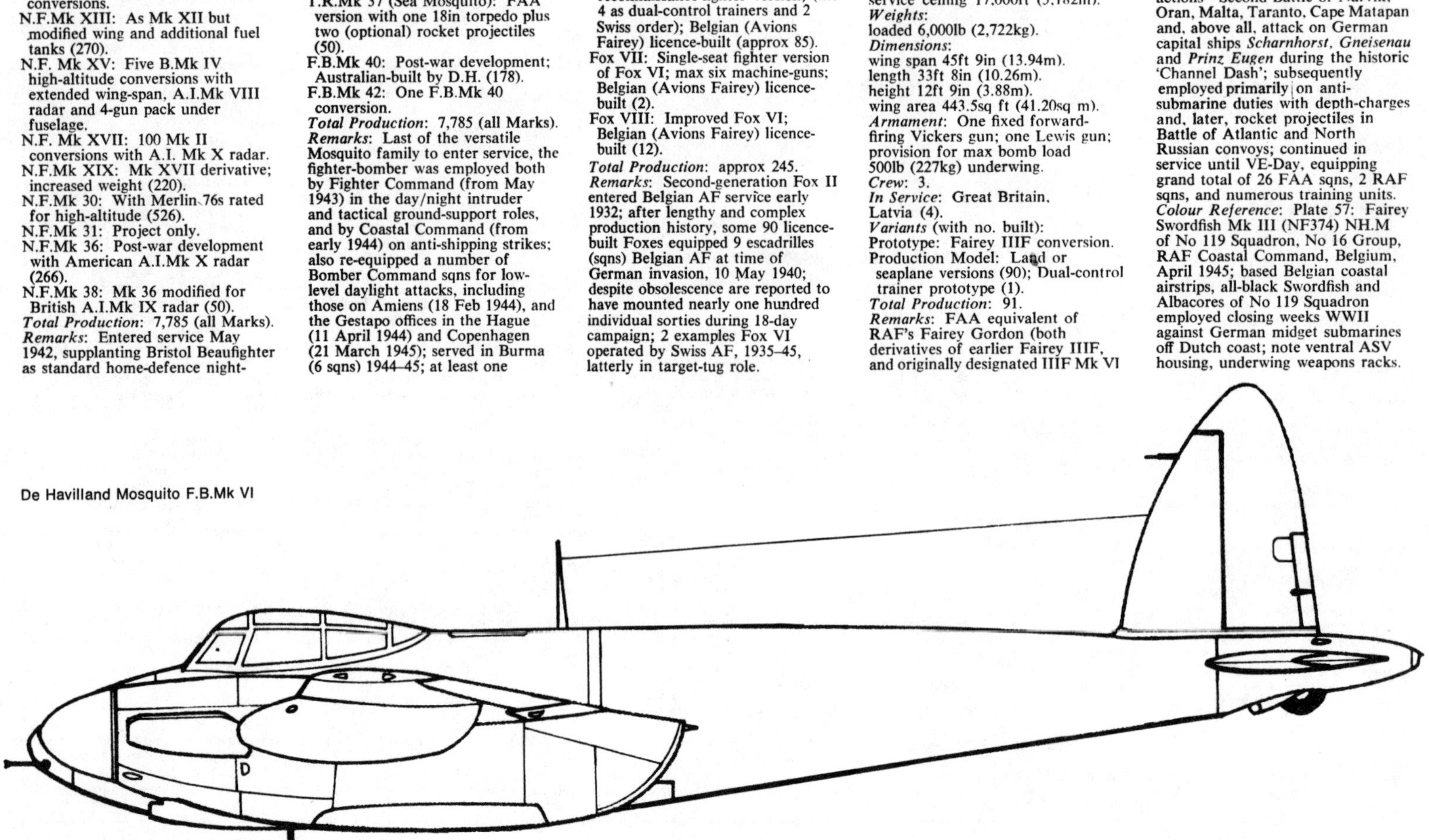

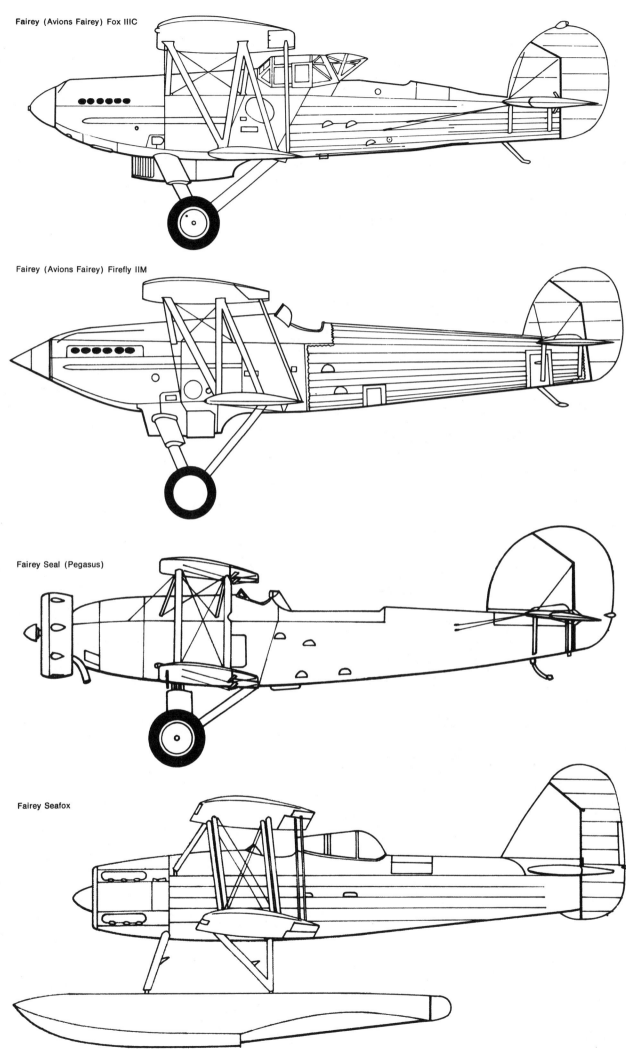

Manufacturer: Fairey.
Model: Battle Mk III.
Type: Light bomber.
Power Plant: One 1,440hp Rolls-Royce Merlin III.
Performance:
maximum speed at sea level
  210mph (338km/hr).
maximum speed at 15,000ft (4,572m)
  257mph (414km/hr).
maximum range 1,000 miles
  (1,609km).
time to 5,000ft (1,524m) 4min 6sec.
service ceiling 25,000ft (7,620m).
Weights:
empty 6,647lb (3,015kg).
loaded 10,792lb (4,895kg).
Dimensions:
wing span 54ft 0in (16.46m).
length 42ft 2in (12.9m).
height 15ft 6in (4.72m).
wing area 422sq ft (39.20sq m).
Armament: One fixed .303in
Browning gun in starboard wing;
one Vickers 'K' gun in rear
cockpit; max bomb load 1,000lb
(454kg).
Crew: 3.
In Service: Australia (366), Belgium
(18), Canada, Eire (1), Great
Britain (RAF, FAA), Greece (9),
South Africa (190+), Turkey (29).
Variants (with no. built):
Prototype (1).
Battle Mk I/V: Retrospective
 designations of basic model to
 indicate type of powerplant
 (Merlin I/V) installed (many
 subsequently converted to T.T.1s):
 Fairey-built (955); Austin-built
 (863); Belgian licence-built by
 Avions Fairey (18).
Battle (T): Dual-control trainer
 version (100).
T.T.1: Target-tug version; Fairey-
 built (100); Austin-built (166).
Total Production: 2,203.
Remarks: Entered service March
1937; equipped 16 sqns by outbreak
of WWII, of which 10 to France
as major component of AASF;
suffered heavy casualties during
Battle of France (May–June 1940)
lost 35 out of 63 aircraft in one
raid alone; after return to UK
operated by night against German-
occupied Channel and North Sea
ports; later patrolled Northern
Ireland coastline (2 sqns), and
served Coastal Command based
Iceland (1 sqn); subsequently
employed for wide variety of
training roles with RAF, RAAF,
RCAF and SAAF.
Colour Reference: Plate 54: Fairey
Battle (K9254) PM.L of No 103
Squadron, AASF, St. Lucien Ferme,
France, May 1940; note overpainted
canopy centre section and unusual
aft fuselage positioning of hastily
hand-painted roundels.

Manufacturer: Fairey.
Model: Seafox.
Type: Spotter-reconnaissance
seaplane.
Power Plant: One 395hp Napier
Rapier VI.
Performance:
maximum speed at sea level
  120mph (193km/hr).
maximum speed at 5,860ft (1,786m)
  124mph (200km/hr).
cruising speed 106mph (171km/hr).
range 440 miles (708km).
time to 5,000ft (1,524m)
  10min 24sec.
service ceiling 11,000ft (3,353m).
Weights:
empty 3,805lb (1,726kg).
loaded 5,420lb (2,459kg).
Dimensions:
wing span 40ft 0in (12.19m).
length 35ft 5½in (10.81m).
height 12ft 1in (3.68m).
wing area 434sq ft (40.32sq m).
Armament: One .303in Lewis gun
in rear cockpit; provision for light
bombs underwing.
Crew: 2.
In Service: Great Britain (FAA).
Variants (with no. built):
Prototypes: Open pilot's cockpit;
 enclosed rear observer's canopy;
 one with wheeled undercarriage (2).
Production model: Ship-borne
 seaplane (63); wheeled undercarriage version (1).
Total Production: 66.
Remarks: Served from outbreak
of WWII until mid-1943; equipped
1 operational sqn, 2 training sqns,
and 5 Catapult-Flights; employed
as spotter throughout Battle of
River Plate (13 Dec 1939), and on
reconnaissance-watch until 'Graf
Spee' scuttled herself off
Montevideo harbour four days
later.

Manufacturer: Fairey.
Model: Albacore.
Type: Carrier-borne/shore-based
torpedo-bomber.
Power Plant: One 1,065hp Bristol

Fairey (Avions Fairey) Fox IIIC

Fairey (Avions Fairey) Firefly IIM

Fairey Seal (Pegasus)

Fairey Seafox

Fairey Albacore

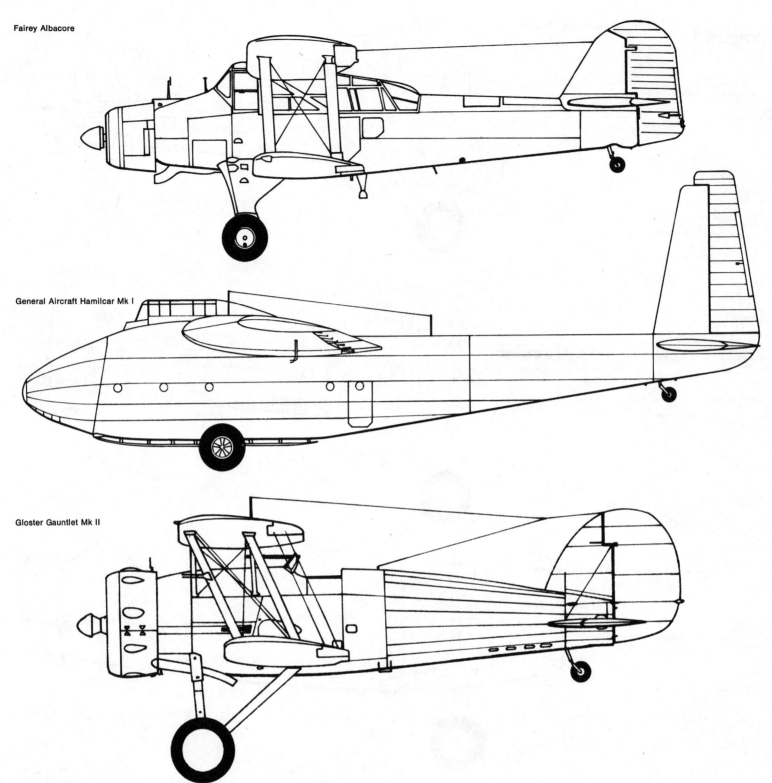

General Aircraft Hamilcar Mk I

Gloster Gauntlet Mk II

Taurus II or one 1,130hp Taurus
XII.
Performance:
maximum speed at 4,000ft (1,219m)
161mph (259km/hr).
cruising speed 126mph (203km/hr).
normal range 820 miles (1,319km).
time to 6,000ft (1,829m) 8min 0sec.
service ceiling 20,700ft (6,309m).
Weights:
empty 7,200lb (3,266kg).
maximum 12,600lb (5,715kg).
Dimensions:
wing span 50ft 0in (15.24m).
length 39ft 9½in (12.13m).
height 15ft 3in (4.65m).
wing area 623sq ft (57.88sq m).
Armament: One fixed forward-
firing .303in Vickers machine-gun;
twin .303in Vickers 'K' guns in
rear cockpit; provision for one 18in
torpedo under fuselage or six
250lb (113kg) or four 500lb (227kg)
bombs underwing.
Crew: 3.
In Service: Canada, Great Britain
(RAF, FAA).
Variants (with no. built):
Prototypes: One landplane, one
floatplane (2).
Production model: Landplane
version (798).

Total Production: 800.
Remarks: Entered service March
1940; initially UK shore-based for
cross-Channel and North Sea
operations; carrier-borne by 1941,
participated Battle of Cape
Matapan; subsequently employed
N Russian convoys, Mediterranean,
Atlantic and Indian Oceans; also
as night-bomber in Western Desert;
took part invasions of North Africa,
Sicily, Italy and Normandy (latter
with RCAF).

Manufacturer: Fairey.
Model: Fulmar I.
Type: Carrier-borne fighter-
reconnaissance.
Power Plant: One 1,080hp Rolls-
Royce Merlin VIII.
Performance:
maximum speed 280mph
(450km/hr).
cruising speed 235mph (378km/hr).
range 800 miles (1,287km).
initial rate of climb 1,200ft/min
(366m/min).
service ceiling 26,000ft (7,925m).
Weights:
empty 6,915lb (3,187kg).
loaded 9,800lb (4,445kg).
Dimensions:

wing span 46ft 4½in (14.13m).
length 40ft 3in (12.27m).
height 14ft 0in (4.27m).
wing area 342sq ft (31.77sq m).
Armament: Eight fixed wing-
mounted Browning machine-guns;
one optional .303in Vickers 'K'
gun in rear cockpit.
Crew: 2.
In Service: France (Vichy, 1
captured), Great Britain (RAF,
FAA).
Variants (with no. built):
Prototype (1).
Mk I: Initial production model
(250).
Mk II prototype: One Mk I
conversion.
Mk II: One 1,300hp Merlin XXX;
tropicalised; some as night-fighter
version (350).
Total Production: 601.
Remarks: Entered service mid-1940;
early actions included defence of
Malta convoys, Taranto, and
Crete; also operated above Arctic
Circle (FAA attack on Petsamo,
July 1944), and as fighter defence of
Suez and Ceylon; participated
invasions North Africa and Sicily;
last employed as night-fighter during
Russian convoys 1944–45; equipped

total of 19 FAA sqns, plus one
RAF.
Colour Reference: Plate 62:
Fairey Fulmar Mk I (N1877) 'H'
flown by Sub-Lt, S. G. Orr of
No 806 Squadron, Fleet Air Arm,
HMS *Illustrious*, Mediterranean,
Oct 1940; note 'Black Panther'
squadron emblem; (Lt-Cdr Orr
ended war with 12 'kills' as FAA's
third-ranking Ace.)

Manufacturer: Fairey.
Model: Barracuda Mk II.
Type: Carrier-borne torpedo-
bomber/dive-bomber.
Power Plant: One 1,640hp Rolls-
Royce Merlin 32.
Performance:
maximum speed at 1,750ft (533m)
228mph (367km/hr).
cruising speed 172mph (277km/hr).
maximum range 1,150 miles
(1,850km).
time to 5,000ft (1,524m) 6min 0sec.
service ceiling 16,600ft (5,060m).
Weights:
empty 9,350lb (4,241kg).
maximum 14,100lb (6,396kg).
Dimensions:
wing span 49ft 2in (14.99m).
length 39ft 9in (12.11m).

height 15ft 1in (4.60m).
wing area 367sq ft (34.09sq m).
Armament: Two .303 Vickers 'K'
guns in rear cockpit; one 1,620lb
(735kg) torpedo, or four 450lb
(204kg) depth-charges, or six 250lb
(113kg) bombs.
Crew: 3.
In Service: Great Britain (FAA).
Variants (with no. built):
Prototypes (2).
Mk I: One 1,260hp Merlin 30;
three-blade propeller (23).
Mk II prototype: One Mk I
conversion.
Mk II: Main production model;
uprated engine; four-blade
propeller; A.S.V. Mk IIN radar;
Fairey-built (225); Blackburn-built
(700); Boulton-Paul-built (692);
Westland-built (18).
Mk III prototype: One Mk II
conversion.
Mk III: Modified Mk II torpedo-
reconnaissance version; A.S.V.
Mk X radar (912).
Mk V: Post-war variant (30).
Total Production: 2,602.
Remarks: FAA's first monoplane
torpedo-bomber; first saw action
during Salerno landings, Sept 1943;
engaged against *Tirpitz*, April–

Aug 1944, inflicted heavy damage; subsequently served in Pacific theatre; equipped 17 operational sqns in WWII, plus 7 training sqns.
Colour Reference: Plates 58, 59: Fairey Barracuda Mk II (BV952) '4S', of No 826 Squadron, Fleet Air Arm, HMS *Indefatigable*, July 1944; '4S' returned safely from Operation 'Mascot', strike on Tirpitz, 17 July 1944, but was damaged beyond repair in hangar fire on *Indefatigable* following day.

Manufacturer: Fairey.
Model: Firefly F.Mk I.
Type: Carrier-borne fighter-reconnaissance.
Power Plant: One 1,730hp Rolls-Royce Griffon IIB or 1,990hp Griffon XII.
Performance:
maximum speed at 14,000ft (4,267m) 316mph (508km/hr).
maximum range 1,300 miles (2,092km).
time to 5,000ft (1,524m) 2min 30sec.
service ceiling 28,000ft (8,534m).
Weights:
empty 9,750lb (4,423kg).
loaded 14,020lb (6,360kg).
Dimensions:
wing span 44ft 6in (13.56m).
length 37ft 7¼in (11.46m).
height 13ft 7in (4.14m).
wing area 328sq ft (30.47sq m).
Armament: Four fixed 20mm cannon in wings; provision for eight 60lb (27kg) rockets, or two 1,000lb (454kg) bombs underwing.
Crew: 2.
In Service: Great Britain (FAA).
Variants (with no. built):
Prototypes (4).
F.Mk I: Initial production model; Fairey-built (F.Mk I and F.R. Mk I) (805); General-Aircraft-built (132).
F.R.Mk I: Modified F.Mk I; ASH radar.
F.Mk IA: F.Mk I conversions to F.R.Mk I standard; ASH radar.
N.F.Mk I: Night-fighter version; F.R.Mk I conversions; exhaust shrouds.
N.F.Mk II; Night-fighter version; lengthened nose; A.I.Mk 10 radar (37).
F.R.4/A.S.6. Post-war variants (645).
Total Production: 1,623.
Remarks: First action during attacks on Tirpitz, July 1944; subsequently served with East Indies and later, British Pacific Fleets against Japanese; first FAA aircraft over Japan, July 1945; immediate post-war weeks engaged in supply-drops to POW camps on Japanese mainland; equipped four WWII sqns in Pacific (inc one of night-fighters).
Colour Reference: Plates 60, 61: Fairey Firefly F.Mk I (MB 522) 279.'Y', of No 837 Squadron, Fleet Air Arm, HMS *Glory*, British Pacific Fleet, Aug 1945; note distinctive US-style barred BPF roundels carried port upper/starboard lower wing stations only, (compare location/size with British East Indies Fleet markings, see Grumman Avenger, plate 141).

Manufacturer: Foster Wikner (Wicko).
Model: G.M.1 Warferry.
Type: Liaison/communications.
Power Plant: One 130hp de Havilland Gipsy Major.
Performance:
maximum speed 140mph (224km/hr).
cruising speed 120mph (192km/hr).
normal range 500 miles (800km).
initial rate of climb 800ft/min (244m/min).
service ceiling 20,000ft (6,100m).
Weights:
empty 1,255lb (569kg).
loaded 2,000lb (908kg).
Dimensions:
wing span 31ft 6in (9.60m).
length 23ft 3in (7.09m).
height 6ft 1in (1.86m).
wing area 153sq ft (14.2sq m).
Crew/Accommodation: 1/2.
In Service: Great Britain, New Zealand (1).
Variants (with no. built):
Wicko F.W.1: Prototype (rebuilt as F.W.2) (1).
F.W.3: 150hp Blackburn Cirrus Major (1).
G.M.1: Production model (9).
Total Production: 11.
Remarks: Pre-war high-wing monoplane; majority impressed into RAF service as Warferry; one into RNZAF; employed on communications and liaison duties.

Manufacturer: General Aircraft.
Model: Monospar S.T.12.
Type: Communications.
Power Plant: Two 140hp de Havilland Gipsy Major I.
Performance:
maximum speed 160mph (257km/hr).
cruising speed 144mph (232km/hr).
normal range 410 miles (659km).
initial rate of climb 1,233ft/min (376m/min).
service ceiling 21,000ft (6,400m).
Weights:
empty 1,840lb (835kg).
maximum 2,875lb (1,304kg).
Dimensions:
wing span 40ft 2in (12.24m).
length 26ft 4in (8.02m).
height 7ft 10in (2.16m).
wing area 217sq ft (20.16sq m).
Crew/Accommodation: 1/3.
In Service: Great Britain.
Variants (with no. built):
Prototype: Re-engined S.T.10; built 1935 (1).
Production model: (9).
Total Production: 10.
Remarks: Two of four British-registered S.T.12s impressed for communications and liaison duties early WWII; earlier General Aircraft products likewise impressed inc S.Ts 4, 6 and 10.

Manufacturer: General Aircraft.
Model: Monospar S.T.25 Universal.
Type: General-purpose transport.
Power Plant: Two 95hp Pobjoy Niagara III.
Performance:
maximum speed 131mph (211km/hr).
cruising speed 115mph (185km/hr).
range 419 miles (674km).
initial rate of climb 710ft/min (216m/min).
service ceiling 14,000ft (4,267m).
Weights:
empty 1,818lb (825kg).
maximum 2,875lb (1,304kg).
Dimensions:
wing span 40ft 2in (12.24m).
length 26ft 4in (8.02m).
height 7ft 10in (2.16m).
wing area 217sq ft (20.16sq m).
Crew/Accommodation: 1/3–4.
In Service: Great Britain.
Variants (with no. built):
S.T.25 Jubilee: 5-seat cabin monoplane; Niagara IIs; prototype (1); production model (9).
S.T.25 Jubilee Freighter: Starboard loading hatch (4).
S.T.25 Jubilee Ambulance: provision for one stretcher, hatch as above (6).
S.T.25 Universal: Twin fins and rudders; 4/5 seat; prototype (1); production model (39).
Total Production: 60.
Remarks: Universal first flown 1936; many foreign sales; some to RAF pre-war; others (12+) impressed for communications duties early WWII.

Manufacturer: General Aircraft.
Model: Cygnet II.
Type: Communications.
Power Plant: 130hp de Havilland Gipsy Major.
Performance:
maximum speed at sea level 135mph (218km/hr).
cruising speed 115mph (187km/hr).
maximum range 600 miles (965km).
initial rate of climb 800ft/min (244m/min).
service ceiling 15,000ft (4,580m).
Weights:
empty 1,400lb (635kg).
maximum 2,100lb (952kg).
Dimensions:
wing span 34ft 6in (10.52m).
length 23ft 3in (7.09m).
height 6ft 0in (1.83m).
wing area 179sq ft (16.63sq m).
Crew: 2.
In Service: Great Britain.
Variants (with no. built):
C.W. Cygnet: Original single-fin model; built by Chronander Waddington 1937 (1).
Cygnet II: General Aircraft-built production model (10).
Total Production: 10 (plus C.W.-built prototype).
Remarks: Five British impressments; served as trainers and on communications duties.

Manufacturer: General Aircraft.
Model: Hamilcar Mk I.
Type: Tank-carrying glider.
Performance:
Towing speed 150mph (240km/hr).
Weights:
empty 19,500lb (8,845kg).
loaded 36,000lb (16,783kg).
Dimensions:
wing span 110ft 0in (33.53m).
length 68ft 0in (20.72m).
height 20ft 3in (6.17m).
wing area 1,658sq ft (153.98sq m).
Crew/Payload: 2/max load 17,500lb (7,940kg).
In Service: Great Britain.
Variants (with no. built):
Prototypes (2).
Mk I: Production model (inc 390 sub-contracted) (410).
Mk X: Powered version; two 965hp Bristol Mercury 31s; twenty-two Mk I conversions.
Total Production: 412.
Remarks: Hinged-nose tank-carrying glider capable of transporting a British Tetrarch or US Locust light tank, two Bren-gun carriers or two scout-cars, or SP Bofors gun; first operation 6 June 1944—Normandy beach-head; also participated Battle of Arnhem; usual tug—Halifax A.Mk III.

Manufacturer: Gloster.
Model: A.S. 31.
Type: General-purpose biplane.
Power Plant: Two 525hp Bristol Jupiter XI.
Performance:
maximum speed 131mph (211km/hr).
cruising speed 110mph (177km/hr).
range 495 miles (796km).
time to 10,000ft (3,048m) 7min 25sec.
service ceiling 23,200ft (7,071m).
Weights:
empty 5,615lb (2,547kg).
maximum 8,570lb (3,888kg).
Dimensions:
wing span 61ft 0in (18.59m).
length 48ft 6in (14.78m).
height 18ft 9in (5.71m).
wing area 1,025sq ft (95.22sq m).
Crew: 2.
In Service: South Africa (1).
Variants (with no. built):
D.H. 67: Two 450hp Bristol Jupiter VI; project only.
D.H. 67: Two 480hp Bristol Jupiter XI; project only.
A.S. 31: Prototypes; Gloster-built (2).
Total Production: 2.
Remarks: Original de Havilland design study; extensively modified version built by Gloster; one sold to SAAF May 1935; in service (general duties) until 1942.

Manufacturer: Gloster.
Model: Gauntlet Mk II.
Type: Fighter.
Power Plant: One 640hp Bristol Mercury VIS2.
Performance:
maximum speed at 15,800ft (4,816m) 230mph (370km/hr).
range 455 miles (732km).
initial rate of climb 2,300ft/min (701m/min).
time to 20,000ft (6,096m) 9min 0sec.
service ceiling 33,500ft (10,210m).
Weights:
empty 2,775lb (1,259kg).
loaded 3,970lb (1,800kg).
Dimensions:
wing span 32ft 9½in (9.99m).
length 26ft 5in (8.05m).
height 10ft 3in (3.12m).
wing area 315sq ft (29.26sq m).
Armament: Two Vickers Mk.V machine-guns; optional underwing bomb racks.
Crew: 1.
In Service: Australia, Denmark (1 pattern, 17 licence-built), Finland (25), Great Britain, South Africa, Southern Rhodesia.
Variants (with no. built):
Prototype (1).
Mk I: Initial production model (24).
Mk II: Modified Mk I; different (Hawker) rear fuselage and wing-spar structure (204).
Danish licence-production (Army Air Service) (17).
Total Production: 246.
Remarks: Entered RAF service 1935; still equipped two UK sqns early weeks of WWII; supplied to Finland Feb 1940; employed by 3 RAF and 1 RAAF sqn in Middle East, 1940; also by SAAF against Italians in East Africa, 1940–42.

Manufacturer: Gloster.
Model: Gladiator Mk I.
Type: Fighter.
Power Plant: One 840hp Bristol Mercury IX.
Performance:
maximum speed at sea level 210mph (338km/hr).
maximum speed at 14,500ft (4,420m) 253mph (407km/hr).
normal range 428 miles (689km).
time to 10,000ft (3,048m) 4min 40sec.
service ceiling 32,800ft (9,997m).
Weights:
empty 3,217lb (1,459kg).
loaded 4,592lb (2,083kg).
Dimensions:
wing span 32ft 3in (9.83m).
length 27ft 5in (8.36m).
height 11ft 9in (3.63m).
wing area 323sq ft (30.01sq m).
Armament: Two fixed .303in Browning machine-guns in fuselage sides; two .303in Browning, Vickers or Lewis guns under lower wing.
Crew: 1.
In Service: Australia (ex-RAF), China (36 Mk I), Belgium (22+ Mk I), Egypt (45 Mk II), Eire (4 Mk I), Finland (30 Mk II), Great Britain (RAF, FAA), Greece (19 Mk I, 6 Mk II), Iraq (9 Mk I), Latvia (26 Mk I), Lithuania (14 Mk I), Norway (6 Mk I, 6 Mk II), Portugal (15 Mk II), Sweden (37 Mk I, 18 Mk II), USSR (ex-Latvian and Lithuanian Mk Is).
Variants (with no. built):
Prototype (1).
Mk I: Initial production model (378).
Mk II: Modified Mk I; Mercury VIIIA or VIII AS; tropicalised (inc 38 converted to interim Sea Gladiator) (311).
Sea Gladiator: Carrier-borne fighter version; arrester hook, catapult points, fairing for dinghy (60).
Swedish Gladiator (J 8A): Modified Mk II; Nohab Mercury VIIIS.3 (18).
Total Production: 768.
Remarks: Entered service 1937; both RAF's and FAA's (Sea Gladiator) last biplane fighter; participated many historic wartime actions—Battle of France, Battle of Britain, Norway (operating from frozen surface of Lake Lesjaskog), Western Desert, Defence of Malta; also saw extensive foreign use—Sino-Japanese conflict 1938–39, Russo-Finnish War of 1939–40 (both Finnish and Swedish AFs), German invasions of Norway (April 1940), Belgium (May 1940), and Greece (April 1941); after withdrawal from first-line service employed by numerous RAF Meteorological Flights both at home and abroad, 1942–44.
Colour Reference: Plate 63: Gloster Gladiator Mk II (J 8A) of Flygflottilj F 19, Swedish volunteer squadron, Lake Kemi, Northern Finland, Jan 1940; attached Finnish AF for Winter War operations, all twelve Swedish Gladiators of F 19 (individual aircraft letters 'A'–'L') had Swedish AF triple-crown insignia overpainted with solid black disc; unofficial F 19 squadron emblem was skull-and-crossbones (applied either to fuselage disc or on vertical tail surfaces), wing motif on Gladiator 'F' personal marking.

Manufacturer: Gloster.
Model: Meteor Mk I.
Type: Interceptor fighter.
Power Plant: Two 1,700lb s.t. Rolls-Royce Welland I.
Performance:
maximum speed at sea level 385mph (619km/hr).
maximum speed at 30,000ft (9,144m) 410mph (660km/hr).
initial rate of climb 2,155ft/min (657m/min).
time to 30,000ft (9,144m) 15min 0sec.
service ceiling 40,000ft (12,192m).
Weights:
empty 8,140lb (3,692kg).
loaded 13,800lb (6,260kg).
Dimensions:
wing span 43ft 0in (13.11m).
length 41ft 3in (12.57m).
height 13ft 0in (3.96m).
wing area 374sq ft (34.74sq m).
Armament: Four 20mm Hispano Mk III cannon.
Crew: 1.
In Service: Great Britain, USA (1).
Variants (with no. built):
Prototypes (8).
Mk I: Initial production model (8).
Mk II: Project only (20).
Mk III: Modified Mk I; 2,000lb s.t. Rolls-Royce Derwent I (First 15 with Welland I) (280).
Mks IV–U.21: Multi-role post-war variants (3,237).
Total Production: 3,545.
Remarks: Only Allied jet aircraft to see operational service in WWII; equipped 1 sqn from Aug 1944 to end of war; initially engaged UK flying anti-"Diver" patrols against incoming V1s, scoring 13 confirmed 'flying-bomb' kills by end Sept; New Year 1945 one flight detached to join 2nd TAF on Continent; based Belgium as defence against German Me 262 jets; no confrontation recorded; flight was forbidden to overfly enemy-occupied territory for security reasons; restriction lifted end of March when joined by rest of sqn; spent last three weeks of war attacking enemy road transport; extensive post-war development/production.
Colour Reference: Plates 64, 65: Gloster Meteor Mk III (EE239) YQ.Q of No 616 'South Yorkshire' Squadron, RAF, on detachment Melsbroek, Belgium, March 1945; temporary overall white finish (obscuring all codes) instant recognition aid in attempt to reduce risk from friendly anti-aircraft gunners (to whom every approaching jet was much publicised Messerschmitt Me 262, see plate 50).

Manufacturer: Handley Page.
Model: HP42E.
Type: Transport.
Power Plant: Four 550hp Bristol Jupiter XIF.
Performance:
maximum speed 120mph (193km/hr).
cruising speed 100mph (161km/hr).
initial rate of climb 790ft/min (241m/min).
Weights:
maximum 28,000lb (12,700kg).
Dimensions:
wing span 130ft 0in (39.62m).
length 89ft 9in (27.35m).
height 27ft 0in (8.23m).
wing area:
upper 1,999sq ft (185.7sq m).
lower 990sq ft (92sq m).
Payload/Accommodation: 3/7,000lb (3,175kg)/18.
In Service: Great Britain (RAF/FAA).
Variants (with no. built):
HP42E (Eastern-type): Civil airliner specifically intended for routes east of Suez (4).
HP42W (Western-type): Civil airliner for London/European services; 550hp Jupiter X (FBM)s; 38 passengers (4).
Total Production: 8.
Remarks: Pre-war Imperial Airways airliners, 'Hannibal' (E) and 'Heracles' (W) classes; all four of former, and two of latter, impressed for wartime transport duties.

Manufacturer: Handley Page.
Model: Harrow Mk II.
Type: Interim bomber/transport.
Power Plant: Two 925hp Bristol Pegasus XX.
Performance:
maximum speed at 10,000ft (3,048m) 200mph (322km/hr).
cruising speed 163mph (262km/hr).
maximum range 1,840 miles (2,960km).
initial rate of climb 710ft/min (216m/min).
service ceiling 22,800ft (6,950m).
Weights:
empty 13,600lb (6,169kg).
loaded 23,000lb (10,433kg).
Dimensions:
wing span 88ft 5in (26.95m).
length 82ft 2in (25.04m).
height 19ft 5in (5.92m).
wing area 1,090sq ft (101.26sq m).
Armament: One .303in machine-gun each in nose turret and dorsal position; two .303in machine-guns in tail turret.
Crew/Accommodation: 5/20.
In Service: Canada (1), Great Britain.
Variants (with no. built):
Mk I: Initial production version; single hand-held Lewis guns in nose, tail and dorsal positions; 830hp Pegasus Xs (38).
Mk II: Re-engined Mk I; increased defensive armament (62).
Sparrow: Unarmed transport; at least 12 converted from above.
Total Production: 100.
Remarks: Equipped 5 pre-war bomber sqns; Winter 1940–41 employed by one sqn as aerial mine-layer, using Pandora aerial mine equipment against Luftwaffe night bombers; but served mainly as transport (Sparrow); in North Africa, UK, and NW Europe; and from Sept 1944 (Arnhem) until end of war as air ambulances.

Manufacturer: Handley Page.
Model: Hampden Mk I.
Type: Medium bomber.
Power Plant: Two 980hp Bristol Pegasus XVIII.
Performance:
maximum speed at 15,500ft (4,724m) 265mph (426km/hr).
cruising speed 167mph (269km/hr).
maximum range 1,990 miles (3,202km).
initial rate of climb 980ft/min (299m/min).
time to 15,000ft (4,572m) 18min 55sec.
service ceiling 22,700ft (6,919m).
Weights:
empty 11,780lb (5,343kg).
loaded 18,756lb (8,508kg).
maximum 21,000lb (9,526kg).
Dimensions:
wing span 69ft 2in (21.08m).
length 53ft 7in (16.33m).
height 14ft 9in (4.49m).
Armament: One fixed .303in Browning machine-gun and one flexible .303in Vickers 'K' gun in nose; twin .303in Vickers 'K' guns in

Handley Page Hampden Mk I

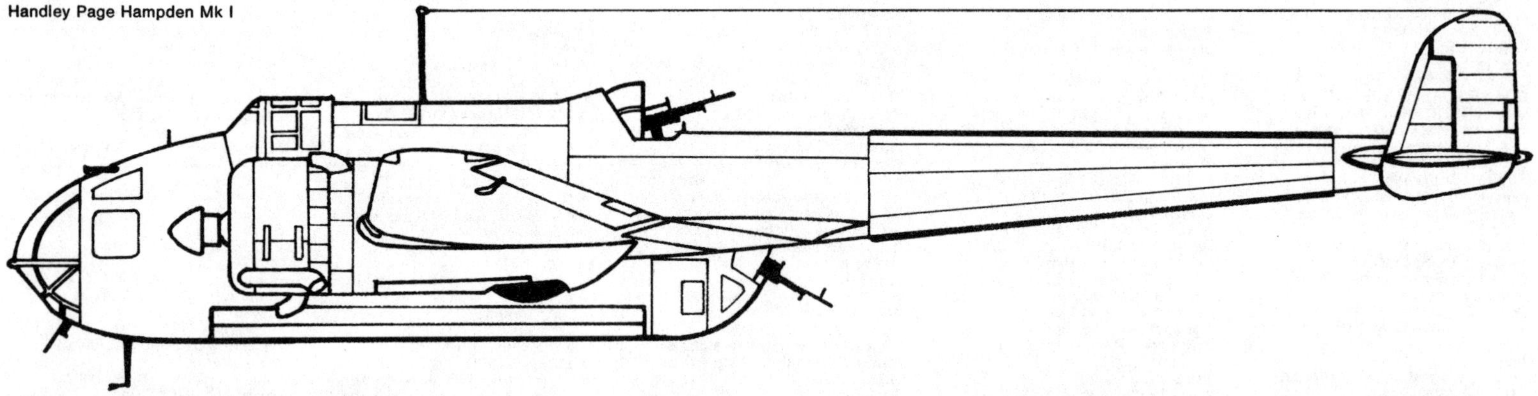

dorsal and ventral positions; max bomb load 4,000lb (1,814kg).
Crew: 4.
In Service: Australia, Canada, Great Britain, New Zealand, Sweden (one P5), USSR (10+ T.B.Mk I).
Variants (with no. built):
HP52: Hampden prototype (1).
HP53: Hereford prototype (1).
Mk I: Production model; Handley Page-built (500); English Electric-built (770); Canadian licence-built by CAA (160).
T.B.Mk I: Torpedo-bomber version; one 18in torpedo plus two 500lb (227kg) bombs; (141 Mk I conversions).
Mk II: Two Mk I conversions with 1,100hp Wright Cyclones.
Hereford: 1,000hp Napier Dagger VIIIs, 9 converted to Hampdens (100).
Total Production: 1,532 (inc Hereford).
Remarks: Although the latest and fastest of RAF's immediate pre-war trio of 'heavy' bombers, operational debut disappointing; grounded after early daylight raids, it rejoined night offensive with improved armament; served 1940–42; subsequently with Coastal Command as torpedo-bomber (4 sqns); 2 sqns based N Russia for attacks on traffic off Norwegian coast; aircraft handed over to USSR; also employed on meteorological reconnaissance; Dagger-engined Hereford not used operationally.

Manufacturer: Handley Page.
Model: Halifax B.Mk III.
Type: Heavy bomber.
Power Plant: Four 1,615hp Bristol Hercules XVI.
Performance:
speed at 13,500ft (4,115m) 282mph (454km/hr).
cruising speed 215mph (346km/hr).
normal range 1,985 miles (3,194km).
initial rate of climb 960ft/min (293m/min).
time to 20,000ft (6,096m) 37min 30sec.
service ceiling 24,000ft (7,315m).
Weights:
empty 38,240lb (17,346kg).
maximum 65,000lb (29,484kg).
Dimensions:
wing span 98ft 10in (30.12m).
length 71ft 7in (21.82m).
height 20ft 9in (6.32m).
wing area 1,250sq ft (116.13sq m).
Armament: One flexible .303in Vickers 'K' gun in nose; four .303in Browning machine-guns each in dorsal and tail turrets (some with one flexible .5in Browning gun in ventral 'blister') max bomb load 13,000lb (5,897kg).
Crew: 7.
In Service: Australia, Canada, Great Britain.
Variants (with no. built):
Prototypes: Four 1,280hp Rolls-Royce Merlin IXs (2).
B.Mk I: Series I; initial production version; four Merlin X.
Series II: stressed for extra weight; four Merlin X.
Series III: increased tankage; four Merlin X or XX (84).
B.Mk II: Series I; as B.Mk I series III, 1,390hp Merlin XXS or XXII; some with 4-gun dorsal turret (Mk II series I (Special); Series IA; 1,390hp Merlin 22; dorsal turret, one .303in Vickers 'K' gun in perspex nose; some converted to G.R.Mk II; Handley Page-built (615); London Aircraft-built (450); Rootes-built (12); English Electric-built (900); Series II: As Series I: Four Merlin 65 (1 conversion).
B.Mk III: Prototypes; Hercules XVIs; one Mk II conversion (*1*); Production model: Handley Page-built (326); London Aircraft-built (260); Rootes-built (279); Fairey-built (326); English Electric-built (900).
A.Mk III: Mk III conversions to glider-tug.
C.Mk III: Mk III conversions to transport (24 troops).
Mk IV: Project only.
Mk V: Modified Mk II; built in series I, IA, and series I (Special); corresponding to Mk II series; some converted to maritime and G.R. Rootes-built (658); Fairey-built (246).
Total Production: 6,178 (all Marks).
Remarks: The Halifax, although overshadowed by the Avro Lancaster (which equipped 68, compared with 34, Bomber Command sqns, and made 150,000+ sorties compared with 75,000) played a major part in the Allies' night bomber offensive over Germany from March 1941 until April 1945; participated in first Pathfinder operation, Flensburg, Aug 1942; first RAF machine to be equipped with H2S blind-bombing radar; also employed by Coastal Command (9 sqns), Transport Command (9 sqns) for paratroop and glider-tug duties, and by two Special Duties sqns for parachuting agents and arms to European resistance movements.
Colour Reference: Plate 67: Handley Page Halifax B.Mk II Series IA (JP275) 'N' of No 614 'County of Glamorgan' Squadron, RAF, Celone, Italy, March 1944; re-numbered from No. 462 Squadron, RAAF (first Middle East Halifax squadron), No 614 employed pathfinder duties southern Europe until re-equipment with Consolidated Liberator early 1945; note standard night finish undersides with Middle East dark earth/mid-stone upper surfaces.

Manufacturer: Handley Page.
Model: Halifax C.Mk VIII.
Type: Military transport.
Power Plant: Four 1,675hp Bristol Hercules 100.
Performance:
maximum speed at 15,000ft (4,572m) 280mph (451km/hr).
normal range 3,360 miles (5,406km).
Weights:
empty 37,250lb (16,897kg).
maximum 68,000lb (30,845kg).
Dimensions:
wing span 104ft 2in (31.75m).
length 71ft 7in (21.82m).
height 20ft 9in (6.32m).
wing area 1,275sq ft (118.45sq m).
Crew/Payload/Accommodation: 5/8,000lb (3,629kg)/11.
In Service: Australia, Canada, Great Britain.
Variants (with no. built):
B.Mk VI: Modified Mk III; increased tankage; filters; 1,675hp Hercules 100s; Handley Page-built (142); English Electric-built (325).
C.Mk VI: Mk VI conversions to transport (24 troops).
B.Mk VII: Final bomber version; as Mk VI but Hercules XVIs; Handley Page-built (15); Fairey-built (20).
A.Mk VII: Glider-tug version; Handley Page-built (167); Rootes-built (121); Fairey-built (90).
C.Mk VII: Mk VII conversions to transport (24 troops).
C.Mk VIII: Transport version; 11 passengers (96).
A.Mk IX: Post-war variant (145).
Total Production: 6,178 (all Marks).
Remarks: Last two bomber variants of Halifax, B.Mks VI and VII, intended for Far Eastern operations; equipped instead mainly Canadian and French sqns of Bomber Command; C.Mk VIII entered service with Transport Command just prior to end of war; operated by 5 sqns; detachable ventral pannier for 8,000lb (3,629kg) freight; many subsequently converted for civil use as Haltons.

Manufacturer: Hawker.
Model: Hart.
Type: Light day bomber.
Power Plant: One 525hp Rolls-Royce Kestrel IB or 510hp Kestrel XDR.
Performance:
maximum speed at 5,000ft (1,524m) 184mph (296km/hr).
range 470 miles (756km).
time to 10,000ft (3,048m) 8min 20sec.
service ceiling 21,350ft (6,507m).
Weights:
empty 2,530lb (1,148kg).
loaded 4,554lb (2,066kg).
Dimensions:
wing span 37ft 3in (11.35m).
length 29ft 4in (8.94m).
height 10ft 5in (3.17m).
wing area 348sq ft (32.33sq m).
Armament: One forward-firing .303in Vickers Mk II or III machine-gun; one .303in Lewis gun in rear cockpit; max bomb load 520lb (236kg).
Crew: 2.
In Service: Estonia (8), Germany (1+ captured), Great Britain, South Africa (Hart/Hart (Special); 320+), Sweden (46).
Variants (with no. built);
Prototype (1).
Bombers (inc Hart I (India), (Special), and SEDB): Hawker-built (151); Vickers-built (110); Armstrong Whitworth-built (149); Gloster-built (40).
Communications: Hawker-built (3); Vickers-built (2); Armstrong Whitworth-built (4).
Trainers (inc Series 2/2A and Interim); Hawker-built (58); Armstrong Whitworth-built (303); Vickers-built (114); Gloster-built (32).
2-seat fighter (6).
Experimental (4).
Estonian Hart (8).
Swedish Hart: Bristol Pegasus IM2 radial engine; Hawker-built (4).
Swedish Hart (B 4): 550hp Nohab Pegasus IU2 radial engine; Swedish licence-built by State Aircraft Factory (42).
Total Production: 1,031.
Remarks: RAF bombers withdrawn from UK front-line service 1938; some Specials (tropicalised bombers) served in Middle East early WWII; SAAF machines employed in communications duties North Africa and Italy, 1940–43; Swedish AF B 4s used by volunteer sqn fighting for Finland during Russo-Finnish War, Jan 1940.

Manufacturer: Hawker.
Model: Fury Mk II.
Type: Interceptor fighter.
Power Plant: One 640hp Rolls-Royce Kestrel VI.
Performance:
maximum speed at 16,500ft (5,029m) 223mph (359km/hr).
range 270 miles (434km).
time to 10,000ft (3,048m) 3min 50sec.
service ceiling 29,500ft (8,992m).
Weights:
empty 2,734lb (1,240kg).
loaded 3,609lb (1,637kg).
Dimensions:
wing span 30ft 0in (9.14m).
length 26ft 9in (8.15m).
height 10ft 2in (3.10m).
wing area 252sq ft (23.41sq m).
Armament: Two forward-firing .303in Vickers Mk V machine-guns; provision for underwing light bomb racks.
Crew: 1.
In Service: Great Britain, Persia (22), Portugal (3), South Africa (30+), Spain (3), Yugoslavia (16).
Variants (with no. built):
Mk I: Initial production model; 525hp Kestrel IIS (inc intermediate Fury trials machine) (118).
Mk II: Modified Mk I; Hawker-built (23); General Aircraft-built (75).
Yugoslav Fury: (6 Series IA) Kestrel IIS and (10 series II) Kestrel XVI (16).
Norwegian Fury: Modified Mk I; 530hp Armstrong Siddeley Panther IIIA (1).
Persian Fury: Modified Mk I; 750hp Pratt & Whitney Hornet S2B1G(16) and Bristol Mercury VISP(6) (22).
Portuguese Fury: Modified Mk I; Kestrel IIs (3).
Spanish Fury: Improved Mk I 700hp Hispano-Suiza 12Xbrs (3).
High Speed Fury: Private venture; engine trials (1).
Total Production: 262.
Remarks: RAF Fury I and II equipped 6 sqns between 1931 and Jan 1939; subsequently to SAAF; equipped 3 sqns in East Africa; Spanish Furies employed by both Republican and Nationalist AFs during course of Civil War (in which at least one Portuguese machine also destroyed); Yugoslav Furies saw action during German invasion, April 1941; Persian machines employed on border patrol duties 1942.

Manufacturer: Hawker.
Model: Nimrod II.
Type: Naval interceptor fighter.
Power Plant: One 608hp Rolls-Royce Kestrel VFP.
Performance:
maximum speed at 14,000ft (4,267m) 193mph (311km/hr).
cruising speed 115mph (185km/hr).
time to 10,000ft (3,048m) 5min 0sec.
service ceiling 28,000ft (8,778m).
Weights:
empty 3,115lb (1,413kg).
loaded 4,059lb (1,841kg).
Dimensions:
wing span 33ft 6¾in (10.23m).
length 26ft 6½in (8.09m).
height 9ft 10½in (3.01m).
wing area 301sq ft (27.96sq m).
Armament: Two forward-firing .303in Vickers Mk III machine-guns; provision for four 20lb (9kg) bombs.
Crew: 1.
In Service: Denmark (Navy, 12), Great Britain (FAA), Japan (1 Mk II), Portugal (1 Mk II).
Variants (with no. built):
Prototype: Private venture (initially as Norn) (1).
Mk I: 477hp Kestrel IIS; inter-changeable wheel or float under-carriage; several subsequently modified to Mk II standard (57).
Mk II: Modified Mk I; first 3 of stainless steel construction; majority later models with 608hp Kestrel V (inc 1 each to Japan and Portugal) (30).
Danish Nimrods: Modified Mk II; Pattern aircraft; Kestrel III (2).
Mk II Nimrodderne: Danish licence-built by Royal Danish Dockyard as Type L.B.V. (10).
Total Production: 100.
Remarks: Few FAA machines still in service (as trainers) early months WWII; Danish Naval Nimrodderne in use until German invasion/occupation, April 1940.

Manufacturer: Hawker.
Model: Osprey IV.
Type: Carrier-borne reconnaissance-fighter.
Power Plant: One 640hp Rolls-Royce Kestrel IV.
Performance:
maximum speed at 6,560ft (2,000m) 161mph (259km/hr).
cruising speed 109mph (175km/hr).
initial rate of climb 1,625ft/min (495m/min).
service ceiling 25,000ft (7,620m).
Weights:
empty 3,405lb (1,545kg).
loaded 4,950lb (2,245kg).
Dimensions:
wing span 37ft 0in (11.28m).
length 29ft 4in (8.94m).
height 10ft 5in (3.17m).
wing area 339sq ft (31.49sq m).
Armament: One fixed forward-firing .303in Vickers III gun; one .303in Lewis gun on rear cockpit mounting.
Crew: 2.
In Service: Spain, Great Britain (FAA).
Variants (with no. built):
Mks I–IV: Pre-war FAA models, inc 2 prototypes (131).
Swedish Osprey: Swedish-built Nohab Mercury engines (4).
Portuguese Osprey: Rolls-Royce Kestrel IIMS (2).
Spanish Osprey: Hispano-Suiza 12Xbrs (Originally Kestrel V-engined Company demonstrator) (1).
Total Production: 138.
Remarks: FAA Ospreys employed towards end of 1932–40 service career on target-tug and ancillary duties; single Spanish Osprey served RepAF early months of Civil War.

Manufacturer: Hawker.
Model: Audax I.
Type: Army co-operation.
Power Plant: One 530hp Rolls-Royce Kestrel IB or one 580hp Kestrel X.
Performance:
maximum speed at 2,400ft (732m) 170mph (274km/hr).
time to 10,000ft (3,048m) 8min 39sec.
service ceiling 21,500ft (6,553m).
Weights:
empty 2,938lb (1,333kg).
loaded 4,386lb (1,990kg).
Dimensions:
wing span 37ft 3in (11.35m).
length 29ft 7in (9.01m).
height 10ft 5in (3.17m).
wing area 348sq ft (32.33sq m).
Armament: One fixed forward-firing .303in Vickers Mk III or V machine-gun; one .303in Lewis gun on rear cockpit mounting; underwing racks for eight 20lb (9kg) bombs.
Crew: 2.
In Service: Australia, Egypt (24), Great Britain, Iran (56), Iraq (34), Malaya (MVAF, 2), South Africa (80+).
Variants (with no. built):
Prototype: One Hawker Hart conversion.
Audax I: Initial production model; Hawker-built; inc 2 with Kestrel V as Audax (Singapore) (173); Avro-built; inc 25 tropicalised (287); Bristol-built (141); Westland-built (43); Gloster-built tropicalised as Audax (India) (25).
Persian Audax: 30 with Pratt & Whitney Hornet S2B; 26 with Bristol Pegasus IIM or IIM2 (56).
Canadian Audax: Modified Mk I (1).
Iraqi Audax: 24 with Bristol Pegasus IIM2 and 10 with VIP8 (34).
Egyptian Audax, Avro 674: 6 with 750hp Armstrong Siddeley Panther VIA and 18 with Panther X; Avro-built (24).
Total Production: 784.
Remarks: Served on communications and glider-tug duties in UK early WWII; overseas operated against Italians in East Africa and during Iraqi rebellion at least once against Iraqi Audaxes! Iranian AF Audaxes employed during Anglo-Soviet occupation of Iran, Aug 1941; the 2 Audax (Singapore) models incorporated into Malayan Volunteer AF; operated during Malayan campaign; Egyptian Audaxes limited service army co-operation/liaison role.

Manufacturer: Hawker.
Model: Hardy.
Type: General-purpose.
Power Plant: One 530hp Rolls-Royce Kestrel IB3, or one 581hp Kestrel X.

Performance:
maximum speed at sea level
161mph (259km/hr).
time to 10,000ft (3,048m)
10min 12sec.
service ceiling 17,500ft (5,334m).
Weights:
empty 3,195lb (1,449kg).
loaded 5,005lb (2,270kg).
Dimensions:
wing span 37ft 3in (11.35m).
length 29ft 7in (9.01m).
height 10ft 7in (3.22m).
wing area 348sq ft (32.33sq m).
Armament: One fixed forward-
firing .303in Vickers machine-gun;
one .303in Lewis gun on rear
cockpit mounting; four 20lb (9kg)
bombs or flares underwing.
Crew: 2.
In Service: Great Britain.
Variants (with no. built):
Prototype: One Hawker Hart
conversion.
Production model: Tropicalised for
overseas service; Gloster-built (47).
Total Production: 47.
Remarks: The Hardy was basically
a development of the Audax,
equipped for desert service; with
one exception it served exclusively
in Middle East; operated against
Italian forces in East Africa June
1940–March 1941; participated
Battle of Keren; several subsequently
employed on communications
duties.

Manufacturer: Hawker.
Model: Hartbees.
Type: Ground-support.
Power Plant: 608hp Rolls-Royce
Kestrel VFP.
Performance:
maximum speed at 6,000ft (1,829m)
176mph (283km/hr).
time to 10,000ft (3,048m)
8min 24sec.
service ceiling 22,000ft (6,706m).
Weights:
empty 3,150lb (1,429kg).
loaded 4,787lb (2,717kg).
Dimensions:
wing span 37ft 3in (11.35m).
length 29ft 7in (9.01m).
height 10ft 5in (3.17m).
wing area 348sq ft (32.33sq m).
Armament: One fixed forward-
firing .303in Vickers gun; one
.303in Lewis gun on rear cockpit
mounting; provision to carry light
bombs.
Crew: 2.
In Service: South Africa.
Variants (with no. built):
Hartbees: Hawker-built pattern
aircraft (4).
Hartbees II: South African licence-
built (65).
Total Production: 69.
Remarks: Audax development for
tropical-climate service; intended
specifically for South African use;
equipped 4 SAAF sqns; operated
in Kenya and against Italian forces
in East Africa 1940; subsequently
relegated to training duties in
Southern Rhodesia and South
Africa, 1940–46.

Manufacturer: Hawker.
Model: Hind.
Type: General-purpose light
bomber.
Power Plant: One 640hp Rolls-
Royce Kestrel V.
Performance:
maximum speed at 16,400ft (4,999m)
186mph (299km/hr).
time to 10,000ft (3,048m) 8min 6sec.
service ceiling 24,450ft (7,452m).
Weights:
empty 3,251lb (1,475kg).
loaded 5,298lb (2,403kg).
Dimensions:
wing span 37ft 3in (11.35m).
length 29ft 3in (8.91m).
height 10ft 7in (3.22m).
wing area 348sq ft (32.33sq m).
Armament: One forward-firing
.303in Vickers Mk III or V machine-
gun; one .303in ring-mounted
Lewis gun on rear cockpit; max
bomb load 510lb (231kg).
Crew: 2.
In Service: Afghanistan (20, inc
12 ex-RAF), Eire (6), Great
Britain, India, Kenya (2), Latvia,
New Zealand, Persia (35),
Portugal (4), South Africa (120+),
Switzerland (1), Yugoslavia (2).
Variants with no. built):
Prototype: Private venture (1).
Mk I: Production model; many as
trainers with Kestrel VDR (527).
Swiss Hind: Unarmed Mk I
communications version (1).
Portuguese Hind: As Mk I; two
bomber, two trainer models (4).
Yugoslav Hind: Modified Mk I; 2
with Kestrel XVI, one with
Gnome-Rhône Mistral K–9 (3).
Persian Hind: Modified Mk I;
Bristol Mercury VIII (35).
Afghan Hind: As Mk I; 4 with

Kestrel V, four with Kestrel VDR
(8).
Latvian Hind: Trainer version;
Bristol Mercury IX (3).
Total Production: 582.
Remarks: RAF Hinds all relegated
to training, communications and,
later, glider-tug duties by outbreak
of WWII; Latvian aircraft believed
seized by USSR; Afghan and
Persian (Iranian) Hinds employed
until late forties.

Manufacturer: Hawker.
Model: Hector.
Type: Army co-operation.
Power Plant: 805hp Napier Dagger
IIIMS.
Performance:
maximum speed at 6,560ft (2,000m)
187mph (300km/hr).
time to 10,000ft (3,048m)
5min 40sec.
service ceiling 24,000ft (7,315m).
Weights:
empty 3,389lb (1,537kg).
maximum 4,910lb (2,227kg).
Dimensions:
wing span 36ft 11½in (11.26m).
length 29ft 9¾in (9.08m).
height 10ft 5in (3.17m).
wing area 346sq ft (32.14sq m).
Armament: One fixed forward-

firing .303in Vickers Mk V
machine-gun; one .303in Lewis gun
mounted on rear cockpit; provision
for two 112lb (50kg) bombs or
flares underwing.
Crew: 2.
In Service: Eire (13), Great Britain.
Variants (with no. built):
Prototype: Napier Dagger III (1).
Production model: Westland-built
(178).
Total Production: 179.
Remarks: Designed as Audax
replacement; equipped 7 Army
Co-operation sqns, 1937–39; also 5
Auxiliary sqns; used as dive-bomber
during siege of Calais, May 1940;
subsequently on communications
and glider-tug duties.

Manufacturer: Hawker.
Model: Hurricane Mk I.
Type: Interceptor Fighter.
Power Plant: One 1,030hp Rolls-
Royce Merlin II.
Performance:
maximum speed at sea level
260mph (418km/hr).
maximum speed at 10,000ft (3,048m)
308mph (496km/hr).
maximum range 525 miles (845km).
time to 10,000ft (3,658m)
4min 15sec.

service ceiling 33,400ft (10,180m).
Weights:
empty 4,743lb (2,151kg).
loaded 6,218lb (2,820kg).
Dimensions:
wing span 40ft 0in (12.19m).
length 31ft 4in (9.55m).
height 13ft 4½in (4.07m).
wing area 258sq ft (23.97sq m).
Armament: Eight wing-mounted
.303in Browning machine-guns.
Crew: 1.
In Service: Australia, Belgium (22),
Canada, Eire (4), Finland (12),
Germany (1+ captured), Great
Britain, Iran (2), Italy (1+ ex-
Yugoslav), Netherlands (NEIAF,
12), Rumania (12), South Africa (30+),
Turkey (15), Yugoslavia (40+).
Variants (with no. built):
Prototype: Private venture; 1,025hp
Merlin C (1).
Mk I: Early models; 2-blade
propeller (600); late models 1,029hp
Merlin III. Rotol or D.H.; 3-blade
propeller; some tropicalised;
Hawker-built (inc some completed
as Mk IIA) (1,300); Gloster-built
(inc some completed as Mk IIA)
(1,819); Canadian licence-built by
Canadian Car and Foundry (later
redesignated Mk X) (140).

Belgian Mk I: Export model; as
early Mk I; provision for two
.5in and two 7.7mm machine-guns
(20); licence-built by Avions Fairey;
four 12.65mm Colt Brownings (2).
Yugoslav Mk I: Export order (plus
one ex-RAF model) (25); licence-
built by Rogožarski and Ikarus
(15+).
Total Production: 14,232
(all Marks).
Remarks: Entered RAF service late
1937; equipped 19 sqns by outbreak
of WWII; 4 to France with AASF
and Air Component; achieved first
RAF 'kill', 30 Oct 1939; 1 sqn to
Norway, April 1940; fired opening
rounds of Battle of Britain, 8
Aug 1940 (currently equipping 29
sqns); formed backbone of Fighter
Command strength throughout
Battle; engaged Italian raid over
East Coast 11 Nov 1940; entered
service in Middle East, Autumn
1940; participated Greek and
Syrian campaigns; also served in
Far East; Singapore, Burma and
East Indies; foreign operational
service inc Finland (Winter War
1939–40), Belgium (May 1940) and
Yugoslavia (April 1941).
Colour Reference: Plate 68:
Hawker Hurricane Mk I (Z4177) 'Q'

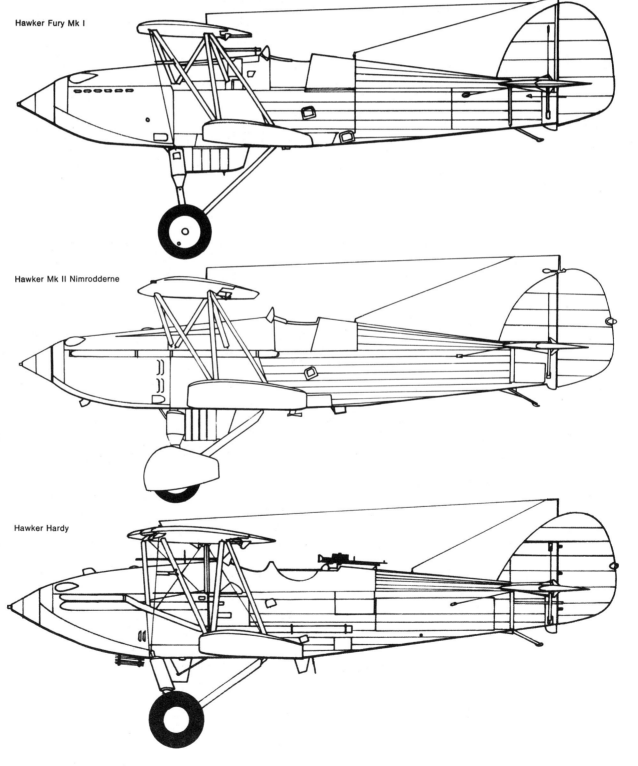

Hawker Fury Mk I

Hawker Mk II Nimrodderne

Hawker Hardy

of No 806 Squadron, Fleet Air Arm, Sidi Haneish (LG 102), Egypt, Oct 1941; component of Royal Naval Fighter Squadron posted ashore and operating in support RAF in Western Desert after damage to carrier HMS *Formidable* previous May; Hurricane Flight (formed from No 806 Squadron) in standard temperate day fighter scheme; note individual aircraft letter 'Q', serial, and 'Royal Navy' in dark blue; (compare with overall azure blue of Grumman Martlet Flight, see plate 145).

Manufacturer: Hawker.
Model: Hurricane IIC.
Type: Fighter/fighter-bomber.
Power Plant: One 1,280hp Rolls-Royce Merlin XX.
Performance:
maximum speed at 18,000ft (5,486m) 329mph (529km/hr).
maximum range 920 miles (1,480km).
initial rate of climb 2,750ft/min (838m/min).
time to 30,000ft (9,144m) 12min 30sec.
service ceiling 35,600ft (10,850m).
Weights:
empty 5,658lb (2,569kg).
maximum 8,044lb (3,649kg).
Dimensions:
wing span 40ft 0in (12.19m).
length 32ft 2¼in (9.81m).
height 13ft 1in (3.98m).
wing area 257.6sq ft (23.93sq m).
Armament: Four wing-mounted 20mm Hispano cannon; two 250lb (113kg) or two 500lb (227kg) bombs, or two drop tanks, or eight 3in rocket-projectiles underwing.
Crew: 1.
In Service: Australia, Canada, Egypt (20 Mk IIB and C), Eire (12 Mk IIB and C), Finland (1), France (FFNAF, NAF), Great Britain, India (200 Mk II, 30 Mk IV, 70 Mk XII), New Zealand, South Africa (150+), Turkey (14 Mk IIC), USSR (SovAF, SovNAF, 2,952+ despatched).
Variants (with no. built):
Mk IIA: As Mk I; 1,280hp Merlin

XX; Series 1: Mk I conversions; Series 2: Lengthened nose.
Mk IIB: Modified Mk IIA with twelve .303in Browning machine-guns in wings, plus underwing stores.
Mk IIC: As Mk IIB with four 20mm Hispano cannon in wings.
Mk IID: Two 40mm Rolls-Royce B.F. or Vickers Type S anti-tank guns in underwing fairings, plus two .303in Brownings.
(Total Mk II: Hawker-built (approx 5,425), Gloster-built (931), Austin-built: 300).
Mk IV: Universal wing; two .303in Brownings and provision for alternative 40mm anti-tank guns, or bombs, or rocket projectiles underwing (approx 2,575).
Mk V: Two Mk IV conversions with Merlin 32 and four-blade propeller; later reverted to Mk IV configuration.
Mk X, XI, XII, XIIA: Canadian licence-production by Canadian Car and Foundry; Packard Merlins (inc some completed as Sea Hurricane Mk XIIA) (937).
Total Production: 14,232 (all Marks).
Remarks: Mk IIA first entered service September 1940; employed as night-fighter during Winter 1940–41 'Blitz'; subsequently participated early cross-Channel offensive sweeps, Spring 1941; two sqns to N Russia, Aug 1941; aircraft later handed over to USSR (further deliveries direct from UK and Canada via North Atlantic and Middle East, many lost en route); Mk IIC primary UK-based variant 1942–44; Mk IID served in tank-busting/ground-attack roles North Africa (5 sqns), and Burma (3 sqns); also widely used by Indian AF in latter theatre; Mk IV employed Sicily and Italy 1943–44; many earlier Marks operated by ASR and Met units towards end of war; altogether equipped a staggering 87 (Mk II) and 11 (Mk IV) RAF fighter sqns
Colour Reference: Plates 69, 70; Hawker Hurricane Mk IIC (HV538)

'B' of No 3 Squadron, Indian Air Force, Assam, Dec 1943; forming part No 167 Wing, Indian AF (Nos 2 and 3 Squadrons on Hurricanes, No 7 Squadron on Vultee Vengeance), participated Second Arakan, Dec 1943–Jan 1944; standard SEAC finish; note white wing/tail bands and Tiger's Head personal insignia.

Manufacturer: Hawker.
Model: Sea Hurricane Mk IIC.
Type: Carrier-borne fighter.
Power Plant: One 1,460hp Rolls-Royce Merlin XX.
Performance:
maximum speed at 22,000ft (6,706m) 342mph (550km/hr).
cruising speed 212mph (341km/hr).
normal range 460 miles (740km).
time to 20,000ft (6,096m) 9min 6sec.
service ceiling 35,600ft (10,850m).
Weights:
empty 5,880lb (2,667kg).
loaded 8,100lb (3,674kg).
Dimensions:
wing span 40ft 0in (12.19m).
length 32ft 3in (3.99m).
height 13ft 1in (3.98m).
wing area 257.5sq ft (23.92sq m).
Armament: Four wing-mounted 20mm Oerlikon cannon.
Crew: 1.
In Service: Canada (RCN), Great Britain (FAA).
Variants (with no. built):
Sea Hurricane Mk I: One Hurricane Mk I conversion; catapult spools and arrester hook.
Sea Hurricane Mk IA: 50 Hurricane conversions; catapult spools only; specially produced for 'Cat-fighter' scheme—launching from CAM-ships (Catapult Aircraft Merchantmen).
Sea Hurricane Mk IB: 300 Hurricane Mk I (Merlin III) and 25 Mk IIA Series 2 conversions; catapult spools and arrester hook (MAC-ship service).
Sea Hurricane Mk IC: Hurricane Mk I conversions with four-cannon wings; catapult spools and arrester hook.
Sea Hurricane Mk IIC: With

arrester hook and naval radio equipment.
(Total Sea Hurricane Mk IC and Mk IIC: approx 450 conversions).
Sea Hurricane Mk XIIA: Canadian-built navalised Mk XII; Packard-Merlin XXIX.
Total Production: all conversions (except small quantity Mk XIIA).
Remarks: Operated 1941–1944, initially aboard CAM-ships (Mk IA): first success 3 Aug 1941, Focke-Wulf Fw 200 destroyed over Gibraltar convoy route; from Oct 1941 aboard converted merchantmen (MAC-ships) for protection of Russian convoys; also aboard Escort Carriers, Fleet Carriers, and land-based Malta and Western Desert; participated Malta Convoy action, Aug 1942; served in Far East and North Atlantic 1943–44.

Manufacturer: Hawker.
Model: Typhoon IB.
Type: Interceptor fighter/fighter-bomber.
Power Plant: One 2,260hp Napier Sabre IIC.
Performance:
maximum speed at 19,000ft (5,791m) 412mph (663km/hr).
maximum range 510 miles (821km).
time to 15,000ft (4,572m) 5min 50sec.
service ceiling 35,200ft (10,729m).
Weights:
empty 8,840lb (4,010kg).
maximum 13,980lb (6,341kg).
Dimensions:
wing span 41ft 7in (12.67m).
length 31ft 11½in (9.74m).
height 15ft 4in (4.67m).
wing area 279sq ft (25.92sq m).
Armament: Four 20mm Hispano cannon; provision for eight 3in rocket projectiles or two 1,000lb (454kg) bombs underwing.
Crew: 1.
In Service: Canada, Great Britain, New Zealand.
Variants (with no. built):
Prototypes: 2,020hp Napier Sabre I (2).
Typhoon (Centaurus): Prototype;

later re-designated Tempest II (I).
Mk IA: Initial production model; 2,100hp Sabre I; twelve .303in Browning machine-guns; built by Hawker and Gloster.
Mk IB: Modified Mk I; built by Hawker and Gloster.
1st series: four 20mm cannon; 2,180hp Sabre IIA.
2nd series: four 20mm cannon; 2,200hp Sabre IIB.
Late series: four 20mm cannon; 2,260hp Sabre IIC.
F.R.IB: Fighter reconnaissance version of standard Mk IB with either two vertical cameras in rear fuselage, or cine-camera replacing port inner wing cannon (2).
N.F.IB: Single night-fighter model; A.I. Mk IV radar.
Total Production: 3,270.
Remarks: Envisaged as 12-gun successor to Hurricane; first 15 (Mk IA/Bs) built by Hawker, remainder (3,253) produced by Gloster; wholly unsatisfactory in intended role of interceptor fighter, but developed into an excellent close-support fighter-bomber; formed the backbone of 2nd TAF's ground-attack wings during the Allied advance from Normandy to Germany; equipped total of 27 RAF and Commonwealth fighter sqns.
Colour Reference: Plates 71–72; Hawker Typhoon Mk IA (R7596) US. M of No 56 Squadron, RAF, Duxford, Cambs, Oct 1941; standard day fighter finish; note early Type A1 fuselage roundels, 'solid' canopy aft fairing, and twelve wing machine-guns.

Manufacturer: Hawker.
Model: Tempest Mk V.
Type: Fighter-bomber.
Power Plant: 2,180hp Napier Sabre IIA, B or C.
Performance:
maximum speed at 18,500ft (5,639m) 426mph (685km/hr).
maximum range 1,530 miles (2,462km).
time to 15,000ft (4,572m) 5min 0sec.
service ceiling 36,500ft (11,125m).

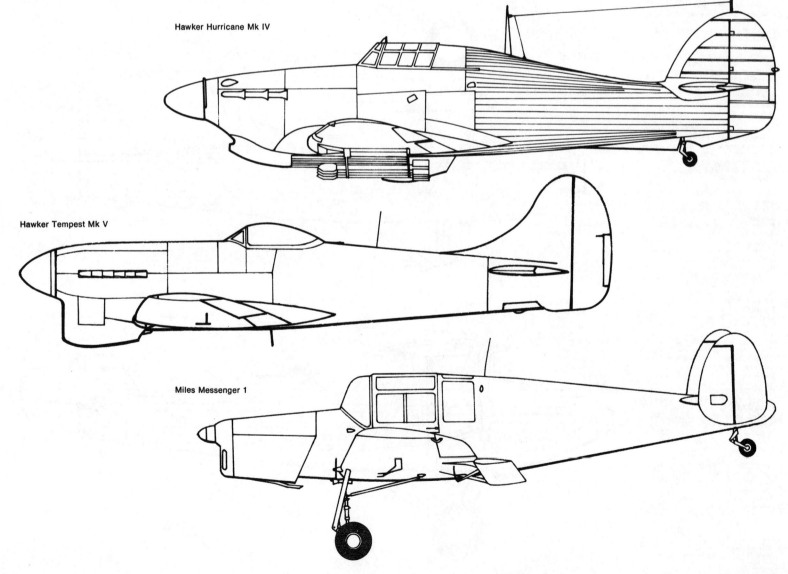

Hawker Hurricane Mk IV

Hawker Tempest Mk V

Miles Messenger 1

Weights:
empty 9,000lb (4,082kg).
loaded 13,000lb (5,897kg).
Dimensions:
wing span 41ft 0in (12.50m).
length 33ft 8in (10.26m).
height 16ft 1in (4.90m).
wing area 302sq ft (28.06sq m).
Armament: Four 20mm Hispano Mk V cannon; provision for two 500lb (227kg) or two 1,000lb (454kg) bombs underwing.
Crew: 1.
In Service: Great Britain, New Zealand.
Variants (with no. built):
Prototype: Mk I (previously as Typhoon Mk II); Napier Sabre IV (1).
Prototypes: Mk II; Bristol Centaurus IV (2).
Mk I: Post-war service model (472).
Prototypes: Mks III and IV; one completed as post-war Fury prototype; one cancelled.
Prototype: Mk V; Napier Sabre II (1).
Mk V: Wartime service model (Series 1 and 2) (800).
Prototype: Mk VI (Prototype Mk V conversion); Napier Sabre V.
Mk VI: Post-war service model (142).
Total Production: 1,418.
Remarks: Entered service January 1944; operated April–June 1944 on cross-Channel fighter-bomber sweeps; thereafter employed by 8 sqns in defence of UK against V1 attack; claimed total of 638 'flying bombs' destroyed June–Sept 1944; subsequently transferred to Continent (9 sqns) as part 2nd TAF in support advancing Allied armies and as air-superiority fighter; both roles highly successful, attacked enemy transportation, destroyed many German aircraft, inc number of Me 262 jet fighters.

Manufacturer: Heston.
Model: Phoenix.
Type: Communications.
Power Plant: One 200hp de Havilland 'Gipsy Six' Series II.
Performance:
maximum speed 150mph (241km/hr).
cruising speed 135mph (217km/hr).
normal range 500 miles (805km).
initial rate of climb 700ft/min (213m/min).
service ceiling 15,500ft (4,700m).
Weights:
empty 2,140lb (970kg).
loaded 3,300lb (1,497kg).
Dimensions:
wing span 40ft 4in (12.29m).
length 30ft 2in (9.19m).
height 8ft 7in (2.62m).
wing area 272sq ft (25.26sq m).
Crew/Accommodation: 1/4.
In Service: Great Britain.
Variants:
Phoenix: Gipsy Six Series I; fixed-pitch propeller.
Phoenix: Gipsy Six Series II; variable-pitch propeller.
Remarks: Pre-war 5-seat high-wing cabin monoplane; at least three (one Series I, two Series II) Brtish impressments; employed in communications/liaison role.

Manufacturer: Miles.
Model: M.2F Hawk Major.
Type: Liaison/communications.
Power Plant: One 130hp de Havilland Gipsy Major.
Performance:
maximum speed 150mph (241km/hr).
cruising speed 135mph (217km/hr).
initial rate of climb 1,080ft/min (329.2m/min).
service ceiling 20,000ft (6,100m).
Weights:
empty 1,150lb (522kg).
maximum 1,800lb (816kg).
Dimensions:
wing span 33ft 0in (10.06m).
length 24ft 0in (7.32m).
height 6ft 8in (2.03m).
wing area 169sq ft (15.7sq m).
Crew/Accommodation: 1/1.
In Service: Australia (2 M.2H), Great Britain.
Variants (with no. built):
M.2, M.2A/B, M.2D Hawk: Initial production models; 1/3-seat cabin/open cockpit civil tourers; various power plants (55).
M.2F Hawk Major: Improved Hawk; one 120hp Gipsy III (prototype) and 130hp Gipsy Major (production); trousered under-carriage (17).
M.2G Hawk Major: 3-seat cabin version (1).
M.2H Hawk Major: As M.2F; wing flaps (39).
M.2M Hawk Major: 3-seat (open cockpit/2-seat cabin) version (1).
M.2P Hawk Major: As M.2H; increased wing span/weight; modified cockpits (2).
M.2R Hawk Major de Luxe (Hawk Trainer): As M.2P; later re-engined Menasco Pirate C4) (1).
M.2S/T Hawk Major: Single-seat long-range versions; Gipsy/Cirrus Majors resp (1/2) (3).
M.2W/X/Y Hawk Trainer: As M.2P; enlarged cockpits; increased rudder area (M.2X/Y) (4/9/13) (26).
Total Production: 145 (excl Indian/Spanish licence production).
Remarks: First of long line Miles light aircraft, twenty M.2 Hawk/Hawk Major series impressed RAF after outbreak WWII, variety ancillary communications/training and instructional duties; Hawk Trainer subsequently developed into M.14 Magister; 2 pre-war exports impressed RAAF communications role, 1940–45.

Manufacturer: Miles.
Model: M.3D Falcon Six.
Type: Liaison/communications.
Power Plant: One 200hp de Havilland Gipsy Six.
Performance:
maximum speed at sea level 180mph (290km/hr).
maximum range 560 miles (901km).
initial rate of climb 1,000ft/min (305m/min).
service ceiling 17,000ft (5,180m).
Weights:
empty 1,550lb (703kg).
loaded 2,525lb (1,145kg).
Dimensions:
wing span 35ft 0in (10.67m).
length 25ft 0in (7.62m).
wing area 174.3sq ft (16.19sq m).
Crew/Accommodation: 1/2.
In Service: Australia (1 M.3A, 1 M.3D), Great Britain (RAF 8, FAA 1).
Variants (with no. built):
M.3A Falcon Major: Initial production model; 3-seat cabin monoplane; one de Havilland Gipsy Major (19).
M.3B/E Falcon Six: Re-engined M.3A (17).
Total Production: 36.
Remarks: Enlarged development earlier M.2 Hawk Major, number M.3 Falcon Major/Falcon Six series (3 latter served pre-war RAF experimental duties) impressed after outbreak WWII for communications role; 6 in UK (inc one to FAA); 2 in Australia.

Manufacturer: Miles.
Model: Merlin.
Type: Liaison/communications.
Power Plant: One 200hp de Havilland Gipsy Six.
Performance:
maximum speed at 155mph (250km/hr).
cruising speed 140mph (225km/hr).
Weights:
empty 1,576lb (715kg).
loaded 3,000lb (1,360kg).
Dimensions:
wing span 35ft 0in (10.67m).
length 25ft 10in (7.87m).
height 7ft 5½in (2.27m).
Crew/Accommodation: 1/4.
In Service: Australia.
Total Production: 4.
Remarks: 5-seat cabin monoplane, one M.4 Merlin impressed RAAF communications duties, 1940–45.

Manufacturer: Miles.
Model: Nighthawk.
Type: Instrument trainer/communications.
Power Plant: 200hp de Havilland Gipsy Six.
Performance:
maximum speed 180mph (290km/hr).
cruising speed 160mph (257km/hr).
Weights:
empty 1,650lb (748kg).
maximum 2,400lb (1,089kg).
Dimensions:
wing span 35ft 0in (10.67m).
length 25ft 0in (7.62m).
wing area 181sq ft (16.81sq m).
Crew/Accommodation: 1/2.
In Service: Great Britain.
Total Production: 6.
Remarks: Pre-war dual-control instrument trainer; M7 Nighthawk served early months of war in communications role.

Manufacturer: Miles.
Model: Whitney Straight.
Type: Light communications.
Power Plant: 130hp de Havilland Gipsy Major.
Performance:
maximum speed 145mph (233km/hr).
cruising speed 130mph (209km/hr).
normal range 570 miles (918km).
initial rate of climb 850ft/min (259m/min).
Weights:
empty 1,275lb (578kg).
maximum 1,896lb (860kg).
Dimensions:
wing span 35ft 8in (10.87m).
length 25ft 0in (7.62m).
height 6ft 6in (1.98m).
wing area 187sq ft (17.37sq m).
Crew/Accommodation: 1/1.
In Service: Great Britain, New Zealand.
Total Production: 50.
Remarks: 2-seat light monoplane, M11 achieved extensive pre-war foreign sales; 20 subsequently impressed UK, and 3 RNZAF, for communications and liaison duties.

Manufacturer: Miles.
Model: Mohawk.
Type: Liaison/communications.
Power Plant: One 250hp Menasco Buccaneer B6S.
Performance:
maximum speed 190mph (306km/hr).
cruising speed 170mph (274km/hr).
Weights:
empty 1,605lb (728kg).
maximum 2,620lb (1,207kg).
Dimensions:
wing span 35ft 0in (10.67m).
length 25ft 6in (7.77m).
Crew/Accommodation: 1/1.
In Service: Great Britain.
Total Production: 1.
Remarks: Built to specification of Col Charles Lindbergh; sole M12 Mohawk completed impressed RAF communications duties, 1941–44.

Manufacturer: Miles.
Model: Magister I.
Type: Elementary trainer/interim light bomber.
Power Plant: One 130hp de Havilland Gipsy Major I.
Performance:
maximum speed at 1,000ft (305m) 132mph (212km/hr).
cruising speed 123mph (198km/hr).
range 380 miles (611km).
initial rate of climb 850ft/min (259m/min).
service ceiling 18,000ft (5,490m).
Weights:
empty 1,286lb (583kg).
loaded 1,900lb (862kg).
Dimensions:
wing span 33ft 10in (10.30m).
length 24ft 7½in (7.50m).
height 6ft 8in (2.02m).
wing area 176sq ft (16.35sq m).
Armament: Eight 25lb (11.3kg) bombs.
Crew/Accommodation: 1/1.
In Service: Estonia (1), Great Britain (RAF, FAA).
Variants (with no. built):
Mks I–III: Elementary trainers (1,293).
Total Production: 1,293.
Remarks: Basic trainer, M14 Magister saw world-wide use; 15 British examples modified as interim light bombers in June 1940 at height of post-Dunkirk invasion scare; others later diverted to Middle East as light liaison aircraft

Manufacturer: Miles.
Model: Mentor.
Type: Trainer/communications.
Power Plant: 200hp de Havilland Gipsy Six.
Performance:
maximum speed 156mph (251km/hr).
initial rate of climb 780ft/min (238m/min).
service ceiling 13,800ft (4,206m).
Weights:
empty 1,978lb (897kg).
maximum 2,710lb (1,229kg).
Dimensions:
wing span 34ft 9½in (10.60m).
length 26ft 1¾in (7.96m).
height 9ft 8in (2.94m).
wing area 181sq ft (16.81sq m).
Crew/Accommodation: 1/2.
In Service: Great Britain.
Total Production: 45.
Remarks: Dual-control trainer; M.16 Mentor also employed on communications duties.

Manufacturer: Miles.
Model: Monarch.
Type: Light communications.
Power Plant: 130hp de Havilland Gipsy Major.
Performance:
maximum speed 140mph (225km/hr).
cruising speed 125mph (201km/hr).
maximum range 910 miles (1,464km).
initial rate of climb 850ft/min (259m/min).
service ceiling 17,400ft (5,304m).
Weights:
empty 1,390lb (631kg).
maximum 2,150lb (975kg).
Dimensions:
wing span 35ft 7in (10.84m).
length 25ft 11¾in (7.91m).
height 8ft 9¼in (2.67m).
wing area 180sq ft (16.72sq m).
Crew/Accommodation: 1/2.
In Service: Great Britain.
Total Production: 8.
Remarks: Improved 3-seat version of earlier M.11 Whitney Straight; only eight M.17 Monarchs built before outbreak of war, of which four impressed for communications and liaison duties.

Manufacturer: Miles.
Model: Master II.
Type: Advanced trainer/communications.
Power Plant: One 870hp Bristol Mercury XX.
Performance:
maximum speed at sea level 221mph (356km/hr).
maximum range 393 miles (632km).
initial rate of climb 2,120ft/min (646.18m/min).
service ceiling 25,100ft (7,650m).
Weights:
empty 4,293lb (1,947kg).
loaded 5,573lb (2,528kg).
Dimensions:
wing span 39ft 0in (11.89m).
length 29ft 6in (8.99m).
height 9ft 3in (2.82m).
wing area 235sq ft (21.83sq m).
Crew/Accommodation: 1/1.
In Service: Great Britain (RAF, FAA), South Africa (approx 420).
Variants (with no. built):
M.9 Master I: Prototype and initial production model; one 715hp Rolls-Royce Kestrel XXX.
Master IA: As Mk I; improved windscreen.
(Total M.9 Master I and IA: 875).
M.19 Master II: Re-engined Master I (1,799).
M.24: Modified Master I; single-seat six-gun emergency fighter version (25).
M.27 Master III: Re-engined Master II; one 825hp Pratt & Whitney Wasp Junior (603).
M.31 Master IV: Modified Master III; raised rear cockpit; project only.
Total Production: 3,302.
Remarks: Standard advanced trainer, considerable numbers also subsequently employed ancillary liaison/communications and glider-tug duties; sold/supplied various foreign AFs inc Egypt, Portugal, South Africa, USA (1).

Manufacturer: Miles.
Model: Martinet.
Type: Target-tug.
Power Plant: One 870hp Bristol Mercury XX or XXX.
Performance:
maximum speed at sea level 221mph (356km/hr).
cruising speed 199mph (320km/hr).
range 694 miles (1,117km).
time to 5,000ft (1,524m) 3min 30sec.
Weights:
empty 4,640lb (2,105kg).
maximum 6,750lb (3,062kg).
Dimensions:
wing span 39ft 0in (11.89m).
length 30ft 11in (9.42m).
height 11ft 7in (3.53m).
wing area 242sq ft (22.48sq m).
Crew: 2.
In Service: Great Britain, Sweden.
Variants (with no. built):
Prototypes (2).
M.25 Martinet: Standard service version (1,724).
M.50 Queen Martinet: Radio-controlled pilotless target aircraft (65).
Martinet Trainer: Post-war trainer version; prototypes (2).
Total Production: 1,793.
Remarks: Designed specifically as target-tug; equipped 16 Anti-aircraft Co-operation sqns RAF; also performed ASR duties (1 sqn).

Manufacturer: Miles.
Model: Messenger 1.
Type: Light liaison/communications.
Power Plant: One 140hp de Havilland Gipsy Major.
Performance:
maximum speed 116mph (187km/hr).
cruising speed 95mph (153km/hr).
range 260 miles (418km).
initial rate of climb 660ft/min (201m/min).
Weights:
empty 1,518lb (689kg).
maximum 1,900lb (862kg).
Dimensions:
wing span 36ft 2in (11.02m).
length 24ft 0in (7.32m).
height 9ft 6in (2.89m).
wing area 191sq ft (17.74sq m).
Crew/Accommodation: 1/3.
In Service: Great Britain.
Variants (with no. built):
Prototype (1).
Messenger 1: Initial RAF production version (21).
Messenger 2A/C, 3, 4, 4A: Post-war models (58).
Total Production: 80.
Remarks: Originally designed for AOP duties; served mainly in light-liaison and VIP communications roles.

Manufacturer: Parnall.
Model: Hendy Heck 2C.
Type: Communications.
Power Plant: One 205hp de Havilland Gipsy Six 2.
Performance:
maximum speed 185mph (298km/hr).
cruising speed 160mph (258km/hr).
range 620 miles (998km).
initial rate of climb 1,100ft/min (335m/min).
ceiling 16,700ft (5,090m).
Weights:
empty 1,750lb (794kg).
loaded 2,600lb (1,180kg).
Dimensions:
wing span 31ft 6in (9.60m).
length 26ft 1½in (7.96m).
height 8ft 6in (2.59m).
wing area 105.2sq ft (9.77sq m).
Crew/Accommodation: 1/2.
In Service: Great Britain.
Variants (with no. built):
Prototype: Hendy 3308; 2-seat low-wing cabin monoplane; Westland-built (1).
Heck 2C: Improved 3-seat version; revised cabin (6).
Total Production: 6 (+ Westland prototype).
Remarks: Several Mk IICs impressed for communications, liaison and experimental duties early WWII.

Manufacturer: Percival.
Model: Proctor IV.
Type: Trainer/communications.
Power Plant: One 210hp de Havilland Gipsy Queen II.
Performance:
maximum speed at sea level 160mph (257km/hr).
cruising speed 140mph (225km/hr).
range 500 miles (805km).
initial rate of climb 700ft/min (213m/min).
service ceiling 14,000ft (4,267m).
Weights:
empty 2,370lb (1,075kg).
loaded 3,500lb (1,588kg).
Dimensions:
wing span 39ft 6in (12.04m).
length 28ft 2in (8.58m).
height 7ft 3in (2.21m).
wing area 202sq ft (18.78sq m).
Crew/Accommodation: 1/3.
In Service: Germany (1), Great Britain (RAF, FAA), USA.
Variants (with no. built):
Mk I: Military version of civil Vega Gull light touring aircraft; Percival-built (RAF: 122, FAA: 100 Mk IA) (222); Hills-built (25).
Mk II, IIA: Radio-trainer versions, Percival-built (RAF: 50, FAA: 50 Mk IIA) (100); Hills-built (FAA: Mk IIA) (100).
Mk III: Radio-trainer version; Prototype (1); Production: Hills-built (437).
Mk IV: (Preceptor); 4-seat radio-trainer version; lengthened fuselage; Percival-built (8); Hills-built (250).
Many subsequently converted to communications.
Total Production: 1,143.
Remarks: Served from 1940–45 with RAF and FAA; extensively used in training and for communications duties; 20+ Vega Gulls impressed, inc 5 Middle East and India; one captured by Germany and evaluated before re-sale to Sweden as AA target-tug.

Manufacturer: Percival.
Model: Q.6 (Petrel).
Type: Communications.
Power Plant: Two 205hp de Havilland Gipsy Six II.
Performance:
maximum speed 195mph (314km/hr).
range 700 miles (1,126km).
service ceiling 21,000ft (6,400m).
Weights:
empty 3,500lb (1,588kg).
loaded 5,550lb (2,517kg).
Dimensions:
wing span 46ft 8in (14.22m).
length 32ft 3in (9.83m).
height 9ft 9in (2.97m).
wing area 278sq ft (25.82sq m).
Crew/Accommodation: 2/4.
In Service: Great Britain (RAF, FAA).
Variants (with no. built):
Q.6: Civil light (executive) transport (20).
Petrel: Popular name for military version (7).
Total Production: 27.
Remarks: Served throughout WWII: at least 12 civil Q.6 impressments

Saro London II

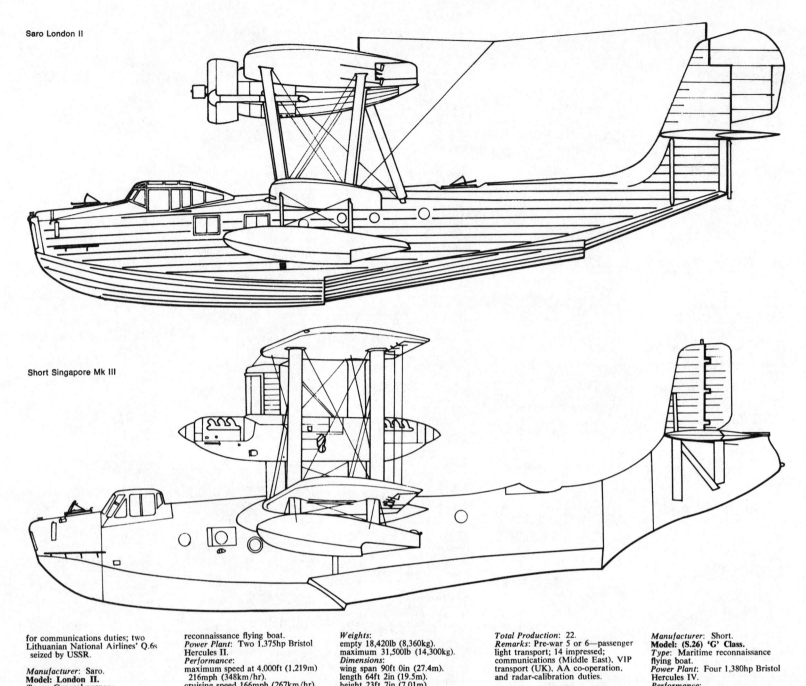

Short Singapore Mk III

for communications duties; two Lithuanian National Airlines' Q.6s seized by USSR.

Manufacturer: Saro.
Model: London II.
Type: General-purpose reconnaissance flying boat.
Power Plant: Two 920hp Bristol Pegasus X.
Performance:
maximum speed at sea level 142mph (228km/hr).
cruising speed 137mph (220km/hr).
maximum range 1,740 miles (2800km).
initial rate of climb 1,180ft/min (360m/min).
service ceiling 19,900ft (6,066m).
Weights:
empty 11,100lb (5,035kg).
maximum 18,400lb (8,346kg).
Dimensions:
wing span 80ft 0in (24.38m).
length 56ft 9.5in (17.31m).
height 18ft 9in (5.71m).
wing area 1,425sq ft (132.38sq m).
Armament: Three .303in Lewis machine-guns in bow, dorsal and tail positions; max load of bombs, depth-charges or mines 2,000lb (907kg).
Crew: 6.
In Service: Great Britain.
Variants (with no. built):
Prototype: 750hp Pegasus IIIs; later converted to London II (1).
London I: Initial production model (10).
London II: Improved version with Pegasus Xs (38).
Total Production: 49.
Remarks: Served with 3 Coastal Command sqns during early part of WWII; employed on anti-submarine and convoy-escort duties in Mediterranean (1sqn) and for patrolling North Sea (2 sqns); withdrawn from service 1941.

Manufacturer: Saro.
Model: Lerwick.
Type: Medium-range general-

reconnaissance flying boat.
Power Plant: Two 1,375hp Bristol Hercules II.
Performance:
maximum speed at 4,000ft (1,219m) 216mph (348km/hr).
cruising speed 166mph (267km/hr).
initial rate of climb 880ft/min (268m/min).
service ceiling 14,000ft (4,267m).
Weights:
loaded 28,500lb (12,928kg).
maximum 33,200lb (15,060kg).
Dimensions:
wing span 80ft 10in (24.63m).
length 63ft 7½in (19.39m).
height 20ft 0in (6.10m).
wing area 845sq ft (78.50sq m).
Armament: One .303in Vickers gun in nose turret; twin .303in Browning guns in dorsal turret; four .303in Brownings in tail turret; four 500lb (227kg) or eight 250lb (113kg) bombs.
Crew: 6.
In Service: Canada, Great Britain.
Variants (with no. built):
Prototypes (3).
Production model, inc 8 with Hercules IV engines (18).
Total Production: 21.
Remarks: Brief service with one Coastal Command sqn, late 1940 May 1941, then relegated to training duties; declared obsolete 1942.

Manufacturer: Short.
Model: Scion II.
Type: Light transport.
Power Plant: Two 90hp Pobjoy Niagara III.
Performance:
maximum speed 126mph (203km/hr).
cruising speed 105mph (169km/hr).
range 390 miles (624km).
service ceiling 13,000ft (3,960m).
Weights:
empty 1,875lb (850kg).
maximum 3,200lb (1,452kg).
Dimensions:
wing span 42ft 0in (12.8m).
length 31ft 4in (9.56m).
height 10ft 4½in (3.16m).
wing area 256sq ft (23.8sq m).
Crew/Accommodation: 1/6.
In Service: Great Britain.
Variants (with no. built):
Prototype: Land-, alternative floatplane (1).
Mk I: Initial production model (4).
Mk II: Improved version (11).
Pobjoy-Scion: Pobjoy-built Mk II (6).

Manufacturer: Short.
Model: Singapore.
Type: General-reconnaissance flying boat.
Power Plant: Four 730hp Rolls-Royce Kestrel VIII/IX tractor/pusher engines.
Performance:
maximum speed at 2,000ft (610m) 145mph (233km/hr).
cruising speed 105mph (169km/hr).
normal range 1,000miles (1,609km).
initial rate of climb 700ft/min (213m/min).
service ceiling 15,000ft (4,570m).

Weights:
empty 18,420lb (8,360kg).
maximum 31,500lb (14,300kg).
Dimensions:
wing span 90ft 0in (27.4m).
length 64ft 2in (19.5m).
height 23ft 7in (7.01m).
wing area 1,834sq ft (170.5sq m).
Armament: Three .303in Lewis guns in open bow, dorsal and tail positions; bomb load 2,000lb (907kg).
Crew: 6.
In Service: Great Britain, New Zealand.
Variants (with no. built):
Mk I: Original twin-engined 1926 model (1).
Mk II: Prototype only (pusher/tractor) (1).
Mk III: Production model (37).
Total Production: 39.
Remarks: Built 1934–1937; served in Middle East 1939–40, and with RNZAF (4 machines) 1941–45.

Manufacturer: Short.
Model: (S.23 Empire) C-Class.
Type: Maritime reconnaissance flying boat.
Power Plant: Four 920hp Bristol Pegasus XC.
Performance:
maximum speed at 5,500ft (1,676m) 200mph (322km/hr).
cruising speed 164mph (264km/hr).
normal range 760 miles (1,245km).
initial rate of climb 950ft/min (290m/min).
service ceiling 20,000ft (6,096m).
Weights:
empty 23,500lb (10,670kg).
maximum 40,500lb (18,380kg).
Dimensions:
wing span 114ft 0in (34.7m).
length 88ft 0in (26.8m).
height 31ft 9.75in (9.69m).
wing area 1,500sq ft (139.5sq m).
Armament: (S.23M) eight .303in Browning machine-guns in dorsal and tail turrets; 2,000lb (907kg) bombs; provision for six 430lb (195kg) depth-charges.
Crew: 6–7.
In Service: Australia, Great Britain.
Variants (with no. built):
S.23: Civil flying boat (31).
S.23M: Military impressments (2) of above; armed and equipped with A.S.V. radar.
S.30: Four Bristol Perseus XIIC (9).
S.33: Strengthened hull (2).
Total Production: 42.
Remarks: Two impressed S.30s destroyed, Norway May 1940; replaced by two impressed S.23s; employed by Coastal Command on maritime patrol; 4 Qantas machines impressed into RAAF, 3 destroyed.

Total Production: 22.
Remarks: Pre-war 5 or 6—passenger light transport; 14 impressed; communications (Middle East), VIP transport (UK), AA co-operation, and radar-calibration duties.

Manufacturer: Short.
Model: (S.26) 'G' Class.
Type: Maritime reconnaissance flying boat.
Power Plant: Four 1,380hp Bristol Hercules IV.
Performance:
maximum speed at 5,500ft (1,676m) 209mph (336km/hr).
range 3,200 miles (5,120km).
Weights:
empty 37,705lb (17,100kg).
maximum 74,500lb (33,800kg).
Dimensions:
wing span 134ft 4in (40.9m).
length 103ft 2in (31.4m).
wing area 2,160sq ft (201sq m).
Armament: Three Boulton Paul turrets, two dorsal, and one tail, each with four .303in Browning machine-guns; eight 500lb (227kg) bombs underwing; plus smoke-, floats, flame-floats and reconnaissance flares.
Crew: 7–8.
In Service: Great Britain.
Variants (with no. built):
S.26: Original civil design (3).
S.26M: Military impressments of above.
Total Production: 3.
Remarks: Modified and enlarged 'C' Class flying boat intended for non-stop Atlantic Mail Services; all three impressed 1940 for maritime reconnaissance; equipped with ASV radar; one lost off Cape Finisterre, June 1941; other two subsequently returned to BOAC.

Manufacturer: Short.
Model: Sunderland V.
Type: Long-range general-reconnaissance/anti-submarine flying boat.
Power Plant: Four 1,200hp Pratt & Whitney Twin Wasp R–1830.
Performance:
maximum speed at sea level 207mph (333km/hr).
maximum speed at 5,000ft (1,524m)

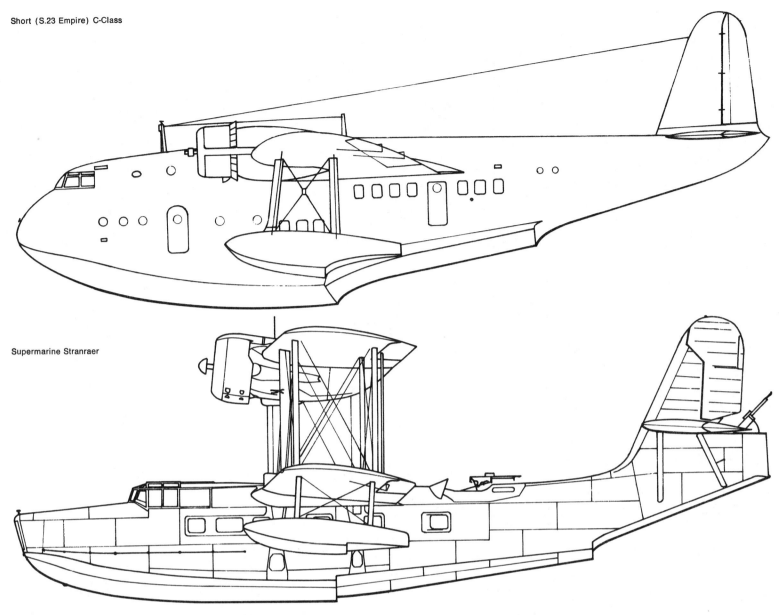

Supermarine Stranraer

213mph (343km/hr).
cruising speed 133mph (214km/hr).
maximum range 2,980 miles
(4,795km).
initial rate of climb 840ft/min
(256m/min).
service ceiling 17,900ft (5,456m).
Weights:
empty 37,000lb (16,783kg).
maximum 65,000lb (29,482kg).
Dimensions:
wing span 112ft 9½in (34.36m).
length 85ft 4in (26m).
height 32ft 10½in (10.01m).
wing area 1,482sq ft (138.1sq m).
Armament: Four fixed forward-
firing .303in machine-guns; plus
two in power-operated bow turret
and four in power-operated tail
turret; two manually-operated .5in
beam guns (in place of dorsal
turret); max bomb load 4,960lb (2,250kg)
(bombs, mines and/or depth-
charges).
Crew: 10.
In Service: Australia, Canada,
Great Britain, New Zealand.
Variants with no. built):
Mk I: Initial production version
with four 1,010hp Bristol Pegasus
XXII and two additional dorsal
Vickers 'K'-guns; Short-built (75);
Blackburn-built (15).
Mk II: As Mk I but Pegasus
XVIII engines and new dorsal and
tail turrets; some with ASV. Mk
II radar; Short-built (38);
Blackburn-built (5).
Mks III and IIIA: As Mk II but
with faired main step; some fitted
with ASV. Mk III radar (Mk
IIIA); Short-built (286);
Blackburn-built (170).
Mk IV (Seaford): Heavier, more
powerfully-armed post-war model;
Two prototypes and eight pro-
duction models; 7 later converted
as Solent 3 civil transports (10).
Mk V: With under-wingtip A.S.V.
Mk VIc radar; Short-built (100);
Blackburn-built (50).
Total Production: 749.

Remarks: First entered service 1938;
remained standard Coastal
Command flying boat throughout
war years; provided convoy-escort
and anti-submarine patrols in UK.
Middle East and Far East; scored
Coastal's first U-Boat 'kill'; participated evacuations of Norway,
Greece and Crete; by war's end
equipped 28 RAF sqns; finally
withdrawn 1959; continued in
service with French Navy until 1960
and RNZAF until 1967.
Colour Reference: Plate 76: Short
Sunderland Mk III (JM673) 'P'
flown by Wg Cdr D. K. Bednall,
CO No 230 Squadron, No 222
Group, RAF, Koggala, Ceylon,
1944–45; unique all-black JM673
(known to squadron as 'Black
Peter') so camouflaged for dawn/
dusk anti-shipping patrols Bay of
Bengal.

Manufacturer: Short.
Model: Stirling III.
Type: Heavy bomber.
Power Plant: Four 1,650hp Bristol
Hercules XVI.
Performance:
maximum speed at 14,500ft (4,420m)
270mph (434km/hr).
maximum range 2,010 miles
(3,240km).
service ceiling 17,000ft (5,181m).
Weights:
empty 46,900lb (21,200kg).
maximum 70,000lb (31,790kg).
Dimensions:
wing span 99ft 1in (30.2m).
length 87ft 3in (26.5m).
height 22ft 9in (6.93m).
wing area 1,460sq ft (135.6sq m).
Armament: Two .303in guns each
in nose and dorsal turrets; four
.303in guns in tail turret; max
bomb load 14,000lb (6,350kg).
Crew: 7–8.
In Service: Great Britain.
Variants (with no. built):
Prototypes (2).
Mk I: Initial production; four

1,595hp Hercules XI (756).
Mk II: 1,600hp Wright Cyclones
(2).
Mk III: Revised dorsal turret (875).
Mk IV: Glider-tug/paratroop
transport; nose and dorsal turrets
deleted (579).
Mk V: Unarmed transport (160).
Silver Stirling: Civil transport.
Total Production: 2,374 (inc 618
by Austin Motors).
Remarks: RAF's first four-engined
monoplane heavy bomber; entered
service Aug 1940; first operation Feb
1941; by 1943–44 being phased out
in favour of Lancaster and Halifax;
last Bomber Command raid Sept
1944; then main role was glider-
tug/transport; D–Day, Arnhem
and Rhine Crossing.
Colour Reference: Plates 74, 75:
Short Stirling Mk IV (LK117) V8.F
of No 570 Squadron, No 38 Group,
RAF, Harwell, Berks, Sept 1944;
participated Operation 'Market-
Garden', Arnhem assault and
back-up supply sorties; note under-
fuselage invasion striping and four
daggers below cockpit, symbol
employed by squadron to indicate
number of special operations supply
missions; pink square port upper
wing surface marks dinghy stowage.

Manufacturer: Short.
Model: Stirling V.
Type: Long-range transport.
Power Plant: Four 1,650hp Bristol
Hercules XVI.
Performance:
maximum speed at 6,000ft (1,829m)
280mph (451km/hr).
cruising speed 233mph (375km/hr).
range 3,000 miles (4,827km).
initial rate of climb 800ft/min
(244m/min).
service ceiling 18,000ft (5,486m).
Weights:
empty 43,500lb (19,731kg).
maximum 70,000lb (31,790kg).
Dimensions:
wing span 99ft 1in (30.20m).

length 87ft 3in (26.59m).
height 22ft 9in (6.93m).
wing area 1,460sq ft (135.6sq m).
Crew/Accommodation: 5/40 troops
or paratroops.
In Service: Great Britain.
Remarks: Built August 1944–
Nov 1945; equipped three Transport
Command squadrons prior to VJ–
Day; mainly on long-distance routes
to India and Far East.

Manufacturer: Supermarine.
Model: Stranraer.
Type: General-purpose
reconnaissance flying boat.
Power Plant: Two 875hp Bristol
Pegasus X.
Performance:
maximum speed at sea level
150mph (241km/hr).
maximum speed at 6,000ft (1,829m)
165mph (268km/hr).
cruising speed 105mph (169km/hr).
range 1,000 miles (1,609km).
initial rate of climb 1,350ft/min
(411m/min).
time to 10,000ft (3,048m)
10min 0sec.
service ceiling 18,500ft (5,639m).
Weights:
empty 11,250lb (5,103kg).
loaded 19,000lb (8,618kg).
Dimensions:
wing span 85ft 0in (25.91m).
length 54ft 10in (16.71m).
height 21ft 9in (6.63m).
wing area 1,457sq ft (135.36sq m).
Armament: Three .303in Lewis
machine-guns in nose, dorsal and
tail positions; max bomb load
1,000lb (454kg).
Crew: 6.
In Service: Canada, Great Britain.
Variants (with no. built):
Prototype: Redesignated
Southampton V; Pegasus IIIM
engines (1).
Production model: Supermarine-
built (17); Canadian licence-built
by Vickers (40).
Total Production: 58.

Remarks: Equipped two Coastal
Command sqns in Scotland in
early months of WWII; served with
RCAF on coastal reconnaissance
duties until 1943.

Manufacturer: Supermarine.
Model: Walrus II.
Type: Air/sea-rescue amphibian.
Power Plant: One 775hp Bristol
Pegasus VI.
Performance:
maximum speed at sea level
124mph (200km/hr).
maximum speed at 4.750ft (1.448m)
135mph (217km/hr).
cruising speed 95mph (153km/hr).
maximum range 600 miles
(965km).
initial rate of climb 1,050ft/min
(320m/min).
service ceiling 18,500ft (5,639m).
Weights:
empty 4,900lb (2,223kg).
loaded 7,200lb (3,266kg).
Dimensions:
wing span 45ft 10in (13.97m).
length 37ft 7in (11.45m).
height 15ft 3in (4.65m).
wing area 610sq ft (56.67sq m).
Armament: One .303in Vickers 'K'
gun in nose and dorsal positions;
bombs and depth-charges underwing.
Crew: 4.
In Service: Australia (26 Seagull V),
Eire (1 Mk II), Great Britain (RAF,
FAA), New Zealand (1 Mk II).
Variants (with no. built):
Seagull V: Prototype; one 635hp
Pegasus IIM2; initial private
venture (1); Production model for
RAAF (26).
Walrus Mk I: Redesignated Seagull
V for FAA and RAF; some fitted
with A.S.V. radar; Supermarine-
built (281); Saro-built (270).
Mk II: Modified Mk I. Uprated
engine; wooden hull; Saro-built
(183).
Total Production: 761 (inc Seagull
V).
Remarks: Metal-hulled Mk I

Supermarine Walrus Mk II

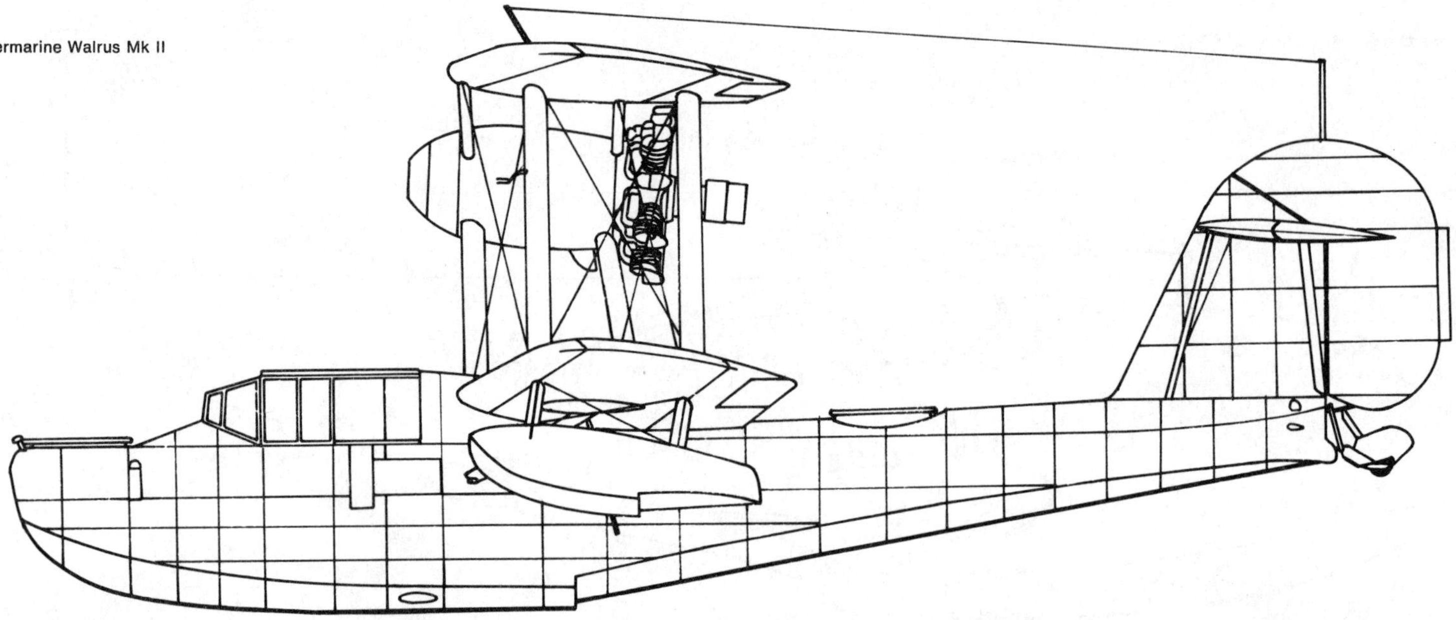

shipboard observation amphibian used primarily by FAA as fleet spotter; RAF Mk IIs performed heroic work in ASR role with 7 UK-based and 4 Middle Eastern-based sqns; also reconnaissance, mine-spotting and—on one memorable occasion—dive-bombing duties!

Manufacturer: Supermarine.
Model: Sea Otter II.
Type: Air/sea-rescue amphibian.
Power Plant: One 855hp Bristol Mercury XXX.
Performance:
maximum speed at 5,000ft (1,524m) 150mph (241km/hr).
cruising speed 100mph (161km/hr).
range 725 miles (1,167km).
initial rate of climb 870ft/min (265m/min).
service ceiling 16,000ft (4,877m).
Weights:
empty 6,805lb (3,087kg).
maximum 10,830lb (4,912kg).
Dimensions:
wing span 46ft 0in (14.02m).
length 39ft 2in (11.94m).
height 16ft 2in (4.93m).
wing area 610sq ft (56.67sq m).
Armament: Two Scarff-mounted Vickers 'K' guns in dorsal position and one Vickers 'K' gun in nose.
Crew: 3–4.
In Service: Great Britain (RAF, FAA).
Variants (with no. built):
Prototypes (2).
Mk I: Amphibian; optional underwing bombs or depth-charges; Saro-built (250).
A.S.R.Mk II: Air/sea-rescue version; modified Mk I; Saro-built (40).
Total Production: 292.
Remarks: Aerodynamically-improved successor to Walrus; entered service with FAA, Nov 1944; equipped 5 home-based RAF sqns and 3 Air/Sea-Rescue Flights (Mk II) in Far East; sterling work throughout final stages Burma campaign.

Manufacturer: Supermarine.
Model: Spitfire Mk IA.
Type: Interceptor fighter.
Power Plant: One 1,030hp Rolls-Royce Merlin III.
Performance:
maximum speed 362mph (582km/hr).
cruising speed 210mph (338km/hr).
normal range 395 miles (636km).
initial rate of climb 2,530ft/min (771m/min).
time to 20,000ft (6,096m) 9min 24sec.
service ceiling 31,900ft (9,723m).
Weights:
empty 4,810lb (2,182kg).
normal 5,784lb (2,624kg).
Dimensions:
wing span 36ft 10in (11.22m).
length 29ft 11in (9.11m).
height 8ft 10in (2.69m).
wing area 242sq ft (22.48sq m).
Armament: Eight .303in Browning machine-guns.
Crew: 1.
In Service: Australia, Canada, Germany (1+ captured), Great Britain, New Zealand, Turkey (3 Mk IA).
Variants (with no. built):
Prototype: Various Merlin installations; later converted to Mk I standard (1).
Mk IA: Initial production model; Supermarine-built (1,533); Westland-built (50).
Mk IB: Thirty Mk IA conversions; two 20mm Hispano cannon and four .303in Brownings.
Mk I (P.R.): Types 'A'–'D'; Photo-reconnaissance; Mk I conversions; later redesignated P.R.Mk III.
Mk IIA: Modified Mk IA; integral armour; 1,175hp Merlin XII (750).
Mk IIB: Modified Mk IIA; two 20mm Hispano and four .303in Brownings (170).
Mk IIC: Air-Sea Rescue; fifty Mk II conversions; later redesignated A.S.R.II; eight .303in Brownings.
Mk III: Several experimental conversions; 1,390hp Merlin XX; also Merlin 60 and 61.
Total Production: 20,351 (all Marks).
Remarks: First models of long and illustrious Spitfire line entered service August 1938; equipped 10 sqns by outbreak of WWII, 19 by beginning of Battle of Britain, (latter action earning it undying fame); very few Mk IIs in Battle, first appeared in numbers in Fighter Command's first 'lean towards France' in December 1940; bore brunt of early 'Rhubarbs' (cross-Channel offensive sweeps) until replaced by Mk V; withdrawn from front-line sqns, but Mks I and II continued to serve in many secondary roles, inc ASR (6 sqns Mk IIC), training, and communications; altogether operated by 62 RAF and Commonwealth fighter sqns.

Manufacturer: Supermarine.
Model: Spitfire L.F. Mk VB.
Type: Low-altitude fighter.
Power Plant: One 1,470hp Rolls-Royce Merlin 45M, 50M or 55M.
Performance:
maximum speed at sea level 332mph (534km/hr).
maximum speed at 6,000ft (1,829m) 357mph (574km/hr).
cruising speed 272mph (438km/hr).
maximum range 470 miles (756km).
initial rate of climb 4,750ft/min (1,448m/min).
service ceiling: 35,500ft (10,820m).
Weights:
empty 5,050lb (2,291kg).
loaded 6,650lb (3,016kg).
Dimensions:
wing span (clipped): 32ft 2in (9.80m).
length 29ft 11in (9.11m).
height 9ft 11in (3.02m).
wing area (clipped): 231sq ft (21.46sq m).
Armament: Two 20mm Hispano cannon; four .303in Browning guns; some modified to carry max bomb load of 500lb (227kg).
Crew: 1.
In Service: Australia (245 Mk VC, 410 Mk VIII), Canada, Egypt (12 Mk VC), France (FAF, FFAF, Mk VB/C), Germany (5+ captured, inc one Mk.F.VB experimentally fitted with Daimler-Benz DB 605A), Great Britain (RAF/FAA 100 Mk V), Greece (Mk VB/C), Italy (ICoAF Mk VB), New Zealand, Portugal (48+ Mk VB), South Africa, Turkey (Mk VB), USA (100+ Mk VB/C, 7 Mk VIII), USSR (143 Mk VB).
Variants (with no. built):
Mk IV: 1,735hp Rolls-Royce Griffon IIB (experimental prototype version only) later modified to prototypes Mk XII and Mk XX).
P.R.Mk IV: Unarmed photo-reconnaissance Mk V (Type 'D') version; some tropicalised (229).
Mk VA: (F.VA and L.F.VA; medium and low altitude versions respectively); Mk II development; eight .303in Brownings; Merlin 45 (94).
Mk VB: F.VB and L.F.VB; as VA with two Hispanos and four Brownings; Supermarine-built (3,783); Westland-built (140).
Mk VC: (F.VC, L.F.VC and H.F.VC medium, low and high altitude versions respectively); as Mk VA but with 'universal' wing allowing for 'A' or 'B'-type armament (as above) or four 20mm Hispanos; Supermarine-built (1,952); Westland-built (495).
P.R.Mk V: Photo-reconnaissance (Type 'C') version; later redesignated P.R.Mk IV, some converted to Types 'E' and 'F' (15).
H.F.Mk VI: As H.F.Mk V with pressurised cabin; Merlin 47 and extended wing (100).
Mk VII: F.VII and H.F.VII; redesigned Mk VI with Merlin 61, 64, 71 or 71S (140).
P.R.Mk VII: Photo-reconnaissance Mk V service conversions; eight .303in Brownings.
Mk VIII: F.VIII, L.F.VIII, H.F.VIII; modified Mk VII; unpressurised; all tropicalised (1,658).
Mk VIII Trainer: Post-war 2-seat trainer; armament optional; Mk VIII conversions.
Total Production: 20,351 (all Marks).
Remarks: Mk V most numerous Spitfire variant, entered service Feb 1941, equipped over one hundred RAF and Commonwealth fighter sqns, and many foreign units; backbone of RAF's cross-Channel offensive sweeps during critical 1941 and early 1942 period until appearance of Mk IX; by Aug 1942 three sqns Mk V operational in Western Desert; subsequent extensive Mediterranean service (Mks V and VIII) with many AFs; 1943 served in Australia (defence of Darwin) and Burma; 30 sqns operated tropicalised Mk VIII in Middle and Far East; Soviet Spitfire Vs flown in defence of Moscow; also equipped Italian Co-Belligerent AF units.
Colour Reference: Plate 77: Supermarine Spitfire Mk VB (AB502) IR.G flown by Wg Cdr Ian Richard Gleed, DFC, CO No 244 Wing, Desert Air Force, Tunisia, April 1943; standard Middle East finish; Abouqir filter; in addition to distinctive Wing Commander's markings (pennant beneath cockpit and initials (IR.G) in place of normal squadron code), AB502 also carried Gleed's personal 'Figaro the Cat' emblem on starboard side of fuselage below windscreen; 'Widge' Gleed failed to return from patrol Cap Bon area, 16 April 1943 (shot down by Messerschmitt Bf 109s of JG 77); 'Figaro' panel later recovered from crash-site and now in possession RAF Museum Hendon.
Plates 78, 79: Supermarine Spitfire H.F.VIII (JF404) GZ.M of No 32 Squadron, RAF, Foggia-Main, Italy, April 1944; Aero-Vee filter; note extended wingtips, enlarged fin and rudder, reduced span ailerons; special high-altitude finish comprising medium sea grey upper surfaces, PRU-blue undersides; no underwing roundels.

Manufacturer: Supermarine.
Model: Spitfire F.Mk IX.
Type: Fighter/fighter-bomber.
Power Plant: One 1,565hp Rolls-Royce Merlin 61 or one 1,650hp Merlin 63.
Performance:
maximum speed at 25,000ft (7,620m) 408mph (655km/hr).
cruising speed 324mph (521km/hr).
maximum range 980 miles (1,576km).
initial rate of climb 3,950ft/min (1,204m/min).
service ceiling 43,000ft (12,106m).
Weights:
empty 5,610lb (2,545kg).
maximum 9,500lb (4,309kg).
Dimensions:
wing span 36ft 10in (11.22m).
length 31ft 0in (9.46m).
height 12ft 7¾in (3.85m).
wing area 242sq ft (22.48sq m).
Armament: Two 20mm Hispano cannon and four .303 guns; some modified to carry max bomb load of 1,000lb (454kg).
Crew: 1.
In Service: Australia, Canada, Great Britain (RAF/FAA), New Zealand, South Africa, USA (16 Mk IX, 8 P.R.Mk XI), USSR (1,186 L.F.Mk IX, 2 H.F.Mk IX).
Variants (with no. built):
Mk IX: F.IX, L.F.IX, H.F.IX; medium, low and high altitude versions respectively; modified Mk V with strengthened engine mounting for Merlin 61 series; Supermarine-built (561); Westland-built (5,104).
Mk IXE: F.IXE, L.F.IXE, H.F.IXE; versions as above, but with 'E'-type wing with two 20mm Hispano cannon and two .5in Browning machine-guns; production figures included in Mk IX totals above.
Mk IX Trainer: Post-war 2-seat trainer; armament optional; Mk IX conversions.
P.R.Mk IX: Unarmed photo-reconnaissance; service modification of Mk IX.
P.R.Mk X: Unarmed photo-reconnaissance; pressurised cabin; Merlin 77 (16).
P.R.Mk XI: Unarmed photo-reconnaissance; modified Mk IX (309 tropicalised) (471).
Total Production: 20,351 (all variants).
Remarks: Spitfire Mk IX entered service June 1942, initially interim answer to Luftwaffe's Focke Wulf Fw 190, but eventually equipped nearly 100 RAF and Commonwealth fighter sqns; at war's end (May 1945) still flown by eight UK home-defence sqns, five 2nd TAF sqns in Europe (destroyed several Me 262 jets), and 22 sqns of the Desert and Balkan AFs; supplied in large numbers to USSR; also to USAAF; extensive post-war Commonwealth and foreign use.

Manufacturer: Supermarine.
Model: Spitfire F. Mk XIV.
Type: Interceptor fighter/fighter-bomber.
Power Plant: One 2,035hp Rolls-Royce Griffon 65 or 66.
Performance:
maximum speed at sea level 375mph (603km/hr).
maximum speed at 26,000ft (7,925m) 448mph (721km/hr).
cruising speed 362mph (582km/hr).
initial rate of climb 4,580ft/min (1,396m/hr).
time to 20,000ft (6,096m) 7min 0sec.
service ceiling 43,000ft (13,106m).
Weights:
loaded 9,000lb (4,082kg).
maximum 10,280lb (4,663kg).
Dimensions:
wing span 36ft 10in (11.22m).
length 32ft 8in (9.95m).
height 12ft 8in (3.86m).
wing area 244sq ft (22.67sq m).
Armament: Two 20mm Hispano Mk II cannon; two .5in Browning machine-guns; provision for one 500lb (227kg) bomb or Mk IX rocket projectiles.
Crew: 1.
In Service: Australia, Canada, Great Britain, New Zealand.
Variants (with no. built):
Mk XII: Rolls-Royce Griffon III or VI; clipped wing, faired engine cowling (100).
P.R.Mk XIII: Photo-reconnaissance; eighteen Mk V conversions; Merlin 32; four .303in Brownings.
F.Mk XIV/XIVE: Modified Mk VIII; universal or 'E'-type wing; lengthened nose; increased fin and rudder area; some with all-round vision canopy (527).
F.R.Mk XIV/XIVE: Fighter reconnaissance; modified F.Mk XIV; all with cut-down rear fuselage and all-round vision canopy (430).
L.F.Mk XVI: Low-altitude fighter; 1,580hp (Packard-built) Merlin 266-engined Mk IX (1,054).
F./F.R.Mk XVIII: Fighter (100) and fighter-reconnaissance (200) developments of Mk XIV; redesigned wing (300).
P.R.M XIX: Unarmed photo-reconnaissance; modified Mk XIV; most with pressurised cabin and tropicalised (225).
F.21, 22, 24: Post-war fighter variants (454).
Total Production: 20,351 (all Marks).
Remarks: Mks XIV, XVI first major production models of Griffon-engined, last of Merlin-engined, Spitfires respectively; Mk XIV entered sqn service January 1944, was among first RAF fighters in action against German V1s, claimed 300+ 'Flying Bombs' during four-month offensive; subsequently served with 2nd TAF on Continent (20 sqns); scored first German Me 262 jet to be destroyed by Allies; about to enter service in Far East as war ended; Mk XVI equipped 27 UK-based sqns (plus 7 AAC sqns), served as ground-attack fighter with 2nd TAF (operated by 11 sqns at war's end); both Marks saw post-war foreign as well as RAF service.

Manufacturer: Supermarine.
Model: Seafire L.F. Mk III.
Type: Low-altitude carrier-borne fighter/fighter-bomber.
Power Plant: One 1,583hp Rolls-Royce Merlin 55M or 1,645hp Merlin 32.

Performance:
maximum speed at 6,000ft (1,829m) 341mph (549km/hr).
maximum range 770 miles (1,239km).
initial rate of climb 3,250ft/min (990m/min).
service ceiling 32,000ft (9,754m).
Weights:
empty 5,450lb (2,472kg).
maximum 8,600 (3,900kg).
Dimensions:
wing span 36ft 10in (11.22m).
length 29ft 11in (9.11m).
height 9ft 11in (3.02m).
wing area 231sq ft (21.46sq m).
Armament: Two 20mm Hispano Mk II cannon; four .303in Browning machine-guns; provision for one 500lb (227kg) or two 250lb (113kg) bombs or eight 60lb (27kg) rocket projectiles.
Crew: 1.
In Service: Great Britain (FAA).
Variants (with no. built):
Prototype: One Spitfire Mk VB conversion with deck-arrester hook.
Mk IB: 166 Spitfire VB conversions; Rolls-Royce Merlin 45 or 46; two Hispanos and four Brownings.
Mk IIC: (F.Mk IIC, L.(F.)Mk IIC and F.R.Mk IIC; medium, low altitude and reconnaissance-fighter versions respectively); Spitfire Mk VC conversions with 'Universal' wing; Supermarine-built (262); Westland-built (110).
Mk III: (F.Mk III, L.(F.)Mk III and F.R.Mk III); as Mk IIC variants above, with folding wings; Westland-built (870); Cunliffe-Owen built (350).
Mk III (Hybrid): Westland-built model with normal non-folding wings; Merlin 55; redesignated as L.(F.)Mk IIC (30).
Mk XV, XVII, 45, 46, 47: Griffon-engined post-war variants (786).
Total Production: 2,408 (all variants).
Remarks: Entered service June 1942; participated Operation 'Torch' Allied invasion of North Africa (November 1942), scoring first victories against Vichy French D.520s; subsequent landings at Salerno and invasion of Southern France; also operated from Normandy beach-head, June–July 1944, and in attacks on 'Tirpitz' in Norway; by 1945 equipped 8 sqns in Far Eastern waters; participated invasions of Rangoon and Penang; escorted strikes against Japanese in East Indies, South-Western, and Central Pacific and, in closing weeks of war, over Japan itself.

Manufacturer: Vickers.
Model: Vildebeest IV.
Type: Torpedo-bomber.
Power Plant: One 825hp Bristol Perseus VIII.
Performance:
maximum speed at 5,000ft (1,524m) 156mph (251km/hr).
normal range 1,625 miles (2,615km).
initial rate of climb 840ft/min (256m/min).
service ceiling 19,000ft (5,791m).
Weights:
empty 4,724lb (2,142kg).
maximum 8,500lb (3,856kg).
Dimensions:
wing span 49ft 0in (14.94m).
length 37ft 8in (11.48m).
height 14ft 8in (4.47m).
wing area 728sq ft (67.63sq m).
Crew: 2–3.
In Service: Great Britain, New Zealand (27 Mk III), Spain (Navy).
Variants (with no. built):
Prototypes (inc one private venture) (2).
Mks I, II: Pegasus-engined pre-war production models (39).
Mk III: 3-seat version (125).
Mk IV: Cowled engine; three-blade Rotol propeller (18).
Spanish Vildebeest: Floatplane; licence-built by CASA (25).
Total Production: 209.
Remarks: Obsolete by beginning of WWII, but performed gallantly in defence of Singapore, Dec 1941, and subsequent retreat through East Indies, in which all aircraft lost; also served on Ceylon 1941–42.

Manufacturer: Vickers.
Model: Vincent.
Type: General-purpose.
Power Plant: One 635hp Bristol Pegasus IIM3.
Performance:
maximum speed at 5,000ft (1,524m) 142mph (229km/hr).
maximum range 1,250 miles (2,012km).
initial rate of climb 765ft/min (233m/min).
service ceiling 19,000ft (5,791m).
Weights:
empty 4,229lb (1,918kg).
maximum 8,100lb (3,674kg).

Dimensions:
wing span 49ft 0in (14.94m).
length 36ft 8in (11.17m).
height 17ft 9in (5.41m).
wing area 728sq ft (67.63sq m).
Armament: One .303in Vickers gun forward; one .303in Lewis gun aft; bomb load 1,000lb (454kg).
Crew: 3.
In Service: Great Britain.
Variants (with no. built):
Prototype: Converted Vildebeest Mk I (1).
Production model, inc both new airframes and Vildebeest conversions (196).
Total Production: 197.
Remarks: Vildebeest development for Middle East general-purpose duties; saw action against Italians in East Africa, 1940–41, and during Iraqi rebellion, May–June 1941.

Manufacturer: Vickers.
Model: Valentia.
Type: Troop-carrier.
Power Plant: Two 635hp Bristol Pegasus IIM3.
Performance:
maximum speed at 5,000ft (1 524m) 120mph (193km/hr).
cruising speed 117mph (188km/hr).
range 800 miles (1,287km).
initial rate of climb 700ft/min (213m/min).
service ceiling 16,250ft (4,953m).
Weights:
empty 10,994lb (4,987kg).
maximum 19,500lb (8,845kg).
Dimensions:
wing span 87ft 4in (26.62m).
length 59ft 6in (18.13m).
height 17ft 9in (5.41m).
wing area 2,178sq ft (202.34sq m).
Armament: Optional underwing bomb-racks; max load 2,200lb (998kg).
Crew/Accommodation: 2/22.
In Service: Great Britain.
Variants (with no. built):
Prototype: Re-engined Victoria

Mk V.
Victoria Mk VI: Pegasus-engined Victoria Mk V airframe (conversion 1).
Valentia Mk I: As above; structural improvements (conversion 2).
(Total Victoria Mk VI, Valentina Mk I conversions: 54).
Valentia Mk I: Production Model; (660hp Pegasus IIL3 or 635hp Pegasus IIM3) (28).
Total Production: 82.
Remarks: Middle East troop-transport; entered service 1934; participated in evacuation of Habbaniyah during Iraqi rebellion, May 1941; night-bomber in Western Desert; communications role until 1943.

Manufacturer: Vickers.
Model: Wellesley I.
Type: Medium bomber.
Power Plant: One 925hp Bristol Pegasus XX.
Performance:
maximum speed at sea level 178mph (286km/hr).
cruising speed 188mph (303km/hr).
maximum range 2,590 miles (4,168km).
initial rate of climb 1,200ft/min (366m/min).
service ceiling 33,000ft (10,058m).
Weights:
empty 6,369lb (2,889kg).
maximum 11,100lb (5,035kg).
Dimensions:
wing span 74ft 7in (22.73m).
length 39ft 3in (11.96m).
height 12ft 4in (3.76m).
wing area 630sq ft (58.5sq m).
Armament: One .303in Vickers gun forward; one .303 Vickers 'K' gun in rear cockpit; max bomb load 2,000lb (907kg).
Crew: 2.
In Service: Great Britain.
Variants (with no. built):
Prototype: Private venture (1).
Mk I: Standard service variant (inc

6 conversions to special long-range model with Pegasus XXII) (176).
Mk II: Service designation to distinguish Mk I models fitted with continuous (inter-cockpit) glazed canopy.
Total Production: 177.
Remarks: First of Vickers geodetic designs in RAF service; broke world's long-distance record 1938; early WWII operated against Italian forces in East African campaigns, Italian Somaliland and Western Desert; subsequently (1941) employed on maritime reconnaissance duties.

Manufacturer: Vickers.
Model: Wellington IC.
Type: Medium bomber.
Power Plant: Two 1,000hp Bristol Pegasus XVIII.
Performance:
maximum speed at 15,500ft (4,724m) 235mph (378km/hr).
maximum range 2,550 miles (4,104km).
initial rate of climb 1,120ft/min (341m/min).
service ceiling 18,000ft (5,486m).
Weights:
empty 18,556lb (8,417kg).
maximum 28,500lb (12,928kg).
Dimensions:
wing span 86ft 2in (26.26m).
length 64ft 7in (19.68m).
height 17ft 5in (5.31m).
wing area 840sq ft (78.04sq m).
Armament: Two .303in machine-guns each in power-operated nose and tail turrets; two manually-operated beam guns; max bomb load: 4,500lb (2,041kg).
Crew: 5–6.
In Service: Australia, Canada, Germany, (evaluation), Great Britain.
Variants (with no. built):
Prototype (1).
Mk I: Initial production model; at least 11 converted to DWI (magnetic mine destroyers) (181).

Mk IA: Nash and Thompson gun turrets; at least 6 converted to DWI (187).
C.Mk IA: Transport conversion of above; later designated Mk XV.
Mk IC: Most numerous Pegasus-powered variant; ventral turret deleted, replaced by beam guns; 138 delivered as torpedo-bombers; 1 converted to DWI (2,685).
C.Mk IC: Transport conversion of above; later designated Mk XVI.
Mk II: Two 1,145hp Rolls-Royce Merlin X (401).
Mk III: Two 1,375hp Bristol Hercules III or 1,425hp Hercules XI; introduction of 4-gun tail-turret (1,519).
Mk IV: Two 1,050hp Pratt & Whitney Twin Wasps (220).
Mk V: High-altitude bomber; pressurised; Hercules VIII or XIs; 2 prototypes, 1 production (3).
Mk VI: As Mk V; 1,600hp Merlin 60 or 62 (inc 18 Mk V conversions) (64).
Mk VII: Merlin XX-powered conversion; prototype only.
Total Production: 11,462 (all Marks).
Remarks: Mainstay of Bomber Command's early night offensive; equipped 6 sqns on outbreak of war, rising to 21 during Winter 1941–42; first operation against German naval units 4 Sept 1939; provided over half the attacking force for first 1,000-bomber raid on Cologne, 30 May 1942; phased out late 1943, having delivered nearly half a million tons of bombs on Axis targets in Europe; at least one known to have been captured intact and evaluated by Luftwaffe.

Manufacturer: Vickers.
Model: Wellington G.R.Mk VIII.
Type: General reconnaissance/torpedo-bomber.
Power Plant: 1,050hp Bristol Pegasus XVIII.
Performance:

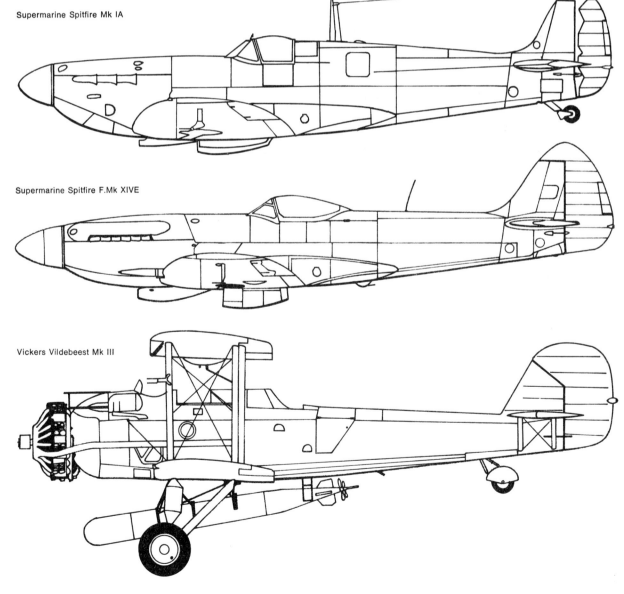

Supermarine Spitfire Mk IA

Supermarine Spitfire F.Mk XIVE

Vickers Vildebeest Mk III

Order of Battle April-May 1945

BRITISH PACIFIC FLEET (Okinawa Support Operations)

TF 57 British Carrier Force

TG 57.2 First Aircraft Carrier Squadron

Fleet Carriers:

HMS *Indomitable*	857 Sqn.	15 Grumman Avenger
	1839 Sqn.	15 Grumman Hellcat
	1844 Sqn.	14 Grumman Hellcat
HMS *Victorious*	849 Sqn.	14 Grumman Avenger
	1834 Sqn.	19 Vought Corsair
	1836 Sqn.	18 Vought Corsair
	Ship's Flight	2 Supermarine Walrus
HMS *Illustrious*	854 Sqn.	16 Grumman Avenger
	1830 Sqn.	18 Vought Corsair
	1833 Sqn.	18 Vought Corsair
HMS *Indefatigable*	820 Sqn.	20 Grumman Avenger
	887 Sqn.	20 Supermarine Seafire
	894 Sqn.	20 Supermarine Seafire
	1770 Sqn.	9 Fairey Firefly
HMS *Formidable**	848 Sqn.	15 Grumman Avenger
	1841 Sqn.	18 Vought Corsair
	1842 Sqn.	18 Vought Corsair

* (Replaced HMS *Illustrious* mid-April.)

TF 112 British Fleet Train

TG 112.2 Logistic Support Group:

Escort Carriers:

HMS *Speaker*	1840 Sqn.	24 Grumman Hellcat

(Fleet Train Fighter Cover to 10 May, 1945)

HMS *Ruler*	885 Sqn.	24 Grumman Hellcat

(Fleet Train Fighter Cover from 9 May, 1945)

HMS *Slinger*	Replenishment
HMS *Striker*	Replenishment
HMS *Chaser*	Ferry Duties
HMS *Fencer*	Ferry Duties

Light Fleet Carrier:

HMS *Unicorn*	Repair and Maintenance

Arrived/en route BPF prior VJ-Day

Fleet Carriers:

HMS *Implacable*	828 Sqn.	21 Grumman Avenger
	801 Sqn.	24 Supermarine Seafire
	880 Sqn.	24 Supermarine Seafire
	1771 Sqn.	12 Fairey Firefly

Light Fleet Carriers:

HMS *Colossus*	
HMS *Glory*	
HMS *Venerable*	11th Aircraft Carrier Squadron
HMS *Vengeance*	

Escort Carriers:

HMS *Arbiter*	Replenishment
HMS *Reaper*	Ferry Duties
HMS *Vindex*	Ferry Duties

BRITISH EAST INDIES FLEET

HMS *Ameer*	804 Sqn.	20 Grumman Hellcat
	888 Sqn.	4 Grumman Hellcat PR.II
	1700 Sqn.	1 Supermarine Sea Otter
HMS *Attacker*		
(August)	879 Sqn.	30 Supermarine Seafire
HMS *Emperor*	800 Sqn.	16 Grumman Hellcat
	1700 Sqn.	1 Supermarine Sea Otter
HMS *Empress*		
(August)	896 Sqn.	24 Grumman Hellcat
HMS *Hunter*		
(August)	807 Sqn.	30 Supermarine Seafire
	1700 Sqn.	1 Supermarine Sea Otter
HMS *Khedive*	808 Sqn.	24 Grumman Hellcat
HMS *Shah*	800 Sqn.	8 Grumman Hellcat
	845 Sqn.	4 Grumman Avenger
	851 Sqn.	8 Grumman Avenger
HMS *Stalker*	809 Sqn.	30 Supermarine Seafire

(Arrived/en route British East Indies Fleet prior VJ-Day)

HMS *Pursuer*	898 Sqn.	24 Grumman Hellcat
HMS *Searcher*	882 Sqn.	24 Grumman Wildcat VI
HMS *Activity*		
HMS *Begum*		
HMS *Fencer*	Assault and Fighter Escort	
HMS *Smiter*		
HMS *Trumpeter*		
HMS *Trouncer*	Ferry Duties	

maximum speed 235mph (378km/hr).
maximum range 2,550 miles (4,104km).
service ceiling 19,000ft (5,790m).
Weights:
empty 21,118lb (9,579kg).
maximum 30,000lb (13,080kg).

Dimensions:
wing span 86ft 2in (26.26m).
length 64ft 7in (19.68m).
height 17ft 8in (5.38m).
wing area 840sq ft (78.04sq m).
Armament: As Mk IC, but with two 420lb (191kg) depth-charges or two torpedoes (day) version or

---

Leigh-light (night) version.
Crew: 6–7.
In Service: Australia, Canada, Great Britain.
Variants (with no. built):
Mk VIII: Coastal Command version of basic Mk IC bomber, ASV Mk II radar; produced in both day (bomber and torpedo-bomber) and night (Leigh-light) variants (394).
Mk IX: Troop-carrier version of Mk IA (1).
Mk X: Medium bomber; strengthened for higher gross weight; two 1,675hp Hercules VI or XVIs; most numerous variant (3,803).
G.R.Mk XI: Coastal Command daylight version of Mk X; ASV Mk II or III radar (180).
G.R.Mk XII: Anti-submarine variant of above; ASV Mk III radar and Leigh-light (58).
G.R.Mk XIII: 1,735hp Hercules XVII-powered daylight torpedo-bomber with ASV Mk II radar (844).
G.R.Mk XIV: Leigh-light and ASV Mk III radar-equipped night version of above (841).
C.Mk XV: Mk IA unarmed transport conversion.
C.Mk XVI: C.Mk IC transport conversion.
T.Mk XVII: Night-fighter crew trainer conversion of Mk XI.
T.Mk XVIII: Flying classroom; Mosquito-type nose with radar (80).
T.Mk XIX: Post-war basic trainer; conversion of Mk X.
Total Production: 11,462 (all Marks).
Remarks: G.R.Mk VIII entered service Spring 1942; first of five radar-equipped Coastal Command variants; remained in service until end of war, equipping fourteen UK-based sqns; Mk X bomber served in Middle and Far East; also employed by Transport Command (Mks XV and XVI), and for night-reconnaissance duties with 2nd TAF; altogether comprised largest total of any British bomber ever produced.
Colour Reference: Plate 80: Vickers Wellington Mk X (HZ950) 'Z' of No 99 'Madras Presidency' Squadron on detachment from Jessore, India, to Burma for emergency supply-dropping duties with Troop Carrier Command during Japanese siege of Imphal, May–June 1944; standard night bomber finish, SEAC-style roundels.

Manufacturer: Vickers.
Model: Warwick A.S.R. Mk I.
Type: Air/sea-rescue.
Power Plant: Two 1,850hp Pratt & Whitney Double Wasp R–2800–S1A4–G.
Performance:
maximum speed at 3,600ft (1,097m) (224mph (360km/hr).
range 2,300 miles (3,701km).
initial rate of climb 660ft/min (201m/min).
time to 10,000ft (3,048m) 16min 6sec.
service ceiling 21,500ft (6,553m).
Weights:
loaded 45,000lb (20,412kg).
Dimensions:
wing span 96ft 8½in (29.47m).
length 72ft 3in (22.02m).
height 18ft 6in (5.56m).
wing area 1,006sq ft (93.46sq m).
Armament: Twin .303in guns in nose and dorsal turrets; four .303in guns in tail turret.
Crew: 7.
In Service: Great Britain.
Variants (with no. built):

Prototypes (2).
B.Mk I: Initial bomber version (16).
C.Mk I: Civil transports (modified B.Mk Is) transferred to RAF (14).
Bomber/A.S.R.: Interim A.S.R. version (inc conversions) (40).
A.S.R. (Stage A): Equipped with lifeboat Mk I (10).
A.S.R. (Stage B): As above plus ASV radar and tail turret (20).
A.S.R. (Stage C): Subsequently designated A.S.R. Mk I.
A.S.R. Mk I: Finalised A.S.R. version; lifeboat Mks I or II (56).
B.Mk I: Prototype (1).
G.R.Mk II: 2,500hp Bristol Centaurus VI (inc fourteen G.R.Mk II Met) (132).
C.Mk III: Transport/freighter version (100).
C.Mk IV: One transport conversion of Mk II.
G.R.Mk V: Development of G.R.Mk II with Leigh-light equipment; two beam guns in lieu of dorsal turret (210).
A.S.R.Mk VI: As Mk I with Double Wasp R–2800–2SBGs (94).
Total Production: 845 (inc one experimental).
Remarks: Designed as twin-engined heavy bomber parallel to highly successful Wellington; superseded by RAF's four-engined heavies; instead served in air/sea-rescue role, equipped 7 UK-based Coastal Command sqns, 4 in Middle East and 1 in Far East; also employed general-reconnaissance (3 sqns) and transport (5 sqns) duties.

Manufacturer: Westland.
Model: Wapiti III.
Type: General-purpose.
Power Plant: One Bristol Jupiter VIIIF or one Armstrong Siddeley Jaguar VI.
Performance:
maximum speed at 5,000ft (1,525m) 140mph (225km/hr).
maximum range 660 miles (1,060km).
time to 5,000ft (1,525m) 4min 18sec.
service ceiling 20,600ft (6,300m).
Weights:
empty 3,180lb (1,442kg).
loaded 5,400lb (2,450kg).
Dimensions:
wing span 46ft 5in (14.1m).
length 32ft 6in (9.9m).
height 11ft 10in (3.6m).
wing area 488sq ft (45.4sq m).
Armament: One fixed forward-firing .303in Vickers gun; one .303in Lewis gun in rear cockpit; max bomb load 580lb (263kg).
Crew: 2.
In Service: Australia (8 Mk IA, 20 Mk IIA), Canada (25 ex-RAF), China (4 Mk VIII), Great Britain, South Africa (31 Mk III).
Variants (with no. built):
Prototype (1).
Mks I, IA, II, IIA: Pre-war RAF/RAAF/RCAF models (483).
Mk III: South African variant. Westland-built (Jupiter IXF) (4); S.A.A.F.-built (Jaguar VI) (27).
Mk IV: Project only.
Mks V–VI: Pre-war RAF models (51).
Mk VII: Wallace Prototype.
Mk VIII: Chinese export variant (4).
Total Production: 570.
Remarks: Retired from operational service by outbreak of WWII in all but SAAF; coastal reconnaissance duties 1939–40; subsequently served in East Africa in communications role.

Manufacturer: Westland.
Model: Wallace II.
Type: General-purpose.
Power Plant: One 680hp Bristol

Pegasus IV.
Performance:
maximum speed at 15,000ft (4,572m) 158mph (254km/hr).
cruising speed 135mph (217km/hr).
range 470 miles (756km).
initial rate of climb 1,350ft/min (411m/min).
service ceiling 24,100ft (7,346m).
Weights:
empty 3,840lb (1,742kg).
loaded 5,750lb (2,608kg).
Dimensions:
wing span 46ft 5in (14.15m).
length 34ft 2in (10.41m).
height 11ft 6in (3.50m).
wing area 488sq ft (45.34sq m).
Armament: One fixed forward-firing Vickers gun; one Lewis gun; max bomb load 580lb (263kg).
Crew: 2.
In Service: Great Britain.
Variants (with no. built):
Prototype: Private venture; Wapiti VII (1).
Mk I: Twelve Wapiti conversions; lengthened fuselage, wheel spats; 570hp Pegasus IIM3; initial production (8).
Mk II: Modified Mk I; enclosed canopy (104).
Total Production: 113 (+12 Wapiti conversions).
Remarks: Served mainly as target-tugs, 1939–43; also general-purpose duties.

Manufacturer: Westland.
Model: Lysander Mk III.
Type: Army co-operation.
Power Plant: One 870hp Bristol Mercury XX.
Performance:
maximum speed at sea level 209mph (336km/hr).
maximum speed at 5,000ft (1,524m) 212mph (341km/hr).
range 600 miles (965km).
time to 5,000ft (1,524m) 4min 6sec.
service ceiling 21,500ft (6,553m).
Weights:
empty 4,365lb (1,980kg).
loaded 6,318lb (2,865kg).
Dimensions:
wing span 50ft 0in (15.24m).
length 30ft 6in (9.29m).
height 14ft 6in (4.42m).
wing area 260sq ft (24.15sq m).
Armament: Two fixed .303in Browning machine-guns mounted in wheel spats; two .303in Browning machine-guns in rear cockpit; sixteen 20lb (9kg) bombs, or four 112lb (51kg), or 120lb (54kg) bombs, or two 250lb (113kg) bombs on rear fuselage racks and detachable stub wing carriers.
Crew: 2.
In Service: Australia, Canada, Egypt (19 Mk I, 1 Mk III), Eire (6 Mk II), Finland (10 Mk I, 1 Mk II), France (FAF/FFAF), Great Britain (RAF/FAA), Portugal (8 Mk IIIA), South Africa, Turkey (36 Mk II), USA 3 Mk IIIA).
Variants (with no. built):
Prototypes (2).
Mk I: Initial production model, 890hp Mercury XII (169).
Mk II: 950hp Bristol Perseus XII, Westland-built (442).
Mk II: 905hp Canadian licence-built by National Steel Car Corp (75).
Mk III: Westland-built (367).
Mk III: Canadian licence-built (150).
Mk IIIA: Modified Mk III (347).
T.T.Mk I: Target-tug; fourteen Mk I conversions.
T.T.Mk II: Target-tug; five Mk II conversions.
T.T.Mk III: Target-tug; seven Mk I, sixteen Mk II, and twenty-eight Mk III conversions.

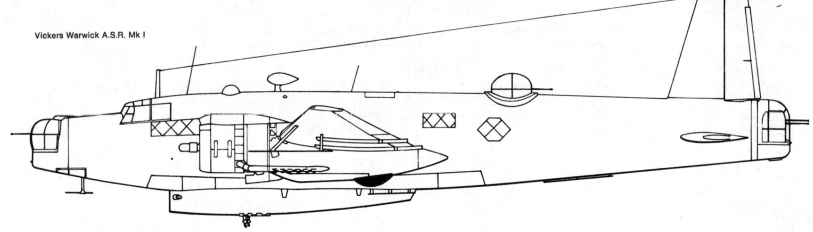

Vickers Warwick A.S.R. Mk I

T.T.Mk IIIA: Mk IIIA target-tug version (100).
Total Production: 1,652.
Remarks: Standard Army co-operation aircraft at outbreak of WWII, equipping 7 sqns; heavy losses during Battle of France (May–June 1940); subsequently served with four sqns in Middle East and two in Far East; widely employed UK and Canada as target-tugs; ASR and radar-calibration; equipped two 'Special Duties' sqns for clandestine operations in Occupied Europe 1941–44.

Manufacturer: Westland.
Model: Whirlwind.
Type: Long-range fighter/fighter-bomber.
Power Plant: Two 885hp Rolls-Royce Peregrine I.
Performance:
maximum speed at 15,000ft (4,572m) 360mph (579km/hr).
initial rate of climb 1,550ft/min (472m/min).
time to 15,000ft (4,572m) 5min 48sec.
service ceiling 30,000ft (9,144m).
Weights:
empty 8,310lb (3,770kg).
maximum 11,400lb (5,171kg).
Dimensions:
wing span 45ft 0in (13.72m).
length 32ft 6in (9.90m).
height 10ft 6in (3.30m).
wing area 250sq ft (23.23sq m).
Armament: Four fixed 20mm Hispano Mk I cannon in nose; two 250lb (113kg), or 500lb (227kg) bombs under wing.
Crew: 1.
In Service: Great Britain.
Variants (with no. built):
Prototypes: One experimentally fitted with twelve .303in Browning machine-guns (2).
Production model: From 1942 fitted with bomb racks (114).
Total Production: 116.
Remarks: RAF's first single-seat twin-engined fighter; delayed entry into service (July 1940) further exacerbated by power plant teething troubles; initially employed as long-range escort fighter (one sqn), subsequently modified as fighter-

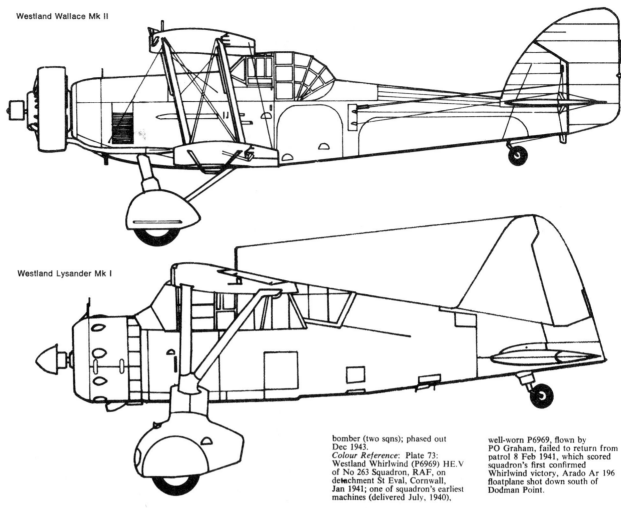

Westland Wallace Mk II

Westland Lysander Mk I

bomber (two sqns); phased out Dec 1943.
Colour Reference: Plate 73: Westland Whirlwind (P6969) HE.V of No 263 Squadron, RAF, on detachment St Eval, Cornwall, Jan 1941; one of squadron's earliest machines (delivered July, 1940),

well-worn P6969, flown by PO Graham, failed to return from patrol 8 Feb 1941, which scored squadron's first confirmed Whirlwind victory, Arado Ar 196 floatplane shot down south of Dodman Point.

HUNGARY

Manufacturer: Manfred Weiss.
Model: WM 16B Budapest II.
Type: Tactical reconnaissance.
Power Plant: One 860hp (licence-built) Gnome-Rhône 14K Mistral-Major.
Performance:
maximum speed 174mph (280km/hr).
Weights:
loaded 5,732lb (2,600kg).
Dimensions:
wing span 50ft 2¼in (15.30m).
length 31ft 11¾in (9.75m).
height 11ft 9½in (3.6m).
wing area 423.02sq ft (39.30sq m).
Crew: 2.
In Service: Hungary.
Variants (with no. built):
WM16A Budapest I: Prototype and initial production model; 2-seat tactical reconnaissance biplane; one 550hp (licence-built) Gnome-Rhône 9K Mistral (8)
WM 16B Budapest II: Re-engined WM 16A (4).
Total Production: 12.
Remarks: Designed to supplement 1928 Manfred Weiss licence-built Fokker C.V.–Ds in tactical reconnaissance role, prototypes of WM 16A/B indigenous derivatives first flown 1934–35 resp; produced in far fewer numbers, relegated second-line ancillary duties by close thirties before final withdrawal from service 1942, year prior eventual retirement last C.V.–D.

Manufacturer: Manfred Weiss.
Model: WM 21 Sólyom (Falcon).
Type: Reconnaissance.
Power Plant: One 870hp WM K-14.
Performance:
maximum speed 199mph (320km/hr).
cruising speed 171mph (275km/hr).
range 373 miles (600km).
time to 10,500ft (3,200m) 7min 0sec.
service ceiling 26,250ft (8,000m).
Weights:
empty 5,400lb (2,450kg).
maximum 7,750lb (3,450kg).

Manfred Weiss WM 21 Sólyom

Dimensions:
wing span upper 42ft 4in (12.9m).
wing span lower 30ft 10in (9.4m).
length 31ft7½in (9.64m).
height 11ft 5½in (3.5m).
wing area 352.31sq. ft (32.73sq m).
Armament: Two fixed forward-firing 7.9mm Gebauer machine-guns; one flexible 7.9mm Gebauer machine-gun in rear cockpit; provision for light bombs underwing.
Crew: 2.
In Service: Hungary.
Variants (with no. built):
WM 21 Sólyom: 2-seat reconnaissance biplane, Manfred Weiss, State Wagon Factory- and MAVAG-built (128).
Total Production: 128.
Remarks: One of number foreign-built developments based upon

highly successful Fokker C.V.–D, WM 21, evolved via WM-produced C.V.–D/WM 16 Budapest derivative, entered Hungarian AF service 1938; equipped number short-range reconnaissance sqns, upon Hungarian declaration of war on USSR (27 June 1941)), one of these accompanying Hungarian AF Brigade's advance into Soviet Union, July–Dec 1941; thereafter gradually relegated homeland second-line communications/training duties until withdrawn from service 1943.

Manufacturer: Repülögépgyàr.
Model: Levente II.
Type: Liaison/trainer.
Power Plant: One 105hp (MAVAG-built) Hirth HM 504A–2.
Performance:

maximum speed 112mph (180km/hr).
cruising speed 99mph (160km/hr).
normal range 404 miles (650km).
initial rate of climb 985ft/min (300m/min).
service ceiling 14,800ft (4,511m).
Weights:
empty 1,040lb (470kg).
loaded 1,655lb (750kg).
Dimensions:
wing span 31ft 0in (9.45m).
length 19ft 11½in (6.08m).
height 8ft 3¾in (2.53m).
wing area 145.31sq ft (13.5sq m).
Crew/Accommodation: 1/1.
In Service: Hungary.
Variants (with no. built):
Levente I: Initial prototype; para-sol-wing 2-seat primary trainer (1).
Levente II: Prototype and production model; modified Levente

I(100).
Total Production: 101
Remarks: Named after Hungarian national hero, prototype Levente I first flew Oct 1940; modified Levente II entered Hungarian AF service exactly three years later; intended for training role majority in fact assigned operational sqns, for liaison/communications duties; remained in use until cessation hostilities.

ITALY

Ambrosini S.A.I.207

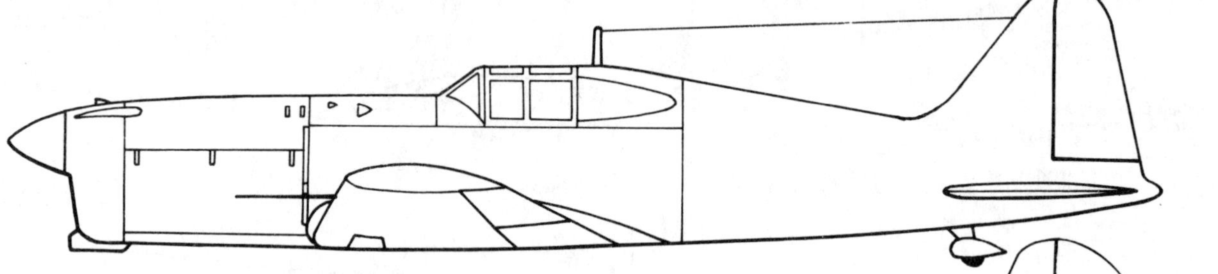

Breda Ba 65bis

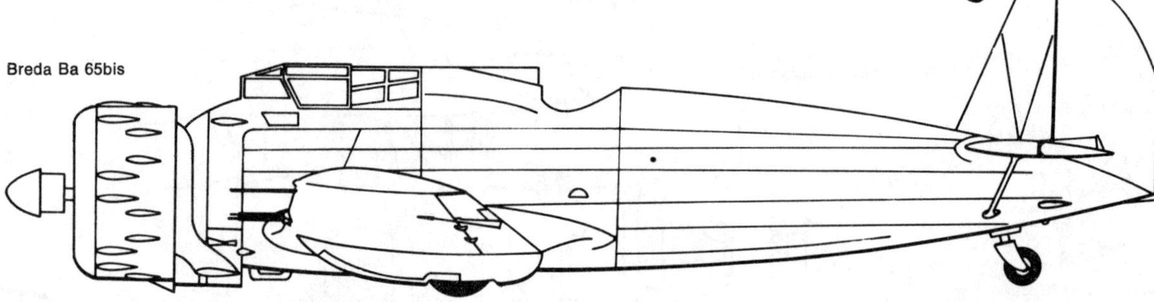

Manufacturer: Ambrosini.
Model: S.A.I.2S.
Type: Liaison/communications.
Power Plant: One 200hp Alfa Romeo 115-I.
Performance:
maximum speed 155mph (250 km/hr).
cruising speed 134mph (215km/hr).
maximum range 603 miles (970km).
service ceiling 19,685ft (6,000m).
Weights:
empty 1,958lb (888kg).
loaded 3,124lb (1,417kg).
Dimensions:
wing span 34ft 11in (10.64m).
length 25ft 6in (7.77m).
height 9ft 2in (2.8m).
wing area 193sq ft (17.93sq m).
Crew/Accommodation: 1/3.
In Service: Italy (IAF, RSIAF, ICoAF).
Variants (with no built):
S.A.I.2: Initial production model; 5-seat civil tourer; one 140hp Fiat A.54.
S.A.I.2S: S.A.I.2 development; 4-seat civil tourer; re-engined; wing slots and flaps (approx 4).
Remarks: Number S.A.I.2S, originally designed/built for 1937 Italian Air Races, impressed wartime military liaison/communications duties IAF, RSIAF and ICoAF; returned civil registry post-war, several still flying early sixties; other pre-war Ambrosini designs, 2-seat S.A.I.3/S.A.I.10, also reportedly used limited scale military liaison/'hack' roles.

Manufacturer: Ambrosini.
Model: S.A.I.207.
Type: Lightweight interceptor-fighter.
Power Plant: One 750hp Isotta-Fraschini Delta RC 40.
Performance:
maximum speed 388mph (625km/hr).
cruising speed 304mph (490km/hr).
normal/range 590 miles (950km).
time to 6,560ft (2,000m) 2min 19sec.
service ceiling 33,464ft (10,200m).
Weights:
empty 3,858lb (1,750kg).
loaded 5,324lb (2,415kg).
Dimensions:
wing span 29ft 6½in (9.0m).
length 26ft 3¾in (8.02m).
height 7ft 10½in (2.4m).
wing area 149.62sq ft (13.9sq m).
Armament: Two 12.7mm Breda-SAFAT machine-guns.
Crew: 1.
In Service: Italy.
Variants (with no. built):
S.A.I.7: Initial 2-seat light sports plane model; one 280hp Hirth HM 508D;fully faired streamlined windscreen (1).
S.A.I.7: 2-seat fighter trainer model; one 280hp Isotta-Fraschini Beta RC 10; orthodox canopy; increased dimensions (1).
S.A.I.107: Prototype; experimental single-seat lightweight fighter version; one 540hp Isotta-Fraschini Gamma; increased length (1).
S.A.I.207: Prototype and pre-production models; operational lightweight fighter version; uprated engine; armed (14).
S.A.I.403 Dardo (Dart): Prototype; improved S.A.I.207; one 750hp Isotta-Fraschini Delta RC 21/60; increased dimensions; modified vertical tail surfaces; various cannon and/or machine-gun armament for altn lightweight interceptor, general purpose, or long-range fighter versions (1).
Total Production: 18 (excl post-war).
Remarks: Developed from record-breaking pre-war S.A.I.7 light sports plane, S.A.I.207 first flown 1942; only thirteen pre-production models built (out of order for 2,000), three of which assigned operational fighter Stormo immediately prior Italian Armistice; none of superseding order for 3,000 S.A.I.403s completed; one S.A.I.7 trainer on strength RSIAF; production improved S.A.I.7 resumed post-war as S.7 and Supersette.

Manufacturer: Ansaldo.
Model: A.120 Ady.
Type: Reconnaissance/light bomber.
Power Plant: One 700hp Fiat A.24R.
Performance:
maximum speed 158mph (255km/hr).
time to 9,840ft (3,000m) 12min 28sec.
service ceiling 22,970ft (7,000m).
Weights:
empty 3,583lb (1,580kg).
loaded 6,261lb (2,840kg).
Dimensions:
wing span 45ft 5¼in (13.85m).
length 29ft 0in (8.84m).
height 10ft 6in (3.2m).
wing area 322.92sq ft (30.0sq m).
Armament: One or two fixed forward-firing Vickers machine-guns, one flexible Lewis gun in rear cockpit; provision for light bombs.
Crew: 2.
In Service: Lithuania.
Variants (with no. built):
A.120/120bis: Prototypes; 2-seat fighter-reconnaissance/reconnaissance versions; one 400hp Lorraine/Fiat A.20–A resp (2).
A.120 Ady: Production model; reconnaissance/light-bomber version; uprated engine; enlarged radiator; (number export orders, inc Austria, Lithuania) (57).
Total Production: 59.
Remarks: Prototypes first flown 1925; served IAF reconnaissance role late twenties/early thirties; long obsolete by outbreak WWII; export model still equipped 2 light-bomber sqns Lithuanian AF at time of Soviet annexation, Summer 1940.

Manufacturer: A.V.I.A.
Model: FL.3.
Type: Liaison.
Power Plant: One 80hp C.N.A. D-4.
Performance:
maximum speed 110mph (177km/hr).
cruising speed 93mph (150km/hr).
maximum range 509 miles (820km).
initial rate of climb 600ft/min (183m/min).
service ceiling 16,400ft (5,000m).
Weights:
empty 660lb (300kg).
loaded 1,157lb (525kg).
Dimensions:
wing span 32ft 3¾in (9.85m).
length 20ft 10¾in (6.36m).
height 5ft 7¼in (1.71m).
wing area 154.4sq ft (14.34sq m).
Crew/Accommodation: 1/1.
In Service: Germany, Italy (IAF, RSIAF, ICoAF).
Variants:
FL.3: Protype and production model(s); civil 2-seat light-plane; pre-war (A.V.I.A.) and post-war (Lombardi/Meteor) production.
Total Production: approx 400.
Remarks: Pre-war light sports-plane, number examples impressed military liaison role during WWII, particularly post-Armistice by RSIAF (27); also employed, minus propellers, as cargo-glider pilot trainers; but vast majority (accounting for well over half total 591 Italian civil-registered types requisitioned) seized by Germany.

Manufacturer: Breda.
Model: Ba 25.
Type: Trainer/liaison.
Power Plant: One 200hp Alfa Romeo Lynx.
Performance:
maximum speed 127mph (205km/hr).
cruising speed 100mph (160km/hr).
normal/range 250 miles (400 km).
time to 16,400ft (5,000m) 29min 0sec.
service ceiling 16,075ft (4,900m).
Weights:
empty 1,653lb (750kg).
loaded 2,205lb (1,000kg).
Dimensions:
wing span 32ft 9½in (10.0m).
length 26ft 3in (8.0m).
height 9ft 6¼in (2.9m).
wing area 269.1sq ft (25sq m).
Crew: 2.
In Service: Italy (IAF, RSIAF, ICoAF).
Variants:
Ba 25: 2-seat trainer version; one 240hp Alfa Romeo D2 Lynx; various altn power plants inc 230hp Walter Castor; some as single-seat advanced trainers.
Ba 25 idro: 2-seat floatplane version of Ba 25; enlarged rudder.
Total Production: approx 700.
Remarks: Standard thirties trainer (subject considerable export orders), used by Italian AF throughout WWII in number addn ancillary roles inc liaison/communications; remained in service both sides post-Armistice; several captured examples employed as unofficial 'hacks' by Allied sqns in Italy.

Manufacturer: Breda.
Model: Ba 39.
Type: Liaison.
Power Plant: One 140hp Colombo S.63.
Performance:
maximum speed 137mph (220km/hr).
maximum range 560 miles (900km).
time to 13,120ft (4,000m) 21min 0sec.
service ceiling 19,685ft (6,000m).
Weights:
empty 1,235lb (560kg).
loaded 1,852lb (840kg).
Dimensions:
wing span 34ft 2in (10.41m).
length 24ft 5in (7.44m).
height 9ft 8in (2.94m).
wing area 188.5 sq ft (17.51sq m).
Crew/Accommodation: 1/1.
In Service: Italy (IAF, RSIAF, ICoAF).
Variants (with no built):
Ba 33: Initial production model; 2-seat civil tourer; 120hp de Havilland Gipsy III.
Ba 33S: Modified Ba 33; single-seat. (Total Ba 33/S: 10+).
Ba 39: Improved Ba 33; re-engined; increased dimensions; wing slots and flaps (64).
Ba 42: Ba 39 development; one 180hp cowled Fiat A.70S.
Remarks: Popular pre-war sports tourer series, number examples (specifically Ba 39) employed military liaison/communications roles.

Manufacturer: Breda.
Model: Ba 44.
Type: Transport.
Power Plant: Two 200hp de Havilland Gipsy VI.
Performance:
maximum speed 124mph (200km/hr).
cruising speed 109mph (175km/hr).
normal range 372 miles (600km).
service ceiling 15,585ft (4,750m).
Weights:
empty 2,976lb (1,350kg).
loaded 4,784lb (2,170kg).
Dimensions:
wing span 43ft 8½in (13.32m).
length 34ft 2in (10.42m).
height 10ft 1in (3.1m).
wing area 431.3sq ft (40.07sq m).
Crew/Payload/Accommodation: 2/661lb (300kg)/6–8.
In Service: Italy.
Variants (with no. built):
Ba 44: Prototype; civil transport version; two 145hp Alfa Romeo Colombo S.63 (1).
Ba 44: Production model; as prototype; altn power plants—two de Havilland Gipsy Six, or two 205hp Walter Major (re-engined); (approx 14).
Total Production: approx 15.
Remarks: First flown 1934, majority Ba 44 airliners operated African colonial routes; several examples impressed military transport duties during Italian occupation of Albania, April 1939; similar small-scale employment opening months WWII.

Manufacturer: Breda.
Model: Ba 65.
Type: Ground-attack/reconnaissance.
Power Plant: One 900hp Isotta-Fraschini K.14.
Performance:
maximum speed at 16,400ft (5,000m) 258mph (415km/hr).
normal range 342 miles (550km).
time to 13,120ft (4,000m) 8min 40sec.
service ceiling 25,590ft (7,800m).
Weights:
empty 4,290lb (1,950kg).
loaded 5,512lb (2,500kg).
Dimensions:
wing span 39ft 0½in (11.9m).
length 31ft 6in (9.6m).
height 10ft 6in (3.2m).
wing area 252.95sq ft (23.5sq m).
Armament: Two 12.7mm and two 7.7mm Breda-SAFAT machine-guns in wings; max bomb load 2,205lb (1,000kg).
Crew: 1.
In Service: Iraq (2 Ba 65, 13 Ba 65bis), Italy, Portugal (10 Ba 65bis).
Variants (with no. built):
Ba 65: Prototype; single-seat ground-support aircraft; one 1,000hp Fiat A.80 RC 41 (1).
Ba 65: Production model; altn power plant—one 900hp Isotta-Fraschini K.14 (licence-built Gnome-Rhône 14 Kdrs) (approx 80).
Ba 65bis: 2-seat version; dorsal position (or turret) with one addn 12.7mm Breda-SAFAT machine-gun (approx 140).
Total Production: approx 220.
Remarks: Direct development of earlier Ba 64 (withdrawn from service immediately prior outbreak WWII), Ba 65/65bis, first flown 1935, subject number export orders inc Hungary, Iraq, Paraguay, Portugal, and USSR; flown by Italian Legion during Spanish Civil War; 154 examples operational upon Italy's entry into war, June 1940; brief unspectacular participation early months North African, and Balkan campaigns.

Manufacturer: Breda.
Model: Ba 88 Lince (Lynx).
Type: Attack-bomber.
Power Plant: Two 1,000hp Piaggio P.XI RC 40.
Performance:
maximum speed at 13,120ft (4,000m) 304mph (490km/hr).
maximum range 1,020 miles (1,640km).
time to 9,840ft (3,000m) 7min 30sec.
max ceiling 26,250ft (8,000m).
Weights:
empty 10,252lb (4,650kg).
maximum 14,881lb (6,750kg).
Dimensions:
wing span 51ft 2in (15.6m).
length 35ft 5in (10.79m).
height 10ft 2¼in (3.0m).
wing area 358.5sq ft (33.3sq m).
Armament: Three 12.7mm Breda-SAFAT machine-guns in nose; one flexible 7.7mm Breda-SAFAT machine-gun in rear cockpit; max bomb load 2,205lb (1,000kg).
Crew: 2.
In Service: Italy (IAF, RSIAF).
Variants (with no. built):
Ba 88: Prototype; two 900hp Isotta-Fraschini K.14 (licence-built Gnome-Rhône K.14); single fin and rudder (1).
Ba 88: Production model; uprated engines; twin fin and rudder;early models with one 7.7mm Breda-SAFAT machine-gun in dorsal turret; Breda-and IMAM-built (148).
Ba 88M: Dive-bomber version; two 840hp Fiat A.74 RC 38; one addn 12.7mm Breda-SAFAT machine-gun in nose; increased wing span; lengthened fuselage (3).
Total Production: 152.
Remarks: Highly publicized 1936 design, winner of pre-war international speed records, Ba 88 failed to live up to early promise under combat conditions; brief service one Gruppo opening rounds Western Desert campaign; despite lack of success twenty-three examples still serving post-armistice RSIAF, inc three Ba 88M dive-bombers; latter reportedly subsequently seized by Luftwaffe.

Manufacturer: CANSA (Fiat).
Model: FC.20bis.
Type: Ground-attack.

Power Plant: Two 870hp Fiat A.74 RC 38.
Performance:
maximum speed 261mph (420km/hr).
cruising speed 211mph (340km/hr).
range 715 miles (1,150km).
service ceiling 22,970ft (7,000m).
Weights:
empty 10,417lb (4,725kg).
loaded 15,035lb (6,820kg).
Dimensions:
wing span 52ft 5¾in (16.0m).
length 39ft 11⅔in (12.18m).
height 12ft 6in (3.81m).
wing area 430.5sq ft (40.0sq m).
Armament: One fixed forward-firing 37mm Breda cannon in nose; two 12.7mm Breda-SAFAT machine-guns in wings; one 12.7mm Breda-SAFAT machine-gun in dorsal turret; max bomb load (internal and external) 1,262lb (572kg).
Crew: 2.
In Service: Italy (IAF, RSIAF).
Variants (with no. built):
FC.20: Prototype; reconnaissance-bomber version; two 840hp Fiat A.74 RC 38; glazed nose (1).
FC.20bis: Pre-production model; ground-attack version; redesigned solid nose; increased armament (11).
FC.20ter: Reconnaissance version; re-engined FC.20; two 1,000hp Fiat A.80 RC 41; project only.
FC.20quater: Re-engined FC.20ter; two Fiat RA.1000 (licence-built DB 601A); revised armament; project only.
Total Production: 12.
Remarks: Designed and first flown 1941 as reconnaissance-bomber, production/service confined to limited series experimental ground-attack version; brief use strategic reconnaissance/convoy escort roles in weeks immediately prior Italian armistice; three examples subsequently on strength RSIAF.

Manufacturer: CANT.
Model: Z.501 Gabbiano (Seagull)
Type: Reconnaissance flying boat.
Power Plant: One 900hp Isotta-Fraschini Asso XI R2 C15.
Performance:
maximum speed at 8,200ft (2,500m) 171mph (275km/hr).
cruising speed 150mph (240km/hr).
maximum range 1,490 miles (2,400km).
time to 13,120ft (4,000m) 18min 0sec.
service ceiling 22,965ft (7,000m).
Weights:
empty 8,488lb (3,850kg).
maximum 15,342lb (7,050kg).
Dimensions:
wing span 73ft 9¾in (22.5m).
length 46ft 11in (14.3m).
height 14ft 6in (4.4m).
wing area 667.36sq ft (62.0sq m).
Armament: One 7.7mm Breda-SAFAT machine-gun each in open bow, semi-enclosed dorsal hull and overwing engine nacelle positions; max bomb load 1,410lb (640kg).
Crew: 4–5.
In Service: Great Britain (1 captured), Italy (IAF, RSIAF, ICoAF), Rumania, Spain (SpanNAF).
Variants (with no. built):
Z.501: Prototype and production model; reconnaissance flying boat; open bow gun position subsequently replaced by enclosed (unarmed) observer station (445).
Total Production: 445.
Remarks: First flown 1934, over two hundred Z.501s still in service at time of Italy's entry WWII June 1940; operated maritime (coastal) patrol/ASR duties throughout hostilities, post-1943 with both pro-Allied and Axis air arms; (pre-war deliveries Spain and Rumania similarly employed Mediterranean/Black Sea areas resp); continued limited use post-war IAF.

Manufacturer: CANT.
Model: Z.506B Airone (Heron).
Type: Reconnaissance-bomber float-plane.
Power Plant: Three 750hp Alfa Romeo 126 RC 34.
Performance:
maximum speed 227mph (365km/hr).
cruising speed 202mph (325km/hr).
normal range 1,243 miles (2,000km).
time to 13,120ft (4,000m) 14min 0sec.
service ceiling 26,240ft (8,000m).
Weights:
empty 18,298lb (8,300kg).
loaded 27,116lb (12,300kg).
Dimensions:
wing span 86ft 11⅓in (26.5m).
length 63ft 1⅔in (19.24m).
height 24ft 5½in (7.45m).
wing area 928.49sq ft (86.26sq m).
Armament: One 12.7mm Breda-SAFAT machine-gun in dorsal turret; one flexible 7.7mm Breda-SAFAT machine-gun at rear of ventral gondola; max bomb load; 2,204lb (1,000kg) or one 1,764lb (800kg) torpedo.
Crew: 5.
In Service: Germany (ex-Italy), Great Britain (3 captured), Italy (IAF, RSIAF, ICoAF), Poland (1).
Variants (with no. built):
Z.506: Prototype and initial civil transport floatplane versions; three Pratt & Whitney Hornet, 750hp Wright Cyclone (Z.506A), or 750/800hp Alfa Romeo 126 (Z.506C); 3 crew, 15 passengers (approx 20).
Z.506B Airone (Heron): Military reconnaissance-bomber floatplane versions; stepped (raised cockpit) dorsal contours; ventral bomb (torpedo)-bay gondola; number subsequent modifications inc (Serie XII) two addn 7.7mm Breda-SAFAT beam machine-guns, plus replacement Breda dorsal turret by Caproni turret with one 12.7mm Scotti machine-gun; increased max bomb load 2,645lb (1,200kg); CANT and Piaggio-built (324).
Z.506S: Air/sea-rescue version; Z.506B conversions.
Total Production: approx 344.
Remarks: Development of successful Z.506A civil floatplane, militarized Z.506B entered service 1938; brief operational use some half-dozen examples Spanish Civil War (Italian Legion); 95 produced by time Italian entry WWII (inc 29 ex-Polish order);initially employed bombing role French, Balkan campaigns, and against British Mediterranean Fleet, subsequently assigned maritime reconnaissance, convoy escort, and anti-submarine duties; also ASR (Z.506S); of 40+ serviceable post-Armistice, 29 to ICoAF (23 Z.506B, 5 Z.506S, plus one civil transport ex-Servizi Aerei Speciali), and three (Z.506B) to RSIAF; others (10+) seized by Luftwaffe for E Med /Balkan ambulance/transport operations; continued post-war ASR use until 1959–60.

Manufacturer: CANT.
Model: Z.511.
Type: Long-range transport float-plane.
Power Plant: Four 1,500hp Piaggio P.XII RC 35.
Performance:
maximum speed at 13,120ft (4,000m) 261mph (420km/hr).
cruising speed 205mph (330km/hr).
time to 13,120ft (4,000m) 16min 0sec.
service ceiling 22,965ft (7,000m).
Weights:
empty 45,106lb (20,460kg).
loaded 73,987lb (33,560kg).
Dimensions:
wing span 131ft 2¾in (39.86m).
length 93ft 6in (28.5m).
height 36ft 1in (11.0m).
wing area 2,098.96sq ft (195.0sq m).
Crew/Payload/Accommodation: 4–5 freight and/or troops.
In Service: Italy (RSIAF).
Variants (with no. built):
Z.511: Prototype; transatlantic passenger/freight transport (1).
Total Production: 1.
Remarks: World's largest floatplane, Z.511 designed specifically for South Atlantic mail routes; completed instead as military transport and first flown 8 Sept 1943, very day on which Armistice was made known; impressed RSIAF, destroyed at moorings shortly thereafter by Allied strafing; second prototype, with provision for defensive armament, seized by German forces prior completion and scrapped.

Manufacturer: CANT.
Model: Z.1007bis Alcione (Kingfisher).
Type: Medium bomber.
Power Plant: Three 1,000hp Piaggio P.XIbis RC 40.
Performance:
maximum speed 283mph (455km/hr).
maximum range 1,115 miles (1,795) km.
time to 19,685ft (6,000m) 16min 8sec.
service ceiling 24,600ft (7,500m).
Weights:
empty 20,715lb (9,396kg).
loaded 30,029lb (13,621kg).
Dimensions:
wing span 81ft 4⅓in (24.8m).
length 60ft 2½in (18.35m).
height 17ft 1½in (5.22m).
wing area 753.47sq ft (70.0sq m).
Armament: One 12.7mm Breda-SAFAT, or Scotti, machine-gun each in dorsal turret and ventral step; two 7.7mm Breda-SAFAT machine-guns in beam positions; max bomb load 2,645lb (1,200kg) or two torpedoes.
Crew: 5.
In Service: France (FFAF 1 Z.1007bis ex-Italy), Germany (ex-Italy), Italy (IAF, RSIAF, ICoAF).
Variants (with no. built):
Z.1007: Prototypes (2) and initial production model; three 840hp Piaggio P.XI; four 7.7mm Breda-SAFAT machine-guns (approx 35).
Z.1007bis: Modified Z.1007; major production version; uprated engines; redesigned engine cowlings; increased dimensions; revised armament; single (Serie I–III) or twin (Serie IV–IX) fin and rudder. CANT-, Piaggio-, and IMAM-built.
Z.1007ter: Improved Z.1007bis; three 1,175hp Piaggio P.XIX; reduced 2,205lb (1,000kg) bomb load.
(Total Z.1007bis/ter: 526).
Z.1015: Modified Z.1007; long-range civil mailplane; three 1,500hp Piaggio P.XII RC 35; military development project only.
Total Production: approx 564.
Remarks: Prototype first flown March 1937; improved Z.1007bis production model entered service 1938–39; second only to numerically far superior S.M.79 as standard IAF medium bomber of WWII; 55 on strength, June 1940; widespread employment Greek/Balkan campaigns, Metropolitan Italy/Mediterranean (as torpedo-bomber); also used in North Africa (Libya), plus brief appearances Channel and Eastern (Russian) Fronts; Z.1007ter produced 1942–43, both types subsequently serving pro-Allied and Axis AFs until cessation of hostilities in Europe.

Manufacturer: CANT.
Model: Z.1011.
Type: Medium bomber/transport.
Power Plant: Two 1,680hp Isotta-Fraschini Asso XI RC 15.
Performance:
maximum speed at 14,760ft (4,500m) 230mph (370km/hr).
cruising speed 193mph (310km/hr).
time to 9,840ft (3,000m) 11min 42sec.
service ceiling 26,240ft (8,000m).
Weights:
empty 12,540lb (5,690kg).
Dimensions:
wing span 92ft 0in (28.0m).
length 55ft 9in (17.0m).
height 17ft 2⅔in (5.25m).
wing area 860.8sq ft (80.0sq m).
Armament: One flexible machine-gun in nose; two machine-guns each in dorsal and ventral turrets.
In Service: Italy.
Variants (with no. built):
Z.1011: Prototypes; medium bomber version; two Isotta-Fraschini Asso RC 15 or 800hp Isotta-Fraschini K.14 (5).
Total Production: 5.
Remarks: Built, but rejected, as medium bomber, Z.1011 prototypes employed by IAF in VIP-transport role.

Manufacturer: CANT.
Model: Z.1012.
Type: Light transport.
Power Plant: Three 170hp Alfa Romeo 115.
Performance:
maximum speed 199mph (320km/hr).
cruising speed 162mph (260km/hr).
maximum range 621 miles (1,000km).
time to 6,560ft (2,000m) 10min 0sec
service ceiling 19,685ft (6,000m).
Weights:
empty 5,060lb (2,295kg).
loaded 6,820lb (3,094kg).
Dimensions:
wing span 49ft 2½in (15.0m).
length 32ft 9½in (10.0m).
height 11ft 11in (3.63m).
wing area 269sq ft (25.0sq m).
Crew/Accommodation: 1/4–6.
In Service: Italy.
Variants:
Z.1012: 4/6-passenger light transport monoplane; altn three 120hp Alfa Romeo 110–I or three 170hp Alfa Romeo 115 power plants.
Remarks: Introduced 1938, CANT Z.1012s served in limited numbers liaison/VIP-transport duties early years WWII.

Manufacturer: CANT.
Model: Z.1018 Leone (Lion).
Type: Medium bomber.
Power Plant: Two 1,320hp Piaggio P.XII RC 35 or 1,350hp Alfa Romeo 135 RC 32 Tornado.
Performance:
maximum speed 330mph (530km/hr).
normal range 746 miles (1,200km).
time to 6,560ft (2,000m) 3min 10sec.
service ceiling 24,600ft (7,500m).
Weights:
empty 19,400lb (8,800kg).
loaded 24,580lb (11,150kg).
Dimensions:
wing span 73ft 9¾in (22.5m).
length 57ft 9in (17.6m).
height 19ft 8¼in (6.0m).
wing area 679.2sq ft (63.1sq m).
Armament: One 12.7mm machine-gun each in starboard wing, dorsal turret, and ventral position; two 7.7mm machine-guns in beam positions; max bomb load 3,310lb (1,500kg).
Crew: 4–6.
In Service: Italy (IAF, RSIAF, ICoAF).
Variants (with no. built):
Z.1018: Prototypes; medium bomber version; two 1,500 Piaggio P.XII RC 35, 1,400hp P.XV RC 45, 1,400hp Alfa Romeo 135 RC 32 or 1,475hp Fiat R.A.1050 RC 58 Tifone (Typhoon); single or twin fin and rudder; various (experimental) modifications; first six all-wood construction (approx 12).
Z.1018: Production model; two Piaggio P.XII RC 35 or Alfa Romeo 135 RC 32; all-metal construction; lengthened nose; single fin and rudder (5).
Z.1018: Heavy day- and night-fighter version; seven fixed forward-firing 20mm MG 151/20 cannon in nose, plus three 12.7mm machine-guns; night-fighter version with FuG Lichtenstein SN–2 radar; projects only.
Total Production: approx 17.
Remarks: First flown 1940, highly promising Z.1018 (first Italian medium bomber design comparable in performance and armament to contemporary Allied types and arguably best bomber produced in Italy during WWII) entered service too late materially to affect course of war; operational debut early 1943 supplementing Z.1007bis Alciones one Gruppo; two flown by RSIAF post-Armistice, others with ICoAF.

Manufacturer: Caproni.
Model: Ca.100.
Type: Trainer/liaison.
Power Plant: One 90hp Blackburn Cirrus Minor.
Performance:
maximum speed 103mph (165km/hr).
cruising speed 87mph (140km/hr).
normal range 310 miles (500km).
time to 3,280ft (1,000m) 7min 40sec.
ceiling 13,120ft (4,000m).
Weights:
empty 1,146lb (520kg).
loaded 1,664lb (755kg).
Dimensions:
wing span 32ft 9⅔in (10.0m).
length 23ft 11½in (7.3m).
height 9ft 0¼in (2.75m).
wing area 242.19sq ft (22.5sq m).
Crew/Accommodation: 1/1.
In Service: Italy.
Variants:
Ca.100: 2-seat light civil/military sports plane/trainer; one 85hp de Havilland Gipsy; various altn power plants, inc 90hp Blackburn Cirrus Minor; dual controls; some as bombing trainers with uprated (130hp) engine and provision for four light bombs; Caproni (and Peruvian licence)-built.
Ca.100 idro: 2-seat amphibian float-plane version.
Total Production: approx 700.
Remarks: Built under licence from de Havilland and based upon D.H.60 Moth, Ca.100 produced in large numbers early thirties; pre-war exports inc Peru and Portugal; considerable use comunications/liaison duties by IAF during WWII.

Manufacturer: Caproni.
Model: Ca.101.
Type: Transport/medium bomber.
Power Plant: Three 240hp Alfa Romeo D.2.
Performance:
maximum speed at 3,280ft (1,000m) 103mph (165km/hr).
range 1,243 miles (2,000km).
time to 16,400ft (5,000m) 40min 30sec.
service ceiling 20,013ft (6,100m).
Weights:
empty 7,221lb (3,275kg).
loaded 10,968lb (4,975kg).
Dimensions:
wing span 64ft 6¾in (19.68m).
length 47ft 1¾in (14.37m).
height 12ft 9¼in (3.89m).
wing area 664sq ft (61.69sq m).
Armament: One flexible 7.7mm machine-gun in dorsal position; one or two 7.7mm machine-guns in ventral position; provision for max bomb load 1,102lb (500kg).
Crew/Accommodation: 3/8 (transport).
In Service: Great Britain (1+ Ca.101 captured), Italy, Hungary (20 Ca.101, 2 Ca.102).
Variants:
Ca.101: Civil transport and military transport/bomber versions; various altn power plants; majority military production three 240hp Alfa Romeo D.2.
Ca.102: Modified Ca.101; two 500hp Bristol Jupiter.
Ca.102quater: As Ca.102; four (tandem pair)-engined; prototype only.
Remarks: Enlarged development of earlier Ca.97, military Ca.101s served pre-war IAF colonial/night bomber sqns; operational transport/ancillary

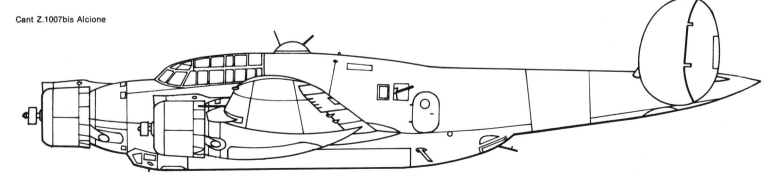

Cant Z.1007bis Alcione

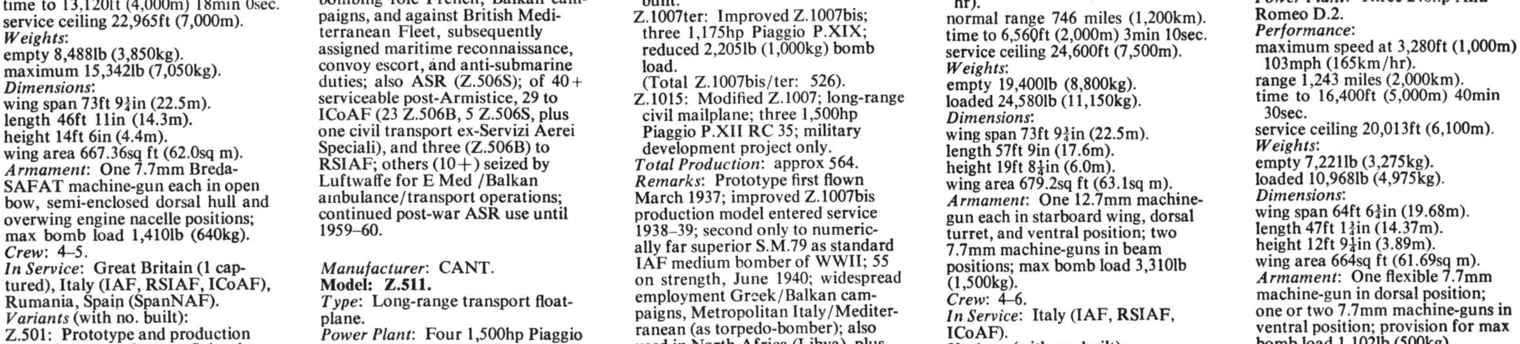

roles early months WWII; Hungarian AF examples in use as transports (employed Russian Front) until 1943.

Manufacturer: Caproni.
Model: Ca.111.
Type: Long-range reconnaissance.
Power Plant: One 950hp Isotta-Fraschini Asso 750 RC.
Performance:
maximum speed 185mph (298km/hr).
cruising speed 158mph (255km/hr).
maximum range 1,243 miles (2,000km).
time to 3,280ft (1,000m) 5min 22sec.
service ceiling 21,982ft (6,700m).
Weights:
loaded 11,795lb (5,350kg).
Dimensions:
wing span 64ft 6½in (19.68m).
length 50ft 2½in (15.3m).
height 12ft 7½in (3.85m).
wing area 661.7sq ft (61.47sq m).
Armament: One machine-gun each in dorsal, ventral and two lateral positions; provision for light bombs (internally and externally).
Crew: 2–4.
In Service: Italy.
Variants (with no. built):
Ca.111: Prototype; modified (single-engined) Ca.101 (1).
Ca.111bis/bis RC: Production models; reconnaissance versions; one 750hp Fiat or 950hp Asso 750 RC; later models with reduced wing span.
Ca.111bis idro: Floatplane (torpedo-bomber) version of Ca.111bis RC. (Total Ca.111bis/bis RC and idro: 152).
Ca.112: Strategic (colonial) reconnaissance version; modified Ca.111 (1).
Total Production: 154.
Remarks: Single-engined long-range (strategic) reconnaissance development of Ca.101 bomber/transport, Ca.111 supplied pre-war Chinese and Peruvian AFs; IAF machines

participated army ground-support role conquest Abyssinia (Ethiopia), 1935–36; several still in use outbreak WWII, employed transport/anti-partisan bombing operations Balkans, 1941–42.

Manufacturer: Caproni.
Model: Ca.113.
Type: Advanced trainer/multi-purpose.
Power Plant: One 370hp Piaggio P.VIII C 35 Stella.
Performance:
maximum speed 155mph (250km/hr).
normal range 186 miles (300km).
time to 16,400ft (5,000m) 11min 15sec.
service ceiling 24,000ft (7,300m).
Weights:
empty 1,870lb (850kg).
loaded 2,420lb (1,100kg).
Dimensions:
wing span 34ft 5in (10.5m).
length 23ft 11in (7.3m).
height 8ft 11in (2.71m).
wing area 290.5sq ft (26.9sq m).
Crew/Accommodation: 1/1.
In Service: Bulgaria (Ka.B.3).
Variants:
Ca.113: Prototype and production model/s; 2-seat advanced trainer biplane; prototype and early models with one 240hp Walter Castor.
Ka.B.3: Bulgarian designation for Ca.113 development; 2-seat multi-purpose biplane; altn power plants, inc one 260hp Walter Castor II, or one 430hp Piaggio P.VII CD; Bulgarian (Ka.B) licence-built.
Remarks: Original Ca.113 first flown 1931; improved version selected as first product newly-established (Caproni-financed) Bulgarian Ka.B.plant, 1938; named Tchout-chouliga (Lark), approx fifty Ka.B.3s equipped Bulgarian AF, Spring 1940; served variety training, liaison, and ancillary roles.

Manufacturer: Caproni.
Model: Ca.133.
Type: Bomber-transport.
Power Plant: Three 460hp Piaggio Stella P.VII C 16.
Performance:
maximum speed 165mph (265km/hr).
cruising speed 143mph (230km/hr).
maximum range 838 miles (1,350 km).
service ceiling 18,044ft (5,500m).
Weights:
empty 9,240lb (4,190kg).
loaded 14,740lb (6,700kg).
Dimensions:
wing span 68ft 8in (21.24m).
length 50ft 4½in (15.36m).
height 13ft 1in (4.00m).
wing area 699.65sq ft (65.0sq m).
Armament: One 7.7mm machine-gun each in dorsal turret, ventral and two lateral positions; max bomb load 1,102lb (500kg).
Crew/Accommodation: 3/18 troops (transport).
In Service: Germany (Ca.148), Italy (IAF, RSIAF, ICoAF), South Africa (1 Ca.133 captured ex-Italy), Spain (Nat.AF approx 10 Ca.133).
Variants (with no. built):
Ca.133: Prototype and production models; military bomber-transport and 16-passenger civil transport versions; three Piaggio Stella P.VII C 16.
Ca.133S: Ambulance version; Ca.133 conversions.
Ca.133T: Transport version; reduced armament; Ca.133 conversions. (Total Ca.133/S/T: 419).
Ca.148: 18-passenger transport version; modified fuselage; strengthened undercarriage (106).
Total Production: 525.
Remarks: Direct development of Ca.101, improved Ca.133's operational debut Ethiopian campaign 1936; also served Spanish Civil War, and Italian invasion of Albania (as paratroop transport), 1939;

obsolescent by Italian entry WWII, suffered heavily East African/Western Desert theatres; relegated transport/ambulance roles also supported Italian operations on Eastern (Russian) Front; served both RSIAF/ICoAF after Armistice, as did impressed Ca.148s; several latter continued post-war IAF use.

Manufacturer: Caproni.
Model: Ca.164.
Type: Trainer/reconnaissance.
Power Plant: One 185hp Alfa Romeo 115–I.
Performance:
maximum speed 135mph (217km/hr).
cruising speed 114mph (185km/hr).
maximum range 329 miles (530km).
time to 6,560ft (2,000m) 9min 10sec.
service ceiling 13,943ft (4,250m).
Weights:
empty 1,720lb (780kg).
loaded 2,270lb (1,030kg).
Dimensions:
wing span 31ft 11½in (9.75m).
length 25ft 4½in (7.74m).
height 9ft 10in (3.0m).
wing area 241.11sq ft (22.4sq m).
Crew/Accommodation: 1/1.
In Service: Italy.
Variants:
Ca.164: 2-seat tourer/trainer.
Remarks: Limited production Ca.164 served IAF trainer/liaison roles; at least one example employed anti-partisan operations (short-range reconnaissance/spotter) over Croatia, 1942; several captured machines used as sqn 'hacks' by Allied AFs Sicily/Italy, 1943–44.

Manufacturer: Caproni-Bergamaschi.
Model: Ca.135/P.XI.
Type: Medium bomber.
Power Plant: Two 1,000hp Piaggio P.XI RC 40.
Performance:
maximum speed at 15,750ft (4,800m) 273mph (440km/hr).

cruising speed 230mph (370km/hr).
maximum range 1,240 miles (2,000km).
time to 13,120ft (4,000m) 13min 20sec.
service ceiling 22,965ft (7,000m).
Weights:
empty 13,450lb (6,100kg).
loaded 21,164lb (9,600kg).
Dimensions:
wing span 61ft 8½in (18.8m).
length 47ft 2in (14.38m).
height 11ft 1½in (3.4m).
wing area 645.84 sq ft (60.0sq m).
Armament: One 12.7mm Breda-SAFAT machine-gun in dorsal turret; one 12.7mm, or 7.7mm, Breda-SAFAT machine-gun each in nose and ventral positions; max bomb load 3,527lb (1,600kg).
Crew: 4.
In Service: Hungary (approx 100 Ca.135bis), Italy, Peru.
Variants (with no. built):
Ca.135: Prototype; medium bomber; two 800hp Isotta-Fraschini Asso XI; retractable dorsal and ventral turrets (1).
Ca.135 tipo Spagna: Initial production model; two 836hp Asso XI RC 40; increased weight and fuel capacity (14).
Ca.135 tipo Peru: Peruvian order/s; two 815hp Asso XI RC 45 or (late models) 900hp Asso XI RC 40; modified nacelles; revised armament (32).
Ca.135/A.80: Re-engined tipo Spagna; two 1,000hp Fiat A.80 RC 41.
Ca.135/P.XI (Ca.135bis): Major production model; two Piaggio P.XI RC 40; modified nose; increased length; revised armament; Hungarian order/s, plus 1 Service Trials model (approx 100).
Total Production: approx 150.
Remarks: Prototype first flown April 1935; intended combat evaluation with Italian Legion in Spanish Civil War (tipo Spagna) not realised; re-

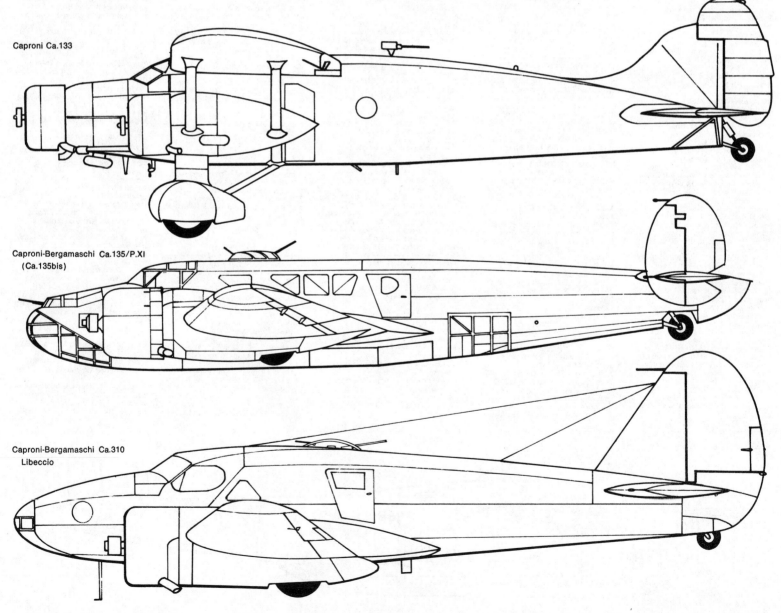

Caproni Ca.133

Caproni-Bergamaschi Ca.135/P.XI
(Ca.135bis)

Caproni-Bergamaschi Ca.310
Libeccio

engined Ca.135/A.80 served IAF solely bombing-trainer role; majority production supplied Hungarian AF as Ca.135bis; participated 1941 Balkans campaign, and against Soviets on southern sector Eastern (Russian) Front latter half 1941 and again in Summer 1942; subsequently withdrawn operations and relegated bombing-training duties.

Caproni-Vizzola F.5

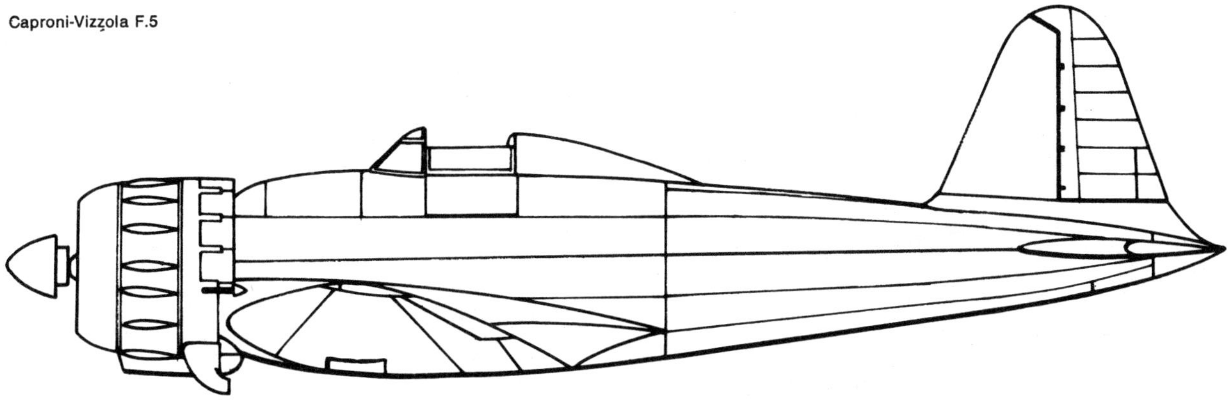

Manufacturer: Caproni Bergamaschi.
Model: Ca.310 Libeccio (South-West Wind).
Type: Light reconnaissance-bomber.
Power Plant: Two 470hp Piaggio P.VII C 35.
Performance:
maximum speed at 9,840ft (3,000m) 227mph (365km/hr).
cruising speed 200mph (320km/hr).
normal range 1,025 miles (1,650km).
time to 13,120ft (4,000m) 12min 30sec.
service ceiling 22,965ft (7,000m).
Weights:
empty 6,730lb (3,053kg)
loaded 10,252lb (4,650kg).
Dimensions:
wing span 53ft 1¾in (16.2m).
length 40ft 0¼in (12.2m).
height 11ft 7in (3.52m).
wing area 416.57sq ft (38.7sq m).
Armament: Two 7.7mm machine-guns in wings; one 7.7mm machine-gun in dorsal turret; max bomb load 882lb (400kg).
Crew: 3.
In Service: Croatia (Ca.310. Ca.311, Ca.312), France (5 Ca.313), Germany (19 Ca.313), Hungary (36 Ca.310), Italy (IAF, RSIAF, ICoAF), Norway (4 Ca.310), Sweden (31 Ca.313), Yugoslavia (12 Ca.310).
Variants (with no. built):
Ca.308 Borea (North Wind): Initial production; 6/7-passenger light civil transport; alt 185/200hp Walter Major, 185hp Alfa Romeo 115, or 200hp de Havilland Gipsy Six; fixed trousered undercarriage (7).
Ca.309 Ghibli (Desert Wind): Light colonial reconnaissance-bomber/military transport versions (Serie I–VI); two 185hp Alfa Romeo 115; fixed spatted undercarriage; three 7.7mm machine-guns, plus max 440lb (200kg) bomb load; Serie VI close-support version with one or two fixed forward-firing 20mm cannon in nose (243).
Ca.310 Libeccio: Improved Ca.309; uprated (radial) engines; dorsal turets; retractable undercarriage (312).
Ca.310 idro: Floatplane version of Ca.310; prototype only (1)
Ca.310bis (Ca.311 prototype): Modified Ca.310; two 500hp Piaggio P.VII C 35; redesigned (unstepped) glazed nose (1 Ca.310 Serie II conversion).
Ca.311: Production model; light reconnaissance-bomber.
Ca.311M: Late production Ca 311; lengthened nose; stepped windscreen.
(Total Ca.311/M: 320+).
Ca.312: Communications version; improved Ca.310; original Norwegian order; two 700hp Piaggio P.XVI RC 35; armament and nose contours as Ca.310.
Ca.312M: Unarmed flying-classroom/crew trainer version; nose as Ca.311M.
(Total Ca.312/M: approx 25).
Ca.312bis, 312 IS: Proposed export and torpedo-bomber floatplane versions resp; projects only.
Ca.313 RPB1: Improved Ca.311; light reconnaissance-bomber version; two 710hp Isotta-Fraschini Delta RC 35; unstepped nose as Ca.311; three 12.7mm plus two 7.7mm machine-guns; max bomb load 1,102lb (500kg).
Ca.313 RPB2: Modified Ca.313 RPB1; stepped-windscreen nose as Ca.311M.
Ca.313 RPB/S: Prototypes; reconnaissance/torpedo-bomber version (7 Ca.313 RPB conversions).
Ca.313 RA: Reconnaissance/torpedo-bomber version; modified Ca.313 RPB2; one 450mm torpedo under fuselage (subsequently redesignated Ca.314).
(Total Ca.313 RPB1—313RA: 271).
Ca.313G: Prototypes; crew trainer version; revised nose; German order (3).
Ca.314A(Ca.314S): Convoy-escort version; modified Ca.313 RPB2; uprated (730hp) Isotta-Fraschini Delta RC 35; armoured.
Ca.314B: Torpedo-bomber version; initial models as Ca.313 RA; late production with uprated Delta RC 35 Serie III.
Ca.314C: Assault-bomber/close-support version; Delta RC 35 Serie III; increased (underwing 12.7mm machine-gun) armament/armour.
(Total Ca.314 A, B, C: 425).
Ca.315, 316: Liaison/trainer and reconnaissance floatplane versions resp; prototypes only.
Total Production: 1,600+.
Remarks: Complex and prolific series of light reconnaissance-bomber designs/derivatives all stemming from seven light transports of 1936; subject numerous export orders (totalling some 2,750) inc, uniquely, large contracts from both Great Britain (400 Ca.311/313) and Germany (905 Ca.313G); but majority of contracts either unfulfilled, uncompleted, cancelled or returned due to lack of performance; major foreign user Sweden, thirty-one Ca.313s (out of reported total eighty-four ordered) serving 1940–46 initially as B 16 bomber, and subsequently as S 16 reconnaissance (and Tp 16 transport) aircraft; remainder production taken over by IAF; operated throughout WWII wide variety first- and second-line roles, and on all fronts inc North Africa and Russia; served both RSIAF and ICoAF after Sept 1943; continued post-war IAF use until early fifties.

Manufacturer: Caproni-Vizzola.
Model: F.5.
Type: Fighter.
Power Plant: One 870hp Fiat A.74 RC 38.
Performance:
maximum speed 317mph (510km/hr).
cruising speed 295mph (475km/hr).
maximum range 620 miles (1,000km).
time to 21,325ft (6,500m) 6min 30sec.
service ceiling 31,170ft (9,500m).
Weights:
empty 4,079lb (1,850kg).
loaded 5,000lb (2,270kg).
Dimensions:
wing span 37ft 0¾in (11.3m).
length 25ft 11in (7.9m).
height 9ft 10in (3.0m).
wing area 187.29sq ft (17.4sq m).
Armament: Two 12.7mm Breda-SAFAT machine-guns in upper cowling.
Crew: 1.
In Service: Italy.
Variants (with no. built):
F.5: Prototype; fighter version; one 870hp Fiat A.74 RC 38 (1).
F.5: Pre-production model; as prototype; modified cockpit canopy, enlarged vertical tail surfaces; increased fuel capacity (14).
F.5bis: Re-engined F.5; one 1,175hp Alfa Romeo R.A.1000 RC 44—1a (licence-built DB 601A–1); project only.
F.5 Gamma: Single/2-seat trainer versions; one 540hp Isotta-Fraschini Gamma RC 35 IS; project only.
F.6: Re-engined F.5; one 1,475hp DB 605A (1 conversion).
F.6M: Prototypes; as F.6; all-metal construction.
F.6MZ: Prototype; one 1,250hp Isotta-Fraschini Zeta RC 25/60.
Total Production: 15 (excl F.6).
Remarks: Prototype F.5 first flown early 1938; pre-production models employed night-fighter defence Rome area early months WWII; subsequently re-assigned day fighter/interceptor role.

Manufacturer: Fiat.
Model: CR.20.
Type: Fighter.
Power Plant: One 400hp Fiat A.20.
Performance:
maximum speed 172mph (276km/hr).
normal range 466 miles (750km).
time to 16,400ft (5,000m) 13min 38sec.
service ceiling 24,606ft (7,500m).
Weights:
empty 2,161lb (980kg).
loaded 2,998lb (1,360kg).
Dimensions:
wing span 32ft 1¾in (9.8m).
length 21ft 11¾in (6.7m).
height 9ft 0¼in (2.75m).
wing area 276.1sq ft (25.65sq m).
Armament: Two .303in Vickers machine-guns in upper cowling.
Crew: 1.
In Service: Lithuania.
Variants (with no. built):
CR.20: Initial production model; single-seat fighter biplane; one 400hp Fiat A.20 (127).
CR.20B: 2-seat trainer version of CR.20.
CR.20 idro: Fighter floatplane version of CR.20; CMASA-built (16).
CR.20bis: Improved CR.20; reduced wing area (226).
CR.20AQ: High altitude fighter version; one 425hp Fiat A.25AQ.
CR.20 Asso: Re-engined CR.20; one 450hp Isotta-Fraschini Asso Caccia; CMASA-built (approx 200).
Total Production: approx 600.
Remarks: First flown 1926, CR.20 subject pre-war export orders, inc Austria (16 CR.20bis) and Hungary (26 CR.20B/bis); also extensive mid-thirties employment by IAF, inc colonial campaigns Libya and Abyssinia; by outbreak WWII all withdrawn first-line service except one fighter sqn Lithuanian AF, these remaining in use until Soviet annexation of Baltic states, Summer 1940.

Manufacturer: Fiat.
Model: CR.30.
Type: Fighter.
Power Plant: One 600hp Fiat A.30 RA.
Performance:
maximum speed 217mph (350km/hr).
normal range 528 miles (850km).
time to 13,120ft (4,000m) 8min 30sec.
service ceiling 28,540ft (8,700m).
Weights:
empty 2,965lb (1,345kg).
loaded 4,178lb (1,895kg).
Dimensions:
wing span 34ft 5½in (10.5m).
length 25ft 8¼in (7.83m).
height 8ft 7⅔in (2.63m).
wing area 297.09sq ft (27.6sq m).
Armament: Two 7.7mm (or 12.7mm) Breda-SAFAT machine-guns in upper cowling.
Crew: 1.
In Service: Italy (IAF, RSIAF).
Variants (with no. built):
CR.30: Prototype; single-seat fighter biplane; one Fiat A.30 RA (1).
CR.30: Production model; modified fin (124).
CR.30B: 2-seat fighter trainer version.
CR.30 idro: Floatplane version of CR.30 (1).
Remarks: Much improved and modernized design in comparison with earlier CR.20 series, CR.30, first flown 1932, overshadowed by externally similar, but smaller, CR.32 of following year; nonetheless supplied several foreign AFs, inc Paraguay, China, Hungary, and Austria (latter's aircraft, together with CR.20s, seized by Germany 1938); production CR.30s equipped both home- and Libyan-based prewar IAF units, a few remaining on strength, in secondary roles, up to and beyond Italian armistice of Sept 1943.

Manufacturer: Fiat.
Model: CR.32bis.
Type: Fighter.
Power Plant: One 600hp Fiat A.30 RAbis.
Performance:
maximum speed at sea level 206mph (332km/hr).
maximum speed at 9,840ft (3,000m) 224mph (360km/hr).
normal range 466 miles (750km).
time to 16.400ft (5,000m) 9min 0sec.
service ceiling 25,256ft (7,700m).
Weights:
empty 3,210lb (1,455kg).
normal/loaded 4,350lb (1,975kg).
Dimensions:
wing span 31ft 2¼in (9.5m).
length 24ft 6in (7.47m).
height 7ft 9in (2.36m).
wing area 237.88sq ft (22.10sq m).
Armament: Two 12.7mm Breda-SAFAT machine-guns in upper cowling; two 7.7mm Breda machine-guns in (lower) wings; max (provisional) bomb load 220lb (100kg).
Crew: 1.
In Service: China (24), Hungary (approx 50 CR.32), Italy (IAF, RSIAF, ICoAF), South Africa (1+ captured ex-Italy), Spain (NatAF: approx 380 inc Italian Legion, SpanAF 100+ inc licence-production).
Variants (with no. built):
CR.32: Prototype and initial production model; single-seat fighter biplane; one 600hp Fiat A.30 RAbis; two 7.7mm (12.7mm) Breda-SAFAT (or Vickers) machine-guns, in upper cowling (inc export orders approx 350).
CR.32bis: Close-support fighter version; modified CR.32; increased armament; provision for two 110lb (50kg) bombs under fuselage (283).
CR.32ter: Modified CR.32; improved equipment; revised undercarriage (150).
CR.32 quater: Modified CR.32ter; reduced weights; late models with radio equipment (337).
HA-132-L 'Chirri' (Chirper): Spanish designation for CR.32quater; inc 40 subsequently converted as C.1 2-seat trainers; Hispano-Suiza licence-built (100+).
Total Production: 1,312 (inc licence-production).
Remarks: CR.30 development, smaller CR.32 likewise purchased by number foreign AFs, European and South American; participated several pre-WWII actions; defence of Shanghai during second Sino-Japanese conflict (Chinese AF), Gran Chaco war (Paraguayan AF), Carpathian dispute (Hungarian AF), and Spanish Civil War (Italian Legion/Spanish NatAF); numerically most important IAF fighter of late thirties, CR.32 in process of replacement at time of Italian entry WWII, June 1940, when approx 300 examples equipped units ranging from Metropolitan Italy to Sardinia, Sicily, the Aegean, Albania, North and East Africa; considerable use early months hostilities (particularly Greek/East African campaigns) in night-fighter and close-support roles before gradual relegation training and ancillary duties.
Colour Reference: Plate 83: Fiat CR.32quater (M.M.4666) '10' of 160ª squadriglia, 12° gruppo assalto, Regia Aeronautica, Tobruk, Italian Cyrenaica, Oct 1940; standard North African desert dapple finish.

Manufacturer: Fiat (CMASA).
Model: G.8.
Type: Trainer/liaison.
Power Plant: One 135hp Fiat A.54.
Performance:
maximum speed 133.7mph (215km/hr).
cruising speed 116.2mph (187km/hr).
normal range 478 miles (770km).
time to 9,840ft (3,000m) 17min 41sec.
service ceiling 16,400ft (5,000m).
Weights:
empty 1,256lb (570kg).
loaded 1,874lb (850kg).
Dimensions:
wing span 28ft 9in (8.76m).
length 22ft 5in (6.83m).
height 8ft 6¾in (2.61m).
wing area 204sq ft (18.91sq m).
Crew/Accommodation: 1/1.
In Service: Italy (IAF, RSIAF, ICoAF).
Variants:
G.8: 2-seat civil touring/military training biplane.
Remarks: First flown 1934, number G.8 trainers served IAF in liaison/communications roles after outbreak WWII; several similarly employed post-Armistice by both RSIAF/ICoAF, as well as captured examples, reportedly, by USAAF.

Manufacturer: Fiat.
Model: BR.20M Cicogna (Stork).
Type: Medium bomber.
Power Plant: Two 1,000hp Fiat A.80 RC 41.
Performance:
maximum speed at sea-level 273mph (440km/hr).
cruising speed 211mph (340km/hr).
maximum range 1,709 miles (2,750km).
time to 19,685ft (6,000m) 25min 0sec.
service ceiling 26,240ft (8,000m).
Weights:
empty 14,330lb (6,500kg).
loaded 22,270lb (10,100kg).
Dimensions:
wing span 70ft 8¾in (21.56m).
length 54ft 8in (16.68m).
height 15ft 7in (4.75m).
wing area 796.54sq ft (74.0sq m).
Armament: One 12.7mm Breda-SAFAT machine-gun each in nose, dorsal turret, and ventral gun position; max bomb load 3,528lb (1,600kg).
Crew: 5.
In Service: Italy (IAF, RSIAF, ICoAF), Japan (IJAAF 85), Spain (Italian Legion/NatAF 20).
Variants (with no. built):
BR.20 Cicogna: Prototype and initial production model; medium bomber version; two 1,000hp Fiat A.80 RC 41; one 12.7mm Breda-SAFAT machine-gun in retractable dorsal turret, plus one 7.7mm Breda-SAFAT machine-gun each in nose and (retractable) ventral position; max bomb load 3,528lb (1,600kg) (inc Japanese (85) and Venezuelan (1) orders (320).
BR.20A/L: Civil competition models (A: 2); (L: 1).
BR.20M: Modified BR.20; improved nose contours; revised armament; increased armour (inc 1 with experimental tricycle undercarriage) (264).
BR.20bis: Improved BR.20M; two 1,250hp Fiat A.82 RC 42S; redesigned nose; two addn 7.7mm Breda-SAFAT machine-guns in lateral blisters; power-operated dorsal turret (15).
Total Production: 602.
Remarks: Designed 1935 and first flown early following year, BR.20 perhaps best remembered as subject of export barter arrangement with Japan, 85 being delivered against return consignments soya beans; unsatisfactory performance with IJAAF (as Army Type I Model 100 Heavy Bomber) during

Fiat BR.20 Cicogna

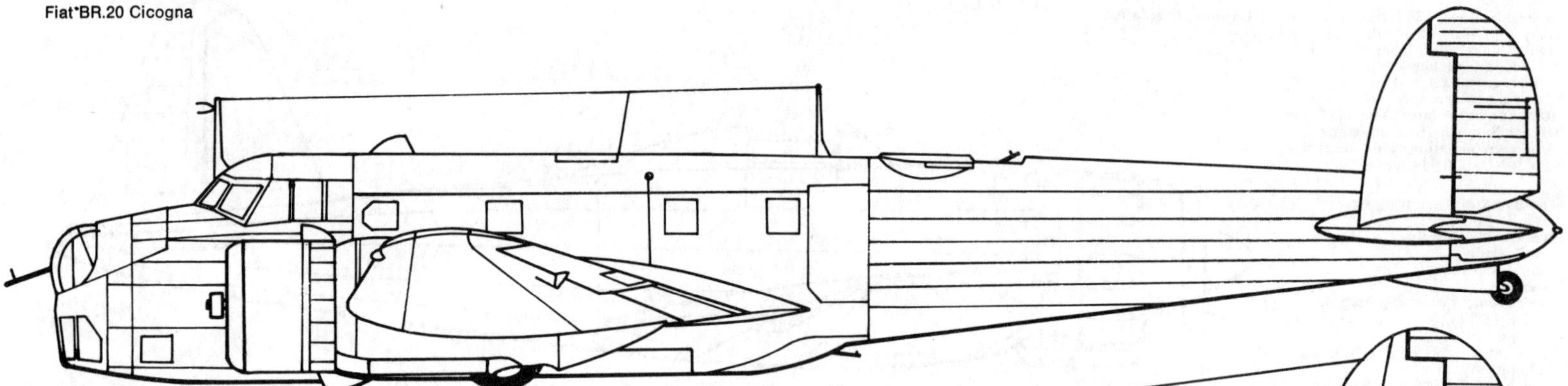

Fiat CR.25bis

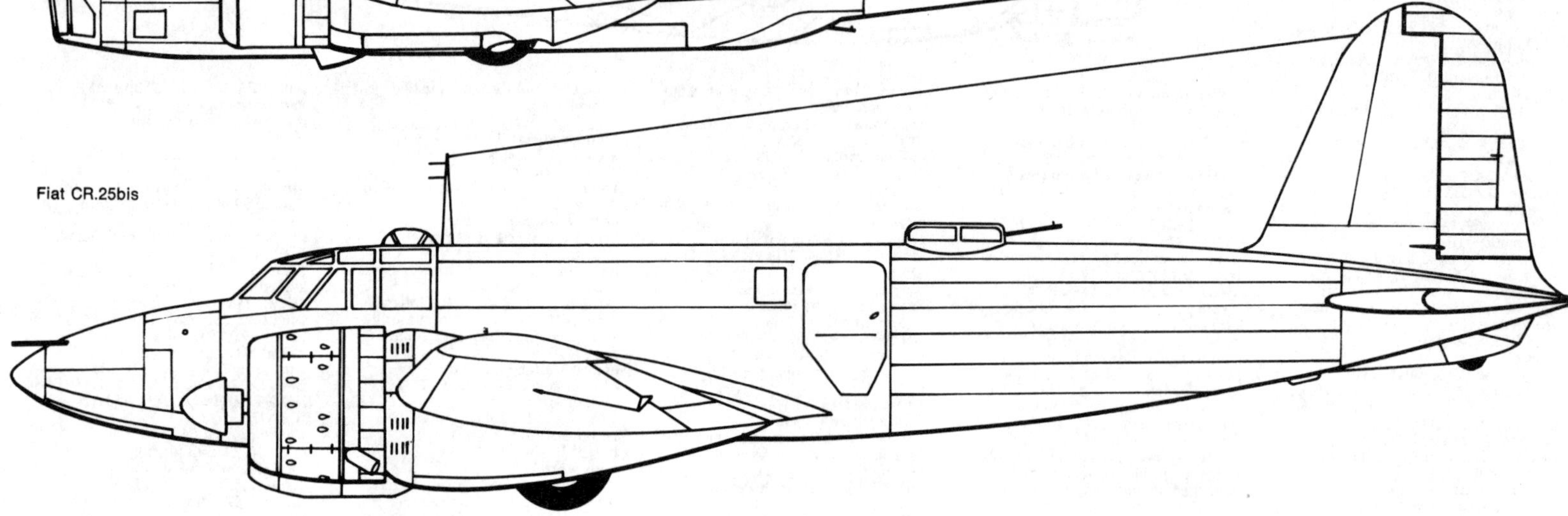

second Sino-Japanese conflict, 1938–39; similar experience early examples despatched Spain resulted in appearance improved BR.20M, 1939; some 160+ BR.20/20Ms on strength IAF, June 1940; participated Italian attack on France and operations against UK (based Belgium), Winter 1940–41; equipping total fifteen Gruppi, subsequently deployed Balkan, Western Desert campaigns; also operated in reconnaissance role southern (Black Sea) sector of Russian Front latter half 1942, plus night bombing attacks Malta, and Mediterranean convoy escort duties; by September 1943 only 67 BR.20 types operational, reports indicating that both RSIAF/ICoAF each had just one example on strength post-Armistice.

Manufacturer: Fiat.
Model: G.18V.
Type: Transport.
Power Plant: Two 1,000hp Fiat A.80 RC 41.
Performance:
maximum speed at 15,088ft (4,600m) 249mph (400km/hr).
cruising speed 211mph (340km/hr).
maximum range 1,025 miles (1,650km).
time to 9,840ft (3,000m) 10min 25sec.
service ceiling 26,902ft (8,200m).
Weights:
empty 15,873lb (7,200kg).
loaded 23,809lb (10,800kg).
Dimensions:
wing span 82ft 0¼in (25.0m).
length 61ft 8½in (18.81m).
height 16ft 5in (5.0m).
wing area 950sq ft (88.26sq m).
Crew/Accommodation: 3/18.
In Service: Italy (IAF, RSIAF).
Variants (with no. built):
G.18: Prototype; civil transport; two 770hp Pratt & Whitney S1EG; subsequently re-engined 700hp Fiat A.59Rs (1).
G.18: Production model; as re-engined prototype; revised vertical tail surfaces (2).
G.18V: Improved G.18; uprated engines; modified fin and rudder; increased weight (6).
Total Production: 9.
Remarks: Bearing striking resemblance to Douglas DC-2, prototype G.18 first flown March 1935; operating pre war internal and Eastern European routes, eight of nine models built incorporated into Servizi Aerei Speciali for para-military airline/communications duties after Italian entry WWII; one G.18V employed by RSIAF post-Armistice.

Manufacturer: Fiat.
Model: G.50bis Freccia (Arrow).
Type: Fighter/fighter-bomber.
Power Plant: One 840hp Fiat A.74 RC 38.
Performance:
maximum speed at 14,765ft (4,500m) 293mph (470km/hr).
normal range 420 miles (676km).
time to 19,685ft (6,000m) 7min 45sec.
ceiling 35,106ft (10,700m).
Weights:
empty 4,443lb (2,015kg).
loaded 5,560lb (2,522kg).
Dimensions:
wing span 36ft 0¾in (10.9m).
length 25ft 7in (7.8m).
height 9ft 8¼in (2.95m).
wing area 196.45sq ft (18.25sq m).
Armament: Two fixed forward-firing 12.7mm Breda-SAFAT machine-guns in fuselage; max bomb load 660lb (300kg).
Crew: 1.
In Service: Croatia (9 G.50bis), Finland (35 G.50bis), Italy (IAF, RSIAF, ICoAF), Spain (11 G.50 ex-Italian Legion).
Variants (with no. built):
G.50 Freccia: Prototype (1) and initial production model; single-seat fighter; one Fiat A.74 RC 38; enclosed cockpit; two 12.7mm Breda-SAFAT machine-guns; many subsequently converted with semi-enclosed cockpit (inc 35 Finnish order); CMASA-built (246).
G.50bis: Improved G.50; semi-enclosed cockpit; increased fuel capacity; improved radio equipment; modified wing (inc 9 Croatian order); Fiat-and CMASA-built (421).
G.50bis/A: Carrier-borne 2-seat fighter-bomber version; increased wing span; two addn 12.7mm Breda-SAFAT machine-guns in underwing fairings; arrester gear; prototype only; CMASA-built (1).
G.50B: Unarmed dual-control trainer version; CMASA-built (108).
G.50ter: Modified G.50B; 1,000hp Fiat A.76 RC 40; not completed.
G.50V: Re-engined G.50; one 1,050hp Daimler-Benz DB 601A; prototype only; CMASA-built (1).
G.51,52: Re-engined G.50; Fiat A.75 RC 53/DB 601N resp; projects only.
Total Production: 777.
Remarks: IAF's first all-metal retractable undercarriage monoplane fighter, G.50's operational debut closing stages Spanish Civil War (15 early examples despatched Jan 1939, survivors subsequently passed to SpanAF); 118 G.50s on IAF strength upon Italian entry WWII; limited employment against France (escorting raids on Corsica), and along Channel/North Sea coasts, Oct 1940–April 1941; also participated Greek and Western Desert campaigns, latterly in fighter-bomber role, before relegation second-line/local-defence duties; final actions Tunisia/Sicily; 48 aircraft remaining at time of Armistice, 10 (G.50/50bis) to RSIAF, others to ICoAF; no confirmed operational use Croatian AF models; Finnish AF examples entered service 1940; took part Continuation War, 1941–44, thereafter relegated training role (retired 1947).
Colour Reference: Plate 88: Fiat (CMASA) G.50bis Serie IV 20° gruppo, 56° stormo caccia terrestre (fighter group) of the Corpo Aereo Italiano, Maldeghem, Belgium, Oct 1940; part of Italian Corps based Belgium for abortive aerial assault on UK, Oct 1940–April 1941; note yellow tactical recognition markings, 'Black Cat' unit badge on tail fin, and Commandante di Gruppo pennant below cockpit.

Manufacturer: Fiat (CMASA).
Model: RS.14B.
Type: Reconnaissance-bomber floatplane.
Power Plant: Two 870hp Fiat A.74 RC 38.
Performance:
maximum speed at sea level 242mph (390km/hr).
maximum speed at 13,120ft (4,000m) 254mph (408km/hr).
cruising speed 205mph (330km/hr).
maximum range 1,553 miles (2,500km).
service ceiling 16,400ft (5,000m).
Weights:
empty 12,125lb (5,500kg).
loaded 17,637lb (8,000kg).
Dimensions:
wing span 64ft 1in (19.54m).
length 46ft 3in (14.1m).
wing area 538.2sq ft (50.0sq m).
Armament: One 12.7mm Scotti machine-gun in dorsal turret; two 7.7mm Breda-SAFAT machine-guns in beam hatches; max bomb load 880lb (400kg) or two 353lb (160kg) depth-charges.
Crew: 5.
In Service: Italy (IAF, RSIAF, ICoAF), Germany ex-Italy.
Variants (with no. built):
R.14A: Prototypes; unarmed reconnaissance floatplane version; two 840hp Fiat A.74 RC 38 (2).
RS.14B: Initial production model; reconnaissance-bomber version; modified nose; dorsal turret; ventral tray for bombs or depth-charges.
RS.14C: Air/sea-rescue/reconnaissance version; modified RS.14B; ventral tray deleted. (Total RS.14B, C: 184).
AS.14: Ground-attack landplane version; modified RS.14; retractable undercarriage; one 45mm cannon, seven 12.7mm machine-guns, plus two 7.7mm machine-guns; prototype only (1).
Total Production: 187.
Remarks: Entering service 1941, RS.14B arguably one of best floatplanes of WWII; initially operated Central and Eastern Mediterranean/Aegean areas maritime reconnaissance and convoy-escort duties, also called upon to perform naval support and defensive fighter roles; by time Italian surrender majority relegated ASR units; subsequently served both RSIAF, ICoAF before resumption post-war IAF service; remained in use until late forties.

Manufacturer: Fiat.
Model: CR.25bis.
Type: Escort-fighter/reconnaissance.
Power Plant: Two 870hp Fiat A.74 RC 38.
Performance:
maximum speed 304mph (490km/hr).
maximum range 1,305 miles (2,100km).
service ceiling 26,575ft (8,000m).
Weights:
empty 8,600lb (3,900kg).
loaded 13,625lb (6,180kg).
Dimensions:
wing span 52ft 6in (16.0m).
length 44ft 5¾in (13.56m).
wing area 421.95sq ft (39.2sq m).
Armament: Two fixed forward-firing 12.7mm Breda-SAFAT machine-guns in nose; one 12.7mm Breda-SAFAT machine-gun in dorsal turret; max bomb load 1,100lb (500kg).
Crew: 3.
In Service: Italy.
Variants (with no. built):
CR.25: Prototypes; escort-fighter/reconnaissance version; two Fiat A.74 RC 38; four 7.7mm plus one one 12.7mm Breda-SAFAT machine-guns (2).
CR.25bis: Pre-production model; revised armament; provision for addn bomb load or auxiliary fuel tanks (9).
CR.25D: VIP transport version; modified CR.25 (1).
CR.25quater: Improved CR.25bis; increased armament/wing area; not completed.
Total Production: 12.
Remarks: Departure from long (and continuing) line single-engined fighters, Fiat's twin-engined CR.25bis, initially intended for strategic reconnaissance, saw brief service convoy escort role Sicily-mainland Italy during latter half 1942; inadequate armament/servicing difficulties hastened relegation light transport duties; sole CR.25D employed as personal transport Italian Air Attaché in Berlin.

Manufacturer: Fiat.
Model: CR.42AS Falco (Falcon).
Type: Assault-fighter.
Power Plant: One 840hp Fiat A.74 RC 38.
Performance:
maximum speed at sea level 213mph (343km/hr).
maximum speed (280mph (450km/hr).
normal range 480 miles (775km).
time to 19,685ft (6,000m) 7min 0sec.
max ceiling 34,450ft (10,500m).
Weights:
empty 3,792lb (1,720kg).
normal 5,060lb (2,295kg).
Dimensions:
wing span 31ft 9¾in (9.7m).
length 27ft 1in (8.26m).
height 10ft 11¾in (3.35m).
wing area 241.1sq ft (22.4sq m).
Armament: Two 12.7mm Breda-SAFAT machine-guns in upper cowling; max bomb load 440lb (200kg).
Crew: 1.
In Service: Belgium (23), Germany (100+), Great Britain (1 captured ex-Italy/evaluation), Hungary (approx 70), Italy (IAF, RSIAF, ICoAF), South Africa (2 captured ex-Italy), Sweden (72).
Variants:
CR.42 Falco: Prototype and initial production model; fighter biplane version; one Fiat A.74R RC 38; one 12.7mm and one 7.7mm Breda-SAFAT machine-guns; prototype with fully retractable tailwheel (inc original Hungarian (50) and Belgian (34) orders).
CR.42AS: Assault-fighter version; provision for two 220lb (100kg) underwing bombs; revised armament; tropicalized.
CR.42bis: Modified CR.42; two 12.7mm machine-guns; Swedish order (as J 11).
CR.42B: Re-engined CR.42; one 1,010hp Daimler-Benz DB 601; prototype only.
CR.42CN: Night-fighter version; modified CR.42; two searchlights in underwing fairings; radio equipment.
CR.42ter: As CR.42bis; two addn 12.7mm machine-guns in underwing fairings.
ICR.42: Fighter floatplane version; modified CR.42; prototype/s only; CMASA-built.
Total Production: 1,780+.
Remarks: World's last single-seat fighter biplane, CR.42 first flown early 1939; exported Belgium, Hungary, and Sweden; former first

to see action, 23 (of 34 ordered) equipping two Escadrilles Belgian AF at time of German invasion; over half destroyed on ground in initial assault, survivors playing limited part remainder of campaign; Hungarian AF machines operated Eastern Front opening months invasion USSR, 1941; Swedish examples in service (as J 11), 1940–45; over 300 CR.42s equipped IAF units upon Italian entry WWII, June 1940; first employed attack on (Southern) France, subsequent brief appearance Belgium for abortive raids on UK, autumn 1940; also participated Greek and East African theatres, but widest use North Africa, 1940–43, initially fighter role, latterly day/night ground-attack; operated night defence Northern Italy (CR.42CN); post-Armistice served both RSIAF/ICoAF limited numbers (4 and 15 resp), majority remainder seized by Germany for Luftwaffe night-ground attack Staffeln (sqns) N Italy/Balkans, 1944–45.
Colour Reference: Plates 84, 85: Fiat CR.42 Falco (No 26) of 4/II/2 (4e Escadrille, II Groupe, 2e Régiment d'Aéronautique (chasse)); Brusthem (nr St Trond), 10 May 1940; one of six CR.42s evacuated to France towards close Belgian campaign, No 26 subsequently damaged during Luftwaffe bombing raid on Chartres; standard Italian-style dapple finish; individual aircraft number on rudder, repeated under lower wing ('R' starboard/'26' port); 4e Escadrille red 'Cocotte' insignia on fuselage.

Manufacturer: Fiat.
Model: G.12T.
Type: Transport.
Power Plant: Three 770hp Fiat A.74 RC 42.
Performance:
maximum speed at 16,400ft (5,000m) 242mph (390km/hr).
cruising speed 192mph (310km/hr).
normal range 1,428 miles (2,300km).
service ceiling 27,890ft (8,500m).
Weights:
empty 20,460lb (9,280kg).
loaded 33,050lb (15,000kg).
Dimensions:
wing span 93ft 10in (28.6m).
length 65ft 11¼in (20.1m).
height 16ft 1in (4.9m).
wing area 1,215.9sq ft (122.96sq m).
Armament: Two 7.7mm machine-guns.
Crew/Accommodation: 4/22 troops (or cargo).
In Service: Germany (12 G.12T), Hungary (4 G.12), Italy (IAF, RSIAF, ICoAF.
Variants (with no. built):
G.12C: Initial production model; high-altitude civil transport version; three 770hp Fiat A.74 RC 42; 14 passengers (3).
G.12GA, LGA: Long-range civil transport versions; three 860hp Alfa Romeo 128 RC 18 or 750hp Alfa Romeo 126 RC 34 resp.
G.12RT (Roma-Tokio), RTbis: Long-range civil transport versions; three 895hp Alfa Romeo RC 18. G.12RTbis increased weight and fuel capacity; range 5,592 miles (9,000km); prototypes only (2).
G.12T: Military cargo and troop transport version; modified G.12C.
G.12 Gondar: Long-range military cargo transport version; modified G.12C; increased weight; range 3,606 miles (5,800km).
G.12CA, L, LA, LB, LP: Post-war civil developments; 16–22 passengers; various power plants.
G.12 Aula Volante (Flying Classroom): Post-war military trainer.
Remarks: Prototype first flown Oct 1940, limited wartime production military G.12T and G.12 Gondar (latter named after Abyssinian provincial capital, one of main objectives of 1935 war); served alongside impressed civil models long-range transport duties, inc supply/evacuation Tunisia, Spring 1943; thirteen G.12Ts on strength RSIAF post-Armistice, majority of which impressed Luftwaffe and employed Eastern (Russian) Front in transport role flown by Italian crews; considerable post-war development and use.

Manufacturer: Fiat.
Model: G.55/I (Serie I) Centauro (Centaur).
Type: Fighter/fighter-bomber.
Power Plant: One 1,475 Fiat RA.1050 RC 58 Tifone (Typhoon) (licence-built DB 605A–1).
Performance:
maximum speed 385mph (620km/hr).
cruising speed 348mph (560km/hr).
maximum range 1,025 miles (1,650km).
time to 19,685ft (6,000m) 7min 12sec.
service ceiling 41,830ft (12,750m).
Weights:
empty 5,798lb (2,630kg).
loaded 7,760lb (3,520kg).
Dimensions:
wing span 38ft 10½in (11.85m).
length 30ft 9in (9.37m).
height 10ft 4¾in (3.17m).
wing area 227.23sq ft (21.11sq m).
Armament: One 20mm MG 151 cannon firing through propeller hub, two 20mm MG 151 cannon in wings; two 12.7mm Breda-SAFAT machine-guns in fuselage; provision for max bomb load 706lb (320kg).
Crew: 1.
In Service: Germany (G.55/56 evaluation), Italy (IAF, RSIAF).
Variants (with no. built):
G.55 Centauro: Prototypes; single-seat fighter version; one 1,475hp Daimler-Benz DB 605A–1 (3).
G.55/O (Serie O): Pre-production model; one engine-mounted 20mm MG 151 cannon, plus two 12.7mm machine-guns each in wings and fuselage (8).
G.55/I (Serie I): Initial (and major) production model; as G.55/O; revised armament; detail improvements (approx 185).
G.55/II (Serie II): Bomber interceptor version; modified G.55/I; five 20mm MG 151 cannon; none completed.
G.55S: Torpedo strike-fighter version; modified G.55/I; lengthened tailwheel leg; 12.7mm fuselage guns deleted; repositioned radiator; provision for one 2,050lb (930kg) torpedo under fuselage (inc 1 conversion, approx 10).
G.55A,B: Single-seat fighter/fighter-trainer, and 2-seat advanced trainer versions resp; post-war developments (85).
G.56: Re-engined G.55/I; one 1,750hp DB 603A; prototype only (1).
G.57: Re-engined G.55; one 1,250hp Fiat A.83 RC 24–52; project only.
Total Production: approx 200 (exc G.55A/B).
Remarks: First flown Spring 1942, early examples G.55/O and /I entered service immediately prior Italian Armistice; reported small-scale use of individual aircraft by IAF Milan area; production continued 1943–44, approx total 170 on strength RSIAF for operations alongside Luftwaffe in defence Northern Italy, 1943–45.

Manufacturer: Macchi.
Model: MC.94.
Type: Transport flying boat.
Power Plant: Two 800hp Alfa Romeo 126 RC 10.
Performance:
maximum speed 181mph (292km/hr).
cruising speed 153mph (246km/hr).
normal range 925 miles (1,490km).
time to 6,560ft (2,000m) 7min 58sec.
service ceiling 19,685ft (6,000m).
Weights:
empty 11,353lb (5,150kg).
loaded 18,077lb (8,200kg).
Dimensions:
wing span 75ft 2¾in (22.93m).
length 53ft 0¾in (16.17m).
height 17ft 10½in ((5.45m).
wing area 818.06sq ft (76.0sq m).
Crew/Accommodation: 3/12.
In Service: Italy, Germany (ex-Italy).
Variants (with no. built):
MC.94 anfibio: Prototype; 12-passenger civil transport amphibian; two 750hp Wright Cyclone SGR–1820–F52 (1).
MC.94: Production model; 12-passenger civil transport flying boat; two 700hp Piaggio Stella, 750hp Wright Cyclone SGR–1820–F52, or 800hp Alfa Romeo 126 RC 10; increased dimensions; reduced weight (approx 11).
MC.99: Reconnaissance-bomber flying boat; enlarged MC.94 development; two 836hp Isotta-Fraschini Asso XI RC 15; twin fin and rudder; four machine-guns; max bomb load 3,308lb (1,500kg); prototype only (1).
MC.100: 26-passenger civil transport flying boat; enlarged MC.94 development; three 800hp Alfa Romeo 126 RC 10; twin fin and rudder; 4 crew (3).
Total Production: approx 12 (exc MC.99/100).
Remarks: Built limited numbers latter half thirties, several MC.94 civil flying boats inducted into Servizi Aerei Speciali upon Italian entry WWII; post-Armistice Sept 1943 eight surviving MC.94s (inc prototype) assigned German authorities, single MC.100 placed at disposal Luftwaffe HQ Mediterranean for military transport duties.

Manufacturer: Macchi.
Model: MC.200 Saetta (Lightning).
Type: Interceptor fighter.
Power Plant: One 870hp Fiat A.74 RC 38.
Performance:
maximum speed at 14,765ft (4,500m) 312mph (502km/hr).
cruising speed 283mph (455km/hr).
maximum range 540 miles (870km).
time to 9,840ft (3,000m) 3min 24sec.
service ceiling 29,200ft (8,900m).
Weights:
empty 3,902lb (1,800kg).
loaded 4,850lb (2,200kg).
Dimensions:
wing span 34ft 8½in (10.58m).
length 26ft 10½in (8.19m).
height 11ft 6¼in (3.51m).
wing area 180.8sq ft (16.8sq m).
Armament: Two 12.7mm Breda-SAFAT machine-guns in upper cowling.
Crew 1.
In Service: Italy (IAF, RSIAF, ICoAF).
Variants (with no. built):
MC.200 Saetta: Prototypes; single-seat interceptor fighter; one 850hp Fiat A.74 RC 38; enclosed cockpit; retractable tailwheel (2).
MC.200: Production model; uprated engine; later models with open, and final version with semi-enclosed, cockpit; some with two addn 7.7mm Breda-SAFAT machine-guns in modified (MC.202-type) wings.
MC.200AS: As MC.200; tropicalized.
MC.200CB: Fighter-bomber version; provision for max 706lb (320kg) bomb load, or (as escort-fighter) two auxiliary fuel tanks, underwing.
MC.200 production (in 25 series); Macchi-, Breda- and SAI-Ambrosini-built (approx 1,100).
MC.201: Improved MC.200; proposed one 1,000hp Fiat A.76 RC 40; modified fuselage and cockpit canopy; prototype only (flown with 870hp Fiat A.74 RC 38) (1).
Total Production: 1,153.
Remarks: Service debut Oct 1939, over 150 MC.200s on IAF strength (of which approx half serviceable) upon Italian entry WWII, June 1940; first combat missions flown against Malta (as bomber/dive-bomber escorts), Autumn 1940; subsequently participated Balkan/Western Desert campaigns; was to serve in North Africa from April 1941, until final Axis defeat in Tunisia 3 years later; initially operated solely as fighter, from early 1942 also employed in fighter-bomber role against both land and coastal targets (responsible for sinking HM destroyer *Zulu* off Tobruk, Sept 1942); equipped two Gruppi during eighteen months' operations along southern sector of Eastern (Russian) Front, claiming 88 Soviet aircraft destroyed; flown by total twenty Gruppi, only 33 MC.200s serviceable at time of Armistice; equipped both RSIAF (9) and ICoAF (23) as trainers.
Colour Reference: Plate 89: Macchi MC.200 Saetta of 362a squadriglia, 22° gruppo autonomo, CSIR (Italian Expeditionary Corps in Russia), Zaporozhe, Ukraine, Aug 1941; standard Regia Aeronautica finish; yellow cowling, wingtip, and fuselage band theatre markings applicable all Axis aircraft operational Eastern Front, white wing leading edge chevrons unique CSIR fighters; note abbreviated tail cross and uncommon position Spauracchio (Scarecrow) gruppo insignia.

Manufacturer: Macchi.
Model: MC.202 Folgore (Thunderbolt).
Type: Fighter.
Power Plant: One 1,175hp Alfa Romeo AR.1000 RC 41–I Monsone (Monsoon (licence-built DB 601A–1).
Performance:
maximum speed at 16,400ft (5,000m) 370mph (595km/hr).
cruising speed 360mph (580km/hr).
normal range 475 miles (765km).
time to 19,685ft (6,000m) 5min 55sec.
service ceiling 37,730ft (11,500m).
Weights:
empty 5,196lb (2,357kg).
loaded 6,475lb (2,937kg).
Dimensions:
wing span 34ft 8½in (10.58m).
length 29ft 0½in (8.85m).
height 9ft 11in (3.02m).
wing area 180.84sq ft (16.8sq m).
Armament: Two 12.7mm Breda-SAFAT machine-guns in upper cowling; provision for two 7.7mm Breda-SAFAT machine-guns in wings.
Crew: 1.
In Service: Germany (12 ex-Italy), Italy (IAF, RSIAF, ICoAF).
Variants (with no. built):
MC.202 Folgore: Prototype; single-seat fighter version; re-engined MC.200 airframe; one 1,175hp Daimler-Benz DB 601A–1; retractable tailwheel (1).
MC.202: Production model; as prototype; altn Alfa Romeo licence-built power plant; modified cockpit; fixed tailwheel; initial models with two 12.7mm machine-guns in upper cowling; from Serie VI two addn 7.7mm Breda-SAFAT machine-guns in wings; one example tested with two 20mm MG 151 cannon in underwing fairings.
MC.202AS: Modified MC.202; tropicalized.
MC.202CB: Fighter-bomber version (Serie XI); provision max 706lb (320kg) bomb load, or (as escort-fighter) two auxiliary fuel tanks underwing.
MC.202D: Modified C.202; repositioned (chin) radiator; experimental only.
MC.202 production (in 11 series): Macchi-, and Breda-built (approx 1,100).
Total Production: approx 1,100.
Remarks: First flown Aug 1940, MC.202 entered service mid-1941; best IAF wartime fighter to serve in any number, MC.202 arrived Libya late 1941; participated remainder North African campaign, from El Alamein to final surrender in Tunisia; also took part air offensives against Malta, and Mediterranean supply convoy actions, as well as limited presence on Russian Front supporting ground movements before Stalingrad, Winter 1942–43; after withdrawal Africa played vital role daylight defence Sicily/Southern Italy against incursions USAAF heavy bombers; having equipped total 19 Gruppi, only some hundred serviceable C.202s available immediately prior Allied invasion Sicily, this figure—despite constant replacement—being halved by time of Armistice; of these, 19 subsequently served RSIAF, others operating with ICoAF; only two MC.202s known to have survived into post-war years.

Manufacturer: Macchi.
Model: MC.205V Veltro (Greyhound).
Type: Fighter/fighter-bomber.

Fiat G.55/I Centauro

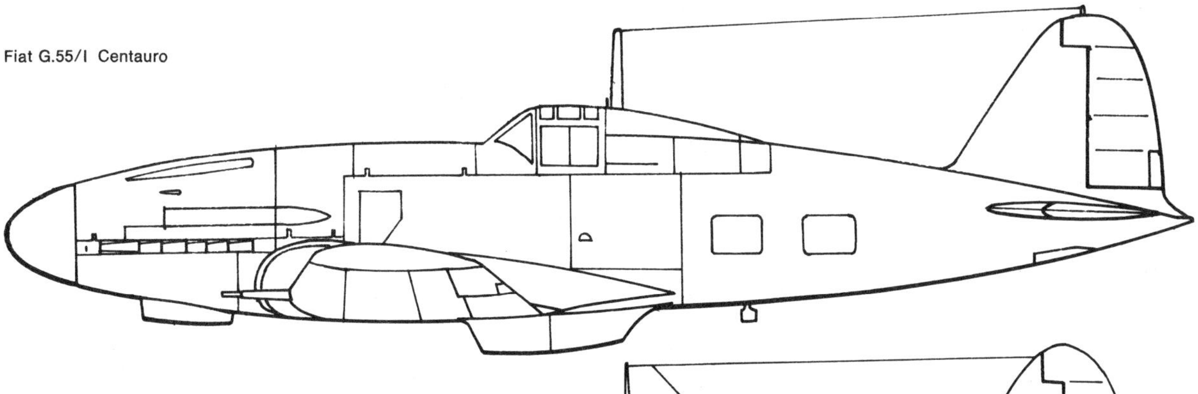

Macchi MC.202 Folgore

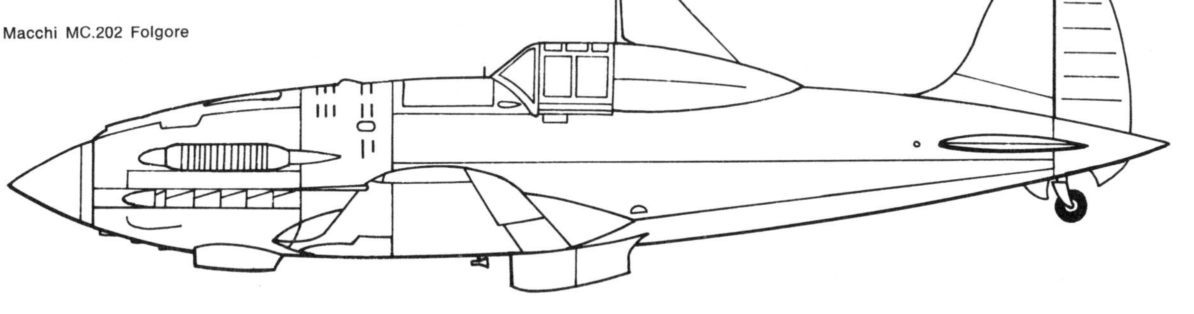

Power Plant: One 1,475hp Fiat RA.1050 RC 58 Tifone (Typhoon) (licence-built DB 605A–1).
Performance:
maximum speed at 23,620ft (7,200m) 399mph (642km/hr).
cruising speed 310mph (500km/hr).
normal range 646 miles (1,040km).
time to 9,840ft (3,000m) 2min 40sec.
service ceiling 36,090ft (11,000m).
Weights:
empty 5,564lb (2,524kg).
loaded 7,108lb (3,224kg).
Dimensions:
wing span 34ft 8½in (10.58m).
length 29ft 0½in (8.85m).
height 9ft 10¾in (3.02m).
wing area 180.84sq ft (16.8sq m).
Armament: Two 12.7mm Breda-SAFAT machine-guns in upper cowling; two 7.7mm Breda-SAFAT machine-guns in wings; max bomb load 706lb (320kg).
Crew: 1.
In Service: Germany (25+ ex-Italy), Italy (IAF, RSIAF, ICoAF).
Variants (with no. built):
MC.205: Prototype; single-seat fighter version; re-engined MC.202 airframe; one Fiat RA.1050 RC 58 (licence-built Daimler-Benz DB 605A); two 12.7mm plus two 7.7mm Breda-SAFAT machine-guns (1).
MC.205V Veltro (Greyhound): Production model; as prototype; late models (Serie III) with two 20mm MG 151 cannon in place of 7.7mm wing machine-guns (262).
MC.205N–1 Orione (Orion): High-altitude interceptor version; modified (increased span) wing; one engine-mounted 20mm MG 151 cannon, plus four fuselage-mounted 12.7mm Breda-SAFAT machine-guns; prototype only (1).
MC.205N–2: As MC.205N–1; two fuselage (side-mounted) 12.7mm Breda-SAFAT machine-guns replaced by two 20mm MG 151 wing cannon; prototype only (1).
MC.206/207: As MC.205N–2; one 1,510hp DB 603A; increased span; armament as MC.205N–2/four 20mm MG 151 wing cannon resp; prototypes only; not completed.
Total Production: 265.
Remarks: Final development of wartime line Macchi single-seat fighters, MC.205V, first flown April 1942, entered combat over Pantelleria, July 1943; served in limited numbers daylight defence Sicily/Southern Italy alongside MC.202. Of sixty-six examples operational at time of Armistice, Sept 1943, only six joined ICoAF; remainder, plus subsequent production, brought RSIAF strength to 140+; continued to oppose Allied daylight air offensive against Northern Italy; considered the equal of contemporary Allied fighters, also equipped one Luftwaffe Gruppe, Winter 1943–44; remained in IAF service post-war years, several exported Egypt late forties.
Colour Reference: Plates 90,91: Macchi MC.205V Veltro (White '17') of II.JG 77, Viterbo, Central Italy, Nov 1943; only Luftwaffe Jagdgruppe to operate MC.205V; standard Regia Aeronautica mirror wave finish; note unusual incorporation German cross into white fuselage band, non-standard (narrow-width) tail swastika, II.Gruppe horizontal bar identification, and typical Luftwaffe spinner spiral.

Manufacturer: Meridionali.
Model: Ro.37bis.
Type: Reconnaissance/light bomber.
Power Plant: One 560hp Piaggio P.IX RC 40.
Performance:
maximum speed at 16,400ft (5,000m) 205mph (330km/hr).
cruising speed 155mph (250km/hr).
maximum range 696miles (1,120km).
time to 6,560ft (2,000m) 4min 10sec.
service ceiling 23,616ft (7,200m).
Weights:
empty 3,498lb (1,587kg).
loaded 5,335lb (2,420kg).
Dimensions:
wing span 36ft 4¼in (11.08m).
length 28ft 1¼in (8.56m).
height 10ft 4in (3.15m).
Armament: Two fixed forward-firing 7.7mm Breda-SAFAT machine-guns; one flexible 7.7mm Breda-SAFAT machine-gun in rear cockpit; max bomb load 396lb (180kg).
Crew: 2.
In Service: Hungary (approx 6 Ro.37bis), Italy, Spain (NatAF approx 20 Ro.37bis).
Variants (with no. built):
Ro.37: Prototype and production model; reconnaissance/light bomber; one 550hp Fiat A.30 RAbis (162).
Ro.37bis: Re-engined Ro.37; altn 560hp Piaggio P.IX or 700hp P.XR (475+).
Total Production: 637+.
Remarks: Built 1934, Ro.37/37bis exported pre-war Hungary, Afghanistan, Central and South America; employed Spanish Civil War and Abyssinia (Ethiopia); 275+ on strength Italian entry WWII, June 1940; equipped number observation Gruppi in Balkans, North and East African campaigns; after withdrawal first-line service, operated variety ancillary roles inc anti-partisan; all retired prior Armistice.

Manufacturer: Meridionali.
Model: Ro.41.
Type: Interceptor-fighter.
Power Plant: One 390hp Piaggio P.VII C 45.
Performance:
maximum speed 180mph (325km/hr).
cruising speed 180mph (290km/hr).
normal range 373 miles (600km).
time to 13,210ft (4,000m) 6min 25sec.
service ceiling 26,900ft (8,200m).
Weights:
empty 2,160lb (980kg).
loaded 2,756lb (1,250kg).
Dimensions:
wing span 28ft 10¾in (8.81m).
length 21ft 11¾in (6.7m).
height 8ft 8¼in (2.65m).
wing area 206.13sq ft (19.15sq m).
Armament: Two fixed forward-firing 7.7mm Breda-SAFAT machine-guns.
Crew: 1.
In Service: Germany (ex-Italy/evaluation), Hungary (5 Ro.41, 3 Ro.41B), Italy (RSIAF).
Variants:
Ro.41: Prototype and production model; single-seat advanced trainer/fighter biplane; one Piaggio P.VII C.45; fixed undercarriage; some completed as 2-seat advanced trainers (Ro.41B) with one 7.7mm machine-gun.
Total Production: 437.
Remarks: First flown 1935, Ro.41 compared unfavourably with contemporary Fiat prototypes (culminating in CR.42); did not enter IAF operational service but served solely training/ancillary liaison duties; several exported Hungary prior outbreak WWII; nine examples appeared on strength RSIAF post-Armistice, Sept 1943; also reportedly employed post-war IAF.

Manufacturer: Meridionali.
Model: Ro.43.
Type: Ship-borne reconnaissance/fighter floatplane.
Power Plant: One 700hp Piaggio P.XR.
Performance:
maximum speed at 8,200ft (2,500m) 186mph (300km/hr).
cruising speed 155mph (250km/hr).
normal range 932 miles (1,500km).
time to 13,120ft (4,000m) 11min 0sec.
service ceiling 21,650ft (6,600m).
Weights:
empty 3,924lb (1,780kg).
loaded 5,290lb (2,400kg).
Dimensions:
wing span 38ft 4¾in (11.6m).
length 31ft 10¼in (9.71m).
height 11ft 5¾in (3.5m).
wing area 359.09sq ft (33.36sq m).
Armament: One fixed forward-firing 7.7mm Breda-SAFAT machine-gun; one flexible 7.7mm Breda-SAFAT machine-gun in rear cockpit.
Crew: 2.
In Service: Italy (INAF), Spain (NAF).
Variants (with no. built):
Ro.43: Prototype; 2-seat reconnaissance/fighter floatplane; one Piaggio P.XR (1).
Ro.43: Production model; as prototype; modified engine cowling; arrester gear (150+).
Ro.44: Single-seat fighter floatplane version; modified Ro.43; two fixed forward-firing 7.7mm Breda-SAFAT machine-guns; rear cockpit/fuselage side windows deleted 35.
Total Production: Approx 200.
Remarks: Standard INAF ship-borne (catapult-launched) floatplane, 100+ Ro.43s available upon Italian entry WWII, June 1940; served aboard most major units Regia Marina duration pro-Axis hostilities; 48 still on strength at Armistice, having seen relatively little action; both Ro.43 and single-seat Ro.44 fighters also deployed shore-based defence of Aegean islands; SpanNAF examples employed ASR duties WWII.

Manufacturer: Meridionali.
Model: Ro.57.
Type: Interceptor-fighter.
Power Plant: Two 840hp Fiat A.74 RC 38.
Performance:
maximum speed 310mph (500km/hr).
cruising speed 242mph (390km/hr).
normal range 1,930 miles (1,200km).
time to 19,685ft (6,000m) 9min 30sec.
service ceiling 25,590ft (7,800m).
Weights:
empty 7,694lb (3,490kg).
loaded 11,000lb (4,990kg).
Dimensions:
wing span 41ft 0¼in (12.5m).
length 28ft 10½in (8.8m).
height 9ft 6in (2.9m).
wing area 247.6sq ft (23.0sq m).
Armament: Two fixed forward-firing 12.7mm Breda-SAFAT machine-guns in nose.
Crew: 1.
In Service: Italy.
Variants (with no. built):
Ro.57: Prototype and initial production model; single-seat interceptor-fighter version; (subsequently modified as dive-bomber) (1).
Ro.57bis: Dive-bomber version; two addn 20mm cannon; provision for max 1,102lb (500kg) bombs under fuselage; dive brakes (50+).
Total Production: 51+.
Remarks: Ro.57 was designed (in 1939) and initially operated (from 1942) as interceptor-fighter, but inadequate performance at altitude led to redeployment in fighter-bomber/dive-bomber roles; saw limited action defence of Sicily/Southern Italy, July–Sept 1943.

Manufacturer: Meridionali.
Model: Ro.63.
Type: AOP/liaison.
Power Plant: One 280hp Hirth HM 508D.
Performance:
maximum speed 126mph (203km/hr).
normal range 560 miles (900km).
Weights:
loaded 2,337lb (1,060kg).
Dimensions:
wing span 44ft 3½in (13.5m).
height 7ft 8¾in (2.35m).
Crew/Accommodation: 1/1–2.
In Service: Italy.
Variants (with no. built):
Ro.63: Unarmed high-wing light observation/liaison monoplane (6).
Total Production: 6.
Remarks: Inspired by Germany's Fieseler Fi 156 Storch, number of which supplied to IAF, indigenous Ro.63 built early 1943; several initial pre-production batch reportedly employed closing stages Tunisian campaign and in Sicily; production plans halted by Armistice.

Manufacturer: Nardi.
Model: FN.305.
Type: Trainer/liaison.
Power Plant: One 190hp Alfa-Romeo 115–I.
Performance:
maximum speed 193mph (310km/hr).
cruising speed 180mph (290km/hr).
normal range 311 miles (500km).
time to 13,120ft (4,000m) 13min 40sec.
service ceiling 21,320ft (6,500m).
Weights:
empty 1,323lb (600kg).
normal/loaded 1,984lb (900kg).
Dimensions:
wing span 27ft 9½in (8.47m).
length 22ft 11½in (7.0m).
height 6ft 10¾in (2.10m).
wing area 129.17sq ft (12.0sq m).
Crew/Accommodation: 1/1.
In Service: Germany (10 FN.315), Italy (IAF, RSIAF, ICoAF), Hungary (12 FN.305, 12 FN.315), Rumania (approx 20 FN.315), Switzerland (2 FN.315).
Variants:
FN.305: 2-seater military trainer version; one Alfa Romeo 115–I; some with one (or two) 7.7mm machine-guns; Nardi-and Piaggio-built.
FN.305D: Initial production model; one- or two-seat civil light tourer; one 205hp Fiat A.70 S; various fuselage modifications; some with lengthened nose.
FN.315: 2-seat military trainer or civil tourer versions; re-engined FN.305; one 280hp Hirth HM 508D; modified cowling; some trainers with one (or two) 7.7mm machine-guns; tourer version with addn glazed side panels; Nardi- and Piaggio-built.
Remarks: First flown early 1935, FN.305 (and later FN.315) served IAF considerable numbers fighter trainer role; also employed lesser extent liaison/communications duties; at least one example participated Balkan anti-partisan actions 1942; limited operation both sides after Armistice, continuing with IAF post-war; subject several pre-war export orders, inc Hungary, Rumania, and Switzerland; latter in use until 1950.

Manufacturer: Nardi.
Model: FN.310.
Type: Light transport/ambulance.
Power Plant: One 205hp Fiat A.70 S.
Performance:
maximum speed 186mph (300km/hr).
normal range 870 miles (1,400km).
service ceiling 19,685ft (6,000m).
Weights:
empty 1,430lb (650kg).
loaded 2,530lb (1,148kg).
Dimensions:
wing span 32ft 9½in (10.0m).
length 22ft 11½in (7.0m).
height 7ft 2¾in (2.2m).
wing area 172.2sq ft (16.0sq m).
Crew/Accommodation: 1/3 (or 1 litter plus 1 medic).
In Service: Italy.
Variants:
FN.310: 4-seat civil tourer/ambulance.
Remarks: Produced 1938, several FN.310s employed military liaison and ambulance duties early months Italian participation WWII.

Manufacturer: Piaggio.
Model: P.32/I.F.
Power Plant: Two 825hp Isotta-Fraschini Asso XI RC 40.
Performance:
maximum speed at 16,400ft (5,000m) 248mph (400km/hr).
time to 13,120ft (4,000m) 15min 0sec.
service ceiling 22,960ft (7,000m).
Weights:
loaded 2,530lb (1,148kg).
empty 12,650lb (5,740kg).
loaded 16,170lb (7,335kg).
Dimensions:
wing span 59ft 0¾in (18.00m).
length 53ft 5½in (16.30m.)
height 16ft 8¾in (5.10m).
wing area 645.84sq ft (60.00sq m).
Armament: Twin 7.7mm Breda machine-guns each in retractable dorsal and ventral turrets; max bomb load 3,527lb (1,600kg).
Crew: 5.
In Service: Italy.
Variants (with no. built):
P.32: Prototype; twin-engined medium bomber; two 825hp Isotta-Fraschini Asso XI RC 40; retractable dorsal and ventral turret; faired nose contours (1).
P.32/I.F.: Initial production model; as prototype (16).
P.32/P.XI: Re-engined P.32/I.F.; two 1,020hp Piaggio P.XI RC 40; one addn 7.7mm Breda machine-gun in non-retractable nose turret (12).
Total Production: 29.
Remarks: Prototype first flown early 1936, small series P.32/I.F. and /P.XI models completed 1937–38 resp; equipped one Gruppo late thirties, but rejected for first-line service prior Italian declaration of hostilities, June 1940; brief employment ancillary roles before final scrapping/destruction as ground-targets 1941–42.

Manufacturer: Piaggio.
Model: P.108B.
Type: Long-range heavy bomber.
Power Plant: Four 1,500hp Piaggio P.XII RC 35.
Performance:
maximum speed at 13,780ft (4,200m) 267mph (430km/hr).
cruising speed 199mph (320km/hr)
normal range 2,187 miles (3,520km).
time to 16,400ft (5,000m) 21min 8sec.
service ceiling 27,890ft (8,500m).
Weights:
empty 38,195lb (17,325kg).
loaded 65,885lb (29,885kg).
Dimensions:
wing span 104ft 11¾in (32.0m).
length 73ft 1½in (22.29m).
height 19ft 8¼in (6.0m).
wing area 1,453.14sq ft (135.0sq m).
Armament: One 12.7mm Breda-SAFAT machine-gun each in nose and (semi-retractable) ventral turrets and two beam hatches; two 12.7mm Breda SAFAT machine-guns each in two remotely-controlled wing-mounted (outboard nacelle) turrets; max bomb load 7,716lb (3,500kg) or three 450mm torpedoes.
Crew: 7.
In Service: Germany (17+ P.108A,B,C,T), Italy (IAF, RSIAF).
Variants (with no. built):
P.108: Prototype; long-range heavy bomber; four 1,500hp Piaggio P.XII RC 35 (1).
P.108A: Anti-shipping version; modified P.108B prototype; redesigned nose with one 102mm cannon (1 conversion).
P.108B: Pre-production and initial production models; long-range heavy bomber version; improved P.108; some modified as night bombers with flame dampers and revised nose (reduced glazing and turret deleted) (approx 20).
P.108C: Civil transport version; redesigned fuselage; increased wing span; 32 passengers—inc 15 military impressments re-equipped for 56 troops (24).
P.108M: Modified P.108B; nose armament increased to one 20mm cannon plus four 7.7mm machine-guns (1).
P.108T: Military freight transport version; modified P.108C. 2,471cu.ft (69.97cu.m) capacity; side/ventral loading doors/hatch; prototype only (1).
P.108T2: Proposed post-war 48/60-passenger or cargo transport version; project only.
P.133: Improved P.108B; uprated engines; increased bomb load; not completed.
Remarks: Italy's only four-engined operational heavy bomber, P.108B entered service late 1942; mounted night-raids on Gibraltar and on Anglo-American supply ports North Africa (Algeria); also attacked Allied Mediterranean convoys; suffered heavy attrition, only two examples (plus sole P.108A) surviving to appear on post-Armistice RSIAF strength; latter subsequently seized by Germany; employed experimental purposes only; but number other versions likewise commandeered and used Luftwaffe long-range transport roles.

Manufacturer: Caproni-Reggiane.
Model: Re.2000 Series I Falco I (Falcon I).
Type: Interceptor-fighter.
Power Plant: One 986hp Piaggio P.XI RC 40.
Performance:
maximum speed at 16,400ft (5,000m) 329mph (530km/hr).
maximum range 870 miles (1,400km).
time to 13,120ft (4,000m) 6min 10sec.
service ceiling 34,450ft (10,500m).
Weights:
empty 4,608lb (2,090kg).
loaded 6,283lb (2,850kg).
Dimensions:
wing span 36ft 1in (11.0m).
length 26ft 2½in (7.99m).
height 10ft 6in (3.2m).
wing area 219.59sq ft (20.4sq m).
Armament: Two 12.7mm Breda-SAFAT machine-guns in upper cowling.
Crew: 1.
In Service: Italy (IAF, INAF), Hungary (261 inc licence production), Sweden (60).
Variants (with no. built):
Re.2000: Initial prototype; single-seat fighter version; one 986hp Piaggio P.XI RC 40 (1).
Re.2000 Serie I; Prototype and production model; modified engine cowling and windscreen; minor equipment changes; inc. 60 Swedish and 70 Hungarian orders (157).
Re.2000 Serie II: Ship-borne fighter version; 1,025hp Piaggio P.XIbis; arrester gear; 10 Serie I conversions.
Re.2000 (GA) Serie III: Long-range fighter version; 1,025hp Piaggio P.XIbis; redesigned cockpit; increased fuel capacity; provision for auxiliary fuel tank or 4,410lb (2,000kg) bomb load under fuselage; 12 Serie I conversions.
Héja I (Hawk I): Hungarian designation for Re.2000 Serie I.
Héja II (Hawk II): Hungarian designation for licence-produced Serie I; one 986hp WMK 14 (Manfred Weiss-built Gnome-Rhône Mistral Major K14); 12.7mm Breda-SAFAT machine-

guns replaced by two Hungarian 12.7mm Gebauer machine-guns; MAVAG-built (191).
Total Production: 349.
Remarks: Initially rejected for Italian service (although subsequently operated in limited nubers on Mediterranean convoy escort duties by both IAF/INAF), over 80% Reggiane production for export Sweden and Hungary; former, under Swedish designation J 20, served 1941–46; during WWII hostilities, as fastest Swedish AF fighter available, employed to intercept and escort Allied/Axis aircraft overflying neutral Swedish airspace; one shot down by Luftwaffe Do 24 closing month of war; Hungarian AF machines served Eastern (Russian) Front latter half 1941 (six-aircraft Flight), and again 1942–43 as part Independent Fighter Group; also equipped home-defence unit until Autumn 1943; bulk Hungarian licence-production employed advance fighter-trainer role, with numbers reportedly operational in all-out effort to stem 1944 Soviet Army drive across Hungary.
Colour Reference: Plates 86, 87: Caproni-Reggiane Re.2000 Serie I (Héja I) (V.417) of special Héja Flight attached to Air Force Brigade in support Hungarian Fast Corps' advance across Ukraine, June-Dec 1941; compare early style Hungarian national markings with post-1941 insignia (see Focke-Wulf Fw 190F, Plates 30–31).

Manufacturer: Reggiane.
Model: Re.2001 Serie III Falco II (Falcon II).
Type: Fighter.
Power Plant: One 1,175hp Alfa Romeo RA 1000 RC 41–Ia Monsone (Monsoon) (licence-built DB 601A–1).
Performance:
maximum speed at sea level 273mph (440km/hr).
maximum speed at 13,120ft (4,000m) 337mph (542km/hr).
cruising speed 291mph (469km/hr).
maximum range 684 miles (1,100km).
time to 16,400ft (5,000m) 6min 20sec.
service ceiling 36,090ft (11,000m).
Weights:
empty 5,500lb (2,495kg).
loaded 7,231lb (3,280kg).
Dimensions:
wing span 36ft 1in (11.0m).
length 27ft 5in (8.36m).
height 10ft 4in (3.15m).
wing area 219.58sq ft (20.4sq m).
Armament: Two 12.7mm Breda-SAFAT machine-guns in upper cowling; two 7.9mm Breda-SAFAT machine-guns in wings.
Crew: 1.
In Service: Italy (IAF, RSIAF, ICoAF).
Variants (with no. built):
Re.2001: Prototypes; single-seat fighter version; one 1,050hp Daimler-Benz DB 601A–1; second prototype with redesigned (three-spar) wing, modified canopy, and fixed tailwheel (2).
Re.2001: Pre-production model; one 1,050hp Alfa Romeo RA 1000 RC 41–Ia Monsone (10).
Re.2001 Serie I: As pre-production model; two fuselage-mounted 12.7mm Breda-SAFAT machine-guns; inc 39 as Re.2001CB fighter-bombers with one 1,410lb (640kg) bomb or torpedo, 12 as land-based carrier trainers with arrester gear, and 2 experimental lightweight versions for land-based catapult tests (100).
Re.2001 OR Serie II: Proposed ship-borne fighter version; completed as Re.2001 CN Serie II night-fighters with two addn 7.9mm Breda-SAFAT machine-guns in wings or two 20mm MG 151 cannon in underwing fairings (50).
Re.2001 CN Serie III: Night-fighter; as production Serie II.
Re.2001 CN Serie IV: Night-fighter/fighter-bomber version; as Serie III; provision for one 1,410lb (640kg) bomb, or auxiliary drop-tank under fuselage. (Total Re.2001 CN Serie III, IV: 74).
Re.2001 G/H: Torpedo-fighter with lengthened tailwheel leg/anti-tank aircraft with two 20mm cannon resp; experimental only; 2 Serie IV conversions.
Re.2001 Delta: Re-engined Re.2001; one 840hp Isotta-Fraschini Delta RC 16/48 (1).
Re.2001bis: Experimental; re-

positioned (flush leading-edge) radiators; 1 Re.2001 (prototype) conversion.
Total Production: 237.
Remarks: Re-engined development of Re.2000, improved Re.2001 subject to lengthy and complex trials programmes; first operational models (Serie I) entered service early Summer 1942; participated attacks on Malta; majority employed night-fighter role, equipping total five Gruppi for defence Central and Northern Italy; twenty-one examples serviceable at time of Armistice, Sept 1943, eight joining ICoAF, one to RSIAF.

Manufacturer: Reggiane.
Model: Re.2002 Ariete (Ram).
Type: Fighter-bomber.
Power Plant: One 1,180hp Piaggio P.XIX RC 45 Turbine B.
Performance:
maximum speed at sea level

267mph (430km/hr).
maximum speed at 18,045ft (5,500m) 329mph (530km/hr).
cruising speed 248mph (400km/hr).
normal range 684 miles (1,100km).
time to 6,560ft (2,000m) 1min 4sec.
service ceiling 36,090ft (11,000m).
Weights:
empty 5,269lb (2,390kg).
loaded 7,143lb (3,240kg).
Dimensions:
wing span 36ft 1in (11.0m).
length 26ft 9¾in (8.165m).
height 10ft 4in (3.15m).
wing area 219.58sq ft (20.4sq m).
Armament: Two 12.7mm Breda-SAFAT machine-guns in upper cowling; two 7.7mm Breda-SAFAT machine-guns in wings; max bomb load 2,095lb (950kg), or one torpedo under fuselage plus 706lb (320kg) bombs under-wing.
Crew: 1.
In Service: Germany (76+ Serie II), Italy (IAF, RSIAF, ICoAF).

Variants (with no. built):
Re.2002: Initial prototype; single-seat fighter version; re-engined development of Re.2000 Serie III; one 1,180hp Piaggio P.XIX RC 45 Turbine B; modified engine cowling; lengthened fuselage (1).
Re.2002 Serie I: Production prototype (1) and initial production model; fighter-bomber version; increased diameter engine cowling; enlarged spinner; revised cockpit canopy; non-retractable tailwheel; bomb-racks (100).
Re.2002 Serie II: Improved Serie I; pre-Armistice production for IAF (48), post-Armistice for Germany (76) (124).
Re.2002bis: Ship-borne fighter version; modified Re.2002; wing as Re.2005; arrester gear; 1 conversion.
Re.2003: Experimental 2-seat reconnaissance-bomber; modified Re.2000 Serie III; one 1,025hp

Piaggio P.XIbis RC 40; second model with definitive Re.2002-type cowling and spinner; prototypes only (2).
Total Production: 227.
Remarks: Reverting to radial engine, Re.2002 entered IAF service late 1942; based Sicily, opposed Allied landings following year; equipping one assault Stormo and two Gruppi, only sixteen examples serviceable by time of Armistice; subsequent limited-scale use both RSIAF/ICoAF; remainder production completed post-Armistice for Germany, employed by Luftwaffe ground-attack Staffeln for anti-partisan operations in Occupied France, 1944.

Manufacturer: Reggiane.
Model: Re.2005 Sagittario (Archer).
Type: Fighter/fighter-bomber.
Power Plant: One 1,475hp Fiat

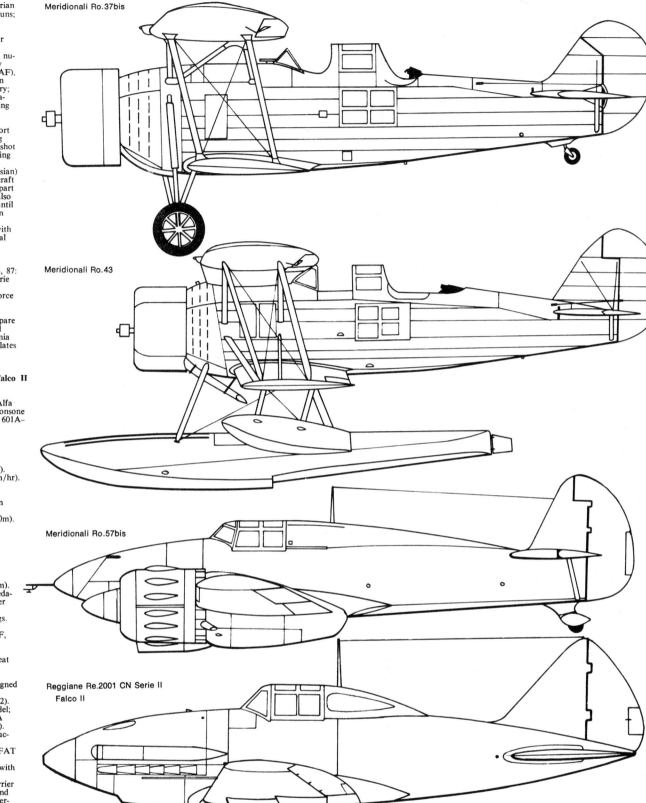

Meridionali Ro.37bis

Meridionali Ro.43

Meridionali Ro.57bis

Reggiane Re.2001 CN Serie II Falco II

R.A. 1050 RC 58 Tifone (Typhoon) (licence-built DB 605A-1).
Performance:
maximum speed at 6,560ft (2,000m) 421mph (678km/hr).
cruising speed 320mph (515km/hr).
maximum range 777 miles (1,250km).
time to 6,560ft (2,000m) 1min 35sec.
service ceiling 39,370ft (12,000m).
Weights:
empty 5,730lb (2,600kg).
loaded 7,960lb (3,610kg).
Dimensions:
wing span 36ft 1in (11.0m).
length 28ft 7½in (8.73m).
height 10ft 4in (3.15m).
wing area 219.58sq ft (20.4sq m).
Armament: Two 12.7mm Breda-SAFAT machine-guns in upper cowling; one 20mm MG 151

cannon firing through propeller hub; two 20mm MG 151 cannon in wings; max bomb load 2,205lb (1,000kg).
Crew: 1.
In Service: Germany (approx 20), Italy (IAF, RSIAF).
Variants (with no. built):
Re.2005: Prototypes; one 1,475hp Daimler-Benz DB 605A-1 (2).
Re.2005: Pre-production model; as prototype; one 1,475hp Fiat RA. 1050 RC 58 Tifone; inc 6 completed for Germany (35).
Re.2005 Serie I: Proposed initial production model (750); none completed.
Re.2005R: Modified Re.2005; rear fuselage-mounted auxiliary centrifugal compressor; project

only.
Total Production: 37.
Remarks: Final, and finest, model of Reggiane line to be built, prototype Re.2005 first flew Sept 1942; externally similar to predecessors, featured much redesign inc, for first time, outward (rather than rearward)-retractable main undercarriage; at least twenty pre-production models operated by IAF from May 1943, in defence Rome/Naples area; eight subsequently despatched Sicily to combat Allied invasion; upon Armistice one captured by USAAF, three to RSIAF, majority of remainder (approx 13) seized by Germany; refitted original DB 605A power plants,

and reportedly employed by Luftwaffe in defence of Berlin.

Manufacturer: SAIMAN.
Model: 200.
Type: Trainer/communications.
Power Plant: One 195hp Alfa Romeo 115-I.
Performance:
maximum speed 137mph (220km/hr).
cruising speed 116mph (187km/hr).
normal range 310 miles (500km).
service ceiling 19,685ft (6,000m).
Weights:
empty 1,653lb (750kg).
loaded 2,315lb (1,050kg).
Dimensions:
wing span 28ft 10½in (8.8m).
length 23ft 7½in (7.2m).

height 8ft 2½in (2.5m).
wing area 236.8sq ft (22.0sq m).
Crew: 1/1.
In Service: Croatia (12), Italy (IAF, ICoAF).
Variants:
SAIMAN 200: 2-seat light sports plane/trainer.
Remarks: First produced mid-thirties, considerable numbers SAIMAN 200 2-seat trainers employed by IAF in communications/liaison roles; captured examples performed similar functions with many Allied AF sqns in Sicily and Italy.

Manufacturer: SAIMAN.
Model: 202.
Type: Liaison/communications.

Order of Battle 8 September 1943

ITALIAN AIR FORCE (Regia Aeronautica)

1a Squadra Aerea Milan
13° Stormo da combattimento:
30° Gruppo
(squa. 55, 56) Bresso — 21 Caproni-Bergamaschi Ca.314

16° Stormo B.T.:
50° Gruppo (squa. 210, 211) Cameri — 5 CANT Z.1007bis
50° Stormo d'Assalto: Lonate Pozzolo 13 Fiat G.50
158° Gruppo (squa. 236, 387, 388) Lonate Pozzolo re-equ. Reggiane Re.2002
159° Gruppo (squa. 389, 390, 391) Lonate Pozzolo 6 Fiat G.50 / 10 Reggiane Re.2002
53° Stormo C.T.: Casselle 1 Fiat G.55
151° Gruppo (squa. 366, 367, 368) Caselle re-equ. Fiat G.55
153° Gruppo (squa. 372, 373, 374) Caselle 12 Fiat G.55/1
2° Gruppo Autonomo Intercettori (squa. 152) Sarzana 6 Reggiane Re.20001 / 12 Fiat CR.42
—(squa. 358) Albenga 6 Reggiane Re.2001 / 12 Fiat CR.42
3° Gruppo Autonomo C.T. (squa. 153, 154, 155) Caselle re-equ. Messerschmitt Bf 109G
8° Gruppo C.T. (squa. 92, 93, 94) Sarzana 18 Macchi MC.200
59° Gruppo Autonomo Intercettori Notturni (squa. 232, 233) Venegono 2 Messerschmitt Bf 110C-4 / 8 Reggiane Re.2001 / 8 Dornier Do 217J / 5 Fiat CR.42
60° Gruppo Autonomo Intercettori Notturni
—(squa. 234) Lonate Pozzolo 11 Reggiane Re.2001 / Venegono 3 Fiat CR.42
—(squa. 235) Lonate Pozzolo 2 Dornier Do 217J
99° Gruppo (squa. 242, 243) Lonate Pozzolo 18 Savoia-Marchetti S.M.84
103° Gruppo Autonomo Tuffatori Lonate Pozzolo 3 Breda Ba 88
150° Gruppo C.T. (squa. 364, 365) Caselle re-equ. Messerschmitt Bf 109G

2a Squadra Aerea Padua
1° Stormo C.T.: Gorizia re-equ. Macchi MC.205
6° Gruppo (squa. 79, 81, 88) Ronchi re-equ. Macchi MC.205
17° Gruppo (squa. 71, 72, 80) Ronchi re-equ. Macchi MC.205
8° Stormo B.T.:
27° Gruppo (squa. 18, 52) Bologna 6 CANT Z.1007bis
10° Stormo B.T.:
32° Gruppo (squa. 57, 58) Iesi re-equ. Junkers Ju 88
33° Gruppo (squa. 59, 60) Iesi re-equ. Junkers Ju 88
35° Stormo B.T.:
95° Gruppo (squa. 230, 231) Bologna 7 CANT Z.1007bis
47° Stormo B.T.:
107° Gruppo (squa. 262, 263) Vicenza 7 CANT Z.1007bis / 1 CANT Z.1018

3a Squadra Aerea Rome
3° Stormo C.T.:
18° Gruppo (squa. 83, 85, 95) Cerveteri 15 Macchi 202 / 8 Macchi 205
8° Stormo B.T.:
28° Gruppo (squa. 10, 19) Perugia 4 CANT Z.1007bis
9° Stormo B.T.:
29° Gruppo (squa. 62, 63) Viterbo 10 Junkers Ju 88
51° Gruppo (squa. 212, 213) Viterbo (re-equ. Junkers Ju 88)
15° Stormo d'assalto:
46° Gruppo (squa. 20, 21) Firenze 28 Fiat CR.42
47° Gruppo (squa. 53, 54) Firenze (re-equ. Reggiane Re.2002)
16° Stormo B.T.:
88° Gruppo (squa. 265) Perugia 4 CANT Z.1007bis
35° Stormo B.T.:
86° Gruppo (squa. 190, 191) Perugia 6 CANT Z.1007bis

47° Stormo B.T.:
106° Gruppo (squa. 260, 261) Perugia 8 CANT Z.1007bis
13° Gruppo Autonomo C.T. (squa. 77, 78) Metato 10 Fiat CR.42 / 8 Macchi 202
20° Gruppo C.T. (squa. 151, 352) Foligno 6 Macchi 202 / 4 Macchi 205
—(squa. 353) Ciampino-Sud 12 Fiat G.55
22° Gruppo Autonomo C.T.
(squa. 150) Capua 20 Macchi 202
(squa. 359) Capodichino 7 Reggiane Re.2005
(squa. 362) Capua 1 Reggiane Re.2001
(squa. 369) Capodichino
24° Gruppo Autonomo C.T. (squa. 354, 355, 370) Metato 13 Dewoitine D.520 / 3 Macchi 202
41° Gruppo Autonomo A.S. (squa. 204, 205) Siena/Ampugnano 14 Savoia-Marchetti S.M.79
104° Gruppo Autonomo A.S. (squa. 252, 253) Siena/Ampugnano 12 Savoia-Marchetti S.M.79
108° Gruppo Autonomo A.S. (squa. 256, 257) Pisa 12 Savoia-Marchetti S.M.79
131° Gruppo Autonomo A.S. (squa. 279, 284) Siena/Ampugnano 13 Savoia-Marchetti S.M.79
132° Gruppo Autonomo A.S. (squa. 278, 281) Littoria 9 Savoia-Marchetti S.M.79
150° Gruppo C.T. (squa. 363) Ciampino 4 Messerschmitt Bf 109G
161° Gruppo C.T. (squa. 162, 163, 164) Castiglione del Lago 2 Ambrosini S.A.I.207 / 1 Macchi 202
167° Gruppo Autonomo Intercettori (squa. 300, 303) Littoria 14 Reggiane Re.2001
172ª Squadriglia Ricognizione Strategica Viterbo 4 Junkers Ju 88
274ª Squadriglia Autonomo BGR Foligno 3 Piaggio P.108
310ª Squadriglia Autonoma Aerofotografica Guidonia 6 Macchi 205
Sezione Autonoma Aerosiluranti Capodichino 1 Savoia-Marchetti S.M.79
Transports:
18° Stormo A.T. Orvieto 198 Savoia-Marchetti S.M.73, S.M.74, S.M.75, S.M.81, S.M.81S, S.M.82, S.M.83
44° Stormo A.T. Ferrara
45° Stormo A.T. Rimini
48° Stormo A.T. Fano 31 Caproni Ca.133, Ca.148P
Gruppo Compl.re A.T. Marcigliana/Roma 12 Fiat G.12
Scuola Paracadutisti Viterbo

Aeronautica Egeo (Air Forces Aegean):
30° Stormo B.T.:
90° Gruppo (squa. 194, 195) 13 CANT Z.1007bis
154° Gruppo Autonomo C.T. (squa. 395, 396) Marizza 19 Fiat CR.42 / 13 Fiat G.50 / 8 Macchi 202
Sezione Autonoma Intercettori 5 Fiat CR.42

Aeronautica Grecia (Air Forces Greece):
30° Stormo B.T.:
87° Gruppo (squa. 192, 193) Kalamaki 6 CANT Z.1007bis / 16 Macchi 200
385ª Squadriglia Autonoma C.T. Araxos 3 Fiat G.50
Sezione Autonoma Intercettori Tatoi 4 Fiat CR.42

Aeronautica Albania (Air Forces Albania):
13° Stormo da combattimento:
43° Gruppo (squa. 3, 5) Devoli 18 Caproni Ca.314
38° Stormo B.T.:
40° Gruppo (squa. 202, 203) Scjak 18 Fiat BR.20
42° Gruppo (squa. 200, 201) 13 Fiat BR.20
376ª Squadriglia Autonoma C.T. Tirana 7 Fiat G.50 / 2 Macchi 200
392ª Squadriglia Autonoma C.T. 11 Fiat CR.42 / 5 Fiat G.50

Aeronautica Slovenia/Dalmazia (Air Forces Slovenia/Dalmatia):
51ª Squadriglia Autonoma B.T. Zara 8 Fiat BR.20
69ª Squadriglia Autonoma B.T. Scutari 6 Fiat BR.20
383ª Squadriglia d'Assalto Zara 16 Fiat CR.42
Sezione distaccata (squa. 383) Altura di Pola 6 Fiat CR.42

Aviazione Ausiliaria per l'Esercito (Army Air Force)
France:
19° Stormo da Osservazione Aerea: Menton 8 Caproni Ca.313
64° Gruppo (squa. 136 O.A.) Hyères 6 Caproni Ca.313
64° Gruppo (squa. 122 O.A.) Cuers 14 Caproni Ca.313
20° Stormo da Osservazione Aerea (squa. 36 O.A.) Capannori 10 Caproni Ca.314
71° Gruppo (squa. 38, 116 O.A.) Venaria Reale 5 Caproni Ca.311
76° Gruppo (squa. 30, 127 O.A.) Le Luc 14 Caproni Ca.313
65° Gruppo (squa. 124 O.A.) Ajaccio (Corsica) 1 Caproni Ca.313 / 5 Caproni Ca.313
65° Gruppo (squa. 131 O.A.) Bastia (Corsica) 18 Caproni Ca.314
137ª Squadriglia O.A. Albenga 9 Caproni Ca.313
Greece:
72° Gruppo (squa. 31 O.A.) Araxos 11 Fiat BR.20
(squa. 35 O.A.) Larissa 9 Caproni Ca.311 / 1 Caproni Ca.313
Albania:
61° Gruppo (squa. 25, 34 O.A.) Scutari 5 Caproni Ca.311 / 7 Caproni Ca.314
70° Gruppo (squa. 114, 123 O.A.) Valona 12 Caproni Ca.311 / 6 Caproni Ca.314
73° Gruppo (squa. 24 O.A.) Scjak 10 Caproni Ca.313
(squa. 115 O.A.) Devoli 8 Caproni Ca.314
Slovenia/Dalmatia:
21° Stormo da Osservazione Aerea Sussak
5° Gruppo (squa. 128 O.A.) Zara 3 Caproni Ca.311
5° Gruppo (squa. 33 O.A.) Mostar 12 Caproni Ca.314
63° Gruppo (squa. 119 O.A.) Altura di Pola 11 Fiat BR.20
63° Gruppo (squa. 41, 113 O.A.) Lubljana 1 Caproni Ca.313 / 11 Caproni Ca.314
68° Gruppo O.A. Lavariano 2 Caproni Ca.311
(squa. 39 O.A.) Iesi 2 Caproni Ca.313
(squa. 121 O.A.) Pescara 15 Caproni Ca.314

Aviazione Ausiliaria per la Marina (Navy Air Force)
Upper Tyrrhenian:
84° Gruppo (squa. 140, 145 R.M.) Torre del Lago 15 Fiat RS.14 / 4 CANT Z.501 / 3 CANT Z.506
171ª Squadriglia R.M. Tolone 7 CANT Z.501 / 3 CANT Z.506
187ª Squadriglia R.M. La Spezia 11 CANT Z.501 / 1 CANT Z.506
Lower Tyrrhenian:
144ª Squadriglia R.M. Orbetello 6 CANT Z.501 / 6 CANT Z.506
148ª Squadriglia R.M. Vigna di Valle 1 CANT Z.501 / 3 CANT Z.506 / 4 Fiat RS.14
182ª Squadriglia R.M. Nisida 2 CANT Z.501 / 6 CANT Z.506
Upper Adriatic:
143ª Squadriglia R.M. Venezia 3 CANT Z.501 / 3 CANT Z.506
149ª Squadriglia R.M. Kumbor 10 CANT Z.501
183ª Squadriglia R.M. Divulje 6 CANT Z.501 / 1 CANT Z.506
Navy Air Forces Greece:
82° Gruppo (squa. 39 R.M.) Prevesa 6 CANT Z.501 / 3 CANT Z.506
(squa. 184 R.M.) Pola 7 CANT Z.501 / 6 CANT Z.506
147ª Squadriglia R.M. Lero 4 CANT Z.501 / 6 CANT Z.506

Power Plant: One 130hp Alfa Romeo 110.
Performance:
maximum speed at sea level 143mph (230km/hr).
normal range 435 miles (700km).
time to 13,120ft (4,000m) 24min 0sec.
service ceiling 16,400ft (5,000m).
Weights:
empty 1,390lb (630kg).
loaded 2,050lb (930kg).
Dimensions:
wing span 35ft 3¼in (10.75m).
length 25ft 3¼in (7.7m).
height 6ft 6¾in (2.0m).
wing area 193.75sq ft (18.0sq m).
Crew/Accommodation: 1/1.
In Service: Croatia (12 SAIMAN 202), Germany (ex-Italy), Great Britain (1 SAIMAN 202 impressment), Italy (IAF, RSIAF, ICoAF).
Variants (with no. built):
SAIMAN 202: 2-seat light civil tourer; various cabin arrangements; some with rear quarter windows; majority with spatted undercarriage.
SAIMAN 202M: Military trainer/liaison version (390).
SAIMAN 204: 4-seat light civil tourer; modified SAIMAN 202; one 185hp Alfa Romeo 115–I; lengthened fuselage; redesigned canopy.
Remarks: Popular pre-war light tourers, SAIMAN 202/204s impressed for IAF military communications duties duration WWII; served both RSIAF/ICoAF post-Armistice; also employed by Luftwaffe and RAF (latter operating single impressment in UK); continued post-war use military and civil.

Manufacturer: Savoia-Marchetti.
Model: S.M.62bis.
Type: Bomber/reconnaissance flying boat.
Power Plant: One 750hp Isotta-Fraschini Asso.

Reggiane Re.2002 Serie II Ariete

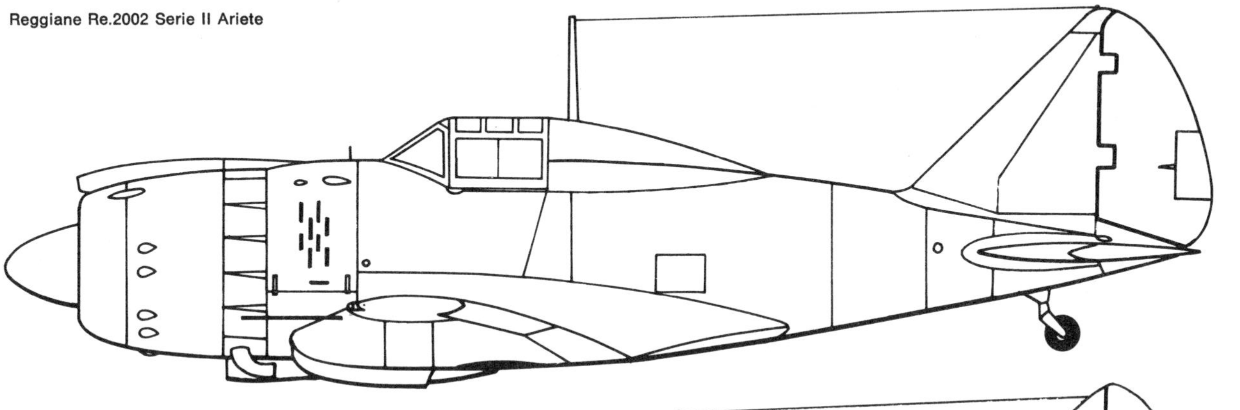

Reggiane Re.2005 Sagittario

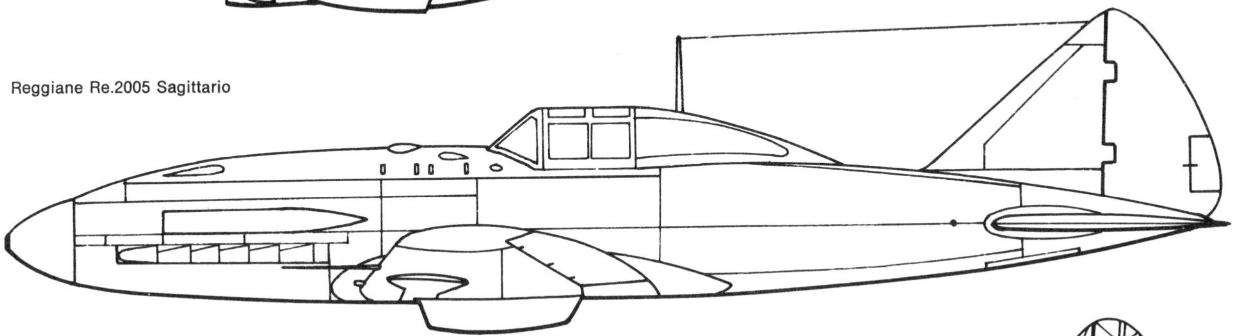

Savoia-Marchetti S.M.82 Marsupiale

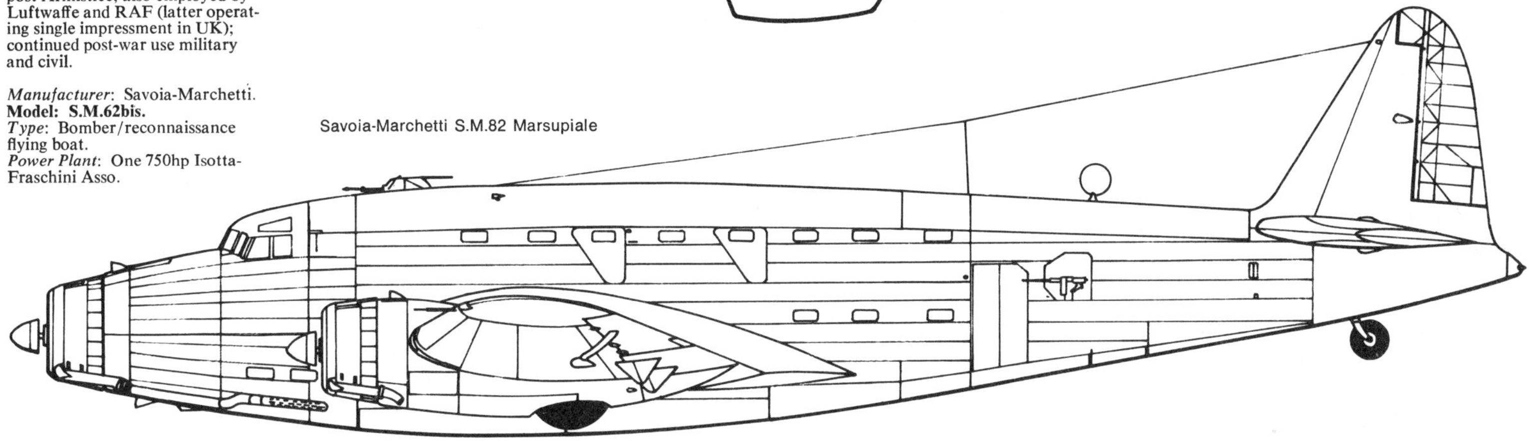

Performance:
maximum speed 137mph (220km/hr).
cruising speed 112mph (180km/hr).
maximum range 746 miles (1,200km).
time to 9,840ft (3,000m) 20min 20sec.
service ceiling 14,760ft (4,500m).
Weights:
empty 5,798lb (2,630kg).
loaded 8,885lb (4,030kg).
Dimensions:
wing span 54ft 5½in (16.60m).
length 41ft 2½in (12.56m).
height 13ft 9¼in (4.20m).
wing area 742.72sq ft (69sq m).
Armament: One (or twin) 7.9mm Lewis gun/s each in open bow position and dorsal turret; provision for light bombs underwing.
Crew: 3.
In Service: Italy (INAF), Rumania, Spain (SpanNAF 20), USSR (SovNAF 24 plus approx 50 licence-production).
Variants:
S.M.62: Prototype and initial production model; 3-seat bomber flying boat; one 500hp Isotta-Fraschini Asso.
S.M.62C: 2-crew/4-passenger civil version.
S.M.62bis: Modified S.M.62; increased weight/dimensions; uprated engine.
MBR–4: USSR designation for S.M.62bis licence-production.
Remarks: First flown 1926, S.M.62 series widely exported ensuing years, inc South America, Japan, Spain, Rumania, and USSR; remained in service latter two Naval Air Arms (training/liaison and reconnaissance roles resp) until well after Axis invasion of USSR, June 1941.

Manufacturer: Savoia-Marchetti.
Model: S.M.71.
Type: Transport.
Power Plant: Three 390hp Piaggio Stella P.VII C 45.
Performance:
maximum speed 168mph (270km/hr).
cruising speed 143mph (230km/hr).
maximum range 2,735 miles (4,400km).
time to 3,280ft (1,000m) 2min 54sec.
Weights:
empty 7,315lb (3,318kg).
normal/loaded 11,353lb (5,150kg).
Dimensions:
wing span 69ft 6½in (21.19m).
length 45ft 11in (14.0m).
wing area 645.6sq ft (60.0sq m).
Crew/Accommodation: 2/8–10.
In Service: Germany.
Variants (with no. built):
SM.71: Civil transport; three 240hp Walter Castor; subsequently re-engined with Piaggio P.VII C 45; various detail design modifications (approx 6).
Total Production: approx 6.
Remarks: First flown late 1930, one SM.71 airliner placed at disposal Luftwaffe HQ Mediterranean post-Italian Armistice, Sept 1943, for military transport/communications duties.

Manufacturer: Savoia-Marchetti.
Model: S.M.74.
Type: Transport.
Power Plant: Four 700hp Piaggio Stella P.X RC.
Performance:
maximum speed at sea level 205mph (330km/hr).
cruising speed 186mph (300km/hr).
normal range 621 miles (1,000km).
time to 3,280ft (1,000m) 2min 48sec.
service ceiling 22,965ft (7,000m).
Weights:
empty 21,164lb (9,600kg).
loaded 30,865lb (14,000kg).
Dimensions:
wing span 97ft 4½in (29.68m).
length 70ft 1in (21.36m).
wing area 1,275.95sq ft (118.54sq m).
Crew/Payload/Accommodation: 4/5,291lb (2,400kg)/24–27.
In Service: Italy.
Variants (with no. built):
S.M.74: Civil transport; four 700hp Stella P.X RC; final model with four 845hp Alfa Romeo Pegasus III (3).
Total Production: 3.
Remarks: Development of 1934 tri-motor transport/bomber (20 examples supplied Chinese AF), S.M.74s built 1934–35; all three impressed IAF war time military transport role.

Manufacturer: Savoia-Marchetti.
Model: S.M.75 Marsupiale (Marsupial) /Canguro (Kangaroo).
Type: Transport.
Power Plant: Three 750hp Alfa Romeo 126 RC 34.
Performance:
maximum speed at 10,070ft (3,070m) 229mph (368km/hr).
cruising speed 202mph (325km/hr).
maximum range 1,417 miles (2,280km).
service ceiling 22,965ft (7,000m).
Weights:
empty 20,900lb (9,500kg).
loaded 31,967lb (14,500kg).
Dimensions:
wing span 97ft 5¼in (29.7m).
length 70ft 10½in (21.6m).
height 16ft 8¼in (5.09m).
wing area 1,276.6sq ft (118.6sq m).
Crew/Accommodation: 3/24–30.
In Service: Germany (approx 10 ex-Italy), Hungary (5), Italy (IAF, RSIAF, ICoAF).
Variants (with no. built):
S.M.75: Civil transport version; three 750hp Alfa Romeo 126 RC 34 or three 1,000hp Piaggio P.XI RC 40; inc 5 with three 986hp Gnome-Rhône Mistral Major K14 for Hungary; detail design changes; some subsequently modified for military service with revised fin and rudder.
S.M.75bis: Military transport version; militarized S.M.75; abbreviated (S.M.82-type) vertical tail surfaces; dorsal turret. (Total S.M.75/75bis: 94).
S.M.87: Civil transport floatplane version; modified S.M.75; three 1,350hp Alfa Romeo 135 RC 32; 24 passengers (4).
Total Production: 98.
Remarks: Enlarged development of earlier highly-successful S.M.73 (see S.M.81), prototype S.M.75 first flown November, 1937; 12+ civil models impressed IAF military transport duties upon Italian entry WWII, June 1940; all 5 Hungarian models likewise served military role, 1940–44; S.M.75/75bis equipped IAF 1940–43, subsequently employed limited numbers by both RSIAF/ICoAF; at time of Armistice approx 10 remaining civil models taken over by Luftwaffe, plus at least one to DLH.

Manufacturer: Savoia-Marchetti.
Model: S.M.78.
Type: Reconnaissance flying boat.
Power Plant: One 900hp Isotta-Fraschini Asso 750 RC 35.
Performance:
maximum speed 153.5mph (245km/hr).
cruising speed 124mph (200km/hr).
maximum range 1,554 miles (2,500km).
time to 13,120ft (4,000m) 28min 0sec.
Weights:
empty 6,504lb (2,950kg).
loaded 11,133lb (5,050kg).
Dimensions:
wing span 54ft 8in (16.66m).
length 40ft 2¾in (12.26m).
wing area 748.1sq ft (69.50sq m).
Armament: One flexible 7.7mm machine-gun each in open bow and dorsal positions; max bomb load 1,323lb (600kg).
Crew: 3.
In Service: Italy (INAF).
Variants:
S.M.78: Prototype and production model; 3-seat reconnaissance flying boat.
Remarks: First flown 1934, S.M.78 essentially a cleaned-up more powerful development of earlier S.M.62bis; operated limited scale by INAF latter half thirties, number remained on strength after outbreak WWII for second-line liaison/training duties.

Manufacturer: Savoia-Marchetti.
Model: S.M.79–I Sparviero (Sparrow-hawk).
Type: Bomber.
Power Plant: Three 780hp Alfa Romeo 126 RC 34.
Performance:
maximum speed at 13,120ft (4,000m) 267mph (430km/hr).
cruising speed 233mph (375km/hr).
normal range 1,180 miles (1,900km).
time to 3,280ft (1,000m) 3min 28sec.
service ceiling 21,320ft (6,500m).
Weights:
loaded 23,100lb (10,480kg).
Dimensions:
wing span 69ft 6¾in (21.2m).
length 51ft 10in (15.8m).
height 14ft 1½in (4.31m).
wing area 664.14sq ft (61.7sq m).
Armament: One fixed forward-firing 12.7mm Breda-SAFAT machine-gun above pilot's cockpit; one flexible 12.7mm Breda-SAFAT machine-gun each in dorsal and ventral positions; one 7.7mm Lewis machine-gun in either of two lateral hatches; max bomb load 2,750lb (1,250kg).
Crew: 4–5.
In Service: Croatia (S.M.79K ex-Yugoslavia), Germany (S.M.79–II, S.M.83 ex-Italy), Great Britain (1 S.M.79 captured, 4 S.M. 79K ex-Yugoslavia), Iraq (4 S.M.79B), Italy (IAF, RSIAF, ICoAF), Rumania (24 S.M.79B, 40 S.M.79JR),South Africa (1 S.M.79 captured), Spain (Italian Legion/NatAF approx 85 S.M.79), Yugoslavia (45 S.M.79K).
Variants (with no. built):
S.M.79P: Prototype; 8-passenger civil transport version; three 610hp Piaggio Stella; re-engined three 780hp Alfa Romeo 125 RC 35/126 RC 34 (1).
S.M.79–I Sparviero: Prototype and initial production model; bomber version; re-engined S.M.79P; modified cockpit; ventral gondola; side windows deleted; some with three 1,350hp Alfa Romeo RC 32.
S.M.79B: Twin-engined export version; modified S.M.79–I; redesigned (glazed) nose; Brazilian order of 3 with two 930hp Alfa Romeo 128 RC 18, Iraqi

order of 4 with two 1,030hp Fiat A.80 RC 41, and Rumanian order of 24 with two 1,000hp Gnome-Rhône Mistral-Major K14 (31).
S.M.79C: Special prestige version; modified S.M.79–I; three 1,000hp Piaggio P.XI RC 40; armament, dorsal and ventral fairings deleted (16 conversions).
S.M.79JR: Second Rumanian order; re-engined S.M.79B; two 1,120hp Junkers Jumo 211Da; Savoia Marchetti-built (24); Rumanian (IAR) licence-built (16).
S.M.79K: As S.M.79–I; Yugoslav order (45).
S.M.79T: Long-range prestige version; modified S.M.79C; three Alfa Romeo 126 RC 34; increased fuel capacity; S.M.79–I conversion/s.
S.M.79–II: Torpedo-bomber version of S.M.79–I; three 1,000hp Piaggio P.XI RC 40 or three 1,030hp Fiat A.80 RC 41; provision for two 450mm torpedoes.
S.M.79–III(S.M.579): Improved S.M.79–II; ventral gondola deleted; forward-firing 12.7mm Breda-SAFAT machine-gun replaced by 20mm cannon.
(Total Savoia-Marchetti S.M.79–I/III production: approx 1,230).
S.M.83, S.M.83A, S.M.83T: Civil transport versions of S.M.79; three 750hp Alfa Romeo 126 RC 34; 10-passenger/mixed 6-passenger and mail/mailplane versions resp; successively increased fuel capacity (approx 23).
Total Production: approx 1,370 (all Marks).
Remarks: Arguably most famous Italian war-plane of WWII, S.M.79 bomber prototype built 1935; combat debut over Spain two years later; by time Italian entry WWII, close on 600 S.M.79–I/IIs (equipping total 14 Gruppi) accounted for over 60% IAF's first line bomber strength; early actions inc campaigns against France (and French Colonial Africa), Greece, Yugoslavia, and East Africa; also engaged North African land campaigns, but more importantly as torpedo-bomber in Mediterranean naval actions, responsible over four-year period (latterly serving RSIAF) for sinking considerable numbers Allied naval (inc five destroyers) and merchant vessels, and for damaging many more; also performed variety other roles, inc reconnaissance, ground-support, transport, and even (when much modified) used as the world's first operational radio-controlled flying bomb; post-Armistice 22 S.M.79s served ICoAF, while some 100+ (inc new S.M.79–III production) operated by RSIAF; retained post-war IAF transport role until early fifties; details wartime foreign use meagre; majority Yugoslav AF examples destroyed during 1941 Axis invasion, remainder to Croatian AF; Rumanian AF S.M.79B/JRs served Eastern Front 1941–44, some dozen latter still on strength after Rumanian declaration of war on Germany, Aug 1944.
Colour Reference: Plates 92,93: Savoia-Marchetti S.M.79–II (mod) Sparviero (No '5') of 2° gruppo, 3° stormo trasporto, Regia Aeronautica cobelligerante, Lecce-Galatina, Southern Italy, Nov 1944; standard RA mid-green overall; note overpainted wing fasces, rear fuselage band, and tail cross; (compare with near-contemporary S.M.81 transport of RSIAF (below).

Manufacturer: Savoia-Marchetti.
Model: S.M.81 Pipistrello (Bat).
Type: Bomber/transport.
Power Plant: Three 700hp Piaggio P.X. RC 35.
Performance:
maximum speed at 3,280ft (1,000m) 211mph (340km/hr).
maximum range 1,243 miles (2,000km).
time to 9,840ft (3,000m) 12min 0sec.
service ceiling 22,965ft (7,000m).
Weights:
loaded 20,503lb (9,300kg).
Dimensions:
wing span 78ft 9in (24.0m).
length 58ft 4¾in (17.8m).
height 14ft 7¼in (4.45m).
wing area 1,000.7sq ft (93.0sq m).
Armament: Two 7.7mm Breda-SAFAT machine-guns each in dorsal and ventral turrets; one 7.7mm Breda-SAFAT machine-gun in either of two lateral hatches; max bomb load 4,410lb (2,000kg).
Crew/Accommodation: 6/18 troops.
In Service: Great Britain (7 S.M.73 ex-Belgium/impressed), Italy (IAF, RSIAF, ICoAF), Spain (Italian Legion/NatAF 55).
Variants (with no. built):
S.M. 73: Prototype and initial production model; civil transport version; three 760hp Wright GR–1820 Cyclone; 4 crew, 18 passengers; various altn power plants; detail design changes (inc one delivered IAF); Savoia-Marchetti- and Belgian (SABCA) licence-built (7) (48).
S.M.81: Bomber/transport version; modified S.M.73; three 650hp Gnome-Rhône 14K, 650hp or 900hp Alfa Romeo 125 RC 35 or 126 RC 34, or 700hp Piaggio P.X RC 35 (inc one modified as personal transport Benito Mussolini); Savoia-Marchetti-, CMASA-, and Piaggio-licence-built (535).
S.M.81B: Experimental version; modified S.M.81; two 840hp Isotta-Fraschini Asso XI RC; third engine replaced by glazed (bombardier) nose section; prototype only (1).
Total Production: 584 (all Marks).
Remarks: Contemporary development of S.M.73 civil airliner (Italian-registered examples, of which either operated by wartime Servizi Aerei Speciali; or 13 impressed IAF as military transport; 7 Belgian machines similarly employed by RAF); S.M.81 bomber/transport first flown 1934; participated conquest Abyssinia, 1935–36; first Italian aircraft despatched Spain, Summer 1936, ferrying Franco troops from North Africa before playing major part Nationalist bombing campaign; over 300 S.M.81s equipped fourteen Gruppi (inc two transport) based Metropolitan Italy, Aegean Islands, Albania, North and East Africa upon Italian entry WWII, June 1940; wartime combat debut latter campaign, subsequently serving Western Desert (transport/night-bomber roles), against British Mediterranean Fleet, Tunisia, Russia, and Sicily; also employed anti-submarine patrol, transport, glider-tug duties; post-Armistice 4 S.M.81s to ICoAF, 40+ to RSIAF for transport operations under German control.
Colour Reference: Plate 94: Savoia-Marchetti S.M.81 Pipistrello (M.M.24147) 8Q+FK of 1° gruppo aerotrasporti 'Terracciano', Aeronautica Nazionale Repubblicana; Riga-Spilve, Latvia, June 1944; RSIAF transport group operating under Luftwaffe control (as 1.Staffel/Transportfliegergruppe 10(ital)), Northern/Baltic Sector of Russian Front; standard RA mid-green overall; Luftwaffe-style national markings and unit codes, plus RSIAF tricolour aft of cockpit.

Manufacturer: Savoia-Marchetti.
Model: S.M.82 Marsupiale (Marsupial)/Canguro (Kangaroo).
Type: Heavy bomber/transport.
Power Plant: Three 950hp Alfa Romeo 128 RC 21.
Performance:
maximum speed 230mph (370km/hr).
cruising speed 186mph (300km/hr).
normal/range 1,864 miles (3,000km).
time to 9,840ft (3,000m) 18min 0sec.
service ceiling 19,685ft (6,000m).
Weights:
empty 23,260lb (10,550kg).
normal/loaded 39,286lb (17,820kg).
Dimensions:
wing span 97ft 4½in (29.68m).
length 75ft 1¾in (22.9m).
height 19ft 8¼in (6.0m).
wing area 1,276.6sq ft (118.6 sq m).
Armament: (Bomber) one 7.7mm Breda-SAFAT machine-gun each in nose, ventral gondola and two lateral positions; one 12.7mm Breda-SAFAT machine-gun in dorsal turret; max bomb load 8,820lb (4,000kg).
Crew/Payload/Accommodation: (Transport) 3/8,820lb (4,000kg)/40 troops.
In Service: Germany (approx 3), Italy (IAF, RSIAF, ICoAF).
Variants (with no. built):
S.M.82: Prototype and production model; heavy bomber/transport version; three Alfa Romeo 128 RC 21; post-war conversions with three 1,215hp Pratt & Whitney Twin Wasps (approx 400).
Total Production: approx 400.
Remarks: First flown 1938, S.M.82 was further development of S.M.75 with enlarged (deepened) fuselage; 12 transports on strength IAF upon Italian entry WWII, June 1940; employed both trooper/freighter duties, in latter configuration able to transport complete (dismantled) Fiat CR.42 fighter biplane; entered service 1941, bomber versions saw limited use; transport role continued post-Armistice, approx 50 operated by RSIAF Gruppi under German control (and in Luftwaffe markings) primarily Eastern (Baltic) Front, and 30 joining ICoAF for pro-Allied transport duties; post-war IAF use (30+) until early sixties.

Manufacturer: Savoia-Marchetti.
Model: S.M.84.
Type: Torpedo-bomber.
Power Plant: Three 1,000hp Piaggio P.XI RC 40.
Performance:
maximum speed at sea level 266mph (428km/hr).
cruising speed 247mph (397km/hr).
normal range 1,137 miles (1,830km).
service ceiling 29,512ft (9,000m).
Weights:
empty 19,504lb (8,847kg).
loaded 29,295lb (13,288kg).
Dimensions:
wing span 69ft 6⅞in (21.2m).
length 58ft 4¾in (17.8m).
height 14ft 9¼in (4.5m).
wing area 656.6sq ft (61.0sq m).
Armament: One 12.7mm Breda-SAFAT machine-gun each in dorsal turret, ventral gondola, and two lateral positions; max bomb load 4,410lb (2,000kg) or two torpedoes.
In Service: Italy (IAF, RSIAF, ICoAF), Slovakia (10 S.M.84bis).
Variants (with no. built):
S.M.84 (S.M. 79bis): Prototype; torpedo-bomber development of S.M.79; three 850hp Alfa Romeo 128 RC 21; lengthened fuselage; twin fins and rudders (1).
S.M.84: Production model; as prototype; three Piaggio P.XI RC 40 (approx 100).
S.M.84bis: As S.M.84; export model (Slovakian order) (10).
Total Production: approx 110.
Remarks: Not to be confused with 1935 civil transport prototype which bore identical designation, S.M.84 torpedo-bomber (initially known as S.M.79bis) first flew three years later; based Sicily, employed primarily against Allied Mediterranean convoys, Nov 1941—Aug 1942; also in use as bomber in Aegean theatre, in attacks on Malta, and against Allied invasion Sicily; 15 examples serviceable at time of Italian Armistice, of which two subsequently operated by RSIAF; limited post-war IAF deployment transport role; ten S.M.84bis (of reported 20 ordered) supplied Slovakian AF circa 1942; details of operational career obscure, at least two surviving as part Insurgent AF's Combined Sqn, Autumn 1944.

Manufacturer: Savoia-Marchetti.
Model: S.M.85.
Type: Dive-bomber.
Power Plant: Two 500hp Piaggio P.VII RC 35.
Performance:
maximum speed at 13,120ft (4,000m) 229mph (368km/hr).
cruising speed 193mph (310km/hr).
maximum range 514 miles (827km).
time to 13,120ft (4,000m) 13min 40sec.
service ceiling 1,981ft (6,500m).
Weights:
empty 6,504lb (2,950kg).
loaded 9,237lb (4,190kg).
Dimensions:
wing span 45ft 11in (14.0m).
length 34ft 1½in (10.4m).
height 10ft 10in (3.3m).
wing area 277.71sq ft (25.8sq m).
Armament: One fixed forward-firing 12.7mm, or 7.7mm Breda-SAFAT, machine-gun in nose; max bomb load 1,102lb (500kg).
Crew: 1.
In Service: Italy.
Variants (with no. built):
S.M.85: Prototypes; twin-engined single-seat dive-bomber (2).
S.M.85: Production model (32).
S.M.86: Prototypes; improved S.M.85; redesigned fuselage; revised tail surfaces; two 520hp Walter Sagitta or two 540hp Isotta-Fraschini Gamma RC 35 IS (2).
Total Production: 36.
Remarks: Prototype S.M.85 first flown Dec 1936; despite wide publicity, no production undertaken until Spring 1939; equipping one dive-bomber Gruppo, three S.M.85s mounted single abortive raid against Royal Navy units reported off Malta; failure to locate vessels and subsequent jettisoning of bomb-load resulted in only confirmed kills of so-called 'Winged Banana's' brief career—a wide assortment of fish; withdrawn from service soon after, to be replaced by Junkers Ju 87 Stuka.

Manufacturer: Savoia-Marchetti.
Model: S.M.95.
Type: Transport.
Power Plant: Four 850hp Alfa Romeo 128 RC 18.
Performance:
maximum speed at 9,840ft (3,000m) 224mph (360km/hr).
cruising speed 196mph (315km/hr).
normal range 1,242 miles (2,000km).
service ceiling 20,830ft (6,350m).
Weights:
empty 29,982lb (13,600kg).
loaded 47,641lb (21,610kg).
Dimensions:
wing span 112ft 5½in (34.28m).
length 72ft 11in (22.22m).
height 17ft 2⅝in (5.25m).
wing area 1,381sq ft (128.3sq m).
Crew/Accommodation: 4/18.
In Service: Germany, Italy (RSIAF).
Variants (with no. built):
S.M.95: Prototype; 18-passenger civil airliner; four 780hp Alfa Romeo RC 34 (1).
S.M.95: Pre-production model; as prototype (1).
S.M.95GA: Second pre-production model; lengthened fuselage; increased fuel capacity (1).
S.M.95B: Prototype; long-range bomber version; redesigned (deepened) fuselage; four 12.7mm Breda-SAFAT machine-guns (1).
S.M.95: Post-war production model; as S.M.95GA; enlarged flight deck; 20–38 passengers; altn power plants, inc four 930hp Alfa Romeo 128 RC 18, 1,000hp Bristol Pegasus 48, or 1,065hp Pratt & Whitney R–1830–S1C3G Twin Wasp (12).
Total Production: 16.
Remarks: Last of long line Savoia-Marchetti airliners, prototype S.M.95 first flown four months prior Italian armistice; subsequent brief service RSIAF, before reported seizure by Germany and employment as Luftwaffe military transport, alongside other similarly sequestrated Italian multi-engined types.

JAPAN

Manufacturer: Aichi.
Model: D1A2 'Susie'.
Type: Carrier-borne dive-bomber.
Power Plant: One 730hp Nakajima Hikari 1.
Performance:
maximum speed at 10,500ft (3,200m) 192mph (309km/hr).
cruising speed 138mph (222km/hr).
normal range 576 miles (927km).
time to 9,840ft (3,000m) 7min 51sec.
service ceiling 22,900ft (6,980m).
Weights:
empty 3,342lb (1,516kg).
maximum 5,754lb (2,610kg).
Dimensions:
wing span 37ft 4¾in (11.4m).
length 30ft 6in (9.3m).
height 11ft 2¼in (3.41m).
wing area 373.506sq ft (34.7sq m).
Armament: Two fixed forward-firing 7.7mm Type 92 machine-guns in upper cowling; one flexible 7.7mm Type 92 machine-gun in rear cockpit; max bomb load 683lb (310kg).
Crew: 2.
In Service: Japan (IJNAF).
Variants (with no built):
Prototype: Re-engined and modified Heinkel He66.
D1A1,Navy Type 94 Carrier Bomber: Initial production model; 580hp Nakajima Kotobuki 2 Kai 1 or Kotobuki 3; modified wings; fixed tailwheel (162).
D1A2,Navy Type 96 Carrier Bomber: Improved D1A1; wheelspats; uprated engine (428).
Total Production: 590.
Remarks: Developed from imported Heinkel He 66 single-seat dive-bomber, Aichi D1A1/2s saw action during second Sino-Japanese conflict; responsible for sinking of US river gunboat *Panay* in Yangtze during evacuation of Nanking, 12 Dec 1937; by outbreak of Pacific War four years later, D1A1s serving solely in training role and only 60+ D1A2s remaining on second-line strength.

Manufacturer: Aichi.
Model: E10A1 'Hank'.
Type: Night reconnaissance flying boat.
Power Plant: One 620hp Hiro Type 91.
Performance:
maximum speed at sea level 128mph (206km/hr).
cruising speed 65mph (105km/hr).
maximum range 930 miles (1,500km).
time to 9,840ft (3,000m) 17min 42sec.
service ceiling 13,517ft (4,120m).
Weights:
empty 4,630lb (2,100kg).
loaded 7,275lb (3,300kg).
Dimensions:
wing span 50ft 10¼in (15.50m).
length 36ft 9¾in (11.22m).
height 14ft 9in (4.50m).
wing area 560.8sq ft (52.10sq m).
Armament: One flexible 7.7mm machine-gun mounted in open bow position.
Crew: 3.
In Service: Japan (IJNAF).
Variants (with no. built):
Prototypes and production models, Navy Type 96 Reconnaissance Seaplane (15).
Total Production: 15.
Remarks: Mid-thirties design, number E10A1s employed coastal reconnaissance/liaison roles early months WWII; also reportedly still serving aboard several second-line cruisers at time of Pearl Harbor.

Manufacturer: Aichi.
Model: D3A1 'Val'.
Type: Carrier-borne dive-bomber.
Power Plant: One 1,000hp Mitsubishi Kinsei 43 or 1,080hp Kinsei 44.
Performance:
maximum speed at 9,840ft (3,000m) 240mph (386km/hr).
cruising speed 184mph (296km/hr).
maximum range 915 miles (1,472km).
time to 9,840ft (3,000m) 6min 27sec.
service ceiling 30,050ft (9,300m).
Weights:
empty 5,309lb (2,408kg).
loaded 8,047lb (3,650kg).
Dimensions:
wing span 47ft 2in (14,365m).
length 33ft 5¼in (10.195m).
height 12ft 7½in (3,847m).
wing area 375.66sq ft (34.9sq m).
Armament: Two fixed forward-firing 7.7mm Type 97 machine-guns in engine cowling plus one flexible 7.7mm Type 92 machine-gun in rear cockpit; max bomb load 813lb (370kg).
Crew: 2.
In Service: Japan (IJNAF).
Variants (with no. built):
Prototypes: Different power plants; modified wings and tail surfaces (2).
D3A1 Service Trials models: 840hp Kinsei 3 (6).
D3A1, Navy Type 99 Carrier

Bomber, Model 11: Initial production; uprated Mitsubishi Kinsei 43 or 44; large dorsal fin (470).
D3A2, Model 12: Prototype; 1,300hp Kinsei 54; increased fuel tankage; redesigned rear canopy (1).
D3A2, Model 22: Production model Aichi-built (815); Showa Hikoki Kogyo-built (201).
D3A2-K, Navy Type 99 Bomber Trainer, Model 12: Trainer version; D3A1/2 conversions.
Total Production: 1,495.
Remarks: IJNAF's standard carrier-borne dive-bomber during opening months of Pacific War; participated Pearl Harbor attack; sank number of RN warships in Indian Ocean, inc two cruisers and carrier Hermes, with her escort, off Ceylon 9 April 1942; only British carrier lost to air attack in WWII; obsolescent D3As suffered heavy attrition Battles of Coral Sea and Midway, May–June 1942; thereafter gradually reassigned to land-based units (8 Kokutais), before relegation to second-line and training duties; re-appeared during US recapture of Philippines, Oct 1944, and again, towards close of war, in Kamikaze role.
Colour Reference: Plates 95,96: Aichi D3A1 'Val'(Navy Type 99 Carrier Bomber, Model 11) No 31 aboard IJN carrier Soryu, Second Koku Sentai for attack on Pearl Harbor, 7 December 1941; overall sky grey finish; tail code: B=Second Koku Sentai, I=First Carrier (Soryu), 2=Carrier Bomber.

Performance:
maximum speed at 7,155ft (2,180m) 234mph (377km/hr).
cruising speed 138mph (222km/hr).
maximum range 1,298 miles (2,088km).
time to 9,840ft (3,000m) 6min 5sec.
service ceiling 28,640ft (8,730m).
Weights:
empty 5,825lb (2,642kg).
maximum 12,192lb (4,000kg).
Dimensions:
wing span 47ft 7in (14.5m).
length 37ft 1in (11.3m).
height 15ft 5in (4.7m).
wing area 387.5sq ft (36.0sq m).
Armament: One flexible 7.7mm Type 92 machine-gun in rear cockpit; max bomb load 551lb (250kg) or depth-charges.
Crew: 3.
In Service: Japan (IJNAF).
Variants (with no. built):
E13A1, Navy Type O Reconnaissance Seaplane, Model 1: Prototypes and initial production model; subsequently re-designated Model 11.
E13A1–K: Dual-control trainer version.
E13A1a,Model 11A: Modified E13A1; re-designed float bracings; improved radio equipment; some as night version with exhaust flame dampers.
E13A1b, Model 11B: As Model 11A. Air-to-surface radar; some as night version with exhaust flame dampers.
E13A1a/b anti-patrol boat version: Modified Models 11A and 11B with flexible downward-firing ventral 20mm cannon.

Production all versions: Aichi-built (133); Watanabe (Kyushu)-built (1,127); Hiro Naval Air Arsenal-built (48).
Total Production: 1,418.
Remarks: Numerically most important IJN floatplane; entered service late 1941 over China, operating from seaplane-tenders and cruisers; subsequently reconnoitred Pearl Harbor; first encountered USN, Battles of Coral Sea and Midway; remained in service throughout Pacific war; performed convoy escort, coastal patrol, anti-shipping, liaison, staff transport, ASR, and many other roles in addition to primary reconnaissance function; employed in Kamikaze attacks end of war; at least one example operated post-war by FNAF in Indo-China.

Manufacturer: Aichi.
Model: H9A1.
Type: Training/anti-submarine flying boat.
Power Plant: Two 780hp Nakajima Kotobuki 41.
Performance:
maximum speed at 9,840ft (3,000m) 197mph (317km/hr).
cruising speed 138mph (222km/hr).
maximum range 1,335 miles (2,150km).
time to 9,840ft (3,000m) 11min 14sec.
service ceiling 22,245ft (6,780m).
Weights:
empty 10,803lb (4,900kg).
maximum 16,535lb (7,500kg).
Dimensions:
wing span 78ft 8½in (24.0m).

length 55ft 7½in (16.95m).
height 17ft 2½in (5.25m).
wing area 681.35sq ft (63.3sq m).
Armament: One flexible 7.7mm Type 92 machine-gun each in open bow and dorsal positions; max bomb load 551lb (250kg) or depth-charges.
Crew: 5 (8 as trainer).
In Service: Japan (IJNAF).
Variants (with no. built):
Prototypes (3).
Production model, Navy Type 2 Training Flying Boat, Model 11: Aichi-built (24); Nippon Hikoki-built (4).
Total Production: 31.
Remarks: Designed as flying boat crew trainer; entered service mid-1942; during closing stages of Pacific war employed in secondary role of anti-submarine patrol bomber over Japanese coastal waters; existence unknown to Allies until revealed by aerial reconnaissance Spring 1945, consequently did not receive Allied code-name.

Manufacturer: Aichi.
Model: E16A1 Zuiun 'Paul'.
Type: Twin-float reconnaissance seaplane.
Power Plant: One 1,300hp Mitsubishi Kinsei 51 or 54.
Performance:
maximum speed at 18,045ft (5,500m) 273mph (439km/hr).
cruising speed 207mph (333km/hr).
maximum range 1,504 miles (2,420km).
time to 9,840ft (3,000m) 4min 40sec.
service ceiling 32,810ft (10,000m).

Weights:
empty 6,493lb (2,945kg).
maximum 10,038lb (4,553kg).
Dimensions:
wing span 42ft 0½in (12.81m).
length 35ft 6½in (10.83m).
height 15ft 8½in (4.79m).
wing area 301.389sq ft (28.0sq m).
Armament: Two fixed wing-mounted 20mm Type 99 Model 2 cannon; one flexible 13mm Type 2 machine-gun in rear cockpit; max bomb load 551lb (250kg).
Crew: 2.
In Service: Japan (IJNAF).
Variants (with no. built):
E16A1: Prototypes; 1,300hp Kinsei 51 (3).
E16A1 Zuiun (Auspicious Cloud), Navy Reconnaissance Seaplane, Model 11: Production model; majority with Kinsei 54; Aichi-built (193); Nippon Hikoki-built (59).
E16A2: Prototype; 1,560hp Kinsei 62 (1).
Total Production: 256.
Remarks: Heavily armed reconnaissance floatplane, E16A1's operational debut late 1944 during Philippines campaign; committed to both reconnaissance and dive-bombing roles in face of overwhelming US air superiority, suffered severe losses; majority surviving examples subsequently used in Kamikaze missions against Allied forces in Okinawa area.

Manufacturer: Aichi.
Model: B7A2 Ryusei 'Grace'.
Type: Carrier-borne torpedo/dive-bomber.

Aichi E11A1 'Laura'

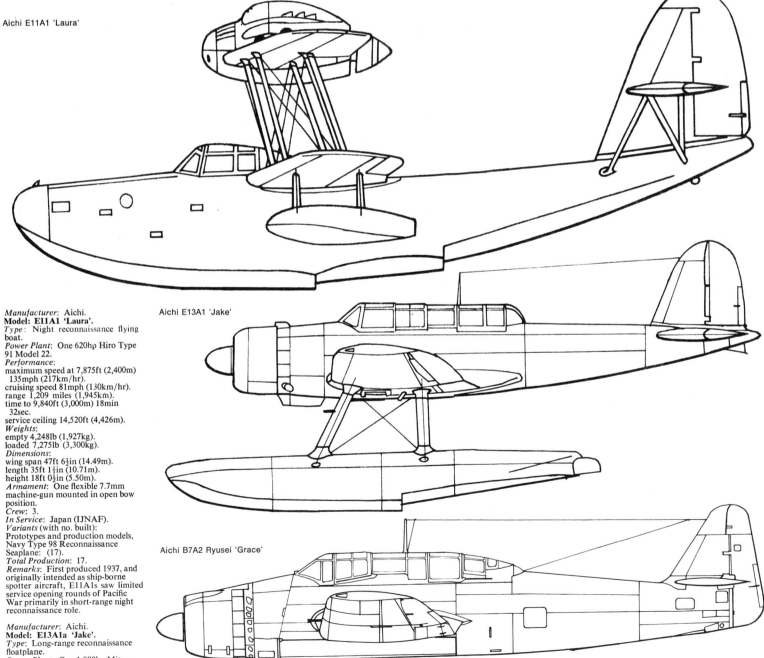

Manufacturer: Aichi.
Model: E11A1 'Laura'.
Type: Night reconnaissance flying boat.
Power Plant: One 620hp Hiro Type 91 Model 22.
Performance:
maximum speed at 7,875ft (2,400m) 135mph (217km/hr).
cruising speed 81mph (130km/hr).
range 1,209 miles (1,945km).
time to 9,840ft (3,000m) 18min 32sec.
service ceiling 14,520ft (4,426m).
Weights:
empty 4,248lb (1,927kg).
loaded 7,275lb (3,300kg).
Dimensions:
wing span 47ft 6½in (14.49m).
length 35ft 1½in (10.71m).
height 18ft 0½in (5.50m).
Armament: One flexible 7.7mm machine-gun mounted in open bow position.
Crew: 3.
In Service: Japan (IJNAF).
Variants (with no. built):
Prototypes and production models, Navy Type 98 Reconnaissance Seaplane: (17).
Total Production: 17.
Remarks: First produced 1937, and originally intended as ship-borne spotter aircraft, E11A1s saw limited service during opening rounds of Pacific War primarily in short-range night reconnaissance role.

Manufacturer: Aichi.
Model: E13A1a 'Jake'.
Type: Long-range reconnaissance floatplane.
Power Plant: One 1,080hp Mitsubishi Kinsei 43.

Aichi E13A1 'Jake'

Aichi B7A2 Ryusei 'Grace'

Power Plant: One 1,825hp Nakajima NK9C Homare 12 or 2,000hp NK9H–S Homare 23.
Performance:
maximum speed at 21,490ft (6,550m) 352mph (566km/hr).
maximum range 1,888 miles (3,038km).
time to 13,120ft (4,000m) 6min 55sec.
service ceiling 36,910ft (11,250m).
Weights:
empty 8,400lb (3,810kg).
maximum 14,330lb (6,500kg).
Dimensions:
wing span 47ft 3in (14.4m).
length 37ft 8⅓in (11.49m).
height 13ft 4½in (4.075m).
wing area 381.04sq ft (35.4sq m).
Armament: Two 20mm Type 99 Model 2 cannon in wings plus one flexible 7.92mm Type 1 machine-gun in rear cockpit; or two wing-mounted 20mm cannon plus one flexible 13mm Type 2 machine-gun in rear cockpit; max bomb load 1,896lb (860kg) or one 1,764lb (800kg) torpedo.
Crew: 2.
In Service: Japan (IJNAF).
Variants (with no. built):
B7A1, Navy Experimental 16-Shi Carrier Attack Bomber: Prototype; one 1,800hp NK9B Homare 11 (9).
B7A2 Ryusei (Shooting Star), Navy Carrier Attack Bomber: Production model; uprated engine (inc one with 2,000hp Homare 23) Aichi-built (80); Omura Naval Air Arsenal-built (25).
B7A3: Improved version; project only.
Total Production: 114.
Remarks: Beginning to enter service latter half of 1944—by which time majority IJN's carrier fleet already at bottom of Pacific—intended carrier-borne B7A (multi-role attack/dive/torpedo-bomber) brief service career limited to operating with two land-based Kokutais; low rate of production brought to complete halt by destruction of Aichi plant in earthquake, May 1945.

Manufacturer: Aichi.
Model: M6A1 Seiran.
Type: Attack bomber (detachable) twin-float seaplane.
Power Plant: One 1,400hp Aichi Atsuta 32.
Performance:
maximum speed at 17,060ft (5,200m) 295mph (475km/hr).
cruising speed 184mph (296km/hr).
range 739 miles (1,190km).
time to 9,840ft (3,000m) 5min 48sec.
service ceiling 32,480ft (9,900m).
Weights:
empty 7,277lb (3,301kg).
maximum 9,800lb (4,445kg).
Dimensions:
wing span 40ft 2¾in (12.262m).
length 38ft 2¼in (11.64m).
height 15ft 0⅓in (4.58m).
wing area 290.62sq ft (27.0sq m).
Armament: One flexible 13mm Type 2 machine-gun in rear cockpit; max bomb load 1,874lb (850kg).
Crew: 2.
In Service: Japan (IJNAF).
Variants (with no. built):
M6A1: Prototypes; 1,400hp Atsuta 30 or 31; detachable floats (8).
M6A1 Seiran (Mountain Haze), Navy Special Attack Bomber: Production model (18).
M6A1—K Nanzan (Southern Mountain): Trainer prototypes; retractable wheeled under-carriage (2).
Total Production: 28.
Remarks: Specifically designed for submarine-borne operations, M6A1 featured elaborate wing and tail swivel and fold mechanism for stowage in watertight deck hangar; original plan of attack was bombing of Panama Canal lock gates, but switched to strike against USN Ulithi Atoll anchorage; IJN 1st Submarine Flotilla (four submarines carrying ten M6A1s) en route Ulithi at cessation of hostilities.

Manufacturer: Hitachi.
Model: LXG1.
Type: Liaison/communications.
Power Plant: One 150hp Tokyo Gasu Denki Jimpu 3.
Performance:
maximum speed 134mph (215km/hr).
cruising speed 112mph (180km/hr).
maximum range 447 miles (720km).
service ceiling 15,420ft (4,700m).
Weights:
empty 1,213lb (550kg).
loaded 2,160lb (980kg).
Dimensions:
wing span 30ft 2¼in (9.20m).
length 24ft 11¼in (7.60m).
height 8ft 10¼in (2.70m).
wing area 193.75sq ft (18.00sq m).
Crew/Accommodation: 1/3.
In Service: Japan (IJNAF).
Variants:
Chidori-Go (Plover II): Civil 4-seat cabin biplane; Tokyo Gasu Denki-built.
LXG1: IJNAF designation for impressed Chidori-Go.
Remarks: Built in two variants, 1933–35 resp, by Tokyo Gasu Denki (Tokyo Gas and Electrical Engineering Co), number Chidori-Go civil tourers impressed by IJNAF upon outbreak of hostilities for carrier-to-shore staff transport/liaison duties.

Manufacturer: Kawanishi.
Model: E7K2 'Alf'.
Type: Ship-borne reconnaissance floatplane.
Power Plant: One 870hp Mitsubishi Zuisei 11.
Performance:
maximum speed at 6,560ft (2,000m) 171mph (275km/hr).
cruising speed 115mph (185km/hr).
range 1,147 miles (1,845km).
time to 9,840ft (3,000m) 9min 6sec.
service ceiling 23,165ft (7,060m).
Weights:
empty 4,630lb (2,100kg).
loaded 7,275lb (3,300kg).
Dimensions:
wing span 45ft 11¼in (14.0m).
length 34ft 5⅓in (10.5m).
height 15ft 10½in (4.85m).
wing area 469.31sq ft (43.6sq m).
Armament: One fixed forward-firing 7.7mm Type 92 machine-gun plus one flexible 7.7mm Type 92 machine-gun each in rear cockpit and (downward-firing) ventral position; max bomb load 264lb (120kg).
Crew: 3.
In Service: Japan (IJNAF).
Variants (with no. built):
E7K1: Prototypes; 500hp Hiro Type 91 (2).
E7K1, Navy Type 94 Reconnaissance Seaplane, Model 1: Initial production model; later models with uprated 600hp Type 91; Kawanishi-built (126); Nippon Hikoki-built (57).
E7K2: Prototype (1).
E7K2, Model 2 (Model 12): Modified Model 1; uprated Mitsubishi engine; Kawanishi-built (287); Nippon Hikoki-built (approx 57).
Total Production: approx 530.
Remarks: Entering service 1935, E7K1 relegated to training role by outbreak of Pacific War; radial-engined E7K2 remained in first-line service 1941–43, being widely used for both ship-borne and shore-based reconnaissance duties, inshore convoy escort and anti-submarine patrols; subsequently served in liaison, training and other secondary roles; both types reappeared end of war, pressed into service for Kamikaze attacks.

Manufacturer: Kawanishi.
Model: H6K4 'Mavis'.
Type: Long-range maritime reconnaissance/bomber flying boat.
Power Plant: Four 1,070hp Mitsubishi Kinsei 43 or 46.
Performance:
maximum speed at 13,120ft (4,000m) 211mph (340km/hr).
cruising speed 138mph (222km/hr).
maximum range 3,779 miles (6,080km).
time to 16,400ft (5,000m) 13min 31sec.
service ceiling 31,530ft (9,610m).
Weights:
empty 25,810lb (11,707kg).
maximum 47,399lb (21,500kg).
Dimensions:
wing span 131ft 2¾in (40.0m).
length 84ft 0¾in (25.63m).
height 20ft 6¾in (6.27m).
wing area 1,829.86sq ft (170.0sq m).
Armament: One 7.7mm Type 92 machine-gun each in open bow, forward turret, 2 beam blisters and open dorsal positions; one 20mm Type 99 Model 1 cannon in tail turret; max bomb load 2,205lb (1,000kg) or two 1,764lb (800kg) torpedoes.
Crew: 9.
In Service: Japan (IJNAF).
Variants (with no. built).
H6K1: Prototypes; four Hikari 2s (4).
H6K1, Navy Type 97 Flying Boat, Model 1: 3 prototypes re-engined with 1,000hp Mitsubishi Kinsei 43s.
H6K2, Model 11: Initial production model (inc 2 modified as transport prototypes) (10).
H6K4, Model 22: Modified H6K2; revised armament; some with 930hp Kinsei 46s (inc 2 subsequently converted to H6K4–L) (127).
H6K5, Model 23: 1,300hp Kinsei 51 or 53s; forward turret in place of open bow position (36).
Total Production: 215 (all Marks).
Remarks: Entered service Jan 1938; only long-range maritime reconnaissance flying boat operated by IJN on outbreak of Pacific War (66 examples serving with four Kokutais); enjoyed some success early months of war in NEI and SWPA; initially employed in both reconnaissance and bombing roles, soon forced to abandon latter in face of increasing Allied fighter presence; continued to serve in long-range patrol capacity until advent of H8K in 1943; majority subsequently converted to troop-transport configuration.

Manufacturer: Kawanishi.
Model: H6K2–L.
Type: Transport flying boat.
Power Plant: Four 1,000hp Mitsubishi Kinsei 43.
Performance:
maximum speed at 8,565ft (2,610m) 207mph (333km/hr).
cruising speed 150mph (241km/hr).
normal range 2,690 miles (4,300km).
Weights:
empty 26,511lb (12,025kg).
maximum 50,706lb (23,000kg).
Dimensions:
wing span 131ft 2¾in (40.0m).
length 81ft 8⅓in (24.9m).
height 20ft 6¾in (6.27m).
wing area 1,829.86sq ft (170sq m).
Crew/Accommodation: 8/10–18.
In Service: Japan (IJNAF).
Variants (with no. built):
H6K2–L, Navy Type 97 Transport Flying Boat: Unarmed transport version of H6K4; Kinsei 43s (16).
H6K3: VIP staff-transport version of modified H6K2 (2).
H6K4–L: As H6K2–L; Kinsei 46s (20).
Total Production: 215 (all Marks).
Remarks: Unarmed military/civil versions of H6K reconnaissance/bomber flying boat; used by both IJN in staff-transport and communications roles, and by the Overseas (Ocean) Division of Japan Air Lines (Dai Nippon Koku KK) on their Central and Western Pacific routes—several falling to Allied air attack; remained in service until end of war; IJNAF machines based Netherlands East Indies seized post-war by Indonesian nationalists.

Manufacturer: Kawanishi.
Model: E11K1.
Type: Utility transport flying boat.
Power Plant: One 750hp Hiro Type 91.
Performance:
maximum speed 144mph (232km/hr).
cruising speed 129mph (208km/hr).
time to 9,840ft (3,000m) 22min 0sec.
service ceiling 13,780ft. (4,200m).
Weights:
empty 5,996lb (2,720kg).
maximum 8,510lb (3,860kg).
Dimensions:
wing span 53ft 1⅓in (16.50m).
length 38ft 8¾in (11.80m).
height 14ft 5¼in (4.40m).
wing area 409.029sq ft (38.00sq m).
Armament: One flexible 7.7mm machine-gun in open bow position.
Crew: 3.
In Service: Japan (IJNAF).
Variants (with no. built):
E11K1 Prototypes, Navy Type 96 Transport Flying Boat (3).
Total Production: 3.
Remarks: Designed to same requirement as Aichi E11A1; latter selected for production; E11K1 prototypes later modified for IJN service in utility transport role during war years.

Manufacturer: Kawanishi.
Model: H8K2 'Emily'.
Type: Long-range maritime reconnaissance/bomber flying boat.
Power Plant: Four 1,850hp Mitsubishi Kasei 22.
Performance:
maximum speed at 16,400ft (5,000m) 290mph (467km/hr).
cruising speed 185mph (298km/hr).
maximum range 4,460 miles (7,180km).
time to 13,120ft (3,990m) 7min 56sec.
service ceiling 28,740ft (8,760m).
Weights:
empty 40,521lb (18,380kg).
maximum 71,650lb (32,500kg).
Dimensions:
wing span 124ft 8in (38.0m).

Kawanishi H6K5 'Mavis'

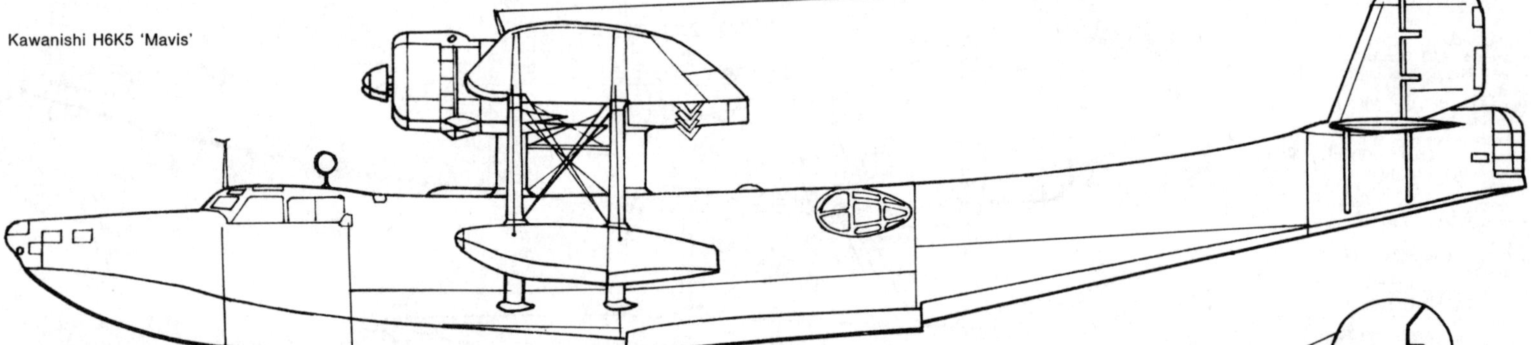

Kawanishi H8K2 'Emily'

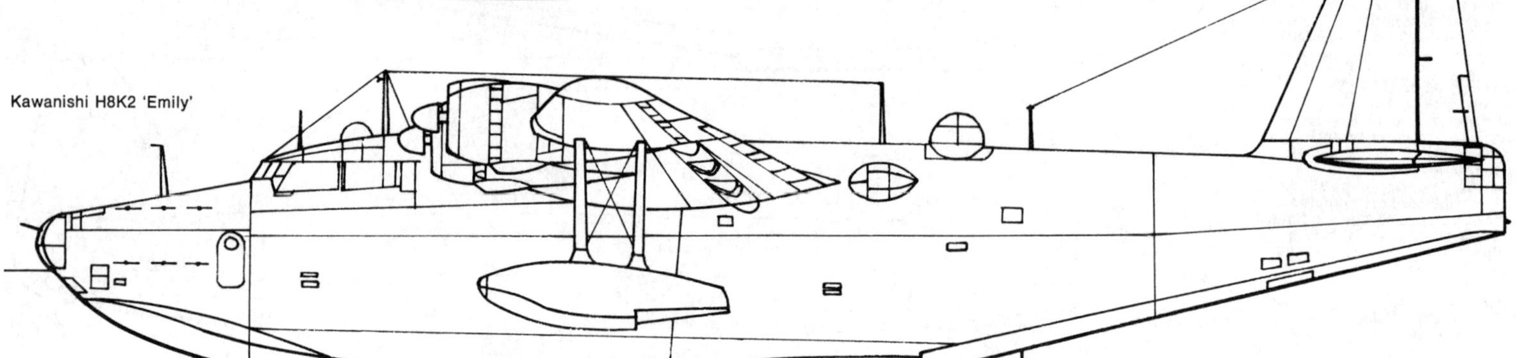

length 92ft 4in (28.13m).
height 30ft 0in (9.15m).
wing area 1,722sq ft (160sq m).
Armament: One 20mm Type 99
Model 1 cannon each in bow,
dorsal and tail turrets and in two
beam blisters; plus four 7.7mm
Type 92 hand-held machine-guns
in cockpit, ventral and side hatches;
max bomb load 4,408lb (2,000kg),
or two 1,764lb (800kg) torpedoes,
or depth-charges.
Crew: 10.
In Service: Japan (IJNAF).
Variants (with no. built):
H8K1: 1 prototype; 2 modified
pre-production models (3).
H8K1, Navy Type 2 Flying Boat,
Model 11: Initial production
model (14).
H8K2, Model 12: Uprated engines;
increased armament; some with
ASV radar (120).
H8K2-L Seiku (Clear Sky),
Model 32: 2-gun transport
version of H8K1; 29–64 passengers
(36).
H8K3, Model 22: Experimental
version; modified H8K2; retractable wing-tip floats; addn armour
plate (2).
H8K4, Model 23: Re-engined
H8K3; 2 conversions.
Total Production: 175.
Remarks: Fastest flying boat of
WWII, heavily-armed H8K entered
service early 1942; combat debut
night attack on Oahu Island
(Hawaii), 4/5 March 1942; daring
raid, carried out at extreme range
and made possible only by
rendezvous with refuelling submarine, but poor results due to
heavy cloud obscuring target
area; H8K2 model, entering service
1943, remained standard IJNAF
long-range maritime reconnaissance flying boat for duration of
war; arguably the best flying boat
produced by any combatant nation
of WWII, and accorded a healthy
respect whenever encountered by
Allied fighter pilots, H8K2s operated
throughout Pacific in reconnaissance, bombing and torpedo-
bombing roles; equipped six
Kokutais, plus two transport
Kokutais (H8K2-L).

Manufacturer: Kawanishi.
Model: N1K1 Kyofu 'Rex'.
Type: Interceptor-fighter floatplane.
Power Plant: One 1,460hp Mitsubishi **MK4C Kasei** 13 or one
1,530hp Mitsubishi MK4E Kasei 15.
Performance:
maximum speed at 18,700ft
(5,700m) 304mph (489km/hr).
cruising speed 230mph (370km/hr).
maximum range 1,036 miles
(1,700km).
time to 16,400ft (5,000m) 5min
32sec.
service ceiling 34,645ft (10,560m).
Weights:
empty 6,067lb (2,752kg).
maximum 8,184lb (3,712kg).
Dimensions:
wing span 39ft 4½in (12.0m).
length 34ft 8½in (10.59m).
height 15ft 7½in (4.75m).
wing area 252.95sq ft (23.5sq m).
Armament: Two 7.7mm Type 97
machine-guns in upper cowling;
two wing-mounted 20mm Type 99
Model 1 cannon.
Crew: 1.
In Service: Japan (IJNAF).
Variants (with no. built):
Prototypes and pre-production
models: 1,460hp Kasei 14 or
13 (8).
N1K1 Kyofu (Mighty Wind),
Navy Fighter Seaplane, Model 11:
Production model (89).
Total Production: 97.
Remarks: Intended as forward air-
superiority fighter to protect
amphibious assault forces from
land-based enemy air power,
ambitious N1K programme—
designed to be most powerful and
advanced floatplane in the world—
was overtaken by progress of
war; served instead in defensive
interception role, first based
Netherlands East Indies, later
operating from Lake Biwa on
Honshu for home defence duties;
production halted in favour of
conventional land-based derivative, N1K1-J—destined to develop
into best IJNAF fighter of WWII.

Manufacturer: Kawanishi.
Model: E15K1 Shiun 'Norm'.
Type: High-speed reconnaissance
floatplane.
Power Plant: One 1,850hp Mitsubishi MK4S Kasei 24.
Performance:
maximum speed at 18,700ft
(5,700m) 291mph (468km/hr).
cruising speed 184mph (296km/hr).

range 2,095 miles (3,370km).
time to 19,685ft (6,000m) 10min
0sec.
service ceiling 32,250ft (9,830m).
Weights:
empty 6,978lb (3,165kg).
maximum 10,803lb (4,900kg).
Dimensions:
wing span 45ft 11½in (14.0m).
length 38ft 0¼in (11.59m).
height 16ft 2¾in (4.95m).
wing area 322.92sq ft (30.0sq m).
Armament: One flexible 7.7mm
Type 92 machine-gun in rear
cockpit; max bomb load 264lb (120kg).
Crew: 2.
In Service: Japan (IJNAF).
Variants (with no. built):
Prototypes and Service Trials
models (6).
E15K1 Shiun (Violet Cloud),
Navy Type 2 High-Speed reconnaissance Seaplane, Model 11:
Production model (9).
Total Production: 15.
Remarks: Kawanishi's last float-
plane, E15K1 designed specifically
for reconnaissance in enemy-
dominated airspace; emphasis on

speed of escape; two-blade contra-
rotating propellers and central-
float jettison mechanism;
protracted and troublesome development; six examples sent to Palau,
South Pacific, for combat evaluation; float jettison complete failure,
all six soon caught and destroyed
by Allied fighters; production
cancelled.
Manufacturer: Kawanishi.
Model: N1K1-J Shiden 'George'.
Type: Interceptor fighter.
Power Plant: One 1,990hp Nakajima NK9H Homare 21.
Performance:
maximum speed at 17,716ft
(5,400m) 363mph (584km/hr).
cruising speed 230mph (370km/hr).
range 890 miles (1,432km).
time to 19,685ft (6,000m) 7min
50sec.
service ceiling 41,010ft (12,500m).
Weights:
empty 6,387lb (2,897kg).
maximum 9,526lb (4,321kg).
Dimensions:
wing span 39ft 4½in (12.0m).

length 29ft 2in (8.885m).
height 13ft 4in (4.06m).
wing area 252.95sq ft (23.5sq m).
Armament: Two 7.7mm Type 97
machine-guns in nose, two wing-
mounted 20mm Type 99 Model 2
cannon; two 20mm Type 99 Model
2 cannon in underwing gondolas;
max bomb load 264lb (120kg).
Crew: 1.
In Service: Japan (IJNAF), USA
(1 + captured).
Variants (with no. built):
N1K1-J prototypes: Development
of N1K1 Kyofu floatplane;
1,820hp Homare 11 (9).
N1K1-J Shiden (Violet Lightning),
Navy Interceptor Fighter
Model 11: Initial production
model; uprated engine; increased
armament; modified engine
cowling.
N1K1-Ja, Model 11A: Fuselage-
guns deleted; four 20mm cannon
in wings.
N1K1-Jb, Model 11B: As Model
11A; two 551lb (250kg) bombs;
improved wing armament.
N1K1-Jc, Model 11C: Fighter-

bomber version of N1K1-Jb; four
underwing bomb-racks.
(Total N1K1-J,a,b,c: 1,098).
N1K1-J KAI: Experimental
rocket-boosted interceptor version;
one Model 11 conversion.
N1K1-J KAI Shiden, Model
11KAI: Dive-bomber version;
large ventral pannier with one
551lb (250kg) bomb and six
rocket projectiles; N1K1-J
conversions.
Total Production: 1,435 (all
Marks).
Remarks: Unique in being only
land-based fighter aircraft to be
developed from an earlier floatplane fighter design (nearest
parallel being Spitfire's illustrious
Schneider Trophy forbears),
N1K1-J was initiated as a private
venture by Kawanishi; after lengthy
flight trials plagued by power plant
and undercarriage teething troubles,
Shiden entered IJNAF service
early 1944; first major action in
defence of Philippines, Oct 1944;
despite continuing engine unreli-
ability, proved the equal of most

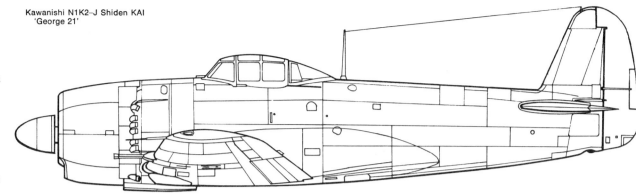

Kawanishi N1K2-J Shiden KAI
'George 21'

Order of Battle December 1941
IMPERIAL JAPANESE AIR FORCES

Imperial Japanese Army Air Force (Malayan and Philippine Campaigns)
3rd Hikoshidan (Air Division) Malaya:

3rd Hikodan (Wing):	
27th Sentai	Mitsubishi Ki-51 'Sonia'
59th Sentai	Nakajima Ki-43 'Oscar'
	Nakajima Ki-27 'Nate'
75th Sentai	Kawasaki Ki-48 'Lily'
90th Sentai	Kawasaki Ki-48 'Lily'
7th Hikodan (Wing):	
12th Sentai	Mitsubishi Ki-21 'Sally'
60th Sentai	Mitsubishi Ki-21 'Sally'
64th Sentai	Nakajima Ki-43 'Oscar'
	Nakajima Ki-27 'Nate'
98th Sentai	Mitsubishi Ki-21 'Sally'
12th Hikodan (Wing):	
1st Sentai	Nakajima Ki-27 'Nate'
11th Sentai	Nakajima Ki-27 'Nate'
81st Sentai	Mitsubishi Ki-15 'Babs'
	Mitsubishi Ki-46 'Dinah'
15th Dokuritsu Hikotai (Independent Wing):	
50th Dokuritsu Dai Shijugo Chutai	Mitsubishi Ki-15 'Babs'
	Mitsubishi Ki-46 'Dinah'
51st Dokuritsu Dai Shijugo Chutai	Mitsubishi Ki-15 'Babs'
	Mitsubishi Ki-46 'Dinah'
21st Dokuritsu Hikotai (Independent Wing):	
82nd Dokuritsu Dai Shijugo Chutai	Mitsubishi Ki-30 'Ann'
84th Dokuritsu Dai Shijugo Chutai	Nakajima Ki-27 'Nate'

5th Hikoshidan (Air Division) Philippines:

4th Hikodan (Wing):	
8th Sentai	Kawasaki Ki-48 'Lily'
	Mitsubishi Ki-30 'Ann'
14th Sentai	Mitsubishi Ki-21 'Sally'
50th Sentai	Nakajima Ki-27 'Nate'
10th Hikodan (Wing):	
31st Sentai	Mitsubishi Ki-30 'Ann'
62nd Sentai	Mitsubishi Ki-21 'Sally'
77th Sentai	Nakajima Ki-27 'Nate'
16th Sentai	Mitsubishi Ki-30 'Ann'
10th Dokuritsu Hikotai (Independent Wing):	
52nd Dokuritsu Dai Shijugo Chutai	Mitsubishi Ki-51 'Sonia'
74th Dokuritsu Dai Shijugo Chutai	Tachikawa Ki-36 'Ida'
76th Dokuritsu Dai Shijugo Chutai	Mitsubishi Ki-51 'Sonia'
11th Hiko Chutai	Mitsubishi Ki-57 'Topsy'

Imperial Japanese Navy Air Force
(Pearl Harbor Attack and Philippine Campaign)
First Koku Kantai (Air Fleet) Carrier-borne:

1st Koku Sentai (Carrier Division):	
CV Akagi	18 Mitsubishi A6M2 'Zeke'
	18 Aichi D3A1 'Val'
	27 Nakajima B5N2 'Kate'
CV Kaga	18 Mitsubishi A6M2 'Zeke'
	18 Aichi D3A1 'Val'
	27 Nakajima B5N2 'Kate'
2nd Koku Sentai (Carrier Division):	
CV Soryu	18 Mitsubishi A6M2 'Zeke'
	18 Aichi D3A1 'Val'
	18 Nakajima B5N2 'Kate'
CV Hiryu	18 Mitsubishi A6M2 'Zeke'
	18 Aichi D3A1 'Val'
	18 Nakajima B5N2 'Kate'
4th Koku Sentai (Carrier Division):	
CV Ryujo	22 Mitsubishi A5M4 'Claude'
	18 Nakajima B5N2 'Kate'
5th Koku Sentai (Carrier Division):	
CV Zuikaku	18 Mitsubishi A6M2 'Zeke'
	27 Aichi D3A1 'Val'
	27 Nakajima B5N2 'Kate'
CV Shokaku	18 Mitsubishi A6M2 'Zeke'
	27 Aichi D3A1 'Val'
	27 Nakajima B5N2 'Kate'

Eleventh Koku Kantai (Air Fleet) Land-based:

21st Koku Sentai (Air Flotilla):	
1st Kokutai	48 Mitsubishi G4M1 'Betty'
Kanoya Kokutai	72 Mitsubishi G4M1 'Betty'
Toko Kokutai	24 Kawanishi 'Mavis'
22nd Koku Sentai (Air Flotilla):	
Mihoro Kokutai	43 Mitsubishi G3M2 'Nell'
Genzan Kokutai	48 Mitsubishi G3M2 'Nell'
Koku Sentai Attachment	6 Mitsubishi C5M2 'Babs'
	36 Mitsubishi A6M2 'Zeke'
23rd Koku Sentai (Air Flotilla):	
3rd Kokutai	92 Mitsubishi A6M2 'Zeke'
	12 Mitsubishi C5M2 'Babs'
Tainan Kokutai	92 Mitsubishi A6M2 'Zeke'
	12 Mitsubishi C5M2 'Babs'
Takao Kokutai	72 Mitsubishi G3M2 'Nell'

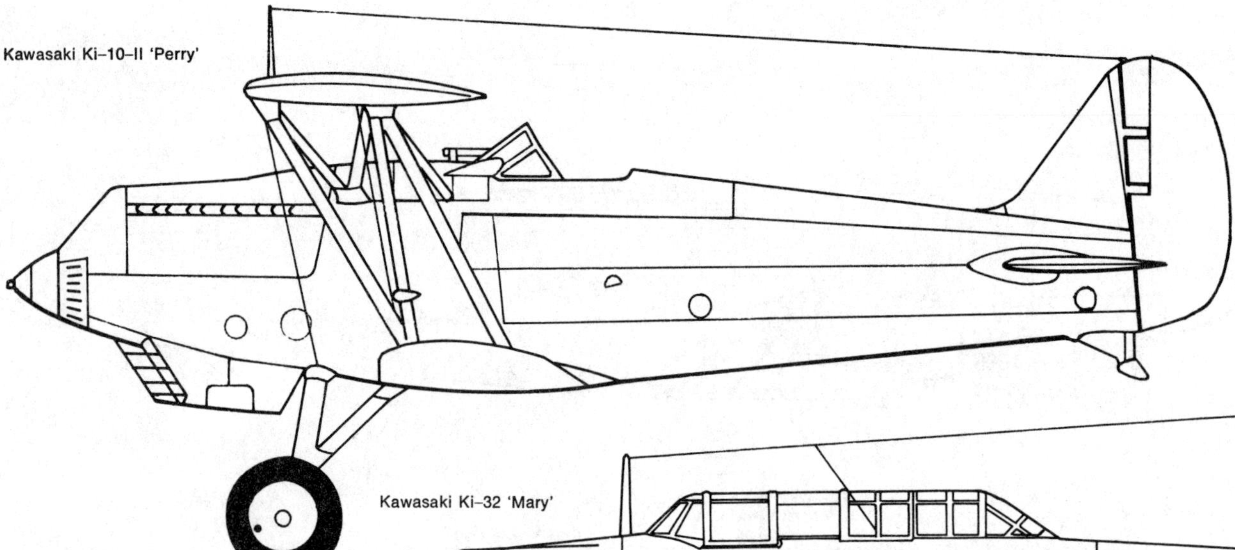

Kawasaki Ki–10–II 'Perry'

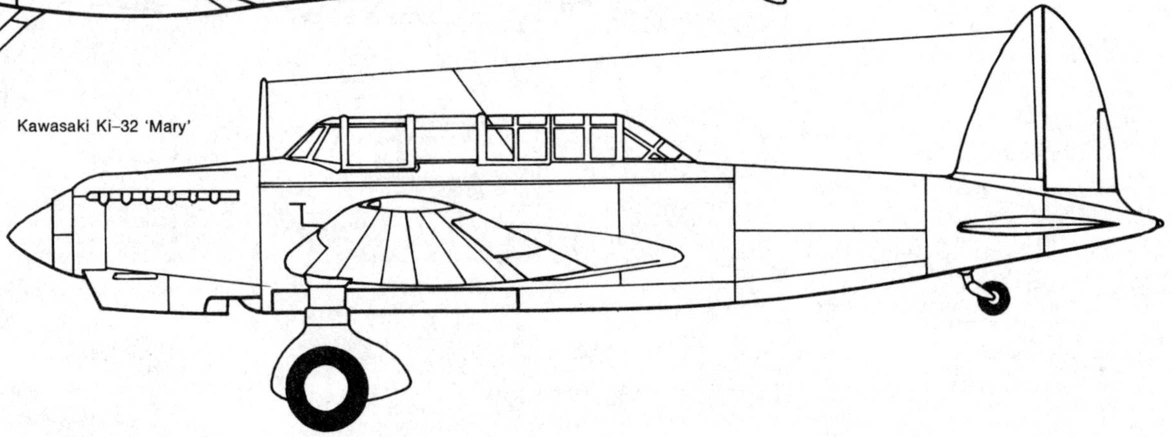

Kawasaki Ki–32 'Mary'

contemporary US fighters; encountered throughout remaining months of Pacific war, inc invasion of Okinawa, finally being employed in Kamikaze role.

Manufacturer: Kawanishi.
Model: N1K2–J Shiden KAI 'George 21'.
Type: Interceptor fighter.
Power Plant: One 1,990hp Nakajima NK9H Homare 21.
Performance:
maximum speed at 18,375ft (5,600m) 369mph (594km/hr).
cruising speed 230mph (370km/hr).
maximum range 1,293 miles (2,080 km).
time to 19,685ft (6,000m) 7min 22sec.
service ceiling 35,300ft (10,760m).
Weights:
empty 5,858lb (2,657kg).
maximum 10,714lb (4,860kg).
Dimensions:
wing span 39ft 4½in (12.0m).
length 30ft 8in (9.345m).
height 13ft 0in (3.96m).
wing area 252.95sq ft (23.5sq m).
Armament: Four 20mm Type 99 Model 2 cannon in wings; max bomb load 1,102lb (500kg).
Crew: 1.
In Service: Japan (IJNAF).
Variants (with no. built):
N1K2–J prototypes: Redesigned N1K1–Jb; low wing; revised cowling and undercarriage; redesigned fuselage and tail (8).
N1K2–J Shiden Kai (Violet Lightning, Modified), Navy Interceptor Fighter, Model 21: Production model.
N1K2–Ja, Model 21A: Fighter-bomber version; four 551lb (250kg) bombs; N1K2–J/–Ja: Kawanishi-built (393); Mitsubishi-built (9); Aichi-built (1); Showa Hikoki-built (1); Omura Naval Air Arsenal-built (10); Hiro Naval Air Arsenal-built (1).
N1K2–K Shiden Kai Rensen (Violet Lightning, Modified Fighter Trainer): 2-seat trainer; N1K2–J conversions.
N1K3–J Shiden Kai 1, Model 31: Prototypes; engine moved forward; two fuselage-mounted 13.2mm Type 3 machine-guns (2).
N1K3–A Shiden Kai 2, Model 41: Carrier-borne version of N1K3–J; project only.
N1K4–J Shiden Kai 3, Model 32: Prototypes; 2,000hp Homare 23 (2).
N1K4–A Shiden Kai 4, Model 42: Carrier-borne version of N1K4–J; prototype (1).
N1K5–J Shiden Kai 5, Model 25: Projected high-altitude interceptor fighter version.
Total Production: 1,435 (all Marks).
Remarks: Ultimate in N1K series development, N1K2–J was basically a much modified, but simplified, redesign of Shiden predecessor; major external differences inc repositioning wing from mid- to low-fuselage, lengthened aft fuselage, and entirely new vertical tail surfaces; entering IJNAF service at close of 1944 with specially-activated Kokutai comprised of only the most experienced pilots, N1K2–J spent last eight months of war in home-defence role; invariably outnumbered, Shiden Kai proved outstanding combat fighter (during one oft-quoted action a single N1K2–J engaged twelve USN F6Fs, destroying four of the Hellcats and forcing other eight to retire); despite some loss of performance at high altitudes, also accounted for considerable number of B–29 Superfortress bombers.

Manufacturer: Kawasaki.
Model: Type 88–II (KDA–2).
Type: Light bomber/reconnaissance.
Power Plant: One 600hp Kawasaki-built BMW VI.
Performance:
maximum speed at sea level 130mph (210km/hr).
time to 9,840ft (3,000m) 18min 0sec.
service ceiling 17,060ft (5,200m).
Weights:
empty 4,189lb (1,900kg).
loaded 6,834lb (3,100kg).
Dimensions:
wing span 49ft 10½in (15.20m).
length 40ft 3½in (12.28m).
height 11ft 1½in (3.40m).
wing area 516.67sq ft (48.0sq m).
Armament: One fixed forward-firing 7.7mm machine-gun; single or twin 7.7mm Type 89 machine-gun/s in rear cockpit; max bomb load 440lb (200kg).
Crew: 2.
In Service: Manchuria.
Variants: (with no. built):
KDA–2: Private venture prototypes; one 600hp BMW VI (3).
Army Type 88–I Reconnaissance plane: as prototypes; increased wing span; licence-built power plant; Kawasaki-built (520); Tachikawa-built (187).
Army Type 88–II Light Bomber: Modified Type 88–I; redesigned nose; underslung radiator; underwing bomb racks (407).
KDC–2: Four-passenger civil transports; modified Type 88–II; redesigned (cabin) fuselage; alt float undercarriage (2).
Total Production: 1,119.
Remarks: Entered IJAAF service 1928, participating first Sino-Japanese conflict (inc 'Shanghai Incident') early thirties; supplied to Manchurian AF; operated reconnaissance/light bomber roles until replaced by Kawasaki Ki–32 'Mary' in 1943.

Manufacturer: Kawasaki.
Model: Ki–3.
Type: Light bomber/liaison.
Power Plant: One 800hp licence-production BMW IX.
Performance:
maximum speed 162mph (260km/hr).
time to 9,840ft (3,000m) 12min 0sec.
service ceiling 22,960ft (7,000m).
Weights:
empty 3,639lb (1,650kg).
loaded 6,820lb (3,100kg).
Dimensions:
wing span 42ft 8in (13.0m).
length 32ft 9¾in (10.0m).
height 9ft 10in (3.0m).
wing area 409.02sq ft (38.0sq m).
Armament: One fixed forward-firing 7.7mm machine-gun; one flexible 7.7mm machine-gun in rear cockpit; max bomb load 1,102lb (500kg).
Crew: 2.
In Service: Japan.
Variants (with no. built):
Prototype: Private venture (KDA–6) reconnaissance biplane; 500hp Kawasaki-built BMW VI (1).
Army Type 93 Single-Engine Light Bomber: Production model; Kawasaki-or Mitsubishi-built BMW IX; revised engine cowling (Kawasaki- and Tachikawa-built 243).
Total Production: 243.
Remarks: Extensive use early stages Sino-Japanese conflict; by outbreak of WWII few examples still operating mainland China in liaison/general duties roles.

Manufacturer: Kawasaki.
Model: Ki–10–II 'Perry'.
Type: Fighter.
Power Plant: One 850hp Kawasaki Ha–9–IIa.
Performance:
maximum speed at 9,840ft (3,000m) 249mph (400km/hr).
normal range 684 miles (1,100km).
time to 16,400ft (5,000m) 5min 0sec.
service ceiling 37,730ft (11,500m).
Weights:
empty 2,998lb (1,360kg).
loaded 3,836lb (1,740kg).
Dimensions:
wing span 32ft 10½in (10.02m).
length 24ft 9¼in (7.55m).
height 9ft 10in (3.0m).
wing area 247.57sq ft (23sq m).
Armament: Two fixed forward-firing 7.7mm Type 89 machine-guns in upper cowling.
Crew: 1.
In Service: Japan.
Variants (with no. built):
Ki–10: Prototypes (4).
Ki–10–I, Army Type 95 Fighter, Model 1: Initial production model (300).
Ki–10–II prototype: Modified Model 1; lengthened fuselage; increased wingspan (1).
Ki–10–II, Model 2: Production model (280).
Ki–10–I KAI: Prototype; improved Ki–10–I; repositioned radiator (1).
Ki–10–II KAI: Prototypes; aerodynamically improved Ki–10–II as Ki–10–I KAI; 850hp Kawasaki Ha–9–IIb (2).
Total Production: 588.
Remarks: Widespread IJAAF service, inc action in China and Manchuria during Sino-Japanese hostilities and against Russo-Mongolian forces in Nomonhan Incident; relegated to training and other secondary roles by outbreak of Pacific War, but returned to brief first-line service for patrol and reconnaissance duties over both Home Islands and mainland China early months 1942.

Manufacturer: Kawasaki.
Model: Ki–32 'Mary'.
Type: Light bomber.
Power Plant: One 950hp Kawasaki Ha–9–IIb, Army Type 98.
Performance:
maximum speed at 12,925ft (3,940m) 263mph (423km/hr).
cruising speed 186mph (300km/hr).
maximum range 1,218 miles (1,960km).
time to 16,400ft (5,000m) 10min 55sec.
service ceiling 29,265ft (8,920m).
Weights:
empty 5,179lb (2,349kg).
maximum 8,294lb (3,762kg).
Dimensions:
wing span 49ft 2½in (15.0m).
length 38ft 2¼in (11.64m).
height 9ft 6¼in (2.9m).
wing area 365.97sq ft (34.0sq m).
Armament: One fixed forward-firing 7.7mm Type 89 machine-gun in upper cowling; one flexible 7.7mm Type 89 machine-gun in rear cockpit; max bomb load 992lb (450kg).
Crew: 2.
In Service: Japan, Manchuria.
Variants (with no. built):
Prototypes: (8).
Ki–32, Army Type 98 Single-Engined Light Bomber: Production model (846).
Total Production: 854.
Remarks: Entered service 1938–39; participated second Sino-Japanese conflict and Nomonhan Incident; obsolescent by outbreak of Pacific War, taking part briefly in attacks on Hong Kong before being relegated to training role early 1942; supplied to Manchurian AF; remained sole Manchurian bomber equipment throughout remaining war years.

Manufacturer: Kawasaki.
Model: Ki–45 KAIa Toryu 'Nick'.
Type: Heavy fighter.
Power Plant: Two 1,050hp Nakajima Ha–25, Army Type 99.
Performance:
maximum speed at 22,965ft (7,000m) 340mph (547km/hr).
cruising speed 232mph (373km/hr).
normal range 1,404 miles (2,260km).
time to 16,400ft (5,000m) 6min 17sec.
service ceiling 35,200ft (10,730m).
Weights:
empty 8,679lb (3,982kg).
loaded 12,081lb (5,480kg).
Dimensions:
wing span 49ft 3½in (15.02m).
length 34ft 9¼in (10.6m).
height 12ft 1½in (3.7m).
wing area 344.44sq ft (32.0sq m).
Armament: Two fixed forward-firing 12.7mm Ho–103 machine-guns in nose; one 20mm Ho–3 cannon in ventral tunnel; plus one flexible 7.92mm Type 98 machine-gun in rear cockpit.
Crew: 2.
In Service: Japan.
Variants (with no. built):
Ki–45 prototypes: 730hp Nakajima Ha–20bs (3).
Improved Type 1 Ki–45 prototypes: Nacelle modifications; 950hp Nakajima Ha–25s (8).
Ki–45 KAI prototypes: Redesigned fuselage, wing and tail surfaces; improved armament (3).
Ki–45 KAI pre-production: (12).
Ki–45 KAIa Toryu (Dragon-Slayer), Army Type 2 two-seat Fighter, Model A: Initial production model.
Ki–45 KAIb, Model B: Ground-attack/anti-shipping aircraft; lengthened nose; revised armament; late models: 1,050hp Mitsubishi Ha–102s.
(Total Ki–45 KAIa,b,d: 1,198).
Total Production: 1,701 (all Marks).
Remarks: First flown early 1939, Ki–45's combat debut not until Autumn 1942; equipped two Sentais China/Burma theatres; originally designed as strategic heavy fighter (prompted in part by advent of Germany's Bf 110), used primarily in tactical ground-attack and anti-shipping roles; widely employed South-West and Central Pacific areas (New Guinea, Philippines); subject of several field modifications, mainly to armament, inc provision for bombs; four aircraft so modified made first recorded suicide attack of war during Allied invasion Biak Island, Dutch New Guinea, 27 May 1944; one USN sub-chaser damaged.

Manufacturer: Kawasaki.
Model: Ki–45 KAIc Toryu 'Nick'.
Type: Night-fighter.
Power Plant: Two 1,080hp Mitsubishi Ha–102, Army Type 1.
Performance:
maximum speed at 22,965ft (7,000m) 340mph (547km/hr).
cruising speed 235mph (378km/hr).
maximum range 1,243 miles (2,000km).
time to 16,400ft (5,000m) 6min 7sec.

Kawasaki Ki-48-I 'Lily'

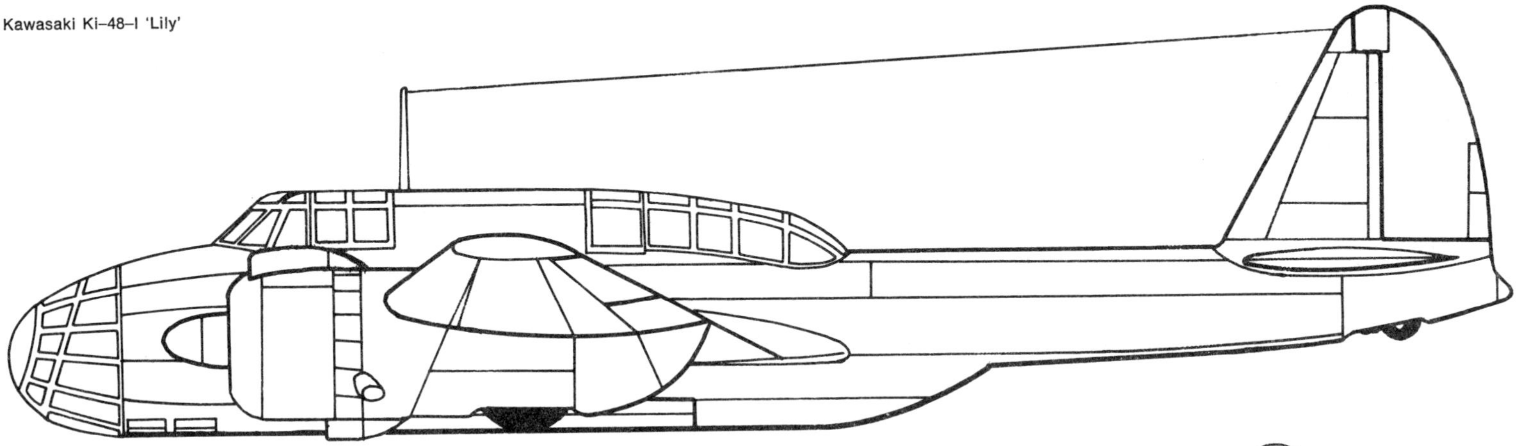

Kawasaki Ki-100-16

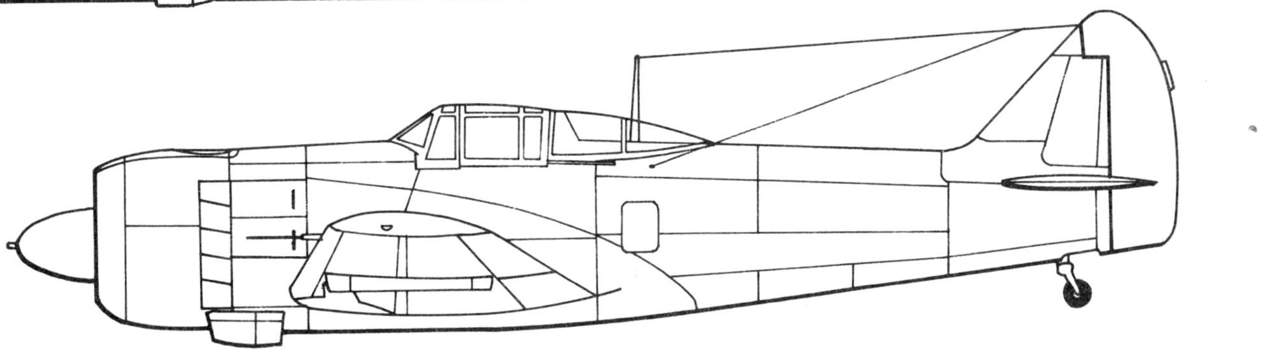

service ceiling 32,810ft (10,000m).
Weights:
empty 8,818lb (4,000kg).
loaded 12,125lb (5,500kg).
Dimensions:
wing span 49ft 3¼in (15.02m).
length 36ft 1in (11.0m).
height 12ft 1¾in (3.7m).
wing area 344.44sq ft (32.0sq m).
Armament: One 37mm Ho-203 cannon in ventral tunnel; two fixed oblique upward-firing 20mm Ho-5 dorsal cannon; plus (early production models only) one flexible 7.92mm Type 98 machine-gun in rear cockpit.
Crew: 2.
In Service: Japan.
Variants (with no. built):
Ki-45 KAIc, Model C: Night-fighter version; modified Model B; revised armament; pointed nose for centimetric radar; not fitted (477).
Ki-45 KAId: Anti-shipping version; modified Model C; two 20mm nose and one 37mm ventral cannon, one 7.92mm machine-gun, plus two 551lb (250kg) bombs.
Ki-45-II: Project only (completed as Ki-96 experimental prototype).
Total Production: 1,701 (all Marks).
Remarks: Specialized night-fighter development; radar equipment unavailable due to production difficulties; sole IJAAF aircraft operational night defence of Home Islands, equipping four Sentais Autumn 1944 until end of war; achieved considerable success, one Sentai alone claiming over 150 victories; downed eight B-29 Superfortresses in first encounter.
Colour Reference: Plates 99,100: Kawasaki Ki-45 KAIc Toryu 'Nick' (Army Type 2 2-seat Fighter, Model C) of 3rd Chutai, 53rd Sentai, IJAAF, Matsudo (Chiba Prefecture), NW of Tokyo, Winter 1944-45; white ground to national markings (Hinomaru) indicates home-defence deployment.

Manufacturer: Kawasaki.
Model: Ki-48-II 'Lily'.
Type: Light bomber.
Power Plant: Two 1,150hp Nakajima Ha-115, Army Type 1.
Performance:
maximum speed at 18,375ft (5,600m) 314mph (505km/hr).
maximum range 1,491 miles (2,400km).
time to 16,400ft (5,000m) 8min 30sec.
service ceiling 33,135ft (10,100m).
Weights:
empty 10,030lb (4,550kg).
maximum 14,880lb (6,750kg).
Dimensions:
wing span 57ft 3in (17.45m).
length 41ft 10in (12.75m).
height 12ft 5⅔in (3.8m).
wing area 430.56sq ft (40.0sq m).
Armament: One flexible 7.7mm Type 89 machine-gun each in nose, dorsal and ventral positions; max bomb load 1,764lb (800kg).
Crew: 4.
In Service: Japan.
Variants (with no. built):
Ki-48 prototypes: 950hp Ha-25s (4).
Ki-48 pre-production models: Modified tail surfaces (5).
Ki-48-Ia, Army Type 99 Twin-engined Light Bomber, Model 1A: Initial production model.
Ki-48-Ib, Model 1B: As Model 1A; minor equipment changes, improved gun mountings.
(Total Ki-48-Ia,b: 557).
Ki-48-II prototypes: Uprated engines; lengthened fuselage; addn armour plating; increased bomb-load (3).
Ki-48-IIa, Model 2A: As prototypes; strengthened fuselage; late models with dorsal fin fillet.
Ki-48-IIb, Model 2B: Dive-bomber version; retractable dive-brakes; late models with dorsal fin fillet.
Ki-48-IIc, Model 2C: Improved armament.
(Total Ki-48-II,a,b,c: 1,408).
Ki-48II KAI, Special Attack plane: Taiatari suicide model; Ki-48-II conversions; 1,764lb (800kg) bombs.
Total Production: 1,977.
Remarks: Light bomber design spurred by first encounters during Sino-Japanese conflict with Soviet-built Chinese AF SB-2s; replacing earlier Ki-32 single-engined light bombers, Ki-48's operational debut Northern China; Autumn 1940; widely employed early weeks Pacific War against US forces in Philippines, British and Commonwealth in Malaya and Burma, and in Netherlands East Indies; slow and poorly armed, Ki-48-I replaced by IIa/c variants; despite only marginal improvements, latter continued until invasion of Okinawa, April 1945, where majority expended in suicide role, some as specially-modified Ki-48-II KAI models with nose-mounted percussion-rod contact fuses.

Manufacturer: Kawasaki.
Model: Ki-56 'Thalia'.
Type: Freight transport.
Power Plant: Two 990hp Nakajima Ha-25, Army Type 99.
Performance:
maximum speed at 11,480ft (3,500m) 249mph (400km/hr).
time to 9,840ft (3,000m) 12min 38sec.
service ceiling 26,250ft (8,000m).
Weights:
empty 10,791lb (4,895kg).
loaded 17,692lb (8,025kg).
Dimensions:
wing span 65ft 6in (19.96m).
length 48ft 10½in (14.9m).
height 11ft 9¾in (3.6m).
wing area 551.117sq ft (51.2sq m).
Crew/Payload: 4/5,290lb (2,400kg).
In Service: Japan.
Variants (with no. built):
Prototypes: Indigenous redesign of Army Type LO Transport (licence-produced Lockheed 14) (2).
Ki-56, Army Type 1 Freight Transport: Production model (119).
Total Production: 121.
Remarks: Already producing the civil Lockheed 14 under licence for the IJAAF as the Army Type LO transport, Kawasaki were instructed to modify the basic design as a freight transport; with increased cabin volume and cargo-loading door, plus engine and wing design changes, Ki-56 first flew 1940; participated invasion of Netherlands East Indies, Feb 1942; subsequently operated all major theatres in support Japanese ground and air forces; in service until end of war.

Manufacturer: Kawasaki.
Model: Ki-61-Ib Hien 'Tony'.
Type: Fighter.
Power Plant: One 1,175hp Kawasaki Ha-40, Army Type 2.
Performance:
maximum speed at 15,945ft (4,860m) 368mph (592km/hr).
cruising speed 249mph (400km/hr).
maximum range 684 miles (1,100km).
time to 16,400ft (5,000m) 5 min 31sec.
service ceiling 37,730ft (11,600m).
Weights:
empty 4,872lb (2,210kg).
maximum 7,165lb (3,250kg).
Dimensions:
wing span 39ft 4½in (12.0m).
length 28ft 8½in (8.75m).
height 12ft 1¾in (3.7m).
wing area 215.28sq ft (20.0sq m).
Armament: Two 12.7mm Ho-103 machine-guns in fuselage; two 12.7mm Ho-103 (or two 20mm Mauser MG 151/20 cannon) in wings; max bomb load 1,102lb (500kg).
Crew: 1.
In Service: Japan.
Variants (with no. built):
Ki-61 prototypes and pre-production models (12).
Ki-61-Ia Hien (Swallow), Army Type 3 Fighter, Model 1a: initial production model; two 7.7mm wing-guns (or 20mm Mauser cannon); plus two 12.7mm machine-guns in fuselage.
Ki-61-Ib, Model 1b: Revised armament.
(Total Ki 61-Ia,b: 1,380).
Ki-61-I KAIc: Lengthened fuselage, fixed tailwheel; underwing stores pylons; two 20mm Ho-5 cannon in fuselage plus two 12.7mm or 7.7mm wing-guns.
Ki-61-I KAId: 12.7mm Ho-103 machine-guns in fuselage; two 30mm Ho-105 cannon in wings.
(Total Ki-61-I KAIc,d: 1,274).
Total Production: 3,078 (all Marks).
Remarks: Only operational Japanese fighter to be powered by liquid-cooled engine, Ki-61's combat debut New Guinea, Spring 1943; early production Ia/b models armed with machine-guns only; 388 later examples modified with wing-mounted cannon; saw extensive service in South and South-West Pacific areas, Philippines, Okinawa and, finally, as home-defence interceptor; good performance, heavy firepower, and improved pilot protection made Ki-61 formidable opponent; equipped some fifteen IJAAF Sentais, plus number of training units; captured examples used post-war by Chinese AF.
Colour Reference: Plates 102,103: Kawasaki Ki-61-I KAI Hien 'Tony' (Army Type 3 Fighter, Model 1) of HQ Chutai (Flight), 244th Sentai, IJAAF, Chofu (Tokyo Prefecture), Aug 1945; fuselage/tail lightning flashes are Chutai/Sentai markings, all-red tail indicates HQ Chutai; note white home-defence wing bands do not extend over aileron upper surfaces.

Manufacturer: Kawasaki.
Model: Ki-61-II KAIa Hien 'Tony'.
Type: Interceptor fighter.
Power Plant: One 1,500hp Kawasaki Ha-140.
Performance:
maximum speed at 19,685ft (6,000m) 379mph (610km/hr).
maximum range 995 miles (1,600km).
time to 16,400ft (5,000m) 6min 0sec.
service ceiling 36,090ft (11,000m).
Weights:
empty 6,261lb (2,840kg).
maximum 8,433lb (3,825kg).
Dimensions:
wing span 39ft 4½in (12.0m).
length 30ft 0½in (9.16m).
height 12ft 1¾in (3.70m).
wing area 215.28sq ft (20.0sq m).
Armament: Two 20mm Ho-5 cannon in fuselage; two 12.7mm Ho-103 machine-guns in wings; max bomb load 1,102lb (500kg).
Crew: 1.
In Service: Japan.
Variants (with no. built):
Ki-61-II prototypes: Re-engined Ki-61-I KAI; increased wing area; redesigned rear canopy (8).
Ki-61-II KAI prototypes and pre-production models: Lengthened fuselage; enlarged rudder; standard wing (30).
Ki-61-II KAIa, Army Type 3 Fighter, Model 2a: Production model; Model 2b: four 20mm Ho-5 cannon.
(Total Ki-61-II KAI, KAIa (inc 275 completed as Ki-100): 374).
Ki-61-III, Model 3: Project only; one prototype; Ki-61-II KAI conversion.
Total Production: 3,078 (all Marks).
Remarks: Specifically developed as high-altitude interceptor, Ki-61-II KAI plagued by power plant teething troubles; less than one hundred of 374 completed airframes fitted with uprated Ha-140 before B-29 Superfortress raid brought engine production to a halt; 30 further examples destroyed on ground before delivery; consequently only 60+ entered IJAAF service; limited use in home-defence role, Spring/Summer 1945; engine permitting, gave good account against high-flying B-29s; 275 engine-less airframes subsequently fitted with Mitsubishi radials as Ki-100.

Manufacturer: Kawasaki.
Model: Ki-100-Ib.
Type: Fighter/fighter-bomber.
Power Plant: One 1,500hp Mitsubishi (Ha-33) 62 or Ha-112-II, Army Type 4.
Performance:
maximum speed at 32,810ft (10,000m) 332mph (535km/hr).
cruising speed 249mph (400km/hr).
maximum range 1,367 miles (2,200km).
time to 32,810ft (10,000m) 20min 0sec.
service ceiling 36,090ft (11,000m).
Weights:
empty 5,567lb (2,525kg).
loaded 7,705lb (3,495kg).
Dimensions:
wing span 39ft 4½in (12.0m).
length 28ft 11¼in (8.82m).
height 12ft 3½in (3.75m).
wing area 215.278sq ft (20.0sq m).
Armament: Two 12.7mm Ho-103 Type 1 machine-guns in wings; two fuselage-mounted 20mm Ho-5 cannon; max bomb load 1,102lb (500kg).
Crew: 1.
In Service: Japan.
Variants (with no. built):
Ki-100 prototypes: Re-engined and modified Ki-61-II KAIs; three conversions.
Ki-100-Ia, Army Type 5 Fighter, Model 1a: Initial production; 272 Ki-61-II Kai conversions.
Ki-100-Ib, Model Ib: Improved version; all-round-vision canopy (118).
Ki-100-II prototypes: 1,500hp Ha-112-II Ru turbo-supercharged engine (3).
Total Production: 121 (+275 modified Ki-61-II KAI).
Remarks: Stop-gap measure, mating of 1,500hp Mitsubishi radial engine to stockpiled Ki-61-II KAI airframes resulted in highly successful interceptor fighter, arguably best IJAAF oper-

tional aircraft of entire war; first delivered March 1945, Ki–100–Ia proved match for all incursions Japanese airspace, whether high-altitude attack by B–29s or forays by USN carrier-based fighters; all-new Ki–100–Ib in production final weeks of war; together equipped five home-defence Sentais.

Manufacturer: Kawasaki.
Model: Ki–102b 'Randy'.
Type: Ground-attack.
Power Plant: Two 1,500hp Mitsubishi Ha–112–II, Army Type 4.
Performance:
maximum speed at 19,685ft (6,000m) 360mph (580km/hr).
normal range 1,240 miles (2,000km).
time to 16,400ft (5,000m) 6min 54sec.
service ceiling 32,810ft (10,000m).
Weights:
empty 10,913lb (4,950kg).
loaded 16,094lb (7,300kg).
Dimensions:
wing span 51ft 1in (15.57m).
length 37ft 6¾in (11.45m).
height 12ft 1⅛in (3.7m).
wing area 365.97sq ft (34.0sq m).
Armament: One 57mm Ho–401 cannon in nose; two 20mm Ho–5 ventral cannon; plus one flexible 12.7mm Ho–103 machine-gun in rear cockpit; max bomb load 1,102lb (500kg).
Crew: 2.
In Service: Japan.
Variants (with no. built):
Ki–102 prototypes: Development of Ki–96 experimental heavy fighter; 1,500hp Ha–112–II (3).
Ki–102 pre-production models (20).
Ki–102b, Army Type 4 Assault Plane: Production model; lengthened tailwheel strut (215).
Ki–102a prototypes: High-altitude fighter version; 1,500hp Ha–112–II Ru supercharged engines; revised armament; six Ki–102 pre-production model conversions.
Ki–102a production model: 20 production Ki–102b conversions.
Ki–102c prototypes: Night-fighter version; major redesign-fuselage, cockpit, wing and tail surfaces; interception radar in dorsal radome; ventral and dorsal/oblique cannon; supercharged Ha–112–II Ru engines; two Ki–102b conversions.
Total Production: 238.
Remarks: Few Ki–102b ground-attack aircraft participated Okinawa campaign; majority held in reserve in Japan as counter-invasion force; 15 Ki–102a high-altitude interceptors delivered IJAAF before end of war.

Manufacturer: Kayaba.
Model: Ka–1.
Type: Observation/anti-submarine autogyro.
Power Plant: One 240hp Kobe-built Argus As 10c.
Performance:
maximum speed 103mph (165km/hr).
cruising speed 72mph (115km/hr).
normal range 174 miles (280km).
time to 3,280ft (1,000m) 3min 20sec.
service ceiling 11,485ft (3,500m).
Weights:
empty 1,709lb (775kg).
loaded 2,579lb (1,170kg).
Dimensions:
rotor diameter 40ft 0½in (12.2m).
length 30ft 2⅛in (9.2m).
Armament: Two 132lb (60kg).
depth-charges (anti-submarine version).
Crew: 2/1.
In Service: Japan.
Variants (with no. built):
Ka–1: Production model; based on US Kellet KD–1A (approx 240).
Ka–1 KAI: Rotor tips fitted with powder rockets for increased load-carrying; 1 Ka–1 conversion.
Ka–2: Ka–1 with 240hp Jacobs L–4MA–7; 1 conversion.
Total Production: approx 240.
Remarks: World's first armed operational rotary-wing aircraft; developed from imported civil Kellet KD–1A; first flew May 1941; delivered to Japanese Army for AOP and liaison duties; also served aboard Army light escort carrier, as single-seater and armed with depth-charges, on inshore anti-submarine patrol.

Manufacturer: Kokusai.
Model: Ki–59 'Theresa'.
Type: Light transport.
Power Plant: Two 510hp Hitachi Ha–13a, Army Type 98.
Performance:
cruising speed at 6,560ft (2,000m) 186mph (300km/hr).

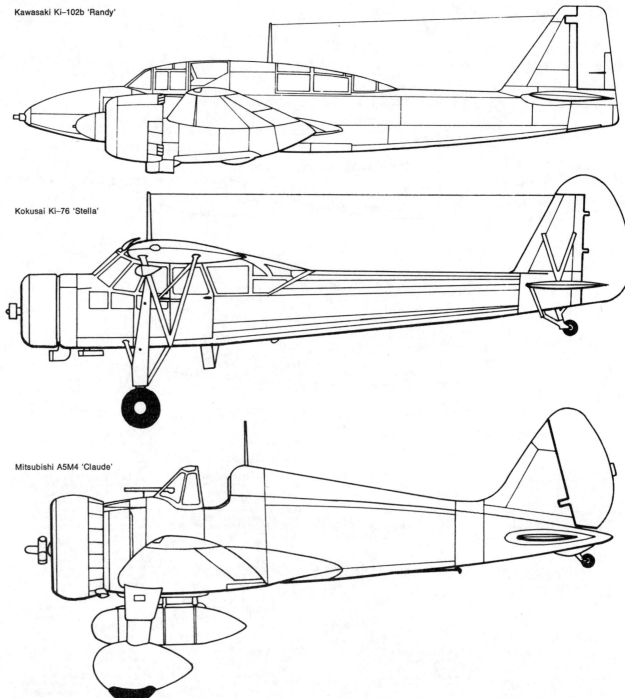

Kawasaki Ki–102b 'Randy'

Kokusai Ki–76 'Stella'

Mitsubishi A5M4 'Claude'

Weights:
empty 6,349lb (2,880kg).
maximum 9,350lb (4,240kg).
Dimensions:
wing span 55ft 9¼in (17.0m).
length 41ft 0in (12.5m).
height 10ft 0in (3.05m).
wing area 413.33sq ft (38.4sq m).
Crew/Accommodation: 2 or 3/8.
In Service: Japan.
Variants (with no. built):
Ki–59 prototypes: Militarized civil TK–3 transport.
Ki–59, Army Type 1 Transport: Production model; redesigned nose and undercarriage fairings; enlarged vertical tail surfaces (59, inc prototypes).
Total Production: 59.
Remarks: First produced 1941, Ki–59 saw brief operational service in light transport role with IJAAF before being replaced by Tachikawa Ki–54; one airframe modified as experimental glider (see (Ku–8–II).

Manufacturer: Kokusai.
Model: Ki–76 'Stella'.
Type: Liaison/anti-submarine patrol aircraft.
Power Plant: One 310hp Hitachi Ha–42.
Performance:
maximum speed 111mph (178km/hr).
normal range 466 miles (750km).
service ceiling 18,470ft (5,630m).
Weights:
empty 2,447lb (1,110kg).

maximum 3,571lb (1,620kg).
Dimensions:
wing span 49ft 2½in (15.0m).
length 31ft 4½in (9.56m).
height 9ft 6½in (2.90m).
wing area 316.46sq ft (29.4sq m).
Armament: One flexible 7.7mm Type 89 machine-gun in rear cockpit; (anti-submarine version) two 132lb (60kg) depth-charges.
Crew: 2.
In Service: Japan.
Variants:
Ki–76, Army Type 3 Command Liaison Plane: Prototypes and majority of production models land-based liaison/observation aircraft; number modified as carrier-borne anti-submarine version.
Remarks: Based upon successful German Fieseler Fi 156 Storch concept, Ki–76 first flew May 1941; after lengthy trials, production commenced late 1942; extensive use in AOP and liaison roles until end of war; late 1943 converted for anti-submarine patrol duties aboard Army escort carrier; equipped with deck arrester hook and depth-charge racks.

Manufacturer: Kokusai.
Model: Ku–8–II 'Gander'.
Type: Transport glider.
Performance:
maximum towing speed 139mph (224km/hr).
Weights:
empty 3,748lb (1,700kg).

loaded 7,716lb (3,500kg).
Dimensions:
wing span 76ft 1½in (23.2m).
length 43ft 8in (13.31m).
wing area 545.73sq ft (50.70sq m).
Crew/Payload/Accommodation:
2/light artillery piece and gun crew/20 troops.
In Service: Japan.
Variants (with no. built):
Ku–8–I: Modified Ki–59 airframe; landing skids; fixed nose (1).
Ku–8–II, prototype: Modified Ku–8–I; hinged nose section (1).
Ku–8–II, Army Type 4 Large-size Transport Glider: Production model.
Remarks: Japan's only operational transport glider; in production early 1944–March 1945; first encountered by Allied forces during invasion of Philippines, Oct 1944; usually towed by Mitsubishi Ki–21–II.

Manufacturer: Kyushu.
Model: K10W1 'Oak'.
Type: Trainer/communications.
Power Plant: One 600hp Nakajima Kotobuki 2 Kai.
Performance:
maximum speed at 6,825ft (2,080m) 175mph (282km/hr).
cruising speed 138mph (222km/hr).
range 652 miles (1,050km).
time to 16,400ft (5,000m) 17min 13sec.
service ceiling 23,950ft (7,300m).
Weights:
empty 3,254lb (1,476kg).

maximum 4,615lb (2,093kg).
Dimensions:
wing span 40ft 6½in (12.36m).
length 29ft 0in(8.84m).
height 9ft 3½in (2.84m).
wing area 240.034sq ft (22.3sq m).
Armament: One flexible 7.7mm Type 97 machine-gun in rear cockpit.
Crew: 2.
In Service: Japan (IJNAF).
Variants (with no. built):
Prototypes: Two North American NA–16 advanced trainer pattern aircraft; evaluated by IJNAF as KXA1/2.
K10W1 prototype: Re-engined; modified vertical tail surfaces; Watanabe (later Kyushu)- built (1).
K10W1, Navy Type 2 Intermediate Trainer: Production model; Watanabe (Kyushu)-built (25); Nippon Hikoki-built (150).
Total Production: 176.
Remarks: Re-engined and extensively modified development of imported North American NA–16 advanced trainer; supplemented numerically far superior Yokosuka K5Y (5,770 built) as IJNAF intermediate trainer, 1943–45; also employed in liaison-communications roles.

Manufacturer: Kyushu.
Model: K11W1 Shiragiku.
Type: Crew trainer/suicide-attack.
Power Plant: One 515hp Hitachi GK2B Amakaze 21.

Performance:
maximum speed at 5,580ft (1,700m) 143mph (230km/hr).
cruising speed 127mph (204km/hr).
maximum range 1,093 miles (1,760km).
time to 9,840ft (3,000m) 19min 35sec.
service ceiling 18,440ft (5,620m).
Weights:
empty 3,697lb (1,677kg).
maximum 6,173lb (2,800kg).
Dimensions:
wing span 49ft 1¾in (14.98m).
length 33ft 7¼in (10.24m).
height 12ft 10¾in (3.93m).
wing area 328.298sq ft (30.5sq m).
Armament: One flexible 7.7mm Type 92 machine-gun in rear cockpit; max bomb load (trainer) 132lb (60kg); (Kamikaze) 551lb (250kg).
Crew: 5 (1).
In Service: Japan (IJNAF).
Variants (with no. built):
K11W1 prototype (1).
K11W1 Shiragiku (White Chrysanthemum), Navy Operations Trainer, Model 11: Initial production model.
K11W2: Modified all-wood transport/anti-submarine patrol version (797).
(Total K11W1 Model II, K11W2: 797).
Q3W1 Nankai (South Sea) prototype: 2-seat K11W2 development specialised anti-submarine patrol version (1).
Total Production: 799 (inc Q3W1).
Remarks: Single-engined IJNAF bomber-crew trainer, K11W1 entered service mid-1943; number of examples modified towards close of war for Kamikaze role; K11W2 development saw limited employment transport and anti-submarine patrol duties; sole Q3W1 prototype crash-landed maiden flight.

Manufacturer: Kyushu.
Model: Q1W1 Tokai 'Lorna'.
Type: Anti-submarine patrol.
Power Plant: Two 610hp Hitachi GK2C Amakaze 31.
Performance:
maximum speed at 4,395ft (1,340m) 200mph (322km/hr).
cruising speed 150mph (241km/hr).
range 834 miles (1,340km).
time to 6,560ft (2,000m) 8min 44sec.
service ceiling 14,730ft (4,490m).
Weights:
empty 6,839lb (3,102kg).
maximum 11,724lb (5,318kg).
Dimensions:
wing span 52ft 6in (16.0m).
length 39ft 7¾in (12.085m).
height 13ft 6in (4.12m).
wing area 411.287sq ft (38.21sq m).
Armament: One flexible rearward-firing 7.7mm Type 92 machine-gun; provision for one (or two) 20mm Type 99 cannon in nose; max bomb load 1,102lb (500kg) or depth-charges.
Crew: 3.
In Service: Japan (IJNAF).
Variants (with no. built):
Q1W1 Prototype (1).
Q1W1 Tokai (Eastern Sea), Navy Patrol Plane, Model 11; Initial production model.
Q1W2, Model 21: Modified Q1W1; wooden rear fuselage.
(Total Q1W1 Model 11 and Model 21: 151).
Q1W1-K Tokai Ren (Eastern Sea Trainer): 4-seat trainer version; all-wood construction; prototype only (1).
Total Production: 153.
Remarks: Limited service 1944–45 convoy-escort/anti-submarine patrol duties East China, Yellow Sea and Sea of Japan; wholly inadequate performance/defensive armament for such operations in face of ever-widening areas of Allied air superiority; no confirmed submarine sinkings.

Manufacturer: Mansyu.
Model: Hayabusa I (Peregrine Falcon).
Type: Transport/communications.
Power Plant: One 460hp Nakajima Kotobuki 2 Kai 1.
Performance:
maximum speed 149mph (240km/hr).
Weights:
loaded 5,950lb (2,700kg).
Dimensions:
wing span 42ft 7¾in (13.00m).
length 32ft 9⅔in (10.00m).
Crew/Accommodation: 1/6.
In Service: Manchuria.
Variants:
Hayabusa I: Prototype and initial production model; six-passenger low-wing civil light transport monoplane; fixed undercarriage.
Hayabusa II: Improved Hayabusa I; revised cowling/cockpit canopy; provision for wheel spats.
Hayabusa III: Modified Hayabusa II; increased wing span; shortened fuselage; retractable undercarriage.
Total Production: 30+.
Remarks: First product of newly-established Manchurian Aircraft Manufacturing Co, Hayabusa entered commercial service 1938; approx 30 examples operated by para-military national airline (alongside licence-built Fokker Super-Universals and imported Junkers Ju 86s and de Havilland D.H.80A Puss Moths), as well as 3+ delivered Manchurian AF for VIP-transport/communications duties; several reportedly utilized post-war Soviet/Communist Chinese AFs.

Manufacturer: Mansyu.
Model: Ki-79a.
Type: Advanced trainer/communications.
Power Plant: One 510hp Hitachi Ha–13a.
Performance:
maximum speed at 211mph (340km/hr).
normal range 572 miles (920km).
Weights:
empty 2,866lb (1,300kg).
Dimensions:
wing span 37ft 8¾in (11.5m).
length 25ft 9in (7.85m).
Armament: One forward-firing 7.7mm Type 89 machine-gun.
Crew: 1.
In Service: Japan, Thailand.
Variants:
Ki–79a, Army Type 2 Advanced Trainer: Redesigned Nakajima Ki–27 fighter; initial single-seat all-metal trainer version.
Ki–79b: 2-seat (tandem) trainer version.
Ki–79c: As Ki–79a; Hitachi (Ha–23) 22; mixed wood and steel construction.
Ki–79d: As Ki–79b; Hitachi (Ha–23)24; mixed wood and steel construction.
Remarks: Manchurian-built IJAAF advanced trainer; developed from licence-produced Ki–27 single-seat fighter; also supplied to Thai AF; utilized in secondary liaison/communications roles.

Manufacturer: Mitsubishi.
Model: Ki–1–I.
Type: Heavy bomber/transport.
Power Plant: Two 944hp Ha–2–II.
Performance:
maximum speed 137mph (220km/hr).
range 684 miles (1,100km).
Weights:
loaded 17,857lb (8,100kg).
Dimensions:
wing span 86ft 11¼in (26.5m).
length 48ft 6⅔in (14.80m).
wing area 976.73sq ft (90.74sq m).
Armament: One 7.7mm machine-gun each in nose, dorsal, and ventral positions; max bomb load 2,205lb (1,000kg).
Crew: 4.
In Service: Japan.
Variants (with no. built):
Ki–1: Prototype; two 825hp Rolls-Royce Buzzard (1).
Ki–1–I, Army Type 93 Heavy bomber, Model 1: Initial production model; two 944hp Ha–2–II.
Ki–1–II, Model 2: Improved Model 1; redesigned fuselage; modified undercarriage; two 970hp Ha–2–III.
(Total Ki–1–I,II: 117).
Total Production: 118.
Remarks: Prototype built 1933; after limited service opening stages Sino-Japanese conflict, both Ki–1 (and contemporary Mitsubishi Ki–2, Army Type 93 Light bomber) relegated bombing-training role prior outbreak Pacific War; former also served second-line transport duties, 1941–42.

Manufacturer: Mitsubishi.
Model: K3M3–L 'Pine'.
Type: Utility transport.
Power Plant: One 580hp Nakajima Kotobuki 2 KAI 2.
Performance:
maximum speed at 3,280ft (1,000m) 146mph (235km/hr).
normal range 497 miles (800km).
time to 16,400ft (5,000m) 9min 30sec.
service ceiling 20,965ft (6,390m).
Weights:
empty 2,998lb (1,360kg).
loaded 4,850lb (2,200kg).
Dimensions:
wing span 51ft 9¼in (15.78m).
length 31ft 3⅔in (9.54m).
height 12ft 6⅓in (3.82m).
wing area 371.354sq ft (34.5sq m).
Armament: One flexible 7.7mm Type 92 machine-gun in rear cockpit; max bomb load 264lb (120kg).
Crew/Accommodation: 1/4–5 (or light cargo).
In Service: Japan (IJNAF).
Variants (with no. built):
K3M1 Prototypes (4).
K3M2, Navy Type 90 Crew Trainer, Model 1: 340hp Hitachi Amakaze 11; Mitsubishi-built (70); Aichi-built (247).
K3M3, Model 2: Re-engined and modified K3M2; enlarged tail surfaces; Watanabe-built (301).
K3M3–L: Utility transport version; K3M3 conversions.
Ki–7: Modified K3M2s Mitsubishi/Nakajima radials; IJAAF order; one subsequently adapted as civil transport (MS–1) (2).
Total Production: 624.
Remarks: Single-engined crew trainer dating back to early thirties; brief pre-war IJAAF interest; extensive service IJNAF wartime training role; also employed as personnel/light-cargo utility transport.

Manufacturer: Mitsubishi.
Model: A5M4 'Claude'.
Type: Carrier-borne fighter.
Power Plant: One 785hp Nakajima Kotobuki 41 or 41 KAI.
Performance:
maximum speed at 9,840ft (3,000m) 270mph (434km/hr).
maximum range 746 miles (1,200km).
time to 9,840ft (3,000m) 3min 35sec.
service ceiling 32,150ft (9,800m).
Weights:
empty 2,681lb (1,216kg).
loaded 3,684lb (1,671kg).
Dimensions:
wing span 36ft 1¼in (11.0m).
length 24ft 9¾in (7.565m).
height 10ft 8¾in (3.27m).
wing area 191.597sq ft (17.8sq m).
Armament: Two 7.7mm Type 89 machine-guns; max bomb load 132lb (60kg).
Crew: 1.
In Service: Japan (IJNAF).
Variants (with no. built):
Prototypes (Ka–14): Various engines and design modifications (6).
A5M1, Navy Type 96 Carrier Fighter, Model 1: Initial production model; 580hp Kotobuki 2 KAI 1.
A5M2a, Model 2–1: Uprated engine.
A5M2b, Model 2–2: 640hp Kotobuki 3; early models enclosed cockpit; NACA cowling.
A5M3a prototypes: 610hp Hispano-Suiza 12Xcrs; 20mm cannon (2).
A5M4, Model 24 (ex-Model 4): Re-engined A5M2b; open cockpit; auxiliary drop tank; late prod. models (Model 34) with Kotobuki 41 Kai.
(A5M1–A5M4 Mitsubishi-built (780); A5M4 Watanabe-built (39); A5M4 Omura Naval Air Arsenal-built (161)).
A5M4–K: 2-seat trainer version; Omura Naval Air Arsenal-built (103)
Ki–18 prototype: IJAAF equivalent of A5M1; 550hp Kotobuki 5 (1).
Ki–33 prototypes: Modified and re-engined Ki–18; enclosed cockpit (2).
Total Production: 1,094.
Remarks: IJNAF's first monoplane fighter, A5M's combat debut in second Sino-Japanese conflict assured Japanese forces complete air superiority for remainder of pre-war campaign; initial IJAAF interest in Ki–18/33 derivative rejected in favour of Nakajima Ki–27; by outbreak of Pacific War A5M4 equipped two Koku Sentais aboard three light carriers; limited participation invasion of Philippines, Dec 1941; subsequently relegated training and other secondary roles; surviving A5M4 and A5M4–K trainers expended at war's end in Kamikaze sorties against Allied shipping off Home Islands.

Manufacturer: Mitsubishi.
Model: G3M2 'Nell'.
Type: Bomber.
Power Plant: Two 1,075hp Mitsubishi Kinsei 41, 42 or 45.
Performance:
maximum speed at 13,715ft (4,180m) 232mph (373km/hr).
cruising speed 173mph (278km/hr).
maximum range 2,722 miles (4,380km).
time to 9,840ft (3,000m) 8min 19sec.
service ceiling 29,950ft (9,130m).
Weights:
empty 10,936lb (4,965kg).
loaded 17,637lb (8,000kg).
Dimensions:
wing span 82ft 0¼in (25.0m).
length 53ft 11½in (16.45m).
height 12ft 1in (3.69m).
wing area 807.3sq ft (75.0sq m).
Armament: One flexible 20mm Type 99 Model 1 cannon in dorsal turret; one flexible 7.7mm Type 92 machine-gun each in lateral blisters and retractable ventral turret; one hand-held 7.7mm Type 92 machine-gun in cockpit; max bomb load 1,764lb (800kg) or one torpedo.
Crew: 7.
In Service: Japan (IJNAF).
Variants (with no. built):
Prototypes (Ka–15): 750hp Hiro Type 91s, 830hp Kinsei 2s or 910hp Kinsei 3s; glazed or solid nose (21).
G3M1, Navy Type 96 Attack Bomber, Model 11; initial production model; enlarged cockpit, revised canopy; some with fixed-pitch propellers (34).
G3M1a/c: Redesignated prototypes; Hiro Type 91-powered, Kinsei powered, and glazed nose versions resp.
G3M1–L: Armed military transport version; 1,075hp Kinsei 45s; G3M1 conversions.
G3M2, Model 21: Uprated engines; increased fuel capacity; differing dorsal turret design; Mitsubishi-built (343); G3M2 (and G3M3) Nakajima-built (412).
G3M2, Model 22: Modified Model 21; retractable ventral and rear dorsal turrets replaced by single large dorsal 'turtle-back' turret; addn side 'blisters' (238).
Total Production: 1,048 (all Marks).
Remarks: First flown July 1935, G3M's combat debut exactly two years later—attacks across East China Sea by Formosan- and Japanese-based Kokutais on mainland China; first strategic transoceanic bombing raids in history of air warfare; subsequently based China, G3M2 units participated Sino-Japanese conflict until mid-1941; although obsolescent by outbreak of Pacific War, IJNAF deployed 200+ first-line G3Ms; operated Central Pacific and Philippine campaigns; also played leading part sinking of HMS *Prince of Wales* and *Repulse* off east coast Malaya; after 1943 majority relegated secondary roles, inc glider tug, crew-trainer and transport.
Colour Reference: Plates 104, 105: Mitsubishi G3M2 'Nell' (Navy Type 96 Attack Bomber, Model 22) No 23 of Mihoro Kokutai (Mihoro Naval Air Corps), 22nd Koku Sentai, IJNAF; Saigon, French Indo-China, Dec 1941; participated sinking *Prince of Wales* and *Repulse*, South China Sea; tail code: M=Mihoro (Naval Air Corps), —3=Attack Bomber.

Manufacturer: Mitsubishi.
Model: G3M3 'Nell'.
Type: Long-range bomber.
Power Plant: Two 1,300hp Mitsubishi Kinsei 51.
Performance:
maximum speed at 19,360ft (5,900m) 258mph (415km/hr).
maximum range 3,871 miles (6,230km).
time to 9,840ft (3,000m) 5min 29sec.
service ceiling 33,730ft (10,280m).
Weights:
empty 11,551lb (5,243kg).
loaded 17,637lb (8,000kg).
Dimensions:
wing span 82ft 0¼in (25.0m).
length 53ft 11½in (16.45m).
height 12ft 1in (3.685m).
wing area 807.3sq ft (75.0sq m).
Armament: As G3M2 Model 22.
Crew: 7.
In Service: Japan (IJNAF).
Variants (with no. built):
G3M3, Model 23: Improved G3M2, Model 22; uprated engines; increased fuel capacity; Nakajima-built (see G3M2).
L3Y1, Navy Type 96 Transport, Model 11: Armed transport conversion of G3M1.
L3Y2, Model 12: Armed transport conversion of Kinsei 45-powered G3M2.
Total Production: 1,048 (all Marks).
Remarks: Introduced 1941, G3M3 variant, produced solely by Nakajima, fastest of series; remained in first-line service only two years; post-1943, utilizing excellent long-range performance, many converted to maritime reconnaissance role with search radar; earlier G3M1/2 models modified as L3Y1/2 personnel transports.

Manufacturer: Mitsubishi.
Model: Ki–15–II 'Babs'.
Type: Reconnaissance.
Power Plant: One 900hp Mitsubishi Ha–26–I, Army Type 99 Model 1.
Performance:
maximum speed at 14,205ft (4,330m) 317mph (510km/hr).
time to 16,400ft (5,000m) 6min 49sec.
Weights:
empty 3,510lb (1,592kg).
maximum 5,470lb (2,481kg).
Dimensions:
wing span 39ft 4½in (12.0m).
length 28ft 6½in (8.7m).
height 10ft 11½in (3.34m).
wing area 219.152sq ft (20.36sq m).
Armament: One flexible rearward-firing 7.7mm Type 89 machine-gun.
Crew: 2.
In Service: Japan.
Variants (with no. built):
Ki–15 prototypes: One military, one civil (Karigane I—Wild Goose I) model (2).
Ki–15–I, Army Type 97 Command Reconnaissance Plane, Model 1: Initial production model; 550hp Nakajima H–8.
Ki–15–II, Model 2: Modified Ki–15–I; uprated engine (inc 2+ civil Karigane IIs).
(Total Ki–15–I, II: 435).
Ki–15–III prototypes: 1,050hp Mitsubishi Ha–102 (2).
C5M1/2: IJNAF equivalent/development of Ki–15–II.
Total Production: 439 (exc C5M).
Remarks: High-speed reconnaissance/communications aircraft; second (civil) prototype, christened 'Kamikaze' (Divine Wind), set pre-war Japan-England record; military Ki–15s among earliest aircraft engaged second Sino-Japanese conflict; also operated against Russo-Mongolian forces during Nomonham Incident; employed in reconnaissance role opening months Pacific War; subsequently relegated communications duties; the name 'Kamikaze' was also later used to refer to all suicide attacks and at end of war Ki–15s some used for this purpose.

Manufacturer: Mitsubishi.
Model: C5M2 'Babs'.
Type: Reconnaissance.
Power Plant: One 950hp Nakajima Sakae 12.
Performance:
maximum speed at 14,930ft (4,550m) 303mph (487km/hr).
maximum range 691 miles (1,110km).
time to 9,840ft (3,000m) 3min 58sec.
service ceiling 31,430ft (9,580m).
Weights:
empty 3,781lb (1,715kg).
loaded 5,170lb (2,345kg).
Dimensions:
wing span 39ft 4½in (12.0m).
length 28ft 6½in (8.7m).
height 11ft 4⅓in (3.465m).
wing area 219.152sq ft (20.36sq m).
Armament: One flexible rearward-firing 7.7mm Type 92 machine-gun.
Crew: 2.
In Service: Japan (IJNAF).
Variants (with no. built):
C5M1, Navy Type 98 Reconnaissance Plane, Model 11: IJNAF equivalent of Ki–15–II; 875hp Mitsubishi Zusei 12; naval equipment (20).
C5M2, Model 12: Modified C5M1; uprated engine; increased weight (addn equipment (30).
Total Production: 50.
Remarks: IJNAF adaptation of Army's Ki–15; serving with two Koku Sentais outbreak of Pacific War; initial sighting by C5M2 led to destruction of HMS *Prince of Wales* and *Repulse* off east coast Malaya, Dec 1941; served latter part of war in communications and training roles.

Manufacturer: Mitsubishi.
Model: F1M2 'Pete'.
Type: Observation/general-purpose floatplane.
Power Plant: One 875hp Mitsubishi MK2 Zusei 13.
Performance:
maximum speed at 11,285ft (3,440m) 230mph (370km/hr).
cruising speed 127mph (204km/hr).
maximum range 460 miles (740km).
time to 9,840ft (3,000m) 5min 4sec.
service ceiling 30,970ft (9,440m).
Weights:
empty 4,251lb (1,928kg).
maximum 6,296lb (2,855kg).
Dimensions:
wing span 36ft 1in (11.0m).
length 31ft 2in (9.5m).

height 13ft 1¾in (4.0m).
wing area 317.965sq ft (29.54sq m)
Armament: Two fixed forward-firing 7.7mm Type 97 machine-guns; one flexible 7.7mm Type 92 machine-gun in rear cockpit; max bomb load; 264lb (120kg).
Crew: 2.
In Service: Japan (IJNAF), Thailand (RTNAF).
Variants (with no. built):
F1M1 Prototypes: 820hp Nakajima Hikari 1 (4).
F1M2, Navy Type O Observation Seaplane, Model 11: Re-engined; Re-designed wings and engine cowling; Mitsubishi-built (524); Sasebo Naval Air Arsenal-built (590).
F1M2–K: Advanced trainer version; F1M2 conversions.
Total Production: 1,118.
Remarks: Excellent performance, employed extensively throughout Pacific War both ship- and shore-based; originally designed as catapult-launched observation seaplane, saw service in many other roles inc convoy escort, coastal patrol, even as interceptor fighter and dive-bomber in support of amphibious operations; also supplied Thai NAF for coastal/anti-submarine patrol duties.

Manufacturer: Mitsubishi.
Model: Ki–21–IIb 'Sally'.
Type: Heavy bomber.
Power Plant: Two 1,500hp Mitsubishi Ha-101, Army Type 100.
Performance:
maximum speed at 15,485ft (4,720m) 302mph (486 km/hr).
cruising speed 236mph (380km/hr).
maximum range 1,680 miles (2,700km).
time to 19,685ft (6,000m) 13min 13sec.
service ceiling 32,810ft (10,000m).
Weights:
empty 13,382lb (6,070kg).
maximum 23,391lb (10,610kg).
Dimensions:
wing span 73ft 9¾in (22.5m).
length 52ft 6in (16.0m).
height 15ft 11in (4.85m).
wing area 749.165sq ft (69.6sq m).
Armament: One flexible 7.7mm Type 89 machine-gun each in nose, tail, ventral and two beam positions; one 12.7mm Type 1 machine-gun in dorsal turret; max bomb load 2,205lb (1,000kg).
Crew: 5–7.
In Service: Japan, Thailand (9 Ki–21–I).
Variants (with no. built):
Ki–21: Prototypes and service trials aircraft; various engines and armament (8).
Ki–21–Ia, Army Type 97 Heavy bomber, Model 1A: Initial production model; 850hp Nakajima Ha–5 KAIs; Mitsubishi-built (143); Nakajima Hikoki-built (inc Ki–21–1b and –1c) (351).
Ki–21–Ib, Model 1B: One addn 7.7mm machine-gun each in tail and fuselage side positions; enlarged bomb-bay and landing flaps; redesigned horizontal tail surfaces; Mitsubishi-built (120).
Ki–21–Ic, Model 1C: One addn 7.7mm machine-gun; increased fuel capacity; Mitsubishi-built (160).
Ki–21–II: Service trials aircraft; improved Ki–21–Ic; re-engined; modified engine nacelles (4).
Ki–21–IIa, Model 2A: Production model (590).
Ki–21–IIb, Model 2B: Modified Model 2A; dorsal 'greenhouse' replaced by turret (688).
MC–21: Unarmed civil freighter/transport version; Ki–21–Ia conversion.
Total Production: 2,064.
Remarks: Perhaps best-known IJAAF bomber of WWII; operational debut Sino-Japanese conflict; also participated Nomonhan Incident; outbreak of Pacific War employed principally campaigns in Malaya, Burma and Netherlands East Indies; attacked targets in India; also remained in action mainland China; early successes, but soon outclassed by advent superior Allied fighter presence; introduction of Ki–21–IIb with bicycle pedal-powered dorsal turret did little to remedy situation; nevertheless remained in first-line service until end of war; also used in transport role (both civil and military), as bomber trainer, communications aircraft, and for suicide and special commando-attack missions; 9 Ki–21–Is supplied to Thai AF; known as Nagoya, type saw action against Vichy AF over French Indo-China.
Colour Reference: Plate 110: Mitsubishi Ki–21–IIb 'Sally' (Army Type 97 Heavy Bomber, Model 2B) of 1st Chutai, 14th Sentai, IJAAF, Philippines, June 1944); olive green dapple over natural metal; note stylized '14' Sentai insignia across vertical tail surfaces.

Manufacturer: Mitsubishi.
Model: Ki–30 'Ann'.
Type: Light bomber.
Power Plant: One 960hp Nakajima Ha–5 KAI, Army Type 97.
Performance:
maximum speed at 13,120ft (4,000m) 263mph (423km/hr).
cruising speed 236mph (380km/hr).
maximum range 1,056 miles (1,700 km).
time to 16,400ft (5,000m) 10min 36sec.
service ceiling 28,120ft (8,570m).
Weights:
empty 4,916lb (2,230kg).
loaded 7,324lb (3,322kg).
Dimensions:
wing span 47ft 8¾in (14.55m).
length 33ft 11in (10.34m).
height 11ft 11½in (3.65m).
wing area 329.16sq ft (30.58sq m).
Armament: One 7.7mm Type 89 wing-gun plus one flexible 7.7mm Type 89 machine-gun in rear cockpit; max bomb load 882lb (400kg).
Crew: 2.
In Service: Japan, Thailand (9).
Variants (with no. built):
Ki–30 prototypes: 825hp Mitsubishi Ha–6 or 850hp Ha–5 KAI (2).
Ki–30 Service Trials models: Revised armament (16).
Ki–30 Army Type 97 Light Bomber: Production model; Mitsubishi-built (618); Tachikawa Army Air Arsenal-built (68).
Total Production: 704.
Remarks: Operated primarily mainland China; participated Nomonhan conflict; WWII saw brief service latter stages Japanese invasion of Philippines; subsequently employed as crew-trainer; nine supplied Thai AF; in action against Vichy forces in French Indo-China; end of war reappeared in Kamikaze role.

Manufacturer: Mitsubishi.
Model: B5M1.
Type: Carrier-borne attack-bomber.
Power Plant: One 1,000hp Mitsubishi Kinsei 43.
Performance:
maximum speed at 7,220ft (2,200m) 237mph (381km/hr).
normal range 1,367 miles (2,200km).
service ceiling 27,100ft (8,260m).
Weights:
loaded 8,818lb (4,000kg).
Dimensions:
wing span 50ft 2½in (15.3m).
length 33ft 10½in (10.23m).
height 13ft 11in (4.24m).
Armament: One flexible 7.7mm machine-gun in rear cockpit; max bomb load 1,764lb (800kg) or one torpedo.
Crew: 3.
In Service: Japan (IJNAF).
Variants:
B5M1, Navy Type 97 Carrier Attack-Bomber Model 2: Production model, inc prototype.
Total Production: 125.
Remarks: Fixed, spatted undercarriage torpedo/attack-bomber produced to same specification as Nakajima B5N; saw brief service early months Pacific War, mainly shore-based South-East Asia area; subsequently relegated second-line duties.

Manufacturer: Mitsubishi.
Model: A6M2 Model 21 Reisen 'Zeke' ('Zero').
Type: Carrier-borne fighter/fighter-bomber.
Power Plant: One 950hp Nakajima NK1C Sakae 12.
Performance:
maximum speed at 14,930ft (4,550m) 332mph (534km/hr).
cruising speed 207mph (333km/hr).
maximum range 1,930 miles (3,105km).
time to 19,685ft (6,000m) 7min 27sec.
service ceiling 32,810ft (10,000m).
Weights:
empty 3,704lb (1,680kg).
maximum 6,164lb (2,796kg).
Dimensions:
wing span 39ft 4½in (12.0m).
length 29ft 8¾in (9.06m).
height 10ft 0in (3.05m).
wing area 241.541sq ft (22.44sq m).
Armament: Two 20mm Type 99 cannon in wings; two 7.7mm Type 97 machine-guns in upper fuselage decking; bomb load 264lb (120kg).
Crew: 1.
In Service: China (1+ captured), Japan (IJNAF), USA (2+ evaluation).
Variants (with no. built):
A6M1 Prototypes: 780hp Mitsubishi Zuisei 13 (2).
A6M2 Prototype: 940hp Nakajima Sakae 12 (1).
A6M2 Reisen (Zero Fighter), Navy Type O Carrier Fighter, Model 11: Initial production model; redesigned wing structure (64).
A6M2, Model 21: Modified Model 11; manually-folding wing tips; late models with aileron tab balance; Mitsubishi-built (740); Nakajima-built (A6M2–A6M7) (6,570).
A6M2–N: Interceptor floatplane version (see Nakajima A6M2–N) (327).
A6M2–K Zero-Reisen (Zero Fighter-Trainer): 2-seat trainer version; wing armament deleted; Omura (Sasabo) Naval Air Arsenal-built (236); Hitachi-built (272).
Total Production: approx 11,283 (all Marks).
Remarks: Synonymous with Japanese wartime airpower, name 'Zero' remains to this day best-known of all Japanese aircraft; early models' operational debut Sino-Japanese conflict, Autumn 1940; excellent performance/kill-ratio largely unnoticed by Western Allies; by outbreak of Pacific War A6M2s comprised over 60 per cent IJNAF's carrier-fighter force; burst upon unsuspecting US-Allied forces, sweeping length and breadth Pacific and Indian Ocean war zones; participated Pearl Harbor and Wake Island attacks, escorted bombing raids Australia and Ceylon, and supported land campaigns Philippines and Netherlands East Indies; suffered first severe reversals Battle of Midway, June 1942, subsequently relinquishing initiative to newer US designs; early model recovered overturned but intact by US forces in Aleutians proved invaluable intelligence prize; number of elderly A6M2s also operated post-war by Thai AF.
Colour Reference: Plates 107, 108: Mitsubishi A6M2 Reisen 'Zero' (Navy Type O Carrier Fighter, Model 21) No 08 aboard IJN carrier Ryujo, Fourth Koku Sentai, Aleutians attack force, June 1942; flown by Flight Petty Officer Tadayoshi Koga, No 08 participated attack on Dutch Harbor, Unalaska Island, 4 June 1942; with oil-pressure gauge indicator line severed by single bullet from PBY Catalina, Koga attempted wheels-down landing nearby Akutan Island; machine recovered intact by US Navy team one month later; tail code: D=Fourth Koku Sentai, I=First Carrier (Ryujo), –1= Carrier Fighter.

Manufacturer: Mitsubishi.
Model: A6M3 Model 22 Reisen 'Zeke 32' ('Zero').
Type: Carrier-borne fighter/fighter-bomber.
Power Plant: One 1,130hp Nakajima Sakae 21.
Performance:
maximum speed at 19,685ft (6,000m) 336mph (540km/hr).
cruising speed 220mph (354km/hr).
Weights:
empty 4,107lb (1,863kg).
loaded 5,906lb (2,679kg).
Dimensions:
wing span 39ft 4½in (12.0m).
length 29ft 8¾in (9.06m).
height 11ft 6½in (3.51m).
wing area 241.541sq ft (22.44sq m).
Armament: Two 20mm Type 99 Model 1 cannon in wings; two 7.7mm Type 97 machine-guns in upper fuselage decking; bomb load 264lb (120kg).
Crew: 1.
In Service: Japan (IJNAF).
Variants (with no. built):
A6M3 Reisen (Zero Fighter), Navy Type O Carrier Fighter, Model 32: Modified and re-engined A6M2; redesigned cowling; clipped wings (folding wingtips deleted); reduced fuel capacity; Mitsubishi-built (343); also Nakajima-built.
A6M3, Model 22: Folding wingtips restored as A6M2; addn fuel capacity; 3+ with 30mm cannon in wings; Mitsubishi-built (inc Model 22a) (560); also Nakajima-built.
A6M3a, Model 22a: As Model 22. Two 20mm Type 99 Model 2 wing cannon.
A6M4: Experimental conversions two A6M2 with supercharged Sakae.
Total Production: approx 11,283 (all Marks).
Remarks: Entered service late Spring/early Summer 1942 in SWPA, A6M3 featured uprated engine, but only at expense of fuel capacity; consequent lack of range serious drawback for long over-water distances involved Summer 1942 Solomons campaign; models 22/22a redressed balance, but unable to regain superiority lost to modern Allied fighters introduced post-Guadalcanal; despite limitations remained in service until end of war, number being expended in Kamikaze role.

Manufacturer: Mitsubishi.
Model: A6M5 Model 52 Reisen 'Zeke' ('Zero').
Type: Carrier-borne fighter/fighter-bomber.
Power Plant: One 1,130hp Nakajima NKIF Sakae 21.
Performance:
maximum speed at 19,685ft (6,000m) 351mph (565km/hr).
cruising speed 230mph (370km/hr).
maximum range 1,194 miles (1,920km).
time to 19,685ft (6,000m) 7min 1sec.
service ceiling 38,520ft (11,740m).
Weights:
empty 4,136lb (1,876kg).
loaded 6,025lb (2,733kg).
Dimensions:
wing span 36ft 1in (11.0m).
length 29ft 11in (9.12m).
height 11ft 6¼in (3.51m).
wing area 229.271sq ft (21.3sq m).
Armament: Two 20mm Type 99 cannon in wings plus two 7.7mm Type 97 machine-guns in upper fuselage decking; bomb load 264lb (120kg).
Crew: 1.
In Service: Japan (IJNAF).
Variants (with no built):
A6M5 Reisen (Zero Fighter), Navy Type O Carrier Fighter, Model 52: Modified A6M3; redesigned wings (non-folding tips); individual exhaust stacks; main production model; Mitsubishi-built (747) also Nakajima-built.
A6M5a, Model 52A: Improved version; modified wings; belt-fed 20mm cannon; built by Mitsubishi and Nakajima.
A6M5b, Model 52B: Armour protection; one 7.7mm fuselage machine-gun plus one 13.2mm Type 3 fuselage machine-gun; Mitsubishi and Nakajima-built.
A6M5c, Model 52C: Heavy fighter version; addn fuel capacity, armament, armour and bomb-racks; Mitsubishi-built (93).
A6M5d–S: Night-fighter conversion of A6M5s; one oblique-firing 20mm cannon in rear fuselage.
A6M5–K Zero-Rensen (Zero Fighter-Trainer), Model 22: Experimental 2-seat trainer version; Hitachi-built (7).
Total Production: approx 11,283 (all Marks).
Remarks: Due to failure of both experimental A6M4 and intended A7M replacement, interim A6M5 version remained in production throughout final two years of Pacific war; operational debut Autumn 1943, early models still suffered basic 'Zero' weakness: inadequate armament and pilot/fuel tank protection; appearance heavier Model 52C, with additional pair wing machine-guns, helped rectify fault; but A6M5s nonetheless decimated in US liberation of Philippines 1944–45; many employed in Kamikaze attacks against US fleet; successes inc escort carrier sunk off Leyte; field-modified A6M5s (unofficial designation A6M5d–S) participated night home defence close of war.

Manufacturer: Mitsubishi.
Model: A6M6c 'Zeke' ('Zero').
Type: Interceptor fighter/fighter-bomber.
Power Plant: One 1,130hp Nakajima NK1P Sakae 31.
Performance:
maximum speed at sea level 289mph (465km/hr).
maximum speed at 19,685ft (6,000m) 346mph (557km/hr).
cruising speed 201mph (323km/hr).
maximum range 1,130 miles (1,818km).
initial rate of climb 3,140ft/min (957m/min).
service ceiling 35,100ft (10,700m).
Weights:
empty 3,920lb (1,778kg).
maximum 6,507lb (2,950kg).
Dimensions:
wing span 36ft 1in (11.6m).
length 30ft 3¾in (9.24m).
height 11ft 11¼in (3.64m).
wing area 229.271sq ft (21.3sq m).
Armament: Two 20mm Type 99 cannon and two 13.2mm Type 3 machine-guns in wings; one 13.2mm Type 3 machine-gun in upper fuselage decking; bomb load 264lb (120kg), plus eight 22lb (10kg) or two 132lb (60kg) rockets.
Crew: 1.
In Service: Japan (IJNAF).
Variants (with no. built):
A6M6 prototype: Re-engined A6M5c; Mitsubishi-built (1).
A6M6c Reisen (Zero Fighter), Model 53C: Production model; self-sealing wing tanks; Nakajima-built.
A6M7, Model 63: Dive-bomber version; ventral bomb rack; max bomb load 1,102lb (500kg); underwing drop tanks; reinforced tailplane; built by Mitsubishi and Nakajima.
A6M8, Model 64: Prototypes; re-engined A6M7 airframes (2); 1,560hp Mitsubishi MK8P Kinsei 62; fuselage armament deleted.
Total Production: approx 11,283 (all Marks).
Remarks: A6M5c development with water-methanol boosted Sakae 31, A6M6 entered service end 1944–early 45; final operational fighter variant of series; A6M7, specialised dive-bomber version, appeared closing weeks of Pacific War; A6M8, first Mitsubishi-powered model since original A6M1 prototypes, about to enter mass-production (6,300 ordered) at cessation of hostilities; throughout war years A6M fighters served aboard every IJN carrier; equipped nearly thirty Kokutais in all; numerically most important Japanese aircraft of either army or navy AFs, 'Zero' shared fate of many lesser brethren, ending career as suicide-attack bomber.

Manufacturer: Mitsubishi.
Model: G4M1 Model 11 'Betty'.
Type: Medium bomber.
Power Plant: Two 1,530hp Mitsubishi MK4A Kasei 11.
Performance:
maximum speed at 13,780ft (4,200m) 266mph (428km/hr).
cruising speed 196mph (315km/hr).
maximum range 3,748 miles (6,030km).
time to 22,965ft (7,000m) 18min 0sec.
Weights:
empty 14,991lb (6,800kg).
loaded 20,944lb (9,500kg).
Dimensions:
wing span 82ft 0¼in (25.0m).
length 65ft 7½in (20.0m).
height 19ft 8¼in (6.0m).
wing area 840.927sq ft (78.125sq m).
Armament: One 7.7mm Type 92 machine-gun each in nose and dorsal blister; two 7.7mm Type 92 machine-guns in beam blisters; plus one 20mm Type 99 Model 1 cannon in tail position; max bomb load 1,764lb (800kg) or one torpedo.
Crew: 7.
In Service: Japan (IJNAF).
Variants (with no. built):
G4M1 prototypes: Land-based attack bomber (2).
G6M1, Navy Type 1 Wingtip Convoy Fighter: Initial production model. Heavy escort fighter version; one 20mm cannon each in fuselage (either side) and tail positions, one 7.7mm nose machine-gun, plus two 20mm cannon in ventral gondola (30).
G6M1–K, Navy Type 1 Large Land Trainer: Trainer version; G6M1 conversions.
G6M1–L2, Navy Type 1 Transport: Transport version; G6M1–K conversions.
G4M1, Navy Type 1 Attack Bomber, Model 11: Main production model; bomber version.
G4M1, Model 12: 1,530hp MK4E Kasei 15s; modified tail-cone and beam blisters. (Total G6M1–K, –L2, Model 11 and Model 12; 1,200).
Total Production: 2,446 (all Marks)
Remarks: Initial versions of Japan's most famous and numerically most important wartime bomber; G4M1 served throughout Pacific War from very first day of hostilities, attacking US forces in Philippines, until very last, ferrying Japanese surrender delegation to Io Shima en route to Nichols Field, Luzon; operational debut early Summer 1941 over mainland China;

outbreak Pacific War 120 IJNAF G4M1s divided between Philippines and South-East Asia theatres; participated sinking *Prince of Wales* and *Repulse*; subsequently engaged NEI, New Guinea, and Solomons campaigns; by Autumn 1942 lack of crew armour and fuel tank protection proved severe weakness in face of stiffening Allied fighter opposition; G4M1 gradually relegated to maritime-reconnaissance, transport and training duties upon introduction of newer models; two G4M1 transports carrying IJN Admiral Yamamoto, architect of Pearl Harbor attack, and staff on inspection tour of South Pacific intercepted and shot down over Bougainville by USAAF P-38 Lightnings, 18 April 1943.
Colour Reference: Plates 40, 41: Mitsubishi G4M1 'Betty' (Navy Type 1 Attack Bomber, Model 11) No 39 of 1st Kokutai, 21st Koku Sentai, IJNAF; Formosa, Dec 1941; standard early style camouflage scheme dark green/tan upper surfaces (separated by narrow light blue strips), light grey undersides; participated attack on Philippines across Luzon Strait; Tail code: Z=1st Kokutai, —7 =Naval land-based Attack Bomber.

Manufacturer: Mitsubishi.
Model: G4M2 Model 22 'Betty'.
Type: Medium bomber.
Power Plant: Two 1,800hp Mitsubishi MK4P Kasei 21.
Performance:
maximum speed at 15,090ft (4,600m) 272mph (438km/hr).
cruising speed 196mph (315km/hr).
maximum range 3,270 miles (5,260km).
time to 26,245ft (8,000m) 30min 24sec.
service ceiling 29,365ft (8,950m).
Weights:
empty 17,990lb (8,160kg).
loaded 27,558lb (12,500kg).
Dimensions:
wing span 82ft 0¼in (25.0m).
length 65ft 7½in (20.0m).
height 19ft 8¼in (6.0m).
wing area 840.927sq ft (78.125sq m).
Armament: Two 7.7mm Type 92 machine-guns each in nose and fuselage beam positions; one 20mm Type 99 Model 1 cannon each in dorsal and tail turrets; max bomb load 2,205lb (1,000kg), or one 1,764lb (800kg) torpedo.
Crew: 7.
In Service: Japan (IJNAF), USA (1+ evaluation).
Variants (with no. built):
G4M2, Navy Type 1 Attack Bomber, Model 22: Re-engined G4M1; revised armament; enlarged tailplane; increased nose glazing, laminar flow wing.
G4M2, Model 22A: Two 20mm Type 99 Model 1 cannon in lieu of 7.7mm beam guns.
G4M2, Model 22B: As Model 22A; four 20mm Type 99 Model 2 cannon.
(Total G4M2 Models 22, 22A, 22B: 350).
G4M2a, Model 24: Modified Model 22; 1,850hp MK4T Kasei 25s; bulged bomb-bay doors (14).
G4M2a, Model 24A/B: Armament as Model 22A and 22B resp.
G4M2a, Model 24C: As Model 24B: addn 13mm Type 2 machine-gun in nose.
(Total G4M2a Models 24A, B, C: 790).
G4M2b, Model 25: One G4M2a conversion; 1,825hp MK4T-B Kasei 25b's; experimental.
G4M2c, Model 26: Turbosupercharged 1,825hp MK4T-B Ru Kasei 25b Ru's; two G4M2a conversions.
G4M2d, Model 27: One G4M2 conversion; 1,795hp MK4V Kasei 27s.
G4M2e, Model 24J: Special carrier version for Ohka (Baka) piloted suicide missile; G4M2a Model 24B and 24C conversions.
Total Production: 2,446 (all Marks).
Remarks: Entering service mid-1943, G4M2 offered improved performance and heavier defensive armament, but only at expense of earlier models' phenomenal range; nor was any attempt made to remedy G4M1's propensity to burst into flames if hit by enemy fire; both variants consequently suffered severe losses during final two years of Pacific War, particularly in defence of Philippines, Marianas, and Okinawa; G4M2e operations, the aerial launching of Navy Suicide Attacker Ohka Model 11 missiles, commenced on 21 March 1945; first mission complete failure (see Yokosuka MXY7 Ohka 11); further attacks achieved little material success—no Allied capital ship was sunk by G4M/Ohka combination—but resulted in heavy casualties among overladen G4M 'mother' aircraft.

Manufacturer: Mitsubishi.
Model: G4M3 Model 34 'Betty'.
Type: Bomber.
Power Plant: Two 1,825hp Mitsubishi MK4T Kasei 25.
Performance:
maximum speed at 16,895ft (5,150m) 292mph (470km/hr).
cruising speed 196mph (315km/hr).
maximum range 2,694 miles (4,335km).
time to 22,965ft (7,000m) 20min 10sec.
service ceiling 30,250ft (9,220m).
Weights:
empty 18,409lb (8,350kg).
loaded 27,558lb (12,500kg).
Dimensions:
wing span 82ft 0¼in (25.0m).
length 63ft 11¾in (19.5m).
height 19ft 8¼in (6.0m).
wing area 840.927sq ft (78.125sq m).
Armament: As G4M2 Model 22.
Crew: 7.
In Service: Japan (IJNAF).
Variants (with no. built):
G4M3, Model 34: Redesigned G4M2; armour plating; self-sealing fuel tanks; redesigned wing; dihedral tailplane; modified tail turret (60).
G4M3a, Model 34A: Transport and anti-submarine version; revised armament; project only.
G4M3, Model 36: Prototypes turbosupercharged 1,825hp Kasei 25b Ru's; two Model 34 conversions.
Total Production: 2,446 (all Marks).
Remarks: G4M3, last of the 'Betty' line, represented belated attempt to cure chronic inflammability which had earned earlier versions nickname of 'Flying Lighter'; too late, and far too few, to affect outcome of war, G4M3 partially equipped one Kokutai for operational test purposes; in all, G4M series had been mainstay of Japan's bomber arm throughout Pacific campaign, equipping grand total of over twenty Kokutais.

Manufacturer: Mitsubishi.
Model: Ki-46-II 'Dinah'.
Type: High-altitude reconnaissance.
Power Plant: Two 1,080hp Mitsubishi Ha-102, Army Type I.
Performance:
maximum speed at 19,030ft (5,800m) 375mph (604km/hr).
cruising speed 249mph (400km/hr).
maximum range 1,537 miles (2,474km).
time to 26,250ft (8,000m) 17min 58sec.
service ceiling 35,170ft (10,720m).
Weights:
empty 7,194lb (3,263kg).
maximum 12,787lb (5,800kg).
Dimensions:
wing span 48ft 2¾in (14.7m).
length 36ft 1in (11.0m).
height 12ft 8¾in (3.88m).
wing area 344.4sq ft (32.0sq m).
Armament: One flexible 7.7mm Type 89 machine-gun in rear cockpit.
Crew: 2.
In Service: Japan (IJAAF, IJNAF), USA (1 evaluation).
Variants (with no. built):
Ki-46: Prototype.
Ki-46-I, Army Type 100 Command Reconnaissance Plane, Model 1: Initial production; 900hp Mitsubishi Ha-26-Is. (Total Ki-46, Ki-46-I, Model 1: 34).
Ki-46-II, Model 2: Main production model; uprated engines (1,093).
Ki-46-II KAI, Army Type 100 Operation Trainer: Three-seat radio-navigation trainer version; redesigned cockpit with stepped dorsal extension; Ki-46-II conversions.
Total Production: 1,742 (all Marks).
Remarks: Initial batch Model 1s used solely for training/service trials purposes; Model 2 entered service Summer 1941 over China and Manchuria; equipped seven Direct Command Chutais; also flew unauthorised reconnaissance projected landing zones in Malaya prior to Japanese invasion; early months Pacific War covered South-East Asia/Indian Ocean areas; limited employment by IJNAF over northern coastline Australia; remained in front-line service until end of war, supplemented post-1943 by improved Model 3.

Manufacturer: Mitsubishi.
Model: Ki-46-III KAI 'Dinah'.
Type: High-altitude interceptor fighter.
Power Plant: Two 1,500hp Mitsubishi Ha-112-II, Army Type 4.
Performance:
maximum speed at 19,685ft (6,000m) 391mph (630km/hr).
time to 26,250ft (8,000m) 19min 0sec.
service ceiling 34,450ft (10,500m).
Weights:
empty 8,446lb (3,831kg).
loaded 13,730lb (6,228kg).
Dimensions:
wing span 48ft 2¾in (14.7m).
length 37ft 8¼in (11.49m).
height 12ft 8¾in (3.88m).
wing area 344.44sq ft (32sq m).
Armament: Two 20mm Ho-5 cannon in nose; one oblique upward-firing 37mm Ho-203 cannon in dorsal position.
Crew: 2.
In Service: Japan.
Variants (with no. built):
Ki-46-III prototypes: Modified Ki-46-II; re-engined; streamlined unstepped canopy; re-designed fuel system; no armament (2).
Ki-46-III, Army Type 100 Command Reconnaissance Plane, Model 3: Production model (609).
Ki-46-III KAI, Army Type 100 Air Defence Fighter: Interceptor fighter conversions of Ki-46-III; two 20mm and one 37mm cannon in lieu of photographic equipment.
Ki-46-IIIb, Army Type 100 Ground-Attack Aircraft: Modified Ki-46-III KAI; dorsal 37mm cannon deleted.
Ki-46-IIIc: Project only.
Ki-46-IV prototypes: Reconnaissance plane; two turbosupercharged 1,100hp Ha-112-II Ru; increased fuel capacity (4).
Ki-46-IVa/b: Reconnaissance/fighter production models; projects only.
Total Production: 1,742 (all Marks).
Remarks: Interceptor fighter development of basic high-altitude reconnaissance model intended to combat B-29 raids on Japanese homeland; poor climbing speed and vulnerability to bombers' defensive fire precluded success in new role; nevertheless remained in service Nov 1944 until end of war, equipping two Sentais plus number of Direct Command units.
Colour Reference: Plate 98: Mitsubishi Ki-46-III 'Dinah' (Army Type 100 Command Reconnaissance Plane, Model 3) of 3rd Chutai, 81st Sentai, IJAAF; Burma, Aug 1944; overall brown, deep yellow wing leading edge panels.

Manufacturer: Mitsubishi.
Model: Ki-51 'Sonia'.
Type: Ground-attack.
Power Plant: One 940hp Mitsubishi Ha-26-II, Army Type 99 Model 2.
Performance:
maximum speed at 9,840ft (3,000m) 263mph (424km/hr).
maximum range 660 miles (1,060km).
time to 16,400ft (5,000m) 9min 55sec.
service ceiling 27,130ft (8,270m).
Weights:
empty 4,129lb (1,873kg).
maximum 6,415lb (2,920kg).
Dimensions:
wing span 39ft 8¼in (12.1m).
length 30ft 2¼in (9.21m).
height 8ft 11¼in (2.73m).
wing area 258.55sq ft (24.02sq m).
Armament: Two 7.7mm Type 89, or (late production) two 12.7mm Type 1 machine-guns in wings; one flexible 7.7mm Type 89 machine-gun in rear cockpit; max bomb load 441lb (200kg).
Crew: 2.
In Service: Japan.
Variants (with no. built):
Ki-51 Prototypes (2).
Ki-51 Service Trials Models: Hinged or sliding canopies (11).
Ki-51, Army Type 99 Assault Plane: Production model; Mitsubishi-built (1,459); Tachikawa Army Air Arsenal-built (913).
Ki-51a Prototype: Reconnaissance model; one Ki-51 Service Trials model conversion.
Ki-71, Army Experimental Tactical Reconnaissance Plane: Prototypes; improved retractable undercarriage reconnaissance version of Ki-51; 1,500hp Mitsubishi Ha-112-II; two 20mm Ho-5 wing cannon; Tachikawa Army Air Arsenal-built (3).
Total Production: 2,388 (inc Ki-71).
Remarks: Scaled-down ground-attack version of earlier Ki-30 light bomber design, Ki-51's combat debut Sino-Japanese conflict; subsequently served throughout Pacific War, during closing stages with 551lb (250kg) bomb load in Kamikaze role; examples abandoned NEI used post-war by Indonesian AF in hostilities against Dutch.

Manufacturer: Mitsubishi.
Model: Ki-57-I 'Topsy'.
Type: Personnel transport.
Power Plant: Two 950hp

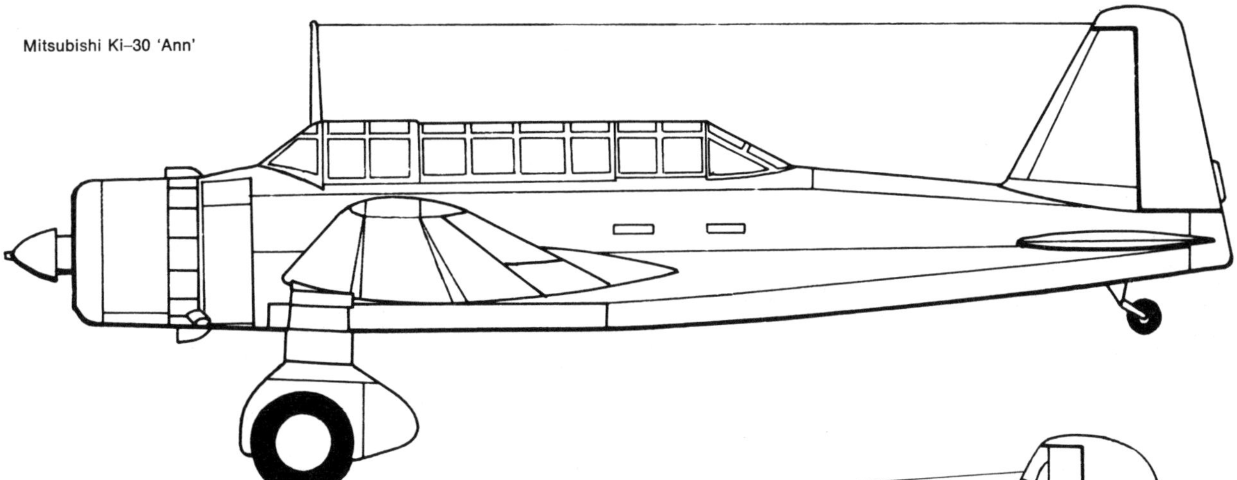
Mitsubishi Ki-30 'Ann'

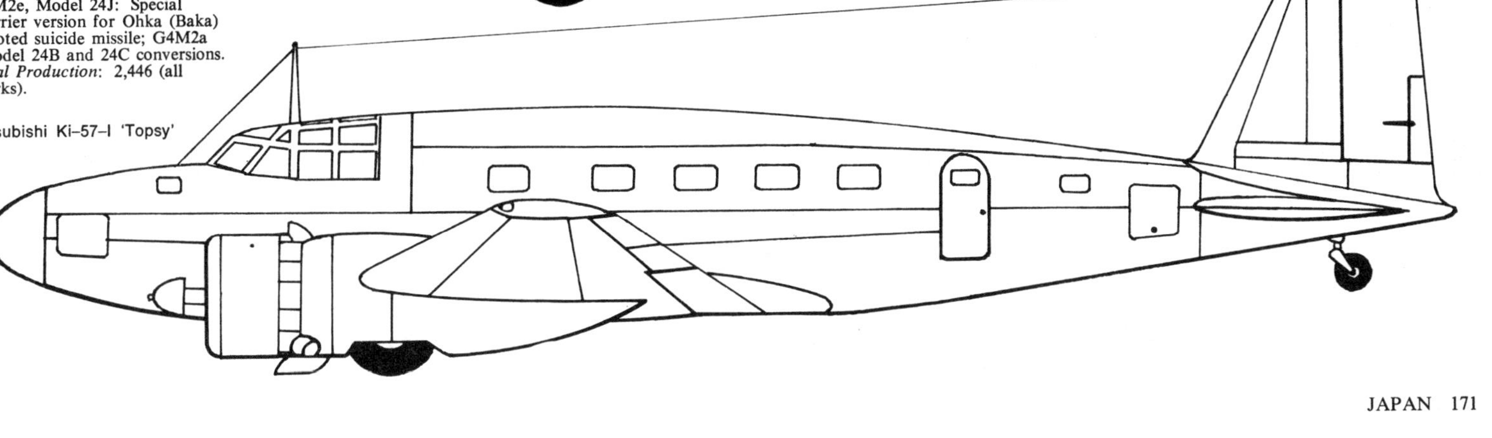
Mitsubishi Ki-57-I 'Topsy'

Nakajima Ha–5 KAI, Army Type 97.
Performance:
maximum speed at 11,155ft (3,400m) 267mph (430km/hr).
cruising speed 199mph (320km/hr).
maximum range 1,865 miles (3,000km).
time to 16,400ft (5,000m) 12min 10sec.
service ceiling 22,965ft (7,000m).
Weights:
empty 12,174lb (5,522kg).
maximum 18,600lb (8,437kg).
Dimensions:
wing span 74ft 1¾in (22.6m).
length 52ft 10in (16.1m).
height 15ft 7¾in (4.77m).
wing area 754.332sq ft (70.08sq m).
Crew: 4/11 troops.
In Service: Japan (IJAAF, IJNAF).
Variants (with no. built):
Ki–57: Prototype; civil (MC–20) and military transport version of Ki–21–I heavy bomber (1).
Ki–57–I, Army Type 100 Transport, Model 1: Initial production model, inc civil MC–20–Is (100).
Ki–57–II, Model 2: Modified Ki–57–I. 1,050hp Mitsubishi Ha–102s inc civil MC–20–IIs (406).
L4M1, Navy Type O Transport, Model 11: IJNAF equivalent of Ki–57–I; several transferred ex-IJAAF.
Total Production: 507 (inc civil MC–20s).
Remarks: In production 1940–45, Ki–57 transport development of Ki–21 heavy bomber was IJAAF's standard troop-carrier; manufactured in parallel with MC–20 civil airliner versions, served in personnel/paratroop transport, liaison, and communications roles both IJAAF and IJNAF; participated airborne assault Palembang oil refineries, Feb 1942.

Manufacturer: Mitsubishi.
Model: J2M3 Raiden 'Jack'.
Type: Interceptor fighter.
Power Plant: One 1,800hp Mitsubishi MK4R–A Kasei 23a.
Performance:
maximum speed at 17,880ft (5,450m) 363mph (584km/hr).
cruising speed 219mph (352km/hr).
normal range 1,180 miles (1,900km).
initial rate of climb 3,838ft/min (1,170m/min).
service ceiling 38,385ft (11,700m).
Weights:
empty 5,489lb (2,490kg).
maximum 8,120lb (3,683kg).
Dimensions:
wing span 35ft 5¼in (10.8m).
length 32ft 7¼in (9.94m).
height 12ft 11¼in (3.945m).
wing area 215.816sq ft (20.05sq m).
Armament: Two 20mm Type 99 Model 1; two 20mm Type 99 Model 2 cannon in wings; max bomb load 264lb (120kg).
Crew: 1.
In Service: Japan (IJNAF).
Variants (with no. built):
J2M1: Prototypes; 1,430hp MK4C Kasei 13; low-drag curved windscreen (3).
J2M2, Raiden (Thunderbolt), Navy Interceptor Fighter, Model 11: Initial production model; Kasei 23a; two fuselage machine-guns, two wing cannon; shortened nose, conventional windscreen (155).
J2M3, Model 21: Two 20mm Type 99 Model 1, plus two Model 2 cannon in strengthened wings; fuselage guns deleted (260).
J2M3a, Model 21A: Four 20mm Type 99 Model 2 cannon (21).
Total Production: 476+.
Remarks: Designed by same team as responsible for 'Zero', J2M Raiden failed to live up to famous forbear; lengthy development and slow rate of production plagued by technical and planning problems; performance of early versions only marginal; apart from brief appearance in battle for Philippines, late 1944, J2M served solely as home-defence interceptor.
Colour Reference: Plate 109: Mitsubishi J2M3 Raiden 'Jack' (Navy Interceptor Fighter, Model 21) 02 of 302nd Kokutai, IJNAF; Yokosuka (Tokyo Prefecture), Aug 1945; standard dark green/light grey finish (note IJNAF machines did not follow IJAAF practice of marking home-defence aircraft with white wing/fuselage bands around Hinomaru stations, see plates 99–100 and 102–103); late style tail code identifies Kokutai (ヨD), indicates naval land-based interceptor fighter (1100-series), and individual aircraft number.

Manufacturer: Mitsubishi.
Model: J2M5 Raiden 'Jack'.
Type: High-altitude interceptor fighter.
Power Plant: One 1,820hp Mitsubishi MK4U–4 Kasei 26a.
Performance:
maximum speed at 22,310ft (6,800m) 382mph (615km/hr).
cruising speed 230mph (370km/hr).
normal range 783 miles (1,260km).
time to 19,685ft (6,000m) 6min 20sec.
service ceiling 36,910ft (11,250m).
Weights:
empty 5,534lb (2,510kg).
loaded 7,676lb (3,482kg).
Dimensions:
wing span 35ft 5¼in (10.8m).
length 32ft 7¼in (9.94m).
height 12ft 11¼in (3.945m).
wing area 215.816sq ft (20.05sq m).
Armament: Two 20mm Type 99 Model 1; two 20mm Type 99 Model 2 cannon in wings.
Crew: 1.
In Service: Japan (IJNAF).
Variants (with no. built):
J2M4, Model 34: Prototypes; high-altitude version; modified J2M3; 1,820hp turbosupercharged MK4R–C Kasei 23c; two oblique upward-firing dorsal cannon (2).
J2M5, Model 33: J2M4 airframe with 1,820hp MK4U–A Kasei 26a with three-stage supercharger; armament as J2M3; some with armament as J2M3a(J2M5a); Mitsubishi-built (34); also Koza Naval Air Arsenal-built.
J2M6, Model 31: Modified J2M3; enlarged cockpit with domed canopy as J2M5 (1).
J2M6a, Model 31A: As J2M6 but armament as J2M3a; project only.
J2M7/7a: Projects only.
Total Production: 476+.
Remarks: High-altitude development of basic J2M, Model 33s served alongside earlier Model 21s in defence of homeland during closing months of war; improved performance, good pilot protection, and all-cannon armament made J2M3/5 highly successful bomber destroyer; many field-modified with oblique upward-firing cannon (20mm Type 99 Model 1) as originally tested on J2M4.

Manufacturer: Mitsubishi.
Model: Ki–67–I Hiryu 'Peggy'.
Type: Heavy bomber/torpedo-bomber.
Power Plant: Two 1,900hp Mitsubishi Ha–104, Army Type 4.
Performance:
maximum speed at 19,685ft (6,000m) 334mph (537km/hr).
cruising speed 249mph (400km/hr).
maximum range 2,360 miles (3,800km).
time to 19,685ft (6,000m) 14min 30sec.
service ceiling 31,070ft (9,470m).
Weights:
empty 19,068lb (8,649kg).
loaded 30,347lb (13,765kg).
Dimensions:
wing span 73ft 9¾in (22.5m).
length 61ft 4¼in (18.7m).
height 25ft 3¼in (7.7m).
wing area 708.86sq ft (65.85sq m).
Armament: One flexible 12.7mm Type 1 machine-gun each in nose and two beam blisters; one (two on late models) 12.7mm Type 1 machine-gun/s in tail turret; plus one flexible 20mm Ho–5 cannon in dorsal turret; max bomb load 1,765lb (800kg), or one 1,764lb (800kg), or 2,359lb (1,070kg) torpedo.
Crew: 6–8.
In Service: Japan (IJAAF, IJNAF).
Variants (with no. built):
Ki–67–I prototypes and Service Trials models: Various armament (19).
Ki–67–I Hiryu (Flying Dragon), Army Type 4 Heavy Bomber, Model 1: Production model; majority (420+) modified as torpedo-bombers (also inc 3 experimental versions: 2 with turbosupercharged Ha–104 Ru engines, and one as I–Go–1A guided-missile carrier) Mitsubishi-built (587); Kawasaki-built (91); Tachikawa First Army Air Arsenal-built (1).
Ki–67–I KAI Army Type 4 Special Attack Plane: 3-seat suicide attack version; turrets removed; nose-rod percussion fuse; two 1,764lb (800kg) bombs or 6,393lb (2,900kg) of explosives; Ki–67–I conversions.
Ki–67–II prototypes: 2,400hp Mitsubishi Ha–214 radials; two Ki–67–I conversions.
Yasakuhi (Shrine to an Unknown Warrior): IJNAF equivalent of Ki–67–I torpedo-bomber version; transferred from IJAAF.
Total Production: 698.
Remarks: Best Japanese bomber of WWII, Ki–67 entered service in face of overwhelming Allied air superiority, and far too late materially to affect outcome of war; operational debut mid-Oct 1944, both IJAAF and IJNAF torpedo-bombers being employed against US 3rd Fleet's strikes on Formosa and Ryukus; subsequently participated battle for Okinawa; served in conventional heavy bomber role over mainland China and against B–29 bases on Saipan, Tinian, and Guam; excellent performance all but nullified by paucity of trained crews; modified Ki–67–I KAIs expended end of war in Kamikaze role.
Colour Reference: Plate 106: Mitsubishi Ki–67–I KAI Hiryu 'Peggy' (Army Type 4 Special Attack Plane) No. 05 of 1st Chutai, 7th Sentai, IJAAF; Formosa, April 1945; standard olive green/light grey finish; employed Kamikaze role against Okinawan invasion forces, April–July 1945.

Manufacturer: Mitsubishi.
Model: Ki–109.
Type: Heavy interceptor.
Power Plant: Two 1,900hp Mitsubishi Ha–104, Army Type 4.
Performance:
maximum speed at 19,980ft (6,090m) 342mph (550km/hr).
maximum range 1,367 miles (2,200km).
Weights:
empty 16,367lb (7,424kg).
loaded 23,810lb (10,800kg).
Dimensions:
wing span 73ft 9¾in (22.5m).
length 58ft 10¾in (17.95m).
height 19ft 1in (5.8m).
wing area 708.80sq ft (65.85sq m).
Armament: One fixed forward-firing 75mm Type 88 cannon in nose; one flexible 12.7mm Ho–103 Type 1 machine-gun in tail-turret.
Crew: 4.
In Service: Japan.
Variants (with no. built):
Prototypes: Modified Ki–67–Is; solid nose with fixed 75mm anti-aircraft cannon; one experimentally with 1,900hp turbosupercharged Ha–104 Ru engines (2).
Ki–109: Production model; dorsal turret, ventral blisters and bomb-bay deleted; revised tail armament (20).
Total Production: 22.
Remarks: Heavy interceptor development of Ki–67 which latter, despite heavy bomber classification, was in fact medium-sized and highly manoeuvrable; originally envisaged as two aircraft bomber-destroyer night hunter/killer team (109a and b versions, with armament and radar/searchlight resp), project subsequently simplified to single cannon-armed day interceptor; equipped one Sentai; minimal success as, by time of operational debut, USAAF B–29s had been reassigned from high-altitude daylight, to low-level night raids.

Manufacturer: Nakajima.
Model: Type 91 (NC).
Type: Fighter.
Power Plant: One 500hp Nakajima-built Bristol Jupiter VII.
Performance:
maximum speed at 6,560ft (2,000m) 186mph (300km/hr).
maximum range 373 miles (600km).
time to 9,840ft (3,000m) 4min 0sec.
service ceiling 29,528ft (9,000m).
Weights:
loaded 3,420lb (1,550kg).
Dimensions:
wing span 36ft 1in (11.0m).
length 23ft 11in (7.29m).
height 9ft 10in (3.0m).
wing area 215.3sq ft (20.0sq m).
Armament: Two fixed forward-firing 7.7mm machine-guns in upper decking.
Crew: 1.
In Service: Manchuria.
Variants (with no. built):
Prototypes (2) and pre-production machines (7).
Army Type 91 Fighter: Production models (343).
Total Production: 352.
Remarks: Parasol-wing fighter monoplane; entered IJAAF service early thirties, participating first Sino-Japanese incidents; long obsolete by outbreak of Pacific War; equipped Manchurian AF fighter units until replaced by Mansyu-built Ki–27 'Nate'.

Manufacturer: Nakajima.
Model: E4N2.
Type: Reconnaissance floatplane.
Power Plant: One 580hp Nakajima Kotobuki.
Performance:
maximum speed 144mph (232km/hr).
cruising speed 92mph (148km/hr).
time to 9,840ft (3,000m) 10min 34sec.
service ceiling 18,832ft (5,740m).
Weights:
empty 2,760lb (1,252kg).
loaded 3,968lb (1,800kg).
Dimensions:
wing span 36ft 0¼in (10.98m).
length 29ft 1in (8.87m).
height 13ft 0¼in (3.97m).
wing area 319.26sq ft (29.66sq m).
Armament: One fixed forward-firing 7.7mm Type 92 machine-gun; one flexible 7.7mm machine-gun in rear cockpit; max bomb load; 132lb (60kg).
Crew: 2.
In Service: Germany, Japan (IJNAF).
Variants:
E4N1: Prototype.
E4N2, Navy Type 90–2. Reconnaissance Floatplane, Model 1: Initial production model; twin-float 2-seat reconnaissance catapult floatplane; one 420hp Nakajima Kotobuki.
E4N2, Model 2: Modified Model 1; single float; uprated engine; reduced span/length dimensions.
E4N2–C, Model 3: Landplane version.
E4N3: As E4N2, altn float/landplane.
Total Production: 152.
Remarks: Based upon Vought V–50/90 series Corsair, prototype E4N1 first flown 1930; E4N2 retired IJNAF first-line service prior outbreak Pacific War; at least one example supplied/embarked upon German blockade runner during stop-over Home Islands.

Manufacturer: Nakajima.
Model: Ki–4.
Type: Reconnaissance/dive-bomber.
Power Plant: One 640hp Nakajima Ha–8.
Performance:
maximum speed at 7,875ft (2,400m) 186mph (300km/hr).
time to 9,840ft (3,000m) 9min 0sec.
service ceiling 26,240ft (8,000m).
Weights:
empty 3,560lb (1,615kg).
loaded 5,755lb (2,616kg).
Dimensions:
wing span 39ft 4½in (12.00m).
length 25ft 4¼in (7.73m).
height 11ft 5¾in (3.50m).
wing area 319.69sq ft (29.7sq m).
Armament: Two forward-firing 7.7mm machine-guns; single or twin 7.7mm Type 89 machine-gun/s in rear cockpit; provision (dive-bomber version) for max 110lb (50kg) bomb load.
Crew: 2.
In Service: Japan.
Variants:
Ki–4, Army Type 94 Reconnaissance Plane: Production models; individual exhausts/wheel spats (Model Ko) or exhaust collector ring/unspatted mainwheels (Model Otsu); alt (experimental) float undercarriage/floatation equipment.
Total Production: 516.
Remarks: Pre-war IJAAF service in reconnaissance/light bomber roles; participated second Sino-Japanese conflict and Nomonhan Incident, Summer 1939; relegated to second-line duties by outbreak Pacific War.

Manufacturer: Nakajima.
Model: E8N2 'Dave'.
Type: Short-range reconnaissance floatplane.
Power Plant: 630hp Nakajima Kotobuki 2 KAI 2.
Performance:
maximum speed at 9,840ft (3,000m) 186mph (300km/hr).
cruising speed 115mph (185km/hr).
maximum range 559 miles (900km).
time to 9,840ft (3,000m) 6min 31sec.
service ceiling 23,850ft (7,270m).
Weights:
empty 2,910lb (1,320kg).
loaded 4,189lb (1,900kg).
Dimensions:
wing span 36ft 0¼in (10.98m).
length 28ft 10¾in (8.81m).
height 12ft 7¼in (3.84m).
wing area 285.24sq ft (26.5sq m).
Armament: One fixed forward-firing 7.7mm machine-gun; one flexible 7.7mm machine-gun in rear cockpit; max bomb load 132lb (60kg).
Crew: 2.
In Service: Japan (IJNAF).
Variants (with no. built):
E8N1 Prototypes: (7).
E8N1, Navy Type 95 Reconnaissance Floatplane, Model 1: Initial production model; 580hp 2 KAI 1; Nakakima-built inc E8N2s (700); Kawanishi-built inc E8N2s (48).
E8N2: As E8N1; uprated engine.
Total Production: 755.
Remarks: Catapult-launched ship-borne floatplane, saw extensive pre-war use aboard IJN capital ships and aircraft tenders; in action during Sino-Japanese conflict; WWII service restricted opening months, inc Battle of Midway; subsequently relegated shore-based second-line roles.

Manufacturer: Nakajima.
Model: A4N1.
Type: Carrier-borne fighter.
Power Plant: One 730hp Hikari.
Performance:
maximum speed at 10,500ft (3,200m) 219mph (352km/hr).
cruising speed 145 mph (233km/hr).
maximum range 526 miles (846km).
time to 9,840ft (3,000m) 3min 30sec.
service ceiling 25,393ft (7,740m).
Weights:
empty 2,813lb (1,276kg).
loaded 3,880lb (1,760kg).
Dimensions:
wing span 32ft 9¾in (10.00m).
length 21ft 9½in (6.64m).
height 10ft 1in (3.07m).
wing area 246.39sq ft (22.89sq m).
Armament: Two fixed forward-firing 7.7mm Type 92 machine-guns; provision for max 132lb (60kg) bomb load.
Crew: 1.
In Service: Japan (IJNAF).
Variants (with no. built):
A4N1, Navy Type 95 Carrier Fighter: Prototype and production model; single-seat fighter biplane (221).
Total Production: 221.
Remarks: IJNAF's last fighter biplane, A4N1 produced 1935–40; participated opening stages Sino-Japanese conflict; relegated second-line advanced training/liaison duties by outbreak Pacific War.

Manufacturer: Nakajima.
Model: Ki–27a 'Nate'.
Type: Light fighter.
Power Plant: One 710hp Nakajima Ha–1b, Army Type 97.
Performance:
maximum speed at 11,480ft (3,500m) 292mph (470km/hr).
cruising speed 217mph (350km/hr).
maximum range 1,060 miles (1,710km).
time to 16,400ft (5,000m) 5min 22sec.
service ceiling 40,190ft (12,250m).
Weights:
empty 2,447lb (1,110kg).
loaded 3,946lb (1,790kg).
Dimensions:
wing span 37ft 1¼in (11.31m).
length 24ft 8½in (7.53m).
height 10ft 8in (3.25m).
wing area 199.777sq ft (18.56sq m).
Armament: Two 7.7mm Type 89 machine-guns in upper fuselage decking; provision for max 220lb (100kg) bomb load.
Crew: 1.
In Service: Cochin China, (Nat 1+ captured), Japan, Manchuria (Ki–27b), Thailand (12).
Variants (with no. built):
Type P.E: Prototype; private venture (1).
Ki–27 prototypes: Minor design changes; differing wing areas (2).
Ki–27 pre-production models: Modified clear-vision canopy; increased wing span (100).
Ki–27a, Army Type 97 Fighter, Model A: Uprated engine; metal-faired canopy.
Ki–27b, Model B: Modified Model A; Provision for four 55lb (25kg) bombs; clear-vision canopy re-introduced; Ki–27a and b: Nakajima-built (2,005); Ki–27a and b: Mansyu-built (1,379).
Ki–27, Army Type 97 Fighter Trainer: Ki–27 conversions.
Ki–27 KAI prototypes: Experimental lightweight

Nakajima Ki-49-I Donryu 'Helen'

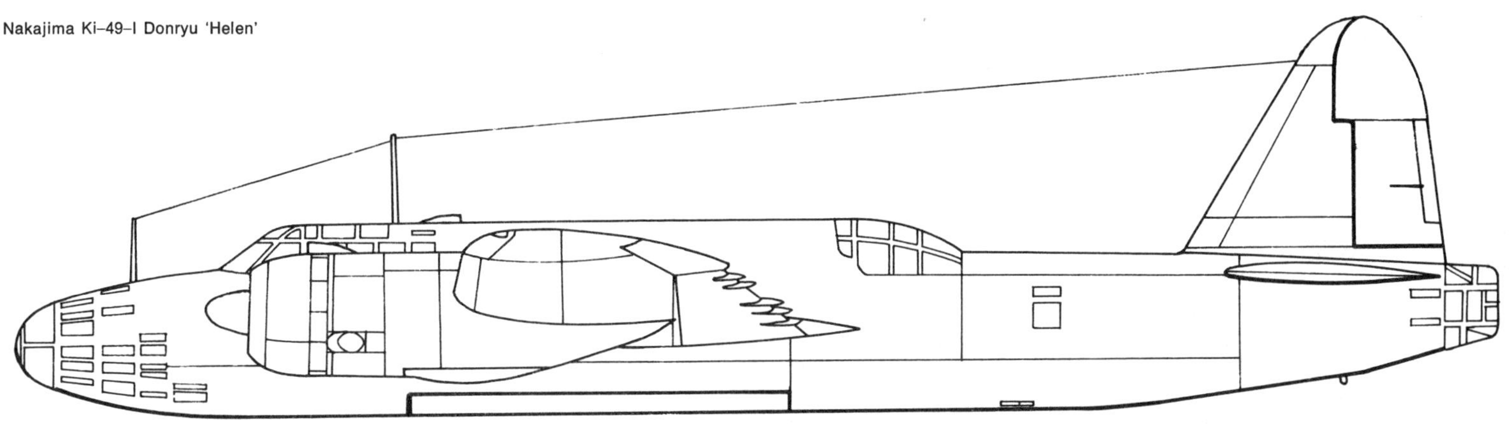

version; improved performance (2).
Total Production: approx 3,499.
Remarks: Combat debut Spring 1938, Sino-Japanese conflict; also participated as principal IJAAF fighter in Nomonhan Incident following year; outbreak Pacific War obsolescent but highly manoeuvrable Ki–27 supported invasions Philippines, NEI, Malaya and Burma; subsequently redeployed home defence role 1941–43, thereafter relegated training duties; some trainers equipped 1,102lb (500kg) bomb load for suicide missions end of war; Manchurian (Mansyu)-produced models provided first-line fighter strength Manchurian AF throughout war years; twelve examples also supplied Thai AF.
Colour Reference: Plate 101: Nakajima Ki–27b 'Nate' (Army Type 97 Fighter, Model B) of Manchurian Air Force, Mukden, Manchoukuo, Sept 1942; overall light grey finish; Manchurian AF roundels upper and lower wing stations; one of number Ki–27s purchased by public donations, fuselage inscription reads 'Defence of the Homeland, Anto (Province) No 4'.

Manufacturer: Nakajima.
Model: Ki–34 'Thora'.
Type: Personnel transport.
Power Plant: Two 780hp Nakajima Kotobuki 41 or two Nakajima Ha–1b.
Performance:
maximum speed at 11,025ft (3,360m) 224mph (360km/hr).
cruising speed 193mph (310km/hr).
normal range 750 miles (1,200km).
time to 9,840ft (3,000m) 6min 38sec.
service ceiling 22,970ft (7,000m).
Weights:
empty 7,716lb (3,500kg).
loaded 11,574lb (5,250kg).
Dimensions:
wing span 65ft 0in (19.92m).
length 50ft 2¼in (15.3m).
height 13ft 7¼in (4.15m).
wing area 529.582sq ft (49.2sq m).
Crew/Accommodation: 3/8.
In Service: China (Cochin), Japan (IJAAF, IJNAF).
Variants (with no. built):
AT–2 prototype: Civil transport; two 580hp Nakajima Kotobuki 2–1 (1).
AT–2 production model: Civil transport; uprated engines (32).
Ki–34, Army Type 97 Transport: IJAAF equivalent of AT–2; Nakajima-built (19); Tachikawa-built (299).
L1N1, Navy Type AT–2 Transport: IJNAF equivalent of Ki–34; transferred ex-IJAAF.
Total Production: 351.
Remarks Pre-war civil light airliner; used by both Japan and Manchurian Airlines, 1937–45; military variants (Ki–34 and L1N1) served IJAAF and IJNAF respectively in paratroop training, communications and transport roles; several Ki–34s also supplied puppet Cochin Chinese AF, 1942.

Manufacturer: Nakajima.
Model: B5N2 'Kate'.
Type: Carrier-borne torpedo-bomber.
Power Plant: One 1,000hp Nakajima NK 1B Sakae 11.
Performance:
maximum speed at 11,810ft (3,600m) 235mph (378km/hr).
cruising speed 161mph (260km/hr).
maximum range 1,237 miles (1,990km).
time to 9,840ft (3,000m) 7min 40sec.
service ceiling 27,100ft (8,260m).
Weights:
empty 5,024lb (2,279kg).
maximum 9,039lb (4,100kg).
Dimensions:
wing span 50ft 11in (15.52m).
length 33ft 9½in (10.3m).
height 12ft 0½in (3.7m).
wing area 405.798sq ft (37.7sq m).
Armament: One flexible 7.7mm Type 92 machine-gun in rear cockpit; max bomb load 1,764lb (800kg) or one torpedo.
Crew: 3.
In Service: Japan (IJNAF).
Variants (with no. built):
B5N1 prototypes: 700hp Nakajima Hikari 2 or 770hp Hikari 3; various modifications (2).
B5N1, Navy Type 97 Carrier Attack Bomber, Model 11: initial production model; 770hp Hikari 3.
B5N1–K: Advanced trainer (Total Nakajima-built B5N1, B5N1–K, B5N2: 667).
B5N2, Model 12: Re-engined B5N1; modified cowling; Aichi-built (200); Hiro 11th Naval Air Arsenal-built (280); also Nakajima-built.
Total Production: 1,149.
Remarks: B5N1 operational debut second Sino-Japanese conflict; replaced by B5N2 by outbreak of Pacific War; main instrument of Pearl Harbor attack force; May–Oct 1942 responsible for sinking three US carriers—*Lexington* (Coral Sea), *Yorktown* (Midway) and *Hornet* (Santa Cruz); remained in first-line service, both carrier and land-based, until Philippines campaign, late 1944; subsequently re-deployed in secondary roles, inc maritime reconnaissance (some equipped with ASV radar), anti-submarine (MAD-equipped), glider- and target-towing, and training.
Colour Reference: Plate 97: Nakajima B5N2 'Kate' (Navy Type 97 Carrier Attack Bomber, Model 12) No 15 aboard IJN carrier *Kaga*, First Koku Sentai Battle of Midway, June 1942; dark green upper surfaces, light grey undersides; tail code: A = First Koku Sentai, II = Second Carrier (*Kaga*, sunk during battle), –3 = Carrier Attack Bomber.

Manufacturer: Nakajima.
Model: Ki–43–Ia Hayabusa 'Oscar'.
Type: Fighter/fighter-bomber.
Power Plant: One 980hp Nakajima Ha–25, Army Type 99.
Performance:
maximum speed at 13,120ft (4,000m) 308mph (495km/hr).
cruising speed 199mph (320km/hr).
maximum range 745 miles (1,200km).
time to 16,400ft (5,000m) 5min 30sec.
service ceiling 38,500ft (11,750m).
Weights:
empty 3,483lb (1,580kg).
maximum 5,695lb (2,583kg).
Dimensions:
wing span 37ft 6¼in (11.44m).
length 28ft 11¾in (8.83m).
height 10ft 8¾in (3.27m).
wing area 236.805sq ft (22.0sq m).
Armament: Two 7.7mm Type 89 machine-guns in upper cowling; max bomb load 66lb (30kg).
Crew: 1.
In Service: China (1+ captured), Japan, Thailand (12+).
Variants (with no. built):
Ki–43 Prototypes: Solid aft canopy section (3).
Ki–43 Service Trials models: All-round-vision canopy; minor modifications (10).
Ki–43–Ia Hayabusa (Peregrine Falcon), Army Type 1 Fighter, Model 1A: Initial production model; combat flaps, cowling gills; fixed-pitch wooden, or (later models) two-pitch metal, two-blade propeller.
Ki–43–Ib, Model 1B: As late Model 1A; one 12.7mm Ho–103 and one 7.7mm Type 89 machine-guns.
Ki–43–Ic, Model 1C: Two 12.7mm Ho–103 machine-guns. (Total Ki–43–Ia, b, c: 716).
Total Production: 5,919 (all Marks).
Remarks: Numerically IJAAF's most important fighter (equipped over 30 Sentais, plus 12 Chutais and training establishments), Ki–43's operational debut concurrent with opening weeks Pacific War; scoured Burma, Malaya and NEI of all early Allied fighter opposition; also operated CBI theatre; subsequently served over every major front contested by IJAAF until war's end, although latterly completely out-classed by newer Allied types; many expended in suicide attacks; Thai AF machines reportedly saw action against USAAF over Southern China border areas.
Colour Reference: Plates 112, 113: Nakajima Ki–43–Ia Hayabusa 'Oscar' (Army Type 1 Fighter, Model 1A) of Royal Thai Air Force; Chiengmai, Northern Thailand, Summer 1944; brown/light blue dapple over standard IJAAF olive green finish; national insignia as carried during period of Japanese occupation only.

Manufacturer: Nakajima.
Model: Ki–43–IIa Hayabusa 'Oscar'.
Type: Interceptor fighter/fighter-bomber.
Power Plant: One 1,150hp Nakajima Ha–115, Army Type 1.
Performance:
maximum speed at sea level 289mph (465km/hr).
cruising speed 273mph (440km/hr).
maximum range 1,990 miles (3,200km).
time to 16,400ft (5,000m) 5min 49sec.
service ceiling 36,750ft (11,200m).
Weights:
empty 4,211lb (1,910kg).
maximum 6,450lb (2,925kg).
Dimensions:
wing span 35ft 6¾in (10.84m).
length 29ft 3¼in (8.92m).
height 10ft 8¾in (3.27m).
wing area 230.37sq ft (21.4sq m).
Armament: Two 12.7mm Ho–103 machine-guns in upper cowling; max bomb load 1,102lb (500kg).
Crew: 1.
In Service: Japan, Manchuria, USA (evaluation).
Variants (with no. built):
Ki–43–II prototypes: Modified Ki–43–Ic; two-speed supercharged engine; three-blade propeller (5).
Ki–43–II Service Trials models (3).
Ki–43–IIa, Model 2A: Reduced wing span; modified canopy; increased bomb load; armour plating.
Ki–43–IIb, Model 2B: Minor equipment changes.
Ki–43–II KAI: Airframe modifications; individual exhaust stacks.
(Total prod Ki–43–IIs: Nakajima-built (2,492); Ki–43–IIa: Tachikawa First Army Air Arsenal-built (49); prod Ki–43–II and Ki–43–IIIa; Tachikawa-built (2,629)).
Ki–43–IIIa prototypes: 1,230hp Nakajima Ha–115–II (10).
Ki–43–IIIa, Model 3A: Production model; Tachikawa-built.
Ki–43–IIIb prototypes: Interceptor version; re-engined Model 3A; cannon armament; Tachikawa-built (2).
Total Production: 5,919 (all Marks).
Remarks: Improved Model 2s entered service late 1942 II–KAIs mid-1943, and Model 3A early Summer 1944; gradually replacing Model 1s, these later versions bore brunt of Allied offensives throughout SEAC, SWPA and CBI theatres; also operated over Formosa and in home defence role; like Model 1, Ki–43–II/IIIs also employed as suicide attack aircraft at war's end; limited post-war service with both Indonesian and French AFs, latter in Indo-China (two Groupes) against Communist insurgents.

Manufacturer: Nakajima.
Model: G5N2–L Shinzan 'Liz'.
Type: Freight transport.
Power Plant: Four 1,530hp Mitsubishi Kasei 12.
Performance:
maximum speed at 13,450ft (4,100m) 261mph (420km/hr).
cruising speed 230mph (370km/hr).
time to 6,560ft (2,000m) 5min 17sec.
service ceiling 24,440ft (7,450m).
Weights:
empty 44,313lb (20,100kg).
maximum 70,768lb (32,000kg).
Dimensions:
wing span 138ft 3in (42.14).
length 101ft 9¾in (31.02m).
wing area 2,172.15sq ft (201.8sq m).
Armament: One 20mm Type 99 Model 1 cannon each in dorsal and tail turrets; plus one 7.7mm Type 97 machine-gun each in nose, ventral and lateral beam positions; max bomb load 8,818lb (4,000kg) (bomber configuration).
Crew/Payload: 7(10)/25,000 + lb (11,340 + kg) transport version.
In Service: Japan (IJNAF).
Variants (with no. built):
G5N1: Bomber prototypes; based upon imported DC–4E civil transport; redesigned fuselage and tail surfaces; four 1,870hp Nakajima NK7A Mamoru 11 (4).
G5N2: Modified G5N1; 1,530hp Mitsubishi Kasei 12s; prototypes (2).
G5N2–L Shinzan-Kai (Mountain Recess) Model 12 Transport: Two G5N2 and two re-engined G5N1 conversions (4).
Ki–68: IJAAF version of re-engined G5N2; project only.
Total Production: 6.
Remarks: Intended as long-range heavy bomber; based upon unsuccessful US design, G5N1 suffered poor performance allied to power plant teething troubles; four examples subsequently modified and utilized general-purpose freight transport duties.

Manufacturer: Nakajima.
Model: Ki–44–IIb Shoki 'Tojo'.
Type: Interceptor fighter.
Power Plant: One 1,520hp Nakajima Ha–109, Army Type 2.
Performance:
maximum speed at sea level 323mph (520km/hr).
maximum speed at 17,060ft (5,200m) 376mph (605km/hr).
cruising speed 249mph (400km/hr).
maximum range 1,050 miles (1,690km).
time to 16,400ft (5,000m) 4min 17sec.
service ceiling 36,745ft (11,200m).
Weights:
empty 4,643lb (2,106kg).
maximum 6,598lb (2,993kg).
Dimensions:
wing span 31ft 0in (9.45m).
length 28ft 10in (8.785m).
height 10ft 8in (3.25m).
wing area 161.46sq ft (15.0sq m).
Armament: Two 12.7mm Ho–103 machine-guns in upper cowling plus two in wings; provision for two 220lb (100kg) bombs.
Crew: 1.
In Service: Japan.
Variants (with no. built):
Ki–44 prototypes: One 1,250hp Nakajima Ha–41 (3).
Ki–44 pre-production models: Modified cowling and cockpit canopy; redesigned rudder; subsequently to IJAAF as Army Type 2 single-seat Fighter, Model 1 (7).
Ki–44–Ia Shoki (Demon), Army Type 2 Single Seat Fighter, Model 1A: Initial production model; two 12.7mm wing-guns plus two 7.7mm machine-guns in cowling.
Ki–44–Ib, Model 1B: Four 12.7mm machine-guns.
Ki–44–Ic, Model 1C: Modified mainwheel fairings. (Total Ia, b, c: 40).
Ki–44–II prototypes: 1,520hp Nakajima Ha–109 (5).
Ki–44–II pre-production models (3).
Ki–44–IIa, Model 2A: Armament as Model 1A.
Ki–44–IIb, Model 2B: Armament as Model 1B; major production model.
Ki–44–IIc, Model 2C: Four 20mm Ho–3 cannon, or two 12.7mm Ho–103 machine-guns plus two 40mm Ho–301 (or 37mm Ho–203) cannon.
Ki–44–IIIa, Model 3A: 2,000hp Ha–145; increased wing area and tail surfaces; four 20mm Ho–5 cannon.
Ki–44–IIIb, Model 3B: As Model 3A; two 20mm Ho–5 and two 37mm Ho-203 cannon. (Total IIa, b, IIIa, b: 1,167).
Total Production: 1,225.
Remarks: IJAAF's first interceptor fighter designed as such from outset; all nine Model 1s (seven pre-production, plus two final prototypes) equipped experimental Chutai based mainland China, Summer 1942; more powerful Model 2s, primarily 2B, operated NEI (in defence of Sumatran oilfields), SEAC and CBI theatres, as well as in home-defence role; cannon-armed 2C employed against high-altitude B–29 attacks on Japanese homeland; also operated by specially formed suicide Chutai for aerial ramming attacks in defence of Tokyo; equipping eight Sentais at peak, Ki–44s in process of replacement by Ki–84 at war's end.
Colour Reference: Plate 114: Nakajima Ki–44–IIb Shoki 'Tojo' (Army Type 2 Single Seat Fighter, Model 2B) of Shinten (Sky Shadow) air superiority flight of 47th Sentai, 10th Hikoshidan, IJAAF, Narimasu (Tokyo Prefecture), Winter 1944–45; 47th Home Defence Sentai formed special Shinten flight late 1944 for aerial ramming attack against USAAF B–29 bombers; note red fuselage flash and Shinten emblem, stylized '47' Sentai insignia across vertical tail surfaces.

Manufacturer: Nakajima.
Model: Ki–49–IIa Donryu 'Helen'.
Type: Heavy bomber.
Power Plant: Two 1,450hp Nakajima Ha–109, Army Type 2.
Performance:
maximum speed at 16,400ft (5,000m) 306mph (492km/hr).
cruising speed 217mph (350km/hr).
maximum range 1,833 miles (2,950km).
time to 16,400ft (5,000m) 13min 39sec.

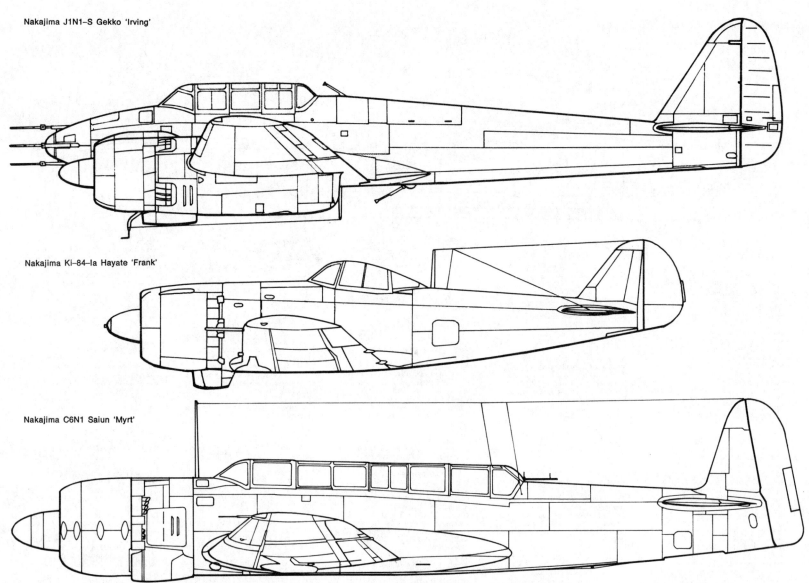

Nakajima J1N1–S Gekko 'Irving'

Nakajima Ki–84–Ia Hayate 'Frank'

Nakajima C6N1 Saiun 'Myrt'

service ceiling 30,510ft (9,300m).
Weights:
empty 14,396lb (6,530kg).
maximum 25,133lb (11,400kg).
Dimensions:
wing span 67ft 0in (20.42m).
length 54ft 1½in (16.5m).
height 13ft 11½in (4.25m).
wing area 743.245sq ft (69.05sq m).
Armament: One flexible 7.7mm
Type 89 machine-gun each in
nose, ventral, tail and two beam
positions; one flexible 20mm Ho–1
cannon in dorsal turret; max
bomb load 2,205lb (1,000kg).
Crew: 8.
In Service: Japan.
Variants (with no. built):
Ki–49 prototypes: 950hp
Nakajima Ha–5 KAIs or
1,250hp Ha–41s (3).
Ki–49 pre-production models:
Ha–41s; minor modifications (7).
Ki–49–I, Donryu (Storm Dragon),
Army Type 100 Heavy Bomber,
Model 1: Initial production
(129).
Ki–49–II prototypes: Re-engined
and modified Model 1; increased
armour (2).
Ki–49–IIa, Model 2A: Production
model.
Ki–49–IIb, Model 2B: 12.7mm
Ho–103 machine-guns.
(Total Ki–49–IIa, b:
Nakajima-built 617,
Tachikawa-built 50).
Ki–49–III prototypes: 2,420hp
Ha–117s (6).
Ki–58 prototypes: Escort fighter
version of Ki–49–I; Ha–109s;
five 20mm Ho–1 cannon, three
12.7mm Ho–103 machine-guns
(3).
Ki–80 prototypes: Proposed
formation lead-aircraft;
subsequently as test-beds for
2,420hp Ha–117s (2).
Total Production: 819 (inc
Ki–58 and 80).
Remarks: Model 1's operational
debut over China, subsequently
serving SWPA, inc attacks on
Australia; Model 2 also confined
mainly South-West Pacific, New

Guinea and Philippines; Ki–49s
unsatisfactory performance meant
it was unable to fulfil intended
role of Ki–21 replacement; many
expended in suicide attacks during
US liberation of Philippines
(aircraft so employed flown by
crew of two, stripped of all
armament, and with 3,527lb
(1,600kg) bomb load); others
modified for night-fighter,
anti-submarine, and troop
transport duties.

Manufacturer: Nakajima.
Model: J1N1–C 'Irving'.
Type: Long-range reconnaissance.
Power Plant: Two 1,130hp
Nakajima NK1F Sakae 21/22.
Performance:
maximum speed at 19,685ft
(6,000m) 329mph (530km/hr).
cruising speed 173mph (278km/hr).
normal range 1,678 miles
(2,700km).
time to 13,120ft (4,000m)
5min 37sec.
service ceiling 33,795ft (10,300m).
Weights:
empty 10,697lb (4,852kg).
maximum 16,594lb (7,527kg).
Dimensions:
wing span 55ft 8½in (16.98m).
length 39ft 11½in (12.18m).
height 14ft 11½in (4.526m).
wing area 430.555sq ft (40.0sq m).
Armament: One flexible 13mm
Type 2 machine-gun at rear of
forward cockpit.
Crew: 3.
In Service: Japan (IJNAF).
Variants (with no. built):
J1N1, Navy Experimental 3-seat
Escort Fighter: Prototypes; two
1,130hp Nakajima Sakae handed
engines (one Sakae 21 and one
Sakae 22); opposite rotating
propellers; one cannon and two
machine-guns in nose, plus four
machine-guns in two remote-
controlled dorsal barbettes (2).
J1N1–C prototypes:
Reconnaissance version;
simplified J1N1; unhanded
Sakae 21s; reduced weight;

single machine-gun (7).
J1N1–C, Navy Type 2
Reconnaissance Plane:
Production model (approx 50).
J1N1–C KAI: 2-seat night-fighter
version; revised armament as
J1N1–S; J1N1–C conversions.
J1N1–R: Redesignated J1N1–Cs;
some with 13mm machine-gun
replaced by one 20mm cannon
in spherical dorsal turret (J1N1–F).
Total Production: 479 (all Marks).
Remarks: Originally envisaged as
heavily-armed long-range fighter;
complicated handed engine/dorsal
barbette arrangements led to
abandonment of project;
resuscitated as reconnaissance
aircraft; operational debut Autumn
1942, South Pacific; participated
Solomons campaign; examples
based Rabaul field-modified for
night-fighter sorties by installing
four cannon in rear cockpit;
early successes against USAAF
B–24s led to official adoption of
revised armament arrangement
and new role.

Manufacturer: Nakajima.
Model: J1N1–S Gekko 'Irving'.
Type: Night fighter.
Power Plant: Two 1,130hp
Nakajima NK1F Sakae 21.
Performance:
maximum speed at 19,160ft
(5,840m) 315mph (509km/hr).
cruising speed 207mph (333km/hr).
range 2,348 miles (3,757km).
time to 16,400ft (5,000m) 9min
35sec.
service ceiling 30,610ft (9,320m).
Weights:
empty 10,670lb (4,840kg).
maximum 18,043lb (8,184kg).
Dimensions:
wing span 55ft 8½in (16.98m).
length 41ft 10½in (12.77m).
height 14ft 11½in (4.562m).
wing area 430.555sq ft (40.0sq. m).
Amament: Four fuselage-mounted
20mm Type 99 cannon; two oblique
upward-firing, plus two oblique
downward-firing.
Crew: 2.

In Service: Japan (IJNAF).
Variants (with no. built):
J1N1–S Gekko (Moonlight),
Model 11: Night-fighter version;
modified J1N1–C; revised armament; unstepped aft fuselage
decking; some with AI radar.
J1N1–Sa, Model 11A: As J1N1–S;
downward-firing 20mm cannon
deleted; majority with AI radar
(or nose searchlight); some with
nose-mounted 20mm Type 99
Model 2 cannon.
(Total J1N1–S, SA: approx 420).
Total Production: 479 (all Marks).
Remarks: Night-fighter development of J1N1–C/R reconnaissance
aircraft; third crew-member
replaced by battery of four
obliquely-mounted cannon; entered
service late 1943; initially successful
against 5th and 7th AFs' B–24s
in South-West and Central Pacific,
less so against B–29s when
deployed in home-defence role;
by war's end most J1N1 models
expended in kamikaze attacks
(carrying 1,102lb (500kg) bomb
load).

Manufacturer: Nakajima.
Model: B6N2 Tenzan 'Jill'.
Type: Carrier-borne torpedo-
bomber.
Power Plant: One 1,850hp
Mitsubishi MK4T Kasei 25.
Performance:
maximum speed at 16,075ft
(4,900m) 299mph (481km/hr).
cruising speed 207mph (333km/hr).
maximum range 1,892 miles
(3,045km).
time to 16,400ft (5,000m)
10min 24sec.
service ceiling 29,660ft (9,040m).
Weights:
empty 6,636lb (3,010kg).
maximum 12,456lb (5,650kg).
Dimensions:
wing span 48ft 10½in (14.894m).
length 35ft 7½in (10.865m).
height 12ft 5½in (3.8m).
wing area 400.416sq. ft (37.2sq. m).
Armament: One flexible 7.7mm
Type 97 machine-gun in rear

cockpit; one flexible 7.7mm Type
97 machine-gun in ventral turret;
max bomb load 1,764lb (800kg) or
one torpedo.
Crew: 3.
In Service: Japan (IJNAF).
Variants (with no. built):
B6N1 prototypes: 1,870hp
Nakajima NK7A Mamoru 11;
four-blade propeller (2).
B6N1 Tenzan (Heavenly
Mountain), Navy Carrier Attack
Bomber, Model 11: Initial
production model; modified, inc
local strengthening and addn
ventral armament (133).
B6N2, Model 12: Re-engined;
non-retractable tailwheel.
B6N2, Model 12A: Dorsal 7.7mm
Type 97 machine-gun replaced
by 13mm Type 2 machine-gun.
(Total B6N2, N2a: 1,133).
B6N3, Model 13: Prototypes;
1,850hp Mitsubishi MK4T-C
Kasei 25c; modified undercarriage
for projected land-based version;
two B6N2a conversions.
Total Production: 1,268.
Remarks: Designed to replace
earlier B5N 'Kate', B6N was
distinguished by forward rake of
vertical tail surfaces; after
protracted and troublesome trials,
initial models finally entered
service late 1943; operational
debut in South Pacific, 1944;
participated Battle of Philippine
Sea in defence of Marianas, June
1944; subsequently engaged Iwo
Jima and Okinawa operations,
during latter both by night and in
Kamikaze role; lack of skilled crews
and losses among IJN's larger fleet
carriers, only vessels capable of
operating B6N, precluded full use
being made of 'Jill's' improved
performance.

Manufacturer: Nakajima.
Model: A6M2–N 'Rufe'.
Type: Interceptor fighter/fighter-
bomber floatplane.
Power Plant: One 950hp Nakajima
NK1C Sakae 12.
Performance:

maximum speed at 16,400ft (5,000m) 270mph (435km/hr).
cruising speed 184mph (296km/hr).
maximum range 1,107 miles (1,780km).
time to 16,400ft (5,000m) 6min 43sec.
service ceiling 32,810ft (10,000m).
Weights:
empty 4,235lb (1,912kg).
maximum 6,349lb (2,880kg).
Dimensions:
wing span 39ft 4½in (12.0m).
length 33ft 1⅔in (10.1m).
height 14ft 1⅓in (4.3m).
wing area 241.54sq ft (22.44sq m).
Armament: Two 7.7mm Type 97 machine-guns in upper cowling; two 20mm Type 99 cannon in wings; max bomb load 264lb (120kg).
Crew: 1.
In Service: Japan (IJNAF).
Variants (with no. built):
A6M2–N prototype: Modified Mitsubishi A6M2, Model 11; float installation; enlarged vertical tail surfaces (1).
A6M2–N, Navy Type 2 Floatplane Fighter, Model 11: production model (326).
Total Production: 327.
Remarks: Floatplane development of basic A6M 'Zero' intended for offensive operations in support of amphibious landings; overtaken by course of war, A6M2–N forced into mainly defensive role; served in both Southern (Solomons) and Northern (Aleutians) Pacific areas; towards close of war released from training and pressed into occasional service for home-defence duties; equipped total of six Kokutais.

Manufacturer: Nakajima.
Model: Ki–84–Ia Hayate 'Frank'.
Type: Fighter/fighter-bomber.
Power Plant: One 1,900hp Nakajima Ha–45, Army Type 4; 1,800hp Ha–45–11, 1,825hp Ha–45–12, or 1,990hp Ha–45–21.
Performance:
maximum speed at sea level 325mph (523km/hr).
maximum speed at 20,080ft (6,120) 392mph (631km/hr).
cruising speed 277mph (445km/hr).
maximum range 1,347 miles (2,167km).
initial rate of climb 3,790ft/min (1,155m/min).
time to 16,400ft (5,000m) 5min 54sec.
service ceiling 36,090ft (11,000m).
Weights:
empty 5,864lb (2,660kg).
maximum 8,576lb (3,890kg).
Dimensions:
wing span 36ft 10½in (11.24m).
length 32ft 6½in (9.92m).
height 11ft 1¼in (3.39m).
wing area 226.04sq. ft (21.0sq m).
Armament: Two 12.7mm Ho–103 machine-guns in upper cowling; two 20mm Ho–5 cannon in wings; max bomb load 1,102lb (500kg).
Crew: 1.
In Service: Japan.
Variants (with no built):
Ki–84 prototypes (2).
Ki–84 Service Trials models: Progressive minor modifications to vertical tail and fuselage; some with underwing bomb racks (83).
Ki–84 pre-production model: Individual exhaust stacks; fuselage rack deleted (42).
Ki–84–Ia Hayate (Gale), Army Type 4 Fighter, Model 1A: Initial production model.
Ki–84–Ib, Model 1B: Four 20mm Ho–5 cannon.
Ki–84–Ic, Model 1C: Bomber-destroyer version; two 20mm Ho–5 cannon plus two wing-mounted 30mm Ho–105 cannon; Total Ki–84–I (and Ki–84–II): Nakajima-built (3,288); Ki–84–I: Mansyu-built (94).
Total Production: 3,514 (inc derivatives).
Remarks: Intended replacement for Ki–43 'Oscar', heavier armed and armour-protected Ki–84 proved to be finest IJAAF fighter of Pacific War; combat debut over China, based Hankow, Aug 1944; subsequently fought in defence of Philippines (10 Sentais); good record despite overwhelming Allied air superiority and maintenance difficulties; also operated South-East Asia, Formosa, Okinawa (inc fighter-bomber attacks by night), and in home-defence role; hampered by production problems, lack of aviation fuel and experienced pilots, Ki–84 continued effectively to oppose Allied forces until very end of war.

Manufacturer: Nakajima.
Model: Ki–84–II Hayate 'Frank'.
Type: Fighter/fighter-bomber.
Power Plant: One 1,990hp Nakajima Ho–45–21, Army Type 4, 1,900hp Ha–45–23, or 2,000hp Ha–45–25.
Performance:
maximum speed 416mph (670 km/hr).
Weights:
loaded 8,495lb (3,855kg).
Dimensions:
wing span 36ft 10½in (11.24m).
length 32ft 6½in (9.92m).
height 11ft 1¼in (3.39m).
wing area 226.04sq ft (21.0 sq m).
Armament: Four 20mm Ho–5 cannon in fuselage and wings, or two wing-mounted 30mm He–105 cannon; two fuselage-mounted 20mm Ho–5 cannon; max bomb load 1,102lb (500kg).
Crew: 1.
In Service: Japan.
Variants (with no. built):
Ki–84–II (IJAAF design. Ki–84–Ib or Ic): As Ki-84-Ib or Ic; wooden rear fuselage and fittings; re-engined; (prod figs inc in Model 1).
Ki–84–III: Turbosupercharged high-altitude version; project only.
Ki–84N/P/R: High-altitude versions; project only.
Ki–106 prototypes: Modified Ki–84; all-wooden construction; Tachikawa-built (3).
Ki–113 prototype: As Ki–84–Ib; part steel construction (1).
Ki–116 prototype: Modified Ki–84–1; 1,500hp Mitsubishi (Ha–33) (62).
Ki–117: Re-designation of projected Ki–84N.
Total Production: 3,514 (inc derivatives).
Remarks: Identified by manufacturer's designation Ki–84–II but remaining Ki–84–Ib or Ic to IJAAF, represented late-war production of standard Ki–84 utilizing wooden components in attempt to conserve Japan's dwindling aluminium stocks; entered service Spring 1945; operated alongside conventional all-metal models during closing months of war; in all, Ki–84s equipped total of twenty-five Sentais plus original experimental Service Trials Chutai.

Manufacturer: Nakajima.
Model: C6N1 Saiun 'Myrt'.
Type: Carrier-borne reconnaissance.
Power Plant: One 1,990hp Nakajima NK9H Homare 21.
Performance:
maximum speed at 20,015ft (6,100m) 379mph (610 km/hr).
cruising speed 242mph (390 km/hr).
maximum range 3,300 miles (5,310km).
time to 19,685ft (6,000m) 8min 9sec.
service ceiling 35,236ft (10,470m).
Weights:
empty 6,543lb (2,968kg).
maximum 11,596lb (5,260kg).
Dimensions:
wing span 41ft 0in (12.5m).
length 36ft 1in (11.0m).
height 13ft 0in (3.96m).
wing area 274.479sq ft (25.5sq. m).
Armament: One flexible 7.92mm Type 2 machine-gun in rear cockpit.
Crew: 3.
In Service: Japan (IJNAF).
Variants (with no. built):
C6N1 prototypes and pre-production models: 1,820hp. Homare 11 or 1,990hp Homare 21 (19).
C6N1 Saiun (Painted Cloud), Navy Carrier Reconnaissance Plane, Model 11: Production model (443).
C6N1–B Saiun, Model 21: Projected carrier-borne attack-bomber version.
C6N1–S: Two-seat night fighter; two oblique-mounted 20mm Type 99 cannon; C6N1 conversions.
C6N2 prototype: Turbosupercharged NK9K–L Homare 24 (1).
C6N3 Saiun KAI 1, C6N4 Saiun KAI 2, C6N5 Saiun KAI 3 and C6N6 Saiun KAI 4: Projects only.
Total Production: 463.
Remarks: Specialised carrier-borne long-range reconnaissance; operational debut mid-1944; participated Battle of Marianas; performed important service throughout remaining months of war, shadowing USN Task Forces with little fear of interception (C6N1's speed only marginally slower than that of contemporary US carrier-borne fighters); some converted to night-fighter role; as such, fastest aircraft committed to nocturnal defence of homeland, but hampered by lack of radar; historical footnote—C6N1 can claim dubious honour of providing last confirmed aerial 'kill' of WWII, an example being shot down by USN fighters just five minutes prior to official cessation of hostilities in Pacific.

Manufacturer: Nihon.
Model: L7P1.
Type: Light transport amphibian.
Power Plant: Two 710hp Nakajima Kotobuki.
In Sevice: Japan (IJNAF).
Variants (with no. built):
Prototypes: Navy Experimental 13-Shi Small Amphibious Transport; all-wood construction (2).
Total Production: (2).
Remarks: Two prototypes completed Spring/Summer 1942; subsequently employed Yokosuka First Naval Air Technical Arsenal for liaison/local transport duties; no production.

Manufacturer: Showa/Nakajima.
Model: L2D2 'Tabby'.
Type: Personnel/cargo transport.
Power Plant: Two 1,080hp Mitsubishi Kinsei 43.
Performance:
maximum speed at 7,875ft (2,400m) 220mph (354km/hr).
cruising speed 161mph (260km/hr).
normal range 2,000 miles (3,220km).
time to 16,400ft (5,000m) 20min 36sec.
service ceiling 35,760ft (10,900m).
Weights:
empty 15,708lb (7,125kg).
loaded 24,030lb (10,900kg).
Dimensions:
wing span 95ft 0in. (28.95m).
length 64ft 8¼in (19.72m).
height 24ft 5¾in (7.46m).
wing area 985.97sq ft (91.6sq m).
Crew/Payload/Accommodation: 3–5/9, 920lb (4,500kg)/21 passengers.
In Service: Japan (IJNAF).
Variants (with no built):
L2D1, Navy Type D Transport: Prototypes; 2 Douglas DC–3 pattern aircraft; assembled by Showa; 1,000hp Pratt & Whitney SB3Gs.
L2D2, Navy Type O Transport, Model 11: Initial production model; modified L2D1; re-engined; Nakajima-built (71).
L2D2–1: Cargo transport version; modified L2D2; cargo-doors, strengthened floor.
L2D3, Navy Type O Transport, Model 22: Personnel transport; additional flight deck windows; 1,300hp Kinsei 51s.
L2D3a: As L2D3. 1,300hp Kinsei 53s.
L2D3–1: Cargo transport version of L2D3.
L2D3–1a: Cargo transport version of L2D3a.
L2D4/L2D4–1, Navy Type O Transport, Model 32: Experimental armed personnel/cargo transport versions; dorsal turret with flexible 13mm Type 2 machine-gun plus two hand-held 7.7mm Type 92 machine-guns.
L2D5, Navy Type O Transport, Model 33: Modified L2D4; part wood/steel construction; uncompleted.
(Total L2D2–L2D4: Showa-built: 414).
Total Production: 485.
Remarks: Developed from pre-war DC–3 imports (20); military variants saw extensive use throughout Pacific War in personnel/cargo transport roles.

Manufacturer: Tachikawa.
Model: Light ambulance.
Power Plant: One 130hp Cirrus Hermes IV.
Performance:
maximum speed 112mph (180km/hr).
cruising speed 96mph (155km/hr).
time to 6,560ft (2,000m) 14min 0sec.
service ceiling 14,760ft (4,500m).
Weights:
empty 1,328lb (604kg).
loaded 2,294lb (1,043kg).
Dimensions:
wing span 32ft 9½in (10.00m).
length 25ft 10in (7.90m).
height 7ft 9½in (2.38m).
wing area 236.7sq ft (22.00sq m).
Crew/Accommodation: 1/2 litters plus 1 medic.
In Service: Japan.
Variants:
Prototype and production: Single-engined civil cabin biplane.
Remarks: First produced (by Ishikawajima) in 1933, at least three examples donated IJAAF for light ambulance duties.

Manufacturer: Tachikawa.
Model: Ki–9 'Spruce'.
Type: Trainer/reconnaissance.
Power Plant: One 350hp Hitachi Ha–13a, Army Type 95.
Performance:
maximum speed 150mph (240km/hr).
cruising speed 93mph (150km/hr).
time to 3,280ft (1,000m) 4min 55sec.
service ceiling 19,030ft (5,800m).
Weights:
empty 2,238lb (1,015kg).
loaded 3,142lb (1,425kg).
Dimensions:
wing span 33ft 10¼in (10.32m).
length 24ft 8¼in (7.53m).
height 9ft 10in (3.0m).
wing area 263.715sq ft (25.4sq m).
Crew: 2.
In Service: China (Cochin), Japan, Manchuria, Thailand (Thai NAF).
Variants (with no. built):
Prototypes: One primary (150hp Nakajima NZ) and two intermediate (350hp Hitachi Ha–13a) trainer versions (3).
Army Type 95–1 Medium Grade Trainer, Model A: Production model; shortened fuselage; Tachikawa-built (2,395); Tokyo Koku-built (220).
Total Production: 2,618.
Remarks: Standard IJAAF intermediate trainer; also supplied satellite Thai, Manchurian and Cochin Chinese AFs; limited reconnaissance/communications duties; abandoned examples employed post-war by Indonesia.

Manufacturer: Tachikawa.
Model: Ki–17 'Cedar'.
Type: Trainer/liaison.
Power Plant: One 150hp Hitachi Ha–12, Army Type 95.
Performance:
maximum speed 106mph (170 km/hr).
cruising speed 81mph (130km/hr).
service ceiling 17,390ft (5,300m).
Weights:
empty 1,362lb (618kg).
loaded 1,984lb (900kg).
Dimensions:
wing span 32ft 2½in (9.82m).
length 25ft 7in (7.8m).
height 9ft 8¼in (2.95m).
wing area 280.076sq ft (26.02sq m).
Crew: 2.
In Service: Japan.
Variants (with no. built):
Prototypes (2).
Army Type 95–3 Primary Trainer: Production model; upper wing ailerons deleted (558).
Total Production: 560.
Remarks: Standard IJAAF basic trainer; also employed liaison/communications roles.

Manufacturer: Tachikawa.
Model: Ki–36 'Ida'.
Type: Army co-operation.
Power Plant: One 510hp Hitachi Ha–13a, Army Type 98.
Performance:
maximum speed at 5,905ft (1,800m) 216mph (348km/hr).
cruising speed 147mph (236 km/hr).
maximum range 767 miles (1,235km).
time to 9,840ft (3,000m) 6min 39sec.
service ceiling 26,740ft (8,150m).
Weights:
empty 2,749lb (1,247kg).
loaded 3,660lb (1,660kg).
Dimensions:
wing span 38ft 8½in (11.8m).
length 26ft 3in (8.0m).
height 11ft 11⅓in (3.64m).
wing area 215.277sq ft (20.0sq. m).
Armament: One forward-firing

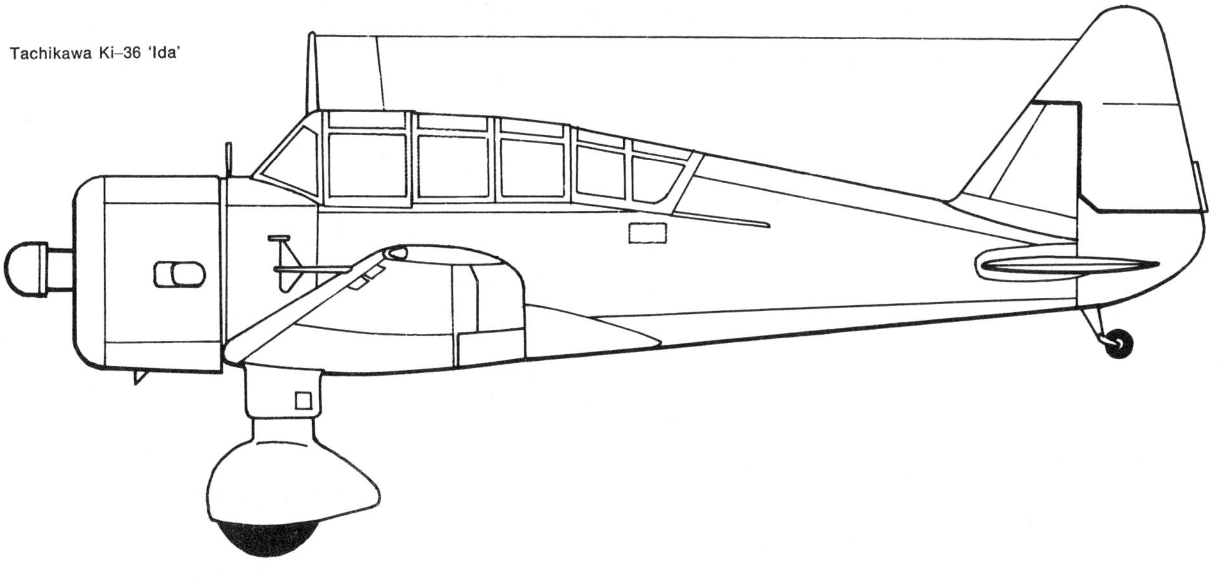
Tachikawa Ki–36 'Ida'

7.7mm Type 89 machine-gun in engine cowling plus one flexible 7.7mm Type 89 machine-gun in rear cockpit; max bomb load 330lb (150kg).
Crew: 2.
In Service: Japan, Thailand.
Variants (with no built):
Ki–36 prototypes (2).
Ki–36, Army Type 98 Direct Co-operation Plane: Production model, Tachikawa-built (860); Kawasaki-built (472).
Ki–55: Advanced trainer version (see Ki–55).
Ki–72: Re-engined Ki–36; retractable undercarriage; project only.
Total Production: 1,334.
Remarks: Operating in close liaison with Japanese Army ground forces, Ki–36's combat debut during second Sino–Japanese conflict; participated Nomonhan Incident Summer 1939; limited service early months Pacific War; easy prey for Allied fighters; post–1943 restricted mainland China; at close of war number expended in suicide role with single 551lb (250kg) or single 1,102lb (500kg) bomb; also supplied to Thai AF.

Manufacturer: Tachikawa.
Model: Type LO 'Thelma'.
Type: Personnel transport.
Power Plant: Two 900hp Mitsubishi Ho–26–I, Army Type 99.
Performance:
maximum speed at 11,700ft (3,570m) 260mph (418km/hr).
Weights:
empty 10,906lb (4,947kg).
loaded 15,653lb (7,100kg).
Dimensions:
wing span 65ft 6in (19.97m).
length 49ft 2½in (13.42m).
height 11ft 5½in (3.49m).
wing area 552.193sq ft (51.3sq m).
Crew/Accommodation: 3/12.
In Service: Japan.
Variants (with no. built):
(Prototype): Imported Lockheed Model 14–38 civil transports; 900hp Wright R–1820–G3Bs; allied code-name 'Toby' *(30)*.
Army Type LO Transport: Modified Lockheed Model 14–38; re-engined, Tachikawa-built (64); Kawasaki-built (55).
SS–1: Experimental version for cabin pressurization tests; modified Type LO, 1,080hp Mitsubishi Ha–102s (1).
Total Production: 120 (inc SS–1).
Remarks: Civil US Lockheeds used throughout war on Japan–China routes; licence-produced Type LO employed by IJAAF as personnel transport; modified passenger/cargo development built by Kawasaki as Ki–56 'Thalia'.

Manufacturer: Tochikawa.
Model: Ki–54 'Hickory'.
Type: Light transport anti-submarine patrol.
Power Plant: Two 510hp Hitachi Ha–13a, Army Type 98.
Performance:
maximum speed at 6,560ft (2,000m) 234mph (376km/hr).
cruising speed 149mph (240km/hr).
normal range 597 miles (960km).
time to 16,400ft (5,000m) 20min 18sec.
service ceiling 23,555ft (7,180m).
Weights:
empty 6,512lb (2,954kg).
loaded 8,591lb (3,897kg).
Dimensions:
wing span 58ft 8¾in (17.9m).
length 39ft 2in (11.94m).
height 11ft 9in (3.58m).
wing area 430.55sq ft (40.0sq m).
Armament: Four flexible 7.7mm Type 89 machine-guns (gunnery trainer); 1,058lb (480kg) depth-charges (anti-submarine patrol).
Crew: 5–9.
In Service: Japan, Manchuria.
Variants (with no. built):
Ki–54 prototype: (1).
Ki–54a, Army Type 1 Advanced Trainer, Model A: Initial production model.
Ki–54b, Army Type 1 Operations Trainer, Model B: Armed crew-trainer version of Model A; four gunnery stations.
Ki–54c, Army Type 1 Transport, Model C: 8-seat transport/communications version (Civil designation Y–59).
Ki–54d, Army Type 1 Patrol Bomber, Model D: Anti-submarine version.
(Total Ki–54a, b, c, d: 1,367).
Ki–110: All-wood construction Ki–54c; destroyed before completion.
Ki–111 and Ki–114: Flying tanker/advanced Ki–110; projects only.
Total Production: 1,368.
Remarks: Designed as multi-purpose trainer; subsequently also produced in light transport (military and civil) and anti-submarine versions; extensive employment former roles, but only limited service as anti-submarine patrol bomber.

Manufacturer: Tachikawa.
Model: Ki–55 'Ida'.
Type: Advanced trainer/suicide attack.
Power Plant: One 510hp Hitachi Ha–13a, Army Type 98.
Performance:
maximum speed at 7,220ft (2,200m) 217mph (349km/hr).
cruising speed 146mph (235km/hr).
normal range 659 miles (1,060km).
time to 9,840ft (3,000m) 6min 55sec.
service ceiling 26,900ft (8,200m).
Weights:
empty 2,848lb (1,292kg).
loaded 3,794lb (1,721kg).
Dimensions:
wing span 38ft 8½in (11.8m).
length 26ft 3in (8.0m).
height 11ft 11⅓in (3.64m).
wing area 215.277sq ft (20.0sq m).
Armament: One forward-firing 7.7mm Type 89 machine-gun in engine cowling; max bomb load (suicide attack) one 551lb (250kg) or one 1,102 (500kg) bomb.
Crew: 2.
In Service: Cochin China, Japan, Manchuria, Thailand (9).
Variants (with no. built):
Ki–55 prototype: Modified Ki–36 army co-operation aircraft (1).
Ki–55, Army Type 99 Advanced Trainer: Tachikawa-built (1,077); Kawasaki-built (311).
Total Production: 1,389.
Remarks: Development of Ki–36, stripped of all unnecessary weight and distinguishable by unspatted mainwheels, Ki–55 performed standard advanced training role; during closing months of war number fitted with single bomb for suicide-attack sorties; trainer examples supplied satellite AFs; also employed post-war by Indonesian AF.

Manufacturer: Watanabe.
Model: E9W1 'Slim'.
Type: Submarine-borne observation floatplane.
Power Plant: One 300hp Hitachi GK2 Tempu II.
Performance:
maximum speed 144mph (232km/hr).
cruising speed 92mph (148km/hr).
time to 9,840ft (3,000m) 9min 41sec.
service ceiling 22,100ft (6,750m).
Weights:
empty 1,940lb (880kg).
loaded 2,756lb (1,250kg).
Dimensions:
wing span 32ft 9¾in (10.0m).
length 26ft 3in (8.0m).
height 12ft 2in (3.70m).
wing area 252.95sq ft (23.50sq m).
Armament: One flexible 7.7mm machine-gun in rear cockpit.
Crew: 2.
In Service: Japan (IJNAF).
Variants (with no. built):
Prototypes: (3).
E9W1, Navy Type 96 Reconnaissance Seaplane, Model 11: production model (32).
Total Production: 35.
Remarks: First flown early 1935, E9W1 employed during second Sino–Japanese conflict against blockade-runners along China Sea coast; obsolescent by outbreak Pacific War, operated early months only, Japanese coastal waters; replaced by Yokosuka E14Y1 'Glen'.

Manufacturer: Yokosuka.
Model: B4Y1 'Jean'.
Type: Carrier-borne torpedo-bomber.
Power Plant: One 840hp Nakajima Hikari 2.
Performance:
maximum speed 173mph (278 km/hr).
maximum range 917 miles (1,475km).
time to 9,840ft (3,000m) 14min 0sec.
service ceiling 19,685ft (6,000m).
Weights:
empty 4,410lb (2,000kg).
loaded 7,937lb (3,600kg).
Dimensions:
wing span 49ft 2½in (15.00m).
length 33ft 3½in (10.15m).
height 14ft 3⅔in (4.36m).
wing area 538.2sq ft (50.00sq m).
Armament: One flexible 7.7mm Type 92 machine-gun in rear cockpit; max bomb load 1,102lb (500kg), or one 1,764lb (800kg) torpedo.
Crew: 3.
In Service: Japan (IJNAF).
Variants (with no. built): —
Initial prototype: New fuselage/tail mated to Kawanishi E7K wing; one 600hp Hiro Type 91 (1).
Prototypes: Alt one 640hp Nakajima Kotobuki 3 (Nos 2/3) or one 840hp Nakajima Hikari 2 (Nos 4/5) power plants (4).
B4Y1, Navy Type 96 Carrier Attack Bomber: Production model; as prototypes (Nos 4/5); addn rear cockpit canopy; Mitsubishi-built (135); Nakajima-built (37); Hiro 11th Naval Air Arsenal-built (28).
Total Production: 205.
Remarks: Prototype first flown late 1935; widespread service latter half thirties, still equipping one first-line sqn aboard light carrier at time of Pearl Harbor, Dec 1941; subsequently relegated training role.

Manufacturer: Yokosuka.
Model: H5Y1 'Cherry'.
Type: Maritime reconnaissance flying boat.
Power Plant: Two 1,200hp Mitsubishi MK1A Shinten 21.
Performance:
maximum speed at 3,280ft (1,000m) 188mph (302km/hr).
maximum range 2,940 miles (4,730km).
time to 9,840ft (3,000m) 24min 0sec.
service ceiling 17,320ft (5,280m).
Weights:
empty 15,666lb (7,106kg).
loaded 25,353lb (11,500kg).
Dimensions:
wing span 103ft 6¾in (31.57m).
length 67ft 3.1in (20.5m).
height 22ft 0in (6.71m).
wing area 1,159.27sq ft (107.7sq m).
Armament: One or two flexible 7.7mm machine-guns in bow; one 7.7mm machine-gun in tail turret; max bomb load 1,102lb (500kg).
Crew: 6.
In Service: Japan (IJNAF).
Variants (with no. built):
Prototypes: (2).
H5Y1, Navy Type 99 Flying Boat, Model 11: Production model (approx 18).
Total Production: approx 20.
Remarks: Built by Hiro 11th Naval Air Arsenal, H5Y was basically scaled-down, twin-engined version of Kawanishi H6K 'Mavis'; poor performance halted production; limited employment early months Pacific War as anti-submarine coastal patrol bomber; subsequently relegated ancillary transport/communications duties.

Manufacturer: Yokosuka.
Model: E14Y1 'Glen'.
Type: Submarine-borne reconnaissance floatplane.
Power Plant: One 340hp Hitachi Tempu 12.
Performance:
maximum speed at sea level 153mph (246km/hr).
cruising speed 104mph (167km/hr).
normal range 548 miles (882km).
time to 9,840ft (3,000m) 10min 11sec.
service ceiling 17,780ft (5,420m).
Weights:
empty 2,469lb (1,119kg).
maximum 3,527lb (1,600kg).
Dimensions:
wing span 36ft 1in (11.0m).
length 28ft 0½in (8.54m).
height 12ft 5½in (3.8m).
wing area 204.514sq ft (19.0sq m).
Armament: One flexible 7.7mm Type 92 machine-gun in rear cockpit; max bomb load 132lb (60kg).
Crew: 2.
In Service: Japan (IJNAF).
Variants (with no. built):
Prototype: Yokosuka 1st Naval Air Technical Arsenal-built (1).
E14Y1, Navy Type O Small Reconnaissance Seaplane, Model 11: Production model (125).
Total Production: 126.
Remarks: Replacing earlier E9W1 biplane, E14Y1 monoplane featured detachable wings/floats and detachable/folding tail

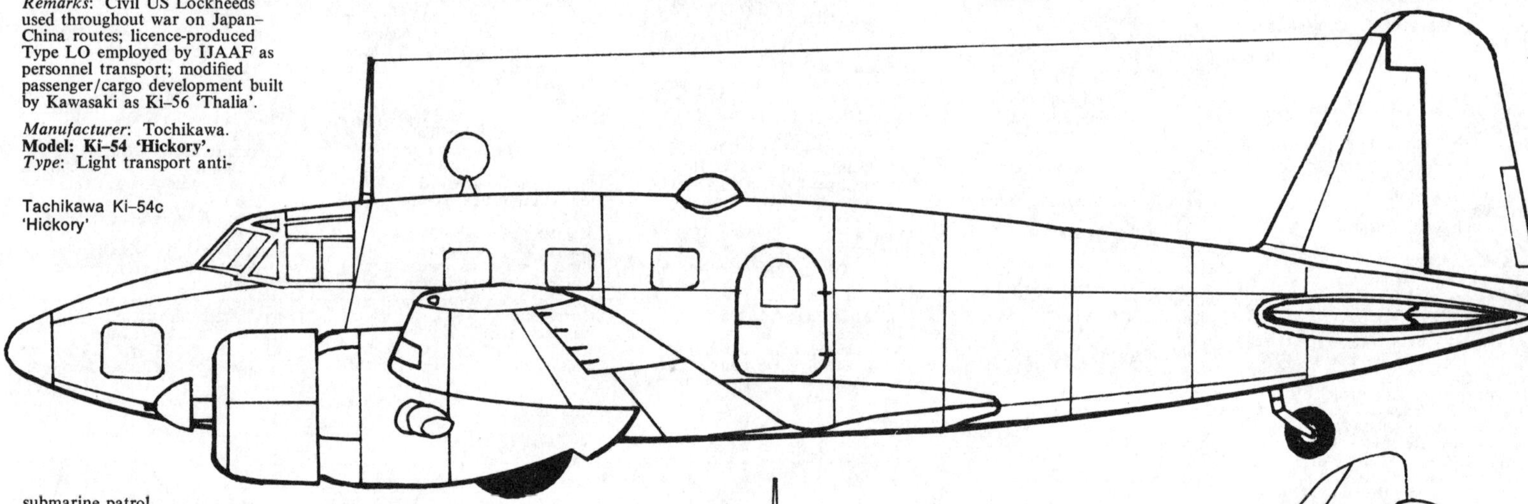

Tachikawa Ki-54c 'Hickory'

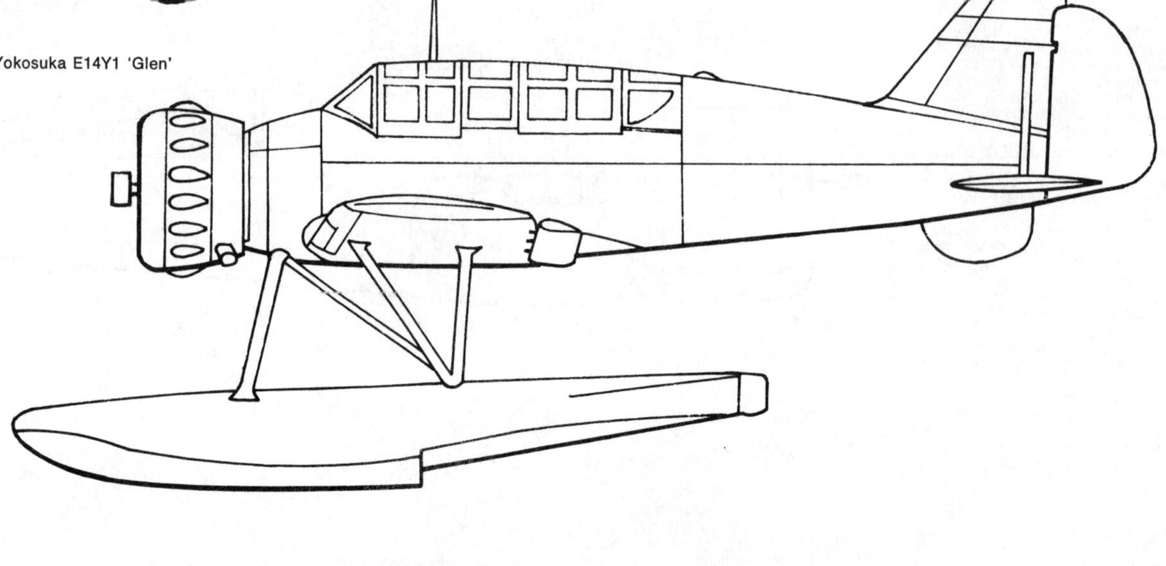

Yokosuka E14Y1 'Glen'

Yokosuka P1Y1 Ginga 'Frances'

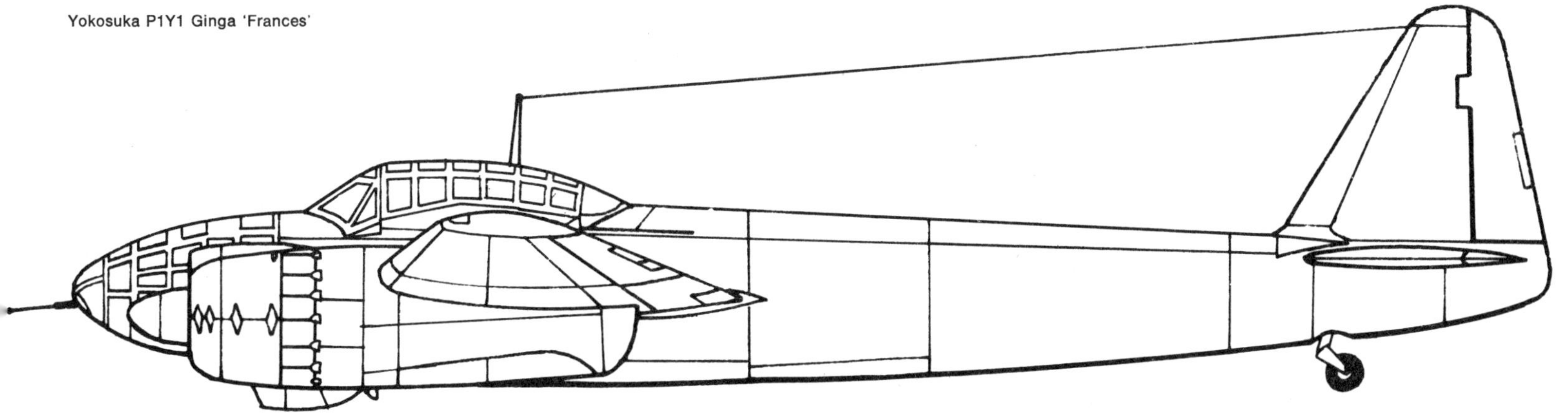

surfaces for stowage in watertight hangar aboard IJN's *I-7, I-9*, large, and *I-15, I-16*, small patrol-class submarines (26 vessels); operational debut (from *I-7*) reconnaissance Pearl Harbor ten days after Japanese attack; subsequently reconnoitred Australasian, African, American Pacific and Aleutian coasts; only enemy aircraft to bomb mainland USA—single E14Y1 (from *I-25*), dropping incendiaries on to Oregon forest.

Manufacturer: Yokosuka.
Model: D4Y1 Suisei 'Judy'.
Type: Carrier-borne dive-bomber/reconnaissance.
Power Plant: One 1,200hp Aichi AE1A Atsuta 12.
Performance:
maximum speed at 15,585ft (4,750m) 343mph (552km/hr).
cruising speed 265mph (426km/hr).
maximum range 978 miles (1,575km).
time to 9,840ft (3,000m) 5min 14sec.
service ceiling 32,480ft (9,900m).
Weights:
empty 5,379lb (2,440kg).
maximum 9,370lb (4,250kg).
Dimensions:
wing span 37ft 8¾in (11.5m).
length 33ft 6½in (10.22m).
height 12ft 0¼in (3.675m).
wing area 254.027sq ft (23.6sq m).
Armament: Two 7.7mm Type 97 machine-guns in cowling; one flexible 7.92 Type 1 machine-gun in rear cockpit; max bomb load 683lb (310kg).
Crew: 2.
In Service: Japan (IJNAF).
Variants (with no. built):
Prototype: Dive-Bomber; 960hp Daimler-Benz DB 600G (5).
D4Y1: Pre-production model; 1,200hp Aichi AE1A Atsuta 12.
D4Y1-C, Navy Type 2 Carrier Reconnaissance Plane, Model 11: Initial production model; reconnaissance version; one K-8 camera in rear fuelage.
D4Y1 Suisei (Comet), Carrier Bomber, Model 11: as pre-production model; strengthened wing spars, modified dive brakes.
D4Y1 KAI: D4Y1 conversions; catapult equipment; D4Y1s: Aichi-built (660); D4Y1, D4Y2 and D4Y3s; Hiro 11th Naval Air Arsenal-built (215).
D4Y2, Model 12: 1,400hp AE1P Atsuta 32.
D4Y2, Model 12A: As D4Y2; 7.92mm Type 1 machine-gun replaced by 13mm Type 2.
D4Y2-C/-Ca: Reconnaissance versions of D4Y2/D4Y2a resp.
D4Y2 KAI, Model 22//D4Y2a KAI, Model 22A: As D4Y2/D4Y2a resp; catapult equipment.
D4Y2-S Susei-E, Night Fighter: modified D4Y2s; rear armament, bomb racks, deck-landing equipment deleted; single obliquely-mounted upward-firing 20mm Type 99 Model 2 cannon; some with underwing air-to-air rocket racks.
(Total Aichi-built D4Y2 Model 12 to D4Y2a-S: 326).
Total Production: 2,038 (all Marks).
Remarks: Based upon German He 118 design, D4Y1 developed as carrier-borne bomber but served initially in reconnaissance role; D4Y1 pre-production examples played minor part Battle of Midway, June 1942; continued to operate on reconnaissance until war's end; dive-bomber variant first entered service late 1943; participated air-sea engagement off Marianas, June 1944; suffered heavy losses; D4Y2s took part defence of Philippines; again heavy casualties in face of Allied air superiority; number expended in kamikaze role after Rear Admiral Arima, CO of 26th Koku Sentai, took off on what is believed to be first deliberate suicide-attack mission of war, crashing his D4Y 'Suisei' into US carrier *Franklin*, 15 October 1944.

Manufacturer: Yokosuka.
Model: D4Y4 Suisei 'Judy'.
Type: Suicide attack bomber.
Power Plant: One 1,560hp Mitsubishi MK8P Kinsei 62.
Performance:
maximum speed at 19,355ft (5,900m) 350mph (563km/hr).
cruising speed 230mph (370km/hr).
maximum range 1,610 miles (2,590km).
time to 16,400ft (5,000m) 9min 22sec.
service ceiling 27,725ft (8,450m).
Weights:
empty 5,809lb (2,635kg).
maximum 10,463lb (4,746kg).
Dimensions:
wing span 37ft 8¾in (11.5m).
length 33ft 6½in (10.22m).
height 12ft 3¼in (3.72m).
wing area 254.027sq ft (23.6sq m).
Armament: Two 7.7mm Type 97 machine-guns in cowling; max bomb load; one 1,764lb (800kg) bomb (semi-external).
Crew: 1.
In Service: Japan (IJNAF).
Variants (with no. built):
D4Y3 Suisei, Carrier Bomber, Model 33: Improved D4Y2; 1,560hp Mitsubishi MK8P Kinsei 62 radial; modified cowling (late models RATOG-equipped).
D4Y3a, Model 33A: As D4Y3. Armament as D4Y2a.
D4Y3/3a: Aichi-built (536); also Hiro 11th Naval Air Arsenal-built (see D4Y1 above).
D4Y4 Suisei, Special Attack Bomber, Model 43: Single-seat suicide bomber version; RATOG; Aichi-built (296).
D4Y5 Carrier Bomber: Project only.
Total Production: 2,038 (all Marks).
Remarks: D4Y3 radial-engined development of earlier D4Y2; more reliable power plant, but still suffered basic weakness—lack of crew armour/fuel tank protection (faults to have been rectified on D4Y5, Model 54); final production comprised specialized D4Y4 kamikaze version; first used against US Third Fleet off Formosa, Jan 1945; heavily committed in defence of Okinawa; mounted last recorded suicide sortie of Pacific War: seven D4Ys, led by Admiral Ugaki, set out to attack Okinawa, 15 Aug 1945; all disappeared without trace.

Manufacturer: Yokosuka.
Model: P1Y1 Ginga 'Frances'.
Type: Medium bomber.
Power Plant: Two 1,825hp Nakajima NK9C Homare 12.
Performance:
maximum speed at 19,355ft (5,900m) 340mph (547km/hr).
cruising speed 230mph (370km/hr).
maximum range 3,338 miles (5,370km).
time to 9,840ft (3,000m) 4min 15sec.
service ceiling 30,840ft (9,400m).
Weights:
empty 16,017lb (7,265kg).
maximum 29,760lb (13,500kg).
Dimensions:
wing span 65ft 7¼in (20.0m).
length 49ft 2½in (15.0m).
height 14ft 1¼in (4.3m).
wing area 592.013sq ft (55.0sq m).
Armament: One flexible 20mm Type 99 cannon in nose; one flexible rear-firing 20mm Type 99 cannon in dorsal position; max bomb load 2,205lb (1,000kg), or one 1,764lb (800kg) torpedo.
Crew: 3.
In Service: Japan (IJNAF).
Variants (with no. built):
Prototypes: 1,820hp NK9C Homare 11s (6).
P1Y1 Ginga (Milky Way), Navy Bomber, Model 11: Initial production model; extensive detailed design changes; revised armament; re-engined; Nakajima-built.
P1Y1-S, Byakko (White Light), Navy Night Fighter: Night-fighter version; modified P1Y1; one pair obliquely-mounted 20mm Type 99 cannon forward of cockpit, plus one pair aft of cockpit; one flexible rear-firing 13mm Type 2 machine-gun. Nakajima-built.
(Total P1Y1, -S, inc P1Y1a-c: 996).
P1Y2-S Kyokko (Aurora), Navy Night Fighter: Night-fighter development of P1Y1; two 1,850hp Mitsubishi MK4T-A Kasei 25a; two obliquely-mounted 20mm Type 99 cannon in fuselage; nose cannon deleted; Kawanishi-built; (96, inc P1Y2a/c).
P1Y2, Model 16: Bomber version of P1Y2-S; obliquely-mounted cannon deleted; armament as P1Y1 (conversions).
P1Y1a/P1Y2a: As P1Y1/P1Y2; one 20mm Type 99 cannon in nose plus one flexible rear-firing 13mm Type 2 machine-gun.
P1Y1b/P1Y2b: As P1Y1/P1Y2; dorsal turret with twin 13mm Type 2 machine-guns plus 20mm Type 99 cannon in nose.
P1Y1c/P1Y2c: As P1Y1b/P1Y2b; nose cannon replaced by one flexible 13mm Type 2 machine-gun.
P1Y3-P1Y6: Various power plants; projects only.
Total Production: 1,098.
Remarks: First flown late Summer 1943, P1Y1's troublesome trials and development programme delayed combat debut until closing six months of Pacific War; equipping five Kokutais, saw limited service medium bomber role; night-fighter versions lacked performance; many expended as Kamikazes against USN surface vessels off Okinawa.

Manufacturer: Yokosuka.
Model: MXY7 Ohka 11 'Baka'.
Type: Suicide attack aircraft.
Power Plant: Three Type 4 Mark 1 Model 20 solid-propellant rockets with 1,764lb (800kg) total thrust.
Performance:
maximum speed at 11,485ft (3,500m) 403mph (648 km/hr).
terminal dive speed 576mph (927km/hr).
range 23 miles (37km).
Weights:
empty 970lb (440kg).
loaded 4,718lb (2,140kg).
Dimensions:
wing span 16ft 9½in (5.12m).
length 19ft 10¾in (6.07m).
height 3ft 9¾in (1.16m).
wing area 64.58sq ft (6.0sq m).
Armament: One 2,646lb (1,200kg) warhead in nose.
Crew: 1.
In Service: Japan (IJNAF).
Variants (with no. built):
MXY7 Ohka (Cherry Blossom), Navy Suicide Attacker, Model 11: Initial production model (inc 1 with steel wings); First Naval Air Technical Arsenal (Yokosuka)-built (155); First Naval Air Arsenal (Kasumigaura)-built (600).
Ohka, Model 21: Modified Model 22 with rockets as Model 11; project only.
Ohka, Model 22: Improved version; one 551lb (200kg) s.t. Tsu-11 turbojet; reduced wingspan; 1,323lb (600kg) warhead; to be carried by Yokosuka P1Y1 bomber (50).
Ohka, Model 33, 43A/B: Enlarged versions; 33 to be carried by Nakajima G8N1, 43A/B to be catapult-launched from surfaced submarine/underground (cave) installations resp; projects only.
Ohka Model 53: One 1,047lb 475kg) s.t. Ne-20 turbojet; towed version; project only.
Ohka, Model K-1: Unpowered trainer version; water ballast in lieu of warhead (45).
Ohka, Model 43 K-1 KAI Wakazakura (Young Cherry): Two-seat trainer version; one 573lb (260kg) Type 4 Mark 1 Model 20 rocket (2).
Total Production: 852.
Remarks: Brainchild of IJNAF transport pilot, MXY7 envisaged as coastal defence/anti-invasion weapon; ordered into full production before completion of flight trials, wood and alloy Ohka, soon to be dubbed 'Baka' (Idiot) by USN personnel, thrown into action against heavily-defended US Task Forces; intercepted by US Navy fighters, overburdened parent aircraft (Mistubishi G4M2e) often forced to release piloted missile well outside target range; such was case on first mission, flown 21 March 1945, against Task Force 58 retiring after carrier strikes on Kyushu; all eighteen Ohkas, released prematurely, crashed into sea; all eighteen G4M 'Mother' aircraft shot down by USN Hellcats; some limited success subsequently achieved during invasion of Okinawa inc battleship *West Virginia* slightly damaged on first day landings, 1 April 1945, and destroyer *Mannert L. Abele* sunk on radar-picket duty off NE Okinawa twelve days later.

LATVIA

Manufacturer: V.E.F. (State Electro-technical Factory).
Model: I-12.
Type: Trainer/liaison.
Power Plant: One 90hp Cirrus Minor.
Performance:
maximum speed 143mph (230km/hr).
cruising speed 123mph (198km/hr).
maximum range 360 miles (580km).
service ceiling 13,120ft (4,000m).
Weights:
empty 1,010lb (458kg).
loaded 1,500lb (680kg).
Dimensions:
wing span 30ft 6¼in (9.3m).
length 23ft 3¼in (7.1m).
height 6ft 2¾in (1.9m).
wing area 121.63sq ft (11.3sq m).
Crew/Accommodation: 1/1.
In Service: Latvia.
Variants (with no. built):
I-11: Prototype; two-seat monoplane; enclosed cockpit; fixed undercarriage (1).
I-12: Improved I-11; two-seat civil light tourer/military trainer; redesigned wing; stressed for aerobatics (12).
Total Production: 12 (exc I-11).
Remarks: Apart from single examples (prototypes) I-15a/b advanced trainers, the six I-12s which entered service in 1937 are believed only indigenous aircraft operated by Latvian AF; several converted as single-seat fighter trainers, others served liaison/light communications roles; subsequent deployment post-Soviet annexation unknown.

LITHUANIA

Manufacturer: Army Aircraft Factory.
Model: Anbo 41.
Type: Reconnaissance/observation.
Power Plant: One 800hp Bristol Pegasus XI.
Performance:
maximum speed 200mph (320km/hr).
cruising speed 165mph (265km/hr).
Weights:
empty 3,307lb (1,500kg).
loaded 5,070lb (2,300kg).
Dimensions:
wing span 43ft 3¾in (13.2m).
length 28ft 10¼in (8.8m).
wing area 312.16sq ft (29.0sq m).
Armament: 1 2 machine-guns.
Crew: 2.
In Service: Lithuania.
Variants:
Anbo IV: Prototype and initial production model; parasol wing two-seat day/night observation monoplane; one 600hp Bristol Pegasus L.2.
Anbo 41: Improved Anbo IV; uprated engine.
Remarks: Only indigenous combat design/s to enter operational service, Anbo IV/41 equipped one/two reconnaissance sqns at Soviet annexation.

NETHERLANDS

Manufacturer: Fokker.
Model: S.II.
Type: Trainer/liaison.
Power Plant: One 110hp Le Rhône.
Performance:
maximum speed 86mph (139km/hr).
cruising speed 81mph (130km/hr).
Weights:
empty 1,803lb (818kg).
loaded 2,650lb (1,202kg).
Dimensions:
wing span 36ft 9¾in (11.22m).
length 23ft 7¾in (7.21m).
height 9ft 1¾in (2.79m).
Crew/Accommodation: 1/1.
In Service: Netherlands.
Variants (with no. built):
S.II: Two-seat trainer version; one 110hp Le Rhône (or Thulin X) (12).
S.IIA: Ambulance version; modified S.II; one 218hp Armstrong Siddeley Lynx; redesigned (enlarged) fuselage; enclosed cockpit; provision for two litters; 1 conversion.
Total Production: 12.
Remarks: 1922-vintage S.II trainers long obsolete prior outbreak WWII (replaced by S.IV/S.IX); sole S.IIA ambulance conversion entered service mid-1932; operated up to and including, 'five-day war.'

Manufacturer: Fokker.
Model: S.IV.
Type: Trainer/liaison.
Power Plant: One 130hp Armstrong Siddeley Mongoose.
Performance:
maximum speed 93mph (150km/hr).
cruising speed 81mph (130km/hr).
normal range 435 miles (700km).
service ceiling 9,840ft (3,000m).
Weights:
empty 1,653lb (750kg).
normal 2,271lb (1,030kg).
Dimensions:
wing span 36ft 9in (11.20m).
length 27ft 10½in (8.50m).
height 10ft 6in (3.20m).
wing area 297.09sq ft (27.60sq m).
Crew/Accommodation: 1/1.
In Service: Netherlands.
Variants:
S.IV: Two-seat basic training biplane; subsequent various alt power plants inc Armstrong Siddeley Puma, Bristol Lucifer, Clerget, Mercedes, Oberursel, and Siemens.
Total Production: 31.
Remarks: Entering service mid-twenties (inc one example to NEIAF), at least four S.IVs still on NethAF strength at time of German invasion, May 1940; pressed into emergency liaison and evacuation roles during, and upon cessation, hostilities.

Manufacturer: Fokker.
Model: C.V–D.
Type: Escort fighter/light bomber/reconnaissance.
Power Plant: One 450hp Hispano-Suiza.
Performance:
maximum speed 140mph (225km/hr).
cruising speed 114mph (184km/hr).
normal range 478 miles (770km).
service ceiling 18,050ft (5,500m).
Weights:
empty 2,756lb (1,250kg);
normal/loaded 4,080lb (1,850kg).
Dimensions:
wing span 41ft 0¼in (12.5m).
length 31ft 2in (9.5m).
height 11ft 5¾in (3.50m).
wing area: 310sq ft (28.8sq m).
Armament: One or two fixed forward-firing 7.9mm machine-guns in fuselage; one or two flexible 7.9mm machine-guns in rear cockpit; one (optional) machine-gun in ventral hatch; provision for sixteen 17.6lb (8kg) light bombs or four 110lb (50kg) mines.
Crew: 2.
In Service: Denmark (DAF; 18 C.V–B (IR); DNAF; 24 C.V–D/E (IIR/IIIR)), Finland (2 C.V–D, 17 C.V–E), Germany (approx 15 C.V ex-Denmark), Hungary (approx 60 C.V–D), Netherlands (NethAF, 69 C.V–D; NethNAF, 14 C.V–E, 10 C.V–W, NEIAF; 26 C.V–D/E), Norway (27 C.V–D, 20 C.V–E), Sweden (48 C.V–D/E (J 3/S 6), Switzerland (11 C.V–D, 53 C.V–E).
Variants (with no. built):
C.V: Prototype and production models; various (interchangeable) power plants, inc BMW, Hispano-Suiza, and Lorraine-Dietrich; also altn (interchangeable) wings (as C.V–A, C.V–B, and C.V–C); Fokker and Danish (Army) licence-built (13 C.V–B).
C.V–D, E: Improved versions; redesigned wing; abbreviated lower span; altn power plants inc Armstrong Siddeley Jaguar, Pratt & Whitney Hornet or Wasp, Napier Lion, Bristol Jupiter or Pegasus, or Rolls-Royce Kestrel.
C.V–W: Floatplane version of C.V–C; advanced trainer.
C.VI: Modified C.V–D; 350hp Hispano-Suiza or 450hp Armstrong Siddeley Jaguar; 26 conversions.
C.V production: Fokker-built (154); Danish (Army) licence-built (as I/IIIR) (approx 40); Italian (Meridionali) licence-built (as Ro–1/1 bis) (349); Hungarian (WM approx 50, KRG 9) licence-built (C.V–D) (approx 60); Norwegian (Army) licence-built (C.V–D/E) (40); Swedish (State) licence-built (as J 3, S 6) (46); Swiss (EKW, Dornier) licence-built (C.V–D/E) (58).
Total Production: 850+.
Remarks: Highly successful between-wars general-purpose design available in multiplicity versions and subject extensive licence-production; although obsolete by outbreak WWII still serving second-line capacities in considerable numbers; employed as light bomber during Dutch 'five-day war'; Finnish AF examples (some ex-Sweden and Norway) operational throughout Winter and Continuation Wars; number Danish machines seized by Germany and re-engined for night ground-attack use by Luftwaffe Estonian-volunteer Staffel (sqn) on Eastern Front, May–Sept 1944.

Manufacturer: Fokker.
Model: F.VIIb–3m/M.
Type: Bomber/ transport.
Power Plant: Three 325hp Wright R–975 Whirlwind.
Performance:
maximum speed at 9,840ft (3,000m) 129mph (207km/hr).
normal range 528 miles (850km).
service ceiling 10,171ft (3,100m).
Weights:
empty 6,722lb (3,050kg).
loaded 11,442lb (5,190kg).
Dimensions:
wing span 71ft 0in (21.7m).
length 47ft 8¾in (14.55m).
height 12ft 9½in (3.9m).
Armament: One flexible 7.7mm machine-gun each in dorsal and ventral positions; max bomb load 2,205lb (1,000kg) or one torpedo.
Crew/Accommodation: 3/10 paratroops or 6 litters.
In Service: Finland (1 F.VIIa), Netherlands (NethAF, 1 F.VIIa–3m/M, 2 F.VIIb–3m/M; NEIAF, 2 F.VIIb–3m/M), Poland (21 F.VIIb–3m/M), Spain (RepAF, approx 7 F.VIIb–3m; RepAF/NatAF, 4 F.VIIb–3m/M). RepAF/NatAF, 4 F.VIIb–3m/M).
Variants (with no. built):
F.VII, F.VIIa, F.VIIa–3m, F.VIIb–3m: Civil transport versions; single– (F.VII/VIIa) and three-engined resp; various power plants; wing modifications: detail design changes Fokker, plus Belgian (SABCA), Czech (Avia), Italian (Meridionali), Polish (Lublin), UK (Avro), and USA (F–10, F–10A) licence-built (approx 220).
F.VIIa–3m/M: Military bomber/transport version; three 200hp Armstrong Siddeley Lynx.
F.VIIb–3m/M: Modified F.VIIa–3m/M; re-engined; increased wing span; Fokker, plus (21) Polish (Lublin) and (3) Spanish licence-built.
(Total F.VIIa–3m/b–3m: approx 35).
Total Production: approx 255 (civil and military).
Remarks: Hugely successful between-wars series of civil airliners, F.VIIa/b failed transition to military bomber/transport; of relatively few such examples built some saw service Spanish Civil War and after; Skoda-powered Polish licence-built models relegated paratroop transport role late thirties; several still in use on outbreak WWII; NethAF's three machines, employed transport/aerial survey duties, all destroyed during German invasion of 10 May 1940; few individual civil models impressed for military transport service, inc one Finnish AF example (gift from Denmark) used during Continuation War, 1941–43, plus possible Manchurian para-military employment.

Manufacturer: Fokker.
Model: F.VIII.
Type: Transport.
Power Plant: Two 480hp Gnome–Rhône Jupiter VI.
Performance:
maximum speed 124mph (200km/hr).
cruising speed 106mph (170km/hr).
normal range 649 miles (1,045km).
service ceiling 18,050ft (5,500m).
Weights:
empty 8,124lb (3,685kg).
loaded 12,566lb (5,700kg).
Dimensions:
wing span 75ft 5½in (23.0m).
length 54ft 11¾in (16.75m).
height 13ft 10in (4.21m).
wing area 893.4sq ft (83.0sq m).
Crew/Accommodation: 2/15.
In Service: Finland (1), Sweden (1).
Variants (with no. built):
F.VIII: Prototype; 15-passenger civil transport version; two 480hp Gnome–Rhône Jupiter VI (1).
F.VIII: Production model; as prototypes; several subsequently re-engined; Hungarian models 13 passengers only; Fokker-built (7); Hungarian (Manfred Weiss) licence-built (2).
F.VIIIa: Modified F.VIII; two 690hp Wright Cyclones; repositioned engines; 1 conversion.
Total Production: 10.
Remarks: Enlarged twin-engined development of original single-engined F.VII/VIIa civil transport series, prototype F.VIII first flown March 1927; two ex-KLM machines sold to Sweden 1934 and 1939; former to Swedish AF (as Tp 10), Aug 1942; latter donated to Finnish AF, 1940; employed in Continuation War against Soviets following year.

Manufacturer: Fokker (Corp).
Model: Super Universal.
Type: Transport.
Power Plant: One 450hp (Nakajima-built) Bristol Jupiter.
Performance:
cruising speed 118mph (190km/hr).
normal range 675 miles (1,090km).
service ceiling 18,000ft (5,480m).
Weights:
loaded 5,271lb (2,391kg).
Dimensions:
wing span 50ft 7¾in (15.44m).
length 36ft 7in (11.15m).
wing area 370sq ft (34.37sq m).
Crew/Accommodation: 1 or 2/6.
In Service: Manchuria.
Variants (with no. built):
Model 4 Universal: Prototype and initial production models; civil transport version; one 200hp Wright J4, 220hp J5, or (later models) 330hp J6 Whirlwind; 1 or 2 crew, 4–6 passengers; Fokker (USA)—and Atlantic Aircraft Corp-built (45).
Model 8 Super Universal: Improved version; one 420hp Pratt and Whitney Wasp; enclosed cockpit; modified wing; lengthened fuselage; 1–2 crew, 6 passengers; Fokker (USA)-built (81); Canadian (Vickers) licence-built (14); Japanese (Nakajima) licence-built with 450hp Bristol Jupiter (inc 22 for IJAAF as Ki–6 crew-trainers (20) ambulance (2), and 20 for (IJNAF as C2N1 transport and liaison) (approx 50).
F.XI Universal: Modified US Universal/super Universal; one 240hp Lorraine 7Aa (1), or 480hp Gnome–Rhône Jupiter (2); 2 crew, 4 passengers; Fokker (Netherlands)-built (3).
Total Production: approx 193 (all Marks).
Remarks: Product of US Fokker Aircraft Corp, Model 4 Universal civil airliner designed 1925; improved Super Universal appeared late 1927; latter licence-produced in Japan (by Nakajima) as military transport; served IJAAF pre-war; number subsequently supplied puppet Manchurian (Manchukuo) AF; operated in transport role early years Pacific War.

Manufacturer: Fokker.
Model: C.VII–W.
Type: Light reconnaissance/trainer.
Power Plant: One 225hp Armstrong Siddeley Lynx.
Performance:
maximum speed 100mph (160km/hr).
cruising speed 81mph (130km/hr).
maximum range 625 miles (1,000km).
time to 6,560ft (2,000m) 27min 0sec.
service ceiling 7,870ft (2,400m).
Weights:
empty 2,643lb (1,200kg).
normal 3,776lb (1,700kg).
Dimensions:
wing span 42ft 4in (12.90m).
length 31ft 2in (9.50m).
height 13ft 2in (4.00m).
wing area 398sq ft (37.00 sq m).
Armament: One fixed forward-firing 7.9mm machine-gun; one or two flexible 7.9mm Lewis gun/s in rear cockpit; provision for light bombs under aft fuselage.
Crew: 2
In Service: Netherlands NethNAF, 18; NEINAF, 12).
Variants (with no. built):
C.VII–W: Two-seat light reconnaissance/advanced training twin-float biplane; late production models with alt one 280hp Lorraine–Dietrich Mizar or one 340hp Armstrong Siddeley Double–Mongoose (30).
Total Production: 30.
Remarks: Prototype first flown 1926, C.VII–Ws operated both Europe and East Indies; several still employed ancillary duties upon outbreak WWII.

Manufacturer: Fokker.
Model: T.IVa.
Type: Torpedo-bomber/reconnaissance floatplane.
Power Plant: Two 768hp Wright Cyclone SR–1820–F2.
Performance:
maximum speed at 2,624ft (800m) 161mph (260km/hr).
cruising speed 135mph (215km/hr).
normal range 970 miles (1,560km).
time to 3,280ft (1,000m) 3min 6sec.
service ceiling 19,360ft (5,900m).
Weights:
empty 10,284lb (4,665kg).
loaded 15,873lb (7,200kg).
Dimensions:
wing span 85ft 11¼in (26.2m).
length 57ft 9in (17.6m).
height 19ft 8¼in (6.0m).
wing area 1,052.7sq ft (97.8sq m).
Armament: One flexible 7.9mm FN–Browning machine-gun each in bow, dorsal, and ventral positions; max bomb load (internal) 1,764lb (800kg), or one torpedo under fuselage.
Crew: 4.
In Service: Netherlands (NEINAF).
Variants (with no. built):
T.IV: Prototype and initial production model; four-seat torpedo-bomber/reconnaissance floatplane version; two 450hp Lorraine–Dietrich 'W'; open cockpit; subsequently modified to T.IVa standard (12).
T.IVa: Improved version; re-engined; redesigned nose; enclosed cockpit; late models with bow and dorsal turrets (12).
Total Production: 24.

Fokker C.V–D

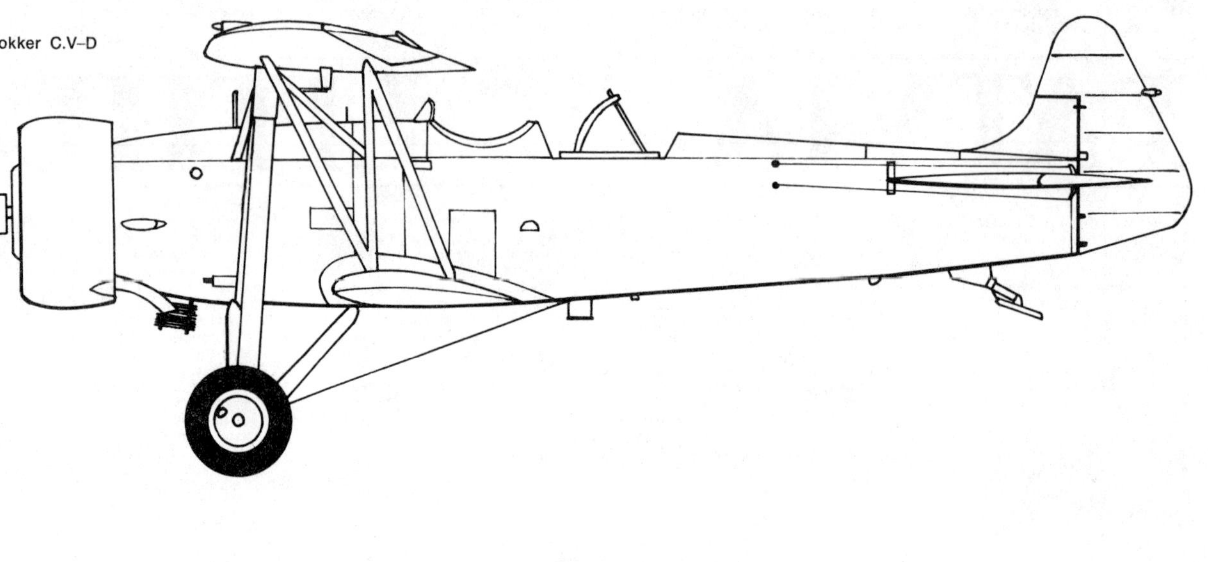

Fokker F.VIIa

Fokker F.VIII

Fokker C.X

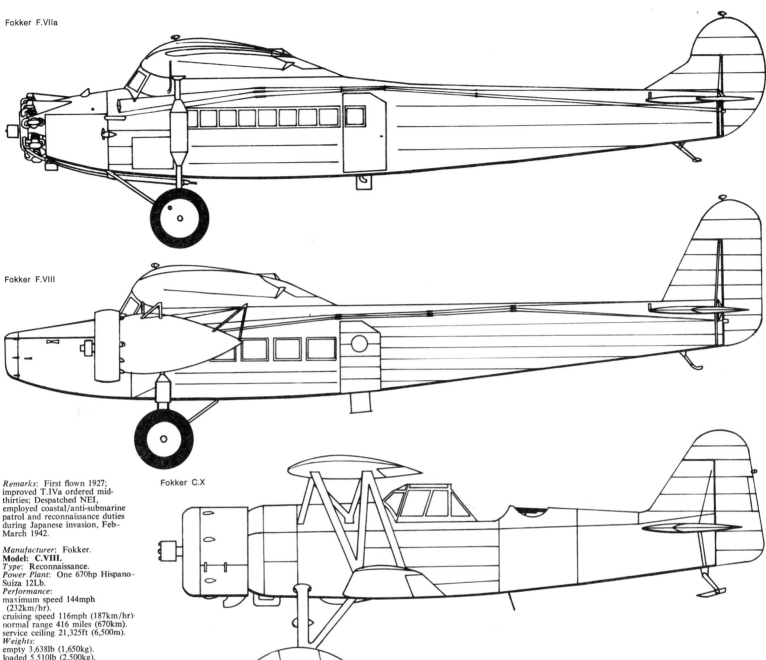

Remarks: First flown 1927;
improved T.IVa ordered mid-
thirties; Despatched NEI,
employed coastal/anti-submarine
patrol and reconnaissance duties
during Japanese invasion, Feb–
March 1942.

Manufacturer: Fokker.
Model: C.VIII.
Type: Reconnaissance.
Power Plant: One 670hp Hispano-
Suiza 12Lb.
Performance:
maximum speed 144mph
  (232km/hr).
cruising speed 116mph (187km/hr)
normal range 416 miles (670km).
service ceiling 21,325ft (6,500m).
Weights:
empty 3,638lb (1,650kg).
loaded 5,510lb (2,500kg).
Dimensions:
wing span 46ft 0½in (14.03m).
length 34ft 9½in (10.6m).
height 10ft 4in (3.15m).
wing area 376.74sq ft (35.0sq m).
Armament: One downward-firing
7.9mm machine-gun in floor of
rear cockpit; one flexible 7.9mm
twin machine-gun in middle
cockpit.
Crew: 3.
In Service: Netherlands (NethAF,
1 C.VIII; NethNAF, 9 C.VIII–W).
Variant (with no. built):
C.VIII: Three-seat reconnaissance
version; one Hispano-Suiza 12Lb;
two searchlights underwing;
subsequently with increased wingspan (1).
C.VIII–W: Maritime recon-
naissance floatplane version; one
450hp Lorraine–Dietrich;
lengthened fuselage (9).
Total Production: 10.
Remarks: C.VIII/C.VIII–W
entered NethAF/NethNAF
service 1928–30 resp; served
strategic/maritime (high-seas)
reconnaissance roles; majority
(inc sole C.VIII) still operational
at time of German invasion,
10 May 1940; engaged neutrality
patrol had forced down Luftwaffe
Do 18 over Dutch coast late 1939;
five C.VIII–Ws escaped to UK
prior capitulation.

Manufacturer: Fokker.
Model: F.39.
Type: Bomber.
Power Plant: Three 450hp
Walter Jupiter.
Performance:
maximum speed at sea level
  130mph (210km/hr).
normal range 373 miles (600km).
service ceiling 14,800ft (4,500m).

Weights:
loaded 20,194lb (9,160kg).
Dimensions:
wing span 89ft 0½in (27.14m).
length 63ft 6½in (19.37m).
height 15ft 8½in (4.79m).
Armament: Twin Mk 28 (or Mk
30) machine-guns in dorsal
position; one machine-gun each
in ventral step (or retractable
turret), in floor of forward
ventral gondola, and in fuselage
lateral positions; max bomb load
3,305lb (1,500kg).
Crew: 4–5.
In Service: Yugoslavia.
Variants (with no. built):
F.IX: Prototype and one production model; civil transport
versions; 18- and 20-passenger
resp; three 500hp Gnome–
Rhône Jupiter XIs; prototype
subsequently re-engined; production model with modified
(lengthened) nose, Fokker-built
(2).
F.IXD: Civil transport version;
improved F.IX; three 580hp
Walter Pegasus II.M2; 20-
passenger; inc one as VIP
transport; Czech (Avia)
licence-built (approx 3).
F.39: Bomber version; modified
F.IX; three 450hp Walter
Jupiter; various detail modifications; some with retractable
ventral turret; inc 2 Yugoslav
order with three 560hp Gnome–
Rhône Jupiter; Czech (Avia)
licence-built (14).
Total Production: approx 19.
Remarks: Prototype first flown

1929; Avia-built F.IXD/F.39
civil airliner/bomber versions
delivered CSA/CzAF mid/early
thirties resp; two bombers also
supplied Yugoslav AF; former
seized by Germany, March 1939,
subsequent disposition unknown;
latter reportedly in service until
outbreak WWII.

Manufacturer: Fokker.
Model: D.XVII.
Type: Fighter.
Power Plant: One 595hp Rolls-
Royce Kestrel IIS.
Performance:
maximum speed 208mph (335km/hr).
cruising speed 174mph (280km/hr).
normal range 528 miles (850km).
service ceiling 28,710ft (8,750m).
Weights:
empty 2,425lb (1,100kg).
loaded 3,262lb (1,480kg).
Dimensions:
wing span 31ft 6in (9.6m).
length 23ft 7½in (7.2m).
height 9ft 10in (3.0m).
wing area 215.28sq ft (20.0sq m).
Armament: Two fixed forward-
firing 7.9mm M.36 machine-guns
in upper cowling.
Crew: 1.
In Service: Netherlands.
Variants (with no. built):
D.XVI: Prototype; single-seat
fighter biplane; one 450hp
Armstrong Siddeley Jaguar (1).
D.XVI: Production model;
modified D.XVI prototype; two
7.5mm machine-guns; Townend
ring; inc Chinese (1), Hungarian
(4) with Bristol Jupiter engine,

and Italian (1) orders (20).
D.XVI: Prototype, modified
(experimental) D.XVI; one
Curtiss V–1570 Conqueror;
redesigned forward fuselage (1).
D.XVII: Production model; one
Rolls-Royce Kestrel IIS; alt
power plants, 790hp Lorraine
Petrel, or 690hp Hispano-Suiza
12Xbrs (11).
D.XVIIB: Improved D.XVII;
enclosed cockpit; one Hispano–
Suiza 12Ycrs; increased (cannon)
armament; project only.
Total Production: 33 (all Marks).
Remarks: First flown 1929–31
resp, both D.XVI and D.XVII
obsolete by outbreak WWII;
six examples of latter, ex-training
establishment, pressed into
emergency service as fighter-
escort for C.V/C.X bombing
raids on German columns during
five-day war, 10–14 May, 1940.

Manufacturer: Fokker.
Model: C.X.
Type: Reconnaissance.
Power Plant: One 830hp Rolls-
Royce Kestrel V.
Performance:
maximum speed 199mph
  (320km/hr).
cruising speed 168mph (270km/hr).
maximum range 516 miles (830km).
service ceiling 27,230ft (8,300m).
Weights:
empty 3,196lb (1,450kg).
loaded 4,960lb (2,250kg).
Dimensions:
wing span 39ft 4in (12.0m).
length 29ft 6½in (9.0m).

height 10ft 10in (3.3m).
wing area 341.3sq ft (31.7sq m).
Armament: Two fixed forward-
firing 7.9mm machine-guns in
upper cowling; one flexible
7.9mm machine-gun in rear
cockpit; max bomb load
(external); 880lb (400kg).
Crew: 2.
In Service: Finland (39),
Netherlands (NethAF, NEIAF).
Variants (with no. built):
C.X: Two-seat reconnaissance/
light ground-attack aircraft;
one Rolls-Royce Kestrel V or
(1) 925hp Hispano-Suiza 12Ycrs;
late models with enclosed
cockpit; inc 4 Finnish order
with 835hp Bristol Pegasus
XXI; Fokker-built (36); Finnish
(VL) licence-built (35).
Total Production: 71.
Remarks: Intended as C.V
successor, prototype C.X first
flown 1934; pre-war service both
NethAF and NEIAF; ten of
former still on strength at time of
German invasion, employed
reconnaissance, light bombing,
and ground-attack sorties initial
phases five-day war; sole export
order, four examples supplied
Finland (as Series I), 1936;
subsequent licence-production
(series II/IV) 1936–37 and 1942;
served Finnish AF throughout
Winter and Continuation Wars,
last machine written off 1958.

Manufacturer: Fokker.
Model: C.XI-W.
Type: Reconnaissance floatplane.

Fokker C.XIV–W

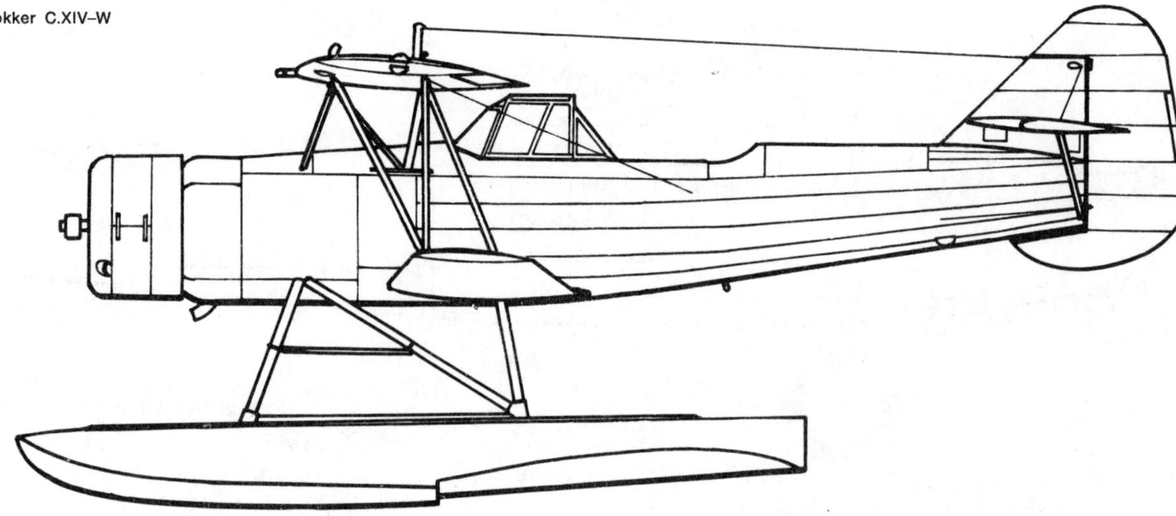

Power Plant: One 775hp Bristol Pegasus.
Performance:
maximum speed at 5,750ft (1,750m) 174mph (280km/hr).
cruising speed 146mph (235km/hr).
normal range 453 miles (730km).
time to 3,280ft (1,000m) 2min 24sec.
service ceiling 20,990ft (6,400m).
Weights:
empty 3,792lb (1,720kg).
loaded 5,622lb (2,550kg).
Dimensions:
wing span 42ft 8in (13.0m).
length 34ft 1in (10.4m).
height 14ft 9in (4.5m).
wing area 430.4sq ft (40.0sq m).
Armament: One fixed forward-firing 7.9mm FN–Browning machine-gun; one flexible 7.9mm FN–Browning machine-gun in rear cockpit.
Crew: 2.
In Service: Netherlands (NEINAF).
Variants:
C.XI–W: Prototype and production model; reconnaissance floatplane; one 775hp Wright Cyclone SR–1820–F.52 or Bristol Pegasus III; stressed for catapult launching.
Total Production: 14.
Remarks: Designed for both ship-borne and shore-based operations, C.XI–W entered service 1938; majority despatched NEI; operated in reconnaissance role during Japanese invasion, none surviving fall of Java, March 1942.

Manufacturer: Fokker.
Model: F.XVIII.
Type: Long-range transport.
Power Plant: Three 420hp Pratt and Whitney Wasp C.
Performance:
maximum speed 149mph (240km/hr).
cruising speed 130mph (210km/hr).
normal range 1,131 miles (1,820km).
service ceiling 15,748ft (4,800m).
Weights:
empty 10,192lb (4,623kg).
normal/loaded 16,645lb (7,550kg).
Dimensions:
wing span 80ft 4½in (24.5m).
length 60ft 8¼in (18.5m).
wing area 904.16sq ft (84.0sq m).
Crew/Payload/Accommodation: 3–4/4,078lb (1,850kg)/13.
In Service: Netherlands (NethAF, 1), Spain (RepAF, 1).
Variants:
F.XVIII: Long-range civil transport; 12–13 passenger or 4-berth sleeper.
Total Production: 5.
Remarks: Last of long line traditional Fokker tri-motors, F.XVIII built 1932 for Amsterdam–Batavia route; two examples later based West Indies, one of which chartered/impressed 1940–41; militarized with dorsal Lewis gun position, and equipped with depth-charge racks, F.XVIII served in anti-submarine patrol role Caribbean area; one other F.XVIII reportedly operated as military transport by RepAF during Spanish Civil War, as was sole F.XX, Fokker's ultimate tri-motor.

Manufacturer: Fokker.
Model: T.V.
Type: Medium bomber.
Power Plant: Two 925hp Bristol Pegasus XXVI.
Performance:
maximum speed 259mph (416km/hr).
cruising speed 214mph (345km/hr).
normal range 1,012 miles (1,630km).
time to 3,280ft (1,000m) 2min 30sec.
service ceiling 25,260ft (7,700m).
Weights:
empty 10,230lb (4,640kg).
loaded 15,950lb (7,235kg).
Dimensions:
wing span 68ft 10in (21.0m).
length 52ft 6in (16.0m).
height 16ft 5in (5.0m).
wing area 712.6sq ft (66.2sq m).
Armament: One fixed forward-firing 20mm Solothurn cannon (or twin 7.9mm machine-guns) in nose; one flexible 7.9mm machine-gun each in dorsal, ventral, and lateral hatches and in glazed tail-cone; max bomb load 2,205lb (1,000kg).
Crew: 5.
In Service: Netherlands.
Variants:
T.V.: Production model; medium bomber.
Total Production: 16.
Remarks: Designed as both medium bomber and long-range fighter, but lacking performance to fulfil latter role, T.V. (first flown Oct 1937) equipped NethAF's sole bomber sqn at time of German invasion, 10 May 1940, all nine serviceable examples destroyed within four days fighting.

Manufacturer: Fokker.
Model: D.XXI.
Type: Interceptor fighter.
Power Plant: One 830hp Bristol Mercury VIII.
Performance:
maximum speed at 16,730ft (5,100m) 286mph (460km/hr).
cruising speed 240mph (385km/hr).
normal range 528 miles (850km).
time to 26,250ft (8,000m) 12min 36sec.
service ceiling 33,135ft (10,100m).
Weights:
empty 3,197lb (1,450kg).
loaded 4,519lb (2,050kg).
Dimensions:
wing span 36ft 1in (11.0m).
length 26ft 10¾in (8.2m).
height 9ft 8in (2.95m).
wing area 174.38sq ft (16.2sq m).
Armament: Four 7.9mm FN–Browning M–36 machine-guns in wings; provision for light bombs underwing.
Crew: 7.
In Service: Denmark (12), Finland (97), Netherlands.
Variants (with no. built):
D.XXI: Prototype; single-seat fighter version; one 645hp Bristol Mercury VI–S (1).
D.XXI: Production model; modified prototype; uprated engine; inc 7 Finnish order and 2 Danish order; Fokker-built (44); Danish licence-built; two 8mm DISA machine-guns, plus (1 only) two 20mm Madsen cannon (10); Finnish (VL) licence-built; thirty-five as Series II/III with one 830hp (Tampella-built) Bristol Mercury VII; fifty as Series IV/V with 825hp Pratt & Whitney Twin Wasp Junior SB4–C/–G; five assembled from spares (90).
Total Production: 145.
Remarks: First flown 1936, D.XXI was standard NethAF fighter at time of German invasion, 10 May 1940; twenty-nine of thirty-six examples delivered participated 'five-day war'; suffered heavy losses both in air and on ground during opening hours; majority destroyed; Finnish AF machines employed throughout Winter and Continuation Wars, latterly in fighter-reconnaissance role; finally withdrawn from service 1948.
Colour Reference: Plates 115, 116: Fokker D.XXI (No 241) of 1e Ja.V.A. (1st Fighter Group), L.V.A. (Netherlands Air Force), De Kooy (nr Den Helder), 10 May 1940; flown by Luitenant-vlieger (Fl Lt) Bosch, No 241 destroyed by Luftwaffe Bf 109Es while attempting to land at De Kooy on first day of hostilities; note post-Oct 1939 national insignia (compare with Fokker G.IA below), and 'Three White Mice' Group insignia on engine cowling.

Manufacturer: Fokker.
Model: C.XIV–W.
Type: Trainer/reconnaissance.
Power Plant: One 450hp Wright R–975E–3.
Performance:
maximum speed 143mph (230km/hr).
cruising speed 120mph (195km/hr).
normal range 590 miles (950km).
time to 3,280ft (1,000m) 3min 48sec.
service ceiling 17,720ft (5,400m).
Weights:
empty 2,930lb (1,330kg).
loaded 4,300lb (1,950kg).
Dimensions:
wing span 39ft 5in (12.0m).
length 31ft 2in (9.5m).
height 13ft 11in (4.24m).
wing area 341.22sq ft (31.70sq m).
Armament: Provision for one fixed forward-firing 7.9mm machine-gun, one flexible 7.9mm machine-gun in rear cockpit.
Crew: 2.
In Service: Netherlands (NethNAF, NEINAF).
Variants:
C.XIV–W: Prototype and production model; unarmed advanced trainer floatplane; provision for two 7.9mm machine-guns.
Total Production: 24.
Remarks: Dual-purpose advanced trainer/light reconnaissance C.XIV–W saw limited service coastal patrol duties opening hours German invasion of Netherlands, 10 May 1940; evacuated UK, via France, prior capitulation, eleven examples subsequently despatched NEI; all later destroyed during Japanese invasion.

Manufacturer: Fokker.
Model: S.IX.
Type: Trainer/liaison.
Power Plant: One 165hp Armstrong Siddeley Genet Major.
Performance:
maximum speed 118mph (190km/hr).
cruising speed 99mph (160km/hr).
normal range 404 miles (650km).
service ceiling 14,764ft (4,500m).
Weights:
empty 1,543lb (700kg).
normal 2,150lb (975kg).
Dimensions:
wing span 31ft 2in (9.50m).
length 24ft 11¼in (7.60m).
height 9ft 6in (2.90m).
wing area 247.57sq ft (23.00sq m).
Crew/Accommodation: 1/1.
In Service: Netherlands (NethAF, 21 S.IX/1, NethNAF, 15 S.IX/2).
Variants (with no. built):
S.IX/1: Prototype and initial production model; two-seat initial/aerobatic training biplane (24).
S.IX/2: Re-engined S.IX/1; one 168hp Menasco Buccaneer; 27 ordered by NethNAF (15).
Total Production: 39.
Remarks: First flown Autumn 1937, S.IX standard NethAF/NAF basic trainer; still in production at time of German invasion, May 1940, number S.IXs both services employed emergency liaison/evacuation duties closing hours of five-day compaign.

Manufacturer: Fokker.
Model: T.VIII–W/G.
Type: Torpedo-bomber/reconnaissance floatplane.
Power Plant: Two 450hp Wright Whirlwind R–975–E3.
Performance:
maximum speed at 9,840ft (3,000m) 177mph (285km/hr).
cruising speed 137mph (220km/hr).
maximum range 1,275 miles (2,050km).
service ceiling 22,310ft (6,800m).
Weights:
empty 6,834lb (3,100kg).
loaded 11,023lb (5,000kg).
Dimensions:
wing span 59ft 0½in (18.0m).
length 42ft 7¾in (13.0m).
height 16ft 4¾in (5.0m).
wing area 473.61sq ft (44.0sq m).
Armament: One fixed forward-firing 7.9mm FN–Browning machine-gun in portside of nose; one flexible 7.9mm FN–Browning machine-gun in rear cockpit; max bomb load 1,334lb (606kg), or one torpedo.
Crew: 3.
In Service: Germany (8 T.VIII–W/G, 12 T.VIII–W/M, 5 T.VIII–W/C), Great Britain (8 T.VIII–W/G ex-NethNAF), Netherlands (NethNAF, 11 T.VIII–W/G).
Variants (with no. built):
T.VIII–W/G: Initial production model; three-seat torpedo-bomber/reconnaissance float-plane version; part-wood and fabric fuselage construction (19).
T.VIII–W/M: As T.VIII–W/G; all-metal rear fuselage (12).
T.VIII–W/C: Modified T.VIII–W/M; original Finnish order; two 890hp Bristol Mercury XI; increased dimensions; one with wheeled undercarriage (T.VIII–W/L) (5).
Total Production: 36.
Remarks: Designed as replacement for obsolescent T.IVa torpedo-bomber floatplane T.VIII–W/G first flown 1938; eleven delivered NethNAF prior German invasion, 10 May 1940 (inc one forced down in error by Luftwaffe Do 18 in Sept 1939); engaged in coastal patrol opening days of campaign before evacuation to France, and subsequently U.K.; eight examples formed Dutch-manned RAF Coastal Command sqn, operating May–Sept 1940; remaining production completed for Germany; operated by Luftwaffe in maritime reconnaissance/convoy-escort roles North Sea and Mediterranean areas.

Manufacturer: Fokker.
Model: G.IA.
Type: Heavy fighter.
Power Plant: Two 830hp Bristol Mercury VIII.
Performance:
maximum speed at 9,020ft (2,750m) 295mph (475km/hr).
cruising speed 221mph (355km/hr).
normal range 876 miles (1,410km).
time to 16,400ft (5,000m) 8min 0sec.
service ceiling 30,510ft (9,300m).
Weights:
empty 7,440lb (3,375kg).
loaded 10,582lb (4,800kg).
Dimensions:
wing span 56ft 3¼in (17.15m).
length 35ft 9in (10.9m).
height 11ft 2in (3.4m).
wing area 412.26sq ft (38.3sq m).
Armament: Eight 7.9mm FN–Browning machine-guns in nose; one flexible 7.9mm FN–Browning machine-gun in tail cone; max bomb load 881lb (400kg).
Crew: 3.
In Service: Germany, Netherlands.
Variants (with no. built):
G.I. prototype: Two-seat interceptor/bomber version; private venture; two 750hp Hispano–Suiza 80–02; subsequently re-engined with two 750hp Pratt and Whitney Twin Wasp Junior SB4G; two 20mm Madsen cannon plus three 7.9mm machine-guns; max bomb load 881lb (400kg) (1).
G.IA: Initial production model; three-seat heavy fighter/close-support version; uprated engines; increased dimensions; revised armament, inc 1 with hydraulic dive brakes, and 1 with ventral observation cupola (approx 36).
G.IB: Export version; two-seat heavy fighter/close-support version; as prototype; two 750hp Pratt and Whitney Twin Wasp Junior SB4G; original Spanish (12), Swedish (18), Finnish (26), and Danish orders; none delivered (approx 25).
Total Production: approx 62.
Remarks: One of relatively few twin-boom configuration operational aircraft of WWII, prototype G.I first flew in March 1937; twenty-three NethAF G.IAs operational at time of German invasion, 10 May 1940; all but one destroyed by close of 'five-day war'; three of export G.IBs also pressed into service; remainder G. IB production completed for Germany; employed by Luftwaffe fighter-training role.
Colour Reference: Plate 117: Fokker G.IA (No 313) of 4e Ja.V.A. (4th Fighter Group), L.V.A. (Netherlands Air Force), Bergen, Oct 1939; No 313 (shown here in early style national markings prior re-painting as Fokker D.XXI above) destroyed in hangar during Luftwaffe bombing attack on Bergen, 10 May 1940.

Manufacturer: Koolhoven.
Model: F.K.41.
Type: Liaison/communications.
Power Plant: One 115hp Cirrus Hermes.
Performance:
maximum speed 108mph (173km/hr).
cruising speed 91mph (146km/hr).
time to 3,000ft (915m) 5min 0sec.
service ceiling 13,780ft (4,200m).
Weights:
empty 1,014lb (460kg).
loaded 1,653lb (750kg).
Dimensions:
wing span 34ft 5½in (10.50m).
length 24ft 11¼in (7.60m).
height 7ft 0½in (2.15m).
Crew/Accommodation: 1/2.
In Service: Finland, Great Britain.
Variants (with no. built):
F.K.41: Prototype and initial production model; three-seat high-wing civil tourer; alt 90hp Cirrus III or 115hp Cirrus Hermes.
Desoutter Mk I: British licence-production of F.K.41; one 90hp Cirrus III (28).
Desoutter Mk II: Improved Mk I; reduced dimensions; alt power plants (13).
Remarks: Several British-built Desoutters impressed mid-war years for R.A.F. general communications/liaison duties; one Mk II previously exported to Denmark subsequently donated to Finland; served Finnish AF throughout Continuation War, 1941–44, in similar communications role.

Manufacturer: Koolhoven.
Model: F.K.46.
Type: Trainer/communications.
Power Plant: One 130hp de Havilland Gipsy Major.
Performance:
maximum speed 108mph (175km/hr).
cruising speed 100mph (160km/hr).

maximum range 404 miles
(650km).
service ceiling 13,780ft (4,200m).
Weights:
empty 1,257lb (570kg).
loaded 1,918lb (870kg).
Dimensions:
wing span 26ft 3in (8.0m).
length 23ft 11½in (7.3m).
height 9ft 4¼in (2.85m).
wing area 258.34sq ft (24.0sq m).
Crew/Accommodation: 1/1.
In Service: Netherlands.
Variants:
F.K.46: Initial production model;
two-seat trainer/sports biplane.
F.K.46L: Lightweight version;
one 95hp Walter Minor.
Total Production: 16.
Remarks: Popular pre-war sports/
trainer; one acquired by NethAF
1936; one on strength during
'five-day war'; served liaison role.

Manufacturer: Koolhoven.
Model: F.K.49.
Type: Aerial survey/ambulance.
Power Plant: Two 130hp de
Havilland Gipsy Major.
Performance:
maximum speed 126mph
(202km/hr).
cruising speed 103mph (165km/hr).
normal range 292 miles (470km).
service ceiling 14,107ft (4,300m).
Weights:
empty 2,932lb (1,330kg).
loaded 6,020lb (2,730kg).
Dimensions:
wing span 52ft 6in (16.0m).
length 38ft 4¼in (11.7m).
height 9ft 10in (3.0m).
wing area 376.74sq ft (35.0sq m).
Crew/Accommodation: 2 or 4/
provision for litters.
In Service: Netherlands (1),
Turkey (1).
Variants:
F.K.49: Cartographic survey
aircraft; alt 285hp Hirth 508C/
305hp Ranger power plants
(Finnish/Turkish orders resp);
both export models with modified
(stepped) nose.
Total Production: 3.
Remarks: NethAF's first twin-
engined machine, and first non-
Fokker since WWI, F.K.49
entered service 1935; initially
engaged photographic survey
duties, subsequently also employed
ambulance role; destroyed on
ground during German invasion,
10 May 1940; single examples also
supplied Finland and Turkey;
former operated civil-registered
Coast Guard, 1939–48, latter as
military transport.

Manufacturer: Koolhoven.
Model: F.K.51.
Type: Advanced trainer/
reconnaissance.
Power Plant: One 350hp
Armstrong Siddeley Cheetah IX.
Performance:
maximum speed at 7,462ft
(2,280m) 146mph (235km/hr).
cruising speed 133mph (215km/hr).
normal range 454 miles (730km).
time to 3,280ft (1,000m) 3min
12sec.
service ceiling 18,370ft (5,600m).
Weights:
empty 2,227lb (1,010kg).
loaded 3,527lb (1,600kg).
Dimensions:
wing span 29ft 6¼in (9.0m).
length 25ft 9¼in (7.85m).
height 9ft 4¼in (2.85m).
wing area 290.63sq ft (27.0sq m).
Armament: Provision for two
7.9mm machine-guns in wings;
one flexible 7.9mm machine-gun
in rear cockpit.
Crew/Accommodation: 1/1.
In Service: Germany (approx 3
ex-NethAF), Netherlands (NethAF,
NethNAF, NEIAF), Spain
(RepAF/NatAF), approx 30
F.K.51, F.K.51bis).
Variants:
F.K.51: Two-seat advanced
trainer; one 270/350hp
Armstrong Siddeley Cheetah V
or IX, 450hp Pratt and Whitney
Wasp, or (Spanish order) 400hp
Armstrong Siddeley Jaguar;
provision for max three 7.9mm
machine-guns and one camera.
F.K.51bis: Re-engined F.K.51;
one 450hp Wright Whirlwind
975–E–3.
Total Production: 134+.
Remarks: Numerically most
important Koolhoven, F.K.51
trainers saw extensive service
Netherlands and NEI late
thirties; pressed into emergency
operational use, employed in
reconnaissance role during German
invasion of Low Countries, May
1940, and for coastal patrol/
maritime reconnaissance duties
during Japanese assault on NEI,
Feb–March 1942; also served in
Spanish Civil War and after.

Manufacturer: Koolhoven.
Model: F.K.52.
Type: Escort fighter.
Power Plant: One 840hp Bristol
Mercury VIII.
Performance:
maximum speed at sea level
192mph (308km/hr).
maximum speed at 15,600ft
(4,750m) 230mph (370km/hr).

normal range 703 miles (1,130km).
initial rate of climb 1,970ft/min
(600m/min).
service ceiling 30,180ft (9,200m).
Weights:
empty 2,976lb (1,350kg).
loaded 5,512lb (2,500kg).
Dimensions:
wing span 32ft 1in (9.8m).
length 27ft 3in (8.3m).
height 10ft 10in (3.3m).
wing area 305.6sq ft (28.4sq m).
Armament: Provision for two
20mm cannon in upper wing;
plus one flexible machine-gun in
rear cockpit; max bomb load
253lb (115kg) under fuselage.
Crew: 2.
In Service: Finland (2).
Variants (with no. built):
F.K.52: Prototype; two-seat escort
fighter biplane; one 645hp Bristol
Mercury VI–S (1).
F.K.52: Production model; uprated
engine; modified cowling;
redesigned vertical tail surfaces (5).
Total Production: 6.
Remarks: Intended as potential
Fokker C.V–D replacement,
prototype F.K.52 first flown Feb
1937; failure to gain official
NethAF order allowed private
purchase two examples for
donation to Finnish AF, 1940,
employed Winter and Continuation
Wars, 1940 and 1941–43, in
training, liaison, and ancillary
roles; one lost while engaged on
leaflet dropping sortie; reported
use as ground-attack aircraft by
RepAF during Spanish Civil War
not substantiated.

Manufacturer: Koolhoven.
Model: F.K.56.
Type: Trainer/reconnaissance.
Power Plant: One 420hp Wright
Whirlwind R–975.
Performance:
maximum speed 186mph (300km/hr).
cruising speed 171mph (275km/hr).
normal range 497 miles (800km).
time to 6,560ft (2,000m) 5min
18sec.
service ceiling 23,950ft (7,300m).
Weights:
empty 2,332lb (1,058kg).
loaded 3,527lb (1,600kg).
Dimensions:
wing span 37ft 8¾in (11.5m).
length 25ft 9in (7.85m).
height 7ft 6½in (2.3m).
wing area 215.3sq ft (20.0sq m).
Armament: One fixed forward-
firing machine-gun in starboard
wing; one flexible machine-gun
in rear cockpit.
Crew/Accommodation: 1/1.
In Service: Belgium (8), Netherlands.

Variants (with no. built):
F.K.56: Prototypes; two-seat
trainer/reconnaissance version;
fixed (1) and retractable (1)
undercarriage; gull wing; enclosed
cockpits (2).
F.K.56: Production model;
modified (straight) wing;
retractable undercarriage; open
rear cockpit; inc 8 Belgium
order (14).
Total Production: 16.
Remarks: Prototype first flown
June 1938; neither Dutch nor
Belgian orders (for 15/20 resp)
completed prior German invasion,
10 May 1940; several of former
(6 delivered) reportedly employed
emergency reconnaissance/liaison
duties during 'five-day war'.

Manufacturer: Koolhoven.
Model: F.K.58.
Type: Interceptor-fighter.
Power Plant: One 1,030hp
Gnome-Rhône 14N39.
Performance:
maximum speed at 16,400ft
(5,000m) 295mph (475km/hr).
cruising speed 267mph (430km/hr).
maximum range 466 miles (750km).
time to 16,400ft (5,000m) 7min
12sec.
service ceiling 32,810ft (10,000m).
Weights:
empty 4,255lb (1,930kg).

maximum 6,063lb (2,750kg).
Dimensions:
wing span 36ft 1⅛in (11.0m).
length 28ft 6½in (8.7m).
height 9ft 10in (3.0m).
wing area 186.21sq ft (17.30sq m).
Armament: Four 7.9mm FN–
Browning machine-guns in
underwing fairings.
Crew: 1.
In Service: France.
Variants (with no. built):
F.K.58: Prototypes; single-seat
fighter; one 1,080hp Hispano-
Suiza 14AA (2).
F.K.58: Production model; first
four as prototypes; subsequent
models re-engined Gnome-
Rhône 14N39, commencing
No 6 redesigned engine cowling;
smaller spinner; French order;
Fokker-built (17); French
(Nevers)—assembled (1).
Total Production: 20.
Remarks: Prototype first flown
Sept 1938; French order for 50
aircraft delayed by non-delivery
specified French power plants;
only 18 examples reached FAF;
intended for Far East service, in
fact employed metropolitan
defence during Battle of France
flown by Polish volunteer pilots;
none of last-minute Dutch order
for 36 Bristol Taurus-powered
F.K.58s completed.

1e Luchtvaartregiment (1st Air Regiment):

Strategic Group:
Reconnaissance

Squadron	Bergen	10 Fokker C.X
Bomber Squadron	Schiphol	9 Fokker T.V
Jachtgroep (Fighter Group):		
1e Fighter Squadron	De Kooy	11 Fokker D.XXI
2e Fighter Squadron	Schiphol	9 Fokker D.XXI
3e Fighter Squadron	Waalhaven	11 Fokker G.IA
4e Fighter Squadron	Bergen	12 Fokker G.IA

2e Luchtvaartregiment (2nd Air Regiment):

Ie Reconnaissance		1 Fokker C.X
Wing	Hilversum	4 Fokker C.V
		4 Koolhoven F.K.51
IIe Reconnaissance		7 Fokker C.V
Wing	Ypenburg	5 Koolhoven F.K.51
IIIe Reconnaissance		9 Fokker C.V
Wing	Ruigenhoek	4 Koolhoven F.K.51
IVe Reconnaissance		7 Fokker C.V
Wing	Gilze-Rijen	3 Koolhoven F.K.51
Jachtgroep (Fighter Group):		
1e Fighter Squadron	Ypenburg	8 Fokker D.XXI
3e Fighter Squadron	Ypenburg	11 Douglas DB–8A–3N

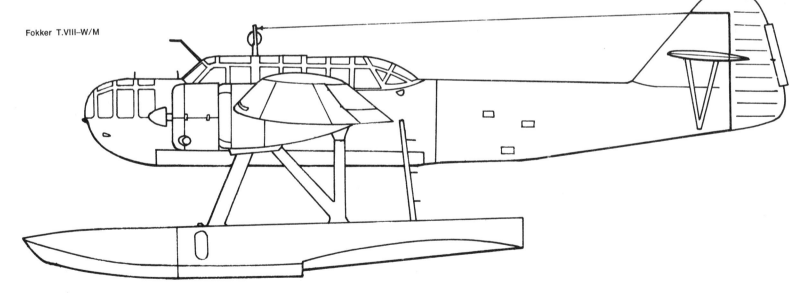

Fokker T.VIII–W/M

NORWAY

Manufacturer: Høver.
Model: M.F.11.
Type: Reconnaissance floatplane.
Power Plant: One licence-built
575hp Armstrong Siddeley

Panther II.
Performance:
maximum speed at sea level
133mph (214km/hr).
maximum speed at 2,790ft

(850m) 146mph (235km/hr).
cruising speed 106mph (170km/hr).
time to 3,280ft (1,000m). 3min
5sec.
service ceiling 16,400ft (5,000m).

Weights:
empty 4,078lb (1,850kg).
loaded 6,283lb (2,850kg).
Dimensions:
wing span 50ft 6¼in (15.4m).

length 38ft 1⅛in (11.62m).
height 14ft 7in (4.44m).
wing area 575.87sq ft (53.5sq m).
Armament: Two fixed forward-
firing .3in Browning machine-

guns; one flexible .3in Colt Browning machine-gun in rear cockpit; max bomb load 660lb (300kg).
Crew: 3.
In Service: Finland (3 ex-NorNAF), Germany (10+ inc captured ex-NorNAF), Norway (NorNAF).
Variants (with no. built):
M.F.11: Prototype; three-seat twin-float biplane; one Armstrong Siddeley Panther (1).
M.F.11: Production model; as prototype; majority with (licence-built) Armstrong Siddeley Panther II; inc 4 completed during German occupation (29).
Total Production: 30.
Remarks: Prototype first flown 1931; twenty-five on strength NorNAF at time of German invasion, April 1940; operational throughout campaign, inc abortive bombing attacks German naval units; some half-dozen captured (plus four under construction) and reportedly employed Luftwaffe coastal patrol; three escapees, interned Finland, subsequently operated by Finnish AF during Soviet–Finnish Continuation War, 1941–44.

Høver M.F.11

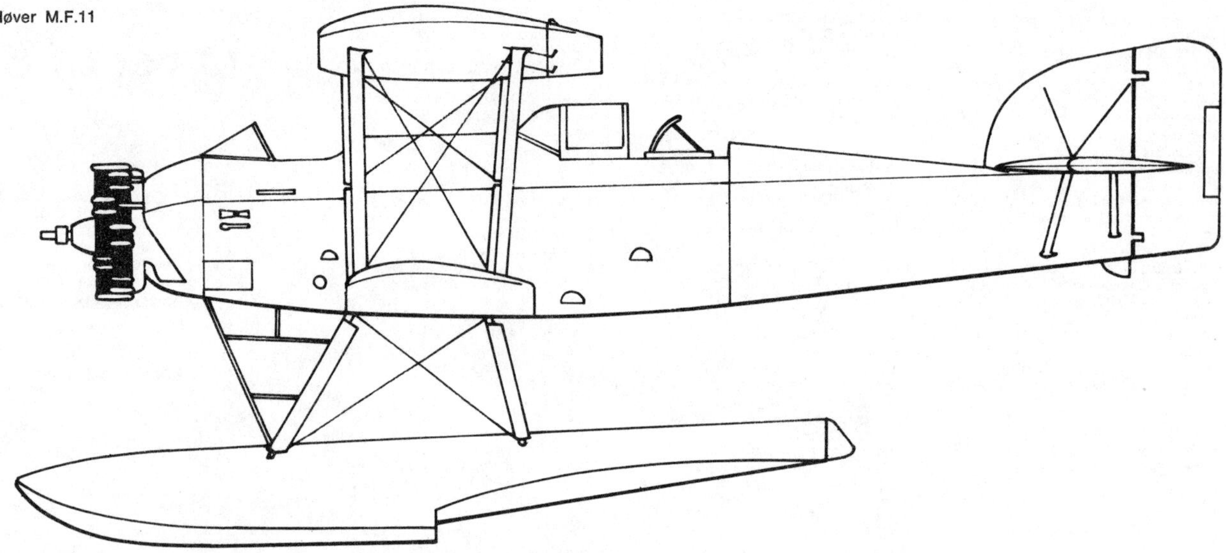

POLAND

Manufacturer: Lublin.
Model: R–VIIIbis.
Type: Reconnaissance-bomber floatplane.
Power Plant: One 760hp Lorraine-Dietrich.
Performance:
maximum speed at sea level 137mph (220km/hr).
normal range 497 miles (800km).
service ceiling 13,120ft (4,000m).
Weights:
empty 6,435lb (2,919kg).
maximum 11,020lb (5,000kg).
Dimensions:
wing span 55ft 9¼in (17.0m).
length 39ft 7in (12.06m).
height 17ft 6in (5.33m).
wing area 822.3sq ft (76.4sq m).
Armament: One fixed forward-firing machine-gun; twin machine-guns in rear cockpit; max bomb load 2,205lb (1,000kg).
Crew: 2–3.
In Service: Poland (PolNAF).
Variants (with no. built):
R–VIII: Prototypes (2) and pre-production model (5); single-engined reconnaissance-bomber biplane; various power plants (7).
R–VIIIG: Modified R–VIII; PolNAF order (1).
R–VIIIbis: Twin-float seaplane version of R–VIII; one 760hp Lorraine–Dietrich or one 740hp Hispano–Suiza; modified rudder; naval equipment; three R–VIII conversions.
R–IX: Modified R–VIII; 6-passenger civil transport version; prototype only (1).
R–XXII: Coastal-patrol floatplane version; modified R–VIIIbis; project only.
Total Production: 9 (all Marks).
Remarks: Initial prototype first flown 1928; R–VIIIbis floatplane conversions entered PolNAF service mid-1933; two examples still on first-line strength outbreak WWII; operated coastal patrol/reconnaissance duties opening days Sept campaign.

Order of Battle 1 September 1939

POLISH AIR FORCE (Lotnictwo Wojskowe)

Dispositional Air Force	
Pursuit Brigade (Fighter Wings):	
III/1 (111, 112 Sqns.)	20 P.Z.L. P.11
IV/1 (113, 114 Sqns.)	20 P.Z.L. P.11
III/2 (123 Sqn.)	10 P.Z.L. P.7a
Bomber/Reconnaissance Brigade:	
X/1 (211, 212 Sqns.)	18 P.Z.L. P.37 Łoś
XV/1 (216, 217 Sqns.)	18 P.Z.L. P.37 Łoś
II/2 (21, 22 Sqns.)	20 P.Z.L. P.23 Karaś
VI/6 (64, 65 Sqns.)	20 P.Z.L. P.23 Karaś
Observation:	
16 Sqn.	7 Lublin R–XIII
Liaison:	
I Sqn.	3 RWD 8
II Sqn.	3 RWD 8
IV Sqn.	3 RWD 8
XII Sqn.	3 RWD 8
Armies' Air Force	
Army 'Pomorze':	
III/4 (141, 142 Sqns.)	22 P.Z.L. P.11
II/4 (42 Sqn.)	10 P.Z.L. P.23 Karaś
43, 46 Sqns.	14 Lublin R–XIII
7, 8 Sqns.	7 RWD 8
Army 'Poznan':	
III/3 (131, 132 Sqns.)	22 P.Z.L. P.11
III/3 (34 Sqn.)	10 P.Z.L. P.23 Karaś
33, 36 Sqns.	14 Lublin R–XIII
6 Sqn.	3 RWD 8
Army 'Lodz':	
III/6 (161, 162 Sqns.)	12 P.Z.L. P.11
	10 P.Z.L. P.7a
III/6 (32 Sqn.)	10 P.Z.L. P.23 Karaś
63, 66 Sqns.	7 RWD 14 Czapla
	7 Lublin R–XIII
10 Sqn.	3 RWD 8
Army 'Krakow':	
III/2 (121, 122 sqns.)	20 P.Z.L. P.11
III/2 (24 Sqn.)	10 P.Z.L. P.23 Karaś
23, 26 Sqns.	7 RWD 14 Czapla
	7 Lublin R–XIII
3 Sqn.	3 RWD 8
Army 'Modlin':	
III/5 (152 Sqn.)	10 P.Z.L. P.11
III/5 (41 Sqn.)	10 P.Z.L. P.23 Karaś
53 Sqn.	7 RWD 14 Czapla
11 Sqn.	3 RWD 8
Army 'Karpaty':	
31 Sqn.	10 P.Z.L. P.23 Karaś
56 Sqn.	7 Lublin R–XIII
5 Sqn.	3 RWD 8
Group 'Narew':	
151 Sqn.	10 P.Z.L. P.7a
51 Sqn.	10 P.Z.L. P.23 Karaś
13 Sqn.	7 RWD 14 Czapla
9 Sqn.	3 RWD 8

Manufacturer: Lublin.
Model: R–XIIID.
Type: Observation/liaison.
Power Plant: One 220hp (Skoda-built) Wright J5 Whirlwind.
Performance:
maximum speed at sea level 121mph (195km/hr).
normal range 373 miles (600km).
time to 9,840ft (3,000m) 15min 50sec.
service ceiling 14,600ft (4,450m).
Weights:
empty 1,956lb (887kg).
loaded 2,932lb (1,330kg).
Dimensions:
wing span 43ft 4in (13.2m).
length 27ft 9¼in (8.46m).
height 9ft 0¾in (2.76m).
wing area 263.7sq ft (24.5sq m).
Armament: One or two flexible 7.7mm machine-gun/s in rear cockpit.
Crew: 2.
In Service: Poland (PolAF, PolNAF), Rumania (17 interned ex-Poland).
Variants (with no. built):
R–XIII: Prototype; two-seat parasol-wing observation/liaison monoplane; one 220hp (Skoda-built) Wright Whirlwind (1).
R–XIIIA: Initial production model; gun-ring mounting; modified dorsal decking (30).
R–XIIIB: As R–XIIIA; modified gun-mounting (inc 5 R–XIIIA/B civil conversions) (20).
R–XIIIbis: Prototype; floatplane version (1 R–XIII conversion).
R–XIIIbis: Production model; altn float, wheel, or ski-under carriage (3).
R–XIIIC: Modified R–XIIIB; improved equipment (inc some subsequently modified to R–XIIID) (48).
R–XIIID: Improved R–XIIIC (95).
R–XIIIter/hydro: Floatplane version; modified R–XIIID; altn float, wheel undercarriage (10).
R–XIIIE: Prototype; re-engined R–XIIIC; one 360hp Gnome–Rhône 7K Titan-Major; experimental only (1).
R–XIIIF: Prototype; re-engined R–XIIIC; one 340hp (Polish) Skoda G.1620 Mors (1).
R–XIIIF: Production model; as prototype, some with one 420hp supercharged (Polish) Skoda G.1620A Mors A; modified rear fuselage (inc 50 L.W.S.-built) (57).
R–XIIIG: Re-engined R–XIIIF; one 220hp (Skoda-built) Wright Whirlwind (1).
R–XIIIG/hydro: Floatplane version; interchangeable floats (6).
R–XIIIt: Blind-flying/navigational trainer version; faired-in front cockpit; raised dorsal decking (2/6 R–XIIIA/B conversions).
R–XIX: Modified R–XIII prototype; experimental Vee-tail; private venture; 1 conversion.
R–XXIII (R–XIIIDr): Long-range competition tourer; modified civil R–XIIIB; increased fuel capacity; 1 conversion.
Total Production: 273.
Remarks: First flown mid-1931, prototype R–XIII forerunner successful but complex series PolAF/PolNAF observation land/floatplanes; outbreak WWII equipped seven PolAF observation sqns (50+), plus PolNAF liaison/co-operation units (10+), both arms operational throughout Sept campaign in reconnaissance/liaison roles; suffered heavy losses both enemy and friendly ground-fire; seventeen examples escaped Rumania close of hostilities; subsequently impressed Rumanian AF.

Manufacturer: Lublin.
Model: R–XVIB.
Type: Transport.
Power Plant: One 220hp (Skoda-built) Wright J5 Whirlwind.
Performance:
maximum speed at sea level 118mph (190km/hr).
maximum speed at 13,120ft (4,000m) 104mph (168km/hr).
normal range 497 miles (800km).
time to 3,280ft (1,000m) 6min 30sec.
service ceiling 14,632ft (4,460m).
Weights:
empty 2,535lb (1,150kg).
loaded 3,593lb (1,630kg).
Dimensions:
wing span 49ft 0in (14.93m).
length 33ft 1¼in (10.08m).
height 9ft 8½in (2.96m).
wing area 328.3sq ft (30.5sq m).
Crew/Accommodation: 1/2 stretchers plus 1 medic.
In Service: Poland.
Variants (with no. built):
R–XVI: Prototype; single-engine high-wing light 4-passenger transport; subsequently modified as ambulance; strengthened fuselage; fixed-pitch propeller (1).
R–XVIB: Production model; ambulance version; modified fuselage and cockpit canopy; variable-pitch propeller (5).
Total Production: 6.
Remarks: Prototype first flown early 1932; all six examples still in service at time of German invasion; employed medical evacuation duties September campaign.

Manufacturer: L.W.S.
Model: 3 Mewa (Gull).
Type: Reconnaissance.
Power Plant: One 730hp Gnome–Rhône 14MO5 Mars.
Performance (approx):
maximum speed at sea level 186mph (300km/hr).
maximum speed at 11,810ft (3,600m) 224mph (360km/hr).
time to 3,280ft (1,000m) 1min 40sec.
service ceiling 27,890ft (8,500m).
Weights (approx):
empty 3,854lb (1,748kg).
loaded 5,335lb (2,420kg).
Dimensions (approx):
wing span 44ft 1½in (13.45m).
length 31ft 2½in (9.5m).
height 8ft 8¼in (2.65m).
wing area 290.6sq ft (27.0sq m).
Projected armament: Two fixed forward-firing machine-guns in wheel spats; twin flexible (retractable) machine-guns in rear cockpit.
Crew: 2.
In Service: Bulgaria (7 Ka.B.11), Poland.
Variants (with no. built):
L.W.S.3/I–III: Prototypes; two-seat shoulder-wing reconnaissance monoplane; one 715hp Gnome–Rhône 14MO1 Mars; one fixed machine-gun in each wheel spat plus one flexible machine-gun in rear cockpit; L.W.S.3/II with experimental (manually-operated) movable vertical tail; L.W.S.3/III with refined cockpit canopy and simplified structure; unarmed (3).
L.W.S.3 Mewa A: Production model; as L.W.S.3/III; uprated engine; projected armament increase (approx 10).
L.W.S.3 Mewa B: Re-engined Mewa A; one 860hp Fiat A.74 RC; three blade variable-pitch propeller; modified equipment; Bulgarian order (60); none completed.
L.W.S.7 Mewa 2: Improved L.W.S.3; one 900hp P.Z.L. Legwan (Iguana) or 918 P.Z.L.-built Bristol Pegasus XX; modified fuselage; tapering wings; project only.
Ka.B.11: Modified Mewa B/2; one 860hp Fiat A.74; redesigned fuselage; re-positioned (high-wing) tapering mainplane; increased cockpit (side) glazing; Bulgarian (CBSA)-built (approx 7).
Total Production: approx 20.
Remarks: Initial prototype first flown Autumn 1937; initial production Mewa A's first flight second morning of war; two examples assigned operational sqn closing stages Sept campaign; no record of use; bulk of technical files evacuated Bulgaria, basis for subsequent production much-modified Ka.B.11 for Bulgarian AF;

first flown following Spring, several later serving operational reconnaissance role.

Manufacturer: P.W.S.
Model: 26.
Type: Trainer/liaison.
Power Plant: One 220hp (P.Z.L.- or Avia-built) Wright J5 Whirlwind.
Performance:
maximum speed at sea level 134.8mph (217km/hr).
cruising speed 112mph (180km/hr).
normal range 286 miles (460 km).
time to 3,280ft (1,000m) 3min 45sec.
service ceiling 15,157ft (4,620m).
Weights:
empty 1,874lb (850kg).
loaded 2,561lb (1,162kg).
Dimensions:
wing span 29ft 6½in (9.0m).
length 23ft 0¾in (7.03m).
height 9ft 0in (2.74m).
wing area 258.3sq ft (24.0sq m).
Armament: One fixed forward-firing 7.7mm machine-gun in fuselage; provision for max 26.5lb (12kg) bomb load underwing.
Crew/Accommodation: 1/1.
In Service: Germany, Poland, Rumania, USSR.
Variants (with no. built):
P.W.S.16, 16bis: Two-seat intermediate/aerobatic trainer biplane versions; unarmed; cowling/undercarriage modifications (40+).
P.W.S.26: Improved P.W.S.16bis; structural strengthening; one 7.7mm machine-gun; provision for two 26.5lb (12kg) bombs underwing; refined undercarriage (250).
P.W.S.27, 28: Modified P.W.S.26; redesigned wings; P.W.S.28 with uprated engine; projects only.
Total Production: 300 (all Marks).
Remarks: Earlier P.W.S.16/16bis supplanted by improved P.W.S.26 late thirties as standard basic/intermediate trainer PolAF; several latter employed Sept 1939 campaign emergency reconnaissance/liaison duties; considerable number captured by Germany; limited service Luftwaffe training role (plus 28 sold to Rumania); some also reportedly seized by USSR and subsequently used ancillary duties.

Manufacturer: P.W.S.
Model: 24bis.
Type: Photographic-survey.
Power Plant: One 420hp Pratt and Whitney Wasp Junior TB.
Performance:
maximum speed at sea level 140mph (225km/hr).
cruising speed 119mph (191km/hr).
service ceiling 18,045ft (5,500m).
Weights:
empty 2,630lb (1,193kg).
loaded 4,800lb (2,177kg).
Dimensions:
wing span 49ft 2½in (15.0m).
length 31ft 8in (9.65m).
height 9ft 8¼in (2.95m).
wing area 341.22sq ft (31.7sq m).
Crew/Accommodation: 1/4 (as transport).
In Service: Poland.
Variants (with no. built):
P.W.S.24T: Prototype; single-engined high-wing civil transport; one 220hp (Skoda-built) Wright J5A Whirlwind (1).
P.W.S.24: Initial production model; detail design improvements; reduced weight (5).
P.W.S.24bis (P.W.S.24WJ): Re-engined P.W.S.24 (5).
Total Production: 11.
Remarks: Early thirties feederliner, withdrawn from commercial service Spring 1936; one P.W.S.24bis to PolAF; two each P.W.S.24/24bis refitted photographic-survey duties; two still in use outbreak WWII; employed emergency transport role close Sept campaign.

Manufacturer: P.W.S.
Model: 35 Ogar (Hound).
Type: Trainer/liaison.
Power Plant: One 130hp P.Z. Inz Major.
Performance:
maximum speed at sea level 124mph (200km/hr).
cruising speed 100mph (160km/hr).
normal range 404 miles (650km).
service ceiling 16,400ft (5,000m).
Weights:
loaded 1,896lb (860kg).
Dimensions:
wing span 26ft 3in (8.0m).
length 22ft 11½in (7.0m).
height 8ft 2½in (2.5m).
wing area 148.6sq ft (13.8sq m).
Crew: 1/1.

Lublin R-VIIIbis

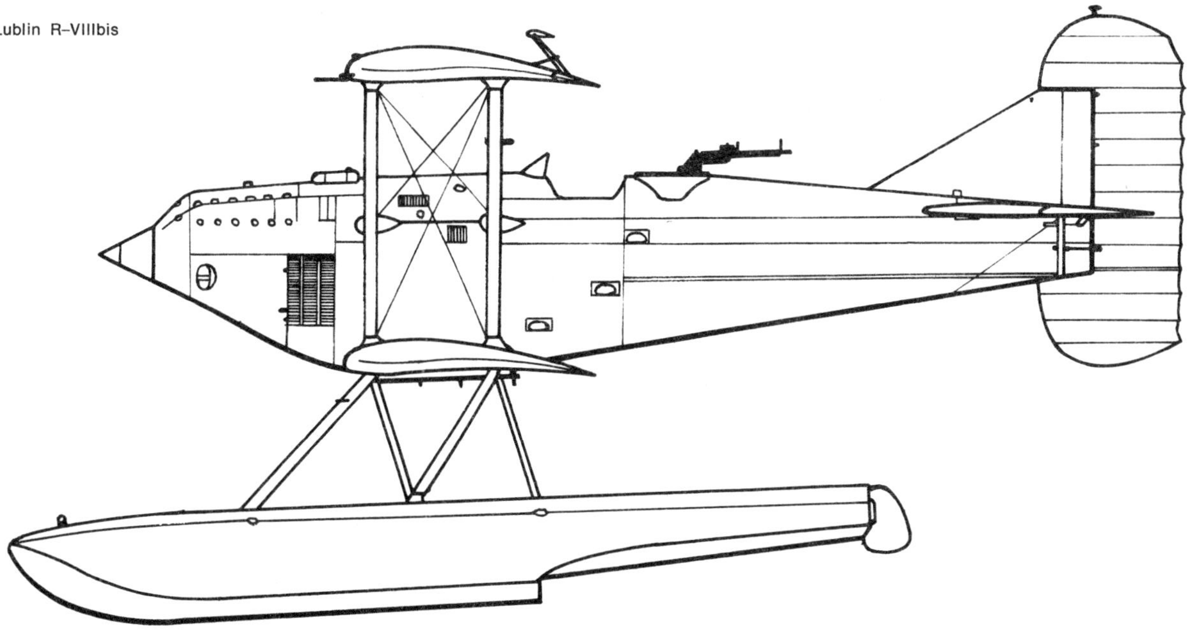

Lublin R-XIIID

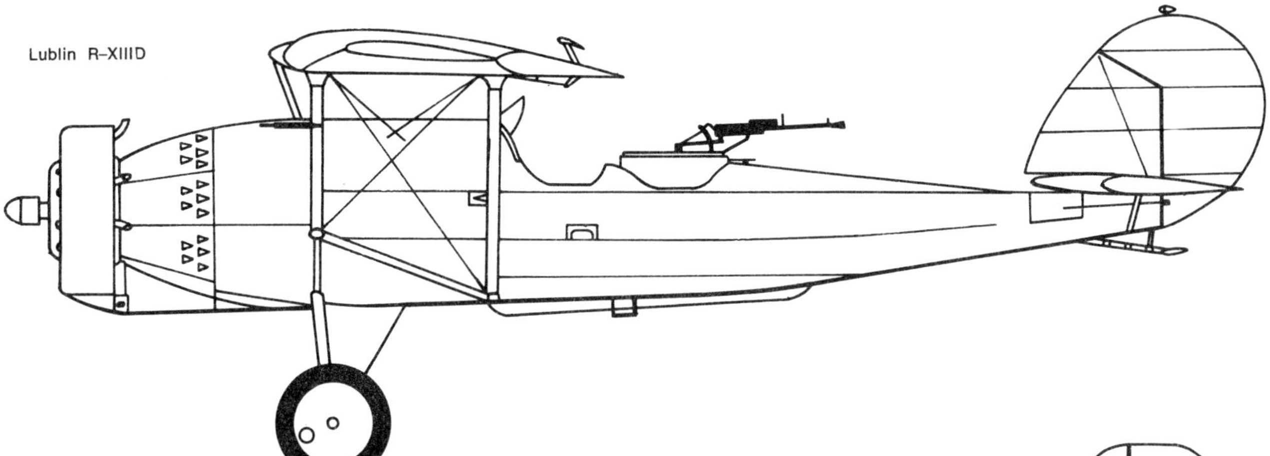

P.Z.L. P.7a

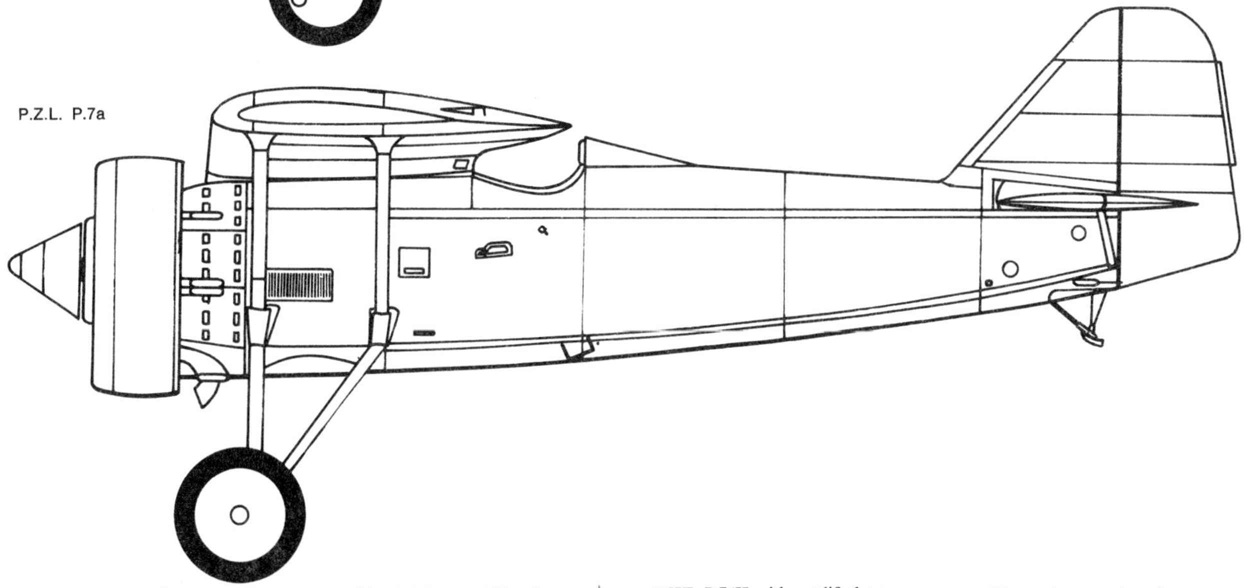

In Service: Poland.
Variants (with no. built):
P.W.S. 35/I, II: Prototypes; two-seat dual-control trainer biplane (2).
P.W.S.35: Production model; as prototype; modified fuselage; reduced weight (approx 2).
Total Production: approx 4.
Remarks: Prototype first flown late Summer 1938, P.W.S.35 under construction for PolAF at time of German invasion; at least one example reportedly operated emergency liaison role during September campaign.

Manufacturer: P.Z.L.
Model: P.7a.
Type: Interceptor-fighter.
Power Plant: One 485hp (Skoda-built) Bristol Jupiter VIIF.
Performance:
maximum speed at sea level 171mph (276km/hr).
maximum speed at 13,120ft (4,000m) 197mph (317km/hr).
normal range 348 miles (560km).
time to 3,280ft (1,000m) 1min 38sec.
service ceiling 27,148ft (8,275m).
Weights:
empty 2,226lb (1,010kg).
loaded 3,106lb (1,409kg).
Dimensions:
wing span 33ft 9½in (10.3m).
length 23ft 6in (7.16m).
height 9ft 0½in (2.75m).
wing area 185.3sq ft (17.2sq m).
Armament: Two forward-firing 7.7mm Vickers E machine-guns in fuselage.
Crew: 1.
In Service: Germany (approx 50), Poland, Rumania (10).
Variants (with no. built):
P.6/I,/II: Prototypes; single-seat high (gull)-wing fighter monoplane; one 450hp Bristol Jupiter VIFH (2).
P.7/I,/II: Prototypes; single-seat high (gull)-wing fighter monoplane; one 485hp Bristol Jupiter

VIIF; P.7/II with modified rear fuselage and redesigned engine cowling (2).
P.7a: Pre-production and production models; licence-built power plant; engine ring cowling; modified cockpit and tail surfaces; revised ailerons (149).
Total Production: 153 (all Marks).
Remarks: Entering service Winter 1932–33, P.7a established Polish AF claim as world's first fighter arm entirely to be equipped with all-metal single-seat interceptor fighter monoplanes; although long obsolete by outbreak WWII, still equipped three operational fighter sqns; employed both fighter and reconnaissance roles opening rounds September campaign; of some hundred survivors approx half escaped Rumania (number subsequently impressed Rumanian AF), remainder seized by Germany, many of which utilized training and ancillary duties (inc

possible employment invasion USSR, June 1941).

Manufacturer: P.Z.L.
Model: P.11c.
Type: Interceptor-fighter.
Power Plant: One 645hp (Skoda-built) Bristol Mercury VIS.2.
Performance:
maximum speed at sea level 185mph (300km/hr).
maximum speed at 18,050ft (5,500m) 242mph (390km/hr).
normal range 435 miles (700km).
time to 16,400ft (5,000m) 6min 0sec.
service ceiling 26,250ft (8,000m).
Weights:
empty 2,529lb (1,147kg).
maximum 3,968lb (1,800kg).
Dimensions:
wing span 35ft 2in (10.72m).
length 24ft 9½in (7.55m).
height 9ft 4½in (2.85m).
Armament: Two 7.7mm KM Wz 33 machine-guns each in fuselage

and (some late models only) in wings; max bomb load 110lb (50kg) underwing.
Crew: 1.
In Service: Latvia, Poland, Rumania (120 P.11b/P.11f, plus 28 interned/impressed ex-Poland).
Variants (with no. built):
P.11/I–III: Prototypes; single-seat high (gull)-wing interceptor-fighter monoplane; one 515hp Gnome–Rhône Jupiter IXASb P.11/I), and one 530hp Bristol Mercury IVA (P.11/II and /III) resp; P.11/II subsequently re-engined with one 525hp Gnome–Rhône 9K Mistral (3).
P.11a: Production model; as late P.11b; one 517hp (Skoda-built) Bristol Mercury IVs.2; two 7.7mm machine-guns in forward fuselage (30).
P.11b: Initial production model; as re-engined P.11/III; one 525hp (IAR-built) Gnome–Rhône 9K; late models with revised engine cowling, wing and tail modifications; Rumanian order (50).
P.11c: Prototype; improved P.11a; one 600hp Gnome–Rhône 9Krse; subsequently re-engined one 517hp (Skoda-built) Bristol Mercury IVS.2; trials aircraft (1).
P.11c: Production model; improved P.11a; one 560hp (Skoda-built) Bristol Mercury VS.2 or (late models) one 645hp (Skoda-built) Mercury VIS.2; redesigned inboard wing sections, vertical tail surfaces; modified rear fuselage; provision for increased armament, bomb-racks (175).
P.11d,e: Proposed navalized P.11c; project/s only.
P.11f: Modified P.11c; one 595hp (IAR-built) Gnome–Rhône 9Krse; revised engine cowling; Rumanian (IAR) licence-built (approx 80).
P.11g Kobutz (Hobby): Improved P.11c; one 840hp (P.Z.L.-built) Bristol Mercury VIII; strengthened fuselage; four 7.7mm machine-guns in wings; enclosed cockpit; prototype only; 1 P.11c conversion.
Total Production: approx 330 (all Marks).
Remarks: Direct development of earlier P.7, prototype P.11/I first flown Aug 1931; subject various pre-war export orders (those fulfilled inc Rumania, Latvia); obsolescent by outbreak WWII (production plans for 400 updated P.11g underway by mid-1939); 185 P.11s provided PolAF's first-line fighter strength Sept 1939; claimed first Luftwaffe aircraft (Ju 87 dive-bomber) to be destroyed in combat during WWII; further 125 confirmed victories accredited before end of campaign, at which time 28 P.11 fighters evacuated Rumania; all impressed Rumanian AF, P.11 still equipping 5 sqns upon Axis invasion USSR (June 1941), but seeing no service Russian Front.
Colour Reference: Plates 118, 119: P.Z.L. P.11c (8.13) No 3 of unidentified operational fighter unit, Polish Air Force (Lotnictwo Wojskowe); Sept 1939; note three-tone 'splinter' camouflage finish reportedly being applied Polish AF fighter squadrons immediately prior outbreak WWII, also assymmetrical upper wing insignia.

Manufacturer: P.Z.L.
Model: P.23B Karaś B (Crucian).
Type: Light bomber/reconnaissance.
Power Plant: One 680hp (P.Z.L.-built) Bristol Pegasus VIII.
Performance:
maximum speed at sea level 170mph (274km/hr).
maximum speed at 6,560ft (2,000m) 186mph (299km/hr).
normal range 782 miles (1,260km).
time to 6,560ft (2,000m) 4min 45sec.
service ceiling 23,950ft (7,300m).
Weights:
empty 4,250lb (1,928kg).
loaded 7,716lb (3,500kg).
Dimensions:
wing span 45ft 9¼in (13.95m).
length 31ft 9¼in (9.68m).
height 10ft 10in (3.3m).
wing area 288.5sq ft (26.8sq m).
Armament: One fixed forward-firing 7.7mm KM Wz 33 machine-gun in fuselage; one flexible 7.7mm Vickers F machine-gun each in (retractable) dorsal position and ventral gondola; max bomb load 1,543lb (700kg) underwing.
Crew: 3.
In Service: Bulgaria (46 P.43A/B), Germany (1 P.43B ex-Poland/evaluation), Poland, Rumania (30 P.23A/11 P.23B ex-Poland).
Variants (with no. built):
P.Z.L.13: Six-passenger civil transport version; project only.
P.23/I–III: Prototypes; light bomber/reconnaissance version; development of P.Z.L.13; one 590hp Bristol Pegasus IIM2; P.23/II and /III with modified cockpit/canopy, repositioned (lowered) engine, and internal bomb-bay replaced by underwing racks (3).
P.23A Karaś A: Initial production model; one 590hp (P.Z.L.-built) Bristol Pegasus IIM2; subsequently converted as dual-control trainers (40).
P.23B: Prototype; re-engined P.23/III; one 680hp Bristol Pegasus VIII; 1 conversion.
P.23B Karaś B: Major production model (210).
P.42: Prototype; one (P.Z.L.-built) Bristol Pegasus VIIIA; retractable ventral gondola; twin fins and rudders; experimental only; 1 P.23B conversion.
P.43A Tchaika (Seagull): Modified P.23B; one 930hp Gnome–Rhône 14Kfs; two 7.7mm KM Wz 36 machine-guns in fuselage, plus one flexible 7.7mm Vickers F machine-gun each in dorsal position and ventral gondola; lengthened fuselage; modified cockpit; Bulgarian order (12).
P.43B: Improved P.43A; one 970hp Gnome–Rhône 14NO1; Bulgarian order (inc 9 initially retained by Poland) (42).
Total Production: 307 (all Marks).
Remarks: Designed to meet army co-operation requirement, yet seemingly inappropriately named after member of the carp family, Karaś A/B both first flown 1936; former restricted operational training, latter (plus five sequestrated Bulgarian P.43Bs) equipped twelve operational sqns during September 1939 campaign, five as part Bomber Brigade, seven for reconnaissance duties under direct army control, sustained heavy losses both roles; eleven surviving P.23Bs evacuated Rumania, plus thirty P.23As; impressed Rumanian AF, continued resp reconnaissance/training functions throughout WWII; Bulgarian AF P.43s equipped four bomber-reconnaissance sqns; limited-scale operational service.
Colour Reference: Plates 121, 122: P.Z.L. P.43A Tchaika of 1st Orliak (Air Regiment), Royal Bulgarian Air Force, Sofia-Bojourishté, Sept 1939; early style fuselage/wing markings with non-standard rudder tricolour striping; (see Dewoitine D.520, plate 12, for 1940–44 pro-Axis period national insignia).

Manufacturer: P.Z.L.
Model: P.24F.
Type: Interceptor fighter.
Power Plant: One 970hp Gnome–Rhône 14NO7.
Performance:
maximum speed at sea level 214mph (345km/hr).
maximum speed at 14,760ft (4,500m) 267mph (430km/hr).
normal range 435 miles (706km).
time to 16,400ft (5,000m) 5min 40sec.
service ceiling 34,450ft (10,500m).
Weights:
empty 2,937lb (1,332kg).
maximum 4,410lb (2,000kg).
Dimensions:
wing span 35ft 0¼in (10.68m).
length 24ft 11¼in (7.6m).
height 8ft 10¼in (2.69m).
Armament: Two fixed forward-firing 20mm Oerlikon FF cannon, two 7.9mm Browning machine-guns in wings; max bomb load 88lb (40kg) underwing.
Crew: 1.
In Service: Bulgaria (56), Greece (36), Poland, Rumania (approx 56), Turkey (approx 140).
Variants (with no. built):
P.24/I–III: Prototypes; single-seat high (gull)-wing fighter monoplane; one 760hp Gnome–Rhône 14Kds and (P.24/III) one 900hp Gnome–Rhône 14Kfs resp; two 20mm Oerlikon FF cannon plus two machine-guns; P.24/II and /III with modified cowling and structural strengthening; altn designation P.24/II and /III—Super P24 and Super P.24bis resp (3).
P.24: Pre-production model; various uprated Gnome–Rhône, Renault, and Fiat power plants; enclosed cockpit; modified wings; redesigned tail surfaces; revised armament (6).
P.24A: Initial production model; as pre-production model; one 900hp Gnome–Rhône 14Kfs; two 20mm Oerlikon FF cannon in wing-strut fairings, plus two 7.9mm Browning machine-guns in wings; max bomb load 88lb (40kg); Turkish (14) and Greek (5) orders; P.Z.L.-built (10); plus Turkish licence-built.
P.24B: As P.24A; modified wheel spats; max bomb load 110lb (50kg); Bulgarian order (14).
P.24C: As P.24A; four 7.9mm Browning machine-guns in wings; max bomb load 220lb (100kg); Turkish (26) and Bulgarian (20) orders (46).
P.24E: Re-engined P.24A; one 900hp (IAR-built) Gnome–Rhône 14KIIc32 or (late models) 940hp (IAR-built) 14KMc36; Rumanian order P.Z.L.-built (6); Rumanian (IAR) licence-built (approx 50).
P.24F, G: Improved versions of P.24A; uprated engine; redesigned (NACA) cowling; modified forward fuselage; armour plating; two cannon plus two machine-guns, and four machine-guns resp; Greek (25 P.24F and 6 P.24G) and Bulgarian (26 P.24F) orders; P.Z.L.-built (approx 57); Turkish licence-built (inc P.24A) (approx 100).
P.24H: Proposed Polish variant; one 1,050hp Gnome–Rhône 14N21; two 20mm Wz 38 cannon, plus two 7.7mm KM Wz 36 machine-guns; or two cannon only.
Total Production: approx 300.
Remarks: Re-engined export development of earlier P.11, initial P.24/I prototype first flown Spring, 1933; subject extensive pre-war export sales/licence-production; first ordered Turkey; served Turkish AF from 1936 until post-WWII, latterly as fighter-trainers re-engined Pratt and Whitney Twin Wasp; also delivered Rumania, Greece (1937) and Bulgaria (1938); backbone Greek AF fighter strength, P.24s heavily committed interceptor role Axis invasions, 1940–41; equipped three Rumanian AF sqns opening rounds Eastern (Soviet) Front campaign, subsequently employed home-defence duties until 1944 capitulation; limited Bulgarian AF service, majority grounded lack of spares by mid-1940; belated Polish order (70 P.24H) cancelled immediately prior outbreak WWII; only one (pre-production) P.24 participated September Campaign, claimed destruction two Luftwaffe machines.
Colour Reference: Plate 120: P.Z.L. P.24G (Delta 127) of 22 Mira (sqn), EVA (Royal Hellenic AF); Ptolemaïs, Greece, Dec 1940; standard olive green/sand-brown finish; saw extensive action against Regia Aeronautica aerial defence Salonika, Winter 1940–41.

Manufacturer: P.Z.L.
Model: P.37B Łoś B (Elk).
Type: Medium bomber.
Power Plant: Two 918hp (P.Z.L.-built) Bristol Pegasus XX.
Performance:
maximum speed at sea level 242mph (390km/hr).
maximum speed at 11,150ft (3,400m) 277mph (445km/hr).
maximum range 2,796 miles (4,500km).
service ceiling 30,347ft (9,250m).
Weights:
empty 9,436lb (4,280kg).
maximum 19,620lb (8,900kg).
Dimensions:
wing span 58ft 10in (17.93m).
length 42ft 4¾in (12.92m).
height 16ft 8in (5.08m).
wing area 575.9sq ft (53.5sq m).
Armament: One flexible 7.7mm KM Wz 37 machine-gun each in nose, dorsal, and ventral positions; max bomb load 5,688lb (2,580kg).
Crew: 4.
In Service: Germany (1 ex-Polish, evaluation), Poland, Rumania (40 approx ex-Polish), USSR (2 ex-Polish).
Variants (with no. built):
P.37/I/III: Prototypes; twin-engine medium bomber; two 873hp Bristol Pegasus XII, 925hp Pegasus XX and 970hp Gnome–Rhône 14N07 resp; P.37/II and P.37/III with redesigned cockpit, twin fins and rudders, twin-wheel main undercarriage; unarmed (3).
P.37A Łoś A: As P.37/I; two 873hp (P.Z.L.-built) Bristol Pegasus XIIB (10).
P37Abis Łoś Abis: As Łos A; twin fins and rudders; detail design improvements; both Łos A/Abis subsequently converted as dual-control trainers (20).
P.37B Łoś B: As P.37/11; two supercharged (P.Z.L.-built) Bristol Pegasus XX; inc approx 20 not fully equipped (approx 60).
P.37C: Export version; two 970hp Gnome–Rhône 14NO7; Yugoslav (20) and Bulgarian (15) orders; none completed.
P.37D: Export versions; two 1,050hp Gnome–Rhône 14N 20/21; Rumanian (30) and Turkish (25) orders; none completed.
P.49/I Miś (Teddy Bear): Prototype; improved P.37; uprated 1,200–1,600hp engines; increased armament; not completed.
Total Production: approx 95.
Remarks: Pride of PolAF and best operational aircraft in service upon outbreak WWII, prototype P.37/1 had first flown mid-1936; subject number (unfulfilled) export contracts; initial production P.37As relegated conversion training duties; of some 40 examples later P.37B actively engaged reconnaissance and bombing attacks against invading German forces over 25 lost to enemy action by close September campaign; 39 withdrawn Rumania subsequently served Rumanian AF early months advance into USSR, late summer 1941; later relegated second-line duties, final (target-tug) models not withdrawn until mid-fifties.
Colour Reference: Plate 123: P.Z.L. P.37B Łoś B of 1st Air Regiment, Polish Air Force (Lotnictwo Wojskowe) Warsaw–Okecie, Sept 1939.

Manufacturer: P.Z.L.
Model: P.46/I Sum (Sheatfish).
Type: Light bomber/reconnaissance.
Power Plant: One 918hp Bristol Pegasus XX.
Performance (approx):
maximum speed at sea level 217mph (350km/hr).
maximum speed at 11,810ft (3,600m) 264mph (425km/hr).
normal range 807 miles (1,300km).
service ceiling 25,260ft (7,700m).
Weights:
empty 4,393lb (1,995kg).
loaded 7,827lb (3,550kg).
Dimensions:
wing span 47ft 10¾in (14.6m).
length 34ft 5½in (10.5m).
height 10ft 10in (3.3m).
wing area 290.6sq ft (27.0sq m).
Armament: Four fixed forward-firing 7.7mm KM Wz 36 machine-guns in wings; one flexible 7.7mm KM Wz 36 machine-gun each in (retractable) dorsal position and (retractable) ventral gondola; max bomb load 1,323lb (600kg).
Crew: 3.
In Service: Poland.
Variants with no. built):
P.46/I, II: Prototypes; three-seat light bomber/reconnaissance monoplane; one supercharged Bristol Pegasus XX; four 7.7mm KM Wz 36 machine-guns in wings plus one each in dorsal position and retractable ventral gondola (2).
P.46A Sum A: Production model; as initial prototypes; two 7.7mm KM Wz 36 machine-guns in dorsal position; none completed.
P.46/III: Prototype for proposed export version (P.46B); one 1,030hp Gnome–Rhône 14N21; not completed.
Total Production: 2.
Remarks: Designed as P.23 replacement, via one-off P.42, and perpetuating former's piscine appellation, P.46/I first flown late 1938; P.46/II evacuated Rumania towards close Sept campaign; returned Warsaw at very end, landing under fire of German ground forces, to bring last-minute orders to capital's defenders (initiating underground army).

Manufacturer: RWD (D.W.L.).
Model: 8.
Type: Trainer/liaison.
Power Plant: One 110hp P.Z.Inż Junior or 120hp P.Z.Inż Major.
Performance:
maximum speed at sea level 109mph (175km/hr).
cruising speed 90mph (145km/hr).
range 270 miles (435km).
time to 3,280ft (1,000m) 4min 15sec.
service ceiling 16,400ft (5,000m).
Weights:
empty 1,058–1,102lb (480–500kg).
normal 1,653lb (750kg).
Dimensions:
wing span 36ft 1in (11.0m).
length 26ft 3in (8.0m).
height 7ft 6½in (2.3m).
wing area 215.3sq ft (20.0sq m).
Crew/Accommodation: 1/1.
In Service: Germany (ex-Poland), Poland, Rumania (30 escapees ex-Poland), USSR (ex-Poland).
Variants (with no built):
RWD 8: Protypes; two-seat parasol-wing trainer/touring monoplane; one 115hp Cirrus Hermes II and one Walter Junior resp; D.W.L.-built (2).
RWD 8: Production model; various power plants inc 120hp de Havilland Gipsy Major, 110hp Walter (or P.Z.Inż) Junior, 120hp Walter or P.Z.Inż) Major, and 120hp (Polish) Skoda G.594; modified wings; P.W.S.-built models with modified cockpits (inc some as blind-flying trainers with sliding-hooded rear cockpit); wing-strut and undercarriage fairings deleted; D.W.L.-built (approx 100); Estonian (Tallinn) licence-built (1); Yugoslav (Rogožarski) licence-built.
RWD 8a: As RWD 8. Increased fuel capacity.
(Total RWD 8/8a production (P.W.S.-built): approx 500).
Total Production: 600+.
Remarks: Highly successful pre-war trainer/tourer, prototype RWD 8 first flown late 1932; approx 100 examples (inc approx 60 impressed civil models) participated September campaign variety liaison/communications, observation, and ancillary duties; some fitted defensive light machine-gun in rear cockpit; one flight (two RWD 8 plus single P.W.S. 26), continued offensive operations, attacking German troops with hand-grenades, into first week Oct (well beyond official surrender Warsaw) as last Polish aircraft in action; numbers (60+, inc over 40 civil examples) previously evacuated Rumania, of which half impressed into Rumanian AF; served training role, as did others captured Germany/USSR at cessation of hostilities.

Manufacturer: RWD (D.W.L.).
Model: 13.
Type: Liaison.
Power Plant: One 130hp de Havilland Gipsy Major.
Performance:
maximum speed at sea level 130mph (210km/hr).
cruising speed 112mph (180km/hr).
normal range 560 miles (900km).
time to 3,280ft (1,000m) 4min 20sec.
service ceiling 13,780ft (4,200m).
Weights:
empty 1,168lb (530kg).
loaded 1,962lb (890kg).
Dimensions:
wing span 37ft 9in (11.5m).
length 25ft 9in (7.85m).
height 6ft 9in (2.05m).
wing area 172.2sq ft (16.0sq m).
Crew/Accommodation: 1/2.
In Service: Germany (ex-Poland/Yugoslavia), Poland, Rumania (approx 35 ex-Poland), Spain (NatAF: 4), Sweden (1 ex-Poland), Yugoslavia.
Variants (with no. built):
RWD 13: Prototype and initial production model; three-seat high-wing civil tourer; various power plants inc 130hp Walter Major and de Havilland Gipsy Major I (inc 4 Spanish order); D.W.L.-built (approx 110); Yugoslav (Rogožarski) licence-built.
RWD 13S: Ambulance version; modified RWD 13; provision for one stretcher plus one medic (inc 3 Polish order); D.W.L.-built (15); Yugoslav (Rogožarski) licence-built.
Total Production: approx 125 (exc licence-production).
Remarks: First flown early 1935, considerable number popular RWD 13 executive/club tourers exported pre-war (plus Yugoslav licence-manufacture); participated Spanish Civil War liaison role; several impressed civil models performed similar duties, plus specialized RWD 13S medical-evacuation, during German invasion of Poland, September 1939; 40+ evacuated Rumania (inc 3+ RWD 13S), majority employed Rumanian AF liaison/ambulance roles duration WWII; one Baltic escapee likewise impressed Swedish AF (as Tp 11 transport).

Manufacturer: RWD (D.W.L.).
Model: 14 Czapla (Heron).
Type: Reconnaissance/observation.
Power Plant: One 470hp P.Z.L. G.1620B Mors B.
Performance:
maximum speed at sea level 154mph (247km/hr).
maximum speed at 6,560ft (2,000m) 148mph (238km/hr).
cruising speed 129mph (208km/hr).
maximum range 360 miles (580km).
time to 6,560ft (2,000m) 7min 0sec.
service ceiling 16,400ft (5,000m).
Weights:
empty 2,542lb (1,153kg).
loaded 3,747lb (1,700kg).
Dimensions:
wing span 39ft 0¾in (11.9m).
length 29ft 6¾in (9.0m).
height 9ft 10¼in (3.0m).
wing area 236.8sq ft (22.0sq m).
Armament: One fixed forward-firing 7.7mm KM Wz33 machine-gun in nose; one flexible 7.7mm Vickers F machine-gun in rear cockpit.
Crew: 2.
In Service: Poland, Rumania (11 ex-Poland).
Variants (with no. built):
RWD 14: Initial prototype; two-seat parasol-wing reconnaissance/observation monoplane; one 420hp Pratt & Whitney Wasp Junior (1).
RWD 14a: Protoypes; modified RWD 14; one 420hp P.Z.L. G.1620A Mors A; improved fuselage design; folding wings; second model with redesigned tail surfaces (2).
RWD 14b: Prototype; modified RWD 14a; one 470hp P.Z.L. G.1620B Mors B; detail design improvements (1).
RWD 14B Czapla: Production model; as prototype; one ventral camera; minor modifications; L.W.S.-built (65).
Total Production: 69.
Remarks: Designed to replace Lublin R-XIII, RWD 14b equipped five PolAF observation sqns (compared with latter's seven) upon outbreak WWII; suffered heavy losses Sept campaign, especially from friendly ground-fire; approx 11 survivors evacuated Rumania, 1 to Hungary; former subsequently impressed Rumanian AF.

RWD 14b Czapla

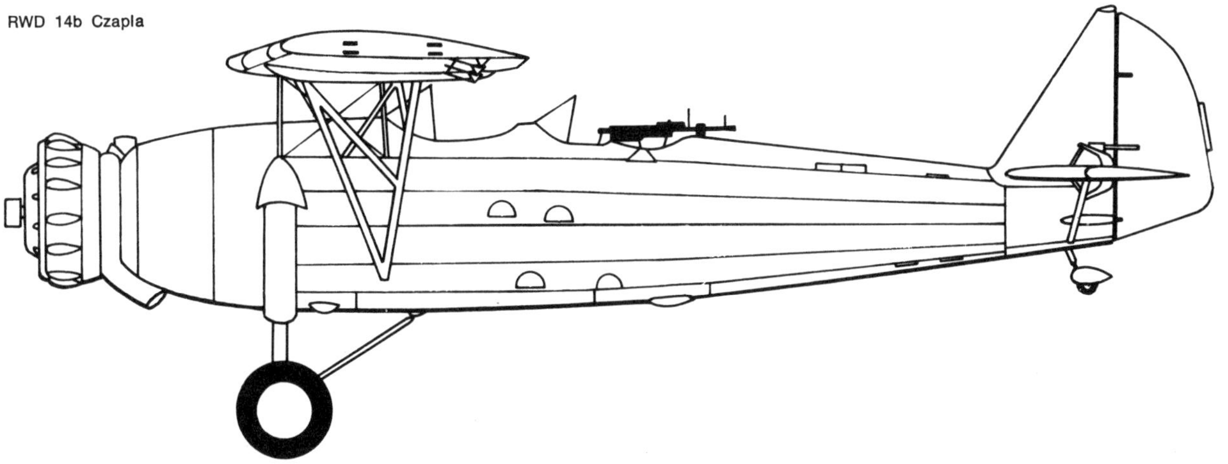

Manufacturer: RWD (D.W.L.).
Model: 17.
Type: Trainer/liaison.
Power Plant: One 130hp P.Z.Inż Major.
Performance:
maximum speed at sea level 121mph (195km/hr).
cruising speed 103mph (165km/hr).
normal range 423 miles (680km).
time to 3,280ft (1,000m) 4min 10sec.
service ceiling 16,400ft (5,000m).
Weights:
empty 1,120lb (520kg).
loaded 1,786lb (810kg).
Dimensions:
wing span 32ft 9¾in (10.0m).
length 25ft 3¼in (7.7m).
height 7ft 6¾in (2.3m).
wing area 201.3sq ft (18.7sq m).
Crew/Accommodation: 1/1.
In Service: Poland.
Variants (with no built):
RWD 17: Prototype; two-seat parasol-wing aerobatic trainer/touring monoplane; one 130 P.Z.Inż Major (1).
RWD 17 Series I: Initial production model; as prototype (approx 18).
RWD 17bis: Floatplane version of RWD 17; one 160hp Bramo Sh 14A4; 2 RWD 17 conversions.
RWD 17w: Two-seat primary/single-seat aerobatic military (naval) trainer floatplane version; one Bramo Sh 14A4. Altn wheel undercarriage; 12 on order (1).
RWD 17 Series II: Military (aerobatic) trainer version; improved RWD 17 Series I; redesigned wings; 120 on order; none completed.
Total Production: approx 20.
Remarks: Primarily designed as aerobatic trainer, prototype RWD 17 first flown mid-1937; several impressed Sept 1939 campaign, for emergency liaison duties.

Manufacturer: Samolot (Bartel).
Model: BM 4a.
Type: Trainer/liaison.
Power Plant: One 80hp Le Rhône.
Performance:
maximum speed at sea level 78mph (125km/hr).
time to 3,280ft (1,000m) 9min 42sec.
service ceiling 9,251ft (2,820m).
Weights:
empty 1,186lb (538kg).
loaded 1,744 (791kg).
Dimensions:
wing span 33ft 5in (10.18m).
length 23ft 8¼in (7.22m).
height 9ft 10¼in (2.93m).
wing area 269.1sq ft (25.0sq m).
Crew/Accommodation: 1/1.
In Service: Poland.
Variants (with no. built):
BM 4b, d: Factory prototypes; two-seat military trainer biplane; one 85hp Walter and one 80hp Zalewski Avia W.Z.7 resp; BM 4d subsequently re-engined with one 80hp Le Rhône; Samolot-built (2).
BM4a: Initial production model; as re-engined BM 4d; one 80hp Le Rhône; subsequently modified with redesigned wing-tips, tail surfaces, and improved undercarriage; Samolot-built (22).
BM 4c: Light touring/liaison version; one 110hp Lorraine; increased fuel capacity; Samolot-built (1).
BM 4e: Re-engined BM 4d; one 85hp Peterlot; redesigned undercarriage; 1 conversion.
BM 4f, g, h: Re-engined BM 4a versions; one 120hp (Polish) Skoda G.594, one 100hp de Havilland Gipsy I, and one 105hp Walter Junior resp; 3 BM 4a conversions.
BM 4h: Production model; two-seat trainer version; one 105hp Walter (or P.Z.Inż-built) Junior, or one 120hp de Havilland Gipsy III; P.W.S.-built (50).
Total Production: 75.
Remarks: Entering service late twenties (first indigenous design to equip PolAF in quantity), last examples (BM 4h) relegated air cadet flying school/civil club use decade later; several returned military employ emergency liaison role after German invasion, Sept 1939.

RUMANIA

Manufacturer: IAR.
Model: 36.
Type: Transport.
Power Plant: One 380hp Armstrong Siddeley Serval.
Performance:
maximum speed 149mph (240km/hr).
cruising speed 134mph (215km/hr).
normal range 435 miles (700km).
time to 9,840ft (3,000m) 17min 0sec.
service ceiling 14,760ft (4,500m).
Weights:
empty 2,976lb (1,350kg).
loaded 4,960lb (2,250kg).
Dimensions:
wing span 50ft 6⅓in (15.4m).
length 32ft 2in (9.8m).
height 9ft 2¼in (2.8m).
wing area 328.3sq ft (30.5sq m).
Crew/Accommodation: 2/6.
In Service: Rumania.
Variants (with no. built):
IAR 36: Prototype; civil transport; single-engined high-wing monoplane; ICAR-built (1).
IAR 36: Production model; civil/military transport (approx 4).
Total Production: approx 5.
Remarks: Messerschmitt-designed civil prototype first flown late 1934; employed Rumanian domestic routes; five examples entered service Rumanian AF 1936; performed staff transport/communications duties late thirties and into opening months WWII.

SET 7K

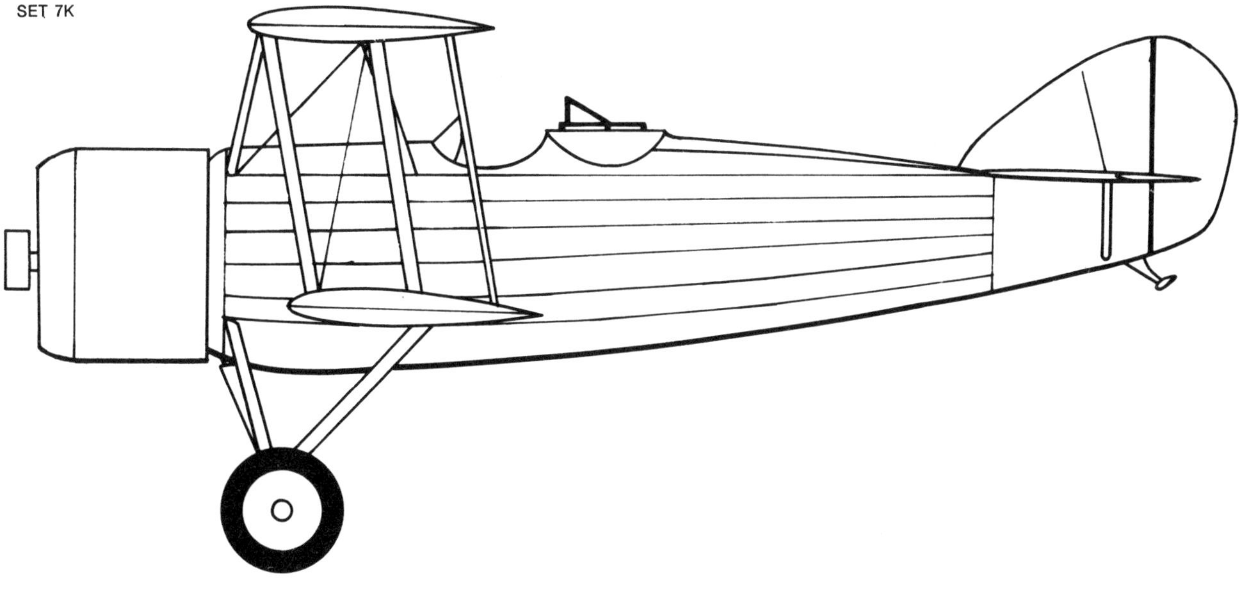

Manufacturer: IAR.
Model: 37.
Type: Light reconnaissance-bomber.
Power Plant: One 870hp IAR 14 KIIc 32.
Performance:
maximum speed at sea level 192mph (310km/hr).
maximum speed at 10,500ft (3,200m) 208mph (335km/hr).
cruising speed 168mph (270km/hr).
normal range 620 miles (998km).
time to 6,560ft (2,000m) 4min 10sec.
service ceiling 26,250ft (8,000m).
Weights:
empty 4,806lb (2,180kg).
loaded 7,628lb (3,460kg).
Dimensions:
wing span 40ft 1in (12.22m).
length 31ft 2in (9.5m).
height 13ft 0¼in (3.97m).
wing area 384.27sq ft (35.7sq m).
Armament: One flexible 7.7mm machine-gun each in rear cockpit and retractable ventral tunnel; max bomb load 1,320lb (600kg) underwing.
Crew: 3.
In Service: Rumania.
Variants (with no. built):
IAR 37: Prototype; three-seat light reconnaissance-bomber biplane; one IAR 14 KIIc 32 (licence-built Gnome–Rhône 14K Mistral–Major) (1).
IAR 37: Production model; as prototype; revised cockpit canopy; mainwheel fairings deleted.
IAR 38, 39: Modified IAR 37; two-seat tactical reconnaissance/light bomber and three-seat close-support versions resp.
Total Production: approx 325.
Remarks: First flown 1938, more than 300 IAR 37/39 series built over next four years; 135 examples equipped fifteen reconnaissance/light bomber sqns at time of Axis invasion of USSR (22 June 1941); saw extensive and continuing service throughout hostilities, post-Aug 1944 capitulation, fought alongside Soviet when German forces retreated; IAR 39 army co-operation/close-support version remained in use until late forties, latterly relegated liaison and ancillary duties.
Colour Reference: Plate 126: IAR 39 (No 204) army co-operation aircraft attached Corpul 1 Aerien (1st Air Corps), FARR (Royal Air Forces of Rumania); Slovakian Front, Jan 1945; now subordinated 5th Soviet Air Force, all machines of Corpul 1 Aerien have had earlier pro-Axis wing/fuselage cross insignia (see IAR 81C above) supplanted by re-introduction pre-war roundels; rudder tricolour striping retained.

Manufacturer: IAR.
Model: 80A.
Type: Fighter.
Power Plant: One 1,025hp IAR (Gnome–Rhône) 14 K115.
Performance:
maximum speed at 13,120ft (4,000m) 317mph (510km/hr).
cruising speed 205mph (330km/hr).
maximum range 584 miles (940km).
time to 14,760ft (4,500m) 5min 40sec.
service ceiling 34,500ft (10,500m).
Weights:
empty 3,930lb (1,783kg).
maximum 5,480lb (2,490kg).
Dimensions:
wing span 34ft 5¼in (10.5m).
length 29ft 2¼in (8.9m).

height 11ft 10in (3.6m).
wing area 171.9sq ft (15.97sq m).
Armament: Six 7.92mm Browning FN machine-guns in wings.
Crew: 1.
In Service: Rumania.
Variants (with no. built):
IAR 80: Prototype and initial production model; single-seat fighter version; prototype with 930hp IAR 14 KIIIc 36 (licence-built Gnome–Rhône 14K Mistral-Major); four 7.92mm machine-guns in wings (51).
IAR 80A: Modified IAR 80; increased armament (90).
IAR 80B: Modified IAR 80A; improved radio equipment; two 7.92mm machine-guns replaced by 13.2mm machine-guns (31).
IAR 80DC: Dual-control two-seat trainer version; post-war conversions.
IAR 81, 81A: Dive-bomber versions; modified IAR 80, 80A.

resp; increased wing span; bomb rack for one 551lb (250kg) bomb under fuselage, plus four 110lb (50kg) bombs and rockets underwing; four 7.92mm or two 7.92mm plus two 13.2mm machine-guns resp.
IAR 81B: Long-range fighter version of IAR 81; two addn 20mm Oerlikon FF or Ikaria cannon in wings.
IAR 81C: Fighter/dive-bomber version; two 20mm MG 151 cannon, plus four 7.92mm Browning FN machine-guns; provision for under fuselage/underwing bombs.
(Total IAR 81, A, B, C: approx 260).
Total Production: approx 437.
Remarks: Embodying rear fuselage and tail assembly of Polish P.Z.L. P.24E (currently under licence-production IAR), prototype IAR 80 designed early 1938; first

production models entered service Rumanian AF four years later; employed Eastern Front close support/fighter bomber roles 1942–43 (inc fighting around Stalingrad) before redeployment home-defence duties (Bucharest, Ploesti oilfields); post-Armistice both IAR 80/81 saw action against German air and ground forces; remained in service until late forties, several IAR 80s being converted as two-seat advanced trainers.
Colour Reference: Plates 124, 125: IAR 81C (No 391) of Grupul 3 picaj (3rd Dive-bomber Group), Corpul 1 Aerien (1st Air Corps), FARR (Royal Air Forces of Rumania), Cioara Dolcesti, Rumania, Aug 1944; subordinated to Luftwaffe Lf1.Kdo.4 (currently headquartered Debrecen, Hungary), IAR 81C No 391 carries pro-Axis wing/fuselage national insignia

(compare with post-Aug 1944 markings on IAR 39 below).

Maufacturer: SET.
Model: 7K.
Type: Observation.
Power Plant: One 420hp IAR 7K–120.
Performance:
maximum speed at sea level 156mph (251km/hr).
maximum speed at 4,920ft (1,500m) 158mph (255km/hr).
range 360 miles (580km).
time to 16,400ft (5,000m) 19min 41sec.
service ceiling 22,310ft (6,800m).
Weights:
empty 2,227lb (1,010kg).
loaded 3,638lb (1,650kg).
Dimensions:
wing span 32ft 2in (9.8m).
length 23ft 5½in (7.15m).
height 10ft 8½in (3.26m).
wing area 286.32sq ft (26.6sq m).

Armament: One fixed forward-firing machine-gun; one (or twin) flexible machine-gun/s in rear cockpit; provision for light bombs under fuselage and light bombs or flares underwing.
Crew: 2.
In Service: Rumania.
Variants:
SET 7K: Prototype and production model/s; two-seat observation biplane; one 420hp IAR 7K–120 (licence-built Gnome–Rhône 7K Titan–Major).
Total Production: approx 100.
Remarks: Entering Rumanian AF service 1926, SET 7K in use throughout pro-Axis period of hostilities; still on first-line strength several observation sqns at time of capitulation (Aug 1944), survivors subsequently relegated training and secondary roles.

SWEDEN

Manufacturer: ASJA.
Model: J 6B 'Jaktfalk II' (Gerfalcon).
Type: Fighter.
Power Plant: One 500hp Armstrong Siddeley Jaguar.
Performance:
maximum speed at 14,764ft (4,500m) 193mph (310km/hr).
normal range 342 miles (550km).
time to 3,280ft (1,000m) 4min 0sec.
service ceiling 30,500ft (9,300m).
Weights:
empty 2,149lb (975kg).
loaded 3,240lb (1,470kg).
Dimensions:
wing span 28ft 10½in (8.8m).
length 24ft 7½in (7.5m).
height 11ft 4½in (3.46m).
wing area 236.81sq ft (22.0sq m).
Armament: Two 8mm machine-guns in upper fuselage.
Crew: 1.
In Service: Finland (1 J 6A, 2 J 6B).
Variants (with no. built):
J 5 'Jaktfalk': Private venture prototype; one 500hp Armstrong Siddeley Jaguar; two 8mm machine-guns; Svenska-built (1).
J 6 'Jaktfalk': Initial production model; re-engined J 5; one 500hp Bristol Jupiter VII F; Svenska-built (7).
J 6A/B 'Jaktfalk II': Modified J 6; one 500hp Bristol Jupiter VIIF (3), or one Armstrong Siddeley Jaguar (7) resp (latter

FFVS J 22B

SAAB B 17A

SAAB B 18B

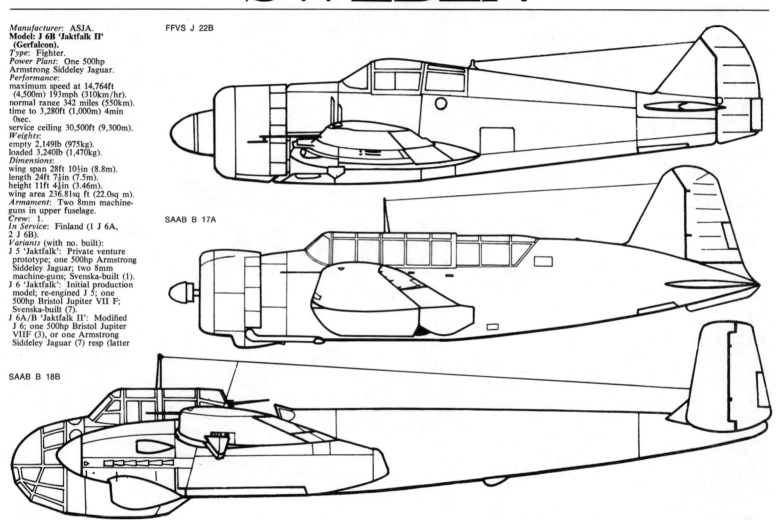

inc one with 530hp Armstrong Siddeley Panther IIIA supplied Norway). ASJA-built (10).
Total Production: 18.
Remarks: Svenska-designed and built J 5/6 entered service 1932, later supplemented by J 6A/B models produced by ASJA; three examples of latter supplied Finnish AF 1939; served throughout Winter and Continuation Wars initially as emergency fighter, subsequently relegated fighter trainer role, 1941–45.

Manufacturer: FFVS.
Model: J 22A.
Type: Fighter.
Power Plant: One 1,065hp SFA-built STWC3–G (Pratt & Whitney SC3–G Twin Wasp).
Performance:
maximum speed at 11,500ft (3,500m) 354mph (570km/hr).
cruising speed 241mph (388km/hr).
maximum range 780 miles (1,270km).
service ceiling 30,000ft (9,300m).

Weights:
empty 4,400lb (2,000kg).
loaded 6,300lb (2,835kg).
Dimensions:
wing span 32ft 9½in (10.0m).
length 25ft 7in (7.8m).
height 8ft 6½in (2.6m).
wing area 172sq ft (16sq m).
Armament: Two 7.9mm M/22F machine-guns; two 13.2mm M/39A machine-guns in wings.
Crew: 1.
In Service: Sweden.
Variants (with no. built):
J 22A: Prototype and initial production model; Swedish-built (unlicensed) copy of 1,065hp Pratt and Whitney Twin Wasp.
J 22B: As J 22 A; revised armament; four 13.2mm M/39A machine-guns; J 22 production: FFVS-built (181); CVA-built (18).
Total Production: 199.
Remarks: Indigenous design prompted by US government embargo on export of fighters to Sweden, J 22 entered service early

1944; equipped total 7 Wings, last examples retiring 1952 upon replacement by de Havilland F.B.50 Vampire jet.

Manufacturer: SAAB.
Model: B 17C.
Type: Dive-bomber.
Power Plant: One 1,020hp Piaggio P.XIbis RC 40D.
Performance:
maximum speed 270mph (435km/hr).
cruising speed 230mph (370km/hr).
Weights:
loaded 8,520lb (3,865kg).
Dimensions:
wing span 44ft 11½in (13.7m).
length 32ft 2in (9.8m).
height 14ft 5½in (4.4m).
wing area 306.77sq ft (28.5sq m).
Armament: Two 13.2mm M/39A machine-guns in wings; one flexible 7.9mm M/22 machine-gun in rear cockpit; max bomb load 1,500lb (680kg).
Crew: 2.
In Service: Denmark (9 B 17C),

Sweden.
Variants (with no. built):
SAAB–17 (L 10): Prototypes; one Nohab-built My XII (Bristol Pegasus XII), or 980hp SFA-built My XXIV (Bristol Pegasus XXIV) (2).
B 17A: Definitive production model; dive-bomber version; one 1,065hp SFA-built STWC3–G (unlicensed Pratt & Whitney SC3–G Twin Wasp) (132).
B 17B: Initial production model; dive-bomber version; 980hp My XXIV.
S 17B: Reconnaissance version of B 17B; camera equipment. (Total B 17B, S 17B: 76).
S 17BS: Maritime patrol (float-plane) version of B 17B (38).
B 17C: Re-engined B 17B; 1,200hp Piaggio P.XIbis (77).
Total Production: 325.
Remarks: First aircraft produced by SAAB, B 17B delivered Swedish AF 1942; remained in service until mid-fifties, latterly second-line ancillary roles;

equipped one Danish vol sqn based Sweden closing weeks WWII; 47 B 17As supplied post-war Ethiopian AF, served 1947 until late sixties.

Manufacturer: SAAB.
Model: B 18A.
Type: Light bomber/dive-bomber.
Power Plant: Two 1,065hp SFA-built Pratt & Whitney R–1830–S1C3–G Twin Wasp.
Performance:
maximum speed at 19,685ft (6,000m) 289mph (465km/hr).
cruising speed 258mph (415km/hr).
maximum range 1,367 miles (2,200km).
service ceiling 26,250ft (8,000m).
Weights:
empty 12,100lb (5,490kg).
loaded 17,946lb (8,140kg).
Dimensions:
wing span 55ft 9½in (17.0m).
length 43ft 5in (13.23m).
height 14ft 3½in (4.35m).
wing area 471sq ft (43.75sq m).

Variants (with no. built):
SAAB–18 (L 11): Prototype; dive-bomber version; two (unlicensed Swedish-built) 1,065hp Pratt & Whitney R–1830 Twin Wasp (2).
B 18A: Initial production model; dive-bomber version; as prototype.
S 18A: Reconnaissance version of B 18A; provision for Ska 5/13 cameras; subsequently equipped with radar.
(Total B 18A, S 18A: 60).
B 18B: Prototype and production model; dive-bomber version; re-engined B 18A; two 1,475hp Daimler–Benz DB 605B; pro-

vision for underwing rocket missiles (121).
T 18B: Original torpedo-bomber proposal; DB 605Bs; delivered as attack-bomber with fixed forward-firing two 29mm, plus one 57mm Bofors, cannon (62).
Total Production: 245.
Remarks: Designed for reconnais-

sance role, SAAB 18 requirement changed prior first flight to that of dive-bomber; both B 18A and S 18A began to enter service mid-1944; former supplemented/supplanted by more powerful B 18B immediate post-war years, latter retained until late fifties.

SWITZERLAND

Manufacturer: EKW.
Model: **C–35.**
Type: Reconnaissance/general-purpose.
Power Plant: One 860hp Hispano–Suiza 12Y 31.
Performance:
maximum speed at 13,120ft (4,000m) 208mph (335km/hr).
time to 16,400ft (5,000m) 8min 30sec.
service ceiling 32,810ft (10,000m).
Dimensions:
wing span 42ft 7¾in (13.0m).
length 30ft 4in (9.25m).
wing area 344.45sq ft (32.0sq m).
Armament: One 20mm Hispano–Suiza cannon firing through propeller hub, two 7.5mm machine-guns in lower wings; one flexible 7.5mm machine-gun in rear cockpit; max bomb load 220lb (100kg) underwing.
Crew: 2.
In Service: Switzerland.
Variants (with no. built):
C–35: Prototypes; two-seat reconnaissance/general-purpose biplane; one (Saurer/SLM licence-built) Hispano–Suiza 12Y 31 (2).
C–35: Production model; as prototypes; inc 8 subsequently assembled from spares (88).
Total Production: 90.
Remarks: Designed as Fokker C.V-E replacement for Swiss AF, indigenous C–35 derivative

EFW C-3603

(developed via licence-manufacture Dutch original) first flown 1936; entering service following year, equipped 6 sqns upon outbreak WWII; last examples retired 1948.

Manufacturer: EFW.
Model: **C–3603.**
Type: Reconnaissance-bomber.
Power Plant: One 1,020hp Hispano–Suiza 12Y 51.
Performance:
maximum speed at sea level 240mph (386km/hr).
maximum speed at 15,750ft (4,800m) 296mph (476km/hr).
time to 16,400ft (5,000m) 8min 0sec.
service ceiling 32,970ft (10,100m).
Weights:
empty 5,009lb (2,272kg).

maximum 8,713lb (3,952kg).
Dimensions:
wing span 41ft 1in (13.74m).
length 33ft 6½in (10.23m).
height 13ft 4in (4.07m).
wing area 308.92sq ft (28.7sq m).
Armament: One 20mm Oerlikon cannon firing through propeller hub, two 7.5mm machine-guns in wings and two flexible 7.5mm machine-guns in rear cockpit; max bomb load 880lb (400kg) underwing, plus (internal) 264lb (120kg) fragmentation bombs, or 132lb (60kg) incendiaries.
Crew: 2.
In Service: Switzerland.
Variants (with no. built):
C–3600: Proposed ground-attack version; single fin and rudder; project only.

C–3601/2: Prototypes; two-seat reconnaissance-bomber version; one 860hp Hispano–Suiza 12Ycrs and 1,000hp HS 12Y 51 resp; twin fins and rudders; fixed undercarriage (2).
C–3603: Production model; one (Saurer/SLM licence-built) Hispano–Suiza 12Y 51; retractable undercarriage; inc 2 completed as dual-control trainers and 6 assembled (post-war) from spares (152).
C–3604: Improved C–3603; one 1,250hp (Saurer/SLIM licence-built) Hispano–Suiza 12Y 52; two addn 20mm Oerlikon cannon in wings; provision for six 75mm rocket projectiles underwing; post-war production (13).

C–3605: Post-war development; target-tug version; one Avco Lycoming T5307A; one C–3603 conversion.
Total Production: 167.
Remarks: Initial prototype first flown early 1939, C–3603 entered service Spring 1942 as replacement earlier C–35 first-line reconnaissance duties; also participated day/night ground-attack/close-support manoeuvres and (1 sqn) flew neutrality patrols Swiss borders; only one recorded instance of actual combat when attacked in error by USAAF P–51 Mustangs, Sept 1944; gradually withdrawn operational service from late forties, number subsequently modified target-tug role; retired 1969.

USA

Manufacturer: Aeronca.
Model: **L–3 Grasshopper.**
Type: Liaison.
Power Plant: One 65hp Continental 0–170–3.
Performance:
maximum speed at sea level 87mph (139km/hr).
cruising speed 79mph (126km/hr).
normal range 190 miles (306km).
initial rate of climb 400ft/min (122m/min).
service ceiling 7,750ft (2,362m).
Weights:
empty 890lb (404kg).
maximum 1,450lb (658kg).
Dimensions:
wing span 35ft 0in (10.67m).
length 21ft 0in (6.40m).
height 7ft 88in (2.33m).
wing area 158sq ft (14.68sq m).
Crew: 2.
In Service: USA.
Variants (with no. built):
L–3: Dual-control trainer; 65hp Continental 0–170–3 (54).
L–3A: Widened fuselage (20).
L–3B: Increased cabin window area; first fully militarized version (875).
L–3C; Reduced weight; modified radio equipment (490).
L–3D/H and J: Dual-control civil tourers; no service modifications; various power plants (48).
TG–5: Glider-trainer version; 3-control seat; modified L–3; inc 3 for USN (253).
Total Production: 1,740.
Remarks: Pre-war civil tandem trainer; original military designation 0–58; saw limited overseas use in liaison role; majority retained in USA and employed in training capacities.

Manufacturer: Beech.
Model: **UC–43 Traveler.**
Type: Light transport/communications.
Power Plant: One 450hp Pratt & Whitney R–985–AN–1 or 3.
Performance:
maximum speed at 5,000ft (1,525m) 195mph (312kmIhr).
range 500 miles (800km).

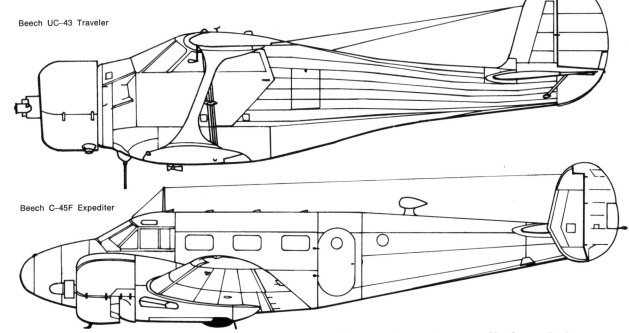

Beech UC-43 Traveler

Beech C-45F Expediter

initial rate of climb 1,500ft/min (455m/min).
service ceiling 20,000ft (6,100m).
Weights:
empty 3,085lb (1,400kg).
maximum 4,700lb (2,132kg).
Dimensions:
wing span 32ft 0in (9.75m).
length 26ft 2in (7.97m).
height 10ft 3in (3.12m).
wing area 296sq ft (27.5sq m).
Crew/Accommodation: 1/4.
In Service: Australia (4 Model 17

impressed), Finland (1 Model 17 impressed), Great Britain (RAF, FAA), USA (USAAF, USN, USMC).
Variants (with no. built):
Model 17: Civil versions; (pre- and post-war production) (248).
YC–43: Civil D–175s purchased for evaluation (3).
UC–43: Standard service variant (207).
UC–43A/H, J and K: Impressed civil models; various power plants (118).

GB–1, GB–2: USN equivalents of UC–43s; 8 civil impressments, plus 63 UC–43s assigned ex-USAAF (423).
Traveller: RAF, FAA equivalent of above; 105 Lend-Lease.
Total Production: 740.
Remarks: Employed by both USAAF and USN/USMC for light communications duties; many civil 'Staggerwings' impressed during early 1942; majority British lend-lease deliveries to FAA.

Manufacturer: Beech.
Model: **C–45 Expediter.**
Type: Light transport.
Power Plant: Two 450hp Pratt & Whitney R–985–AN–1.
Performance:
maximum speed 215 mph (346km/hr).
maximum range 700 miles (1,126km).
time to 10,000ft (3,048m) 8 min 36sec.
service ceiling 20,000ft (6,096m).

Weights:
empty 5,890lb (2,672kg).
maximum 7,850lb (3,560kg).
Dimensions:
wing span 47ft 8in (14.5m).
length 34ft 3in (10.4m).
height 9ft 8in (2.8m).
wing area 349sq ft (32.4sq m).
Crew/Accommodation: 2/6–8.
In Service: Canada, China, Great
Britain (RAF, FAA), USA
(USAAF, USN, USMC).
Variants (with no. built):
Model 18: Civil versions (pre- and
post-war production (approx
1,970).
C–45: C–18s purchased by
USAAF; 450hp Pratt & Whitney
R–985–17 (11).
C–45A: 8-seat version (20).
C–45B Redesigned interior (223).
C–45C/E: Impressed civil variants
(10).
C–45F: 7-seat version; lengthened
nose (1,137).
AT–7A/C and AT–11: Trainer
versions (5,257).
F–2: Civil B–18s; modified
photographic reconnaissance
version; two .3in guns, ten
100lb (45kg) bombs (56).
JRB–1/4 and SNB–1/2: USN/
USMC versions of C–45 (377)
and AT–7/11 (1,364) resp.
Expediter: British and Canadian
designation; 430 Lend-Lease.
deliveries (RAF, FAA).
Total Production: approx 9,100.
Remarks: Development of civil
Beechcraft Model 18 first flown
Jan 1937; standard US bombardier/
navigation trainer of WWII; also
world-wide employment on light
transport and communications
duties; RAF machines used
primarily SEAC theatre.

Manufacturer: Bell.
Model: P–39D Airacobra.
Type: Interceptor fighter.
Power Plant: One 1,150hp
Allison V–1710–35.
Performance:
maximum speed at 5,000ft
(1,524m) 335mph (539km/hr).
maximum range 600 miles
(965km).
time to 5,000ft (1,524m) 1min
54sec.
service ceiling 29,000ft (8,840m).
Weights:
empty 5,462lb (2,478kg).
loaded 7,845lb (3,558kg).
Dimensions:
wing span 34ft 0in (10.36m).
length 30ft 2in (9.19m).
height 11ft 10in (3.60m).
wing area 213sq ft (19.79sq m).
Armament: One 37mm cannon
firing through propeller hub; two
fuselage-mounted .5in guns; two
.3in guns in outer wings; provision
for one 500lb (227kg) bomb.
Crew: 1.
In Service: France (FAF, FFAF),
Great Britain (284), Italy (ICoAF;
149 P–39N/Q), Portugal, USA,
USSR (4,924).
Variants (with no. built):
XP–39: Prototype; B–5 turbo-
supercharger (1).
YP–39: Service test versions; one
without supercharger (YP–39A)
(13).
XP–39B: Converted prototype.
P–39C: Modified YP–39 (20).
P–39D: Fully militarized version;
self-sealing tanks; various
armaments (863).
XP–39E: Experimental version
only (3).
P–39F: With Aeroproducts
propeller (229).
P–39G: Delivered as P–39K/N.
P–39J: Modified P–39F; 1,100hp
V–1710–59 (25).
P–39K/M/N: V1–170–63/83/85
engines respectively (2,545).
P–39L: Curtiss Electric propeller
(250).
P–39Q: 3 versions; 37mm cannon;
two 5in guns each in cowling
and wing fairing; 3- or 4-blade
props (4,905).
P–400 Retained from British order
(179).
Airacobra I: RAF equivalent of
P–39, 212 diverted to USSR
(497).
Total Production: 9,590.
Remarks: Innovatory tricycle
undercarriage, mid-engine design;
limited yet widespread US employment by 13 groups, serving North
(Aleutians) and South Pacific
(Guadalcanal), New Guinea,
Tunisia and Italy; UK-based group
flew just one mission; RAF
employment (one sqn) likewise
restricted to single operation; operated by FFAF in Mediterranean
theatre and Italian Co-Belligerent
AF over Yugoslavia; over half
total production to USSR, widely
used in ground-support role.

Manufacturer: Bell.
Model: P–63A Kingcobra.
Type: Fighter/fighter bomber.
Power Plant: One 1,325hp Allison
V–1710–93.
Performance:
maximum speed at 5,000ft
(1,524m) 361mph (581km/hr).
cruising speed 378mph (608km/hr).
maximum range 2,200 miles
(3,540km).
time to 25,000ft (7,620m) 7min
18sec.
service ceiling 43,000ft (13,106m).
Weights:
empty 6,375lb (2,892kg).
maximum 10,500lb (4,763kg).
Dimensions:
wing span 38ft 4in (11.63m).
length 32ft 8in (9.95m).
height 12ft 7in (3.83m).
wing area 248sq ft (23.04sq m).
Armament: One 37mm and two
.5 in fixed nose guns firing
forward; one .5in gun beneath
each wing; three 500lb (227kg)
bombs.
Crew: 1.
In Service: France (300 P–63),
Great Britain (2 evaluation only),
USA, USSR (2,421).
Variants (with no. built):
XP–63/A: Prototypes; modified
P–39s (3).
P–63A: 6 versions; various bomb/
rocket loads (1,725).
P–63C: V–1710–117 engine;
ventral fin (1,227).
P–63D: Modified wing, 'bubble'
cockpit; V–1710–109 engine (1).
P–63E: As D but standard
cockpit (13).
P–63F: Modified P–63E;
V–1710–135; revised fin and
rudder (2).
RP–63A/C/G: Manned target
aircraft (332).
Kingcobra: RAF equivalent of
P–63; evaluation only (2).
Total Production: 3,305.

Remarks: Evolved from earlier
P–39; entered service Winter
1943–44; limited USAAF service;
300 to France, but two-thirds of
all production delivered to USSR.

Manufacturer: Bellanca.
Model: C–27C.
Type: Transport.
Power Plant: One 750hp Wright
R–1820–25 Cyclone.
Performance:
maximum speed 143mph (230km/hr).
Weights:
empty 5,402lb (2,450kg).
loaded 9,655lb (4,380kg).
Dimensions:
wing span 65ft 0in (18.81m).
length 42ft 9in (13.03m).
wing area 737sq ft (68.47sq m).
Crew/Accommodation: 1/14.
In Service: USA.
Variants (with no. built):
P–100/300 Airbus: Initial produc-
tion; 9- or 15-seat single-engined
civil transport sesquiplane;
various alt power plants.
Y1C–27: Militarized Airbus;
12-seat; cargo loading doors;
one 550hp Pratt & Whitney
R–1860 Hornet (4).
C–27A: Modified Y1C–27; 15-seat;
one 650hp R–1860–19 Hornet (10).
C–27B: Re-engined C–27A; one
675hp Wright R–1820–17 Cyclone;
1 conversion).
C–27C: Re-engined Y1C–27/C-
27A; one 750hp Wright
R–1820–25 Cyclone; 13
conversions.
Remarks: Military development
of civil Airbus series, C–27 entered
USAAC service 1933; several still
employed ZI second-line transport/
ancillary duties early months
WWII.

Manufacturer: Boeing.
Model: F4B–4 (and P–12F).
Type: Fighter.

Power Plant: One 500hp Pratt
& Whitney R–1340–16.
Performance:
maximum speed at 6,000ft
(1,829m) 184mph (296km/hr).
cruising speed 160mph (257km/hr).
range 370 miles (595km).
time to 5,000ft (1,525m) 2min 42sec.
service ceiling 24,800ft (7,559m).
Weights:
empty 2,312lb (1,049kg).
loaded 3,087lb (1,400kg).
Dimensions:
wing span 30ft 0in (9.14m).
length 20ft 4½in (6.22m).
height 9ft 9in (2.97m).
wing area 227.5sq ft (21.13sq m).
Armament: Two fixed forward-
firing .3in machine-guns; or one
.5in and one .3in machine-gun;
provision for two 116lb (53kg)
bombs underwing.
Crew: 1.
In Service: Japan, Thailand, USA
(USAAF, USN, USMC).
Variants (with no. built):
F4B–1/4: Pre-war USN, USMC
service versions (188).
P–12B/F: Pre-war USAAC
service versions (366).
Model 100: Commercial version
of P–12; inc one to Japan (4).
Model 100A: 2-seat Model 100 (1).
Model 100E: Thai order (2).
Model 100F: Engine test bed (1).
Total Production: 562.
Remarks: Both F4Bs and P–12s
long obsolete by outbreak of
Pacific War; but several examples
of former pressed into service for
emergency home-defence duties
during immediate post-Pearl
Harbor period; one Thai machine
taken over by Japan; an all-metal
development of P–12, Model 218,
was taken to China for demonstration purposes, where it became
first US fighter to destroy an
enemy aircraft during Sino-
Japanese conflict; itself subse-

quently shot down during dogfight
near Shanghai.

Manufacturer: Boeing.
Model: P–26A.
Type: Fighter.
Power Plant: One 500hp Pratt
& Whitney R–1340–27.
Performance:
maximum speed at 6,000ft
(1,829m) 234mph (376km/hr).
cruising speed 200mph (322km/hr).
range 360 miles (580km).
initial rate of climb 2,360ft/min
(720m/min).
service ceiling 27,400ft (8,352m).
Weights:
empty 2,196lb (996kg).
loaded 2,955lb (1,336kg).
Dimensions:
wing span 27ft 11½in (8.52m).
length 23ft 10in (7.21m).
height 10ft 5in (3.17m).
wing area 149.5sq ft (13.89sq m).
Armament: Two .3in machine-
guns; or one .3in and one .5in
machine-gun; provision for two
100lb (45kg), or five 30lb (14kg)
bombs under fuselage or underwing.
Crew: 1.
In Service: China (11 Model 281),
Philippines (P–26A), Spain (1
Model 281), USA.
Variants (with no. built):
XP–936: Prototypes (3).
P–26A: Production version (111).
P–26B/C: Modified P–26As (25).
Model 281: Re-engined P–26A;
export version (12).
Total Production: 151.
Remarks: Boeing's famous
'Peashooter' equipped 7 pre-war
USAAC groups; Chinese machines
employed in defence of Nanking
and Shanghai, scoring considerable
success against Japanese bombers;
P–26As of Philippine Air Corps
engaged during Japanese invasion,
8 Dec 1941, all believed lost.

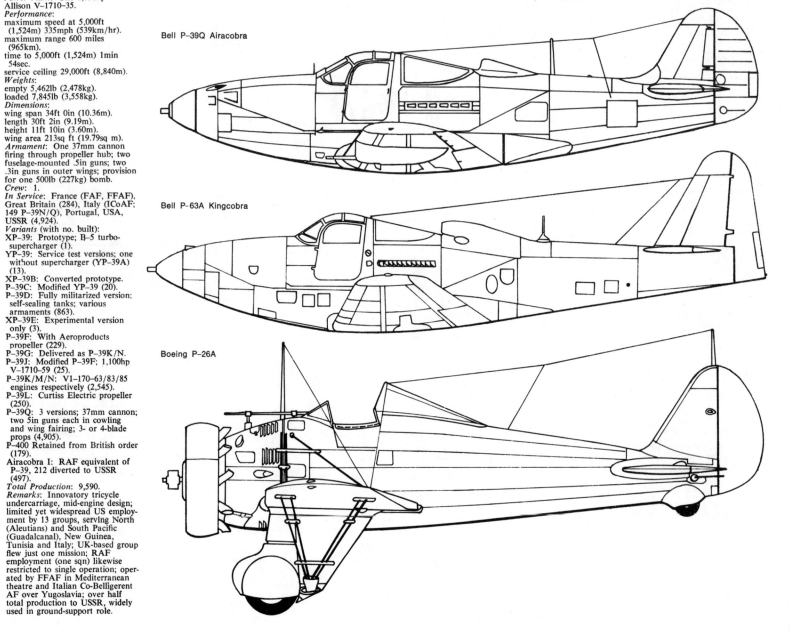

Bell P–39Q Airacobra

Bell P–63A Kingcobra

Boeing P–26A

Manufacturer: Boeing.
Model: 247D (C-73).
Type: Transport.
Power Plant: Two 550hp Pratt & Whitney Wasp S1H-1G.
Performance:
maximum speed 200mph (322km/hr).
cruising speed 189mph (304km/hr).
range 745 miles (1,199km).
service ceiling 18,400ft (5,608m).
Weights:
maximum 13,650lb (6,192kg).
Dimensions:
wing span 74ft 0in (22.56m).
length 51ft 7in (15.72m).
height 12ft 1¾in (3.69m).
wing area 836sq ft (77.66sq m).
Crew/Accommodation: 3/10 (civil version).
In Service: Canada (8), China (1), Great Britain (1), USA (27).
Variants (with no. built):
247: Civil airliner; majority converted to 247D standard (61).
247A: Executive/research model; 625hp Twin Wasps (1).
247D: Modified 247; redesigned windscreen and tail surfaces (13).
247Y: Armed transport; three .303in machine-guns; one 247D conversion.
C-73: USAAF designation for impressed civil 247Ds (27).
Total Production: 75.
Remarks: Operated by USAAF and RCAF as troop/crew transport, later trainer; single RAF example employed on communications/research duties; armed 247Y delivered to China for personal use of Provincial Military Governor; believed destroyed during Sino-Japanese conflict.

Manufacturer: Boeing.
Model: Stratoliner (C-75).
Type: Transport.
Power Plant: Four 1,100hp Wright Cyclone GR-1820.
Performance:
maximum speed at 17,300ft (5,273m) 246mph (396km/hr).
cruising speed 220mph (354km/hr).
range 2,390 miles (3,846km).
Weights:
loaded 42,000lb (19,051kg).
Dimensions:
wing span 107ft 3in (32.69m).
length 74ft 4in (22.66m).
height 20ft 9in (6.32m).
wing area 1,486sq ft (138.05sq m).
Crew/Accommodation: 5/33 (civil version).
In Service: USA.
Variants (with no. built):
Prototype: (1).
S-307: Civil airliner; initial production model (3).
SA-307B: Modified S-307 (5).
SB-307B: Personnel transport; 1,600hp Twin Cyclones (1).
C-75: USAAF designation for

impressed civil SA-307Bs.
Total Production: 10.
Remarks: Three S-307 and five SA-307B impressments; employed by USAAF as VIP-transports, primarily on North and South Atlantic routes, 1942-44.

Manufacturer: Boeing.
Model: Model 314 Clipper (C-98).
Type: Long-range transport flying boat.
Power Plant: Four 1,600hp Wright Double Cyclone R-2600.
Performance:
maximum speed 193mph (311km/hr).
cruising speed 183mph (295km/hr).
range 3,500 miles (5,632km).
Weights:
loaded 82,500lb (37,422kg).
Dimensions:
wing span 152ft 0in (46.33m).
length 106ft 0in (32.31m).
height 27ft 7in (8.40m).
wing area 2,867sq ft (266.3sq m).
Crew/Accommodation: 10/77 (civil version).
In Service: USA (USAAF, USN).
Variants (with no. built):
314: Civil flying-boat airliner; 1,500hp Double Cyclones; five subsequently converted to 314As (6).
314A: Modified 314 (6).
C-98: USAAF designation for impressed civil 314 and 314A.
B-314: USN designation.
Total Production: 12.
Remarks: Three 314A, and one converted 314 impressed by USAAF in 1942 for long-range transport duties as C-98; three later passed to USN, together with two direct ex-PanAm, as B-314.

Manufacturer: Boeing.
Model: XC-105.
Type: Transport.
Power Plant: Four 1,000hp Pratt & Whitney R-1830-11.
Performance:
maximum speed 190mph (306km/hr).
Weights:
maximum 92,000lb (41,731kg).
Dimensions:
wing span 149ft 0in (45.42m).
length 87ft 11in (26.79m).
height 18ft 0in (5.49m).
Crew: 6.
In Service: USA.
Variants (with no. built):
XB-15: Long-range bomber; experimental (1).
XC-105: Transport; XB-15 conversion; cargo-doors and hoist.
Total Production: 1.
Remarks: Originally intended as long-range bomber; single prototype converted in 1943 to utility transport.

Manufacturer: Boeing.
Model: B-17C (Flying) Fortress.
Type: High-altitude heavy bomber.
Power Plant: Four 1,200hp Wright Cyclone R-1820-65.
Performance:
maximum speed at 25,000ft (7,620m) 291mph (468km/hr).
cruising speed 250mph (402km/hr).
maximum range 3,400 miles (5,471km).
time to 10,000ft (3,048m) 7min 30 sec.
service ceiling 37,000ft (11,278m).
Weights:
empty 30,600lb (13,880kg).
maximum 49,650lb (22,520kg).
Dimensions:
wing span 103ft 9in (31.62m).
length 67ft 11in (20.70m).
height 15ft 5in (4.70m).
wing area 1,420sq ft (131.92sq m).
Armament: One 3in machine-gun in nose; two .5in guns in top and ventral positions; one .5in gun in each fuselage side; bomb load 10,496lb (4,761kg).
Crew: 9.
In Service: Great Britain (20), USA.
Variants (with no. built):
Prototype (XB-17): Model 299; private venture (1).
YB-17: Service test model; later re-designated B-17 (13).
YB-17A: As YB-17 but 1,000hp supercharged R-1820-51s; re-designated B-17A (1).
B-17B: Modified B-17A; re-designed nose (39).
B-17C: Re-engined B-17B; increased weight and armament; fuselage-side gun blisters deleted (38).
B-17D: Modified B-17C; one addn crew (42).
Fortress Mk I: RAF equivalent of B-17C (20).
Total Production: 12,731 (all Marks).
Remarks: First operational models of America's most famous WWII bomber; B-17D serving in Philippines on outbreak of Pacific War; over half destroyed on ground during initial Japanese attacks; remainder fought gallant rearguard actions from Philippines, through East Indies, to Australia; one survivor withdrawn to USA early 1942; RAF Fortress Is (one sqn) operational debut, July 1941; easy prey for German fighters—severe losses; four machines subsequently to Middle East as night-bombers, others transferred to Coastal Command for maritime reconnaissance role.

Manufacturer: Boeing.
Model: B-17F Flying Fortress.
Type: High-altitude heavy bomber.
Power Plant: Four 1,200hp

Wright R-1820-97.
Performance:
maximum speed at 25,000ft (7,620m) 325mph (523km/hr).
cruising speed 160mph (257km/hr).
maximum range 4,420 miles (7,112km).
Weights:
empty 35,728lb (16,206kg).
maximum 72,000lb (32,660kg).
Dimensions:
wing span 103ft 9½in (31.63m).
length 74ft 9in (22.78m).
height 19ft 2½in (5.85m).
wing area 1,420sq ft (131.92sq m).
Armament: One .3in Browning machine-gun in nose; twelve .5in Browning machine-guns in dorsal, ventral, waist and tail positions; various bomb arrangements; max bomb load 17,600lb (7,983kg).
Crew: 10.
In Service: Germany (5+), Great Britain (64), USA (USAAF, USN (1 B-17F)).
Variants (with no. built):
B-17E: Modified B-17D; additional armament; redesigned tail surfaces (512).
B-17F: Improved B-17E; frameless Plexiglas nose; various armament. Boeing-built (2,300); Douglas-built (605); Lockheed Vega-built (500).
CB-17: VIP transport versions; various B-17 conversions.
VB-17: Staff transport version; similar to CB-17; B-17 conversions.
X/YB-40: Armed escort version; 21 B-17F conversions.
TB-40: Trainer version; 4 B-17F conversions.
XB-38: Re-engined B-17E; one conversion.
XC-108, 108A/B, YC-108: Various transport versions; B-17E and F conversions (4).
BQ-7: Pilotless flying bomb; approx 25 B-17E and F conversions.
Fortress Mk II: RAF equivalent of B-17F; 19 Lend-Lease.
Fortress Mk IIA: RAF equivalent of B-17E; 45 Lend-Lease.
Total Production: 12,731 (all Marks).
Remarks: Early B-17Es to Pacific to replace Ds; majority to UK to equip newly-constituted 8th AF; operational debut 17 Aug 1942—twelve B-17Es attacked Rouen marshalling-yards; soon supplemented by improved F-model; first attacks against Germany proper, Jan 1943; tempo increased throughout year; also equipped 15th AF based Italy; with introduction of B-17G (late 1943) several 'war-weary' Es and Fs stripped of equipment and used as BQ-7 radio-controlled bombs, Summer 1944; others converted to transport/freighter configura-

tions; RAF Fortress II/IIAs employed predominantly by Coastal Command; a number of US aircraft (Fs and Gs) captured by Germany; used in evaluation, fighter-training, and clandestine roles.
Colour Reference: Plate 155: Boeing B-17F Flying Fortress (41-24587) GN.P 'Bad Check' of 427th Bomb Squadron, 303rd Bomb Group (Heavy) 'Hell's Angels', 8th USAAF, Molesworth, Hunts, late 1943; olive drab upper surfaces with medium green dapple over fuselage and tail surfaces; standard Group (triangle 'C') tail markings and Squadron/aircraft fuselage codes, plus Squadron 'Bugs Bunny' emblem on port side of nose; 'Bad Check' one of ten B-17s lost by 303rd to German defences over Oschersleben, 11 Jan 1944.

Manufacturer: Boeing.
Model: B-17G Flying Fortress.
Type: High-altitude heavy bomber.
Power Plant: Four 1,200hp Wright R-1820-97.
Performance:
maximum speed at 25,000ft (7,620m) 302mph (486km/hr).
cruising speed 160mph (257km/hr).
range 3,400 miles (5,470km).
time to 20,000ft (6,096m) 37min 0sec.
service ceiling 35,600ft (10,850m).
Weights:
empty 36,135lb (16,391kg).
maximum 72,000lb (32,660kg).
Dimensions:
wing span 103ft 9½in (31.62m).
length 74ft 9in (22.78m).
height 19ft 1in (5.82m).
wing area 1,420sq ft (131.92sq m).
Armament: Thirteen .5in Browning machine-guns in chin, cheek, ventral, dorsal. waist and tail positions; max bomb load 17,600lb (7,983kg).
Crew: 10.
In Service: Germany, Great Britain (85), USA (USAAF, USN, 1 B-17G), USSR (1+ sequestrated).
Variants (with no built):
B-17G: Improved B-17F; additional power-operated chin turret; Boeing-built (4,035); Lockheed Vega-built (2,250); Douglas-built (2,395).
B-17H: Air-sea-rescue version; approx 50+ B-17G conversions; re-designated SB-17G.
F-9, 9A/C: Long-range photographic reconnaissance versions 73+ B-17F and G conversions.
TB-17G: Trainer version; B-17 conversions.

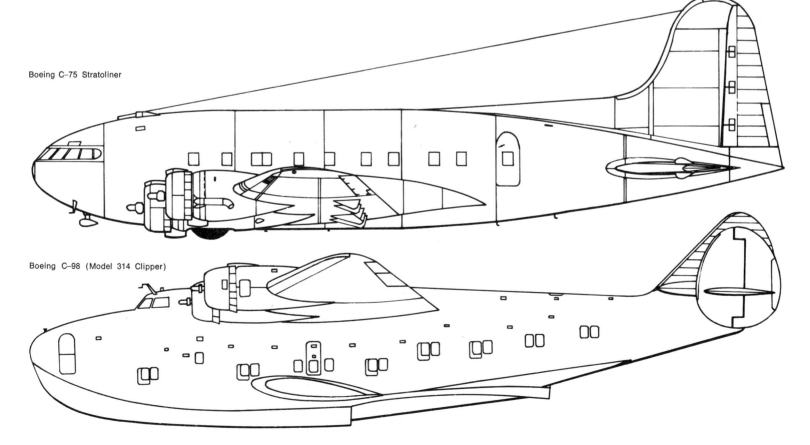

Boeing C-75 Stratoliner

Boeing C-98 (Model 314 Clipper)

Order of Battle June 1944, Northern Europe

UNITED STATES ARMY AIR FORCES

United States 8th Army Air Force (Strategic)

7th Photographic Group (Reconnaissance):
(13, 14 & 22 Sqns.) Mount Farm Lockheed F–5
482nd Bombardment Group (Pathfinder):
(812, 813 & 814 Sqns.)Alconbury Boeing B–17 Flying Fortress
Consolidated B–24 Liberator
801st Bombardment Group (Provisional):
(36, 406, 788 & 850
Sqns.) Harrington Consolidated B–24 Liberator
802nd Reconnaissance Group (Provisional):
(652, 653 & 654 Sqns.)Watton Consolidated B–24 Liberator
De Havilland Mosquito
803rd Reconnaissance Squadron:
(Provisional) Oulton Boeing B–17 Flying Fortress

1st Bombardment Division

1st Combat Bombardment Wing (Heavy):
91st Bombardment Group (H):
(322, 323, 324 & 401
Sqns.) Bassingbourn Boeing B–17 Flying Fortress
381st Bombardment Group (H):
(532, 533, 534 & 535
Sqns.) Ridgewell Boeing B–17 Flying Fortress
398th Bombardment Group (H):
(600, 601, 602 & 603
Sqns.) Nuthampstead Boeing B–17 Flying Fortress
40th Combat Bombardment Wing (Heavy):
92nd Bombardment Group (H):
(325, 326, 327 & 407
Sqns.) Podington Boeing B–17 Flying Fortress
303rd Bombardment Group (H):
(358, 359, 360 & 427
Sqns.) Molesworth Boeing B–17 Flying Fortress
305th Bombardment Group (H):
(364, 365, 366 & 422
Sqns.) Chelveston Boeing B–17 Flying Fortress
306th Bombardment Group (H):
(367, 368, 369 & 423
Sqns.) Thurleigh Boeing B–17 Flying Fortress
41st Combat Bombardment Wing (Heavy):
379th Bombardment Group (H):
(524, 525, 526 & 527
Sqns.) Kimbolton Boeing B–17 Flying Fortress
384th Bombardment Group (H):
(524, 525, 526 & 527
Sqns.) Grafton Underwood Boeing B–17 Flying Fortress
94th Combat Bombardment Wing (Heavy):
351st Bombardment Group (H):
(508, 509, 510 & 511
Sqns.) Polebrook Boeing B–17 Flying Fortress
401st Bombardment Group (H):
(612, 613, 614 & 615
Sqns.) Deenethorpe Boeing B–17 Flying Fortress
457th Bombardment Group (H):
(748, 749, 750 & 751
Sqns.) Glatton Boeing B–17 Flying Fortress

2nd Bombardment Division

2nd Combat Bombardment Wing (Heavy):
389th Bombardment Group (H):
(564, 565, 566 & 567
Sqns.) Hethel Consolidated B–24 Liberator
445th Bombardment Group (H):
(700, 701, 702 & 703
Sqns.) Tibenham Consolidated B–24 Liberator
453rd Bombardment Group (H):
(732, 733, 734 & 735
Sqns.) Old Buckenham Consolidated B–24 Liberator
14th Combat Bombardment Wing (Heavy):
44th Bombardment Group (H):
(66, 67, 68 & 506
Sqns.) Shipdham Consolidated B–24 Liberator
392nd Bombardment Group (H):
(576, 577, 578 & 579
Sqns.) Wendling Consolidated B–24 Liberator
492nd Bombardment Group (H):
(856, 857, 858 & 859
Sqns.) North Pickenham Consolidated B–24 Liberator
20th Combat Bombardment Wing (Heavy):
93rd Bombardment Group (H):
(328, 329, 330 & 409
Sqns.) Hardwick Consolidated B–24 Liberator
446th Bombardment Group (H):
(704, 705, 706 & 707
Sqns.) Bungay Consolidated B–24 Liberator
448th Bombardment Group (H):
(712, 713, 714 & 715
Sqns.) Seething Consolidated B–24 Liberator
95th Combat Bombardment Wing (Heavy):
489th Bombardment Group (H):
(844, 845, 846 & 847
Sqns.) Halesworth Consolidated B–24 Liberator
491st Bombardment Group (H):
(852, 853, 854 & 855
Sqns.) Metfield Consolidated B–24 Liberator
96th Combat Bombardment Wing (Heavy):
458th Bombardment Group (H):
(752, 753, 754 & 755
Sqns.) Horsham St. Faith Consolidated B–24 Liberator
466th Bombardment Group (H):
(784, 785, 786 & 787
Sqns.) Attlebridge Consolidated B–24 Liberator
467th Bombardment Group (H):
(788, 789, 790 & 791
Sqns.) Rackheath Consolidated B–24 Liberator

3rd Bombardment Division

4th Combat Bombardment Wing (Heavy):
94th Bombardment Group (H):
(331, 332, 333 & 410
Sqns.) Bury St. Edmunds Boeing B–17 Flying Fortress
385th Bombardment Group (H):
(548, 549, 550 & 551
Sqns.) Great Ashfield Boeing B–17 Flying Fortress
447th Bombardment Group (H):
(708, 709, 710 & 711
Sqns.) Rattlesden Boeing B–17 Flying Fortress

13th Combat Bombardment Wing (Heavy):
95th Bombardment Group (H):
(334, 335, 336 & 412
Sqns.) Horham Boeing B–17 Flying Fortress
100th Bombardment Group (H):
(349, 350, 351 & 418
Sqns.) Thorpe Abbotts Boeing B–17 Flying Fortress
390th Bombardment Group (H):
(568, 569, 570 & 571
Sqns.) Framlingham Boeing B–17 Flying Fortress
45th Combat Bombardment Wing (Heavy):
96th Bombardment Group (H):
(337, 338, 339 & 413
Sqns.) Snetterton Heath Boeing B–17 Flying Fortress
388th Bombardment Group (H):
(560, 561, 562 & 563
Sqns.) Knettishall Boeing B–17 Flying Fortress
452nd Bombardment Group (H):
(728, 729, 730 & 731
Sqns.) Deopham Green Boeing B–17 Flying Fortress
92nd Combat Bombardment Wing (Heavy):
486th Bombardment Group (H):
(832, 833, 834 & 835
Sqns.) Sudbury Consolidated B–24 Liberator
487th Bombardment Group (H):
(836, 837, 838 & 839
Sqns.) Lavenham Consolidated B–24 Liberator
93rd Combat Bombardment Wing (Heavy):
34th Bombardment Group (H):
(4, 7, 18 & 391
Sqns.) Mendlesham Consolidated B–24 Liberator
490th Bombardment Group (H):
(848, 849, 850 & 851
Sqns.) Eye Consolidated B–24 Liberator
493rd Bombardment Group (H):
(860, 861, 862 & 863
Sqns.) Debach Consolidated B–24 Liberator

VIII Fighter Command

65th Fighter Wing:
4th Fighter Group
(334, 335 & 336
Sqns.) Debden Nth. American P–51 Mustang
56th Fighter Group
(61, 62 & 63 Sqns.) Boxted Republic P–47 Thunderbolt
355th Fighter Group
(354, 357 & 358
Sqns.) Steeple Morden Nth. American P–51 Mustang
356th Fighter Group
(359, 360 & 361
Sqns.) Martlesham Heath Republic P–47 Thunderbolt
479th Fighter Group
(434, 435 & 436
Sqns.) Wattisham Lockheed P–38 Lightning
Detachment B
(ASR Squadron) Boxted Republic P–47 Thunderbolt
66th Fighter Wing:
55th Fighter Group
(38, 338 & 343
Sqns.) Wormingford Lockheed P–38 Lightning
78th Fighter Group
(82, 83 & 84 Sqns.) Duxford Republic P–47 Thunderbolt
339th Fighter Group
(503, 504 & 505 Sqns.) Fowlmere Nth. American P–51 Mustang
353rd Fighter Group
(350, 351 & 352 Sqns.) Raydon Republic P–47 Thunderbolt
357th Fighter Group
(362, 363 & 364 Sqns.) Leiston Nth. American P–51 Mustang
67th Fighter Wing:
20th Fighter Group
(55, 77 & 79 Sqns.) Kingscliffe Lockheed P–38 Lightning
352nd Fighter Group
(328, 486 & 487 Sqns.) Bodney Republic P–47 Thunderbolt
359th Fighter Group
(368, 369 & 370
Sqns.) East Wretham Republic P–47 Thunderbolt
361st Fighter Group
(374, 375 & 376
Sqns.) Bottisham Republic P–47 Thunderbolt
364th Fighter Group
(383, 384 & 385 Sqns.) Honington Lockheed P–38 Lightning

United States 9th Army Air Force (Tactical)

IX Bomber Command

1st Pathfinder Sqn.
(Provisional) Great Saling Martin B–26 Marauder
97th Combat Bombardment Wing (Medium):
409th Bombardment Group (L):
(640, 641, 642 & 643
Sqns.) Little Walden Douglas A–20 Havoc
410th Bombardment Group (L):
(644, 645, 646 & 647
Sqns.) Gosfield Douglas A–20 Havoc
416th Bombardment Group (L):
(668, 689, 670 & 671
Sqns.) Wethersfield Douglas A–20 Havoc
98th Combat Bombardment Wing (Medium):
323rd Bombardment Group (M):
(453, 454, 455 & 456
Sqns.) Horham Martin B–26 Marauder
387th Bombardment Group (M):
(556, 557, 558 & 559
Sqns.) Chipping Ongar Martin B–26 Marauder
394th Bombardment Group (M):
(584, 585, 586 & 587
Sqns.) Boreham Martin B–26 Marauder
397th Bombardment Group (M):
(596, 597, 598 & 599
Sqns.) Rivenhall Martin B–26 Marauder
99th Combat Bombardment Wing (Medium):
322nd Bombardment Group (M):
(449, 450, 451 & 452
Sqns.) Great Saling Martin B–26 Marauder
344th Bombardment Group (M):
(494, 495, 496 & 497
Sqns.) Stansted Martin B–26 Marauder

386th Bombardment Group (M):
(552, 553, 554 & 555
Sqns.) Great Dunmow Martin B–26 Marauder
391st Bombardment Group (M):
(572, 573, 574 & 575
Sqns.) Matching Martin B–26 Marauder

IX Fighter Command

IX Tactical Air Command:
67th Tactical Reconnaissance Lockheed F–5
Group Middle Wallop North American F–6
70th Fighter Wing:
48th Fighter Group
(492, 493 & 494 Sqns.) Ibsley Republic P–47 Thunderbolt
367th Fighter Group
(392, 393 & 394
Sqns.) Stony Cross Lockheed P–38 Lightning
371st Fighter Group
(404, 405 & 406
Sqns.) Bisterne Republic P–47 Thunderbolt
474th Fighter Group
(428, 429 & 430 Sqns.) Moreton Lockheed P–38 Lightning
71st Fighter Wing:
366th Fighter Group
(389, 390 & 391
Sqns.) Thruxton Republic P–47 Thunderbolt
368th Fighter Group
(395, 396 & 397
Sqns.) Chilbolton Republic P–47 Thunderbolt
370th Fighter Group
(401, 402 & 403
Sqns.) Andover Lockheed P–38 Lightning
84th Fighter Wing:
50th Fighter Group
(10, 81 & 313 Sqns.) Lymington Republic P–47 Thunderbolt
365th Fighter Group
(386, 387 & 388 Sqns.) Beaulieu Republic P–47 Thunderbolt
404th Fighter Group
(506, 507 & 508
Sqns.) Winkton Republic P–47 Thunderbolt
405th Fighter Group
(509, 510 & 511
Sqns.) Christchurch Republic P–47 Thunderbolt
XIX Tactical Air Command:
10th Photographic Douglas F–3A
Group Lockheed F–5
(Reconnaissance) Chalgrove North American F–6
100th Fighter Wing:
354th Fighter Group
(353, 355 & 356
Sqns.) Lashenden Nth. American P–51 Mustang
358th Fighter Group
(365, 366 & 367
Sqns.) High Halden Republic P–47 Thunderbolt
362nd Fighter Group
(377, 378 & 379
Sqns.) Headcorn Republic P–47 Thunderbolt
363rd Fighter Group
(380, 381 & 382
Sqns.) Staplehurst Nth. American P–51 Mustang
303rd Fighter Wing:
36th Fighter Group
(22, 23 & 53 Sqns.) Kingsnorth Republic P–47 Thunderbolt
373rd Fighter Group
(410, 411 & 412
Sqns.) Woodchurch Republic P–47 Thunderbolt
406th Fighter Group
(512, 513 & 514
Sqns.) Ashford Republic P–47 Thunderbolt

IX Troop Carrier Command

50th Troop Carrier Wing:
439th Troop Carrier Group:
(91, 92, 93 & 94
Sqns.) Upottery Douglas C–47 Skytrain
440th Troop Carrier Group:
(95, 96, 97 & 98
Sqns.) Exeter Douglas C–47 Skytrain
441st Troop Carrier Group:
(99, 100, 301 & 302
Sqns.) Merryfield Douglas C–47 Skytrain
442nd Troop Carrier Group:
(303, 304, 305 & 306
Sqns.) Fulbeck Douglas C–47 Skytrain
Douglas C–53 Skytrooper
52nd Troop Carrier Wing:
61st Troop Carrier Group:
(14, 15, 53 & 59
Sqns.) Barkston Douglas C–47 Skytrain
313th Troop Carrier Group:
(29, 47, 48 & 49 Folkington
Sqns.) Douglas C–47 Skytrain
Douglas C–53 Skytrooper
314th Troop Carrier Group:
(32, 50, 61 & 62 Saltby Douglas C–47 Skytrain
Sqns.) Douglas C–53 Skytrooper
315th Troop Carrier Group:
(34, 43, 309 & 310 Spanhoe Douglas C–47 Skytrain
Sqns.) Douglas C–53 Skytrooper
316th Troop Carrier Group:
(36, 37, 44 & 45 Cottesmore Douglas C–47 Skytrain
Sqns.) Douglas C–53 Skytrooper
53rd Troop Carrier Wing:
434th Troop Carrier Group:
(71, 72, 73 & 74
Sqns.) Aldermaston Douglas C–47 Skytrain
435th Troop Carrier Group:
(75, 76, 77 & 78 Welford Park Douglas C–47 Skytrain
Sqns.) Douglas C–53 Skytrooper
436th Troop Carrier Group:
(79, 80, 81 & 82
Sqns.) Membury Douglas C–47 Skytrain
437th Troop Carrier Group:
(83, 84, 85 & 86
Sqns.) Ramsbury Douglas C–47 Skytrain
438th Troop Carrier Group:
(87, 88, 89 & 90
Sqns.) Greenham Common Douglas C–47 Skytrain

PB–1W/G: USN/USCG early-warning/ASR conversions of B–17G (*47*).
Fortress Mk III: RAF equivalent of B–17G; 85 Lend-Lease.
Total Production: 12,731 (all Marks).
Remarks: Entered service late 1943; backbone of Allied strategic daylight bomber offensive for remainder of European war; at peak, Aug 1944, USAAF deployed 4,574 B–17s; equipped some 26 UK-based Groups (8th AF), plus 6 in Italy (15th AF); also used in photo-reconnaissance role; RAF Fortress IIIs employed by both Coastal (maritime reconnaissance) and Bomber (radio-counter-measures/clandestine/decoy duties) Commands; served USN/USCG as early-warning aircraft in immediate post-war years; many other post-war conversions plus extensive foreign use.

Manufacturer: Boeing.
Model: B–29 Superfortress.
Type: Long-range very heavy bomber.
Power Plant: Four 2,000hp Wright R–3350–23.
Performance:
maximum speed at 25,000ft (7,620m) 358mph (576km/hr).
cruising speed 230mph (370km/hr).
maximum range 5,600 miles (9,010km).
time to 20,000ft (6,096m) 38min 0sec.
service ceiling 31,850ft (9,708m).
Weights:
empty 70,140lb (31,816kg).
loaded 124,000lb (56,250kg).
Dimensions:
wing span 141ft 3in (43.05m).
length 99ft 0in (30.18m).
height 29ft 7in (9.01m).
wing area 1,736sq ft (161.27sq m).
Armament: Two .5in guns each in four remotely-controlled turrets; two .5in guns or (early production) one 20mm cannon in tail; max bomb load 20,000lb (9,072kg).
Crew: 11.
In Service: USA, USSR (3 sequestrated).
Variants (with no built):
XB–29: Prototypes (3).
YB–29: Pre-production model (14).
B–29: Initial production model, Boeing-built (1,570); Bell-built (352); Martin-built (536).
B–29A: Re-designed wing centre section; 4-gun forward turret; R–3350–57 or 59s (1,119).
F–13A: Camera-equipped reconnaissance version; B–29 conversions.
B–29B: Modified B–29; increased bomb load; tail armament only; Bell-built (311).
YB–29J: B–29 conversions with fuel injection engines (*5+*).
FB–29J: Photo-reconnaissance version of above.
Total Production: 3,905.
Remarks: Operational debut 5 June 1944; attack on Bangkok from bases in India; second operation against Japanese home-land ten days later; subsequently based in Marianas (20th AF) for concentrated VHB offensive against Japan, Nov 1944–Aug 1945; initially employed as high-altitude precision bombers, B–29s later switched to low-level incendiary night raids; first such operation, 9 March 1945 against Tokyo, proved most destructive single raid of war; during Pacific campaign B–29s dropped over 170,000 tons of conventional bombs (25 times the total of all otherUS aircraft combined), but even this staggering figure pales before the Superfortress' one great claim to notoriety—the delivery of the world's first atomic bombs.

Manufacturer: Brewster.
Model: F2A–3 Buffalo.
Type: Carrier/land-based interceptor/fighter-bomber.
Power Plant: One 1,200hp Wright R–1820–40.
Performance:
maximum speed at sea level 284mph (457km/hr).
maximum speed at 16,500ft (5,030m) 321mph (516km/hr).
cruising speed 161mph (259km/hr).
maximum range 965 miles (1,650km).
initial rate of climb 2,290ft/min 698 m/min).
service ceiling 33,200ft (10,119m).
Weights:
empty 4,732lb (2,146kg).
maximum 7,159lb (3,247kg).
Dimensions:
wing span 35ft 0in (10.67m).
length 26ft 4in (8.02m).
height 12ft 1in (3.68m).
wing area 208.9sq ft (19.41sq m).
Armament: Two fixed forward-firing .5in Browning guns in fuselage plus two .5in Browning wing guns; max bomb load 200lb (91kg).
Crew: 1.
In Service: Australia, Finland, Great Britain (RAF, FAA), Japan (1+ evaluation), Netherlands (NEIAF), New Zealand, USA (USAAF, USN, USMC).
Variants (with no built):
XF2A–1: Prototype (1).
F2A–1: Production model; 940hp R–1820–34; carrier-borne (11).
F2A–2: Modified F2A–1; uprated engine; redesigned rudder (43).
F2A–3: Improved F2A–2; increased armour; lengthened nose (108).
Model B–239: Export equivalent of F2A–1; Finnish order (44).
Model B–339B: Land-based version of B–239; Belgian order, inc 38 to RAF (40).
Model B–339D: As B–339; Netherlands East Indies order (72).
Model B–339E: As B–339; British order (170).
Model B–439: Export version of F2A–3; Netherlands East Indies order; all to USAAF, 17 subsequently to RAAF (20).
Buffalo I: RAF, FAA designation for B–339 (*208*).
Humu: Finnish-built design development; all metal fuselage; wooden wing; reduced armament; prototype only.
Total Production: 509.
Remarks: Disappointing yet colourful fighter whose operational history—with only one exception—is synonymous with gallant defeat; equipped 3 US sqns (two USN, one USMC) on outbreak of Pacific War; operational debut Battle of Midway, 13 out 19 destroyed; subsequently relegated to training role; 7 Allied sqns (RAF, RAAF, RNZAF) deployed Malaya and Burma similarly overwhelmed by Japanese aggression; survivors joined NEIAF in continued retreat through East Indies; only Finnish AF operated Buffalo with considerable success, opposing Soviet forces June 1941–Sept 1944, and thereafter their erstwhile ally, Germany, Sept 1944–Jan 1945, after signing Russian surrender terms; one minor WWII anomaly was discovery of Belgian Buffalo (with full 1940 military markings) in Germany at war's end.
Colour Reference: Plate 127: Brewster Buffalo I (W8153) GA.P of No 21 Squadron, RAAF; shown in late NEIAF markings (roundels overpainted with Dutch tricolour flag) as captured by Japanese forces upon occupation Netherlands East Indies; Andir (Bandoeng), Java, March 1942.

Manufacturer: Brewster.
Model: SB2A–2 Buccaneer.
Type: Scout-bomber.
Power Plant: One 1,700hp Wright R–2600–8.
Performance:
maximum speed at sea level 259mph (417km/hr).
cruising speed 161mph (259km/hr).
maximum range 1,675miles (2,695km).
initial rate of climb 2,080ft/min (634m/min).
service ceiling 24,900ft (7,590m).
Weights:
empty 9,924lb (4,502kg).
maximum 14,289lb (6,481kg).
Dimensions:
wing span 47ft 0in (14.33m).
length 39ft 2in (11.94m).
height 15ft 5in (4.70m).
wing area 379sq ft (35.21sq m).
Armament: Two fixed forward-firing .5in guns in nose plus two .3in guns in wings and two in dorsal position; max bomb load (internal) 1,000lb (454kg).
Crew: 2.
In Service: Great Britain, USA (USN, USMC).
Variants (with no. built):
XSB2A–1: Prototype (1).
SB2A–1: Production model, Lend-lease to RAF (approx 468).
SB2A–2: Initial USN order; reduced armament (80).
SB2A–3: Carrier-based version; folding wings, arrester gear (60).
SB2A–4: Similar to SB2A–2; eight .3in guns; repossessed Dutch order (162).
Bermuda I: RAF equivalent of SB2A–1; approx 468 Lend-lease.
Total Production: approx 771.
Remarks: Entered US service 1942–43; employed principally in training roles by both USN and USMC; of 750 originally ordered by Great Britain only some 468 delivered under Lend-Lease; adapted for target-towing duties.

Manufacturer: Cessna.
Model: UC–77C.
Type: Liaison.
Power Plant: One 145hp Warner R–500 Scarab.
Performance:
maximum speed 162mph (260km/hr).
cruising speed 143mph (230km/hr).
maximum range 525 miles (845km).
initial rate of climb 1,000ft/min (305m/min).
service ceiling 18,900ft (5,760m).
Weights:
empty 1,315lb (596kg).
loaded 2,250lb (1,021kg).
Dimensions:
wing span 34ft 2in (10.41m).
length 24ft 7in (7.49m).
wing area 182sq ft (16.91sq m).
Crew/Accommodation: 1/3.
In Service: Australia (1 C–34), Finland (1 C–37), USA.
Variants:
DC–6A/B: Initial civil production; 4-seat single-engined high-wing monoplane; one 300/250ph Wright R–975/–760 resp.
C–34, –37, –145, –165 Airmaster: Subsequent civil series; alt Warner Scarab/Super Scarab power plants.
UC–77: USAAF designation impressed DC–6A (*4*).
UC–77A: USAAF designation impressed DC–6B (*4*).
UC–77B: USAAF designation impressed C–34 (*2*).
UC–77C/D: USAAF designations impressed C–37 (*1/3*).
UC–94/C–94: USAAF designations impressed C–165 (*2/1*).
Remarks: UC–77/–94 generic military designations for two entirely separate civil series (DC–6A/B of 1929, and C–34/165 Airmasters of 1935–41), seventeen of which impressed USAAF liaison/communications duties 1942; in addition, two pre-war Airmaster exports impressed foreign AFs: one C–37 employed by Finnish AF during Winter and Continuation Wars, 1939–43, and one C–34 serving RAAF communications role, 1941–45.

Manufacturer: Cessna.
Model: UC–78 Bobcat.
Type: Light personnel transport.
Power Plant: Two 245hp Jacobs R–755–9.
Performance:
maximum speed at sea level 195mph (314km/hr).
cruising speed 175mph (282km/hr).
normal range 750 miles (1,200km).
initial rate of climb 1,325ft/min (404m/min).
service ceiling 22,000ft (6,706m).
Weights:
empty 3,500lb (1,588kg).
loaded 5,700lb (2,588kg).
Dimensions:
wing span 41ft 11in (12.8m).
length 32ft 9in (10.0m).
height 9ft 11in (3.03m).
wing area 295sq ft (27.5sq m).
Crew/Accommodation: 1/4.
In Service: Canada, USA (USAAF, USN).
Variants (with no built):
AT–8: Trainer; service equivalent of T–50 civil transport (33).
AT–17/A–D: Trainer versions (780).
UC–78: Transport version (1,287).
UC–78A: Impressed civil T–50s (17).
UC–78B/C: As UC–78; minor equipment changes (2,133).
JRC–1: USN equivalent of UC–78 (*67*).
Crane I: RCAF equivalent of AT–8 (640).
Crane IA: RCAF equivalent of AT–17A (550 Lend-Lease).
Total Production: 4,890.
Remarks: Originally ordered as advanced trainer; from 1942 adopted as light personnel transport; extensive use in communications and liaison role.

Manufacturer: Consolidated.
Model: P2Y–3.
Type: Maritime reconnaissance flying boat.
Power Plant: Two 750hp Wright R–1820–90.
Performance:
maximum speed at 4,000ft (1,219m) 139mph (224km/hr).
cruising speed 117mph (188km/hr).
normal range 1,180 miles (1,900km).
initial rate of climb 650ft/min (198m/min).
service ceiling 16,100ft (4,907m).
Weights:
empty 12,769lb (5,792kg).
maximum 25,266lb (11,461kg).
Dimensions:
wing span 100ft 0in (30.48m).
length 61ft 9in (18.82m).
height 19ft 1in (5.82m).
wing area 1,514sq ft (140.65sq m).
Armament: One flexible .3in Browning machine-gun each in bow and two lateral hatches.
Crew: 5.
In Service: USA (USN).
Variants (with no built):
XP2Y–1: Prototype; XPY–1 development; twin-engined sesquiplane flying boat; two 575hp Wright R–1820E below upper wings; originally flown with third engine mounted above wing (1).
P2Y–1: Initial production model (23).
XP2Y–2: Prototype; modified P2Y–1; re-positioned (wing leading edge) engines; two Wright R–1820–88; 1 conversion.
P2Y–2; As XP2Y–2; 20+ P2Y–1 conversions.
P2Y–3: As XP2Y–2; uprated engines (23).
Total Production: 47.
Remarks: Service debut 1933, P2Y–2/–3 remained in first-line use until early months WWII; withdrawn from overseas operational units prior Pearl Harbor attack, Dec 1941 subsequently employed Stateside ancillary duties.

Manufacturer: Consolidated.
Model: PBY–5 Catalina.
Type: Patrol bomber flying-boat.
Power Plant: Two 1,200hp Pratt and Whitney R–1830–82.
Performance:
maximum speed at 5,700ft (1,737m) 200mph (322km/hr).
cruising speed 115mph (185km/hr).
range 1,895 miles (3,049km).
initial rate of climb 990ft/min (302m/min).
service ceiling 21,600ft (6,584m).
Weights:
empty 17,400lb (7,893kg).
maximum 33,389lb (15,145kg).
Dimensions:
wing span 104ft 0in (31.7m).
length 63ft 10in (19.45m).
height 18ft 11in (5.76m).
wing area 1,400sq ft (130.06sq m).
Armament: One .5in machine-gun each in nose and turret; two .3in Browning machine-guns in waist blisters; four depth-charges, two torpedoes or four 1,000lb (454kg) bombs.
Crew: 7–9.
In Service: Australia (169), Brazil, Canada (228+), France (FNAF), Great Britain (650+), Netherlands (NEIAF 6, NEINAF 53), New Zealand, South Africa, USA (USAAF, USN, USMC), USSR (SovNAF 189+ GST).
Variants (with no. built):
XP3Y–1: Prototype; subsequently modified, re-designated XPBY–1 (1).
PBY–1: Initial production model; waist hatches (60).
PBY–2 Modified PBY–1 (50).
PBY–3: 1,000hp R–1830–66s (66).
PBY–4: 1,050hp R–1830–72s; some with waist blisters (33).
PBY–5: Uprated engines; waist blisters; different armament, inc 33 finished as PBY–5A; Consolidated-built (1,040); Canadian Boeing-built (17).
XPBY–5A: Amphibious PBY–4 conversion; tricycle undercarriage (*1*).
PBY–5A: Amphibious PBY–5; various armament (USN, USMC) (761).
PBY–5B: Modified PBY–5; all to RAF (225).
PBY–6A: As PBN–1; amphibious undercarriage; different armament; enlarged tail, inc 48 to USSR, 75 to USAAF (235).
PBN–1 (Nomad): Modified PBY–5A; increased fuel capacity and weight; enlarged tail; different armament; 138 Lend-Lease to USSR; NAF-built (156).
PB2B–1: As PBY–5; Canadian Boeing-built (240).
PB2B–2: As PB2B–1 with PBN tail; Canadian Boeing-built (50).
PBV–1A: As PBY–5A; all to USAAF; Canadian Vickers-built (230).
OA–10: USAAF designation for ASR version of PBY–5A (*56*).
OA–10A: USAAF designation for PBY–1A (*230*).
OA–10B: USAAF designation for PBY–6A (*75*); post-war.
Canso: RCAF service designation for PBY–5As; Canadian Vickers-built (55); Canadian Boeing-built (149).
Catalina I: RAF equivalent of PBY–5; 6 to RCAF and 19 to RAAF (118).
Catalina IA: RAF designation for

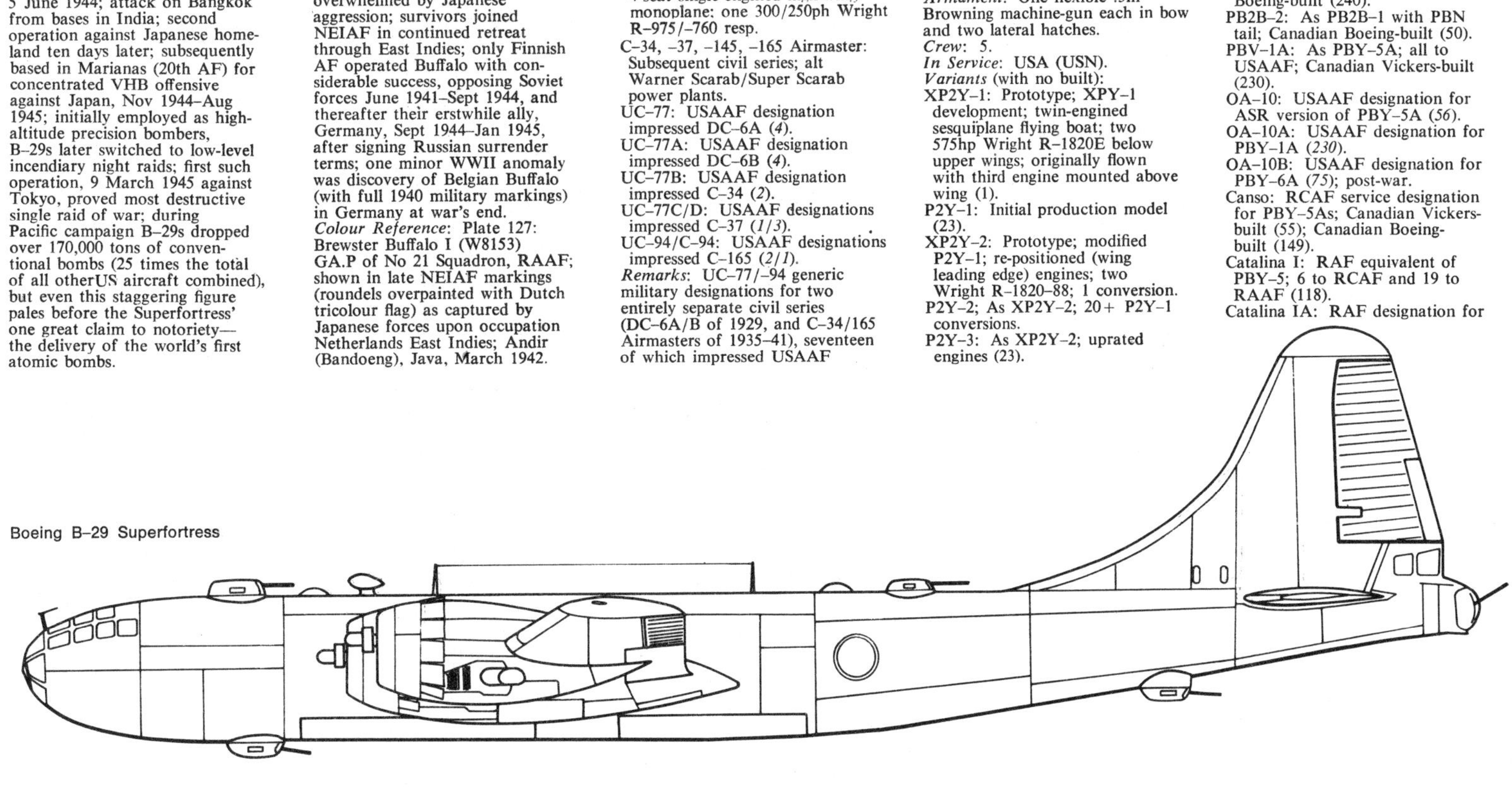

Boeing B–29 Superfortress

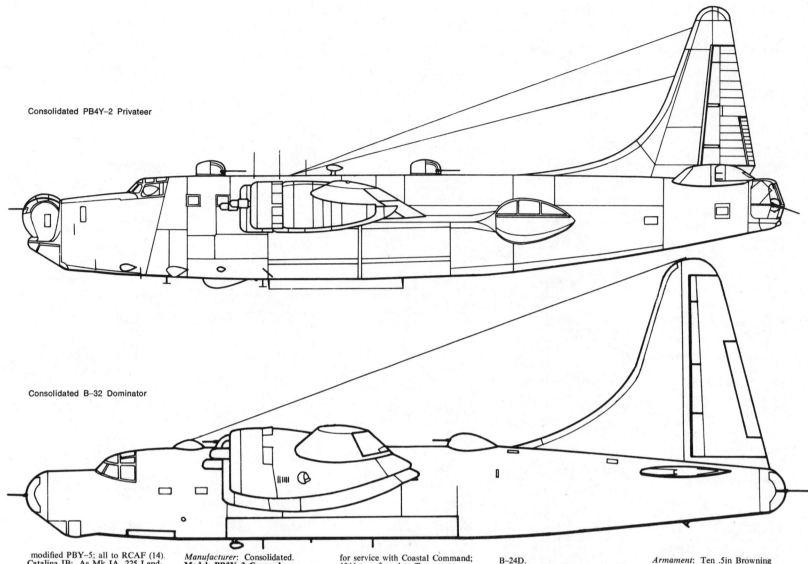

Consolidated PB4Y–2 Privateer

Consolidated B–32 Dominator

modified PBY-5; all to RCAF (14).
Catalina IB: As Mk IA, 225 Lend-Lease (inc 2 for BOAC).
Catalina II: As Mk I, NAF-built (7).
Catalina IIA: RCAF version of PBY-5; transferred to RAF (36).
Catalina III: RAF designation for PBY-5; 12 Lend-Lease (inc 1 to USN).
Catalina IVA: RAF designation for general-reconnaissance version of PBY-5; 97 Lend-Lease.
Catalina IVB: RAF designation for PB2B-1; some as ASR; 193 Lend-Lease (inc 3 to BOAC).
Catalina VI: RAF designation for PB2B-2; 50 Lend-Lease; all to RAAF.
Catalina GST: USSR designation of PBY-3; USSR licence-built (approx 3).
Total Production: 3,290.
Remarks: Most successful and numerous flying-boat of WWII; extensive use by Allied AFs in all theatres; entered service USN late 1936, equipping 21 patrol sqns by outbreak of Pacific War; played prominent part throughout Pacific campaigns, performing bombing, minelaying, anti-submarine and ASR roles (latter also undertaken by USAAF as OA-10); RAF Coastal Command service from 1941; participated hunt for *Bismarck*, Battle of Atlantic, European, Mediterranean and Indian Ocean theatres; also based Russia for Arctic convoy duty; scored last Coastal Command U-boat 'kill', 7 May 1945. Also served Netherlands East Indies and SWPA; Soviet use until mid-fifties; extensive post-war foreign service.
Colour Reference: Plates 131, 132: Consolidated (Vickers) OA-10A Catalina (44-33882) of 2nd ERS (Emergency Rescue Squadron), 13th USAAF, Middelburg Island, Netherlands New Guinea, late 1944; relatively rare example of AAF aircraft sporting naval-style colour scheme, ERS Catalinas usually finished either dark-blue upper surfaces as illustrated (Pacific theatre), or white overall (Pacific/European theatres).

Manufacturer: Consolidated.
Model: PB2Y-3 Coronado.
Type: Long-range patrol bomber flying boat.
Power Plant: Four 1,200hp Pratt and Whitney R-1830-88.
Performance:
maximum speed at sea level 199mph (320km/hr).
maximum speed at 20,000ft (6,096m) 213mph (343km/hr).
cruising speed 140mph (227km/hr).
normal range 1,370 miles (2,204km).
initial rate of climb 570ft/min (174m/min).
service ceiling 20,900ft (6,370m).
Weights:
empty 41,031lb (18,612kg).
loaded 68,000lb (30,845kg).
Dimensions:
wing span 115ft 0in (35.05m).
length 79ft 3in (24.2m).
height 27ft 6in (8.38m).
wing area 1,780sq ft (175.4sq m).
Armament: Eight .5in machine-guns in bow, tail and dorsal turrets and beam positions; max bomb load (internal) 8,000lb (3,629kg); bombs or depth-charges (external) 4,000lb (1,814kg).
Crew: 10.
In Service: Great Britain, USA (USN).
Variants (with no. built):
XPB2Y-1: Prototype (1).
PB2Y-2: Improved XPB2Y-1; increased armament (6).
PB2Y-3: Modified PB2Y-2; self-sealing fuel tanks; increased armament; some with ASV radar (210).
PB2Y-3B: Export version (10).
PB2Y-3R: Transport version; re-engined PB2Y-3 conversions (31).
XPB2Y-4: Re-engined PB2Y-2 conversion (1).
PB2Y-5, 5H, R: Low-altitude versions; re-engined PB2Y-3 conversions; -5H provision for 25 litters.
Coronado I: RAF equivalent of PB2Y-3B; 10 Lend-Lease.
Total Production: 227.
Remarks: Employed by USN on reconnaissance and anti-submarine patrol duties, 1941-45; British Coronado Is originally intended

for service with Coastal Command; 1944 transferred to Transport Command, initially as freighters on North Atlantic routes, subsequently flying passenger services North and South Atlantic.

Manufacturer: Consolidated.
Model: B-24D Liberator.
Type: Heavy bomber.
Power Plant: Four 1,200hp Pratt & Whitney R-1830-43 or 65.
Performance:
maximum speed at 25,000ft (7,620m) 303mph (488km/hr).
cruising speed 200mph (322km/hr).
range 2,850 miles (4,586km).
time to 20,000ft (6,096m) 22min 0sec.
service ceiling 32,000ft (9,754m).
Weights:
empty 32,605lb (14,790kg).
loaded 60,000lb (27,215kg).
Dimensions:
wing span 110ft 0in (33.53m).
length 66ft 4in (20.22m).
height 17ft 11in (4.46m).
wing area 1,048sq ft (97.36sq m).
Armament: Two .5in Browning machine-guns each in dorsal, tail and retractable ventral turrets; two .5in guns in nose plus two waist guns; max bomb load 8,800lb (3,992kg).
Crew: 10.
In Service: Australia (12), Germany (1+ evaluation), Great Britain, Italy, Rumania (1+ evaluation), USA (USAAF, USN, USMC), USSR (1).
Variants (with no. built):
XB-24: Prototype (1).
YB-24: Service test model; six converted to B-24Ds (7).
B-24A: Increased weight; .5in machine-guns in tail (9).
XB-24B: Prototype; converted XB-24.
B-24C: 1,200hp R-1830-41s; three power turrets (9).
B-24D: R-1830-43s; various armament, inc 10 with radar bomb-sights; Convair-built (2,728); Douglas-built (10).
B-24E: As B-24D but different props; various engines; Convair-built (144); Ford-built (480); Douglas-built (167).
XB-24F: Prototype; 1 converted

B-24D.
B-24G: As B-24D; first variant to introduce nose turret; North American-built (430).
Liberator I: RAF equivalent of B-24A; Coastal Command; some with ASV radar and ventral gun tray (20).
LB-30A: Unarmed transport version of above (6).
Liberator II: Coastal Command; inc unarmed transport version: LB-30; 75 repossessed by USAAF (139).
Liberator III: Similar to II; first Lend-Lease variant (260).
Liberator B.V., G.R.V.: Bomber and Coastal Command versions of II and III; 112 Lend-Lease.
Total Production: 18,482 (all Marks).
Remarks: First operational models of the second standard US heavy bomber of WWII; despite being built in far greater numbers, the Liberator never enjoyed the same public acclaim as was bestowed upon the more glamorous Fortress; operational debut, 11-12 June 1942, attacking Rumanian oilfields from base in Egypt, incidentally the first US bombing raid on the continent of Europe; subsequently served all major theatres, Europe and Middle East, North and South Pacific, CBI; also employed by USN/USMC as land-based patrol bomber, and by RAF Bomber and Coastal Commands.

Manufacturer: Consolidated.
Model: B-24J Liberator.
Type: Heavy bomber.
Power Plant: Four 1,200hp Pratt and Whitney R-1830-65.
Performance:
maximum speed at 30,000ft (9,144m) 300mph (483km/hr).
range 2,100 miles (3,380km).
time to 20,000ft (6,096m) 25min.
service ceiling 28,000ft (8,534m).
Weights:
empty 36,500lb (16,556kg).
normal/loaded 56,000lb (25,400kg).
Dimensions:
wing span 110ft 0in (33.53m).
length 67ft 2in (20.47m).
height 18ft 0in (5.49m).
wing area 1,048sq ft (97.36sq m).

Armament: Ten .5in Browning machine-guns in nose, dorsal, ventral, tail and waist positions; max bomb load 8,800lb (3,992kg).
Crew: 8-12.
In Service: Australia (275), Canada, Germany (1+ evaluation), Great Britain, USA (USAAF, USN), USSR (1+ sequestrated).
Variants (with no. built):
B-24H: With Emerson nose turret, Convair-built (738); with Consolidated nose turret, Ford-built (1,780); Douglas-built (582).
B-24J: Modified B-24H; later models with autopilot and bombsight, Convair-built (4,350); Douglas-built (205); North American-built (536, Ford-built (1,587).
XB-24K: Large single fin and rudder; one B-24D conversion.
B-24L: As B-24J; two manually-controlled .5in guns in lieu of tail-turret; Convair-built (417); Ford-built (1,250).
B-24M: Modified B-24J; Convair-built (916); Ford-built (1,677).
XB-24N: Revised armament; single fin; Ford-built (1).
YB-24N: Service evaluation model; Ford-built (7).
RB-24L: Trainer version; B-24 conversions.
XB-41: Armed escort version; one B-24D conversion.
F-7: Photo-reconnaissance version; B-24 D/H conversions.
F-7A/B: Photo-reconnaissance versions; B-24J conversions.
PB4Y-1: USN/USMC equivalents of B-24D, G, H and J (977).
Liberator VI and VIII: RAF equivalents of B-24J; Bomber (B) and Coastal (G.R.) versions; some with ventral ball-turret and ASV radome respectively; 1,668 Lend-Lease.
Total Production: 18,482 (all Marks).
Remarks: Major Liberator variant, B-24J entered service Aug 1943; soon operating in all theatres; equipped 46 bomber groups, plus two PRGs and various special sqns; at peak, Sept 1944, USAAF had 6,043 Liberators on strength; although somewhat overshadowed by Fortress in European and Mediterranean theatres (8th and

15th AFs), Liberators of USAAF and USN formed backbone of Pacific strategic bombing campaign throughout most of war; also operated by 41 RAF sqns (Mks VI and VIII) and by 4 RAAF sqns in Far East; continued post-war use, both by US and various foreign AFs.
Colour Reference: Plate 154: Consolidated B-24H Liberator (42–52106) 'Sunshine' of 716th Bomb Squadron, 449th Bomb Group (Heavy), 15th USAAF, Grottaglie, Italy, March 1944; standard olive drab finish; early style 15th AF rudder markings: upper triangle denoting 47th Bomb Wing, lower '3' Group (449th) within Wing, plus individual aircraft number '5' on rudder (note evidence of over-painting on tailfin); 'Sunshine' captured intact after landing in error at Venegono airfield (25 miles n. Milan), April 1944; subject much propaganda footage before repainting in German markings for clandestine service with Luftwaffe's KG 200.

Manufacturer: Consolidated.
Model: C-87 Liberator.
Type: Transport.
Power Plant: Four 1,200hp Pratt and Whitney R-1830–43.
Performance:
maximum speed 306mph (492km/hr).
cruising speed 200mph (322km/hr).
normal range 2,900 miles (4,666km).
time to 20,000ft (6,096m) 20min 54sec.
service ceiling 31,000ft (9,449m).
Weights:
empty 31,935lb (14,486kg).
loaded 56,600lb (25,674kg).
Dimensions:
wing span 110ft 0in (33.53m).
length 66ft 4in (20.22m).
height 18ft 0in (5.49m).
wing area 1,048sq ft (97.36sq m).
Armament: One .5in Browning machine-gun in tail.
Crew/Payload/Accommodation:
5/8,800lb (3,992kg)/25.
In Service: Australia (2), Great Britain, USA (USAAF, USN).
Variants (with no. built):
C-87: Transport version of B-24D (280).
C-87A: Executive transport; 10 berths (6).
C-87B/C: Projects only.
C-109: Fuel carrier; B-24D and E conversions.
AT-22: Flying classroom; five C-87 conversions, subsequently redesignated TB-24.
RY-1: USN equivalent of C-87A (3).
RY-2: USN equivalent of C-87 (5).
Liberator C.Mk VII: RAF equivalent of C-87; 24 Lend-Lease.
Total Production: 18,482 (all Marks).
Remarks: Transport and tanker versions/conversions of basic B-24 Liberator bomber; C-87 become USAAF's principal long-range heavy transport aircraft, in use throughout war years; C-109 converted as flying tanker to ferry fuel over the 'Hump' from India to China to supply B-29s attacking Japan from advanced bases in China; RAF Mk VIIs operated by 3 sqns Transport Command as troopers on Far Eastern trunk routes, 1944–45 (for earlier RAF transport versions LB-30/30A, see B-24D).

Manufacturer: Convair.
Model: PB4Y-2 Privateer.
Type: Patrol bomber.
Power Plant: Four 1,350hp Pratt and Whitney R-1830–94.
Performance:
maximum speed at 13,700ft (4,176m) 237mph (381km/hr).
cruising speed 140mph (225km/hr).
range 2,800 miles (4,505km).
initial rate of climb 1,090ft/min (332m/min).
service ceiling 20,700ft (6,309m).
Weights:
empty 37,485lb (17,003kg).
loaded 65,000lb (29,484kg).
Dimensions:
wing span 110ft 0in (33.53m).
length 74ft 7in (22.73m).
height 30ft 1in (9.17m).
wing area 1,048sq ft (97.36sq m).
Armament: Twelve .5in Browning machine-guns in turrets and waist positions; max bomb load 1,600lb (726kg).
Crew: 10–11.
In Service: Great Britain, USA (USN, USMC).
Variants (with no. built):

XPB4Y-2: Prototype; three B-24D conversions.
PB4Y-2: Initial production version (736).
PB4Y-2S: Post-war anti-submarine conversions.
RY-3: Transport version (46).
Liberator C.Mk IX: RAF equivalent of RY-3; 27 Lend-Lease.
Total Production: 782.
Remarks: Single-finned and lengthened Liberator developed specifically for USN; limited employment during closing months of Pacific War, inc one sqn equipped with underwing ASM-N-2 Bat anti-shipping radar-homing glide bombs; RAF Mk IXs operated by Transport Command out of Canada on trans-Pacific routes to SEAC.

Manufacturer: Convair.
Model: B-32 Dominator.
Type: Heavy bomber.
Power Plant: Four 2,200hp Wright R-3350–23.
Performance:
maximum speed at 25,000ft (7,620m) 360mph (576km/hr).
range 3,800 miles (6,080km).
service ceiling 35,000ft (10,680m).
Weights:
empty 60,272lb (27,365kg).
maximum 111,500lb (50,576kg).
Dimensions:
wing span 135ft 0in (41.2m).
length 82ft 1in (25.02m).
height 32ft 2in (9.8m).
wing area 1,422sq ft (132sq m).
Armament: Ten .5in guns in five turrets; max bomb load 20,000lb (9,080kg).
Crew: 8.
In Service: USA.
Variants (with no. built):
XB-32: Prototypes; pressurized, remote-control turrets; first two with twin fins and rudders (3).
B-32: Single fin and rudder; unpressurized; power-operated manned turrets (115).
TB-32: Trainer version; modified B-32s (40).
Total Production: 118.
Remarks: Developed in parallel with Boeing B-29 Superfortress, Convair's Dominator was completely overshadowed by its highly successful competitor, only fifteen examples seeing action

with one Philippines-based heavy bomber group during closing weeks of Pacific War.

Manufacturer: Curtiss.
Model: Hawk III.
Type: Carrier-borne fighter-bomber.
Power Plant: One 785hp Wright R-1820–F53.
Performance:
maximum speed at 11,500ft (3,505m) 240mph (387km/hr).
cruising speed 204mph (328km/hr).
maximum range 790 miles (1,270km).
initial rate of climb 2,000ft/min (609m/min).
service ceiling 25,800ft (7,864m).
Weights:
empty 3,213lb (1,457kg).
maximum 4,645lb (2,107kg).
Dimensions:
wing span 31ft 5in (9.58m).
length 23ft 5in (7.14m).
height 9ft 9½in (2.98m).
wing area 262sq ft (24.33sq m).
Armament: Two .3in Browning machine-guns in fuselage; max bomb load 474lb (215kg).
Crew: 1.
In Service: Argentina (10 Hawk III, 1 Hawk IV), China (60 Hawk I, 210 Hawks II and III), Thailand (37 Hawk III), Turkey (24 Hawk II).
Variants (with no. built):
XBFC-1/2: Prototypes (2).
BFC-2 (Goshawk): Initial USN production model; fixed under-carriage; open cockpit (27).
XBF2C-1: Prototype; modified BFC-2; retractable under-carriage (1).
BF2C-1: USN production model; semi-enclosed cockpit (27).
Hawk I: Export version of BFC-2; Chinese order (60).
Hawk II: As Mk I; increased fuel capacity; exported to Bolivia, China, Columbia, Cuba, Germany (2), Turkey (24).
Hawk III: Export version of BF2C-1: to Argentina, China and Thailand; 37, inc 25 Thai-assembled.
(Total Hawk II, III: 190).
Hawk III (Chinese): Chinese (Central Govt) licence-built (80).
Hawk IV: Improved Mk III; 745hp R-1820–F56; enclosed cockpit; to Argentina (1).

Total Production: 388.
Remarks: Limited USN service; provided backbone of Chinese AF's fighter arm on outbreak of Sino-Japanese conflict, July 1937; fought over Peking and Shanghai; withdrawn first-line service, 1941; Thai Hawk IIIs in action against both French (invasion of Indo-China, Jan 1941) and Japanese forces (Dec 1941); served until late forties, latterly as advanced trainer.

Manufacturer: Curtiss.
Model: O-1G Falcon.
Type: Observation.
Power Plant: One 435hp Curtiss V-1150–5.
Performance:
maximum speed 146mph (234km/hr).
cruising speed 116mph (187km/hr).
initial rate of climb 1,060ft/min (323m/min).
service ceiling 16,750ft (5,105m).
Weights:
empty 3,143lb (1,426kg).
loaded 4,488lb (2,035kg).
Dimensions:
wing span 38ft 0in (11.58m).
length 27ft 4in (8.33m).
height 9ft 11in (3.02m).
wing area 349sq ft (32.42sq m).
Armament: Two fixed forward-firing .3in machine-guns in upper cowling; twin flexible .3in machine-guns in rear cockpit.
Crew: 2.
In Service: Philippines.
Variants (with no. built):
XO-1: Prototype; two-seat observation biplane; one 400hp Liberty; re-engined with one 510hp Packard IA-1500 (1).
O-1: Initial production model; one 435hp Curtiss V-1150 (D-12) (10).
O-1A: Modified O-1; one 420hp Liberty; deepened fuselage; 1 conversion.
O-1B: Improved O-1; one 430hp Curtiss D-12 (25).
O-1C: Modified O-1B; unarmed VIP-transport version; widened rear cockpit; 4 conversions.
O-1E: Improved O-1B; one 435hp V-1150–5; refined cowling contours (37).
O-1F: Modified (unarmed) O-1E (1).
XO-1G: Prototype; improved

(streamlined) O-1E; modified rear cockpit; 1 conversion.
O-1G: As XO-1G (30).
Total Production: 104.
Remarks: Prototype first flown 1924, O-1 was forerunner prolific series USAAC observation types; long obsolete by outbreak Pacific War, at least one example survived in Philippines AF service for photographic-reconnaissance Japanese positions during final days defence of Bataan Peninsula.

Manufacturer: Curtiss.
Model: A-12 Shrike.
Type: Attack bomber.
Power Plant: One 775hp Wright SR-1820F-52.
Performance:
maximum speed at sea level 182mph (293km/hr).
cruising speed 171mph (275km/hr).
normal range 481 miles (774km).
service ceiling 20,700ft (6,309m).
Weights:
empty 4,024lb (1,825kg).
loaded 5,925lb (2,688kg).
Dimensions:
wing span 44ft 0in (13.41m).
length 31ft 5in (9.57m).
height 9ft 4in (2.84m).
wing area 284sq ft (26.38sq m).
Armament: Four .3in machine-guns mounted in landing gear; one .3in machine-gun in observer's cockpit; max bomb load 488lb (221kg).
Crew: 2.
In Service: China (20), USA.
Variants (with no. built):
X/YA-8, YA-10, A-12: Pre-war USAAC service test and production models (60).
Export Shrike: Re-engined A-12; Chinese order (20).
Total Production: 80.
Remarks: Obsolete by outbreak of Pacific War; several based Hawaii at time of Japanese attack on Pearl-Harbor, Dec 1941; Chinese Shrikes operational during opening phases Sino-Japanese conflict.

Manufacturer: Curtiss.
Model: SOC-1 Seagull.
Type: Scout-observation floatplane.
Power Plant: One 600hp Pratt and Whitney R-1340–18.
Performance:

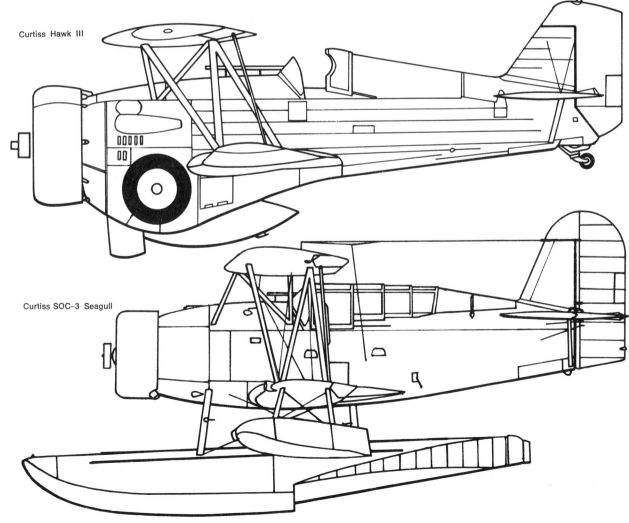

Curtiss Hawk III

Curtiss SOC-3 Seagull

maximum speed at sea level 157mph (253 km/hr).
maximum speed at 5,000ft (1,525m) 165mph (265km/hr).
cruising speed 133mph (214km/hr).
maximum range 954 miles (1,535km).
initial rate of climb 880ft/min (268m/min).
service ceiling 14,900ft (4,542m).
Weights:
empty 3,508lb (1,591kg).
maximum 5,341lb (2,423kg).
Dimensions:
wing span 36ft 0in (10.97m).
length 31ft 8in (9.65m).
height 14ft 1in (4.29m).
wing area 348sq ft (32.33sq m).
Armament: One fixed forward-firing .3in Browning machine-gun in wing; one flexible .3in Browning in rear cockpit.
Crew: 2.
In Service: USA (USN, USMC, USCG).
Variants (with no. built):
XO3C-1 (XSOC-1): Prototype; alternative land/seaplane (1).
SOC: 1 Initial production model; re-engined (135).
SOC-2: Uprated SOC-1; land-based (40).
SOC-3: As SOC-2; some with arrester gear (SOC-3A) (83).
SON-1, -1A: As SOC-3; equipped with arrester gear; NAF-built (44).
SOC-4: USCG version; subsequently to USN; modified to SOC-3A (3).
Total Production: 306.
Remarks: Extensive service as catapult floatplanes aboard USN battleships and cruisers; operated Pacific, Atlantic and Mediterranean theatres; participated Guadalcanal campaign and attack on Wake Island, Oct 1943.

Manufacturer: Curtiss.
Model: SBC-4 Helldiver.
Type: Carrier-borne scout-bomber.
Power Plant: One 950hp Wright R-1820-34.
Performance:
maximum speed at 15,200ft (4,633m) 237mph (381km/hr).
cruising speed 127mph (204km/hr).
normal range 590 miles (949km).
initial rate of climb 1,860ft/min (567m/min).
service ceiling 27,300ft (8,321m).
Weights:
empty 4,841lb (2,196kg).
maximum 7,632lb (3,462kg).
Dimensions:
wing span 34ft 0in (10.36m).
length 28ft 4in (8.63m).
height 12ft 7in (3.83m).
wing area 317sq ft (29.45sq m).
Armament: One fixed forward-firing .3in gun; one flexible .3in gun in rear cockpit; one 500lb (227kg) or 1,000lb (454kg) bomb under fuselage.
Crew: 2.
In Service: France (45), Great Britain, USA (USN, USMC).
Variants (with no. built):
XSBC-1/3: Prototype; various power plants (1).
SBC-3: Initial production model; Pratt & Whitney R-1535-94 (83).
XSBC-4: Re-engined SBC-3; 1 conversion.
SBC-4: Production model; increased bomb load; inc 50 transferred to France (224).
Cleveland I: RAF equivalent of SBC-4; 5 of above French order; ground instruction only.
Total Production: 308.
Remarks: Last US-built combat biplane; withdrawn from service shortly after Pearl Harbor; majority of French order held aboard aircraft carrier *Béarn* at Martinique in West Indies after fall of France, June 1940; 5 diverted to RAF as instructional airframes.

Manufacturer: Curtiss.
Model: A-18 Shrike.
Type: Attack bomber.
Power Plant: Two 600hp Wright R-1820-47 Cyclone.
Performance:
maximum speed at 3,500ft (1,067m) 238mph (383mph/hr).
Weights:
loaded 12,679lb (5,751kg).
Dimensions:
wing span 59ft 6in (18.13m).
length 42ft 4in (12.9m).
height 15ft 0in (4.57m).
wing area 526sq ft (48.86 sq m).
Armament: Four fixed forward-firing machine-guns; one flexible machine-gun in rear cockpit; max bomb load 654lb (297kg).
Crew: 2.
In Service: USA.

Variants (with no. built):
Model 76: Private venture prototype; twin-engined two-seat attack bomber; two Curtiss XR-1510 (1).
XA-14: Re-engined Model 76; two 735hp Wright R-1670-5.
Y1A-18: As XA-14; two 600hp Wright R-1820-47; subsequently redesignated A-18 (13).
Total Production: 14.
Remarks: Despite repetition of name, A-18 completely different design from earlier single-engined A-8/-12 series; entering USAAC service 1938, thirteen Y1A-18 service test models accepted as A-18 following year; remained on USAAF strength into opening years WWII, latterly relegated ancillary/support roles.

Manufacturer: Curtiss.
Model: SO3C-2 Seamew.
Type: Scout/patrol floatplane.
Power Plant: One 600hp Ranger V-770-6.
Performance:
maximum speed at sea level 150mph (241km/hr).
cruising speed 117mph (188km/hr).
maximum range 940 miles (1,512km).
initial rate of climb 720ft/min (220m/min).
service ceiling 16,500ft (5,029m).
Weights:
empty 4,995lb (2,266kg).
maximum 7,000lb (3,175kg).
Dimensions:
wing span 38ft 0in (11.58m).
length 34ft 9in (10.59m).
height 14ft 2in (4.32m).
wing area 293sq ft (27.22sq m).
Armament: One fixed forward-firing .3in Brownig machine-gun; one flexible .3in gun in rear cockpit; two 100lb (45kg) bombs or 325lb (147kg) depth-charges underwing; max bomb load under fuselage 500lb (227kg).
Crew: 2.
In Service: Great Britain (FAA), USA (USN).
Variants (with no. built):
XSO3C-1: Prototype; alternative land/seaplane (1).
SO3C-1: Initial production model; Ranger V-770-6; underwing bomb- or depth-charge racks; many subsequently converted to target drones (SO3C-1K) (300).
SO3C-2: Modified SO3C-1; arrester gear; addn bomb rack under fuselage (landplane version) (206).
SO3C-2C: Re-engined SO3C-2; revised electrics; hydraulic brakes; Lend-Lease to FAA (250).
SO3C-3: Improved SO3C-2; Ranger V-770-8 (39).
Seamew Mk I: FAA equivalent of SO3C-2C; 250 Lend-Lease allocations, 100+ delivered.
Queen Seamew: FAA equivalent of SO3C-1K; 30 Lend-Lease.

Total Production: 794.
Remarks: Designed to replace earlier SOC Seagull; served eighteen months with USN (July 1942- early 1944), before poor performance record forced withdrawal; replaced by restoring SOC to operational status; FAA Seamew Mk Is employed solely in training role (UK and Canada).

Manufacturer: Curtiss.
Model: O-52 Owl.
Type: Observation.
Power Plant: One 600hp Pratt and Whitney R-1340-51.
Performance:
maximum speed at 3,000ft (914m) 208mph (335km/hr).
cruising speed 180mph (290km/hr).
range 700 miles (1,126km).
service ceiling 19,500ft (5,944m).
Weights:
empty 4,230lb (1,919kg).
loaded 5,307lb (2,407kg).
Dimensions:
wing span 43ft 10in (13.36m).
length 25ft 5in (7.75m).
height 9ft 3⅓in (2.83m).
wing area 210sq ft (19.51sq m).
Armament: One .5in Browning machine-gun in rear cockpit.
Crew: 2.
In Service: USA, USSR (19).
Variants:
O-52: Sole production. High-wing, strut-braced monoplane.
Total Production: 203.
Remarks: Used as trainers by USAAF; 30 supplied to USSR Lend-Lease via Arctic Convoy route; 11 lost at sea; others employed by SovAF on northern and central sectors of Eastern Front, Spring-Summer 1943; at least one shot down by German fighters.

Manufacturer: Curtiss.
Model: Hawk 75.
Type: Interceptor/fighter-bomber.
Power Plant: One 875hp Wright Cyclone GR-1820-G3.
Performance:
maximum speed at 10,700ft (3,261m) 280mph (451km/hr).
cruising speed 240mph (386km/hr).
maximum range 1,210 miles (1,947km).
time to 2,340ft (713m) 1min 0sec.
service ceiling 31,800ft (9,693m).
Weights:
empty 3,975lb (1,803kg).
maximum 6,618lb (3,002kg).
Dimensions:
wing span 37ft 4in (11.38m).
length 28ft 7in (8.71m).
height 9ft 4in (2.84m).
wing area 236sq ft (21.92sq m).
Armament: One .5in and one .3in machine-gun in cowl; two .3in wing guns; max bomb load 300lb (136kg).
Crew: 1.
In Service: Argentina, Brazil, China, Thailand.
Variants (with no. built):
Hawk 75 H: Demonstration

models (2).
75 M: Chinese order (112).
75 N: Thai order; 12+ with 23mm Madsens (25).
75 O: Argentine order; six .3in wing guns; Curtiss-built (30); Argentine licence-built (200).
Total Production: 1,424 (all Marks).
Remarks: Simplified export version of Model 75; fixed spatted undercarriage; one demonstration model to China (personal craft of General Claire Chennault), one to Argentina; 75 Ms saw limited service Sino-Japanese conflict; 75 Ns offered brief resistance to Japanese invasion of Thailand, 8 Dec 1941.

Manufacturer: Curtiss.
Model: P-36A (Hawk 75A) Mohawk.
Type: Fighter.
Power Plant: One 1,050hp Pratt & Whitney R-1830-13.
Performance:
maximum speed at 10,000ft (3,048m) 300mph (483km/hr).
cruising speed 270mph (434km/hr).
maximum range 825 miles (1,327km).
time to 3,400ft (1,036m) 1min 0sec.
service ceiling 33,000ft (10,058m).
Weights:
empty 4,567lb (2,072kg).
maximum 6,010lb (2,726kg).
Dimensions:
wing span 37ft 4in (11.38m).
length 28ft 6in (8.68m).
height 12ft 2in (3.71m).
wing area 236sq ft (21.92sq m).
Armament: Two .3in machine-guns; or one .5in and one .3in machine-gun in cowling.
Crew: 1.
In Service: China, Finland (44), France (FAF, FFAF, VFAF), Germany, Great Britain, Netherlands (NEIAF 20), Norway (30), Peru (28), Portugal, South Africa (72), USA.
Variants (with no built):
Hawk 75, 75A, 75B: Prototype; various power plants (1).
Y1P-36: Pre-production model (3).
P-36A: Initial production model, inc 2 conversions to XP-40 and XP-42 (178).
P-36B: Re-engined P-36A (1).
P-36C: Modified P-36A; two .3in wing guns (31).
XP-36D/F: Experimental 36A conversions; various armament.
P-36G: 30 retained from second Norwegian order; 28 subsequently to Peru under Lend-Lease.
Hawk 75A-1/4: French orders; various power plants and armament; French (metric) equipment (730).
75A-5: Pattern model to China (1).

75A-6: Initial Norwegian order; four 7.9mm Brownings (24).
75A-7: Netherlands order; diverted to NEIAF (20).
75A-8: Second Norwegian order; two 12.7mm nose guns; 6 to Norwegian forces in Canada; 30 impressed by USAAF as P-36G (36).
75A-9: As A-4; to Iran; seized by RAF as Mohawks (10).
Mohawk I-IV: RAF equivalents of Hawk 75A-1/4 resp (227); Mk IV six .3in machine-guns plus provision for 400lb (181kg) bombs underwing.
Indian Hawk: Indian licence-built 75A by Hindustan Acft; 1 impressed as Mohawk (5).
Hawk 75I: Experimental; re-designated XP-37 and YP-37 (14).
75R: Supercharged engine; prototype only (1).
Total Production: 1,424 (all Marks).
Remarks: P-36A formed principal fighter defence of Hawaii at time of Japanese attack on Pearl Harbor, Dec 1941; first USAAC fighter to destroy Japanese aircraft in WWII; subsequently relegated to training duties, as was P-36G before delivery to Peru; similarly, H75A-1 was first French fighter to destroy German aircraft in WWII, Sept 1940; after French collapse H75As either to Vichy, seized by Germany, or to RAF; used by Luftwaffe as fighter-trainer; 37 later sold to Finland, plus 7 ex-Norwegian H75A-6s; RAF machines (either ex-FAF or direct US delivery) refitted with British equipment and employed in Burma and India (three sqns) and East Africa (one SAAF sqn); some also to Portuguese AF; Dutch H75A-7s served in NEI against Japanese.
Colour Reference: Plate 133: Curtiss Mohawk IV (BS798) 'B' of 'A'-Flight, No 155 Squadron, Agartala, Bengal, Aug 1943; participated Imphal fighting Feb-March 1943, subsequently engaged dive-bomber Army support duties India/Burma theatre, May-Dec 1943, early style SEAC insignia; note retention sky rear fuselage band.

Manufacturer: Curtiss.
Model: P-40B Tomahawk IIA.
Type: Fighter.
Power Plant: One 1,040hp Allison V-1710-33.
Performance:
maximum speed at 15,000ft (4,572m) 352mph (566km/hr).
cruising speed 273mph (439km/hr).
maximum range 1,230 miles (1,980km).
rate of climb 2,860ft/min (872m/min).
service ceiling 32,400ft (9,875m).

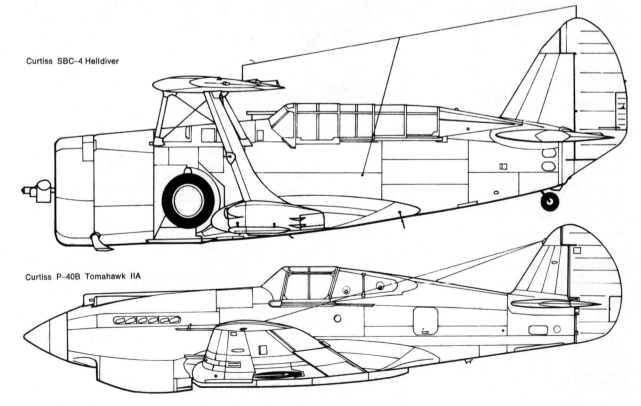

Curtiss SBC-4 Helldiver

Curtiss P-40B Tomahawk IIA

Weights:
empty 5,590lb (2,536kg).
maximum 7,600lb (3,447kg).
Dimensions:
wing span 37ft 4in (11.38m).
length 31ft 8¾in (9.67m).
height 10ft 7in (3.22m).
wing area 236sq ft (21.92sq m).
Armament: Two .5in guns in engine cowling; two .3in wing-mounted guns.
Crew: 1.
In Service: Australia, Canada, China (36 Tomahawk IIB, +90 to AVG), Egypt (6 Tomahawk IIB), Great Britain, South Africa, Turkey, USA, USSR (24 P–40B, 195 P–40C).
Variants (with no built):
XP–40: Prototype; one re-engined P–36A; 1,160hp V–1710–19 (1).
P–40: Initial production model; supercharged engine (199).
P–40B: Modified P40; two addn .3in machine-guns (131).
P–40C: Re-designed fuel system (193).
RP–40: Reconnaissance fighter; P–40 conversion.
Tomahawk I: RAF equivalent of P–40; two addn .303in Browning machine-guns in wings (140).
Tomahawk IIA: RAF equivalent of P–40B (110).
Tomahawk IIB: RAF equivalent of P–40C (930).
Total Production: 13,740 (all Marks).
Remarks: Limited USAAF use; majority of 73 Hawaiian-based P–40Bs and Cs destroyed on ground during Pearl Harbor attack, others managed to score some of earliest AAF victories of Pacific War; also based in Iceland; British and Commonwealth UK-based sqns served solely in low-level tactical reconnaissance role; main theatre of operations North Africa and Middle East, operated by Desert Air Force during winter of 1941–42; superseded by Kittyhawk April 1942 onwards; most famous of all the Tomahawks were the shark-mouthed aircraft flown by the 'Flying Tigers'—General Claire Chennault's American Volunteer Group (AVG) based in China and Burma, Dec 1941–June 1942.

Manufacturer: Curtiss.
Model: P–40E Kittyhawk IA.
Type: Fighter-bomber.
Power Plant: One 1,150hp Allison V–1710–39.
Performance:
maximum speed at 5,000ft (1,524m) 335mph (539km/hr).
maximum range 850 miles (1,368km).
time to 10,000ft (3,048m) 4min 48sec.
service ceiling 29,000ft (8,840m).
Weights:
empty 6,350lb (2,880kg).
maximum 9,200lb (4,173kg).
Dimensions:
wing span 37ft 4in (11.38m).
length 31ft 2in (9.50m).
height 10ft 7in (3.22m).
wing area 236sq ft (21.92sq m).
Armament: Six .5in wing guns; one 500lb (227kg) bomb under fuselage; two 100lb (45kg) bombs underwing.
Crew: 1.
In Service: Australia (848 Kittyhawk IA), Canada (Kittyhawk IA), China (AVG), France (FAF, FFAF), Great Britain, Japan (1+ P–40E, evaluation), Netherlands (NEIAF 38 P–40E/F), South Africa, USA, USSR.
Variants (with no built):
P–40D: Re-designed P–40C; shortened fuselage and undercarriage; Allison V–1710–39 (22).
P–40E: As P–40D; two addn wing guns (2,320).
Kittyhawk I: Re-designed Tomahawk; no fuselage guns (560).
Kittyhawk IA: RAF equivalent of P–40E; 1,500 Lend-Lease.
Total Production: 13,740 (all Marks).
Remarks: Became operational with British and Commonwealth sqns in Middle East, April 1942; many subsequently converted to carry bombs; highly successful against Axis troops and armour in Western Desert; also operated by French AF, NW Africa; P–40E equipped number of USAAF sqns in Middle East theatre, 1942; approx 30 also supplied to AVG to replace earlier Tomahawks; others to NEIAF and to USSR.

Manufacturer: Curtiss.
Model: P–40N–20 Warhawk.
Type: Fighter-bomber.

Curtiss SB2C–3 Helldiver

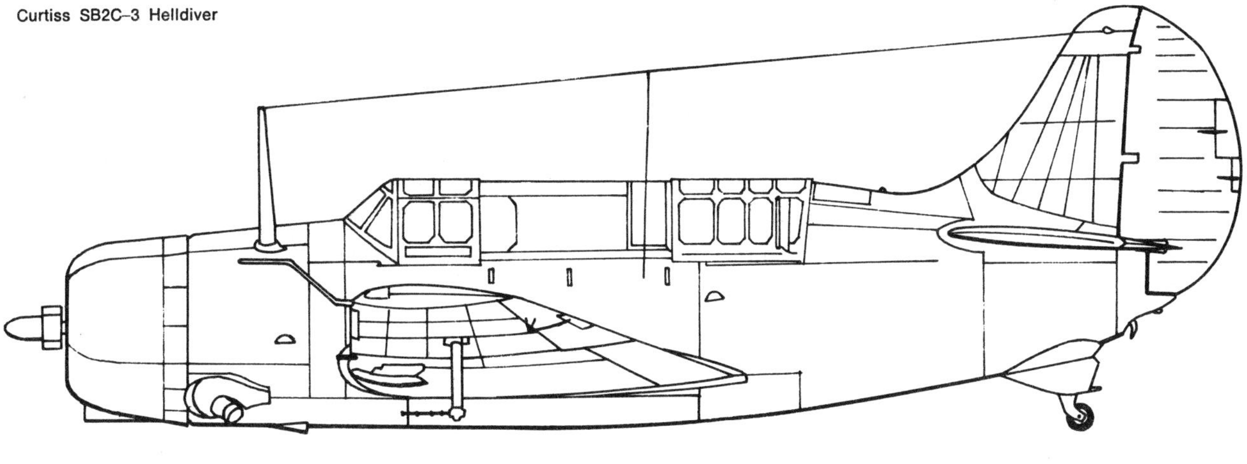

Power Plant: One 1,200hp Allison V–1710–81, 99 or 115.
Performance:
maximum speed at 16,400ft (5,000m) 350mph (563km/hr).
cruising speed 290mph (466km/hr).
maximum range 3,100 miles (4,988km).
time to 14,000ft (4,267m) 7min 18sec.
service ceiling 31,000ft (9,450m).
Weights:
empty 6,200lb (2,812kg).
maximum 11,400lb (5,171kg).
Dimensions:
wing span 37ft 4in (11.38m).
length 33ft 4in (10.16m).
height 12ft 4in (3.76m).
wing area 236sq ft (21.92sq m).
Armament: Six .5in machine-guns in wings; one 500lb (227kg) bomb.
Crew: 1.
In Service: Australia, Brazil, Canada, Chile, China (377 Lend-Lease), Finland (1), France (FAF), Great Britain, Netherlands (NEIAF 77 P–40N), New Zealand, South Africa (approx 80), USA, USSR (2,097 P–40s, all Marks).
Variants (with no built):
XP–40F: Converted P–40D; supercharged Rolls-Royce Merlin 28.
YP–40F: Service test models; Packard Merlin V–1650–1 (3).
P–40F (Warhawk): Production model; lengthened fuselage, 260 with early P–40 fuselage (1,311).
P–40G: One P–40 conversion; six-gun wings.
P–40H/J: Projects only.
P–40K: As P–40F; 1,325hp Allison V–1710–73, some with short fuselage (1,300).
P–40L: As P–40F; two wing guns removed (700).
P–40M: As P–40K; 1,200hp V–1710–81 (600).
P–40N–1/15: Modified P–40L and P–40M; new lightweight structure; four wing guns (1,977).
P–40N–20/35: 1,200hp V–1710–99; six wing guns; one bomb (3,022).
P–40N–40: 1,200hp V–1710–115; three bombs (220).
XP–40Q: Modified P–40N; four blade prop; 'Bubble' canopy (1).
P–40R: Re-engined P–40F and L conversions (300).
Kittyhawk II: RAF equivalent of P–40F; 250 Lend-Lease, inc 100 to USSR, some to France (FFAF) and some retained by USA.
Kittyhawk III: RAF equivalent of 21 P–40K and 595 P–40M; Lend-Lease; majority to RAAF and RNZAF.
Kittyhawk IV: RAF equivalent of P–40N; 586 Lend-Lease.
Total Production: 13,740 (all Marks).
Remarks: Ultimate operational developments of Curtiss' Hawk family; employed by USAAF in Middle East and Pacific theatres; majority supplied under Lend-Lease to Great Britain and Allied AFs—Commonwealth, USSR and China; primarily operated in Far East by RAAF and RNZAF; in Middle East by RAF, RAAF and SAAF; also to FAF (NW Africa), and to NEIAF; many later Marks subsequently relegated to training role.
Colour Reference: Plates 134, 135: Curtiss P–40N Warhawk (42–105120?) '51' of 80th Fighter Group, 10th USAAF, Nagaghuli (Upper Assam), India, May 1944; although less well-known than famous P–40s of 'Flying Tigers', each 80th FG machine bore individual interpretation of Group's macabre grinning skull marking; few examples were as elaborately shaded or as extensive (joining across top of carburettor intake fairing) as that carried by No 51; note also over-painted fin and rudder, evidence of previous ownership.

Manufacturer: Curtiss.
Model: SB2C–4 Helldiver.
Type: Carrier-borne scout bomber.
Power Plant: One 1,900hp Wright R–2600–20.
Performance:
maximum speed at sea level 270mph (434km/hr).
cruising speed 158mph (254km/hr).
range 1,235 miles (1,987km).
initial rate of climb 1,800ft/min (549m/min).
service ceiling 29,100ft (8,870m).
Weights:
empty 10,547lb (4,784kg).
maximum 16,616lb (7,537kg).
Dimensions:
wing span 49ft 9in (15.16m).
length 36ft 8in (11.17m).
height 13ft 2in (4.01m).
wing area 422sq ft (39.20sq m).
Armament: Two fixed forward-firing 20mm cannon in wings; two .3in machine-guns in rear cockpit; max (internal) bomb load 1,000lb (454kg), plus eight .5in rocket projectiles, or 1,000lb (454kg) bomb load underwing.
Crew: 2.
In Service: Australia (10 A–25), Great Britain (FAA), USA (USAAF, USN, USMC).
Variants (with no built):
XSB2C–1: Prototype (1).
SB2C–1: Initial production model; increased armament; enlarged fin and rudder (200).
SB2C–1C: As SB2C–1; altered armament plus two addn .3in guns in rear cockpit; bomb load 1,000lb (454kg) (778).
XSB2C–2: Floatplane prototype; one SB2C–1 conversion.
SB2C–3: 1,900hp R–2600–20 (1,112).
SB2C–4: As SB2C–3; addn underwing rockets or bombs; some with radar (SB2C–4E) (2,045).
XSB2C–5: Prototype; one SB2C–1C conversion.
SB2C–5: Increased fuel capacity (970).
XSB2C–6: Prototypes; two SB2C–3 conversions.
XSBF–1, SBF–1, 3, 4E: As XSB2C 1, SB2C–1, 3, 4E; Canadian Fairchild-built (300).
SBW–1, 3, 4, 4E, 5: As SB2C–1, 3, 4, 4E, 5; Canadian Car and Foundry-built (894).
A–25A: USAAF equivalent of SB2C–1; many to USMC as SB2C–1A (900).
Helldiver I (SBW–1B): FAA equivalent of SBW–1; 26 Lend-Lease.
Total Production: 7,200.
Remarks: Operational debut 11 Nov 1943, carrier strike against Rabaul; combat record of early versions regarded in official circles as no more than adequate; but after Battle of Philippine Sea, 19–20 June 1944, Helldiver quickly became standard USN scout-bomber for remainder of Pacific War; also employed by USMC; USAAFs A–25s (initially known as Shrike) relegated to training and other second-line duties; 10 delivered to RAAF; FAA's Helldiver Is equipped one sqn, no operational service.

Manufacturer: Curtiss.
Model: C–46A Commando.
Type: Transport.
Power Plant: Two 2,000hp Pratt and Whitney R–2800–51.
Performance:
maximum speed at 15,000ft (4,572m) 269mph (433km/hr).
cruising speed 183mph (294km/hr).
range 1,200 miles (1,930km).
initial rate of climb 1,300ft/min (396m/min).
service ceiling 27,600ft (8,412m).
Weights:
empty 32,400lb (14,697kg).
loaded 56,000lb (25,402kg).
Dimensions:
wing span 108ft 1in (32.94m).
length 76ft 4in (23.26m).
height 21ft 9in (6.63m).
wing area 1,360sq ft (126.34sq m).
Crew/Payload/Accommodation: 4/10,000lb (4,536kg)/50 troops, or 33 litters and 4 medics.
In Service: Great Britain (1), USA (USAAF, USMC), USSR (1).
Variants (with no. built):
C–46: Military version of CW–20 commercial transport (25).
C–46A: Uprated engines; large cargo door in rear fuselage; Curtiss-built (1,489); Higgins-built (2).
XC–46B: One C–46A conversion.
XC–46C: Prototypes only (2).
C–46D: Re-designed nose; double cargo doors (1,410).
C–46E: Re-designed C–46D; single cargo door; stepped windscreen (17).
C–46F: Modified C–46E; double cargo doors; blunt wing tips (234).
C–46G: Re-engined C–46E (1).
C–55: Military designation of original CW–20 civil prototype; purchased for evaluation; subsequently Lend-Lease to Great Britain (1).
R5C–1: USMC equivalent of C–46A (160).
Total Production: 3,341.
Remarks: Extensive USAAF service 1942–45, primarily Pacific theatre; distinguished record in CBI ferrying supplies over the 'Hump' from India to China; limited employment during closing months of European war with 9th AF Troop Carrier Command; used by USMC in South Pacific Campaign; sole British example flown by British Overseas Airways, 1941–43.
Colour Reference: Plate 138: Curtiss C–46A Commando (41–12322) of Air Transport Command, USAAF, assigned CBI theatre for operations over 'Hump', Kunming, Western China, Summer 1944; standard olive-drab finish, no unit markings.

Manufacturer: Curtiss.
Model: SC–1 Seahawk.
Type: Shipboard scout/anti-submarine patrol floatplane.
Power Plant: One 1,350hp Wright R–1820–62.
Performance:
maximum speed at sea level 238mph (383km/hr).
cruising speed 125mph (201km/hr).
range 1,090 miles (1,754km).
initial rate of climb 2,500ft/min (762m/min).
service ceiling 37,300ft (11,369m).
Weights:
empty 6,320lb (2,867kg).
maximum 9,000lb (4,082kg).
Dimensions:
wing span 41ft 0in (12.5m).
length 36ft 4½in (11.09m).
height 18ft 0in (5.49m).
wing area 280sq ft (26.01sq m).
Armament: Two fixed forward-firing .5in Browning machine-guns; underwing bomb-racks; max bomb load 650lb (295kg) plus bomb-cells in central float (optional).
Crew: 1.
In Service: USA (USN).
Variants (with no. built):
XSC–1, 1A, 2: Prototypes (6).
SC–1: Production version; landplane; provision for conversion to float-plane (approx 561).
SC–2: Modified SC–1, post-war (10).
Total Production: approx 577.
Remarks: Last USN scout-type aircraft designed for alternative battleship, carrier or land-based service; first deliveries Oct 1944; first reported in action June 1945 during invasion of Borneo; limited post-war use.

Manufacturer: Curtiss-Wright.
Model: BT–32 Condor II.
Type: Bomber/ transport.
Power Plant: Two 760hp Wright SGR–1820–F52.
Performance:
maximum speed at 7,000ft (2,134m) 180mph (288km/hr).
cruising speed 160mph (258km/hr).
normal range 840 miles (1,352km).
service ceiling 20,000ft (6,100m).
Weights:
empty 11,762lb (5,335kg).
loaded 18,500lb (8,392kg).
Dimensions:
wing span 82ft 0in (24.99m).
length 49ft 6in (15.1m).
height 16ft 4in (4.98m).
wing area 1,208sq ft (122.2sq m).
Armament: Five .3in Browning machine-guns in front and dorsal turrets, ventral and lateral hatches; max bomb load 3,968lb (1,800kg).
Crew/Accommodation: 4/15.
In Service: Argentina, China, Colombia, Japan, Peru, USA (USAAC, USN, USMC).
Variants (with no. built):
T–32: Civil airliner; various power plants, inc 2 to USAAC (20).
AT–32A/E: Modified T–32; day/night transport versions; various power plants, inc 2 to USN (13).
CT–32: Freighter/ambulance version, inc 3 to Argentine Navy; 24 troops or 10 litters and 1 medic (4).
BT–32: Bomber version (8).
YC–30: USAAC designation for T–32 (2).
R4C–1: USN/USMC designation for AT–32E (2).
Total Production: (45).
Remarks: Pre-war civil airliner; many subsequently sold to Central and South American airlines and AF; six to China as civil freighters; five destroyed in Japanese attack on Hong Kong, Dec 1941, sixth captured; BT–32 bomber-demonstrator also to China; used as personal armed transport by Generalissimo Chiang Kai-Shek.

Manufacturer: Curtiss–Wright.
Model: CW–21B Demon.
Type: Light interceptor fighter.
Power Plant: One 1,000hp Wright R–1820–G5.
Performance:
maximum speed at 12,200ft (3,709m) 314mph (505km/hr).
cruising speed 282mph (454km/hr).
normal range 630 miles (1,014km).
time to 13,120ft (4,000m) 4min 0sec.
service ceiling 34,300ft (10,455m).
Weights:
empty 3,382lb (1,534kg).

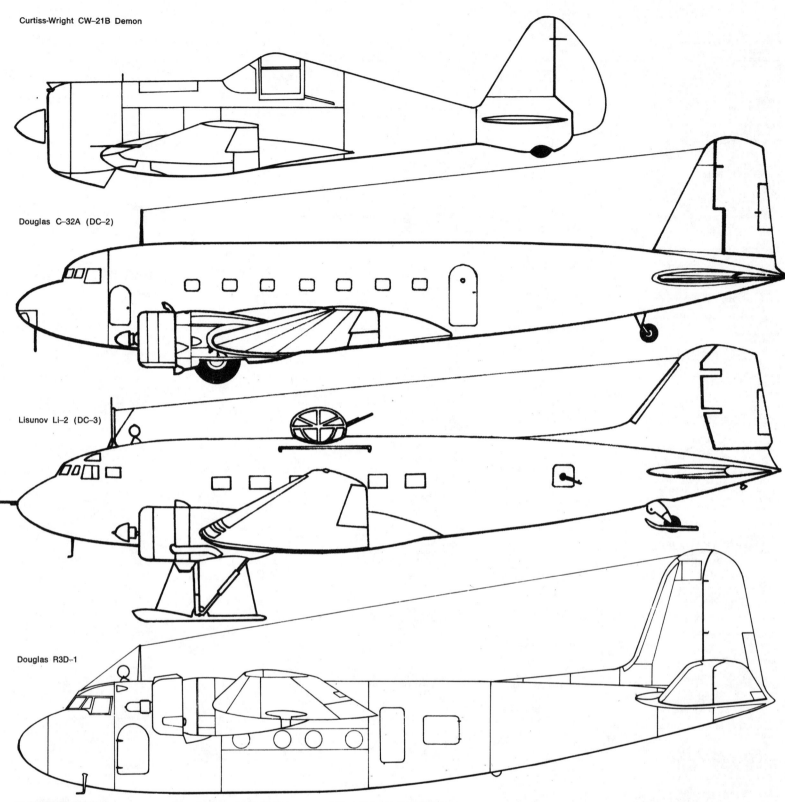

Curtiss-Wright CW–21B Demon

Douglas C–32A (DC–2)

Lisunov Li–2 (DC–3)

Douglas R3D–1

loaded 4,500lb (2,041kg).
Dimensions:
wing span 35ft 0in (10.67m).
length 27ft 2in (8.28m).
height 8ft 11in (2.71m).
wing area 174sq ft (16.16sq m).
Armament: One .3in plus one
.5in machine-gun in fuselage.
Crew: 1.
In Service: Netherlands
(NEIAF 24).
Variants (with no. built):
Prototypes: (2).
CW–21: Initial production model;
Chinese order, inc 32 component
sets for licence-assembly
(approx 35).
CW–21B: Dutch order (NEIAF);
four 7.7mm or two 12.7mm
machine-guns (27).
Total Production: approx 64.
Remarks: 24 of Dutch order
delivered to NEI; saw intensive
action against Japanese over Java,
Feb-March 1942; suffered severe
losses; remaining three of original
order diverted to AVG in Burma;
all lost on ferry flight to China;
details of actual Chinese order/
manufacture unconfirmed.

Manufacturer: Curtiss-Wright.
Model: SNC–1 Falcon.
Type: Trainer/communications.
Power Plant: One 420hp Wright
R–974.
Performance:
maximum speed 215mph
(346km/hr).
cruising speed 195mph (314km/hr).
normal range 515 miles (829km).
Weights:
loaded 3,626lb (1,645kg).
Dimensions:
wing span 35ft 0in (10.66m).
length 28ft 6in (8.68m).
height 8ft 11in (2.71m).
wing area 174sq ft (16.16sq m).
Crew: 2.
In Service: Great Britain (1),
Japan (1+), Netherlands (NEIAF
24), USA (USN, USMC).
Variants (with no. built):
CW–22 Prototype: Two-seat
trainer version of CW–21.
CW–22/3 Production: Trainer
version—to Turkey, USA;
fighter version—to Bolivia, Peru,
Turkey; reconnaissance version
to Colombia, Netherlands.
(NEIAF).

SNC–1 (Falcon): USN/USMC
designation for CW–22 trainer
(305).
Remarks: Low-powered, two seat
development of CW–21, USN/
USMC machines, ordered as
advanced combat trainers, also
served in liaison and glider-tug
roles; basic design exported in
variety of versions; NEIAF's
Falcons employed against
Japanese forces; initially for
reconnaissance, later fitted with
two 7.7mm machine-guns and
racks for two 100lb (45kg)
bombs; nearly all destroyed in
defence of Java, but at least one
example captured and evaluated
by Japanese; one other CW–22,
ex-Burmese VolAF, operated by
RAF prior to outbreak of Pacific
War.

Manufacturer: Douglas.
Model: RD–2.
Type: Transport amphibian.
Power Plant: Two 450hp Pratt
and Whitney R–1340–96.
Performance:
maximum speed at sea level

153mph (246km/hr).
normal range 770 miles (1,240km).
time to 5,000ft (1,525m) 7min
18sec.
service ceiling 15,900ft (4,846m).
Weights:
empty 6,377lb (2,893kg).
loaded 9,387lb (4,258kg).
Dimensions:
wing span 60ft 0in (18.29m).
length 45ft 2in (13.77m).
height 15ft 2in (4.62m).
wing area 592sq ft (55.0sq m).
Crew/Accommodation: 1/7.
In Service: Australia (4 impressed),
USA (USN, USCG).
Variants (with no. built):
RD: Military designation for
Dolphin civil transport
(USCG) (3).
XRD–1: Prototype; militarized
version of RD (USN) (1).
RD–2: Initial production model
(3).
RD–3: Modified RD–2 (6).
RD–4: USCG version of RD–3
(10).
C–21 (OA–3)/C–26(OA–4):
pre-war USAAC series (24).
Total Production: 47 (military

production).
Remarks: Undertook US coastal
patrol duties during early months
WWII.

Manufacturer: Douglas.
Model: DF.
Type: Long-range transport
flying boat.
Power Plant: Two 850hp Wright
R–1820–G2 Cyclone.
Performance:
maximum speed at 6,800ft
(2,073m) 178mph (286km/hr).
cruising speed 160mph (257km/hr).
normal range 2,700 miles
(4,344km).
initial rate of climb 800ft/min
(244m/min).
service ceiling 13,900ft (4,237m).
Weights:
empty 16,500lb (7,480kg).
loaded 28,500lb (12,927kg).
Dimensions:
wing span 95ft 0in (28.96m).
length 70ft 0in (21.34m).
wing area 1,295sq ft (120.31sq m).
Crew/Accommodation: 3–4/
32–48.
In Service: Japan (IJNAF), USSR.

Variants (with no. built):
Prototype (1).
Production model (4).
Total Production: 5.
Remarks: Designed 1935; two delivered to Japan, tested by IJN as Navy Experimental Type D Flying Boat; two others to USSR; initially employed as commercial transports, subsequently (1940–41) as military troopers.

Manufacturer: Douglas.
Model: O–46A.
Type: Observation.
Power Plant: One 725hp Pratt and Whitney R–1535–7.
Performance:
maximum speed 200mph (322km/hr).
Weights:
loaded 6,135lb (2,783kg).
Dimensions:
wing span 45ft 9in (13.94m).
length 34ft 10in (10.61m).
Armament: One fixed forward-firing .3in machine-gun in starboard wing; one flexible .3in machine-gun in rear cockpit.
Crew: 2.
In Service: USA.
Variants (with no. built):
Y10–43: Redesignated Y10–31C; one 675hp Curtiss V–1570–59 (5).
O–43A: Production model; as Y10–43 (24).
XO–46: Re-engined O–43A; one 725hp Pratt & Whitney R–1535–7; 1 conversion.
O–46A: Production model; as XO–46; modified aft fuselage decking (90).
Total Production: 119.
Remarks: Continuation of O–31 series (prototype first delivered 1930); both O–43A/46A models (debuts 1933/35 resp) obsolescent by outbreak WWII; number latter still equipped one observation sqn, US FEAF based Philippines at time of Japanese attack.

Manufacturer: Douglas.
Model: B–18A Bolo.
Type: Medium bomber.
Power Plant: Two 1,000hp Wright R–1820–53.
Performance:
maximum speed at 10,000ft (3,048m) 215mph (346km/hr).
cruising speed 167mph (269km/hr).
time to 10,000ft (3,048m) 9min 54sec.
service ceiling 23,900ft (7,285m).
Weights:
empty 16,321lb (7,403kg).
maximum 27,673lb (12,552kg).
Dimensions:
wing span 89ft 6in (27.28m).
length 57ft 10in (17.62m).
height 15ft 2in (4.62m).
wing area 965sq ft (89.65sq m).
Armament: Three .3in machine-guns in nose, dorsal and ventral positions; max bomb load 6,500lb (2,948kg).
Crew: 6.
In Service: Brazil (2 B–18C), Canada (20 Digby I), USA.
Variants (with no. built):
B–18: Militarized derivative of DC–2 commercial transport, inc prototype (DB–1) and 1 equipped with power-operated nose turret (DB–2) (133).
B–18A: Modified B–18; re-designed nose, power-operated dorsal turret (217).
B–18B: 76 B–18A conversions; re-modelled nose; Magnetic Airborne Detection (MAD) tail boom.
B–18C: 2 conversions as above, to Brazil.
C–58: Transport version; two B–18A conversions.
Digby I: As B–18A; Canadian order (20).
Total Production: 370.
Remarks: In first-line service on outbreak of Pacific War; many Hawaiian-based machines destroyed in Pearl Harbor attack; phased out 1942; subsequently employed (as B–18B) on anti-submarine patrols in Caribbean; RCAF Digby I also operated mainly convoy escort and anti-submarine duties.

Manufacturer: Douglas.
Model: C–32A.
Type: Troop carrier/transport.
Power Plant: Two 760hp Wright Cyclone SGR–1820F–52.
Performance:
maximum speed 210mph (338km/hr).
cruising speed 190mph (306km/hr).
initial rate of climb 1,000ft/min (305m/min).
service ceiling 22,450ft (6,843m).
Weights:
empty 12,408lb (5,628kg).
loaded 18,560lb (8,419kg).
Dimensions:
wing span 85ft 0in (25.91m).
length 61ft 11¾in (18.89m).
height 16ft 3¾in (4.97m).
wing area 939sq ft (87.23sq m).
Crew/Accommodation: 2/14–16.
In Service: Australia (10), Finland (3), Germany (6+), Great Britain, Japan (1 impressment), USA (USAAF, USN, USMC).
Variants (with no. built):
DC–2: Original civil model, inc 21 RAF impressments (138).
XC–32: Military prototype (1).
C–32A: 24 civil DC–2 impressments (USAAF).
C–33: Modified XC–32; enlarged tail and cargo door (18).
YC–34: As XC–32; different interior (2).
C–38: C–33 conversion with DC–3 tail (*1*).
C–39 Redesigned C33 with DC–3 centre section and tail (35).
C–41, 41A, 42: Personnel carrier versions; modified C–39s; various engines (3).
R2D–1: USN/USMC equivalents of DC–2 (5).
DC–2: Japanese licence-built by Nakajima, inc one from US components (6).
Total Production: 208.
Remarks: Military versions of civil DC–2 airliner of 1934; entered USAAC service 1936; employed early months of war, inc evacuation of Philippines; RAF impressments operated primarily India and Burma theatres; many other civil machines impressed for temporary war service, inc Finland's 'Hanssin-Jukka', unique in being converted into bomber complete with underwing bomb-racks and dorsal gun position; sole DC–1 served in transport role during Spanish Civil War.

Manufacturer: Douglas.
Model: C–47 Dakota.
Type: Troop/cargo transport.
Power Plant: Two 1,200hp Pratt and Whitney R–1830–92.
Performance:
maximum speed at 7,500ft (2,290m) 229mph (368km/hr).
cruising speed 185mph (296km/hr).
normal range 1,500 miles (2,400km).
initial rate of climb 1,130ft/min (345m/min).
service ceiling 23,200ft (7,076m).
Weights:
empty 16,970lb (7,705kg).
loaded 26,001b (11,805kg).
Dimensions:
wing span 95ft 0in (28.9m).
length 64ft 5½in (19.63m).
height 16ft 11in (5.2m).
wing area 987sq ft (91.7sq m).
Crew/Payload/Accommodation: 3/10,000lb (4,536kg)/28 troops or 18 litters.
In Service: Australia (4 DC–3, 124 C–47), Canada, Germany (4+ captured/impressed), Great Britain, India, Japan (licence-production), Rumania (DC–3), USA (USAAF, USN, USMC), USSR (709 Lend-Lease, + licence production).
Variants (with no. built):
DC–3/DST: Pre-war civil airliners; numerous impressments (455).
C–47 (Skytrain): Personnel/cargo transport; militarized DC–3; cargo door and strengthened floor (953).
C–47A: As C–47; revised electrical system (4,931).
C–47B: Re-engined C–47A; high altitude blowers, inc 133 TC–47B trainer versions (3,241).
XC–47C: Floatplane; one C–47 conversion.
C–47D, E, YC–47F: Post-war conversions.
C–48, –48A/C: Impressed civil DC–3A, DST and DC–3s; various engines (*36*).
C49, –49A/H, J, K: Impressed civil DC–3s, some ex-factory; various engines (*138*).
C–50, –50A/D: Civil impressments as C–49; altered interiors; various engines (*14*).
C–51: One civil DC–3 impressment; trooper.
C–52; 52A/C: Civil DC–3 impressments; troopers; 1,200hp Pratt & Whitney R–1830–51 (*5*).
C–53, –53B/D (Skytrooper): Personnel transports (370).
XC–53A: One C–53 conversion; full-span wing flaps.
C–68: Civil DC–3 impressments (*2*); 21 passengers.
C–117A, B: Modified C–47B; personnel transports (17).
XCG–17: One C–47 glider conversion.
R4D–1: USN/USMC equivalents of C–47 (106).
R4D–2 (R4D–2F): USN equivalent of C–49; VIP transport; redesignated R4D–2Z (2).
R4D–3, 4: USN/USMC equivalents of C–53, –53C (30).
R4D–5, 6: USN/USMC cargo transport equivalents of C–47A, B (200).
R4D–7, 8: USN/USMC equivalents of TC–47B, YC–47F (43).
DC–3: 8 RAF impressments.
Dakota Mk I: RAF equivalent of C–47; 52 Lend-Lease; 1 built from spares.
Dakota Mk II: Civil DC–2, 3 impressments (7).
Dakota Mk III RAF equivalent of C–47A; 12 ex-USAAF; 950 Lend-Lease.
Dakota Mk IV: RAF equivalent of C–47B; 1 ex-USAAF glider pick up; 895 Lend-Lease.
Lisunov Li–2: DC–3 licence-built in USSR by State Aircraft Plant; some with dorsal armament (*2,000+*).
Showa (Nakajima) L2D1–4: DC–3 licence-built in Japan (*485*).
Total Production: 10,349 (excl Japanese and USSR licence-production).
Remarks: Backbone of the Allies' transport and troop-carrier commands, C–47/Dakota series served in every combat theatre throughout the world; equipped 34 USAAF groups and over 50 RAF and Commonwealth sqns; licence-produced machines also extensively employed by both Japan and USSR; continued post-war service both military (inc Korea, Berlin/Airlift and Vietnam) and civilian up to present day, a 40-year service career unequalled in aviation history.
Colour Reference: Plates 136, 137: Douglas Dakota Mk III (KG496) of No 267 'Pegasus' Squadron, RAF, Bari, Italy, Oct 1943; standard Middle East camouflage scheme; note squadron badge on nose; employed in support SOE operations in Balkans.

Manufacturer: Douglas.
Model: R3D–1.
Type: General-purpose transport.
Power Plant: Two 1,000hp Wright R–1820–44.
Performance:
maximum speed 221mph (356km/hr).
cruising speed 195mph (314km/hr).
Weights:
loaded 19,582lb (8,882kg).
Dimensions:
wing span 78ft 0in (23.77m).
length 62ft 2in (18.95m).
height 19ft 10in (6.04m).
wing area 824sq ft (76.55sq m).
Crew/Accommodation: 2/14.
In Service: Japan (1 evaluation), USA (USAAF, USN, USMC).
Variants (with no. built):
DC–5: Civil transport (5).
R3D–1: USN service model of DC–5 (3).
R3D–2: Trainer version (USMC) (4).
R3D–3: One civil DC–5 impressment (USN).
C–110: USAAF designation; 3 impressments.
Total Production: 12.
Remarks: Limited US service, as troop-carrier/transports by USAAF and USN, and as paratroop trainers by USMC; four civil examples employed by KLM in Dutch East Indies, one of which captured and test-flown by Japanese.

Manufacturer: Douglas.
Model: XB–19A.
Type: Bomber/transport.
Power Plant: Four 2,600hp Allison V–3420–11.
Performance:
maximum speed at 20,000ft (6,096m) 265mph (426km/hr).
cruising speed 185mph (298km/hr).
maximum range 4,200 miles 6,760km).
service ceiling 39,000ft (11,887m).
Weights:
empty 92,400lb (41,913kg).
loaded 140,230lb (63,608kg).
Dimensions:
wing span 212ft 0in (64.62m).
length 132ft 2in (40.23m).
height 42ft 9in (13.03m).
wing area 4,285sq ft (398.08sq m).
Crew/Payload: 4–5/20,000lb (9,072kg).
In Service: USA.
Variants (with no. built):
XB–19: Bomber prototype; 2,000hp Wright R–3350–5s (1).
XB–19A: Re-engined XB–19; transport (*1*).
Total Production: 1.
Remarks: Initially designed and flown as heavy bomber; later stripped of all armament (two 37mm, five .5in and six .3in guns) and re-engined for service as long-range transport.

Manufacturer: Douglas.
Model: B–23 Dragon.
Type: Medium bomber.
Power Plant: Two 1,600hp Wright R–2600–3.
Performance:
maximum speed at 12,000ft (3,658m) 282mph (454km/hr).
cruising speed 210mph (338km/hr).
normal range 1,455 miles (2,341km).
service ceiling 31,600ft (9,632m).
Weights:
empty 19,059lb (8,645kg).
maximum 30,500lb (13,835kg).
Dimensions:
wing span 92ft 0in (28.04m).
length 58ft 4in (17.78m).
height 18ft 6in (5.64m).
wing area 993sq ft (92.25sq m).
Armament: Three .3in machine-guns in nose, dorsal and ventral positions; one .5in machine-gun in tail.
Crew: 4–5.
In Service: USA.
Variants (with no. built):
B–23: Production model; development of B–18A (38)
UC–67: Transport/glider-tug conversions (*12*).
Total Production: 38.
Remarks: Saw limited service on coastal patrol duties along US west coast after outbreak of Pacific War; subsequently relegated to training and other secondary roles.

Manufacturer: Douglas.
Model: TBD–1 Devastator.
Type: Carrier-based torpedo-bomber.
Power Plant: One 900hp Pratt and Whitney R–1830–64.
Performance:
maximum speed at 8,000ft (2,438m) 206mph (331km/hr).
cruising speed 128mph (206km/hr).
normal range 435 miles (700km).
initial rate of climb 720ft/min (219m/min).
service ceiling 19,500ft (5,944m).
Weights:
empty 5,600lb (2,540kg).
maximum 10,194lb (4,624kg).
Dimensions:
wing span 50ft 0in (15.24m).
length 35ft 0in (10.67m).
height 15ft 1in (4.6m).
wing area 422sq ft (39.20sq m).
Armament: One fixed forward-firing .3in machine-gun; one flexible .5in machine-gun in rear cockpit; one 1,000lb (454kg) torpedo under fuselage.
Crew: 3.
In Service: USA (USN).
Variants (with no. built):
XTBD–1: Prototype; upward folding wings; 800hp R–1830–60 (1).
TBD–1: Production model; modified cowling and raised canopy (129).
TBD–1A: Floatplane version; one TBD–1 conversion.
Total Production: 130.
Remarks: Equipped four USN torpedo sqns on outbreak of Pacific War; saw action early 1942 in Central Pacific; during Battle of Midway, 4 June 1942, one sqn completely destroyed attempting to attack Japanese carrier force, a second severely mauled; remaining Devastators relegated to training roles shortly thereafter.

Manufacturer: Douglas.
Model: SBD–5 Dauntless.
Type: Carrier-borne scout and dive-bomber.
Power Plant: One 1,200hp Wright R–1820–60.
Performance:
maximum speed at 15,800ft (4,816m) 245mph (394km/hr).
cruising speed 139mph (224km/hr).
service ceiling 24,300ft (7,407m).
Weights:
empty 6,533lb (2,963kg).
maximum 10,700lb (4,855kg).
Dimensions:
wing span 41ft 6¼in (12.65m).
length 33ft 0in (10.06m).
height 13ft 7in (4.14m).
wing area 325sq ft (30.19sq m).
Armament: Two fixed forward-firing .5in machine-guns; two flexible .3in machine-guns in rear cockpit; max bomb load 1,600lb (726kg) under fuselage, plus 650lb (295kg) underwing.
Crew: 2.
In Service: France (FAF 40+ A–24B; FNAF 32 SBD–5), Great Britain (FAA), Mexico, New Zealand (68 SBD–3/5), USA (USAAF, USN, USMC).
Variants (with no. built):
XBT–2: Prototype; Northrop BT–1 conversion (*1*).
SBD–1: Initial production model (USMC) (57).
SBD–2: Addn armament and fuel capacity (87).
SBD–3: Two .5in guns in lieu of .3in gun in cowling; self-sealing

Douglas TBD–1 Devastator

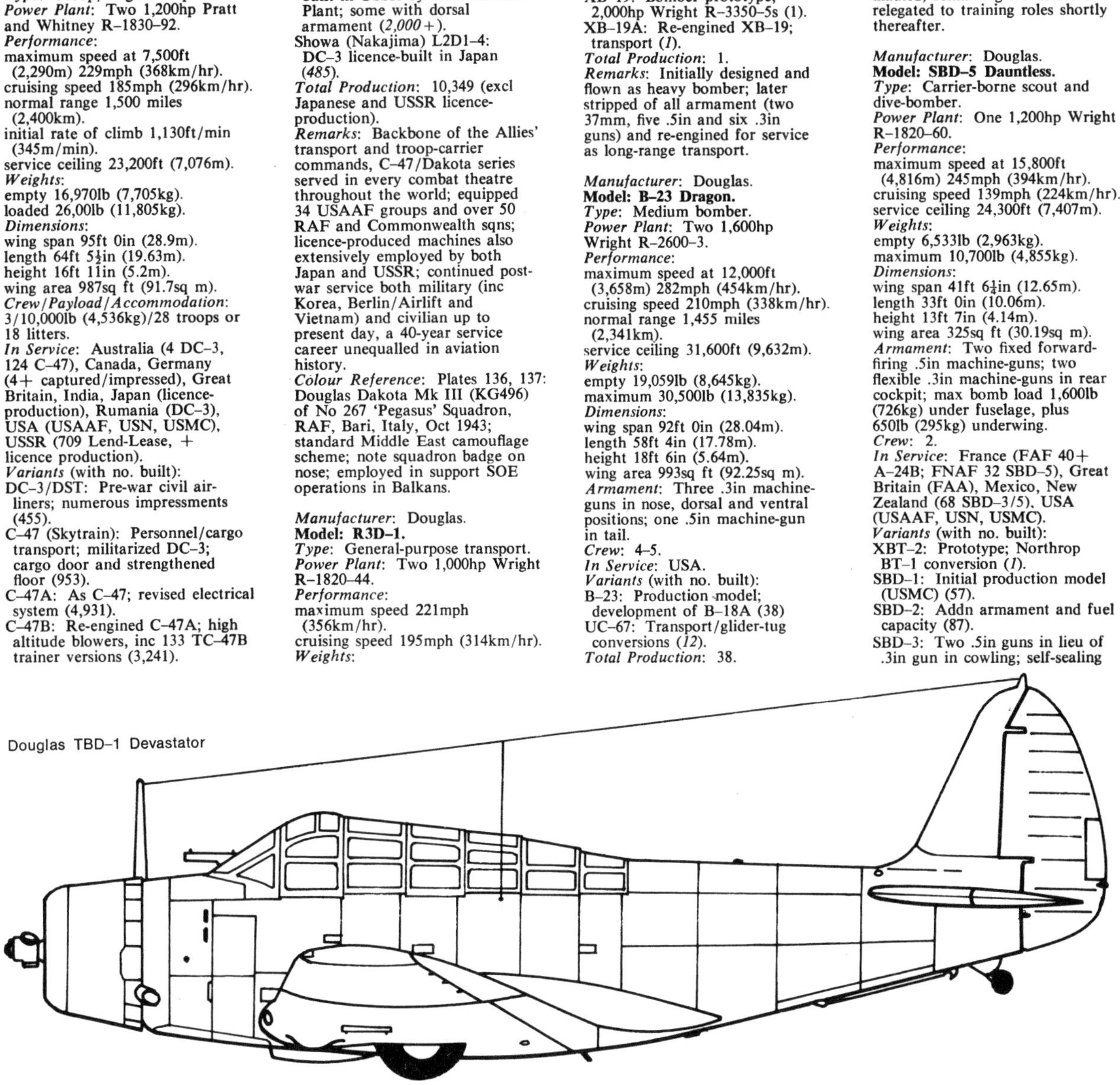

tanks (584).
SBD-4: Revised electrics (780).
SBD-5: Uprated engine; inc 60 SBD-5A (3,025).
SBD-6: Re-engined SBD-5 (451).
A-24: USAAF equivalent of SBD-3(A) (168).
A-24A: USAAF equivalent of SBD-4(A) (170).
A-24B: USAAF equivalent of SBD-5; (615).
Dauntless I: FAA equivalent of SBD-5; 9 Lend-Lease.
Total Production: 5,937.
Remarks: In action from very outset of Pacific War, both USN and USMC sqns being caught by Japanese at Pearl Harbor; balance more than redressed during ensuing months, Dauntless sqns participating both Coral Sea and Midway actions; remained in front-line service until Battle of Philippine Sea, June 1944; also employed by USAAF and RNZAF in limited numbers; and by French AF/NAF units in ground-support role against German forces on French Atlantic Coast, 1944-45; Mexican A-24Bs undertook anti-submarine patrols in Caribbean; British FAA, no operational service.
Colour Reference: Plates 139, 140: Douglas SBD Dauntless (No '3') of VS-6 aboard carrier USS *Enterprise* (CV-6), prior raid on Marcus Island, Central Pacific, 4 March 1942; standard late-1941 blue/grey finish; note earlier red/white rudder striping over-painted, also deletion ship's number from fuselage ship/mission/aircraft number coding (full code would previously have read 6-S-3), and variation in size wing upper surface markings.

Manufacturer: Douglas.
Model: DB-7B Boston.
Type: Light bomber.
Power Plant: Two 1,500hp Wright R-2600-A5B.
Performance:
maximum speed at sea level 311mph (500km/hr).
cruising speed 273mph (439km/hr).
normal range 525 miles (845km).
initial rate of climb 2,000ft/min (6,096m/min).
service ceiling 25,170ft (7,672m).
Weights:
empty 15,051lb (6,827kg).
maximum 21,580lb (9,790kg).
Dimensions:
wing span 61ft 4in (18.69m).
length 47ft 3in (14.40m).
height 18ft 1in (5.51m).
wing area 464sq ft (43.11sq m).
Armament: Four fixed .303in Browning machine-guns in nose;

twin flexible .303in guns in dorsal position; one .303in Vickers gun in ventral position; max bomb load 2,000lb (907kg).
Crew: 3.
In Service: Brazil (21), Canada, France (FAF, FVAF, FFAF), Great Britain, Netherlands, South Africa, USA, USSR (Boston III).
Variants (with no. built):
Model 7B: Prototype (1).
DB-7: Initial French order; 1,100hp Pratt & Whitney R-1830-SC3Gs or 1,200hp -S3C4-Gs (270).
DB-7A: As DB-7; Wright R-2600-A5Bs; French order (100).
DB-7B: Modified DB-7A; re-designed; enlarged fin and rudder; British order, inc 62 repossessed by USAAF (300).
DB-7B: Final French order (as DB-7B); undelivered; 453 taken over by RAF; 28 to USSR; Douglas-built (241); Boeing-built (240).
DB-7C: Dutch order; 14 delivered (as RA-20A); 34 repossessed by USAAF (48).
Boston I: RAF equivalent of DB-7; 20 taken over from French order.
II: RAF equivalent of DB-7B; 146 taken over from French order; all converted to Havoc I.
III: RAF designation of DB-7B; British/exFrench order and USAAF A-20Cs (*781*).
Havoc I: Boston II conversions to night fighter/intruder; inc 31 to Havoc I Turbinlite.
Havoc II: 99 DB-7A conversions to night-fighter/intruder inc 39 to Havoc II Turbinlite.
Total Production: 7,478 (all Marks).
Remarks: Initial versions of what was to become numerically most important of all USAAF's light-bomber 'Attack' types; originally ordered by France; only limited FAF service prior to French capitulation, June 1940; subsequently employed by Vichy AF; remainder of French orders diverted to RAF as Boston I/III; majority of Mks I and II converted into Havoc night-fighter/intruders; 70 examples equipped with high-powered searchlight in nose as Turbinlite I and II; others fitted to carry Pandora aerial mines; Boston Mk III employed in light day-bomber role, UK and Western Desert.

Manufacturer: Douglas.
Model: A-20B Havoc (Boston).
Type: Light bomber.
Power Plant: Two 1,600hp Wright

R-2600-11.
Performance:
maximum speed at 12,000ft (3,658m) 350mph (563km/hr).
cruising speed 278mph (447km/hr).
maximum range 2,300 miles (3,700km).
time to 10,000ft (3,048m) 5min 0sec.
service ceiling 28,600ft (8,717m).
Weights:
empty 14,830lb (6,727kg).
maximum 23,800lb (10,795kg).
Dimensions:
wing span 61ft 4in (18.69m).
length 48ft 0in (14.63m).
height 18ft 1in (5.51m).
wing area 464sq ft (43.11sq m).
Armament: Two fixed .5in nose guns, one flexible .5in upper gun, twin rearward-firing .3in guns in engine nacelles; max bomb load 2,600lb (1,179kg).
Crew: 3.
In Service: Australia (9 A-20A, 31 A-20C), Canada, Great Britain, Netherlands (NAF 6), USA (USAAF, USN, USMC), USSR (inc 665 A-20B, 48 A-20C, all Lend-Lease).
Variants (with no. built):
A-20: Initial USAAF order (variant of French DB-7B) (63).
A-20A: Re-engined A-20; unsupercharged (143).
XA-20B: Modified A-20A; three power turrets (1 conversion).
A-20B: USAAF equivalent of DB-7A (999).
A-20C: Modified A-20A with British equipment; Douglas-built (808); Boeing-built (140).
A-20E: 17 A-20A conversions with A-20B engines.
XA-20F: One A-20A conversion; different armament.
DB-7B: British order repossessed by USAAF (62).
F-3: Photo-reconnaissance conversion of A-20 (3).
XP-70: Prototype night-fighter conversion of A-20 (1).
P-70: Night-fighter conversion of A-20 (59).
P-70A-1: Night-fighter conversion of A-20C (*13*).
BD-1: USN equivalent of A-20A (1).
BD-2: USN/USMC equivalent of A-20B (8).
Boston IIIA: RAF equivalent of A-20C; 200 Lend-Lease.
Total Production: 7,478 (all Marks).
Remarks: Early USAAF versions; A-20A entered service 1941; A-20C first variant to see combat, based UK 1942; also served in North Africa and Pacific; USAAF P-70s employed primarily as

radar-equipped night-fighter trainers; RAF Boston IIIAs used in tactical day-bomber role; participated D-Day landings, specially equipped with smoke-laying apparatus to screen Normandy beach-heads.

Manufacturer: Douglas.
Model: A-20G Havoc (Boston).
Type: Light bomber.
Power Plant: Two 1,600hp Wright R-2600-23.
Performance:
maximum speed at 12,400ft (3,780m) 339mph (545km/hr).
cruising speed 272mph (438km/hr).
normal range 1,090 miles (1,754km).
time to 10,000ft (3,048m) 7min 6sec.
service ceiling 25,800ft (7,864m).
Weights:
empty 15,984lb (7,250kg).
maximum 27,200lb (12,338kg).
Dimensions:
wing span 61ft 4in (18.69m).
length 48ft 0in (14.63m).
height 17ft 7in (5.36m).
wing area 464sq ft (43.11sq m).
Armament: Six fixed .5in guns (or four 20mm); two .5in nose guns; one .5in hand-held gun in rear cockpit (or two .5in guns in power-operated turret); one .5in gun in ventral position; max bomb load 4,000lb (1,814kg).
Crew: 3.
In Service: Australia (29 A-20G), Canada, Great Britain, South Africa, USA, USSR (SovAF, SovNAF 3, 125 Bostons, Havocs, all Marks).
Variants (with no. built):
A-20G: Modified A-20D; solid nose; various armament; Series 1/3 (2,850).
A-20H: As A-20G; uprated engines (412).
A-20J: As A-20G; frameless transparent nose (450).
A-20K: As A-20H; frameless transparent nose (413).
F-3A: Photo-reconnaissance conversions of A-20J/K (46).
P-70A-2: Night-fighter conversions of A-20G (26).
Boston IV: RAF equivalent of A-20J; 169 Lend-Lease.
Boston V: RAF equivalent of A-20K; 90 Lend-Lease, inc 11 to RCAF.
Total Production: 7,478 (all Marks).
Remarks: A-20G most numerous and principal operational variant of entire series; served in European (9th AF), Mediterranean (12th AF) and Pacific (5th AF) theatres, primarily in low-altitude attack role; Boston IV entered RAF service Aug 1944; together

with Boston V employed in tactical close-support of Allied armies in Northern Europe (2nd TAF) and Italy (DAF) until VE-Day; almost half of all production supplied to USSR; extensively used in ground-support, and on anti-shipping strike missions, from Black Sea to North Cape.
Colour Reference: Plates 142, 143: Douglas A-20G Havoc (42-54255) of Soviet Air Force, Tula, Central (Moscow) Sector, Russian Front, March 1944; representative of the many thousands Allied aircraft supplied to the Soviet AF during WWII; note (local) dorsal turret modification, also overpainting US bars four of six stations; white tail tip and rudder tab tactical/unit marking; rudder motifs, corresponding to rank and branch badges as worn by Colonel of Soviet AF, presumably indicate pilot's status/rank.

Manufacturer: Douglas.
Model: A-26B Invader.
Type: Attack bomber.
Power Plant: Two 2,000hp Pratt and Whitney R-2800-27 or 79.
Performance:
maximum speed at 15,000ft (4,572m) 355mph (571km/hr).
cruising speed 284mph (457km/hr).
normal range 1,800 miles (2,896km).
time to 10,000ft (3,048m) 8min 6sec.
service ceiling 31,300ft (9,450m).
Weights:
empty 22,850lb (10,365kg).
loaded 35,000lb (15,880kg).
Dimensions:
wing span 70ft 0in (21.35m).
length 50ft 9in (15.47m).
height 18ft 6in (5.64m).
wing area 540sq ft (50.17sq m).
Armament: Six fixed .5in machine-guns in nose; two .5in machine-guns each in dorsal and ventral remotely-controlled turrets; optional eight .5in guns in additional underwing and cheek packages; max bomb load 4,000lb (1,815kg) internally, plus 2,000lb (907kg) underwing bombs or rockets.
Crew: 3.
In Service: Great Britain, USA.
Variants (with no. built):
XA-26: Prototype; bomber version (1).
XA-26A: Prototype; night-fighter version (1).
XA-26B: Prototype; night-fighter version; re-designed nose with one 75mm cannon (1).
A-26B: Initial production model (1,355).

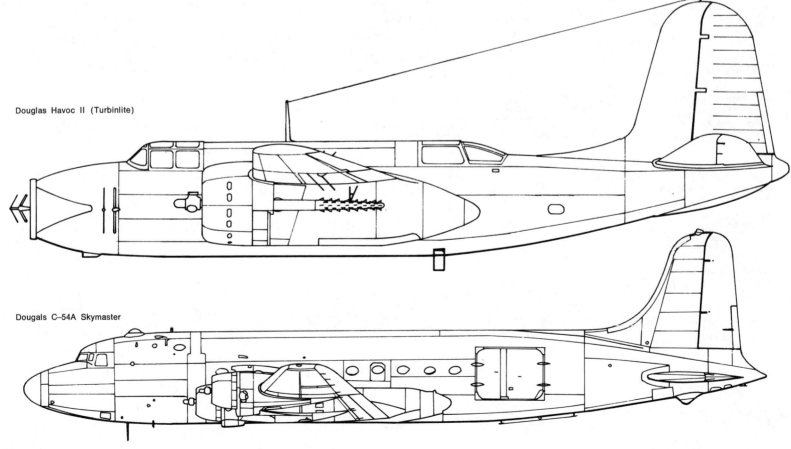

Douglas Havoc II (Turbinlite)

Dougals C-54A Skymaster

A-26C: Transparent 'bombardier' nose; widened fuselage; dual controls (1,091).
FA-26C: Post-war reconnaissance version; one A-26C conversion.
XA-26D: Prototype only; eight-gun nose, plus six in wing (1).
XA-26F: Engine test-bed (*1*).
B-26K: Post-war COIN conversions (*70+*).
Total Production: 2,450.
Remarks: Last important USAAF 'A' (Attack)-category aircraft to be produced in quantity, Invader entered service ETO, Nov 1944; equipped four Groups of 9th AF; also operational with 5th AF (one Group) on Okinawa during closing weeks of war with Japan; extensive post-war service, inc Korea and Vietnam.
Colour Reference: Plate 144: Douglas A-26B Invader (41-39272) AN.V of 553rd Bomb Squadron, 386th Bomb Group (Medium), 9th USAAF; St Trond, Belgium, April 1945; natural metal finish; horizontal yellow tail band (outlined in black) group marking; fuselage code (AN) and yellow engine cowlings indicate squadron.

Manufacturer: Douglas.
Model: C-54A Skymaster.
Type: Long-range general-purpose transport.
Power Plant: Four 1,290hp Pratt & Whitney R-2000-7.
Performance:
maximum speed 275mph (442km/hr).
range 3,900 miles (6,275km).
time to 10,000ft (3,048m) 14min 48sec.
service ceiling 22,000ft (6,706m).
Weights:
empty 37,000lb (16,783kg).
maximum 62,000lb (28,123kg).
Dimensions:
wing span 117ft 6in (35.81m).
length 93ft 10in (28.6m).
height 27ft 6in (8.38m).
wing area 1,460sq ft (135.63sq m).
Crew/Accommodation: 6/30-50.
In Service: Great Britain (23), USA (USAAF, USN, USMC).
Variants (with no. built):
C-54: USAAF designation for impressed DC-4A civil transports (24).
C-54A: Re-engined C-54; strengthened floor for heavy loads; cargo doors; convertible passenger/troop configuration (207).
C-54B: As C-54A; increased weight; provision for stretchers (220).
C-54C: VIP transport; one C-54A conversion.
C-54D: Re-engined C-54B (350).
C-54E: Long-range cargo/passenger transport version (75).
C-54G: Re-engined C-54E; high density passenger interior (76).
XC-54F, C-54H, J: Projects only.
XC-54K: Modified long-range C-54E (1).
XC-114, 116: Post-war variants; Allison V-1710-131 inline engines (2).
R5D-1/4: USN/USMC equivalent of C-54, -54A, D, G (211).
Skymaster I: RAF equivalent of of C-54B (*1*) and C-54D (*22*); Lend-Lease 1944/45.
Total Production: 1,122.
Remarks: Entered service with US Air Transport Command late 1942; soon established regular world-wide routes—transatlantic, across Pacific from USA to Australia, over Indian Ocean from Australia to Ceylon; in just under 80,000 wartime ocean crossings only three C-54s lost; also served North Africa, Alaska/Aleutians and over 'Hump' from India to China; sole C-54C was US Presidential transport fitted with State and conference rooms, plus electrically-operated elevator for use of President Roosevelt; likewise single Lend-Lease C-54B was for personal use of Prime Minister Churchill; both USAAF and USN/USMC Skymasters saw extensive post-war use, inc Korea and Berlin Airlift.

Manufacturer: Fairchild.
Model: 91 'Baby Clipper'.
Type: Transport amphibian.
Power Plant: One 750hp Pratt and Whitney Hornet S2E-G.
Performance:
maximum speed at sea level 161mph (259km/hr).
cruising speed 150mph (241km/hr).
maximum range 665 miles (1,070km).
initial rate of climb 840ft/min (256m/min).
service ceiling 15,600ft (4,755m).

Fairchild 91 'Baby Clipper'

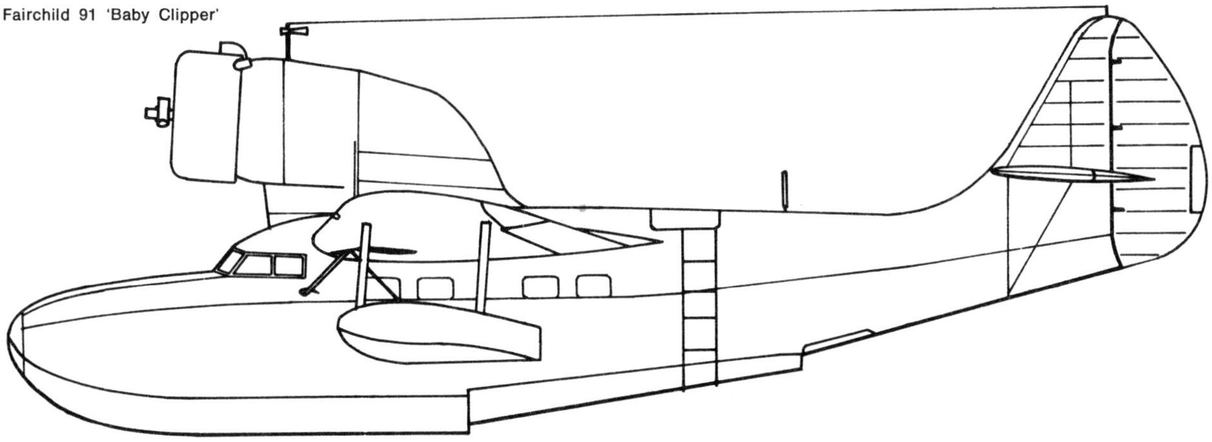

Weights:
empty 6,596lb (2,992kg).
loaded 10,500lb (4,763kg).
Dimensions:
wing span 56ft 0in (17.06m).
length 46ft 8¼in (14.22m).
height 14ft 8in (4.47m).
wing area 483sq ft (44.87sq m).
Crew/Accommodation: 2/9.
In Service: Great Britain (1), Japan (1), Spain (NatAF 1, RepAF 2).
Variants (with no. built):
Model 91: Production model; Panair do Brasil (2); Japan (IJN) (1); Spain (3).
Total Production: 6.
Remarks: Original PanAm order; two to Brazilian subsidiary; one to IJN for evaluation as Type F Amphibious Transport; three to Republican Spain, two arriving safely, one captured en route by Nationalists; subsequently saw service on both sides during Civil War, performing maritime patrol, liaison, and spotting duties along Spanish Biscay and Mediterranean coasts; both Republican examples destroyed Autumn 1937; one Brazilian machine acquired by British-American Ambulance Corps; operated by RAF along North African coast Nov 1941 until sunk off Benghazi, May 1943.

Manufacturer: Fairchild.
Model: UC-61K Forwarder.
Type: Utility transport/communications.
Power Plant: One 200hp Ranger L-440-7.
Performance:
maximum speed 124mph (198km/hr).
cruising speed 112mph (179km/hr).
normal range 465 miles (745km).
service ceiling 12,700ft (3,873m).
Weights:
empty 1,813lb (823kg).
loaded 2,882lb (1,308kg).
Dimensions:
wing span 36ft 4in (11.7m).
length 23ft 10¾in (7.24m).
height 7ft 7¼in (2.32m).
wing area 193.3sq ft (18.5sq m).
Crew/Accommodation: 1/3.
In Service: Australia (2 Model 24R, 1 Model 24G, 1 Model 24W-40), Canada, Finland (1 Model 24J), Great Britain, USA (USAAF, USN, USMC, USCG).
Variants (with no. built):
Model 24G, J, K, R, W: Initial civil production; 3/4-seat high-wing cabin monoplane.
UC-61: Militarized Model 24W-41 civil light transport; 165hp Warner R-500-1; inc 161 to RAF) (163).
UC-61A: As UC-61; improved radio equipment; inc 364 to RAF (512).
UC-61B/H, J: Impressed civil light transports; various engines (14).
UC-61K: Militarized Model 24-R; all to RAF (306).
GK-1: USN equivalent of UC-61A (13).
J2K-1/2: USCG designations for Model 24-R; (2/2) (4).
J2K-2: Proper USMC designation for impressed Model 24-H, incorrect contemporary designation JK-1 (1).
Argus I: RAF designation for UC-61; 161 Lend-Lease.
Argus II: RAF designation for UC-61A; 364 Lend-Lease.
Argus III: RAF designation for UC-61K; 306 Lend-Lease.
Total Production: 1,008 (military variants).
Remarks: Original Type 24 civil model first appeared 1932; USAAF production initiated 1941; majority delivered to RAF under Lend-Lease; Argus Is to UK (several lost at sea en route); Argus II/IIIs used principally in Middle and Far Eastern theatres, 1943-45; number pre-war civil export models impressed foreign AFs, inc Finland (one 24-J employed HQ communications duties, Winter War 1939-40), Australia (4) and Canada (liaison/communications roles, 1940-45).

Manufacturer: Fairchild.
Model: JK-1.
Type: Light transport/communications.
Power Plant: One 320hp Wright XR-760-6 Whirlwind.
Performance:
maximum speed 168mph (270km/hr).
maximum range 840 miles (1,352km).
service ceiling 19,000ft (5,791m).
Weights:
loaded 19,500lb (8,845kg).
Dimensions:
wing span 39ft 6in (12.04m).
length 30ft 0in (9.14m).
height 8ft 0in (2.44m).
wing area 248sq ft (23.04sq m).
Crew/Accommodation: 1/4.
In Service: USA (USN).
Variants (with no. built):
Fairchild 45: Initial civil production; 5-seat cabin monoplane.
JK-1: USNAF designation; Staff transport (3).
Remarks: Single JK-1 entered USN service 1936 VIP/Staff transport duties; two further civil examples impressed post-Pearl Harbor.

Manufacturer: Fairchild.
Model UC-96.
Type: Photographic survey/transport.
Power Plant: One 450hp Pratt & Whitney R-1340.
Performance:
maximum speed at 5,000ft (1,525m) 142mph (228km/hr).
Weights:
empty 3,296lb (1,495kg).
loaded 5,500lb (2,495kg).
Dimensions:
wing span 50ft 0in (15.24m).
length 33ft 0in (10.06m).
wing area 335sq ft (31.12sq m).
Crew/Accommodation: 3 crew (photog. survey); 1/5 or 6 (transport).
In Service: Canada, USA.
Variants (with no. built):
Model 71: Initial civil production.
UC-96: USAAF designation impressed Model 71 (3).
Remarks: Civil Model 71 one of few types to be re-enlisted USAAF; original service debut (as C-8/F-1 series), 1929; three examples subsequently impressed 1942 (as UC-96) for photographic survey duties; Canadian (Fairchild)-built Models, inc earlier 51, 71, and Super 71, served RCAF communications/light transport roles between early thirties and (Model 51) 1946.

Manufacturer: Ford.
Model: 5-AT-B
Type: Transport.
Power Plant: Three 420hp Pratt & Whitney C-1/SC-1 Wasp.
Performance:
cruising speed 122mph (196km/hr).
normal range 550 miles (885km).
service ceiling 18,500ft (5,639m).
Weights:
normal 13,000lb (5,897kg).
Dimensions:
wing span 77ft 10in (23.72m).
length 49ft 10in (15.19m).
wing area 835.0sq ft (77.57sq m).
Crew/Accommodation: 2/15.
In Service: Australia.
Variants (with no. built):
4-AT: Prototype; civil transport version; three 200hp Wright J4 Whirlwind; open cockpit; 2 crew/8 passengers (1).
4-AT-A: Initial production model (25).
4-AT-B: Modified 4-AT-A; three 220hp J5 Whirlwind; increased wing span; 12 passengers (35).
4-AT-C/F: Re-engined 4-AT-B; various power plants (29).
5-AT-A: Improved 4-AT; three 420hp Pratt & Whitney Wasp; increased wing span; enlarged cabin; 13 passengers (3).
5-AT-B/D: As 5-AT-A; increased passenger seating (114).
6-AT-A: Re-engined 5-AT-C; three 300hp J6 Whirlwind (3).
7-AT, 9-AT, 11-AT: Re-engined 6-AT-A, 4-AT-B, 4-AT-E and 5-AT-D; various power plants.
8-AT: Single-engined freighter version; modified 5-AT-C.
10-AT, 12-A: Projects only.
14-A: 40-passenger transport version; one 1,100hp and two 715hp Hispano-Suiza (1).
C-3/4, -9 USAAC designations for militarised 4-AT-B, 5-AT-B/D (*13*).
Total Production: 225.
Remarks: Ford's famous tri-motored 'Tin Goose' first appeared early twenties; entered USAAC service 1928; two examples (4-AT-E/5-AT-C) impressed RAAF 1942 for ambulance duties/emergency medical evacuation New Guinea combat zone.

Manufacturer: Goodyear.
Model: K-type (K-14 to K-135).
Type: Patrol airship.
Power Plant: Two 550hp Pratt and Whitney R-1340-AN-2.
Performance:
maximum speed 75mph (121km/hr).
cruising speed 47mph (75km/hr).
range 2,000 miles (3,220km).
Dimensions:
volume 425,000cu ft (12,034.75cu m).
length 251ft 8½in (76.72m).
diameter 62ft 6in (19.05m).
Armament: Provision for anti-submarine bombs and/or depth-charges.
Crew: 12.
In Service: USA (USN).
Variants (with no. built):
K-1: Prototype and initial production model; enlarged J-type envelope; 319,900cu ft (9,059.6cu m) capacity; two 330hp Wright J-6-9; training and experimental only (1).
K2: K-1 development; increased volume, 404,000cu ft (11,440cu m); two 550hp Pratt & Whitney R-1340-AN-2 (1).
K-3 to K-13: Modified K-2; increased volume (K-5 to K-8)—416,000cu ft (11,779.87cu m), altn power plant (K-3 to K-8), two 420hp Wright R-975-28; K-3, K-4 and K-7, K-8 training only (11).
K-14 to K-135: Major production model; some subsequently modified to 456,000cu ft (12,912.56cu m) capacity (122).
ZPK: Post-war USN designation for K-type.
ZP2K, ZP3K: Post-war USN designations for modified K-types; subsequently re-designated ZSG-2, ZSG-3 resp.
Total Production: 135.
Remarks: Standard USN patrol airship of WWII; four examples (K-2 to K-5) on strength at time of Pearl Harbor; 111 subsequently employed first-line coastal patrol, shipping-escort, anti-submarine and allied duties, 1942-45; equipped five Fleet Airship Wings (total 13 sqns) deployed US Atlantic, US Pacific, Gulf Caribbean, and Brazilian seaboards; two also operated by Florida-based utility sqn, plus six by independent patrol sqn on detachment to Mediterranean theatre from June 1944; only one airship lost to enemy action, K-74 shot down by German submarine U-134 off Key West, Florida, night of 18 July 1943; no confirmed individual sinkings, but airships participated in destruction number of U-boats, inc *U 853* off New England coast, 6 May 1945.

Manufacturer: Goodyear.
Model: M-type (M-1).
Type: Patrol airship.
Power Plant: Two 600hp Pratt & Whitney R-1340-AN-2.
Performance:
maximum speed 75mph (121km/hr).
Dimensions:
volume 625,000cu ft (17,698.12cu m).
length 310ft 0in (94.49m).
Armament: Provision for anti-submarine bombs and/or depth-charges.
Crew: 10 or 12.
In Service: USA (USN).
Variants (with no. built):
M-1: Prototype and initial production model; articulated car (1).
M-2 to M4: Improved M-1; increased volume-725,000cu ft (20,529.83cu m) (3).
Total Production: 4.
Remarks: First flown Oct 1943, only four M-type airships (out of total twenty-two ordered) delivered to USN; remained in service until Sept 1956.

Manufacturer: Great Lakes.
Model: BG-1
Type: Carrier-borne dive-bomber.
Power Plant: One 750hp Pratt & Whitney R-1535-882 Wasp.
Performance:
maximum speed at 8,900ft (2,713m) 188mph (302km/hr).
normal range 549 miles (883km).
time to 5,000ft (1,525m) 5min 30sec.
service ceiling 20,100ft (6,126m).
Weights:
empty 3,903lb (1,770kg).
maximum 6,347lb (2,879kg).
Dimensions:
wing span 36ft 0in (10.97m).
length 28ft 9in (8.76m).
height 11ft 0in (3.35m).
wing area 384sq ft (35.67sq m).
Armament: One fixed forward-firing .3in machine-gun; one flexible .3in machine-gun in rear cockpit; provision for one 1,000lb (454kg) bomb.
Crew: 2.
In Service: USA (USN, USMC).
Variants (with no. built):
XBG-1: Prototype; single-engined two-seat dive-bomber biplane; one Pratt & Whitney R-1535-64; open cockpits (1).
BG-1: Production model; uprated engine; enclosed cockpits (60).
Total Production: 61.
Remarks: Equipped one USN carrier-based sqn and two USMC sqns late thirties; relegated to secondary liaison/

training roles both services by 1940; 20+ still on strength at time of Pearl Harbor, Dec 1941.

Manufacturer: Grumman.
Model: FF-2 (Goblin).
Type: Fighter.
Power Plant: One 700hp Wright R–1820–78.
Performance:
maximum speed at 4,000ft (1,220m) 207mph (333km/hr).
normal range 921 miles (1,482km).
time to 5,000ft (1,525m) 2min 54sec.
service ceiling 21,100ft (6,430m).
Weights:
empty 3,250lb (1,474kg).
loaded 4,828lb (2,190kg).
Dimensions:
wing span 34ft 6in (10.52m).
length 24ft 6in (7.47m).
height 9ft 5in (2.87m).
wing area 310sq ft (28.8sq m).
Armament: One fixed forward-firing .3in Browning machine-gun; two flexible .3in Brownings in rear cockpit.
Crew: 2.
In Service: Canada, Spain (RepAF, NatAF).
Variants (with no. built):
XFF–1: Fighter prototype (1).
XSF–1: Two seat scout prototype (1).
FF–1: Initial USN production model; Wright R–1820–78 (7).
SF–1: Scout version; Wright R–1820–84 (34).
FF–2: Dual-control version of FF–1 (20).
Model GE–23: Export version of FF–2; 800hp Wright R–1820–F52; Canadian Car and Foundry-built (57).
Goblin: RCAF designation for GE–23 (*17*).
Delfin: Spanish designation for GE–23 (*40*).
Total Production: 120.
Remarks: First USN fighter with retractable undercarriage; withdrawn from service by outbreak of WWII; served with RCAF until April 1941; Spanish examples delivered to Republican AF Winter 1937–38; engaged in Civil War; eight captured by Nationalists, surviving to equip Spanish AF into fifties.

Manufacturer: Grumman.
Model: F3F–3.
Type: Carrier-borne fighter.
Power Plant: One 950hp Wright R–1820–22.
Performance:
maximum speed at 15,200ft (4,633m) 264mph (425km/hr).
maximum range 980 miles (1,577km).
initial rate of climb 2,750ft/min (838m/min).
service ceiling 33,200ft (10,120m).
Weights:
empty 3,285lb (1,490kg).
maximum 4,795lb (2,175kg).
Dimensions:
wing span 32ft 0in (9.75m).
length 23ft 2in (7.06m).
height 9ft 4in (2.84m).
wing area 260sq ft (24.15sq m).
Armament: Two fixed forward-firing .3in machine-guns.
Crew: 1.
In Service: USA (USN, USMC).
Variants (with no. built):
XF2F–1: Prototype; single-seat fighter biplane; one Pratt & Whitney R–1535–44 (1).
F2F–1: Production model; uprated engine (54).
XF3F–1: Prototype; modified F2F–1; increased fuselage length and wing span (1).
F3F–1: Production model; one 650hp Pratt & Whitney R–1535–84 Twin Wasp (54).
XF3F–2; Re-engined F3F–1; one Wright R–1820 (1).
F3F–2: Production model (81).
XF3F–3: Modified F3F–2; one 950hp Wright R–1820–22; 1 conversion.
F3F–3: Production model (27).
Total Production: 219.
Remarks: Scaled-down single-seat development of earlier FF–1, Grumman's 'Flying Barrel' was last US fighter biplane; F2F–1 entered service 1935; F3Fs still on first-line USN/USMC strength upon outbreak WWII, but withdrawn shortly thereafter; some 140 examples all marks still employed ancillary liaison/'hack' roles at time of Pearl Harbor.

Manufacturer: Grumman.
Model: J2F–6 Duck.
Type: General utility amphibian floatplane.
Power Plant: One 1,050hp Wright R–1820–54.
Performance:
maximum speed at sea level 176mph (283km/hr).
cruising speed 155mph (248km/hr).
service ceiling 20,000ft (6,100m).
Weights:
empty 5,445lb (2,470kg).
loaded 7,700lb (3,496kg).
Dimensions:
wing span 39ft 0in (11.9m).
length 34ft 0in (10.37m).
height 12ft 4in (3.76m).
wing area 409sq ft (38.0sq m).
Armament: One .3in Browning machine-gun in rear cockpit; two 100lb (45kg) bombs or 325lb (147kg) depth-charges.
Crew/Accommodation: 2/5 (or 1 litter).
In Service: Argentina (8), USA (USN, USMC, USCG).
Variants (with no. built):
XJF–1: Prototype; 700hp Pratt and Whitney R–1830 (1).
JF–1: Initial production model (27).
JF–2: 750hp Wright Cyclone; 14 to USCG, 1 to USN, 8 to Argentina (23).
JF–3: Similar to JF–2 (5).
J2F–1 (Duck): Modified JF–3; arrester gear, catapult points (29).
J2F–2: With armament; USMC (30).
J2F–3; Supercharged R–1820–36 (20).
J2F–4: Target-tug version (32).
J2F–5: Improved J2F–4; several to USCG, 1 to USAAF (OA–12) test only (144).
J2F–6: Modified J2F–5; alternative utility, PR, TT and anti-submarine versions; Columbia Aircraft Corp licence-built (330).
Total Production: 641.
Remarks: Served throughout WWII; performed multitude of tasks: anti-submarine, coastal patrol, ASR, casualty evacuation, photographic-reconnaissance, target-tug; was instrumental in capture of secret German radio station on Greenland; claimed two U-boats damaged; was last aircraft to leave beleaguered Bataan; later stages of Pacific war extensive use in air-sea rescue role.

Manufacturer: Grumman.
Model: JRF–5 Goose.
Type: Utility transport/photo-reconnaissance amphibian.
Power Plant: Two 450hp Pratt and Whitney R–985–AN–6.
Performance:
maximum speed at 5,000ft (1,525m) 201mph (323km/hr).
cruising speed 191mph (307km/hr).
maximum range 640 miles (1,030km).
initial rate of climb 1,100ft/min (335m/min).
service ceiling 21,000ft (6,405m).
Weights:
empty 5,425lb (2,461kg).
loaded 8,000lb (3,629kg).
Dimensions:
wing span 49ft 0in (14.95m).
length 38ft 6in (11.73m).
height 16ft 2in (4.93m).
wing area 375sq ft (34.8sq m).
Crew/Accommodation: 2/4–7.
In Service: Canada (29 JRF–5), Great Britain, Portugal (PNAF), USA (USAAF, USN, USMC, USCG).
Variants (with no. built):
XJ3F–1: Service test model of civil G–21A amphibian (1).
JRF–1: Modified XJ3F–1; 450hp R–985–SB2 (7).
JRF–1A: Photo-reconnaissance, target-tug version of JRF–1 (5).
JRF–2: Air/sea rescue version (USCG) (7).
JRF–3: As JRF–2, anti-icing equipment (USCG) (3).
JRF–4: Anti-submarine version of JRF–1; bomb-racks for two 250lb (113kg) bombs or depth-charges (12).
JRF–5: Major production model; photo-reconnaissance version; re-engined (185).
JRF–6B: Trainer/ASR version; improved JRF–5 (RAF) (50).
OA–9: USAAC equivalent of JRF–1; civil impressments (31).
OA–13A: Re-engined OA–9 (USAAF) (3).
OA–13B: USAAF equivalent of JRF–5 photo-reconnaissance version (2).
Goose I: RAF equivalent of JRF–5; 5 Lend-Lease.
Goose IA: RAF equivalent of JRF–6B; 50 Lend-Lease.
Total Production: 304 (excl civil models).
Remarks: Original civil utility amphibian; first military use by USAAC, 1938; subsequently adapted by USN; saw widespread service during WWII in transport, reconnaissance, anti-submarine, and ASR roles; British examples served in West Indies and communications duties in U.K.

Manufacturer: Grumman.
Model: J4F Widgeon.
Type: General utility/anti-submarine amphibian.
Power Plant: Two 200hp Ranger L–440–5.
Performance:
maximum speed 153mph (245km/hr).
cruising speed 138mph (221km/hr).
range 920 miles (1,472km).
initial rate of climb 700ft/min (213m/min).
service ceiling 14,600ft (4,453m).
Weights:
loaded 4,500lb (2,043kg).
Dimensions:
wing span 40ft 0in (12.2m).
length 31ft 1in (9.45m).
height 11ft 5in (3.48m).
wing area 245sq ft (22.76sq m).
Armament: One 200lb (91kg) depth-charge.
Crew/Accommodation: 2/3–5.
In Service: Canada, Brazil, Great Britain, Portugal (PNAF), USA (USAAF, USN, USMC, USCG).
Variants (with no. built):
J4F–1: Civil G–44 light amphibian; underwing light bomb-racks (USCG) (25).
J4F–2: Service production; similar to J4F–1 (USN, USMC) (131).
OA–14: USAAF equivalent of J4F–1 (16).
Widgeon I: FAA equivalent of J4F–2; 16 Lend-Lease.
Remarks: Original civil amphibian converted for general utility/coastal patrol roles; major user, USN, employed primarily as utility transport; only USCG aircraft to score confirmed U-boat 'kill' during WWII: U–166 sunk 1 Aug 1942 in Gulf of Mexico; originally known in FAA service as Gosling I, served in communications role principally in West Indies, 1943–45.

Manufacturer: Grumman.
Model: F4F–4 Wildcat.
Type: Carrier-borne fighter.
Power Plant: One 1,200hp Pratt and Whitney R–1830–86.
Performance:
maximum speed at 19,400ft (5,913m) 318mph (512km/hr).
cruising speed 155mph (250km/hr).
normal range 770 miles (1,240km).
initial rate of climb 1,950ft/min (594m/min).
service ceiling 34,900ft (10,637m).
Weights:
empty 5,785lb (2,624kg).
maximum 7,952lb (3,607kg).
Dimensions:
wing span 38ft 0in (11.58m).
length 28ft 9in (8.76m).
height 11ft 10in (3.60m).
wing area 260sq ft (24.15sq m).
Armament: Six fixed forward-firing .5in Browning machine-guns; two 100lb (45kg) bombs.
Crew: 1.
In Service: Canada, Great Britain (FAA), USA (USN, USMC).
Variants (with no. built):
XF4F–1/3: Prototypes (2).
F4F–3: Initial production model; addn armament (285).
F4F–3A: Re-engined F4F–3 (55).
XF4F–4: Prototype; hydraulic folding wings; one F4F–3 conversion.
F4F–4: Production model; manual folding wings (1,169).
FM–1: As F4F–4; General Motors-built (1,140).
XF4F–5, 6, 8: Prototypes; modified F4F–3A, 4s; various engines (5).
F4F–7: Long-range unarmed reconnaissance version (21).
FM–2: As XF4F–8; 1,350hp Wright R–1820–56; heightened fin and rudder; General Motors-built (4,467).
Martlet (Wildcat) I: FAA equivalent of F4F–3A; fixed wings (100).
Wildcat II: As Mk I; folding wings; 2 addn guns (90).
Wildcat III: Modified Mk II; catapult spools; 60 Lend-Lease (original Greek order) (10).
Wildcat IV: FAA equivalent of F4F–4; two addn wing guns; 200 Lend-Lease.
Wildcat V: FAA equivalent of FM–1; 312 Lend-Lease.
Wildcat VI: FAA equivalent of FM–2; 370 lend-Lease.
Total Production: 7,344.
Remarks: Equipped several USMC sqns on outbreak of Pacific war; first action in defence of Wake Island; subsequently equipped all USN carrier-borne fighter sqns; standard US naval fighter 1942–43; participated all major actions, destroying over 900 enemy aircraft in process, before replacement by F6F; purchased by UK as Martlet I/III (inc French and Greek orders), subsequently supplied Lend-Lease Martlet IV, V and Wildcat VI; latter name standardized from Jan 1944; first US fighter in British service to down enemy aircraft (Ju 88 over Scapa Flow, Dec 1940); equipped many RN carrier sqns, also operated in Western Desert.
Colour Reference: Plate 145: Grumman Martlet I (AX730) 'L' of No 805 Squadron, Fleet Air Arm, Sidi Haneish (LG 102), Egypt, Sept 1941; forming one flight of Royal Naval Fighter Squadron in Western Desert, No 805's Martlets finished light azure blue overall; (compare with Hawker Hurricane Mk I, plate 68).

Manufacturer: Grumman.
Model: TBF–1 Avenger.
Type: Torpedo bomber.
Power Plant: One 1,700hp Wright R–2600–8.
Performance:
maximum speed at sea level 251mph (404km/hr).
cruising speed 145mph (233km/hr).
normal range 1,215 miles (1,955km).
initial rate of climb 1,430ft/min (436m/min).
service ceiling 22,400ft (6,828m).
Weights:
empty 10,080lb (4,572kg).
maximum 15,905lb (7,215kg).
Dimensions:
wing span 54ft 2in (16.51m).
length 40ft 0in (12.19m).
height 16ft 5in (5.00m).
wing area 490sq ft (45.52sq m).
Armament: One fixed forward-firing .3in gun; one .5in gun in dorsal, one .3in gun in ventral positions; max bomb or torpedo load 1,600lb (726kg).
Crew: 3.
In Service: Great Britain (FAA), New Zealand (48 TBF–1/–1C), USA (USN, USMC).
Variants (with no. built):
XTBF–1: Prototype (2).
TBF–1: Initial production model, inc subvariants TBF–1D, E, J, L, P (1,525).
TBF–1C: Two addn wing guns and drop tanks, inc P.R. version TBF–1CP (764).
XTBF–2: One conversion with XR–2600–10 Cyclone.
XTBF–3: With Wright R–2600–10 (2).
TBM–1: As TBF–1; General Motors-built (550).
TBM–1C: As TBF–1C; General Motors-built (2,332).
XTBM–3: Prototype as XTBF–3; General Motors-built (4).
TBM–3: Wright R–2600–8; armament as TBF–1C, inc subvariants TBM–3H, J, L, P and TBM–3D/E with centrimetric radar; General Motors-built (4,657).
XTBM–4: Prototypes; similar to TBM–3E; General Motors-built (3).
Tarpon (Avenger) Mk I (TBF–1B): FAA equivalent of TBF–1; 402 Lend-Lease.
Avenger Mk II: FAA equivalent of TBM–1C; 334 Lend-Lease.
Avenger Mk III: FAA equivalent of TBM–3, –3E; 222 Lend-Lease.
Avenger A.S. Mk 4: Post-war FAA equivalent of TBM–3E, 35 Lend-Lease.
Total Production: 9,839.
Remarks: First operation Battle of Midway, five out of six participating Avengers lost to enemy action; nonetheless went on to become standard USN torpedo-bomber of WWII, taking active—often decisive—part in all subsequent major air-sea actions from Guadalcanal to Okinawa; also operated Atlantic and Mediterranean areas, principally, in anti-submarine role; employed by USMC both against ground targets and for anti-submarine patrols; equipped 15 FAA sqns (where initially known as Tarpon), operating Arctic, Atlantic and Pacific theatres; extensive post-war use by US and foreign forces.
Colour Reference: Plate 141: Grumman Avenger Mk II (JZ512) K1.B of No 832 Squadron, Fleet Air Arm; HMS *Begum*, British East Indies Fleet, Indian Ocean, 1944–45; standard FAA dark slate grey/extra dark sea grey/sky finish; note over-painted roundels (six stations) with new reduced diameter SEAC blue/white roundels superimposed; (compare with British Pacific Fleet markings, see Fairey Firefly, plates 60–61).

Manufacturer: Grumman.
Model: F6F–5 Hellcat.
Type: Carrier- and land-based naval fighter.
Power Plant: One 2,000hp Pratt and Whitney R–2800–10W.
Performance:
maximum speed at 23,400ft (7,132m) 380mph (611km/hr).
cruising speed 168mph (270km/hr).
normal range 945 miles (1,520km).
initial rate of climb 2,980ft/min (908m/min).
service ceiling 37,300ft (11,369m).
Weights:
empty 9,238lb (4,190kg).
maximum 15,413lb (6,991kg).
Dimensions:
wing span 42ft 10in (13.05m).
length 33ft 7in (10.23m).
height 13ft 1in (3.99m).
wing area 334sq ft (31.03sq m).
Armament: Six fixed forward-firing .5in Browning wing guns; or two 20mm cannon plus four .5in guns; max bomb load 2,000lb (907kg) or six rocket projectiles underwing.
Crew: 1.
In Service: Great Britain (FAA), USA (USN, USMC).
Variants (with no. built):
XF6F–1, 2: Prototypes; various engines; redesigned and re-designated as XF6F–3, 4 resp (2).
F6F–3: Initial production model (4,423).
F6F–3N: Night-fighter version; APS–6 radar (205).
F6F–3E: As –3N; APS–4 radar (18).
F6F–5: Improved F6F–3; redesigned cowling; provision for bombs or rockets (6,436).
F6F–5N: Night-fighter version; APS–6 radar (1,189).
F6F–5P: Photo-reconnaissance version; F6F–5, –5N conversions.
XF6F–6: 2,100hp R–2800–18W (2).
Hellcat I: RAF equivalent of F6F–3; 252 Lend-Lease.
Hellcat II, N.F.II: RAF equivalents of F6F–5, –5N; 930 Lend-Lease.
Total Production: 12,275.
Remarks: Operational debut Aug 1943; swung balance of Pacific naval aviation power firmly and irrevocably to US; during last two years of war credited with 75% of all enemy aircraft shot down by USN carrier pilots; together with land-based sqns claimed well over 5,000 enemy machines; also used in night-fighter role; equipped fourteen FAA sqns (initially known as Gannet).
Colour Reference: Plates 146, 147: Grumman F6F–5 Hellcat (No 73) of VF–15 aboard carrier USS *Randolph* (CV–15), Task Force 58, off Okinawa, May 1945; representative example late-war white geometrical squadron markings assigned by COM-NAVAIRPAC, 27 Jan 1945, to twenty-eight USN Pacific Fleet carriers, Randolph's squadrons' identifying symbols comprised horizontal bars across tailfin/rudder and solid white ailerons.

Manufacturer: Hall.
Model: PH–3.
Type: Patrol/air/sea rescue flying-boat.
Power Plant: Two 750hp Wright R–1820F–51.
Performance:
maximum speed at sea level 153mph (246km/hr).
maximum speed at 3,200ft (975m) 159mph (256km/hr).
cruising speed 136mph (216km/hr).
normal range 1,937 miles (3,117km).
service ceiling 21,350ft (6,507m).
Weights:
empty 9,614lb (4,361kg).
maximum 17,679lb (8,019kg).
Dimensions:
wing span 72ft 10in (22.20m).
length 51ft 0in (15.54m).
height 19ft 10in (6.04m).
wing area 1,170sq ft (108.69sq m).
Armament: Four flexible .3in Lewis guns; max bomb load 1,000lb (454kg).
Crew: 4–6.
In Service: USA (USN, USCG).

Variants (with no. built):
XPH-1: Prototype; 537hp Wright GR-1750 (1).
PH-1: Initial production model; re-engined XPH-1 (620hp R-1820-86) (9).
PH-2: Modified PH-1 (USCG); uprated engine (7).
PH-3: Modified PH-2; improved cockpit enclosure (7).
Total Production: 24.
Remarks: Last US biplane flying boat, PH-1 first entered service in 1931; Coast Guard variants (PH-2/3) ordered 1936-39 respectively; latter served on anti-submarine patrol duties following Pearl Harbor, subsequently reverting to coastal-patrol/ASR role.

Manufacturer: Harlow.
Model: UC-80.
Type: Liaison.
Power Plant: One 145hp Warner Super Scarab 50-A.
Performance:
maximum speed at sea level 150mph (241km/hr).
cruising speed 135mph (217km/hr).
maximum range 500 miles (805km).
initial rate of climb 660ft/min (201m/min).
service ceiling 15,500ft (4,725m).
Weights:
empty 1,700lb (771kg).
loaded 2,600lb (1,180kg).
Dimensions:
wing span 35ft 7½in (10.86m).
length 23ft 3½in (7.1m).
height 7ft 3in (2.21m).
wing area 185sq ft (17.19sq m).
Crew/Accommodation: 1/3.
In Service: USA.
Variants (with no. built):
PJC-2: Initial civil production model; four-seat cabin monoplane.
UC-80: USAAF designation impressed PJC-2 (4).
Remarks: Four civil tourers impressed USAAF liaison duties 1942.

Manufacturer: Howard.
Model: GH-1 Nightingale.
Type: Ambulance/communications.
Power Plant: One 450hp Pratt and Whitney R-985-AN-12.
Performance:
maximum speed at sea level 165mph (265km/hr).
cruising speed 154mph (248km/hr).
normal range 875 miles (1,130km).
service ceiling 20,000ft (6,100m).
Weights:
empty 3,050lb (1,385kg).
loaded 4,500lb (2,040kg).
Dimensions:
wing span 38ft 0in (11.58m).
length 25ft 8in (7.82m).
height 8ft 4in (2.54m).
wing area 210sq ft (19.5sq m).
Crew/Accommodation: 1/3.
In Service: USA (USAAF, USN, USMC).
Variants (with no. built):
GH-1: Militarised (USN/USMC) version of DGA civil transport (34).
GH-2: Ambulance version; provision for 2 stretchers; enlarged entry door (131).
GH-3: Modified GH-2 (115).
NH-1: Instrument trainer (205).
UC-70, -70A/D: USAAF designations for impressed civil DGA transports; various engines (20).
Total Production: 505 (military variants).
Remarks: USN/USMC variants entered service 1941; used primarily in ambulance/medical-evacuation roles; USAAF impressments 1942 for communications/liaison duties.

Manufacturer: Interstate.
Model: L-6 Grasshopper.
Type: Liaison.
Power Plant: One 102hp Franklin 0-200-5.
Performance:
maximum speed 104mph (167km/hr).
normal range 540 miles (869km).
Weights:
empty 1,103lb (500kg).
loaded 1,650lb (748kg).
Dimensions:
wing span 35ft 6in (10.82m).
length 23ft 5½in (7.15m).
height 7ft 3in (2.6m).
wing area 174sq ft (16.16sq m).
Crew: 2.
In Service: USA.
Variants (with no. built):
XO-63 (XL-6): Prototype; impressed civil Model S-1B Cadet (1).
L-6: Production model (250).

Grumman (C.C.F.) GE-23 Goblin

Grumman J2F-6 Duck

Grumman JRF-6B Goose

Grumman J4F-2 Widgeon

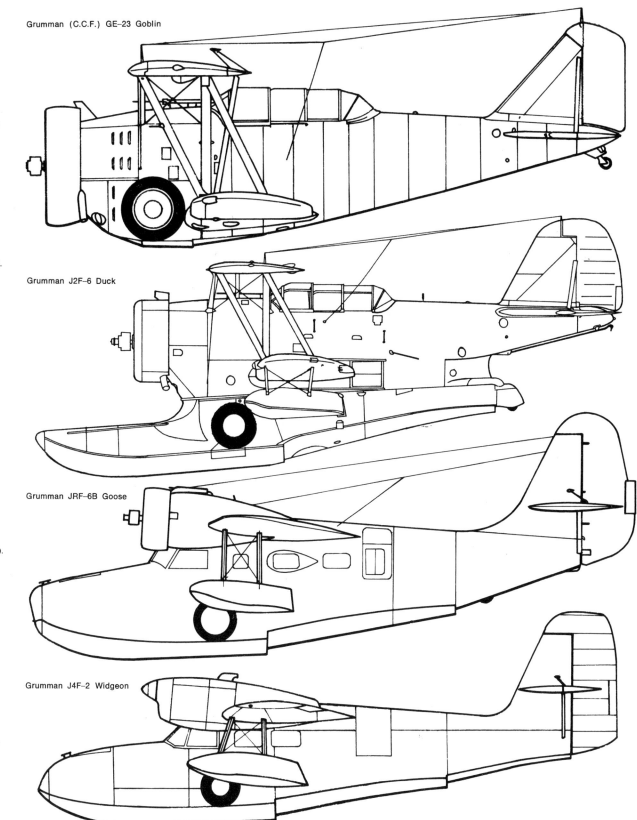

Total Production: 251.
Remarks: Pre-war civil light-plane; entered AAF service late 1943; limited employment in liaison and communications roles; L-8A was similar military derivative of civil Model S-1A Cadet; all eight ex-USAAF delivered to Bolivia.

Manufacturer: Interstate.
Model: TDR-1.
Type: Assault drone.
Power Plant: Two 220hp Lycoming 0-435.
Dimensions:
wing span 45ft 0in (13.72m).
length 30ft 0in (9.14m).
Armament: Bomb or torpedo-load of 2,000lb (907kg).
In Service: USA (USAAF, USN).
Variants (with no. built):
XTDR-1: Prototype (2).
TDR-1: Production model (189).
XBQ-4: USAAF test model; one TDR-1.
Total Production: 191.

Remarks: TV camera- and transmitter-equipped pilotless assault drone employed by USN in attacks on Rabaul, Sept-Oct 1944; marginal success, overwhelming conventional air superiority precluded further use.

Manufacturer: Lockheed.
Model: UC-101.
Type: Communications.
Power Plant: One 450hp Pratt and Whitney Wasp R-1340.
Performance:
maximum speed 190mph (306km/hr).
initial rate of climb 1,000ft/min (305m/min).
service ceiling 19,000ft (5,790m).
Weights:
loaded 4,750lb (2,155kg).
Dimensions:
wing span 41ft 0in (12.50m).
length 27ft 6in (8.38m).
Crew/Accommodation: 1/6.
In Service: Australia, USA.
Variants (with no. built):

Model 5 Vega: Civil production; high-wing seven-seat cabin monoplane.
Model UC-101: USAAF designation for impressed Model 5 (1).
Remarks: Famous early thirties commercial series; Australia and USA each impressed one Model 5 Vega (1941-42 resp) for general-purpose communications duties.

Manufacturer: Lockheed.
Model: UC-36 Electra.
Type: Utility transport.
Power Plant: Two 450hp Pratt and Whitney R-985-13.
Performance:
maximum speed at sea level 192mph (309km/hr).
cruising speed 180mph (290km/hr).
maximum range 880 miles (1,416km).
initial rate of climb 1,000ft/min (305m/min).
service ceiling 19,400ft (5,920m).
Weights:
empty 6,450lb (2,926kg).

loaded 10,500lb (4,762kg).
Dimensions:
wing span 55ft 0in (16.76m).
length 38ft 7in (11.76m).
height 10ft 1in (3.07m).
wing area 460sq ft (42.73sq m).
Crew/Accommodation: 2/10.
In Service: Canada (15), Germany, Great Britain (8+), USA (USAAF, USN, USCG), USSR (1).
Variants (with no. built):
Model 10 Electra: Civil transport (142).
XC-35: Experimental high-altitude version of Model 10 (USAAF) (1).
C-36 (UC-36): USAAF designation for Model 10A; 10 seats (3).
UC-36A/C: Impressed civil transports; Models 10A, E, B; various engines; 10-12 seats (26).
C-37 (UC-37): As UC-36; Militia Bureau (1).
XR20-1: USN designation for Model 10A (1).

XR30-1: USCG designation for Model 10B (1).
Total Production: 149.
Remarks: Original high-speed civil passenger/freight carrier; 100+ delivered to US and foreign airlines prior to outbreak of WWII; USAAF's UC-36/37 employed as utility transports; USN/USCG examples as VIP personnel transports; many other civil machines impressed/sequestrated for temporary war service; 8+ to RAF, inc 3 ex-Yugoslav impressed Middle East for reconnaissance duties; 4 ex-Polish to Rumania (subsequently to Germany), fifth seized by USSR.

Manufacturer: Lockheed.
Model: C-40A.
Type: Utility transport.
Power Plant: Two 450hp Pratt and Whitney Wasp-Junior SB.
Performance:
maximum speed at sea level 214mph (344km/hr).
cruising speed 202mph (325km/hr).
maximum range 1,060 miles (1,705km).
initial rate of climb 1,360ft/min (415m/min).
service ceiling 22,300ft (6,802m).
Weights:
empty 5,960lb (2,703kg).
loaded 8,650lb (3,923kg).
Dimensions:
wing span 49ft 6in (15.10m).
length 36ft 4in (11.12m).
height 9ft 9in (2.98m).
wing area 325sq ft (32.75sq m).
Crew/Accommodation: 2/5.
In Service: Canada (10), Great Britain (17+), Netherlands (NEIAF), USA (USAAF, USN, USMC).
Variants (with no. built):
Model 12/12-A: Civil transports (Electra Junior) (73).
C-40 (UC-40): USAAF designation for Model 12-A; 7 seats (3).
C-40 (UC-40A): As C-40; 5 seats (10).
C-40B: Model 12 with tricycle undercarriage (1).
UC-40D: Impressed civil Model 12A; 8 seats (10).
JO-1: USN designation for Model 12A; 7 seats (3).
JO-2: As JO-1; 6 seats (USN/USMC) (9).
XJO-3: Model 12 with tricycle undercarriage (1).
R30-2: Civil model 12As impressed by USMC (3+).
Model 212: NEIAF order; Crew trainers (16).
Total Production: 114.
Remarks: Smaller version of

Model 10 intended for feeder-line, private and business use; employed as general-purpose transport/liaison throughout WWII by USAAF; at least one USMC JO-2 destroyed on ground by enemy action during Pearl Harbor attack; Dutch Model 212 crew-trainers employed in transport and maritime patrol roles after Japanese invasion of Netherlands East Indies; further Dutch examples (Model 12s) diverted to Ceylon and Australia; impressed by RAF and USAAF; two privately-registered British Model 12-As employed on clandestine photo-reconnaissance of German and Italian installations during months immediately prior to WWII; subsequently formed nucleus of RAF's official PDU (later PRU).

Manufacturer: Lockheed.
Model: A-29 Hudson.
Type: Light bomber/maritime-reconnaissance.
Power Plant: Two 1,200hp Wright R-1820-87.
maximum speed at 15,000ft (4,572m) 253mph (407km/hr).
cruising speed 205mph (330km/hr).
maximum range 2,800 miles (4,505km).
time to 10,000ft (3,048m) 6min 18sec.
service ceiling 26,500ft (8,077m).
Weights:
empty 12,825lb (5,817kg).
maximum 21,000lb (9,526kg).
Dimensions:
wing span 65ft 6in (19.96m).
length 44ft 4in (13.51m).
height 11ft 11in (3.63m).
wing area 551sq ft (51.19sq m).
Armament: Two .3in machine-guns each in nose and power-operated dorsal turret (optional); plus one in lower rear fuselage; max bomb load 1,600lb (726kg).
Crew: 4.
In Service: Australia (247 Mks I, III, IV), Canada, China (3), Great Britain (RAF, FAA), Netherlands (NAF approx 20), New Zealand (Mks IIIA, VI), South Africa (2), USA (USAAF, USN).
Variants (with no. built):
A-28: USAAF designation for militarized civil Model 14 Super Electra; all Lend-Lease to RAF (52).
A-28A: As A-28; uprated engines; all Lend-Lease to RAF (450).
A-29: Re-engined A-28; all Lend-Lease to RAF (416).
A-29A: Troop-carrying version of A-29; all Lend-Lease to RAF (384).

A-29B: Photo-reconnaissance version of A-29/29A; 24 conversions.
AT-18: Trainer version of A-29A; dorsal turret (217).
AT-18A: As AT-18 minus turret (83).
C-111: Utility transport version of impressed civil Model 14 (3).
PBO-1: USN designation for requisitioned RAF Hudson IIIA (20).
Hudson Mk I: RAF designation for militarized civil Model 14 Super Electra (350).
Mk II: As Mk I; different propellers (20).
Mk III: Modified Mk I; 1,200hp Wright GR-1820-G205A; addn armament; some as long-range version (410).
Mk IIIA: RAF designation for A-29/29A; inc 20 requisitioned by USN and approx 300 by USAAF (800).
Mk IV: As Mk III; two Pratt and Whitney Twin Wasps; inc 30 diverted from RAAF order (130).
Mk IVA: RAF designation for A-28; 52 Lend-Lease to RAAF.
Mk V: Re-engined Mk IV; majority long-range (319).
Mk VI: RAF designation for A-28A; 450 Lend-Lease.
Hudson Mks I, III, IV: RAAF equivalent of RAF Hudson Mks I, IIIA, IVa; 147 inc 87 Mk III and 60 Mk IV (Lend-Lease) (100).
Total Production: 2,934.
Remarks: Original civil transport (Model 14 Super Electra) militarized specifically to meet RAF needs for coastal reconnaissance bomber; entered service summer 1939; first RAF aircraft to destroy enemy aircraft in WWII: Do 18 over North Sea; operated during Dunkirk evacuation; maintained anti-U-boat patrols North Sea and Western Approaches; 27 Aug 1941 captured U-boat in North Atlantic; from 1942 flew clandestine missions to enemy-occupied Europe; 1942-43 operated Mediterranean area; first aircraft to sink U-boat by means of underwing rocket projectiles; phased out of first-line service 1943-44, but continued to serve in transport and ASR roles; extensively used by RAAF in Far East; limited service only by US forces, mainly on training duties, but also accounted for first U-boat sunk by USAAF (A-29), and first two by USN (PBO-1).

Manufacturer: Lockheed.
Model: C-60A Lodestar.
Type: Paratroop carrier/troop and freight transport.
Power Plant: Two 1,200hp Wright R-1820-87.
Performance:
maximum speed at 17,000ft (5,185m) 266mph (426km/hr).
cruising speed 200mph (320km/hr).
normal range 1,660 miles (2,660km).
time to 10,000ft (3,048m) 6min 36sec.
Weights:
empty 12,075lb (5,480kg).
loaded 18,500lb (8,400kg).
Dimensions:
wing span 65ft 8in (19.96m).
length 49ft 10in (15.19m).
height 11ft 10¼in (3.60m).
wing area 551sq ft (51.9sq m).
Crew/Accommodation: 2/21 paratroops.
In Service: Australia (10), Great Britain, Netherlands (NEIAF 26), South Africa (26 impressments), USA (USAAF, USN, USMC, USCG).
Variants (with no. built):
C-56: USAAF order; militarized Model 18-50; Wright R-1820-89s (1).
C-56A/E: Impressed civil Model 18s; various engines (35).
C-57: USAAF order; militarized Model 18-14; Pratt & Whitney R-1830-53s (13).
C-57B: Impressed civil Model 18; troop carrier (7).
C-57C/D: Three/one C-60A conversions; various engines.
C-59: Impressed civil Model 18-07 (10).
C-60: Impressed civil Model 18-56 (36).
C-60A: Paratroop version (325).
XC-60B: As C-60A with de-icers; one conversion.
C-66: As civil Model 18-10; 11 passengers (1).
C-111: Impressed civil Model 14-N (see A-29 Hudson) (3).
XR50-1: Prototype, USN (1).
R50-1: Command transport; USN/USCG equivalent of C-56 (3).
R50-2/4: Executive transports, 4-7 passengers (16).
R50-5: Standard 12-14 seat transport version, USN/USMC (41).
R50-6: USN/USMC equivalent of C-60A; 18 paratroopers (35).
Lodestar Mk I: RAF civil purchase Model 18-07/08 (9).
Lodestar Mk IA: RAF equivalent of C-59; 11 Lend-Lease.
Lodestar Mk II: RAF equivalent of C-60; 15 Lend-Lease.

Total Production: 560+.
Remarks: Civil Model 18, an enlarged and improved version of Model 14, first flown early 1940; subsequently militarized for widespread use by USAAF as general-purpose personnel and freight transport, and by USN/USMC as staff and command transport; RAF examples equipped 4 sqns in Middle East for general-purpose and air ambulance duties; many civil machines impressed for temporary war service.

Manufacturer: Lockheed.
Model: PV-1 Ventura.
Type: Patrol-bomber.
Power Plant: Two 2,000hp Pratt & Whitney R-2800-31.
Performance:
maximum speed at sea level 296mph (476km/hr).
cruising speed 164mph (264km/hr).
normal range 1,660 miles (2,670km).
initial rate of climb 2,230ft/min (6,797m/min).
service ceiling 26,300ft (8,016m).
Weights:
empty 20,197lb (9,161kg).
maximum 31,077lb (14,097kg).
Dimensions:
wing span 65ft 6in (19.96m).
length 51ft 9in (15.77m).
height 11ft 11in (3.63m).
wing area 551sq ft (51.19sq m).
Armament: Two .5in machine-guns each in nose and dorsal turret; two .3in in ventral position; internal bomb or torpedo-load 3,000lb (1,361kg), max underwing bomb load 2,000lb (907kg).
Crew: 4-5.
In Service: Australia (20 B-34, 41 B-37, 14 PV-1), Canada (Ventura I, G.R.V), Great Britain, South Africa (approx 270), New Zealand (139), USA (USAAF, USN, USMC).
Variants (with no. built):
PV-7: Militarized civil Model 18 for USN/USMC, inc 338 for RAF (1,600).
PV-1P: Photo-reconnaissance conversions of PV-1.
PV-3: USN designation for requisitioned Ventura II (27).
B-34 Lexington: USAAF equivalent of PV-1; all to RAF/RAAF (200).
B-34A/B: USAAF designation of requisitioned RAF Venturas; patrol/trainer versions.
B-37 (O-56): Modified B-34; 1,700hp Wright R-2600-31; 18 requisitioned from RAF order.
Ventura I: RAF designation of purchased Model L-37 (88).
Ventura II: Modified Mk I; re-

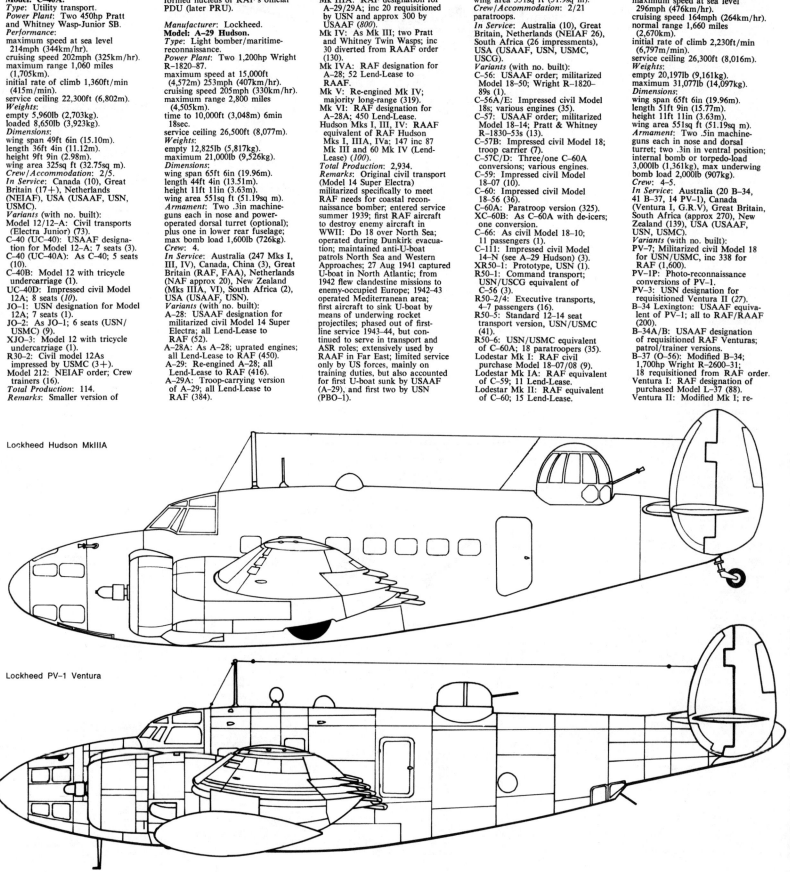

Lockheed Hudson MkIIIA

Lockheed PV-1 Ventura

engined; approx 208 requisitioned by USAAF (B-34A/B), 27 to USN (PV-3) (587).
Ventura IIA: RAF designation for B-34; 200 Lend-Lease.
Ventura G.R.I: Coastal Command designation of original Mk I.
Ventura G.R.V: General-reconnaissance version for Coastal Command; as PV-1; 388 Lend-Lease.
Total Production: 2,475.
Remarks: Military development of civil Model 18 again produced to specific British contract; entered RAF service Oct 1942 as light day-bomber; unsuccessful in this role, and heartily disliked by crews, was subsequently employed by Coastal Command; G.R.V widely used by Commonwealth AFs; limited employment by USAAF as land-based over-water patrol bomber; majority of production to USN/USMC; first deliveries Dec 1942 as PBO Hudson replacements; in service until end of war; PV-1 modified for service as USMC's first night-fighter, scoring first victory Nov 1943 over Solomon Islands.

Manufacturer: Lockheed.
Model: PV-2 Harpoon.
Type: Patrol-bomber.
Power Plant: Two 2,000hp Pratt & Whitney R-2800-31.
Performance:
maximum speed at sea level 271mph (436km/hr).
maximum speed at 13,700ft (4,175m) 282mph (454km/hr).
cruising speed 171mph (275km/hr).
maximum range 2,930 miles (4,714km).
initial rate of climb 1,630ft/min (497m/min).
service ceiling 23,900ft (7,285m).
Weights:
empty 21,028lb (9,538kg).
maximum 36,000lb (16,330kg).
Dimensions:
wing span 75ft 0in (22.86m).
length 51ft 1in (15.57m).
height 13ft 3in (4.04m).
wing area 686 sq ft (63.73sq m).
Armament: Five fixed forward-firing nose guns; two flexible .5in guns each in dorsal turret and ventral position: max bomb load, internal 4,000lb (1,814kg), external 2,000lb (907kg).
Crew: 4–5.
In Service: USA (USN).
Variants (with no. built):
PV-2; Modified PV-1; increased wingspan, fins, rudders and fuel capacity; improved armament (500).
PV-2C: Trainer version; 30 PV-2 conversions.
PV-2D: As PV-2; eight .5in nose guns (35).
Total Production: 535.
Remarks: Basically similar to earlier Ventura, and retaining PV designation, PV-2 Harpoon was first delivered to USN in March 1944; served mainly in Pacific theatre during closing year of war; continued post-war use by both USN Reserve and by USMC.

Manufacturer: Lockheed.
Model: P-38F Lightning.
Type: Long-range fighter/fighter-bomber.
Power Plant: Two 1,250hp Allison V-1710-49/53.
Performance:
maximum speed at 5,000ft (1,524m) 347mph (558km/hr).
maximum range 1,425 miles (2,293km).
time to 5,000ft (1,524m) 1min 48sec.
service ceiling 39,000ft (11,887m).
Weights:
empty 13,600lb (6,169kg).
maximum 20,000lb (9,070kg).
Dimensions:
wing span 52ft 0in (15.85m).
length 37ft 10in (11.52m).
height 9ft 10in (2.99m).
wing area 327.5sq ft (30.42sq m).
Armament: One 20mm Hispano cannon; four .5in Browning machine-guns in nose; max bomb load 2,000lb (907kg).
Crew: 1.
In Service: Australia (3 F-4), France (FAF, FFAF: F-5A/B), Germany (1 P-38E: evaluation/demonstration), Great Britain (3), Italy (1), Portugal, USA.
Variants (with no. built):
XP-38: Prototype; four 23mm Madsen cannon plus four .5in Colt-Browning machine-guns (1).
YP-38: Service test model; modified XP-38; one 37mm Oldsmobile cannon, two .5in plus two .3in machine-guns (13).
P-38: Initial production model; V-1710-27/29; one 37mm

Lockheed P-80A Shooting Star

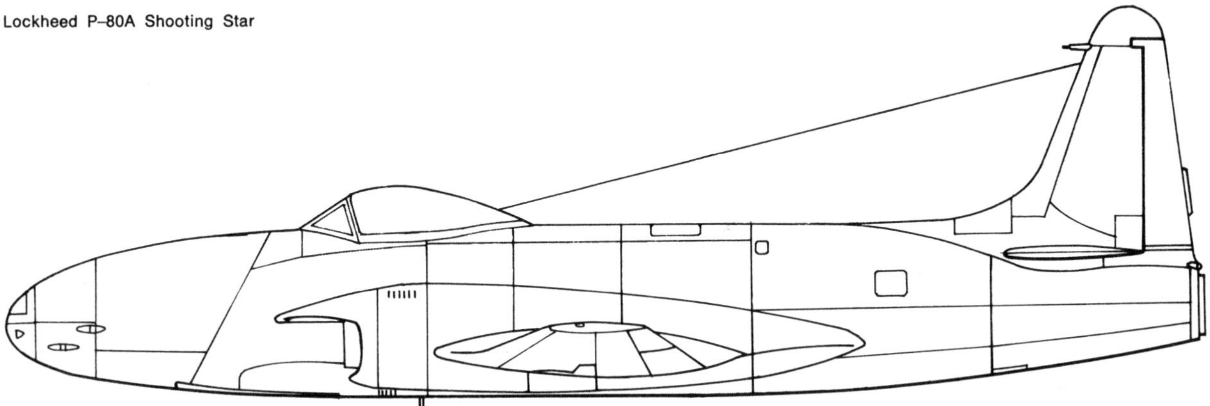

cannon, plus four .5in machine-guns in nose (30).
XP-38A: One P-38 conversion with pressure cabin.
P-38D: Modified P-38; revised tail plane; self-sealing fuel tanks (36).
P-38E: As P-38D; one 20mm Hispano in lieu of 37mm cannon (210).
P-38F: Re-engined P-38E; tropicalized; some converted to two-seat trainers (527).
P-38G: As P-38F; Allison V-1710-51s or 55s; provision for max 2,000lb (907 kg) underwing bomb load (1,082).
P-322: USAAF trainers; 140 retained from original British order.
F-4/-4A: Unarmed photo-reconnaissance P-38E (99) and P-38F (20) conversions.
F-5A: 181 P-38Gs completed as photo-reconnaissance.
F-5B: As F-5A but with inter-coolers (*200*).
Lightning I: RAF equivalent of P-38E; 1,040hp unsupercharged V-1710-C15s; 143 ordered; only 3 tested UK; remainder retained by USAAF as P-322 trainers.
Lighting II: RAF equivalent of P-38F/G; 524 ordered; 495 built; all retained by USAAF.
Total Production: 9,393 (all Marks).
Remarks: Radical twin-tailboom configuration; first operational variant, P-38D, entered service Aug 1941; first kill one year later, Aug 1942; Fw 200 shot down over Atlantic by Icelandic-based Lightning; two USAAF Groups arrived UK mid-1942; no combat, transferring to North Africa (12th AF) before end of year; first large-scale employment NW Africa, Nov 1942; continued operations Mediterranean area with 12th, later 15th, AFs; also served Pacific theatre from late 1942; P-38Gs based Guadalcanal intercepted and destroyed Mitsubishi G4M transport carrying Japanese Admiral Yamamoto off Bougainville, a round flight of some 1,100 miles.

Manufacturer: Lockheed.
Model: P-38J Lightning.
Type: Long-range fighter/fighter-bomber.
Power Plant: Two 1,425hp Allison V-1710-89/91.
Performance:
maximum speed at 25,000ft (7,620m) 414mph (666km/hr).
cruising speed 290mph (467km/hr).
maximum range 2,260 miles (3,636km).
time to 5,000ft (1,524m) 2min 0sec.
service ceiling 44,000ft (13,411m).
Weights:
empty 12,780lb (5,797kg).
maximum 21,600lb (9,798kg).
Dimensions:
wing span 52ft 0in (15.85m).
length 37ft 10in (11.52m).
height 9ft 10in (2.99m).
wing area 327.5sq ft (30.42sq m).
Armament: One 20mm Hispano cannon; four .5in Browning machine-guns in nose; two 500lb (227kg), 1,000lb (454kg) or 1,600lb (726kg) bombs, or ten .5in rockets.
Crew: 1.
In Service: China (F-5), France (F-5, P-38J/L), USA.
Variants (with no. built):
P-38H: Modified P-38G; 1,425hp VC-1710-89/91s; improved supercharger; increased bomb load (601).
P-38J: Improved P-38H; 'Chin' radiators; last 1,400 with increased tankage (2,970).
P-38K: High-altitude version; one P-38J conversion.
P-38L: As P-38J; 1,600hp V-1710-111/113s; underwing rockets; Lockheed-built (3,810); Vultee-built (113).
P-38M: Two-seat night-fighter; ASH radar; P-38L conversions.
TP-38M: Trainer version; P-38L conversions.
F-5C: Photo-reconnaissance P-38H conversions (*128*).
F-5D: One F-5 conversions to two-seater.
F-5E/G: Photo-reconnaissance P-38J/L conversions (*705+*).
Total Production: 9,393 (all Marks).
Remarks: Numerically most important Lightning variants, P-38J and L, first delivered 1943 and 1944 respectively, saw widespread service in Europe, Mediterranean and Pacific areas; based UK, 8th and 9th AFs, flew first bomber escort missions to Berlin, as well as long-range penetration and ground-attack sorties; some fitted with transparent nose-cone and modified to accommodate bomb-aimer (Droopsnoot), others equipped with radar (Pathfinder); P-38's long-range made it ideal for use in Pacific; played important part in island-hopping campaigns of 1944–45; P-38M night-fighter entered service closing weeks of Pacific War; F-4 and F-5 conversions, most numerous reconnaissance aircraft employed by USAAF in WWII, served all major theatres; limited post-war use, inc France, Honduras, Italy, Nationalist China.
Colour Reference: Plates 148, 149: Lockheed P-38L Lighting (No 210) 'Rickie Boy' of 18th Fighter Group, 13th USAAF; Zamboanga (Mindanao), Philippine Islands, June 1945; employed bomber-escort duties length and breadth South China Sea, attacking targets in Borneo, French Indo-China, and Formosa; natural metal overall, light blue Group/Squadron markings, red checker-board trim.

Manufacturer: Lockheed.
Model: C-69 Constellation.
Type: Transport.
Power Plant: Four 2,200hp Wright R-3350-35.
Performance:
maximum speed 330mph (530km/hr).
normal range 2,400 miles (3,860km).
time to 10,000ft (3,048m) 7min 6sec.
service ceiling 25,000ft (7,620m).
Weights:
empty 50,500lb (22,907kg).
loaded 72,000lb (32,660kg).
Dimensions:
wing span 123ft 0in (37.49m).
length 95ft 2in (29.01m).
height 23ft 8in (7.21m).
wing area 1,650sq ft (153.29sq m).
Crew/Accommodation: 4–5/60 troops.
In Service: USA.
Variants (with no. built):
C-69: Initial civil transport (L-49); requisitioned by USAAF (19).
C-69C: VIP transport; 43 passengers (1).
C-69A, B, D: Cancelled wartime trooper/transports.
Total Production: 20 (wartime military).
Remarks: Served as long-range transport during last year of war; subsequently resold to airlines; numerous post-war variants and developments both civil and military.

Manufacturer: Lockheed.
Model: YP-80A Shooting Star.
Type: Interceptor fighter.
Power Plant: One 3,850lb.s.t. General Electric J-33-GE-9 or 11 turbojet.
Performance:
maximum speed at sea level 558mph (898km/hr).
cruising speed 410mph (660km/hr).
normal range 540 miles (869km).
time to 5,000ft (1,524m) 1min 12sec.
service ceiling 45,000ft (13,716m).
Weights:
empty 7,920lb (3,593kg).
maximum 14,500lb (6,577kg).
Dimensions:
wing span 39ft 0in (11.89m).
length 34ft 6in (10.51m).
height 11ft 4in (3.45m).
wing area 238sq ft (22.11sq m).
Armament: Six .5in Browning machine-guns in nose.
Crew: 1.
In Service: USA (USAAF).
Variants (with no. built):
XP-80: Prototype; 2,460lb s.t. de Havilland H-1B turbojet; five .5in guns in nose (1).
XP-80A: Modified XP-80; 3,850lb s.t.; General Electric I-40; increased weight and overall dimensions (2).
YP-80A: Service test version; weight decrease; addn nose gun (13).
P-80A/C, XFP-80A, FP-80A, RF-80C: Post-war developments (1,715).
Total Production: 1,731.
Remarks: USAAF's first operational jet aircraft; first service test models delivered Oct 1944, two arriving in Italy just prior to VE-Day; extensive post-war use, remaining in production (as T-33A) until 1959.

Manufacturer: Martin.
Model: T4M-1.
Type: Torpedo-bomber.
Power Plant: One 525hp Pratt & Whitney R-1690-24 Hornet.
Performance:
maximum speed at sea level 114mph (183km/hr).
cruising speed 98mph (158km/hr).
maximum range 363 miles (584km).
time to 5,000ft (1,525m) 14min 0sec.
service ceiling 10,150ft (3,093m).
Weights:
empty 3,931lb (1,783kg).
maximum 8,071lb (3,661kg).
Dimensions:
wing span 53ft 0in (16.15m).
length 35ft 7in (10.84m).
height 14ft 9in (4.49m).
wing area 656sq ft (60.94sq m).
Armament: One flexible .3in machine-gun in rear cockpit plus provision for bomb/s or torpedo under fuselage.
Crew: 3.
In Service: USA (USN).
Variants (with no. built):
T3M-1: Initial production model; Curtiss SC-1 development, redesigned fuselage; three-seat torpedo-bomber-scout biplane; one 575hp Wright T-3B; alt wheel-, float- undercarriage (24).
T3M-2: Improved T3M-1; increased upper wing span; revised (tandem) cockpit; one 770hp Packard 3A-2500 (100).
XT3M-3/XT3M-4: Re-engined T3M-2; one Pratt & Whitney Hornet/later one Wright Cyclone; 1 conversion.
XT4M-1: Modified XT3M-3; one 525hp Pratt & Whitney Hornet; reduced wing span; revised rudder.
T4M-1: As XT4M-1; production model; alt wheel-, float- undercarriage (102).
TG-1: As T4M-1; uprated engine; modified undercarriage; Great Lakes-built (18).
TG-2: Re-engined TG-1; one 620hp Wright R-1820-86 Cyclone; Great Lakes-built (32).
Total Production: 276.
Remarks: Entering service late 1926, T3M/T4M/TG series standard USN torpedo-bomber of early thirties; although long obsolete by outbreak WWII, number T4M-1 and TG-2 models still on strength in ancillary roles at time of Pearl Harbor attack.

Manufacturer: Martin.
Model: M 130 Clipper.
Type: Long-range transport flying-boat.
Power Plant: Four 800/950hp Pratt & Whitney R-1830.
Performance:
maximum speed at 7,000ft (2,134m) 180mph (290km/hr).
cruising speed 157mph (253km/hr).
maximum range 4,000 miles (6,436km).
Weights:
empty 25,363lb (11,505kg).
maximum 48,000lb (21,773kg).
Dimensions:
wing span 130ft 0in (39.62m).
length 90ft 10½in (27.69m).
height 24ft 7¼in (7.51m).
wing area 2,315sq ft (215.1sq m).
Crew/Accommodation: 7/30.
In Service: USA (USN), USSR (SovNAF, M 156).
Variants (with no. built):
M 130: Civil flying-boat; Pan-AM order (3).
M 156: Larger version of M 130 Clipper; 850hp Wright GR-1820-G2; to USSR (1).
Total Production: 4.
Remarks: M 130 Clippers served with USN 1942–43 on trans-Pacific routes; one lost; sole M 156 purchased by USSR, 1938; militarised and served throughout WWII in patrol-bomber, naval transport roles.

Manufacturer: Martin.
Model: 139W (Model 166).
Type: Medium bomber.
Power Plant: Two 900hp Wright R-1820G-102.
Performance:
maximum speed 200mph (325km/hr).
cruising speed 168mph (270km/hr).
normal range 1,120 miles (1,800km).
initial rate of climb 1,860ft/min (567m/min).
service ceiling 25,200ft (7,680m).
Weights:
empty 10,322lb (4,682kg).
loaded 15,894lb (7,209kg).
Dimensions:
wing span 70ft 10in (21.59m).
length 44ft 2in (13.46m).
height 11ft 7in (3.53m).
wing area 682sq ft (63.4sq m).
Armament: One .3in Browning machine-gun each in nose and rear turrets, and in ventral tunnel; max bomb load 2,260lb (1,025kg).
Crew: 4.
In Service: Argentina (35), China (9), Netherlands (NEIAF 120), Philippines, Thailand (6), Turkey (20), USA, USSR (1).
Variants (with no. built):
XB-907: Prototype (1).
B-10/12/14 Series: Pre-war USAAC models (151).
Model 139: Basic export model (see In Service) (71).
139WH-1/2: Initial Dutch orders; separate cockpit enclosures (39).
139WH-3/3A (Model 166):

Martin 139WH-2

Martin 167F (Maryland)

Martin Baltimore Mk V (A-30A)

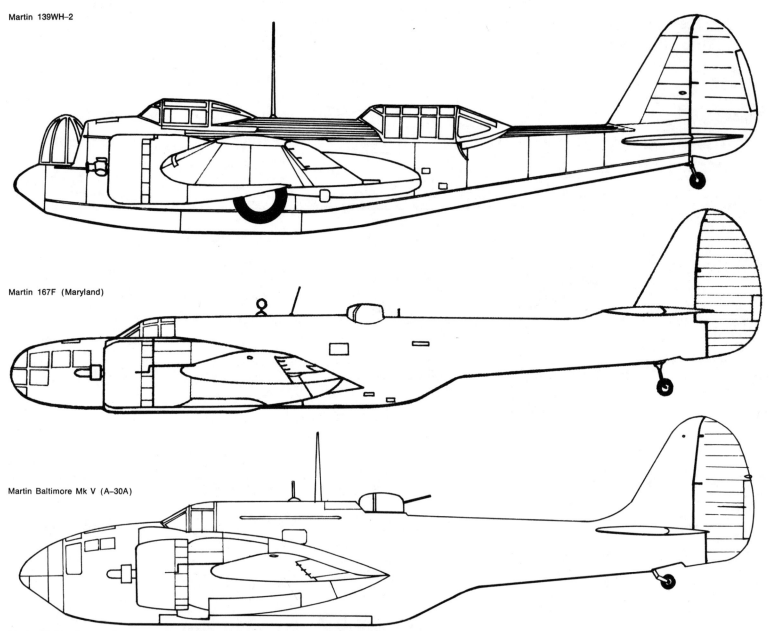

Further Dutch order; one-piece canopy (82).
Total Production: 343.
Remarks: USAAC's first all-metal monoplane bomber, B–10/12 series phased out of service late thirties; Chinese and NEIAF models both saw action against Japanese; former were first enemy aircraft to overfly Japanese homeland, Feb 1938, dropping nothing more lethal than propaganda leaflets; otherwise poor service record; Dutch machines fought in defence of Netherlands East Indies.

Manufacturer: Martin.
Model: Maryland II.
Type: Reconnaissance-bomber.
Power Plant: Two 1,200hp Pratt & Whitney R–1830–S3C4–G.
Performance:
maximum speed at 11,800ft (3,597m) 278mph (447km/hr).
normal range 1,210 miles (1,947km).
initial rate of climb 1,790ft/min (546m/min).
service ceiling 26,000ft (7,925m).
Weights:
empty 11,213lb (5,086kg).
loaded 16,809lb (7,625kg).
Dimensions:
wing span 61ft 4in (18.69m).
length 46ft 8in (14.22m).
height 14ft 11½in (4.55m).
wing area 538.5sq ft (50.03sq m).
Armament: Four .3in Browning wing guns plus one Vickers 'K' gun each in dorsal and ventral positions; max bomb load 2,000lb (907kg).
Crew: 3.
In Service: France (FAF, FNAF, FFAF, FVAF), Great Britain (RAF, FAA), South Africa (72 Maryland II).
Variants (with no. built):
XA–22: USAAF prototype; ground-attack (1).
167F: Initial production model; 950 or 1,100hp Wright R–1820;

French order (115).
167A–3: Bomber version; French order, inc 76 to RAF (Maryland I) with Twin Wasp SC3–G (100).
Maryland I: British order (75).
Maryland II: British order; uprated engines (150).
Total Production: 441.
Remarks: Originally built to French contract; in action during German 'Blitzkrieg' of May–June 1940; survivors to French North Africa; continued service with Vichy AF/NAFs in Middle East; also served with FFAF, and later again with FAF, in Sahara, Tunisia, Southern France and along French Atlantic Coast; outstanding French deliveries taken over by RAF; some to FAA for maritime reconnaissance; majority to Middle East; employed on general-reconnaissance/bombing by RAF (3 sqns) and SAAF (6 sqns), late 1940–42.

Manufacturer: Martin.
Model: Baltimore III.
Type: Light bomber.
Power Plant: Two 1,660hp Wright GR–2600–19.
Performance:
maximum speed at 11,000ft (3,353m) 302mph (486km/hr).
normal range 950 miles (1,530km).
time to 15,000ft (4,572m) 12min 0sec.
service ceiling 24,000ft (7,315m).
Weights:
empty 15,200lb (6,895kg).
loaded 23,000lb (10,433kg).
Dimensions:
wing span 61ft 4in (18.69m).
length 48ft 5½in (14.77m).
height 17ft 9in (5.41m).
wing area 538.5sq ft (50.03sq m).
Armament: Four .303in Browning wing guns (two or four) .303in Browning guns in dorsal turret, and two in ventral position; provision for four fixed rearward-

firing .3in guns; max bomb load 2,000lb (907kg).
Crew: 4.
In Service: Australia, France (FAF, FFAF), Great Britain (RAF, FAA), Greece, Italy (ICoAF), South Africa, Turkey.
Variants (with no. built):
Baltimore Mk I: British order (50).
Baltimore Mk II: As Mk I; twin Vickers guns in lieu of one 'K' gun in dorsal position (100).
Baltimore Mk IIIA (A–30): USAAF order; electrically-operated dorsal turret with two .5in guns; Lend-Lease to RAF (281).
Baltimore Mk IV (A–30A): USAAF order; similar to Mk IIIA; Lend-Lease to RAF (294).
Baltimore Mk V (A–30A): USAAF order; uprated engines; .5in wing guns (600).
Total Production: 1,575.
Remarks: Development of earlier Maryland, specifically to British requirements; Mk Is employed primarily by OTUs; Mk IIs operational Spring 1942; Baltimore served exclusively Mediterranean area, from El Alamein to Tunisia, Sicily and Italy, until VE-Day; also flown by French AF and Italian Co-Belligerant AF, 1944–45, latter operating against Axis targets in Yugoslavia; supplied to Turkey under Lend-Lease.

Manufacturer: Martin.
Model: PBM–3C Mariner.
Type: Maritime reconnaissance flying boat.
Power Plant: Two 1,700hp Wright R–2600–12.
Performance:
maximum speed at 13,000ft (3,962m) 198mph (319km/hr).
normal range 2,137 miles (3,438km).
initial rate of climb 410ft/min

(125m/min).
service ceiling 16,900ft (5,151m).
Weights:
empty 32,378lb (14,687kg).
maximum 58,000lb (26,310kg).
Dimensions:
wing span 118ft 0in (35.97m).
length 80ft 0in (24.38m).
height 27ft 6in (8.38m).
wing area 1,408sq ft (130.80sq m).
Armament: Two flexible .5in machine-guns each in nose and dorsal turrets; plus single .5in machine-gun in tail and two beam positions; max bomb load or depth-charges, 2,000lb (907kg).
Crew: 7–8.
In Service: Great Britain, USA (USN).
Variants (with no. built):
XPBM–1: Prototype; two 1.600hp Wright R–2600–6 Cyclones; retractable floats (1).
PBM–1: Initial production model; 7 crew (20).
XPBM–2: Long-range prototype (1).
PBM–3B, C: Reconnaissance bomber versions; standardised US/British equipment; some with search radar; 25 PBM–3B Lend-Lease to RAF (approx 304).
PBM–3D: Re-engined PBM–3C; improved armament; self-sealing fuel tanks; enlarged, non-retractable floats (201).
PBM–3R: Unarmed transport version; modified PBM–3D; 20 passengers or cargo (50).
PBM–3S: Anti-submarine version; revised armament; addn fuel capacity (156).
PBM–4: Project only.
XPBM–5: Prototypes; improved PBM–3D (2).
PBM–5: Production model; eight .5in machine-guns; AN/APS–15 radar (589).
PBM–5A, E, S: Post-war variants (42).
Mariner G.R.I.: RAF equivalent

of PBM–3B; 25 Lend-Lease; subsequently returned to USA.
Total Production: 1,366.
Remarks: Although overshadowed by numerically superior PBY Catalina, PBM Mariner was less vulnerable and possessed better performance; served USN throughout Pacific War in variety of roles—patrol bomber, anti-submarine ASR, transport and crew trainer; continued in use until end of Korean War; British Lend-Lease deliveries, in contrast, served with only one Coastal Command sqn for just six weeks Oct–Nov 1943.
Colour Reference: Plate 130: Martin PBM–3D Mariner (P–9) of VP–202 'Leeman's Demons', Tarawa, Central Pacific, Jan 1944; named after CO, Commander Leeman, VP–202 was one of first Mariner squadrons to achieve operational status; standard non-specular blue fuselage/white under surfaces; note squadron insignia, winged 'Napoleon' (well-known US canine comic-strip hero) below cockpit.

Manufacturer: Martin.
Model: XPB2M–1 Mars.
Type: Long-range transport/flying boat.
Power Plant: Four 2,200hp Wright R–3350–18 Duplex Cyclone.
Performance:
maximum speed at sea level 205mph (330km/hr).
cruising speed 149mph (240km/hr).
maximum range 4,945 miles (7,957km).
initial rate of climb 440ft/min (134m/min).
service ceiling 14,000ft (4,267m).
Weights:
empty 75,573lb (34,280kg).
maximum 144,000lb (65,318kg).
Dimensions:

wing span 200ft 0in (60.96m).
length 117ft 3in (35.74m).
height 38ft 5in (11.71m).
wing area 3,683sq ft (342.15sq m).
Crew/Payload: 7/20,500lb (9,300kg).
In Service: USA (USN).
Variants (with no. built):
XPB2M–1 Prototype: Bomber version; converted to transport (1).
JRM–1 Production: Post-war; transport version (5).
JRM–2: Increased weight (1).
Total Production: 7.
Remarks: Originally built as maritime reconnaissance bomber; prototype converted to cargo transport, 1943; employed by USN on Pacific routes; ferried 120 tons of plasma to USMC on Iwo Jima, Feb–March 1945.

Manufacturer: Martin.
Model: B–26B Marauder.
Type: Medium bomber.
Power Plant: Two 2,000hp Pratt & Whitney R–2800–41.
Performance:
maximum speed at 14,500ft (4,420m) 317mph (510km/hr).
cruising speed 260mph (418km/hr).
range 1,150 miles (1,850km).
time to 15,000ft (4,572m) 12min 0sec.
service ceiling 23,500ft (7,163m).
Weights:
empty 22,380lb (10,152kg).
loaded 34,200lb (15,513kg).
Dimensions:
wing span 65ft 0in (19.81m).
length 58ft 3in (17.75m).
height 19ft 10in (6.04m).
wing area 602sq ft (55.93sq m).
Armament: One .3in gun each in nose and ventral tunnel, or two .5in beam guns in lieu of tunnel gun; plus two .5in guns each in tail and dorsal turrets; max bomb or torpedo load 5,200lb (2,359kg).
Crew: 7.
In Service: Australia, France (FAF, FFAF), Great Britain, South Africa (100 Marauder II), USA (USAAF, USN, USMC).
Variants (with no. built):
B–26: Initial production model; one .3in gun each in nose and tail positions; two .5in guns in dorsal turret; 1,850hp R–2800–5s (201).
B–26A: Increased weight; four .5in guns, 22in torpedo (139).
B–26B: Re-engined B–26A; spinners deleted; various armament; final 1,242 with increased wing span (71ft) and four 'package' guns in side blisters (commencing B–26B–10 block) (1,883).
B–26C: As B–26B–10; Omaha-built (1,235).
XB–26D: One B–26 conversion; hot air de-icers.
B–26E: One B–26B conversion; dorsal turret moved forward.
AT–23A/B: Target-tug versions; 208 B–26B and 350 B–26C conversions resp.
JM–1: USN/USMC equivalent of AT–23B (255); some converted for reconnaissance duties (JM–1P).
Marauder I: RAF equivalent of B–26A; 77 Lend-Lease.
Marauder IA: RAF equivalent of B–26B; 19 Lend-Lease.
Marauder II: RAF equivalent of B–26C; 100 Lend-Lease; to SAAF.
Total Production: 4,708 (all Marks).
Remarks: Developed in parallel with North American B–25 Mitchell, B–26 Marauder equipped one USAAF group on outbreak of Pacific War; operational debut bombing attack on Rabaul, 5 April 1942; participated Battle of Midway, June 1942, fitted with external torpedo racks; also served North Pacific (Aleutians); subsequently operated primarily European (9th AF) and Mediterranean (12th AF) theatres; disastrous start by UK-based Marauders, all ten aircraft lost during raid on Ijmuiden, 17 May 1943; British and Commonwealth sqns operated exclusively Middle East.
Colour Reference: Plate 153: Martin B–26B Marauder (42–43304) of 444th Bomb Squadron, 320th Bomb Group (Medium), 12th USAAF, Sardinia, Summer 1944; standard olive drab finish; group identification yellow tail band; squadron within Group indicated officially by Battle Number '95' on vertical tail surfaces, and unofficially by Shark's Nose which decorated all 444th Marauders during closing year of war.

Manufacturer: Martin.
Model: B–26G Marauder.
Type: Medium bomber.
Power Plant: Two 2,000hp Pratt & Whitney R–2800–43.
Performance:
maximum speed at 5,000ft (1,524m) 283mph (455km/hr).
maximum range 1,100 miles (1,770km).
initial rate of climb 1,000ft/min (305m/min).
service ceiling 19,800ft (6,035m).
Weights:
empty 25,300lb (11,476kg).
maximum 38,200lb (17,328kg).
Dimensions:
wing span 71ft 0in (21.64m).
length 56ft 1in (17.09m).
height 20ft 4in (6.20m).
wing area 658sq ft (61.13sq m).
Armament: Eleven .5in Browning machine-guns in fixed forward-firing nose and flexible waist positions, and power-operated dorsal and tail turrets; max bomb load 4,000lb (1,814kg).
Crew: 7.
In Service: France, Great Britain, South Africa, USA (USAAF, USN).
Variants (with no. built):
B26F: Modified B–26C; redesigned wing (300).
B–26G: As B–26F; minor equipment changes (893).
TB–26G: Unarmed trainer and target-tug version (57).
XB–26H: 4 wheel bicycle under-carriage; 1 conversion.
JM–2: USN equivalent of TB–26G (*47*).
Marauder III: RAF equivalent of B–26F/G (*200* and *150* resp); Lend-Lease.
Total Production: 4,708 (all Marks).
Remarks: B–26F introduced increased wing incidence angle to improve take-off performance; entering service 1943–44, B–26Fs and Gs remained USAAF's standard tactical air support bomber until close of European war; also operated in Italy and Southern France by 12th and 1st Tactical AFs.

Manufacturer: Naval Aircraft Factory.
Model: SBN–1.
Type: Carrier-borne scout bomber.
Power Plant: One 950hp Wright R–1820–38.
Performance:
maximum speed 254mph (409km/hr).
maximum range 1,015 miles (1,633km).
initial rate of climb 1,970ft/min (600 m/min).
service ceiling 28,500ft (8,687m).
Weights:
empty 4,080lb (1,850kg).
maximum 6,759lb (3,066kg).
Dimensions:
wing span 39ft 0in (11.89m).
length 28ft 3in (9.28m).
height 11ft 1in (3.38m).
wing area 259sq ft (24.06sq m).
Armament: One fixed forward-firing .5in gun plus one flexible .3in gun; max bomb load (internal) 500lb (227kg).
Crew: 2–3.
In Service: USA (USN).
Variants (with no. built):
XSBA–1: Prototype; 2/3-seat mid-wing monoplane; one Wright R–1820–4; Brewster-built (1).
SBN–1: Production model; modified XSBA–1; uprated engine; NAF-built (30).
Total Production: 31.
Remarks: Entered service late 1940; equipped one sqn in scout-bomber/reconnaissance role; subsequently relegated to carrier-borne trainer duties.

Manufacturer: North American.
Model: O–47A.
Type: Reconnaissance.
Power Plant: One 975hp Wright R–1820–49.
Performance:
maximum speed at 4,000ft (1,220m) 221mph (356km/hr).
time to 10,000ft (3,048m) 6min 48sec.
service ceiling 23,200ft (7,071m).
Weights:
empty 5,980lb (2,713kg).
loaded 7,636lb (3,464kg).
Dimensions:
wing span 46ft 4in (14.12m).
length 33ft 7in (10.23m).
height 12ft 2in (3.71m).
wing area 350sq ft (32.52sq m).
Armament: One fixed .3in Browning machine-gun in wing; one flexible .3in Browning in rear cockpit.
Crew: 3.
In Service: USA.
Variants (with no. built):
XO–47: Prototype (1).
O–47A: Initial production model (164).
O–47B: Modified O–47A; 1,060hp Wright R–1820–57 (74).
Total Production: 239.
Remarks: Limited service Far East area early weeks Pacific War; majority employed USA on photo-mapping, training and general liaison duties; also on anti-submarine patrols off California coast and in Canal Zone.

Manufacturer: North American.
Model: A–27.
Type: Light bomber.
Power Plant: One 745hp Wright R–1820–75.
Performance:
maximum speed at 11,500ft (3,505m) 250mph (402km/hr).
cruising speed 220mph (354km/hr).
maximum range 800 miles (1,287km).
service ceiling 28,000ft (8,534m).
Weights:
empty 4,520lb (2,050kg).
maximum 6,700lb (3,039kg).
Dimensions:
wing span 42ft 0in (12.80m).
length 29ft 0in (8.84m).
height 12ft 2in (3.71m).
wing area 258sq ft (23.97sq m).
Armament: Two fixed .3in machine-guns in nose, one in each wing; plus one flexible .3in gun in rear cockpit; max bomb load 400lb (181kg).
Crew: 2.
In Service: Brazil, USA.
Variants:
NA–44/69: Light bomber versions of AT–6 trainer; Brazilian (31)/ Thai (10) orders.
A–27: USAAF service designation of NA–69 (*10*).
Total Production: 41.
Remarks: Thai aircraft intercepted in Philippines during shipment, Oct 1941; commandeered by USAAF and saw brief use opening stages Japanese invasion of islands two months later.

Manufacturer: North American.
Model: P–64.
Type: Fighter-bomber.
Power Plant: One 870hp Wright R–1820–77.
Performance:
maximum speed at 8,700ft (2,652m) 270mph (434km/hr).
cruising speed 235mph (378km/hr).
maximum range 965 miles (1,553km).
service ceiling 27,500ft (8,382m).
Weights:
empty 4,660lb (2,114kg).
maximum 6,800lb (3,085kg).
Dimensions:
wing span 37ft 3in (11.35m).
length 27ft 0in (8.23m).
height 9ft 0in (2.74m).
wing area 227.5sq ft (21.09sq m).
Armament: Two .3in machine-guns in cowling; two 200mm wing cannon; four 100lb (45kg) bombs.
Crew: 1.
In Service: Peru, USA (6).
Variants (with no. built):
NA–50A: Fighter version of NA–16 trainer; two .3in machine-guns; Peruvian order (7).
NA–68: Modified NA–50A; Thai order (6).
P–64: USAAF service designation of NA–68 (*6*).
Total Production: 13.
Remarks: Peruvian NA–50As participated war against Ecuador, 1941; Thai order commandeered by US before shipment; with wing cannon removed served briefly as advanced trainers, subsequently employed as utility aircraft (general duties).

Manufacturer: North American.
Model: B–25D Mitchell.
Type: Medium bomber.
Power Plant: Two 1,700hp Wright R–2600–13.
Performance:
maximum speed at sea level 264mph (425km/hr).
maximum speed at 15,000ft (4,572m) 284mph (457km/hr).
cruising speed 233mph (375km/hr).
normal range 1,500 miles (2,414km).
time to 15,000ft (4,572m) 16min 30sec.
service ceiling 21,200ft (6,462m).
Weights:
empty 20,300lb (9,208kg).
maximum 35,000lb (15,880kg).
Dimensions:
wing span 67ft 7in (20.60m).
length 52ft 11in (16.12m).
height 15ft 10in (4.82m).
wing area 610sq ft (56.67sq m).
Armament: Two .5in nose guns; twin .5in guns each in dorsal and retractable ventral turrets; max bomb load 3,000lb (1,361kg).
Crew: 5.
In Service: Brazil (29 Lend-Lease), Canada, France (FFAF), Great Britain, Netherlands (NAF 20+ B–25B; NEIAF 43+ B–25C/D), USA (USAAF, USN, USMC), USSR.
Variants (with no. built):
Model NA–40: Prototype; 3 crew (1).
B–25: Redesigned NA–40; increased armament; widened fuselage; 5 crew (24).
B–25A: As B–25; self-sealing tanks (40).
B–25B: Dorsal and ventral turrets; tail gun deleted (119).
B–25C: Re-engined B–25B; external bomb racks; later models with additional fuel tanks (1,619).
B–25D: As B–25C (Dallas-built) (2,290).
XB–25E/F: B–25C conversions (2); de-icers.
F–10: Photo-reconnaissance version; ten B–25D conversions.
PBJ–1, –1C/D: USN, USMC equivalents of B–25, –25C/D (*50*/*152*).
Mitchell I: RAF equivalent of B–25B; 23 Lend-Lease.
Mitchell II: RAF equivalent of B–25C and D; 533 Lend-Lease.
Total Production: 9,816 (all Marks).
Remarks: Operational debut early 1942 against Japanese targets in New Guinea and Philippines; most famous B–25 action of entire war, April 1942—sixteen aircraft, led by Lt. Col. James Doolittle, flew from carrier USS *Hornet* to attack Tokyo; little material damage, but enormous propaganda value; Mitchells continued to serve throughout Pacific war with both USAAF and, from 1943, USN/USMC units; also operated by 12th AF in Mediterranean and 10th AF in CBI; employed by RAF in tactical light day-bombing role NW Europe, 1943–45.

Manufacturer: North American.
Model: B–25H Mitchell.
Type: Medium bomber.
Power Plant: Two 1,700hp Wright R–2600–13.
Performance:
maximum speed at 13,000ft (3,962m) 275mph (442km/hr).
cruising speed 230mph (370km/hr).
maximum range 2,700 miles (4,344km).
time to 15,000ft (4,572m) 19min 0sec.
service ceiling 23,800ft (7,254m).
Weights:
empty 19,975lb (9,061kg).
maximum 36,047lb (16,351kg).
Dimensions:
wing span 67ft 7in (20.60m).
length 51ft 0in (15.54m).
height 15ft 9in (4.80m).
wing area 610sq ft (56.67sq m).
Armament: One 75mm cannon plus four .5in guns in nose; four forward-firing .5in guns in fuselage side blisters; two .5in waist guns; two .5in guns each in dorsal turret and powered tail mounting; provision for eight .5in rocket projectiles underwing; max bomb load 3,200lb (1,452kg), or one 2,000lb (907kg) torpedo.
Crew: 5.
In Service: Australia, Canada, China (131 Lend-Lease), France (FAF, FFAF), Great Britain, Netherlands (NEIAF 10 B–25G, 139 B–25C/D/J), USA (USAAF, USN, USMC), USSR (862 B–25B/D, G, J).
Variants (with no. built):
XB–25G: Prototype; one B–25C conversion; solid nose with forward-firing 75mm field gun.
B–25G: Production model (405).
B–25H: As B–25G; dorsal turret moved forward; revised armament (1,000).
B–25J: Modified B–25H; initially with nose glazing as B–25D; first 150 models provision for one 2,000lb (907kg) bomb; late production models with solid eight-gun nose (4,318).
AT–24A, B, C and D: Trainer versions; B–25D, G, C and J conversions resp (60); later redesignated TB–25D, G, C and J.
PBJ–1G, H, J: USN/USMC equivalents of B–25G (*1*), H (*248*), J (*255*).
Mitchell: RAF equivalent of B–25G; 2 for evaluation with 75mm nose gun.
Mitchell III: RAF equivalent of B–25J; 314 Lend-Lease.
Total Production: 9,816 (all Marks).
Remarks: Heavily-armed B–25G/Js employed primarily SWPA/CBI theatres on ground-attack and anti-shipping operations, 1944–45; USMC PBJ–1Js carried out radar-directed night rocket strikes on Japanese shipping in Central Pacific; many delivered Lend-Lease to USSR, saw action from Battle of Stalingrad (B–25B/D) until VE-Day; also employed by NEIAF; extensive post-war use, both US and foreign, inc Communist China, examples captured from Chinese Nationalist forces late forties.
Colour Reference: Plates 151, 152. North American B–25J Mitchell (No 192) of 498th 'Falcon' Squadron, 345th Bomb Group (Medium) 'Air Apaches', 5th USAAF, Clark Field (Luzon), Philippine Islands, May 1945; one of most distinctively marked of all USAAF units, 'Air Apache' Mitchells carried variety colourful nose/fin motifs; Aircraft No 192 brought down by anti-aircraft fire over

North American O–47A

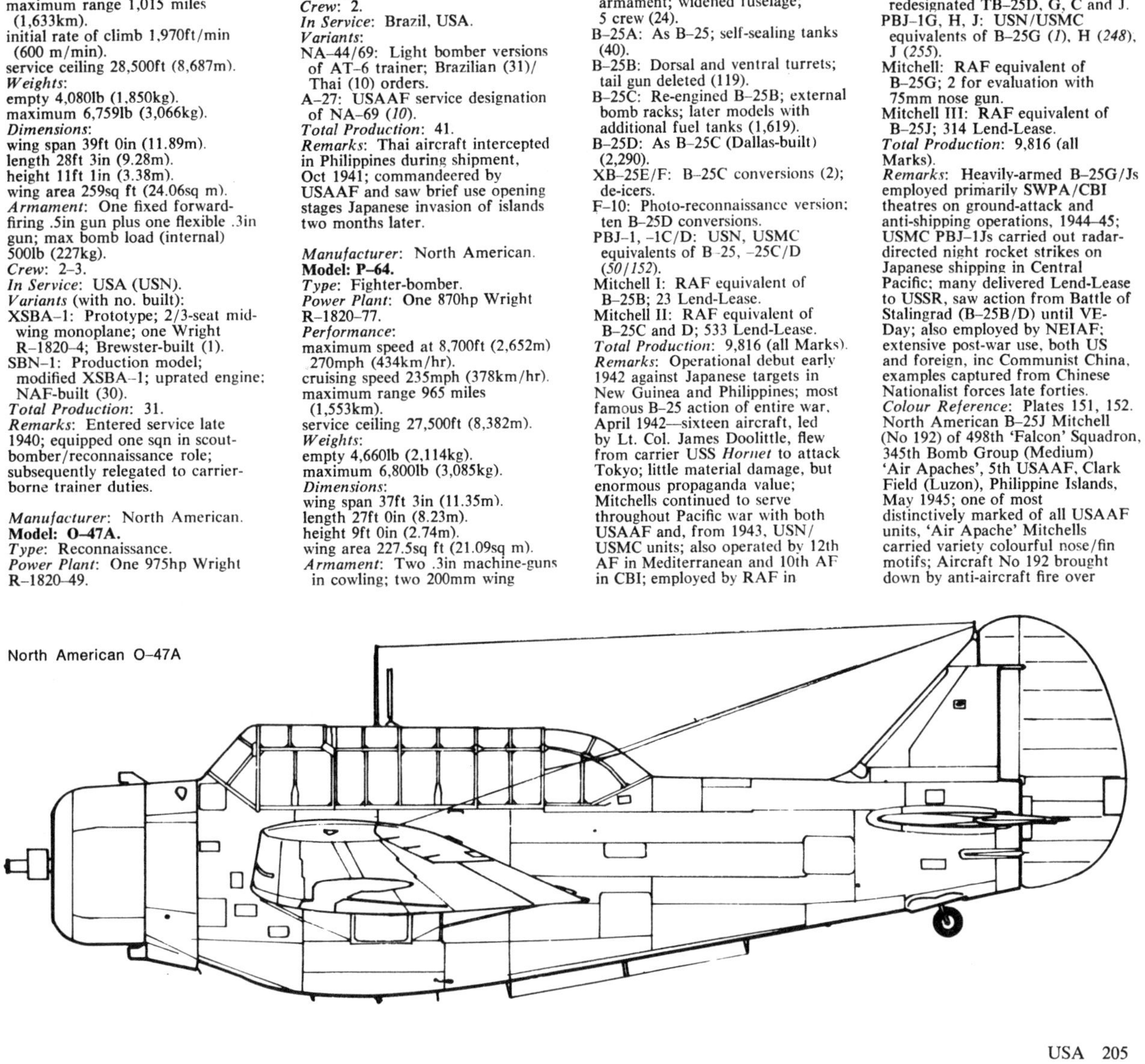

target during low-level attack on Formosan oil refinery, 26 May 1945.

Manufacturer: North American.
Model: Mustang I.
Type: Reconnaissance fighter.
Power Plant: One 1,150hp Allison V–1710–39.
Performance:
maximum speed at 8,000ft (2,438m) 390mph (628km/hr).
normal range 1,050 miles
time to 15,000ft (4,572m) 8min 6sec.
service ceiling 32,000ft (9,754m).
Weights:
empty 6,300lb (2,858kg).
loaded 8,600lb (3,900kg).
Dimensions:
wing span 37ft 0¼in (11.34m).
length 32ft 2½in (9.82m).
height 8ft 8in (2.64m).
wing area 235sq ft (21.83sq m).
Armament: Two .5in machine-guns in lower nose, firing through propeller arc; two .5in and four .3in wing-mounted machine-guns.
Crew: 1.
In Service: Canada, Great Britain, USA.
Variants (with no. built):
NA–73X: Prototype; private venture (1).
Mustang I: Initial production; tactical reconnaissance fighter; four .5in plus four .3in guns; British order; 2 to USAAF as XP–51 (620).
IA: Modified Mk I; four 20mm cannon; Lend-Lease to RAF (*93*).
II: Long-range version of Mk I; uprated engine; four .5in machine-guns; Lend-Lease to RAF (*50*).
X: Mk I fitted with Rolls-Royce Merlin 61 or 65; 4 conversions.
P–51: USAAF equivalent of Mustang IA; 93 to RAF, 57 requisitioned by USAAF (150).
P–51A: USAAF equivalent of Mustang II (275).
F–6A: Tactical reconnaissance version of P–51 (55).
F–6B: Tactical reconnaissance version of P–51A (35).
A–36A: Dive-bomber/ground-attack version of P–51; six .5in wing guns, dive brakes, bomb racks inc 1 to RAF (500).
Total Production: 15,469 (all Marks).
Remarks: Original Allison-powered Mustangs produced to British requirement; employed as low-level tactical reconnaissance fighter, equipping 23 British and Commonwealth sqns; first entered RAF service April 1942; operated mainly NW Europe, participating Dieppe raid, Normandy invasion; few served Mediterranean theatre; USAAF F–6s first employed NW Africa; A–36As took part invasions Pantelleria, Sicily and Italy; P–51As operated CBI theatre; majority requisitioned P–51s retained for US home defence duties post-Pearl Harbor.
Colour Reference: Plate 156: North American Mustang I (AG565) HB.A of No 239 Squadron, RAF; primarily engaged Army co-operation exercises in UK, AG565 failed to return from cross-Channel sortie (crash-landing Occupied Europe) in July 1943, two months prior to Squadron's re-mustering for night-fighter role.

Manufacturer: North American.
Model: P–51B Mustang.
Type: Long-range interceptor fighter.
Power Plant: One 1,400hp Packard Merlin V–1650–3.
Performance:
maximum speed at 30,000ft (9,144m) 440mph (708km/hr).
cruising speed 362mph (582km/hr).
maximum range 2,200 miles (3,540km).
time to 10,000ft (3,068m) 1min 48sec.
service ceiling 42,000ft (12,800m).
Weights:
empty 6,840lb (3,103kg).
maximum 11,200lb (5,080kg).
Dimensions:
wing span 37ft 0¼in (11.89m).
length 32ft 3in (9.83m).
height 8ft 8in (2.64m).
wing area 233sq ft (21.65sq m).
Armament: Four .5in Browning machine-guns; max bomb load 2,000lb (907kg).
Crew: 1.
In Service: Australia, Canada, China (P–51B/C), France (F–6C), Germany (1+ evaluation), Great Britain (RAF), South Africa, Sweden, USA.
Variants (with no. built):
XP–51B: Prototype; P–51 with Packard Merlin V–1650–3; four 20mm cannon (2).
P–51B: Production model; some with bubble hood; four .5in machine-guns (1,988).
P–51C: As P–51B; Dallas built; bubble hood; majority with 1,510hp Packard V–1650–7 (1,750).
F–6C: Tactical reconnaissance version; 71 P–51B and 20 P–51C conversions.
Mustang III: RAF equivalent of P–51B/C; 274 P–51B and 636 P–51C; Lend-Lease.
Total Production: 15,469 (all Marks).
Remarks: First of Packard Merlin variants; served primarily with UK-based US 8th AF as long-range escort fighter; first operation, to Kiel, 13 Dec 1943; first Allied fighters over Berlin, March 1944; flew 'shuttle' missions to USSR; also operated by 9th AF in both fighter and reconnaissance (F–6C) roles; served Mediterranean and CBI theatres; equipped British and Commonwealth sqns in UK, NW Europe (2nd TAF), and Italy (DAF).

Manufacturer: North American.
Model: P–51D Mustang.
Type: Long-range interceptor fighter.
Power Plant: One 1,510hp Packard Merlin V–1650–7.
Performance:
maximum speed at 25,000ft (7,620m) 437mph (703km/hr).
cruising speed 362mph (582km/hr).
maximum range 2,300 miles (3,700km).
service ceiling 41,900ft (12,771m).
Weights:
empty 7,125lb (3,232kg).
maximum 11,600lb (5,262kg).
Dimensions:
wing span 37ft 0¼in (11.89m).
length 32ft 3¼in (9.85m).
height 13ft 8in (4.16m).
wing area 233.2sq ft (21.65sq m).
Armament: Six .5in Browning machine-guns; max bomb load 2,000lb (907kg), or six 5in rocket projectiles.
Crew: 1.
In Service: Australia (inc 215 P–51D, 84 P–51K, + licence production), China (50 P–51D), Germany, (1+ evaluation), Great Britain, Netherlands (41 P–51D/K), New Zealand (30+ P–51D), South Africa, USA.
Variants (with no. built):
P–51D: Modified P–51B; redesigned all-round 'bubble' canopy; cut-down rear fuselage; addn dorsal fin; six .5in wing guns; various series (7,966).
XP–51F/G: Light-weight versions; Packard and Rolls-Royce engines resp, inc 1 each to RAF (5).
P–51H: As XP–51F, inc 1 to RAF (555).
XP–51J: As XP–51F with 1,500hp Allison (2).
P–51K: As P–51D; Aeroproducts propeller (1,337).
P–51M: Re-engined P–51H; V–1650–9A (1).
F–6D: Tactical reconnaissance version; 136 P–51D conversions.
F–6K: Tactical reconnaissance version; 163 P–51K conversions.
Mustang IV: RAF equivalent of P–51D, K; 875 Lend-Lease.
Mustang 20–24 (CA–17/18): RAAF equivalents of P–51D; Australian licence-built by Commonwealth Aircraft (200).
Total Production: 15.469 (all Marks).
Remarks: Numerically most important Mustang variants, USAAF P–51D/Ks operated both European and Pacific theatres; outstanding long-range high-altitude escort/interceptor performance; participated many UK–USSR and UK–North Africa 'shuttle' raids; also employed Italy and SE Europe; closing stages Pacific War, based Iwo Jima, escorted B–29s against Japan; first land-based US fighter over Tokyo; equipped thirteen RAF sqns, plus Commonwealth AFs; continued late- and post-war development for USAAF, inc P–82B Twin Mustang; also world-wide post-war foreign service, inc Communist China; participated Korean war and 1956 Arab–Israeli conflict.
Colour Reference: Plates 157, 158: North American P–51D Mustang (44–14292) QP.A 'Man o'War' of 334th Fighter Squadron, 4th Fighter Group, 8th USAAF, Debden Essex, late 1944; flown by Lt. Col. C. H. Kinnard, 44–14292 featured unusual dark green camouflage pattern over natural metal finish; note also victory scoreboard around canopy frame.

Manufacturer: Northrop (Canadian Vickers).
Model: Delta Mk. II.
Type: Transport.
Power Plant: One 640hp Wright SR–1820–F52 Cyclone.
Performance:
maximum speed at 6,300ft (1,920m) 219mph (351km/hr).
cruising speed 200mph (322km/hr).
maximum range 1,930 miles (3,120km).
initial rate of climb 1,390ft/min (424m/min).
service ceiling 23,400ft (7,130m).
Weights:
empty 4,600lb (2,080kg).
loaded 7,350lb (3,337kg).
Dimensions:
wing span 47ft 7in (14.60m).
length 33ft 1in (10.08m).
wing area 363.0sq ft (33.72sq m).
Crew/Payload/Accommodation: 1/1,100lb (500kg)/8.
In Service: Australia, Canada, Spain (NatAF 2).
Variants (with no. built):
Alpha, Delta, Gamma: Civil transport and mailplane versions; one 420hp Pratt & Whitney Wasp C; 575hp, or 700hp, Wright & Cyclone resp (58+).
Beta: Light civil transport version of Alpha.
YC–19, Y1C–19: USAAC designation for militarised Alpha, 1 and 2 resp (3).
Delta Mk I: RCAF military photographic-survey version; alt wheel-, ski-, or float undercarriage; Canadian Vickers licence-built (3).
Delta Mk II: Improved Mk I; late production; strengthened floor; addn freight door; enlarged vertical tail surfaces; Canadian Vickers licence-built (17).
Total Production: 80+ (all models).
Remarks: Original Northrop civil transport designs (evaluated by USAAC early thirties), one Delta impressed RAAF transport role, 1942–44; licence-built Delta Mk I(Ia)/II served RCAF similar ancillary duties, 1936–45.

Manufacturer: Northrop.
Model: A–17A Nomad.
Type: Attack-bomber.
Power Plant: One 825hp Pratt & Whitney R–1535–13.
Performance:
maximum speed at 2,500ft (762m) 220mph (354km/hr).
cruising speed 170mph (274km/hr).
maximum range 1,195 miles (1,923km).
time to 5,000ft (1,524m) 3min 54sec.
service ceiling (19,400ft (5,913m).
Weights:
empty 5,106lb (2,316kg).
loaded 7,550lb (3,425kg).
Dimensions:
wing span 47ft 9in (14.55m).
length 31ft 8in (9.65m).
height 12ft 0in (3.66m).
wing area 362sq ft (33.63sq m).
Armament: Four fixed forward-firing .3in Browning wing guns; one .3in Browning machine-gun in rear cockpit; max bomb load 400lb (181kg).
Crew: 2.
In Service: Argentina, Canada, France (32), Great Britain (61), Iraq, Netherlands, Norway, Peru, South Africa (47), Sweden, USA.
Variants (with no. built):
Prototype: XA–16 (1).
A–17: Initial production model; re-engined XA–16 (110).
A–17A: Uprated engine; retractable undercarriage (129).
A–17AS: 3-seat command transport; 600hp Pratt & Whitney R–1340–45 (2).
DB–8A: Export production; Douglas-built, inc; DB–8A–1: Swedish order (B–5, B–5A), as A–17 (2); Swedish licence-built (B–5B/D) (102).
DB–8A–5: Iraqi order, as A–17A (15).
DB–8A–3N: Dutch order, as A–17A (20).
DB–8A–3P: Peruvian order; high-altitude version (10).
DB–8A–5: Iraqi order, as A–17A (15).
DB–8A–5: Norwegian order (36).
A–33: Original Peruvian order (8A–5); requisitioned by USAAF (34).
Nomad: RAF equivalent of A–17A; 61 Lend-Lease.
Total Production: 491.
Remarks: Original Northrop-designed pre-war USAAC attack aircraft; A–17s relegated to general duties by WWII; export models (all built by Douglas) fitted with various engines; Dutch 8A–3Ns employed as fighters during German invasion of Netherlands, May 1940; majority destroyed by enemy action; 93 A–17s released to Britain and France, 1940; 47 RAF machines subsequently passed to SAAF; used as trainers; SAAB-built B–5B/D dive-bombers in Swedish AF service until 1950.

Manufacturer: Northrop.
Model: BT–1.
Type: Carrier-borne scout and dive-bomber.
Power Plant: One 825hp Pratt & Whitney R–1535–94.
Performance:
maximum speed at 9,500ft (2,896m) 222mph (357km/hr).
cruising speed 192mph (309km/hr).
maximum range 1,150 miles (1,850km).
initial rate of climb 1,270ft/min (387m/min).
service ceiling 25,300ft (7,710m).
Weights:
empty 4,606lb (2,090kg).
maximum 7,197lb (3,265kg).
Dimensions:
wing span 41ft 6in (12.65m).
length 31ft 8in (9.65m).
height 9ft 11in (3.02m).
wing area 319sq ft (29.64sq m).
Armament: One fixed forward-firing .5in machine-gun plus one flexible .3in gun in rear cockpit; max bomb load 1,000lb (454kg).
Crew: 2.
In Service: USA (USN).
Variants (with no. built):
XBT–1: Prototype; 2-seat carrier-borne scout and dive-bombing monoplane; one 825hp R–1535–94 (1).
BT–1: Production model (54).
XBT–2: Modified BT–1; redesigned undercarriage; revised cockpit canopy and vertical surfaces; served as Douglas SBD prototype, 1 conversion.
Total Production: 55.
Remarks: Entered USN service Spring 1938; still on strength upon outbreak WWII; replaced by first of highly successful Douglas SBD Dauntless series prior Pearl Harbor; subsequently employed ancillary liaison/training roles.

Manufacturer: Northrop.
Model: N–3PB.
Type: Patrol-bomber floatplane.
Power Plant: One 1,100hp Wright GR–1820–G205A.
Performance:
maximum speed at sea level 257mph (414km/hr).
cruising speed 184mph (296km/hr).
normal range 1,000 miles (1,609km).
time to 15,000ft (4,572m) 14min 24sec.
service ceiling 24,000ft (7,392m).
Weights:
empty 6,190lb (2,808kg).
maximum 10,600lb (4,808kg).
Dimensions:
wing span 48ft 11in (14.91m).
length 36ft 0in (10.97m).
height 12ft 0in (3.66m).
wing area 376sq ft (34.93sq m).
Armament: Four fixed forward-firing .5in Browning machine-guns in wings; one flexible .3in gun each in dorsal and ventral positions; max bomb load 2,000lb (907kg).
Crew: 3.
In Service: Great Britain.
Variants:
N–3PB: Norwegian order.
Total Production: 24.
Remarks: Original Norwegian order placed prior to German invasion and occupation; subsequently operated by Norwegian-manned RAF Coastal Command sqn based Iceland, April 1942–Aug 1943, on convoy-escort and anti-submarine duties; relegated to training role after replacement by PBY Catalinas.

Manufacturer: Northrop.
Model: P–61B Black Widow.
Type: Night-fighter.
Power Plant: Two 2,000hp Pratt & Whitney R–2800–65.
Performance:
maximum speed at 20,000ft (6,096m) 366mph (589km/hr).
maximum range 3,000 miles (4,827km).
time to 20,000ft (6,096m) 12min 0sec.
service ceiling 33,100ft (10,089m).
Weights:
empty 22,000lb (9,980kg).
maximum 38,000lb (17,240kg).
Dimensions:
wing span 66ft 0in (20.12m).
length 49ft 7in (15.11m).
height 14ft 8in (4.46m).
wing area 664sq ft (61.69sq m).
Armament: Four fixed forward-firing .5in guns; four 20mm cannon in remote-controlled dorsal turret; four 1,600lb (726kg) bombs underwing.
Crew: 3.
In Service: USA.
Variants (with no. built):
XP–61: Prototype (2).
YP–61: Pre-production model (13).
P–61A: Production model; first 37 delivered with dorsal turret; remainder deleted (200).
P–61B: As P–61A with underwing bomb fittings; final 250 delivered with dorsal turret (450).
P–61C: 2,800hp R–2800–73 engines (41).
XP–61D/E: Four P–61A/B conversions.
P–61G: Unarmed weather-reconnaissance version; sixteen P–61B conversions.
F–15A (RF–61C): Post-war variant; tandem-seat reconnaissance (36).
Total Production: 742.
Remarks: First USAAF night-fighter designed as such from outset; entered service Pacific theatre mid-1944; first recorded victories 6–7 July 1944; became standard USAAF night-fighter during final year of war, equipping all such sqns both Pacific, CBI, and Europe (9th AF) theatres; latter AF's two sqns employed by night against incoming V–1s, July 1944; first Luftwaffe aircraft destroyed over France following month.
Colour Reference: Plate 150: Northrop P–61B Black Widow (42–39405) of 6th Night Fighter Squadron, 7th USAAF, Kagman Field, Saipan, late 1944; overall gloss black finish, individual nose artwork.

Manufacturer: Piper.
Model: L–4 Grasshopper.
Type: Liaison.
Power Plant: One 65hp Continental 0–170–3.
Performance:
maximum speed 85mph (137km/hr).
normal range 190 miles (306km).
time to 5,000ft (1,524m) 14min 0sec.
service ceiling 9,300ft (2,835m).
Weights:
empty 730lb (331kg).
loaded 1,220lb (553kg).
Dimensions:
wing span 35ft 3in (10.74m).
length 22ft 0in (6.71m).
height 6ft 8in (2.01m).
wing area 179sq ft (16.63sq m).
Crew: 2.
In Service: Great Britain, USA (USAAF, USN, USMC).
Variants (with no. built):
YO–59: Service test model; civil model J–3C Cub; re-designated L–4 (4).
O–59 (L–4): Initial production model (140).
O–59A (L–4A): Modified L–4 (948).
L–4B: As L–4A minus radio, inc one UC–83B (981).
L–4C/G: Training glider version; J–3C, F, J and J–5A, B, C impressments (117).
L–4H: Improved L–4B (1,801).
L–4J: As L–4H; controllable-pitch propeller (1,680).
TG–8: Training glider version of L–4 (240).
NE–1: USN, USMC equivalent of L–4 (230).
NE2: Modified NE–1 (26).
XLNP–1: USN/USMC equivalent of TG–8 (3).
HE–1 (AE–1): USN/USMC ambulance version of civil model J–5C (100).
J–4/5: RAF Piper Cub impressments (approx 16).
Total Production: approx 6,280.
Remarks: Development of pre-war Cub, Piper's L–4 proved best 'Liaison' type of WWII; served USAAF in every theatre of war—Mediterranean, European, CBI, Pacific—from late 1942 onwards; both land- and ship (CV, LST)-based; extensive post-war use both US and foreign.

Manufacturer: Republic.
Model: P–43A–1 Lancer.
Type: Fighter-bomber.
Power Plant: One 1,200hp Pratt & Whitney R–1830–57.
Performance:
maximum speed at 20,000ft (6,096m) 356mph (573km/hr).
cruising speed 280mph (450km/hr).
maximum range 1,450 miles (2,333km).
time to 15,000ft (4,572m) 6min 0sec.
service ceiling 36,000ft (10,973m).
Weights:
empty 5,996lb (2,720kg).
maximum 8,480lb (3,847kg).
Dimensions:
wing span 36ft 0in (10.97m).
length 28ft 6in (8.68m).
height 14ft 0in (4.27m).
wing area 233sq ft (21.72sq m).
Armament: Two .5in and two .3in wing guns; max bomb load 200lb (90.7kg).
Crew: 1.
In Service: Australia (4 P–43A, 4 P–43D), China (108+), USA.
Variants (with no. built):
XP–41: Seversky-built prototype; converted P–35; supercharger.

YP–43: Service test model; modified XP–41 (13).

P–43: Initial production model; R–1830–35; two .3in wing guns, plus two .5in guns in cowling (54).

P–43A: As P–43 but 1,200hp R–1830–49 (80).

P–43A–1: Modified P–43; revised armament, inc 108 Lend-Lease to China (125).

P–43B/C: Photo-reconnaissance models; P–43/43A conversions; 150 P–43Bs, 2 P–43Cs.

P–43D/E: Photo-reconnaissance models; P–43/43A–1 conversions.

Total Production: 272.

Remarks: First delivered 1941, all USAAF P–43s subsequently converted to photo-reconnaissance role; Chinese AF machines saw action against Japanese forces 1942–43.

Manufacturer: Republic.
Model: P–47B Thunderbolt.
Type: Interceptor fighter.
Power Plant: One 2,000hp Pratt & Whitney R–2800–21.
Performance:
maximum speed at 27,800ft (8,473m) 429mph (690km/hr).
cruising speed 335mph (539km/hr).
maximum range 1,100 miles (1,770km).
time to 15,000ft (4,572m) 6min 42sec.
service ceiling 42,000ft (12.802m).
Weights:
empty 9,346lb (4,240kg).
maximum 13,360lb (6,060kg).
Dimensions:
wing span 40ft 9in (12.42m).
length 35ft 0in (10.67m).
height 12ft 8in (3.86m).
wing area 300sq ft (27.87sq m).
Armament: Eight fixed .5in Browning wing guns.
Crew: 1.
In Service: USA, USSR (203).
Variants (with no. built):
XP–47/47A: Cancelled.
XP–47B: Prototype (1).
P–47B: Initial production model, inc 1 completed as XP–47E and 1 converted to XP–47F (171).
P–47C: Modified P–47B; new engine mount; fuel tank/bomb shackles (602).
Total Production: 15,634 (all Marks).
Remarks: Early versions of USAAF's last major radial-engined fighter; equipped two UK-based Groups (8th AF), P–47B's operational debut April 1943; poor low altitude performance, rate of climb and manoeuvrability, but excellent at high-altitude, in dive, and ability to absorb battle damage; shortcomings remedied in P–47C, which began long-range escort missions with 8th AF in July 1943.

Manufacturer: Republic.
Model: P–47D Thunderbolt.
Type: Fighter/fighter-bomber.
Power Plant: One 2,300hp Pratt & Whitney R–2800–21 or 2,535hp R–2800–59.
Performance:
maximum speed at 30,000ft (9,144m) 433mph (697km/hr).
cruising speed 350mph (563km/hr).
time to 20,000ft (6,096m) 11min 0sec.
service ceiling 42,000ft (12,800m).
Weights:
empty 9,900lb (4,491kg).
maximum 15,000lb (6,804kg).
Dimensions:
wing span 40ft 9¾in (12.43m).
length 36ft 1¾in (11.01m).
height 14ft 7in (4.44m).
wing area 300sq ft (27.87sq m).
Armament: Six or eight .5in Browning machine-guns; bomb racks with max load 2,500lb (1,134kg), or ten 5in rocket projectiles.
Crew: 1.
In Service: Brazil (50 P–47D), France (FFAF/FAF 446 P–47D), Germany (2+ evaluation), Mexico, Great Britain, USA, USSR (203 P–47D Lend-Lease).
Variants (with no. built):
P–47D: Initially similar to P–47C; subsequent detail design changes, inc increasing warload and introduction of 'bubble' canopy; 6 completed as XP–47K/L and N, and YP–47M (3), 2 converted to XP–47H (12,559).
P–47G: Similar to P–47C (60) and P–47D (294); Curtiss-built (354).
XP–47J: High-speed lightweight experimental (1).
P–47M: High-power version of late-model P–47D; dorsal fin introduced during production (130).
Thunderbolt Mk I: RAF equivalent of P–47D with framed canopy; 240 Lend-Lease.
Thunderbolt Mk II: RAF

North American P–51B Mustang

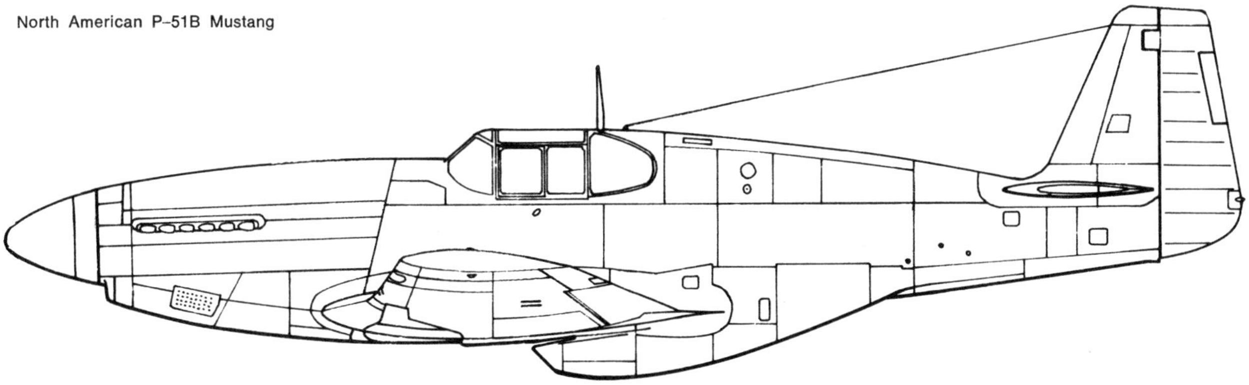

Northrop A–17A Nomad

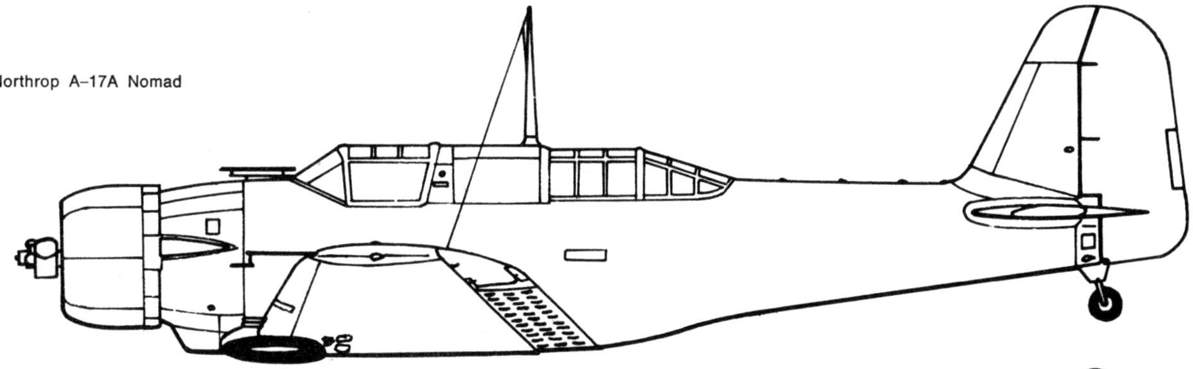

Northrop N–3PB

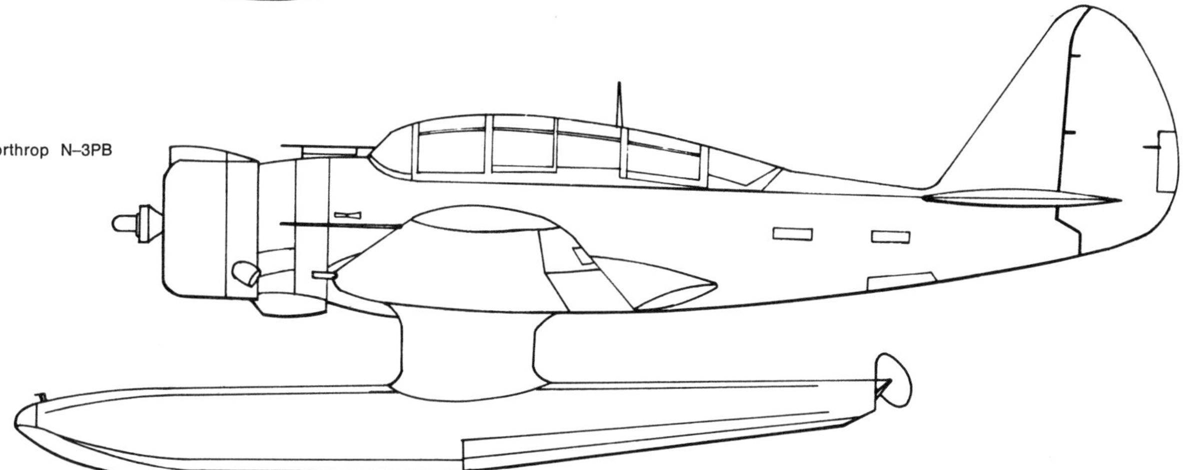

Republic P–43A Lancer

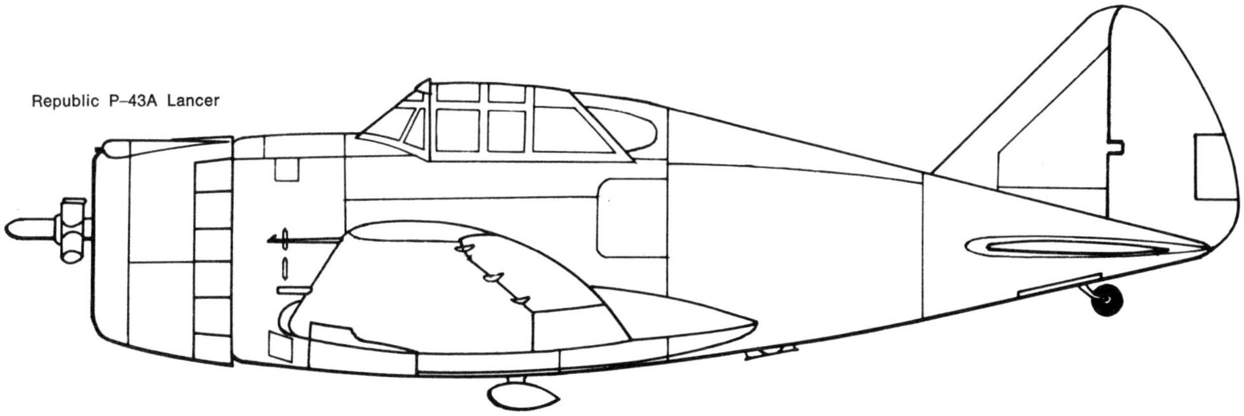

Republic P–47D Thunderbolt

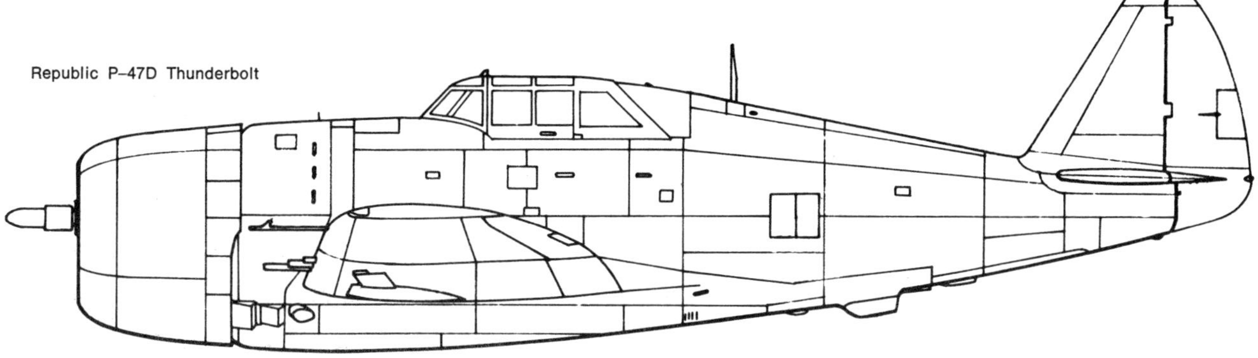

Ryan STM–2

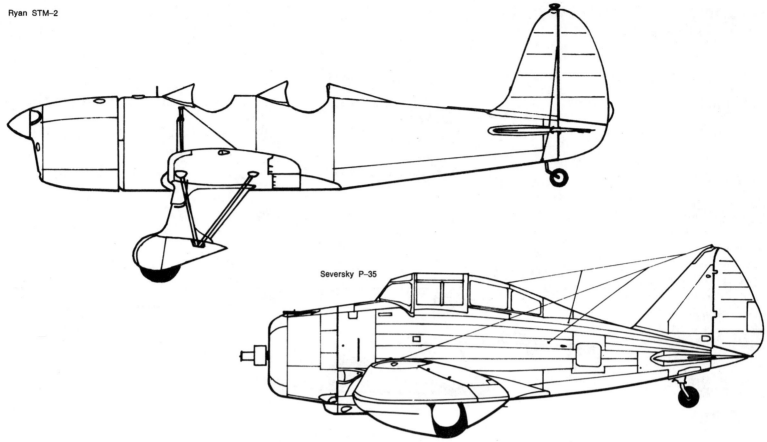

Seversky P–35

equivalent of P-47D with 'bubble' canopy; 590 Lend-Lease.
Total Production: 15,634 (all Marks).
Remarks: Most numerous of all variants, P-47D series accounted for well over 75% of entire Thunderbolt production; type divided almost equally between early framed-canopy 'Razorback' (6,266), and later all-round vision 'bubble' canopy model (6,293); P-47D first variant to serve Pacific theatre, operating with both 5th and 7th AFs; also with 10th and 14th AFs in CBI, and 12th and 15th in Italy; standard long-range escort fighter and fighter-bomber with 8th and 9th AFs in UK, based Europe with latter post-Normandy; entered RAF service Sept 1944, operated exclusively SEAC (16 sqns), with single exception one Middle East OTU; also equipped four French AF Groupes in ETO; Brazilian and Mexican units operated with USAAF in Italy and Philippines respectively; Lend-Lease to USSR; numerous other post-war foreign users; finally phased out US (NAG) service 1955.
Colour Reference: Plate 159: Republic P-47M Thunderbolt (44–21225) UN.K 'Fire Ball' of 63rd Fighter Squadron, 56th Fighter Group, 8th USAAF, Boxted, Essex, early 1945; flown by Lt P. G. Kuhn, 44–21225 finished in distinctive dark blue/sky blue shadow shading camouflage scheme adopted by 63rd FS upon re-equipping with P-47M model; Group's other two squadrons, 61st and 62nd featured overall matt-black and dark green/light grey shadow shading resp.

Manufacturer: Republic.
Model: P-47N Thunderbolt.
Type: Long-range fighter/fighter-bomber.
Power Plant: One 2,800hp Pratt & Whitney R-2800–57, 73 or 77.
Performance:
maximum speed at 32,500ft (9,906m) 467mph (751km/hr).
cruising speed 300mph (482km/hr).
maximum range 2,200 miles (3,540km).
time to 25,000ft (7,620m) 14min 12sec.
service ceiling 43,000ft (13,106m).
Weights:
empty 11,000lb (4,990kg).
maximum 20,700lb (9,390kg).
Dimensions:
wing span 42ft 7in (12.98m).
length 36ft 1in (11.0m).
height 14ft 8in (4.47m).
wing area 322sq ft (29.91sq m).
Armament: Eight .5in Browning machine-guns plus either two

1,000lb (454kg), or three 500lb (227kg) bombs; or ten .5in rocket projectiles.
Crew: 1.
In Service: USA.
Variants (with no. built):
XP-47N: Prototype; one completed from P-47D (*1*).
P-47N: Final model; long-range version; re-designed strengthened wing with internal tankage (1,816).
Total Production: 15,634 (all Marks).
Remarks: Developed specifically for long-range Pacific theatre operations, P-47N entered service closing weeks WWII (four Groups); attacked targets in China, Korea and Japan; also flew B-29 escort missions.
Colour Reference: Plates 160, 161: Republic P-47N Thunderbolt (No 107) 'The Shell Pusher' of 463rd Fighter Squadron, 507th Fighter Group 20th USAAF, Io Shima, Western Pacific, July 1945; all-yellow tail served group identification, blue triangle on both vertical and horizontal surfaces denoted 463rd FS; flown by Capt R. T. Forrest, 'The Shell Pusher' can claim to have carried out one of very last operational missions of WWII, hostilities between Japan and Allies having officially ceased prior to his landing back from patrol over Korea, 14 Aug 1945.

Manufacturer: Ryan.
Model: STM-S2.
Type: Trainer/light fighter floatplane.
Power Plant: One 125hp Menasco L-365-1 or 150hp Menasco C-4S.
Performance:
maximum speed 122mph (196km/hr).
cruising speed 108mph (173km/hr).
normal range 246 miles (396km).
initial rate of climb 700ft/min (213m/min).
service ceiling 12,250ft (3,734m).
Weights:
empty 1,058lb (480kg).
loaded 1,600lb (726kg).
Dimensions:
wing span 29ft 11in (9.11m).
length 21ft 5¼in (6.53m).
height 6ft 11in (2.10m).
wing area 124sq ft (11.52sq m).
Armament: Two forward-firing machine-guns underwing.
Crew: 2.
In Service: Australia (34 ex-NEINAF), China, Netherlands (NEIAF 60, NEINAF 48).
Variants (with no. built):
ST; STA; STB; STW; STM-S2; ST-3KR, -3S, -4: Civil and export trainer series.
XPT-16: Military prototype

(USAAF) (*1*).
YPT-16: Service test model (15).
PT-20/22C: Production models; similar to YPT-16; various engines (1,178).
YPT-25: USAAF designation for ST-4; plywood fuselage; one 185hp Lycoming 0-435-1 (5).
NR-1: USN designation for PT-22 (100).
Total Production: 1,198.
Remarks: Standard WWII primary trainer; extensively used by USAAF (PT-22) and USN (NR-1); numerous export orders/deliveries, inc 60 STM-2 and 48 STM-2 and -S2 land- and floatplanes for Netherlands East Indies AF/NAF respectively; employed on coastal patrol and liaison during Japanese invasion; also, with underwing armament, as emergency light fighter; all NEIAF STM-2 landplanes lost (some captured by Japanese); 34 NEINAF STM-S2 floatplanes shipped to Australia; converted to landplanes for use by RAAF.

Manufacturer: Seversky.
Model: 2PA 'Convoy Fighter'.
Type: Escort fighter.
Power Plant: One 1,000hp Wright Cyclone R-1820.
Performance:
maximum speed at 10,000ft (3,048m) 285mph (489km/hr).
cruising speed 242mph (389km/hr).
maximum range 1,200 miles (1,930km).
initial rate of climb 1,666ft/min (508m/min).
service ceiling 25,000ft (7,620m).
Weights:
empty 4,190lb (1,900kg).
maximum 8,035lb (3,645kg).
Dimensions:
wing span 36ft 0in (10.97m).
length 25ft 4in (7.72m).
height 9ft 6in (2.89m).
wing area 220sq ft (20.44sq m).
Armament: Two .5in or four .3in machine-guns in fuselage; one .3in machine-gun mounted in rear cockpit; provision for two .3in wing guns; max bomb load 500lb (227kg).
Crew: 2.
In Service: Japan (IJNAF), Sweden, USA, USSR.
Variants (with no. built):
2PA: Parallel 2-seat export development of USAAC P-35; prototype (*1*).
2PA-L/A: Russian order; landplane/amphibian; pattern aircraft (*2*).
2PA-204L: Swedish order, inc 50 requisitioned by USAAF as AT-12 Guardsman; Republic-built (52).
2PA-B3: Japanese order (as A8V-1) (20).
Total Production: 75.
Remarks: 2-seat escort fighter;

Japanese examples, IJNAF designation A8V1, Navy Type S 2-seat Fighter (code-name Dick), in action during second Sino-Japanese conflict; all but eight export aircraft to be employed operationally in combat by Japan.

Manufacturer: Seversky.
Model: P-35.
Type: Fighter.
Power Plant: One 950hp Pratt & Whitney R-1830-9.
Performance:
maximum speed at 10,000ft (3,048m) 281mph (452km/hr).
cruising speed 260mph (418km/hr).
maximum range 1,150 miles (1,850km).
time to 5,000ft (1,524m) 2min 3sec.
service ceiling 30,600ft (9,327m).
Weights:
empty 4,315lb (1,957kg).
maximum 6,295lb (2,855kg).
Dimensions:
wing span 36ft 0in (10.97m).
length 25ft 2in (7.67m).
height 9ft 1in (2.77m).
wing area 220sq ft (20.44sq m).
Armament: One .5in and one .3in machine-gun in upper cowling firing through propeller; provision for light fragmentation bombs.
Crew: 1.
In Service: Sweden (60 J9), USA.
Variants (with no. built):
Prototype (AP-1): Private venture (*1*).
P-35: Initial production model (77).
XP-41: One P-35 conversion; 1,200hp supercharged R-1830-19; lengthened fuselage.
EP-106: Swedish export version of P-35; uprated engines; increased armament; inc 60 requisitioned by USAAF as P-35A; Republic-built (120).
Total Production: 198.
Remarks: By late 1941, 48 of USAAC's P-35As based in Philippines; all but eight destroyed within forty-eight hours of first Japanese attacks, 7 Dec 1941, majority on ground; few recorded air combats; those not despatched Philippines eventually delivered Ecuador; Swedish export models (Swedish AF designation J 9) remained in service until 1944.

Manufacturer: Sikorsky.
Model: JRS-1.
Type: Transport amphibian flying boat.
Power Plant: Two 750hp Pratt & Whitney R-1690-52.
Performance:
maximum speed at sea level 178mph (286km/hr).
cruising speed 166mph (267km/hr).
maximum range 775 miles

(1,247km).
initial rate of climb 1,000ft/min (305m/min).
service ceiling 19,000ft (5,795m).
Weights:
empty 12,750lb (5,783kg).
maximum 20,000lb (9,070kg).
Dimensions:
wing span 86ft 0in (26.21m).
length 51ft 2in (15.59m).
height 17ft 8in (5.38m).
wing area 781sq ft (72.55sq m).
Crew/Accommodation: 1/10.
In Service: USA (USAAF, USN; USMC).
Variants (with no. built):
JRS-1: Militarised version of civil S-43; USN (15); USMC (2).
Y10A-8: USAAC equivalent of JRS-1 (5).
OA-11: One civil S-43 impressment; personnel transport (*1*).
Total Production: 23 (military).
Remarks: Basically commercial amphibian flying-boat of 1935 with minor modifications to military standard; employed by all three US services early months WWII on utility transport duties.

Manufacturer: Sikorsky.
Model: JR2S-1.
Type: Long-range patrol/transport flying boat.
Power Plant: Four 1,050hp Pratt & Whitney XR-1830-68 'Twin-Wasp'.
Performance:
maximum speed at 12,000ft (3,658m) 227mph (365.3km/hr).
cruising speed 175mph (282km/hr).
maximum range 4,545 miles (7,313km).
service ceiling 23,100ft (7,040m).
Weights:
empty 26,407lb (11,978kg).
maximum 48,541lb (22,018kg).
Dimensions:
wing span 124ft 0in (37.80m).
length 76ft 2in (23.21m).
height 27ft 7in (8.40m).
wing area 1,670sq ft (155.14sq m).
Armament: One .5in gun each in front and tail turrets; two .3in waist guns.
Crew/Accommodation: 6–11/16.
In Service: USA (USN).
Variants (with no. built):
XPBS-1: Prototype; long-range patrol bomber flying boat, (USN) (*1*).
VS-44A: Civil variant of XPBS-1 (*3*).
JR2S-1: USN designation for impressed VS-44A (*3*).
Total Production: 4.
Remarks: Prototype first flown Aug 1937, experimental only; civil development (VS-44A) subsequently impressed by USN and employed on transatlantic transport duties 1942–45.

Manufacturer: Sikorsky.
Model: R–4B Hoverfly.
Type: General-purpose helicopter.
Power Plant: One 200hp Warner
R–550–3.
Performance:
maximum speed 75mph (120km/hr).
normal range 130 miles (209km).
time to 8,000ft (2,440m)
  45min 0sec.
service ceiling 8,000ft (2,440m).
Weights:
empty 2,011lb (913kg).
loaded 2,540lb (1,153kg).
Dimensions:
rotor diameter 38ft 0in (11.6m).
length 48ft 1in (14.65m).
height 12ft 5in (3.78m).
rotor disc area 1,134sq ft
  (105.3sq m).
Crew: 2.
In Service: Canada (1), Great
Britain (RAF, FAA), USA
(USAAF, USN, USCG).
Variants (with no. built):
XR–4: Prototype; 165hp R–500–3;
  anti-torque tail rotor (1).
YR–4A: Service test model;
  increased main rotor diameter;
  180hp R–550–1 (3).
YR–4B: As YR–4A; increased
  weight; provision for bomb-racks
  or 1 litter (27).
R–4B: Production model; extended
  range (100).
XR–4C: Re-engined XR–4;
  R–550–1.
HNS–1: USN designation of
  YR–4B (3) and R–4B (20 ex-
  AAF) (2).
Hoverfly I: RAF/FAA designation
  of YR–4B (7) and R–4B (45).
Total Production: 133.
Remarks: USAAF's first
operational helicopter; entered
service 1943–44; widespread use
closing months of war in Pacific;
also by USN and USCG (3 YR–4B,
20 R–4B) in ASR, liaison,
reconnaissance and training roles;
equipped one RAF sqn for radar-
calibration duties; also with FAA;
either wheeled or pontoon-float
undercarriage.

Manufacturer: Sikorsky.
Model: R–5A.
Type: Reconnaissance/rescue
helicopter.
Power Plant: One 450hp Pratt &
Whitney R–985–AN–5.
Performance:
maximum speed 105mph
  (169km/hr).
range 360 miles (579km).
time to 10,000ft (3,048m)
  15min 0sec.
service ceiling 14,400ft (4,390m).
Weights:
loaded 5,000lb (2,270kg).
Dimensions:
rotor diameter 48ft 0in (14.6m).
length 57ft 1in (17.4m).
height 13ft 0in (3.96m).
rotor disc area 1,810sq ft (168sq m).
Crew/Accommodation: 2/4
external litters.
In Service: USA (USAAF, USN).
Variants (with no. built):
XR–5: Prototype (5).
XR–5A: Two XR–5 conversions
  with British equipment.
YR–5A: Service test model;
  provision for two litters (26).
R–5A: Production model; to Air
  Rescue Service (34).
R–5D: Modified R–5A; addn
  passenger; rescue hoist; auxiliary
  fuel tank; 21 conversions.
YR–5E: Dual control; 5 YR–5A
  conversions.
HO2S–1: USN equivalent of
  YR–5A (2).
Total Production: 65.
Remarks: First helicopter to be
operated by Air Rescue Service;
entering service close of WWII;
forerunner of long and continuing
line of Sikorsky helicopters to be
used by USAF, USN, USMC.

Manufacturer: Spartan.
Model: UC–71.
Type: Communications/Liaison.
Power Plant: One 400hp Pratt &
Whitney Wasp-Junior R–985–33.
Performance:
maximum speed at 5,000ft (1,525m)
  216mph (348km/hr).
cruising speed 208mph (335km/hr).
maximum range 950 miles
  (1,520km).
maximum rate of climb 1,530ft/min
  (447m/min).
service ceiling 24,200ft (7,372m).
Weights:
empty 2,987lb (1,355kg).
loaded 4,400lb (1,996kg).
Dimensions:
wing span 39ft 0in (11.9m).
length 26ft 10in (8.2m).
height 8ft 5in (2.56m).
wing area 250.8sq ft (23.4sq m).
Crew/Accommodation: 1/4.
In Service: USA.

Variants:
Executive: Pre-war civil light
  aircraft.
UC–71: Military designation;
  16 impressments.
Total Production: 16.
Remarks: Impressed 1942; served
solely within US on communications
/liaison duties.

Manufacturer: Stinson.
Model: YO–54.
Type: Liaison.
Power Plant: One 80hp
Continental 0–170–1.
Performance:
maximum speed 90mph (145km/hr).
Weights:
loaded 1,580lb (717kg).
Dimensions:
wing span 34ft 0in (10.36m).
length 22ft 2in (6.76m).
Armament: Two 100lb (45kg)
depth-charges.
Crew: 2.
In Service: Canada (1 + impressed),
USA.
Variants (with no. built):
YO–54: Military designation of
  civil Model 105 (6).
Remarks: 6 Model 105s purchased
by USAAF; equipped with two
depth-charge racks and assigned to
CAP for inshore coastal patrol; at
least one reported attack made on
German U-Boat; twenty Stinson
10–As similarly equipped and
employed under military designation
L–9.

Manufacturer: Stinson.
Model: Reliant I (UC–81).
Type: Trainer/communications.

Power Plant: One 290hp Lycoming
R–680–13.
Performance:
maximum speed 141mph
  (226km/hr).
service ceiling 14,000ft (4,270m).
Weights:
empty 2,810lb (1,276kg).
loaded 4,000lb (1,816kg).
Dimensions:
wing span 41ft 11in (12.77m).
length 27ft 11in (8.5m).
height 8ft 7in (2.59m).
wing area 258.5sq ft (24sq m).
Crew: 4.
In Service: Australia (1 impressed),
Great Britain (FAA), Norway,
USA.
Variants (with no. built):
UC–81, –81A/H and J/N: Civil
  models impressed for utility
  transport duties (USAAF) (47).
AT–19: Advanced trainer; military
  model (500).
Reliant I: FAA equivalent of
  AT–19; all 500 Lend-Lease.
Remarks: Original civil Reliant of
1938; various models impressed
into USAAF as above; all military
production to FAA; used primarily
in West Indies for navigation-
training and on communications
duties (3 sqns).

Manufacturer: Stinson.
Model: L–1 Vigilant.
Type: Liaison.
Power Plant: One 295hp Lycoming
R–680–9.
Performance:
maximum speed at sea level
  122mph (196km/hr).
normal range 280 miles (450km).

time to 10,000ft (3,048m)
  24min 30sec.
service ceiling 12,800ft (3,900m).
Weights:
empty 2,670lb (1,211kg).
loaded 3,400lb (1,542kg).
Dimensions:
wing span 50ft 11in (15.52m).
length 34ft 3in (10.44m).
height 10ft 2in (3.10m).
wing area 329sq ft (30.56sq m).
Crew: 2.
In Service: Great Britain, USA.
Variants (with no. built):
L–1: Former O–49 (142).
L–1A: Modified L–1; lengthened
  fuselage; former O–49A (182).
L–1B/C: Ambulance conversions
  of above (3 and 113 resp).
L–1D: Glider-pilot trainer; 14
  converted L–1As.
L–1E: Amphibious ambulance;
  7 conversions of L–1s.
L–1F: Amphibious ambulance; 5
  conversions of L–1As.
Vigilant I: RAF equivalent of L–1;
  17 Lend-Lease.
IA: RAF equivalent of L–1A;
  96 Lend-Lease allocations, only
  13+ delivered.
Total Production: 324.
Remarks: First of new 'Liaison'
category, L–1 served in both
European and Pacific theatres,
proving itself particularly well
during Burma campaign; RAF
Vigilants performed liaison and
AOP duties in Mediterranean area
(Tunisia, Sicily and Italy), 1943–44.

Manufacturer: Stinson.
Model: L–5 Sentinel.
Type: Liaison.

Power Plant: One 185hp Lycoming
0–431–1.
Performance:
maximum speed 130mph
  (209km/hr).
normal range 420 miles
  (676km).
time to 5,000ft (1,524m)
  6min 24sec.
service ceiling 15,800ft (4,820m).
Weights:
empty 1,550lb (703kg).
loaded 2,020lb (916kg).
Dimensions:
wing span 34ft 0in (10.37m).
length 24ft 1in (7.33m).
height 7ft 11in (2.41m).
wing area 155sq ft (14.4sq m).
Crew: 2.
In Service: Australia (1), Great
Britain, USA (USAAF, USMC).
Variants (with no. built):
L–5: Former O–62; initial produc-
  tion model (1,731).
L–5A: Modified L–5; revised
  electrics; 668 conversions.
L–5B: Ambulance version (679).
L–5C: Provision for reconnaissance
  camera (200).
L–5E: As L–5C; modified ailerons
  (558).
XL–5F: Re-engined L–5B.
L–5G: Improved L–5E (115).
L–9A: Impressed civil Voyagers (8).
L–5B: Impressed civil Model
  10–As (12).
OY–1: USMC equivalent of L–5
  and L–5A (304).
Sentinel I: RAF equivalent of
  L–5 (40).
Sentinel II: RAF equivalent of
  L–5B (60).
Total Production: 3,700 + .

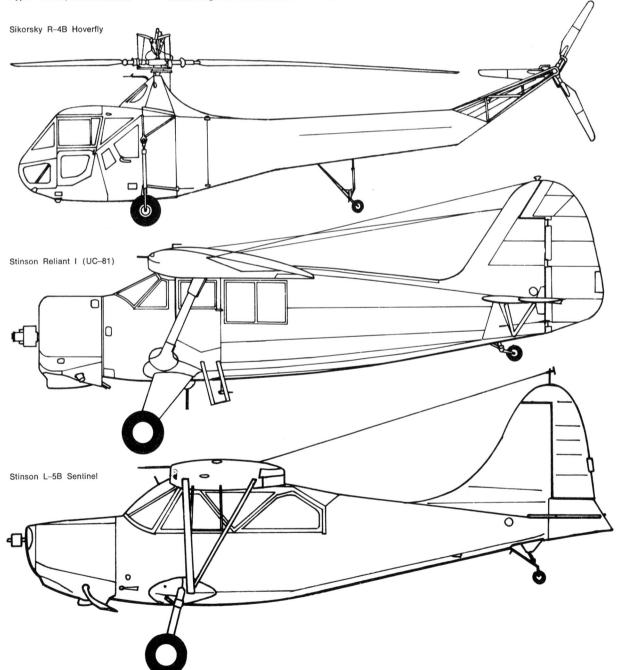

Sikorsky R–4B Hoverfly

Stinson Reliant I (UC–81)

Stinson L–5B Sentinel

Remarks: Development of civil Model V–76 Voyager; entered AAF service 1942, initially as O–62; larger and more advanced than other types of the 'L' series. Stinson's L–5 Sentinel served in all theatres, performing liaison, AOP, reconnaissance and ambulance duties; operated by USMC 1943–45, and by RAF in Burma; extensive post-war USAAF use, inc Korea.

Manufacturer: Taylorcraft.
Model: L–2A Grasshopper.
Type: Liaison.
Power Plant: One 65hp Continental 0–170–3.
Performance:
maximum speed 88mph (142km/hr).
range 230 miles (370km).
time to 5,000ft (1,524m) 14min 12sec.
service ceiling 10,050ft (3,063m).
Weights:
empty 875lb (397kg).
maximum 1,300lb (590kg).
Dimensions:
wing span 35ft 5in (10.79m).
length 22ft 9in (6.93m).
height 8ft 0in (2.44m).
wing area 181sq ft (16.81sq m).
Crew: 2.
In Service: Netherlands (NEIAF, L2–M), USA (USAAF, USN).
Variants (with no. built):
YO–57: Service test examples of civil Model D; subsequently redesignated L–2 (4).
O–57 (L–2): Initial production model (70).
O–57A (L–2A): Modified L–2 (476).
L–2B: Artillery spotter (490).
L–2C/H, J/L: Civil impressments; various models (41).
L–2M: Improved L–2A; wing spoilers (900).
TG–6: Trainer glider; modified L–2 (253).
XLNT–1: Experimental USN equivalent of TG–6 (10).
LNT–1: Service model (25).
Total Production: 2,044.
Remarks: Popularly known as the 'Tee-Cart', Taylorcraft's L–2 (formerly O–57) saw widespread service in liaison, AOP, and communications roles, 1942–44; forerunner of highly successful British Taylorcraft/Auster series.

Manufacturer: Universal.
Model: L–7A.
Type: Liaison.
Power Plant: One 90hp Franklin 0–200–1.
Performance:
maximum speed 120mph (193km/hr).
cruising speed 103mph (166km/hr).
range 580 miles (933km).
initial rate of climb 600ft/min (183m/min).
service ceiling 15,000ft (4,572m).
Weights:
empty 973lb (441kg).
loaded 1,610lb (730kg).
Dimensions:
wing span 32ft 0in (9.75m).
length 22ft 11in (6.98m).
height 6ft 11in (2.10m).
wing area 132.3sq ft (12.29sq m).
Crew: 2.
In Service: France (FFAF).
Variants (with no. built):
L–7A: Military designation of civil Model 90–AF Monocoupe (19).
Remarks: 19 Monocoupes purchased by USAAF, 1942; entire order subsequently Lend-Leased to Free French.

Manufacturer: Vought.
Model: V–65C Corsair.
Type: 2-seat fighter.
Power Plant: One 600hp Pratt & Whitney R–1690–C Hornet.
Performance:
maximum speed 180mph (290km/hr).
initial rate of climb 1,550ft/min (472m/min).
service ceiling 20,000ft (6,096m).
Dimensions:
wing span 36ft 10in (11.02m).
length 26ft 2.9in (8.0m).
height 10ft 8in (3.25m).
wing area 325.6sq ft (30.25sq m).
Armament: One fixed .3in machine-gun in upper wing; plus one flexible .3in gun in rear cockpit; provision for two underwing bomb racks.
Crew: 2.
In Service: China Thailand, USA (USN).
Variants (with no. built):
O2U–1/4; O3U–1, 3, 6; SU–1/4: Pre-war USN variants (622).
V–50/60/70/80/90/ series: Export versions inc: V–65C: Chinese order; Vought-built (42); Cantonese licence-built; V–92C: Chinese order; improved Model

65 (21); V–935: Thai order; Vought-built, Thai (ASW) licence-built (72).
Total Production: 760+.
Remarks: Few late-model USN examples employed in communications role, 1941–43; Chinese machines served as attack aircraft early months Sino-Japanese conflict; Thai models saw action against Vichy French forces over Indo-China; remained in Thai service until late forties; numerous other foreign users inc Argentina, Brazil, Cuba, Germany, Great Britain, Japan, Mexico and Peru.

Manufacturer: Vought.
Model: SBU–1.
Type: Scout bomber.
Power Plant: One 700hp Pratt & Whitney R–1535–80.
Performance:
maximum speed at 8,900ft (2,713m) 205mph (330km/hr).
cruising speed 122mph (196km/hr).
maximum range 548 miles (882km).
initial rate of climb 1,180ft/min (360m/min).
service ceiling 23,700ft (7,224m).
Weights:
empty 3,645lb (1,653kg).
maximum 5,520lb (2,504kg).
Dimensions:
wing span 33ft 3in (10.13m).
length 27ft 10in (8.48m).
height 11ft 11in (3.63m).
wing area 327sq ft (30.38sq m).
Armament: One fixed forward-firing .3in Browning machine-gun; one flexible .3in Browning machine-gun in rear cockpit; max bomb load 500lb (227kg).

Crew: 2.
In Service: USA (USN).
Variants (with no. built):
XF3U–1: 2-seat fighter prototype; one Pratt & Whitney R–1535–64 (1).
XSBU–1: 2-seat scout bomber prototype; redesigned XF3U–1; enlarged wings; increased fuel capacity; uprated engine; 1 conversion.
SBU–1: Production model; as XSBU–1 (84).
SBU–2: Improved SBU–1; one Pratt & Whitney R–1535–98 (40).
Total Production: 125.
Remarks: Entering service late 1935, SBU–1/2 remained on strength (latterly with USNR) until 1941; subsequently employed ancillary liaison/training duties.

Manufacturer: Vought.
Model: SB2U–1 Vindicator.
Type: Carrier-based scout/dive-bomber.
Power Plant: One 825hp Pratt & Whitney R–1535–96.
Performance:
maximum speed at 9,500ft (2,896m) 250mph (402km/hr).
cruising speed 143mph (230km/hr).
maximum range 1,004 miles (1,615km).
initial rate of climb 1,500ft/min (457m/min).
service ceiling 27,400ft (8,352m).
Weights:
empty 4,676lb (2,121kg).
maximum 7,278lb (3,301kg).
Dimensions:
wing span 42ft 0in (12.80m).
length 34ft 0in (10.36m).

height 10ft 3in (3.12m).
wing area 305sq ft (28.33sq m).
Armament: One fixed forward-firing .3in Browning machine-gun; one flexible .3in gun in rear cockpit; max bomb load 1,000lb (454kg).
Crew: 2.
In Service: France (FNAF). Great Britain (FAA). USA (USN. USMC).
Variants (with no. built):
XSB2U–1: Prototype; monoplane (1).
XSB3U–1: Prototype; biplane (1).
SB2U–1: Initial production model of XSB2U–1 (54).
SB2U–2: As SB2U–1; equipment changes (58).
XSB2U–3: Float plane; ventral fin; one SB2U–1 conversion.
SB2U–3: Modified SB2U–1; addn long range fuel capacity, increased armament; 825hp R–1535–02 (57).
V–156F: French export order for SB2U–1 (39).
Chesapeake Mk I: FAA designation, inc residual French order; British modifications (50).
Total Production: 241.
Remarks: USN/USMC sqns operated against Japanese early months Pacific war, inc Battle of Midway, June 1942; V–156Fs equipped two sqns at time of German attack on France, 10 May 1940; one sqn wiped out first day; second fought rearguard action along Channel Coast before withdrawal to Southern France; subsequent brief action against invading Italian forces; British Chesapeake Mk Is served two FAA sqns, training purposes only.

Manufacturer: Vought.
Model: OS2U–3 Kingfisher.
Type: Reconnaissance floatplane.
Power Plant: One 450hp Pratt & Whitney R–985–AN–2.
Performance:
maximum speed at sea level 157mph (253km/hr).
maximum speed at 5,500ft (1,676m) 164mph (264km/hr).
cruising speed 119mph (191km/hr).
maximum range 1,155 miles (1,858km).
time to 10,000ft (3,048m) 29min 6sec.
service ceiling 13,000ft (3,962m).
Weights:
empty 4,123lb (1,870kg).
maximum 6,000lb (2,722kg).
Dimensions:
wing span 35ft 11in (10.94m).
length 33ft 7½in (10.25m).
height 15ft 1in (4.60m).
wing area 262sq ft (24.34sq m).
Armament: One fixed forward-firing .3in Browning machine-gun and one flexible .3in gun in rear cockpit; max bomb load 650lb (295kg).
Crew: 2.
In Service: Argentina, Australia (18 ex-NEINAF), Chile, Great Britain (FAA), Uruguay, USA (USN, USMC).
Variants (with no. built):
XOS2U–1: Prototype (1).
OS2U–1: Initial production model (54).
OS2U–2: As OS2U–1; revised equipment (158).
OS2U–3: Addn fuel tanks in wings, inc Lend-Lease to Argentina (9), Chile (15), Great Britain (FAA

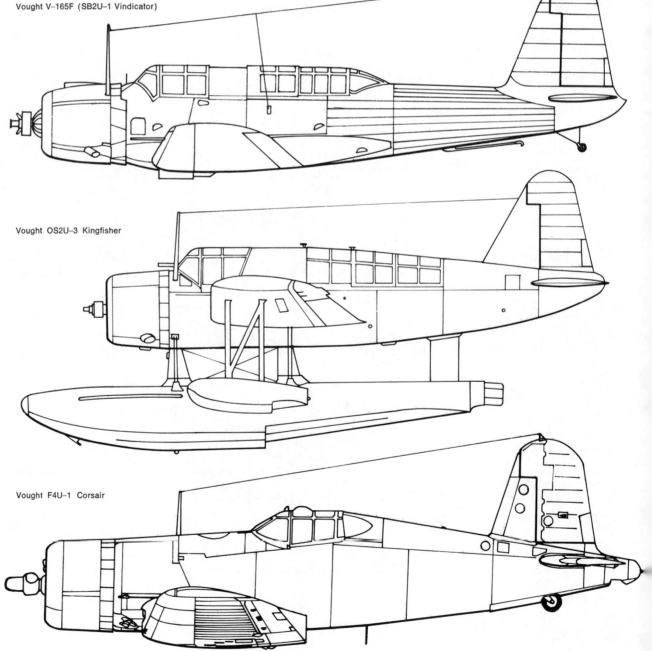

Vought V–165F (SB2U–1 Vindicator)

Vought OS2U–3 Kingfisher

Vought F4U–1 Corsair

100), Netherlands (NEI, 24), Uruguay (6) (1,006).
OSN–1: As OS2U–3; NAF-built (300).
Kingfisher I: FAA designation for Lend-Lease OS2U–3s.
Total Production: 1,519.
Remarks: Standard USN observation-scout floatplane, served throughout Pacific war, from Pearl Harbor to Tokyo Bay; participated all major campaigns, as well as numerous local naval actions, operating in artillery-spotter, dive-bomber, anti-submarine, ASR and many other roles; also served in Atlantic, Mediterranean and Caribbean theatres; operated from battleships, cruisers, even destroyers; FAA Kingfishers flown from AMCs in South Atlantic and Indian Oceans; but majority employed in training role in West Indies; 18 of 24 OS2U–3s destined for NEINAF were diverted to RAAF.
Manufacturer: Vought.
Model: F4U–1 Corsair.
Type: Land-based/carrier-borne fighter.
Power Plant: One 2,000hp Pratt & Whitney R–2800–8.
Performance:
maximum speed at 20,000ft (6,096m) 415mph (668km/hr).
cruising speed 182mph (293km/hr).
normal range 1,015 miles (1,633km).
initial rate of climb 3,120ft/min (951m/min).
service ceiling 37,000ft (11,278m).
Weights:
empty 8,695lb (3,944kg).
maximum 14,000lb (6,350kg).
Dimensions:
wing span 40ft 11¾in (12.48m).
length 33ft 4½in (10.17m).
height 15ft 0¾in (4.59m).
wing area 314sq ft (29.17sq m).
Armament: Six .5in Browning machine-guns in wings.
Crew: 1.
In Service: Great Britain (FAA), New Zealand (425 Lend-Lease: 233 F4U–1A, 131 F4U–1D; 61 FG–1D), USA (USN, USMC).
Variants (with no. built):
XF4U–1: Prototype; one .3in and one .5in gun in fuselage; two .5in wing guns (1).
F4U–1: Initial production model; addn armament.
F4U–1A: Fixed wing model.
F4U–1B: FAA model.
F4U–1C: Four 20mm cannon in wings in lieu of machine-guns.
F4U–1D: Fighter-bomber version; provision for bombs or rockets underwing.
F4U–1P: Photographic equipment. (Total F4U–1 to 1P: 4,669).
FG–1, –1A, D: As F4U–1, –1A, D resp; Goodyear-built (4,014).
F3A–1, –1A, D: As F4U–1, –1A, D resp; Brewster-built (735).
XF4U–2: Prototype; autopilot; AI radar; Twelve F4U–1 night-fighter conversions.
F4U–2: USN night-fighter modification.
XF4U–3: Turbo supercharged Double Wasp, 1 conversion; 2 built.
FG–3: As XF4U Goodyear-built (13).
XF4U–4: Prototype; improved F4U–1; uprated engine, 4-blade propeller, revised cowling (5).
F4U–4: Production model (2,197).
F4U–4C, E, N, P, –5, –5N, NL, P, –7, AU–1: Late- and post-war variants (923).
F2G–1, 2: Low-altitude versions; Goodyear-built (10).
Corsair I: FAA equivalent of F4U–1; 95 Lend-Lease.
II: FAA equivalent of F4U–1; raised cockpit hood; 510 Lend-Lease.
III: FAA equivalent of F3A–1; 430 Lend-Lease.
IV: FAA equivalent of FG–1; 977 Lend-Lease.
Total Production: 12,571.
Remarks: Arguably the best US fighter of WWII; destroyed 2,140 enemy aircraft, achieving an 11-to-1 'kill' ratio; entered service as land-based Marine fighter, Feb 1943; subsequently equipped many USN and USMC sqns throughout rest of Pacific War; first carrier-borne Corsairs operated by FAA during invasion of *Tirpitz*, April 1944; equipped nineteen FAA sqns, majority serving in Far East; RNZAF employment primarily close-support; extensive post-war use, inc Korea and Indo-China (FNAF).
Colour Reference: Plates 128, 129: Vought F4U–1A Corsair (NZ5339) of No 22 Squadron, RNZAF, Bougainville, late 1944; note US-style (barred) RNZAF roundels all six wing/fuselage stations, plus

narrow fin flash unique to RNZAF, and one of few instances of red being used in markings by Allied forces in Pacific area post-1942.

Manufacturer: Vultee.
Model: V–1A.
Type: Transport/liaison.
Power Plant: One 750hp Wright SR–i820–F2.
Weights:

Performance:
maximum speed 225mph (362km/hr).
cruising speed 205mph (330km/hr).
maximum range 1,000 miles (1,609km).
initial rate of climb 1,000ft/min (3,048m/min).
service ceiling 20,000ft (6,096m).
Weights:

empty 5,302lb (2,405kg).
maximum 8,500lb (3,856kg).
Dimensions:
wing span 50ft 0in (15.24m).
length 37ft 0in (11.28m).
height 10ft 2in (3.10m).
wing area 384sq ft (35.67sq m).
Crew/Accommodation: 2/8.
In Service: China (3), Spain (NatAF 4, RepAF 11+).

Variants (with no. built):
V–1 Prototype: Single pilot/ 8 passenger civil transport (1).
V–1A: Production model; various engines; minor customer modifications (26).
Total Production: 27.
Remarks: Vultee's first product. V–1/1A eight-passenger monoplane first flew 1933; at least 18 of total

Order of Battle Assault on Okinawa, March–June 1945

UNITED STATES NAVAL AIR FORCES

TF 58 Fast Carrier Force Pacific Fleet
TG 58.1 Task Group One:
USS *Hornet* (CV–12)
VF–17   61 Grumman F6F–5 Hellcat
  6 Grumman F6F–5P Hellcat
  4 Grumman F6F–5N Hellcat
VB–17   9 Curtiss SB2C–3 Helldiver
  2 Curtiss SB2C–4 Helldiver
  4 Curtiss SBW Helldiver
VT–17   15 Grumman TBM–3 Avenger
USS *Wasp* (CV–18)
VBF–86   36 Vought F4U–1D Corsair
VF–86   28 Grumman F6F–5 Hellcat
  2 Grumman F6F–5E Hellcat
  2 Grumman F6F–5P Hellcat
  2 Grumman F6F–5N Hellcat
VB–86   15 Curtiss SB2C–4 Helldiver
VT–86   15 Grumman TBM–3 Avenger
USS *Bennington* (CV–20)
VF–82   29 Grumman F6F–5 Hellcat
  2 Grumman F6F–5E Hellcat
  2 Grumman F6F–5P Hellcat
  4 Grumman F6F–5N Hellcat
VB–82   15 Curtiss SB2C–4E Helldiver
VT–82   15 Grumman TBM–3 Avenger
VMF–112   18 Vought F4U–1D Corsair
VMF–123   17 Vought F4U–1D Corsair
USS *Belleau Wood* (CVL–24)
VF–30   24 Grumman F6F–5 Hellcat
  1 Grumman F6F–5P Hellcat
VT–30   8 Grumman TBM–3 Avenger
  1 Grumman TBM–3P Avenger
USS *San Jacinto* (CVL–30)
VF–45   24 Grumman F6F–5 Hellcat
  1 Grumman F6F–5P Hellcat
VT–45   9 Grumman TBM–3 Avenger
TG 58.2 Task Group Two:
USS *Enterprise* (CV–6)
VFN–90   11 Grumman F6F–5E Hellcat
  2 Grumman F6F–5P Hellcat
  19 Grumman F6F–5N Hellcat
VTN–90   21 Grumman TBM–3D Avenger
USS *Franklin* (CV–13)
VF–5   2 Grumman F6F–5 Hellcat
  4 Grumman F6F–5N Hellcat
  2 Vought FG–1D Corsair
  30 Vought F4U–1D Corsair
VB–5   15 Curtiss SB2C–4E Helldiver
VT–5   15 Grumman TBM–3 Avenger
USS *Randolph* (CV–15)
VF–12   25 Grumman F6F–5 Hellcat
  2 Grumman F6F–5E Hellcat
  2 Grumman F6F–5P Hellcat
  4 Grumman F6F–5N Hellcat
VBF–12   24 Grumman F6F–5 Hellcat
VB–12   15 Curtiss SB2C–4E Helldiver
VT–12   15 Grumman TBM–3 Avenger
TG 58.3 Task Group Three:
USS *Essex* (CV–9)
VF–83   28 Grumman F6F–5 Hellcat
  2 Grumman F6F–5E Hellcat
  2 Grumman F6F–5P Hellcat
  4 Grumman F6F–5N Hellcat
VBF–83   36 Vought F4U–1D Corsair
VB–83   15 Curtiss SB2C–4 Helldiver
VT–83   15 Grumman TBM–3 Avenger
USS *Bunker Hill* (CV–17)
VF–84   6 Grumman F6F–5P Hellcat
  4 Grumman F6F–5N Hellcat
  27 Vought F4U–1D Corsair
VB–84   2 Curtiss SB2C–4 Helldiver
  13 Curtiss SB2C–4E Helldiver
VT–84   15 Grumman TBM–3 Avenger
VMF–221   18 Vought F4U–1D Corsair
VMF–451   18 Vought F4U–1D Corsair
USS *Hancock* (CV–19)
VF–6   28 Grumman F6F–5 Hellcat
  2 Grumman F6F–5E Hellcat
  2 Grumman F6F–5P Hellcat
  4 Grumman F6F–5N Hellcat
VBF–6   36 Grumman F6F–5 Hellcat
VB–6   5 Curtiss SB2C–3 Helldiver and SB2C–3E Helldiver
  3 Curtiss SB2C–4 Helldiver
  4 Curtiss SBW–3 Helldiver and SBW–4E Helldiver
VT–6   10 Grumman TBM–3 Avenger
USS *Cabot* (CVL–27)
VF–29   25 Grumman F6F–5 Hellcat
VT–29   9 Grumman TBM–3 Avenger
USS *Bataan* (CVL–29)
VF–47   23 Grumman F6F–5 Hellcat
  1 Grumman F6F–5P Hellcat
VT–47   12 Grumman TBM–3 Avenger
TG 58.4 Task Group Four:
USS *Yorktown* (CV–10)
VF–9   40 Grumman F6F–5, F6F–5E, F6F–5P & F6F–5N Hellcat
VBF–9   33 Grumman F6F–5 Hellcat
VB–9   15 Curtiss SB2C–4E Helldiver
VT–9   6 Grumman TBM–3 Avenger
  1 Grumman TBM–3P Avenger
USS *Intrepid* (CV–11)
VF–10   2 Grumman F6F–5P Hellcat
  4 Grumman F6F–5N Hellcat

  1 Vought FG–1 Corsair
  29 Vought F4U–1D Corsair
VBF–10   36 Vought F4U–1D Corsair
VB–10   15 Curtiss SB2C–4E Helldiver
VT–10   15 Grumman TBM–3 Avenger
USS *Langley* (CVL–28)
VF–23   3 Grumman F6F–3 Hellcat
  21 Grumman F6F–5 Hellcat
  1 Grumman F6F–5P Hellcat
VT–23   9 Grumman TBM–1C Avenger
USS *Independence* (CVL–22)
VF–46   24 Grumman F6F–5 Hellcat
  1 Grumman F6F–5P Hellcat
VT–46   8 Grumman TBM–3 Avenger
TG 50.8 Logistics Support Group Fifth Fleet:
USS *Shamrock Bay* (CVE–84)
VC–94   18 Grumman FM–2 Wildcat
  12 Grumman TBM–3 Avenger
USS *Makassar Strait* (CVE–91)
VC–97   12 Grumman FM–2 Wildcat
  12 Grumman TBM–3 Avenger

TF 52 Amphibious Support Force
TG 52.1 Support Carrier Group:
Unit One:
USS *Makin Island* (CVE–93)
VC–84   16 Grumman FM–2 Wildcat
  11 Grumman TBM–3 Avenger
USS *Fanshaw Bay* (CVE–70)
VOC–2   24 Grumman FM–2 Wildcat
  6 Grumman TBM–3 Avenger
USS *Lunga Point* (CVE–94)
VC–85   18 Grumman FM–2 Wildcat
  11 Grumman TBM–3 Avenger
  1 Grumman TBM–3P Avenger
USS *Sangamon* (CVE–26)
Air Group 33   24 Grumman F6F Hellcat
  6 Grumman TBM–3E Avenger
USS *Natoma Bay* (CVE–62)
VC–81   20 Grumman FM–2 Wildcat
  11 Grumman TBM–1C Avenger
  1 Grumman TBM–1CP Avenger
USS *Savo Island* (CVE–78)
VC–91   20 Grumman FM–2 Wildcat
  11 Grumman TBM–1C Avenger
  4 Grumman TBM–3 Avenger
USS *Anzio* (CVE–57)
VC–13   12 Grumman FM–2 Wildcat
  12 Grumman TBM–1C Avenger
Unit Two:
USS *Saginaw Bay* (CVE–82)
VC–88   20 Grumman FM–2 Wildcat
  12 Grumman TBM Avenger
USS *Sargent Bay* (CVE–83)
VC–83   16 Grumman FM–2 Wildcat
  12 Grumman TBM–1C Avenger
USS *Rudyerd Bay* (CVE–81)
VC–96   20 Grumman FM–2 Wildcat
  11 Grumman TBM–1C Avenger
USS *Marcus Island* (CVE–77)
VC–87   20 Grumman FM–2 Wildcat
  12 Grumman TBM–3 Avenger
USS *Petrof Bay* (CVE–80)
VC–93   16 Grumman FM–2 Wildcat
  12 Grumman TBM–3 Avenger
USS *Tulagi* (CVE–72)
VC–92   19 Grumman FM–2 Wildcat
  12 Grumman TBM–3 Avenger
USS *Wake Island* (CVE–65)
VOC–1   26 Grumman FM–2 Wildcat
  6 Grumman TBM–3 Avenger
Unit Three:
USS *Suwannee* (CVE–27)
Air Group 40   17 Grumman F6F Hellcat
  10 Grumman TBM Avenger
USS *Chenango* (CVE–28)
Air Group 25   17 Grumman F6F–5 Hellcat
  1 Grumman F6F–5P Hellcat
  12 Grumman TBM Avenger
USS *Santee* (CVE–29)
Air Group 24   18 Grumman F6F Hellcat
  12 Grumman TBM Avenger
USS *Steamer Bay* (CVE–87)
VC–90   19 Grumman FM–2 Wildcat
  12 Grumman TBM–3 Avenger

Special Escort Carrier Group
USS *Hollandia* (CVE–97)
USS *White Plains* (CVE–66)
USS *Sitkoh Bay* (CVE–86)
USS *Breton* (CVE–23)   Marine Air Groups 31 and 33   192 Vought F4U Corsair
  30 Grumman F6F Hellcat

TG 50.5 Search and Reconnaissance Group
USS *Hamlin* (AV–15) VPB–208   12 Martin PBM–5 Mariner
USS *St. George* (AV–16) VPB–18   12 Martin PBM–5 Mariner
USS *Chandeleur* (AV–10) VPB–21   12 Martin PBM–3 Mariner
USS *Yakutat* (AVP–32)
USS *Onslow* (AVP–48) VPB–27   12 Martin PBM–5 Mariner
USS *Shelikof* (AVP–52)
USS *Bering Strait* (AVP–34) VH–3   6 Martin PBM–3R Mariner

Vultee V-11-GB

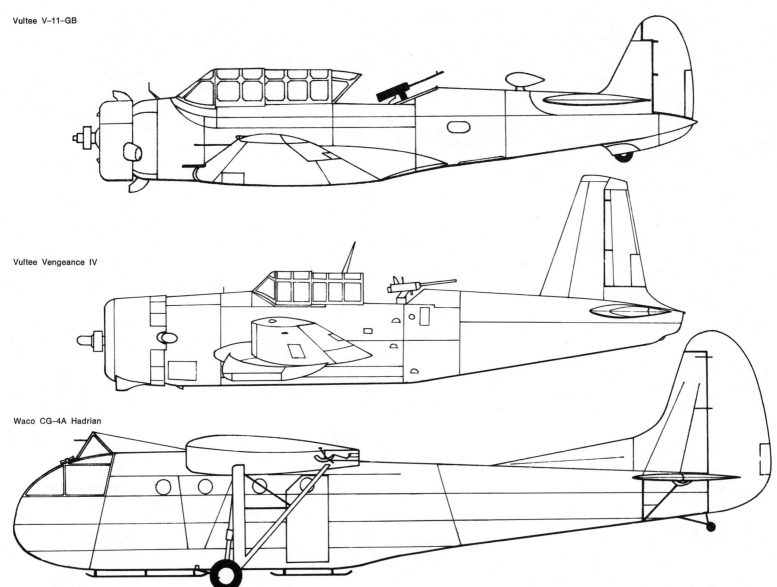

Vultee Vengeance IV

Waco CG-4A Hadrian

production eventually acquired by agents of Spanish Republic; 11+ believed to have reached, and served with RepAF; 4 captured en route, flown by NatAF; 3 to China; all operated in liaison/communications role; one direct to USSR as floatplane.

Manufacturer: Vultee.
Model: V-11-GB.
Type: Attack-bomber.
Power Plant: One 1,000hp Wright SGR-1820-G2.
Performance:
maximum speed at sea level 214mph (344km/hr).
cruising speed 207mph (333km/hr).
normal range 1,225 miles (1,971km).
initial rate of climb 1,285ft/min (392m/min).
service ceiling 23,000ft (7,010m).
Weights:
empty 6,176lb (2,801kg).
maximum 11,437lb (5,188kg).
Dimensions:
wing span 50ft 0in (15.24m).
length 37ft 5½in (11.42m).
height 10ft 0in (3.05m).
wing area 384sq ft (35.67sq m).
Armament: Four fixed forward-firing .3in Browning machine-guns in wings; one flexible .3in Browning each in dorsal and ventral positions; max bomb load 3,000lb (1,361kg).
Crew: 3.
In Service: Brazil, China, Turkey, USA, USSR.
Variants (with no. built):
Prototypes: Development of V-1A transport (2).
V-11-G: Initial production model; Chinese order (30).
V-11-GB: Bomber version; addn crew member; USSR order (1); Turkish order (40); Brazilian order, inc 8 as floatplanes (26).
YA-19: USAAC service test model of V-11-GB; 1,200hp Pratt & Whitney R-1830-17 (7).
XA-19A/C: Engine test-beds; 3 YA-19 conversions.
BSh-1: As V-11-GB; 920hp Wright M-62; USSR licence-built (31).
V-12 Prototype: Improved V-11-

GB; Pratt & Whitney GR-1830-S1C3; revised armament (1).
V-12-C: As V-12; 1,050hp Wright GR-1820-G105B; Chinese order (2 pattern, 24 licence-assembled by CAMCO) (26).
V-12-D: Modified V-12-C; uprated engine; redesigned fuselage, tail and canopy; Chinese order (2 pattern, 50 licence-assembled by CAMCO and HAL) (52).
Total Production: 216.
Remarks: USSR models, built 1937-38 as armoured assault aircraft, served during WWII in transport/liaison role as PS-43; Chinese V-12-C/D deliveries comprised 2 pattern aircraft each model, remainder as component sets for assembly in China; all V-12-Cs so completed; V-12-D assembly switched to HAL, Bangalore, after CAMCO plant bombed by Japanese; exact number delivered unknown.

Manufacturer: Vultee.
Model: P-66 Vanguard.
Type: Light interceptor fighter.
Power Plant: One 1,200hp Pratt & Whitney R-1830-33.
Performance:
maximum speed at 15,100ft (4,602m) 340mph (547km/hr).
cruising speed 290mph (467km/hr).
normal range 850 miles (1,368km).
time to 2,520ft (768m) 1 min 0sec.
Weights:
empty 5,237lb (2,376kg).
maximum 7,384lb (3,349kg).
Dimensions:
wing span 36ft 0in (10.97m).
length 28ft 5in (8.66m).
height 9ft 5in (2.87m).
wing area 197sq ft (18.30sq m).
Armament: Two .5in nose machine-guns; four .3in wing machine-guns.
Crew: 1.
In Service: China (129), USA.
Variants (with no. built):
Models 48/48X: Prototypes (2).
P-66: Service designation for production Vanguard 48C (144).
Total Production: 146.

Remarks: Originally ordered by Sweden; after embargo, taken over by Great Britain; not accepted into RAF service; 129 subsequently to China (Lend-Lease), remaining 15 retained by USAAF as P-66 fighter-trainer; details of operational career Chinese machines obscure.

Manufacturer: Vultee.
Model: A-35B Vengeance.
Type: Dive-bomber.
Power Plant: One 1,700hp Wright R-2600-13.
Performance:
maximum speed at 13,500ft (4,115m) 279mph (449km/hr).
cruising speed 230mph (370km/hr).
normal range 2,300 miles (3,700km).
time to 15,000ft (4,572m) 11min 18sec.
service ceiling 22,300ft (6,797m).
Weights:
empty 10,300lb (4,672kg).
maximum 16,400lb (7,440kg).
Dimensions:
wing span 48ft 0in (14.63m).
length 39ft 9in (12.11m).
height 15ft 4in (4.67m).
wing area 332sq ft (30.84sq m).
Armament: Six forward-firing .5in machine-guns in wings; one .5in machine-gun in rear cockpit; max bomb load 2,000lb (907kg).
Crew: 2.
In Service: Australia (342 Mks I/IV), Brazil (29 A-35B), Great Britain (RAF, FAA), India (30+), USA.
Variants (with no. built):
Vengeance I: Original British order; Vultee-built (200); Northrop-built (200).
Vengeance II: Original British order; inc 243 retained by USAAF as V-72 (300).
Vengeance Ia: (A-31) Lend-Lease to RAF; Northrop-built (200).
Vengeance III: (A-31) Lend-Lease to RAF; Vultee-built (100).
XA-31A/B: Engine test-bed; 1 A-31 conversion.
YA-31C: As XA-31A/B; B-29 development programme; 5 A-31 conversions.

A-35: Improved Vengeance I; 1,600hp Wright R-2600-19 (100).
A-35A: 99 A-35 conversions; four .5in wing guns.
A-35B: Re-engined A-35A; increased armament (831).
Vengeance IV (Series 1): RAF equivalent of A-35B; 104 Lend-Lease.
Vengeance IV (Series 2): RAF equivalent of A-35B; 458 Lend-Lease.
Vengeance T.T.Mk IV: Target-tug conversions of Mk IV.
Total Production: 1,931.
Remarks: RAF's first dive-bomber specifically designed for role from outset; order inspired by success currently being enjoyed by Luftwaffe's Stuka in Poland and France; by time of operational debut, Spring 1943, dive-bomber myth exploded; consequently service restricted to four RAF sqns, plus two Indian AF, in Arakan campaign; remainder mostly converted to target-tugs (10 sqns); USAAF A-35s similarly reassigned.

Manufacturer: Waco.
Model: UC-72M.
Type: Light transport.
Power Plant: One 285hp Jacobs L-5.
Performance:
maximum speed 152mph (245km/hr).
cruising speed 144mph (232km/hr).
initial rate of climb 850ft/min (257m/min).
service ceiling 14,000ft (4,242m).
Weights:
empty 1,981lb (904kg).
loaded 3,250lb (1,474kg).
Dimensions:
wing span 33ft 3in (10.07m).
length 25ft 4in (7.72m).
height 8ft 6in (2.57m).
wing area 244sq ft (22.69sq m).
Crew/Accommodation: 1/3.
In Service: Australia (1 impressed), Canada (1+ impressed), Great Britain, Netherlands (NEIAF, 2+ impressed), USA (USAAF, USN, USCG).
Variants (with no. built):

UC-72, -72A/E, H, J, L: USAAF designations for impressed 5-seat light civil transport; 9 models; various power plants (34).
UC-72F/G, K, M/N, P: USAAF designations for impressed 4-seat light civil transport 6 models; various power plants (9).
J2W: USN/USCG designation for various civil impressments (6+).
Total Production: approx 50 (military only).
Remarks: Generic designations for variety of pre-war civil Waco biplanes impressed for USAAF/USN military service as staff transports and station ferries; others likewise impressed by RAF as general utility transports, inc two used by LRDG in Western Desert.

Manufacturer: Waco.
Model: CG-4A Hadrian.
Type: Transport glider.
Performance:
maximum towing speed 150mph (241km/hr).
Weights:
empty 3,700lb (1,678kg).
maximum 9,000lb (4,082kg).
Dimensions:
wing span 83ft 8in (25.50m).
length 48ft 4in (14.73m).
height 12ft 7in (3.83m).
wing area 852sq ft (79.15sq m).
Crew/Payload/Accommodation: 2/3,800lb (1,725kg)/13 troops.
In Service: Canada, Great Britain, USA (USAAF, USN).
Variants (with no. built):
XCG-4: Prototype; mixed wood and metal construction (2)
CG-4A: Production model; post-war redesignation G-4A; extensive licence production (13,909).
XCG-4B: All wood construction (1)
G-4C: Post-war CG-4A conversions (35).
LRW-1: USN equivalent of CG-4A (13).
Hadrian I, II: RAF equivalent of CG-4A (694).
Total Production: 13,912.
Remarks: Only US transport glider operationally employed by

Allies; capable of carrying standard Jeep, ¼-ton truck or 75mm howitzer with crews; first used invasion of Sicily; subsequently employed Normandy and Southern France invasions, Arnhem, and Rhine crossing; participated second Wingate Chindit operation in Burma.

Manufacturer: Waco.
Model: CG–13A.
Type: Troop/cargo glider.
Performance:
maximum towing speed 190mph (304km/hr).
Weights:
empty 8,700lb (3,946kg).
normal/loaded 18,900lb (8,573kg).
Dimensions:
wing span 85ft 8in (26.13m).
length 54ft 4in (16.57m).
height 20ft 3in (6.2m).
wing area 873sq ft (80.06sq m).
Crew/Accommodation: 2/30–42.
In Service: Great Britain (6 CG–13A), USA.
Variants (with no. built):
XCG–13: Prototype (2).
YCG–13: Service test model; Ford-built (1); Northwestern-built (1).
XCG–13A: Modified YCG–13; redesigned tail, tricycle undercarriage; Ford-built (1); Northwestern-built (2).
CG–13A: Production model; Ford-built, inc 37 as 42-seaters (85); Northwestern-built (47).
Total Production: 139.
Remarks: Entered USAAF service 1943–44; specifically designed to transport heavy loads (double the carrying capacity of CG–4A); continued post-war use.

Manufacturer: Waco.
Model: CG–15.
Type: Troop/cargo glider.
Performance:
maximum towing speed 180mph (290km/hr).
Weights:
empty 4,000lb (1,814kg).
loaded 8,000lb (3,629kg).
Dimensions:
wing span 62ft 2¼in (18.95m).
length 48ft 10in (14.89m).
wing area 623sq ft (57.87sq m).
Accommodation: 15–16.
In Service: USA.
Variants (with no. built):
XCG–15: Prototype; one CG–4A conversion.
XCG–15A: Improved XCG–15 (2).
CG–15: Production model; inc 42 with 16 seats (427).
Total Production: 429.
Remarks: Brief service career 1945 alongside earlier CG–4A; basically aerodynamically refined version of latter.

USSR

Manufacturer: Antonov.
Model: A–7 (RF–8).
Type: Transport glider.
Dimensions:
wing span 62ft 4in (19.0m).
length 37ft 8¾in (11.5m).
Crew/Accommodation: 1/9 troops.
In Service: USSR.
Variants (with no. built):
A–7 (RF–8): Transport glider (approx 400).
Total Production: approx 400.
Remarks: All-wood A–7 was only glider produced in quantity by USSR during WWII; used primarily small-scale sabotage actions behind Axis lines and to supply isolated partisan groups.

Manufacturer: Beriev.
Model: MBR–2bis (Be–2).
Type: Short-range maritime reconnaissance flying boat.
Power Plant: One 860hp Mikulin AM–34NB.
Performance:
maximum speed at 6,560ft (2,000m) 171mph (275km/hr).
normal range 405 miles (650km).
service ceiling 25,920ft (7,900m).
Weights:
maximum 9,359lb (4,245kg).
Dimensions:
wing span 62ft 4in (19.0m).
length 44ft 3½in (13.5m).
wing area 592sq ft (55sq m).
Armament: One 7.62mm ShKAS machine-gun each in open bow position and manually-operated dorsal turret; max bomb load 661lb (300kg), or mines or depth-charges.
Crew: 4–5.
In Service: Finland (2 MBR–2, 3 MBR–2bis), USSR (SovNAF).
Variants:
MBR–2 Prototype: Naval short-range reconnaissance flying boat; one 500hp BMW VIZ.
MBR–2: Initial production model; one 680hp M–17B; open cockpit/gun (7.62mm PV–1) positions; (provision for fixed wheel or ski undercarriage).
MBR–2bis: Improved MBR–2; uprated engine; enclosed cockpit; dorsal turret; increased vertical tail surfaces; provision for underwing bomb load.
MP–1, 1T: 8-passenger civil transport/freighter versions of MBR–2 resp; one 500hp M–17B.
MP–1bis: Civil transport version of MBR–2bis; one 750hp AM–34NB.
Total Production: 1,500+.
Remarks: Produced 1934–1941. MBR–2/2bis served SovNAF (principally Northern and Black Sea Fleets) in considerable numbers for reconnaissance/ASR duties throughout WWII (and long after in fishery protection and allied roles); five captured examples employed by Finnish AF duration Continuation War, 1941–44.

Manufacturer: Beriev.
Model: KOR–1.
Type: Ship-borne observation floatplane.
Power Plant: One 700hp M–25A.
Performance:
maximum speed at 6,560ft (2,000m) 171mph (275km/hr).
normal range 330 miles (530km).
service ceiling 22,966ft (7,000m).
Weights:
empty 3,968lb (1,800kg).
loaded 5,485lb (2,490kg).
Dimensions:
wing span 36ft 1in (11.0m).
length 29ft 1⅔in (8.88m).
height 12ft 6in (3.81m).
wing area 315.39sq ft (29.3sq m).
Armament: Two fixed forward-firing 7.62mm ShKAS machine-guns in upper wing fairings; one flexible 7.62mm ShKAS machine-gun in rear cockpit; max bomb load 220lb (100kg).
Crew: 2.
In Service: USSR (SovNAF).
Variants:
KOR–1: Prototypes and production model.
Remarks: Standard Soviet Navy catapult floatplane upon outbreak WWII, KOR–1 operated coastal reconnaissance and coastal artillery AOP duties (primarily Black Sea area) opening months German invasion USSR; number also subject hasty conversion to landplane configuration for emergency ground-attack role against Rumanian advance on Odessa, June–Oct 1941.

Manufacturer: Beriev.
Model: KOR–2 (Be–4).
Type: Short-range reconnaissance flying boat.
Power Plant: One 900hp M–62.
Performance:
maximum speed 225mph (362km/hr).
normal range 590 miles (950km).
service ceiling 19,685ft (6,000m).
Weights:
empty 4,530lb (2,050kg).
loaded 6,085lb (2,760kg).
Dimensions:
wing span 39ft 4½in (12.0m).
length 34ft 5¼in (10.5m).
height 13ft 3in (4.04m).
wing area 274.48sq ft (25.5sq m).
Armament: One flexible 7.62mm ShKAS machine-gun in dorsal position; max bomb load 661lb (300kg).
Crew: 2.
In Service: USSR (SovNAF).
Variants:
KOR–2 Prototype and production model.
Remarks: Intended successor to KOR–1 ship-borne observation floatplane, few KOR–2s completed prior German occupation, Oct 1941; presumed limited service ensuing months; small-scale production reinstated immediate post-war years.

Manufacturer: Chetverikov.
Model: MDR–6A (Che–2).
Type: Long-range reconnaissance-bomber flying boat.
Power Plant: Two 960hp M–63.
Performance:
maximum speed 267mph (430km/hr).
time to 16,400ft (5,000m) 12min 0sec.
service ceiling 29,530ft (9,000m).
Weights:
empty 9,040lb (4,100kg).
maximum 15,873lb (7,200kg).
Dimensions:
wing span 64ft 11½in (19.8m).
length 48ft 2¾in (14.7m).
wing area 560sq ft (52sq m).
Armament: One 7.62mm ShKAS machine-gun in bow turret; one 12.7mm UBT machine-gun in dorsal turret; max bomb load 1,321lb (600kg), or mines, torpedoes, or depth-charges underwing.
Crew: 4–5.
In Service: USSR (SovNAF).
Variants (with no. built):
MDR–6: Prototype; two 730hp M–25E; long-range reconnaissance-bomber flying boat (1).
MDR–6A: Production model; as prototype; two 960hp M–63 (approx 50).
MDR–6B–1/5: Prototypes; redesigned hull; twin fins and rudders; various power plants (5).
Total Production: approx 56.
Remarks: Prototype first flown mid-1937, fifty MDR–6A (completed 1941) comprised most modern indigenous flying boats available SovNAF at time of German invasion; employed long-range reconnaissance role duration WWII, remaining in service into mid-fifties.

Manufacturer: Kalinin.
Model: K–5.
Type: Transport.
Power Plant: One 450hp M–15 (Bristol Jupiter).
Performance:
cruising speed 118mph (190km/hr).
normal range 590 miles (950km).
service ceiling 15,680ft (4,780m).
Weights:
empty 5,015lb (2,275kg).
maximum 8,267lb (3,750kg).
Dimensions:
wing span 67ft 3in (20.5m).
length 52ft 0¾in (15.87m).
wing area 710.4sq ft (66.0sq m).
Crew/Accommodation: 2/6.
In Service: USSR.
Variants:
K–5: Prototype and production models; alt power plants, inc one 450hp M–15 (Bristol Jupiter), Pratt & Whitney Hornet, 480hp M–22, or 500hp M–17F.
Total Production: approx 260.
Remarks: First appearing 1929, approx 260 K–5s built over next five years; although long obsolete by time German invasion of USSR, June 1941, number employed second-line personnel transport/supply roles early months hostilities

Manufacturer: Ilyushin.
Model: Il–2m3.
Type: Ground-attack.
Power Plant: One 1,770hp Mikulin AM–38F.
Performance:
maximum speed at 4,920ft (1,500m) 251mph (404km/hr).
normal range 475 miles (765km).
time to 16,405ft (5,000m) 12min 0sec.
ceiling 19,690ft (6,000m).
Weights:
empty 9,975lb (4,525kg).
maximum 14,021lb (6,360kg).
Dimensions:
wing span 47ft 10¾in (14.6m).
length 38ft 0½in (11.6m).
height 11ft 2in (3.4m).
wing area 414.4sq ft (38.5sq m).
Armament: Two fixed forward-firing 23mm VYa cannon in wings; two 7.62mm ShKAS machine-guns in forward fuselage; one flexible 12.7mm UBT machine-gun in rear cockpit; max bomb load 1,321lb (600kg), or eight 82mm RS 82 (or 132mm RS 132) rocket projectiles.
Crew: 2.
In Service: Czechoslovakia, Germany (1+ captured/evaluation), USSR (SovAF, SovNAF).
Variants (with no. built):
BSh–2 (TsKB–55): Initial prototypes; 2-seat ground-assault version; one 1,350hp AM–35A; four fixed forward-firing 7.62mm ShKAS machine-guns (2).
TsKB–57: Prototype; single-seat version; one 1,600hp AM–38; two 7.62mm ShKAS machine-guns plus two 20mm ShVAK cannon; increased fuel capacity; addn armour plating; provision for eight underwing rockets (1).
Il–2: Initial production model; as TsKB–57.
Il–2M: Re-engined Il–2; one 1,700hp AM–38F; two 7.62mm ShKAS machine-guns plus two 23mm VYa cannon.
Il–2m3: 2-seat Il–2M; uprated AM–38F; one addn 12.7mm UBT machine-gun in rear cockpit; DAG 10 grenade launcher; increased bomb load; redesigned (two-crew) cockpit.
Il–2m3 (modified): As Il–2m3; VYa wing cannon replaced by 37mm N–37, or P–37, anti-tank cannon; later models with addn 200 PTAB–2, 5–1, or 5 light anti-tank bombs underwing.
Il–2T: Naval version; provision for one 533mm torpedo.
Il–2U: 2-seat trainer version; reduced armament and 882lb (400kg) bomb load.
Il–8: Redesigned Il–2; 2,000hp AM–42; four wing cannon; 2,204lb (1,000kg) max bomb load; prototypes only.
Total Production: approx 36,150.
Remarks: First of famous Shturmoviki (ground-attack) line, single-seat Il–2 entering service at time of German invasion of USSR, mid-1941; after initial reverses proved successful anti-tank weapon, Winter 1941–42, but fell easy prey to Luftwaffe fighters; 2-seat Il–2m3, with rearward defence, quickly supplanted earlier models; combat debut Autumn 1942, provided close-support advancing Soviet armies from Stalingrad to Berlin; also supplied Polish and Czechoslovak units, operational closing months

Beriev MBR–2bis

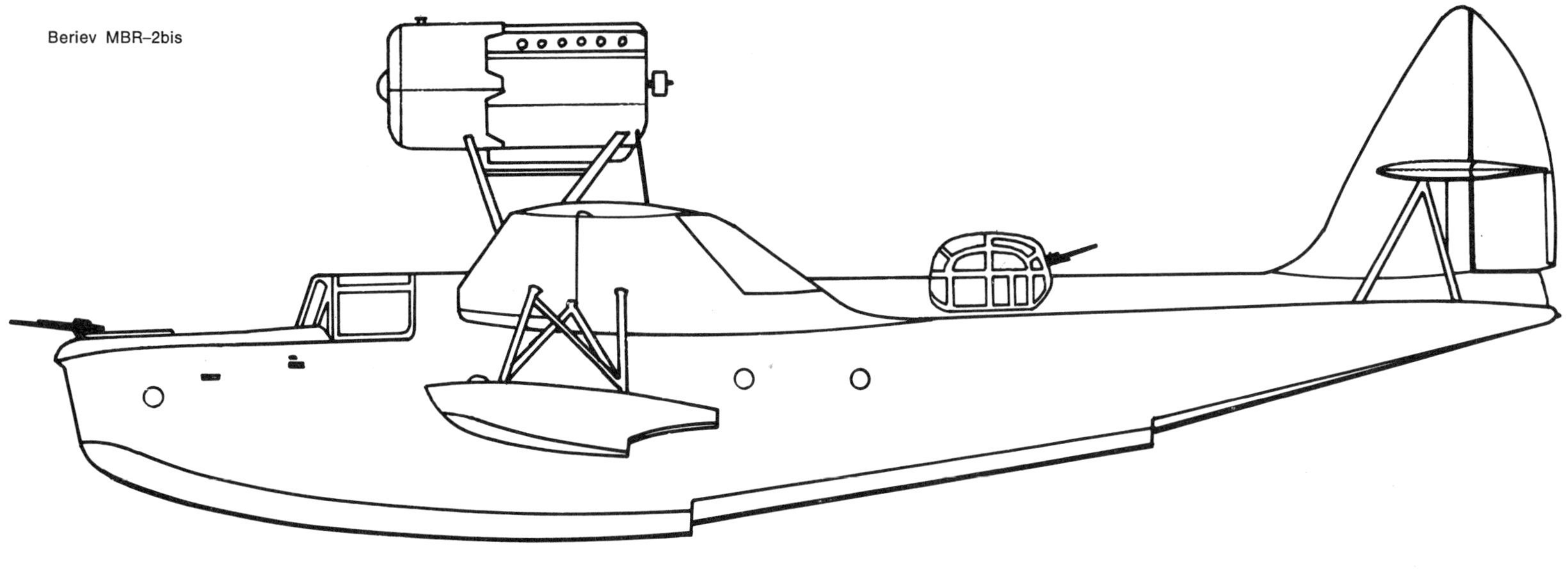

WWII; extensive post-war use Communist satellite AFs.
Colour Reference: Plates 162, 163: Ilyushin Il–2m3 of VVS (Air Forces of the USSR), 1st Belorussian Front (Berlin area), May 1945; note tailfin/rudder tactical/unit markings.

Manufacturer: Ilyushin.
Model: Il–10.
Type: Ground-attack.
Power Plant: One 2,000hp Mikulin AM–42.
Performance:
maximum speed at sea level 315mph (507km/hr).
normal range 621 miles (1,000km).
time to 9,840ft (3,000m) 5min 0sec.
service ceiling 24,606ft (7,500m).
Weights:
empty 9,920lb (4,500kg).
loaded 14,409lb (6,536kg).
Dimensions:
wing span 43ft 11¼in (13.4m).
length 36ft 9in (11.2m).
wing area 322.92sq ft (30.0sq m).
Armament: Two 7.62mm ShKAS machine-guns and two 23mm NS–23 cannon in wings, plus one 20mm cannon in dorsal cupola; provision for 882lb (400kg) bomb load, plus eight 82mm RS 82 (or 132mm RS 132) rocket projectiles.
Crew: 2.
In Service: USSR.
Variants (with no. built):
Il–10: Prototypes and production models; alternative four 23mm NS–23 wing cannon, plus dorsal 12.7mm UBT machine-gun.
Il–10M: Modified Il–10; redesigned wing, horizontal and vertical tail surfaces; rear fuselage-mounted auxiliary rocket motor; prototypes only.
Il–10(U): Unarmed trainer version of Il–10.
B–33/BS–33: Post-war Czechoslovak licence-production of Il–10/Il–10(U).
(Total Ilyushin-built, 4,966; Avia (Czechoslovak licence-built approx 2,000).
Total Production: approx 6,960 (inc licence-production).
Remarks: Slightly smaller but much

more manoeuvrable Il–10 chosen in preference to Il–8 as Il–2 successor; operational debut Feb 1945, supplementing earlier Il–2m3 closing weeks European war; widespread use post-war years many Eastern bloc AFs; also supplied China and North Korea (participated Korean war); last Czech examples retired 1958.

Manufacturer: Ilyushin.
Model: DB–3F (Il–4).
Type: Long-range bomber.
Power Plant: Two 1,100hp M–88B.
Performance:
maximum speed at 22,000ft (6,700m) 267mph (429km/hr).
cruising speed 199mph (320km/hr).
maximum range 2,360 miles (3,800km).
time to 22,000ft (6,700m) 12min 0sec.
service ceiling 31,824ft (9,700m).
Weights:
empty 12,790lb (5,800kg).
loaded 18,975lb (8,380kg).
Dimensions:
wing span 70ft 4in (21.44m).
length 48ft 6¼in (14.80m).
height (approx) 13ft 9in (4,20m).
wing area 718sq ft (66.7sq m).
Armament: One 7.62mm ShKAS (or 12.7mm UBT) machine-gun each in nose, dorsal turret, and ventral positions; max bomb load (internal and external) 5,512lb (2,500kg), or 2,205lb (1,000kg) bombs internally, plus one 2,072lb (940kg) torpedo under fuselage.
Crew: 3.
In Service: Finland (11 DB–3B, 4 DB–3f), Germany (10+ captured/ evaluation), USSR (SovAF, SovNAF).
Variants (with no. built):
TsKB–26 (DB–3): Initial prototypes; two 800hp Gnome-Rhône 14K; two 7.62mm machine-guns; max bomb load 7,715lb (3,500kg).
TsKB–30 (DB–3B): Prototype; two 765hp M–85; redesigned rear fuselage; modified vertical tail surfaces; enclosed cockpit.
DB–3B: Production model; two M–85s or (later models) 960hp

M–86s; one 7.62mm ShKAS machine-gun each in nose, dorsal turret, and ventral position (1,528).
DB–PT: Torpedo-bomber version of DB–3B; twin-float undercarriage; prototypes only.
DB–3F (Il–4): Re-engined DB–3B; two 950hp M–87A or—later models—1,100hp M–88B; redesigned (extended) nose; improved armour; detail design modifications (inc some models with wooden wing spars (5,256).
Total Production: approx 6,800.
Remarks: Produced between 1937 and 1944, DB–3B/DB–3F provided backbone SovAF's long-range bomber arm throughout WWII; former employed Soviet-Finnish Winter War of 1939–40, replaced by improved DB–3F model by time of German invasion USSR, June 1941; first Soviet aircraft to bomb Berlin, 8/9 Aug 1941; also employed as naval torpedo-bomber, in tactical bomber/reconnaissance roles, as troop transport, and glider-tug; Finnish AF examples, both captured and purchased German war booty, used against Soviets during Winter and Continuation Wars 1940–44.

Manufacturer: Kocherigin.
Model: Di–6.
Type: Fighter.
Power Plant: One 720hp M–25.
Performance:
maximum speed at sea level 201mph (324km/hr).
maximum speed at 9,840ft (3,000m) 231mph (372km/hr).
normal range 341 miles (550km).
time to 16,400ft (5,000m) 10min 0sec.
service ceiling 26,245ft (8,000m).
Weights:
empty 3,102lb (1,407kg).
loaded 4,380lb (1,987kg).
Dimensions:
wing span 32ft 9¾in (10.0m).
length 22ft 11¾in (7.0m).
height 10ft 6in (3.2m).
wing area 270.71sq ft (25.15sq m).
Armament: Two or four forward-firing 7.62mm ShKAS machine-guns in wings; one flexible 7.62mm

ShKAS machine-gun in semi-enclosed rear cockpit; provision for max bomb load 88lb (40kg) under fuselage.
Crew: 2.
In Service: USSR.
Variants (with no. built):
TsKB–11: Initial prototype; 2-seat fighter version; one 720hp Wright Cyclone SR–1820–F–3; two 7.62mm ShKAS machine-guns in wings plus one 7.62mm ShKAS machine-gun in rear cockpit (1).
TsKB–11Sh: Prototype; assault-fighter version; armoured; four 7.62mm ShKAS machine-guns in wings; one 720hp Wright Cyclone (1).
DI–6: Initial production model; fighter version; subsequently converted to dual-control trainer.
DI–6Sh: Assault-fighter version; modified DI–6; increased armament.
DI–6bis: Dual-control trainer version of DI–6; 750hp M–25V. (Total DI–6, DI–6Sh, DI–6bis: approx 200).
Total Production: 200 +.
Remarks: Entered service 1937, DI–6 2-seat fighter biplane saw limited use against Japanese forces on Far Eastern Front during Summer 1939; withdrawn first-line service shortly thereafter, many subsequently converted dual-control trainer role.

Manufacturer: Lavochkin.
Model: LaGG–3.
Type: Fighter.
Power Plant: One 1,210hp M–105PF.
Performance:
maximum speed at sea level 308mph (495km/hr).
maximum speed at 16,400ft (5,000m) 348mph (560km/hr).
maximum range 404 miles (650km).
time to 16,400ft (5,000m) 5min 52sec.
service ceiling 31,500ft (9,600m).
Weights:
empty 5,776lb (2,620kg).
loaded 7,032lb (3,190kg).
Dimensions:
wing span 32ft 1¾in (9.8m).

length 28ft 11¼in (8.82m).
wing area 188.37sq ft (17.5sq m).
Armament: One 20mm ShVAK cannon firing through propeller hub; two 12.7mm UBS machine-guns in upper cowling; provision for 440lb (200kg) bomb load, or six 82mm RS 82 rocket projectiles, underwing.
Crew: 1.
In Service: Finland (3), Japan (1 interned/evaluation), USSR.
Variants (with no. built):
I–22 (LaGG–1): Prototype; one 1,100hp M–105P; one 23mm VYa cannon plus one ShKAS machine-guns; all-wood construction (1).
LaGG–3: Production model; one 1,210hp M–105PF; various alt 20/23mm cannon, plus 7.62/12.7mm machine-gun, armament arrangements; reduced weight; provision for auxiliary fuel tanks; (inc number light-weight and higher-powered versions—experimental only) (6,527).
Total Production: 6,528.
Remarks: First of a long line which, together with parallel Yakovlev designs, were to form standard SovAF fighter equipment duration WWII and beyond; least successful of Lavochkin series, LaGG–3 bore brunt initial German onslaught 1941–42; suffered heavily at hands of Luftwaffe's Bf 109s before replacement by improved La–5 commenced late 1942; three captured examples employed by Finnish AF 1943–45.

Manufacturer: Lavochkin.
Model: La–5FN.
Type: Fighter/fighter-bomber.
Power Plant: One 1,850hp Shvetsov Ash–82FN.
Performance:
maximum speed at 21,000ft (6,400m) 403mph (648km/hr).
normal range 475 miles (765km).
time to 16,400ft (5,000m) 4min 42sec.
service ceiling 31,116ft (9,500m).
Weights:
empty 5,743lb (2,605kg).
loaded 7,408lb (3,360kg).

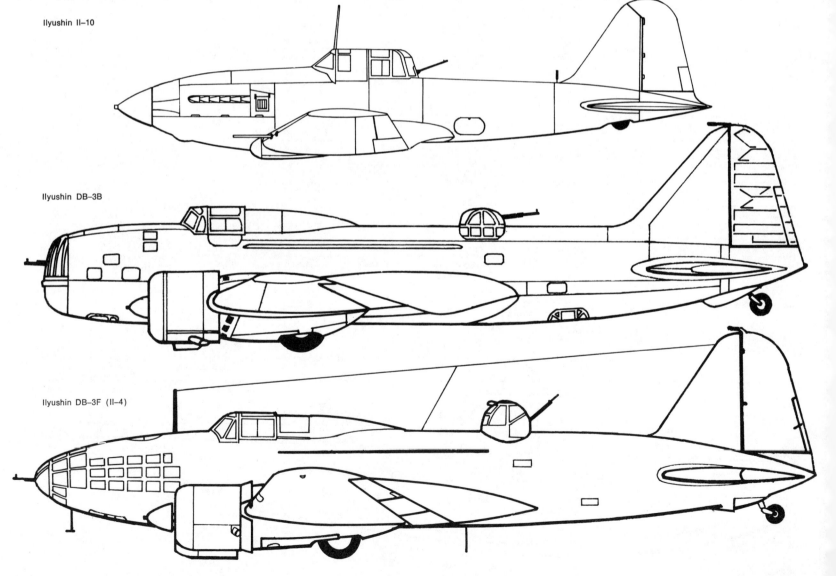

Ilyushin Il–10

Ilyushin DB–3B

Ilyushin DB–3F (Il–4)

Dimensions:
wing span 32ft 2in (9.8m).
length 28ft 5½in (8.67m).
height 8ft 4in (2.54m).
wing area 189.34sq ft (17.59sq m).
Armament: Two 20mm ShVAK, or 23mm NS, cannon in upper cowling; provision for max 662lb (300kg) bombs or rockets underwing.
Crew: 1.
In Service: Czechoslovakia (La–5FN), Germany (1 + captured/evaluation), USSR.
Variants:
La–5: Prototypes and initial production model; re-engined LaGG–3; one 1,330hp Shvetsov M–82F; two 20mm ShVAK cannon in upper cowling; late models with cut-down rear fuselage and revised (improved vision) canopy.
La–5FN: Modified La–5; re-engined; extended air intake; reduced weight; detail design changes.
La–5UTI: 2-seat trainer version; reduced (or deleted) armament.
Total Production: approx 10,000.
Remarks: Progressive (radial-engined) developments of original LaGG–3, La–5/La–5FN's operational debuts Battles of Stalingrad (late 1942) and Kursk (Summer 1943) respectively; among first of new generation Soviet fighters to prove match for contemporary German designs, La–5s (subject continuous modifications to retain equality) served in fighter, fighter-bomber, and ground-attack roles until close of WWII in Europe; also equipped two Czech Regiments final months' hostilities on Eastern Front, inc Slovak National Uprising of Autumn 1944.

Manufacturer: Lavochkin.
Model: La–7.
Type: Interceptor fighter.
Power Plant: One 1,850hp Shvetsov M–82FN.
Performance:
maximum speed 413mph (665km/hr).
range 395 miles (635km).
time to 16.400ft (5,000m) 4min 30sec.

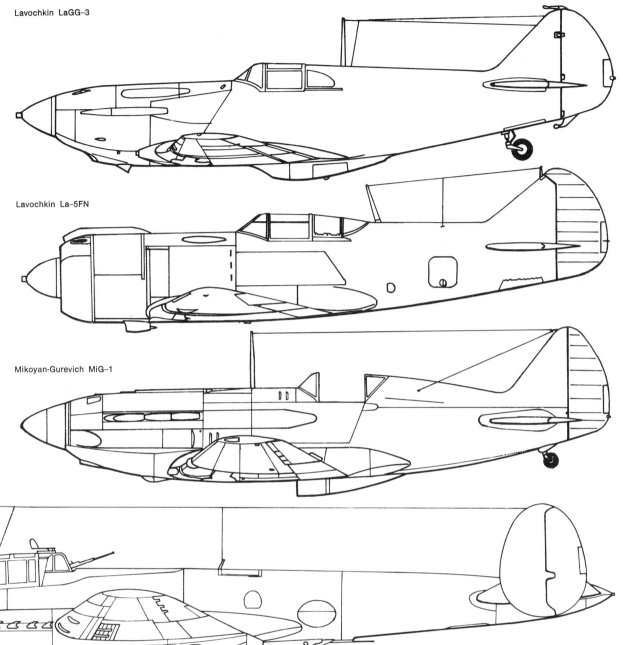

Lavochkin LaGG–3

Lavochkin La–5FN

Mikoyan-Gurevich MiG–1

Petlyakov Pe–2

service ceiling 34,450ft (10,000m).
Weights:
empty 5,816lb (2,638kg).
normal 7,496lb (3,400kg).
Dimensions:
wing span 32ft 1½in (9.8m).
length 28ft 2½in (8.6m).
wing area 188.37sq ft (17.5sq m).
Armament: Two or three 20mm Beresin B–20 cannon in upper cowling; provision for max 441lb (200kg) bombs underwing.
Crew: 1.
In Service: Czechoslovakia (La–7), USSR.
Variants:
La–7: Modified La–5FN; redesigned engine cowling; repositioned (ventral) intake; metal wing spar; minor equipment changes.
La–7UTI: 2-seat trainer/high-speed liaison version; reduced armament.
La–7R: Modified La–7; addn auxiliary booster rocket in tail; experimental only; two La–7 conversions.
La–7TK: High-altitude version; two TK–3 turbo-superchargers; experimental only (one La–7 conversion).
La–9, 11: Post-war developments.
Total Production: 5,753 (exc La–9, 11).
Remarks: La–7 further improvement on basic design, last of series to see operational service WWII, intended specifically as interceptor fighter rather than as La–5FN replacement; supplemented latter in 1944–45 campaigns, La–7 was only

Soviet fighter to claim destruction Luftwaffe jet, downing Me 262 on 15 Feb 1945; also operated by Czechoslovak Regiments at war's end; continued post-war use until replaced by La–9/La–11.
Colour Reference: Plate 167: Lavochkin La–7 (No 47) of 1st Czechoslovak Fighter Regiment, Balice (nr Cracow), Poland, April 1945; note standard Soviet blue/grey shadow shading camouflage scheme and national markings, but no manufacturer's 'La–7' stencils on tailfin tip or engine cowling.

Manufacturer: Mikoyan-Gurevich.
Model: MiG–3.
Type: Interceptor fighter.
Power Plant: One 1,350hp Mikulin AM–35A.
Performance:
maximum speed at 25,590ft (7,800m) 398mph (640km/hr).
normal range 777 miles (1.250km).
time to 16,400ft (5,000m) 5min 42sec.
service ceiling 39,370ft (12,000m).
Weights:
empty 5,721lb (2,595kg).
loaded 7,385lb (3,350kg).
Dimensions:
wing span 33ft 9½in (10.3m).
length 26ft 9in (8.15m).
height 11ft 6in (3.50m).
wing area 187.72sq ft (17.44sq m).
Armament: Two fixed forward-firing 7.62mm ShKAS machine-guns plus one 12.7mm Beresin BS machine-gun in upper cowling; provision for max 440lb (200kg)

bombs or six 82mm RS 82 rocket missiles underwing.
Crew: 1.
In Service: USSR (SovAF, SovNAF).
Variants (with no. built):
MiG–1 (I–200): Prototypes and initial production model; open cockpit or hinged canopy; two 7.62mm and one 12.7mm machine-guns (approx 100).
MiG–3: Improved MiG–1; rearward-sliding canopy; increased fuel capacity; increased outer-wing dihedral; modified radiator; later models subsequently fitted two addn 12.7mm UBS machine-guns underwing plus increased armour (3,322).
Total Production: approx 3,422.
Remarks: Service debut early 1941, initial MiG–1/3s, intended for high-altitude interceptor role, fared badly against Luftwaffe opening months German invasion Soviet Union; despite later equipping with underwing bombs/rockets for medium/low-level operations, never a great success; progressively withdrawn first-line units Winter 1942–43, MiG–3—once show-piece fighter of Moscow defences—ended war relegated rear area duties.
Colour Reference: Plates 165, 166: Mikoyan-Gurevich MiG–3 (No 35) of 12th IAP (Fighter Aviation Regiment), assigned to Moscow Army Region IAP–VO (Anti-aircraft defence Fighter Aviation), Winter 1941–42; note high-visibility wing upper surfaces, intended to facilitate

location downed aircraft, a luxury soon discarded in face of Luftwaffe fighter opposition.

Manufacturer: Nyeman.
Model: R–10.
Type: Reconnaissance-bomber.
Power Plant: One 750hp M–25V.
Performance:
maximum speed at 12,430ft (4,000m) 230mph (370km/hr).
normal range 807 miles (1,300km).
service ceiling 22,965ft (7,000m).
Weights:
empty 4,606lb (2,135kg).
normal 6,338lb (2.875kg).
Dimensions:
wing span 40ft 0in (12.2m).
length 30ft 10½in (9.4m).
wing area 280sq ft (26.81sq m).
Armament: Two fixed 7.62mm ShKAS machine-guns in wings, plus one flexible 7.62mm ShKAS machine-gun in semi-retractable dorsal turret; max bomb load 660lb (300kg).
Crew: 2.
In Service: USSR.
Variants (with no. built):
KhAI–1: Initial six-passenger civil transport version; 480hp M–22 (Bristol Jupiter) (approx 40).
KhAI–5: Military prototype; redesigned KhAI–1; one 750hp M–25V (Wright Cyclone).
R–10: Production model; modified KhAI–5; armoured; late models one 950hp M–63 (PS–5) (approx 500).
Total Production: approx 550 (all Marks).

Remarks: Development of mid-thirties commercial express transport, military R–10 entered service 1937–38; limited employment against Japanese on Far Eastern Front Summer 1939; relegated second-line duties shortly after invasion USSR, June 1941, several falling victim to Luftwaffe fighters during early weeks hostilities.

Manufacturer: Petlyakov.
Model: Pe–2.
Type: Dive-bomber.
Power Plant: Two 1,100hp Klimov M–105R.
Performance:
maximum speed at 16,400ft (5,000m) 336mph (540km/hr).
cruising speed 266mph (428km/hr).
normal range 932 miles (1,500km).
time to 16,400ft (5,000m) 7min 0sec.
service ceiling 28,900ft (8,800m).
Weights:
empty 12,943lb (5,876kg).
maximum 18,730lb (8,496kg).
Dimensions:
wing span 56ft 3½in (17.16m).
length 41ft 6½in (12.66m).
height 13ft 1½in (4.0m).
wing area 436sq ft (40.5sq m).
Armament: Two fixed 7.62mm ShKAS (or one 7.62mm ShKAS and one 12.7mm Beresin UBS) machine-guns in nose; plus one flexible 7.62mm ShKAS (or 12.7mm Beresin UBT) machine-gun each in dorsal and ventral positions; max bomb load 2,645lb (1,200kg).
Crew: 3–4.
In Service: Finland (8), Germany

(evaluation), USSR.
Variants (with no. built):
VI–100: Initial prototypes; high-altitude bomber version; solid nose; dorsal spine; two crew; two 1,100hp M–105R (2).
PB–100: Prototypes; dive-bomber version; glazed nose; redesigned cockpit; tailplane dihedral; underwing dive-brakes; three crew; two 1,100hp M–105R; three 7.62mm machine-guns; altn ski undercarriage (2).
Pe–2: Initial production model; early models as PB–100; subsequently re-engined with two 1,210hp VK–105RF; addn dorsal turret (Pe–2FT); reduced nose glazing.
Pe–2I, 2M: Fighter-bomber versions; modified Pe–2; two 1,620hp VK–107A; increased wing span; extended engine nacelles; two 23mm VYa cannon in unglazed nose, plus one 12.7mm UBT machine-gun in dorsal position; experimental only.
Pe–2R: Photo-reconnaissance version; increased fuel capacity.
Pe–2RD: Addn RD–1 booster rocket in tail; experimental only.
Pe–2Sh: Ground-attack prototype; two ventral 20mm ShVAK cannon and two 12.7mm UBS machine-guns; (one PB–100 conversion).
Pe–2UT: Dual-control trainer version; redesigned (tandem enclosure) cockpit.
(Total Pe–2, 2I, 2M, 2R, 2RD, 2Sh, 2UT: approx 11,000).
Pe–2VI: Single-seat high-altitude interceptor; pressurized cockpit; prototype only.
Pe–3: Multi-purpose fighter variant; modified Pe–2; two 1,100hp M–105R; two fixed forward-firing 12.7mm UBS machine-guns and two 20mm ShVAK cannon, plus one flexible 12.7mm Beresin UBT machine-gun each in dorsal and ventral positions; provision for underwing 132mm RS–132 rocket projectiles (approx 500).
Pe–4: As Pe–2FT; two VK–105PF.
Total Production: 11,427.
Remarks: One of most successful Soviet designs, Pe–2 entered service early 1941; formed backbone Soviet tactical bombing arm throughout war on Eastern Front, initially in defensive role (Moscow, Stalingrad), but subsequently in ever-increasing numbers in support of offensives culminating in capture of Berlin, May 1945; equipped majority fast- and dive-bomber units of SovAF, inc several elite Guards formations; also brief service in Far East against Japanese closing weeks WWII; eight examples employed by Finland (seven purchased from German war booty, plus one captured) 1942–46; continued post-war use, inc number Sov satellite AFs.

Manufacturer: Petlyakov.
Model: Pe–8 (TB–7).
Type: Long-range heavy bomber.
Power Plant: Four 1,350hp Mikulin AM–35A.
Performance:
maximum speed at 24,935ft (7,600m) 272mph (438km/hr).
normal range 2,920 miles (4,700km).
service ceiling 22,965ft (7,000m).
Weights:
loaded 73,469lb (33,325kg).
Dimensions:
wing span 131ft 0½in (39.94m).
length 73ft 8¾in (22.47m).
height 20ft 0in (6.1m).
wing area 2,045sq ft (190.0sq m).
Armament: Two 7.62mm ShKAS machine-guns in nose turrets; one 20mm ShVAK cannon each in dorsal and tail turrets; plus one 12.7mm Beresin machine-gun at rear of each inboard engine nacelle; max bomb load (internal) 8,818lb (4,000kg).
Crew: 10.
In Service: USSR.
Variants (with no. built):
Pe–8: Prototype; long-range heavy bomber; four 1,100hp Mikulin M–105 (subsequently with one addn M–100 within fuselage to drive supercharger) (2).
Pe–8: Production model; four AM–35A; late models with four M–82FN, and with nacelle machine-guns deleted; minor detail modifications alt M–30B diesel and M–82 power plants, test/trials only (79).
Total Production: 81.
Remarks: Only modern four-engined Soviet bomber of WWII, Pe–8 entered service 1940; purported to have participated in first strategic raid on Berlin, night of 9–10 Aug 1941 (this attack, one of only two such raids mounted until closing stages of war, reported by German sources to have been carried out by twin-engined Il–4s); not built in great numbers, Pe–8 continued in limited strategic bombing role throughout war, supplementing rather than supplanting Il–4 (DB–3F) as standard long-range bomber weapon; one of very few machines to venture beyond immediate Soviet sphere during hostilities, single Pe–8 used by Foreign Minister Molotov for flights to UK and Washington in May 1942.
Colour Reference: Plates 172, 173: Petlyakov Pe–8 (TB–7) No 14 of VVS (Air Forces of the USSR), Southern Sector Russian Front, Autumn 1944; standard Soviet AF night-bomber camouflage scheme.

Manufacturer: Polikarpov.
Model: U–2VS (Po–2).
Type: Close-support light bomber.
Power Plant: One 100hp M–11.
Performance:
maximum speed at sea level 93mph (150km/hr).
range 329 miles (530km).
service ceiling 13,123ft (4,000m).
Weights:
empty 1,400lb (635kg).
loaded 1,962lb (890kg).
Dimensions:
wing span
upper 37ft 5in (11.4m).
lower 34ft 11¼in (10.65m).
length 26ft 9in (8.15m).
height 9ft 6¼in (2.9m).
wing area 356.29sq ft (33.1sq m).
Armament: One 7.62mm ShKAS machine-gun in rear cockpit; max bomb load 550lb (250kg) or rocket projectiles underwing.
Crew: 2–3.
In Service: Finland (4 captured ex-USSR), Germany (30+ captured ex-USSR), Rumania (1+ captured ex-USSR), USSR (SovAF, SovNAF).
Variants (with no. built):
U–2 Prototype: 2-seat trainer version.
U–2: Production model; various civil and military versions, inc light transport, observation, and trainer; one 100hp M–11 or (later models) 150hp M–11; open or (civil transport) enclosed cockpit; alt ski undercarriage.
U–2P: Floatplane version.
U–2S: Ambulance version/s; provision for one (internal) or two (wing-mounted) litters (inc Polish licence-built).
U2ShS, U–2SP: Civil transport versions; four/two passenger resp.
U–2VS: Armed close-support light bomber version.
U–2NAK: Night AOP version.
(Total U–2, 33,000+).
CSS–13, CSS–S–13: Post-war Polish production; civil variants.
Total Production: approx 40,000.
Remarks: First flown Jan 1928, over 13,000 U–2s completed prior German invasion USSR, June 1941; served primarily trainer and variety civil (transport, ambulance, forestry) roles; militarised U–2VS pioneered night-harassment 'nuisance' raids; widely employed all sectors of front, inc defence of Stalingrad Winter 1942–43; number captured examples also equipped similar Luftwaffe Staffel manned by ex-SovAF volunteer personnel; post-war (licence) production continued into mid-fifties, many still in use Eastern Europe twenty years later.

Manufacturer: Polikarpov.
Model: R–5.
Type: Reconnaissance-bomber.
Power Plant: One 680hp M–17F.
Performance:
maximum speed at 9,840ft (3,000m) 142mph (228km/hr).
normal range 497 miles (800km).
service ceiling 20,997ft (6,400m).
Weights:
loaded 6,551lb (2,955kg).
Dimensions:
wing span 50ft 10¼in (15.5m).
length 34ft 7¼in (10.56m).
height 10ft 8in (3.25m).
wing area 453.0sq ft (42.0sq m).
Armament: One fixed 7.62mm PV–1 machine-gun in forward fuselage; one flexible 7.62mm DA–1 machine-gun in rear cockpit; max bomb load 882lb (400kg) underwing.
Crew: 2.
In Service: Spain (RepAF), USSR (SovAF, SovNAF).
Variants:
R–5: Initial production model; 2-seat reconnaissance-bomber version; one 500hp M–17B or 680hp M–17F; various armament; altn ski undercarriage.
R–5S: Modified R–5; minor equipment changes; modified wheel fairings; one 680hp M–17F.
R–5T: Torpedo-bomber version; one 680hp M–17F.
R–Z (R–Zet): Assault version; modified R–5; one 750hp AM–34N; five forward-firing 7.62mm PV–1 machine-guns, plus two flexible 7.62mm DA machine-guns in rear cockpit; max 1,102lb (500kg) bomb load.
DI–2: Fighter version; 680hp M–17F; reduced wingspan and length; three 7.62mm machine-guns.
MR–5 (R–5a): Floatplane version; one 500hp M–17B; enlarged vertical tail surfaces.
P–5: Mailplane/cargo-transport version; 881lb (400kg) payload.
P–5bis, PS–5, PR–5: Civil passenger transport versions; modified fuselage; enclosed cockpit; P–5bis with 680hp M–17F.
ARK–5: Civil transport version for Arctic service; ski undercarriage; provision for underwing cargo container.
Total Production: approx 7,000.
Remarks: Late twenties reconnaissance-bomber/general-purpose design, R–5 saw service both Spanish Civil War and against Japanese over Mongolia/Manchuria, 1938–39; employed against Finland during Winter War of 1939–40; still in widespread first-line use at time of German invasion, subsequently relegated ancillary transport, ambulance, and training duties; engaged partisan supply and saboteur/agent-dropping operations (inc experimental version with underwing containers for up to 16 (prone) troops).

Manufacturer: Polikarpov-Grigorovich.
Model: I–5.
Type: Fighter.
Power Plant: One 450hp M–22.
Performance:
maximum speed at sea level 178mph (286km/hr).
normal range 320 miles (530km).
time to 16,400ft (5,000m) 10min 6sec.
service ceiling 26,576ft (8,100m).
Weights:
empty 2,073lb (940kg).
loaded 2,987lb (1,355kg).
Dimensions:
wing span 33ft 7in (10.24m).
length 22ft 3in (6.78m).
wing area 228.74sq ft (21.25sq m).
Armament: Two or (later models) four fixed forward-firing 7.62mm PV–1 machine-guns.
Crew: 1.
In Service: USSR.
Variants (with no. built):
I–5 prototypes: One 450hp M–22 (2).
I–5 production model: Redesigned engine cowling; modified cockpit; alt ski undercarriage (801).
Total Production: 803.
Remarks: First flown Spring 1930, I–5 relegated second-line duties by outbreak WWII; still in use as fighter-trainer June 1941, number encountered opening days German invasion.

Manufacturer: Polikarpov.
Model: I–15bis (I–152).
Type: Fighter.
Power Plant: One 750hp M–25V.
Performance:
maximum speed 230mph (370km/hr).
cruising speed 174mph (280km/hr).
maximum range 497 miles (800km).
Weights:
empty 2,880lb (1,306kg).
maximum 4,189lb (1,900kg).
Dimensions:
wing span 33ft 4¼in (10.18m).
length 20ft 8in (6.3m).
height 7ft 2¼in (2.19m).
wing area 242.51sq ft (22.53sq m).
Armament: Four fixed forward-firing 7.62mm ShKAS machine-guns; max bomb load (optional) 220lb (100kg).
Crew: 1.
In Service: China (I–15, I–15bis), Finland (5 I–15bis), Spain (RepAF, NatAF), USSR.
Variants (with no. built):
TsKB–3: Prototype, one 710hp Wright Cyclone SR–1820–F–3 (1).
I–15: Initial production model; one 635–710/hp (Wright Cyclone) M–25; two (or four) 7.62mm PV–1 machine-guns; fixed or variable-pitch props (approx 733).
I–15bis (I–152): Modified I–15; one 750hp M–25V in long-chord cowling; redesigned upper wing; increased fuel capacity; revised armament; provision for auxiliary fuel tanks underwing (2,408).
Total Production: approx 3,142.
Remarks: Development of earlier I–5, distinctive gull-winged I–15 entered SovAF service 1934; extensive use both Spanish Civil War (RepAF), and second Sino-Japanese conflict (Chinese AF); redesigned I–15bis, service debut 1937, also employed in Spain and against Japanese both in China and during Mongolian incident, Summer 1939; participated Soviet-Finnish war of 1939–40 (five examples captured by Finns subsequently served throughout Continuation War, 1941–44); number Soviet machines, mainly employed in ground-attack role, still in evidence early months German invasion of USSR, Summer 1941.
Colour Reference: Plate 168: Polikarpov I–15 (No 7) of VVS (Air Forces of the USSR) captured intact on advanced landing ground near Kowno (Kaunus), Lithuania, by German 30.I.D. June 1941; standard olive green/light blue scheme.

Manufacturer: Polikarpov.
Model: I–153.
Type: Fighter.
Power Plant: One 1,000hp Shvetsov M–62R.
Performance:
maximum speed at sea level 227mph (366km/hr).
maximum speed at 16,400ft (5,000m) 275mph (443km/hr).
maximum range 547 miles (880km).
time to 9,840ft (3,000m) 3min 0sec.
ceiling 35,105ft (10,700m).
Weights:
empty 3,201lb (1,452kg).
maximum 4,652lb (2,110kg).
Dimensions:
wing span 32ft 9½in (10.0m).
length 20ft 8in (6.3m).
height 7ft 2¼in (2.19m).
wing area 237.88sq ft (22.1sq m).
Armament: Four fixed forward-firing 7.62mm ShKAS machine-guns; max bomb load 220lb (100kg), or six 82mm RS–82 rocket missiles.
Crew: 1.
In Service: China, Finland (22), Germany (captured ex-USSR), USSR.
Variants:
I–153: Prototypes and production model; one 775hp (Wright Cyclone) M–25V or (later models) 1,000hp M–62; four 7.62mm ShKAS or (late models) two 12.7mm BS machine-guns (I–153BS).
I–153P: Modified I–153; two 20mm ShVAK cannon.
I–153V: High-altitude version; pressurised cabin; 2 conversions.
Total Production: 3,437.
Remarks: First flown 1938, improved I–153 reverted to I–15 gull-winged configuration allied to retractable undercarriage; operational debut against Japanese during Nomonhan incident of Summer 1939; extensive use Soviet-Finnish war of 1939–40, and during opening stages German invasion of USSR, June 1941; participated many early defensive actions, inc Leningrad, Sevastopol; relegated second-line duties mid-1943; number examples captured intact by Germany; eleven supplied Finland (plus similar number captured by Finns themselves) in use until 1944.

Manufacturer: Polikarpov.
Model: I–16 Type 24.
Type: Fighter.
Power Plant: One 1,000hp Shvetsov M–62.
Performance:
maximum speed at sea level 326mph (525km/hr).
maximum speed at 14,765ft (4,500m) 286mph (460km/hr).
cruising speed 185mph (298km/hr).
normal range 435 miles (700km).
time to 16,400ft (5,000m) 4min 0sec.
service ceiling 29,530ft (9,000m).
Weights:
empty 3,313lb (1,475kg).
maximum 4,519lb (2,050kg).
Dimensions:
wing span 29ft 6¼in (9.0m).
length 20ft 1¼in (6.13m).
height 8ft 5in (2.57m).
wing area 156.51sq ft (14.54sq m).
Armament: Two 7.62mm ShKAS machine-guns in upper forward fuselage; two 20mm ShVAK cannon in wings; provision for six rockets or two chemical containers.
Crew: 1.
In Service: China (I–16, UTI–4), Finland (6 I–16, 1 UTI–4), Japan (1 evaluation), Rumania (3 captured ex-USSR), Spain (RepAF, NatAF), USSR.
Variants:
CKB 12 (I–16): Prototype; one 450hp (Bristol Jupiter) M–22; two 7.62mm ShKAS machine-guns; enclosed cockpit.
I–16 Type 1: Initial production model; one 480hp M–22.
I–16 bis: Modified I–16; one 700hp M–25.
I–16 Types 4, 5: Re-engined I–16 bis; one 725hp (Wright Cyclone) M–25; type 5 with increased armour plating.
I–16 Type 6: First major production model; one 730hp M–25A or 775hp Wright F.54 Cyclone; increased weight.
I–16 Type 10: Re-engined Type 6; one 750hp M–25B; open cockpit; four 7.62mm ShKAS machine-guns; some with two 20mm ShVAK cannon (I–16P).
I–16 Type 17: Modified Type 10; two 7.62mm ShKAS machine-guns in fuselage plus two 20mm ShVAK cannon in wings.
I–16 Type 18: Improved version; one supercharged 1,000hp M62; four 7.62mm ShKAS machine-guns.
I–16 Type 24, 24B: Modified Type 18; altn power plant, one 1,100hp M–63; two 7.62mm ShKAS machine-guns in fuselage plus two 20mm ShVAK cannon in wings; Type 24B with six 82mm RS–82 rocket projectiles under wing.
SPB: Dive-bomber version; wing armament deleted.
I–16UTI (UTI–4): 2-seat trainer version; modified Type 10; (UTI-4 Type 4 conversion).
Total Production: approx 6,500.
Remarks: Innovatory low-wing retractable undercarriage I–16 first flown Dec 1933; formed mainstay SovAF fighter strength for following decade; extensive pre-war service Spain and China, also Nomonhan incident Summer 1939; participated Soviet-Finnish conflict, 1939–40; widespread use during initial phases German advance into USSR 1941–42; heavy losses during early retreats tempered by some subsequent success with air-to-air and air-to-ground rocket missiles; equipped first ever Guards Fighter Regt; withdrawn first-line service early 1943, continued use trainer and ancillary duties.
Colour Reference: Plates 169, 170: Polikarpov I–16 Type 10 (I–W–20) of Grupo núm 26, Spanish Air Force, Tablada, Summer 1944; light grey fuselage, natural metal cowling, wings, and tail surfaces.

Manufacturer: Polikarpov.
Model: I–17.
Type: Fighter.
Power Plant: One 860hp M–100A.
Performance:
maximum speed at sea level 305mph (491km/hr).
cruising speed 246mph (395km/hr).
normal range 497 miles (800km).
initial rate of climb 3,400ft/min (1,025m/min).
service ceiling 36,090ft (11,000m).
Weights:
empty 3,770lb (1,710kg).
loaded 4,250lb (1,930kg).
Dimensions:
wing span 33ft 5¼in (10.2m).
length 23ft 11¼in (7.3m).
height 8ft 5in (2.56m).
wing area 191.06sq ft (17.75sq m).
Armament: One 20mm ShVAK cannon firing through propeller hub; four 7.62mm ShKAS machine-guns in wings; provision for max 220lb (100kg) bomb load underwing.
Crew: 1.
In Service: USSR.
Variants:
I–17–1: Prototype; one 860hp M–100; two 20mm ShVAK cannon and two 7.62mm ShKAS machine-guns in wings.
I–17–2: Production model; improved I–17–1; revised armament.
I–17–3: Modified I–17–2; reduced weight; three 7.62mm machine-guns; experimental only.
I–17Z: Parasite fighter version; reduced wing area; retracting hook; undercarriage deleted.
Remarks: Limited number I–17s produced late thirties; some reportedly encountered over southern sector of front during opening weeks Axis invasion of USSR, Summer 1941.

Manufacturer: Polikarpov.
Model: I–185I.
Type: Fighter.
Power Plant: One 1,330hp M–82A.
Performance:
maximum speed at sea level 340mph (547km/hr).
maximum speed at 21,490ft (6,550m) 389mph (626km/hr).
maximum range 590 miles (950km).
time to 19,685ft (6,000m) 4min 42sec.
service ceiling 36,090ft (11,000m).
Weights:
empty 5,373lb (2,437kg).
loaded 7,337lb (3,328kg).

Dimensions:
wing span 32ft 1½in (9.8m).
length 26ft 3in (8.0m).
wing area 167.23sq ft (15.53sq m).
Armament: Three fixed forward-
firing 20mm ShVAK cannon in
upper cowling.
Crew: 1.
In Service: USSR.
Variants (with no. built):
I-185R: Initial prototype; not
completed.
I-185RM: Prototype; 1,200hp
M-81; two 7.62mm ShKAS and
two 12.7mm UBS machine-guns(1).
I-185I: Prototypes; 1,330hp M-82A;
revised armament (2).
I-185 (R4): Final prototype;
1,700hp Shvetsov ASh-71; two
UBS machine-guns and two 20mm
ShVAK cannon; provision for
underwing bombs or rockets (1).
Total Production: 4.
Remarks: Final development of
I-16/I-17 series (via unsuccessful
I-180), some confusion surrounds
I-185; reportedly encountered by
Luftwaffe fighter pilots (as I-180)
NW of Moscow late in 1941,
operational career appears to have
been limited to I-185I prototypes
issued to service evaluation unit on
(corresponding) Kalinin Front;
production abandoned in favour of
Lavochkin La-5.

Manufacturer: Shavrov.
Model: Sh-2.
Type: General-purpose amphibian.
Power Plant: One 100hp M-11.
Performance:
maximum speed 87mph (140km/hr).
service ceiling 13,223ft (4,000m).
Weights:
empty 1,455lb (660kg).
loaded 2,061lb (935kg).
Dimensions:
wing span 42ft 7½in (13.0m).
length 26ft 10¾in (8.2m).
wing area 265.87sq ft (24.7sq m).
Crew/Accommodation: 1/1 (or
1 litter).
In Service: Finland (2), USSR.
Variants:
Sh-2: Prototype and production
model/s.
Total Production: approx 700.
Remarks: Sh-2 first flown 1930,
first Soviet amphibian; operated pre-
war civil passenger mailplane
services in conjunction with U-2
landplanes; also employed fishery
patrol and ambulance duties,
continuing latter roles into WWII;
two examples captured 1942
operated by Finnish AF throughout
remainder Continuation War.

Manufacturer: Shcherbakov.
Model: Shche-2.
Type: Troop transport/liaison.
Power Plant: Two 150hp M-11E.
Performance:
maximum speed 96mph (154km/hr).
normal range 400 miles (640km).
service ceiling 9,840ft (3,000m).
Weights:
empty 5,004lb (2,270kg).
loaded 7,495lb (3,400kg).
Dimensions:
wing span 67ft 2½in (20.48m).
length 46ft 9¾in (14.27m).
wing area 687.6sq ft (63.8sq m).
Crew/Accommodation: 2/14 troops
(or 11 litters).
In Service: Poland, USSR.
Variants:
Shche-2 'Shchuka' (Pike):
Prototype and initial production
model; high-wing fixed undercarriage transport; two 100hp
M-11.
Shche-2: Improved version; cabin
windows; modified tailplane; wheel
spats deleted; two 150hp M-11E.
Total Production: approx 750.
Remarks: Prototype first flown
early 1942, Shche-2 (military
designation TS-1) designed
specifically partisan-supply role;
also employed general-purpose
front-line support, liaison,
ambulance duties; operated by
Polish AF units, 1944/45; continued
post-war use both military
(transport/trainer) and civil
(feederliner/survey).

Manufacturer: Sukhoi.
Model: Su-2.
Type: Light (ground-attack)
bomber-reconnaissance.
Power Plant: One 1,000hp M-88B.
Performance:
maximum speed at sea level
235mph (378km/hr).
maximum speed at 14,435ft (4,400m)
283mph (455km/hr).
normal range 746 miles (1,200km).
time to 16,400ft (5,000m)
12min 0sec.
service ceiling 28,870ft (8,800m).
Weights:
empty 6,547lb (2,970kg).
maximum 9,645lb (4,375kg).

intended R-10 replacement,
considerable numbers Su-2 in
first-line service at time of German
invasion USSR, June 1941; no
match for Luftwaffe fighters;
despite later models more
powerful engine and increased
armour/armament, suffered heavy
losses early stages of campaign;
withdrawn from operations end of
1942, subsequently employed
training/ancillary roles.

Manufacturer: Sukhoi.
Model: Su-6.
Type: Anti-tank/ground-attack
aircraft.
Power Plant: One 2,200hp ASh-
71F.
Performance:
maximum speed at sea level
297mph (478km/hr).
maximum speed at 8,202ft (2,500m)
327mph (526km/hr).
normal range 605 miles (973km).
time to 9,840ft (3,000m) 8min 30sec.
service ceiling 26,246ft (8,000m).
Weights:
empty 9,120lb (4,137kg).
loaded 12,229lb (5,547kg).
Dimensions:
wing span 44ft 3½in (13.5m).
length 30ft 3½in (9.24m).
wing area 279.9sq ft (26.0sq m).
Armament: Two 37mm anti-tank
cannon in wings and two 7.62mm
ShKAS machine-guns in wings, plus
one flexible 12.7mm Beresin UBT
machine-gun in rear cockpit;
provision for max 882lb (400kg)
bomb load, or ten rockets
underwing.
Crew: 2.
In Service: USSR.
Variants:
Su-6 (I): Initial model; single-seat
ground-attack version; one 2,000hp
ASh-71; two 23mm cannon plus
two 7.62mm machine-guns in
wings; max bomb load 880lb

(400kg) or ten 82mm RS-82 rocket
missiles.
Su-6 (II): 2-seat anti-tank/ground-
attack version; uprated engine;
two 37mm anti-tank wing cannon;
addn 12.7mm Beresin UBT
machine-gun in rear cockpit.
Su-6 (III): One 2,000hp AM-42;
revised undercarriage; armament as
Su-6 (II).
Remarks: Completely overshadowed
by parallel Il-2 development.
limited number 2-seat Su-6 anti-
tank/ground-attack aircraft
produced 1942-43 relegated service
Far Eastern Front.

Manufacturer: TsAGI.
Model: A-7bis.
Type: Observation/liaison autogyro.
Power Plant: One 480hp M-22.
Performance:
maximum speed 130mph
(210km/hr).
cruising speed (minimum)

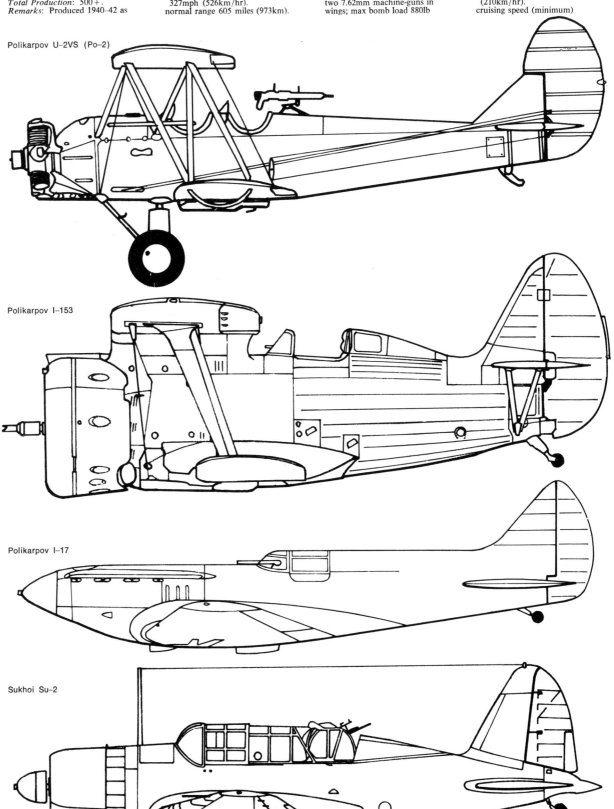

Polikarpov U-2VS (Po-2)

Polikarpov I-153

Polikarpov I-17

Sukhoi Su-2

Tupolev Tu-2S

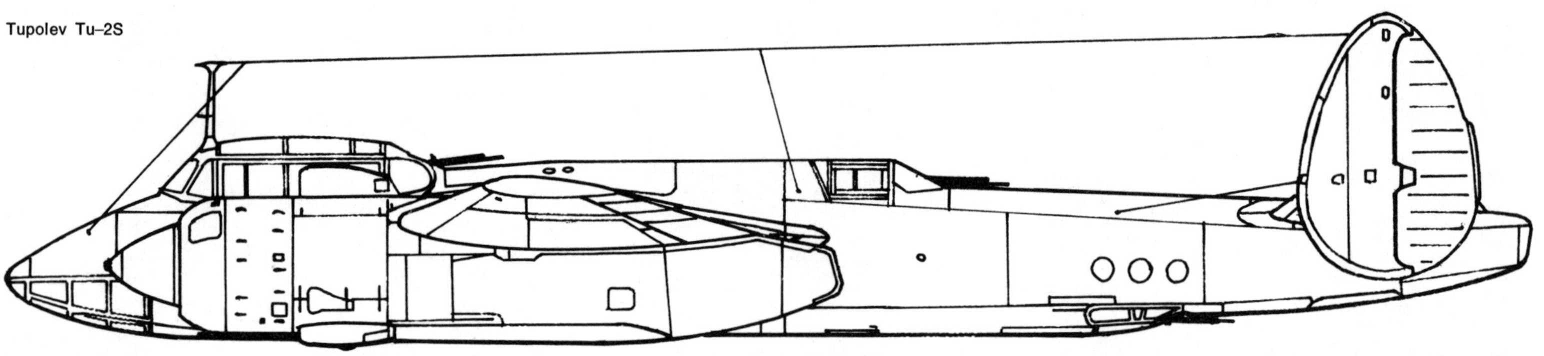

25mph (40km/hr).
maximum ceiling 13,120ft (4,000m).
Weights:
empty 2,965lb (1,345kg).
loaded 4,354lb (1,975kg).
Dimensions:
rotor diameter 49ft 9½in (15.18m).
Armament: One machine-gun.
Crew/Accommodation: 1/1.
In Service: USSR.
Variants:
A-7: Initial production model.
A-7bis: Improved A-7; modified stabilizer.
Remarks: Mid-thirties Kamov design; number A-7bis autogyros employed by Soviet Army for AOP/liaison duties Smolensk area at time of German invasion USSR, June 1941.

Manufacturer: Tupolev.
Model: TB-1 (ANT-4).
Type: Heavy bomber.
Power Plant: Two 680hp M-17.
Performance:
maximum speed at sea level 123mph (198km/hr).
normal range 621 miles (1,000km).
service ceiling 15,419ft (4,700m).
Weights:
loaded 15,036 (6,820kg).
maximum 17,144lb (7,777kg).
Dimensions:
wing span 86ft 11¼in (26.5m).
length 59ft 0½in (18.0m).
height 19ft 11¾in (6.08m).
Armament: Six flexible 7.62mm DA-2 machine-guns in open nose and fuselage positions; max bomb load 6,615lb (3,000kg).
Crew: 6.
In Service: USSR (SovAF, SovNAF).
Variants (with no. built):
ANT-4: Prototype (1).
TB-1: Production model; heavy bomber and transport versions.
MTB-1: Maritime reconnaissance-bomber floatplane; provision for bomb-load or torpedo.
(Total TB-1 and MTB-1, 215).
Total Production: 216.
Remarks: First flown 1925, TB-1 set number payload/distance records, inc 1929 Moscow-New York flight; still employed general-purpose/transport duties at time of German invasion of USSR, June 1941.

Manufacturer: Tupolev.
Model: TB-3 (ANT-6).
Type: Heavy bomber.
Power Plant: Four 970hp M-34 FRN.
Performance:
maximum speed 179mph (288km/hr).
normal range 1,939 miles (3,120km).
service ceiling 25,393ft (7,740m).
Weights:
empty 24,154lb (10,956kg).
maximum 42,990lb (19,500kg).
Dimensions:
wing span 132ft 10½in (40.5m).
length 83ft 0in (25.3m).
height 27ft 8¾in (8.45m).
wing area 2,475.7sq ft (230.0sq m).
Armament: Two flexible 7.62mm ShKAS machine-guns each in open nose, dorsal and tail positions; max bomb load (internal and external) 8,818lb (4,000kg).
Crew: 4-6.
In Service: USSR.
Variants (with no. built):
ANT-6: Prototype; four 600hp Curtiss Conqueror; subsequently re-engined with four 730hp BMW VI (1).
TB-3: Production model; four 715hp M-17F, 830hp M34, M-34R, 900hp M-34FRN, or supercharged 970hp M-34RN; latter version with increased 12,787lb (5,800kg) bomb load; orig version ten DA-2 machine-guns, variations until final version with three 7.62mm ShVAK machine-guns in nose and dorsal turrets and position behind tailplane (817).
G-2: Transport version; modified TB-3.
Total Production: approx 820.
Remarks: Greatly enlarged 4-engined development of earlier TB-1 (ANT-4), prototype TB-3 first flown late 1930; progressively modified/improved, served extensively heavy bomber, troop/paratroop and civil transport roles; saw action against Japanese forces in Mongolian/Manchurian incidents 1938-39; participated Soviet-Finnish war of 1939-40, and as night-bomber early phases German invasion of Soviet Union, Summer 1941; remained in large-scale transport service throughout WWII.
Colour Reference: Plate 171: Tupolev TB-3 (ANT-6) No 9 bomber-transport of VVS (Air Forces of the USSR) abandoned intact in woods outside Smolensk, Central Sector Russian Front, Aug 1941; black/green camouflage scheme, early style fuselage/wing insignia; note outlined Red Star on extreme nose.

Manufacturer: Tupolev.
Model: Kr-6 (ANT-7).
Type: Heavy fighter.
Power Plant: Two 680hp M-17.
Performance:
maximum speed at sea level 150mph (240km/hr).
service ceiling 19,849 (6,050m).
Weights:
loaded 11,553lb (5,240kg).
Dimensions:
wing span 76ft 1⅓in (23.2m).
length 48ft 4⅔in (14.75m).
Armament: Four flexible 7.62mm Darne machine-guns in nose, dorsal and ventral positions.
Crew: 3.
In Service: USSR (SovAF, SovNAF).
Variants:
ANT-7: Prototype; redesigned ANT-4.
Kr-6: Production model; escort-fighter version.
R-6: Long-range reconnaissance version; modified ANT-7; same as floatplane (R-6P).
P-6, MP-6 (ANT-7): Civil land and floatplane versions resp.
Total Production: 400.
Remarks: Development of earlier ANT-4, prototype ANT-7 first flown Sept 1929; number Kr-6 multi-seat escort-fighter/R-6 reconnaissance aircraft still used for second-line duties at time of German invasion of USSR twelve years later; several captured intact; civil examples employed in transport role throughout WWII and after.

Manufacturer: Tupolev.
Model: ANT-9-M-17 (PS-9).
Type: Transport.
Power Plant: Two 680hp M-17.
Performance:
maximum speed 147mph (237km/hr).
cruising speed 109mph (175km/hr).
service ceiling 14,763ft (4,500m).
Weights:
empty 9,700lb (4,400kg).
loaded 13,668lb (6,200kg).
Dimensions:
wing span 77ft 10¼in (23.73m).
length 55ft 9¼in (17.0m).
wing area 904.2sq ft (84.0sq m).
Crew/Accommodation : 2/9.
In Service: Turkey, USSR.
Variants (with no. built):
ANT-9: Prototype; civil transport version; three 230hp Gnome-Rhône Titan (1).
ANT-9: Initial production model; three 300hp M-26 or 365hp Wright J6 Whirlwind; latter version with modified rudder; reduced length; alt wheel or ski undercarriage.
ANT-9-M-17: Modified ANT-9; two 680hp M-17 (BMW VI licence prod) increased weight.
(Total ANT-9 and ANT-9-M-17: approx 70).
Total Production: 70+.
Remarks: First flown 1929, ANT-9 numerically among most important pre-war Soviet transports (several examples supplied Turkish AF, 1933); both 3-engined ANT-9 and twin-engined ANT-9-M-17 development mobilized for wartime Aeroflot service in military transport/general-purpose roles.

Manufacturer: Tupolev.
Model: ANT-20bis (PS-124).
Type: Long-range transport.
Power Plant: Six 1,100hp M-100, or 1,250hp M-34FRN.
Performance:
maximum speed 186mph (300km/hr).
cruising speed 129mph (208km/hr).
range 1,864 miles (3,000km).
service ceiling 22,965ft (7,000m).
Weights:
loaded 102,955 (46,700kg).
Dimensions:
wing span 206ft 8¼in (63.0m).
length 109ft 11⅔in (33.52m).
wing area 5,233.46sq ft (486.2sq m).
Crew/Accommodation: 8-9/60-64.
In Service: USSR.
Variants (with no. built):
ANT-20: Prototype; propaganda aircraft; eight 900hp AM-34R; 20 crew/43 passenger (1).
ANT-20bis: Improved ANT-20; long-range transport (1).
Total Production: 2.
Remarks: ANT-20 'Maxim Gorki', world's largest aircraft at time of appearance in 1934, destroyed in aerial collision following year; improved ANT-20 transport entered service 1940; reportedly operated long-range rear-area transport duties during WWII.

Manufacturer: Tupolev.
Model: ANT-35 (PS-35).
Type: Transport.
Power Plant: Two 850hp M-85.
Performance:
maximum speed approx 268mph (approx 432km/hr).
cruising speed 217mph (350km/hr).
maximum range 1,243 miles (2,000km).
service ceiling 27,887ft (8,500m).
Weights:
loaded 14,594lb (6,620kg).
Dimensions:
wing span 68ft 3in (20.8m).
length 49ft 2½in (15.0m).
wing area 624.3sq ft (58.0sq m).
Crew/Accommodation: 2/10.
In Service: USSR.
Variants:
ANT-35 prototype: Civil transport version; two 850hp M-35.
ANT-35 (PS-35): Production model; minor equipment changes—special cold-weather cowlings and addn spinners for Winter service; two 850hp (Gnome-Rhône 14N) M-85.
Remarks: Entered Aeroflot service 1937; employed trooper/transport duties during Soviet-Finnish Winter War 1939-40; fully mobilised upon German invasion USSR, June 1941. PS-35s participated number supply/relief operations inc Leningrad, Stalingrad, and Crimea.

Manufacturer: Tupolev.
Model: SB-2.
Type: Bomber.
Power Plants: Two 830hp M-100.
Performance:
maximum speed at 13,125ft (4,000m) 255mph (410km/hr).
normal range 746 miles (1,200km).
service ceiling 27,887ft (8,500m).
Weights:
loaded 12,636lb (5,732kg).
Dimensions:
wing span 66ft 8¾in (20.33m).
length 40ft 3¼in (12.27m).
height 10ft 8in (3.25m).
wing area 559.19sq ft (51.95sq m).
Armament: Two 7.62mm ShKAS machine-guns in nose; one flexible 7.62mm ShKAS machine-gun each in dorsal hatch (or turret) and rear ventral position; max bomb load 2,205lb (1,000kg).
Crew: 3.
In Service: China (SB-2, SB-2bis), Bulgaria (42 ex-Czech via Germany), Finland (1 SB-2, 23 SB-2bis: majority ex-Czech/USSR via Germany), Germany (ex-Czech/USSR), Slovakia (1, ex-Czech), Spain (RepAF, NatAF), USSR.
Variants (with no. built):
ANT-40: Prototypes; two 730hp M-25/830hp M-100 resp (2).
SB-2: Initial production model; two M-100 or 860hp M-100A; fixed or variable-pitch props.
SB-2bis: Modified SB-2; two 960hp M-103; increased fuel capacity.
PS-40, 41: Civil transport versions of SB-2, SB-2bis resp.
(Total SB-2, SB-2bis, PS-40, 41: approx 6,654).
SB-RK (Ar-2): Dive-bomber version; two supercharged 1,100hp M-105R; modified SB-2bis; reduced wing area (200).
B 71: Czech equivalent of SB-2; two 860hp Hispano-Suiza 12Ydrs; Avia and Acro licence-built (111).
(Avia-Katusa) M-8: Bulgarian AF designation for B 71.
Total Production: 6,967.
Remarks: First flown Oct 1934. SB-2's SovAF service debut early 1936; 30 examples supplied Czechoslovakia 1937, subsequently subject to licence-production; extensive pre-war use Spanish Civil War (200 delivered RepAF), and in second Sino-Japanese conflict (Chinese AF); SovAF machines participated Soviet-Finnish war of 1939-40, also opening stages German invasion of USSR, primarily in night-bombing role; later relegated trainer/target-tug duties; all Czech examples seized by Germany, March 1939; many likewise employed by Luftwaffe in target-tug role; others passed to Bulgarian and Finnish AFs, latter in use throughout Continuation War, 1941-44, inc two local trainer conversions.
Colour Reference: Plate 164: Tupolev SB-2bis (0202) of Nationalist Chinese Air Force; standard Soviet AF olive green/light blue camouflage finish; the pilot of this particular aircraft defected to Japanese-controlled Cochin China in Nov 1941.

Manufacturer: Tupolev.
Model: ANT-44 (MTB-2).
Type: Long-range maritime reconnaissance flying boat.
Power Plant: Four 950hp M-87A.
Performance:
maximum speed 221mph (355km/hr).
maximum range 2,795 miles (4,500km).
ceiling 21,325ft (6,500m).
Weights:
loaded 40,785lb (18,500kg).
maximum 47,399lb (21,500kg).
Dimensions:
wing span 119ft 7in (36.45m).
length 82ft 0¼in (25.0m).
wing area 1,557.55sq ft (144.7sq m).
Armament: 7.62mm machine-guns in manually operated nose and tail turrets and dorsal position.
In Service: USSR (SovNAF).
Variants (with no. built):
ANT-44: Prototypes; long-range reconnaissance flying boat; four 810hp M-85; subsequently modified as amphibian; twice re-engined—four 950hp M-87, and M-87A; second prototype with dorsal gun position replaced by turret (2).
Total Production: 2.
Remarks: First flown Spring 1937, both Ant-44 prototypes employed on emergency supply/special-duties operations over Crimea/Black Sea areas during WWII.

Manufacturer: Tupolev.
Model: Tu-2S.
Type: Bomber.
Power Plant: Two 1,850hp Mikulin M-82FN.
Performance:
maximum speed at 17,750ft (5,400m) 340mph (547km/hr).
cruising speed 275mph (442km/hr).
normal range 1,243 miles (2,000km).
time to 16,400ft (5,000m) 9min 30sec.
service ceiling 31,170ft (9,500m).
Weights:
empty 18,200lb (8,260kg).
maximum 28,219lb (12,800kg).
Dimensions:
wing span 61ft 10½in (18.86m).
length 45ft 3¼in (13.8m).
height 14ft 11in (4.56m).
wing area 525.28sq ft (48.8sq m).
Armament: Two 20mm ShVAK cannon in wing-roots; one flexible 12.7mm UBT machine-gun each in two dorsal and one ventral positions; max bomb load 6,614lb (3,000kg).
Crew: 4.
In Service: USSR (SovAF, SovNAF).
Variants (with no. built):
ANT-58: Initial prototype; 3-seat bomber version; two 1,400hp Mikulin AM-37 (1).
ANT-59, 60: Prototypes; 4-seat bomber versions; modified ANT-58; lengthened fuselage; increased weight; ANT-60 with two 1,330hp M-82 (2).
Tu-2: Pre-production model; as ANT-60; max bomb load 4,410lb (2,000kg); late models with two ASh-82FNV.
Tu-2S: Modified Tu-2; Uprated engines; increased bomb load; twin 7.62mm machine-guns in dorsal and ventral positions replaced by single 12.7mm UBT machine-gun.
Tu-2D, R: Long-range and reconnaissance versions resp; increased wing span; modified nose; Tu-2R with vertical and oblique cameras.
Tu-2Sh, T, and U: Ground-attack, torpedo-bomber and crew-trainer versions resp; post-war developments.
ANT-63 SDB: Prototype; 3-seat escort-fighter version; re-engined Tu-2; two 1,870hp AM-39; 1 conversion.
Tu-1: Production model; 3-seat escort fighter; four fixed forward-firing 23mm ShVAK cannon.
ANT-64/65, -67/69: Post-war experimental and service (Tu-8, -10) developments.
Total Production: 2,500+ (inc post-war production).
Remarks: ANT-58 first flown Jan 1941; Tu-2 saw front-line combat evaluation, Autumn 1942, before first Tu-2S deliveries early 1944; over one thousand examples completed prior end of WWII; extensive service attack-bomber/ground-support roles in final advances on Germany; continued post-war production and service, inc Polish and Communist Chinese AFs, latter participating Korean War.

Manufacturer: Yakovlev.
Model: UT-1 (AIR-14).
Type: Trainer/light ground-attack.
Power Plant: One 120hp M-11G.
Performance:
maximum speed 160mph (257km/hr).
range 323 miles (520km).
service ceiling 23,360ft (7,120m).
Weights:
empty 948lb (430kg).
loaded 1,318lb (598kg).
Dimensions:
wing span 23ft 11½in (7.3m).
length 18ft 11½in (5.78m).
wing area 89.34sq ft (8.30sq m).
Armament: Provision for two wing-mounted 7.62mm ShKAS machine-guns plus four rockets.
Crew: 1.
In Service: USSR (SovNAF).
Variants:
Ya-14: Prototype and initial production model; single-seat (aerobatic) trainer; one 120hp M-11G.
UT-1: Modified Ya-14; one 120hp

M–11G or 150hp M–11E; military version.
UT–1P (Ya–15): Floatplane version of UT–1.
Total Production: 1,241.
Remarks: Development of contemporary 2-seat Ya–10 (see UT–2), number single-seat UT–1 trainers pressed into service emergency ground-attack and anti-shipping roles by Black Sea Fleet NAF, Spring/Summer 1942.

Manufacturer: Yakovlev.
Model: UT–2 (AIR–20).
Type: Trainer/(night) ground-attack.
Power Plant: One 150hp M–11E.
Performance:
maximum speed at sea level 120mph (192km/hr).
maximum speed 143mph (230km/hr).
normal range 311 miles (500km).
service ceiling 11,480ft (3,500m).
Weights:
empty 1,358lb (616kg).
loaded 1,772lb (804kg).
Dimensions:
wing span 33ft 4¾in (10.18m).
length 23ft 3in (7.1m).
wing area 185.14sq ft (17.2sq m).
Armament: Provision for light bombs.
Crew: 2.
In Service: Germany (ex-USSR), Rumania (ex-USSR), USSR.
Variants:
Ya–10: Prototype; 2-seat trainer; one 100hp M–11.
UT–2: Modified Ya–10; one 100hp M–11 or 150hp M–11E; increased wing area.
VT–2: Float-plane version of UT–2; one 120hp GAZ.
Total Production: 7,243.
Remarks: Entering service 1938, UT–2 employed as standard SovAF trainer throughout WWII; number captured examples operated alongside U–2 (Po–2) biplanes by single Luftwaffe night-harassment Staffel composed of Russian volunteers; brief service northern (Baltic) sector of Eastern Front, Winter 1943–44.

Manufacturer: Yakovlev.
Model: Yak–1.
Type: Fighter/fighter-bomber.
Power Plant: One 1,100hp Klimov M–105PA.
Performance:
maximum speed at sea level 311mph (500km/hr).
maximum speed at 16,400ft (5,000m) 360mph (580km/hr).
cruising speed 149mph (240km/hr).
maximum range 528 miles (850km).
time to 16,400ft (5,000m) 4min 30sec.
service ceiling 32,810ft (10,000m).
Weights:
empty 5,137lb (2,330kg).
loaded 6,217lb (2,820kg).
Dimensions:
wing span 32ft 9¾in (10.0m).
length 27ft 9½in (8.47m).
height 8ft 8in (2.64m).
wing area 184.6sq ft (17.15sq m).
Armament: One 20mm ShVAK cannon firing through propeller hub; two 7.62mm ShKAS machine-guns in upper cowling; max bomb load 440lb (200kg), or six 82mm RS–82 rocket projectiles.
Crew: 1.
In Service: France (FFAF: Yak–1M), Germany (1+ Yak–1 evaluation), Poland (PVolAF: Yak–1M), USSR.
Variants (with no. built):
I–26: Prototype; fighter version; one M–105PA; two 7.62mm ShKAS machine-guns (1).
I–26: Pre-production model; repositioned oil radiator; revised vertical tail surfaces and under-carriage; provision for underwing bombs or rockets.
Yak–1 (I–26): Initial production model; early models as I–26; increased armament; subsequent models with one 1,210hp VK–105PF with power booster; reduced weight; two 7.62mm ShKAS machine-guns replaced by single 12.7mm Berezin UB machine-gun.
Yak–1M: Modified Yak–1; improved all-round vision canopy; cut-down rear fuselage.
(Total Yak–1 (I–26) and Yak 1M: 8,720).
UTI–26: 2-seat trainer version; modified Yak–1; subsequently redesignated Yak–7V (inc several Yak–1 conversions).
Total Production: approx 8,720.
Remarks: Prototype I–26 was forerunner of highly successful single-seat fighter series; first flew early 1940; entered service (as Yak–1) before end of year, some four hundred available at time of German invasion of USSR, June 1941; operated in large numbers duration WWII, latterly being progressively replaced by improved Yak–3; formed initial operational equipment of unique all-woman fighter Regt, Oct 1941, of French 'Normandie-Niémen' volunteer unit, Jan–Nov 1943, and of first of four Polish volunteer units, 1943–45.
Colour Reference: Plate 174: Yakovlev Yak–1 (No 2) of V–VS (Air Forces of the USSR), Leningrad Front, Spring 1942; standard black/green shadow shading camouflage scheme.

Manufacturer: Yakovlev.
Model: Yak–3.
Type: Interceptor fighter.
Power Plant: One 1,300hp Klimov VK–105PF.
Performance:
maximum speed at sea level 370mph (595km/hr).
maximum speed at 1,080ft (3,300m) 407mph (655km/hr).
maximum range 560 miles (900km).
time to 16,400ft (5,000m) 4min 6sec.
service ceiling 35,430ft (10,800m).
Weights:
empty 4,641lb (2,105kg).
maximum 5,864lb (2,660kg).
Dimensions:
wing span 30ft 2¼in (9.2m).
length 27ft 10¼in (8.49m).
height 7ft 11¼in (2.42m).
wing area 159.63sq ft (14.83sq m).
Armament: One 20mm ShVAK cannon firing through propeller hub; two 12.7mm Berezin UBS machine-guns in upper cowling.
Crew: 1.
In Service: France (FFAF, Yak–3), USSR.
Variants:
Yak–3: Prototype; modified Yak–1M; one 1,300hp VK–105PF; redesigned (reduced span) wing; repositioned radiator; improved canopy; reduced weight.
Yak–3: Pre-production and initial production model; as prototype.
Yak–3U: Re-engined Yak–3; one 1,650hp VK–107A; all-metal construction; structural strengthening; one 37mm cannon in nose, plus two 20mm ShVAK cannon in upper cowling.
Yak–3TK, –3R: Experimental versions; modified Yak–3U; addn TsIAM turbo-supercharger, and RD–1KhZ booster rocket resp.
Total Production: 4,848.
Remarks: Yak 3 high-level/interceptor development of modified Yak–1M, entered service latter half 1943; although produced in far fewer (relative) numbers than parallel Yak–9, quickly established enviable reputation, displaying marked superiority over Luftwaffe's Bf 109s and Fw 190s in many respects; remained in service until close of WWII and after; flown by French 'Normandie-Niémen' Regt during third and final 1945 campaign in East Prussia; returned France June 1945 with 37 (out of 40) Yak–3s presented as gift by Soviet Government in recognition of Groupe's 273 confirmed victories.
Colour Reference: Plates 175, 176: Yakovlev Yak–3 (No 11) of 1ère Escadrille, Normandie-Niémen, East Prussia, Germany, May 1945; French volunteer unit attached VVS (Air Forces of the USSR), Normandie-Niémen machines finished dark earth/olive green upper surfaces with Soviet national insignia on fuselage and wing undersides; note French tricolour spinner markings, but absence white Cross of Lorraine on tailfin as normally carried by fighters operated by unit.

Manufacturer: Yakovlev.
Model: Yak–4.
Type: Light attack-bomber.
Power Plant: Two 1,100hp M–105R.
Performance:
maximum speed at 16,400ft (5,000m) 335mph (540km/hr).
normal range 497 miles (800km).
service ceiling 28,870ft (8,800m).
Weights:
maximum 11,465lb (5,200kg).
Dimensions:
wing span 45ft 11in (14.0m).
length 33ft 4½in (10.17m).
wing area 344.45sq ft (32.0sq m).
Armament: One or two fixed forward-firing 7.62mm ShKAS machine-guns; one flexible 7.62mm ShKAS machine-gun in rear cockpit; max bomb load (internal and external) 1,323lb (600kg).
Crew: 2.
In Service: USSR.
Variants:
BB–22: Prototype; two 960hp M–103.
Yak–4: Initial production model; one fixed forward-firing 7.62mm ShKAS machine-gun in nose plus one flexible 7.62mm ShKAS machine-gun in rear cockpit.
Yak–4: Late production; two M–105R; minor equipment design changes; armour plating; modified undercarriage; some with addn forward-firing 7.62mm ShKAS machine-gun.
R–12: Reconnaissance version; modified Yak–4.
Remarks: Designed as recon-naissance-fighter, adoption of Yak–4 as short-range bomber proved unsuccessful; limited service opening months German invasion USSR, Summer 1941; subsequently relegated communications/reconnaissance duties.

Manufacturer: Yakovlev.
Model: Yak–6.
Type: Light transport.
Power Plant: Two 150hp M–11E.
Performance:
maximum speed at sea level 112mph (180km/hr).
normal range 547 miles (880km).
service ceiling 16,400ft (5,000m).
Weights:
normal 5,180lb (2,350kg).
Dimensions:
wing span 45ft 11¼in (14.0m).
length 33ft 11in (10.34m).
wing area 318.61sq ft (29.6sq m).
Armament: Provision for one or two flexible 7.62 ShKAS machine-guns in dorsal position plus max (external) 1,102lb (500kg) bomb load.
Crew/Accommodation: 2/6 (or 1,213lb (500kg) freight, or litters plus medic/s).
In Service: USSR.
Variants:
Yak–6: Prototypes and production models; alt basic light bomber/transport versions.
Yak–8: Improved Yak–6; increased dimensions; transport version; prototype/s only.
Remarks: Yak–6 designed as night-harassment bomber to supplement/supplant U–2 (Po–2), entered service 1943; served variety addn roles, inc light transport, communications/liaison, ambulance, and crew trainer; remained in use until close of WWII and after, latterly supplied number Soviet satellite AFs.

Manufacturer: Yakovlev.
Model: Yak–7B.
Type: Fighter/fighter-bomber.
Power Plant: One 1,210hp Klimov VK–105PF.
Performance:
maximum speed at sea level 339mph (545km/hr).
maximum speed at 16,400ft (5,000m) 381mph (613km/hr).
maximum range 513 miles (825km).
time to 16,400ft (5,000m) 4min 55sec.
service ceiling 33,464ft (10,200m).
Weights:
empty 5,467lb (2,480kg).
loaded 6,636lb (3,010kg).
Dimensions:
wing span 32ft 9¾in (10.0m).
length 27ft 9½in (8.47m).
wing area 184.6sq ft (17.15sq m).
Armament: One 20mm ShVAK cannon firing through propeller hub, plus one 12.7mm Berezin UBS machine-gun in upper cowling; max bomb load 440lb (200kg), or six 82mm RS–82 rocket projectiles.
Crew: 1.
In Service: France (FFAF, Yak–7V), USSR.
Variants:
Yak–7V: 2-seat trainer version (UTI–26); modified Yak–1; 1,210hp VK–105PF with power booster; redesigned undercarriage; radio removed; armament reduced/deleted.
Yak–7A: Single-seat (night) fighter version; one 20mm ShVAK cannon plus two 12.7mm UBS machine-guns; provision for underwing bombs or rockets; radio reinstated; improved equipment.
Yak–7B: As 7A; improved rearward-vision cockpit; revised equipment.
Yak–7DI: Prototype; long-range fighter version; modified 7B; wooden wing spars replaced by dural spars; increased fuel capacity (produced as Yak–9).
Yak–7PVRD: Two addn underwing DM–4C ram-jets; experimental only.
Total Production: 6,399.
Remarks: Developed from original Yak–1 (via interim UTI–26 2-seat conversion trainer), Yak–7 entered service 1942; extensively used in low-level fighter and ground-attack roles during mid-war years, Yak–7's career overshadowed by numerically far superior Yak–9; subsequently relegated second-line training and liaison roles (Yak–7V trainers utilized to familiarize newly-arrived French 'Normandie-Niémen' volunteers prior equipment with Yak–1M).

Manufacturer: Yakovlev.
Model: Yak–9D.
Type: Long-range fighter.
Power Plant: One 1,360hp Klimov VK–105PF–3.
Performance:
maximum speed at sea level 332mph (535km/hr).
maximum speed at 6,560ft (2,000m) 374mph (602km/hr).
maximum range 876 miles (1,410km).
time to 16,400ft (5,000m) 5min 42sec.
service ceiling 34,775ft (10,600m).
Weights:
empty 6,107lb (2,770kg).
maximum 6,790lb (3,080kg).
Dimensions:
wing span 32ft 11½in (9.74m).
length 28ft 0¾in (8.55m).
height 9ft 10in (3.0m).
Armament: One 20mm ShVAK cannon firing through propeller hub, plus one 12.7mm Berezin UB machine-gun in upper cowling.
Crew: 1.
In Service: France (FFAF Yak–9, –9T), Poland (PVolAF Yak–9), USSR.
Variants:
Yak–9: Modified Yak–7DI; one 1,300hp VK–105PF–1 or 1,360hp VK–105PF–3; one 20mm ShVAK cannon in nose, plus one or two 12.7mm UB machine-guns in upper cowling.
Yak–9B: Fighter-bomber version; three 12.7mm UB machine-guns; max bomb load (internal and external) 1,325lb (600kg).
Yak–9D: Modified Yak–9; long-range (escort) fighter; one 1,360hp VK–105PF–3; increased fuel capacity; some with addn drop tank (Yak–9DD).
Yak–9DK: Special anti-tank version; one 45mm NS–P–45 cannon in nose.
Yak–9L: Re-engined Yak–9; one 1,200hp supercharged VK–105RD; revised armament; prototype only.
Yak–9P: Interceptor-fighter version; improved Yak–9U; one 1,650hp VK–107A; post-war development.
Yak–9PVO: Night interceptor-fighter version; modified Yak–9; improved equipment; searchlights.
Yak–9R: Reconnaissance version of Yak–9B.
Yak–9T–37: Close-support version; modified Yak–9; one 37mm NS–11–P–37 cannon in nose, plus one 12.7mm UB machine-gun in upper cowling; provision for PTAB anti-armour bombs underwing.
Yak–9T–45: Close-support version; As –37; one 45mm NS–P–45 cannon in nose.
Yak–9U: Improved (all-metal) Yak–9; one 1,650hp VK–107A; redesigned canopy; modified (lengthened) fuselage; one 23mm VYa–23V cannon in nose, plus two 12.7mm UBS machine-guns in upper cowling.
Yak–9UF: Reconnaissance version of Yak–9U.
U–Yak–9U: Dual-control trainer version.
Total Production: 16.769.
Remarks: Yak 9 most numerous and by far most prolific of entire Yak series, continued basic low-level fighter/ground-attack development of original Yak–1; also performed variety of other roles; entered service late 1942 at time of Battle of Stalingrad; long-range Yak–9D/–9DDs used to escort USAAF heavy bomber shuttle raids; one regt Yak–9DDs based Italy, Winter 1944–45 in support Yugoslav Communist partisans; Yak–9 also equipped French 'Normandie-Niémen' Regt during second (1944) campaign, and four Polish volunteer units; post-war Yak–9P employed by number Soviet satellite AFs, and by Communist Chinese and North Korean AFs; at least one of latter captured by USAF during Korean War and returned US for evaluation.

Manufacturer: Yermolayev.
Model: Yer–2.
Type: Long-range bomber.
Power Plant: Two 1,100hp Klimov M–105.
Performance:
maximum speed at sea level 245mph (395km/hr).
maximum speed at 19,685ft (6,000m) 311mph (500km/hr).
normal range 2,548 miles (4,100km).
service ceiling 32,810ft (10,000m).
Weights:
loaded 24,912lb (10,973kg).
Dimensions:
wing span 75ft 5½in (23.0m).
length 54ft 1½in (16.5m).
wing area 775sq ft (72.0sq m).
Armament: One forward-firing 12.7mm BT machine-gun in nose; one 7.62mm ShKAS machine-gun each in dorsal turret and ventral position; max bomb load 2,205lb (1,000kg).
Crew: 4.
In Service: USSR.
Variants (with no. built):
DB–240: Prototypes; long-range bomber; two 1,100hp M–105 (2+).
Yer–2: Initial production model; two 1,100hp Klimov M–105; offset (port) cockpit canopy (approx 300).
Yer–2: Test models; two 1,200hp Mikulin AM–35 (1) or AM–37s (5); experimental only (6 con-versions).
Yer–2: Definitive production model; two 1,500hp (Charomsky) ACh–30B diesels; increased wing span/area; symmetrical canopy; 5 crew; one 20mm ShVAK cannon in nose plus 12.7mm UB dorsal and ventral machine-guns.

Yakovlev Yak–9U

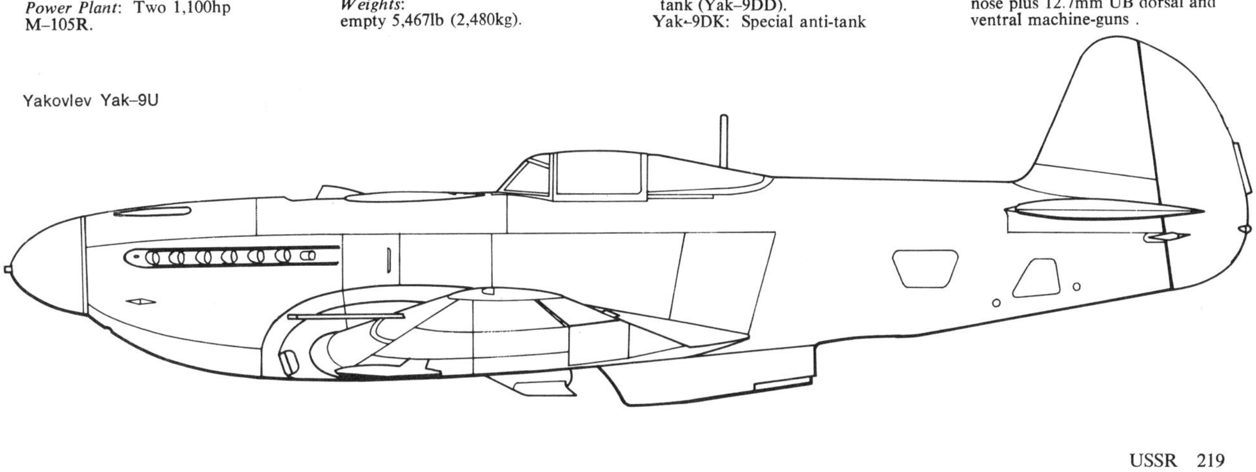

Yermolayev Yer-2

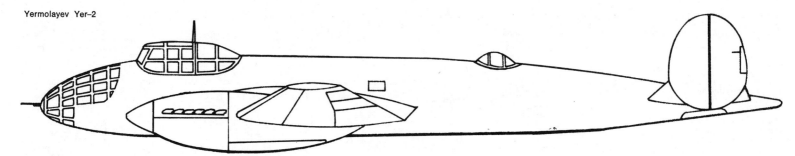

Yer-2 ON: Long-range communications/9-passenger transport version; two 1,500hp ACh-30B (Yer-2 conversions).

Yer-4: Prototype; improved Yer-2; two ACh-30BF; modified radiators; enlarged tailplane (1).
Total Production: approx 320.

Remarks: Developed from experimental Stal-7 civil transport, DB-240 prototype first flown mid-1940; first production Yer-2s served

opening months German invasion in tactical close-support role (often straight from assembly lines), suffered heavy losses in process;

subsequently reverted true role strategic long-range bomber; limited employment as such remainder of war.

YUGOSLAVIA

Manufacturer: Ikarus.
Model: IK-2.
Type: Fighter.
Power Plant: One 860hp Hispano-Suiza 12Ycrs.
Performance:
maximum speed at sea level 224mph (360km/hr).
maximum speed 270mph (435km/hr).
cruising speed 155mph (250km/hr).
normal range 435 miles (700km).
time to 16,400ft (5,000m) 5min 25sec.
maximum service ceiling 34,450ft (10,500m).
Weights:
empty 3,311lb (1,502kg).
loaded 4,094lb (1,857kg).
Dimensions:
wing span 37ft 4½in (11.4m).
length 25ft 10½in (7.88m).
height 12ft 7in (3.84m).
wing area 193.75sq ft (18.0sq m).
Armament: One 20mm Hispano-Suiza HS 404 cannon firing through propeller hub; two 7.92mm Darne machine-guns in engine cowling.
Crew: 1.
In Service: Croatia (approx 4 ex-Yugoslav), Yugoslavia.
Variants (with no. built):
IK-L1(01)-02: Prototypes; single-seat high-wing monoplane fighter; one 860hp Hispano-Suiza 12Ybrs; IK-01 unarmed; IK-02 with one 20mm Hispano-Suiza HS 404 (subsequently replaced by Oerlikon FF), plus two 7.7mm Darne machine-guns; private venture (2).
IK-2: Initial production model; modified IK-02 (12).
IK-4: 2-seat trainer/reconnaissance version of IK-2; project only.
Total Production: 14.
Remarks: Prototype first flown 1935; entering service 1939, eight of twelve production models operational at time of Axis invasion Yugoslavia, 6 April 1941; active throughout week-long campaign, surviving machines rendered inoperable; several subsequently repaired and flown by Croatian AF.

Manufacturer: Rogožarski.
Model: Fizir.
Type: Reconnaissance.
Power Plant: One 240hp Walter Castor.
Performance:
maximum speed 134mph (215km/hr).
time to 16,400ft (5,000m) 34min 0sec.
service ceiling 19,685ft (6,000m).
Weights:
loaded 3,219lb (1,460kg).
Dimensions:
wing span 34ft 7½in (10.55m).
length 24ft 9½in (7.55m).
height 10ft 0in (3.05m).
wing area 290.63sq ft (27.0sq m).
Armament: Provision for machine-gun/s and/or light bombs.
Crew: 2.
In Service: Italy, Yugoslavia.
Variants:
Fizir: 2-seat light reconnaissance biplane.
Remarks: Named after designer, Fizir produced early thirties; several examples captured by Italians after Axis invasion of Yugoslavia, April 1941, and subsequently employed by Italian AF on anti-partisan operations.

Manufacturer: Rogožarski.
Model: PVT.
Type: Trainer/liaison.

Ikarus IK-2

Power Plant: One 420hp Gnome-Rhône 7K.
Performance:
maximum speed at sea level 149mph (239km/hr).
initial rate of climb 1,493ft/min (455m/min).
service ceiling 22,966ft (7,000m).
Weights:
empty 2,132lb (967kg).
loaded 2,892lb (1,312kg).
Dimensions:
wing span 36ft 9in (11.20m).
length 28ft 0½in (8.54m).
height 9ft 2½in (2.81m).
wing area 237.88sq ft (22.1sq m).
Armament: Provision for machine-gun/s and/or light bombs.
Crew/Accommodation: 1/1.
In Service: Italy, Yugoslavia (YAF, YNAF).
Variants:
PVT: 2-seat advanced training parasol monoplane.
PVT-H: Twin-float seaplane version of PVT.
Remarks: PVT/PVT-H employed by YAF/YNAF for advanced trainer (and latterly liaison) duties from mid-thirties until Axis invasion of Yugoslavia, April 1941; number PVTs then seized by occupying Italian forces and later pressed into active service during anti-partisan campaigns of 1941-43.

Manufacturer: Rogožarski.
Model: SIM-XIV-H Series 1.
Type: Coastal reconnaissance floatplane.
Power Plant: Two 270hp Argus As 10E.
Performance:
maximum speed at sea level 151mph (243km/hr).
cruising speed 118mph (190km/hr).
normal range 522 miles (840km).
time to 3,280ft (1,000m) 4min 30sec.
service ceiling 14,240ft (4,340m).
Weights:
empty 4,916lb (2,230kg).
loaded 7,386lb (3,350kg).
Dimensions:

wing span 49ft 10½in (15.2m).
length 36ft 9in (11.19m).
height 14ft 8½in (4.48m).
wing area 404.73sq ft (37.6sq m).
Armament: One 7.5mm Browning-FN machine-gun each in nose and rear cockpit; max bomb load 440lb (200kg) or mines.
Crew: 3 or 6.
In Service: Great Britain (1 ex-YNAF), Yugoslavia (YNAF).
Variants (with no. built):
SIM-XIV-H: Prototype; 3-seat coastal reconnaissance floatplane; two 240hp Argus As 10C; one 7.5mm Browning-FN machine-gun each in retractable nose turret and rear cockpit (1).
SIM-XIV-H Series O: Pre-production model; redesigned vertical tail surfaces; modified tailplane and wingroot fairings; nose turret deleted (6).
SIM-XIV-H Series 1: Production model; uprated engines; unbraced (cantilever) wing; redesigned rear fuselage; revised tail bracing; modified nose; increased cockpit framing; 12 with 450hp Argus As 410s not completed (6).
Total Production: 13.
Remarks: Twin-float seaplane first flown Feb 1938, SIM-XIV-H employed by YNAF Adriatic coastal patrol/reconnaissance duties early months WWII; saw action anti-shipping role during Axis invasion, April 1941; two escapees subsequent brief service under RAF control based North Africa for Mediterranean reconnaissance.

Manufacturer: Rogožarski.
Model: IK-3.
Type: Fighter.
Power Plant: One 980hp Hispano-Suiza 12Ycrs.
Performance:
maximum speed at sea level 262mph (421km/hr).
maximum speed at 17,715 (5,400m) 328mph (527km/hr).
cruising speed 249mph (400km/hr).
normal range 488 miles (785km).

time to 16,400ft (5,000m) 7min 0sec.
service ceiling 30,800ft (9,460m).
Weights:
empty 4,560lb (2,068kg).
loaded 5,799lb (2,630kg).
Dimensions:
wing span 33ft 9½in (10.3m).
length 26ft 3in (8.0m).
height 10ft 8in (3.25m).
wing area 177.5sq ft (16.5sq m).
Armament: One 20mm Oerlikon FF cannon firing through propeller hub; two 7.92mm Browning-FN machine-guns in upper cowling.
Crew: 1.
In Service: Yugoslavia.
Variants (with no. built):
IK-3: Prototype; single-seat low-wing monoplane fighter; one 910hp Hispano-Suiza 12Y 29; private venture (1).
IK-3: Production model; one (Avia-built) Hispano-Suiza 12Ycrs; structural strengthening; modified rear fuselage and (reinforced) cockpit canopy; 1 (first model) with radio equipment (12).
IK-3/2: Dual-control trainer version of IK-3; project only.
Total Production: 13.
Remarks: First flown early Summer 1938, IK-3 entered service two years later; ambitious production/development programme hampered by component supply problems; six machines serviceable at time of Axis invasion, 6 April 1941; fought alongside Yugoslav AF Bf 109s in defence of capital, Belgrade, opening days of week-long campaign; scored considerable success against German bombers but suffered badly in process; surviving examples destroyed to prevent falling into enemy hands, together with 25 others currently under construction.

Manufacturer: Rogožarski.
Model: R-313.
Type: Light bomber/reconnaissance.
Power Plant: Two 500hp Walter

Sagitta I-SR.
Performance:
maximum speed at sea level 234mph (376km/hr).
maximum speed at 13,120ft (4,000m) 286mph (460km/hr).
time to 6,560ft (2,000m) 3min 54sec.
Weights:
empty 6,504lb (2,950kg).
loaded 9,414lb (4,270kg).
Dimensions:
wing span 42ft 8in (13.0m).
length 36ft 1in (11.0m).
height 8ft 9½in (2.68m).
wing area 284.17sq ft (26.4sq m).
Armament: One fixed forward-firing 20mm Hispano-Suiza cannon in nose; one flexible 7.5mm Browning-FN machine-gun in rear cockpit; max bomb load (internal) 882lb (400kg).
Crew: 2.
In Service: Yugoslavia.
Variants:
R-313: Prototype; 2-seat light bomber/reconnaissance.
Total Production: 1.
Remarks: Completed late 1939, sole prototype assumed operational status weeks prior Axis invasion Yugoslavia, 6 April 1941; no details available use during seven-day campaign, wrecked on take-off evacuation Greece towards close.

ABBREVIATIONS AND GLOSSARY

A	Attack, light bombardment (designation prefix, US).
A3	Armée (3-seat tactical-reconnaissance/army co-operation designation suffix, France).
A–A	Anti-aircraft.
AAC	Anti-aircraft co-operation (Great Britain).
AASF	Advanced Air Striking Force (Great Britain).
AB2	Assaut Bombardment (2-seat attack bomber designation suffix, France).
AC	Army co-operation (Great Britain).
ADF	Air Defence Force.
A.D.G.B.	Air Defence of Great Britain.
A.D.L.S.	Air Despatch Letter Service (Great Britain).
Aé.M	Aéronautique Militaire (Belgian Air Force).
AF	Air Force.
A.I.	Airborne Interception (radar).
AIAA	Atelier Industriel de l'Aéronautique d'Alger (Algerian Aviation Workshop).
AMC	Armed Merchant Cruiser (Great Britain).
ANF	Ateliers de Constructions de Nord de la France (Northern France Workshops).
AOP	Air Observation Post.
ARK	Arkticheskii (Arctic coastal reconnaissance prefix, USSR).
A.S.	Aerosiluranti (aerial torpedo-bomber, Italy).
A.St.	Aufklärungsstaffel (reconnaissance squadron, Germany).
ASJA	Aktiebolaget Svenska Jarnvagsverkstadernas Aeroplanavdelning (Swedish Railway Workshops Company Aircraft Division).
ASR	Air/sea-rescue.
ASV	Air to surface-vessel (radar).
A.T.	Aerotrasporti (transport aircraft, Italy).
ATA	Air Transport Auxiliary (Great Britain).
AV	Seaplane tender (USN).
AVG	American Volunteer Group ('Flying Tigers').
A.V.I.A.	Azionaria Vercellese Industrie Aeronautiche (Vercelli Aviation Company, Italy).
AVP	Small seaplane tender (USN).
B	Bombardment (designation prefix, US).
B	Bombardirovshchik (bomber designation suffix, USSR).
B.	Bomber designation prefix (Great Britain).
B3	Bombardement (3-seat bomber designation suffix, France).
BAF	Balkan Air Force (Great Britain).
BB	Blizhnii Bombardirovshchik (short-range close-support bomber designation prefix, USSR).
BEF	British Expeditionary Force.
BF1Gr.	Bordfliergergruppe (shipboard wing, Germany).
BMW	Bayerische Motorenwerke (Bavarian Engine Works).
BN4	Bombardement de Nuit (4-seat night-bomber designation suffix, France).
BOAC	British Overseas Airways Corporation.
Bp2	Bombardement en Piqué (2-seat dive-bomber designation suffix, France).
BQ	Controllable (guided ground-launched) bomb, (designation prefix, US).
Bramo	Brandenburgische Motorenwerke (Brandenburg Engine Works).
BSh	Bronirovanny Shturmovik (armoured assault aircraft designation prefix, USSR).
B.T.	Bombardieri Terrestri (landplane bombers, Italy).
Bulg.	Bulgarien Bulgarian unit designation prefix, Germany).
C	Cargo transport (designation prefix, US).
C	Commercial (civil conversion designation suffix, France).
C.	Cargo transport designation prefix (Great Britain).
C1	Chasse (single-seat fighter designation suffix, France).
CAC	Commonwealth Aircraft Corporation (Australia).
CAMCO	Central Aircraft Manufacturing Company (China).
C.A.M.S.	Chantiers Aéro–Maritimes de la Seine (Seine Maritime Aviation Yards).
CAM-ship	Catapult Aircraft Merchant-ship, Catapult Armed Merchantman (Great Britain).
CANSA	Costruzioni Aeronautiche Novaresi S.A. (Novaresi Aviation Manufacturing Co., Italy).
CANT	Cantieri Riuniti dell'Adriatico (United Adriatic Shipyards, Italy).
CAP	Civil Air Patrol, also Combat Air Patrol (US).
CASA	Construcciones Aeronáuticas Sociedad Anónima (Aviation Manufacturing Company, Spain).
CBI	China–Burma–India Theater (US).
CBSA	Caproni Bulgara Societa Anonima (Bulgarian Caproni Company).
CCF	Canadian Car and Foundry Company.
CG	Troop-cargo glider (designation prefix, US).
C-in-C	Commander-in-Chief.
CKD	Ceskomoravska–Kolben–Danek (Czecho–Moravian engine manufacturers).
CMASA	Costruzioni Meccaniche Aeronautiche S.A. (Aviation Mechanical Manufacturing Co., Italy).
C.N.	Caccia Notturna (night-fighter, Italy).
CN2	Chasse de Nuit (2-seat night-fighter designation suffix, France).
CO	Commanding Officer.
compl.re	Complementare (supplementary, Italy).
CSA	Ceskoslovenske Statni Aerolinie (Czechoslovak State Airlines).
C.T.	Caccia Terrestre (landplane fighter, Italy).
CV	Fleet carrier (USN).
CVE	Escort carrier (USN).
CVL	Light fleet carrier (USN).
D	Dalny (long-range, designation suffix, USSR).
DA	Degtyarev Aviatsionny (Degtyarev aircraft machine-gun, USSR).
DAF	Desert Air Force (Great Britain).
DAP	Department of Aircraft Production (Australia).
DAR	Dalnyi Arkticheskü Razvedchik (Arctic long-range reconnaissance, USSR).
D.A.R.	Darjavna Aeroplanna Rabotilnitza (State Aircraft Workshop, Bulgaria).
DB	Dalny Bombardirovshchik (long-range bomber designation prefix, USSR).
DD	Dalny Deistviya (ultra long-range, designation suffix, USSR).
Det.	Detachment.

DFS	Deutsches Forschungsinstitut für Segelflug (German Research Institute for Gliding).
DI	Dvuchmestnii Istrebitel' (2-seat fighter, USSR).
DI	Dalny Istrebitel' (long-range fighter designation suffix, USSR).
DLH	Deutsche Lufthansa (German Airlines).
D.W.L.	Doswiadczalne Warsztaty Lotnicze (Aeronautical Experimental Workshops, Poland).
EA	Enemy aircraft.
ECD	Escadrille de Chasse de Défense (local fighter defence squadron, France).
ECMJ	Escadrille de Chasse multiplace de Jour (multi-seat day-fighter squadron, France).
ECN	Escadrille de Chasse de Nuit (night-fighter squadron, France).
EFW	Eidgenössisches Flugzeugwerk (Federal Aircraft Factory, Switzerland).
Eis.	Eisenbahn (lit. railway; train-busting unit designation suffix, Germany).
EKW	Eidgenössisches Konstruktions Werkstätte (Federal Assembly Workshops, Switzerland).
ERC	Escadrille Régionale de Chasse (regional (auxiliary) fighter squadron, France).
ETO	European Theater of Operations (US).
F	Reconnaissance (photographic) designation prefix (US).
F.	Fighter designation prefix (Great Britain).
(F)	Fern (long-range strategic reconnaissance designation suffix, Germany).
FA	Force Aérienne (Ground Army attached air unit, France).
FAA	Fleet Air Arm (Great Britain).
FAF	French Air Force (Armée de l'Air).
FAGr.	Fernaufklärungsgruppe (long-range strategic reconnaissance wing, Germany).
F.B.	Fighter-bomber designation prefix (Great Britain).
FEAF	Far East Air Force (US).
FFAF	Free French Air Force.
FFI	Forces Françaises de l'Intérieur (French Forces of the Interior).
FFNAF	Free French Naval Air Force.
FFVS	Flygförvaltningens (Air Board Workshops, Sweden).
Fl.Fü.	Fliegerführer (Flying-leader (command), Germany).
FN	Forsirovannii Nyeposredstvenny (power-boosted, designation suffix, USSR).
FNAF	French Naval Air Force (Aéronavale).
FPAF	Free Polish Air Force (in France).
FT	Frontovoye Trebovaniye (lit. front-line requested), designation suffix, USSR.
FuG	Funkgerät (radio (radar) equipment, Germany).
FVAF	French Vichy Air Force (Armée de l'Air de l'Armistice).
FVNAF	French Vichy Naval Air Force (Aéronavale de l'Armistice).
GAM	Groupe Aérien Mixte (Composite wing, France).
GAO	Groupe Aérien d'Observation (tactical-reconnaissance/observation wing, France).
GAR	Groupe Aérien Régional (regional (auxiliary) wing, France).
GB	Groupe de Bombardement (bomber wing, France).
GBA	Groupe de Bombardement d'Assaut (attack-bomber wing, France).
GC	Groupe de Chasse (fighter wing, France).
GR	Groupe de Reconnaissance (strategic reconnaissance wing, France).
GR(G.R.)	General reconnaissance (designation prefix, Great Britain).
GST	Gidro Samolet Transportnii (Transport seaplane, USSR).
(H)	Heavy; bombardment group designation suffix (US).
(H)	Heer (lit. army; tactical reconnaissance/army co-operation unit designation suffix, Germany).
–H	Hidroavion (seaplane designation suffix, Yugoslavia).
HAL	Hindustan Aircraft Ltd (India).
H.F.	High-altitude fighter designation prefix (Great Britain).
HLeLv	Hävittäjälentolaivue (fighter squadron, Finland).

HMS	His Majesty's Ship (Great Britain).
HMS/M	His Majesty's Submarine (Great Britain).
HQ	Headquarters.
hydro	Hydroplan (seaplane designation suffix, Poland).
I	Istrebitel' (fighter designation prefix, USSR).
IAF	Italian Air Force (Regia Aeronautica).
IAR	Industria Aeronautica Româna (Rumanian Aircraft Factory).
ICAR	Intreprindere pentru Contructii Aeronautice Romane (Rumanian Aircraft Manufacturing Company).
ICoAF	Italian Co-belligerant Air Force (Aeronautica cobelligerante del Sud).
I.D.	Infanterie-Division (Germany).
idro	Idrovolante (seaplane designation suffix, Italy).
IJAAF	Imperial Japanese Army Air Force.
IJN	Imperial Japanese Navy.
IJNAF	Imperial Japanese Navy Air Force.
INAF	Italian Navy Air Force (Aviazione Ausiliaria per la Marina).
Ins.	Instructions (training aircraft designation suffix, France).
Ins.AF	Insurgent Air Force (Slovakia).
Int.	Interim (Great Britain).
(J)	Jagd (fighter unit designation suffix, Germany).
Jabo	Jagdbomber (fighter-bomber designation suffix, Germany).
Jafü	Jagdfüher (Fighter-leader (command), Germany).
JG	Jagdgeschwader (fighter group, Germany).
JGr.	Jagdgruppe (fighter wing, Germany).
JSt.	Jagdstaffel (fighter squadron, Germany).
K	Krupnyi kalibr (heavy calibre, fighter designation suffix, USSR).
(K)	Kampf (bomber unit designation suffix, Germany).
Ka.B	Designation prefix of CBSA's (see above) Kazanluk plant (Bulgaria).
KAI	Kaizo (modified/modification, designation suffix, IJAAF).
KG	Kampfgeschwader (bomber group, Germany).
KGr.	Kampfgruppe (bomber wing, Germany).
KhAI	Kharkovskii Aviatsionny Institut (Kharkov Aviation Institute, USSR).
Ki	Kitai (airframe designation prefix, IJAAF).
KLM	Koninklijke Luchtvaart Maatschappij (Royal Dutch Airlines).
KOR	Korabelnii (shipboard designation prefix, USSR).
Kr	Kreyser (lit. cruiser), heavy escort fighter, USSR.
Kroat.	Kroatien (Croatian unit designation prefix, Germany).
KSt.	Kampfstaffel (bomber squadron, Germany).
Ku	Guraida (glider designation prefix, IJAAF).
KüFlGr.	Küstenfliegergruppe (coastal wing, Germany).
L	Liaison, designation prefix, US).
L	Legkii (light (-weight) fighter designation suffix, USSR).
(L)	Light, bombardment group designation suffix (US).
LAZ	Designation prefix after designer Pro.-Ing.Lazarov (see D.A.R. above, Bulgaria).
L.F.	Low-altitude fighter designation prefix (Great Britain).
LG	Landing ground (Great Britain).
LG	Lehrgeschwader (Operational training and Development Group, Germany).
LRDG	Long-range Desert Group.
LST	Landing ship, tank (USN).
(LT)	Lufttorpedo (air-launched torpedo, bomber unit designation suffix, Germany).
L.W.S.	Lubelska Wytwórnia Samolotów (Lublin Aircraft Manufacturing Company, Poland).
M	Morskoy (seaplane, USSR).
M	Modifikatsirovannii (modified, designation suffix, USSR).
M	Marin (navalized, designation suffix, France).
(M)	Medium, bombardment group designation suffix (US).
(M)	Marine (lit. navy; maritime tactical reconnaissance/naval co-operation unit designation suffix, Germany).
MA	Morskoy Amfibiya (amphibian, USSR).

MAC	Manufacture d'Armes de Chatellerault (France).
MAC-ship	Merchant Aircraft Carrier (Great Britain).
MAD	Magnetic Airborne Detector.
MAVAG	Magyar Allami Vaggon és Gépgyár (Hungarian State Wagon and Engineering Factory).
MBR	Morskoy Blizhnii Razvedchik (naval short-range reconnaissance, USSR).
MDR	Morskoy Dalnyi Razvedchik (naval long-range reconnaissance, USSR).
Met.	Meteorological.
M.F.	Marinens Flyvebatfabrikk (Naval Flying-boat Factory, Norway).
MG	Maschinengewehr (machine-gun, Germany).
MK	Maschinenkanone (machine cannon, Germany).
Mod.	modified/modification.
MP	Morskoy Passazhirskii (Naval transport seaplane, USSR).
MR	Morskoy Razvedchik (Naval reconnaissance seaplane, USSR).
MT	Motor transport.
MTB	Marskoy Torpedonosez Bombardirovshchik (naval torpedo bomber, USSR).
MTO	Mediterranean Theater of Operations (US).
(Mz)	Mehrzweck (maritime multi-purpose unit designation suffix, Germany).
(N)	Nacht (night; unit designation suffix, Germany).
NAF	Navy Air Force.
NAG	National Air Guard (US).
NAGr.	Nahaufklärungsgruppe (tactical reconnaissance wing, Germany).
NAK	Nochnoy Artillerüskü Korrekitrovshchik (night AOP designation suffix, USSR).
NASt.	Nahaufklärungsstaffel (tactical reconnaissance squadron, Germany).
Nat.AF	Nationalist Air Force (China, Spain).
NB	Nochnoy Bombardirovshchik (night bomber, USSR).
NEI	Netherlands East Indies.
NF (N.F.)	Night-fighter (designation prefix, Great Britain).
NJG	Nachtjagdgeschwader (night-fighter group, Germany).
NJGr.	Nachtjagdgruppe (night-fighter wing, Germany).
NJSt.	Nachtjagdstaffel (night-fighter squadron, Germany).
NSGr.	Nachtschlachtgruppe (night ground-attack wing, Germany).
NSt.	Nachtstaffel (night (strategic reconnaissance) squadron, Germany).
O	Observation (designation prefix, US).
OA	Observation amphibian (designatian prefix, US).
O.A.	Osservazione Aerea (tactical reconnaissance, Italy).
ON	Osobovo Naznacheniya (special-purpose, designation suffix, USSR).
OTU	Operational Training Unit (Great Britain).
P	Pursuit (fighter designation prefix, US).
P	Pushechny (cannon (-armed) fighter designation suffix, USSR).
PB	Pikirupuschii Bombardirovshchik (dive-bomber designation prefix, USSR).
PDU	Photographic Development Unit (Great Britain).
PFF	Pathfinder (Great Britain, US).
PLeLv	Pommituslentolaivue (bomber squadron, Finland).
PoW	Prisoner-of-war.
PR (P.R.)	Photographic-reconnaissance (designation prefix, Great Britain).
PRG	Photographic-reconnaissance group (US).
PRU	Photographic-reconnaissance Unit (Great Britain).
PS	Passazhirskii Samolet (passenger airliner, designation prefix, USSR).
PT	Poplavkovii Torpedonosez (torpedo floatplane, designation suffix, USSR).
PV	Pulemot Vozdushny (aerial machine-gun, USSR).
PVO	Protivovozdushnaya Oborona (Air Defence, designatian suffix, USSR).
PVRD	Pryamotochnii Vozdushno Reaktivnii Dvigatel (ramjet, designation suffix, USSR).
PVT	Prototip Vazduhoplavstvo Tehnicki (Aerial-navigation Technical Prototype, Yugoslavia).

P.W.S.	Podlaska Wytwórnia Samalotów (Podlasian Aircraft Manufacturing Company, Poland).
(Pz)	Panzer (lit. tank), anti-tank unit designation suffix, Germany.
P.Z.Inz.	Panstowe Zaklady Inzynierji (State Engineering Institute, Poland).
P.Z.L.	Panstwowe Zaklady Lotnicze w Warszawie (State Aircraft Establishments, Poland).
R	Rotary-wing (helicopter designation prefix, US).
R	Razvedchik (reconnaissance designation prefix/suffix, USSR).
R	Raketny (rocket (-boosted) designation suffix, USSR).
R2	Reconnaissance (2-seat reconnaissance designation suffix, France).
RAAF	Royal Australian Air Force.
RAF	Royal Air Force.
RAN	Royal Australian Navy.
RB4	Reconnaissance-bombardement (4-seat reconnaissance-bomber designation suffix, France).
RCAF	Royal Canadian Air Force.
RCN	Royal Canadian Navy.
Rep.AF	Republican Air Force (Spain).
R.M.	Regia Marina (Royal Italian Navy).
RNZAF	Royal New Zealand Air Force.
RSIAF	Republican Socialist Italian Air Force (Aeronautica Nazionale Repubblicana).
RSV	Renard design (Stampe-et-Vertongen) designation prefix (Belgium).
Rum.	Rumänien (Rumanian unit designation prefix, Germany).
RWD	Designers Messrs. Rogalski, Wigura, and Drzewiecki (see D.W.L., Poland).
SAAB	Svenska Aeroplan Aktiebolaget (Swedish Aircraft Company).
SAAF	South African Air Force.
SABCA	Société Anonyme Belge de Constructions Aéronautiques (Belgian Aviation Manufacturing Company).
SAGr.	Seeaufklärungsgruppe (maritime reconnaissance wing, Germany).
S.A.I.	Società Aeronautica Italiana (Italian Aviation Company).
SAIMAN	Società Anonima Industrie Meccaniche Aeronautiche Navali (Maritime Aviation and Mechanical Industries).
SB	Skorostnoi Bombardirovshchik (fast bomber designation prefix, USSR).
(Schl.)	Schlacht (ground-attack unit designation suffix, Germany).
SD	Special Duties (Great Britain).
SEAC	South-East Asia Command (Great Britain).
(See)	Sea, maritime unit designation suffix (Germany).
SET	Societatea pentru exploatâri technice (Technical Development Company, Rumania).
SFA	Svenska Flygmotor Aktiebolaget (Swedish Aircraft Engine Company).
SG	Schlachtgeschwader (ground-attack group, Germany).
SGr.	Schlachtgruppe (ground-attack wing, Germany).
Sh	Shturmovik (ground-attack designation prefix/suffix, USSR).
ShKAS	Shpital'ny-Komaritsky Aviatsionny Skorostrelny (Shpital'ny-Komoritsky fast-firing aircraft gun, USSR).
ShR	Shturmovik Razvedchik (ground-attack reconnaissance, USSR).
ShVAK	Shpital'ny-Vladimirov Aviatsionnays Krupno-kalibrnaya (Shpital'ny-Vladimirov large-calibre aircraft gun, USSR).
SIM	Designation prefix, after designer Sima Milutinovic (Yugoslavia).
SIPA	Société Industrielle pour L'Aéronautique (Industrial Aviation Company, France).
SKG	Schnellkampfgeschwader (fast-bomber group, Germany).
SKSt.	Schnellkampstaffel (fast-bomber squadron, Germany).
SNCAC	Société Nationale de Constructions Aéronautiques du Centre (State Aircraft Manufacturers Central, France).
SNCAM	Société Nationale de Constructions Aéronautiques du Midi (State Aircraft Manufacturers Midi, France).

SNCAN	Société Nationale de Constructions Aéronautiques du Nord (State Aircraft Manufacturers North, France).	V.E.F.	Valsts Elektrotechniska Fabrika (State Electro-technical Factory, Latvia).
SNCAO	Société Nationale de Constructions Aéronautiques de l'Ouest (State Aircraft Manufacturers West, France).	VF	Fighter squadron (USN).
		VFN	Night-fighter squadron (USN).
SNCASE	Société Nationale de Constructions Aéronautiques de Sud-Est (State Aircraft Manufacturers South-East, France).	VH	Hospital (medical evacuation) squadron (USN).
		VHB	Very heavy bomber (US).
		VI	Vysotnyi Istrebitel (high-altitude fighter designation suffix, USSR).
SNCASO	Société Nationale de Constructions Aéronautiques de Sud-Ouest (State Aircraft Manufacturers South-West, France).	VIT	Vozdushnii Istrebitel Tankov (airborne tank-fighter designation prefix, USSR).
Sov.AF	Soviet Air Force (Voenno-vozdushniye Sily).	VJ–Day	Victory over Japan, 15 August 1945.
Sov.NAF	Soviet Navy Air Force (Morskaya Aviatsiya).	VL	Valtion Lentokonetehdas (State Aircraft Factory, Finland).
SPAD	Société Anonyme Pour l'Aviation et ses Dérivés (Aviation and Ancillaries Company, France).	VMF	Fighter squadron (USMC).
SPB	Skorostnoi Pikiruyushchii Bombardirovshchik (fast dive-bomber designation prefix, USSR).	VO	Observation squadron (USN).
		VOC	Observation (composite) squadron (USN).
SS	Samolyot Svyazi (liaison aircraft, USSR).	vol.	Volunteer.
S.St.	Schlachtstaffel (ground-attack squadron, Germany).	VPB	Patrol bomber squadron (USN).
St.	Staffel (squadron, Germany).	VS	Voyskovaya Seriya (military series, designation suffix, USSR).
(St.)	Sturzkampf (dive-bomber unit designation prefix, Germany).		
		VT	Torpedo-bomber squadron (USN).
St.G	Sturzkampfgeschwader (dive-bomber group, Germany).	VTN	Night torpedo-bomber squadron (USN).
St.Gr.	Sturzkampfgruppe (dive-bomber wing, Germany).		
STOL	Short take-off and land.	WNF	Wiener-Neustädter Flugzeugwerke (Wiener-Neustadt Aircraft Works, Greater Germany).
SWPA	South-West Pacific Area (US).		
		WWII	Second World War.
T	Transportnii (transport designation suffix, USSR).		
T	Tyazhely (heavy (-armament) designation suffix, USSR).	X	Prototype designation prefix (US/USN).
T	Travail (lit. work), general-purpose/army co-operation unit designation suffix, France).	Y	Pre-production and evaluation designation prefix (US).
TAF	Tactical Air Force (Great Britain, US, Free France).	Z	lighter-than-air squadron prefix (USN).
TB	Tchazhelyi Bombardirovshchik (heavy bomber designation prefix, USSR).	(Z)	Zerstörer (unit designation suffix, Germany).
		zbV	Zur besonderen Verwendung (for special employment, unit designation suffix, Germany).
T.B.	Torpedo-bomber designation prefix (Great Britain).		
TF	Task Force (USN).	(Zerst.)	Zerstörer (lit. destroyer; heavy-fighter, Germany).
T.F.	Torpedo-strike fighter designation prefix (Great Britain).	ZG	Zerstörergeschwader (heavy-fighter wing, Germany).
		ZI	Zone of the Interior (US).
TG	Task Group (USN).	ZP	Airship squadron (USN).
TG	Transportgeschwader (transport group, Germany).		
TGr.	Transportgruppe (transport wing, Germany).		
TLeLv	Tiedustelulaivue (close-support squadron, Finland).		
TOE	Théâtres des Opérations Extérieures (overseas territories, designation suffix, France).		
TrGr.	Trägergruppe (carrier wing, Germany).		
TsAGI	Tsentralny Aerogidrodinamichesky Institut (Central Aero and Hydro-dynamic Institute, USSR).		
Tsh	Tyashelyi Shturmovik (heavy ground-attack, USSR).		
TsKB	Tsentralny Konstruktorskoye Byuro (Central Design Bureau, USSR).		
T.T.	Target-tug designation prefix (Great Britain).		
TU	Task Unit (USN).		
U	Uchebno (trainer designation prefix, USSR).		
U	Usilenny (strengthened, designation suffix, USSR).		
U	Usovershenstvovannyi (improved, designation suffix, USSR).		
UC	Utility cargo (designation prefix, US).		
UK	United Kingdom.		
Ung.	Ungarn (Hungarian unit designation prefix, Germany).		
USAAC	United States Army Air Corps.		
USAAF	United States Army Air Force.		
USCG	United States Coast Guard.		
USMC	United States Marine Corps.		
USN	United States Navy.		
USNR	United States Naval Reserve.		
USS	United States Ship.		
USSR	Union of Soviet Socialist Republics.		
UT	Uchebno Trenirovochnyi (advanced training designation prefix/suffix, USSR).		
UTI	Uchebno-Trenirovochny Istrebitel (advanced training fighter designation prefix/suffix, USSR).		
V	Heavier-than-air squadron prefix (USN).		
V	Vyvoznoy (lit. assistance), dual-control trainer designation suffix, USSR.		
VB	Bomber squadron (USN).		
VBF	Fighter-bomber squadron (USN).		
VC	Composite squadron (USN).		
VE–Day	Victory in Europe, 8 May 1945.		

In addition to the various abbreviations of aircraft role or function prefixes listed above (e.g., Boeing *B*–17 Flying Fortress), three other systems of nomenclature were in common use during the war years. The first of these simply gave the name of the aircraft alone (e.g., Westland *Whirlwind*), which offered no indication of type or duties (other than whatever connotations could be drawn from names such as 'Fury' or 'Messenger'). The second was to use the designer's and/or manufacturer's initials (e.g., Dornier *Do*–17), which did even less to explain function, unless, of course, it was accompanied by an equally informative (but often unofficial) name such as the Junkers Ju 352 *Herkules*. Lastly, both the United States and the Imperial Japanese Navy Air Forces shared a unique letter/figure/letter/figure combination which explained all to those conversant with the code. In both services, the first letter indicated the aircraft's primary function; the following figure denoted the numerical order of acceptance into service (in the case of the USN delineated by manufacturer, but irrespective of producer in the IJNAF system); the second code-letter identified the manufacturer; and the final figure the Mark or Model number. For example, the code for the Vought *F4U–1* Corsair, is explained thus: F=fighter; 4=the fourth type of (Vought) fighter to enter USN service under this system; U=Vought; and 1=the first Model of the Corsair series.

In order to better understand the designations of the two major combatant naval air arms in the Pacific, the following lists contain the various code-letters relevant to the types of aircraft described in this book.

United States Navy Air Force
Function:

A	Ambulance.	JR	Utility transport.
B	Bomber.	LN	Training glider.
BT	Bomber-torpedo.	LR	Transport glider.
F	Fighter.	N	Trainer.
G	Single-engined transport.	O	Observation.
H	Hospital.	OS	Observation scout.
HN	Training helicopter.	P	Patrol.
HO	Observation helicopter.	PB	Patrol bomber.
J	General utility.	R	Transport.

S	Scout.	SO	Scout observation.
SB	Scout bomber.	TB	Torpedo-bomber.
SN	Scout trainer.		

Manufacturer:

A	Brewster, Noorduyn.	O	Lockheed.
B	Boeing, Beech.	P	Piper.
C	Curtiss, Cessna.	Q	Stinson, Fairchild.
D	Douglas.	R	Aeronca, Interstate, Ryan.
E	Piper, Bellanca.		
F	Grumman.	S	Sikorsky.
G	Great Lakes, General Motors (Goodyear).	T	Northrop, Taylorcraft.
		U	Vought.
H	Hall, Howard.	V	Lockheed, Vultee, Canadian Vickers.
J	North American.		
K	Fairchild, Kinner.	W	Waco; Canadian Car & Foundry.
L	Bell.		
M	Martin, General Motors.	Y	Consolidated (Convair).
N	Naval Air Factory.		

Imperial Japanese Navy Air Force
Function:

A	Carrier fighter.	L	Transport.
B	Carrier attack bomber.	M	Special floatplane.
C	Reconnaissance.	Mx	Special-purpose.
D	Carrier bomber.	N	Fighter seaplane.
E	Reconnaissance seaplane.	P	Bomber.
F	Observation seaplane.	Q	Patrol.
G	Attack bomber.	R	Land-based reconnaissance.
H	Flying boat.		
J	Land-based fighter.	S	Night-fighter.
K	Trainer.		

Manufacturer:

A	Aichi.	N	Nakajima.
G	Hitachi.	P	Nihon.
H	Hiro.	W	Watanabe.
K	Kawanishi.	Y	Yokosuka.
M	Mitsubishi.		

As the literal translation of many foreign air force units does not correspond to the RAF's organizational equivalent, the tables below may be of assistance in the study of the 'orders of battle'. It must be borne in mind, however, that numbers of aircraft differed considerably even between the nearest equivalent units of the various air forces, and that a direct translation of the chain of command from any one Allied to Axis air force (or vice versa) cannot therefore be regarded as truly representative.

French Air Force (Armée de l'Air)
Basic unit	Escadrille.
Two Escadrilles	One Groupe.
Several Groupes	One Groupement.

German Air Force (Luftwaffe)
Basic unit	Staffel.
Three (later four) Staffeln	One Gruppe.
Three (later four or five) Gruppen	One Geschwader.

British and Commonwealth Air Forces
Basic unit	Squadron.
Three to five Squadrons	One Wing.
Several Wings	One Group.

Italian Air Force (Regia Aeronautica)
Basic unit	Squadriglia.
Three Squadriglie	One Gruppo.
Three Gruppi	One Stormo.

Imperial Japanese Army Air Force
Basic unit	Chutai.
Three Chutais	One Sentai.
Several Sentais	One Hikodan.

United States Army Air Forces
Basic unit	Squadron.
Three (fighter) or four (bomber) squadrons	One Group.
Several Groups	One Wing.

GLOSSARY

Aerofotografica	Aerial photographic (Italy).
Autonomo	Autonomous (Italy).
Behelfsnachtkampfstaffel	Auxiliary night-bomber (ground-attack) squadron (Germany).
da combattimento	Combat (designation suffix, Italy).
d'Assalto	Assault (designation suffix, Italy).
distaccata	Detached (Italy).
Hikodan	Air Brigade (IJAAF).
Hikoshidan	Air Division (IJAAF).
Industrie–Schutzstaffel	Factory defence squadron (Germany).
Intercettori	Interceptor fighter (Italy).
Kamikaze	(Lit. 'Divine Wind'), suicide-attack (Japan).
Koku Kantai	Air Fleet.
Koku Sentai	Carrier Division, or (land-based) Air Flotilla (IJNAF).
Kokutai	Naval Air Corps (IJNAF).
Leigh-light	Airborne anti-submarine searchlight (Great Britain).
Mira	Squadron (Greece).
Mistel	(Lit. mistletoe), fighter/bomber pick-a-back combination (see Ju 88, Germany).
Paracadutisti	Parachutists (Italy).
Raggruppamento	Concentration (of aircraft, Italy).
Rammkommando	Aerial ramming unit (Germany).
Regia Marina	Royal Navy (Italy).
Ricognizione Strategica	Strategic reconnaissance (designation suffix; Italy).
Schräge Musik	(Lit. 'Jazz Music'), oblique upward (or downward) – firing armament installation (Germany).
Schleppgruppe	(Lit. tow-group), i.e., Glider Wing (Germany).
Scuola	School (Italy).
Servizi Aerei Speciali	Special (auxiliary) Air Transport Service (Italy).
Sezione	Section (Italy).
Störkampfstaffeln	(Night) ground-harassment squadrons (Germany).
Sturm	(Lit. storm), anti-bomber aerial ramming unit designation suffix (Germany).
Tuffatori	Dive-bomber (Italy).
Turbinlite	Airborne night-fighter searchlight (employed in conjunction with accompanying fighter, Great Britain).
Wilde Sau	(Lit. Wild Boar), single-engined night-fighter visual interception programme (Germany).
Zahme Sau	(Lit. Tame Boar), twin-engined night-fighter ground-control vector interception programme (Germany).

BIBLIOGRAPHY

The following bibliography has been arranged, as far as possible, into national sections for ease of reference. It is biased towards those books dealing primarily with specific aircraft types and/or manufacturers, and their service and operational careers. With the latter in mind, a number of campaign, single action, and Air Force/Command histories have also been included. Unit histories, of Group level and below, and personal narratives have not generally been included unless it was felt that they provided additional background material not adequately covered elsewhere. Several standard works of reference on the subject of markings are also to be found.

International

Angle, G. D. (ed.) *Aerosphere – 1939*, New York 1940.
Barbieri, C. *I bombardieri della seconda guerra mondiale*, Parma 1971.
Barbieri, C. *I caccia della seconda guerra mondiale*, Parma 1971.
Beaubois, H. *Airships (An Illustrated History)*, London 1974.
Bowman, G. *War in the Air*, London 1956.
Brookes, A. J. *Photo Reconnaissance*, London 1975.
Brown, D. *Carrier Fighters 1939–1945*, London 1975.
Brown, D. *Carrier Operations in World War II* (Vol 2: The Pacific Navies – December 1941–February 1943), London 1974.
Emde, H. *Conquerors of the Air* (The evolution of aircraft 1903–1945), London 1968.
Green, W. *Famous Fighters of the Second World War*, London 1957.
Green, W. *Famous Fighters of the Second World War* (Second Series), London 1962.
Green, W. *Famous Bombers of the Second World War*, London 1959.
Green, W. *Famous Bombers of the Second World War*, (Second Series), London 1960.
Green, W. *Warplanes of the Second World War: Fighters* (Volume One: Austria, Belgium, Bohemia-Moravia, Finland, France, Germany), London 1960.
Green, W. *Warplanes of the Second World War: Fighters* (Volume Two: Great Britain, Italy), London 1961.
Green, W. *Warplanes of the Second World War: Fighters* (Volume Three: Japan, Netherlands, Poland, Rumania, Soviet Union), London 1961.
Green, W. *Warplanes of the Second World War: Fighters* (Volume Four: United States, Yugoslavia), London 1961.
Green, W. *Warplanes of the Second World War: Flying Boats* (Volume Five), London 1962.
Green, W. *Warplanes of the Second World War: Floatplanes* (Volume Six), London 1962.
Green, W. *Warplanes of the Second World War: Bombers and Reconnaissance Aircraft* (Volume Seven: Australia, Belgium, Bohemia-Moravia, Bulgaria, Canada, Finland, France), London 1967.
Green, W. *Warplanes of the Second World War: Bombers and Reconnaissance Aircraft* (Volume Eight: France, Germany), London 1967.
Green, W. *Warplanes of the Second World War: Bombers and Reconnaissance Aircraft* (Volume Nine: Germany), London 1968.
Grey, C. G. (ed.) et al. *Jane's All the World's Aircraft*, London 1928–1946.
Gruss, R. *Les Flottes de l'Air en 1938*, Paris 1938.
Gunston, B. *Night Fighters (A Development & Combat History)*, Cambridge 1976.
Gurney, G. *The War in the Air (A Pictorial History of World War II Air Forces in Combat)*, New York 1962.
Jablonski, E. *Air War* (Vols I–IV), New York 1971–1972.
Lambermont, P. and Pirie, A. *Helicopters and Autogyros of the World*, London 1958.
M.O.I. (Air Min.) *There's Freedom in the Air (The Official Story of the Allied Air Forces from the Occupied Countries)*, London 1944.
Mrazek, J. E. *The Glider War*, London 1975.
Munson, K. *Aircraft of World War II*, London 1962.
Munson, K. *Airliners between the Wars 1919–1939*, London 1972.
Munson, K. *Bombers between the Wars 1919–1939*, London 1970.
Munson, K. *Fighters between the Wars 1919–1939*, London 1970.
Muson, K. *Flying-boats and Seaplanes since 1910*, London 1971.
Munson, K. *Helicopters and other Rotorcraft since 1907*, London 1973.
Price, A. *Battle over the Reich*, London 1973.
Price, A. *Instruments of Darkness (The Struggle for Radar Supremacy)*, London 1967.
Price, A. *The Bomber in World War II*, London 1976.
Russell, D. A. (ed.) et al. *Aircraft of the Fighting Powers* (Vols 1–7), Leicester 1940–1946.
Schnitzler, R. (ed.) et al. *Handbuch der Luftfahrt*, Munich, Berlin, 1939.
Shores, C. and Ring, H. *Fighters over the Desert*, London 1969.
Shores, C., Ring, H. and Hess, W. M. *Fighters over Tunisia*, London 1975.
Stroud, J. *European Transport Aircraft since 1910*, London 1966.
Sunderman, J. F. (ed.) *World War II in the Air: Europe*, New York 1963.
Sunderman, J. F. (ed.) *World War II in the Air: Pacific*, New York.
Taylor, J. W. R. (ed.) *Combat Aircraft of the World*, London 1969.

Australia

Francillon, R. J. *The Royal Australian Air Force & Royal New Zealand Air Force in the Pacific*, Fallbrook, Calif., 1970.
Gillison, D. *Royal Australian Air Force 1939–1942*, Canberra 1962.
Herington, J. *Air War against Germany and Italy 1939–1943* (Australia in the War of 1939–1945, Series 3 (Air) Vol III), Canberra 1954.
Herington, J. *Air Power over Europe 1944–1945* (Australia in the War of 1939–1945, Series 3 (Air) Vol IV), Canberra 1963.
Johnson, F. (ed.) R.A.A.F. over Europe, London 1946.
Odgers, G. *Air War against Japan 1943–1945*, Canberra 1957.
Odgers, G. *The Royal Australian Air Force (An Illustrated History)*, Sydney 1965.
Pentland, G. *Aircraft & Markings of the R.A.A.F. 1939–45*, Melbourne 1970.
Pentland, G. and Malone, P. *Aircraft of the R.A.A.F. 1921–71*, Melbourne 1971.
R.A.A.F. Directorate of Public Relations (ed.) *These Eagles (Story of the R.A.A.F. at War)*, Canberra 1942.
R.A.A.F. *Log (Story of the R.A.A.F. at War)*, Canberra 1943.
R.A.A.F. *Saga (Story of the R.A.A.F. at War)*, Canberra 1944.
Victory Roll (Story of the R.A.A.F. at War), Canberra 1946.

Belgium

Mangin, J. A. and Champagne, J. P. *L'Aviation Militaire Belge: Insignes et Traditions*, Arlon 1972.

Canada

Gordon, J. *. . . of Men and Planes* (Vol II: Fighters, World War II), Ottawa 1968.
Gordon, J. *. . . of Men and Planes* (Vol III: RCAF, RCN, Canadian Army (Air)), Ottawa 1968.
Gordon, J. *The R.C.A.F. Overseas (The First Four Years)*, Toronto 1944.
Gordon, J. *The R.C.A.F. Overseas (The Fifth Year)*, Toronto 1945.
Griffin, J. A. *Canadian Military Aircraft Serials and Photographs*, Ottawa 1969.
Kealy, J. D. F. and Russel, E. C. *A History of Canadian Naval Aviation 1918–1962*, Ottawa 1965.
Roberts, L. *Canada's War in the Air*, Montreal 1942.
Roberts, L. *There shall be Wings (A History of the Royal Canadian Air Force)*, London 1960.
Vincent, C. *Canada's Wings* (Vol 1: The Blackburn Shark), Stittsville, Ont. 1974.

Croatia

Rauchwetter, G. *'U' über der Ostfront*, Zagreb 1943.

Czechoslovakia

Benes, B. *Wings in Exile*, London 1942.
Titz, Z. *Czechoslovakian Air Force 1918–1970*, Reading, Berks. 1971.

Denmark

Kofoed, H. *Danske Militaerfly gennem 50 Ar 1912–1962*, Copenhagen 1962.

Finland

Keskinen, K. *Suomen Ilmavoimien Lentokoneet 1939–72*, Tampere 1972.
Luukkanan, E. *Fighter over Finland*, London 1963.

France

Achard, A. and Tribot-Laspierre, J. *Répertoire des Aéronefs de construction Française pour la période 1890–1967*, Paris 1968.
Bonte, L. *L'Histoire des Essais en Vol (1914–1940)*, Paris 1974.
Brindley, J. F. *French Fighters of World War Two* (Vol 1), Windsor, Berks. 1971.
Cuny, J. and Danel, R. *l'Aviation de chasse française 1918–1940*, Paris 1974.
Cot, P. *L'Armée de l'Air 1936–1938*, Paris 1939.
Danel, R. and Curry, J. *Le Dewoitine D.520*, Paris 1975.
Haute, A. van *Pictorial History of the French Air Force* (Vol 1: 1909–1940), London 1974.
Haute, A. van *Pictorial History of the French Air Force* (Vol 2: 1941–1974), London 1975.
Jackson, R. *Air War over France 1939–40*, London 1974.
Sauvage, R. *Un du Normandie-Niémen*, Givors, Rhône 1950.

Germany

Adler, H. *Ein Buch von der neuen Luftwaffe*, Stuttgart 1938.
Adler, Maj. H. *Wir greifen England an!*, Berlin 1940.
Anttonen, O. and Valtonen, H. *Luftwaffe Suomessa (in Finland) 1941–1944* (Vol 1), 1976.
Bartz, K. *Swastika in the Air*, London 1956.
Baumbach, W. *Zu spät?*, Munich 1949.
Beaman, J. R. *Last of the Eagles*, Greensboro, N. C. 1976.
Bekker, C. *Angriffshöhe 4000 – Kriegstagebuch der deutschen Luftwaffe*, Oldenburg 1964.
Beumelburg, W. *Kampf um Spanien (Die Geschichte der Legion Condor)*, Oldenburg 1939.
Bley, W. *Das Buch der Spanienflieger*, Leipzig 1939.
Borelli, G., Borgotti, A., Caruana, R., Pini, G., and Gori, C. *Junkers Ju 87 Stuka*, Modena 1974.
Conradis, H. *Design for Flight (The Kurt Tank Story)*, London 1960.
Craig, J. F. *The Messerschmitt Bf 109*, New York 1968.
Dahl, W. *Rammjäger*, Heusenstamm (bei Offenbach) 1961.
Deichmann, Gen.d.Flieger a.D.P. *German Air Force Operations in Support of the Army* (USAF Historical Studies: No. 163), New York 1962.
Dettmann, F. *40000 Kilometer Feindflug*, Berlin 1940.
Drum, Gen.d.Flieger a.D.K. *Airpower and Russian Partisan Warfare* (USAF Historical Studies: No. 177), New York 1962.
Ebert, H. J. *Messerschmitt Bolkow Blohm–111 MBB Flugzeuge 1913–1973*, Stuttgart 1974.
Feist, U. and Francillon, R. J. *Luftwaffe in World War II*, Fallbrook, Calif., 1968.
Feuchter, G. W. *Geschichte des Luftktieges*, Bonn 1954.
Galland, A., Ries, K., Ahnert, A. *Die deutsche Luftwaffe 1939–1945 (Eine Dokumentation in Bildern)*, Bad Nauheim.
Galland, A. *Die Ersten und die Letzten*, Darmstadt 1953.
Girbig, W. *Im Anflug auf die Reichshauptstadt*, Stuttgart 1970.
Girbig, W. *Start im Morgengrauen (Eine Chronik vom Untergang der deutschen Jagdwaffe im Westen 1944/1945)*, Stuttgart 1973.
Grabler, J. *Mit Bomben und MGs über Polen*, Gütersloh 1942.
Green, W. *Augsburg Eagle (The Story of the Messerschmitt 109)*, London 1971.
Green, W. *The Warplanes of the Third Reich*, London 1970.
Hahn, F. *Deutsche Geheimwaffen 1939–1945*, Heidenheim 1963.
Heinkel, E. *Stürmisches Leben*, Stuttgart 1953.
Hitchcock, T. H. *Messerschmitt 'O-Nine' Gallery*, Acton, Mass., 1973.
Hove, A. von *Achtung Fallschirmjäger (Eine Idee bricht sich Bahn)*, Leoni am Starnberger See 1954.
Ishoven, A. van *Messerschmitt Aircraft Designer*, London 1975.
Kens, K. and Nowarra, H. J. *Die deutschen Flugzeuge 1933–1945*, Munich 1961.
Kohl, Maj. H. *Wir fliegen gegen England*, Reutlingen 1940.
Krausskopf, Oberltn. *Zerstörer am Nördlichen Himmel*, Berlin 1943.
Langsdorff, W. von *Handbuch der Luftfahrt*, Munich, Berlin 1939.
Lee, A. *The German Air Force*, London 1946.
Legion Condor (ed.) *Deutsche kämpfen in Spanien*, Berlin 1939.
Loewenstern, E. von *Luftwaffe über dem Feind*, Berlin 1941.
Lusar, R. *Die deutschen Waffen und Geheimwaffen des 2.Weltkrieges und ihre Weiterent-wicklung*, Munich 1956.
Matthias, J. *Alarm! Deutsche Flieger uber England*, Berlin 1940.
Meier-Welcker, H. *Abwehrkämpfe am Nordflügel der Ostfront 1944–1945*, Stuttgart 1963.
Menge-Genser, M. *Das Auge der Armee (Kampf und Sieg eines Fernaufklärers)*, Berlin 1943.
Merrick, K. A. *Luftwaffe Colors* (Vol 1: 1935–1940), Melbourne 1973.
Mizrahi, J. V. *Knights of the Black Cross*, Granada Hills, Calif., 1972.
Möhlenbeck, O. and Leihse, M. *Ferne Nachtjagd (Aufzeichnungen aus den Jahren 1940–1945)*, Stuttgart 1975.

Morzik, Genmaj. a.D. F. *German Air Force Airlift Operations* (USAF Historical Studies: No. 167), New York 1961.
Morzik, F. and Hümmelchen, G. *Die deutschen Transportflieger im zweiten Weltkrieg*, Frankfurt 1966.
Murawski, E. *Der deutsche Wehrmachtsbericht 1939–1945*, Boppard am Rhein 1962.
Nowarra, H. J. *Heinkel und seine Flugzeuge*, Munich 1975.
Nowarra, H. J. *The Focke-Wulf 190: A Famous German Fighter*, Letchworth, Herts., 1965.
Nowarra, H. J. *The Messerschmitt 109: A Famous German Fighter*, Letchworth, Herts., 1963.
Osterkamp, T. *Durch Höhen and Tiefen jagd ein Herz*, Heidelberg 1952.
Paquier, P. and Postel, C. *La Bataille Aérienne de L'Allemagne*, Paris 1947.
Philpott, B. *Luftwaffe Camouflage of World War 2*, London 1975.
Plocher, Genltn. H. *The German Air Force versus Russia, 1941, 1942, and 1943* (USAF Historical Studies: No. 153, 154, and 155), New York 1965–1967.
Price, A. *German Air Force Bombers of World War Two* (Vols 1 and 2), Windsor, Berks., 1968–1969.
Pritchard, A. *Messerschmitt*, London 1975.
Ries jr., K. *Die Maulwürfe 1919–1933*, Finthen b.Mainz 1974.
Ries jr., K. *Dora Kurfürst und rote 13 (Bild-band: Flugzeuge der Luftwaffe 1933–1945)* (Vols 1–4), Finthen b.Mainz 1964–1969.
Ries jr., K. *Luftwaffen-Story 1935–1939*, Finthen b.Mainz 1974.
Ries jr., K. *Markings and Camouflage Systems of Luftwaffe Aircraft in World War II* (Vols 1–4), Finthen b.Mainz 1963–1969.
Ries jr., K. *Photo-Collection Luftwaffen Embleme 1935–1945*, Finthen b. Mainz 1976.
Rohden, H. von *Die Luftwaffe ringt um Stalingrad*, Wiesbaden 1950.
Rudel, H. U. *Stuka Pilot*, Dublin 1952.
Rumpf, H. *Luftkrieg über Deutschland (eine Bilanz des Zweiten Weltkrieges)*, Oldenburg 1953.
Schellmann, H. *Die Luftwaffe und das 'Bismarck' – Unternehmen im Mai 1941*, Frankfurt 1962.
Schmidt, H. *Die Fallschirmjäger von Dombas*, Berlin 1941.
Schliephake, H. *The Birth of the Luftwaffe*, London 1971.
Shepherd, C. *German Aircraft of World War II*, London 1975.
Shores, C. F. *Pictorial History of the Mediterranean Air War* (Vol III: Axis Air Forces 1940–1945), London 1974.
Smith, J. R. *Focke-Wulf – An Aircraft Album*, London 1973.
Smith, J. R. *Messerschmitt – An Aircraft Album*, London 1971.
Smith, J. R. and Kay, A. *German Aircraft of the Second World War*, London 1972.
Smith, J. R. and Gallaşpy, J. D. *Luftwaffe Camouflage & Markings 1935–45* (Vol. 2), Melbourne 1976.
Smith, P. C. *Stuka at War*, London 1971.
Stackelberg, K. G. von *Jagdfliegergruppe G. (Gentzen) Jäger an Polens Himmel*, Graz 1943.
Strohmeyer, C. *Stukas (Erlebnis eines Fliegerkorps)*, Berlin 1940.
Supf, P. *Luftwaffe von Sieg zu Sieg – Von Norwegen bis Kreta*, Berlin 1941.
Supf, P. *Luftwaffe schlägt zu!*, Berlin 1939.
Swanborough, G. and Green, W. *The Focke-Wulf Fw 190*, London 1976.
Turner, P.St.J. *Heinkel – An Aircraft Album*, London 1970.
Turner, P.St.J. and Nowarra, H. J. *Junkers – An Aircraft Album*, London 1971.
Völker, K–H. *Die Deutsche Luftwaffe 1933–1939*, Stuttgart 1967.
Windrow, M. C. *German Air Force Fighters of World War Two* (Vols 1 & 2), Windsor, Berks., 1968–1970.
Wundshammer, B. *Flieger-Ritter-Helden (Mit dem Haifischgeschwader in Frankreich)*, Gütersloh 1942.
Ziegler, M. *Raketenjäger Me 163*, Stuttgart 1961.
Air Ministry (comp.) *The Rise and Fall of the German Air Force (1933 to 1945)*, London 1948.
O.K.W. (comp.) *Die Wehrmacht (Das Buch des Krieges 1939/40)*, Berlin 1940.
O.K.W. (comp.) *Die Wehrmacht (Das Buch des Krieges 1940/41)*, Berlin 1941.
O.K.W. (comp.) *Die Wehrmacht 1942*, Berlin 1942.
O.K.W. (comp.) *Die Wehrmacht 1943*, Berlin 1943.
– *Shell-Führer für Flieger*, Hamburg 1935.
– *Klemm-Merkbuch*, Boeblingen 1939.

Great Britain

Air Ministry *The Air Offensive against Germany*, London 1941.
Air Ministry *The Battle of Britain August–October 1940*, London 1941.
Allward, M. *Hurricane Special*, London 1975.
Anderson, W. *Pathfinders*, London 1946.
Andrews, C. F. *Vickers Aircraft since 1908*, London 1969.
Austin, A. B. *Fighter Command*, London 1941.
Barker, R. *The Ship-Busters (The Story of the R.A.F. Torpedo-Bombers)*, London 1957.
Barker, R. *The Thousand Plan (The Story of the First Thousand Bomber Raid on Cologne)*, London 1965.
Barnes, C. H. *Bristol Aircraft since 1910*, London 1970.
Barnes, C. H. *Shorts Aircraft since 1910*, London 1967.
Bishop, E. *Mosquito: Wooden Wonder*, London 1971.
Bowyer, C. *Hurricane at War*, London 1974.

Bowyer, C. *Mosquito at War*, London 1973.
Bowyer, C. *Sunderland at War*, London 1976.
Bowyer, M. J. F. *Fighting Colours (RAF Fighter Camouflage and Markings 1937–1969)*, London 1969.
Bowyer, M. J. F. *Bombing Colours (RAF Bomber Camouflage and Markings 1937–1973)*, Cambridge 1973.
Bowyer, M. J. F. *2 Group R.A.F.*, London 1974.
Branson, A. and Birch, N. *The Tiger Moth Story*, London 1965.
Brickhill, P. *The Dam Busters*, London 1951.
Brown, D. *The Seafire*, London 1973.
Brown, D. L. *Miles Aircraft since 1925*, London 1970.
Brown, J. D. *Carrier Operations in World War II* (Vol 1: The Royal Navy), London 1968.
Bushby, J. *Air Defence of Great Britain*, London 1973.
Cameron, I. *Wings of the Morning*, London 1962.
Chilton, C. E. (ed.) *Coastal Command's war record 1939–1945*, Northwood, Middx., 1957.
Clayton, D. C. *Handley Page – An Aircraft Album*, London 1970.
Collier, B. *The Battle of Britain*, London 1962.
Collier, R. *Eagle Day*, London 1966.
Donahue, A. G. *Tally-Ho! Yankee in a Spitfire*, London 1941.
Duval, G. R. *British Flying-boats and Amphibians 1909–1952*, London 1966.
Duval, G. R. *British Flying-boats (A Pictorial Survey)*, Truro, Cornw., 1973.
Ellison, N. *British Gliders and Sailplanes 1922–1970*, London 1971.
Gardner, C. *A.A.S.F.*, London 1940.
Goulding, J. and Moyes, P. *RAF Bomber Command and its Aircraft 1936–1940*, London 1975.
Griffith, H. *R.A.F. in Russia*, London 1942.
Guedalla, P. *Middle East 1940–1942 (A Study in Air Power)*, London 1944.
Hall, A. W. *RAF Fighters in World War 2*, London 1975.
Hall, A. W. and Taylor, E. *Avro Anson Marks I, III, IV, & X*, New Malden, Surrey, 1972.
Halley, J. J. *Famous Fighter Squadrons of the R.A.F.* (Vol. 1), Windsor, Berks., 1971.
Halley, J. J. *Famous Maritime Squadrons of the R.A.F.*, Windsor, Berks., 1973.
Halley, J. J. *Royal Air Force Unit Histories* (Vol 1: Nos. 1 to 200 Squadrons), Brentwood, Essex, 1969.
Halley, J. J. *Royal Air Force Unit Histories* (Vol 2: Nos. 201 to 1435 Squadrons), Brentwood, Essex, 1973.
Harlin, E. A. and Jenks, G. A. *Avro – An Aircraft Album*, London 1973.
Harris, Sir A. *Bomber Offensive*, London 1947.
Highham, R. (ed.) *A Guide to the Sources of British Military History*, London 1972.
Hoare, J. *Tumult in the Clouds (A Story of the Fleet Air Arm)*, London 1976.
Horsley, T. *Find, Fix and Strike*, London 1945.
Houghton, G. W. *They Flew through Sand (The Western Desert Notes of an R.A.F. Officer)*, London 1942.
Howard-Williams, J. *Night Intruder*, Newton Abbott, Devon, 1976.
Hunt, L. *Twenty-One Squadrons (The History of the Royal Auxiliary Force 1925–1957)*, London 1972.
Jackson, A. J. *Avro Aircraft since 1908*, London 1965.
Jackson, A. J. *Blackburn Aircraft since 1909*, London 1968.
Jackson, A. J. *British Civil Aircraft since 1919* (Vols 1–3), London 1973–1974.
Jackson, A. J. *De Havilland Aircraft since 1915*, London 1962.
Jackson, R. *Before the Storm (The Story of Bomber Command, 1939–1942)*, London 1972.
Jackson, R. *Storm from the Skies (The Strategic Bomber Offensive, 1943–1945)*, London 1974.
Jackson, R. *Strike from the Sea*, London 1970.
James, D. N. *Gloster Aircraft since 1917*, London 1971.
James, D. N. *Hawker – An Aircraft Album*, London 1972.
Joubert de la Ferté, Air Chief Marshall Sir P. *Birds and Fishes (The Story of Coastal Command)*, London 1960.
King, H. F. *Armament of British Aircraft 1909–1939*, London 1971.
Lawrence, W. J. *No. 5 Bomber Group R.A.F. (1939–1945)*, London 1951.
Lewis, P. *Squadron Histories: R.F.C., R.N.A.S., and R.A.F. 1912–1959*, London 1959.
Lewis, P. *The British Bomber since 1914*, London 1967.
Lewis, P. *The British Fighter since 1912*, London 1967.
Lloyd, Air Marshal Sir H. *Briefed to Attack (Malta's Part in African Victory)*, London 1949.
Lloyd, F. H. M. *Hurricane – The Story of a Great Fighter*, Leicester 1945.
Lumsden, A. *Wellington Special*, London 1974.
Macmillan, Capt. N. *The Royal Air Force in the World War* Vols I–IV, London 1942–1950.
MacClure, V. *Gladiators over Norway*, London 1942.
Mason, F. K. *Battle over Britain*, London 1969.
Mason, F. K. *British Fighters of World War Two* (Vol 1), Windsor, Berks., 1970.
Mason, F. K. *Hawker Aircraft since 1920*, London 1961.
Mason, F. K. *The Gloster Gladiator*, London 1964.
Mason, F. K. *The Hawker Hurricane*, London 1962.
Middlebrook, M. *The Nuremberg Raid 30–31 March 1944*, London 1973.
M.O.I. (Adm.) *Fleet Air Arm*, London 1943.

M.O.I. (Air Min.) *The Air Battle of Malta (June 1940 to November 1942)*, London 1944.
M.O.I. (Air Min.) *Atlantic Bridge*, London 1945.
M.O.I. (Air Min.) *The Battle of Britain (An Air Ministry Account of the Great Days from 8th August–31st October 1940)*, London 1941.
M.O.I. (Air Min.) *Bomber Command*, London 1941.
M.O.I. (Air Min.) *Bomber Command Continues*, London 1942.
M.O.I. (Air Min.) *Coastal Command*, London 1942.
M.O.I. (Air Min.) *R.A.F. Middle East (The Official Story of Air Operations in the Middle East from February 1942 to January 1943)*, London 1945.
M.O.I. (Air Min.) *Wings of the Phoenix*, London.
Monks, N. *Fighter Squadrons (The Epic Story of two Hurricane Squadrons in France)*, Sydney 1941.
Moss, P. W. *Impressments Log* (Vols 1–3), Southend, Essex, 1962–1964.
Moyes, P. J. R. *Bomber Squadrons of the R.A.F. and their Aircraft*, London 1964.
Moyes, P. J. R. *British Bombers of World War Two* (Vol 1), Windsor, Berks., 1968.
Moyes, P. J. R. *Royal Air Force Bombers of World War Two* (Vol 2), Windsor, Berks., 1968.
Musgrove, G. *Pathfinder Force (A History of 8 Group)*, London 1976.
Narracott, A. H. *Unsung Heroes of the Air*, London 1943.
Netherwood, G. *Desert Squadron (The Royal Air Force in Egypt and Libya)*, Cairo 1944.
Nicholl, G. W. R. *The Supermarine Walrus*, London 1966.
Oughton, J. D. *Bristol – An Aircraft Album*, London 1973.
Owen, R. *The Desert Air Force*, London.
Poolman, K. *Flying Boat (The Story of the Sunderland)*, London 1962.
Poolman, K. *The Catafighters*, London 1970.
Price, A. *Aircraft versus Submarine*, London 1973.
Price, A. *Spitfire at War*, London 1974.
Rawlings, J. D. R. *Pictorial History of the Fleet Air Arm*, London 1973.
Rawlings, J. *Fighter Squadrons of the R.A.F. and their Aircraft*, London 1969.
Rawnsley, C. F. and Wright, R. *Night Fighter*, London 1957.
Reed, A. and Beamont, R. *Typhoon and Tempest at War*, London 1974.
Richards, D. *Royal Air Force 1939–1945* (Vol I: The Fight at Odds), London 1953.
Richards, D. and Saunders, H. St.G. *Royal Air Force 1939–1945* (Vol II: The Fight Avails), London 1954.
Robertson, B. *Beaufort Special*, London 1976.
Robertson, B. *British Military Aircraft Serials 1911–1971*, London 1971.
Robertson, B. *Spitfire – The Story of a Famous Fighter*, Letchworth, Herts., 1960.
Robertson, B. *Lancaster – The Story of a Famous Bomber*, Letchworth, Herts., 1964.
Russel, W/Cdr. W. W. *Forgotten Skies (The Air Forces in India and Burma)*, London 1945.
Saunders, H. St.G. *Royal Air Force 1939–1945* (Vol III: The Fight is Won), London 1954.
Shacklady, E. *The Gloster Meteor*, London 1962.
Sharp, C. M. and Bowyer, M. J. F. *Mosquito*, London 1967.
Shores, C. F. *Pictorial History of the Mediterranean Air War* (Vol 1: RAF 1940–43), London 1972.
Shores, C. F. *Pictorial History of the Mediterranean Air War* (Vol 2: RAF 1943–45), London 1973.
Shores, C. F. *2nd T.A.F.*, Reading, Berks., 1970.
Shorrick, N. *Lion in the Sky (The Story of Seletar and the Royal Air Force in Singapore)*, Singapore 1968.
Smith, P. *Task Force 57 (The British Pacific Fleet 1944–1945)*, London 1969.
Spaight, J. M. *The Battle of Britain 1940*, London 1941.
Sutton, H. T. *Raiders Approach!*, Aldershot, Hants., 1956.
Tanner, J. (ed.) *British Aviation Colours of World War Two*, London 1976.
Tanner, J. (ed.) *The Hurricane II Manual*, London 1976.
Tanner, J. (ed.) *The Lancaster Manual*, London 1977.
Tanner, J. (ed.) *The Spitfire V Manual*, London 1976.
Tapper, O. *Armstrong Whitworth Aircraft since 1913*, London 1973.
Taylor, H. A. *Airspeed Aircraft since 1931*, London 1970.
Taylor, H. A. *Fairey Aircraft since 1915*, London 1974.
Taylor, H. A. *Test Pilot at War*, London 1970.
Taylor, J. W. R. and Moyes, P. J. R. *Pictorial History of the R.A.F.* (Vol 2: 1939–1945), London 1969.
Taylor, J. W. R. and Allward, M. F. *Spitfire*, Leicester 1946.
Taylor, J. W. R. and Allward, M. F. *Westland 50*, London 1965.
Thetford, O. *Aircraft of the Royal Air Force since 1918*, London 1957.
Thetford, O. *British Naval Aircraft since 1912*, London 1958.
Townsend, P. *Duel of Eagles*, London.
Wallace, G. *RAF Biggin Hill*, London 1957.
Webster, C. and Frankland, N. *The Strategic Air Offensive against Germany* (Vols 1–4), London 1961.
Winton, J. *The Forgotten Fleet*, London 1969.
Wisdom, T. H. *Wings over Olympus (The Story of the Royal Air Force in Libya and Greece)*, London 1942.
Wood, D. and Dempster, D. *The Narrow Margin*, London 1961.
Wright, L. *The Wooden Sword (The Untold Story of the Gliders in World War II)*, London 1967.

Italy

Arena, N. *Battaglie nei cieli d'Italia 1943–1945 (storia dell'aviazione della R.S.I.)*, Genoa 1971.

Arena, N. *l'Aeronautica Nazionale Repubblicana 1943–1945* (Vols I–II), Modena 1974.

Bignozzi, G. and Catalanotto, B. *Storia degli Aerei d'Italia dal 1911 al 1961*, Rome 1962.

Borgiotti, A. and Gori, C. *La Guerra Aerea in Africa Settentrionale 1942–1943 (assalto dal cielo)*, Modena 1974.

Emiliani, A., Ghergo, G. F., and Vigna, A. (ed.) *Immagini e storia dell' Aeronautica Italiana 1935–1945 (Regia Aeronautica: Balcani e Fronte Orientale)*, Milan 1974.

Emiliani, A., Ghergo, G. F. and Vigna, A. (ed.) *Immagini e storia dell'Aeronautica Italiana 1935–1945 (Spagna 1936–39: l'Aviazione Legionaria)*, Milan 1973.

Emiliani, A., Ghergo, G. F., and Vigna, A. (ed.) *Immagini e storia dell' Aeronautica Italiana 1935–1945 (Regia Aeronautica: periodo prebellico e fronte occidentali*, Milan 1975.

Emiliani, A., Ghergo, G. F., and Vigna, (ed.) *Immagini e storia dell'Aeronautica Italiana 1935–1945 (Regia Aeronautica: Colori e Insegne 1935–1943)*, Milan 1974.

Garello, G. *Regia Aeronautica e Armée de l'Air 1940–1943*, Rome 1975.

Malizia, N. *Il 51 Stormo Caccia*, Rome 1975.

Mondini, A., and Pafi, B. *Aeronautica Militare Italiana 1923–1973*, Rome 1973.

Prato, P. *I Caccia Caproni-Reggiane 1938–1945*, Genoa 1968.

Pricolo, F. *La Regia Aeronautica nella Seconda Guerra Mondiale (novembre 1939–novembre 1941)*, Milan 1971.

Santoro, G. *l'Aeronautica Italiana nella Seconda Guerra Mondiale* (Vols 1 and 2), Milan 1957.

Thompson, J. *Italian Civil and Military Aircraft 1930–1945*, Los Angeles, Calif., 1963.

Tosco, V. *C.R.D.A. CANT Z 1007/1007bis 'Alcione'* (Vol 1: caratteristiche tecniche), Milan 1975.

Vergnano, P. *The Fiat Fighters 1930–1945*, Genoa 1969.

India

Gupta, S. C. *History of the Indian Air Force 1933–45 (Official History of the Indian Armed Forces in the Second World War 1939–45)*, New Delhi 1961.

Singh, P. *Aircraft of the Indian Air Force 1933–73*, New Delhi 1974.

Japan

Flanagan, D. N. and Oishi, Y. *Color Schemes of Japanese Aircrafts in World War II*, Takatsuki/Shiga 1964.

Francillon, R. J. *Imperial Japanese Navy Bombers of World War Two*, Windsor, Berks, 1969.

Francillon, R. J. *Japanese Aircraft of the Pacific War*, London 1970.

Inoguchi, R., Nakajima, T., and Pineau, R. *The Divine Wind (Japan's Kamikaze Force in World War II)*, London 1959.

Kohri, K., Komori, I., Naito, I. *The Fifty Years of Japanese Aviation 1910–1960* (2 Vols), Tokyo 1961.

Millot, B. *Divine Thunder (The Life and Death of the Kamikazes)*, London 1971.

Nozawa, T. *A Pictorial History of Aviation in Japan 1910–1960*, Tokyo 1960.

Nozawa, T. (ed.) *Encyclopedia of Japanese Aircraft 1900–1945* (Vols 1–5), Tokyo.

Okumiya, M. Horikoshi, J., and Caidin, M. *Zero! (The Story of the Japanese Navy Air Force 1937–1945)*, London 1957.

Sekigawa, E. *Pictorial History of Japanese Military Aviation*, London 1974.

Sonokawa, K. (ed.) *The Japanese Naval Air Arm*, photo illustrated, Tokyo 1970.

Stroud, J. *Japanese Aircraft*, Letchworth, Herts., 1945.

Thorpe, D. W. *Japanese Army Air Force Camouflage and Markings World War II*, Fallbrook, Calif., 1968.

Webber, B. *Retaliation: Japanese Attacks and Allied Countermeasures on the Pacific Coast in World War II*, Oregon, 1975.

'Aireview' (comp.) *General View of Japanese Military Aircraft in the Pacific War*, Tokyo 1956.

The Japanese Army Wings of the Second World War (pictorial), Tokyo 1972.

Netherlands

Hegener, H. *Fokker: The Man and the Aircraft*, Letchworth, Herts., 1961.

Hooftman, H. *Van Brik tot Starfighter (Vijftig jaar Luchtmachtvliegtuigen)* (Vols 1 and 2), Zwolle 1962.

Hooftman, H. *Van Farman tot Neptune (De vliegtuigen van die Marine Luchtvaartdienst)* Vols. 1 and 2, Zwolle 1964.

Hooftman, H. *Van Glenn Martins en Mustangs (Alle vliegtuigen die gevlogen hebben bij het K.N.I.L. in de Indische Militaire Luchtvaart)* Vols. 1 and 2, Zwolle 1967.

Molenaar, Kol. F. J. *De luchtverdediging in de meidagen 1940* (Vols I–II), 's-Gravenhage 1970.

Tammes, J. *Het Wapen der Militaire Luchtvaart in de Engelse Periode 1940–1945*, 's-Gravenhage 1961.

New Zealand

Bentley, G. *RNZAF, A Short History*, Wellington 1969.

Thompson, H. L. *New Zealanders with the Royal Air Force* (Vols 1 and 2), Wellington 1956.

Poland

Arct, B. *W pogoni za Luftwaffe*, Edinburgh 1946.

Committee (ed.) *Destiny Can Wait – The Polish Air Force in the Second World War*, London 1949.

Cynk, J. B. *History of the Polish Air Force 1918–1968*, Reading, Berks., 1972.

Cynk, J. B. *Polish Aircraft 1893–1939*, London 1971.

Kurowski, A. *Lotnictwo Polskie w 1939 roku*, Warszawa 1962.

Marsh, L. G. *Polish Wings over Britain*, London 1943.

Morgala, A. *Polskie Samoloty Wojskowe 1918–1939*, Warszawa 1972.

South Africa

Brown, J. A. *A Gathering of Eagles* (Vol II: The Campaigns of the South African Air Force in Italian East Africa June 1940–November 1941), Cape Town 1970.

Brown, J. A. *Eagles Strike* (Vol IV: The Campaigns of the South African Air Force in Egypt, Cyrenaica, Libya, Tunisia, Tripolitania and Madagascar 1941–1943), Cape Town 1974.

Sweden

Norrbohm, Col. G. and Skogsberg, B. *Att Flyga är Leva Flygvapnet 1926–1976*, Höganas 1976.

Switzerland

Urech, J. *The Aircraft of the Swiss Air Force since 1914*, Stäfa, Zürich 1975.

USA

Beaman, J. R. *The Unknown Mustangs*, Greensboro, N.C. 1975.

Berry, P., Dunstall, T., Ford, M. and Whittle, J. A. (comp.) *The Douglas DC–4*, Brentwood, Essex, 1967.

Birdsall, S. *Hell's Angels (B–17 Combat Markings)*, Canoga Park, Calif., 1969.

Birdsall, S. *Log of the Liberators*, Garden City, N.Y., 1973.

Birdsall, S. *The B–17 Flying Fortress*, Dallas, Texas, 1965.

Birdsall, S. *The B–24 Liberator*, New York 1969.

Blue, A. G., Borelli, G., Borgiotti, A., Gori, C., and Pini, G. *North American P–51 Mustang 1940–45 (le Macchine e la Storia)*, Modena 1973.

Bowers, P. M. *Boeing Aircraft since 1916*, London 1966.

Bozung, J. H. (ed.) *The 5th over the Southwest Pacific*, Los Angeles, Calif., 1947.

Bozung, J. H. (ed.) *The 8th sees England*, Los Angeles, Calif., 1946.

Bozung, J. H. (ed.) *The 9th sees France and England*, Los Angeles, Calif., 1947.

Bozung, J. H. (ed.) *The 12th over the Mediterranean*, Los Angeles, Calif., 1946.

Bozung, J. H. (ed.) *The 15th over Italy*, Los Angeles, Calif., 1947.

Caidin, M. *Black Thursday (The Flying Fortress attack on Schweinfurt, October 14, 1943)*, New York 1960.

Caidin, M. *Flying Forts (The B–17 in World War II)*, New York 1968.

Caidin, M. *The Ragged, Rugged Warriors (The Heroic Story of the Early Air War against Japan in the Far East and Pacific)*, New York 1966.

Caras, R. A. *Wings of Gold (The Story of United States Naval Aviation)*, New York and Philadelphia 1965.

Carpenter, D. B. and Mayborn, M. *Ryan Guidebook*, Dallas, Texas, 1975.

Collison, T. *Flying Fortress (The Story of the Boeing Bomber)*, New York 1943.

Combs, V/Adm. J. S. *United States Naval Aviation 1910–1960*, Washington 1960.

Craven, W. F. and Cate, J. L. (ed.) *The Army Air Forces in World War II*, (Vols 1–7), Chicago, Ill., 1948–1958.

AAF – The Official Guide to the Army Air Forces (A Directory, Almanac and Chronicle of Achievement), New York 1944.

Delear, F. J. *Igor Sikorsky – His Three Careers in Aviation*, New York 1969.

Dial, J. F. *United States Camouflage WWII (T.O.No. 07–1–1)*, Arlington, Texas, 1964.

Doll, T. E. *Flying Leathernecks in World War II*, Fallbrook, Calif., 1971.

Doll, T. E. *U.S. Navy Markings WWII – Pacific Theatre*, 1967.

Dornbusch, C. E. (comp.) *Unit Histories of the United States Air Forces*, Hampton Bays, N.Y., 1958.

Dugan, J. and Stewart, C. *Ploesti (The Great Ground-Air Battle of 1 August 1943)*, London 1963.

Duval, G. R. *American Flying Boats*, Truro, Cornw., 1974.

Fahey, J. C. *U.S. Army Aircraft (Heavier-than-Air) 1908–1946*, New York 1946.

Farley, E. J. *U.S. Army Air Force Fighter Planes P–1 – F–107*, Los Angeles, Calif., 1961.

Francillon, R. J. *American Fighters of World War Two* (Vol. 1), Windsor, Berks., 1968.

Francillon, R. J. *U.S. Army Air Forces in the Pacific*, Fallbrook, Calif., 1969.

Francis, D. *Mr. Piper and his Cubs*, Ames, Iowa, 1973.
Freeman, R. A. *American Bombers of World War Two*, Windsor, Berks., 1973.
Freeman, R. A. *Camouflage and Markings of the United States Army Air Force 1937–1945*, London 1974.
Freeman, R. A. *Mustang at War*, London 1974.
Freeman, R. A. *Republic Thunderbolt*, London.
Freeman, R. A. *The Mighty Eighth: Units, Men and Machines (A History of the US 8th Army Air Force)*, London 1970.
Fry, G. L. *The Debden Eagles (4th Fighter Group in World War II)*, USA 1970.
Garfield, B. *The Thousand-Mile War (World War II in Alaska and the Aleutians)*, Garden City, N.Y., 1969.
Glines, Lt. Col. C. V. *Doolittle's Tokyo Raiders*, Princetown, N.J., 1964.
Glines, C. V. and Moseley, W. F. *The DC-3 (The Story of a Fabulous Airplane)*, Philadelphia and New York, 1966.
Gruenhagen, R. W. *Mustang (The Story of the P-51 Fighter)*, New York 1969.
Gurney, G. *Journey of the Giants (The Story of the B-29 – the weapon that won the war in the Pacific)*, New York 1961.
Hager, A. R. *Wings for the Dragon (The Air War in Asia)*, New York 1945.
Hall, A. W. *American Fighters of World War 2*, Cambridge 1976.
Hess, W. N. *Fighting Mustang (The Chronicle of the P-51)*, New York 1970.
Hess, W. N. *Pacific Sweep (The 5th and 13th Fighter Commands in World War II)*, Garden City, N.Y., 1974.
Howard, C. and Whitley, J. *One Damned Island After Another – The Saga of the Seventh (Air Force)*, Chapel Hill, N.C., 1946.
Ingells, D. J. *The Plane that Changed the World (A biography of the DC-3)*, Fallbrook, Calif., 1966.
Jablonski, E. *Flying Fortress (The Illustrated Biography of the B-17s and the Men Who Flew Them)*, Garden City, N.Y., 1965.
Jones, L. S. *US Fighters 1925 to 1980s*, Fallbrook, Callif., 1975.
Jones, L. S. *US Bombers B-1 (1928) to B-1 (1980s)*, Fallbrook, Calif., 1974.
Jupter, J. P. *US Civil Aircraft (Vol 6)*, Fallbrook, Calif., 1974.
Larkins, W. T. *US Marine Corps Aircraft 1914–1959*, Concord, Calif., 1959.
Lawson, T. D. *30 Seconds over Tokyo*, London 1943.
Maurer, M. (ed.) *Air Force Combat Units of World War II*, New York 1959.
Mayborn, M. and Pickett, B. *Cessna Guidebook* (Vol 1), Dallas, Texas, 1973.
McCravy, J. R. and Sherman, D. E. *First of the Many (A Journal of Action with the Men of the Eighth Air Force)*, New York 1944.
McDaniel, W. H. *The History of Beech*, Wichita, Kansas, 1971.
McDowell, E. R. *The P-40 Kittyhawk*, New York 1968.
Mills, S. E. *Arctic War Birds (Alaska Aviation of WWII)*, Seattle, Wash., 1971.
Mizrahi, J. V. *U.S. Navy Dive and Torpedo Bombers*, Northridge, Calif., 1967.
Mizrahi, J. V. *Carrier Fighters* (Vols 1 and 2), Northridge, Calif., 1969.
Mizrahi, J. V. (ed.) *North American B-25 (The Full Story of World War II's Classic Medium)*, Hollywood, Calif., 1965.
Mondey, D. *Pictorial History of the US Air Force*, London 1971.
Morgan, L. *The Douglas DC-3*, Dallas, Texas, 1964.
Morgan, L. *The P-47 Thunderbolt*, Dallas, Texas, 1963.
Morison, S. E. *History of United States Naval Operations in World War II* (15 Vols), Boston, Mass., 1947–1960.
Morrison, W. H. *Hellbirds (The Story of the B-29s in Combat)*, New York 1960.
Munday, E. A. *Fifteenth Air Force Combat Markings 1943–1945*, London.
Munson, K. and Swanborough, G. *Boeing – An Aircraft Album*, London 1972.
Naval Airship Training and Experimental Command (comp.) *They Were Dependable – Airship Operation in World War II*, Lakehurst, N.J., 1946.
Pearcy jr., A. A. *The Dakota*, London 1972.
Peasley, B. J. *Heritage of Valor (The Eighth Air Force in World War II)*, Philadelphia and New York 1964.
Price, A. *World War II Fighter Conflict*, London 1975.
Redding, J. M. and Leyshon, H. I. *Skyways to Berlin (with the American Flyers in England)*, London 1943.
Robertson, B. (ed.) *United States Army and Air Force Fighters 1916–1961*, Letchworth, Herts., 1961.
Robertson, B. (ed.) *United States Navy and Marine Corps 1918–1962*, Letchworth, Herts., 1962.
Rubenstein, M. and Goldman, R. M. *To Join with the Eagles (Curtiss-Wright Aircraft 1903–1965)*, New York 1974.
Rust, K. C. *The 9th Air Force in World War II*, Fallbrook, Calif., 1967.
Rust, K. C. *Fifth Air Force Story*, Temple City, Calif., 1973.
Rust, K. C. *Twelfth Air Force Story*, Temple City, Calif., 1975.
Shamburger, P. and Christy, J. *The Curtiss Hawks*, Kalamazoo, Mich., 1972.
Sherrod, R. *History of Marine Corps Aviation in World War II*, Washington, D.C., 1952.
Swanborough, G. *North American – An Aircraft Album*, London 1973.
Swanborough, F. G. and Bowers, P. M. *United States Military Aircraft since 1908*, London 1963.
Swanborough, F. G. and Bowers, P. M. *United States Navy Aircraft since 1911*, London 1968.
Thorne, B. K. *The Hump (The Great Himalayan Airlift of World War II)*, Philadelphia and New York 1965.
Turnbull, A. D. and Clifford, L. L. *History of United States Naval Aviation*, New York 1972.
Underwood, J. W. *The Stinsons*, 1969.
USAAF *Target: Germany (The Official Story of the VIII Bomber Command's First Year over Europe)*, Washington, D.C., 1944.
Wagner, R. *American Combat Planes (A History of Military Aircraft in the USA)*, London 1961.
Whelan, R. *The Flying Tigers*, London 194?
Willoughby, M. F. *US Coast Guard in World War I*, Annapolis, Md., 1957.
Wordell, M. T. and Seiler, E. N. *Wildcats over Casablanca*, Boston, Mass., 1943.

USSR
Alexander, J. *Russian Aircraft since 1940*, London 1975.
Boyd, A. *The Soviet Air Force since 1918*, London 1977.
Jackson, R. *The Red Falcons*, Brighton, Sussex, 1970.
Lee, A. *The Soviet Air Force*, London 1950.
Lee, A. (ed.) *The Soviet Air & Rocket Forces*, London 1959.
MacDonald, H. *Aeroflot: Soviet Air Transport since 1923*, London 1975.
Němeček, V. *Sowjet-Flugzeuge*, Steinbach-Wörthsee 1976.
Nowarra, H. J., Duval, G. R. *Russian Civil and Military Aircraft 1884–1969*, London 1971.
Stroud, J. *The Red Air Force*, London 1943.
Wennerström, S. *Röda vingar*, Malmö 1946.
Yakovlev, A. *The Aim of a Lifetime*, Moscow 1972.